THE OXFORD HANDBOOK OF

CONTEXTUAL
POLITICAL
ANALYSIS

THE OXFORD HANDBOOKS OF POLITICAL SCIENCE

GENERAL EDITOR: ROBERT E. GOODIN

The *Oxford Handbooks of Political Science* is a ten-volume set of reference books offering authoritative and engaging critical overviews of all the main branches of political science.

The series as a whole is under the General Editorship of Robert E. Goodin, with each volume being edited by a distinguished international group of specialists in their respective fields:

POLITICAL THEORY
John S. Dryzek, Bonnie Honig & Anne Phillips

POLITICAL INSTITUTIONS
R. A. W. Rhodes, Sarah A. Binder & Bert A. Rockman

POLITICAL BEHAVIOR
Russell J. Dalton & Hans-Dieter Klingemann

COMPARATIVE POLITICS
Carles Boix & Susan C. Stokes

LAW & POLITICS
Keith E. Whittington, R. Daniel Kelemen & Gregory A. Caldeira

PUBLIC POLICY
Michael Moran, Martin Rein & Robert E. Goodin

POLITICAL ECONOMY
Barry R. Weingast & Donald A. Wittman

INTERNATIONAL RELATIONS
Christian Reus-Smit & Duncan Snidal

CONTEXTUAL POLITICAL ANALYSIS
Robert E. Goodin & Charles Tilly

POLITICAL METHODOLOGY
Janet M. Box-Steffensmeier, Henry E. Brady & David Collier

This series aspires to shape the discipline, not just to report on it. Like the Goodin–Klingemann *New Handbook of Political Science* upon which the series builds, each of these volumes will combine critical commentaries on where the field has been together with positive suggestions as to where it ought to be heading.

THE OXFORD HANDBOOK OF

CONTEXTUAL

POLITICAL

ANALYSIS

Edited by

ROBERT E. GOODIN

and

CHARLES TILLY

OXFORD

UNIVERSITY PRESS

This book has been printed digitally and produced in a standard specification
in order to ensure its continuing availability

OXFORD
UNIVERSITY PRESS

Great Clarendon Street, Oxford OX2 6DP

Oxford University Press is a department of the University of Oxford.
It furthers the University's objective of excellence in research, scholarship,
and education by publishing worldwide in

Oxford New York

Auckland Cape Town Dar es Salaam Hong Kong Karachi
Kuala Lumpur Madrid Melbourne Mexico City Nairobi
New Delhi Shanghai Taipei Toronto
With offices in
Argentina Austria Brazil Chile Czech Republic France Greece
Guatemala Hungary Italy Japan South Korea Poland Portugal
Singapore Switzerland Thailand Turkey Ukraine Vietnam

Oxford is a registered trade mark of Oxford University Press
in the UK and in certain other countries

Published in the United States
by Oxford University Press Inc., New York

ISBN 978-0-19-954844-6

Contents

PART VII   PLACE MATTERS

PART VIII   POPULATION MATTERS

PART IX TECHNOLOGY MATTERS

PART X OLD AND NEW

About the Contributors

Louise Antony is Professor of Philosophy at the University of Massachusetts, Amherst.

David E. Apter is Henry J. Heinz II Professor of Political and Social Development Emeritus and Senior Research Scholar at Yale University.

Dominique Arel is Associate Professor in the School of Political Studies at the University of Ottawa.

Aleida Assmann is Professor of English in the Fachbereich Literaturwissenschaft of the University of Konstanz.

Javier Auyero is Associate Professor of Sociology at the State University of New York, Stony Brook.

Rod Aya is Assistant Professor of Anthropology at the University of Amsterdam.

Pamela Ballinger is Associate Professor of Anthropology at Bowdoin College.

Wiebe E. Bijker is Professor of Technology and Society at the University of Maastricht.

Samuel Bowles is Research Professor and Director of the Behavioral Sciences Program of the Santa Fe Institute and Professor of Economics at the University of Siena.

Daniel Cefaï is Associate Professor of Sociology at the University of Paris X—Nanterre and Researcher at the Institut Marcel Mauss, Ecole des Hautes Etudes en Sciences Sociales.

Lee Clarke is Professor of Sociology at Rutgers University.

Ruth Berins Collier is Professor of Political Science at the University of California, Berkeley.

Neta C. Crawford is Professor of Political Science and African American Studies at Boston University and Adjunct Professor of International Relations at the Watson Institute for International Studies at Brown University.

Bruce Curtis is Professor of Sociology and Anthropology at Carleton University.

James N. Druckman is Associate Professor of Political Science at Northwestern University.

Richard J. Ellis is Mark O. Hatfield Professor of Politics at Willamette University.

Roberto Franzosi is Professor of Sociology at the University of Reading.

Gary P. Freeman is Professor of Government at the University of Texas at Austin.

Susan Gal is Mae and Sidney G. Metzl Distinguished Service Professor of Anthropology and Linguistics at the University of Chicago.

Herbert Gintis is a member of the External Faculty of the Santa Fe Institute, and Professor, Central European University.

Robert E. Goodin is Distinguished Professor of Social & Political Theory and Philosophy at the Research School of Social Sciences, Australian National University.

Colin Hay is Professor of Political Analysis at the University of Birmingham.

Jeffrey Herbst is Provost, Miami University.

M. Kai Ho is a Ph.D. candidate in Sociology at Columbia University.

Jennifer L. Hochschild is Henry LaBarre Jayne Professor of Government and Professor of African and African American Studies at Harvard University.

Patrick Thaddeus Jackson is Assistant Professor of International Relations in the School of International Service at American University.

Sheila Jasanoff is Pforzheimer Professor of Science and Technology Studies at the John F. Kennedy School of Government, Harvard University.

James M. Jasper having previously taught at Berkeley, Columbia, Princeton and New York University now edits *Contexts* magazine.

Courtney Jung is Assistant Professor in the Department of Political Science at The New School for Social Research.

Don Kalb is Associate Professor of Sociology and Social Anthropology at the Central European University, Budapest, and researcher in the Department of Anthropology, Utrecht University.

David I. Kertzer is Paul Dupee, Jr. University Professor of Social Science and Professor of Anthropology and Italian Studies at Brown University.

David Levine is Professor of Theory and Policy Studies at the Ontario Institute for Studies in Education, University of Toronto.

Paul Lichterman is Associate Professor of Sociology at University of Southern California and Associate Professor (on leave) at the University of Wisconsin-Madison.

Arthur Lupia is Professor of Political Science and Senior Research Scientist at the Center for Political Studies of the University of Michigan.

James Mahoney is Associate Professor of Political Science and Sociology at Northwestern University.

Sebastián Mazzuca is a Ph.D. candidate in Political Science at the University of California, Berkeley.

Kathleen M. McGraw is Professor of Political Science at Ohio State University.

Philip Pettit is L. S. Rockefeller University Professor of Politics and Human Values at Princeton University.

Francesca Polletta is Associate Professor of Sociology at Columbia University.

Richard Price is Associate Professor of Political Science at the University of British Columbia.

Lucian Pye is Emeritus Professor of Political Science at MIT.

Dietrich Rueschemeyer is Charles C. Tillinghast Jr. Professor of International Studies, Emertius, Waston Institute for International Studies, Brown University.

Daniel Schensul is a Ph.D. candidate in Sociology at Brown University.

Wim A. Smit is Associate Professor of Science, Technology and Society and Director of the Centre for Studies on Science, Technology and Society at the University of Twente.

Göran Therborn is a Director of the Swedish Collegium for Advanced Study in the Social Sciences at Uppsala.

Michael Thompson is Visiting Fellow at the James Martin Institute for Science and Civilization at the University of Oxford; Senior Researcher at the Stein Rokkan Centre, University of Bergen; and Institute Scholar at the International Institute for Applied Systems Analysis, Laxenburg, Austria.

Nigel J. Thrift is Professor of Geography and Pro-Vice-Chancellor (Research) at Oxford University.

Charles Tilly is Joseph L. Buttenwieser Professor of Social Science at Columbia University.

Marco Verweij is Associate Professor of Political Science at the Singapore Management University.

Judy Wajcman is Professor of Sociology in the Research School of Social Sciences, Australian National University.

R. Bin Wong is Professor of History and Director of the Asia Institute at UCLA.

PART I

INTRODUCTION

CHAPTER 1

....

IT DEPENDS

....

CHARLES TILLY
ROBERT E. GOODIN

1 OVERTURE

....

CAST of characters:

- Sivu, pseudonym for a peasant in Aurel Vlaicu (Vlaicu for short), a Transylvanian village of about 820 people living in 274 houses
- Agron, the local land commission's agronomist
- Map, the land commission's surveyor
- Com't, a member of the land commission from Vlaicu
- Katherine Verdery, American anthropologist and long-time observer of life in Vlaicu

Time: Spring 1994.

In 1994, the Romanian government and the people of Vlaicu faced a knotty problem: how to privatize the village collective farm set up under Romania's state socialism. Before socialism, Vlaicu had maintained its own form of private property with some collective controls over land, animals, and agricultural products. That system lasted until the Russian takeover of 1945. Between then and 1959, however, Romania's socialist authorities went from organizing cooperatives to coercing collectivization; they created both a state farm and a collective farm. In contrast to the government-owned and centrally managed state farm, Vlaicu's households acquired provisional shares of the collective farm's lands, on condition of using its facilities and producing their quotas of its crops.

Over the thirty years between 1959 and the collapse of Romanian socialism in 1989, numerous villagers whose families had previously held land left for city jobs, families that stayed in the village waxed or waned, and shares in the collective farm shifted accordingly. As the old regime collapsed, villagers often claimed the land they were then working, sold it, shared it with other family members, or passed it on to heirs. In 1994, then, the land commission had to decide which rights, whose rights, and as of what date, established claims to the land now being privatized. Hence the drama, as recorded in Verdery's field notes:

Sivu comes in and is very noisy about what terrible things he's going to do if his case isn't settled. He has a piece in Filigore, claims it must be measured, Map says it already has been—they repeat this several times. Map gets mad because people want remeasuring: "We'll never finish this job if people make us remeasure all the time!" One woman wants him to go measure in Lunca; he says, "We already did it there, if we have to go back we won't get out for two weeks." Sivu says loudly, "I don't want anything except what's *mine*!" He accosts Com't: "Look into my eyes, you're my godfather, I'm not asking for anything except what's *mine*. I bought it from Gheorghe, it's next to Ana and to Constantin. If you don't give it to me, I'll ... I'll do what no one's done in all of Vlaicu."   (Verdery 2003, 117)

The village drama enacts politics as most ordinary people experience politics most of the time: not as grand clashes of political theories or institutions, but as local struggle for rights, redress, protection, and advantage in relation to local officials. Here, as elsewhere, how political processes actually work and what outcomes they produce depend heavily on the contexts in which they occur.

Property figured centrally in the Vlaicu drama, but not as the abstract property of constitutions and treatises. Sivu bought Gheorghe's plot, which neighbored those of Ana and Constantin; he wanted the authorities to record and legitimate his right to exactly that piece of land. He insisted that the surveyor and the agronomist set down the land's boundaries so that Ana and Constantin (who may well have been encroaching on Gheorghe's parcel as they plowed) would recognize where their fields ended and his began. Looking on, professional political analysts witness an encounter about which they often theorize: between state-defined rights and obligations, on one side, and local social relations, on the other.

Political analysts are not, however, simply observing the clash of two discordant principles; they are watching the continuous creation and re-creation of rights through struggle. As Verdery (2003, 19) puts it, "I have proposed treating property as simultaneously a cultural system, a set of social relations, and an organization of power. They all come together in social processes." Verdery reports that in reckoning rights to collectivized property the Romanian government adopted a formal, genealogical conception of rights in land, ignoring who had actually worked various plots under socialism, who had invested care in older former proprietors, and so on. From the government's perspective, any individuals who occupied similar positions within the genealogy—two brothers, two cousins, two aunts—had equal rights to shares in privatizing property over which a household or kin group had a legal claim. That formalistic reasoning clashed with local moral codes. According to Verdery:

Villagers, however, had not understood kinship that way; for them, it was performative. To be kin meant *behaving* like kin. It meant cooperating to create marriage, baptismal and death rituals; putting flowers on relatives' graves; helping out with money or other favors; and caring for the elderly (who might not even be one's parents) in exchange for inheriting their land.   (Verdery 2003, 165)

When Sivu demanded what was rightfully his, he appealed to his godfather, the local commissioner, for confirmation of his rights. He was calling on a different code from the one written into Romanian national law.

In the case at hand, Verdery found that—to the dismay of most villagers—the actual distribution of privatized land reproduced the local hierarchy prevailing at the terminus of the socialist regime. The pyramid of land ownership ended up "with state farm directors at the top, collective farm staff below them, and village households at the bottom, holding very few resources for surviving in the new environment" (Verdery 2003, 11). As happened widely elsewhere in the collapse of state socialist regimes, people used their knowledge of the expiring system to capture their pieces of what remained (Solnick 1998). That fact offered tremendous advantages to people who had already been running factories, bureaucracies, security services, or state farms under socialism. But ordinary peasants also used memories, connections, arguments and threats as best they could.

2   CONTEXT MATTERS

Note the immediate importance of context. No one who imagined that privatization simply followed the laws of the market—or of the jungle—could describe or explain what actually happened: Through incessant negotiation, resources that had existed (or had come into being) under governmental control became private property. The negotiation, the character of the contested resources, the privatization process, Verdery's collection of evidence on all three, and our own capacity to describe and explain what was going on in Vlaicu at the time all depend on local and national context.

The context immediately in question here consisted chiefly of previously established relations between villagers and a variety of state officials. But as we step back from Vlaicu's local disputes toward the more general problem of relations between political power and property at large, we begin to see the relevance of other contexts: historical, institutional, cultural, demographic, technological, psychological, ideological, ontological, and epistemological. We cannot dismiss the question "What is property?" with Pierre-Joseph Proudhon's famous reply: "Property is theft." As analysts of political processes, we have no choice: we must place rights to resources in context.

Property obviously does not stand alone in this regard. Political scientists' inquiries into democratization and de-democratization, civil and international war, revolution and rebellion, nationalism, ethnic mobilization, political participation, parliamentary behavior, and effective government all raise contextual questions: when, where, in what settings, on what premises, with what understandings of the processes under investigation? Viable answers to questions of this sort require serious attention to the contexts in which the crucial political processes operate.

This handbook provides a survey of relevant contexts. Against the most reductive versions of parsimony, it argues that attention to context does not clutter the description and explanation of political processes, but, on the contrary, promotes systematic knowledge. Against the most exaggerated versions of postmodernism, it argues that context and contextual effects lend themselves to systematic description and explanation, hence their proper understanding facilitates discovery of true regularities in political processes. Between those extreme positions, it examines the multiple ways in which context affects analysts' understanding of political processes, the extent and sort of evidence available concerning political processes, and the very operation of political processes. In our brief introduction to the handbook's varied discussions of these issues, we concentrate on showing the importance for systematic political knowledge of getting context right.

Here is another way of putting our main point: In response to each big question of political science, we reply "It depends." Valid answers depend on the context in which the political processes under study occur. Valid answers depend triply on context, with regard to understandings built into the questions, with regard to the evidence available for answering the questions, and with regard to the actual operation of the political processes. We take this position not as a counsel of despair, but as a beacon of hope. We pursue the hope that political processes depend on context in ways that are themselves susceptible to systematic exploration and elaboration.

The hope applies both to description and to explanation. On the side of description, political scientists make significant contributions to knowledge simply by getting things right—developing reliable means of identifying the major actors in political conflicts, clarifying where and when different sorts of electoral systems succeed or fail, verifying the factual premises of governmental doctrines, and so on.

On the side of explanation, superior cause–effect accounts of political processes not only serve the advance of political science as a discipline but also permit more accurate forecasts of the effects likely to result from a given political intervention. Better description and explanation improve both theory and practice.

We have therefore organized the handbook to show how and why a variety of contexts matter to systematic description and explanation of political processes. The contexts that we and our contributors examine range from abstractly philosophical to concretely local. Together they allow us to distinguish three classes of contextual effects:

1. On analysts' understanding of political processes.
2. On the evidence available for empirical examination of political processes.
3. On the processes themselves.

Thus an analyst's understanding of electoral campaigns derives in part from the analyst's own involvement or lack of involvement in electoral campaigns, evidence concerning electoral campaigns comes in part from campaign participants' public declarations of who they are, and electoral campaigns vary significantly in form as a function of their locations in time and space. To be sure, the three interact: participant observation of electoral campaigns not only shapes the analyst's understanding and gives the analyst access to certain sorts of evidence other analysts can rarely acquire, but also makes the analyst a cause, however slight, of what actually happens in the election. Nevertheless, we will do well to maintain broad distinctions among the three kinds of contextual effects. The chapters that follow typically deal with one or two of them, but not all three at once.

2.1   Alternative Approaches

Although any thinking political analyst makes some allowances for context, two extreme positions on context have received surprisingly respectful attention from political scientists during recent decades: the search for general laws, and postmodern skepticism.

The Search for General Laws. On one side, we have context as noise, as interference in transmission of the signal we are searching for. In that view, we must clear away the effects of context in order to discover the true regularities in political processes. In a spirited, influential, and deftly conciliatory synthesis of quantitative and qualitative approaches to social science, Gary King, Robert Keohane, and Sidney Verba begin by making multiple concessions to complexity and interpretation, but end up arguing that the final test for good social science is its identification of casual effects, defined as:

the difference between the systematic component of observations made when the explanatory variable takes one value and the systematic component of comparable observations when the explanatory variable takes on another value. (King, Keohane, and Verba 1994, 82)

This seemingly bland claim turns out to be the thin edge of the wedge, the camel's nose under the tent, or the elephant in the room—choose your metaphor! It initiates a remarkable series of moves including the assimilation of scientific inference to the world-view contained in statistics based on the general linear model, assumption that the fundamental causes of political processes do, indeed, consist of variables, consequent rejection of mechanisms as causes, and advice for making small-N studies look more like large-N studies, all of which commit the authors more firmly to explanation as the identification of general laws that encompass particular cases.

Postmodern Skepticism. On the other side, we have context as the very object of political analysis, the complex, elusive phenomenon we must interpret as best we can. In this second view, the first view's "regularities" become illusions experienced by political interpreters who have not yet realized that systematic knowledge is impossible and that they only think otherwise because they have fallen victim to their own immersion in a particular context. Anthropologist Clifford Geertz has written some of the most eloquent and influential statements of the view; indeed, King, Keohane, and Verba (1994, 38–40) quote Geertz's ideas as an often-cited but even more often misunderstood objection to their own approach. Here is Geertz on how law works:

Law, I have been saying, somewhat against the pretensions encoded in woolsack rhetoric, is local knowledge; local not just as to place, time, class and variety of issue, but as to accent—vernacular characterizations of what happens connected to vernacular imaginings of what can. It is this complex of characterizations and imaginings, stories about events cast in imagery about principles, that I have been calling a legal sensibility. This is doubtless more than a little vague, but as Wittgenstein, the patron saint of what is going on here, remarked, a veridical picture of an indistinct object is not after all a clear one but an indistinct one. Better to paint the sea like Turner than attempt to make of it a Constable cow.   (Geertz 1983, 215)

Much more fun than the "systematic component of comparable observations," Geertz's argument comes close to saying that the systematic component does not exist, and would not be worth looking for if it did. Like the King–Keohane–Verba manual, this handbook came into existence largely because political analysts steeped in Geertzian skepticism have offered serious objections to standard social scientific portrayals of political processes, but have not—sometimes on principle—systematized their knowledge of context, cultural variability, and social construction (Hacking 1999). It ends up, however, much more concerned about those objections than King, Keohane, and Verba.

Something in Between. Political scientists rarely line up in disciplined armies under the banners of General Laws and Skepticism to do open battle with each other. Yet the two flags define the limits of a terrain across which political analysts regularly deploy their forces. From differing bases within the terrain, polemicists often venture out for struggle to control one piece or another of the territory. Some observers speak of choices between positivism and constructivism, between covering laws and hermeneutics, between general and local knowledge, or between reductionism and holism. Regardless of the terminology, at one end of the range we find claims for universal principles that cut across particular social contexts, at the other claims that attempts to describe and explain political phenomena have no means of escaping particular social contexts.

Certainly limiting cases exist in which each approach applies in a relatively extreme form. On the one hand, seekers of General Laws can sometimes find fairly robust law-like regularities. Consider the relationship between inflation and un-employment traced by the Phillips Curve (at least the shape of that curve seems constant, even if its actual values have to be recalibrated in every period: Friedman 1977). Another might be Duverger's Law: how plurality voting rules give rise to and sustain two-party electoral systems (Riker 1982). We can also sometimes find clear cases where the acts in question are literally constituted by speech and the shared understandings embodied in it; constitution writing provides a compelling example (Searle 1969, 1995; Skinner 1969, 2002; Tully 1988). Political actors weave legal fictions like sovereignty of just such stuff (Walker 1993; Wendt 1999). Around them, distinctive "standpoints," perspectives, and discourses of different social groupings coalesce.[1] If part of what exists in our world, ontologically, comes into being through these sorts of social construction, then we need an epistemology suited to understanding those mechanisms of social construction—the "how" of constructivism rather than merely the "if ... then" of positivism, "knowing how" rather than merely "knowing that" (Ryle 1949; Foucault 1981; Rose and Miller 1992).

Although we can clearly find cases where one or the other approach captures the whole story, more typically some mixed strategy is required (Archer et al. 1998; Hay 2002, ch. 3). Most of this handbook's chapters offer arguments, at least implicitly, in defense of one position within the range and against others. Readers who consult the handbook on the way to pursuing their own descriptions and explanations of political processes face the same choices. But we hope that having been duly sensitized to the effects of context, none of our readers will ever again find themselves in the position of Ashford's (1992, 27) "analyst of French communal budgets [who], laboring to extend a data bank to 1871, was mystified [by the paucity of data] until someone told him of the Franco-Prussian War."

---

[1] See e.g. Smith 1987; Antony and Witt 1993; Hajer 1995; Finnemore and Sikkink 2001; Jackson 2004.

2.2   Ontologies

Leaving much finer distinctions to the handbook's contributors, let us distinguish three aspects of the unavoidable choices: ontology, explanatory logic, and mechanisms. Within political science, major *ontological* choices concern the sorts of social entities whose coherent existence analysts can reasonably assume. Major alternatives include holism, methodological individualism, phenomenological individualism, and relational realism. *Holism* is the doctrine that social structures have their own self-sustaining logics. In its extreme form—once quite common in political science but now unfashionable—a whole civilization, society, or culture undergoes a life of its own. Less extreme versions attribute self-reproducing powers to major institutions, treat certain segments of society as subordinating the rest to their interests, represent dominant mentalities, traditions, values, or cultural forms as regulators of social life, or assign inherent self-reproducing logics to industrialism, capitalism, feudalism, and other distinguishable varieties of social organization.

Methodological individualism insists on human individuals as the basic or unique social reality. It not only focuses on persons, one at a time, but imputes to each person a set of intentions that cause the person's behavior. In more economistic versions of methodological individualism, the person in question contains a utility schedule and a set of assets, which interact to generate choices within well-defined constraints. In every such analysis, to be sure, figures a market-like allocative structure that operates externally to the choice-making individual—but it is astonishing how rarely methodological individualists examine by what means those allocative structures actually do their work.

The less familiar term *phenomenological individualism* refers to the doctrine that individual consciousness is the primary or exclusive site of social life. Phenomenological individualism veers into solipsism when its adherents argue that adjacent minds have no access to each other's contents, therefore no observer can escape the prison of her own awareness. Even short of that analytically self-destructive position, phenomenological individualists tend to regard states of body and mind—impulses, reflexes, desires, ideas, or programs—as the chief motors of social action. In principle, they have two ways to account for large-scale political structures and processes: (1) as summed individual responses to similar situations; (2) as distributions and/or connections among individual actions.

In the first case, political scientists sometimes constitute collective actors consisting of all the individuals within a category such as peasant or woman. In the second case, they take a leaf from those political scientists who see national political life as a meeting-place, synthesis, and outcome of that shifting distribution of attitudes we call public opinion or from the social psychologists who see individual X's action as providing a stimulus for individual Y's action. Even there, they hold to the conception of human consciousness as the basic site of social life.

Relational realism, the doctrine that transactions, interactions, social ties, and conversations constitute the central stuff of social life, once predominated in social science. Classical economists, Karl Marx, Max Weber, and Georg Simmel all emphasized social relations, regarding both individuals and complex social structures as products of regularities in social relations. During the twentieth century, however, relational realism lost much of its ground to individualism and holism. Only in American pragmatism, various versions of network analysis, and some corners of organizational or labor economics did it prevail continuously. Only with the breakdown of structural Marxism has it once again come to the fore elsewhere. Relational realism concentrates on connections that concatenate, aggregate, and disaggregate readily, forming organizational structures at the same time as they shape individual behavior. Relational analysts follow flows of communication, patron–client chains, employment networks, conversational connections, and power relations from the small scale to the large and back. A case in point is the way in which democracy emerged through networks of workers forming and reforming effervescent "workers commissions" in the interstices of the rigid, formal mechanisms of corporatist intermediation in Franco's Spain (Foweraker 1989).

Intellectual genetic engineers can, of course, create hybrids of the four basic ontologies. A standard combination of phenomenological individualism and holism portrays a person in confrontation with society, each of the elements and their very confrontation having its own laws. Methodological individualists usually assume the presence of a self-regulating market or other allocative institution. Individualists vary in how much they allow for emergents—structures that result from individual actions but once in existence exert independent effects on individual actions, much as music-lovers enter a concert hall one by one, only to see the audience's distribution through the hall affect both the orchestra's performance and their own reactions to it. Relational analysts commonly allow for partly autonomous individual processes as well as strong effects on interaction by such collectively created structures as social categories and centralized organizations. Nevertheless, the four ontologies lead to rather different accounts of political processes.

They also suggest distinctive starting points for analysis. A holist may eventually work her way to the individuals that live within a given system or the social relations that connect individuals with the system, but her starting point is likely to be some observation of the system as a whole. Methodological individualists can treat social ties as products of individual calculation, but above all they must specify relevant individual actors before launching their analyses. Phenomenological individualists likewise give priority to individuals, with the two qualifications that (1) their individuals are sites of consciousness rather than of calculating intentions and (2) they frequently move rapidly to shared states of awareness, at the limit attributing shared orientations to all members of a population. Relational realists may begin with existing social ties, but to be consistent and effective they should actually start with transactions among social sites, then watch when and how transactions bundle into more durable, substantial, and/or consequential relations among sites.

2.3   Explanatory Strategies

As this book's individual chapters illustrate amply, some of political science's fiercest disagreements involve *logics of explanation*. At the risk of fierce disagreement, let us distinguish five competing positions: skepticism, law-seeking accounts, propensity analyses, systemic analyses, and mechanism-based accounts. *Skepticism* considers political processes to be so complex, contingent, impenetrable, or particular as to defy explanation. Short of an extreme position, however, even a skeptic can hope to describe, interpret, or assign meaning to processes that are complex, contingent, particular, and relatively impenetrable. Thus political science skeptics continue to describe, interpret, and assign meaning to the Soviet Union's collapse without claiming to have explained that momentous process.

Law-seeking accounts consider explanation to consist of subjecting robust empirical generalizations to higher and higher-level generalizations, the most general of all standing as laws. In such accounts models are invariant, i.e. work the same in all conditions. Investigators search for necessary and sufficient conditions of stipulated outcomes, those outcomes often conceived of as "dependent variables." Studies of co-variation among presumed causes and presumed effects therefore serve as validity tests for proposed explanations; investigators in this tradition sometimes invoke John Stuart Mill's (1843) Methods of Agreement, Differences, Residues, and Concomitant Variation, despite Mill's own doubts of their applicability to human affairs. Thus some students of democratization hope to state the general conditions under which any non-democratic polity whatsoever becomes democratic.

In contemporary political science, however, few analysts propose flat laws in the form "All Xs are Y." Instead, two modified versions of law-seeking explanations predominate. The first lays out a principle of variation, often stated as a probability. The proposed law often takes the form "The more X, the more Y"—for example, the higher national income the more prevalent and irreversible is democracy.[2] In this case, the empirical demonstration often rests on identifying a partial derivative that stands up robustly to "controls" for such contextual matters as region and predominant religion. The second common version of law-seeking explanations consists instead of identifying necessary and/or sufficient conditions for some

---

[2] As argued, variously, by Burkhart and Lewis-Beck 1994; Muller 1995; Przeworski, Alvarez, Cheibub, and Limongi 2000.

outcome such as revolution, democracy, or civil war, typically through comparison of otherwise similar positive and negative cases (Ragin 1994).

Propensity accounts consider explanation to consist of reconstructing a given actor's state at the threshold of action, with that state variously stipulated as motivation, consciousness, need, organization, or momentum. The actors in question may be individuals, but analysts often construct propensity accounts of organizations or other collective actors. Explanatory methods of choice then range from sympathetic interpretation to reductionism, psychological or otherwise. Thus some students of contentious politics compare the experiences of different social groupings with structural adjustment in an effort to explain why some groupings resist, others suffer in silence, and still others disintegrate under pressure (Auyero 2003; Walton and Seddon 1994).

Although authors of law-seeking and propensity accounts sometimes talk of systems, *systemic* explanations strictly speaking consist of specifying a place for some event, structure, or process within a larger self-maintaining set of interdependent elements, showing how the event, structure, or process in question serves and/or results from interactions among the larger set of elements. Functional explanations typically qualify, since they account for the presence or persistence of some element by its functions—its positive consequences for some coherent larger set of social relations or processes. Nevertheless, systemic accounts can avoid functionalism by making more straightforward arguments about the effects of certain kinds of relations to larger systems. Thus some students of peasant revolt explain its presence or absence by peasants' degree of integration into society as a whole.

Mechanism-based accounts select salient features of episodes, or significant differences among episodes, and explain them by identifying within those episodes robust mechanisms of relatively general scope. As compared with law-seeking, propensity, and system approaches, mechanism-based explanations aim at modest ends: selective explanation of salient features by means of partial causal analogies. Thus some students of nationalism try relating its intensity to the extent and character of competition among ethnic entrepreneurs. In such accounts, the entrepreneurs' competition for political constituencies becomes a central (but not exclusive or sufficient) mechanism in the generation of nationalism.

Systemic explanations still recur in international relations, where the views called "realism" generally attribute great causal efficacy to locations of individual states within the international system. Otherwise, they have lost ground in political science since the heyday of David Easton's *Political System* (1953). When today's political scientists fight about explanation, however, they generally pit law-seeking against propensity accounts, with the first often donning the costume of Science and the second the garb of Interpretation. (Nevertheless, the search for microfoundations in rational choice approaches to political science involves a deliberate attempt to locate general laws in the choice-making propensities of individuals.) Explanation by means of robust causal mechanisms has received much less self-conscious attention from social science methodologists than have law-seeking, propensity, and systemic explanations. Let us therefore say a bit more about mechanistic explanations.

2.4 Mechanisms

Satisfactory law-seeking accounts require not only broad empirical uniformities but also mechanisms that cause those uniformities.[3] For all its everyday employment in natural science, the term "mechanism" rarely appears in social-scientific explanations. Its rarity probably results partly from the term's disquieting suggestion that social processes operate like clockwork, but mainly from its uneasy coexistence with its explanatory competitors: skepticism, law-seeking accounts, propensity analyses, and systemic analyses.

Without much self-conscious justification, most political scientists recognize one or another of these—especially individual or group dispositions—as genuine explanations. They grow uneasy when someone identifies mechanisms as explanations. Even sympathetic analysts often distinguish between mechanisms as "how" social processes work and dispositions as "why" they work. As a practical matter, however, social scientists often refer to mechanisms as they construct partial explanations of complex structures or processes. Mechanisms often make anonymous appearances when political scientists identify parallels within classes of complex structures or processes. In the study of contentious politics, for example, analysts frequently invoke the mechanisms of brokerage and coalition formation (McAdam, Tarrow, and Tilly 2001). If those mechanisms appear in essentially the same form with the same small-scale consequences across a wide range of circumstances, we can call them "robust."

How will we know them when we see them? We choose a level of observation: individual thoughts, individual actions, social interactions, clusters of interactions, durable social ties, or something else. At that level of observation, we can recognize as robust social mechanisms those events that:

1. Involve indistinguishably similar transfers of energy among stipulated social elements.
2. Produce indistinguishably similar rearrangements of those social elements.
3. Do so across a wide range of circumstances.

The "elements" in question may be persons, but they also include aspects of persons (e.g. their jobs), recurrent actions of persons (e.g. their amusements), transactions

---

[3] As emphasized in different ways by: Brady 1995; Laitin 1995; Tilly 2000; 2001; cf. King, Keohane, and Verba 1994.

among persons (e.g. Internet communications between colleagues), and configurations of interaction among persons (e.g. shifting networks of friendship).

To the extent that mechanisms become uniform and universal, their identification starts to resemble a search for general laws. Yet two big differences intervene between law-seeking and mechanism-based explanations. First, practitioners of mechanistic explanation generally deny that any strong, interesting recurrences of large-scale social structures and processes occur.[4] They therefore deny that it advances inquiry to seek law-like empirical generalizations—at whatever level of abstraction—by comparing big chunks of history. Second, while mechanisms have uniform immediate effects by definition, depending on initial conditions and combinations with other mechanisms, their aggregate, cumulative, and longer-term effects vary considerably. Thus brokerage operates uniformly by definition, always connecting at least two social sites more directly than they were previously connected. Yet the activation of brokerage does not in itself guarantee more effective coordination of action at the connected sites; that depends on initial conditions and combinations with other mechanisms.

Let us adopt a simple distinction among mechanisms, processes, and episodes:

- *Mechanisms* form a delimited class of events that change relations among specified sets of elements in identical or closely similar ways over a variety of situations.
- *Processes* are frequently occurring combinations or sequences of mechanisms.
- *Episodes* are continuous streams of social life.

Social mechanisms concatenate into social processes: combinations and sequences of mechanisms producing relatively similar effects. A process we might call identity enlargement, for example, consists of broadening and increasing uniformity in the collective answers given by some set of persons to the question, "Who are you?" Identity enlargement typically results from interaction of two mechanisms: brokerage and social appropriation—the latter activating previously existing connections among subsets of the persons in question. Thus in collective action, enlargement of relevant identities from neighborhood membership to city-wide solidarity emerges from the concatenation of brokerage with social appropriation.

Mechanisms and processes compound into episodes, bounded and connected sequences of social action. Episodes sometimes acquire social significance as such because participants or observers construct names, boundaries, and stories corresponding to them: this revolution, that emigration, and so on. More often, however, analysts chop continuous streams of social life into episodes according to conventions of their own making, thus delineating generations, social movements, fads,

---

[4] See e.g. Bunge 1997; Elster 1999; Hedström and Swedberg 1998; Little 1998; Stinchcombe 1991; Tilly 2000.

and the like. The manner in which episodes acquire shared meanings deserves close study. But we have no a priori warrant to believe that episodes grouped by similar criteria spring from similar causes. In general, analysts of mechanisms and processes begin with the opposite assumption. For them, uniformly identified episodes provide convenient frames for comparison, but with an eye to detecting crucial mechanisms and processes within them. Choice of episodes, however, crucially affects the effectiveness of such a search. It makes a large difference, for example, whether students of generational effects distinguish generations by means of arbitrary time periods or presumably critical events.

Mechanisms, too, entail choices. A rough classification identifies three sorts of mechanism: environmental, cognitive, and relational:

- *Environmental mechanisms* mean externally generated influences on conditions affecting social life; words like "disappear," "enrich," "expand," and "disintegrate"—applied not to actors but their settings—suggest the sorts of cause–effect relations in question.
- *Cognitive mechanisms* operate through alterations of individual and collective perception; words like "recognize," "understand," "reinterpret," and "classify" characterize such mechanisms.
- *Relational mechanisms* alter connections among people, groups, and interpersonal networks; words like "ally," "attack," "subordinate," and "appease" give a sense of relational mechanisms.

Here we begin to detect affinities among ontologies, explanatory strategies, and preferred mechanisms. Methodological individualists, for example, commonly adopt propensity accounts of social behavior and privilege cognitive mechanisms as they do so. Holists lean toward environmental mechanisms, as relational realists give special attention to relational mechanisms. Those affinities are far from absolute, however. Many a phenomenological individualist, for example, weaves accounts in which environmental mechanisms such as social disintegration generate cognitive mechanisms having relational consequences in their turn. In principle, many permutations of ontology, explanatory strategy, and preferred mechanisms should be feasible.

Review of mechanisms identifies some peculiarities of rational choice theory's claims to constitute a—or even *the*—general explanation of social life. Rational choice theory centers on situations of choice among relatively well-defined alternative actions with more or less known costs and consequences according to previously established schedules of preference. It focuses attention on mental processes, and therefore on cognitive mechanisms.

From that focus stem three problems: upstream, midstream, and downstream. Upstream, rational choice theory lacks a plausible account of how preferences, available resources, choice situations, and knowledge of consequences form or change. Midstream, the theory incorporates a dubious account of how people make decisions when they actually confront situations of choice among relatively well defined alternative actions with more or less known costs and consequences according to previously established schedules of preference. Both observational and experimental evidence challenge the rational choice midstream account, confining its scope to very special conditions (Kahneman 2003). Those special conditions rest on historically developed knowledge, preferences, practices, and institutions (Kuran 1991, 1995). They depend on context.

Downstream, the theory lacks an account of consequences, in two senses of the word. First, considering how rarely we human beings execute actions with the flair we would prefer, the theory leaves unclear what happens between a person's choice to do something and the same person's action in response to that choice. Second, considering how rarely we human beings anticipate precisely the effects of our less-than-perfect actions, it likewise remains unclear what links the theory's rationally chosen actions to concrete consequences in social life. In fact, error, unintended consequences, cumulative but relatively invisible effects, indirect effects, and environmental reverberations occur widely in social life. Any theory that fails to show how such effects of human action occur loses its claim to generality.

3   The Nature of Social Explanation

3.1   Explanatory Stories

In dealing with social life in general and political processes in particular, we face a circumstance that distinguishes most of social science from most other scientific inquiries: the prominent place of explanatory stories in social life (Ryan 1970). Explanatory stories provide simplified cause–effect accounts of puzzling, unexpected, dramatic, problematic, or exemplary events. Relying on widely available knowledge rather than technical expertise, they help make the world intelligible. They often carry an edge of justification or condemnation. They qualify as a special sort of narrative, which a standard manual on narrative defines as "the representation of an event or a series of events" (Abbott 2002, 12). This particular variety of narrative includes actors, their actions, and effects produced by those actions. The story usually gives pride of place to human actors. When the leading characters are not human—for example, when they are animals, spirits, organizations, or features of the physical environment such as storms—they still behave mostly like humans. The story they enact accordingly often conveys credit or blame.

Political science's explanatory stories generally reify collective agents and arti-facts—states (Allison and Zelikow 1999), parties (Lawson 1990; Strøm 2001), classes, societies, and corporations. They treat them as if they were unified inten-tional agents, with goals of their own and the capacity to pursue them, and who therefore should be held to the same standards of credit and blame. The ubiquity of explanatory stories in everyday life makes the logical slippage all the easier.

Of course, even natural scientists resort to explanatory stories, at least in telling their tales to lay audiences: this ball hit that, and then that in turn; this electron got excited and jumped into a higher shell; this infectious agent penetrated that cell's membrane. And in those explanatory stories that natural scientists tell lay audi-ences, objects in the story are anthropomorphized and ascribed a sort of quasi-agency. Sophisticated observers might balk at that way of talking about objects they know to be inanimate or with no will of their own. But couching our explanations in terms of such stories comes quite naturally in the human sciences, where we are confident that the actors are genuine agents with wills of their own, however constrained they may be in acting on them.

Aristotle's *Poetics* presented one of the West's first great analyses of explanatory stories. Speaking of tragedy, which he singled out as the noblest form of creative writing, Aristotle described the two versions of a proper plot:

Plots are either simple or complex, since the actions they represent are naturally of this twofold description. The action, proceeding in the way defined, as one continuous whole, I call simple, when the change in the hero's fortunes takes place without Peripety or Discovery; and complex, when it involves one or the other, or both. These should each of them arise out of the structure of the Plot itself, so as to be the consequence, necessary or probable, of the antecedents. There is a great difference between a thing happening *propter hoc* and *post hoc*.   (Aristotle 1984, 1452a)

A "peripety," for Aristotle, was a complete reversal of a state, as when the messenger who comes to comfort Oedipus actually reveals to him the identities of his father and mother. A "discovery" was a fateful change from ignorance to knowledge, an awful or wonderful recognition of something previously concealed; in the story of Oedipus, a discovery (the messenger's announcement) produced a peripety (Oedi-pus' unmasking as a man who killed his father and bedded his mother). Aristotle caught the genius of the explanatory story: one or a few actors, a limited number of actions that cause further actions through altered states of awareness, continuity in space and time, an overall structure leading to some outcome or lesson.

By attributing their main effects to specific actors (even when those actors are unseen and/or divine), explanatory stories follow common rules of individual respon-sibility: X did it, and therefore deserves the praise or blame for what happened as a result. Their dramatic structure separates them from conventional giving of reasons: traffic was heavy, my watch stopped, I have a bad cold, today's my lucky day, and so on. In fact, explanatory stories more closely resemble classical dramas. They generally maintain unity of time and place instead of jumping among temporal and geographic settings. They involve limited casts of characters whose visible actions cause all the subsequent actions and their major effects. They often have a moral. On the whole, however, they represent causal processes very badly: they radically reify and simplify the relevant actors, actions, causes, and effects while disregarding indirect effects, environmental effects, incremental effects, errors, unanticipated consequences, and simultaneous causation (Mills 1940; Scott and Lyman 1968; Ross 1977).

Many political scientists implicitly recognize the inadequacy of explanatory stories for political phenomena by adopting formal representations whose causal logics break decisively with the logic of storytelling: multidimensional scaling, simultaneous equations, input-output tables, syntactic analyses of texts, and much more. These non-narrative models, however, prevail much more regularly in the processing of evidence than in either the initial framing of arguments or the final interpretation of results. At those two ends, explanatory stories continue to predominate.

Explanatory stories matter visibly, even vitally to our study of context. They intervene in all three sorts of contextual effect:

- Analysts' understanding of political processes commonly takes the form of stories; as teachers of formal modeling soon learn, it takes heroic efforts to produce students who do not customarily cast descriptions and explanations as stories and who habitually recognize simultaneous equations or flow charts as helpful representations of political processes.
- Evidence concerning political processes arrives in the form of stories told by participants, observers, respondents, journalists, historians, or other political analysts; even survey research regularly transforms respondents' stories into a questionnaire's fixed alternatives.
- Storytelling frequently looms large within important political processes; just think of how nationalists, revolutionaries, and candidates for public office wield stories about who they are and what they are doing.

Thus one important element of getting context right consists of identifying, describing, and explaining the operation of explanatory stories.

3.2 Other Elements of Context

Of course, other influences than the prevalence of explanatory stories produce contextual effects on our knowledge of political processes. As contributors to this volume show in detail, assumptions built into non-story models likewise deeply affect political scientists' acquisition of knowledge. The bulk of the statistics routinely used by political scientists, for example, assume a world of linear relationships among discrete variables that in nature conform to regular distributions.

Once again the influence of those assumptions appears in all three varieties of contextual effect: shaping analysts' understandings of how the world works, pervading the practices of data collection and measurement employed by analysts, and fitting political phenomena themselves with widely varying degrees of appropriateness (Jackson 1996; Jervis 1997; Kuran 1991, 1995).

Other contributors alert us to a quite different source of contextual effects: the fact that political structures and processes have constraining histories. Participants in revolutions emulate earlier revolutions, acquire legitimacy or illegitimacy from those earlier revolutions, and use institutions, ideas, organizations, and social relations set in place by those earlier revolutions. Electoral contests generate laws, memories, rifts, and alliances that affect subsequent elections. Property rights gain historical force through long use even when they originate in outright predation or deceit.

Our stress on context meshes badly with the view that the ultimate aim of political science is to identify general laws of political process that cut across the details of time, place, circumstance, and previous history. Often political scientists seek to specify extremely general necessary or sufficient conditions for some phenomenon such as democracy or polarization. The specification often concerns co-variation: How X varies as a function of Y.

On that issue, we take three provisional positions (not necessarily shared by all of this *Handbook*'s contributors):

- *First*, the program of identifying simple general laws concerning political structures and processes has so far yielded meager results. It has most likely done so because its logical underpinnings and routine practices conform badly to the way politics actually works.
- *Second*, what strength that program of seeking simple general laws has achieved lies in its identification of empirical regularities to be explained, not in its provision or verification of explanations.
- *Third*, regularities certainly occur in political life, but not at the scale of whole structures and processes. Political scientists should shift their attention away from empirically grounded general laws to repeated processes, and toward efficacious causal mechanisms that operate at multiple scales but produce their aggregate effects through their concatenation, sequences, and interaction with initial conditions.

4   CONTEXT AS PIECES OF A PUZZLE

Explanatory stories are offered in response to puzzlement. Why do Southeast Asian peasants refuse to plant "wonder rice," when its average yield is so much greater?

Because the variability of yield is also greater, and peasants living at the margins of subsistence cannot afford a bad harvest in even a single year (Scott 1976). Why did Margaret Thatcher retain her popularity while presiding over a period of unprecedented economic decline? Because Britons had expected the decline to be even more severe (Alt 1979). Why did Gorbachev do so little to stop the collapse of Communism in Eastern Europe? Perhaps because he was incompetent or the world was just too complicated; but more plausibly because "decisive inaction" was an effective way to shed the Soviet Union's strategically irrelevant and economically costly client states, despite the internal factions that profited from them (Anderson 2001).

As actors, when choosing our own actions, we are highly sensitive to the peculiarities of our own particular desires and the rich particulars of our own mental processes. But in trying to make sense of the social world, we tend (at least as a first approximation) to impute to others broadly the same sort of psychology, broadly the same sorts of beliefs and desires, that we ourselves possess. Not only are we "folk psychologists" (Jackson and Pettit 1990; Pettit 1996); we are also "folk situationalists," assuming (until further investigation reveals otherwise) that the context in which others are acting is broadly the same as our own.[5] When that model fails to fit, we go looking for which bits are to blame: in what ways the actors, or situations, are peculiar. We "make sense" of an otherwise puzzling phenomenon by finding some special features about it which, when taken into account, allow us to assimilate that case to our standard model of how the world works (Grofman 2001).

Sometimes what we need to solve the puzzle is a relatively simple piece of information. To understand why politics takes the peculiar form it does in Senegal, we need to understand that the primary connotation of "demokaraasi" is not so much competition as solidarity (Schaffer 1998). To understand why Kerala is so far ahead of the rest of India and indeed the whole developing world, when it comes to female literacy and related aspects of social progress (Drèze and Sen 1995), it helps to know that Kerala was historically a matrilineal society. To understand why there was so little take-up of Keynesianism in interwar France, we need to understand that there was already a rich "tradition of government measures to alleviate unemployment that went back to at least 1848, ... closely related to the self-understanding of the republican order in general" (Wagner 2003; see further Rosanvallon 1989).

---

[5] The latter is one source (among many: see Gilbert and Malone 1995) of what social psychologists know as the "fundamental attribution bias." Experimental subjects are much more likely to attribute other people's "odd" behavior to discreditable attitudes and dispositions, rather than to assume that there must have been some peculiar situational factors at work, in the absence of any particular information about those other people. When subjects are told of the particular constraints under which others' "odd" behavior was generated, they are much more mixed in that judgment (Jones and Harris 1967, 6; Gilbert, Pelham, and Krull 1988).

Sometimes what we need to appreciate is how the situation looks from the actor's perspective, the actor's "frame" or "standpoint."[6] Other times what we need to appreciate are the options and constraints on action, structures thus channelling agency (Wendt 1987; Hay 2002, ch. 3). Those structures themselves often represent the accretion of past practice, ways of doing things and ways of seeing things that have grown up over time, under the intentional or unintentional influence of agents who stood to benefit from those ways of doing or seeing things (Bourdieu 1977; Foucault 1981).

Yet other times what we have to understand is "agency gone wrong." Sometimes the explanation is simply that intentional actors did something stupid, or something that seemed like a good idea but that backfired, perhaps because of misinformation, miscommunication, or the contrary intentions of other intentional agents. Stories couched in terms of the "unintended consequences of purposive social action" (Merton 1936) are very much explanatory stories with human intention at their heart. We cannot understand what "went wrong" without understanding what they were *trying* to do.

In the process of puzzle-solving, generalists and contextualists proceed in surprisingly similar and ultimately complementary ways. Where one starts leaves a residue, and it shapes one's presentation at the margins. Those who start from the more formal, abstract end of the continuum couch their discussion in one language, that of technical terminology and formal representations (Bates et al. 1998*a* and *b*; Strøm 2001); those who start from the more nuanced end of the continuum tend more toward "thick description" (Geertz 1973, ch. 1). But neither type of craft can do its work without at least *some* of the other's kit.

Popkin's (1979) account of peasant behavior, however "rationalist," nonetheless needs to be firmly rooted in situational aspects of Southeast Asian peasant existence. Equally, Scott's competing account of peasant behavior (1976), however rooted in particulars of Southeast Asian peasant culture, nevertheless must appeal to general ways of understanding the world that we too share. Contextualist narratives must be "analytical" in that minimal sense, if they are to be intelligible to us at all. Conversely, rational choice theorists must "acknowledge that their approach requires a complete political anthropology" and that they "must 'soak and poke' and acquire much the same depth of understanding as that achieved by those who offer 'thick' descriptions" (Bates et al. 1998*b*, 628; see further Bates et al. 1998*a*; Ferejohn 1991, 281). In that sense, at least, the "rational choice wars" within political science seem considerably overblown, however problematic we otherwise might find the bolder claims of rational-choice modelers.[7]

---

[6] On "frames" see Kahneman 2003; Kahneman and Tversky 2000; Kahneman, Slovic, and Tversky 1982. On "standpoints" see Smith 1987; Antony and Witt 1993.

[7] Key texts in that controversy are Green and Shapiro 1994; Friedman 1996; Monroe 2004.

Some advocates anxiously seek explanations that are *simple* in form, others ones that are *general* in their applicability. Concrete explanation, however, typically requires compromise. We might be able to find a valid law that is relatively simple in form (in the sense that it has few subordinate clauses), provided we confine its range of application sufficiently narrowly; alternatively, we might be able to find some valid law that is relatively general in its applicability, provided we are prepared to make it sufficiently complex by writing lots of "if" clauses into it. Naturally, if we go too far down the latter track, writing *all* the particulars of the case at hand into our "if" clauses, we end up not with an explanation of the phenomenon but rather with a mere redescription of the same phenomenon. That is a pointless exercise; if that is all social science can do, then it becomes intellectually redundant and socially ineffectual (Walby 1992; cf. Flyvbjerg 2001). But we must not be overly fond of Occam's razor, either. Explanatory accounts that are too stark, providing too little insight into the actual mechanisms at work, might predict but they cannot truly explain (cf. Friedman 1953). If we want explanations that are of general applicability, then we simply must be prepared to complicate our explanations a little by indexing more to context as necessary. Any sensible social scientist should surely agree (King, Keohane, and Verba 1994, 20, 29–30, 104).

5   CONTEXT IN ITS PLACE

The variety of different contexts in which political action occurs is, for some, a cherished part of the rich tapestry of political life. For others bent on the pursuit of parsimonious generalizations, contextual effects subvert their ambitions toward austerity. Still, acount for them they must. They can do so in either of two ways: by designing their studies in such a way as to "control for context," in effect eliminating contextual variability in their studies; or they can try to "correct for context," taking systematic account of how different contexts might actually matter to the phenomena under study. The latter is obviously a more ambitious strategy. But even the former requires rich contextual knowledge, if only of what contexts might matter in order to bracket them out in the research design.

5.1   Controlling for Context

Some wit described the field of study known as "American politics" as "area studies for the linguistically challenged." It can also be a refuge for the contextually tone-deaf. It is not as if American politics is context-free, of course. It is merely that, operating within a large internal market where broadly the same context is widely shared, context can by and large be taken for granted and pushed into the background.

Of course, even within a single country and a single period, context matters. In generalizing about *The American Voter*, Campbell et al. (1960, ch. 15) had to admit that farmers were different—the best predictor of their votes being, not party identification like the rest of Americans, but rather the price received for last year's crop. So too were Southern politics different, at least in the era of the one-party South (Key 1949). And of course even in country contexts that we think we know well, we are still capable of being surprised: American political development looks very different once you notice the lingering effects there of the feudal law of masters and servants (Orren 1991; Steinfeld 2001).

Still, by focusing on a country where so much of the context is familiar to both writers and readers, most of the context can remain unspoken most of the time. Comparative US state politics is often said to be a wonderful natural experiment, in that sense, in which federalism means that a few things vary while so much of the background is held constant.

Controlling for context does not mean ignoring context, though. We need to know what aspects of context might matter, to make sure that they do indeed hold constant in the situation under study. What things have to be controlled for, in order to get the limited sorts of generalizations in which social scientists such as Campbell et al. (1960) pride themselves? Well, all those that this *Handbook* covers: philosophical self-understandings of society, psychology, culture, history, demography, technology, and so on. As long as none of those things actually vary among the cases you are considering, then you are safe to ignore them.

Ideally, you should use that as a diagnostic checklist in advance. But you can also use it as a troubleshooting guide, after the fact. If generalizations fail you, running down that checklist might be a good place to start in trying to figure out why. Which bit of the contextual ground has shifted under your feet?

In many interesting cases, those factors are pretty well held constant. But even in single-country studies of limited duration, there are cultural differences, rooted in history, that matter. Remember V. O. Key on *Southern Politics* (1949). Every time we put an "urban/rural" variable into an equation predicting voting behavior we are gesturing toward a contextual factor (demographic or perhaps technological) that affects the phenomenon under study.

In cross-national and/or cross-time comparisons, especially, contextual variation always forms a large part of the explanation. Different cleavages have been frozen into different party systems, over time (Lipset and Rokkan 1967). There are different levels of technological development, different demographic divisions that are socially salient (Patterson 1975).

5.2   Correcting for Context

Where context varies, we have to take those differences into account, as systematically as possible. We do not have, and cannot realistically aspire to, any perfectly general laws telling us fully when and how each of those contextual factors will affect the life of a society. But we can aspire to "theories of the middle range" (Merton 1957) explicating in a fairly systematic way the workings of at least some of the key mechanisms. We do have have at least partial understandings of how many of these contextual effects work: theories, for example, about the "demographic transition" from high birth rates in developing countries to much lower ones, as infant mortality declines and female education increases (Caldwell, Reddy, and Caldwell 1989; Drèze and Sen 1995).

So context matters, and context often varies. But these contextual effects are not random. There are patterns to be picked out, and understood from within each distinct historical, cultural, and technological setting. That understanding itself may or may not lend itself to generalization in ways that will allow them to be fit into overarching "laws." Sometimes it might; often it will not. But contrary to the assumptions of more extreme skeptics, there are "rules of the game" within each of those contextual milieux to which such skeptics quite rightly say our explanations need to be indexed. Skeptics are right that our generalizations need to be indexed to particular contexts; they are wrong to deny that, once those indexicals are in place, we can have something that might approximate "systematic understanding" of the situation.

Besides, we do not need a completely comprehensive account of context to use it as a corrective; in this regard, contextual analysis differs fundamentally from the search for general laws. Contextualist accounts typically work by helping us get a grip on some puzzling phenomenon. The contextualist account provides one or two keys, given which someone coming to the story form the outside will say, "Of course: *now* I get it!" In the Vlaicu story of property rights in transition with which we began, the thing you need to realize is that in Vlaicu kinship is a social and not merely a blood relation: someone who took care of your grandmother in her old age is kin, whatever the blood tie may be. To understand how social power is exercised you need to understand both technology (Mann 1986, 1993; Wittfogel 1957; Wacjman 1991) and ideas or strategy (Freedman 1981; Scott 1998). To understand why certain social forms are widely acceptable in one time and place but not another, you may need to understand differing social ontologies—things like "the king's two bodies" (Kantorowicz 1957) or "the West" (Jackson 2004)—and you need to understand the way different languages code and embody them (Bernstein 1974; Bourdieu 1977; Foucault 1981; Laitin 1992; Wagner 2003).

6   THIS HANDBOOK

Remember the three kinds of contextual effects we are seeking to analyze:

1. On analysts' understanding of political processes.
2. On the evidence available for empirical examination of political processes.
3. On the processes themselves.

In this *Handbook*, we take broad views of these effects. Instead, for example, of concentrating on how local knowledge (Geertz 1983; Scott 1998) shapes understandings, evidence, and political processes, we—or, rather, our contributors—range widely across different sorts of contexts. With no grand theory of context in mind, we sought authors who in previous writings had reflected deeply and critically on contextual questions in their areas of expertise. We gave preference to authors who could help Anglophone political analysts, especially but not exclusively political scientists, take better account of context in their own work. As represented in an author's previous work, we balanced among three different configurations of expertise: (1) extensive knowledge of a certain contextual area, with no particular concentration on politics; (2) extensive knowledge of a certain set of political phenomena, with considerable sensitivity to context; (3) deliberate attempts to analyze the impact of certain kinds of contexts on knowledge of certain political phenomena.

Negotiating among these configurations, plausible distinctions among topics, substantial spread, and our own necessarily partial knowledge of relevant scholarship, we arrived at a commonsense division of contextual areas: philosophy, psychology, ideas, culture, history, place, population, technology, and general reflections. With this general plan, we recruited the best authors we could find. We end up proud of the quality and variety of specialists who accepted our invitations, and happy with the multiple ways that the book as a whole puts context on the agenda of political analysis. The book's major divisions run as follows:

Philosophy Matters. Outside of political theory, political scientists often tremble at the injection of philosophical issues into what had seemed concrete comparisons of arguments and evidence. But so many disputes and confusions in political analysis actually pivot on epistemology, ontology, logic, and general conceptions of argument that philosophy demanded its place at the contextual table. Political science could benefit from a band of philosophical ethnographers who would observe the ways that specialists in political processes make arguments, analyze evidence, and drawn inferences about causes; the section's chapters provide a foretaste of what those ethnographers would report.

Psychology Matters. Political scientists often speak of psychological matters as "micro-foundations." We have not used that term for two reasons. First, the term itself suggests a preference for methodological individualism and analogies with economic analysis—serious presences in political science, but by no means the only regards in which psychology matters to political analysis. Second, enough political analysts employ conceptions of collective psychology (for example, collective memory) that readers deserve serious reflection on relations between individual psychological processes and those collective phenomena.

Ideas Matter. Some readers will suppose that together philosophy and psychology exhaust the analysis of ideas as contexts for political analysis. The three topics certainly overlap. The *Handbook* gives ideas separate standing because so many political analysts attribute autonomous importance, influence, and histories to ideas as such: ideas of justice, of democracy, of social order, and much more. We sought authors who could make us all think about proper ways of taking ideas into account as contexts for analysts' understanding of political processes, evidence available for empirical examination of political processes, and influences on or components of the processes themselves.

Culture Matters. Many objections to broad inferences and comparisons across polities rest on the argument that culturally embedded ideas, relations, and practices profoundly affect the operation of superficially similar political processes. Even within the same polities, analysts sometimes object that linguistic, ethnic, religious, and regional cultures differ so dramatically that all efforts to detect general political principles in those polities must fail. Instead of brushing aside such objections by pointing to empirical generalizations that do hold widely, here our contributors look seriously at culture, asking how political analysts can take it into account without abandoning the search for systematic knowledge.

History Matters. Since one of us (Tilly) has written the introduction to this *Handbook*'s section on history, we need not anticipate his more detailed arguments here. Suffice it to say that in all three types of contextual effects—on analysts' understanding of political processes, on the evidence available for empirical examination of political processes, and on the processes themselves—history figures significantly. We do not claim that those who fail to study history are condemned to repeat it, but we do claim that knowledge of historical context provides a means of producing more systematic knowledge of political processes.

Place Matters. In some definitions, history as location in space and time exhausts the influence of place. Yet geographically attuned political analysts detect effects of adjacency, distance, environment, and climate that easily escape historians who deal with the same times and places. This section of the *Handbook* gathers analysts of political processes who have worked seriously on just such effects generally, comparatively, and/or in particular time–place settings. They provide guidance for taking place into account without succumbing entirely to the charms of localism.

Population Matters. The contents of this section may surprise *Handbook* readers. One might turn to it for inventories of demographic tools that can advance political analysis. The discipline of demography does indeed offer a number of formal techniques such as life tables and migration-stream analyses that bear directly on political processes and suggest valuable analogies for political analysis. But we have pointed our contributors in rather a different direction: toward reflection on how population processes affect or constitute political processes. Thus they look hard at demographic change and variation as contexts for politics.

Technology Matters. In contemporary political analysis, technology often appears as a black box, a demonic force, or an exogenous variable that somehow affects politics but does not belong to politics as such. Such a view is hard to sustain, however, when the subject is war or economic imperialism. In fact, technologies of communication, of production, of distribution, of organization, and of rule pervade political processes, and receive insufficient attention for their special properties. In this section, skilled analysts of different technologies and technological processes offer ideas on how political scientists can (and must) take technological contexts into account.

Old and New. We have deliberately avoided giving ourselves the last word about the *Handbook*'s subject and contents. In fact, in the *Handbook*'s very open-ended spirit we offer no last word at all. The final section does not contain syntheses and conclusions from the individual chapters, but more general reflections on context and political processes from two distinguished senior practitioners: David Apter and Lucian Pye. They raise old and new questions that you, our readers, can take up for yourselves. If the materials in this *Handbook* help you accomplish new work that takes better account of the contexts in which political processes unfold, it will have served its purpose.

References

ABBOTT, H. P. 2002. *The Cambridge Introduction to Narrative.* Cambridge: Cambridge University Press.

ALLISON, G. T., and ZELIKOW, P. 1999. *The Essence of Decision.* 2nd edn. Reading, Mass.: Longman.

ALT, J. E. 1979. *The Politics of Economic Decline.* Cambridge: Cambridge University Press.

ANDERSON, R. D., Jr. 2001. Why did the socialist empire collapse so fast—and why was the collapse a surprise? Pp. 85–102 in *Political Science as Puzzle Solving,* ed. B. Grofman. Ann Arbor: University of Michigan Press.

ANTONY, L., and WITT, C. (eds.) 1993. *A Mind of One's Own: Feminist Essays on Reason and Objectivity.* Boulder, Colo.: Westview Press.

ARISTOTLE. 1984 edn. Poetics. Vol. 2, pp. 2316–40 in *The Complete Works of Aristotle,* ed. J. Barnes. Princeton, NJ: Princeton University Press.

ARCHER, M., BASHKAR, R., COLLIER, A., LAWSON, T., and NORRIE, A. (eds.) 1998. *Critical Realism: Essential Readings.* London: Routledge.

Ashford, D. E. 1992. Historical context and policy studies. Pp. 27–38 in *History & Context in Comparative Public Policy,* ed. D. E. Ashford. Pittsburgh, Pd.: University of Pittsburgh Press.

AUYERO, J. 2003. Relational riot: austerity and corruption protest in the neoliberal era. *Social Movement Studies*, 2: 117–46.

BATES, R. H, GREIF, A., LEVI, M., J ROSENTHAL, J.-L., and WEINGAST, B. R. 1998a. *Analytic Narratives*. Princeton, NJ: Princeton University Press.

—— de Figueiredo, Jr., R. J. P., and Weingast, B. R. 1998b. The politics of interpretation: rationality, culture and transition. *Politics & Society*, 26: 603–42.

BERNSTEIN, B. B. 1974. *Class, Codes and Control*. London: Routledge & Kegan Paul.

BOURDIEU, P. 1977. *Outline of a Theory of Practice*. Cambridge: Cambridge University Press

BRADY, H. 1995. Doing good and doing better. *Political Methology*, 6: 11–19.

BUNGE, M. 1997. Mechanism and explanation. *Philosophy of the Social Sciences*, 27: 410–65.

BURKHART, R. E., and LEWIS-BECK, M. S. 1994. Comparative democracy: the economic development thesis. *American Political Science Review*, 88: 903–10.

CALDWELL, J. C., REDDY, P. H., and CALDWELL, P. 1989. *The Causes of Demographic Change*. Madison: University of Wisconsin Press.

CAMPBELL, A., CONVERSE, P. E., MILLER, W., and STOKES, D. 1960. *The American Voter*. New York: Wiley.

DRÈZE, J., and SEN, A. 1995. *India: Economic Development and Social Opportunity*. Delhi: Oxford University Press.

EASTON, D. 1953. *The Political System: An Inquiry Into the State of Political Science*. New York: Knopf.

ELSTER, J. 1999. *Alchemies of the Mind: Rationality and the Emotions*. Cambridge: Cambridge University Press.

FEREJOHN, J. A. 1991. Rationality and interpretation: parliamentary elections in early Stuart England. Pp. 279–305 in *The Economic Approach to Politics*, ed. K. R. Monroe. New York: HarperCollins.

FINNEMORE, M., and SIKKINK, K. 2001. Taking stock: the constructivist research program in international relations and comparative politics. *Annual Review of Political Science*, 4: 391–416.

FLYVBJERG, B. 2001. *Making Social Science Matter: Why Social Inquiry Fails and How it Can Succeed Again*. New York: Cambridge University Press.

FOUCAULT, M. 1981. *Power/Knowledge*. New York: Pantheon.

FOWERAKER, J. 1989. *Making Democracy in Spain: Grass-roots Struggle in the South, 1955–1975*. Cambridge: Cambridge University Press.

FREEDMAN, L. 1981. *The Evolution of Nuclear Strategy*. London: Macmillan.

FRIEDMAN, J. (ed.) 1996. *The Rational Choice Controversy: Economic Models of Politics Reconsidered*. New Haven, Conn.: Yale University Press.

FRIEDMAN, M. 1953. *Essays in the Methodology of Positive Economics*. Chicago: University of Chicago Press.

——1977. Nobel lecture: inflation and unemployment. *Journal of Political Economy*, 85: 451–72.

GEERTZ, C. 1973. *The Interpretation of Cultures*. New York: Basic Books.

——1983. *Local Knowledge*. New York: Basic Books.

GILBERT, D. T., and MALONE, P. S. 1995. The correspondence bias. *Psychological Bulletin*, 117: 21–38.

—— PELHAM, B. W., and KRULL, D. S. 1988. On cognitive business: when person perceivers meet persons perceived. *Journal of Personality and Social Psychology*, 54: 733–40.

GREEN, D. P., and SHAPIRO, I. 1994. *The Pathologies of Rational Choice*. New Haven, Conn.: Yale University Press.

GROFMAN, B. (ed.) 2001. *Political Science as Puzzle Solving*. Ann Arbor: University of Michigan Press.

HACKING, I. 1999. *Social Construction of What?* Cambridge, Mass.: Harvard University Press.

HAJER, M. A. 1995. *The Politics of Environmental Discourse*. Oxford: Clarendon Press.

HAY, C. 2002. *Political Analysis*. Basingstoke: Palgrave.

HEDSTRÖM, P., and SWEDBERG, R. (eds.) 1998. *Social Mechanisms*. Cambridge: Cambridge University Press.

JACKSON, F., and PETTIT, P. 1990. In defence of folk psychology. *Philosophical Studies*, 57: 7–30.

JACKSON, J. E. 1996. Political methodology: an overview. Pp. 717–48 in *A New Handbook of Political Science*, ed. R. E. Goodin and H.-D. Klingemann. Oxford: Oxford University Press.

JACKSON, P. T. 2004. Defending the West: occidentalism and the formation of NATO. *Journal of Political Philosophy*, 11: 223–52.

JERVIS, R. 1997. *System Effects: Complexity in Political and Social Life*. Princeton, NJ: Princeton University Press.

JONES, E. E., and HARRIS, V. A. 1967. The attribution of attitudes. *Journal of Experimental Social Psychology*, 3: 1–24.

KAHNEMAN, D. 2003. Nobel lecture: maps of bounded rationality: psychology for behavioral economics. *American Economic Review*, 93: 1449–75.

——— SLOVIC, P., and TVERSKY, A. (eds.) 1982. *Judgment under Uncertainty: Heuristics and Biases*. Cambridge: Cambridge University Press.

——— and TVERSKY, A. (eds.) 2000. *Choices, Values and Frames*. Cambridge: Cambridge University Press.

KANTOROWICZ, E. 1957. *The King's Two Bodies*. Princeton, NJ: Princeton Univeristy Press.

KEY, V. O., JR. 1949. *Southern Politics*. New York: Knopf.

KING, G., KEOHANE, R. O., and VERBA, S. 1994. *Designing Social Inquiry: Scientific Inference in Qualitative Research*. Princeton, NJ: Princeton University Press.

KURAN, T. 1991. Now out of never: the element of surprise in the East European revolution of 1989. *World Politics*, 44: 7–48.

——— 1995. The inevitability of future revolutionary surprises. *American Journal of Sociology*, 100: 1528–51.

LAITIN, D. D. 1992. *Language Repertoires and State Construction in Africa*. Cambridge: Cambridge University Press.

——— 1995. Disciplining political science. *American Political Science Review*, 89: 454–6.

LAWSON, K. 1990. Political parties: inside and out. *Comparative Politics*, 23: 105–19.

LIPSET, S. M., and ROKKAN, S. (eds.) 1967. *Party Systems and Voter Alignments*. New York: Free Press.

LITTLE, D. 1998. *On the Philosophy of the Social Scienes. Microfoundations, Method, and Causation*. New Brunswick, NJ: Transaction.

MANN, M. 1986; 1993. *The Sources of Social Power*, 2 vols. Cambridge: Cambridge University Press.

McADAM, D., TARROW, S., and TILLY, C. 2001. *Dynamics of Contention*. Cambridge: Cambridge University Press.

MERTON, R. K. 1936. The unintended consequences of purposive social action. *American Sociological Review*, 1: 894–904

—— 1957. *Social Theory and Social Structure*. Glencoe, Ill.: Free Press.

MILL, J. S. 1843. *A System of Logic*. London: Parker.

MILLS, C. W. 1940. Situated actions and vocabularies of motive. *American Sociological Review*, 5: 904–13.

MONROE, K. R. (ed.) 2004. *Perestroika, Methodological Pluralism, Governance and Diversity in Contemporary American Political Science*. New Haven, Conn.: Yale University Press.

MULLER, E. N. 1995. Economic determinants of democracy. *American Sociological Review*, 60: 966–82.

ORREN, K. 1991. *Belated Feudalism: Labor, the Law and Liberal Development in the United States*. Cambridge: Cambridge University Press.

PATTERSON, O. 1975. Context and choice in ethnic allegiance: a theoretical framework and Caribbean case study. Pp. 305–49 in *Ethnicity*, ed. N. Glazer and D. P. Moynihan. Cambridge, Mass.: Harvard University Press.

PETTIT, P. 1996. *The Common Mind*, 2nd edn. New York: Oxford University Press.

POPKIN, S. L. 1979. *The Rational Peasant*. Berkeley: University of California Press.

PRZEWORSKI, A., ALVAREZ, M. E., CHEIBUB, J. A., and LIMONGI, F. 2000. *Democracy and Development. Political Institutions and Well-Being in the World, 1950–1990*. Cambridge: Cambridge University Press.

RAGIN, C. C. 1994. *Constructing Social Research: The Unity and Diversity of Method*. Thousand Oaks, Calif.: Pine Forge.

RIKER, W. 1982. The two-party system and Duverger's law: an essay on the history of political science. *American Political Science Review*, 76: 753–66.

ROSANVALLON, P. 1989. The development of Keynesianism in France. Pp. 171–93 in *The Political Power of Economic Ideas: Keynesianism across Nations*, ed. P. Hall. Princeton, NJ: Princeton University Press.

ROSE, N., and MILLER, P. 1992. Political power beyond the state: problematics of government. *British Journal of Sociology*, 43: 172–205.

ROSS, L. 1977. The intuitive psychologist and his shortcomings. Vol. 10, pp. 173–220 in *Advances in Experimental Social Psychology*, ed. L. Berkowitz. San Diego, Calif.: Academic Press.

RYAN, A. 1970. *The Philosophy of the Social Sciences*. London: Macmillan.

RYLE, G. 1949. *The Concept of Mind*. London: Hutchinson.

SCHAFFER, F. C. 1998. *Democracy in Translation: Understanding Politics in an Unfamiliar Culture*. Ithaca, NY: Cornell University Press.

SCOTT, J. C. 1976. *The Moral Economy of the Peasant*. New Haven, Conn.: Yale University Press.

—— 1998. *Seeing Like a State*. New Haven, Conn.: Yale University Press.

SCOTT, M. B., and LYMAN, S. M. 1968. Accounts. *American Sociological Review*, 33: 46–63.

SEARLE, J. R. 1969. *Speech Acts*. Cambridge: Cambridge University Press.

—— 1995. *The Construction of Social Reality*. New York: Free Press.

SKINNER, Q. 1969. Meaning and understanding in the history of ideas. *History & Theory*, 8: 1–53.

—— 2002. *Visions of Politics*. Cambridge: Cambridge University Press.

SMITH, D. E. 1987. *The Everyday World as Problematic: A Feminist Sociology*. Boston: Northeastern University Press.

SOLNICK, S. L. 1998. *Stealing the State: Control and Collapse in Soviet Institutions*. Cambridge, Mass.: Harvard University Press.

STEINFELD, R. J. 2001. *Coercion, Contract, and Free Labor in the Nineteenth Century.* Cambridge: Cambridge University Press.

STINCHCOMBE, A. L. 1991. The conditions of fruitfulness of theorizing about mechanisms in social science. *Philosophy of the Social Sciences*, 21: 367–88.

STRØM, K. 2001. Why did the Norwegian Conservative Party shoot itself in the foot? Pp. 13–42 in *Political Science as Puzzle Solving*, ed. B. Grofman. Ann Arbor: University of Michigan Press.

TILLY, C. 2000. Processes and mechanisms of democratization. *Sociological Theory*, 18: 1–16.

—— 2001. Mechanisms in political processes. *Annual Review of Political Science*, 4: 21–41.

TULLY, J. (ed.) 1988. *Meaning and Context: Quentin Skinner and His Critics.* Princeton, NJ: Princeton University Press.

VERDERY, K. 2003. *The Vanishing Hectare: Property and Value in Postsocialist Transylvania.* Ithaca, NY: Cornell University Press.

WAJCMAN, J. 1991. *Feminism Confront Technology.* Oxford: Polity.

WAGNER, P. 2003. As intellectual history meets historical sociology: historical sociology after the linguistic turn. In *Handbook of Historical Sociology*, ed. G. Delanty, E. Isin, and M. Somers. London: Sage.

WALBY, S. 1992. Post-post-modernism: theorizing social complexity. Pp. 31–52 in *Destabilizing Theory*, ed. M. Barratt and A. Phillips. Oxford: Polity.

WALKER, R. B. J. 1993. *Inside/Outside: International Relations as Political Theory.* Cambridge: Cambridge University Press.

WALTON, J., and SEDDON, D. 1994. *Free Markets & Food Riots: The Politics of Global Adjustment.* Oxford: Blackwell.

WENDT, A. E. 1987. The agent–structure problem in international relations theory. *International Organization*, 41: 335–70.

—— 1999. *Social Theory of International Politics.* Cambridge: Cambridge University Press.

WITTFOGEL, K. A. 1957. *Oriental Despotism.* New Haven, Conn.: Yale University Press.

PART II

PHILOSOPHY MATTERS

CHAPTER 2

WHY AND HOW PHILOSOPHY MATTERS

PHILIP PETTIT

In order to introduce the question of why and how philosophy matters to politics, I begin with a short discussion of the nature of philosophy in general and the prospect for a philosophy of politics. Then I look at a range of questions that are central to the philosophy of politics, seeking to emphasize their importance in any scheme of thought and the variations possible in response to them. The questions covered bear on the nature of persons, the possibilities for personal relationships, the people and the state, and the role of political values.

1   FROM PHILOSOPHY TO POLITICS

Philosophy is an attempt to think explicitly and rationally about matters on which one cannot help but have implicit commitments (Pettit 2004). To talk or think about questions in any domain, or just to act on the basis of beliefs about those matters, will always be to work with certain presuppositions; in the nature of the case not everything can ever be spelled out explicitly. And to do philosophy in that domain will be to try and lift out the most general presuppositions operative, to examine them properly, and if necessary to revise or replace them. Where philosophy goes, one's presuppositions will always have gone already. And how one's presuppositions have gone may not be how one will wish to go on reflection. Philosophy involves the unmasking of presuppositions and, if needed, the remaking of them.

Consider the manner in which we treat one another as responsible for this or that action and the presupposition, built into that mode of treatment, that we are or can be free in a way in which inanimate processes or non-human animals cannot be. We treat people as responsible and free so far as we entertain attitudes of resentment or gratification towards them, for example (Strawson 1982). But we never treat the weather or the dog that way; or if we do, then we won't long defend the stance: we will admit it's silly or have to suffer some considerable embarrassment. But is the presupposition about the responsibility and freedom of people defensible? What exactly should it be seen as involving? And can we really believe in it, given what science tells us about our own mundane construction? These are typical philosophical questions (Pettit 2001c, chs. 1–4).

What is true of philosophy in general is true of philosophy in the domain of politics. No matter what our involvement in politics, whether it be that of the politician or political scientist or the regular member of a political public, we invariably think and talk and act on the basis of a plethora of presuppositions: a layer of assumption that sustains the beliefs and desires we form, the evaluations we make, and the initiatives we adopt. And the role of a philosophy of politics is to try and spell out those presuppositions or prejudgments, to hold them up to the light of critical reflection, and to make up our minds on whether or not they should be maintained.

What body of information or theory will be deployed in the exercise of reflecting critically on those presuppositions? There is no limit to what may be introduced as a basis for critique so that it is bound to be a variable from culture to culture. The more robust findings of science, as in the sorts of findings that make a belief in free will seem initially puzzling, provide an obvious basis of critique in our age and culture. The same goes for more established observations that are accepted as a matter of common sense. And for some of us the same may go for theses of an avowedly religious or ideological provenance. As there are scientific and common sense philosophies of free will—or philosophies that claim to be both at once—so there can be a Christian or Islamic philosophy too.

Consistently with this general view of philosophical reasoning, we can distinguish five or six domains of inquiry.

- *The philosophy of reason* explicates and examines the presuppositions we make as to what follows from what when we reason on any topic whatsoever, whether of the kind related to deductive or inductive logic, epistemology, or the philosophy and methodology of science.

- *The philosophy of nature* studies the presuppositions that govern our thought about the natural world, including assumptions about space and time, about events, processes, and substances, and about relations of causation, possibility, and necessity.
- *The philosophy of mind* targets the presuppositions encoded in our "folk psychology," to do with belief and desire and action, intentionality and rationality, reasoning and free will, consciousness and personhood, and the like.
- *The philosophy of society* deals with presuppositions about the nature of conventions, norms, and laws, about the possibility of joint intention, communal life, and group agency, and about the character of the citizenry, democracy, and the state.
- *The philosophy of value* starts from the presuppositions we make in aesthetic, ethical, and political discussion about the meaning of goodness and obligation in general, the role of more substantive values—autonomy, welfare, respect, liberty, etc.—in relation to those categories, and the ideal shape of normative argument.

As this categorization suggests, the philosophy of politics spreads across a number of these areas. The presuppositions we make in politics that are likely to attract philosophical attention will figure mainly in the domains of the philosophy of society and the philosophy of value. But presuppositions about what follows from what, about what is involved in causal relations, and about the nature of minds and persons are also wont to make an appearance, so that the philosophy of politics can take us right across the spectrum of philosophical concern.

There are a number of reasons why the philosophy of politics, understood in this manner, is inevitably going to vary over time, making it more unlikely that there will ever be a philosophy of politics for all time. It will vary, first of all, to the extent that formations like the citizenry and the state have changed dramatically in the course of history, depending on size and prosperity and the mode of organization of populations as well on their institutional and other technologies. It will vary, secondly, so far as different bases of critique are activated at different times in the attempt to examine current presuppositions. And it will vary, thirdly, as a result of the fact that previous explications of crucial ideas will have fed back into political life and become part of the philosophy of politics that is given institutional and ideological prominence in a society.

But though the philosophy of politics is likely to vary greatly from time to time, that is no reason for making a sharp divide between studying the philosophies of the past and attempting to work out a philosophy for one's own time. The nature of the enterprise is hard to appreciate without a good sense of the different forms it has taken in figures as varied in location as Aristotle and Cicero, Machiavelli and Harrington, Hobbes and Bentham, Locke and Montesquieu, and Rousseau. But even more important, it may well turn out that there are ideas to be wrested from the study of the past, perhaps ideas common to a range of past figures, that have become hard to identify in reflection on one's own place and tradition. Some of those ideas may be worth trying to resuscitate. I have myself been arguing in common with a number of others, for example, that one finds a republican idea of freedom as non-domination present in a variety of past contexts, that the idea disappeared under local, ideological pressure in the early nineteenth century, and that there is every reason to try and rework it for the contemporary world (Pettit 1997b; Skinner 1998; Richardson 2002; Viroli 2002; Maynor 2003).

These remarks are sufficient, I hope, to introduce my understanding of what philosophy is and of how it promises in general to connect with issues of politics. In the remaining sections I hope to identify a range of issues that I think philosophers can usefully address in the political realm, pointing to variations in the way quite central presuppositions can be explicated or recast.

There are four broad areas where we work with presuppositions that are of the first importance for the stance we adopt in politics, whether this be as a participant—at whatever level—or as a scientific observer. I now proceed to look over those areas, indicating where I think that much turns on how precisely we interpret relevant presuppositions and how far we endorse or revise them. The areas in question involve the nature of persons; the possibilities for personal relationships; the nature of the people and the state; and the role of political values.

2   THE NATURE OF PERSONS

Perhaps the most basic level at which we are bound to make certain philosophically interesting presuppositions in political life and political science—henceforth I shall simply say, politics—is in connection with the nature of human beings and the sort of relationships of which they are capable. Those presuppositions have become matters of explicit attention and formulation within social and political thought and two very different images have emerged. These images represent rival philosophies of person, and of personal relationships, and are right at the heart of many current disputes in politics. They can be associated, on the one side, with decision theory or rational choice theory and, on the other, with what is best described as discourse theory—I once referred to it as inference theory (Pettit 1993, ch. 5). I proceed now to offer a characterization of these two pictures of the person and I then go on in the next section to look at the significance of the different images for the nature of human relationships.

2.1   The Decision-theoretic Image

The dominant image of the human subject in contemporary social and political thought, certainly in thought of a more or less economistic cast, is the picture of agency projected in decision theory, particularly decision theory in the broad tradition of Bayes (Eells 1982, ch. 1). This picture depicts the human agent as a locus at which two different sorts of states interact in the production of decision and action. On the one hand, there are the agent's credences or degrees of belief, and on the other his or her utilities or degrees of preference. These are defined over different states of the world—possible ways the world may be—and correspond to how the agent takes and wants the world to be.

The Bayesian picture makes three claims about these credences and utilities. First, any agent who satisfies certain conditions of rationality, intuitively understood, can be represented as acting on the basis of a well-behaved credence function: a function that evolves under new evidence in such a way—to take the standard version of Bayesianism—that the unconditional credence given to any event in the wake of finding that evidence is the same as the credence that used to be given to the event conditional on the appearance of the evidence; the function evolves so as to satisfy what is known as conditionalization. Second, any agent who satisfies intuitive conditions of rationality can be represented as having such a credence function and such a utility function that for any option involving different possible outcomes the agent will attach a degree of utility to that option—a degree of expected utility—which reflects the utility of each possible outcome and the credence given to its coming about in the event of the option being chosen; different Bayesian theories tell different stories about the exact way this is defined. And, third, as between different options with different degrees of expected utility, any agent of that intuitively rational kind will prefer the option with the highest degree of expected utility and choose accordingly; the agent will maximize expected utility.

The Bayesian image of the human agent is rather formally and artificially constructed but the basic elements correspond fairly well to aspects of our make-up that are recognized in common sense; in this way it represents an explication of presuppositions we make in our ordinary dealings with one another, political and non-political. Utility functions correspond to goal-seeking states of desire, probability functions to fact-construing states of belief, and the idea of acting so as to maximize expected utility is a formal version of acting so as to pursue one's desired goals according to one's beliefs about the facts.

There are some striking gulfs between folk psychology and decision theory. For example, folk psychology depicts us as forming judgments as well as forming degrees of preference and credence, where judgments are on–off commitments; we don't judge in degrees, though we may judge that a scenario has this or that degree of probability. And folk psychology also depicts us as forming degrees of preference for different ways the world may be, on the basis of judgments as to the properties of those scenarios (Pettit 1991). But nevertheless there is a fairly good fit between common sense and the basic thrust of decision theory.

This fit is so good, indeed, that much of what is assumed about human agents in the broad reach of social and political thought, particularly in more analytical traditions, sits well with essentially a decision-theoretic image. People are depicted as moved essentially by their preferences or utility functions, being guided towards the satisfaction of those preferences by the nature of their beliefs. They are preference-driven, credence-directed centers of rational agency. That assumption is often made more substantial, of course, so far as the driving preferences are taken to be essentially self-regarding in character, but this is a dispensable aspect of the standard package.

2.2   The Discourse-theoretic Image

But if decision theory gives a picture of human psychology that picks out many elements already recognized about human agents in common sense—beliefs, desires, actions, and so on—there is one broad aspect of human peformance that it overlooks. Human beings may be decision-theoretic subjects who act on the basis of beliefs and desires that can be modeled, however approximately, in certain credence and utility functions. But they are not just that (Pettit 1993, ch. 5). They are, more specifically, decision-theoretic subjects whose beliefs and desires evolve under the influence of reasoning or discourse, in particular discourse with one another (Habermas 1984, 1989).

Like many non-human animals, we human beings form beliefs and desires and act so as to satisfy our desires according to our beliefs, or at least we do so under intuitively favorable conditions and within intuitively feasible constraints; this is what gives application to the decision-theoretic image. But unlike non-human animals, we also give intentional expression to the ways things present themselves as being in the light of our beliefs and our desires. We don't just have the ability to believe that p; we can assert that p: we can use a voluntary sign, in Locke's phrase, to represent how things present themselves as being, given that belief (Locke 1975, bk. 3, ch. 2). We don't just have the desire that q; we can assert that the prospect that q is attractive or desirable or whatever: we can use a voluntary sign to represent how things present themselves as being, given that desire. We can express our beliefs in regular, content-specifying sentences and we can express our desires in sentences that predicate attraction or desirability or something similar of the contents desired.

The fact that we are articulate believers and desirers in this sense means that we can do something that marks us off very sharply from mute animals. All agents of the kind modelled in decision theory will have reasons to believe and to desire those things that it is rational for them to believe and desire according to the theory. Thus if an agent has a very high credence in "q" conditionally on "p", and comes to give full credence to "p", then he or she has reason to give a very high credence to "q". Or if the agent gives full credence to the claim that there are two options available—to A or not to A—and assigns a higher expected utility to A-ing, then the agent will have reason to A rather than not to A. But that agents have such theoretical or practical reasons for believing and desiring things does not mean that they can articulate or see the reasons they have for making such responses, recognizing them as reasons. The states in virtue of which they have reasons may operate within them without their having any beliefs—any credences—to the effect that there are such and such reasons available or, equivalently, to the effect that it is right or appropriate or rational for them to believe that q, or to A. Thus the agents may be unable to form beliefs about what reasons they have and what it is right, therefore, for them to believe or desire; they may lack the normative concepts required.

This is likely to change, however, if the agents are articulate in the relevant domains. Articulate agents who have the reasons illustrated will be able to give expression to those reasons as such. They will be able to say to themselves in the first case: "p, and if p, very probably q"—assuming, for convenience, that this is the way to express such credences. They will find themselves disposed in virtue of having the beliefs thereby expressed to believe and say that it is very probable that q. And they will thereby put themselves in a position to register that the fact, as they believe it to be, that p and that if p, very probably q, is a reason for believing that it is very probable that q; it makes it right or appropriate or rational, as decision theory implies, to believe that q.

Although it is sketchy, this line of thought should prove generally persuasive; the controversy comes in the details of how it is to be filled out. Assuming that it is correct, it means that articulate subjects will be able to see as such the reason that they have—and had all along—for giving a high credence to "q": viz., that p and that if p, very probably q. And on a similar basis they will be able to see that the inconsistency of two propositions gives them reason not to believe both, that the perceptual evidence that something is the case gives them reason, though perhaps only defeasible reason, to believe that it is indeed the case, and so on.

By a parallel train of reasoning, articulate agents will also be able in this sense to see the reason that they have in a practical case, not just to have that reason in the fashion of mute animals. They will be able to say: there are two options, to A or not to A and it is more attractive to A, assuming that "attractive" expresses higher utility. And saying this, they will be able to register that that fact, so expressed, makes it right or appropriate or rational for them, at least in the decision-theoretic sense, to A. Not only indeed will they be able to think about their options and related outcomes in terms of how far they are attractive. They will also be able to think about them in terms of how far they are consistent, for example, with other things they desire; about how far they represent scenarios that, going on past experience, deliver the goods that they promise to deliver and do not go stale in the mouth (Milgram 1997); about how far perhaps they have properties that serve for them as indices or determinants of what is attractive (Pettit 1991); and so on. In short, they will in some sense be able to consider the options and outcomes for how "desirable" they are, where "desirable" determines what they ought to be attracted by but not necessarily what in fact attracts them: weakness of will or such a pathology may always strike (Smith 1994).

The possibility of forming higher-order beliefs about the reasons they have for holding by various attitudes or for performing various actions should enable people to achieve a higher degree of rationality, even in the decision-theoretic sense. Suppose I find myself prompted by perception to take it to be the case that p, where I already take it to be the case that r. While my psychology may serve me well in this process, it may also fail; it may lead me to believe that p, where "p" is inconsistent with "r". But imagine that in the course of forming the perceptual belief I raise the question of what I should believe at the higher-order level about the candidate fact that p and the other candidates facts I already believe. If I do that then I will put myself in a position, assuming my psychology is working well, to notice that "p" and "r" are inconsistent, and so my belief-forming process will be forced to satisfy the extra check of being squared with this higher-order belief—a crucial one, as it turns out—before settling down.

In this example, I search out a higher-order belief that is relevant to my fact-construing processes and that imposes a further constraint on where they lead. But the higher-order belief sought and formed in the example could equally have had an impact on my goal-seeking processes; it would presumably have inhibited the simultaneous attempt, for example, to act so as to make it the case both that p and that r.

The enterprise of seeking out higher-order beliefs with a view to imposing further checks on one's fact-construing and goal-seeking processes—with a view to promoting one's own rationality—is what we naturally describe as reasoning or deliberation. Not only do we human beings show ourselves to be rational agents, as we seek goals, construe facts, and perform actions in the fashion mapped by decision theory. We also often deliberate about what goals we should seek, about how we should construe the facts in the light of which we seek them, and about how therefore we should go about that pursuit: about what opportunities we should exploit, what means we should adopt, and so on. We do this when we try to ensure that we will form suitably constraining higher-order beliefs about the connections between candidate goals and candidate facts.

That we are creatures of this deliberative kind, however, should not be taken to suggest that we are relentlessly reflective. When I draw on deliberation in full explicit mode, I will certainly ask after the higher-order connections that obtain between candidate facts and candidate goals. But I may be subject to deliberative control without always explicitly deliberating in this sense. Suppose that without explicit deliberation I tend to go where such deliberation would lead me and that if I do not—if my habits take me in intuitively the wrong direction—then the "red lights" generally go on and I am triggered to engage deliberative pilot. Under such a regime, deliberation will "virtually" control the evolution of my beliefs and desires; it will ride herd on the process, being there as a factor that intervenes only on a need-to-act basis (Pettit 2001c, ch.2). I will be in deliberative control of what I do but I may not be particularly reflective in the way I conduct my mental life.

3   The Possibilities for Personal Relationships

The two images of human subjects can be usefully summarised as follows.

- Under the decision-theoretic image human beings:
    have degrees of credence that update suitably under new evidence;
    have degrees of utility for different ways the world may be; and
    act so as to maximize expected utility—more colloquially, act so as to satisfy their desires according to their beliefs.
- Under the discourse-theoretic image human beings:
    can articulate the things they believe and desire;
    can see as such the reasons they have for those attitudes; and
    can be moved by the reasons to improve their performance.

The distinction between these images of human beings is of sharp significance for our view of the relationships that people may form. The decision-theoretic picture suggests that all relationships must ultimately involve a sort of attitudinal manipulation, whether with purpose benign or malign. The discourse-theoretic picture holds out the possibility of a sort of relationship in which others can relate to one in a co-reasoning fashion that is as unmanipulative as reasoning with oneself.

3.1   Decision-theoretic Adaptation

Suppose that we think of human beings in purely decision-theoretic terms, without supposing any ability to reason. They will act perfectly rationally under this image, forming beliefs and desires and intentions in a rational manner and acting rationally in the light of those attitudes. And as part of that rational performance they may act so as to influence one another on the basis of beliefs they form about the attitudes and capacities of others; thus they may act so as to obstruct or intimidate or channel the responses of others, shaping the real or apparent environment in which others have to act. But they may also do more. Having access to linguistic resources, they may intentionally reveal their states of belief and desire and intention to one another—and make it manifest that they are doing this—giving others the opportunity to form beliefs about those attitudes: say, about their beliefs or desires or intentions, including conditional desires or intentions to the effect "I am disposed, should you do such and such, to reply by doing so and so." And so human beings in the decision-theoretic image may also pursue another sort of influence. They may reveal their attitudes to one another with the purpose, perhaps manifest to all, of getting others to change their beliefs in response to seeing what they perceive or believe—the message is "I perceive or believe that p, and I'm in a position to know"—or of coercing others with the prospect of penalties, coaxing them with the prospect of rewards, and thereby securing personally or mutually attractive patterns of accommodation.

Under the decision-theoretic picture, then, it is clear that people can relate to one another in a range of ways. They can shape the parametric environment of others, real or apparent, expecting others to form beliefs about that environment and adjust to it. They can shape the strategic environment of others, real or apparent, letting others discern opportunities for usefully adapting to them or enabling others to create opportunities for reciprocal accommodation. And they can shape the evidential environment of others, real or apparent, by letting others form beliefs about what they perceive or believe, in a situation where others are likely to be evidentially affected by that.

For all this variety of relationship, however, there is one common theme in the decision-theoretic picture of possibilities. That is that since human beings, under this picture, do not have any beliefs about reasons for forming attitudes, or performing actions, they cannot have beliefs about giving one another reasons for responding in those ways and, to anticipate the next section, they cannot set out to reason with one another. Thus they have to think of what they do in making overtures to one another in different, purely causal terms. This implies that they can only conceive of the interactions surveyed, and they can only intend those interactions as means of causally affecting one another; in particular, as means of affecting one another that happen to appeal to them, in virtue of their own particular preferences. Putting the lesson in a word, they have to think of what they attempt, and of what others attempt in their regard, as a variety of attitudinal and behavioral manipulation: an attempt to engineer and tune, to their own satisfaction, the way that others are. The exercise may be welcomed by the manipulated as well as the manipulating but it still remains manipulation: a sort of tampering, one-way or two-way, that cannot be recommended or embraced as something supported by mutually endorsed reason.

3.2   Discourse-theoretic Co-reasoning

With this point made, we can see why the discourse-theoretic image of human beings opens up the possibility of a different sort of relationship between human beings. The fact that we human beings reason or deliberate means that not only can we be moved by goal-seeking and fact-construing states—by the belief that p or the desire that q—in the manner of unreasoning, if rational, animals. We can also reflect on the fact, as we believe it to be, that p, asking if this is indeed something we should believe. And we can reflect on the goal we seek, that q, asking if this is indeed something that we should pursue. We will interrogate the fact believed in the light of other facts that we believe, or other facts that perceptions and the like incline us to believe, or other facts that we are in a position to inform ourselves about; a pressing question, for example, will be whether or not it is consistent with them. We may interrogate the goal on a similar basis, since the facts we believe determine what it makes sense for us to pursue. Or we may interrogate it in the light of other goals that also appeal to us; in this case, as in the case of belief, a pressing question will be whether or not it is consistent with such rival aims.

Nor is this all. Apart from drawing on deliberation to interrogate the facts we take to be the case, and the goals we seek, we can ask after what actions or other responses we ought to adopt in virtue of those facts and goals. Not only can we ask after whether they give us a reliable position at which to stand; we can ask after where they would lead us, whether in espousing further facts or goals, or in resorting to action. We may be rationally led in the manner of non-human animals, for example, to perform a given action as a result of taking the facts to be thus and so and treating such and such as a goal. But we can also reason or deliberate our way to that action—we can reinforce our rational inclination with a deliberative endorsement—by arguing that the facts, as we take them to be, are thus and so, the goals such and such, and that this makes one or another option the course of action to take; it provides support for that response.

But if we are reasoning creatures in this sense, and if we are aware in common of being such creatures—we are each aware of our reasoning capacities, each aware that we are each aware, and so on—then the relational possibility that suddenly opens up is that we can reason together: that we can relate as co-reasoners. This process is going to involve an exercise in which I collaborate with you, or you with me, or each of us with the other, in exploring the respective reasons we have for holding by this or that attitude, or acting in this or that manner (Pettit 2001c, ch. 4; Pettit and Smith 2004).

That I explore your reasons with you for thinking or wanting or doing something—that I behave as a co-reasoner—is going to mean, intuitively, that

- I communicate my own beliefs about those reasons to you;
- I do so openly and honestly, not hiding anything about myself or the world;
- I do so as fully and fairly as your reasoning appears to require;
- I am open to your taking a different view and to your persuading me of it;
- I allow you go where by your judgment the reasons lead.

That I explore your reasons with you, in other words, means that I relate to you in much the way that you relate to yourself when you reason as to what you ought to think or want or do. I am a presence in your mental life of a kind that ought to be wholly welcome, since it serves to advance the epistemic ends that you yourself pursue whenever you try to reason in that way. And this is something that we are both in a position to see. More generally, we are all able to recognize that ratiocinative shaping is something each of has reason to welcome, that each of us is able to recognize that we all recognize this, and so on in the usual hierarchy of common awareness. We are all able to recognize that it is a shared ideal.

This ratiocinative shaping of one another that people can pursue under the discourse-theoretic image of human beings is quite different from the parametric or strategic or evidential shaping possible under the bare decision-theoretic picture. Those forms of shaping remain possible, of course, but they stand in contrast to this newer mode of influence. Where they have to be seen as a merely causal kind of manipulation, ratiocinative shaping can be seen as something quite novel: as a form of relationship that everyone has reason to welcome, and that everyone can believe as a matter of common awareness that everyone has reason to welcome. It may be possible under the rival image for people to achieve a level of mutual accommodation that everyone welcomes and that everyone can believe as a matter of common awareness that everyone welcomes. But it will not be possible for them to believe as a matter of common awareness that everyone has a reason to welcome this, given that they have no beliefs about reasons. And so it will not be possible for them to hail it as an ideal, let alone to hail it as an ideal in common with others.

I should stress that the co-reasoning relationships envisaged here are perfectly consistent with the decision-theoretic image of how human beings are motivated. What becomes possible under the discourse-theoretic image is a new sort of option, not a new sort of motivation. The resort to co-reasoning—the resort to an exercise in which I put my self-interest offline and become a servant of my partner's interests—may make perfect sense in terms of the sorts of motives, even perhaps self-interested motives, that decision theory recognizes.

3.3   The Upshot

The two images of the human person and the associated pictures of potential relationships support quite different views of politics. Let people be cast in the bare decision-theoretic mould, and we will be forced to think of all human life, and politics in particular, as a matter of manipulating one another to more or less mutually beneficial effect. It will be natural to prioritize the notion of human welfare, then, however that is conceptualized; to think of human beings as potential beneficiaries on this front; and to envisage institutional political design as a matter of finding the most benign possible form of treatment. Let people be cast in the discourse-theoretical mould, however, and we are immediately directed to the ideal under which they are treated as co-reasoners: in effect, they are treated with what can count intuitively as respect (Darwall 1977). It will be much more natural on this account, not to focus on human welfare alone, as if people were just the passive objects of treatment, but to pay attention rather to how they can be incorporated into arrangements where they are able to assume their full status as ratiocinative agents and interlocutors.

4   THE PEOPLE AND THE STATE

Politics is not just a matter of individual persons and their relationships, of course, but also of the collective formations that we posit when we speak of the people or citizenry, the state, and the system—as we shall assume, the democratic system—that establishes the relationship between them. Whenever we speak of government, and of the ideals of government, we have to put in place certain presuppositions about the nature of these entities. And political philosophies vary insofar as they offer quite different accounts of how to regiment or recast those presuppositions.

The main issue that I see in this area is how to think of the people for, depending on how this issue is resolved, the state and democracy will naturally be understood in one or another fashion. There are two distinctively different ways in which the notion of the people can be taken, and has been taken, and it may be useful to set these out briefly and then to comment on how they connect with variant understandings of the nature of the state and the nature of democracy.

4.1   The People as a Corporate Body

I describe the first model of the people as solidarist in character; it represents the people—or more accurately, the citizenry that comprises the full-status members of the polity—as a corporate body. The best way of approaching this model is to imagine how any corporate body of individuals might form and what it would require of its members. With the abstract possibility sketched, we can then look at the history of thinking about the people or citizenry as a body of just that kind.

Suppose that a collection of people jointly intend to promote a certain set of purposes in common, however the notion of joint intention is analyzed (see Tuomela 1995; Bratman 1999; Velleman 2000; Gilbert 2001; Miller 2001). Suppose in addition that they jointly intend, implicitly or explicitly, that the actions which are taken on behalf of the collectivity in support of those ends should be directed by one and the same set of canonical, collectively endorsed judgments—say, at a first approximation, the set of judgments supported by majority voting or by some such procedure (Hobbes 1994, ch. 5, §§ 15–17). And suppose, finally, that when any of them acts on behalf of the collectivity—when they act in a representative role, in the group's name—they allow their actions to be guided, not by their own particular beliefs, but by the canonical judgments.

When conditions of this kind are fulfilled, it is perfectly reasonable to say that the collectivity constitutes a corporate agent (Pettit 2001b, 2003). The collectivity will have a set of judgments and a set of purposes—something like a system of belief and desire—that is distinct from the systems of belief and desire that its members individually instantiate; if you like, it will have a single vision by which it operates (Rovane 1997). And when individual members act in its name, they will act on the basis of that system of judgment and purpose, not in expression of their own particular attitudes. The entity in question may be an ad hoc organization of activists, a parish council, the editorial board of a journal, or whatever. And of course it may be part of an organizationally complex entity, like a company or church or university: an entity that is itself articulated out of many corporate sub-agents, each designed to have a province of action of its own.

Why suggest, as I did above, that majority voting will only indicate at a first approximation the sort of thing required for enabling a group to establish canonical judgments? Because majority voting may produce an inconsistent set of judgments for the group to endorse, even if everyone voting is individually consistent (Pettit 2001c, ch. 5). Suppose, to take a simple illustration, that there are three members in the group, A, B, and C, and that they have to make judgments on whether p, whether q, and, at the same or a later time, whether p and q. A and B may vote that p, C against; B and C that q, A against; and A and C that not p-and-q, with only B opposing. Majority voting in such a case would lead to the group holding that p, that q, and that not p-and-q, and would disable it as an agent; after all, inconsistency in judgment means, at some margin, paralysis in decision. The problem here is quite general. A recent impossibility theorem shows that there is no way of reliably generating consistent group judgments over a set of connected issues out of individually consistent judgments; at least not, to put the conditions roughly, if the method used treats all issues independently and all individuals even-handedly (List and Pettit 2002, 2005; Dietrich 2003; Pauly and Van Hees 2003).

The possibility that the judgments endorsed by the group may come apart on any issue from the judgments endorsed by individuals raises a question as to how far they may be allowed to drift away from individual judgments, and yet count as the judgments of the group that those individuals comprise. The line I take is that however the judgments are made, they will count as the group's judgments so far as this answers to the joint intention of the members on the matter. This can even make room for the position defended, notoriously, by Hobbes (1994). He argued that when a sovereign speaks for a people, with each of its members acquiescing in this arrangement, then that sovereign's judgments just are the judgments of the people; and this, even when the sovereign is a single man or woman, as in Hobbes's preferred monarchy, who may pay no attention to what other individuals think.

The possibility of a corporate agent of roughly this kind came to be identified in medieval legal theory, as the idea of the corporation was developed in order to cope with the realities of guilds, universities, cities, and the like (Coleman 1974; Canning 1980). And, unsurprisingly, this idea of the corporation was applied quite early on to the political citizenry. Fourteenth-century scholars like Bartolus of Sassoferrato and Baldus de Ubaldis (Canning 1983) used it to characterize the citizenries of a number of Italian city-states in their own time. They argued that de facto if not strictly *de jure*—as a matter of conventional if not statutory law—these cities had the status of corporations in their relationships with their own residents, with outsiders, with bodies like guilds and universities, and with the great powers represented by Church and Empire.

This medieval tradition of representing the people was very influential, according to recent scholarship (Skinner 2002), in shaping the emergence of the notion of the people in early modern political theory. The high point of its influence was probably in the work of Jean-Jacques Rousseau (1973). He argued that the people are indeed a corporate body and that in matters of legislation, if not administration, it has to represent itself, coming together in assembly and forming its intentions and judgments—the general will—as a group agent. His way of thinking may still have a certain influence on contemporary thought, as in communitarian and related models of political participation that one finds in writers as diverse as Hannah Arendt (1958), Michael Sandel (1996), and Jed Rubenfeld (2001). It may even be part of the common sense of democracy as an ideal of popular sovereignty: an ideal of government in which the pre-formed will of the quasi-corporate people is imposed via referendum or representation.

4.2   The People as a Mere Aggregate

But a more recent tradition of thinking asserts that it makes no sense to posit group agents proper. There are only agents of an individual kind and the idea of group attitudes or group actions, even the attitudes or actions of an organised corporate body, is mere metaphor (Quinton 1975, 17); there are only singular agents, no plural ones. We can describe the view as 'singularism'(Gilbert 1989, 12).

Singularism had a powerful impact in the nineteenth century, partly in reaction to the Romantic excesses to which those who hailed group agencies were prone. The line was that groups count as agents "only by figment, and for the sake of brevity of discussion" (Austin 1869, 364). That line survived into twentieth century social and political thought, particularly in English-speaking countries. It was briefly interrupted by the enthusiasm for legal persons—akin to the corporate entities of medieval thought—that was sparked by translations of the German medieval historian, Otto Gierke (Hager 1989; Runciman 1997). And it was never fully embraced by leftist thought. But it undoubtedly achieved the status of an orthodoxy. The apogee of the approach may have come with the famous remark of Margaret Thatcher: "There is no such thing as society."

The rise of singularism, as might be expected, had an enormous influence on thinking about the citizenry. It naturally led political thought from the Rousseauvian, solidarist extreme to the very opposite end of the spectrum: to a view under which there are citizens but not in any distinct sense a citizenry; there are persons but not in any distinct sense a people. Under the solidarist view, the individuals who constitute the citizenry have relationships with one another of such a kind that they constitute a group agent, establishing a single system of belief and desire. Under the singularist alternative, there are no particular relationships, or none of any particular importance, that individuals in the same citizenry have to bear to one another. The only distinctive relationships they have with one another will be contractual liaisons together with those relationships that make them subjects of the same political system and the same government. For all that belonging to the same citizenry requires, people may relate to one another in just about any fashion; they may be as heterogeneous and disconnected as the set of individuals who live at the same latitude.

But won't the individuals represented by government be united in virtue of that representation, as Hobbes (1994) had envisaged? Not so far as they each think of government as representing them—representing them at the same time that it represents others—in their individual capacity. Given that they each think of government in this way, there will be no question of their jointly intending, as in the Hobbesian picture, that the government's judgments count as their judgments. They will see the government, as they might see an attorney they commission in a class action, as an independent entity that acts in representation of their individual purposes or interests according to its own judgments.

4.3   The State and Democracy

In the history of political philosophy, solidarism and singularism have been very prominent doctrines and have suggested very different pictures of the nature of the state and the nature of democracy. Under solidarism the people are going to be or constitute the state—*l'État, c'est nous!*—and democracy is going to be the ideal whereby the people as a corporation freely forms and enacts its will; the people is autonomous or self-determining, whatever the mode in which it determines its decisions. Under singularism the state is going to be an entity—in practice, a corporate entity—distinct from the people, and democracy is going to be an ideal under which the state is forced to be sensitive in a suitable measure to the individual will of each; this sensitivity will be achieved via regular elections in which different candidates and parties compete on equal terms to attract the votes of citizens and win a term in office (Shumpeter 1984).

Neither image of the state or democracy has an irrefutable claim to the allegiance of citizens. Whether one goes for the decision-theoretic or discourse-theoretic picture of persons and their relationships, the coercive, non-contractual aspect of the state—even the democratic state—raises a serious question about its normative status. Proponents of the solidarist people and state have argued, like Rousseau, that citizens share individually in the identity of the people and state—it represents their general, corporate will—and that this makes it possible for the state to respect individual freedom; but few go along. Proponents of the singularist people have argued, for example like Buchanan and Tullock (1962), that a suitably constitutional democratic state can be represented as an arrangement that would have been chosen by everyone, had there been a moment of constitutional choice; but again, not many have been won over.

Where then to go? Do we have to see the state as a brute force in our lives—even if it is a force, as most will think, for overall good? Or can we find a basis for thinking of it as an entity that is fully coherent—or would be fully coherent, if reformed in this or that manner—with our nature as human beings and our best relational possibilities? Starting from the discourse-theoretic image of the human being, political philosophers in the broadly deliberative tradition of democratic thought have begun to argue that such a basis may yet prove to be available (see e.g. Bohman and Rehg 1997; Elster 1998).

The best version of the guiding idea in this approach, as I take it, holds that the people or the citizenry should be seen as something more than an aggregate entity but something less than a corporate one. It should be seen as a community in which common ideas get established in the course of discussing public affairs and achieve the status of what John Rawls describes as public reasons (Rawls 1993, 1999, 2001). These, roughly, are considerations that are openly acknowledged as relevant to public decision-making on all sides—this, perhaps, as an inevitable byproduct of public debate (Habermas 1984, 1989; 1996)—even if they are weighted differently and taken to support different judgments and policies. What should democratic institutions be designed to achieve, then, for such an ideationally, if not judgmentally, unified people?

One line would be that they should impose such electoral and constitutional constraints as will force the state, first, to recognize the need to justify its decisions on the basis of those shared ideas and, second, to make room for impartially adjudicated, effective contestation as to how far the justifications work (Pettit 2000). Democracy on this account would not empower any imagined corporate will. Nor would it be of its essence to ensure sensitivity to the individual wills or preferences—perhaps the self-seeking wills—of individuals. Rather it should serve to empower the reasons and concerns that everyone in the community is disposed to recognize as relevant to public business, however differently they may weigh them. Those considerations will not often serve to determine concrete issues of policy uniquely, but they will rule out a variety of policy alternatives—they will make them unthinkable—and they can determine procedures whereby remaining questions are to be settled.

This line of thought points us towards a third model of democracy, on a par with the earlier two. I think that the three models identify attractive aspects of a political constitution and that the ideal of a full democracy should incorporate all those dimensions. I mention the models here, however, not with a view to arguing that point, but just to illustrate the different directions in which background, often unexamined presuppositions may take us in political design.

5   THE ROLE OF VALUES

The discussion so far should illustrate the wide range of issues on which we invariably make presuppositions when we think about political matters. Furthermore, it should display the implications of construing those presuppositions, now in this way, now in that. The exercise of showing how philosophy has an unavoidable presence in political life and thought might be continued indefinitely across further and further questions, but there is space to comment only on the sorts of presuppositions about matters of value that also have an impact in politics.

Any theory of value, any explication of the presuppositions we make in this area, will have to underwrite a number of different stories. First, a metaphysical account of what sort of entities give rise to the human experience of value; I shall assume here that the experience of value reflects human practices and sentiments in some way, rather than directing us to a domain of transcendent claims. Second, a semantic story as to how those practices and sentiments are reflected in judgments and statements of value; on this matter I shall assume that they report how the world presents itself in the light of those practices and sentiments, in particular those that we expect one another to share. And third, an epistemological account of how it is that we become aware of values, conceptualise them, and resolve disputes. Here I think that while we may be attuned to values in a quasi-intuitive way—in virtue of our practice- and sentiment-bound responses—the confirmation of a value judgment always involves recourse to implicit or explicit generalization (Jackson, Pettit, and Smith 2000; Pettit 2001a). If we can speak of a method for arguing about matters of value, it probably corresponds to what John Rawls (1971) describes as that of seeking a reflective equilibrium between our judgments of particular cases and our more general principles and assumptions.

I just mention these positions in meta-ethics because, while political philosophers need to adopt one or another view about the issues involved, it is not clear how great a political difference will be made by adopting one or another theory. But there is a further meta-ethical issue that does arise in politics and that generates significant debate. This is the question about how value or goodness relates to rightness: say, the rightness of doing this or that action, or of instituting this or that arrangement (Scheffler 1988; Pettit 1997a). Consequentialism holds that for any neutral value or values that people contemplate in common, the right option among any set of alternatives on which they bear is that option or option-set that does as well as possible—and so at least as well as any other—in promoting the realization of the value or values. Non-consequentialism holds that this need not be the case: that whether an option is the right alternative for an individual or people or state may depend, not on how far it promotes the relevant values—or not just on that—but on how far it exemplifies them: on how far espousing that alternative bears witness, as it were, to those values. Thus whereas pacifists in the consequentialist camp might think that the cause of peace justifies occasionally going to war, pacifists of the non-consequentialist persuasion may not; they may argue that it is wrong not to exemplify peace, even if the resort to violence would make for more peace overall. And whereas liberals in the consequentialist camp might think that the cause of freedom will occasionally require repression—say, the repression of a fascist group—liberals of a non-consequentialist stamp may not be willing to agree.

It is very important, I think, for political philosophers to be clear about this issue, since the decision on how to resolve it—the decision on how to interpret the widely shared presupposition that rightness is distinct from but connected with goodness—will impact on what one thinks is required to justify a constitution or policy. Go consequentialist and the question will be whether the constitution or policy produces or promotes the goods—however those goods are counted. Go non-consequentialist and one may think that it is equally, even perhaps uniquely, important that the goods be instantiated and exemplified in the state's performance, at whatever cost to overall promotion.

My own preference is for the consequentialist line—all the more so, in matters of politics (Pettit 2001*b*)—but I won't try to defend it here. One conciliatory remark worth making is that provided they agree on what the relevant political values are, consequentialists and non-consequentialists will often converge in practice on concrete issues. Thus even consequentialists may be willing to admit that since war tends to lead to war by lowering resistance to arms and by activating a desire for revenge, the chance of war bringing peace is usually so slim that there is no live debate among pacifists. And consequentialists may take a similar line on the issue about freedom, invoking the common wisdom that the state will almost always represent a sharper threat to freedom than any group it might repress, so that it is never sensible to allow it to have resort to repressive measures.

This takes us finally to the question of what values—what goods—are relevant in politics. Here it is important, straight off, to distinguish between the values that argue for designing a political system in one way or another—call these, designer values—and the values that participants within the political system may invoke in the attempt to persuade other participants, and ultimately government, to go in one or another direction; call these, participant values. There is a bad tradition in political philosophy of failing to make this distinction and of assuming the stance of a super-legislator in dictating both the constitution and the policies of the ideal state (Walzer 1981). But no one of a democratic stamp—in almost any variant on the democratic ideal—can reflectively endorse this.

Suppose I invoke certain designer values to argue for the third model of democracy distinguished earlier, in which the important point is to empower people's shared ideas about the polity; a plausible base for supporting that model, as indicated, might be that it is the only feasible way in which the state can give recognition to people as co-reasoners, treating them with what we natur- ally regard as respect. I am hardly going to go on and argue in the same designer voice that the policies adopted within such a polity ought to take this or that form. I will surely recognize that when I begin to argue about policies—as of course I may naturally want to do—I move to the role of participant, and that in this second role I have to think of myself as constrained in a different way by the ideas valorized in the community to which I belong. The designer values on the basis of which I recommend the democratic regime envisaged will have to have a resonance in the culture for which I am designing the regime, if it is to have any chance of gaining roots there. But the participant values I invoke will have to figure explicitly or implicitly in the society—they may of course be subject to various interpretations—or purport to extrapolate from values that figure there.

What values are candidates for figuring in the designer and participant argu- ments of philosophers? There is no hope of documenting these here, let alone of doing them proper justice. Suffice it to mention that they will include the usual gamut of considerations invoked under tags like "justice," "equality," "freedom," and "welfare." One of the most important jobs that philosophy does for politics is to provide different versions in which these ideals can be cast, generating well-tested, well-honed terms for political debate. Philosophy is well-known for its contributions on this front, however, and I hope that that may justify having concentrated here on other areas where it makes and is required to make a contribution.

There is no possibility of a rich and vibrant politics without a full repertoire of values being engaged in people's debates, and for that reason it is important that philosophy is there to explicate such values and to provide a framework for political life and political science. But equally, and perhaps less obviously, there is no possibility of a rich and vibrant politics without a shared image of human beings, without an ideal of the relationships to which human beings may aspire, and without a model of how they come together to form a people and a state. Philosophy matters to politics because it is the discipline in which the views we take for granted on these issues get to be explicated and explored. The philosophically unexamined life is not worth living, so we are told. It may equally be that the philosophically unexamined politics is not worth practicing.

REFERENCES

ARENDT, H. 1958. *The Human Condition.* Chicago: University of Chicago Press.

AUSTIN, J. 1869. *Lectures on Jurisprudence, or the Philosophy of Positive Law.* London: John Murray.

BOHMAN, J., and REHG, W. (eds.) 1997. *Deliberative Democracy: Essays on Reason and Politics.* Cambridge, Mass.: MIT Press.

BRATMAN, M. 1999. *Faces of Intention: Selected Essays on Intention and Agency.* Cambridge: Cambridge University Press.

BUCHANAN, J., and TULLOCK, G. 1962. *The Calculus of Consent.* Ann Arbor: University of Michigan Press.

CANNING, J. P. 1980. The corporation in the political thought of the Italians Jurists of the thirteenth and fourteenth century. *History of Political Thought,* 1: 9–32.

——1983. Ideas of the state in thirteenth and fourteenth century commentators on the Roman law. *Transactions of the Royal Historical Society,* 33: 1–27.

COLEMAN, J. 1974. *Power and the Structure of Society.* New York: Norton.

DARWALL, S. 1977. Two kinds of respect. *Ethics,* 88: 36–49.

DIETRICH, F. 2003. Judgment aggregation: (im)possibility theorems. Mimeo, Group on Philosophy, Probability and Modeling, University of Konstanz.

EELLS, E. 1982. *Rational Decision and Causality.* Cambridge: Cambridge University Press.

ELSTER, J. (ed.) 1998. *Deliberative Democracy.* Cambridge: Cambridge University Press.

GILBERT, M. 1989. *On Social Facts.* Princeton, NJ: Princeton University Press.

——2001. Collective preferences, obligations, and rational choice. *Economics and Philosophy,* 17: 109–20.

HABERMAS, J. 1989. *A Theory of Communicative Action*, vols.1 and 2. Cambridge: Polity Press; originally published 1984.

——1996. *Between Facts and Norms: Contributions to a Discourse Theory of Law and Democracy.* Cambridge, Mass.: MIT Press.

HAGER, M. M. 1989. Bodies politic: the progressive history of organizational "real entity" theory. *University of Pittsburgh Law Review,* 50: 575–654.

HOBBES, T. 1994. *Leviathan.* Indianapolis: Hackett.

JACKSON, F., PETTIT, P., and SMITH, M. 2000. *Moral Particularism*, ed. B. Hooker and M. Little. Oxford: Oxford University Press.

LIST, C., and PETTIT, P. 2002. The aggregation of sets of judgments: an impossibility result. *Economics and Philosophy,* 18: 89–110.

————2005. Aggregating sets of judgments: two impossibility results compared. *Synthese,* 140: 207–35.

LOCKE, J. 1975. *An Essay Concerning Human Understanding.* Oxford: Oxford University Press.

MAYNOR, J. 2003. *Republicanism in the Modern World.* Cambridge: Polity Press.

MILGRAM, E. 1997. *Practical Induction.* Cambridge, Mass.: Harvard University Press.

MILLER, S. 2001. *Social Action: A Teleological Account.* Cambridge: Cambridge University Press.

PAULY, M., and VAN HEES, M. 2003. Some general results on the aggregation of individual judgments. Dept. of Computer Science, University of Liverpool.

PETTIT, P. 1991. Decision theory and folk psychology. In *Essays in the foundations of Decision Theory,* ed. M. Bacharach and S. Hurley. Oxford: Blackwell; reprinted in Pettit 2002.

——1993. *The Common Mind: An Essay on Psychology, Society and Politics,* 2nd edn 1996. New York: Oxford University Press.

——1997a. A consequentialist perspective on ethics. In *Three Methods of Ethics: A Debate,* ed. M. Baron, M. Slote, and P. Pettit Oxford: Blackwell.

——1997b. *Republicanism: A Theory of Freedom and Government.* Oxford: Oxford University Press.

——2000. Democracy, electoral and contestatory. *Nomos,* 42: 105–44.

——2001a. Embracing objectivity in ethics. Pp. 234–86 in *Objectivity in Law and Morals,* ed. B. Leiter. Cambridge: Cambridge University Press.

——2001b. Non-consequentialism and political philosophy. Pp. 83–104 in *Nozick,* ed. D. Schidmtz. Cambridge: Cambridge University Press.

——2001c. *A Theory of Freedom: From the Psychology to the Politics of Agency.* Cambridge: Polity.

——2002. *Rules, Reasons, and Norms.* Oxford: Oxford University Press.

——2003. Groups with minds of their own. Pp. 167–93 in *Socializing Metaphysics,* ed. F. Schmitt. New York: Rowman and Littlefield.

——2004. Existentialism, quietism and philosophy. Pp. 234–86 in *The Future for Philosophy,* ed. B. Leiter. Oxford: Oxford University Press.

——and SMITH, M. 2004. The truth in deontology. Pp. 153–75 in *Reason and Value: Themes from the Moral Philosophy of Joseph Raz,* ed. R. J. Wallace, P. Pettit, S. Scheffler, and M. Smith. Oxford: Oxford University Press.

QUINTON, A. 1975. Social objects. *Proceedings of the Aristotelian Society,* 75:

RAWLS, J. 1971. *A Theory of Justice.* Cambridge, Mass.: Harvard University Press.

——1993. *Political Liberalism.* New York: Columbia University Press.

—— 1999. *The Law of Peoples*. Cambridge, Mass.: Harvard University Press.

—— 2001. *Justice as Fairness: A Restatement*. Cambridge, Mass.: Harvard University Press.

RICHARDSON, H. 2002. *Democratic Autonomy*. New York: Oxford University Press.

ROUSSEAU, J.-J. 1973. *The Social Contract and Discourses*. London: J. M. Dent & Sons Ltd.

ROVANE, C. 1997. *The Bounds of Agency: An Essay in Revisionary Metaphysics*. Princeton, NJ: Princeton University Press.

RUBENFELD, J. 2001. *Freedom and Time: A Theory of Constitutional Self-government*. New Haven, Conn.: Yale University Press.

RUNCIMAN, D. 1997. *Pluralism and the Personality of the State*. Cambridge: Cambridge University Press.

SANDEL, M. 1996. *Democracy's Discontent: America in Search of a Public Philosophy*. Cambridge, Mass.: Harvard Universty Press.

SCHEFFLER, S. (ed.) 1988. *Consequentialism and its Critics*. Oxford: Oxford University Press.

SHUMPETER, J. A. 1984. *Capitalism, Socialism and Democracy*. New York: Harper Torchbooks.

SKINNER, Q. 1998. *Liberty Before Liberalism*. Cambridge: Cambridge University Press.

—— 2002. *Visions of Politics*. Vol. 2, *Renaissance Virtues*. Cambridge: Cambridge University Press.

SMITH, M. 1994. *The Moral Problem*. Oxford: Blackwell.

STRAWSON, P. 1982. Freedom and resentment. *Free Will*, ed. G. Watson. Oxford: Oxford University Press.

TUOMELA, R. 1995. *The Importance of Us*. Stanford, Calif.: Stanford University Press.

VELLEMAN, D. 2000. *The Possibility of Practical Reason*. Oxford: Oxford University Press.

VIROLI, M. 2002. *Republicanism*. New York: Hill and Wang.

WALZER, M. 1981. Philosophy and democracy. *Political Theory*, 9: 379–99.

CHAPTER 3

THE SOCIALIZATION
OF EPISTEMOLOGY

LOUISE ANTONY

DRAGNET was a TV cop show, popular in the United States during the 1950s and 1960s. Each week viewers would watch as Los Angeles Police Sgt. Joe Friday and his partner investigated a single crime. Sgt. Friday, played in scrupulous deadpan by the mellifluously voiced actor Jack Webb, usually conducted the interrogations. Every so often, an overly eager witness would venture a personal opinion about the case. Friday would immediately interrupt: "Just the facts, Ma'am."

Probably no one ever took this show seriously as a portrayal of big city police work. Nonetheless, I think the figure of Joe Friday gave pretty adequate expression to a popular conception of *objectivity*—one that is still current today. The notion is that a good investigator—whether scientist, historian, journalist, or everyday citizen—will do as Sgt. Friday did, and discipline herself to consider *just the facts*—the raw, undisputed data of the matter, unadorned with personal speculation and uncorrupted by emotional interest in the case. Only by taking this studiedly neutral, disinterested viewpoint can an investigator hope to uncover the plain truth.

But this conception of objectivity is seriously flawed. Not only because no living, breathing human being could ever hope to live up to the gold standard set by the stony Joe Friday—this will be readily conceded on all sides; but objectivity so conceived—call it "*Dragnet Objectivity*"—offers an inappropriate ideal for human epistemic activity. Given the kind of creatures we are, with the faculties and abilities we happen to possess, the attainment of Dragnet Objectivity would lead to *less* knowledge rather than more. This much can be established—or so I shall argue—on the basis of considerations internal to contemporary analytic epistemology. But I believe the critique I will develop has wider significance—*political* significance. In my own society (I speak as a member of the upper middle class in the United States in 2004), there is not only widespread, if tacit, allegiance to the ideal of Dragnet Objectivity, there is a general and uncritical belief that the ideal is actually *satisfied* by at least some individuals and institutions in the United States. This latter belief is, I believe, actively fostered by powerful, well-monied interest groups, groups that hold inordinate sway over the organs of government, so that the promulgation of Dragnet Objectivity functions ideologically to safeguard and reinforce the political status quo. Those of us who are alarmed by the erosion of democratic participation and control in as powerful a nation as the United States would therefore do well to gain a more sophisticated understanding of human epistemic achievements, and the norms that ought to govern them.

This is a lot to unpack. But before I start, I would like to make clear what I am *not* going to argue. I am not going to claim that there is no such thing as objectivity. Specifically, I am not joining extreme "social constructionists"[1] and other advocates of "Strong Program" sociology in charging that "objectivity" and other cognitive virtues are chimeras, that there can be no rational assessment of theories on the basis of evidence or argument. While I will agree with Strong Program partisans that non- and even irrational factors typically play an important causal role in determining which theories scientists and other investigators come to accept and defend, I will also insist that this fact in no way undermines the possibility of rational assessment of theories, nor diminishes the prospects for objectivity in human epistemic endeavors. Indeed, those who draw such conclusions from the "situatedness" of human knowledge claims actually rely for their inference on precisely the concept of objectivity it is my object to criticize. Latour (1987), along with David Bloor (1981) and Karin Knorr-Cetina (1983), essentially set up a false dilemma: either objectivity has to be a wholly disinterested standpoint accessing a transparent "Nature," or it can be nothing at all (Schmaus, Segestrale,

---

[1] For an excellent systematization of the various meanings of "social construction," see Haslanger (1993/2002; 1995); also see Hacking (1999). The terms "social construction" and "social constructionists" are used with a variety of meanings through a wide range of disciplinary discourses. Generally, though, the term is relativized; one can be a social constructionist about Xs without being a social constructionist about Ys. I myself am a social constructionist about gender: I believe that the categories of "man" and "woman," with their attendant norms of physical appearance, dress, and behavior, are the result of social conventions. I am not a social constructionist about biological sex, however, which means that I believe that the (largely but not fully) dimorphic distribution of human beings into those with male and those with female bodies is not the result of social conventions. Sometimes "social constructionism" is taken to be opposed to realism, so that to be a social constructionist about X is to believe that there is no such thing as X. Many Critical Race Theorists take this to be true about race, arguing that racial classifications are based on false biological beliefs. Strong Program sociologists like Bruno Latour (1987) are, in this sense, social constructionists about concepts like truth, objectivity, and rationality.

and Jesseph 1992). I am as interested in refuting this dilemma as in criticizing the concept of objectivity that features in its first horn. I beseech the reader to keep this in mind while reading this chapter for what I have to say, as I have indicated, will support some of the premises of their arguments.

The central problem with the ideal of Dragnet Objectivity is that it ignores the fact that human knowledge is, as I termed it above, "situated."[2] This means two things: first, that human knowledge, like all human productions, has a *causal* history, even if it also has a rational structure. But secondly, and more importantly, it means that its status *as* knowledge is dependent upon its possessors' being located in a particular kind of situation. To a much larger extent than is generally realized, our *reasons* for believing what we believe only count as *good* reasons because of a certain propitious fit between our beliefs and features of our environment. In other words, *jusitification*—traditionally regarded as a prerequisite for knowledge—is often contingent on the would-be knower's occupying the right kind of context. As I will argue below, this is easiest to see in connection with features of our sensory and cognitive systems, which evolution has presumably honed to function efficiently in a particular range of physical environments. But for self-conscious inquirers like ourselves, it is no less true with respect to our reflective methodologies, which, in a perfectly analogous way, take advantage of our locations in certain sorts of *social* environments. Understanding human knowledge crucially involves understanding not only *that* we rely on each other for knowledge, but that such reliance is essential to *our* epistemic progress. This will, in turn, underwrite a different conception of objectivity—a turn away from the static requirement of individual divestiture inherent in Dragnet Objectivity, and toward dynamic and largely social desiderata.

1   EPISTEMOLOGY GETS REAL: NATURALIZING THE STUDY OF KNOWLEDGE

For a good part of the twentieth century, analytic epistemology displayed a studied indifference to the actual circumstances of human knowers. Its methodology was a prioristic, not empirical, and its aims were normative, not descriptive. With

---

[2] The term became current through the work of Donna Haraway. For a general explanation of the concept, together with Haraway's reflections on the relation between the concepts of situated knowledge and objectivity, see Haraway (1991, 183–201). I embrace her concept, but do not endorse all of her conclusions.

respect to scientific knowledge, a sharp distinction was drawn between the "context of discovery" and the "context of justification," between, that is, the factors on the one hand that *had actually caused* a given theorist to invent or adopt a given hypothesis, which might include events or states with no probative value (like the apocryphal fallen apple), and the factors on the other hand that *would rationally justify* belief in such a hypothesis. The logical positivist program of "rational reconstruction" was scientific epistemology in this mold: the aim of the exercise was to demonstrate how theoretical claims could, *in principle*, be rationally justified on the basis of sensory experience. The idea was to display extant scientific knowledge as forming a confirmational hierarchy, with primitive observation reports ("red here now") as the foundation, and proceeding upwards through statements about observable, middle-sized objects, to the higher reaches of scientific theories about unobservable objects and forces. The levels were linked inferentially, via rules of inductive reasoning, so that statements at each higher level were guaranteed to be empirically warranted by statements lower down, and ultimately, by pure sensory data. If existing bodies of theory and data could be made to fit within such a model, then it would vindicate the scientific practice that produced them, regardless of how the theories were discovered.

While it should be emphasized that the positivists themselves were not trying either to describe existing scientific method, or to prescribe reforms, their philosophy nonetheless encouraged a certain picture of how good scientific investigation ought to proceed. On this common view, dubbed "naive inductivism" by the turncoat positivist C. G. Hempel (1966), the scientist first accumulates data, unburdened by any prior theoretical commitments. Gradually regularities emerge and hypotheses suggest themselves. These are then submitted to focused experimental tests; if they fail, they are discarded, and the process begins anew. If they pass, then they are accepted, provisionally, while the whole process is repeated with new, additional data.

It is easy to see how faith in naive inductivism might give rise to the picture of the ideal inquirer inherent in Dragnet Objectivity. Because the proper role of the researcher is passively to collect and mechanically to assess data that are simply "given" to her through her senses, a good scientist will limit her role in the development of theory to observation and calculation, and will put aside anything that would interfere with these functions—emotions, values, interests, and above all, prior opinions as to the outcome of her research. To the extent that she is able to achieve this divestiture, she is counted *objective*. To the extent that she fails, she is *biased*. This notion of "bias" will figure importantly in what follows.

In the second half of the century, positivism came increasingly under attack. The most prominent of its critics, W. v. O. Quine (1969), argued against rational reconstruction and other a prioristic epistemological programs, partly on the grounds that no idealized model of human knowledge-gathering could address the question most in need of answer: how is it that embodied creatures such as ourselves, situated in the physical world as we are, come up with theories that appear to be reasonably close to true, a reasonable amount of the time? The only possible way of answering this question, Quine argued, was to attend to the *actual* conditions under which human knowledge develops—to treat knowledge as a naturally occurring phenomenon, and to study, by familiar scientific methods, the processes that produce it.

Quine called his new approach "naturalized epistemology." The proposal sparked immediate and intense controversy, controversy that continues to this day. Quine was charged with abandoning normative epistemological goals in favor of mere chronicling of the causal history of belief (Haack 1993; Kim 1994). Quine's aim, though, was not to cut off critical scrutiny of epistemic activity, but rather to take settled epistemic achievements—like the extraordinary success of modern science—as data to be explained. If our ordinary practice turned out to be deficient from some idealized point of view, then our task would be figuring out how we manage, nonetheless, to acquire or develop robustly useful theories of the world.

Quine impressed upon us the sobering truth that our fundamental epistemic challenge is to pare down the overwhelmingly large set of hypotheses consistent with any body of data, and in a non-arbitrary and truth-conducive way. This is done, he thought, by means of various evolutionarily honed "biases"—built-in prejudices for attending to some data more than to others, or for generalizing in some ways rather than in others—so that our ability to extract truth from our experience is the result of a co-evolution of mind and environment. Cognitive scientists open to the possibility of innate ideas—to which Quine, the recidivist empiricist, was not—inferred by similiar considerations the existence of highly specific and elaborate native cognitive structures facilitating such mundane human cognitive miracles as language acquisition, face recognition, and knowledge of other minds. Because of the way we are built, we cannot help but hear certain patterns of sound as speech, see certain visual patterns as visages, or think of certain patterns as the actions of intentional agents. Note that "open-mindedness" about the meaning of such patterns would have been fatal in the ancestral environment, and still constitutes extreme disability today.[3]

To speak of "biases" in this connection is not mere metaphor. The cognitive mechanisms we rely on for early sensory processing appear to utilize substantive assumptions about spatial and other features of our distal environment. When these assumptions occasionally turn out false, as they do in certain kinds of atypical situations, we fall victim to perceptual illusions.[4] Our ability to garner information

---

[3] One current theory of autism, for example, conceives the disorder to involve absence of an innate "theory of mind." See Frith (1989).

[4] For an informative—and entertaining—demonstration and explanation of forty well-known visual illusions, visit the website of Michael Bach (2004a). In particular, see the demonstration of the Mueller-Lyre illusion, and the explanation in terms of "assumptions" the visual system makes about the significance of inward and outward opening angles (Bach 2004b).

about our external environment by means of our senses is thus *contingent*—we have to be in the right kind of situation in order for our perceptual mechanisms to do their jobs. For this reason, our sensory knowledge counts as situated knowledge: our ability to gain sensory information depends upon contingent but stable features of the knower's situation.

The salutary role of biases in human epistemic activity is not restricted to the largely unconscious perceptual and cognitive processes I have been discussing. Human beings, of course, are not epistemically limited to what our senses and intuitions tell us. We can reflect on what we see and hear, reason about it, and communicate our thoughts to others. We can ask novel questions about the world, and organize ourselves to find the answers. But even when we are most explicit, careful, and reflective in our knowledge-seeking, we are still subject to the limitations entailed by embodiment. As we become more self-conscious and active as knowers, our epistemic selection must, of necessity, become more active as well. We deliberately search out some data, while blithely ignoring others right before our noses. Typically, the necessary focus will be provided by inquirers' provisional *theories* about the phenomenon in question: different theories will dictate looking in different places, for different kinds of evidence. Contrary to the naive inductivist picture, theory drives data collection, not the other way around.

Hempel (1966) makes the point nicely by means of a brief case study: Ignaz Semmelweiss's discovery of germs. Semmelweiss and his colleagues at a Vienna maternity hospital were baffled by the high rate of mortality from childbed fever among doctor-attended laboring women, until an unfortunate accident prompted Semmelweiss to speculate that "putrid material" on the hands of attending physicians was the cause of the maternal illnesses. Guided by this hypothesis, Semmelweiss required all his medical students to rinse their hands in a chlorine solution, and was gratified to observe a precipitous drop in the number of cases of childbed fever.[5] Thomas Kuhn (1962) preached the same lessons, reacting, again, to a popular, a prioristic model of scientific progress: as a gradual evolution of ever better theories, through the methodical testing of older theories against a steady accretion of observational data. Kuhn's careful case studies revealed that the evolution of human scientific knowledge was hardly gradual; that it involved initial periods of virtual intellectual chaos until a satisfactory theoretical picture finally emerged—a "paradigm"—providing researchers with a common understanding of the available data, the central questions, and the outstanding challenges in their field.

This brings us to a second way in which actual human knowledge-seeking differs markedly from the methodology of naive inductivism. On the naive inductivist view, the logic of confirmation is simple: once a hypothesis is formed, it is subjected

[5] For a more detailed account than Hempel's, see Caplan (2004). For his own account, see Semmelweiss (1983).

to experimental test. If the experiment yields the predicted result, the hypothesis survives; if it does not, the hypothesis counts as refuted, and is discarded. Quine points out, however, that hypotheses can never be subjected to such focused, definitive tests. Whenever a researcher tests a hypothesis, she is doing so, necessarily, against the background of many other assumptions. These include assumptions about the normalcy of the experimental conditions (e.g. good lighting, properly working equipment) and common sense truisms (objects don't spontaneously levitate). But the assumptions also include additional theory, from fundamental, highly confirmed principles like the conservation of mass/energy, to more parochial tenets specific to the area in which the researcher is working. It is this whole conjunction of hypothesis and background assumptions that is actually subjected to experimental test. If a predicted result fails to come off, then the logic of the experiment says only that one of the conjoined premises must be false, not which one. A researcher is thus free, as far as *logic* is concerned, to retain her hypothesis and attribute the experimental failing to equipment malfunction or to falsity in some other part of the background theory.

The choices scientists actually make when confronted with recalcitrant data are not arbitrary, but are, once again, shaped by systematic biases. Some of these, once again, may be innate: whether we are investigating the origins of the universe, or the origins of a noise in the attic, we tend to prefer simpler theories to more complicated ones, and we prefer making local, limited changes to our background beliefs to making sweeping or fundamental ones.[6] But a good many of the principles that guide scientific reasoning are not ones we are born with; rather they are *socially* inculcated. As Kuhn has emphasized, it is an integral part of scientific education for young researchers to learn and internalize the consensus about where trouble is likely to lie, should trouble come.

As I explained above, Kuhn (1998) distinguished between pre-paradigm and post-paradigm, or "mature" science: scientific progress vastly accelerates once a paradigm is in place. Paradigms work their magic largely by bringing into being a scientific *community*—a group of researchers who share basic theoretical commitments, and who agree about such matters as which findings and problems are significant, and which are irrelevant "noise." Such agreement creates common vocabulary and common technology, all of which makes possible the sharing of data and the easy promulgation of theoretical innovation. But all of this comes at the cost of a certain kind of open-mindedness. Commitment to a paradigm entails an unwillingness to call certain basic principles into question. In terms of the logic of confirmation, it means that those principles will not be candidates for revision in light of recalcitrant data, that they will be held instead as fixed points. Indeed, Kuhn argues, it is not hyperbolic to say that, within mature science, fundamental tenets of

---

[6] Quine and Ullian called such qualities as simplicity and conservatism "virtues" of hypotheses. For a complete catalog and discussion, see Quine and Ullian (1978).

the theoretical paradigm are taken as *dogma* (Kuhn's own word) by properly trained scientists. This form of "dogmatism," Kuhn emphasizes, is not to be lamented: it is *because* not everything is equally up for grabs that progress in science is possible.

If Kuhn is right, then human knowledge is "situated" in yet another way: it is *socially* situated. Kuhn, of course, is talking about scientific knowledge, but once the point is appreciated, we can see that epistemic co-dependence is ubiquitous. It is not only in science that we rely on our fellow human beings for guidance about what to believe and what to reject. As the old adage ("Fifty million Frenchmen can't be wrong") suggests, we take it as probative that many other people believe something to be true. The naive inductivist model obscures this important feature of our epistemic practice: it treats the fact that a huge proportion of our beliefs come from the testimony of others as an accidental fact, relevant to the context of discovery, but not to the context of justification. The idea is that there is no particular epistemic significance to our reliance on other knowers—we are justified in accepting the testimony of others just to the extent that we are justified in treating them as reliable sources of information, or to the extent that we can find independent justification for the beliefs obtained through social means. But in this, the model displays the same familiar shortcoming. It fails to explain how it is that our de facto reliance on the testimony and judgements of other people reliably produces knowledge. We do not, nor could we, vet the all the sources of information on which we rely. To begin with, we are utterly dependent as small children on the testimony of our older family members—we could not even acquire language if we didn't take it on faith that they were giving us the right names for things! The whole point of testimony is to increase our epistemic efficiency, and that would be impossible if we could only rely on those whose credibility we had antecedently checked.

2   THE SOCIAL ECOLOGY OF OBJECTIVITY

I have been arguing that the picture of human epistemic activity that emerges from taking a naturalized approach to the study of knowledge is sharply at odds with the positivist-flavored methodology of naive inductivism. The salient discrepancy has to do with the role of *biases*. On the naive inductivist picture, biases are bad, and epistemic practice is flawed just to the extent that the agent deviates from the ideal of Dragnet Objectivity. On the naturalistic picture, however, certain kinds of biases are a prerequisite for any kind of epistemic progress on the part of finite, embodied creatures. These biases serve us well to the extent that we employ them in the *situations* for which they are suited. Given our epistemic situations, we are not only incapable of obeying the injunctions of Dragnet Objectivity; we would diminish rather than increase our epistemic success if we did.

But now the question arises: what's become of objectivity? If bias is a good thing, and if Dragnet Objectivity is unsuitable as an epistemic norm for embodied creatures, what epistemic norms are left? I said earlier that a naturalized approach does not entail the abandonment of normative epistemology, and it does not. Rather, the approach bids us take an empirical approach to normative questions themselves: given the ubiquity of bias in human epistemic life, we must discover the conditions under which the effect of bias is salutary, and when it is pernicious. We have already seen that the biases hardwired into our perceptual and cognitive systems are likely to have been shaped by evolutionary pressures to provide reasonably good guidance in a reasonably large range of natural environments. But what about the set of biases that have to do with testimony and popular opinion? We know we are a credulous species—ask a stranger on the street the time of day, and chances are you'll believe her—but we also know that there's a sucker born every minute. We do, frequently, feel confirmed in our beliefs when we learn that they are widely shared, but we sometimes also feel "I'm right and everyone else is wrong." Evolution is not going to save our bacon this time—our time on the planet as a verbal, communicating species has been far too short for us to have much confidence that our inclination to believe other people is as uniformly trustworthy as our inclination to, say, see sharp color gradients as edges. We need, then, in the first instance, a serious critical understanding of testimony and trust—work already begun by many philosophers.[7]

Then, too, there is the whole set of biases that we think of in connection with social injustice—unreasoned biases against people with certain skin color, beliefs in advance of evidence as to the character of individuals from certain parts of town. We certainly do not want an epistemology that licenses us to give free rein to hasty generalizations, nor to—citing another ready source of belief—socially inculcated prejudices. Similarly, we want a way of understanding what is bad about such cases as these: the scientist funded by a company with a financial interest in her findings, the politician who "spins" the data to enhance her political advantage, the disapproving parent who will see no good in a child's romantic choice. Surely naturalistic epistemology does not counsel us to endorse all *these* forms of bias?

It had better not: the challenge is to discover a subtler and more nuanced critique of these—as I'll call them—*bad* biases than what can be provided by the epistemology of Dragnet Objectivity. According to that ideal, the badness of bias lies in the mere possession of belief prior to the gathering of evidence. But *that* is precisely what *cannot* be bad about bad biases; prior opinion is necessary for the human

---

[7] Like Annette Baier (1986); Lorraine Code (1981); C. A. J. Coady (1994); Karen Jones (1996; 1999); Trudy Govier (1997; 1998); and John Hardwig (1985; 1991).

epistemic engine to function. One alternative, however, suggests itself: on analogy with our understanding of perceptual system biases, we might try to identify the situational factors on which the felicitous effects of our biases depend. We might then be able to flag those environments in which our epistemic predilections threaten to lead us away from rather than toward the truth.

Insofar as we focus on those biases that appear to facilitate the acquisition of knowledge by social means, it will be necessary to look at the social contexts in which inquiry takes place. A relatively easy case to start with is the case of credulity. I have speculated that we are built with a bias to believe what other people tell us—suppose I am right. What must our social environment be like in order for such a bias to facilitate, rather than interfere with knowledge-gathering? Clearly it must be an environment in which our fellow epistemic agents are, for the most part, both competent and sincere. If, however, we have the misfortune to be co-situated with people who don't know much, or who are determined to deceive us, we will not come to learn very much by uncritical reliance on testimony. Indeed, whatever the general rule with people in our society, it behooves us to appreciate ignorance and mendacity in any particular case. If we had easy, ready marks of these characteristics, we could breathe a sigh of relief. Our epistemic plan would be clear: believe what you hear unless your witness displays the marks of a fool or a liar. Unfortunately, though, there are no such marks. Despite gamblers' confidence that bluffers always have a "tell," many people can lie without giving any perceptible signs of insincerity. Similarly for ignorance: it may be possible to tell that a testifier is not in a position to know whereof she speaks, but more often it is not. After all, it's the cases where *our* ignorance is greatest that we need to rely most heavily on testimony. And the problem becomes more acute as knowledge becomes more specialized and arcane.

But just because there are no *natural* signs of ignorance or mendacity does not mean that there are no signs at all. Human societies in fact have contrived systems of marking to aid their members in assessing the quality of testimony in areas where the risks of credulity are high. These marking systems ideally serve two functions: first, they help us distinguish good from poor informants, and second, they generate systems of sanctions that can serve to discipline would-be informants to behave. People who lie, and are caught, develop bad reputations; and a bad name in many social milieux carries heavy enough costs that lying is frequently deterred in the first place. Societies mark substantive expertise in many ways. Individuals who are deemed to be especially wise may be authorized to adopt particular modes of dress, or to display special symbols. Doctors and lawyers in my society, for example, are issued diplomas when they complete their courses of study, to be displayed in their offices for all prospective clients to see. Universities mark the expertise of their faculty by giving them offices, by listing their names in official publications, and in myriad other ways, both subtle and overt. Often expertise is marked by means of endorsement by some other recognized expert. Newspapers mark the expertise of political pundits by publishing their columns, or quoting their remarks.

If such systems are sound—if they produce neither too many false positives nor too many false negatives—then individuals have only to attune their credulity to the system's markings to take advantage of the social division of epistemic labor. But if such systems are unsound, then we have a new source of epistemic concern: a bias toward credulity tuned to a system that marks unreliable witnesses as reliable will surely produce a great deal of false belief. It is not the tendency to believe—the bias—that is at fault. The defect, rather, lies in the social situation within which the bias is left to operate. Since the remedy can never be the elimination of bias—it is futile to vow never to trust again—it must be to fix the situation, to reform the system of marking.

One of the social situational requirements for the possibility of testimonial knowledge, then, is the existence of a sound system of reliability-markers. But this is not enough. Recall what Kuhn said about the salutary role of bias in the conduct of mature science: a certain degree of dogmatism is necessary for any particular theoretical program to be developed to any level of specificity. But the worry arises: what if some particular group of paradigm-sharers simply get themselves off on the wrong track; what if their fundamental principles, the ones they treat as dogma, are badly mistaken? Won't their dogmatism keep them from placing the blame where it properly lies, as experiment after experiment fails to work? Kuhn certainly addresses this question, since cases of this sort are ubiquitous in the history of science. He replies that an accumulation of enough "anomalies"—unpredicted or counter-predicted empirical results—will throw a scientific community into "crisis." Crisis is marked by, among other things, an increased willingness on the part of member scientists to scrutinize fundamental elements of theory. Still, he contends, scientists do not abandon an old paradigm unless and until a new paradigm emerges to take its place. A new paradigm must accommodate most of the data explained by the old, but must also sell itself by providing an explanation of the anomalies that threw its predecessor into crisis.

Significantly, new paradigms, according to Kuhn, tend to be invented by members of the newest generation of scientists—youngsters less committed to the old paradigms, less burdened with professional relationships to be preserved, and less indebted, careerwise, to the success of their teachers' views. A healthy environment, then, for the conduct of mature science will always include mechanisms that permit the emergence of novelty. If new ideas are suppressed—whether by directives from the Central Committee or by the exigencies of grantsmanship—the forces that bind scientists to their favorite theories will remain unopposed, for good, or, more likely in the long run, for ill.

But the benefits of novelty, and the diversity of opinion that can result, are not limited to the possibility afforded for the discovery of more adequate theories. Even if a new theory fails to pan out, one's rational confidence in the old theory can be increased if it successfully stands up in competition with the new one. The point is emphasized by J. S. Mill (1859/1995, ch. 2) in *On Liberty*:

There is the greatest difference between presuming an opinion to be true, because, with every opportunity for contesting it, it has not been refuted, and assuming its truth for the purpose of not permitting its refutation. Complete liberty of contradicting and disproving our opinion, is the very condition which justifies us in assuming its truth for purposes of action; and on no other terms can a being with human faculties have any rational assurance of being right.

Note that Mill cites "*liberty* of contradicting and disproving opinion" as the condition that warrants one in trusting one's own opinion. He seems not to be recommending that one actively seek out conflicting opinion against which to test one's ideas. Rather the suggestion is that the normal dynamics of human inquiry will suffice to generate sufficient tests, *provided* no ideas are suppressed. It is perhaps not too anachronistic to read Mill as appreciating the Kuhnian point that too tentative a commitment to one's own views prevents their full development; the scientist too quick to jettison her theoretical commitments in the face of empirical difficulty eschews the epistemic benefits of working within a paradigm.

So let it be supposed that scientists' commitment to their theories is accounted for, in causal/historical terms, by a variety of factors, including non-rational, or even irrational factors like loyalty to colleagues or desire for fame and fortune. And let it be supposed, furthermore, that some such biasing factors are ubiquitous and ineliminable. If Kuhn and Mill are right, the hope that theories that result from these unholy mixes of motivations will approximate truth, lies in the constitution of the social environment. Objectivity, in other words, is not secured by the scrupulousness of individual scientists, but rather by the effects of competition among the ideas of contending groups of theorists. This is what feminist philosophers of science (such as Longino 1990 and Solomon 2001) have in mind in arguing that objectivity must be taken as a *social norm*—a virtuous feature of properly constituted scientific *communities*, rather than of individuals within them.

I have identified, then, two properties a social situation ought to have for human reliance on testimony to function properly: there must be a free play of ideas, with no sanctions against novelty or dissidence, and there must be a sound system for marking expertise. What happens if these requirements are not met?

It has been the burden of feminist epistemologists, together with other radical social critics, to raise alarms about failures in just these areas. Two concerns are paramount. The first problem is that existing systems of expert-marking are inflected by gender, class, and race inequities. White women, men and women of color, and the poor have less access to the mechanisms by which epistemic authority is conferred. It is harder for them to obtain higher education, to gain relevant work experience, or simply to be taken seriously.[8] Furthermore, because for so long

---

[8] True story: the following question was put to me by a professor in my college honors program during an interview for a prestigious study-abroad opportunity: "What's a pretty young thing like you want to go study dusty old philosophy for?"

experts have predominantly been men, characteristics of masculinity have, to some extent, become in themselves markers of epistemic authority: a deep and sonorous voice (like Jack Webb's!), for example, or an imposing physical presence. This undoubtedly leads to false positives—men accorded epistemic authority that is not warranted by their actual level of expertise. All this makes it that much harder for a qualified woman, and much, much harder for a qualified woman of color, to establish herself as a credible expert.[9] The objectivity of our epistemic community is diminished to the extent that potential experts fail to be properly marked.

The second problem that must be confronted is this: whenever there are serious disparities of power within a society, the more powerful individuals can, and frequently do enforce a monopoly of opinion. The first problem contributes to, and interacts with this second one. I've alleged that members of groups who have been socially marginalized are apt not to be marked as experts, and hence are less likely to be believed or even to be permitted to voice their opinions in any effective forum. But according to *standpoint theory*, the absence of these marginalized voices is a social-epistemic deficiency in its own right.[10] Just as Kuhn argued that breakthrough scientific innovations are most likely to come from individuals slightly outside the dominant paradigm, so do standpoint theorists argue that members of marginalized groups represent a special epistemic resource for society. The reasoning goes like this: in a society stratified by injustice, those in the dominant groups have a strong interest in obscuring the truth about the basis of the stratification, both from the subordinate classes, and from themselves. As a result, *ideologies* develop—stories that falsely present the existing order as either morally or rationally just, or else simply inevitable. Thus white slaveholders in the antebellum South in the US held that the Africans they had enslaved were, by nature, unsuited for any other kind of life. According to Marx, capitalists promote the view that workers, no matter how low their wages or degraded their working conditions, have made a "voluntary" and hence fair contract to sell their labor power. According to feminists, the "natural" submissiveness, maternal feeling, and domesticity of women is held, ideologically, to explain their second-class status in patriarchal societies.

Because the dominant classes are apt to control, to a significant extent, the society's main organs of communication—print and (now) electronic news media, but also schools and universities—the individuals who are apt to be authorized as experts in such societies will tend to be individuals who accept the ideological consensus, either by dint of occupying the upper strata themselves, or by having been educated in accordance with the prevailing ideology. Views consistent with the ideology will come to dominate or completely exclude alternatives. The only individuals likely to recognize the falsity of the ideological view, then, are individuals who have no stake in preserving the status quo; these are the marginalized, the people at the bottom of the heap. Such individuals, according to stand-

[9] See Antony and Hanrahan 2005 for more detail.
[10] See Haraway 1991; Hartsock 1983; 1998; Harding 1991; Smith 1974; and essays in Harding 2003.

point theorists, do not automatically see the truth in virtue of their social positions.[11] Rather, their social positions make available to them a distinctive *standpoint* from which a more accurate view of reality is possible—in order to take up this standpoint, they must come to appreciate the nature of their social position, which is to say, develop *class* consciousness.

As Marx argued in the case of the proletariat, workers are politically marginalized, but at the same time *central* to production. They see very clearly who does the work, who suffers the injuries, who bears the economic risk. Such details of everyday work life are invisible to the ruling elite; that invisibility is part of the reason they can deceive themselves successfully. Workers are thus well placed to appreciate the mismatch between the world depicted in the ideology, and the world in which they actually labor. Their very marginality deprives them of any motive for believing the ideology, even as it positions them to see an alternative reality. Feminist standpoint theorists contend that women are analogously placed: we are socially marginal, but central to *re*production—it is our role in perpetuating the species that is the basis of our exploitation, but that also affords us the possibility of a better view. Lesbian standpoint theorists argue, however, that heterosexual women may have too heavy an investment in particular men to be able to see their own exploitation as such. In this respect, they argue, it is lesbian experience that is most apt to yield a truly feminist standpoint (Frye 1983; Hoagland 1988). Black feminist standpoint theorists have similarly questioned the adequacy of white women's perspective for an understanding of racism (Collins 1990; Lorde 1984).

There are many questions that can be, and have been raised about standpoint theory (Bar On 1993). One has to do with the *net* epistemic benefits of marginality. The socially subordinate, as I observed above, typically have less access to education, and so are apt to be disadvantaged in any areas where literacy and numeracy are required to make sense of social relations; it's not at all obvious that the epistemic deficits one suffers as a result of marginalization are even compensated for, much less outweighed, by the epistemic benefits of occupying a socially subordinate position.

But whether or not standpoint theorists are right about the epistemic advantages of marginality, they are certainly right to raise concerns about forces in stratified society that tend to produce an epistemically unhealthy homogeneity of authorized opinion. I believe that political discourse in my own society is horribly disfigured by such a counterfeit consensus, to the extreme detriment not only of US citizens but also of innocent people around the world. And although the mechanisms for producing and promulgating ideology posited by Marx and other radicals do not require self-conscious mendacity on the part of the ruling elite, I fear that the ruling classes in the United States are knowingly propagating lies. Ironically, one of their most effective tools is the ideological picture of knowledge I sketched at the

[11] Nor, indeed, in virtue of pre-social or "natural" characteristics. Standpoint theory is commonly misread as asserting that women or people of color have, by dint of sex or race, some kind of *intrinsic* epistemic privilege.

beginning of this chapter; Dragnet Objectivity becomes a stick with which to beat off just those dissident views the existence of which is necessary for the achievement of *real* objectivity—the fruit, that is, of a dynamic social process of contention and disputation.

To see how this works, let us make a few assumptions. (I happen to think these assumptions are all true, but I won't be able to defend them here.) Suppose that the economic elite in the US stands to gain enormously if their companies secured control over Iraqi oil. Suppose further that the only feasible way to ensure such control—particularly without having to share it with European nations or with Russia or China—is through a military takeover of the country. Such an adventure would be extremely costly, not just in terms of dollars, but in terms of human life. Since the people who would bear these costs would *not* be the people who would benefit so handsomely from the invasion, there would be an acute need for some story that would simultaneously obscure the real reasons for the invasion and supply new ones, reasons that could be made to seem compelling to those who would have to shoulder the costs. And so a story is developed: the leader of Iraq, obsessed with the destruction of our vital and prosperous democracy, has stock-piled weapons of mass destruction (WMDs) and is collaborating with terrorists, the likes of which perpetrated the atrocities of September 11. He must be deposed and neutralized before he can act against us.

Many, many Americans bought the story. So did almost all of our elected representatives (at least so they said). Now, in the aftermath, second thoughts are being expressed, and controversy about the wisdom of the invasion is growing. But the controversy is strangely limited. There is some debate about whether the pre-war intelligence was faulty (sometime diehard right-wingers insist that the WMDs are there, and that we'll find them eventually), and rather more debate about whose fault the faulty intelligence was. There is some speculation that President Bush may have had personal reasons—avenging his father's honor—for trying to depose Saddam Hussein. There is much debate about the wisdom of trying to "impose democracy" on a country like Iraq. There is vague talk about the war's having to do with oil. What there is not is any sounding of the theory I advanced above—that the whole adventure was rationally undertaken with the goal of preserving US hegemony in the Middle East, a goal that necessitated the telling of a deliberate and massive lie. Such a view, which only attributes to a US leader the kinds of motives and actions routinely attributed to leaders of "enemy" states, is never debated, much less refuted, because it is not even articulated in the mainstream press. No member of the current administration has been challenged by a reporter to refute these charges. Nor are these charges waged by the "opposition" party. (It is a truly striking fact that at a time when the country is embroiled in an expensive and unpopular war, our "two-party system" has not offered us a candidate who is unequivocally opposed to the war.) The view can be found articulated in left-wing magazines like *The Nation* and *In These Times*. But such publications and the people who write for them, if they are not simply invisible, are regarded with great suspicion by the average American. Why?

Because, it is commonly alleged, such authors and such publications are "biased," not "objective." Indeed, such charges are flying fast and furiously these days, and not just against genuinely left-wing sources. Not a week goes by but that my local newspaper (*The Columbus Dispatch*) is accused of displaying bias, either in its choice of columnists, its phrasing of headlines, or its selection of news stories. But what exactly do the complainants take "bias" to be? Apparently, for many letter-writers, it is sufficient to sustain a charge of bias that someone—whether columnist, reporter, or quoted expert—has expressed a substantive point of view. Consider, for example, the following excerpts:

A May 30 story about the Ohio Senate budget bill was an attack on Republicans in the state Senate and on the party as a whole. According to the article, Zach Schiller is from a nonpartisan research group. Yet his statement to *The Dispatch* showed an opinion.   (Hunter 2003)

Or the following:

On Feb. 1, a column by Editor Benjamin J. Marrison gave his liberal views on gays and lesbians being allowed to marry and derided the new concealed-carry law ... The money we pay for our paper should not be used to espouse views at all. It is my opinion, and I believe others will agree with me, that all the readers want is the news of the day.   (Frenier 2004)

These readers object to the paper's carrying anything other than "the news of the day," i.e. just the facts, where these are presumed to be expressible in some way that would be completely neutral as to the import or significance of the facts. The newspaper's editors appear to agree, sheepishly conceding the justice of one such charge:

The morning after responding to about 200 emails from readers regarding our alleged bias against President Bush, I picked up Wednesday's Dispatch and winced. Our lead headline on the front page undoubtedly fueled the sentiment that our news pages are pro-John Kerry. "Edwards adds oomph." The headline accompanied the story about the Massachusetts senator having picked Sen. John Edwards of North Carolina to join him on the Democratic ticket. It came across as boosterish. It should have played the news straight, focusing, as the top of the story did, on Kerry and Edwards' planned visit to Ohio that day.   (Anon. 2004)

The editors saw no reason to issue a similar *mea culpa* for this headline, which introduces a story about what the Bush administration "thinks" it accomplished with recent surveillance work: "Arrests Probably Disrupted Al-Qaida" (*Columbus Dispatch* 2004).

Clearly, the conception of "bias" at work here is the one that derives from the Dragnet conception of Objectivity. This is significant. While I hope that I have convinced you by now that no one can actually fulfill this ideal—that it would be folly for anyone to attempt to report the news without benefit of a host of substantive, organizing assumptions—the point is most definitely *not* clear to either these readers or this editor. In their minds, good reporting can only be presuppositionless reporting, and moreover, such reporting can be and has been achieved, if only intermittently.

The belief that Dragnet Objectivity can be and is sometimes attained by, for example, news reporters can only be sustained if people believe that they can recognize such "objective" reporting when they see it. In that case, then, how is this done? I submit that reporting is construed as Dragnet Objective, when the substantive presuppositions that are in fact present have the status of consensus presuppositions—a status that renders them *invisible as opinions*. It is one of the epistemic habits of human beings, I have argued, to treat the agreement of other human beings as probative. Near unanimity of opinion translates into near certainty—an opinion that everyone shares shifts status, and turns into a "fact."

To return, then, to our hypothetical ruling elite. The power to monopolize opinion, which belongs to those who own newspapers, radio, and television stations, and to those who have unlimited access to these outlets, becomes the power to create "facts." Correlatively, it becomes the power to stigmatize as "opinion," and hence as "bias," any seriously divergent point of view. In this way, the elite can claim for itself the virtue of "objectivity" even as it constricts the acceptable range of opinion, even as it eliminates, in Mill's words, the very "opportunities for contesting" that would warrant a claim of genuine objectivity.

To see the extent to which this process has taken hold in the United States, reflect on this recent case of outright censorship—perpetrated, not by the government, but by a private corporation. The Sinclair Broadcasting Group, owner of 64 ABC network affiliate stations, unilaterally pulled the April 30 episode of the popular news program *Nightline* from several markets, including St. Louis, Missouri; Mobile, Alabama; and Columbus, Ohio. The episode consisted entirely of a sequenced presentation of the pictures and names of all the US military personnel who have been killed in Iraq since the initial US invasion. Sinclair explained in its public statement that: "The ABC Television Network announced on Tuesday that the Friday, April 30 edition of 'Nightline' will consist entirely of Ted Koppel reading aloud the names of U.S. servicemen and women killed in action in Iraq. Despite the denials by a spokeswoman for the show, the action appears to be motivated by a political agenda designed to undermine the efforts of the United States in Iraq" (NorthStar News Staff 2004). If a mere list of names of soldiers killed in the line of duty does not count as "just the facts," I do not see how anything could. And yet Sinclair successfully spun its grotesquely partisan breach of professional responsibility as a *defense* of objectivity.

There is a growing assault on the rights of US citizens to protest the actions of their government, and the rhetoric of "bias" and "objectivity"—always in the Dragnet sense—is functioning ever more overtly as a tactic for destroying the only kind of social environment in which genuine objectivity can be achieved.

Nowhere is this more evident than in the growing harassment of scholars in Middle East studies who have the temerity to criticize either US policy in the region, or the analyses that are supposed to support it. The avidly pro-Zionist policy wonk Daniel Pipes has started a new organization, Campus Watch. Here is the group's mission statement, from its website:

CAMPUS WATCH, a project of the Middle East Forum, reviews and critiques Middle East studies in North America with an aim to improving them. The project mainly addresses five problems: analytical failures, the mixing of politics with scholarship, intolerance of alternative views, apologetics, and the abuse of power over students.   (Campus Watch 2004)

The group carries out this noble mission, however, by recruiting students to inform on professors who teach views the group finds offensive. According to Sara Roy (2004, 24), Pipes told an interviewer:

I want Noam Chomsky to be taught at universities about as much as I want Hitler's writing or Stalin's writing ... These are wild and extremist ideas that I believe have no place in a university.

The US House of Representatives has already passed the "International Studies in Higher Education Act, HR 3077" which, if passed by the Senate, would create an advisory board to oversee the expenditure of federal education dollars earmarked for Middle East studies. One of the Bill's chief architects, Stanley Kurtz of the conservative Hoover Institute, has testified before Congress that work in post-colonialist theory, like that of Edward Said, presents "extreme and one-sided criticisms of American foreign policy," and is the sort of work that shows the need for government oversight (Roy 2004, 24).

One-sided? Most scholars, myself included, pride themselves on being able to understand and appreciate points of view not their own. But it is a kind of childish fantasy for any of us to think that we are not always presenting some particular point of view to our students and to our readers—that we are not, in one way or another, expressing the "one side" that is our own perspective, even as we expound what we take to be the views of others. An individual posture of neutrality can be nothing but a sham; and it is particularly false when the posture serves simply to deliver as "fact" the substantive opinion most pleasing to the powers that be. The best way to expose a student, or a citizen, to a variety of viewpoints is for there to *be* different viewpoints—including especially the viewpoints of the marginal—present and available. Objectivity, let me repeat myself, is a *social* virtue—it emerges only out of a healthy interchange among a host of single "sides."

I have argued that epistemology has political import. If we are to be good knowers, the kind of knowers crucial to the health of a democratic society, we need to attend to the social dimensions of knowing. False epistemologies are not mere academic curiosities—they can be and are used as ideological tools that degrade our social situation. I am not so foolish as to think that an epistemology lesson is all that's needed to stop the current Orwellian juggernaut. But I do think that a proper understanding of bias and objectivity can impede it.

REFERENCES

ANON. 2004. Editorial. *Columbus Dispatch*. 11 June.

ANTONY, L., and HANRAHAN, R. 2005. Because I said so: toward a feminist theory of authority. *Hypatia*, 20: 59–79.

——and WITT, C. (eds.) 1993/2003. *A Mind of One's Own: Feminist Essays on Reason and Objectivity*, 2nd edn. Boulder, Colo.: Westview.

BACH, M. 2004a. 46 optical illusions and visual phenomena. http://www.michaelbach.de/ot/index.html (accessed 13 Sept. 2004).

——2004b. Müller-Lyer illusion. http://www.michaelbach.de/ot/sze_muelue/index.html (accessed 13 Sept. 2004).

BAIER, A. 1986. Trust and anti-trust. *Ethics*, 96: 231–60.

BAR ON, B. 1993. Marginality and epistemic privilege. Pp. 83–100 in *Feminist Epistemologies*, ed. L. Alcoff and E. Potter. New York: Routledge.

BLOOR, D. 1981. The strengths of the strong programme. *Philosophy of the Social Sciences*, 11: 199–213.

CAMPUS WATCH. 2004. About Campus Watch. http://www.campus-watch.org/about.php (accessed 13 Sept. 2004).

CAPLAN, C. E. 2004. The childbed fever mystery and the meaning of medical journalism. http://www.med.mcgill.ca/mjm/issues/v01n01/fever.html (accessed 13 Sept. 2004).

COADY, C. A. J. 1994. *Testimony: a Philosophical Study*. Oxford: Oxford University Press.

CODE, L. 1981. *What Can She Know? Feminist Theory and the Construction of Knowledge*. Ithaca, NY: Cornell University Press.

COLLINS, P. H. 1990. *Black Feminist Thought: Knowledge, Consciousness, and the Politics of Empowerment*. Boston: Unwin Hyman.

Columbus Dispatch 2004. Headline. 9 August.

FRENIER, P. 2004. Letter to the editor. *Columbus Dispatch*, 11 Feb.

FRITH, U. 1989. *Autism: Explaining the Enigma*. Oxford: Blackwell.

FRYE, M. 1983. To be and to be seen: the politics of reality. In Frye, *The Politics of Reality*. Freedom, Calif.: Crossing Press.

GOODMAN, N. 1983. *Fact, Fiction, and Forecast*, 4th edn. Cambridge, Mass.: Harvard University Press.

GOVIER, T. 1997. *Social Trust and Human Communities*. Montreal: McGill-Queens University Press.

——1998. *Dilemmas of Trust*. Montreal: McGill-Queens University Press.

HAACK, S. 1993. *Evidence and Inquiry*. Oxford: Blackwell.

HACKING, I. 1999. *The Social Construction of What?* Cambridge, Mass.: Harvard University Press.

HARAWAY, D. 1988. Situated knowledges: the science question in feminism and the privilege of partial perspective. *Feminist Studies*, 14 (Fall): 575–99. Reprinted as ch. 9 in Haraway, *Simians, Cyborgs, and Women: The Reinvention of Nature*. New York: Routledge, 1991.

HARDING, S. 1991. *Whose Science, Whose Knowledge? Thinking from Women's Lives*. Ithaca, NY: Cornell University Press.

——2003. *The Feminist Standpoint Theory Reader: Intellectual and Political Controversies*. New York: Routledge.

——and HINTIKKA, M. (eds.) 1983. *Discovering Reality*. Dordrecht: Reidel.

HARDWIG, J. 1985. Epistemic dependence. *Journal of Philosophy*, 82: 335–49.

——1991. The role of trust in knowledge. *Journal of Philosophy*, 88: 693–708.

HARTSOCK, N. 1983. The feminist standpoint: developing the ground for a specifically feminist historical materialism. Pp. 283–310 in Harding and Hintikka 1983.

——1998. *The Feminist Standpoint Revisited and Other Essays*. Boulder, Colo.: Westview.

HASLANGER, S. 1993/2002. On being objective and being objectified. Pp. 209–53 in Antony and Witt 1993/2003.

——1995. Ontology and social construction. *Philosophical Topics*, 23 (2): 95–125.

HEMPEL, C. G. 1966. *The Philosophy of Natural Science*. Englewood Cliffs, NJ: Prentice Hall.

HOAGLAND, S. 1988. *Lesbian Ethics*. Palo Alto, Calif.: Institute of Lesbian Studies.

HUNTER, M. 2003. Letter to the editor. *Columbus Dispatch*, 16 June.

JONES, K. 1996. Trust as an affective attitude. *Ethics*, 107: 4–25.

——1999. Second-hand moral knowledge. *Journal of Philosophy*, 96: 55–78.

KIM, J. 1994. What is "naturalized epistemology"? Pp. 33–55 in *Naturalized Epistemology*, ed. H. Kornblith, 2nd edn. Cambridge, Mass.: MIT Press.

KNORR-CITINA, K. 1983. The fabrication of facts: toward a microsociology of scientific knowledge. Pp. 223–44 in *Society and Knowledge: Contemporary Perspectives on the Social Study of Science*, ed. N. Stehr and V. Meja. New Brunswick, NJ: Transaction.

KUHN, T. 1962. *The Structure of Scientific Revolutions*. Chicago: University of Chicago Press.

——1998. The function of dogma in scientific research. Pp. 301–15 in *Scientific Knowledge*, ed. J. Kourany. Toronto: Wadsworth.

LATOUR, B. 1987. *Science in Action*. Cambridge, Mass.: Harvard University Press.

LONGINO, H. 1990. *Science as Social Knowledge: Values and Objectivity in Scientific Inquiry*. Princeton, NJ: Princeton University Press.

LORDE, A. 1984. The master's tools will never dismantle the master's house. In Lorde, *Sister Outsider: Essays and Speeches*. Freedom, Calif.: Crossing Press.

MILL, J. S. 1859/1995. *On Liberty*. London: Longman, Roberts and Green.

NORTHSTAR NEWS STAFF. 2004. Media group pulls Nightline (1 May). www.thenorthstar-network.com/news/topstories/18280311.html (accessed 13 Sept. 2004).

QUINE, W. V. O. 1969. Epistemology naturalized. Pp. 69–90 in Quine, *Ontological Relativity and Other Essays*. New York: Columbia University Press.

——and ULLIAN, J. S. 1978. *The Web of Belief*, 2nd edn. New York: McGraw-Hill.

ROY, S. 2004. Short cuts. *London Review of Books*, 1 April.

SCHMAUS, W., Segerstrale, U., and Jesseph, D. 1992. A manifesto. Symposium on the "Hard Program" in the sociology of scientific knowledge. *Social Epistemology*, 6 (3): 243–65.

SEMMELWEISS, I. 1983. The etiology, concept and prophylaxis of childbed fever. Trans. K. Codell Carter. Reprinted in *Medicine: A Treasury of Art and Literature*, ed A. Carmichael and R. Ratzan. New York: Macmillan, 1991.

SMITH, D. E. 1974. Women's perspective as a radical critique of sociology. *Sociological Inquiry*, 44(1): 7–13.

SOLOMON, M. 2001. *Social Empiricism*. Cambridge, Mass.: MIT Press.

CHAPTER 4

POLITICAL ONTOLOGY

COLIN HAY

The problems of pure philosophical ontology have seemed so deep or confused that philosophers who concentrate primarily on the concept of being as such have acquired an occasionally deserved reputation for obscurity and even incoherence. (Jacquette 2002, xi)

THE terms "political" and "ontology" have, until recently, rarely gone together and, given the above comments, it might seem desirable to maintain that separation. Political scientists, for the most part, have tended to leave ontological issues to philosophers and to those social scientists less encumbered by substantive empirical concerns. Yet as the discipline has become more reflexive and perhaps rather less confident than once it was at the ease with which it might claim a scientific license for the knowledge it generates, so ontological concerns have increasingly come to the fore. In addressing such issues, as I shall argue, political analysts have no so much moved into novel terrain as acknowledged, reflected upon, challenged, and, in some cases, rethought the tacit assumptions on which their analytical enterprises were always premised. No political analysis has ever been ontologically neutral; rather fewer political analysts are prepared to proceed today on the basis of this once unacknowledged and unchallenged presumption.

Consequently, however tempting it might well be to leave ontology to others, that option may not be available to us. The principal aim of the present chapter is to explain why this is so. The argument is, in essence, simple. Ontological assumptions (relating to the nature of the political reality that is the focus of our analytical attentions) are logically antecedent to the epistemological and methodological choices more usually identified as the source of paradigmatic divergence in political science (cf. King, Keohane, and Verba 1994; Monroe 2004). Two points almost immediately follow from this. First, often unacknowledged ontological choices underpin major theoretical disputes within political analysis. Second, whilst such disagreements are likely to be manifest in epistemological and methodological choices, these are merely epiphenomena of more ultimately determinate ontological assumptions. Accordingly, they cannot be fully appreciated in the absence of sustained ontological reflection and debate.

This is all very well in the abstract, but it remains decidedly abstract. The second challenge of this chapter is to demonstrate that "ontology matters" in substantive terms. This may sound like a tall order. However, it is in fact rather more straightforward that might be assumed. First, we might note that political ontology is intimately associated with adjudicating the categories to which legitimate appeal might be made in political analysis. As Charles Tilly and Robert E. Goodin note, "ontological choices concern the sorts of social entities whose consistent existence analysts can reasonably assume" (2005). In other words, whether we choose to conduct our analysis in terms of identities, individuals, social collectivities, states, regimes, systems, or some combination of the above, reflects a prior set of ontological choices and assumptions—most obviously about the character, nature, and, indeed, "reality" of each as ontological entities and (potential) dramatis personae on the political stage.

Second, even where we can agree upon common categories of actors, mechanisms, or processes to which legitimate appeal can be made, ontological choices affect substantively the content of our theories about such entities (and hence our expectations about how the political drama will unfold). A shared commitment to ontological individualism (the view that human individuals are the sole, unique, and ultimate constituents of social reality to which all else is reducible) is no guarantee of a common approach to political analysis, far less to a common account of a specific political drama or context. The substantive content of our ontological individualism will vary dramatically if we regard actors to be self-serving instrumental utility maximizers, on the one hand, or altruistic communitarians, on the other, just as our view of the strategies appropriate to the emancipation of women will vary significantly depending on our (ontological) view as to the biological and/or social character of seemingly "essential" gender differences (compare, for instance, Brownmiller 1975; Daly 1978; Elshtain 1981; Wolf 1993; Young 1990). In these, and innumerable other ways, our ontological choices—whether acknowledged or unacknowledged—have profound epistemological, methodological, and practical political consequences.

Given this, it is pleasing to be able to report that contemporary political analysts are rather more reflexive, ontologically, than many of their immediate predecessors. Representative of contemporary trends in this respect is Alexander Wendt. Ontology, he suggests, is not something that most international relations (IR) scholars spend much time thinking about. Nor should they. The primary task of IR social science is to help to understand world politics, not to ruminate about issues more properly the concern of philosophers. Yet even the most empirically minded students of international politics must "do" ontology.   (1999, 370)

In the brief survey that follows, my aim is to indicate in outline form what "doing" political ontology entails. But it is first important to establish, in somewhat greater detail, what it is and why it is important.

1   POLITICAL ONTOLOGY: WHAT IS IT?

Most standard philosophical treatments of ontology differentiate between two, albeit closely related, senses of the term.[1] The first, and more abstract, is concerned with the nature of "being" itself—what is it to exist, whether (and, if so, why) there exists something rather than nothing, and whether (and, if so, why) there exists one logically contingent actual world. The second sense of the term is concerned with the (specific) set of assumptions made about the nature, essence, and characteristics (in short, the reality) of an object or set of objects of analytical inquiry. However ethereal such issues may nonetheless seem, political analysts have principally concerned themselves with the latter, philosophically more prosaic, set of concerns. In Benton and Craib's (2001) terms, political ontology is a "regional ontology." This chapter replicates that focus.

Thus, whilst ontology is defined, literally, as the 'science' or 'philosophy' of being, within political analysis it has tended to be defined in more narrow and specific terms. Norman Blaikie's definition is here representative. Ontology, he suggests, "refers to the claims or assumptions that a particular approach to social [or, by extension, political] enquiry makes about the nature of social [or political] reality—claims about what exists, what it looks like, what units make it up and how these units interact with one another" (1993, 6). Ontology relates to *being*, to what *is*, to what *exists*, to the constituent units of reality; political ontology, by extension, relates to *political being*, to what *is* politically, to what *exists politically*, and to the units that comprise political reality.

The analyst's ontological position is, then, her answer to the question: What is the nature of the social and political reality to be investigated? Alternatively, what

[1] See e.g. Grossmann 1992; Honderich 1995, 634–5; Jacquette 2002; Schmitt 2003; see also Benton and Craib 2001, 183.

exists that we might acquire knowledge of? As this already implies, ontology logically precedes epistemology. However put, these are rather significant questions whose answers may determine, to a considerable extent, the content of the political analysis we are likely to engage in and, indeed, what we regard as an (adequate) political explanation. Thus, for "ontological atomists," convinced in Hobbesian terms that "basic human needs, capacities and motivations arise in each individual without regard to any specific feature of social groups or social interactions" (Fay 1996, 31), there can be no appeal in political explanation to social interactions, processes or structures. For "ontological structuralists," by contrast, it is the appeal to human needs and capacities that is ruled inadmissible in the court of political analysis. Similarly, for those convinced of a separation of appearance and reality—such that we cannot trust our senses to reveal to us that which is real as distinct from that which merely presents itself to us *as if* it were real—political analysis is likely to be a rather more complex and methodologically exacting process than for those prepared to accept that reality presents itself to us in a direct and unmediated fashion.

Working from this simple definition, a great variety of issues of political ontology can be identified. Adapting Uskali Mäki's thoughtful (and pioneering) reflections on economic ontology (2001, 3; see also Mäki 2002, 15–22) to the political realm, we might identify all of the following as ontological questions:

What is the polity made of? What are its constituents and how do they hang together? What kinds of general principles govern its functioning, and its change? Are they causal principles and, if so, what is the nature of political causation? What drives political actors and what mental capacities do they possess? Do individual preferences and social institutions exist, and in what sense? Are (any of) these things historically and culturally invariant universals, or are they relative to context?

Such questions readily establish a simple analytical agenda for political ontology. They also serve to indicate that no political analysis can proceed in the absence of assumptions about political ontology. That such assumptions are rarely explicit hardly makes them less consequential. Presented more thematically, amongst the ontological issues on which political analysts formulate consequential assumptions are the following:

1. The relationship between structure and agency, context, and conduct.
2. The extent of the causal and/or constitutive role of ideas in the determination of political outcomes.
3. The extent to which social and political systems exhibit organic qualities or are reducible in all characteristics to the sum of their constituent units/parts.
4. The (dualistic or dialectical) relationship between mind and body.
5. The nature of the human (political) subject and its behavioural motivations.
6. The extent to which causal dynamics are culturally/contextually specific or generalizable.

7. The respective characteristics of the objects of the natural and social sciences.
8. Perhaps most fundamentally of all, the extent (if any) of the separation of appearance and reality—the extent to which the social and political world presents itself to us as really it is such that what is real is observable.

Whilst interest in, and reflexivity with respect to, such ontological issues has certainly risen considerably in recent years, coverage of such issues is very uneven. Indeed, it is really only some of these issues—principally the first, second, third, and, to some extent, the fifth—that have prompted sustained ontological reflection to date.[2] It is on these issues that this chapter will concentrate principally.

The crucial point, for now, to note about each of these issues is that none of them can be resolved empirically. Ultimately, no amount of empirical evidence can refute the (ontological) claims of the atomist or the structuralist; neither can it confirm or reject the assumption that there is no separation of appearance and reality.[3] This is all rather disconcerting and perhaps explains the characteristic reluctance of political analysts to venture into debate on, and thereby to lay bare, their ontological assumptions. For to acknowledge an ontological dependence, and hence a reliance upon assumptions that are in principle untestable, may be seen to undermine the rightly cherished and long-fought-for authority of the analyst and the analytical traditions in which her contribution is constructed. Yet, on any sustained reflection, silence is not a very attractive option either. For, whether we like it or not, and whether we choose to acknowledge it or not, we *make* ontological assumptions—in Wendt's terms, we "do" ontology. These assumptions profoundly shape our approach to political analysis and cannot simply be justified by appeal to an evidential base. It is to the consequences of such choices that we now turn.

2   ... And Why Is It Important?

However significant they may be in their own terms, ontological assumptions find themselves increasingly the subject of the political analyst's attentions largely for their epistemological and methodological consequences.

[2] Whilst the appropriate preference function(s) and behavioral assumptions that we should adopt in, for instance, game-theoretic modeling has been a focus of considerable attention, the vast majority of that reflection has failed to acknowledge the ontological character of the issue.

[3] For, clearly, what counts as evidence in the first place depends on one's view of the relationship between that which is observed and experienced, on the one hand, and that which is real, on the other. Where the (archetypal) pluralist sees an open and democratic decision-making process, the (similarly archetypal) elite theorist sees the work of covert agenda-setting processes behind the scenes, and the (no less archetypal) Marxist, evidence of preference-shaping ideological indoctrination.

Again it is important to be precise about our terminology, for confusions abound in the literature.[4]

Epistemology, again defined literally, is the "science" or "philosophy" of knowledge. In Blaikie's terms, it refers "to the claims or assumptions made about the ways in which it is possible to gain knowledge of reality" (1993, 6–7). In short, if the ontologist asks "what exists to be known?", then the epistemologist asks "what are the conditions of acquiring knowledge of that which exists?" Epistemology concerns itself with such issues as the degree of certainty we might legitimately claim for the conclusions we are tempted to draw from our analyses, the extent to which specific knowledge claims might be generalized beyond the immediate context in which our observations were made, and, in general terms, how we might adjudicate and defend a preference between contending political explanations. As this indicates, epistemological assumptions are invariably ontologically loaded—whether knowledge is transferable between different settings for political analysis and hence whether we can legitimately generalize between "cases" (an epistemological consideration) depends on (prior) assumptions about the ontological specificity of such settings.

Yet the implications of ontological choices are not confined to epistemology; they are also methodological.

Methodology relates to the choice of analytical strategy and research design which underpins substantive research. Although methodology establishes the principles which might guide the choice of method, it should not be confused with the methods and techniques of research themselves. Indeed, methodologists frequently draw the distinction between the two, emphasizing the extent of the gulf between what they regard as established methodological principles and perhaps equally well-established methodological practices. What they invariably fail to do is to acknowledge and reflect upon the ontological dependence of methodological choices. For our purposes methodology is best understood as the means by which we reflect upon the methods appropriate to realize fully our potential to acquire knowledge of that which exists.

What this brief discussion hopefully serves to demonstrate is that ontology, epistemology, and methodology, though closely related, are irreducible. Ontology relates to the nature of the social and political world, epistemology to what we can

---

[4] In the much-lauded second edition of their highly respected and influential text on *Theory and Methods in Political Science*, for instance, the editors and contributors display a marked lack of consistency in defining ontology and epistemology. Given that theirs is practically the only entry-level introduction to these topics currently available to students of political science, this is all the more tragic. Thus, in their introductory essay, David Marsh and Gerry Stoker suggest, quite remarkably, that "ontology is concerned with what we can know and epistemology with how we can know it" (2002, 11). Yet in the first substantive chapter of the volume, David Marsh, this time with Paul Furlong, defines ontology (correctly) as "a theory of being" and suggests that epistemology relates to "what we can know about the world" and (more problematically) "how we can know it" (2002, 18–19). Of these, only the second definition of ontology is entirely unproblematic.

know about it, and methodology to how we might go about acquiring that knowledge.

As this perhaps already serves to indicate, their relationship is also directional—ontology logically precedes epistemology which logically precedes methodology (see also Archer 1998; Bhaskar 1989, 49; Gilbert 1989, 440; though cf. Smith 1990, 18). We cannot know what we are capable of knowing (epistemology) until such time as we have settled on (a set of assumptions about) the nature of the context in which that knowledge must be acquired (ontology). Similarly, we cannot decide upon an appropriate set of strategies for interrogating political processes (methodology) until we have settled upon the limits of our capacity to acquire knowledge of such processes (epistemology) and, indeed, the nature of such processes themselves (ontology).

The directional dependence of this relationship is presented schematically and illustrated with respect to postmodernism in Figure 4.1. As this already serves to indicate, to suggest that ontological consideration are both irreducible and logically prior to those of epistemology is most definitely not to suggest that they are unrelated. The degree of confidence that we might have for the claims we make about political phenomena, for instance, is likely to vary significantly depending on our view of the relationship between the ideas we formulate on the one hand and the political referents of those ideas, on the other. In this way, our ontology may shape our epistemology; moreover, both are likely to have methodological implications. If we are happy to conceive of ourselves as disinterested and dispassionate observers of an external (political) reality existing independently of our conceptions of it, then we are likely to be rather more confident epistemologically than if we are prepared to concede that: (1) we are, at best, partisan participant observers; (2) that there is no neutral vantage-point from which the political can be viewed objectively; and that (3) the ideas we fashion of the political context we inhabit influence our behavior and hence the unfolding dynamics of that political context.[5] Such ontological assumptions and their epistemological implications are, in turn, likely to influence significantly the type of evidence we consider and the techniques we deploy to interrogate that evidence. If, for instance, we are keen to acknowledge (ontologically) an independent causal role for ideas in determining the developmental trajectory of political institutions, then we are likely to devote our methodological energies to gauging the understandings of political subjects. If, by contrast, we see ideas as merely epiphenomenal of ultimately determinant material bases (for instance, the self-interest of the actors who hold such ideas), then our methodological attentions will be focused elsewhere.

---

[5] To suggest that our ideas influence our conduct and that our conduct has, in turn, the capacity to reshape our environment is not, of course, to insist that it necessarily does so in any given setting over any particular time-horizon. It is to suggest, however, that insofar as conduct serves to shape and reshape a given political landscape, the ideas held by actors about that context are crucial to any understanding of such a process of political change (see also Rueschemeyer, this volume).

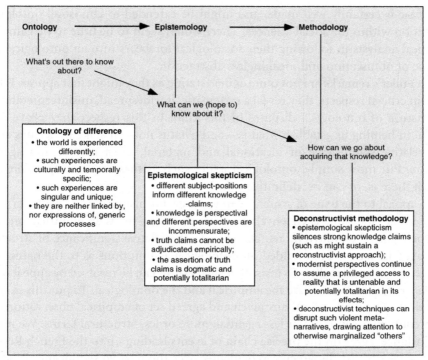

Fig. 4.1 The directional dependence of ontology, epistemology, and methodology: the case of postmodernism
Source: Hay (2002: 227).

3   THE STATUS OF ONTOLOGICAL CLAIMS

Given the sheer volume of literature devoted in recent years to questions of ontology (principally the structure–agency and material–ideational relationships) in political science and international relations, it might be tempting to assume that the need for a series of reflections on this question is relatively undisputed. The reality, however, it somewhat different. For even in sociology, perhaps the natural home of reflection on such issues, there are dissenting voices. In making the case for the centrality of such concerns to political analysis it is perhaps appropriate that we first deal with the potential objections. Among the most vociferous of critics of the "craze" for abstract ontological reflection is Steve Fuller. His central argument is simply stated:

Given the supposedly abortive attempts at solving the structure–agency problem, one is tempted to conclude that sociologists are not smart enough to solve the problem or that the problem itself is spurious. (Fuller 1998, 104)

The case is certainly well made, and might be extended to almost all ontological reflection within the social sciences. There would seem to be little to be gained by political analysts in following their sociological forebears into an ontological cul-de-sac of obfuscation and meaningless abstraction.

Yet Fuller's remarks are not quite as devastating as they might first appear. For, in certain crucial respects, they reveal a systematic, if widespread, misinterpretation of the nature of ontological disputes of this kind. In this respect they prove quite useful in helping us establish what is—and what is not—at stake in debates about the relative significance of ideational and material, or structural and agential factors. Put most simply, ontological issues such as these are not "problems" to which there is, or can be, definitive solutions.

To appeal to the issue of structure and agency, for instance, as a "problem" with a potential "solution" is effectively to claim that the issue is an empirical one that can be resolved definitively. Yet, claims as to the relative significance of structural and agential factors are founded on ontological assumptions as to the nature of a social and political reality. To insist that such claims can be resolved by appeal to the evidence is, then, to conflate the empirical and the ontological. To put this in more practical and prosaic terms, any given and agreed set of empirical observations can be accounted for in more or less agential, more or less structural terms. We might, for instance, agree on the precise chain of events leading up to the French Revolution of 1789 whilst disagreeing vehemently over the relative significance of structural and agential factors in the explanation of the event itself. Evidence alone is not ontologically discriminating, though it is often presented as such.[6]

Two important implications follow directly from the above discussion. First, if the relative significance of structural and agential, ideational, and material factors cannot be established empirically, then we must seek to avoid all claims which suggest that it might. Sadly, such claims are commonplace. Even Wendt himself, doyen both of the "structure–agency problematique" and of constructivism in international relations theory, is not above such conceptual confusions. Consider the following passage from an otherwise exemplary discussion co-written with Ian Shapiro:

The differences among ... "realist" models of agency and structure—and among them and their individualist and holist rivals—are differences about where the important causal mechanisms lie in social life. As such, *we can settle them only by wrestling with the empirical merits of their claims about human agency and social structure ... These are in substantial part empirical questions.*   (Wendt and Shapiro 1997, 181, emphasis added)

---

[6] This is largely because the process of presenting evidence is invariably one which situates it ontologically (with respect to often tacit ontological assumptions, such as the extent, if any, of a separation of appearance and reality).

Wendt and Shapiro are surely right to note that ontological differences such as those between, say, more agency-centered and more structure-centered accounts, tend to resolve themselves into differences about where to look for and, indeed, what counts as important causal mechanisms in the first place. This implies that ontology precedes epistemology. Such a view is entirely consistent with the argument of the previous section—we must decide what exists out there to know about (ontology) before we can consider what knowledge we might acquire of it (epistemology), let alone how we might go about acquiring that knowledge (methodology). Yet having noted this, Wendt and Shapiro almost immediately abandon the logic it implies, suggesting that we might choose between contending ontologies on the basis of what we observe empirically. Surely this now implies that epistemology precedes ontology. If our ontology informs where we look for causal mechanisms and what we see in the first place (as they contend), then how can we rely upon what we observe to adjudicate between contending ontologies?

Wendt and Shapiro's confusion is further compounded in the passage which immediately follows, in which a Popperian logic of falsifiability is invoked:

The advocates of individualism, structuralism and structuration theory have all done a poor job of specifying the conditions under which their claims about the relationship of agency and social structure would be falsified.   (Wendt and Shapiro 1997, 181)

Here again we see direct appeal to the possibility of an epistemological refutation of ontological propositions. The point is that, as ontological positions, individualism, structuralism, and structuration theory *cannot* be falsified—our preference between them has to be adjudicated differently. A similar conflation underpins Wendt's recent prescriptive suggestion that "ontology talk is necessary, but we should also be looking for ways to translate it into propositions that might be adjudicated empirically" (1999, 37). If only this were possible. When, as Wendt himself notes, ontological sensitivities inform what is "seen" in the first place and, for (philosophical) realists like himself, provide the key to peering through the mists of the ephemeral and the superficial to the structured reality beneath, the idea that ontological claims as to what exists can be adjudicated empirically is rendered deeply suspect. Quite simply, perspectives on the question of structure and agency, or any other ontological issue for that matter, cannot be falsified—for they make no necessary empirical claim. It is for precisely this reason that logical positivists (like Popper) reject as meaningless ontological claims such as those upon which realism and structuration theory are premised.[7]

It is important, then, that we avoid claiming empirical license for ontological claims and assumptions. Yet arguably more important still is that we resist the

---

[7] However tempting this strategy may seem, however, it does not provide an escape from ontological issues and choices. For, as indicated earlier, whether we choose to acknowledge them or nor, political analysis necessarily proceeds on the basis of ontological assumptions.

temptation to present positions on, say, the structure–agency question as universal solutions for all social scientific dilemmas. In particular, social ontologies cannot be brought in to resolve substantive empirical disputes. Giddens' structuration theory can no more tell me who will win the next US presidential election than the theory of predestation can tell me whether my train will arrive on time tomorrow. The latter might be able to tell me that the movements of trains is etched into the archaeology of historical time itself, just as the structuration theorist might tell me the next US presidential election will be won and lost in the interaction between political actors and the context in which they find themselves. Neither is likely to be of much practical use to me, nor is it likely to provide much consolation if my train is late and my preferred candidate loses. It is important, then, that we do not expect too much from "solutions" to ontological "problems."

4   ONTOLOGICAL DISPUTES IN POLITICAL ANALYSIS

Of all issues in political ontology, it is the related though by no means interchangeable (see Pettit 1993) questions of the relationship between individuals and social collectivities and between structure and agency that have undoubtedly attracted the most sustained attention and reflection over the longest period of time. A rather more recent set of concerns relates to the question of the relationship between the material and the ideational as (related or independent) dimensions of political reality. In the brief sections which follow, I consider each set of issues in turn.

4.1   The Individual–Group Relationship

In political analysis and the philosophy of the social sciences more broadly there is no more hardy perennial than the question of the relationship between individuals and social collectivities or groups (see Fay 1996, ch. 3; Gilbert 1989; Hollis 1994; Pettit 1993; Ryan 1970, ch. 8). Can collective actors (states, political parties, social movements, classes, and so forth) realistically, or indeed just usefully, be said to exist? If so, do they exhibit organic qualities, such that their character or nature is not simply reducible to the aggregation of the constituent units (generally individual actors) from which they are forged? Are such entities (if that is indeed what they are) appropriate subjects of political analysis and, if so, what if any behavioural characteristics can be attributed to them?

These and other related ontological questions have divided political analysts, and will no doubt continue to divide political analysts, as they have divided philosophers, for centuries. Generally speaking the controversy they have generated has seen protagonists resolve themselves with one of two mutually exclusive positions. These are usually labeled "individualism" and "holism" and they are often defined in mutually antagonistic terms. As Margaret Gilbert explains, ontological individualism is simply the doctrine that "social groups are nothing over and above the individuals who are their members" (1989, 428). It tends to be associated with a further, analytical set of claims, namely that what she terms "everyday collectivity concepts" (states, classes, parties, and other groups) "are analysable without remainder in terms of concepts other than collectivity concepts, in particular, in terms of the concept of an individual person, his [sic] goals, beliefs and so on" (1989, 434–5).

Holism, by contrast, is invariably understood as the simple denial of individualism, the doctrine that "social groups exist in their own right" (1989, 428) or, in Brian Fay's more applied terms, that "the theories which explain social phenomena are not reducible to theories about the individuals which perform them" (1996, 50). In its more extreme variants, however, holism is less a belief in the organic nature of social and political reality than the dogmatic assertion that the task of social and political analysts is exclusively to document the (causal) role of social, i.e. holistic, phenomena, processes, and dynamics (cf. Ryan 1970, 172). In this form, holism, though very much in vogue in the 1970s, is now little more than a term of abuse within contemporary political science. It might be tempting, then, to see the dispute having been resolved in favor of individualism. This, however, would be too rash an inference to draw. For although most analytical routes in political science today lead from individualism, many make considerable concessions, as we shall see, to holism.

The dispute, as already indicated, is a timeless one, with perhaps the most eloquent defender of ontological (and, indeed, methodological) individualism being John Stuart Mill:

The laws of the phenomena of society are, and can be, nothing but the laws of the actions and passions of human being united together in the social state ... Men [sic] are not, when brought together, converted into another kind of substance, with different properties ... Human beings in society have no properties but those which are derived from, and may be resolved into, the laws of nature of individual man. (1970 [1843], 573; cited in Hollis 1994, 10)

Though, as is often noted, Mill was by no means consistent in keeping to the strictures of such an individualism and can be found at various times on the other side of the fence, he is a seemingly obligatory first citation for those asserting or defending their (ontological) individualism.

Unremarkably, the most dogged contemporary defence of individualism is found in rational choice theory. Jon Elster is characteristically incisive in claiming that "the elementary unit of social life is the individual human action." Consequently "to explain social institutions and social change is to show how they arise as the result of the action and interaction of individuals" (1989, 13). What is unusual about this comment is that, unlike most rational choice theory, it seeks to present and defend individualism in ontological, rather than in more narrowly methodological, terms. Yet even rational choice theory, resolutely committed as it remains to methodological individualism, has made significant concessions to the organic qualities of social and political collectivities identified by holists. Indeed, in this respect, the developmental trajectory of rational choice in recent years is suggestive of something of an emerging ontological consensus amongst political analysts. Two points might here be made. First, whilst there have always been those who have presented rational choice theory in such terms (most notably, Friedman 1953, 14–15), many more contemporary rational choice theorists seem prepared to accept the ontological irrealism of rational choice assumptions, defending such premises in terms of their analytical utility not their correspondence to an external reality (for a more sustained discussion, see Hay 2004). Second, the move by many rational choice theorists, particularly so-called rational choice institutionalists, from an absolute towards a "bounded," i.e. context-dependent, conception of rationality significantly qualifies and arguably violates any purist defence of ontological or, indeed, methodological individualism. For, put simply, if the stylized rational actor's utility- and/or preference-function is a product of her context, role, or systemic function (as in much contemporary rational choice institutionalism), then to explain her behavior or to predict the consequences of her behavior in terms of such a utility/preference-function is no longer to subscribe to a methodological individualism.

As this perhaps suggests, however seemingly entrenched holism and individualism have, on occasions, become, a commonsense ground between such antagonistic extremes exists and is inhabited by a growing number of political analysts. Such a position accepts, ontologically, the following: (1) that a social whole is "not merely the sum of its parts"; (2) that there are "holistic properties" of such social wholes; (3) that these "can sensibly be said to belong to the whole and not to any of the parts"; and yet (4) that dismantle the whole and we are left with the parts and "not them and some mysterious property which formerly held the whole thing together" (Ryan 1970, 181).

4.2   The Structure–Agency Relationship

No less classical or disputed an issue in the philosophy of the social sciences is the question of the structure–agency relationship. Though closely related, it is by no means irreducible to the question of the relationship between groups and individuals and has been far more hotly contested than the latter in recent years.

Though space does not permit a detailed review of the literature, the key trends can nonetheless be established relatively simply (for more sustained discussion see Hay 1995; 2002, 89–134):

- The proliferation of interest in the relationship between structure and agency has in fact been remarkably consensual, with scholars in political science and international relations rounding on both structuralist and intentionalist tendencies.[8]
- In so doing they have come to champion a range of perspectives from social theory, notably Giddens' (1984) structuration theory and the critical realists' strategic-relational approach (Bhaskar 1979; 1989; Jessop 1990; 1996).
- What each of these perspectives shares is the attempt to explore the dynamic interplay of structure and agency.

In short, and almost without exception, those who have reflected in a sustained fashion upon the question of structure and agency have done so with an increasing sense of frustration at the tacit intentionalism or, more usually, structuralism of existing mainstream approaches to political analysis. In particular they have found structuralism lurking in some apparently unlikely places. Chief amongst these is rational choice theory.

As a perspective which emphasizes the rationality exhibited by conscious and reflective actors in the process of making choices, it is difficult to imagine an approach that is seemingly more attentive to agency. However, impressions can be deceptive. For, within any rational choice model, we know one thing above all: that the actor will behave rationally, maximizing his or her personal utility. Consequently, any rational actor in a given context will choose precisely the same (optimal) course of action. Actors are essentially interchangeable (Tsebelis 1990, 43). Moreover, where there is more than one optimal course of action (where, in short, there are multiple equilibria), we can expect actors' behavior to be distributed predictably between—and only between—such optima. What this implies is that the agent's "choice" is rendered predictable (and, in the absence of multiple equilbria, entirely predictable) given the context. The implications of this are clear. We need know nothing about the actor to predict the outcome of political behavior. For it is independent of the actor in question. Indeed, it is precisely this which gives rational choice modes of explanation their (much cherished) predictive capacity.

In short, it is only the substitution of a fixed preference function for an indeterminate actor that allows a spurious and naturalist notion of prediction to be retained in rational choice (see also Hay 2004). Render the analytical assumptions

---

[8] See, for instance, Adler 1997; Carlsnaes 1992; Cerny 1990; Dessler 1989; Kenny and Smith 1997; Smith 1998; 1999; Suganami 1999; Wendt 1987. For a review, see Hay 1995.

about the individual actor more complex and realistic (by recognizing some element of contingency) and rational choice models become indeterminate.

This raises a final and important point, something of a leitmotif of this chapter. The rise of political ontology has increasingly led to a series of challenges to naturalism (a belief in the possibility of a unity of method between the natural and social sciences) and to naturalistic political science more specifically. The above paragraphs provide but one example. As they suggest, rational choice theory can deliver a naturalist science of politics only by virtue of the implausible (ontological) assumptions it makes about the universally instrumental, self-serving, and utility-maximizing character of human conduct. These serve, in effect, to empty agency of any content such that the actor becomes a mere relay for delivering a series of imperatives inherent in the context itself. In short, a naturalist science of politics is only possible if we assume what we elsewhere deny—that all actors, in any given context, will act in a manner rendered predictable (in many cases fully determinate) by the context in which they find themselves. Soften the assumptions, or even the universality of the assumptions, and the fragile edifice of naturalism crumbles. With it must go the universal pretensions of much rational choice theory and, indeed, the very possibility of a predictive science of the political.

4.3   The Ideational–Material Relationship

Very similar themes emerge in the burgeoning literature on the relationship between the ideational and the material and the extent to which ideas may be accorded a causal and/or constitutive role in the determination of political outcomes.[9] Here, once more, the key question relates to the limits of naturalism. In particular, it is suggested, the existence of an irredeemably cognitive dimension to the social and political world for which there is no direct equivalent or analogue in the natural world, presents profound ontological impediments to a naturalist social science.

Once again there has been a considerable degree of harmony and consensus amongst those who have addressed these issues in ontological terms. The result is a convergence upon, and consolidation of, a position usually labeled constructivism in international relations theory, and usually seen as a development of historical institutionalism in political science (for a useful review see Blyth 2003). It defines itself in opposition to the materialist and naturalist rump of mainstream political science and international relations.

Like the qualified materialism of many contemporary rational choice institutionalists and neo-realists,[10] constructivists start from the recognition that we

[9] See Hay (2002, 194–215) for a more sustained discussion.
[10] See, for instance, Denzau and North 1994; Goldstein and Keohane 1993; North 1990.

cannot hope to understand political behavior without understanding the ideas actors hold about the environment in which they find themselves. Yet here the materialists and the constructivists part company, with the latter refusing to see such ideas as themselves reducible to ultimately determinant material factors (such as contextually given interests). Consequently, they accord ideas an independent causal role in political explanation. Nonetheless, whilst it is important not simply to reduce the ideational to a reflection, say, of underlying material interests, it is equally important not to subscribe to a voluntarist idealism in which political outcomes might be read off, more or less directly, from the desires, motivations, and cognitions of the immediate actors themselves. What is required, instead, is a recognition of the complex interaction of material and ideational factors. Political outcomes are, in short, neither a simple reflection of actors' intentions and understandings nor of the contexts which give rise to such intentions and understandings. Rather, they are a product of the impact of the strategies actors devise as means to realize their intentions upon a context which favors certain strategies over others and does so irrespective of the intentions of the actors themselves.

Constructivism is, however, a broad church, encompassing a diverse range of positions. At the idealist end of the spectrum we find varieties of "thick" constructivism keen to privilege the constitutive role of ideas whilst not entirely denying the significance of material factors. At the other end of the spectrum we find varieties of critical realism whose rather "thinner" constructivism tends to emphasize instead the constraints the material world places on such discursive constructions.[11] What each of these positions shares, however, is a complex or dialectical view of the relationship between the ideational and the material and a rejection of the possibility of a naturalist social science.

5   CONCLUSION

As the previous sections have sought to demonstrate, the proliferation of literature on political ontology in recent years has produced (or perhaps reflected and reinforced) a remarkable consensus. The vast majority of authors who have interrogated systematically the relationships between structure and agency and the material and the ideational *as ontological issues*, have, for instance, come subsequently to promote a post-naturalist, post-positivist approach to social and political analysis

---

[11] For a variety of different positions within this spectrum compare the various contributions to Christiansen, Jørgensen, and Wiener (2001).

premised upon the acknowledgement of the dynamic interplay of structure and agency and material and ideational factors. In so doing they have pointed to a consistent disparity between the often tacit and normalized analytical assumptions of existing mainstream approaches to political analysis and those which emerge from sustained ontological reflection.

In particular they have challenged the often parsimonious and self-confessedly unrealistic analytical assumptions which invariably make naturalist approaches to political science possible. This is undoubtedly a useful exercise and has already given rise to genuinely novel approaches to political analysis and a series of important insights (the contributions of the new constructivist–institutionalist synthesis being a case in point). Yet it can be taken too far. In one sense it is unremarkable that political ontologists, interested principally in the extent to which the complexity and contingency of the "real world" of social and political interaction might be captured, encourage us to choose complex, credible, and realistic analytical assumptions. Yet this is not a costless move. Simple, elegant, and parsimonious analytical assumptions are unlikely to satisfy the political ontologist, but this may not be sufficient reason to jettison them. However unrealistic they may be, they have an appeal and can certainly be defended in the kind of pragmatic terms that are unlikely to feature prominently in the ontologist's deliberations. Here, as elsewhere, clear trade-offs are involved. Political ontology can certainly help us to appreciate what is at stake in such choices, providing something of a counterbalance to the mainstream's characteristic silence on its most central assumptions, but it cannot be allowed to dictate such choices alone.

References

ADLER, E. 1997. Seizing the middle ground: constructivism in world politics. *European Journal of International Relations*, 3: 319–63.

ARCHER, M. S. 1998. Social theory and the analysis of society. Pp. 69–85 in *Knowing the Social World*, ed. T. May and M. Williams. Buckingham: Open University Press.

BENTON, T., and CRAIB, I. 2001. *Philosophy of Social Science: The Philosophical Foundations of Social Thought*. Buckingham: Open University Press.

BHASKAR, R. 1979. *The Limits of Naturalism*. Brighton: Harvester Wheatsheaf.

—— 1989. *Reclaiming Reality*. London: Verso.

BLAIKIE, N. 1993. *Approaches to Social Enquiry*. Cambridge: Polity.

BLYTH, M. 2003. Structures do not come with an instruction sheet: interests, ideas and progress in political science. *Perspectives on Politics*, 1: 695–706.

BROWNMILLER, S. 1975. *Against Our Will: Men, Women and Rape*. London: Secker and Warburg.

CARLSNAES, W. 1992. The agent–structure problem in foreign policy analysis. *International Studies Quarterly*, 6: 245–70.

CERNY, P. G. 1990. *The Changing Architecture of Politics: Structure, Agency and the Future of the State*. London: Sage.

CHRISTIANSEN, T., JØRGENSEN, K. E., and WIENER, A. 2001. Introduction. Pp. 1–21 in *The Social Construction of Europe*, ed. T. Christiansen et al. London: Sage.

DALY, M. 1978. *Gyn/Ecology: The Metaethics of Radical Feminism*. Boston: Beacon Press.

DENZAU, A. T., and NORTH, D. C. 1994. Shared mental models: ideologies and institutions. *Kyklos*, 47: 3–31

DESSLER, D. 1989. What's at stake in the agent-structure debate? *International Organization*, 43: 441–73.

ELSHTAIN, J. B. 1981. *Public Man, Private Woman: Women in Social and Political Thought*. Princeton, NJ: Princeton University Press.

ELSTER, J. 1989. *Nuts and Bolts for the Social Sciences*. Cambridge: Cambridge University Press.

FAY, B. 1996. *Contemporary Philosophy of Social Science: A Multicultural Approach*. Oxford: Blackwell.

FRIEDMAN, M. 1953. *Essays in Positive Economics*. Chicago: University of Chicago Press.

FULLER, S. 1998. From content to context: a social epistemology of the structure–agency craze. Pp. 92–117 in *What is Social Theory? The Philosophical Debates*, ed. A. Sica. Oxford: Blackwell.

GIDDENS, A. 1984. *The Constitution of Society*. Cambridge: Polity.

GILBERT, M. 1989. *On Social Facts*. Princeton, NJ: Princeton University Press.

GOLDSTEIN, J., and KEOHANE, R. O. (eds.) 1993. *Ideas and Foreign Policy: Beliefs, Institutions and Political Change*. Ithaca, NY: Cornell University Press.

GROSSMANN, R. 1992. *The Existence of the World: An Introduction to Ontology*. London: Routledge.

HAY, C. 1995. Structure and agency. Pp. 189–206 in *Theory and Methods in Political Science*, ed. D. Marsh and G. Stoker. London: Macmillan.

—— 2002. *Political Analysis*. Basingstoke: Palgrave.

—— 2004. Theory, stylised heuristic or self-fulfilling prophecy? The status of rational choice theory in public administration. *Public Administration*, 82: 39–61.

HOLLIS, M. 1994. *The Philosophy of Social Science*. Cambridge: Cambridge University Press.

HONDERICH, T. (ed.) 1995. *The Oxford Companion to Philosophy*. Oxford: Oxford University Press.

JACQUETTE, D. 2002. *Ontology*. Chesham: Acumen.

JESSOP, B. 1990. *State Theory: Putting Capitalist States in their Place*. Cambridge: Polity.

—— 1996. Interpretative sociology and the dialectic of structure and agency. *Theory, Culture and Society*, 13 (1): 119–28.

KING, G., KEOHANE, R. O., and VERBA, S. (eds.) 1994. *Designing Social Inquiry: Scientific Inference in Qualitative Research*. Princeton, NJ: Princeton University Press.

KENNY, M., and SMITH, M. J. 1997. (Mis)Understanding Blair. *Political Quarterly*, 68: 220–30.

MÄKI, U. 2001. Economic ontology: what? why? how? Pp. 3–14 in *The Economic Worldview: Studies in the Ontology of Economics*, ed. U. Mäki. Cambridge: Cambridge University Press.

—— 2002. The dismal queen of the social sciences. Pp. 3–32 in *Fact and Fiction in Economics: Models, Realism and Social Construction*, ed. U. Mäki. Cambridge: Cambridge University Press.

MARSH, D., and FURLONG, P. 2002. A skin not a sweater: ontology and epistemology in political science. Pp. 17–41 in *Theory and Methods in Political Science*, ed. D. Marsh and G. Stoker, 2nd edn. Basingstoke: Palgrave.

——and STOKER, G. 2002. Introduction. Pp. 1–16 in *Theory and Methods in Political Science*, ed. D. Marsh and G. Stoker, 2nd edn. Basingstoke: Palgrave.

MILL, J. S. 1970. *A System of Logic*. London: Longman; originally published 1843.

MONROE, K. R. (ed.) 2004. *Perestroika, Methodological Pluralism, Governance and Diversity in Contemporary American Political Science*. New Haven, Conn.: Yale University Press.

NORTH, D. C. 1990. *Institutions, Institutional Change and Economic Performance*. Cambridge: Cambridge University Press.

PETTIT, P. 1993. *The Common Mind: An Essay on Psychology, Society and Politics*. Oxford: Oxford University Press.

RYAN, R. 1970. *The Philosophy of the Social Sciences*. Basingstoke: Macmillan.

SCHMITT, F. F. 2003. Socialising metaphysics: an introduction. Pp. 1–37 in *Socialising Metaphysics*, ed. F. F. Schmitt. Boulder, Colo.: Rowman and Littlefield.

SMITH, M. J. 1998. Reconceptualising the British state: theoretical and empirical challenges to central government. *Public Administration*, 76: 45–72.

SMITH, M. J. 1999. *The Core Executive in Britain*. London: Macmillan.

SMITH, S. 1990. Positivism and beyond. Pp. 11–46 in *International Theory: Positivism and Beyond*, ed. S. Smith, K. Booth, and M. Zalewski. Cambridge: Cambridge University Press.

SUGANAMI, H. 1999. Agents, structures, narratives. *European Journal of International Relations*, 5: 365–86.

TILLY, C., and GOODIN, R. E. 2006. It depends. Pp. 3–32 in *The Oxford Handbook of Contextual Political Analysis.*, ed. R. E Goodin and C. Tilly. Oxford: Oxford University Press.

TSEBELIS, G. 1990. *Nested Games: Rational Choice in Comparative Politics*. Berkeley: University of California Press.

WENDT, A. 1999. *Social Theory of International Politics*. Cambridge: Cambridge University Press.

——and SHAPIRO, I. 1997. The misunderstood promise of realist social theory. Pp. 166–90 in *Contemporary Empirical Political Theory*, ed. K. R. Monroe. Berkeley: University of California Press.

WOLF, N. 1993. *Fire With Fire: The New Female Power and How to Use It*. New York: Fawcett Combine.

YOUNG, I. M. 1990. *Throwing Like a Girl and Other Essays in Feminist Philosophy and Social Theory*. Bloomington: Indiana University Press.

CHAPTER 5

....

MIND, WILL, AND CHOICE

....

JAMES N. DRUCKMAN

ARTHUR LUPIA

MUCH of what we recognize as political is a function of choice. Political phenomena such as elections, wars, legislation, and protests occur because people choose to take particular actions at particular times. For scholars, the concept of *choice* is important because it primes us to consider not just the existence of an action, but also the volition that produced it. Such priming of volition is why news of important, unusual, or controversial political phenomena is often followed by the question, "Why?"

Scholars answer this question in many ways. Some emphasize attributes of those who make the choices. Others focus on the context in which the choices are made.

Individual-centered and context-based explanations are sometimes posed in opposition to one another—as if the validation of one approach necessarily undermines the other. In this essay, we argue for the benefits of integrating the two approaches. While there are several ways to examine the interactive effects of individual and contextual variables, we base our argument on a particular method of integration. The method entails using tools and concepts often associated with individual-centered analyses to clarify the relationship between context and choice.

* We thank Adam Seth Levine and Elizabeth A. Suhay for helpful comments.

We offer this chapter in response to the editors' invitation to write on "mind, will, and choice" in the domain of contextual political science. We find the invitation interesting for at least two reasons. First, political choices have long been explained as products of *mind* or *will*. Second, advances in several scientific fields shed new light on choice and its cognitive antecedents. Therefore, in what follows, we use the method of integration described above to show that new advances in the study of human thought not only aid individual-centered analysis by challenging old notions of mind and will, but also help scholars study contextual effects more effectively.

Our chapter is organized into five sections: this introduction, three sections respectively entitled "Mind," "Will," and "Choice," and a brief conclusion. In "Mind," we argue that many questions about how context affects choice are better answered by focusing on the brain instead of the mind. In "Will," we make a parallel argument for focusing on preferences instead of wills. The key premise of these two sections is that brains and preferences, as the foci of decades of empirical study, are more amenable to reliable measurement and transparent analysis than are minds and wills—about whose measurability there is much less consensus. The key conclusion of these sections is that incorporating insights about brains and preferences—concepts often associated with individual-level analyses—into context-oriented research designs can provide greater clarity about how, when, and why factors such as time, place, language, and culture affect political choices.

In "Mind" and "Will," most of the studies cited in support of our key conclusion are experimental. These experiments document how deliberately altering specific aspects of a controlled domain affects critical attributes of focal phenomena and can provide excellent vehicles for evaluating causal hypotheses. While social science experiments are tools often associated with research on individual-level phenomena, they can be powerful tools in contextual analyses. If, for example, a specific contextual factor is presumed irrelevant to a particular political interaction, then a well-designed experiment that varies whether or not the named factor is present can be sufficient to reject the hypothesis. Several of the studies we cite have this attribute and, hence, provide an effective means of understanding why certain interactions of context and cognition affect choice.

In the section entitled "Choice," we draw on non-cooperative game theory to complement the perspective of the laboratory experiments cited in "Mind" and "Will." Scholars use this brand of game theory to present two or more situations that differ by perhaps only one attribute. They then work through the variation's logical implications. While this approach (which, we will suggest, is akin to a thought experiment) is not often associated with context-based political analysis, we show that it has been used very effectively to identify key causal attributes of important contextual variables (that have been empirically verified).

In sum, we contend how and when context affects choice is a function not just of traditional contextual variables such as time, place, language, and culture, but also of increasingly well-understood properties of brains and preferences. At the same time, we come to understand that answers to many questions about choice that were once answered strictly in terms of mind and will are not context independent. For a wide range of political inquiries, therefore, constructive and clarifying answers can emerge when we integrate knowledge of context and cognition.

1   MIND

How does context affect choice? Our answer is based on a simple model of human action that follows from scholarly efforts in many disciplines. Following Clark (1997), we describe this model as:

$$\{mind, will, choice\} = f(brain, body, world).$$

Interactions among brain, body, and world create feelings, perceptions, beliefs, and preferences. They determine the range of actions a person thinks he can take and the consequences he associates with his actions.

In this model, the body is the intermediary between brain and world. Unlike the brain, it has direct contact with certain parts of the world. Its physical construction provides a conduit that translates environmental stimuli into electrical impulses and chemical reactions that travel to the brain. It simultaneously converts products of brain activity into embodied actions (e.g. an arm movement or a flight response).

The brain, in turn, "processes information" by receiving, transforming, and manufacturing the impulses and reactions described above. In the brain–body–world correspondence, the brain is distinguished from the mind. The brain is a discrete physical object with measurable attributes. While remaining mysterious in some ways, its basic anatomy and functional properties are increasingly well understood. Indeed, many well-documented tests show how electrical activity and chemical reactions correspond to consciousness and subconscious brain activities.[1]

The *mind*, by contrast, is a centuries-old philosophical construct. Among the concept's problems when applied in an analytic framework is that it is sometimes used to refer to what we now understand as parts of the brain, sometimes refers to the brain itself, and sometimes refers to products of a brain–body–world interaction. Despite this lack of clarity, many political theories, folk theories, and contemporary common wisdoms about social reasoning are based on conjectures

---

[1] For reviews of relevant research, see Kandel, Schwartz, and Jessell (1995), and Cacioppo et al. (2002).

about minds. One problem with this legacy is that twentieth-century research on brains has exposed many of these conjectures as false. Fortunately, these new studies can yield improved measures of cognitive functions that, if attended to by theoreticians, can improve our ability to understand and explain many political interactions.[2]

Consider, for example, the case of deliberative democracy.[3] The idea of deliberative democracy has gained increasing attention in recent years, particularly after the writings of Jürgen Habermas (see, e.g., Fishkin 1991; 1995). Habermas describes a context—the ideal speech environment—in which allocating speech rights in an equal manner increases civic competence. In recent years, the concept of ideal speech environments has moved from a philosophical endeavor to an icon for democratic reformers (see, e.g., Gutmann and Thompson 1996; Ackerman and Fishkin 2004). While seeking uniformly to improve civic competence, many such efforts are based on mind-based predictions about the consequences of deliberation that twentieth-century research on brains contradicts.

For example, many deliberation advocates describe communication as a process where participants will leave privileging certain pieces of information rather than others.[4] But under what conditions would a deliberative encounter lead a participant to favor one claim over another? A necessary condition for such an effect is that the target audience for these critical pieces of information pays attention to them and thinks about them for at least some minimum amount of time.

A challenge for deliberative advocates is the fact that the capacity of the part of the brain where such information would have to be initially processed—working (or short-term) memory—is very small (Kandel, Schwartz, and Jessell 1995, 664). Moreover, the modal decay rate of items that are ever admitted into working memory (i.e. the items to which we pay attention) is best stated in terms of milliseconds. As a consequence, unchangeable physical attributes of working (or short-term) memory force us to ignore everything around us. To get our attention, an utterance must fend off competitors—such as aspects of prior or future events—with which a person may be preoccupied, the simultaneous actions or utterances of others, background noise, and so on. Therefore, people pay attention to only a tiny fraction of the information that is available to them and can later recall only a tiny fraction of the things to which they paid attention.

Moreover, even if a piece of information is attended to, an exercise such as deliberation can increase a participant's competence only if the information is processed in a particular way that leaves *a unique cognitive legacy* in long-term memory (henceforth, LTM). The physical foundation of LTM is found in the

---

[2] See e.g. Churchland and Sejnowski (1992), Schacter (2001), and Pinker (2002). For an efficiently packaged overview of central debates among cognitive scientists, see McCauley (1996).

[3] This example follows from one presented in Lupia (2002).

[4] See e.g. the contrasting descriptions of deliberation by Ackerman and Fishkin (2004), Lupia (2004), and Posner (2004).

distribution of specialized cells throughout the brain. Chemical reactions within and across these cells generate activation potentials for particular kinds of mental responses. You can think of activation potentials as corresponding to probabilities of recalling things you once noticed. What we usually call learning involves changing these activation potentials. The physical embodiment of learning that smoking is highly correlated with lung cancer, for example, is a change in activation potentials that makes you more likely to associate pain and death with smoking. Therefore, if one person's attempt to increase another's competence through deliberation does not lead to a change in another person's activation potentials, the latter person's competence will not increase. However, not any change in activation potentials is sufficient to increase competence—the change must cause participants' LTMs to produce "ideas" that induce them to take different and more competent actions than they would have taken absent deliberation.

An implication of these facts is that claims about the positive impact of deliberation—on individuals or the societies in which they are members—will be true only if they are consistent with physical and biological processes that govern what the target audience will attend to (short-term memory) and remember (LTM) about the event. Many deliberation advocates fail to recognize the existence of such conditions, instead adopting the approach that if people are put into a room together and each given a chance to speak, all participants will walk out enlightened. This practice is tragic because it leads well-intentioned people to invest time and effort in deliberative efforts that are destined to fail even though research on attention, memory, and persuasion make the problems knowable in advance.

Our increasing knowledge of even basic brain functions places ominous clouds over the landscape of claims about deliberative effectiveness. Applied research brings more reason for doubt.

Deliberation is said, for example, to increase engagement, tolerance, and justification for individuals' opinions (see Mendelberg 2002). However, Schkade, Sunstein, and Kahneman (2000, 1139) ran studies on over 500 mock juries and found that "the principal effect of deliberation is often to polarize individual judgments." Hibbing and Theiss-Morse (2002) review a growing literature on the topic that conveys many similar insights.

A parallel claim is that opinions formed via deliberation with conflicting perspectives are presumed to capture better the "will of the people" by ensuring quality opinions that approximate truth, reasonableness, and rationality (Mill 1859, 23; Dewey 1927, 208; Kinder and Herzog 1993, 349; Benhabib 1996, 71; Bohman 1998, 401; Fishkin 1999, 283; Dryzek 2000, 55; Mendelberg 2002, 180). Lupia and McCubbins (1998) use communication models and a range of laboratory experiments to reveal conditions under which communication *decreases* participants' competence (i.e. they identify conditions under which the most knowledgeable people in a room are not the most persuasive). Sanders (1997) reaches a similar conclusion by focusing on how power relationships tip the balance of communicative effectiveness in favor of socially privileged groups. Moreover, Goodin and Nie-meyer's (2003) work casts doubt on empirical claims about the impact of deliber-ation's communicative element. They show that information given to respondents in advance of a deliberative exercise had a far greater impact on participants' attitudes than the communication that followed (also see Parkinson (2006) on limitations to deliberation via mass media).

While studies such as these can be used to criticize the deliberative democracy movement, a more enlightened use for them is to improve it. Deliberative demo-crats are correct in presuming that contextual variations *can* affect when and what citizens communicate to one another. The key to achieving success, and avoiding a waste of the goodwill and human capital devoted to such efforts, is knowing when, why, and how deliberation's effect is beneficial. Approaches that combine knowledge of communicative contexts with rigorously tested principles of human cognition will provide greater clarity about what contextual alterations are neces-sary or sufficient to make deliberation deliver the normative benefits its supporters desire.

2   WILL

How do people decide to choose one candidate, policy, or action rather than another? In many cases, the question is answered by using the concept of will. While framing the volition of individuals, majorities, and collectives in terms of will has been effective in the past, will is problematic as an analytic concept. Chief among the concept's problems is how to measure it.[5] A common response to the problem of measurability is that preferences now play the role once occupied by will in political analysis.

We define a *preference* as "a comparative evaluation of (i.e., a ranking over) a set of objects" (Druckman and Lupia 2000, 2). For example, imagine that an individual faces a choice between two alternatives—Policy A and Policy B. In this case, the individual may prefer Policy A to Policy B, prefer Policy B to Policy A, or be

---

[5] Social choice scholarship including that of Arrow (1963), McKelvey (1976), and Schofield (1983) has convinced many people to question even the existence of collective will. While this work proves that some universal claims about attributes of collective will are logically inconsistent, Lupia and McCubbins (2005) demonstrate that such results are often overinterpreted. Specifically, the proofs are not sufficient to negate all possible propositions about collective intent.

indifferent between Policy A and Policy B.[6] Seen in this light, if a contextual variable is hypothesized to *cause* a choice, then at least one contextual variable must affect an actor's preference in a particular way (e.g. the variable causes the actor to change his revealed preference from some option A to some option ∼A).

While many scholars study political preferences, few focus on how context affects preferences. As Mutz, Suiderman, and Brody (1996, 5) explain, "More often than not, our topics of study and the methods we employ fail to take into systematic account the power of situations to influence political attitudes." Beck et al. (2002, 57) agree, stating "most studies of voting behavior in the United States and other democracies have paid little attention to context, viewing vote choices as the product of a 'personal' rather than a 'social' calculus" (see, e.g., Zaller 1992, 2).

While we concede that the literature on preferences has focused on individual—rather than contextual—differences, we read it as being anything but silent on the matter of contextual effects. To this end, we offer two examples where experiments in contextual variation clarify important attributes of political preferences.[7]

In the first example, careful attention to context influences a long-standing debate about how information affects preferences. The debate regards two prominent models of political preference formation: the memory-based model and the on-line model. The memory-based model's core premise is that, when asked to express a preference, people search their memory for information and base their preference on that information. This search can be extensive (e.g. such as computing relative candidate issue positions over a large number of issues and characteristics; Kelly and Mirer 1974), or it can be haphazard (e.g. the information that happens to be easily accessible in memory at that moment; Zaller 1992). An example of the latter form of memory-based reasoning occurs when an individual bases her preference over two candidates entirely on one attribute that comes easily to her mind because it was just on the news.

The core premise of on-line models, by contrast, is that people form and maintain a running "evaluation counter" of certain objects (e.g. Lodge, McGraw, and Stroh 1989; Lodge, Steenbergen, and Brau 1995). When a person encounters new information, he or she brings an affect-laden "evaluation counter" (i.e. running tally) into working memory, updates it given the new information, and then restores the counter to long-term memory. The new information need not be remembered directly. Therefore, when asked to express a preference, people retrieve the evaluation counter, and, in contrast to memory models, not the discrete events on which the summary evaluation is based.

---

[6] It is worth noting that preference and choice are not one in the same. A person can prefer Kucinich to Kerry among Democratic candidates for president, but vote for Kerry in a primary election because Kucinich is perceived as certain to lose to the Republican nominee. Research in social psychology also shows regular disconnects between preferences and behavior (e.g. Eagly and Chaiken 1993, ch. 4).

[7] We focus on contextual influences beyond the well-known and widely acknowledged direct effects of elite rhetoric and interpersonal conversations (e.g. Berelson et al. 1954).

Initial work in political science either asserted the primacy of one model over the other (see, e.g., Zaller 1992, 279; Lodge, Steenbergen, and Brau 1995, 119) or focused on the moderating role of individual differences such as political sophistication (McGraw, Lodge, and Stroh 1990; McGraw and Pinney 1990; also see Krosnick and Brannon 1993, 965; Jarvis and Petty 1996). There was little attention to context.

Rahn, Aldrich, and Borgida (1994) took a different approach. They pointed out that some political contexts create simple communication environments, such as when candidates give sequential speeches, while others are more complex, such as when candidates debate. Drawing on social cognition research (e.g. Fiske et al. 1983), Rahn, Aldrich, and Borgida (1994) argue that complex settings increase the difficulty of comprehending, integrating, and adding information to an on-line evaluation, especially if the information is unfamiliar and the audience is not motivated. In other words, context matters. They predict that non-sophisticated individuals will not engage in on-line processing in complex contexts, but will do so in simple settings. In contrast, they predict that sophisticates will engage in on-line processing in both contexts.

To test the hypothesis, they implemented an experiment in which some participants watched two candidates offer sequential speeches (simple context) while others watched a two-candidate debate (complex context). The information offered in each context was identical. Their findings support their hypotheses: non-sophisticates engaged in memory-based processing in the complex setting and on-line processing in the simple setting. Sophisticates, by contrast, always processed on-line. Individual differences depend on context, with sophistication only mattering in complex settings. This study shows that the applicability of memory-based and on-line models depends, in part, on attributes of the context in which the information is presented (also see Redlawsk 2001).[8]

In the second example, experiments in contextual variation clarify how framing affects preferences. A framing effect occurs when differently worded, but logically equivalent phrases cause individuals to alter their preferences (Tversky and Kahneman 1981, 1987). An example of such an effect occurs when people reject a policy program after being told that it will result in 5 percent unemployment but prefer it after being told that it will result in 95 percent employment.[9] Many scholars

---

[8] Another dynamic that appears to influence processing strategy is the type of choice under consideration. Specifically, the on-line processing research focuses on candidate evaluation, whereas memory-based work often focuses on survey response more generally. In the former case, people may anticipate evaluating candidates (i.e. they know that they will have to vote), and thus, they form on-line evaluations (see Hastie and Park 1986, 262). In contrast, most people do not anticipate answering survey questions, and thus, they cannot access on-line evaluations when a surveyor surprises them with a question (see Kinder 1998, 813–14; Druckman and Lupia 2000, 11–12). While features of the choice do not directly form part of the context, it is another often understudied dynamic of political preference formation (see Payne, Bettman, and Johnson 1993; Lau and Redlawsk 2001; Taber 2003).

[9] Political communication scholars use the term "framing effects" to refer to situations where by emphasizing a sub-set of potentially relevant considerations, a speaker leads individuals to focus on these considerations when constructing their opinions. For example, if a speaker describes a hate group rally in terms of free speech (or public safety), then the audience will base its rally opinions on

interpret such effects as evidence that citizens do not have well-formed or coherent preferences about important social issues.

Many framing studies, however, pay limited attention to context. While they vary context in one way—by presenting a singular phenomenon in two different ways—few question the extent to which their subjects' reactions are context-dependent.[10] For those who want to claim that results from classic framing studies apply to political actors generally, knowing the answer to such questions is critically important.

Druckman (2004) explores the impact of social contexts on framing. He builds on memory accessibility research (e.g. Fazio and Olson 2003) and behavioral decision theory (e.g. Payne Bettman, and Johnson 1993) to specify the conditions under which framing effects will occur. He tested his predictions with an experiment on more than 500 participants. The experiment involved four classic framing problems with four conditions. The *control* condition mimicked the classic framing experiments—he presented each problem to participants using one of two frames (e.g. either an unemployment frame or an employment frame). The *elite competition* condition added to the control condition a second framing of the problem—specifically, it included a counterclaim where participants received a "re-framing" of the problem (e.g. those who had received the initial unemployment frame received a re-framing with the employment frame). Two intergroup discussion conditions added to the control condition the opportunity to discuss the problem with three other participants. In the *homogeneous discussion* condition, all participants received the same frame. In the *heterogeneous discussion* condition, participants received different frames.

The experiment reveals how contextual attributes moderate or eliminate framing effects (also see, e.g., Bless et al. 1998; Druckman 2001b). The control condition closely replicates the classic studies by showing substantial framing effects. Context matters, however, because the effects disappear or are severely minimized in all of the other experimental conditions. In other words, changing the context to allow elite competition or interpersonal discussion limits or eliminates framing effects (also see Druckman and Nelson 2003). Since such factors are important attributes of many political contexts, it is incorrect to presume that framing affects political preferences generally in ways that the original framing studies suggest.[11] As a result,

---

free speech (or public safety) considerations (e.g. Nelson, Clawson, and Oxley 1997). These types of framing effects are *distinct* since they do not involve logically equivalent ways of making the same statement (see Druckman 2001a).

[10] Since Tversky and Kahneman do not specify a theory of information processing (see Jou, Shanteau, and Harris 1996, 2; Fong and McCabe 1999, 10927), their work provides no direct information about the robustness of their findings to reasonable contextual variations.

[11] Two other findings are of note. First, consistent with other evidence that the nature of the conversational context matters (e.g. Mutz 2002), Druckman finds that, compared to the homogenous discussions, the heterogeneous discussions exhibit a stronger moderating effect on framing. Second, Druckman explores the moderating impact of individual level variables. Echoing Rahn, Aldrich, and

classic framing studies provide little or no evidence about the quality of citizens' attitudes in many important political contexts.

These two examples are part of a growing population of studies (e.g. Kuklinski et al. 2001; Lau and Redlawsk 2001; Sniderman, Hagendoorn, and Prior 2004) that deliver important insights about political preference formation and change. While these studies differ in many ways, they share the attribute of considering psychological processes and contextual variations simultaneously. At their best, such studies demonstrate that the value of a distinctly political psychology, over psychology as traditionally recognized, comes from adding to the psychologists' careful treatment of human cognition special attention to the unique social dynamics and challenges that characterize political settings. The value added comes from contemplating the context.

3   CHOICE

In this section, we turn to research that is useful for identifying contextual effects though it is not typically associated with contextual political science. Specifically, we focus on non-cooperative game theoretic work that falls under the rubric of "The New Institutionalism." Scholars use this research to derive empirical predictions about how certain contextual variables, such as formal and informal bargaining or legislative rules, affect individual perceptions, preferences, and choices (see, e.g., Shepsle 1989; Epstein and O'Halloran 1999; Huber and Shipan 2002).

The typical non-cooperative model built to clarify contextual-institutional variables takes the following form. First, present a political context, complete with a description of the relevant actors, their preferences, the actions available to them, and their beliefs about all aspects just mentioned. Use deductive logic to derive a logically coherent conclusion about what choice every actor will make. Second, vary the context in a specific way and use the same logic to draw a parallel conclusion. Third, compare the two conclusions. If the conclusions are the same, then we would expect the contextual variation to have no impact on the behaviors described in the model. If the conclusions are different, we would expect empirical evidence to show that context matters.

Borgida's (1994) results, he finds that expertise does not have an effect across contexts; rather, it only matters in the homogenous conversation conditions. In this case, the conversations appeared to simulate thought among experts who showed no susceptibility to framing effects. Non-experts were susceptible, however. This is further evidence that individual differences are context specific (also see, e.g., Lau and Redlawsk 2001).

Non-cooperative models have changed the way that many political scientists think about legislatures, elections, and the bureaucracy. In an important sense, the models are akin to thought experiments that can be used to derive robust empirical predictions about context. We offer, as an example, work on coalition formation in parliamentary democracies.

The defining feature of parliamentary democracy is that the viability of the government (i.e. the executive and the cabinet) depends directly on the willingness of all possible legislative majorities to support, or at least to tolerate, its existence. In other words, if any majority of members of parliament votes to replace the existing government, it ends.

In many cases, this requirement places a premium on coalition building and maintenance, since parliamentary democracies rarely contain single parties that control a majority of legislative seats. Questions about how coalitions form and which parties are included in government are among the most important that scholars of parliamentary democracies can pursue. These decisions affect what politicians become powerful, what legislation is passed, and important aspects of the quality of citizens' lives.

Initial coalition formation theories posited parties as seeking to join governments while sharing the spoils of office as narrowly as possible. Using cooperative game theory, they predicted "minimal winning coalitions" in which the governing parties collectively control a majority of parliamentary seats, but only just so (e.g. von Neumann and Morgenstern 1953; Riker 1962). For example, if a hundred-person legislature has three parties, where Party A has 40 seats and Parties B and C have 30 seats each, the minimum winning coalition is one between B and C as no other combination of parties (e.g., "A and B" or "A and C") has a sum of seats less than 60.

Many scholars viewed this approach as unsatisfactory. Chief among their complaints was that the conclusions depended on the assumption that politicians care about gaining office and winning perks rather than policy. A subsequent generation of theories paid greater attention to policy and predicted that governing coalitions would form only among parties who were close ideologically (Axelrod 1970; De Swaan 1973).

While the minimal-winning and policy-aware theories differed in many ways, subsequent research revealed them to share one unfortunate attribute—neither predicted the actual membership of governing coalitions very well (see, e.g., Laver and Schofield 1990, 96). What was missing was a consideration of context. As Strøm et al. (1994, 306) put it, these theories were "operationalized at a level general enough to bear upon a range of political systems...data come from standard sources and are used with no contextual interpretation" (also see Laver and Schofield 1990, 195–216).

This changed as researchers began to use non-cooperative game theory to incorporate contextual variables into coalition formation theories (see, e.g., Laver

1998). Scholars increasingly recognized that countries employ different rules that regulate the coalition formation and policy-making process, and they modeled these differences by specifying coalition outcomes in the presence or absence of different institutions (e.g. Austen-Smith and Banks 1988; Baron 1991; Lupia and Strøm 1995). For example, some countries (e.g. Germany, Italy) require investiture votes such that a majority of legislators must vote in favor of an incoming government, while other countries (e.g. Denmark, Norway) have no such requirement—meaning that a government can assume office as long as a majority does not vote against it. The models show that investiture requirements constrain the formation of minority governments—in which the parties in government do not control a majority of legislative seats. As Laver and Schofield (1990, 207) explain, "an investiture requirement forces an incoming government to survive on the basis of its program and cabinet taken as a whole, rather than on the basis of a package of proposals that can be considered one at a time." Minority governments, by contrast, survive by stringing together varying majorities on different issues, even if a majority does not support its overall existence (see Strøm, Budge, and Laver 1994, 311–12). As Martin and Stevenson (2001, 46) later verified, whether or not a country requires investiture votes is an important determinant of the viability of minority governments.

The investiture vote is just one of many contextual variables that shape coalition governments. Others include the presence of a formateur party, no-confidence votes, electoral rules, powers of parliamentary committees, and bicameral legislatures (e.g. Strøm, Budge, and Laver 1994; Martin and Stevenson 2001; Druckman and Thies 2002). A growing number of scholars are now using non-cooperative game theory first to isolate correspondences among contextual/institutional variables and coalition choices, and then use these findings as the basis for rigorous empirical tests. The combination of these activities has produced much more accurate empirical predictions about many facets of coalition governance (Diermeier and Stevenson 1999; Müller and Strøm 2000). For example, Martin and Stevenson (2001, 47) report that relying only on office and policy preferences leads to an 11 percent success rate in predicting coalition formation whereas models that include institutional features increase the predictive success by an additional 33 percent.[12] In short, empirical and theoretical studies of coalition formation and termination that include key institutional attributes perform dramatically better in terms of predictive success than do studies that neglect these contextual variations.[13]

Explaining and predicting the actions of individuals and groups requires more than knowledge of the actors and their preferences; it also requires an appreciation of the context in which actions are taken. The kinds of complex thought experi-

---

[12] Successfully predicting 44 percent of coalitions formed is impressive when one considers the enormous number of possible configurations of coalitions at a given time.

[13] Experimental studies, such as Fréchette, Kagel, and Lehrer (2003) and Fréchette, Kagel, and Morelli (2005), also validate focal predictions of this approach.

ment facilitated by methods such as non-cooperative game theory offer a powerful method for understanding how different contexts influence actions.

4 CONCLUSION

Choice has always been a focal concept in the study of politics. When the goal of scholarship is to explain choice, volition becomes relevant as well. Advances in many scientific fields are giving researchers more reliable ways to measure important aspects of volition and to evaluate causal hypotheses about choice. Political science has contributed, and will continue to contribute to this endeavor. Our biggest comparative advantage, however, is in our ability to combine other disciplines' ideas with deep knowledge of, and sustained attention to, a set of critically important social contexts. Context, not methodology, is what unites our discipline. It is what causes scholars from distinct intellectual traditions such as philosophy, sociology, economics, and psychology to want to be in a single department, attending each other's research seminars and jointly training graduate students at institutions of higher learning all over the world. Political science is united by the desire to understand, explain, and predict important aspects of contexts where individual and collective actions are intimately and continuously bound. Our comparative advantage is valuable and we should encourage researchers to leverage it whenever they can. At the same time, integrating new knowledge about brains and preferences, and inferential methods that allow strong tests of causal hypotheses, can improve the empirical reliability and substantive relevance of contextual political science. In other words, the desire to highlight the role of context in political analysis and the desire to provide scientifically rigorous explanations of political choice are inherently complementary.

REFERENCES

ACKERMAN, B., and FISHKIN, J. 2004. Righting the ship of democracy. *Legal Affairs*, 3: 34–9.

ARROW, K. J. 1963. *Social Choice and Individual Values*, 2nd edn. New Haven, Conn.: Yale University Press.

AUSTEN-Smith, D., and BANKS, J. 1988. Elections, coalitions, and legislative outcomes. *American Political Science Review*, 82: 405–22.

AXELROD, R. 1970. *Conflict of Interest*. Chicago: Markham.

BARON, D. P. 1991. A spatial bargaining theory of government formation in parliamentary systems. *American Political Science Review*, 85: 137–65.

BECK, P. A., DALTON, R. J., GREENE, S., and HUCKFELDT, R. 2002. The social calculus of voting. *American Political Science Review*, 96: 57–73.

BENHABIB, S. 1996. Toward a deliberative model of democratic legitimacy. In *Democracy and Difference*, ed. S. Benhabib. Princeton, NJ: Princeton University Press.

BERELSON, B. R., LAZARSFELD, P. F., and McPHEE, W. N. 1954. *Voting*. Chicago: University of Chicago Press.

BLESS, H., BETSCH, T., and FRANZEN, A. 1998. Framing the framing effect: the impact of context cues on solutions to the "Asian disease" problem. *European Journal of Social Psychology*, 28: 287–91.

BOHMAN, J. 1998. Survey article: the coming age of deliberative democracy. *Journal of Political Philosophy*, 6: 400–25.

CACIOPPO, J. T., BERNTSON, G. G., ADOLPHS, R., CARTER, C. S., DAVIDSON, R. J., McCLINTOCK, M., McEWEN, B. S., MEANEY, M. J., SCHACTER, D. L., STEINBERG, E. M., SUOMI, S. S., and TAYLOR, S. E. 2002. *Foundations in Social Neuroscience*. Cambridge, Mass.: MIT Press.

CHURCHLAND, P. S., and SEJNOWSKI, T. J. 1992. *The Computational Brain*. Cambridge, Mass.: MIT Press.

CLARK, A. 1997. *Being There: Putting Brain, Body, and World Together Again*. Cambridge, Mass.: MIT Press.

DE SWAAN, A. 1973. *Coalition Theories and Cabinet Formation*. Amsterdam: Elsevier.

DEWEY, J. 1954. *The Public and Its Problems*. Athens, Oh.: Shallow Press; originally published 1927.

DIERMEIER, D., and STEVENSON, R. T. 1999. Cabinet terminations and critical events. *American Political Science Review*, 94: 627–40.

DRUCKMAN, J. N. 2001a. The implications of framing effects for citizen competence. *Political Behavior*, 23: 225–56.

—— 2001b. Using credible advice to overcome framing effects. *Journal of Law, Economics, & Organization*, 17: 62–82.

—— 2004. Political preference formation: competition, deliberation, and the (ir)relevance of framing effects. *American Political Science Review*, 98: 671–86.

—— and LUPIA, A. 2000. Preference formation. *Annual Review of Political Science*, 3: 1–24.

—— and NELSON, K. R. 2003. Framing and deliberation: how citizens' conversations limit elite influence. *American Journal of Political Science*, 47: 728–44.

—— and THIES, M. F. 2002. The importance of concurrence: the impact of bicameralism on government formation and duration. *American Journal of Political Science*, 46: 760–71.

DRYZEK, J. S. 2000. *Deliberative Democracy and Beyond*. Oxford: Oxford University Press.

EAGLY, A. H., and CHAIKEN, S. 1993. *The Psychology of Attitudes*. Fort Worth, Tex.: Harcourt Brace.

EPSTEIN, D., and O'HALLORAN, S. 1999. *Delegating Power*. New York: Cambridge University Press.

FAZIO, R. H., and OLSON, M. A. 2003. Implicit measures in social cognition research. *Annual Review of Psychology*, 54: 297–327.

FISHKIN, J. S. 1991. *Democracy and Deliberation: New Directions for Democratic Reform*. New Haven, Conn.: Yale University Press.

——1995. *The Voice of the People: Public Opinion and Democracy.* New Haven, Conn.: Yale University Press.

——1999. Toward deliberative democracy. In *Citizen Competence and Democratic Institutions*, ed. S. L. Elkin and K. E. Soltan. University Park: Pennsylvania State University Press.

FISKE, S. T., KINDER, D. R., and LARTER, W. M. 1983. The novice and the expert: knowledge-based strategies in political cognition. *Journal of Experimental Social Psychology*, 19: 381–400.

FONG, C., and McCABE, K. 1999. Are decisions under risk malleable? *Proceedings of the National Academy of Sciences*, 96: 10927–32.

FRÉCHETTE, G., KAGEL, J. H., and LEHRER, S. F. 2003. Bargaining in legislatures: an experimental investigation of open versus closed amendment rules. *American Political Science Review*, 97: 221–32.

FRÉCHETTE, G., KAGEL, J. H., and MORELLI, M. 2005. Nominal bargaining power, selection protocol, and discounting in legislative bargaining. *Journal of Public Economics*, 89: 1497–518.

GOODIN, R. E., and NIEMEYER, S. J. 2003. When does deliberation begin? Internal reflection versus public discussion in deliberative democracy. *Political Studies*, 51: 627–49.

GUTMANN, A., and THOMPSON, D. 1996. *Democracy and Disagreement: Why Moral Conflict Cannot Be Avoided in Politics and What Should Be Done About It.* Cambridge, Mass.: Harvard University Press.

HASTIE, R., and PARK, B. 1986. The relationship between memory and judgment depends on whether the judgment task is memory-based or on-line. *Psychological Review*, 93: 258–68.

HIBBING, J. R., and THEISS-MORSE, E. 2002. *Stealth Democracy: Americans' Beliefs about How Government Should Work.* New York: Cambridge University Press.

HUBER, J. D., and SHIPAN, C. R. 2002. *Deliberate Discretion? The Institutional Foundations of Bureaucratic Autonomy.* New York: Cambridge University Press.

JARVIS, W. B. G., and Petty, R. E. 1996. The need to evaluate. *Journal of Personality and Social Psychology*, 70: 172–94.

JOU, J., SHANTEAU, J., and HARRIS, R. J. 1996. An information processing view of framing effects: the role of causal schemas in decision making. *Memory & Cognition*, 24: 1–15.

KANDEL, E. R., SCHWARTZ, J. H., and JESSELL, T. M. 1995. *Essentials of Neural Science and Behavior.* Norwalk, Conn.: Appleton and Lange.

KELLEY, S., JR., and MIRER, T. W. 1974. The simple act of voting. *American Political Science Review*, 68: 572–91.

KINDER, D. R. 1998. Opinion and action in the realm of politics. In *The Handbook of Social Psychology*, ed. D. T. Gilbert, S. T. Fiske, and G. Lindzey, 4th edn. Boston: McGraw-Hill.

——and HERZOG, D. 1993. Democratic discussion. In *Reconsidering the Democratic Public*, ed. G. E. Marcus and R. L. Hanson. University Park: Pennsylvania State University Press.

KROSNICK, J. A., and BRANNON, L. A. 1993. The impact of the Gulf War on the ingredients of presidential evaluations: multidimensional effects of political involvement. *American Political Science Review*, 87: 963–75.

KUKLINSKI, J. H., QUIRK, P. J., JERIT, J., and RICH, R. F. 2001. The political environment and citizen competence. *American Journal of Political Science*, 45: 410–24.

LAU, R. R., and REDLAWSK, D. P. 2001. Advantages and disadvantages of cognitive heuristics in political decision making. *American Journal of Political Science*, 45: 951–71.

LAVER, M. 1998. Models of government formation. *Annual Review of Political Science*, 1: 1–25.

——and SCHOFIELD, N. 1990. *Multiparty Government: The Politics of Coalition in Europe*. Oxford: Oxford University Press.

LODGE, M., McGRAW, K. M., and STROH, P. 1989. An impression-driven model of candidate evaluation. *American Political Science Review*, 83: 399–419.

——STEENBERGEN, M. R., and BRAU, S. 1995. The responsive voter. *American Political Science Review*, 89: 309–26.

LUPIA, A. 2002. Deliberation disconnected: what it takes to improve civic competence. *Law and Contemporary Problems*, 65: 133–50.

——2004. The wrong tack (can Deliberation Day increase civic competence?) *Legal Affairs*, 3: 43–45.

——and McCUBBINS, M. D. 1998. *The Democratic Dilemma: Can Citizens Learn What They Need To Know?* New York: Cambridge University Press.

————2005. Lost in translation: social choice theory is misapplied against legislative intent. *Journal of Contemporary Legal Issues*, 14: 585–617.

——and STRØM, K. 1995. Coalition termination and the strategic timing of parliamentary elections. *American Political Science Review*, 89: 648–65.

McCAULEY, R. N. (ed.) 1996. *The Churchlands and their Critics*. Cambridge, Mass.: Blackwell.

McGRAW, K. M., LODGE, M., and STROH, P. 1990. On-line processing in candidate evaluation: the effects of issue order, issue importance, and sophistication. *Political Behavior*, 12: 41–58.

——and PINNEY, N. 1990. The effects of general and domain-specific expertise on political memory and judgment. *Social Cognition*, 8: 9–30.

McKELVEY, R. D. 1976. Intransitivities in multidimensional voting models and some implications for agenda control. *Journal of Economic Theory*, 2: 472–82.

MARTIN, L. W., and STEVENSON, R. T. 2001. Government formation in parliamentary democracies. *American Journal of Political Science*, 45: 33–50.

MENDELBERG, T. 2002. The deliberative citizen. Vol. 6, pp. 151–93 in *Research in Micropolitics*, ed. M. X. Delli Carpini, L. Huddy, and R. Y. Shapiro. New York: Elsevier.

MILL, J. S. 1989. *On Liberty and Other Writings*, ed. S Collini. New York: Cambridge University Press; originally published 1869.

Müller, W. C., and STRØM, K. (eds.) 2000. *Coalition Governments in Western Europe*. Oxford: Oxford University Press.

MUTZ, D. C. 2002. Cross-cutting social networks. *American Political Science Review*, 96: 111–126.

——SNIDERMAN, P. M., and BRODY, R. A. 1996. Political persuasion: the birth of a field of study. In *Political Persuasion and Attitude Change*, ed. D. C. Mutz, P. M. Sniderman, and R. A. Brody. Ann Arbor: University of Michigan Press.

NELSON, T. E., CLAWSON, R. A., and OXLEY, Z. M. 1997. Media framing of a civil liberties conflict and its effect on tolerance. *American Political Science Review*, 91: 567–583.

PARKINSON, J. 2006. Rickety bridges: using the media in deliberative democracy. *British Journal of Political Science*, 36: 175–83.

PAYNE, J. W., BETTMAN, J. R., and JOHNSON, E. J. 1993. *The Adaptive Decision Maker*. New York: Cambridge University Press.

PINKER, S. 2002. *The Blank Slate: The Modern Denial of Human Nature*. New York: Viking.

POSNER, R. 2004. Smooth sailing (democracy doesn't need Deliberation Day). *Legal Affairs*, 3: 41–2.

RAHN, W. M., ALDRICH, J. H., and BORGIDA, E. 1994. Individual and contextual variations in political candidate appraisal. *American Political Science Review*, 88: 193–9.

REDLAWSK, D. P. 2001. You must remember this: a test of the on-line model of voting. *Journal of Politics*, 63: 29–58.

RIKER, W. 1962. *The Theory of Political Coalitions*. New Haven, Conn.: Yale University Press.

SANDERS, L. M. 1997. Against deliberation. *Political Theory*, 25: 347–76.

SCHACTER, D. L. 2001. *The Seven Sins of Memory: How the Mind Forgets and Remembers*. New York: Houghton Mifflin.

SCHKADE, D., SUNSTEIN, C. R., and KAHNEMAN, D. 2000. Deliberating about dollars: the severity shift. *Columbia Law Review*, 100: 1139–75.

SCHOFIELD, N. 1983. Generic instability of majority rule. *Review of Economic Studies*, 50: 695–705.

SHEPSLE, K. A. 1989. Studying institutions: some lessons from the rational choice approach. *Journal of Theoretical Politics*, 1: 131–147.

SNIDERMAN, P. M., HAGENDOORN, L., and PRIOR, M. 2004. Predispositional factors and situational triggers: exclusionary reactions to immigrant minorities. *American Political Science Review*, 98: 35–49.

STRØM, K., BUDGE, I., and LAVER, M. J. 1994. Constraints on cabinet formation in parliamentary democracies. *American Journal of Political Science*, 38: 303–35.

TABER, C. S. 2003. Information processing and public opinion. In *Political Psychology*, ed. D. O. Sears, L. Huddy, and R. Jervis. Oxford: Oxford University Press.

TVERSKY, A., and KAHNEMAN, D. 1981. The framing of decisions and the psychology of choice. *Science*, 211: 453–8.

——— 1987. Rational choice and the framing of decisions. In *Rational Choice: The Contrast Between Economics and Psychology*, ed. R. M. Hogarth and M. W. Reder. Chicago: University of Chicago Press.

VON NEUMANN, J., and MORGENSTERN, O. 1953. *Theory of Games and Economic Behavior*. Princeton, NJ: Princeton University Press.

ZALLER, J. 1992. *The Nature and Origins of Mass Opinion*. New York: Cambridge University Press.

CHAPTER 6

....

THEORY, FACT, AND LOGIC

....

ROD AYA

SOCIAL as well as physical science is an endless argument where theory explains fact and fact tests theory by way of logic, which connects them as premise to conclusion. The argument is endless because the evidence is never conclusive. Fact does not prove theory true—explanation is always hypothetical—and fact is observed in light of theory. Despite the "underdetermination of theory by evidence," however, science gets results in conformity with ground rules of method that answer four questions:

Are conclusions to be consistent with premises (maybe even follow from them)? Do facts matter? Or can we string together thoughts as we like, calling it an "argument," and make up facts as we please, taking one story to be as good as another? (Chomsky 1992, 52)

The ground rules answer the first two questions "yes" and the last two "no," stipulating "consistency and responsibility to fact" (Chomsky 1992, 52). Postmodern antinomianism gives the opposite answer, celebrating incoherence and "the fact that facts are made" (Geertz 1995, 62). The present article accepts the ground rules, but considers antinomianism at the end.

1   THEORY EXPLAINS FACT, FACT TESTS THEORY

Theory explains fact by some other fact (or facts) given which the fact to be explained follows.[1] Explanation is hypothetico-deductive. Theory is generalization—it asserts "constant conjunction" between some fact (or facts) and the fact to be explained (Ayer 1946; Braithwaite 1953).[2] In effect it claims "whenever this, that" so given "this" it logically implies and explains "that" (Quine 1992). Fact tests theory by observation compared with prediction. Validation is also hypothetico-deductive. Theory implies and predicts "that" given "this" and rules out anything except "that" given "this." So if observation confirms prediction—if when "this" is observed "that" is observed—it confirms theory. But if when "this" is observed anything except "that" is observed, it refutes it. Prediction is prohibition; violation is refutation (Popper 1972).[3]

In sum, theory explains fact and fact tests theory through logic. The watchword is "consistency and responsibility to fact." Since (by the law of contradiction) two contradictory statements cannot both be true, theory that contradicts fact is false. This hypothetico-deductive view of method in physical and social science (Popper 1989; Medawar 1982; Gellner 1974) comes with a few caveats in train.

Theory that binds facts together, explaining "that" by "this," is hypothesis. Predictive success does not prove it true. As Hume pointed out in 1739, to say predictive success proves theory true begs the question whether future observation will oblige: "No matter how many times the results of experiments agree with some theory, you can never be sure that the next time the result will not contradict the theory," whereas "you can disprove a theory by finding even a single observation that disagrees with the predictions of the theory" (Hawking 1988, 10).[4]

---

[1] Classic exemplars include Newton's theory of gravity explaining it by mass and distance and Darwin's theory of evolution explaining it by variation and selection.

[2] Some say "events" instead of "facts" (Beauchamp and Rosenberg 1981). Others use them as synonyms (Braithwaite 1953). That the world "is not the totality of things but of events or *facts*" goes back to Heraclitus (Popper 2002, 594).

[3] The hypothetico-deductive method derives (by *modus ponens*) "that" fact as a conclusion from "whenever this, that" theory plus "this" fact as premises, compares "that" fact with observation, and (if prediction and observation do not match) concludes (by *modus tollens*) that one or more premises are false. "We have premises and a conclusion, and if . . . the conclusion is false . . . and . . . the inference is valid, . . . at least one of the premises must be false" (Popper 1979, 304). Look at a visual aid from any logic textbook where "$p \supset q$" is "if p is true, then q is true," p is "whenever this, that" theory plus "this" fact, and q is "that" fact:

modus ponens	*modus tollens*
$p \supset q$	$p \supset q$
p	$\sim q$
$\therefore q$	$\therefore \sim p$

[4] "Only the falsity of the theory can be inferred from empirical evidence, and this inference is a purely deductive one" (Popper 1989, 55).

Falsification is logically not empirically conclusive, however. Blaming theory or fact for inconsistency between them is guesswork, also because observation of fact is made in light of a "backlog of accepted theory" (Popper 1989; Quine 1992). Uncertainty rules science thanks to the "impossibility of generating unassailable general propositions from particular facts" and to the "tentative and theory-infected character of the facts themselves" (Simon 1983, 6).[5]

Causation of fact by some other fact (or facts) presumes theory that binds the facts together. As Hume also pointed out in 1739, "this" causes "that" only on the theory that "whenever this, that" (Beauchamp and Rosenberg 1981). Causation—Hume's "cement of the universe"—is hypothetical:

We can never be certain...that A is the cause of B...because we can never be certain whether the universal hypothesis in question is true,...[though] the specific hypothesis that A is the cause of B [is] the more acceptable the better we have tested and confirmed the corresponding universal hypothesis.   (Popper 2002, 837)

"True" means corresponding to fact—a theory is true if and only if its predictions fit observed facts.[6] But whether the theory is true is open to doubt so long as the facts are in doubt—empirical evidence can at any moment disprove it. A synonym for "acceptable" is "probable."[7]

Theory that explains fact by some other fact (or facts) often goes unstated where it is common knowledge and interest centers on the fact to be explained and the fact (or facts) that explain it. For example:

Suppose we have set up some "tissue cultures" of living cells, using a variety of media.... Some of the cultures, but not all, have been ruined by bacterial infection, and we naturally wish to find out why. ... Media common to all the cultures cannot have been responsible for introducing the infection. If the infected cultures, and they alone, were set up with a medium from a certain special source, then that medium was almost certainly responsible; and we shall be confirmed in this interpretation [explanation] if we find that the more

---

[5] "There are no absolutely certain empirical propositions....Only tautologies...are certain.... Empirical propositions are one and all hypotheses," also propositions reporting "observations that verify [test] these hypotheses" (Ayer 1946, 93–4). "Even in the advanced sciences almost everything is questionable....Something like 90 percent of the matter in the universe...is called dark matter... because they don't know what it is, they can't find it, but it has to be there or the physical laws don't work" (Chomsky 2002, 152, 99). Dark matter is a hypothetical "this" fact posited to explain (on physical theory) "that" fact of observed stellar and galactic motion (Hawking 1988, 45).

[6] "Facts are what make statements true or false" (Russell 1948, 159). The "prediction of evidence...may be about past facts" (Popper 1989, 248).

[7] Taking "probability in its widest sense" (Keynes 1973, 36) of "likeliness to be true" (Locke, *Essay concerning Human Understanding*, 4.15) given evidence—as in "all our knowledge is only probable and...probability is the guide of life" (Russell 1948, 361)—not probability in the sense of either casino or insurance odds: "'Tis only probable that the sun will rise tomorrow" (Hume, *Treatise of Human Nature*, 1.3.11).

heavily contaminated cultures were those in which a larger quantity of the medium under suspicion had been used. We are taken aback when a fuller study of the records shows that a number of cultures escaped infection although the supposedly infected medium had been used to prepare them, but it turns out that these anomalous cultures differed ... by the use of a bactericidal ingredient which kept the infection down. .... The situation can be made as complicated as we please, but the reasoning which resolves it is straightforward and quite commonplace.   (Medawar 1982, 96)

This "commonplace" reasoning is the experimental (alias, comparative) method of hypothesis testing on which more below. The point here is that the explanation is enthymematic—it leaves the theory that bacteria cause infection unstated.

Explanation is often called "theory" even if no "whenever this, that" generalization, principle, or law—the distinction is purely honorific (Weinberg 2001, 115)—is invoked. Ordinary language calls a detective's reconstruction of a crime, a historian's account of a war, or a sociologist's explanation of a social fact a "theory." Social science jargon also calls it a "model," which needs explication.

2   EXPLANATION BY MODEL

Social theory explains one social fact by another through a model whose elements are people in a social situation trying to solve the problem posed by the situation as available evidence indicates they see it. The fact to be explained is their aggregate social behavior, which consists of observable individual social behavior (Coleman 1990). And the fact that explains it on the theory that (as Hobbes says) "man by nature chooseth the lesser evil" is the social situation they think they are in.[8] Explanation by model where people try to solve a problem posed by their situation as they see it is pervasive in social science and history.[9] To see how it works, consider some examples from classic and modern political theory, starting with a transparent do-it-yourself thought-experiment.

Take a chessboard and pretend it is a neighborhood. Pretend each of the sixty-four squares is a home. Take fifty coins—twenty-five each of two denominations. Pretend each coin is a family and each denomination is an ethnic group. Distribute the coins at random on the chessboard, one to a square. Assume every "family" wants at least half its neighbors to be of its own "ethnic group," and let any "family" move to any unoccupied square. Move the coins at will until every "family" is

[8] Hobbes, *Leviathan*, 1.14.
[9] And everyday life where folk models are "frames" (Goffman 1974).

satisfied. The "equilibrium" where no "family" wants to move will look like apartheid, though segregation is aggregation in a free market where "families" with a preference for own kind can move at will (Schelling 1978, 147–55).

The same thought-experiment predicts another "equilibrium" where a different situation constrains different behavior. Assume every "family" wants at least half its neighbors to be of its own "ethnic group," but let any "family" move to any square that is either unoccupied or else occupied by a "family" from the other "ethnic group" and (if the square is occupied) displace the occupant. The "equilibrium" where no "family" wants to move will look like apartheid with no man's land between "ethnic" enclaves.[10]

The first model explains ethnic segregation; the second model explains ethnic cleansing. How? Each model represents people trying to make the best of their social situation. The situation comprises the actions they think they can take, the results they think these actions will get, and the satisfaction they think those results will give—what can be done, what will result if one thing or another is done, and what result is preferred. Given the situation (which involves other people trying to make the best of their own situation), choice of action follows logically on the theory that people go for the "lesser evil." People in both situations choose the "lesser evil," doing what they think is necessary to get what they want (the result they prefer) in the situation they face.

All depends on the social situation that people think they are in. Their view of the situation—what they can do, what will result if they do it, and what result they prefer—motivates behavior constituent of a social fact they may not intend. Two classics illustrate. In Smith's model of market society, government protects people and keeps them honest so that by trying to "better their own condition" they serve the "public interest" as if "led by an invisible hand."[11] In Hobbes's model of stateless society, no government protects people or keeps them honest so that by trying to ensure "their own conservation" they fight a "war of every man against every man" where "force and fraud are ... the two cardinal virtues" and life is "solitary, poor, nasty, brutish and short."[12] People choosing the "lesser evil" in different social situations create equally unintended social facts: "micromotives" cause "macro-behavior" (Schelling 1978).[13]

Modern model explanations of sociopolitical facts like tribalism, feudalism, organized crime, machine politics, nationalism, and revolution are likewise hypothetico-deductive—they predict what people do from the situation they face

[10] Bosnia suggested this "transformation" of Schelling's model.

[11] Smith, *Wealth of Nations*, 2.3, 4.2. A Nobel laureate calls the "invisible hand" alias "market mechanism" the "key result in economic theory" (Akerlof 1984, 175).

[12] Hobbes, *Leviathan*, 1.13. Often accused of forgetting that people live in groups, Hobbes gives just three examples of war—tribal, civil, and interstate—all fought by organizations.

[13] Another example: "An extensive, complicated, and yet well ordered institution is the outcome of ever so many doings and pursuits, carried on by savages, who ... know their own motives, know the purpose of individual actions and the rules which apply to them, but how, out of these, the whole

on the theory that they choose the "lesser evil." These models include much contextual detail in the description of both the social fact to be explained and the social situation that explains it, but they all work the same way.[14]

Start with a model of tribalism propounded by anthropologists. The social fact to be explained is coalitions of feuding "blood and soil" communities that gang up on similar coalitions of adjacent communities; coalitions of these coalitions that gang up on similar adjacent coalitions; and coalitions of these larger coalitions that gang up on outsiders as "tribes" —coalitions that break up into feuding communities again when their common enemies relent. And the social situation that explains this fact on the "choose the lesser evil" theory is one where people have no police or government (only kinsmen and neighbors) to protect them. They gang up with closer kinsmen and neighbors on more distant ones because (despite local feuding) they fear a smaller opponent less than a larger one—their choice of allies depends on the enemy that confronts them. Every potential attack-and-defense coalition confronts an equal opponent, thus solving (through deterrence) Hobbes's problem of social order without benefit of central government (Evans-Pritchard 1940; Gellner 1969).

Now consider a model of feudalism, also from anthropology. The social fact to be explained is coalitions (instead of class struggle) between landlords and peasants who form patron–client gangs that fight other such gangs. And the social situation that explains it on the "choose the lesser evil" theory is one where landlords and peasants need each other. The landlords want paramilitary manpower; the peasants want protection, work, and housing; so they barter what they have and the other wants for what the other has and they want. Since the peasants can defect, the landlords (to attract them) need more land, which they get by taking it from rival landlords. The more successful landlords are as warlords, the more enemies they make, creating a vicious circle that often closes with their assassination (Barth 1959).

A model of organized crime likewise explains it on the "choose the lesser evil" theory by a social situation where the haves and have-nots need each other. Classical mafia involves absentee landlords who want their estates guarded and a seat in parliament; gangsters who want a front and immunity as well as tribute; and peasants who want protection and work. The trade-off is mafia. The landlords employ the gangsters and (as politicians) obstruct justice; the gangsters protect estates and get the vote out for their patrons; the peasants work and vote as they are told; all keep quiet. The gangsters have to compete for what they want and mostly

collective institution shapes, ... is beyond their mental range," just as a "humble member of any modern institution ... is *of* it and *in* it, but has no vision of the resulting integral action of the whole. ... The Ethnographer has to construct the picture [model] of the big institution ... consisting of thousands of men ... as the physicist constructs his theory from experimental data" (Malinowski 1922, 83–4, 11–12, 92).

[14] The methodological rules are (1) "considérer tout phénomène collectif comme le produit d'actions individuelles" and (2) "interpréter l'action individuelle comme rationnelle" (Boudon 1992, 282–3).

kill each other. Under Fascism (which gives protection and ends elections) mafia withers; after Fascism it revives (Blok 1988).

A model of machine politics explains it as a similar trade-off between vested interests, namely party bosses, businessmen, racketeers, and immigrants. The party bosses take bribes from the businessmen and racketeers in exchange for permits and protection, and provide social services and personal favors for the immigrants who vote the party ticket at elections. Like tribalism, feudalism, and organized crime, machine politics consists of social behavior motivated by "local knowledge" of the social situation. All involved can get what they want in no other way. Choosing the "lesser evil" from their own point of view, they create what outsiders condemn as a greater one (Merton 1968, 124–36).

A model of nationalism explains it as people trying to get their culture its own state (through agitprop, electioneering, and negotiation; or else terrorism, ethnic cleansing, and genocide) in a social situation where (as they see it) culture is destiny. This situation exists where people and governments striving for wealth and power create (or project) a modern economy and bureaucracy staffed by interchangeable, mobile, literate personnel whose culture is like a huge oxygen tent that only the state can maintain through mass education. Who shares this culture can get by and get ahead; who lacks it cannot get decent treatment, much less compete for jobs and promotions. Modern life is interaction with bureaucrats, and if their culture is alien, interaction is humiliation. Where culture is destiny, people are nationalist—they want to avoid humiliation and think they can do so only if the state preserves and protects their culture. If rulers and ruled share the same culture, the model predicts all quiet on the national identity front. If they do not, it predicts assimilation, expulsion, or liquidation to purge states and would-be states of enemy aliens (Gellner 1983).

Models of revolution have a complication called history. The social fact to be explained—people successfully changing (or trying to change) government, regime, or society by means of violence—consists of collective actions and reactions over time. And the social situations that explain these strategic moves and coun-termoves or "échanges de coups" (Dobry 1986) on the "choose the lesser evil" theory also differ over time. Historical model-builders break revolution up into pivotal actions and reactions that are explained by the relevant actors' social situation at each stage of the narrative. Two examples illustrate. In one model, elites usurp the government, subalterns rebel, radicals seize power—and (as a new regime) reconstruct society (Skocpol 1979; 1994). In another model, insurgents claim sovereignty, people back them, the government dithers, government backers defect, insurgents arm, government forces defect, and insurgents seize power (Tilly 1993). In both models, revolution consists of successive actions and reactions, each of which depends on the one that precedes it, helping create the situation people take it in response to. The short list of actions and situations is different, but the theoretical method of explaining revolution by making a "cumulative causal model" whose elements are "people defining problems and trying to work their way out of them" (Stinchcombe 1978, 64, 121) is the same.[15]

Model explanations may be called "laws" when they connect model social situations to model social behavior on the "choose the lesser evil" theory. Such "laws," Weber says, state a "Sinnzusammenhang" or "Beziehung vom Mittel und Zweck," that is, "meaning nexus" or "means–end connection," since the model behavior is the sole means to the end of the "lesser evil" in the model situation.[16] A textbook favorite is the "law of supply and demand," according to which people all trying to buy cheap and sell dear in a market situation buy and sell less at a high price and more at a low price until they hit on an "equilibrium" price where every willing buyer finds a willing seller (Samuelson and Nordhaus 2001). More pertinent examples here are Plato's "law" (no weak government torn by faction, no revolution) and Olson's "law" (no selective incentives, no collective action). Plato's "law" says revolution has no hope of success against a strong, united government; Olson's "law" says collective action does not pay unless by taking part one gets individual rewards beyond the projected "public good," which one makes no difference to achieving and which (if achieved) one enjoys anyway.[17] Both "laws" predict and explain model behavior from a model situation where that behavior is the sole means to the end of the "lesser evil."[18]

3   THE COMPARATIVE METHOD

Testing model explanations uses the comparative method, which is the experimental method *without* controlled conditions just as, conversely, the experimental

[15] To sum up a case argued elsewhere (Aya 2001*a* and *b*).

[16] Weber's theoretical method, "soziales Handeln deutend verstehen und dadurch ursächlich erklären" by "Sinnzusammenhang" or "Beziehung vom 'Mittel' und 'Zweck'" (1964, 1: 3, 6, 7, 8), is perennial: "Men's actions are derived from the opinions they have of the good or evil which from those actions redound unto themselves" (Hobbes, *Leviathan*, 3.42). "The same motives always produce the same actions: The same events follow from the same causes.... A man who at noon leaves his purse full of gold on the pavement at Charing Cross, may as well expect that it will fly away like a feather, as that he will find it untouched an hour after" (Hume, *Enquiry Concerning Human Understanding*, 8.1). The standard mistranslation of "Sinnzusammenhang" as "meaningful complex," "context of meaning," "complex of meaning," or "meaningful system" (Parsons 1968, 2: 642; Weber 1978, 1: 8, 58) not only obscures Weber but ordains hermeneutic mysticism.

[17] Plato, *Republic*, 545d. Olson's "law" (1971) is also perennial: as Pericles told the Athenians in 432–431 BC, "Everyone supposeth that his own neglect of the common estate can do little hurt and that it will be the care of somebody else, ... not observing how by these thoughts of everyone in several the common business is jointly ruined" (Thucydides, *Peloponnesian War*, 1.141).

[18] If "law" has an archaic ring here, try "causal mechanism" as a synonym for constrained choice in similar and recurrent social situations (Hedström and Swedberg 1998).

method is the comparative method *with* controlled conditions (Durkheim 1937, 127; Parsons 1968, 2: 743). In simplest terms, the comparative method says fact confirms "whenever this, that" theory if when "this" is present, "that" is present—and when "this" is absent, "that" is absent too. The method says fact refutes theory if when "this" is present, "that" is absent—and when "this" is absent, "that" is present. The "this, that" and "not this, not that" rules for confirmation are Mill's methods of agreement and difference. Ditto the "this, not that" and "not this, that" rules for refutation.[19]

Where to pin the blame for refutation—inconsistency between theory and fact where observation contradicts prediction—is once again guesswork: theory could be false, but so could observation of "this," "that," or both (Popper 1989). In social science and history, discrepancy between predicted and observed behavior is blamed on the explanatory situational model (Popper 1994). Behavior predicted but not observed, or observed but not predicted means the situation to which that behavior is appropriate is not the one hypothesized. Taking the "choose the lesser evil" theory for granted lets the comparative method test the explanatory model. Insofar as the model is true, predicted and observed behavior will match; insofar as it is false, they will diverge.[20]

Three model explanations confirmed or refuted through the comparative method—one of the sex color bar in colonial society, one of revolutionary violence in 1848, and one of "social" revolution—may illustrate. The first model explanation claims that British colonies where many white women went had sex apartheid, whereas Iberian colonies where few white women went saw rampant miscegenation—like British India before the memsahib (McNeill 1991, 603). Here the methods of agreement and difference confirm the model explanation—colonies with many white women had a sex color bar; those without did not.

The second (Marxist) model explanation claims that the Paris shootout of June 1848 pitted the proletariat against the lumpenproletariat hired by the bourgeoisie—though in fact street fighters on both sides of the barricades had the same class background and, moreover, were a cross section of the manual work force (Traugott 2002). Here the method of difference refutes the model explanation—no class difference between the two sides explains the violence.

The third model explanation claims that "social" revolution has "distinctive, long-term, structural causes," namely "state weakness" plus "solidarity and autonomy" of subaltern communities (Skocpol 1979, 295; 1994, 17, 250)—so that when elites usurp the government, subalterns rebel, letting radicals seize power and reconstruct society. The second "structural" cause does not appear in every case,

[19] Both methods date back to the Scholastics (Losee 2001, 29–31).

[20] Mill's method of concomitant variation—the "more this, more that, less this, less that" version of agreement and difference Durkheim recommends (1937, 128–34)—correlates indicators of social conditions or circumstances and social behavior. The conditions or circumstances are the social situation (Wilson and Herrnstein 1985).

but what does—radicals seizing power and changing society—is not "distinctive," "long-term," or "structural" (Aya 1990). Worse, "social" revolutions since the Second World War share no antecedent "structural conditions" besides weak government torn by faction, but they all see socialist vanguards taking what they think is a shortcut to power and prosperity (Colburn 1994). Here the methods of agreement and difference refute a model explanation they allegedly confirm.

As logic, the comparative method is "straightforward and quite commonplace" (Medawar 1982, 96).[21] Pope Clement VI used the methods of agreement and difference in 1348 to refute those who blamed Jews for the plague (saying they poisoned wells) by observing that it killed Jews too and spread where no Jews lived (Ginzburg 1990, 67). But Polish peasants who had bad harvests after adopting iron plows and went back to wooden ones and Borneo tribals who blamed hot weather on a European also used the method of difference (Keynes 1973, 273). The comparative method tests theory with fact only if theory is falsifiable and explanation is noncircular. Consider a fictional dialogue:

"Why is the sea so rough today?"—"Because Neptune is very angry."—"By what evidence can you support your statement that Neptune is very angry?"—"Oh, don't you *see* how *very* rough the sea is? And is it not always rough when Neptune is angry?"   (Popper 1979, 192)

The "whenever this, that" theory here—whenever Neptune is angry, the sea is rough—is untestable. And the explanation of "that" by "this"—the sea is rough because Neptune is angry—is circular: the only evidence for "this" is "that."

Anthropology books give many examples of superstition verified by the comparative method:

If one of two canoes, both apparently equally well constructed, surpasses the other in some respect, this will be attributed to magic.   (Malinowski 1922, 116)

All a man's hopes of success ... are based on confidence in his magical equipment, exactly as all failure is attributed to lack or impotence in this respect.   (Malinowski 2002a, 315)

Any unaccountable good luck ... the natives attribute to magic; exactly as they attribute unexpected and undeserved bad luck to black magic or to some deficiency in ... their own magic.   (Malinowski 2002b, 1: 77)

The healthy person ... has powerful magic, the sick or deformed or dying person ... has weak magic. ... If one man has sought out another's company too much and for no reason that appears customary, and the latter dies, suspicion falls on his unexplained companion.   (Fortune 1989, 135, 155)

They say that it is very foolish to steal and run the risk of dying from magic, and when I have asked them what proof they have that thieves are so punished they have made some

---

[21] Despite all empirical complications of comparative history (Tilly 1984; Ragin 1987).

such reply as, "There have been many thefts this year. There have also been many deaths from dysentery. It would seem that many debts have been settled through dysentery." (Evans-Pritchard 1976, 201)

Social science is not exempt either. One "revealing exercise in the comparative method" confirms the hypothesis that Fascism "triumphed in those countries that were the weakest links in the capitalist chain" by noting that "none of the strong links snapped under tension, while all the weak ones did" (Parkin 1979, 171). More examples could be cited.

For the comparative method to work, in short, theory has to be falsifiable—it has to imply predictions that observation could contradict: only if given "this" it rules out anything but "that" does it explain "that" by "this." And explanation has to be noncircular—it needs evidence of "this" besides "that." Without these specifications of "consistency and responsibility to fact," the comparative method typifies primitive thought as well as social science.

4   CONCLUSION

Under the ground rules of method, "for an argument to be persuasive, . . . it must be coherent; its conclusions must follow from its premises," so "reasonable people will . . . be troubled if their conclusions contradict their premises" and "try to find the source of error in faulty reasoning or incorrect assumptions" (Chomsky 1987, 169, 187; 1993, 16). In science, conclusions contradict premises if "whenever this, that" theory and "this" fact together predict "that" fact, and "this" fact is observed but "that" fact is not—implying by *modus tollens* (assuming observation is accurate) that the theory is false. In social science, falsification is blamed on the model that (together with the "choose the lesser evil" theory) predicts behavior different from the behavior observed.

The ground rules do not require that scientists refute their own ideas, however. Colleagues do it for them. Objectivity owes to public scrutiny, not private conscience (Popper 2002, 488–93). Something said of anthropology goes for social science generally:

The anthropologist propounds some rather preposterous hypothesis of a very general kind and then puts forward his cases to illustrate the argument. . . . Insight comes from . . . private intuition; the evidence is only put in by way of illustration.   (Leach 2000, 1: 271–2)

The issue is not private intuition, but public testability. Nothing stops critics from searching out facts that refute the propounded theory or from searching out new facts where old facts confirm alternative theories that contradict each other. Neither physical nor social science is inherently circular (Popper 2002, 788, 536, 542–3).[22]

To say theory explains fact and facts tests theory by way of logic is to accept "consistency and responsibility to fact" as ground rules, which postmodern antinomianism rejects, insisting that "everything is a social construction" (Rorty 1999, 48). The laws of physics are like the rules of baseball; science is politics by other means; power produces knowledge; all "perspectives" are "partial" and therefore political, but none of them is privileged—the litany makes "people in many disciplines more relaxed" (Rorty 1999, 181). But if "everything is a social construction," then so is that sentence, which denies its own truth and (by the law of excluded middle) asserts its own falsehood; it contradicts itself and (by the law of contradiction) is logically false. If "everything is a social construction," then "incommensurable paradigms" that various "discourse communities" accept (like magic and physics) are equally valid, though physics (unlike magic) gets testable, cumulative results with applications in technology, which cannot be faked. And if "everything is a social construction," then "consistency and responsibility to fact" do not matter. There is no check on sophistry and humbug; dogmatism and credulity have free rein. No one is obliged to refute opponents with argument—it is enough to dismiss them as "politically suspect," the winner being whoever has the power to compel agreement (Lasch 1995, 13, 188). If postmodern antinomianism is correct, then the hypothetico-deductive "consistency and responsibility to fact" view of rational inquiry is vanity—and vice versa.

References

AKERLOF, G. A. 1984. *An Economic Theorist's Book of Tales.* Cambridge: Cambridge University Press.

AYA, R. 1990. *Rethinking Revolutions and Collective Violence.* Amsterdam: Spinhuis.

—— 2001a. The third man; or, agency in history; or, rationality in revolution. *History and Theory,* 40: 143–52.

—— 2001b. Revolutions, theories of. Pp. 13314–17 in *International Encyclopedia of the Social and Behavioral Sciences,* ed. N. J. Smelser and P. B. Baltes. Oxford: Elsevier Science.

AYER, A. J. 1946. *Language, Truth and Logic.* London: Gollancz; originally published 1936.

---

[22] The "incommensurability" thesis that alternative explanatory theories are "paradigms" between which choice is a leap of faith (Kuhn 1970) has three problems with it. One, it notes "anomalies" that one "paradigm" cannot explain but another "paradigm" predicts, which means fact is not slave to theory. Two, scientific consensus occurs without thought control—evidence decides arguments. Three, applied science yields powerful technology (Gellner 1996, 682, 674).

BARTH, F. 1959. *Political Leadership among Swat Pathans*. London: Athlone.

BEAUCHAMP, T. L., and ROSENBERG, A. 1981. *Hume and the Problem of Causation*. Oxford: Oxford University Press.

BLOK, A. 1988. *The Mafia of a Sicilian Village, 1860–1960*. Prospect Heights, Ill.: Waveland; originally published 1974.

BOUDON, R. 1992. *L'idéologie ou l'origine des idées reçues*. Paris: Fayard; originally published 1986.

BRAITHWAITE, R. B. 1953. *Scientific Explanation*. Cambridge: Cambridge University Press.

CHOMSKY, N. 1987. *The Chomsky Reader*, ed. J. Peck. New York: Pantheon.

—— 1992. Rationality/science. *Z Papers*, 1 (4): 52–7.

—— 1993. Chomsky replies. *Z Papers*, 2 (3): 11–12.

—— 2002. *On Nature and Language*, ed. A. Belletti and L. Rizzi. Cambridge: Cambridge University Press.

COLBURN, F. D. 1994. *The Vogue of Revolution in Poor Countries*. Princeton, NJ: Princeton University Press.

COLEMAN, J. S. 1990. *Foundations of Social Theory*. Cambridge, Mass.: Harvard University Press.

DOBRY, M. 1986. *Sociologie des crises politiques: La dynamique des mobilisations multisectorielles*. Paris: Presses de la Fondation Nationale des Sciences Politiques.

DURKHEIM, É. 1937. *Les règles de la méthode sociologique*. Paris: Presses Universitaires de France; originally published 1894.

EVANS-Pritchard, E. E. 1940. *The Nuer*. Oxford: Oxford University Press.

—— 1976. *Witchcraft, Oracles and Magic among the Azande*, ed. E. Gillies. Oxford: Oxford University Press; originally published 1937.

FORTUNE, R. F. 1989. *Sorcerers of Dobu*. Prospect Heights, Ill.: Waveland; originally published 1932.

GEERTZ, C. 1995. *After the Fact: Two Countries, Four Decades, One Anthropologist*. Cambridge, Mass.: Harvard University Press.

GELLNER. E. 1969. *Saints of the Atlas*. London: Weidenfeld and Nicolson.

—— 1974. *Legitimation of Belief*. Cambridge: Cambridge University Press.

—— 1983. *Nations and Nationalism*. Oxford: Blackwell.

—— 1996. Reply to critics. Pp. 623–86 of *The Social Philosophy of Ernest Gellner*, ed. J. A. Hall and I. C. Jarvie. Amsterdam: Rodopi.

GINZBURG, C. 1990. *Ecstasies: Deciphering the Witches' Sabbath*, trans. R. Rosenthal, ed. G. Elliott. London: Hutchinson.

GOFFMAN, E. 1974. *Frame Analysis: An Essay on the Organization of Experience*. Cambridge, Mass.: Harvard University Press.

HAWKING, S. W. 1988. *A Brief History of Time from the Big Bang to Black Holes*. New York: Bantam.

HEDSTRÖM, P., and SWEDBERG, R. (eds.) 1998. *Social Mechanisms*. Cambridge: Cambridge University Press.

KEYNES, J. M. 1973. *A Treatise on Probability*. London: Macmillan; originally published 1921.

KUHN, T. S. 1970. *The Structure of Scientific Revolutions*. Chicago: University of Chicago Press; originally published 1962.

LASCH, C. 1995. *The Revolt of the Elites and the Betrayal of Democracy*. New York: Norton.

LEACH, E. 2000. *The Essential Edmund Leach*, ed. S. Hugh-Jones and J. Laidlaw, 2 vols. New Haven, Conn.: Yale University Press.

LOSEE, J. 2001. *A Historical Introduction to the Philosophy of Science*, 4th edn. Oxford: Oxford University Press.

MALINOWSKI, B. 1922. *Argonauts of the Western Pacific: An Account of Native Enterprise and Adventure in the Archipelagoes of Melanesian New Guinea*. London: Routledge.

—— 2002a. *The Sexual Life of Savages in North-Western Melanesia*. London: Routledge; originally published 1929.

—— 2002b. *Coral Gardens and Their Magic*, 2 vols. London: Routledge; originally published 1935.

McNEILL, W. H. 1991. *The Rise of the West*. Chicago: University of Chicago Press; originally published 1963.

MEDAWAR, P. 1982. *Pluto's Republic*. Oxford: Oxford University Press.

MERTON, R. K. 1968. *Social Theory and Social Structure*, 3rd edn. New York: Free Press.

OLSON, M. 1971. *The Logic of Collective Action: Public Goods and the Theory of Groups*. Cambridge, Mass.: Harvard University Press; originally published 1965.

PARKIN, F. 1979. *Marxism and Class Theory*. London: Tavistock.

PARSONS, T. 1968. *The Structure of Social Action*, 2 vols. New York: Free Press; originally published 1937.

POPPER, K. R. 1972. *The Logic of Scientific Discovery*. London: Hutchinson; originally published 1934.

—— 1979. *Objective Knowledge*. Oxford: Oxford University Press; originally published 1972.

—— 1989. *Conjectures and Refutations*. London: Routledge; originally published 1963.

—— 1994. Models, instruments and truth: the status of the rationality principle in the social sciences. PP. 154–84 in *The Myth of the Framework*, ed. M. A. Notturno. London: Routledge.

—— 2002. *The Open Society and Its Enemies*. London: Routledge; originally published 1945.

QUINE, W. V. 1992. *Pursuit of Truth*. Cambridge, Mass.: Harvard University Press; originally published 1990.

RAGIN, C. C. 1987. *The Comparative Method*. Berkeley: University of California Press.

RORTY, R. 1999. *Philosophy and Social Hope*. London: Penguin.

RUSSELL, B. 1948. *Human Knowledge: Its Scope and Limits*. London: Allen and Unwin.

SAMUELSON, P. A., and NORDHAUS, W. D. 2001. *Economics*, 17th edn. New York: McGraw-Hill.

SCHELLING, T. C. 1978. *Micromotives and Macrobehavior*. New York: Norton.

SIMON, H. A. 1983. *Reason in Human Affairs*. Oxford: Blackwell.

SKOCPOL, T. 1979. *States and Social Revolutions*. Cambridge: Cambridge University Press.

—— 1994. *Social Revolutions in the Modern World*. Cambridge: Cambridge University Press.

STINCHCOMBE, A. L. 1978. *Theoretical Methods in Social History*. New York: Academic.

TILLY, C. 1984. *Big Structures, Large Processes, Huge Comparisons*. New York: Russell Sage Foundation.

—— 1993. *European Revolutions, 1492–1992*. Oxford: Blackwell.

TRAUGOTT, M. 2002. *Armies of the Poor: Determinants of Working-Class Participation in the Parisian Insurrection of June 1848*. New Brunswick, NJ: Transaction; originally published 1985.

WEBER, M. 1964. *Wirtschaft und Gesellschaft: Grundriss der verstehenden Soziologie*, ed. J. Winckelmann, 2 vols. Cologne: Kiepenheuer & Witsch; originally published 1922, translated as Weber 1978.

WEBER, M. 1978. *Economy and Society: An Outline of Interpretive Sociology,* ed. G. Roth and C. Wittich, 2 vols. Berkeley: University of California Press; originally published 1922, translation of Weber 1964.

WEINBERG, S. 2001. *Facing Up: Science and Its Cultural Adversaries.* Cambridge, Mass.: Harvard University Press.

WILSON, J. Q., and HERRNSTEIN, R. J. 1985. *Crime and Human Nature.* New York: Simon and Schuster.

PART III

PSYCHOLOGY MATTERS

CHAPTER 7

WHY AND HOW PSYCHOLOGY MATTERS

KATHLEEN M. MCGRAW

THE assumption that self-interest plays a central role in how citizens respond to the political world has a long and distinguished history in political theory. However, as a general empirical principle, most—although certainly not all—political scientists would agree with the conclusion that "self-interest is surprisingly unimportant" when it comes to predicting public opinion (Kinder 1998, 801). This general principle proves to be particularly robust in the literature on economic voting, where little evidence of "pocketbook voting," that is, assessments of political candidates based on personal economic well-being, can be found. Rather, voting is strongly linked to national political conditions (or "sociotropic"; Lewis-Beck and Stegmaier 2000). This general principle can be a useful pedagogical tool for understanding, describing, and explaining election outcomes in democratic systems. Nonetheless, the conclusion that economic self-interest never matters, that "all of the people all of the time" are focused on collective economic outcomes, also rings false. In fact, scholars have identified certain conditions under which pocketbook voting is more likely to occur. For example, the propensity to engage in pocketbook voting has been linked to the voter's level of education or sophistication, and to the causal attributions the voter makes for his or her personal economic well-being[1]. Men are more likely to engage in pocketbook voting than

[1] See e.g. Abramowitz, Lanoue, and Ramesh 1988; Delli Carpini and Keeter 1996; Feldman 1982; Gomez and Wilson 2001.

are women (Chaney, Alvarez, and Nagler 1998). When the personal financial stakes are clear, large, and important, pocketbook voting is more likely to occur (Sears and Funk 1991). The information environment, particularly the mass media, have been implicated in both facilitating and inhibiting pocketbook voting (e.g. Mutz 1998; Weatherford 1983).

In short, there are systematic, predictable, and theoretically meaningful exceptions to the general principle that citizens' votes are *not* determined by personal economic self-interest. These exceptions can be broadly construed as contextual effects, as they point to the conditions under which economic self-interest does, and does not, matter. Because these "conditions under which" are systematic and theoretically meaningful, they cannot be treated as noise that obscures our understanding of the economic determinants of voting. Rather, identification of these contingencies enriches scientific knowledge and promotes the further development of even richer and more powerful theories.

The contributions to this volume attest to the value and vibrancy of contextual political analysis. The goal of this chapter is to sketch how psychology might provide guidelines for engaging in productive contextual political analysis. The discipline of psychology covers an enormous amount of territory, bordering on the biological sciences at one end and the social sciences such as political science, anthropology, and sociology at the other. Psychology is typically defined as the scientific study of the human mind and human behavior. For example, according to Zimbardo (1988, 5) the essential concern of psychology is "the scientific study of behavioral and mental processes... [with an interest] in discovering *general laws*" (emphasis mine). As politics is a human endeavor, the science of psychology can contribute considerably to the political scientist's goals of systematically describing and explaining the political world. The task I set for myself here is to delineate one way in which the psychologist's quest for general laws of human thought and behavior can illuminate the contextual underpinnings of political phenomena. Because psychology is such a large field, some limits are necessary. For the most part, the discussion draws on social psychological principles and examples, because of my background and because contemporary political science draws much of its psychological basis from social psychology (Bar-Tal 2002). A psychologist with different training (for example, in clinical psychology or neuroscience) would no doubt put forth a very different set of arguments. In addition, the focus is on understanding the political thoughts and behavior of *individuals*, as opposed to larger collective entities.

The chapter is organized in five sections. First, I outline a general theoretical perspective, originating in Kurt Lewin's (1936) classic work, that proposes that human behavior is a function of both individual and situational forces. As I will relate, this simple explanatory framework has generated a fair amount of controversy within the field of psychology. Second and third, I describe how both individual differences and situational forces, taken separately, have illuminated our understanding of the contextual determinants of political phenomena. Fourth, I consider research that illustrates that the combination of the two—the joint effects of the person and the situation—yields rigorous theorizing and empirical regularities that satisfy the often incompatible scientific goals of understanding the complexity of political life and at the same time developing generalizable laws. I conclude in Section 5 with a few thoughts about the potential tension between a focus on contextual effects and theory development.

1   LEWIN'S FRAMEWORK AND THE PERSON—SITUATION CONTROVERSY

Kurt Lewin, one of the many prominent European social scientists who emigrated to the United States as refugees from Nazi Germany in the 1930s, is widely recognized as the father of modern social psychology. He was trained as a Gestaltist and so the starting point of his theorizing is that perception is largely determined by the context in which the object of perception is embedded. He was also greatly influenced by Einstein and the principles of force-field physics. From this background emerged the theoretical development for which Lewin (1936; 1951) is most renowned, field theory. The "field" is the individual's life space, the space containing the individual and his or her environment. Not limited to a specific domain, Lewin intended field theory to be a set of concepts that would be applicable to all behavioral realms and yet at the same time be precise enough to understand the behavior of a specific person in a concrete situation. The important principle of field theory, for the purposes of this chapter, is reflected in this summary statement:

In general terms, behavior (B) is a function (F) of the person (P) and of his environment (E), $B = F(P, E)$. This statement is correct for emotional outbreaks as well as for "purposive" directed activities; for dreaming, wishing and thinking, as well as for talking and acting. (1951, 239)

As the functional expression suggests, Lewin believed these processes could, and should, be represented mathematically; as the second sentence makes explicit, he felt this explanatory framework can be applied to any domain of human behavior.[2]

---

[2] Field theory is considerably more elaborate and rich than this brief description can convey and it was subject to a fair amount of criticism. Interested readers should see Hall and Lindzey (1957) for an accessible introduction and even-handed critique.

The argument put forth in this chapter, then, is that characteristics of the person (P) and characteristics of the environment (E) can be regarded as contextual factors that should be incorporated into theorizing about political behavior, because such theorizing can illuminate the systematic conditions under which the phenomenon of interest is more or less likely to occur. Many political scientists already make use of contextual theorizing that invokes personal and situational contingencies, as the discussion below will illustrate. However, greater attention to these kinds of contextual contingencies, and the psychological principles that illuminate the mechanisms by which these contingencies operate, will yield a stronger empirical and theoretical foundation for the discipline.

Lewin's explanatory model is, on its face, intuitively pleasing, and some might even charge, obvious. However, the claim that behavior is a function of both the person and the situation has a history of considerable controversy within psychology. Historically, social and personality psychologists have placed more or less (or no) weight on the different elements of the Lewinian equation, social psychologists emphasizing the situational determinants of behavior, personality psychologists emphasizing individual differences. Simmering beneath this intellectual division of labor was an ideological battle, which flared into the open in the 1960s with a situationist attack on the validity and reliability of personality traits. Fueled by Walter Mischel's (1968) devastating critique, the situationists charged that personality traits demonstrate trivial empirical relationships with behavior, yielding little cross-time or cross-situation consistency in behavior. The conclusion that followed is that personality traits and perhaps individual differences more generally are untenable and fictitious theoretical constructs. Rather, as Stanley Milgram (1974, 205) famously concluded, "it is not so much the kind of person a man is as the kind of situation in which he finds himself that determines how he will act."

The concept of *personhood*—the idea that people have essential natures and propensities, and that they operate as causal agents—is fundamental not only to personality psychology, but also to larger philosophical and legal understandings of human nature. From this larger perspective, the situationist critique has profound implications for perspectives on individual responsibility. If the individual does not have an essential and enduring true nature and is simply buffeted by situational forces, then personal responsibility has little meaning.

I have offered this extended bit of psychological history to illustrate that psychology has long wrestled with how to balance the two contextual elements, the person and the situation, into productive theorizing. There is not a comparable history of antagonism among political scientists over the "person versus situation" question. I would go so far as to say there has been relatively little explicit consideration in political science of the relative explanatory value, and normative implications, of theories that emphasize properties of the individual versus properties of the situation. There are exceptions to this broad generalization, of course. For example, theorists of international relations have long debated whether individual leaders matter in the major events that shape the international system or whether international events are largely a result of historic, organizational, and systemic factors (Waltz 1959). Similarly, scholars of judicial behavior have disagreed about the extent to which case decisions are due to external factors such as precedent and institutional and social constraints, as opposed to the ideological values and attitudes of the justices themselves (Segal and Spaeth 1993).

In their introductory chapter to this volume, Tilly and Goodin maintain "in response to each big question of political science, we reply 'It depends.'" They go on to suggest three classes of contextual effects: those that depend upon the analysts' understanding of political processes; those that depend upon the evidence that is available for empirical examination; and those that depend upon the particular temporal and spatial circumstances of the processes. I do not disagree with this tripartite categorization of contextual effects, but instead offer up a different classification scheme that also is capable of yielding productive and systematic understandings of the contextual determinants of political processes. First, empirical regularities in political processes can be linked systematically to properties of the individuals engaged in those processes. Second, empirical regularities in political processes can be linked systematically to properties of the situations in which those processes unfold. And third, empirical regularities in political processes can be linked systematically to the interaction between properties of the individual and of the situation (Snyder and Ickes 1985).

2   IT DEPENDS UPON CHARACTERISTICS OF THE INDIVIDUAL

Research guided by this first principle is based upon the theoretical assumption that meaningful and systematic regularities in political behavior are the result of relatively stable and enduring propensities that reside "within" individuals. However, documenting the variety of "individual differences" that are politically relevant is an impossibly large task, because one might include biological characteristics, social and cultural backgrounds, personal experiences, abilities, motives, personality traits, and attitudes. Of particular note is the personality approach, that is, the study of stable predispositions that lead individuals to act in a particular way, and that are often summarized by trait labels such as authoritarianism, social dominance, self-esteem, neuroticism, etc. The personality approach to politics dominated political psychology in the 1940s and 1950s (McGuire 1993; Sullivan, Rahn, and Rudolph 2002), but is less prominent today.[3] I defer discussion of personality traits until Section 4 below, in agreement with Greenstein's (1969, 143) observation: "rarely do we find simple and direct relationships between some indicator of personality and political behavior—relationships that are present under all circumstances and in all populations. The strong relationships and the theoretically and practically important relationships are likely to take the form of interactions" (see also Winter 2003). Here, I consider two other ways that characteristics of the individual have a robust impact on politics, regardless of the situation. The first is a characteristic of *all* people—members of the mass public and political elites—which illustrates the point that how people perceive the political world depends upon their prior preconceptions and goals. The second points to the role that differences in political sophistication plays in shaping mass public opinion.

2.1   Perceptual Biases

Psychologists have documented many ways in which people "go beyond the information given" (Bruner 1957) in perceiving the social and physical world. Individuals' prior experiences as well as their current expectations and goals determine, and sometimes distort, what is noticed and the inferences that are drawn.[4] Two goals, or motivations, are central to social perception. First, people can be motivated to reach as accurate or correct a judgment as is possible in the situation. Ideally, this is how we would like to see political actors reason. In contrast, directional goals (or, as it is often referred to by political scientists, *motivated reasoning*) lead the perceiver to reach a judgment that is consistent with a preferred, pre-existing conclusion; perceptions are accordingly distorted to support preferences. There is an inherent tension between these two goals, and so the perceptual trick is to achieve a balance, for citizens to "believe both what accounts satisfactorily for the sensory evidence and what suits their purposes" (Fiske 1992).

Political scientists have long recognized that citizens with different political orientations reach very different conclusions about the same set of facts. Partisan attachments, in particular, have been linked to distorted reasoning: "Identification with a party," Campbell et al. contended (1960, 133), "raises a perceptual screen through which the individual tends to see what is favorable to his partisan orientation." Many psychological process mechanisms have been identified as playing a role in biased reasoning. What is clear as a general principle is that when people are faced with undesirable evidence, they work hard—invest cognitive resources—to

---

[3] Greenstein (1969), Simonton (1990), and Winter (2003) provide good overviews of the personality and politics literature.

[4] The literature on bias in perception and decision-making is enormous, and so here I limit myself to a single example that is of particular relevance to political scientists.

undermine the implications of the evidence (Festinger 1957). In fact, motivated political reasoning seems most likely to occur among citizens who are knowledgeable about political matters and so mostly likely to possess the necessary cognitive resources (Lodge and Taber 2000; Zaller 1992). Ironically, then, it is those who are most attentive to the political world who are most likely to develop distorted beliefs and opinions.

Because people start with different preferences and predispositions, biased political reasoning can aggravate disagreement and conflict. People have a pronounced tendency to see bias more readily in others than in themselves. This has been linked to a broader epistemic stance dubbed *naive realism*, "the defining feature of which is the conviction that one sees and responds to the world objectively, or 'as it is,' and that others therefore will see it and respond to it differently only to the extent that their behavior is a reflection of something other than that reality" (Pronin, Gilovich, and Ross 2004, 781). If others disagree with us, according to this model, we assume either that they are uninformed or that they are biased by ideological and other values. When one is confident that he or she is objective, viewing the world as "black and white," portrayals in shades of grey will be seen as biased in favor of the other side. This is the psychological mechanism underlying the *hostile media phenomenon*, that is, the tendency for ideological partisans to believe that media coverage is biased against their particular side of the issue (Vallone, Ross, and Lepper 1985).

The implications of naive realism for intergroup and international conflict in the twenty-first century are sobering indeed. In the service of balance and evenhandedness, I will resist pointing to specific contemporary examples. As a general principle, the conviction that *I* am right, that *my* party, *my* group, *my* country has a monopoly on objectivity, and that *they* refuse to see the world as it really is has a number of ramifications for national and international conflict. The convictions of naive realism can lead both parties to feel that the other side is too biased to be reasoned with; when grievances are aired, the other party is charged with being biased, "strategic," or irrational; and the gap between antagonists is viewed as larger than it really is, contributing even more to pessimism about resolving the conflict (Pronin, Gilovich, and Ross 2004).

2.2   Political Sophistication and Public Opinion

An informed citizenry is an essential precondition for an ideal democracy, and so the mass public's fitness for democratic life, in terms of their cognitive capabilities, plays a crucial role in political science theorizing, and in particular in the study of public opinion. In fact, Zaller (1990, 125) argued "political awareness deserves to rank alongside party identification and ideology as one of the central constructs of the public opinion field.''[5] There is little doubt that differences in the extent to which individuals are interested in and knowledgeable about the political world has a pervasive impact on political judgment and choice, although it is also true that additional theorizing is necessary to specify with more precision when and why sophistication matters (McGraw 2000). As noted above, sophisticated citizens are more likely to engage in motivated political reasoning, in the service of reaching judgments that are consistent with pre-existing preferences. A second theoretical principle appears to be quite robust. Specifically, the opinions of citizens who are less sophisticated about political matters tend to be heavily influenced by immediate affective considerations—for example, moods and emotions. In contrast, the opinions of more sophisticated citizens tend to be derived from more enduring core beliefs and values (Delli Carpini and Keeter 1996; Goren 2001; Isbell and Wyer 1999; McGraw, Hasecke, and Conger 2003; McGraw and Steenbergen 1995; Ottati and Isbell 1996; Pollock, Lillie, and Vittes 1993; Rahn 2000; Sniderman, Brody, and Tetlock 1991). The implication here is that the opinions of sophisticated citizens are more constrained by politically relevant principles (Converse 1964), are more stable, and so are more likely to correspond to images of the ideal democratic citizen. In contrast, the opinions of the less sophisticated are more strongly influenced by contemporary feelings and passions, which are easily subject to manipulation by political and other elites, an unflattering portrait of citizenship which has occupied theorists since the ancient Greeks (but see Marcus, Neuman, and MacKuen 2000 for a very different argument).

3   IT DEPENDS ON THE SITUATION

In this section, I turn to evidence supporting the second contextual principle, namely that meaningful and systematic regularities in political behavior are caused by situational factors that are "outside" of the individual. A word of warning: Human beings—ordinary people and scholarly analysts—have a robust tendency to favor dispositional explanations of behavior over explanations that point to the power of situational forces. This over-emphasis on personal qualities, without careful consideration of relevant situational factors, is so pervasive and so central to our thinking about other people that it has been dubbed the "fundamental

---

[5] There is a fair amount of disorder in the literature regarding the labeling, conceptualization, and measurement of "sophistication," which is variously labeled expertise, awareness, and knowledge. Space does not permit a discussion of these issues in this chapter; see Price (1999) for a recent review.

attribution error" by social psychologists (Ross 1977).[6] Consequently, consideration of the possibility that behavior is largely determined by the situation, and not personal attributes, may require a deliberate effort on the reader's part to override this inferential tendency.

3.1   The Situationist Perspective on Obedience and Evil

In 1961, Adolph Eichmann stood trial in a Jerusalem court, charged with causing the deaths of millions of Jews in the Holocaust. Upon conviction, in his final statement to the court, Eichmann pleaded, "I am guilty of having been obedient, having subordinated myself to my official duties and the obligations of war service and my oath of allegiance and my oath of office . . . I am not the monster I am made out to be." The political philosopher Hannah Arendt, who covered the Eichmann trial, controversially agreed, generalizing beyond Eichmann by concluding, "in certain circumstances, the most ordinary decent person can become a criminal." This epitomizes one of the most profound and enduring questions of human existence, asked by generations past and present, namely, does a person who performs evil deeds necessarily possess evil personal qualities? I would anticipate that most people—members of the general public, academics, and political leaders—would answer in the affirmative, not simply because of the fundamental attribution error but because the experience of evil is so far removed from everyday existence. This dispositional orientation—the belief that evil acts are perpetrated by evil people, immoral acts committed by immoral people—understandably has appeal: it supports the illusion of a simple, dichotomous existence, divided between good people (us) and bad people (not us). However, most social psychologists would probably answer the question in the negative, and like Eichmann and Arendt would reject the dispositional explanation of evil. One of the central lessons of social psychology, which added fuel to the situationist critique of personality, points to the power of social situations to overwhelm individual dispositions, to the point of transforming ordinary people into perpetrators of harm and evil.

The most prominent representatives of this literature are familiar to many social scientists.[7] First, Stanley Milgram's (1974) experiments on blind obedience to authority revealed that about two-thirds of his subjects, ordinary residents of New Haven, were willing to give apparently harmful electric shocks—up to 450 volts—to an agonizingly protesting victim, simply because a scientific authority

[6] An important cultural, and so contextual, qualification: the emphasis on dispositional attributes over situational forces is "fundamental" for Americans and Europeans, but much less pervasive for East Asians, who are more likely to invoke situational, contextual, and societal factors when explaining human behavior (Fiske et al. 1998).

[7] Zimbardo (2004) provides a useful literature review coupled with a sharp political point of view.

commanded them to, and in spite of the fact that the victim did not do anything to deserve such punishment. Importantly, compliance with the authority's order to commit harm varied systematically under different circumstances, pointing to the contextual conditions under which blind obedience is more or less likely to occur. For example, obedience in the Milgram paradigm diminishes when the subject must make physical contact with the victim and increases when the victim is remote and not immediately present; obedience dramatically increases when subjects observe someone else obeying and dramatically decreases when a peer defies the authority's command; obedience is maximized when the harm starts with a small, insignificant act and increases gradually; obedience is at its highest level when the subject is only indirectly involved, as an accessory, helping another person who was directly responsible for the harm (see Milgram 1974, for a detailed discussion of other contextual influences). Particularly damaging to the dispositional explanation of evil is the absence of effects attributable to individual differences in the Milgram paradigm: women are as likely to obey as men, Yale undergraduates behaved no differently than New Haven residents, obedience rates are remarkably consistent across cultures (Brown 1986) and time (Blass 1999), and, with one exception, there appear to be no significant personality trait differences that differentiate the maximally obedient from the maximally disobedient (Elms and Milgram 1966). The exception is an important one, because it involves a personality trait that is quite clearly theoretically relevant to obedience to authority: authoritarians (defined as individuals who have a "submissive, uncritical attitude toward idealized moral authorities of the ingroup": Adorno et al. 1950, 228) are more likely to obey, and deliver shocks of greater intensity, than nonauthoritarians (Blass 1991).[8]

A second illustration of the power of the situation over individual predispositions is the Stanford Prison Experiment, conducted by Philip Zimbardo and his colleagues in 1971.[9] In the Stanford Prison Experiment, male college students, who had been pre-screened to limit participation to those who were psychologically and physically healthy, were randomly assigned to role-play prisoners and guards in a simulated prison. Although everyone knew it was just an experiment, behavior quickly spiraled out of control. The "guards" became increasingly cruel and abusive, inflicting sadistic suffering on the prisoners with no apparent moral compunction; the "prisoners," on the other hand, either passively accepted the abuse and dehumanization, or exhibited serious stress disorders that required their immediate release. The planned two-week study was terminated after only six days.

---

[8] Although it would certainly be appropriate and productive to consider obedience to authority within a Person X Situation interaction framework, surprisingly little research that has done so (Blass 1991).

[9] See www.prisonexp.org for information. This work has attracted renewed attention, with media commentators noting parallels between the Prison study and the abuse of Iraqis at the Abu Graib prison.

Because these were psychologically healthy and normal young men who were randomly assigned to the two roles, it is impossible to argue that the guards were innately cruel and the prisoners innately passive. Rather, in Zimbardo's (2004, 40) telling, "The Evil Situation triumphed over the Good People."

Although evil is typically construed as requiring active participation, harm also can result from *non*-action. In the United States, bystanders have no obligation to assist victims of crimes or other disasters who might be in need of assistance, and so cannot be held civilly or criminally liable for inaction. In contrast, many European countries have duty to assist laws that criminalize failure to assist others in obvious peril. Consequently, the legal, if not the moral, imperative response to the failure to aid others in need varies cross-culturally. Research in a variety of contexts indicates that characteristics of the social situation, and in particular the number of other people present, is a significant determinant of a bystander's willingness to come to another's aid (Latane and Darley 1970). Simply, the greater the number of other bystanders (who sit passively by), the lower the probability that any given individual will come to another's assistance. In other words, apathy breeds apathy. Although a number of contributing factors are implicated in this "bystander effect," two seem to be key. The first is informational: we rely on others to help us interpret ambiguous events, and the inaction of others who are present is taken as a cue that the situation does not require intervention, producing a state of pluralistic ignorance. The second involves diffusion of responsibility: when others are present, each individual feels less responsibility to help than if he or she was alone.

The conclusion that social structures and situations can lead ordinary people to commit extra-ordinary acts of harm is not limited to experimental social psychologists. Robert Jay Lifton (1986, 5), who studied the participation of medical doctors in the Nazi death camps, concluded, "The disturbing psychological truth [is] that participation in mass murder need not require emotions as extreme or demonic as would seem appropriate for such a malignant project. Or to put the matter another way, ordinary people can commit demonic acts." Ervin Staub (1989, 13), in his analysis of multiple instances of genocide, concluded, "Human beings have the capacity to come to experience killing other people as nothing extraordinary." If social scientists accept the implications of the situationist perspective on evil and anti-social behavior—and I believe the empirical research compels us to—we face the disquieting paradox of reconciling our understanding of the causal determinants of behavior with moral evaluation—punishing or forgiving—of the behavior. And the discomfort extends to our ability to prevent future evil. One lesson of the situationist perspective on evil is that the prevention, or at least amelioration of evil, cannot fully lie in exhorting individuals to resist the powers of the situation, because those pressures can be experienced so intensely. Rather, the solution requires changes in social, organizational, and political structures, both short- and long-term (Darley 1992).

3.2   Great Leaders are Created by Situations

Tolstoy, in the Epilogue to *War and Peace*, analyzed Napoleon's career and concluded, "A king is history's slave . . . Though Napoleon at that time, in 1812, was more convinced than ever that it depended on him . . . he had never been so much in the grip of inevitable laws." Tolstoy then declared about leaders more generally, "Every act of theirs, which appears to them an act of their own will, is in an historical sense involuntary and is related to the whole course of history and predestined from eternity" (1952, 343–4). This very exaggerated claim that the characteristics of individual leaders are largely irrelevant for understanding world affairs has some support in the research literature. For example, Dean Simonton (1984; 1987; 1990) has attempted to disentangle the impact of personality and situational factors on evaluations of historical political leaders, concluding that the impact of personality factors is "puny in comparison" to the impact of situational factors, and consequently "Tolstoy's theory does not require serious qualification" (Simonton 1990, 682). So, for example, for both European monarchs and United States Presidents, the most powerful predictor of historical judgments of greatness is the reign span or number of years in office. Although a reasonable hypothesis is that tenure duration is itself an indicator of personal leadership factors, in fact the primary predictors of tenure duration are situational rather than individual.

Of course, the conclusion that the great leaders are created by situations and not the intrinsic qualities of the leaders themselves flies in the face of lay intuitions and "great men" scholarly theories. Ordinary people, academics, and pundits find it easy to think of examples where a leader's personal qualities seem to have had an enormous impact on political events: Hitler's personal pathologies, Clinton's lack of self-control, Osama bin Laden's fanaticism, George W. Bush's religious faith. However, this over-emphasis on personal qualities, without careful consideration of the situational factors that constrain a leader's choices and behavior, is a classic example of the fundamental attribution error. I return to this issue below, when I consider evidence that suggests the impact of leaders' personalities depends upon the situation.

3.3   Contextual Influences on Identity

It is a social science truism that identity is fluid and so influenced by contextual factors, although the balance between the fluid and stable aspects of identity, as well as the specific mechanisms underlying the construction of identity is subject to considerable debate. Here, I briefly point to two general principles that support the claim that aspects of identity are influenced by situational factors. First, the salience of a given category—operationally defined as being in a statistical minority— clearly has an impact on the likelihood that category is evoked as central to the self-concept. That is, ethnic and gender identities are more likely to be expressed when the group category is made salient by virtue of minority status (e.g. an individual's identity as an American is more pronounced when she is in France, as opposed to Kansas; McGuire et al. 1978; McGuire and Padawer-Singer 1976; Hogg and Turner 1985). On the other hand, when we are like people who are like ourselves, that aspect of our identity becomes less salient. In addition, category salience promotes the development of ingroup bias (i.e. positive reactions to the ingroup relative to the outgroup), such that ingroup bias is more pronounced among smaller groups (Mullen, Brown, and Smith 1992).

Second, the social context provides feedback about the evaluative worth of our identities and so contributes to the maintenance of self-esteem. Individuals derive psychic benefits when their groups succeed (Cialdini et al. 1976), even when those individuals do not contribute directly to the group's success. The social context can also be a source of threat to the group, given resource scarcity and intergroup conflict in the political, economic, or social realms. The impact of threat on personal and social identity depends upon one's level of commitment to the group. When the group is threatened and the individual's commitment to the group is low, avoidance of identification with the group is the dominant response. On the other hand, when the group is threatened and the individual's commitment to the group is strong, affirmation and renewed loyalty to the group results.[10]

Identity is a central explanatory concept in political science, invoked to explain nationalism, ethnic conflict, group mobilization, and electoral politics. However, political scientists have only just begun to scratch the surface in theorizing about when, why, and how the different components of an individual's identity are politically consequential. The social psychological literature on identity is large and unruly, but to the extent it points to systematic contextual influences on the formation and expression of identity, consideration of that literature should be useful for facilitating productive contextual theorizing about the political significance of this essential explanatory concept.

4   IT DEPENDS ON THE PERSON AND THE SITUATION: $B = F(P, E)$

Lewin's framework can rightfully be interpreted in two distinct ways. The first, invoking the language of statistical analysis, implies two independent main effects: both characteristics of the individual *and* characteristics of the situation have

---

[10] See Ellemers, Spears, and Doosje (2002) for a comprehensive overview.

meaningful and systematic effects on political behavior. In contrast, the second interpretation emphasizes the interaction between the two classes of predictor variables. In other words, the meaningful and systematic effects attributable to characteristics of the individual emerge only in certain situations; or conversely, the meaningful and systematic effects attributable to characteristics of the situation emerge only for certain types of people. Both the main effect and interaction approach provide a framework for productive contextual analysis, as they require political scientists to conceptualize behavior as multiply systematically determined. However, if one accepts the proposition that most political phenomena are highly complex, and that cause and effect relationships are likely to be highly contingent upon other variables present in the social context (Mackie 1974), then the interactive framework is better suited for the accurate description and explanation of political reality. Accordingly, I focus on scholarship demonstrating the fertility of the Person $\times$ Situation approach to political judgment and behavior.

4.1 Information, Predispositions, and Public Opinion

Public opinion is central to our understanding of democratic politics, at least in the modern world. Information is a critical component of democratic citizenship, a "central resource for democratic participation" as it allows "citizens to engage in politics in a way that is personally and collectively constructive" (Delli Carpini and Keeter 1996, 5). The difficulty for the ideal practice of democratic politics, of course, is that the political information environment is complex and many citizens have neither the motivation nor the resources to invest time and energy into learning about politics, "a sideshow in the great circus of life" (Dahl 1961, 305). The difficulty for the empirical analyst is to understand how—if at all—characteristics of the information environment and characteristics of the individual combine to produce regularities in public opinion. Paul Sniderman (1993, 222), upon reviewing the literature, reached an optimistic conclusion about the "new look" in public opinion research, precisely because of the focus on "the interaction of situationally defined alternatives and enduring individual characteristics."

Information must be communicated for it to have an impact on public opinion and to be politically consequential. Perhaps the most productive model of attitude change and persuasion has it roots in the Yale studies of the 1940s and 1950s. Carl Hovland of Yale was commissioned by the Information and Education Division of the United States War Department to conduct research on propaganda during the Second World War; the research continued after the War. Hovland and his colleagues organized their studies of communication around the classic question, "Who say what to whom with what effect?" (Smith, Lasswell, and Casey 1946). So conceptualized, persuasive messages can be broken down into several parameters:

characteristics of the source (such as credibility, attractiveness, power), character-istics of the message itself (such as argument strength, emotional appeals, com-plexity, length), characteristics of the medium (print, audio, video), and characteristics of the recipient (such as intelligence, age, gender, self-esteem). Source, message, and medium effects are external and so can be conceptualized as situational factors, which both independently and in interaction with character-istics of the individual recipient produce systematic effects on attitude change.[11]

William McGuire has been largely responsible for elaborating on the cognitive process mechanisms that contribute to successful and unsuccessful persuasion within the Yale paradigm (1968; 1969; 1985). He proposed that the persuasive impact of any communication is a multiplicative function of the probability of several information processing steps occurring. Shorter and longer lists of the steps have been detailed by McGuire; for our purposes four are critical for successful persua-sion: (1) the individual must *attend* to the message; (2) the individual must *comprehend* the message; (3) the individual must accept, or *yield* to, the conclusions of the message; and (4) for the changed attitude to be consequential, it must persist or be *retained*. The source, message, medium, and recipient characteristics de-scribed above have a systematic impact through their effects on each of these processes. Because each step occurs with a probability of less than one (e.g. perfect comprehension is unlikely), and because the model specifies that successful per-suasion is a multiplicative function of the four steps, the McGuire model makes explicit something practitioners of persuasion have long known: it is difficult to change people's opinions. This model has particular relevance for understanding when and why political attitude change occurs, because citizens vary in the extent to which they attend to and understand political communications, and because their existing values and predispositions can lead them to either accept or resist a persuasive appeal (indeed, Zaller's (1992) model, discussed below, builds on exactly this logic).

McGuire, and those following from the Yale tradition, have been concerned with attitude formation and change as general psychological processes, not unique to the political realm. In contrast, John Zaller (1992, 4) undertook a more focused but still ambitious task: understanding the dynamics of mass public opinion on political issues, and in particular "how citizens use information from the mass media to form political preferences." Zaller's theoretical apparatus is "disarmingly simple" (Kinder 1998, 813), essentially boiling down to three variables. The first is infor-mation, namely the extent to which elite discourse on an issue is largely homoge-neous, where elites are in agreement, or two-sided, characterized by elite disagreement. The other two important theoretical variables are characteristics of individuals, namely political awareness (or attention to and understanding of politics) and political predispositions, such as partisanship and ideology. These

---

[11] See Eagly and Chaiken (1993) and McGuire (1985) for reviews.

three variables are coupled with a micro-psychological model of the mental processes that underlie the expression of an opinion. Zaller's theory, building on
insights provided by Converse (1962; 1964) and McGuire (1968), yields very precise
predictions about the movement of public opinion in response to changes in the
information that is supplied by political elites. Importantly, the magnitude and
direction of that movement depends upon citizens' levels of awareness and their
predispositions. So specified, the model accounts for a remarkable and varied set of
empirical cases (Zaller 1989, 1991, 1992; Zaller and Hunt 1994, 1995).

Arguably, the Yale-McGuire and the Zaller theories are the most sophisticated
and far-reaching conceptual models of public opinion making use of a Person X
Situation framework. However, the interactionist approach has illuminated other
public opinion research programs. Two deserve a brief mention. Paul Sniderman
and his colleagues have promoted, and made creative theoretical use of, the
integration of experimentation within large scale, general population surveys
(Sniderman and Grob 1996; Sniderman, Brody, and Tetlock 1991). This methodological advance allows analysts systematically to manipulate meaningful features of
the policy question or issue in order to understand the interplay between situational factors and individual characteristics in shaping public opinion. Herrmann,
Tetlock, and Visser (1999) have extended this "cognitive-interactionist" framework
to mass public support for military intervention, to understand how individual
predispositions interact with aspects of the strategic geopolitical context.

4.2   The Contingent Effects of Personality

One of the consequences of the situationist critique of personality traits was the
recognition that predictions about the impact of personality are often best phrased
conditionally, as more or less likely to occur in specified situations. Some have gone
so far as to prescribe that personality predictions "must always" be contingent
upon situational factors (Winter 2003, 133). Smith (1968) provided what still
remains as the most sophisticated framework for understanding the contingent
effects of personality in politics, in his "map for the analysis of personality and
politics." In this "declaration of intellectual strategy" (1968, 16), Smith attempted to
summarize the complex interdependencies that exist among personality processes
and three classes of environmental forces: the immediate situation in which the
behavior occurs; the social environment within which the individual is socialized
and develops; and the "distal" environment consisting of historical forces and the
contemporary sociopolitical system. Greenstein (1969) added considerable empirical flesh to Smith's map by reviewing the extant empirical literature on personality
and politics within Smith's framework. The Smith (1968) and Greenstein (1969)
works are gems and remain the single most important guides for theory develop-

ment and research on the impact of personality on political behavior. Here, I consider more recent developments in our understanding of mass public personality (specifically, authoritarianism) and elite personality that make use of a Person × Situation framework.

4.2.1   Authoritarianism and Threat

The landmark *The Authoritarian Personality* (Adorno et al. 1950) identified a personality syndrome that is central to understanding mass political behavior; the subsequent literature was, and continues to be, voluminous. The authoritarian personality consists of a set of covarying traits, including submissiveness to authorities, intolerance of outgroups and minorities, pressure to social conformity, and a rejection of unconventional behavior and beliefs. The original formulation was subject to substantial methodological and theoretical critique; much of that is familiar and so need not be rehashed here (see, e.g., Christie and Jahoda 1954; Brown 1965). Yet, in the face of considerable scholarly controversy, widespread agreement remains that the basic notion of authoritarianism is sound: that citizens vary in the extent to which they possess authoritarian traits and that this variation is politically consequential.

Many scholars have argued that conditions of threat or anxiety produce higher levels of authoritarianism, which in turn has consequences for political judgment and behavior. (See e.g.: Doty, Peterson, and Winter 1991; Fromm 1941; Rokeach 1960; Sales 1972; 1973.) In other words, this model posits that threatening situational circumstances have an impact on personality, which in turn has consequences for behavior (E → P → B, using the Lewinian shorthand). Surprisingly, there is little empirical evidence, particularly at the individual level, that supports this sequence of events, nor is that sequence easily accommodated within extant theories of authoritarianism. Stenner (2005; Feldman and Stenner 1997) proposes an alternative interaction model, namely that the manifestations of authoritarianism—intolerance, hostility, aggression—depend upon the interaction between the predisposition and the environment, and in particular conditions of threat (be that threat naturally experienced, subjectively perceived, or experimentally manipulated). Stenner (2005) identifies "threats to the normative order" as critical, described as "the experience or perception of disobedience to group authorities (*or* authorities unworthy of respect), non-conformity with group norms (*or* norms proving questionable), and in general, diversity and freedom "run amok." Stenner (2005; Feldman and Stenner 1997) brings together a truly impressive body of evidence, from multiple research methodologies, demonstrating the significant impact of the predicted Authoritarian Personality × Threat interaction on a host of politically important attitudinal and behavioral measures. In other words, neither authoritarianism by itself, nor threat by itself, are the critical predictors of racism, intolerance, and punitiveness. Rather it is the combination of the two that is politically consequential. Intriguingly, this research also makes it clear that collective threat is what is necessary to activate, and make politically consequential, authoritarian predispositions. Personal threats (e.g. family financial distress, criminal victimization, personal trauma) actually dampen the effects of authoritarian predispositions. Stenner (2005) concludes, "overall, it is clear that authoritarians are oriented to collective rather than individual conditions, concerned more with the fate of the normative order than their personal fortunes, and greatly aggravated by perceptions both of belief diversity and failed political leadership: broken rules and unfit rulers."

4.2.2   Personality of Political Elites

Here I return to the question raised earlier, namely the extent to which the personalities of political leaders have an influence on their performance and policy choices, and ultimately, then, the strategies and actions of the state. Extreme and simplistic views abound in the literature, with some arguing that political outcomes are fully determined by personalities and others that individual personalities have no effect at all. A more balanced and theoretically fruitful approach posits that the impact of elite personalities depends upon situational factors, an approach for which there is considerable empirical support. For example, David Winter, drawing on the inaugural addresses of all of the United States' presidents, has documented differences in the fundamental motivations of the need for power (the drive to control and influence others), the need for achievement (the quest for excellence and accomplishment), and the need for affiliation (the desire for friendship and love) (Winter 2003). In order to test the hypothesis that candidates are more likely to be successful if their personal characteristics are congruent with society's, i.e. that a match between the leader and the "mood of the people" is critical, Winter (1987) made use of standard cultural documents (e.g. novels, readers, hymns) to obtain similar motive scores for American society, across the course of the nation's history. A higher congruence between the president's and society's motive profile was associated with larger margins of victory and an increased probability of re-election to a second term. In short, electoral success depends upon a match between the leader's motive profile (characteristics of the individual) and the modal profile of the American people (a characteristic of the situation). Ironically, this motive congruence is not associated with more effective leadership, but just the opposite: these popular presidents are generally viewed as inferior by historians (Simonton 1987).

Reviewing a number of studies, Greenstein (1969) concluded that a leader's personality is likely to have an impact under certain specified conditions, including: when the situation is ambiguous or unstable, lacking a clear precedent; when the person is highly emotionally involved; when the decision or behavior is spontaneous; or, when the decision or behavior requires a great deal of effort. Hermann has determined that political leaders are more likely to have an impact on their country's foreign policy in authoritarian regimes, in crisis situations, when advisory structures are formal and hierarchical, and in cultures that value strong and forceful leadership (Hermann 1986; Hermann and Hagan 1998; Hermann and Kegley 1995). Finally, Byman and Pollock (2001) conducted five case studies to examine the impact of the personal characteristics of leaders on international relations outcomes. Beyond concluding that "individual personalities matter to the affairs of nations" (2001, 133), Byman and Pollock argue that a leader's personality is particularly consequential for world affairs when power is concentrated in the hand of an individual leader, when systemic or domestic institutions are in conflict, and in times of great change. Taken together, these research programs provide compelling evidence for the utility of a Person × Situation theoretical framework in the study of political elites and international affairs.

4.3   Emerging Theoretical Developments

Political psychologists, representing different theoretical perspectives and substantive interests, have recently converged on a common plea. Jervis (2002) has called for the unifying the study of signaling and perception in international politics, arguing that "a theory of signaling, then, requires a careful investigation of how signals are perceived" (p. 297), and "what we need, then, are studies that are two-sided in looking at both the actor and the perceiver" (p. 308). In the same volume, Jackman and Sniderman (2002) call for an integration of what they label the *internalist* and *externalist* approaches to political choice. In their analysis, internalist approaches emphasize individual predispositions and psychological processes, whereas an externalist approach emphasizes institutional parameters and strategies that limit the alternatives available to citizens. Institutions, and in particular political parties in democratic politics, coordinate the options that are available, and so a fuller understanding of citizen choice requires an account of how institutions coordinate the alternatives open for consideration. Finally, McGraw (2003) reviewed the two interrelated processes of *impression formation* (specifically, citizens' beliefs and opinions about political leaders) and *impression management* (the activities that political leaders engage in regulate and control the information about themselves that they present to the mass public). I concluded that what is sorely needed is theorizing "that takes seriously what is happening at the intersection of individual citizens' processes of impression formation and elite strategies of impression formation" (2003, 420). All three sets of authors reach the same conclusion: theorizing and empirical research rarely grapple with the explicit connections between the two sides of the related coins.

This emerging perspective is too new to have generated much in the way of robust theoretical or empirical principles. However, it clearly can be recast within a Person × Situation theoretical framework. Perceiving, internalist approaches, and impression formation are all concerned with individual psychological processes; social psychologists and political scientists have both made formidable advances in understanding these processes. Signaling, externalist approaches, and impression management all involve behaviors of other social actors and/or institutions and so can be considered external, situational factors. Because social psychology is so overwhelmingly concerned with individual perception, the advances here are more clearly within the realm of political science, and in particular, perspectives informed by rational choice and game theory. Understanding the two sides of the coin, in each instance, requires studying them—for example, impression formation and impression management—together, and over time in a dynamic fashion. Theoretical challenges abound, and will no doubt benefit from the integration of both psychological and rational choice principles. Nonetheless, a serious commitment to theory and research integrating models of internal psychological processes of political actors with both institutional constraints and the strategic attempts of others to influence those processes holds great promise.

5   CONCLUDING THOUGHTS: CONTEXT AND THEORY DEVELOPMENT

All political behavior occurs in a specific context, at a specific time and place by particular individuals characterized by different backgrounds, preferences, and personalities. Any search for universal regularities in political behavior is doomed for precisely this reason. This volume attests to the variety of approaches that might be adopted to engage in productive contextual analysis. I have argued that systematic consideration of the properties of individuals and properties of the situation, separately and in combination, can be a fruitful strategy for contextual analysis. To support this argument, I have drawn examples from the social and political psychological literatures to illustrate how some of the fundamental concerns of political science—"How do individuals perceive the political world?" "When does personality matter?" "How is information converted into opinion?" "Are evil acts committed by evil people?" "What shapes identity and when is it politically consequential?"—can be understood within a Person × Situation framework. *Psychology matters* because it provides theories and methods for rigorous and systematic empirical research aimed at disentangling the impact of forces residing within the individual and those residing within the situation. In this way, psychology can illuminate the contextual contingencies of important political phenomena.

Underlying the recommendation for the Person × Situation theoretical framework is a preference for a particular epistemology of causation. Although the job of social scientists would be considerably easier if the social world was characterized by simple linear cause and effect relationships, an alternative perspective that emphasizes multiple factors that are causally contingent is arguably more faithful to reality (Mackie 1974). If we accept the premise of contingent causality, then our jobs are considerably more complicated because causal regularities are much more complex than a simple linear regularity theory would propose. The analytic trick is to avoid the simplistic and often sloppy thinking that characterizes the "it depends" thinking of our less sophisticated students. Single, isolated studies of the causal mechanisms involved in specific situations that provide little or no potential for yielding generalizable principles can bring productive theorizing to a grinding halt. Rather, the goal of the contextually aware analyst, cognizant of contingent causality, should be theories of the middle range (Merton 1957) that provide hypotheses than can be confirmed or refuted by empirical investigation. The "middle range" perspective can be further enriched by McGuire's (1983) "contextualist theory of knowledge." McGuire rejects the logical empiricist's tenet that some theories are right and some theories are wrong, and that empirical investigation provides the means to determine which is which. Rather, McGuire argues that *all* (reasonable) theories are true, *at least in some circumstances*, and so provides a fitting closing to this chapter:

In the contextualist vision of science, empirical confrontation is not so much a testing of the hypothesis as it is a continuing revelation of its full meaning made apparent by its pattern of confirmations and disconfirmations in a strategically programmed set of observable situations.... Hence, the scientist should subject his or her a priori theoretical speculations to empirical confrontations, not to test if they are true, but to discover the pattern of contexts in which each adequately represents the observation, thus bringing out more fully the meaning of each theory by making explicit its limiting assumptions and yielding a more sophisticated appreciation of the complex factors operative across the spectrum of situations.   (McGuire 1983, 14)

References

Abramowitz, A. I., Lanoue, D. J., and Ramesh, S. 1988. Economic conditions, causal attributions and political evaluations in the 1984 Presidential elections. *Journal of Politics*, 50: 848–63.

Adorno, T. W., Frenkel-Brunswick, E., Levinson, D. J., and Stanford, R. N. 1950. *The Authoritarian Personality*. New York: Harper and Row.

Bar-Tal, D. 2002. The (social) psychological legacy for political psychology. Pp. 173–92 in *Political Psychology*, ed. K. R. Monroe. Mahwah, NJ: Erlbaum.

BLASS, T. 1991. Understanding behavior in the Milgram obedience experiment: the role of personality, situations and their interactions. *Journal of Personality and Social Psychology*, 60: 398–413.

——1999. The Milgram paradigm after 35 years: some things we now know about obedience to authority. *Journal of Applied Social Psychology*, 29: 955–78.

BROWN, R. 1965. *Social Psychology*. New York: Free Press.

——1986. *Social Psychology*, 2nd edn. New York: Free Press.

BRUNER, J. S. 1957. Going beyond the information given. Pp. 41–69 in *Contemporary Approaches to Cognition*, ed. H. Gruber, K. Hammond, and R. Jesser. Cambridge, Mass.: Harvard University Press.

BYMAN, D. L., and POLLACK, K. M. 2001. Let us now praise great men: bringing the statesman back in. *International Security*, 25: 107–46.

CAMPBELL, A., CONVERSE, P., MILLER, W., and STOKES, D. 1960. *The American Voter*. New York: Wiley.

CHANEY, C. K., ALVAREZ, R. M., and NAGLER, J. 1998. Explaining the gender gap in U.S. Presidential elections, 1980–1992. *Political Research Quarterly*, 51: 311–39.

CHRISTIE, R., and JAHODA, M. 1954. *Studies in the Scope and Method of "The Authoritarian Personality."* New York: Free Press.

CIALDINI, R., et al. 1976. Basking in reflected glory: three (football) field studies. *Journal of Personality and Social Psychology*, 34: 366–75.

CONVERSE, P. E. 1962. Information flow and the stability of partisan attitudes. *Public Opinion Quarterly*, 26: 578–99.

——1964. The nature of belief systems in mass publics. Pp. 206–61 in *Ideology and Discontent*, ed. D. E. Apter. London: Collier-Macmillan.

DAHL, R. 1961. *Who Governs?* New Haven, Conn.: Yale University Press.

DARLEY, J. 1992. Social organization for the production of evil. *Psychological Inquiry*, 3: 199–218.

DELLI CARPINI, M. X., and KEETER, S. 1996. *What Americans Know About Politics and Why It Matters*. New Haven, Conn.: Yale University Press.

DOTY, R. M., PETERSON, B. E., and WINTER, D. G. 1991. Threat and authoritarianism in the United States: 1978–1987. *Journal of Personality and Social Psychology*, 61: 629–40.

EAGLY, A, H., and CHAIKEN, S. 1993. *The Psychology of Attitudes*. Fort Worth, Tex.: Harcourt Brace Jovanovich.

ELLEMERS, N., SPEARS, R., and DOOSJE, B. 2002. Self and social identity. *Annual Review of Psychology*, 53: 161–86.

ELMS, A. C. and MILGRAM, S. 1966. Personality characteristics associated with obedience and defiance toward authoritative command. *Journal of Experimental Research in Personality*, 1: 282–9.

FELDMAN, S. 1982. Economic self-interest and political behavior. *American Journal of Political Science*, 26: 446–66.

——and Stenner, K. 1997. Perceived threat and authoritarianism. *Political Psychology*, 18: 741–70.

FESTINGER, L. 1957. *A Theory of Cognitive Dissonance*. Stanford, Calif.: Stanford University Press.

FISKE, A. P., KITAYAMA, S., MARKUS, H. R., and NISBETT, R. E. 1998. The cultural matrix of social psychology. In Gilbert, Fiske, and Lindzey 1998, 2: 915–81.

FISKE, S. T. 1992. Thinking is for doing: portraits of social cognition from daguerreotype to laserphoto. *Journal of Personality and Social Psychology*, 63: 877–89.

FROMM, E. 1941. *Escape from Freedom*. New York: Holt, Rinehart, and Winston.

GILBERT, D. T., FISKE, S. T., and LINDZEY, G. (eds.) 1998. *The Handbook of Social Psychology*, 4th edn. New York: McGraw-Hill.

GOMEZ, B. T., and WILSON, J. M. 2001. Political sophistication and economic voting in the American electorate: a theory of heterogeneous attribution. *American Journal of Political Science*, 45: 899–914.

GOREN, P. 2001. Core principles and policy reasoning in mass publics: a test of two theories. *British Journal of Political Science*, 31: 159–77.

GREENSTEIN, F. 1969. *Personality and Politics*. Chicago: Markham.

HALL, C. S., and LINDZEY, G. 1957. *Theories of Personality*. New York: Wiley.

HERMANN, M. G. 1986. The ingredients of leadership. Pp. 167–92 in *Political Psychology*, ed. M. G. Hermann. San Francisco: Jossey-Bass.

——and HAGAN, J. D. 1998. International decision making: leadership matters. *Foreign Policy*, 100: 124–37.

——and KEGLEY, C. W. (1995). Rethinking democracy and international peace: perspectives from political psychology. *International Studies Quarterly*, 39: 511–33.

HERRMANN, R., TETLOCK, P., and VISSER, P. 1999. Mass public decisions to go to war: a cognitive-interactionist framework. *American Political Science Review*, 93: 553–73.

HOGG, M. A., and TURNER, J. C. 1985. Interpersonal attraction, social identification and psychological group formation. *European Journal of Social Psychology*, 15: 51–66.

ISBELL, L., and WYER, R. S. 1999. Correcting for mood-induced bias in the evaluation of political candidates: the roles of intrinsic and extrinsic motivation. *Personality and Social Psychology Bulletin*, 25: 237–49.

JACKMAN, S., and SNIDERMAN, P. M. 2002. Institutional organization of choice spaces: a political conception of political psychology. Pp. 209–24 in *Political Psychology*, ed. K. R. Monroe. Mahwah, NJ: Erlbaum.

JERVIS, R. 2002. Signaling and perception: drawing inferences and projecting images. Pp. 293–314 in *Political Psychology*, ed. K. R. Monroe. Mahwah, NJ: Erlbaum.

KINDER, D. R. 1998. Opinion and action in the realm of politics. In Gilbert, Fiske, and Lindzey 1998, 2: 778–865.

LATANE, B., and DARLEY, J. 1970. *The Unresponsive Bystander: Why Doesn't He Help?* New York: Appleon-Century-Crofts.

LEWIS-BECK, M., and STEGMAIER, M. 2000. Economic determinants of electoral outcomes. *Annual Review of Political Science*, 3: 183–219.

LEWIN, K. 1936. *Principles of Topological Psychology*. New York: McGraw-Hill.

——1951. *Field Theory in Social Science*. New York: Harper and Row.

LIFTON, R. J. 1986. *The Nazi Doctors: Medical Killing and the Psychology of Genocide*. New York: Basic Books.

LINDZEY, G., and ARONSON, E. (eds.) 1985. *Handbook of Social Psychology*, 3rd edn. New York: Random House.

LODGE, M., and TABER, C. 2000. Three steps toward a theory of motivated reasoning. In Lupia, McCubbins, and Popkin 2000: 183–213.

LUPIA, A., McCUBBINS, M.D., and POPKIN, S. L. (eds.) 2000. *Elements of Reason: Cognition, Choice and the Bounds of Rationality*. New York: Cambridge University Press.

McGRAW, K. M. 2000. Contributions of the cognitive approach to political psychology. *Political Psychology*, 21: 805–32.

—— 2003. Political impressions: formation and management. Pp. 394–432 in Sears, Huddy, and Jervis 2003.

—— HASECKE, E., and CONGER, K. 2003. Ambivalence, uncertainty and processes of candidate evaluation. *Political Psychology*, 24: 421–48.

—— and STEENBERGEN, M. 1995. Pictures in the head: memory representations of political actors. Pp. 15–42 in *Political Judgment: Structure and Process*, ed. M. Lodge and K. M. McGraw. Ann Arbor: University of Michigan Press.

McGUIRE, W. J. 1968. Personality and susceptibility to social influence. Pp. 1130–87 in *Handbook of Personality Theory and Research*, ed. E. F. Borgatta and W. W. Lambert. Chicago: Rand McNally.

—— 1969. The nature of attitudes and attitude change. Pp. 136–314 in *Handbook of Social Psychology*, ed. G. Lindzey and E. Aronson, 2nd edn. Reading, Mass.: Addison-Wesley.

—— 1983. A contextualist theory of knowledge: its implications for innovation and reform in psychological research. *Advances in Experimental Social Psychology*, 16: 1–48.

—— 1985. Attitudes and attitude change. In Lindzey and Aronson 1985, 2: 233–46.

—— 1993. The poly-psy relationship: three phases of a long affair. Pp. 9–35 in *Explorations in Political Psychology*, ed. S. Iyengar and W. J. McGuire. Durham, NC: Duke University Press.

—— McGUIRE, C., CHILD, P., and FUJIOKA, T. 1978. Salience of ethnicity in the spontaneous self-concept as a function of one's ethnic distinctiveness in the social environment. *Journal of Personality and Social Psychology*, 36: 511–20.

—— and PADAWER-SINGER, A. 1976. Trait salience in the spontaneous self-concept. *Journal of Personality and Social Psychology*, 33: 743–54.

MACKIE, J. L. 1974. *The Cement of the Universe*. Oxford: Oxford University Press.

MARCUS, G. E., NEUMAN, W. R., and MACKUEN, M. 2000. *Affective Intelligence and Political Judgment*. Chicago: University of Chicago Press.

MERTON. R. K. 1957. *Social Theory and Social Structure*. Glencoe, Ill.: Free Press.

MILGRAM, S. 1974. *Obedience to Authority*. New York: Harper and Row.

MISCHEL, W. 1968. *Personality and Assessment*. New York: Wiley.

MULLEN, B., BROWN, R., and SMITH, C. 1992. Ingroup bias as a function of salience, relevance and status: an integration. *European Journal of Social Psychology*, 22: 103–22.

MUTZ, D. C. 1998. *Impersonal Influence*. New York: Cambridge University Press.

OTTATI, V., and ISBELL, L. 1996. Effects on mood during exposure to target information on subsequently reported judgments: an on-line model of misattribution and correction. *Journal of Personality and Social Psychology*, 71: 39–53.

POLLOCK, P. H., LILLIE, S. A., and VITTES, M. E. 1993. Hard issues, core values and vertical constraint: the case of nuclear power. *British Journal of Political Science*, 23: 29–50.

PRICE, V. 1999. Political information. Pp. 591–640 in *Measures of Political Attitudes*, ed. J. P. Robinson, P. R. Shaver, and L. S. Wrightsman. San Diego: Academic Press.

PRONIN, E., GILOVICH, T., and Ross, L. 2004. Objectivity in the eye of the beholder: divergent perceptions of bias in self versus other. *Psychological Review*, 111: 781–99.

RAHN, W. M. 2000. Affect as information: the role of public mood in political reasoning. Pp. 130–52 in Lupia, McCubbins, and Popkin 2000.

ROKEACH, M. 1960. *The Open and Closed Mind*. New York: Basic Books.

Ross, L. 1977. The intuitive psychologist and his shortcomings: distortions in the attribution process. *Advances in Experimental Social Psychology*, 10: 174–221.

Sales, S. M. 1972. Economic threat as a determinant of conversion rates in authoritarian and nonauthoritarian churches. *Journal of Personality and Social Psychology*, 23: 420–28.

—— 1973. Threat as a factor in authoritarianism. *Journal of Personality and Social Psychology*, 28: 44–57.

Sears, D. O., and Funk, C. L. 1991. The role of self-interest in social and political attitudes. *Advances in Experimental Social Psychology*, 24: 1–91.

—— Huddy, L., and Jervis, R. (eds.) 2003. *Oxford Handbook of Political Psychology*. New York: Oxford University Press.

Segal, J., and Spaeth, H. 1993. *The Supreme Court and the Attitudinal Model*. New York: Cambridge University Press.

Simonton, D. 1984. Leaders as eponyms: individual and situational determinants of monarchal eminence. *Journal of Personality*, 52: 1–21.

—— 1987. *Why Presidents Succeed*. New Haven, Conn.: Yale University Press.

—— 1990. Personality and politics. Pp. 670–92 in *Handbook of Personality*, ed. L. A. Pervin. New York: Guilford Press.

Smith, M. B. 1968. A map for the analysis of personality and politics. *Journal of Social Issues*, 24: 15–28.

Smith, B. L., Lasswell, H. D., and Casey, R. D. 1946. *Propaganda, Communication and Public Opinion*. Princeton, NJ: Princeton University Press.

Sniderman, P. M. 1993. The new look in public opinion research. Pp. 219–46 in *Political Science: The State of the Discipline II*, ed. A. Finifter. Washington, DC: APSA.

—— Brody, R. A., and Tetlock, P. E. 1991. *Reasoning and Choice: Explorations in Political Psychology*. New York: Cambridge University Press.

—— and Grob, D. B. 1996. Innovations in experimental design in attitude surveys. *Annual Review of Sociology*, 22: 377–99.

Snyder, M., and Ickes, W. 1985. Personality and social behavior. In Lindzey and Aronson 1985, 2: 883–948.

Staub, E. 1989. *The Roots of Evil: The Origins of Genocide and Other Group Violence*. New York: Cambridge University Press.

Stenner, K. 2005. *The Authoritarian Dynamic*. New York: Cambridge University Press.

Sullivan, J. L., Rahn, W. M., and Rudolph, T. J. 2002. The contours of political psychology: situating research on political information processing. Pp. 23–50 in *Thinking about Political Psychology*, ed. J. H. Kuklinski. New York: Cambridge University Press.

Tolstoy, L. 1952. *War and Peace*, trans. L. Maude and A. Maude. Chicago: Encyclopedia Britannica; originally published 1865–9.

Vallone, R. P., Ross, L., and Lepper, M. R. 1985. The hostile media phenomenon: biased perception and perceptions of media bias in coverage of the Beirut massacre. *Journal of Personality and Social Psychology*, 49: 577–85.

Waltz, K. N. 1959. *Man, the State and War*. New York: Columbia University Press.

Weatherford, M. S. 1983. Economic voting and the "symbolic politics" argument: a reintepretation and synthesis. *American Political Science Review*, 77: 158–74.

Winter, D. G. 1987 Leader appeal, leader performance and motive profiles of leaders and followers: a study of American presidents and elections. *Journal of Personality and Social Psychology*, 52: 196–202.

—— 2003. Personality and political behavior. Pp. 110–45 in Sears, Huddy, and Jervis 2003.

ZALLER, J. 1989. Bringing Converse back in: modeling information flow in political campaigns. Vol. 1, pp. 181–243 in *Political Analysis*, ed. J. A. Stimson. Ann Arbor: University of Michigan Press.

ZALLER, J. 1990. Political awareness, elite opinion leadership and the mass survey response. *Social Cognition*, 8: 125–53.

——1991. Information, values and opinion. *American Political Science Review*, 85: 1215–37.

——1992. *The Nature and Origins of Mass Opinion*. New York: Cambridge University Press.

——and HUNT, M. 1994. The rise and fall of candidate Perot: unmediated versus mediated politics, part 1. *Political Communication*, 11: 357–90.

————1995. The rise and fall of candidate Perot: the outsider versus the political system, part 2. *Political Communication*, 12: 97–123.

ZIMBARDO, P. G. 1988. *Psychology and Life*. Glenview, Ill.: Scott, Foresman, and Co.

——2004. A situationist perspective on the psychology of evil: understanding how good people are transformed into perpetrators. Pp. 21–50 in *The Social Psychology of Good And Evil*, ed. A. G. Miller. New York: Guilford Press.

CHAPTER 8

MOTIVATION AND EMOTION

JAMES M. JASPER

A truly subtle politician does not wholly reject the conjectures which one can
derive from man's passions, for passions enter sometimes rather openly into,
and almost always manage to affect unconsciously, the motives that propel the
most important affairs of state. (Cardinal de Retz)

WHAT moves people to action, especially political action? Almost anything. As
Weber said of parties, his term for organized strategic efforts, "All the way from
provision for subsistence to the patronage of art, there is no conceivable end which
some political association has not at some time pursued. And from the protection
of personal security to the administration of justice, there is none which *all* have
recognized" (1978, 55).

I shall construe motives and motivation in their broadest, etymological sense, as
whatever moves humans to initiate or continue action. We are conscious of some
motives but not others. Some well up from inside us, others arise outside us. Freud
was the master of unconscious, internal motives, which he labeled drives. Rational
choice traditions derived from microeconomics feature internal but conscious
motives. Sociological, poststructural, and other more "structural" traditions, in
contrast, have focused on motivations that originate outside the individual,
in moral, cognitive, linguistic, and other social systems. A great deal of political

analysis has sought ways of making unconscious system imperatives ("false consciousness") into conscious ones (which can be resisted).

Through the ages, analysts have concentrated on the motivations that are explicit and widely shared. Glory used to motivate wars, money and other resources more local efforts—although in our cynical modern age money is seen as lurking behind all actions. Indeed in the modern world, motivations have become generally murky and unsettled. In cities and markets, we are never entirely certain what moves the stranger with whom we interact. As Luhmann (1987, 121–2) put it, "Traditional societies ascribe motives and do not require much exploration of 'real' motives—either in economic (household) or in political (public) affairs." One result of modernizing processes is an "interest in rules and recipes [for personal interaction] in the seventeenth century and the rather desperate reliance on sentiment, taste, and natural morality in the early eighteenth century." Motives become subject to speculation.

The concept of "interest," so central to economics, was a solution to this uncertainty, intended to pinpoint objective motivations. You have a legal interest (an early usage) and a material interest in an outcome even if you are not aware of them. And of course, any rational actor would be aware of them. For the word implies an element of calculation, one reason it emerged as a third term between passion and reason in the seventeenth century, a constraint on the passions (Hirschman 1977). If you faithfully pursue your interests, others can predict your actions. In nineteenth-century Europe, *homo economicus*—a model of self-interest and materialism—proved a useful simplification for liberal reformers battling aristocratic privilege. After they won their battle, in the twentieth century, the language of interests came to represent the triumph of cynical materialism over other images of humans—which is exactly its limitation. It flatters our rationality but not our motives. Few of us are motivated primarily, much less exclusively, by money and possessions. The precision of having a single metric for human calculation and satisfactions (although even these two do not line up as well as economic models suggest) came at the cost of realism.

This shortcoming of economic theory left an opportunity for sociologists to offer additional motives. Weber, in demonstrating the importance of reputation and power, was partly reviving premodern traditions of glory and honor. Durkheim and Parsons focused on morality as the necessary underpinning of more self-interested actions. With them, motivation migrated from the individual to the social system—in the process becoming unconscious as well. Under the influence of the cognitive revolution, later sociologists continued down this road, turning to shared cultural understandings as the glue holding markets and other institutions together (e.g. Powell and DiMaggio 1991; Fligstein 2001). Like language, these cultural meanings can be made explicit but most of the time operate beneath full awareness as unspoken assumptions. Yet even the most ingrained routine can be brought to awareness—precisely what much social science aims to do.

Explicit interests and implicit morality or routine hardly exhaust human motivation. On the fringes of conscious choice and rationality lie a number of powerful
urges, attachments, and habits which, although hard to model, are central to what we
are as human beings. Debates have raged over whether these feelings can be raised to
consciousness and controlled, whether they derail or aid rational decision-making
(or did at some evolutionary point in the past), whether they are so idiosyncratic to
individuals as to elude systematic analysis. All too often, one type of emotion is taken
as the exemplar for all, distorting our ability to comprehend the many ways that our
feelings attach us to the physical and social worlds around us.

At least since Plato human motivation has been framed as a battle between
reason and the passions (Plato's preference appears even in the terms: there is *one*
correct reason, but *many* unruly passions). Debates over whether humans were
good or evil increasingly gave way in the modern world to controversies over our
rationality. A major category of these have addressed motivation. How rational can
we be if much of our activity lacks articulated goals? Traditions such as realism in
international relations or rational choice approaches derived from microeconomics
emphasize explicit goals and means, in contrast to an even larger number of
frameworks that downplay them. Freudians highlight repressed and unconscious
motives. Many cognitive psychologists see humans as trapped in their information-
processing systems (Bem 1972; Nisbett and Ross 1980), roughly parallel to French
poststructuralists who see language or discourse as a similar constraint (Lacan 1966;
Foucault 1966; 1969). Sociologists have offered "practices" as a fundamental guide
for action that is habitual and not quite conscious (Bourdieu 1977; Giddens 1984, 6;
cf. Turner 1994). In these latter views, systems of action move individuals.

All these traditions get at pieces of the truth about what drives and channels
action: many things do. Giddens usefully distinguishes three levels of awareness:
discursive consciousness, practical consciousness, and the unconscious. The first
level is things we can talk about explicitly; the second things that we know how to
do without fully articulating them. We are moved by impulses originating at all
three levels, often simultaneously. Emotions were traditionally seen as arising from
the unconscious, especially in Freudian frameworks, but at least as often they are
practical and sometimes even discursive. We can articulate our emotions, much of
the time, and even be talked out of inappropriate ones.

To be sure, much human action follows "practical" routines which preclude
discussion of explicit motives. Some may be of our own making, while others are
offered to us by the large organizations that dominate life in modern society. But
many sociologists, in particular, have adopted this as their model of action to such
an extent that they lack a language for discussing purposive action (Campbell
1996). At the extreme, explicit motives are merely rhetorical justification we give
for things we have already done (Mills 1940). It is no wonder the highly calculating
image of rational choice theory often seems the only alternative that recognizes
intention (Smith 2003). The lack of visions that integrate system and intention only

pushes those who reject rational choice models further into the arms of tacit routine and practices.

Emotions are what make us care about the world around us, repelling or attracting us. (The depressed, incapable of many normal emotions, have a largely neutral feeling about the world, and are paralyzed as a result.) More than fifty years ago, Parsons and Shils (1951, 59), defining cathexis as "the various processes by which an actor invests an object with affective significance," argued that "it is through the cathexis of objects that energy or motivation, in the technical sense, enters the system of the orientation of action." But this appears in a footnote, showing how little salience emotion actually had in Parsons' action theory, much less his systems theory.

As the three basic components of culture, emotions, cognition, and morals (both principles and intuitions) operate in similar ways, with similar methodological challenges: they can be observed in individual or collective expressions, and individuals often diverge from "normal" beliefs and feelings. Much has been written—in an elaboration of the "boundedness" of rationality—about cognition in the form of memory, decision heuristics, and so on, as well as about morality. Only in the last few years have emotions been resurrected as a serious analytic tool for understanding politics (Jasper 1997; Holst-Warhaft 2000; Goodwin, Jasper, and Polletta 2001). They are the subject of this chapter, especially since in addition to their own driving force they also permeate cognition and morality. Indeed, in most cases thinking and feeling are inextricably entwined.

To discourage conceptual overextension—a risk for all new tools—I distinguish several different categories of feelings that have often been lumped together. They typically operate by different chemical and neurological pathways, persist for different lengths of time, and affect action in different ways. Discussions of emotions in politics will remain a muddle if we pretend they are one large homogeneous category.

1   URGES

Certain impulses well up from our bodies with such force that they overpower our conscious intentions, propelling us to act. Elster (1999*b*, 2), calling these "strong feelings," includes chemical addictions as well as "hunger, thirst, and sexual desire; urges to urinate, defecate, or sleep; as well as organic disturbances such as pain, fatigue, vertigo, and nausea." These pressing urges are relatively independent of culture and cognition. We tend to ignore other possible goals until we have satisfied the urge.

At one time, most emotions were viewed on this model, as "passions" that propel us without any thought or resistance, as events that happen to us in contrast to willed choice and action, derailing our reason. But overpowering urges are a small subset of human emotion, which perhaps should not even be dignified with that rubric. What is more, such urges come in two forms. One kind, centered on deprivation, focus our attention in such an immediate way that they rarely influence political action—except they suggest how deprivation can crowd out political concerns. Survival needs usually, but not always, crowd out other motivations (the bottom of Maslow's (1954) famous hierarchy). But the other kind are urges that can be satisfied in multiple ways, or via multiple pathways. Immediate lust or addiction may crowd out other concerns, but I may take elaborate steps to get to those final moments of pleasure. Indeed, impressing potential lovers is a central human motivation. Like Scarlett O'Hara, we work to avoid the pain of hunger or fatigue.

A lingering doubt remains: cannot any emotion, felt strongly enough, overpower us in this way? Anger can, and it is the usual exemplar given of an irrational passion (see Harris 2001 on ancient efforts to control it in various social relations). But most forms of anger do not lead us astray, into actions we later regret. Plus, most emotions do not have this power at all. In the sections that follow, I hope to show why affective allegiances, moods, and moral emotions are compatible with reasoning.

2   REFLEXES

One step up from urges are what Griffiths (1997) calls "reflex emotions." These are quick to appear and quick to subside. Anger, fear, joy, sadness, disgust, and surprise may be universal and hardwired into us, operating rapidly through the hypothalamus and amygdala rather than through parts of the cortex that evolved later (Damasio 1994, ch. 7). Neurology plays a big part in these reflexes, but a significant role still remains for culture, which is necessary to explain exactly *what* disgusts or frightens us, as well as *how* we express reflex emotions.

The "affect program" theory is especially suited to reflex emotions. Ekman (1972*b*; 1980), its main proponent, uses the term program for the neurally encoded responses which he says constitute emotions, including facial expressions, body movements such as flinching, vocal changes, shifts in the endocrine system and subsequent hormonal changes, and other modifications of the nervous system. Such packages are automatic, coordinated, complex, and common across cultures. To his original six, he later added contempt (Ekman and Friesen 1971). Others would add shame, evidence of which can be seen in nonhuman primates. Ekman was inspired by Charles Darwin (1965 [1872]), who wrote a compelling book on the parallels in the emotions of humans and other species.

The main evidence for affect program theory comes from photographs of the human face. If you take photos in one culture of people expressing these basic emotional reactions, people of other cultures can immediately identify the emotions expressed. One apparent exception was that Japanese students did not express the negative emotions despite the proper stimuli. But it was discovered that, when authority figures were not present, they displayed the same expressions as people from other cultures. What is more, when videotapes were slowed down, very brief expressions could be detected even when the authority figures were present, covered immediately by a bland smile (Ekman 1972b).

By contrasting the immediate context with broader ones, Frank (1988) and others have suggested a number of advantages that reflex emotions (and other types) confer on strategic actors. Momentary anger may lead to actions later regretted, but a reputation for angry reactions may have wider advantages, encouraging compliance from others. Loyalty, contempt, disgust, and love can also be seen as helping humans keep their commitments. Alliances may be built on reflex emotions as well as on affects (Frank does not distinguish the two). Emotions are partly signals of character.

Nonetheless, reflex emotions seem to play a limited role in politics and conflict. Mostly, we strive to elicit adverse reflexes in opponents. Brave protestors may hope to enrage a police officer so that he lashes out in front of cameras. Forces of order may try to paralyze protestors through fear (Goodwin and Pfaff 2001). But as we shall see, other forms of anger and fear, more abiding than these sudden reflexes, are more central to politics.

3   AFFECTIVE ALLEGIANCES

Affects are another type of emotion, more stable and more tied to cognition. They are often little more than positive or negative clusters of feelings, mere attraction or repulsion. Love and hate are the obvious ones, but trust, respect, ressentiment, and some abiding kinds of fear are also examples. The opposite of reflex responses, affects are relatively enduring orientations to the social and physical worlds. They provide the goals of many of our purposive actions and projects.

In "affect control theory," Heise (1979) and others have shown the importance of affective allegiances in a variety of social processes and socially constructed definitions, especially roles and identities (Smith-Lovin and Heise 1988; MacKinnon 1994). We try to maintain our affective sense of the world, a cognitive as well as emotional orientation. We interpret what happens to us through pre-existing expectations about types of people summed up in roles and identities and situations; specifically we try to confirm our expectations about how good, strong, and active people are (labeled evaluation, potency, and agency). Shocks to our expectations require a great deal of work, and sometimes even a rearrangement of those expectations. Out of such adjustments arise shared cultural meanings (Ridgeway et al. 1998).

In addition to these interpretive goals of confirming our view of the world, affects also provide something close to basic values. Solidarity with various collectives—a nation, organization, family, and so on—consists of affective loyalties surrounded by considerable cognitive reinforcement and interpretation. (Although the literature on collective identity slights its emotional underpinnings: Jasper 1998; Polletta and Jasper 2001.) Trust, for instance, arises out of the interaction between expectations and experience with groups and individuals (Hardin 1993). These positive affects, along with negative ones toward outsiders, enemies, and other threats, motivate or allow much political action. The nationalist banner under which so many Europeans clamored for and marched off to war, especially until 1945, was a complex cluster of positive and negative affects (Berezin 1997).

Affects are not easily changed. We may fall out of love with someone, become disenchanted with our team (although more often with its current leaders), or come to modify our hatred and suspicion of foreigners. Often, we change our affects through some kind of moral shock that forces us to reinterpret our experiences, as we'll see below.

Tightly interwoven with our cognitions, our affects influence how we process information, especially about political leaders (Ottati and Wyer 1993). Most obviously, we remember positive information about (and associate positive character traits with) those leaders whom we like, and negative ones about those we dislike. Negative information tends to be noticed and remembered more than positive, however, so that we have to work harder to maintain positive sentiment (Kinder 1978; 1986). Negative information especially affects "short-term mobilization," but its influence fades over time (Taylor 1991; McGraw et al. 1996). Because so much politics is about group solidarities (Schmitt 1976 [1932]), affects are crucial motivations.

4   MOODS

Moods are another category, typically lasting longer than reflex emotions but not as long as affects (although moods can sometimes be almost permanent, something like aspects of temperament). We usually carry moods with us from one social setting to another, perhaps because of the biochemical states associated with them (one reason that drugs affect them, and one reason individuals differ temperamentally). The obvious contrast is between positive and negative moods, which have been shown to affect judgments (Schwarz and Clore 1983; 1988; Ottati et al. 1989). Moods may also affect our propensity to feel and exhibit other emotions, as in the case of a depressed person inclined to sadness or irritation. (Just as reflex emotions may leave us in a certain mood even after the original triggering emotions fade.) Moods filter our intentions and actions, strengthening or dissolving them, changing their tone or seriousness. If other emotions give our actions direction, moods affect their pace (Geertz 1973, 97).

I suspect that esthetic emotions—those brought on by art—are moods, as we "try on" feelings such as sadness or elation. Nostalgia, often found in artistic appreciation, may be a kind of wistful mood. (In addition to the moods aroused by art through our empathy with characters portrayed or the mysterious influence of music, we also may feel a kind of wonder or awe at the beauty of the work as art—a cognitive accomplishment that is perhaps close to the complex moral emotions described below, and which is useful for understanding how political rhetoric works.)

The example of nostalgia suggests that cultures can embrace certain moods and discourage others. There can be "official" moods, fostered by government, intellectuals, and mass media. Weber believed that ideologies of predestination fostered anxiety. Moods of despair appear frequently, often through the interpretation of economic and political trends (as downward). Widespread fatalism, resignation, and cynicism work against political action, since they entail a loss of a sense of agency. Political efforts will avail little. Optimism and pessimism are possibly moods, with substantial effects on our sense of agency and visions of potential social change. Anxiety, too, is likely to affect the ways we scan the world for dangers.

Certain social settings are designed to affect participants' moods. As crowd theories waned after the 1960s, it was unfashionable to refer to Durkheim's collective effervescence and other processes that gave emotional energy to groups. Nonetheless the joys of crowds (Lofland 1985) have been analyzed, along with the effects of collective marching, dancing, and singing (McNeill 1995). Collins (2001) has recast the emotions of participation as an interaction ritual in which emotional attention is a major reward. (These mobilizing moods have their opposite in efforts to intimidate and paralyze, to demobilize people: Goodwin and Pfaff 2001.)

A great deal of political mobilization appeals to people's fears and anxieties, especially in what have been labeled "moral panics" (Cohen 1972). One tradition views these anxieties as pre-existing moods, for which political leaders find scapegoats (Lipset 1960; Lipset and Raab 1978). Critics, skeptical of pre-existing anxieties, argue that these leaders sustain and transform reflex fears into more cognitive analyses and affects, including the demonization of opponents (Rieder 1985; Edsall and Edsall 1991). Moral shocks are only the beginning. In some cases the media amplify existing moods, in others they seem to create them. If nothing else, protest leaders and elected officials take advantage of what they *perceive* to be citizens' moods (Goodin 1988).

5 MORAL SENTIMENTS

In my final category are complex moral emotions, which require considerable cognitive processing. These include shame and pride, but also compassion, outrage, and more complex forms of disgust, fear, or anger (which are cognitively processed more than the reflex forms: ongoing fear of a nuclear plant has little in common with sudden fright at a lunging shadow).[1] Our anger may begin as a reflex, but sustaining it requires an admixture of hateful affect or moral indignation (Katz 1999). Elster (1999a) has written interestingly about these, especially about humans' ability to have emotions about their emotions. We are ashamed of our anger or fear, say. We monitor our actions, thoughts, and even feelings, in the kind of reflexivity dear to social constructionists.

Post-Kantian theorists distinguish too sharply between morals and emotions, portraying the former as an austere cognitive judgment which mysteriously moves us. Older theorists, including the French "moralists" who took this idea to its cynical extreme, recognized that we only obey moral precepts because of the accompanying emotional pleasures. As in the eighteenth century Spinoza (1989, 277) put it, "Blessedness is not the reward of virtue, but virtue itself; neither do we rejoice therein, because we control our lusts, but contrariwise, because we rejoice therein, we are able to control our lusts." Doing the right thing feels good *directly*; it is not the side effect of other actions. When we do the right thing, it is because we are driven by emotions—not, as Kant would have it, out of a spare recognition of duty.

We do not follow the moral rules of our society automatically, as Parsons' notion of values, into which we are socialized, also seemed to have it. We either obey moral rules because we fear sanctions if we do not, or because it feels good to do the right thing—Spinoza's "rejoicing." The Kantian "deontological" tradition, in which we do what we believe is right simply because of that belief, has discouraged attention to the many satisfactions that accompany this kind of action. We can be proud, sometimes smugly or invidiously so, comparing ourselves to those less righteous.

---

[1] Thomas Scheff believes that shame is a reflex emotion (personal communication), a recategorization I am willing to entertain based on evidence that other primates demonstrate shame behavior such as staring down. This may be a form of submission and acknowledgment of a lower place in the pecking order. In humans shame may have more complex moral sources built upon this simple basis. Guilt, at any rate, seems necessarily to entail complex moral and cognitive judgments.

We may feel relieved to have overcome temptations to act differently. We may get a charge from being agents rather than victims. We get these feelings especially when we obey explicit moral rules recognized by those around us, but also sometimes when we follow vague moral intuitions. And some are especially pleased to follow their own moral rules in the face of opposition. Following moral norms when we have little choice in the matter doesn't have the same satisfactions (although it has others) as when we choose to obey them.

Outrage over unfairness has even begun to make inroads into game theory, as experiments show that people are willing to pay a great deal to remedy perceived injustices. The Ultimatum game is a simple way to measure the price of fairness. One player proposes how to divide up a sum of money provided by experimenters, and the second player can either accept or reject the proposal. If the deal is rejected, neither player gets anything. If responders were out to maximize their gains, they would accept any offer. Most proposers offer half or nearly half (40 percent on average)—already showing some concern for fairness—and responders tend to reject offers of less than 20 percent. The amount they reject shows the price they put on a fair distribution. Countless variations have uncovered variables that affect preferences for fairness, including cultural background, how the interaction is labeled (inequalities are tolerated when the game is labeled a market exchange), how much discretion is attributed to proposers (when they do not choose the amounts they offer, they are not punished for unfair offers), and the number of proposers and responders. Interestingly, players punish unfairness to themselves more than unfairness to others, suggesting that emotions such as anger and vengeance are at work more than abstract norms of fairness. (Camerer 2003, ch. 2 summarizes this literature.) Because it addresses distributional issues like these, fairness is one of the few moral topics that can be inserted into games with monetary payoffs, but there are many other sources of outrage.

Moral emotions are necessarily social, and they are affected by one's place in social hierarchies. As Kemper (1978; 2001) especially has argued, changes in status and power (our own and others') frequently trigger emotions. Increases in our power relative to others (and relative to our expectations) make us feel secure and safe, decreases anxious or fearful (although we may also feel guilty if we think the increase is undeserved). Increases in our status, similarly, lead to emotions such as pride or contentment, decreases to shame, disappointment, or depression. Kemper's scheme is further complicated by factors such as whether we are dealing with someone above or below us in some hierarchy, by whether we were the agents who caused the changes, by the perceived permanence of the changes, and so forth.

Moral emotions are the "hot cognitions," as Gamson called them, which motivate so much protest. Emotions that follow from a sense of threat (anger, indignation, condemnation, hate) are common motivations to engage in politics and other strategic projects—a decision that is otherwise rather daunting. (To be sure, there is also a path that leads to fear and paralysis, often via moods of resignation or cynicism.) When the world proves to be different and more threatening than thought, "moral shocks" frequently lead to action, especially if blame can be attached to human agents, villains and victims and heroes identified, and the infrastructure for action created or commandeered (Jasper 1997). Moral emotions are the core of political rhetoric.

The moral emotions are especially important when we try to build from micro-motives to broader political systems. Kemper shows how our place in hierarchies conditions the emotions we feel, and many emotions arise out of structured strategic interactions in a number of institutional arenas. Many of our moral emotions arise out of our reactions to and beliefs about the social systems in which we live, especially outrage, indignation, and other feelings tied to our sense of justice. (Fairness, in contrast, has more to do with our dealings with other *individuals*, not our sense of the *system*.) Finally, many aspects of our institutions are designed to curb the social effects of individual emotions, for example anger (Harris 2001), love (Goodwin 1997), and disgust (Nussbaum 2004).

Moral emotions can involve evaluations of one's own or someone else's behavior, character, or possession of something valued. We feel guilt over one of our actions, but shame over our general character. We feel contempt for those we believe are morally inferior. We feel malice over someone else's undeserved misfortune, gloating over their deserved misfortune. This class of emotions frequently involve our sense of how good and bad eventualities should be distributed, clearly a moral sensibility. Scheff (1990; 1994) has suggested a range of effects that shame can have on political and strategic action at both the individual and the collective levels.

Morality consists of intuitions as well as principles, and these are even closer to emotions. We often feel moral shock, disgust, or indignation faster than we can articulate our reasons—if we can articulate them at all. Our cognitive, emotional, and moral processes are in many cases inextricable.

Perhaps Hemingway best expressed the difference between moral and reflex emotions when he said, "What is moral is what you feel good after and what is immoral is what you feel bad after." Many reflex emotions lead us into actions that feel right (or inevitable) at the moment, but later leave us with regret. Moral emotions leave us with pride and satisfaction.

6   DECISIONS

Most social life operates through routines, familiar activities about which we rarely stop to think. But politics is one arena where we frequently consider and articulate our goals and choose means to attain them. For whom shall we vote? Shall we join the protest march today? Volunteer to work for the trade union? There are a number of choice points, which in turn influence our daily routines. Sometimes our routines themselves break down, and we are forced to make decisions about new ones.

The motivations that shape our goals and choices are never all entirely conscious. If nothing else, there are too many of them to juggle in our heads. A few are, as Freudians would say, deeply repressed and unconscious. Far more, I suspect, reside in Giddens' practical consciousness and can be brought to awareness when we are puzzled, thwarted, or challenged to give our reasons. Finally, a fair number are explicit. We may know we're angry, and know what we're angry about.

When political researchers have made micromotives central—in the behavioralist revolution of the 1950s or more recently in game theory[2]—they have typically combined this emphasis with empiricist methodological prescriptions and aspirations to universal theories. Neither is necessary. We can and must carve out a thoroughly cultural and interpretative understanding of individual motives, emotions, meanings, and choices (this is not incompatible with recognition of neurological pathways). There is no reason to proceed with a positivist psychology that leaves out most of what we want to understand. If we wish to understand the motivations of political action, we must be prepared to grapple with an extremely diverse lot. Reductionism will only mislead us.

REFERENCES

BAIRD, D. G., GERTNER, R. H., and PICKER, R. C. 1994. *Game Theory and the Law*. Cambridge, Mass.: Harvard University Press.

BEM, D. 1972. Self-perception theory. Vol. 6, pp. 1–62 in *Advances in Experimental Social Psychology*, ed. L. Berkowitz. New York: Academic Press.

BEREZIN, M. 1997. *Making the Fascist Self*. Ithaca, NY: Cornell University Press.

BOURDIEU, P. 1977. *Outline of a Theory of Practice*. Cambridge: Cambridge University Press.

CAMERER, C. F. 2003. *Behavioral Game Theory*. Princeton, NJ: Princeton University Press.

CAMPBELL, C. 1996. *The Myth of Social Action*. Cambridge: Cambridge University Press.

COHEN, S. 1972. *Folk Devils and Moral Panics*. New York: St. Martin's Press.

COLLINS, R. 2001. Social movements and the focus of emotional attention. In Goodwin et al. 2001, 27–44.

DAMASIO, A. R. 1994. *Descartes' Error*. New York: Putnam.

DARWIN, C. 1965. *The Expression of the Emotions in Man and Animals*. Chicago: University of Chicago Press; originally published 1872.

EASTON, D. 1953. *The Political System*. New York: Knopf.

EDSALL, T. B., and EDSALL, M. D. 1991. *Chain Reaction*. New York: W. W. Norton.

---

[2] On the behavioralist revolution see: Easton 1953; Truman 1955; Eulau 1963. On game theory see: Ordeshook 1986; Baird, Gertner, and Picker 1994; Morrow 1994.

EKMAN, P. 1972a. Universals and cultural differences in facial expressions of emotion. Pp. 207–83 in *Nebraska Symposium on Motivation, 1971*, ed. J. K. Cole. Lincoln: University of Nebraska Press.

—— 1972b. *Emotion in the Human Face*. Elmsford, NY: Pergamon.

—— 1980. *The Face of Man*. New York: Garland.

—— and FRIESEN, W. V. 1971. Constants across cultures in the face and emotion. *Journal of Personality and Social Psychology*, 17: 124–9.

ELSTER, J. 1999a. *Alchemies of the Mind*. Cambridge: Cambridge University Press.

—— 1999b. *Strong Feelings*. Cambridge, Mass.: MIT Press.

EULAU, H. 1963. *The Behavioral Persuasion in Politics*. New York: Random House.

FLIGSTEIN, N. 2001. *The Architecture of Markets*. Princeton, NJ: Princeton University Press.

FOUCAULT, M. 1966. *Les Mots et les choses*. Paris: Gallimard.

—— 1969. *L'Archéologie du Savoir*. Paris: Gallimard.

FRANK, R. H. 1988. *Passions within Reason*. New York: W. W. Norton.

GEERTZ, C. 1973. *The Interpretation of Cultures*. New York: Basic Books.

GIDDENS, A. 1984. *The Constitution of Society*. Berkeley: University of California Press.

GOODIN, R. E. 1988. Mood matching and arms control. *International Studies Quarterly*, 32: 473–81.

GOODWIN, J. 1997. The libidinal constitution of a high-risk social movement: affectual ties and solidarity in the Huk rebellion. *American Sociological Review*, 62: 53–69.

—— JASPER, J. M., and POLLETTA, F. A. (eds.) 2001. *Passionate Politics*. Chicago: University of Chicago Press.

—— and PFAFF, S. 2001. Emotion work in high-risk social movements. In Goodwin et al. 2001, 282–302.

Griffiths, P. E. 1997. *What Emotions Really Are*. Chicago: University of Chicago Press.

HARDIN, R. 1993. The street-level epistemology of trust. *Politics and Society*, 21: 505–29.

HARRIS, W. V. 2001. *Restraining Rage*. Cambridge, Mass.: Harvard University Press.

HEISE, D. 1979. *Understanding Events*. Cambridge: Cambridge University Press.

HIRSCHMAN, A. O. 1977. *The Passions and the Interests*. Princeton, NJ: Princeton University Press.

HOLST-WARHAFT, G. 2000. *The Cue For Passion*. Cambridge, Mass.: Harvard University Press.

JASPER, J. M. 1997. *The Art of Moral Protest*. Chicago: University of Chicago Press.

—— 1998. The emotions of protest: affective and reactive emotions in and around social movements. *Sociological Forum*, 13: 397–424.

KATZ, J. 1999. *How Emotions Work*. Chicago: University of Chicago Press.

KEMPER, T. D. 1978. *A Social Interactional Theory of Emotions*. New York: Wiley.

—— 2001. A structural approach to social movement emotions. In Goodwin et al. 2001, 58–73.

KINDER, D. R. 1978. Political person perception: the asymmetrical influence of sentiment and choice on perceptions of presidential candidates. *Journal of Personality and Social Psychology*, 36: 859–71.

—— 1986. Presidential character revisited. Pp. 233–56 in *Political Cognition*, ed. R. R. Lau and D. O Sears. Hillsdale, NJ: Erlbaum.

LACAN, J. 1966. *Ecrits*. Paris: Seuil.

LIPSET, S. M. 1960. *Political Man*. Garden City, NJ: Anchor.

—— and RAAB, E. 1978. *The Politics of Unreason*, 2nd edn. Chicago: University of Chicago Press.

LOFLAND, J. 1985. *Protest.* New Brunswick, NJ: Transaction.

LUHMANN, N. 1987. The evolutionary differentiation between society and interaction. Pp. 112–31 in *The Micro-Macro Link,* ed. J. C. Alexander, B. Giesen, R. Münch, and N. J. Smelser. Berkeley: University of California Press.

MACKINNON, N. J. 1994. *Symbolic Interactionism as Affect Control Theory.* Albany, NY: SUNY Press.

MASLOW, A. H. 1954. *Motivation and Personality.* New York: Harper and Brothers.

MCGRAW, K. M., FISCHLE, M., STENNER, K., and LODGE, M. 1996. What's in a word? Bias in trait descriptions of political leaders. *Political Behavior,* 18: 63–87.

MCNEILL, W. H. 1995. *Keeping Together in Time.* Cambridge: Harvard University Press.

MILLS, C. W. 1940. Situated actions and vocabularies of motive. *American Sociological Review,* 5: 904–13.

MORROW, J. D. 1994. *Game Theory for Political Scientists.* Princeton, NJ: Princeton University Press.

NISBETT, R. E., and ROSS, L. 1980. *Human Inference.* Englewood Cliffs, NJ: Prentice Hall.

NUSSBAUM, M. 2004. *Hiding from Humanity.* Princeton, NJ: Princeton University Press.

ORDESHOOK, P. D. 1986. *Game Theory and Political Theory.* Cambridge: Cambridge University Press.

OTTATI, V. C., RIGGLE, E., WYER, R. S., JR., SCHWARZ, N., and KUKLINSKI, J. 1989. Cognitive and affective bases of opinion survey responses. *Journal of Personality and Social Psychology,* 57: 404–15.

—— and WYER, R. S., JR. 1993. Affect and political judgment. Pp. 296–315 in *Explorations in Political Psychology,* ed. S. Iyengar and W. J. McGuire. Durham, NC: Duke University Press.

PARSONS, T., and SHILS, E. A. (eds.) 1951. *Toward a General Theory of Action.* Cambridge, Mass.: Harvard University Press.

POLLETTA, F., and JASPER, J. M. 2001. Collective identity and social movements. *Annual Review of Sociology,* 27: 283–305.

POWELL, W. W., and DIMAGGIO, P. J. (eds.) 1991. *The New Institutionalism in Organizational Analysis.* Chicago: University of Chicago Press.

RIDGEWAY, C. L., BOYLE, E. H., KUIPERS, K. J., and ROBINSON, D. T. 1998. How do status beliefs develop? The role of resources and interactional experience. *American Sociological Review,* 63: 331–50.

RIEDER, J. 1985. *Canarsie.* Cambridge, Mass.: Harvard University Press.

SCHEFF, T. J. 1990. *Microsociology: Discourse, Emotion, and Social Structure.* Chicago: University of Chicago Press.

—— 1994. *Bloody Revenge: Emotions, Nationalism and War.* Boulder, Colo.: Westview.

SCHMITT, C. 1976. *The Concept of the Political.* New Brunswick, NJ: Rutgers University Press; originally published 1932.

SCHWARZ, N., and CLORE, G. L. 1983. Mood, misattribution, and judgments of well-being: informative and directive functions of affective states. *Journal of Personality and Social Psychology,* 45: 513–23.

—— 1988. How do I feel about it? The informative function of affective states. Pp. 44–62 in *Affect, Cognition and Social Behavior,* ed. K. Fiedler and J. P. Forgas. Toronto: Hogrefe International.

SMITH, C. 2003. *Moral, Believing Animals.* New York: Oxford University Press.

SMITH-LOVIN, L., and HEISE, D. 1988. *Analyzing Social Interaction.* New York: Gordon and Breach Science Publishers.

SPINOZA, B. 1989. *Ethics.* Amherst, NY: Prometheus Books.

TAYLOR, S. E. 1991. Asymmetrical effects of positive and negative events. *Psychological Bulletin,* 110: 67–85.

TRUMAN, D. B. 1955. The impact on political science of the revolution in the behavioral sciences. Pp. 202–32 in *Research Frontiers in Politics and Government,* ed. S. K. Bailey. Washington, DC: Brookings Institution.

TURNER, S. 1994. *The Social Theory of Practices.* Chicago: University of Chicago Press.

WEBER, M. 1978. *Economy and Society.* Berkeley: University of California Press.

CHAPTER 9

SOCIAL PREFERENCES, *HOMO ECONOMICUS*, AND *ZOON POLITIKON*

SAMUEL BOWLES
HERBERT GINTIS

THE rational choice model pioneered by economists is rapidly becoming the standard approach throughout the behavioral sciences. The model is attractive as it allows the mathematical formalization of an essential truth, namely that when people act, they are generally trying to accomplish something, and their efforts are more or less effectively oriented to this end. However, its acceptance in other disciplines coincides with an increasing recognition in economics of the limitations of the behavioral assumptions sometimes summarized by the term *Homo economicus*. While *Homo economicus* is not entailed by any of the axioms of the rational choice model, in both teaching and research three assumptions embracing this behavioral model are commonly treated as integral to the approach.

First, preferences are assumed to be *outcome-regarding*; i.e. agents care about only the quantity and quality of goods and services that they possess and consume, not about the social process through which their economic opportunities are determined. In fact, preferences are also in part *process-regarding*; agents care about how they treat and are treated by others. In evaluating states, people care how those states

* We would like to thank Elisabeth Wood for comments, as well as the John D. and Catherine T. MacArthur Foundation and the Behavioral Sciences Program of the Santa Fe Institute for financial support.

come to be available. In particular, people care about fairness and reciprocity. Second, preferences are assumed to be *self-regarding*: agents are assumed to care only about states experienced by themselves, not by others. In fact, however, preferences are in part *other-regarding*; agents care about the well-being of others, both positively and negatively. In particular, people reward and punish the behavior of others even at a net cost to themselves.

Third, preferences are assumed either to be unchanging, or to evolve under influences external to the social system under consideration. While a handy—even indispensable—assumption for many analytical tasks, the assumption of *exogenous preferences* is strongly counter-intuitive, while the *social formation of preferences*, as we will see, is strongly suggested by recent behavioral experiments.

Since Aristotle introduced the idea of *zoon politikon*, students of political behavior have recognized the importance of process-regarding, other-regarding, and endogenous preferences in explaining such essential aspects of political behavior as the maintenance of social order, collective action to achieve common ends, political violence, and even the simple act of voting. Recent experimental research has confirmed the existence of process-regarding and other-regarding preferences. One such preference, which we call *strong reciprocity* (Gintis 2000; Bowles and Gintis 2004a; Gintis et al. 2004), is a predisposition to cooperate with others, and to punish those who violate the norms of cooperation, at personal cost, even when it is implausible to expect that these costs will be repaid either by others or at a later date.

We here present empirical evidence supporting strong reciprocity as a schema for explaining important forms of political behavior. Although most of the evidence we report is based on behavioral experiments, the same behaviors are regularly observed in everyday life, for example in collective actions such as strikes and insurgencies (Petersen 2002; Goodwin, Polletta, and Jasper 2001; Wood 2003), wage setting by firms (Bewley 2000), tax compliance (Andreoni, Erard, and Feinstein 1998), and cooperation in the protection of local environmental public goods (Acheson 1988; Ostrom 1998; Cardenas, Stranlund, and Willis 2000; Ostrom et al. 2002).

Nothing in the material to be presented casts doubt on the rational actor framework per se. Our concerns address the nature and origins of preferences, not the underlying model of consequentialist choice. Decision theory shows that as long as agents have consistent and complete preferences (meaning that an agent who prefers A to B and prefers B to C also prefers A to C, and any two possible choices can be compared in terms of desirability) over a finite choice set, their actions can be modeled as if maximizing a preference function subject to constraints (Kreps 1988). Studies show that other-regarding preferences fit this framework just as well as the standard selfish preferences of traditional economic theory (Andreoni and Miller 2002). Contrary to a common usage, the fact that an action is other-regarding does not make it "irrational" or even "non-rational."

The reasons for the power of the rational actor model are clear. An agent's preferences, together with the agent's beliefs concerning the means of achieving them and the informational, material, and other constraints the agent faces, have proven remarkably illuminating in accounting for individual actions. Beliefs are an individual's conception of the relationship between an act and an outcome. Preferences are reasons for goal-oriented behavior. Preferences thus include a heterogeneous melange: tastes (food likes and dislikes, for example), habits, emotions (such as shame or anger) and other visceral reactions (such as fear), the manner in which individuals construe situations (or more narrowly, the way they frame a decision), commitments (like promises), socially enforced norms, psychological propensities (for aggression, extroversion, and the like), and one's affective relationships with others. To say that a person acts on her preferences means only that knowledge of the preferences would be helpful in providing a convincing account of the actions—though not necessarily the account which would be given by the actor, for as is well known individuals are sometimes unable or unwilling to provide such an account.

We diverge from the standard preferences–beliefs–constraints model only by positing the importance of other-regarding and process-regarding behavior in accounting for human behavior in strategic interaction, and in taking the preferences accounting for this behavior as endogenous.

1   STRONG RECIPROCITY IN THE LABOR MARKET

We begin with an example of economic behavior in experimental labor markets, as it neatly illustrates the kind of motives that are present in any kind of patron–client relationship or social exchange (Blau 1964). In Fehr, Gächter, and Kirchsteiger (1997), the experimenters divided a group of 141 subjects (college students who had agreed to participate in order to earn money) into a set of "employers" and a larger set of "employees." The rules of the game are as follows. If an employer hires an employee who provides effort e and receives a wage w, the employer's payoff is 100 times the effort e, minus the wage w that he must pay the employee ($\pi = 100e - w$), where the wage is between zero and 100 ($0 \le w \le 100$), and the effort between 0.1 and 1 ($0.1 \le e \le 1$). The payoff u to the employee is then the wage he receives, minus a "cost of effort," $c(e)$ ($u = w - c(e)$). The cost of effort schedule $c(e)$ is constructed by the experimenters such that supplying effort $e = $ 0.1, 0.2, 0.3, 0.4, 0.5, 0.6, 0.7, 0.8, 0.9, and 1.0, cost the employee $c(e) = $ 0, 1, 2, 4, 6, 8, 10, 12, 15, and 18, respectively. All payoffs are converted into real money that the subjects are paid at the end of the experimental session.

The sequence of actions is as follows. The employer first offers a "contract" specifying a wage *w* and a desired amount of effort *e**. A contract is made with the first employee who agrees to these terms. An employer can make a contract *(w,e*)* with at most one employee. The employee who agrees to these terms receives the wage *w* and supplies an effort level *e*, which *need not equal the contracted effort, e**. In effect, there is no penalty if the employee does not keep his promise, so the employee can choose any effort level, *e*∈*[0.1,1]*, with impunity. Although subjects may play this game several times with different partners, each employer–employee interaction is a one-shot (non-repeated) event. Moreover, the identity of the interacting partners is never revealed.

If employees are self-regarding, they will choose the zero-cost effort level, *e = 0.1*, no matter what wage is offered them. Knowing this, employers will never pay more than the minimum necessary to get the employee to accept a contract, which is 1 (assuming only integral wage offers are permitted). The employee will accept this offer, and will set *e = 0.1*. Since *c(0.1) = 0*, the employee's payoff is *u = 1*. The employer's payoff is *π = 0.1 × 100−1 = 9*.

In fact, however, this self-regarding outcome rarely occurred in this experiment. The average net payoff to employees was *u = 35*, and the more generous the employer's wage offer to the employee, the higher the effort provided. In effect, employers presumed the strong reciprocity predispositions of the employees, making quite generous wage offers and receiving higher effort, as a means to increase both their own and the employee's payoff, as depicted in Figure 9.1. Similar results have been observed in Fehr, Kirchsteiger, and Riedl (1993; 1998).

Figure 9.1 also shows that, though most employees are strong reciprocators, at any wage rate there still is a significant gap between the amount of effort agreed upon and the amount actually delivered. This is not because there are a few "bad apples" among

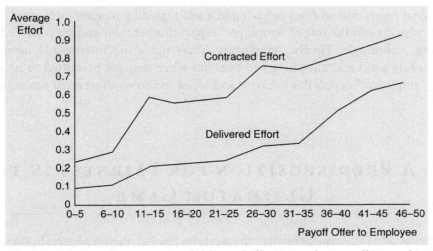

Fig. 9.1 Relation of contracted and delivered effort to worker payoff (141 subjects)
Source: Fehr, Gächter, and Kirchsteiger (1997).

the set of employees, but because only 26 percent of employees delivered the level of effort they promised! We conclude that strong reciprocators are inclined to compromise their morality to some extent, just as we might expect from daily experience.

The above evidence is compatible with the notion that the employers are purely self-regarding, since their beneficent behavior vis-à-vis their employees was effective in increasing employer profits. To see if employers are also strong reciprocators, following this round of experiments, the authors extended the game by allowing the employers to respond reciprocally to the *actual effort choices* of their workers. At a cost of 1, an employer could *increase* or *decrease* his employee's payoff by 2.5. If employers were self-regarding, they would of course do neither, since they would not interact with the same worker a second time. However, 68 percent of the time, employers punished employees that did not fulfill their contracts, and 70 percent of the time, employers rewarded employees who overfulfilled their contracts. Indeed, employers rewarded 41 percent of employees who *exactly* fulfilled their contracts. Moreover, employees *expected* this behavior on the part of their employers, as shown by the fact that their effort levels *increased significantly* when their bosses gained the power to punish and reward them. Underfulfilling contracts dropped from 83 to 26 percent of the exchanges, and overfulfilled contracts rose from 3 to 38 percent of the total. Finally, allowing employers to reward and punish led to a 40 percent increase in the net payoffs to all subjects, even when the payoff reductions resulting from employer punishment of employees are taken into account. Several researchers have predicted this general behavior on the basis of general real-life social observation and field studies, including Homans (1961), Blau (1964), and Akerlof (1982). The laboratory results show that this behavior has a motivational basis in strong reciprocity and not simply long-term material self-interest.

We conclude from this study that the subjects who assume the role of "employee" conform to internalized standards of reciprocity, even when they know there are no material repercussions from behaving in a self-regarding manner. Moreover, subjects who assume the role of "employer" expect this behavior and are rewarded for acting accordingly. Finally, "employers" draw upon the internalized norm of rewarding good and punishing bad behavior when they are permitted to punish, and "employees" expect this behavior and adjust their own effort levels accordingly.

2   A Predisposition for Fairness in the Ultimatum Game

The next set of experiments evokes themes raised by Barrington Moore, Jr. (1978) in his study of obedience and revolt and James Scott (1976) in his study of rebellion in a moral economy: commitments to justice run deep, and violations of fair treatment are likely to be harshly treated. In the Ultimatum game, under conditions of anonymity, two players are shown a sum of money, say $10. One of the players, called the "proposer," is instructed to offer any number of dollars, from $1 to $10, to the second player, who is called the "responder." The proposer can make only one offer. The responder, again under conditions of anonymity, can either accept or reject this offer. If the responder accepts the offer, the money is shared accordingly. If the responder rejects the offer, both players receive nothing.

Since the game is played only once and the players do not know each other's identity, a self-regarding responder will accept any positive amount of money. Knowing this, a self-regarding proposer will offer the minimum possible amount, $1, and this will be accepted. However, when actually played, *the self-regarding outcome is never attained and never even approximated.* In fact, as many replications of this experiment have documented, under varying conditions and with varying amounts of money, proposers routinely offer respondents very substantial amounts (50 percent of the total generally being the modal offer), and respondents frequently reject offers below 30 percent (Camerer and Thaler 1995; Güth and Tietz 1990; Roth et al. 1991).

The ultimatum game has been played around the world, but mostly with university students. We find a great deal of individual variability. For instance, in all of the above experiments a significant fraction of subjects (about a quarter, typically) behave in a self-regarding manner. But, among student subjects, average performance is strikingly uniform from country to country.

To expand the diversity of cultural and economic circumstances of experimental subjects, we (Henrich et al. 2005) undertook a large cross-cultural study of behavior in various games including the ultimatum game. Twelve experienced field researchers, working in twelve countries on four continents, recruited subjects from fifteen small-scale societies exhibiting a wide variety of economic and cultural conditions. These societies consisted of five groups of foragers (some combined with horticulture or trade—the Hadza of Tanzania, the Lamalera of Indonesia, the Ache of Paraguay, the Au and the Gnau of Papua New Guinea), four groups of horticulturists (the Machiguenga, Quichua, Achuar, and Tsimane of South America), four pastoral herding groups (Torguuds and Kazakhs in Central Asia and the Sangu and Orma of East Africa), and two farming groups (the Shona of Zimbabwe, the Mapuche of Chile). Ethnographic and other detailed information on these societies and our experiments are reported in Henrich et al. (2004).

We can summarize our results as follows.

The canonical model of self-regarding behavior is not supported in *any* society studied. In the ultimatum game, for example, in all societies either respondents, or proposers, or both, behaved in a reciprocal manner.

There is considerably more behavioral variability across groups than had been found in previous cross-cultural research. While mean ultimatum game offers in experiments with student subjects are typically between 43 and 48 percent, the mean offers from proposers in our sample ranged from 26 to 58 percent. While modal ultimatum game offers are consistently 50 percent among university students, sample modes with these data ranged from 15 to 50 percent. In some groups rejections were extremely rare, even in the presence of very low offers, while in others, rejection rates were substantial, including frequent rejections of *hyper-fair* offers (i.e. offers above 50 percent). By contrast, the most common behavior for the Machiguenga was to offer zero. The mean offer was 22 percent. The Aché and Tsimané distributions resemble American distributions, but with very low rejection rates. The Orma and Huinca (non-Mapuche Chileans living among the Mapuche) have modal offers near the center of the distribution, but show secondary peaks at full cooperation.

Differences among societies in "market integration" and "cooperation in production" explain a substantial portion of the behavioral variation between groups: the higher the degree of market integration and the higher the payoffs to cooperation, the greater the level of cooperation and sharing in experimental games. The societies were rank-ordered in five categories—"market integration" (how often do people buy and sell, or work for a wage), "cooperation in production" (is production collective or individual), plus "anonymity" (how prevalent are anonymous roles and transactions), "privacy" (how easily can people keep their activities secret), and "complexity" (how much centralized decision-making occurs above the level of the household). Using statistical regression analysis, only the first two characteristics, market integration and cooperation in production, were significant, and they together accounted for 66 percent of the variation among societies in mean Ultimatum game offers.

Individual-level economic and demographic variables did not explain behavior either within or across groups.

The nature and degree of cooperation and punishment in the experiments was generally consistent with economic patterns of everyday life in these societies.

In a number of cases the parallels between experimental game play and the structure of daily life were quite striking. Nor was this relationship lost on the subjects themselves. Here are some examples.

The Orma immediately recognized that the public goods game was similar to the *harambee*, a locally initiated contribution that households make when a community decides to construct a road or school. They dubbed the experiment "the harambee game" and gave generously (mean 58 percent with 25 percent maximal contributors).

Among the Au and Gnau, many proposers offered more than half the pie, and many of these "hyper-fair" offers were rejected! This reflects the Melanesian culture of status-seeking through gift giving. Making a large gift is a bid for social dominance in everyday life in these societies, and rejecting the gift is a rejection of being subordinate.

Among the whale-hunting Lamalera, 63 percent of the proposers in the ulti-matum game divided the pie equally, and most of those who did not, offered more than 50 percent (the mean offer was 57 percent). In real life, a large catch, always the product of cooperation among many individual whalers, is meticulously divided into pre-designated parts and carefully distributed among the members of the community.

Among the Aché, 79 percent of proposers offered either 40 or 50 percent, and 16 percent offered more than 50 percent, with no rejected offers. In daily life, the Aché regularly share meat, which is being distributed equally among all other house-holds, irrespective of which hunter made the kill.

The Hadza, unlike the Aché, made low offers and had high rejection rates in the ultimatum game. This reflects the tendency of these small-scale foragers to share meat, but with a high level of conflict and frequent attempts of hunters to hide their catch from the group.

Both the Machiguenga and Tsimané made low ultimatum game offers, and there were virtually no rejections. These groups exhibit little cooperation, exchange, or sharing beyond the family unit. Ethnographically, both show little fear of social sanctions and care little about "public opinion."

The Mapuche's social relations are characterized by mutual suspicion, envy, and fear of being envied. This pattern is consistent with the Mapuche's post-game interviews in the ultimatum game. Mapuche proposers rarely claimed that their offers were influenced by fairness, but rather by a fear of rejection. Even proposers who made hyper-fair offers claimed that they feared rare spiteful responders, who would be willing to reject even 50/50 offers.

3   Cooperation and Altruistic Punishment in the Public Goods Game

Our final set of experiments illuminates the tension between free riding and civic virtue central to the master works of political theory since Hume and Rousseau. The *public goods game* has been analyzed in a series of papers by the social psychologist Toshio Yamagishi (1986; 1988a), by the political scientist Elinor Ostrom and her co-workers (Ostrom, Walker, and Gardner 1992), and by economists Ernst Fehr and his co-workers (Gächter and Fehr 1999; Fehr and Gächter 2000; 2002). These research-ers uniformly found that *groups exhibit a much higher rate of cooperation than can be expected assuming the standard economic model of the self-regarding actor*, and this is especially the case when subjects are given the option of incurring a cost to themselves in order to punish free riders.

A typical public goods game consists of a number of rounds, say ten. The subjects are told the total number of rounds, as well as all other aspects of the game. The subjects are paid their winnings in real money at the end of the session. In each round, each subject is grouped with several other subjects—say three others—under conditions of strict anonymity. Each subject is then given a certain number of "points," say twenty, redeemable at the end of the experimental session for real money. Each subject then places some fraction of his points in a "common account," and the remainder in the subject's "private account." The experimenter then tells the subjects how many points were contributed to the common account, and adds to the private account of each subject some fraction, say 40 percent, of the total amount in the common account. So if a subject contributes his whole twenty points to the common account, each of the four group members will receive eight points at the end of the round. In effect, by putting the whole endowment into the common account, a player loses twelve points but the other three group members gain in total 24 ($= 8 \times 3$) points. The players keep whatever is in their private account at the end of the round.

A self-regarding player will contribute nothing to the common account. However, only a fraction of subjects in fact conform to the self-interest model. Subjects begin by contributing on average about half of their endowment to the public account. The level of contributions decays over the course of the ten rounds, until in the final rounds most players are behaving in a self-regarding manner (Dawes and Thaler 1988; Ledyard 1995). In a meta-study of twelve public goods experiments, Fehr and Schmidt (1999) found that in the early rounds, average and median contribution levels ranged from 40 to 60 percent of the endowment, but in the final period 73 percent of all individuals ($N = 1042$) contributed nothing, and many of the remaining players contributed close to zero. These results are not compatible with the self-regarding actor model, which predicts zero contribution on all rounds, though they might be predicted by a reciprocal altruism model, since the chance to reciprocate declines as the end of the experiment approaches. However this is not in fact the explanation of moderate but deteriorating levels of cooperation in the public goods game.

The explanation of the decay of cooperation offered by subjects when debriefed after the experiment is that cooperative subjects became angry at others who contributed less than themselves, and retaliated against free-riding low contributors in the only way available to them—by lowering their own contributions (Andreoni 1995).

Experimental evidence supports this interpretation. When subjects are allowed to punish noncontributors, they do so at a cost to themselves (Orbell, Dawes, and Van de Kragt 1986; Sato 1987; Yamagishi 1988a and b; 1992). For instance, in Ostrom, Walker, and Gardner (1992) subjects interacted for twenty-five periods in a public goods game, and by paying a "fee," subjects could impose costs on other subjects by "fining" them. Since fining costs the individual who uses it, but the benefits of increased compliance accrue to the group as a whole, the only Nash equilibrium in this game that does not depend on incredible threats is for no player to pay the fee, so no player is ever punished for defecting, and all players defect by contributing nothing to the common pool. However the authors found a significant level of punishing behavior.

These studies allowed individuals to engage in strategic behavior, since costly punishment of defectors could increase cooperation in future periods, yielding a positive net return for the punisher. Fehr and Gächter (2000) set up an experimental situation in which *the possibility of strategic punishment was removed*. They used six- and ten-round public goods games with groups of size four, and with costly punishment allowed at the end of each round, employing three different methods of assigning members to groups. There were sufficient subjects to run between ten and eighteen groups simultaneously. Under the *Partner* treatment, the four subjects remained in the same group for all ten periods. Under the *Stranger* treatment, the subjects were randomly reassigned after each round. Finally, under the *Perfect Stranger* treatment the subjects were randomly reassigned and assured that they would never meet the same subject more than once. Subjects earned an average of about $35 for an experimental session.

Fehr and Gächter (2000) performed their experiment for ten rounds with punishment and ten rounds without.[1] Their results are illustrated in Figure 9.2. We see that when costly punishment is permitted, cooperation does not deteriorate, and in the Partner game, despite strict anonymity, cooperation increases almost to full cooperation, even on the final round. When punishment is not permitted, however, the same subjects experience the deterioration of cooperation found in previous public goods games. The contrast in cooperation rates between the Partner and the two Stranger treatments is worth noting, because the strength of punishment is roughly the same across all treatments. This suggests that the credibility of the punishment threat is greater in the Partner treatment because in this treatment the punished subjects are certain that, once they have been punished in previous rounds, the punishing subjects are in their group. The prosociality impact of strong reciprocity on cooperation is thus more strongly manifested, the more coherent and permanent the group in question.

---

[1] For additional experimental results and their analysis, see Bowles and Gintis (2002) and Fehr and Gächter (2002).

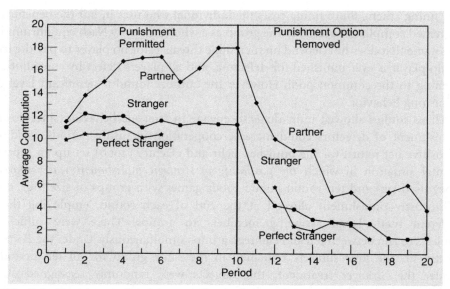

Fig. 9.2 Average contributions over time in the Partner, Stranger, and Perfect Stranger treatments, when the punishment condition is played first
Source: adapted from Fehr and Gächter (2000).

4   CONCLUSION

The evidence for other-regarding, process-regarding, and endogenous preferences is compelling. But, it raises a puzzle, one that we address in greater detail in a related paper (Bowles and Gintis 2006). If many of us are fair-minded and reciprocal, then we must have acquired these preferences somehow, and it would be a good check on the plausibility of the views advanced here and the empirical evidence on which they are based to see if a reasonable account of the evolutionary success of these preferences can be provided. Generosity toward one's biological kin is readily explained (Hamilton 1964). The evolutionary puzzle concerns non-selfish behaviors towards non-kin. Among non-kin, selfish preferences would seem to be favored by any payoff-rewarding evolutionary process, whether genetic or cultural. Thus, the fair-mindedness that induces people to transfer resources to the less well-off, and the reciprocity motives that impel us to incur the costs of punishing those who violate group norms, on this account, are doomed to extinction by long-term evolutionary processes. If other regarding preferences are common, this conventional evolutionary account must be incorrect.

In many cases, the evolutionary success of what appear to be unselfish traits is explained by the fact that when an accounting of long-term and indirect effects is done, the behaviors are payoff maximizing, often representing forms of mutualism. The great hunter who shares his prey may, by advertising his prowess, recruit coalition partners and mates and deter opponents (Gintis, Smith, and Bowles

2001). But, some seemingly generous behaviors are just what they seem. Indeed, the experiments we have cited were designed to study behavior in the *absence* of the indirect or long-term benefits just mentioned. The behaviors observed in these experiments, we think, have become common because they contribute to the success of groups in which the behaviors are common. People in successful groups tend to be copied, either genetically or culturally, and thus genuinely other-regarding preferences can proliferate. Recent theoretical modeling, anthropological studies, and agent-based computer simulations lend some credibility to this account.[2]

The experimental evidence as well as observation of economic and political behavior in natural settings does not lead us to reject the rational actor model, for that model, in its minimalist conception as consistency and completeness of preferences, is perfectly compatible with altruistic, spiteful, or reciprocal motives. Indeed, this versatility is among its merits.

However, an adequate reformulation of the psychological foundations of the behavioral sciences cannot be accomplished by inventing some new *Homo sociologicus* or *zoon politikon* to replace *Homo economicus* as the epitome of intentional behavior. Behavioral experiments and everyday observation make it clear that populations are heterogeneous. Heterogeneity makes a difference in outcomes. But, as the public goods experiments showed, its effects are not adequately captured by a process of simple averaging. The outcome of interaction among a population that is composed of equal numbers of saints and sinners will not generally be the average of the outcomes of two populations with just one type. The reason is that in many settings, the norm-upholding activities of a few saints may induce even the sinners to act civic-mindedly, while in other institutional settings, a few sinners can induce all players to act like *Homo economicus*. Recall, as another example, that in the public-goods-with-punishment game, those with reciprocal preferences not only acted generously themselves, but they apparently also induced the selfish types to act as if they were generous. Indeed, seemingly small differences in institutions can make large differences in outcomes, as illustrated by the following example. Imagine a one-shot Prisoners' Dilemma game played between a self-regarding player, for whom defect is the dominant strategy in the simultaneous moves game, and a strong reciprocator, who prefers to cooperate if the other cooperates and to defect otherwise (Kiyonari, Tanida, and Yamagishi 2000; Fehr and Fischbacher 2001). Suppose the players' types are known to each. If the game is played simultaneously, the reciprocator, knowing that the other will defect, will do the same. The outcome will be mutual defection. If the self-regarding player moves first, however, he will know that the reciprocator will match whatever action he takes, narrowing the possible outcomes to {cooperate, cooperate} or {defect,

---

[2] See Gintis 2000; Boehm 2000; Bowles, Choi, and Hopfensitz 2003; Gintis et al. 2004; Bowles and Gintis 2004*a* and *b*.

defect}, the former yielding both players a higher payoff. The self-regarding first mover will therefore cooperate and mutual cooperation will be sustained as the outcome.

In addition to heterogeneity across individuals, versatility of individuals must also be accounted for. In the ultimatum game, many proposers often offer amounts that maximize their expected payoffs, given the observed relationship between offers and rejections: they behave selfishly but expect responders not to. And they are correct in this belief! The *same individuals*, when in the role of responder, typically reject substantial offers if they appear to be unfair, thus confirming the expectations of the proposer and violating the self-interest axiom.

Finally, as our cross-cultural experiments suggest, culture matters: differences in an individual's preferences often correspond to differences in the way people interact socially in making their living and in other aspects of daily life. This means that populations that experience different structures of social interaction over prolonged periods are likely to exhibit differing behaviors, not simply because the constraints entailed by these institutions are different but also because the structure of social interaction affects the evolution of preferences.

Progress in the direction of a more adequate behavioral foundation for political behavior must take account of these three aspects of people: namely their *heterogeneity*, their *versatility*, and their *plasticity*.

References

ACHESON, J. 1988. *The Lobster Gangs of Maine*. Hanover, NH: New England Universities Press.

AKERLOF, G. A. 1982. Labor contracts as partial gift exchange. *Quarterly Journal of Economics*, 97: 543–69.

ANDREONI, J. 1995. Cooperation in public goods experiments: kindness or confusion. *American Economic Review*, 85: 891–904.

——and MILLER, J. H. 2002. Giving according to GARP: an experimental test of the consistency of preferences for altruism. *Econometrica*, 70: 737–53.

——ERARD, B., and FEINSTEIN, J. 1998. Tax compliance. *Journal of Economic Literature*, 36: 818–60.

BEWLEY, T. F. 2000. *Why Wages Don't Fall During a Recession*. Cambridge: Cambridge University Press.

BLAU, P. 1964. *Exchange and Power in Social Life*. New York: Wiley.

BOEHM, C. 2000. *Hierarchy in the Forest: The Evolution of Egalitarian Behavior*. Cambridge, Mass.: Harvard University Press.

BOWLES, S., and GINTIS, H. 2002. Homo reciprocans. *Nature*, 415: 125–8.

——————2004a. The evolution of strong reciprocity: cooperation in heterogeneous populations. *Theoretical Population Biology*, 65: 17–28.

————— 2004b. The origins of human cooperation. Pp. 430–43 in *Genetic and Cultural Origins of Cooperation*, ed. P. Hammerstein. Cambridge, Mass.: MIT Press.

————— 2006. Evolutionary origins of collective action. In *Oxford Handbook of Political Economy*, ed. D. Wittman and B. Weingast. Oxford: Oxford University Press.

BOWLES, S., CHOI, J.-K., and HOPFENSITZ, A. 2003. The co-evolution of individual behaviors and social institutions. *Journal of Theoretical Biology*, 223: 135–47.

CAMERER, C., and THALER, B. 1995. Ultimatums, dictators and manners. *Journal of Economic Perspectives*, 9: 209–19.

CARDENAS, J. C., STRANLUND, J. K., and WILLIS, C. E. 2000. Local environmental control and institutional crowding-out. *World Development*, 28: 1719–33.

DAWES, R. M., and THALER, R. 1988. Cooperation. *Journal of Economic Perspectives*, 2: 187–97.

FEHR, E., and FISCHBACHER, U. 2001. Why social preferences matter. *Nobel Symposium on Behavioral and Experimental Economics*.

—— and GÄCHTER, S. 2000. Cooperation and punishment. *American Economic Review*, 90: 980–94.

————— 2002. Altruistic punishment in humans. *Nature*, 415: 137–40.

—— GÄCHTER, S., and KIRCHSTEIGER, G. 1997. Reciprocity as a contract enforcement device: experimental evidence. *Econometrica*, 65: 833–60.

—— KIRCHSTEIGER, G., and RIEDL, A. 1993. Does fairness prevent market clearing? *Quarterly Journal of Economics*, 108: 437–59.

———— —— 1998. Gift exchange and reciprocity in competitive experimental markets. *European Economic Review*, 42: 1–34.

—— and SCHMIDT, K. M. 1999. A theory of fairness, competition and cooperation. *Quarterly Journal of Economics*, 114: 817–68.

GÄCHTER, S., and FEHR, E. 1999. Collective action as a social exchange. *Journal of Economic Behavior and Organization*, 39: 341–69.

GINTIS, H. 2000. Strong reciprocity and human sociality. *Journal of Theoretical Biology*, 206: 169–79.

—— SMITH, E. A., and BOWLES, S. 2001. Costly signaling and cooperation. *Journal of Theoretical Biology*, 213: 103–19.

—— BOWLES, S., BOYD, R., and FEHR, E. 2004. *Moral Sentiments and Material Interests: On the Foundations of Cooperation in Economic Life*. Cambridge, Mass.: MIT Press.

GOODWIN, J., POLLETTA, F., and JASPER, J. M. 2001. *Passionate Politics: Emotions and Social Movements*. Chicago: University of Chicago Press.

GÜTH, W., and TIETZ, R. 1990. Ultimatum bargaining behavior: a survey and comparison of experimental results. *Journal of Economic Psychology*, 11: 417–49.

HAMILTON, W. D. 1964. The genetical evolution of social behavior I & II. *Journal of Theoretical Biology*, 7: 1–16, 17–52.

HENRICH, J., BOYD, R., BOWLES, S., CAMERER, C., FEHR, E., GINTIS, H., and McELREATH, R. 2004. *Foundations of Human Sociality: Economic Experiments and Ethnographic Evidence in Fifteen Small-scale Societies*. Oxford: Oxford University Press.

———— ———— ———— ———— and others. 2005. "Economic man" in cross-cultural perspective: behavioral experiments in 15 small-scale societies. *Behavioral and Brain Sciences*.

HOMANS, G. 1961. *Social Behavior*. New York: Harcourt Brace.

KIYONARI, T., TANIDA, S., and YAMAGISHI, T. 2000. Social exchange and reciprocity: confusion or a heuristic? *Evolution and Human Behavior*, 21: 411–27.

KREPS, D. M. 1988. *Notes on the Theory of Choice*. London: Westview.

LEDYARD, J. O. 1995. Public goods: a survey of experimental research. Pp. 111–94 in *The Handbook of Experimental Economics*, ed. J. H. Kagel and A. E. Roth. Princeton, NJ: Princeton University Press.

MOORE, B., JR. 1978. *Injustice: The Social Bases of Obedience and Revolt*. White Plains, NY: M. E. Sharpe.

ORBELL, J. M., DAWES, R. M., and VAN DE KRAGT, J. C., 1986. Organizing groups for collective action. *American Political Science Review*, 80: 1171–85.

OSTROM, E. 1998. A behavioral approach to the rational choice theory of collective action. *American Political Science Review*, 92: 1–21.

——— WALKER, J. and GARDNER, R. 1992. Covenants with and without a sword: self-governance is possible. *American Political Science Review*, 86(2): 14–17.

——— DIETZ, T., DOLSAK, N., STERN, P. C., STONICH, S., and WEBER, E. 2002. *The Drama of the Commons*. Washington, DC: National Academy Press.

PETERSEN, R. D. 2002. *Understanding Ethnic Violence, Fear, Hatred and Resentment in Twentieth-century Eastern Europe*. Cambridge: Cambridge University Press.

ROTH, A. E., PRASNIKAR, V., OKUNO-FUJIWARA, M., and ZAMIR, S. 1991. Bargaining and market behavior in Jerusalem, Ljubljana, Pittsburgh and Tokyo: an experimental study. *American Economic Review*, 81: 1068–95.

SATO, K. 1987. Distribution and the cost of maintaining common property resources. *Journal of Experimental Social Psychology*, 23: 19–31.

SCOTT, J. C. 1976. *The Moral Economy of the Peasant: Rebellion and Subsistence in Southeast Asia*. New Haven, Conn.: Yale University Press.

WOOD, E. J. 2003. *Insurgent Collective Action and Civil War in El Salvador*. Cambridge: Cambridge University Press.

YAMAGISHI, T. 1986. The provision of a sanctioning system as a public good. *Journal of Personality and Social Psychology*, 51: 110–16.

——— 1988a. The provision of a sanctioning system in the United States and Japan. *Social Psychology Quarterly*, 51: 265–71.

——— 1988b. Seriousness of social dilemmas and the provision of a sanctioning system. *Social Psychology Quarterly*, 51: 32–42.

——— 1992. Group size and the provision of a sanctioning system in a social dilemma. Pp. 267–87 in *Social Dilemmas: Theoretical Issues and Research Findings*, ed. W. B. G. Liebrand, D. M. Messick, and H. A. M. Wilke. Oxford: Pergamon.

CHAPTER 10

....

FRAMES AND THEIR CONSEQUENCES

....

FRANCESCA POLLETTA

M. KAI HO

IN 1979, the nuclear reactor at Three Mile Island in Pennsylvania suffered a partial meltdown. Hundreds of thousands of residents fled as radiation leaked into the atmosphere. The resulting media coverage made "Three Mile Island" into an international symbol of the dangers of nuclear energy, prompted nationwide opposition to nuclear power, and shut down the nuclear industry for more than a decade. Yet Three Mile Island was not the first accident of its kind. In 1966, the Fermi reactor outside Chicago experienced a partial meltdown followed by a failure of the automatic shut-down system. Officials discussed evacuation plans for area residents as they tried to avert the possibility of a secondary accident.

The Fermi accident was no secret: the press was alerted as it was happening. But newspapers, including the *New York Times*, gave the episode only perfunctory coverage, mainly repeating company spokespeople's assurances that the reactor would soon be up and running. Why did the Fermi accident not produce the public crisis that Three Mile Island did? Because it was viewed through different frames, according to William Gamson (1988). At the time of the Fermi accident, nuclear power was covered by the press mainly in terms of a "faith in progress" frame that viewed nuclear power as a boon to technological development and human progress. By the time of Three Mile Island, however, media stories about nuclear power were less confident of its safety and effectiveness. The stage was set for a critical and alarmist interpretation of the accident.

What accounts for the shift? In large part, says Gamson, the strategic framing activities of anti-nuclear movement groups. Between 1966 and 1979, groups such as the Union for Concerned Scientists and the environmentalist Friends of the Earth energetically promoted frames that were critical of nuclear power. Protest events such as the nonviolent occupation of a nuclear power plant and a celebrity-studded "No-Nukes" concert attracted media attention and provided framing opportunities for movement spokespeople. Activists' representations of nuclear power as dangerous and the nuclear power industry as unaccountable guided news coverage of Three Mile Island and of nuclear power in its aftermath. That, in turn, contributed to further anti-nuclear mobilization.

Frames matter. The ways in which political actors package their messages affect their ability to recruit adherents, gain favorable media coverage, demobilize antagonists, and win political victories. The ways in which ordinary citizens think about gains and losses shape their political preferences; the ways in which states do so shape their international bargaining strategies. The concept of framing has been used to capture these diverse processes by scholars of the media (Gitlin 1980; Carragee and Roefs 2004), international relations (Bernstein 2002; Berejekian 1997), decision-making (Tversky and Kahneman 1986), policy-making (Schon and Rein 1994), and social movements.

The concept is appealing for several reasons. The term "frame" reminds us that persuasion works in part by demarcating and punctuating important aspects of reality, that is, by making events and circumstances intelligible as much as by advancing a compelling point of view. If we think of a frame as the structure of a building rather than the perimeter of a picture (Gamson 2004), the concept also points to the deeper logics structuring political contention. While actors instrumentally frame situations so as to press their case, their very understanding of what is instrumental is shaped by taken-for-granted frames. In that sense, frames are both strategic and set the terms of strategic action.

In this chapter, we focus on framing in social movements. The theoretical and empirical literature on the topic is now extensive and, in many cases, sophisticated. But it remains thin on the relations between frames and their political and cultural contexts. We do not know enough about why activists choose the frames they do, what aspects of the environment shape frames' effectiveness, and what impacts frames have on institutions outside the movement. Several factors are probably to blame. The single case orientation of much of the work on framing has made it difficult to generalize about causes and effects. A tendency to view frames as emergent, that is, as constructed in and through movement work, has been valuable in capturing the dynamic quality of frames but has discouraged attention to the environmental conditions for frames' plausibility and impact. Where scholars have sought to identify influential aspects of the environment in which framing takes place, they have concentrated more on political factors than on cultural ones.

Certainly, culture is notoriously difficult to study systematically. But the neglect extends also to how frames are shaped in interaction with other cultural forms, such as ideology, discourse, and institutional logics of action.

Our intention here is not to engage in a critique of the framing perspective in social movements.[1] Instead, we draw on the existing literature in order to answer three questions: *What are frames*—and how are they different from ideologies, discourses, and other concepts that have been used to capture the cultural dimensions of movements? *Where do frames come from*—and why do activists choose, modify, and discard particular frames? And finally, *how important are frames in accounting for key movement processes such as movement emergence and impacts*—and what makes for politically effective frames? Where good answers exist within the framing perspective, we synthesize empirical findings from that literature. Where the answers have been incomplete, we draw from literatures outside framing in order to flesh out alternatives. We make two main recommendations for future work on framing. One is to pay more attention to institutionalized relationships and practices as sources of meaning. Familiar relationships, routines, and associational models both provide activists with resources in their framing efforts and levy important constraints on those efforts. Our other recommendation is for a more sophisticated understanding of persuasion, in which ambiguity and inconsistency are sometimes more powerful than clarity and coherence.

1   WHAT ARE FRAMES?

The concepts of *frame* and *framing* entered the sociology of social movements in the 1980s, largely in response to the neglect of social psychological processes by the resource mobilization models that then dominated the field. Resource mobilization theorists had downplayed grievances relative to resources and political opportunities in accounting for protest since grievances were assumed to be ubiquitous (see, for representative treatments, Jenkins and Perrow 1977; McCarthy and Zald 1977). Framing theorists like William Gamson (Gamson, Fireman, and Rytina 1982; Gamson 1988) and David Snow and colleagues (Snow et al. 1986; Snow and Benford 1988; see also Klandermans 1988) countered that how people interpreted their grievances was critical to whether they participated. Indeed, much of the work of movements involved various *frame alignment* processes aimed at linking individual interests, values, and beliefs to those of the movement (Snow et al. 1986; Gamson 1988).

---

[1] For critiques, see Benford 1997; Steinberg 1999*a*; Jasper 1997; Ferree and Merrill 2000; and for good defenses, see Snow and Benford 2000; Snow 2004.

Snow and his colleagues and Gamson drew their conception of framing from Erving Goffman (1974), and they adopted Goffman's interactionist perspective: frames are jointly and continuously constructed and reconstructed by movement actors and their audiences. This contrasts with a view of frames as fixed rather than dynamic and as the property of individuals rather than groups. The latter view has characterized work on framing in other fields, for example in the psychology of decision-making, where frames have been defined both as the manner in which a choice problem is presented and the "norms, habits, and expectancies of the decision maker" that operate in conditions of bounded rationality (Kahneman and Tversky 1986: 257). On the other hand, even within the field of social movements, an interactionist perspective has not been inconsistent with an instrumentalist one. Frames have generally been conceptualized as the interpretive packages that activists develop to mobilize potential adherents and constituents, appeal to authorities, and demobilize antagonists (Snow et al. 1986; Gamson 1988; Snow and Benford 1988; Tarrow 1998). Frames combine a *diagnosis* of the social condition in need of remedy, a *prognosis* for how to effect such a remedy, and a *rationale* for action, a "call to arms" (Snow and Benford 1988; Benford and Hunt 1992).

In effective frames, the diagnostic, prognostic, and motivational components are clearly specified, richly developed, and well integrated (Snow and Benford 1988; Stoecker 1995). Effective frames also make a compelling case for the "injustice" of a targeted condition and the likely effectiveness of collective "agency" in changing that condition. They make clear the "identities" of the contenders, distinguishing "us" from "them" and depicting antagonists as human decision-makers rather than impersonal forces such as industrialization or the demands of the market (Gamson 1988; 1992; also, Hunt and Benford 1994; Hunt, Benford, and Snow 1994; Klandermans 1997). Along with those formal features, finally, frames' resonance with their audiences is crucial to their success. Effective frames accord with available evidence, with people's experiences, and with familiar stories, values, and belief systems (Gamson 1988). That is, they are at once empirically credible, experientially commensurable, and narratively faithful (Snow and Benford 1988; 1992).

Frames are produced in and through movements' signifying practices but they are also often drawn from larger *master frames*, common to a cluster of movements or *cycle of protest* (Snow and Benford 1992; Tarrow 1998; Osa 2003). For example, an "equal rights" frame that became prominent in the southern black freedom movement in the 1950s went on to orient the women's movement and disability activism. The "psychosalvational" frame of Scientology was shared with transcendental meditation (Snow and Benford 1992). Master frames not only provide activists with ideological resources; they also shape activists' tactical choices. For example, groups adhering to a nonviolent master frame have found it difficult to adopt violent tactics. Whether members find violence personally repugnant, adopting it would diminish the group's credibility in the eyes of the public (Snow and Benford 1992).

The concept of frames in movements has proven enormously productive, generating scores of theoretical elaborations, empirical applications, critiques, and defenses (for good recent overviews of the literature, see Benford and Snow 2000; Snow 2004). In the political process models of mobilization that largely eclipsed resource mobilization models, mobilizing frames are, along with political opportunities and indigenous networks, a precondition for mass mobilization (McAdam, McCarthy, and Zald 1996; McAdam, Tarrow, and Tilly 2001). Framing has also come to be seen as central in other movement processes, including activists' selection of strategies and tactics (Snow and Benford 1992), their choice of organizational form (Clemens 1996), movement competition and alliance-building (Caroll and Ratner 1996), movement success (Diani 1996; Cress and Snow 2000), and movement collapse (Voss 1996).

The popularity of the concept has been a double-edged sword. Frames have been conceptualized in diverse and often ambiguous ways even within the subfield of social movements: as beliefs (Klandermans 1992), rhetoric (Diani 1996; Berbrier 1998), and symbolizing actions (McAdam, McCarthy, and Zald 1996). They have also been treated as particular to individuals (Klandermans et al. 2001; Snow et al. 1986; Johnston 2002), organizations (Tarrow 1998; Gerhards and Rucht 1992), and the political discourse that spans movements, opponents, and authorities (McCarthy 1994). The problem is not just one of specificity. Treating frames as the properties both of individuals and of groups may obscure the question of just how a frame is shared by members of a group: do people have identical conceptions or do they share rules for linking idea elements? In other words, is a shared frame more like a shared mental schema or more like a shared language?

The overextension of the framing concept has also been a problem. Made to stand in for a variety of cultural processes, framing has been treated in ways that neglect the differences between and relations among those processes (Benford 1997; Oliver and Johnston 2000; Zald 1996; Ferree and Merrill 2000). For example, treating frames as synonymous with ideologies obscures the socialization processes through which movement participants become steeped in an ideological tradition—but not in a frame (Oliver and Johnston 2000). Treating identities as constructed in and through movement framing work obscures the cultural processes that give rise to mobilizing identities before the existence of any organized movement (Polletta 1998).

How, then, should we conceptualize frames in relation to, say, ideologies, discourses, and identities—three other concepts used to capture the cultural dimensions of contentious politics? Whereas a *frame* can be seen as a delimited ideational package, *discourse* is the sum total of talk produced by an organization, institution, or society at a given point in time (Johnston 2002).[2] So we can talk about the "NAACP's discourse" or "medical discourse" or "1950s gender discourse." Discourses have a greater diversity of idea elements, more conflict, and more inconsistencies than frames (Ferree and Merrill 2000). Ideologies, on the other hand, are

---

[2] Steinberg (1999a, 743) describes it as "language in social use."

usually conceptualized as complex systems of belief. They are more encompassing and elaborated than frames and are explicitly normative (Oliver and Johnston 2000; Westby 2002; Ferree and Merrill 2000; Zald 1996). Frames are derived from ideologies, but they are also oriented to the strategic demands of making claims effectively (Westby 2002). So, Oliver and Johnston (2000) note that pro-life and pro-choice activists subscribe to very different ideologies but have used an identical frame of individual rights in promoting their opposing positions. Finally, collective identity is the subjective perception of a collective bond. Some minimal level of collective identity is usually necessary for the emergence of movements but once underway, movements devote considerable work to affirming, transforming, and securing recognition for collective identities (Taylor and Whittier 1992; Polletta and Jasper 2001).

These distinctions make sense, but they raise as many questions as they answer. Consider just the ideology/frame distinction. Are formal ideologies the only cultural sources of movement frames? How do we account for frames that seem to break with existing ideological traditions? Activists are undoubtedly ideological actors as well as strategic ones, as framing theorists point out. But where do activists' notions of what is strategic come from—as well as their notions of what is moral, what is political, what is a resource, and so on? Treating activists as balancing ideological commitments with instrumental ones in their framing efforts misses the cultural processes that shape activists' very criteria of instrumental rationality. Although it is conceptually awkward, the notion of frames as both persuasive devices and interpretive frameworks does alert us to the fact that such frameworks are both evolving and, at any point in time, limiting.

Finally, treating ideologies as the coherent world-views of the audiences to whom activists pitch their message underplays the internal contradictions in people's world-views (Snow 2004; Billig et al. 1988). That, in turn, suggests that consistency and clarity may not be necessary to effective appeals. Persuasion may work in more complex ways. We highlight these three features of framing—the diverse sources from which frames are drawn; the logics of appropriateness that govern activists' framing choices; and the complex dynamics by which frames resonate—as we discuss frames' sources and impacts.

2   WHERE DO FRAMES COME FROM?

With frames often treated as strategic persuasive devices (McAdam, McCarthy, and Zald 1996; Tarrow 1998), one strand of research on frames' content has focused on the organizational and political conditions that make some frames more likely to be effective than others. A second strand has treated activists as *ideological* actors as much as *instrumental* ones and has traced activists' framing choices to longstanding and more recent political traditions. After rehearsing research findings from each perspective, we identify certain cultural influences on framing choices that have been neglected by both.

Far from existing in isolation, activists operate in a *multiorganizational field* made up of allies, competitors, antagonists, authorities, and third parties (Curtis and Zurcher 1973; Klandermans 1992; Caroll and Ratner 1996; Evans 1997). They invent and modify frames to take advantage of strategic opportunities and demands created by those other actors. While *allies* may compel movement groups to adopt more encompassing, universalistic frames (Caroll and Ratner 1996; and see Ferree and Roth (1998) on how organizational insularity produces exclusivist frames), *opponents*, too, shape movement frames. Since ignoring rival frames puts a group at risk of seeming off-topic or evasive, movement groups often find themselves forced to counter, debunk, co-opt, or conform to opponents' frames in their own public statements (Evans 1997; Esacove 2004). For example, anti-abortion activists have adopted an individual rights frame, championing the fetus's "right to life," even though many of them recoil at the overemphasis on rights in American society and are much more attuned to duties than rights (Williams 2004). In a common dynamic, the we/they opposition that develops as groups challenge rivals' frames may lead to increasingly absolutist frames on both sides—which in turn may alienate potential supporters (Mansbridge 1986). In other words, the pressure to respond to opponents by no means guarantees that doing so will be without cost.

Where a challenging group's targets are relatively independent of it, challengers are likely to engage in the kind of *frame extension* (Snow et al. 1986) that can bring them new allies and adherents. So, the American Federation of Labor began to call for the social welfare legislation that would benefit union members and non-members alike at a time when employers were less dependent on unions for a supply of labor (Cornfield and Fletcher 1998).

If relations among movement groups' allies, opponents, and targets shape frames' content, so too should other features of the political context in which they operate. Shrewd activists will match their rhetoric to the kinds of political opportunities that are available. Mario Diani (1996) draws on variables commonly associated with a *political opportunity structure* to argue that where traditional political alignments are in crisis and the political system has openings for independent citizen action, activists can afford to adopt a "realignment frame" that calls for a restructuring of the polity without completely rejecting existing polity members and procedures. By contrast, where political alignments are stable and the system is closed to outsiders (the worst case scenario for activists) challengers are limited to "revitalization" frames, in which they call for changes from within the system. In between those two poles, challengers do best using "anti-system" frames during a period of elite crisis, since there is some prospect for an overhaul of the whole system.

While acknowledging the importance of the institutional political context in shaping activists' strategic framing choices, other researchers have pointed to additional variables in defining that context. They have also suggested that activists have considerable flexibility in responding to their political contexts. For example, when movement groups are largely shut out of positions of power, they may respond not by adopting the revitalization frame that Diani describes, but by targeting their framing to a narrower constituency, seeking to sustain the cause until a more favorable period. This is what Mary Bernstein (1997) found in her analysis of campaigns for local gay rights ordinances. The frames that gay and lesbian activists adopted when they faced a closed political system were highly critical of dominant normative values and celebrated their differences from heterosexuals rather than their similarities. When activists target non-state institutions such as medicine, art, or the educational system, they may tailor their frames to the values and beliefs of institutional insiders rather than the public simply because the public has relatively little influence on policy decisions (Binder 2004). The Afro-centrists and Creationists who challenged American school curricula in the 1980s downplayed radical critiques of American culture as, respectively, racist and godless, instead advancing pluralistic arguments about the importance of ensuring that no student felt culturally marginalized (Binder 2004). These arguments were not expected to resonate with the public but they were expected to play well with the school officials who were in charge of setting curricula, largely independent of public opinion.

Where activists operate in political regimes that strictly control their access to the public, they may frame their messages in "disguised, coded, implied" ways, Maryjane Osa argues (2003: 18). The artists, writers, and actors who have often led the opposition in contexts like these have the discursive skills to frame dissent in indirect ways, using irony, satire, subtexts, and ellipses to convey messages to potential supporters that are counter-hegemonic but difficult for authorities to suppress.[3]

Finally, Ferree et al. (2002) identify factors such as the status of religion in society, the particular cleavages around which injustice claims tend to be organized, and media reporting practices, claiming that all contribute to a *discursive opportunity structure* that activists seek to exploit in their framing efforts. That structure includes, in addition to the political components that Diani stresses, sociocultural and mass media components: party, state, and judicial structures; public beliefs about politics and contention; and routine news reporting practices. So, comparing abortion discourse in Germany and the United States, Ferree et al. found that Americans' wariness of the state was responsible for the prominence of an anti-state interventionist frame among pro-choice activists, a frame that was largely absent among their German counterparts. The discursive opportunity structure also

---

[3] See also Noonan (1995) on Chilean women's appropriation of a hegemonic maternalist frame to challenge the repressive Pinochet regime.

influenced what ideas were considered radical: with individual privacy arguments advantaged in the United States, arguments for abortion cast in terms of the moral obligation of the state were considered radical. Precisely the opposite was the case in Germany (Ferree 2003).

In sum, research suggests that activists engaged in training efforts should pay attention to the openness of the political system to challengers, the degree to which public discourse is controlled by the regime, the media practices that favor some themes and actors over others, the extent to which targets are dependent on the challenging group or insulated from public criticism, and the political clout of allies and opponents. These factors make for frames that are more or less extensive in the issues they address, more or less elaborated in their normative vision, and more or less critical of the current regime.

While activists are strategic in their framing choices, they are also committed to certain normative values. In a second vein of research, scholars have traced activists' frames to prior ideological traditions, often those associated with other movements in a cycle of protest (Snow and Benford 1992; Valocchi 1994; Babb 1996). For example, gay liberationists in the 1960s took from the radical feminist and black power movements an orientation to transforming cultural perceptions of a stigmatized self and crafted a "gay is good" frame (Valocchi 1994). Frames may also come from longer-standing traditions of dissent. A non-violence frame migrated from Gandhian direct action in pre-independence India to the post-Second World War American pacifist movement, the 1960s civil rights movement, and the 1970s and 1980s anti-nuclear movements (Chabot and Duyvendak 2002).

Frames' indebtedness to political traditions does not mean that such traditions are unchanging, with later movements simply reproducing the claims and rhetoric of earlier ones. To the contrary, the influence is often reciprocal. Moreover, frames derived from preexisting ideologies are invariably modified in the light of participants' experiences (although Steinberg (1999a) and Gamson and Meyer (1996) criticize a tendency in the framing literature to see frames as fixed rather than evolving). In her study of the pre- and post-civil war labor movement's support for labor greenbackism, a soft-currency scheme, Sarah Babb (1996) argues that labor activists could sustain for only so long the contradictions that existed between the producerist ideology underpinning the greenback frame and workers' experience of employers as antagonists rather than as fellow toilers. Eventually, the frame and then the ideology was abandoned.[4] Similar dynamics of selective appropriation and adaptation operate across movements separated by geography rather than time. Along with targets and tactics, frames diffuse across national boundaries. Here, too, the influence is reciprocal, and ideas, images, and claims made in one context are altered as they are imported into another.

---

[4] See also Snow and Benford (2000) on the remedial work done by framing when ideology comes up against experience, and Ellingson (1995) on the dialectic of discourse and events.

While activists often select among, combine, and adapt previous protest trad-itions, they sometimes invent new frames. The women who launched a movement for liberation in the late 1960s could not draw on an ideological tradition of radical challenge to everyday gender norms. The dissidents who overthrew the Communist regime in Poland had no obvious master frames at their disposal. How do we account for the frames they produced? One answer is that people are able to capitalize on the relative autonomy that some institutions are granted in repressive societies, developing within them insurgent ideas and networks. These are the *free spaces* that scholars have seen as seedbeds for dissent: institutions like the Black Church for the civil rights movement and literary circles for opposition to the Soviet regime (Morris 1984; Johnston and Snow 1998). What is important about such institutions, though often missed in discussions of free spaces, is not that they are somehow empty of ideas but that they enjoy relative freedom from the scrutiny and control of authorities (Polletta 1999). So, for example, mosques played a crucial role in Kuwaiti opposition to Iraqi occupation because of their long-standing right to challenge the state (Tetreault 1993, 278).

This raises a larger point about the specifically *institutional* sources of movement frames. If, following Philip Selznick (1957, 6–7), we think of structures and practices as institutionalized when they are "infuse[d] with value beyond the technical requirements of the task at hand," then we can see that myriad practices, relationships, and structures in society offer models for action and interaction. People may derive frames for attacking one institution from the operation of another institution. For example, the striking hospital workers whom Karen Brod-kin Sacks (1988) studied invoked the relations between parents and grown children to describe the acknowledgment and care they expected from hospital management. A familiar associational form adapted from another institutional sphere provided an idiom for formulating opposition. Poles drew on a moral idiom from Catholicism to challenge the Communist regime. Local activists in the Southern civil rights move-ment talked frequently about their "God-given rights," using a religious idiom where a legal one fell short (Polletta 2000).

Institutionalized routines and relationships shape frames in another sense, defining the kinds of claims that are considered feasible and legitimate to make. Charles Tilly's notion of a "repertoire" of contentious claims-making is relevant here. Tilly writes, "existing repertoires incorporate collectively-learned shared understandings concerning what forms of claim-making are possible, desirable, risky, expensive, or probable, as well as what consequences different possible forms of claim-making are likely to produce. They greatly constrain the contentious claims political actors make on each other and on agents of the state" (1999).

To be sure, since anything is, in principle, thinkable, activists can break with existing repertoires. They can exploit silences and contradictions in dominant discourses and can attach new meanings to old words (Steinberg 1999b). However, the risks in challenging conventions of claims-making are substantial and the gains uncertain. For example, feminists who challenged workplace discrimination in court in the 1980s were encouraged to supply stories of individuals unfairly barred from hiring or promotion. This was despite the fact that a few such stories could not, on their own, demonstrate patterns of disparate treatment. Feminists could have refused to frame their claims in terms of individuals' experience of discrimination. Those who did, however, were much more likely to lose their cases (Schultz 1990). The problem was that the same framing strategy that won the movement legal victories may also have alienated potential recruits who were unwilling to see themselves as the victims that judges required (Bumiller 1988).

So, institutional conventions shape frames' content. It is hardly surprising, moreover, that such conventions enter into activists' own tactical calculations. The animal rights activists whom Julian Groves (2001) studied discouraged women from serving in leadership positions because they believed that women were seen by the public as prone to the kind of emotionalism that would cost the movement credibility. Activists spent little time debating whether women were prone to emotionalism, however, or whether emotional accounts rather than rational arguments were in fact a bad framing strategy (Jasper 1999). The logic behind activists' framing choices here is neither one of ideological consistency nor one of instrumental rationality but one of appropriateness. Ideology understood as a coherent set of normative principles held by activists does not capture this kind of cultural influence on frames' content.

Again, the frames that predominate in a movement at a particular time reflect activists' strategic bids to mobilize public opinion as well as their efforts to balance the demands of catering to public opinion with those of staying loyal to their ideological commitments. But dominant frames also reflect the institutional common sense that defines some claims and ways of making claims as feasible, appropriate, even rational.

3   How Important are Frames in Accounting for Key Movement Processes Outcomes?

It is surprising, given the theoretical attestations to frames' importance, that studies systematically assessing frames' impacts remain relatively few. How important are frames in accounting for why movements emerge when they do and for how successful they are in realizing their goals? And what features of frames best predict their influence? In the following, we draw on comparative studies where they exist, along with more fragmentary evidence, in order to identify some of the conditions for frames' impact.

In the political process models that dominate the field, effective frames are a critical variable in accounting for movement emergence. In the absence of frames making obvious the necessity and viability of protest, the presence of political opportunities and powerful mobilizing networks will come to nought (McAdam, Tarrow, and Tilly 2001). For example, the emergence of a northern black voting bloc to which federal officials were beholden supplied the objective political opportunity for a postwar Southern civil rights movement. Without a compelling set of arguments for the urgency of fighting Jim Crow, however, the movement would have remained small, elite, and probably ineffectual (McAdam 1982).

But if effective frames depend on their ability to convey the viability of protest, that is, its likelihood of political impact, then the existence of political opportunities should be a precondition for effective frames. This is what Koopmans and Duyendak (1995) argue in their cross-national study of anti-nuclear mobilization. Public opinion that was opposed to nuclear power tended to follow movements' success in winning changes in nuclear energy policy rather than precede it. Even where there was little in the way of public opposition to nuclear power, if the political system was receptive to an anti-nuclear challenge, mobilization was likely. For these authors, then, effective frames are a consequence of political opportunities rather than a variable that exists alongside them.

In her study of American women's suffrage mobilization, Holly McCammon (2001) found something different still: resonant frames spurred protest in the absence of political opportunities. Between 1886 and 1914, some states seemed much likelier candidates for the formation of state-level suffrage associations than others. With a prior history of state suffrage legislation, influential third parties, and a reform process that was open to outsiders, these states offered the political opportunities that Koopmans and Duyendak found were critical to mobilization. Yet these were not necessarily the states in which suffrage associations were formed. By contrast, the manner in which activists framed their cause did account for where such associations were formed. Where activists argued that women were citizens and therefore just as deserving as men of equal suffrage, they met with deaf ears. Where they argued that women brought special, "womanly" skills to the voting booth, including an ability to solve problems relating to women, children, and families, they were successful in mobilizing suffrage supporters. The kind of equality argument that is familiar to us today was simply too radical to mobilize people effectively.

How, then, should we adjudicate among these possibilities: that mobilization depends on the existence of resonant frames *and* political opportunities (McAdam, Tarrow, and Tilly 2001), or on the existence just of political opportunities (Koopmans and Duyendak 1995), or on the existence just of resonant frames (McCammon 2001)? McCammon suggests that where women lacked the vote, the openness of the state to voters' influence had little import for women's decision to mobilize. So frames may matter more where political opportunities are lacking. In his study of mobilization against drunk driving, John McCarthy (1994) provides another gloss on the relationship between political opportunities and frames. At a time when an "auto safety" frame was hegemonic for talking about automobile-related deaths, agencies within the government were trying to promote a "drunk driving" frame. In the latter, intoxicated drivers rather than poor automobile design was the problem. Government reformers had little luck in gaining public support for that frame, however, until citizen activists began to promote it. Activists were aided by government reformers, and they, in turn, provided the media with tragic stories of drunk drivers and unnecessary deaths. In short order, the drunk driving frame eclipsed the auto safety frame in the public consciousness. More than providing political opportunities, state actors here helped to generate challengers' frames.

Along with a better understanding of the relation between political opportunities and frames, we need a better understanding of the relation between indigenous mobilizing networks and frames. In political process accounts, such networks supply the solidary incentives that persuade people to participate. But McCammon found that mobilization occurred whether or not local networks of dissent existed. Powerful frames may be able to substitute for indigenous networks in spurring protest. More evidence for that proposition: some of the most prominent collective actors in the postwar era—women, the elderly, gays and lesbians, and the disabled—generally had had little day-to-day contact with each other before movements got off the ground. Movement organizations framed collective identities around which people then began to create networks (Minkoff 1997). More evidence still: John Glenn (2001) found that "civil society" was essential to successful democratic transitions in Eastern Europe—but civil society not as actual institutions but as a framing strategy. Successful political challengers in Poland and Czechoslovakia invoked a civil society frame: they argued that the Communist regime was violating citizens' rights and that the solution was change through peaceful negotiation. In both countries, the pitch brought together diverse groups, including some within the government, in a coalition for effective reform.

Like the research on movement emergence, that on movement outcomes points to the influence of framing, here independent not only of the receptiveness of the political system but also of how well resourced and disruptive movement groups are. In their study of homeless mobilization in eight American cities, Cress and Snow (2000) found that homeless groups advancing coherent and focused frames were more likely to succeed in winning representation on city task forces, resources like office space, and new provisions for homeless people. In different combinations, activists' use of disruptive tactics, their access to sympathetic allies, and the existence of city agencies targeting homelessness also mattered. But Cress and Snow consistently found that when groups used diagnostic and prognostic frames that focused on specific problems (for example, shelter conditions rather than "home-lessness"), pinned responsibility on specific groups rather than, say, "the govern-ment," and proposed viable solutions such as the "investigation of shelter conditions," they were more likely to win results.

That some organizations advanced coherent and articulate frames was no acci-dent, say Cress and Snow. Rather, such organizations tended to have existed for some time, had met regularly, and had planned a series of protest events. Their longevity provided activists the time and space to deliberate over framing choices. This raises a larger issue. As we noted, most depictions of framing have activists seeking to match effectively their rhetoric to their political circumstances. What, then, makes activists more or less adept at doing that? As Cress and Snow suggest, features of the organizations doing the framing seem important. McCammon argued that the existence of *indigenous* organizations was not a precondition for mobilization, but that the existence of *national* suffrage organizations was. Such groups supplied not only funding but tactical advice and traveling speakers. McCammon does not say this, but such groups may have been better equipped to figure out what kinds of pitches would resonate with their audiences. Other research suggests that decentralized movement structures may encourage ideological experi-mentation as activists adapt agendas to the needs, aspirations, and skills of local people (Gerlach and Hine 1970; Polletta 2000); and that groups with more hetero-geneous memberships may be less constrained by familiar claims-making strategies (Ganz 2000). These just hint at some of the factors involved in groups' framing skill.

What is it about frames themselves that secure movement groups support, participation, and concessions from those in power? McCammon argues that a frame centered on women's equality was simply foreign to potential supporters' world-view. Cress and Snow found that frames that were more coherent and articulate were likely to win the movement victories. These empirical findings accord with propositions long made by framing theorists. Influential frames are clear and coherent, with diagnostic, prognostic, and motivational elements well integrated. Protagonists and antagonists should be sharply delineated, and the viability, moral necessity, and urgency of protest made indisputable. Frames should seem credible to audiences, as well as consonant with their experiences, and congruent with their beliefs, myths, and world-views. Frame resonance, to continue with the scenario posited by framing scholars, leads to people's participation in and support for the movement and generates pressure on decision-makers to make concessions to it.

These propositions are plausible. But they may miss some of the ways in which frames have political impact. Consider, first, the argument that influential frames are clear and coherent, with a well-specified rationale for participation and a clear distinction between "we" and "they." In her study of the 1960 black student sit-ins, Polletta (1998) found that the stories students told about the protests as they were occurring were remarkably *unclear* about the sources of the protest, vague about antagonists, and downright dismissive of students' own agency. In letters to campus newspapers, editorials, flyers, and personal correspondence, students represented the sit-ins as spontaneous and impulsive. "*No one* started it," one insisted. And yet the stories helped to mobilize thousands of students to participate. Polletta argues that the stories' *failure* to fully explain the protest, their inability to specify the unspecifiable point at which individual action became collective and resistance became opposition, called for more stories, and for more actions to recount. That spurred students to participate. There are two ways to interpret this finding. One is that narratives may operate differently than other discursive forms. To talk about framing as a generic process may miss important differences in how stories, logical arguments, analogies, and other discursive forms work. The other possibility is that the importance of clarity in persuasion may be overrated. We noted earlier research suggesting the internal diversity and indeed, inconsistency in people's ideological beliefs (Billig et al. 1988). It is possible that effective frames may actually combine disparate, even contradictory ideas. They may seem, as a result, both fair-minded and admirably pointed in their claims. Or they may preempt criticism by incorporating what should be discrediting information. In that sense, a perception of frames' coherence may follow from their resonance rather produce it.

Frames' *credibility* may similarly be a consequence rather than a cause of their resonance. Framing theorists, recall, consider frames' empirical credibility and their congruence with familiar myths and world-views to be independent conditions for their effectiveness (Snow and Benford 1988). Narrative theorists argue, to the contrary, that accounts are often thought to be truer the more they resemble familiar stories. That is, they have a beginning, middle, and end, a moral, and a plot derived from a canon of familiar plots (White 1980). We believe particular stories because we have heard them before. If frames' ambiguity functions for activists as a persuasive resource, frames' dependence on canonical plots poses a real constraint. Activists' claims may be dismissed simply on account of their unfamiliarity.

There are other obstacles to activists' ability to get their message across. We noted earlier that conventional assumptions about what kinds of claims are appropriate to make, what kinds of frames are persuasive, and what kinds of people are authoritative, guide political actors' framing efforts. Even if activists manage to concoct an effective message, their ability to get that message to the public depends on the mainstream media. And, as numerous scholars have pointed out, the media are rarely cooperative. Journalists' dependence on official sources, their tendency to pin systemic problems on individuals, and their commitment to presenting both sides of a conflict, even when counter-movement groups are small in number and otherwise uninfluential, diminishes the persuasive power of activists' framing efforts (Gitlin 1980; Smith et al. 2001). Movement scholars have paid special attention to the media's tendency to focus on events rather than conditions (Iyengar 1994). Activists stage demonstrations in order to draw attention to broad social injustices but the press tends to concentrate on the event itself: the number of participants, the number of arrests, the presence of counterdemonstrators, and so on. The point of the demonstration gets lost (Smith et al. 2001).

On the other hand, another body of research, less frequently cited by social movement scholars, presents a more sanguine picture of activists' prospects for favorable coverage. Journalists' reliance on *exemplars* in news stories may serve movements well. Exemplars are the stories, examples, and first-hand accounts that describe an issue from the perspective of an individual (Zillmann and Brosius 2000). Experimental research shows that when presented with exemplars and with information that contradicts the exemplars, audiences tend to see the exemplars as reflecting majority opinion. For example, if audiences are exposed to a statement in a simulated radio broadcast that, "two-thirds of Americans support the war," after they have heard a man on the street express his disapproval of the war, they tend to believe that more people oppose the war. Moreover, audiences are likely to modify their own opinions in line with those of exemplars. This is true even when the issues are controversial ones (Perry and Gonzenbach 1997). What this means for movement groups is that making people affected by the issue in question available to reporters may get the movement's frame into the media. In this sense, personalizing the movement's cause may not undermine it.

At least, this is the case in the United States. The Ferree team (Ferree et al. 2002) found that the American media was much more likely to credit the views of grassroots groups and ordinary people than was the German media, which relied overwhelmingly on state and party representatives as sources. Activists in this country benefit from a populist wariness of experts that extends to media reporting, an attitude that stems at least in part from efforts on the part of movements in the 1960s and 1970s to challenge conventional notions of expertise.

We highlight the latter also because it suggests a way in which frames may be influential that has not been much discussed. On most accounts, frames have impact when their targets accept a frame's definition of the problem and solution. This may mean that policy-makers adopt the specific solutions pressed by a movement group or that they adopt policies that are not inconsistent with the group's frame, as was the case following the successful anti-homelessness campaigns that Cress and Snow (2000) studied. Frame impact may mean, more generally, that the movement's issue is acknowledged as a significant social problem, as, for example, violence against gays and lesbians came to be recognized as a hate crime (Jenness 1995). It may mean that a movement is able to get its issues permanently on the table, as were women activists in the Catholic Church (Katzenstein 1998).

Frames may also have impact by redefining what counts as authoritative knowledge. Here, it is not so much the content of the frame but the manner in which the frame is advanced that is influential. In their framing efforts, movement groups may challenge who counts as a legitimate spokesperson, what issues qualify for public discussion, what kinds of evidence are authoritative. The alternatives they model may influence practices within diverse institutions. So, Ferree et al. (2002) suggest that activists' commitment to the authority of personal experience in the 1960s and 1970s has filtered down to news reporting practices. Another example: in the 1980s, AIDS activists succeeded in gaining formal representation on federal research review committees. But they also gained recognition for AIDS patients' accounts as a form of authoritative knowledge in drug research (Epstein 1996). Again, it is the *how* of movement framing that is important here in altering the *how* of news reporting and the *how* of scientific research.

This returns to our point about institutional logics as both the sources and products of movement frames. In addition to gains such as formal representation and policy reform, movements may change the norms governing how organizations within an institutional sphere operate. Changing organizational culture, in this sense, means changing the rules of the game.

4   CONCLUSION

Frames matter. The devil for social movement scholars is in showing how and when and how much they matter. The thinness of theory on frames' sources and impacts reflects several things: the single-case orientation of much of the research on framing; the difficulty of disentangling causal factors in processes such as movement emergence, trajectories, and impacts; and especially, the difficulty of isolating the independent force of ideas. In this chapter, we have focused on the neglect of the cultural environment in accounting for frames' origins and impacts. Drawing on research from outside the framing perspective as well as from within it, we have highlighted the diverse cultural materials from which frames are drawn. Such materials are not limited to ideological traditions of dissent. We have also sought to elucidate the cultural constraints on activists' framing choices as well as the neglected mechanisms by which frames have political impact. In particular, we have emphasized the role of familiar relationships, routine practices, and institutionalized rules, both in spawning frames and in limiting their reach. And we have drawn attention to the surprising virtues of ambiguity and inconsistency in persuasive efforts.

Much work remains to be done on these and other fronts. If several exemplary studies have recently demonstrated the independent influence of frames in triggering mobilization and in accounting for its outcomes, we still know little about how frames interact with other factors considered important in those processes. If framing theorists have advanced plausible propositions about what makes for effective frames, those propositions can only be strengthened by incorporating the sometimes counterintuitive findings from social and cognitive psychology on how ideas achieve their effects. That activists' messages work in ways unanticipated even by them is unsurprising, but also the source of important insight.

REFERENCES

BABB, S. 1996. A true American system of finance: frame resonance in the U.S. labor movement, 1866 to 1886. *American Sociological Review*, 61: 1033–52.

BAZERMAN, M. H. 1983. Negotiator judgement: a critical look at the rationality assumption. *American Behavioral Scientist*, 27: 211–28.

BENFORD, R. D. 1993a. "You could be the hundredth monkey:" collective action frames and vocabularies of motive within the nuclear disarmament movement. *Sociological Inquiry*, 34: 195–216.

——1993b. Frame disputes within the nuclear disarmament movement. *Social Forces*, 71: 677–701.

——1997. An insider's critique of the social movement framing perspective. *Sociological Inquiry*, 67: 409–30.

——and HUNT, S. 1992. Dramaturgy and social movements: the social construction and communication of power. *Sociological Inquiry*, 62: 36–55.

——and SNOW, D. A. 2000. Framing processes and social movements: an overview and assessment. *Annual Review of Sociology*, 26: 611–39.

BERBRIER, M. 1998. "Half the battle:" cultural resonance, framing processes, and ethnic affectations in contemporary white separatist rhetoric. *Social Problems*, 45: 431–50.

BEREJEKIAN, J. 1997. The gains debate: framing state choice. *American Political Science Review*, 91: 789–805.

BERNSTEIN, M. 1997. Celebration and suppression: the strategic uses of identity by the lesbian and gay movement. *American Journal of Sociology*, 103: 531–65.

BERNSTEIN, S. 2002. International institutions and the framing of domestic policies: the Kyoto Protocol and Canada's response to climate change. *Policy Sciences*, 35: 203

BILLIG, M., CONDOR, C., EDWARDS, D., GANE, M., MIDDLETON, D., and RADLEY, A. 1988. *Ideological Dilemmas: A Social Psychology of Everyday Thinking*. London: Sage.

BINDER, A. J. 2004. *Contentious Curricula: Afrocentrism and Creationism in American Public Schools*. Princeton, NJ: Princeton University Press.

BUMILLER, K. 1988. *The Civil Rights Society: The Social Construction of Victims*. Baltimore: Johns Hopkins University Press.

CARRAGEE, K. M., and ROEFS, W. 2004. The neglect of power in recent framing research. *Journal of Communication*, 54: 214.

CARROLL, W. K., and RATNER, R. S. 1996. Master framing and cross-movement networking in contemporary social movements. *Sociological Quarterly*, 37: 601–25.

CHABOT, S., and DUYVENDAK, J. W. 2002. Globalization and transnational diffusion between social movements: reconceptualizing the dissemination of the Gandhian repertoires and the "coming out" routine. *Theory and Society*, 31: 697–740.

CLEMENS, E. S. 1996. Organizational form as frame: collective identity and political strategy in the American Labor Movement 1880–1920. Pp. 205–26 in *Comparative Perspectives on Social Movements: Political Opportunities, Mobilizing Structures, and Cultural Framings*, ed. D. McAdam, J. D. McCarthy, and M. N. Zald. New York: Cambridge University Press.

CORNFIELD, D. B., and FLETCHER, B. 1998. Institutional constraints on social movement "frame extension:" shifts in the legislative agenda of the American Federation of Labor. *Social Forces*, 76: 1305–21.

CRESS, D., and SNOW, D. A. 2000. The outcomes of homeless mobilization: the influence of organization, disruption, political mediation, and framing. *American Journal of Sociology*, 105: 1063–104.

DIANI, M. 1996. Linking mobilization frames and political opportunities: insights from regional populism in Italy. *American Sociological Review*, 61: 1053–69.

ELLINGSON, S. 1995. Understanding the dialectic of discourse and collective action: public debate and rioting in antebellum Cincinnati. *American Journal of Sociology*, 101: 100–44.

EPSTEIN, S. 1996. *Impure Science: AIDS, Activism, and the Politics of Knowledge*. Berkeley: University of California Press.

ESACOVE, A. W. 2004. Dialogic framing: the framing/counterframing of "partial-birth" abortion. *Sociological Inquiry*, 74: 70–101.

EVANS, J. H. 1997. Multi-organizational fields and social movement organization frame content: the religious pro-choice movement. *Sociological Inquiry*, 67: 451–69.

FERREE, M. M. 2003. Resonance and radicalism: feminist framing in the abortion debates of the United States and Germany. *American Journal of Sociology*, 109: 304–44.

—— and MERRILL, D. 2000. Hot movements, cold cognition: thinking about social movements in gendered frames. *Contemporary Sociology*, 29: 454–62.

—— and ROTH, S. 1998. Gender, class, and the interaction between social movements: a strike of West Berlin day care workers. *Gender and Society*, 12: 626–48.

—— GAMSON, W. A., GERHARDS, J., and RUCHT, D. 2002. *Shaping Abortion Discourse: Democracy and the Public Sphere in Germany and the United States*. Cambridge: Cambridge University Press.

FIREMAN, B., and RYTINA, S. 1982. *Encounters with Unjust Authority*. Homewood, Ill.: Dorsey.

GAMSON, W. A. 1988. Political discourse and collective action. Pp. 219–44 in *International Social Movement Research*, vol. 1, ed. B. Klandermans, H. Kriesi, and S. Tarrow. Greenwich: JAI Press.

—— 1991. Commitment and agency in social movements. *Sociological Forum*, 6: 27–50.

—— 1992. *Talking Politics*. New York: Cambridge University Press.

—— 2004. Bystanders, public opinion, and the media. Pp. 242–61 in *The Blackwell Companion to Social Movements*, ed. D. A. Snow, S. A. Soule, and H. Kriesi. New York: Blackwell.

—— and MEYER, D. S. 1996. Framing political opportunity. Pp. 275–90 in *Comparative Perspectives on Social Movements: Political Opportunities, Mobilizing Structures, and Cultural Framings*, ed. D. McAdam, J. D. McCarthy, and M. N. Zald. New York: Cambridge University Press.

GANZ, M. 2000. Resources and resourcefulness: strategic capacity in the unionization of California agriculture. *American Journal of Sociology*, 105: 1003–62.

GERHARDS, J., and RUCHT, D. 1992. Mesomobilization: organizing and framing in two protest campaigns in West Germany. *American Journal of Sociology*, 98: 555–95.

GITLIN, T. 1980. *The Whole World is Watching: Mass Media in the Making & Unmaking of the New Left*. Berkeley: University of California Press.

GLENN, J. K., III 2001. *Framing Democracy: Civil Society and Civic Movements in Eastern Europe*. Stanford, Calif.: Stanford University Press.

GOFFMAN, E. 1974. *Frame Analysis: An Essay on the Organization of Experience*. New York: Harper and Row.

GROVES, J. 2001. Animal rights and the politics of emotion: folk constructions of emotion in the animal rights movement. Pp. 212–29 in *Passionate Politics: Emotions and Social Movements*, ed. J. Goodwin, J. J. M., and F. Polletta. Chicago: University of Chicago Press.

HART, S. 2001. *Cultural Dilemmas of Progressive Politics: Styles of Engagement among Grass-roots Activists*. Chicago: University of Chicago Press.

HIRSCH, E. L. 1990. Sacrifice for the cause: group processes, recruitment, and commitment in a student social movement. *American Sociological Review*, 55: 243–55.

HUNT, S. A., and BENFORD, R. D. 1994. Identity talk in the peace and justice movements. *Journal of Contemporary Ethnography*, 22: 488–517.

——— and SNOW, D. A. 1994. Identity fields: framing processes and the social construction of movement identities. Pp. 185–208 in *New Social Movements: From Ideology to Identity*, ed. E. Laraña, H. Johnston, and J. R. Gusfield. Philadelphia: Temple University Press.

IMIG, D. R., and TARROW, S. 2001. *Contentious Europeans: Protest and Politics in an Emerging Polity*. Lanham, Md.: Rowman and Littlefield.

IYENGAR, S. 1994. *Is Anyone Responsible? How Television Frames Political Issues*. Chicago: University of Chicago Press.

JASPER, J. M. 1997. *The Art of Moral Protest: Culture, Biography, and Creativity in Social Movements*. Chicago: University of Chicago Press.

——— 1999. Sentiments, ideas, and animals: rights talk and animal protection. Pp.147–57 in *Ideas, Ideologies, and Social Movements*, ed. P. A. Coclanis and S. W. Bruchey. Columbia: University of South Carolina Press.

JENKINS, J. C., and PERROW, C. 1977. Insurgency of the powerless: farm worker movements (1946–1972). *American Sociological Review*, 42: 249–68.

JENNESS, V. 1995. Social movement growth, domain expansion, and framing processes: the gay/lesbian movement and violence against gays and lesbians as a social problem. *Social Problems*, 42: 145–70.

JOHNSTON, H. 2002. Verification and proof in frame and discourse analysis. Pp. 62–91 in *Methods of Social Movement Research*, ed. B. Klandermans and S. Staggenborg. Minneapolis: University of Minnesota Press.

——— and SNOW, D.A. 1998. Subcultures and the emergence of Estonian nationalist opposition, 1945–1990. *Sociological Perspectives*, 41: 473–97.

KATZENSTEIN, M. F. 1998. *Faithful and Fearless: Moving Feminist Protest Inside the Church and Military*. Princeton, NJ: Princeton University Press.

KLANDERMANS, B. 1988. The formation and mobilization of consensus. Pp. 173–97 in *International Social Movement Research*, vol. 1, ed. B. Klandermans, H. Kriesi, and S. Tarrow. Greenwich: JAI Press.

—— 1992. The social construction of protest and multiorganizational fields. Pp. 77–103 in *Frontiers in Social Movement Theory*, ed. A. D. Morris and C. M. Mueller. New Haven, Conn.: Yale University Press.

—— 1997. *The Social Psychology of Protest.* Oxford: Blackwell

—— de WEERD, M., SABUCEDO, J. M., and RODRIGUEZ, M. 2001. Framing contention: Dutch and Spanish farmers confront the EU. In Imig and Tarrow 2001, 77–95.

KOOPMANS, R. and DUYVENDAK, J. W. 1995. The political construction of the nuclear energy issue and its impact on the mobilization of anti-nuclear movements in Western Europe. *Social Problems*, 42: 235–51.

MANSBRIDGE, J. 1986. *Why We Lost the ERA.* Chicago: University of Chicago Press.

MCADAM, D. 1982. *Political Process and the Development of Black Insurgency.* Chicago: University of Chicago Press.

—— 1994. Culture and social movements. Pp. 36–57 in *New Social Movements: From Ideology to Identity*, ed. E. Laraña, H. Johnston, and J. R. Gusfield. Philadelphia: Temple University Press.

—— MCCARTHY, D., and ZALD, M. N. 1996. Introduction: opportunities, mobilizing structures, and framing processes—toward a synthetic, comparative perspective on social movements. Pp. 1–20 in *Comparative Perspectives on Social Movements: Political Opportunities, Mobilizing Structures, and Cultural Framings*, ed. D. McAdam, J. D. McCarthy, and M. N. Zald. New York: Cambridge University Press.

—— TARROW, S. and TILLY, C. 2001. *Dynamics of Contention.* Cambridge: Cambridge University Press.

MCCAMMON, H. 2001. Stirring up suffrage sentiment: the formation of the state woman suffrage organizations, 1866–1914. *Social Forces*, 80: 449–80.

MCCARTHY, J. D. 1994. Activists, authorities, and media framing of drunk driving. Pp. 133–67 in *New Social Movements: From Ideology to Identity*, ed. E. Laraña, H. Johnston, and J. R. Gusfield. Philadelphia: Temple University Press.

—— and ZALD, M. N. 1977. Resource mobilization and social movements: a partial theory. *American Journal of Sociology*, 82: 1212–41.

MINKOFF, D. C. 2001. Social movement politics and organization. Pp. 282–94 in *The Blackwell Companion to Sociology*, ed. J. R. Blau. Malden, Mass.: Blackwell.

MORRIS, A.D. 1984. *The Origins of the Civil Rights Movement: Black Communities Organizing for Change.* New York: Free Press.

NOONAN, R. K. 1995. Women against the state: political opportunities and collective action frames in Chile's transition to democracy. *Sociological Forum*, 10: 81–111.

OLIVER, P., and JOHNSTON, H. 2000. What a good idea! Ideologies and frames in social movement research. *Mobilization*, 5: 37–54.

OSA, M. 2003. *Solidarity and Contention: Networks of Polish Opposition.* Minneapolis: University of Minnesota Press.

PERRY, S. D., and GONZENBACH, W. J. 1997. Effects of news exemplification extended: considerations of controversiality and perceived future opinion. *Journal of Broadcasting and Electronic Media*, 41: 229–45.

POLLETTA, F. 1998. "It was like a fever...": narrative and identity in social protest. *Social Problems*, 45: 137–59.

—— 1999. Free spaces in collective action. *Theory and Society*, 28: 1–38.

—— 2002. *Freedom Is an Endless Meeting: Democracy in American Social Movements.* Chicago: University of Chicago Press.

POLLETTA, F. 2004. Culture is not in your head. Pp. 97–110 in *Rethinking Social Movements: Structure, Meaning, and Emotion*, ed. J. Goodwin and J. M. Jasper. Larham, Md.: Rowman and Littlefield.

——and JASPER, J. M. 2001. Collective identity in social movements. *Annual Review of Sociology*, 27: 283–305.

ROCHON, T. R. 1998. *Culture Moves: Ideas, Activism, and Changing Values*. Princeton, NJ: Princeton University Press.

SACKS, K. B. 1988. Gender and grassroots leadership. Pp. 77–94 in *Women and the Politics of Empowerment*, ed. A. Bookman and S. Morgen. Philadelphia: Temple University Press.

SCHON, D. M., and REIN, M. 1994. *Frame Reflection: Toward the Resolution of Intractable Policy Controversies*. New York: Basic Books.

SCHUDSON, M. 1989. How culture works: perspectives from media studies on the efficacy of symbols. *Theory and Society*, 18: 153–80.

SCHULTZ, V. 1990. Telling stories about women and work: judicial interpretations of sex segregation in the workplace in Title VII cases raising the lack of interest argument. *Harvard Law Review*, 103: 1749–943.

SELZNICK, P. 1957. *Leadership in Administration: A Sociological Interpretation*. New York: Harper and Row.

SMITH, J., McCARTHY, J. D., McPHAIL, C., and AUGUSTYN, B. 2001. From protest to agenda building: description of bias in media coverage of protest events in Washington, D.C. *Social Forces*, 79: 1397–423.

SNOW, D. A. 2004. Framing processes, ideology, and discursive fields. Pp. 380–412 in *The Blackwell Companion to Social Movements*, ed. D. A. Snow, S. A. Soule, and H. Kriesi. Malden, Mass.: Blackwell.

——and BENFORD, R. D. 1988. Ideology, frame resonance and participant mobilization. Pp. 197–217 in *International Social Movement Research*, vol. 1, ed. B. Klandermans, H. Kriesi, and S. Tarrow. Greenwich: JAI Press.

————1992. Master frames and cycles of protest. Pp. 133–55 in *Frontiers in Social Movement Theory*, ed. A. D. Morris and C. M. Mueller. New Haven, Conn.: Yale University Press.

————2000. Clarifying the relationships between framing and ideology. *Mobilization*, 5: 55–60.

——ROCHFORD, E. B., WARDEN, S., and BENFORD, R. 1986. Frame alignment processes, micromobilization, and movement participation. *American Sociological Review*, 51: 464–81.

STEINBERG, M. W. 1998. Tilting the frame: considerations on collective framing from a discursive turn. *Theory and Society*, 27: 845–72.

——1999a. The talk and back talk of collective action: a dialogic analysis of repertoires of discourse among nineteenth-century English cotton-spinners. *American Journal of Sociology*, 105: 736–80.

——1999b. *Words: Working-Class Formation, Collective Action, and Discourse in Early Nineteenth-Century England*. Ithaca, NY: Cornell University Press.

STOECKER, R. 1995. Community, movement organization: the problem of identity convergence in collective action. *Sociological Quarterly*, 36: 111–30.

TARROW, S. 1994. *Power in Movement: Social Movements, Collective Action and Politics*. New York: Cambridge University Press.

——1998. *Power in Movement*, 2nd edn. Cambridge: Cambridge University Press.

TETREAULT, M. A. 1993. Civil society in Kuwait: protected spaces and women's rights. *Middle East Journal*, 47: 275–91.

TILLY, C. 1999. Epilogue. Now where? Pp. 407–19 in *State/Culture: State-Formation After the Cultural Turn*, ed. G. Steinmetz. Ithaca, NY: Cornell University Press.

TVERSKY, A., and KAHNEMAN, D. 1986. Rational choice and the framing of decisions. *Journal of Business*, 59: 251–78.

VALOCCHI, S. 1994. Riding the crest of a protest wave? Collective action frames in the gay liberation movement, 1969–1973. *Mobilization*, 4: 59–73.

VOSS, K. 1996. The collapse of a social movement: the interplay of mobilizing structures, framing, and political opportunities in the Knights of Labor. Pp. 227–58 in *Comparative Perspectives on Social Movements: Political Opportunities, Mobilizing Structures, and Cultural Framings*, ed. D. McAdam, J. D. McCarthy, and M. N. Zald. New York: Cambridge University Press.

WESTBY, D. L. 2002. Strategic imperative, ideology, and frame. *Mobilization*, 7: 287–304.

WHITE, H. 1980. The value of narrativity in the representation of reality. *Critical Inquiry*, 7: 5–27.

WILLIAMS, G. I., and WILLIAMS, R. H. 1995. "All we want is equality": rhetorical framing in the fathers' rights movement. Pp. 191–212 in *Images of Issues: Typifying Contemporary Social Problems*, ed. J. Best. New York: Aldine de Gruyter.

WILLIAMS, R. H. 2004. The cultural contexts of collective action: constraints, opportunities, and the symbolic life of social movements. Pp. 91–115 in *The Blackwell Companion to Social Movements*, ed. D. A. Snow, S. A. Soule, and H. Kriesi. Malden, Mass.: Blackwell.

ZALD, M. N. 1996. Culture, ideology, and strategic framing. Pp. 261–74 in *Comparative Perspectives on Social Movements: Political Opportunities, Mobilizing Structures, and Cultural Framings*, ed. D. McAdam, J. D. McCarthy, and M. N. Zald. New York: Cambridge University Press.

ZILLMAN, D., and BROSIUS, H. 2000. *Exemplification in Communication: The Influence of Case Reports on the Perception of Issues*. Mahwah, NJ: Lawrence Erlbaum.

CHAPTER 11

....

MEMORY, INDIVIDUAL AND COLLECTIVE

....

ALEIDA ASSMANN

Over the last decade, memory has been acknowledged as a "leading concept" of cultural studies. Memory research investigates how we live by our memories, how we are haunted by them, how we use and abuse them. This discourse is quickly expanding; the books and essays that have appeared on the subject already fill whole libraries. Memory research carries the potential of a paradigmatically interdisciplinary project; it includes neuronal, medical, and psychological as well as literary, cultural, social, and political studies. The scientific and scholarly discovery of memory reflects and interacts with a "memory boom" in society and politics. A new concern with the past is expressed by a new wave of memoirs, testimonies, films with historical themes, museums, and monuments. This orientation toward the past is a recent phenomenon. It started only in the late 1980s and developed fully in the 1990s. Possible motivations for this new and acute interest in memory and the past are:

- The breakdown of the so-called "grand narratives" at the end of the cold war that had provided frameworks for the interpretation of the past and future orientation and, together with it, the resurgence of frozen memories that had been contained by the larger ideological formations; with the change of political framework, access was finally possible to the sealed archives of the former Communist countries, which provided a new basis for history and memory.
- The postcolonial situation in which humans that have been deprived of their indigenous history and culture are trying to recover their own narratives and memories.

- The post-traumatic situation after the Holocaust and the two World Wars, the accumulated violence, cruelty, and guilt of which is surfacing only gradually and belatedly after a period of psychic paralysis and silence.
- The decline of a generation of witnesses to these traumas whose experiential memory is now being replaced by translating it in externalized and mediated forms.
- The new digital revolution in communication technology that changes the status of information by creating more efficient ways of storing and circulating information without, however, securing its long-term durability.

1   FOUR MEMORY FORMATS

In everyday discourse, we generally refer to two forms of memory: individual and collective. My argument will be that these two categories do not suffice to describe the complex network of memories in which humans participate. Our personal memories include much more than what we, as individuals, have ourselves experienced.

Individuals' personal and collective memories interact. The term collective memory, however, is too vague and conflates important distinctions. The larger and more encompassing memory of which individuals are part of include the family, the neighborhood, the generation, the society, the state, and the culture we live in. These different dimensions of memory, differing in scope and range, overlap and intersect within the individual who incorporates those memories in various ways. Humans acquire these memories not only via lived experience, but also via interacting, communicating, learning, identifying, and appropriating. It is often not easy to determine where one type of memory ends and another begins. The usual dichotomy of "individual" versus "collective" does little justice to the complex amalgam of memories, which I will try to disentangle by distinguishing four levels or "formats of memory": (1) individual memory; (2) social memory; (3) political memory; and (4) cultural memory.

1.1   Individual Memory

Contemporary neurologists and cognitive psychologists have a rather poor view of human memory capacity. According to these scientists, human memory is not designed for accurate representations of past experiences but is notoriously distorting and unreliable. The German neuroscientist Wolf Singer has defined memories as "data-based inventions" and Daniel Schacter, a psychologist at Harvard, has made a detailed list of what he called "the seven sins of memory" (Schacter 1999). There is also virtue in the vice, however, and Schacter himself emphasizes that the fallibility and notorious unreliability of our memories are perhaps better "conceptualized as by-products of adaptive features of memory than as flaws in system design or blunders made by Mother Nature during evolution" (Schacter, in Tulving 2000, 120).

Whatever our memories may be worth from a scientific point of view or from the point of view of a judge who is interested in a precise testimony, as human beings we have to rely on them, because they are what makes human beings human. The English philosopher John Locke insisted already at the end of the seventeenth century that without this capacity and at least a sense of its reliability, we could not construct a self nor could we communicate with others. Our memories are indispensable because they are the stuff out of which individual experiences, interpersonal relations, the sense of responsibility, and the image of our own identity are made. To be sure, it is always only a small part of our memory that is consciously processed and emplotted in a "story" that we construct as a backbone to our identity (Randall 1995). A large part of our memories, to put it in a Proustian language, "sleeps" within our bodies until it is "awakened" or triggered by some haphazard external stimulus. In such a case, these hitherto wholly somatic memories suddenly rise to the level of consciousness, reclaiming for a moment a sensuous presence, after which they may or may not be symbolically encoded and categorized for further conscious retrieval. There are not only involuntary memories; there are also inaccessible memories. They are "repressed," which means that they are locked up and guarded by taboos or trauma. These memories are too painful or shameful to be recalled to consciousness without external therapeutic help or legal enforcement. For traumatic memories to rise to the surface, a positive social climate of empathy and recognition is necessary.

Psychologists have emphasized the existence and interplay of various memory systems within the human brain (Tulving 2000). There is "procedural" memory that stores body skills and movements that have become habitual, and "semantic" memory that stores the fund of knowledge that is acquired mentally through conscious learning. There is also "episodic" memory that processes autobiographical experiences. The following four general traits characterize episodic memories:

They are perspectival and idiosyncratic. These memories are necessarily bound to a specific stance and thus limited to one perspective, which means that they are neither exchangeable nor transferable. Every living individual occupies a specific place in the world which is not interchangeable. For instance the oldest child in a family has a different vantage point from any other sibling and thus, in addition to a shared fund of memories, owns also a set of exclusive memories.

They are fragmentary. What we recall are, as a rule, cut-out bits and pieces, moments without a before or after. They flash up isolated scenes within a network of seemingly random associations without order, sequence, or cohesion. These latter qualities are acquired only if memories are tied into a larger narrative that retrospectively provides them with a form and a structure. It is through such retrograde strategies of "emplotment" (White 1992) that individual shards of memory gain a retrievable shape and are complemented with meaning.

Fragmented and random though they may be, episodic memories never exist in complete isolation but are connected to a wider network of other memories and, what is even more important, the memories of others. In such networks of association and communication, memories are continuously socially readapted, be it that they are substantiated and corroborated, or challenged and corrected. Due to their connective and adaptive structure, they can be integrated in larger complexes. It is thus that they not only acquire coherence and consistency, but also create social bonds.

They are transient, changing, and volatile. Some undergo changes in the course of time as one grows older and the living conditions are altered; some fade and are lost altogether. As social structures of relevance and individual value systems change, things that used to be important recede into the background and hitherto unheeded things may call for new retrospective attention. Those memories that are tied into narratives and are often rehearsed are best preserved, but even they are limited in time: they are dissolved with the death of the person who owned and inhabited them.

1.2   Social Memory

Individual memory is the dynamic medium for processing subjective experience and building up a social identity. If these memories are to some extent idiosyncratic, this certainly does not mean that they are exclusively private and solipsistic. According to the French sociologist and memory theoretician Maurice Halbwachs (1925), a completely isolated individual could not establish any memory at all. Memories, he argues, and his argument is corroborated by current psychological research, are built up, developed, and sustained in interaction, i.e. in social exchange with significant others. Following Halbwachs, we may say that our personal memories are generated in a milieu of social proximity, regular interaction, common forms of life, and shared experiences. As these are embodied memories, they are defined by clear temporal limits and extinguished with the death of the person. In the shape of stories and anecdotes transmitted in oral communication, some of the episodic memories can transcend the individual person's lifespan. They are recycled within a period of 80–100 years, which is the period within which the generations of a family—three as a rule, but sometimes up to five—exist simultaneously, forming a community of shared experience, stories, and memories.

The grandchildren still share some memories with their grandparents if they are recycled in the family memory. Even if these memories are anecdotalized and regularly rehearsed or stabilized by letters or photographs, they remain volatile and subject to change and fading away. Within that cycle of oral interaction they, as a rule, do not transcend the temporal range of three generations, a span amounting to at most 100 years.

We share our memories not only with members of our family and circles of friends and neighbors, but also with many of our contemporaries whom we may never have met or seen, for instance with the age-cohort to which we happen to belong. One form of social memory is generational memory, the importance of which was outlined by Karl Mannheim in a famous essay in 1928 and is being rediscovered by contemporary social psychologists (Mannheim 1952; Schuhmann and Scott 1989; Becker 2000). As a group of more or less the same age that has witnessed the same incisive historical events, generations share a common frame of beliefs, values, habits, and attitudes. The members of a generation tend to see themselves as different from preceding and succeeding generations. Within a generation, there is much tacit knowledge that can never be made fully explicit to members of another generation. Age separates in an existential way due to the temporality of experience. Avowed or unavowed, this shared generational memory is an important element in the constitution of personal memories, because "once formed, generational identity cannot change" (Conway 1997, 43). While familial generations are indistinguishable on the social level, social generations acquire a distinct profile through shared experience of incisive events as well as through an ongoing discourse of self-thematization. The invisible frame of shared experiences, hopes, values, and obsessions becomes tangible only when it shifts. Such shifts occur after a period of around thirty years when a new generation enters into offices and takes over public responsibility. The change of generations is paramount for the reconstruction of societal memory, the transformation of norms and values, and the renewal of cultural creativity (Singh, Skerrett, and Hogan 1996, introduction).

The generational timespan is also decisive for the belated processing of personal memories, especially when they are of a traumatic character. An interest in public monuments, films, and other forms of attention and commemoration tends to arise only after a lapse of at least fifteen or more years after the event. A comparative study on Dallas and Memphis has investigated how traumatic experiences were processed in different cities. The results were quite striking. In the city of Dallas in which John F. Kennedy was assassinated in 1963, no school and no street was named after the president. The same holds true for Memphis, which saw the assassination of Martin Luther King in 1968. In this city, not one street or school was named after the leader of the civil rights movement. Each city, however, had schools and streets named after the respective other victim. And both cities have established museums after a period of thirty years, documenting and commemorating the murder that occurred in its streets (Pennebaker and Banasik 1997, 11–13).

With the support of symbolic forms of commemoration, be they material such as monuments and museums, or procedural such as rites of commemoration, the limited temporal range of personal and generational memories can be infinitely extended in time. Then, however, they lose the quality of a generational experience and become a much more generalized form of memory that is opened up to members of succeeding generations. The monument of the Vietnam Memorial Wall (1982) with the names of the fallen soldiers is still very much a monument for social and embodied memories, primarily addressing the generation of the surviving soldiers and the families and friends of those who fell in battle. Being situated, however, as it is, in the vicinity of the Lincoln memorial and the Holocaust museum, it forms one of the "lieux de memoire" of a more inclusive national memory and identity.

1.3   Political Memory

To move from individual and social memory to political and cultural memory is to cross a threshold in time. Individual and social memory is embodied; both formats are grounded in lived experience; they cling to and abide with human beings and their embodied interaction. Political and cultural memory, on the other hand, are mediated; both are founded on the more durable carriers of external symbols and material representations; they rely not only on libraries, museums, and monuments, but also on various modes of education and repeated occasions for collective participation. While social forms of memory are *inter*generational, political and cultural forms of memory are designed as *trans*generational. As we pass the shadow-line from short-term to long-term durability, an embodied, implicit, heterogeneous, and fuzzy bottom-up memory is transformed into an explicit, homogeneous, and institutionalized top-down memory. This shift does not go unnoticed and may become the target of criticism and alienation (Novick 1999). However overlapping and intertwined social and political memory may be, they have become the objects of different academic disciplines. The bottom-up social memory is studied by social psychologists, who are interested in the ways in which historical events are perceived and remembered by individuals within their own lifespan. The top-down political memory is investigated by political scientists, who discuss the role of memory on the level of ideology formation and construction of collective identities that are geared towards political action. Social psychologists look at individuals in specific historical situations and investigate how memories are established and how experience is fabricated in the process of communication; political scientists examine collective units such as institutions, states, and nations and ask how memories are used and abused for political action and the formation of group identities (identity politics).

It must be emphasized here that the step from individual to collective memory does not afford an easy analogy. Institutions and groups do not possess a memory like individuals; there is, of course, no equivalent to the neurological system or the anthropological disposition. Institutions and larger social groups, such as nations, states, the church, or a firm do not "have" a memory; they "make" one for themselves with the aid of memorial signs such as symbols, texts, images, rites, ceremonies, places, and monuments. Together with such a memory, these groups and institutions "construct" an identity. Such a memory is based on selection and exclusion, neatly separating useful from not useful, and relevant from irrelevant memories. Hence a political memory is necessarily a mediated memory. It resides in material media, symbols and practices which have to be engrafted into the hearts and minds of individuals. The extent to which they take hold there depends on the efficiency of political pedagogy on the one hand and the level of patriotic or ethnic fervor on the other. An interest in a (national) political memory, for instance, was rather low in postwar Germany and increased only after reunification in 1989 (Olick 2003). Political memory is stronger in ethnically homogeneous groups and nations (such as Israel) as compared with multicultural nations (such as the United States).

Forms of participation in collective memory differ widely between social and political memory. While social memory is based on lived experience and hence on autobiographical memory, each individual will retain slightly different memories due to his or her specific position and perspective. The memory of the Holocaust, for instance, will vary vastly among survivors depending on whether they endured the torments of the concentration camps, hid in secret places, or managed to escape the perpetrators into exile. For the second and third generation of the survivors, however, as well as for the participants of other nations, this memory will be much more homogeneous as it is reconstructed by historians and represented by public narratives, images, and films. Individual access to collective memory occurs via various channels. They involve mental activities such as cognitive learning (or semantic memory) about the past, imaginative and emotive identification with images, roles, values, and narratives, and various forms of action such as celebrations, processions, and demonstrations. *History* turns into *memory* when it is transformed into forms of shared knowledge and collective identification and participation. In such cases, "history in general" is reconfigured into a particular and emotionally charged version of "our history," absorbing it as part of a collective identity. Collective participation in national memory is enforced in totalitarian states coercively via indoctrination and propaganda, and in democratic states via popular media, public discourse, and "liberal representation" (Williams 1998). In both cases, however, it relies on effective symbols and rites that enhance emotions of empathy and identification.

In order to transform ephemeral social memory into long-term collective memory, it has to be organized and elaborated. Some of the ways of organizing and elaborating collective memory are:

- emplotment of events in an affectively charged and mobilizing narrative;
- sites and monuments that present palpable relics;
- visual and verbal signs as aids of memory;
- commemoration rites that periodically reactivate the memory and enhance collective participation.

In this way, a political memory is stabilized and can be transmitted from generation to generation. Beyond these differences, there are also some similarities between personal and collective memory. Both are limited in scope and perspective. Selection and forgetting are as constitutive of individual as they are of collective memory. To emphasize this point, Nietzsche has introduced a term from optics, speaking of "the horizon" of memory which separates the known from the unknown, the relevant from the irrelevant (Nietzsche 1957 [1872], 64). Another term that he used was "plastic power," by which he meant the capacity to erect such boundary-lines between remembering and forgetting, between the significant and the insignificant, between what is of vital "interest" and what is merely "interesting". Without this filter, Nietzsche argued, there is no creation of identity (he used the term "character") and no possibility of an orientation for future action. Zygmunt Bauman has underscored this streamlining effect in the construction of national memory. He points out that national states "construct joint historical memories and do their best to discredit or suppress such stubborn memories as cannot be squeezed into shared traditions—now redefined in the state-appropriate quasi-legal terms, as 'our common heritage'" (1991, 64). It is this very process of exclusion that may later gives rise to new formations of subnational ethnic countermemories.

As my example for social memory has been generational memory, my example for political memory will be mainly national memory. It is not difficult to define the criteria for selection that have determined the construction of collective memory and identity in the past. Most conspicuous in this respect have been the memory constructions of nation states. Within this frame, only those historical referents were selected which strengthened a positive self-image and supported specific goals for the future. What did not fit into this heroic pattern was passed over and forgotten. For a hegemonic nation, victories are much easier to remember than defeats. Streets and metro-stations in Paris commemorate Napoleonic victories, but none of his defeats. In London, however, in the country of Wellington, there is a station with the name "Waterloo:" an obvious example of the selectivity of national memory. If we move from hegemonic nations to minority nations, however, we find that their memories are not those of winners but of losers, crystallizing around devastating defeats. Experiences of defeat can be erected into seminal cores for collective memory provided that they are emplotted in the martyriological narrative of the tragic hero (Giesen 2004). Defeats are commemorated with great pathos and ceremonial expense by nations who founded their identity on the consciousness of victims, whose whole aim it is to keep awake the memory of a suffered iniquity in order to mobilize heroic counteraction or to legitimate claims to redress. A conspicuous case in point is that of the Serbs, who have canonized the tragic heroes of the lost battle in the Kosovo against the Ottoman Turks in 1389, commemorating them in their annual religious calendar, singing their praises in extended oral epics, and using them as fuel for renewed ethnic battles (Volkan 1997). The citizens of Quebec commemorate the 1759 defeat of General Montcalm against colonial British rule. "Je me souviens," is written on the license plates of their cars. But also hegemonic nations and states have their reasons to remember assaults and defeats when they wish to consolidate their power by a sense of imminent danger. In this way, the English "remember, remember the 5th of November," the attempted assault on parliament in the Catholic uprising in 1605, and the Texans continue to "remember the Alamo." Another example is the history of Massada, which was incorporated into Israeli national memory in the 1960s (Lewis 1975). The message connected with this memory is: we will never more be victims! It serves as an invigorating heroic memory in a political situation which is under severe external pressure.

Collective national memory, in other words, is receptive to historical moments of triumph and defeat, provided they can be integrated into the semantics of a heroic or martyriological narrative. What cannot be integrated into such a narrative are moments of shame and guilt, which threaten and shatter the construction of a positive self-image. In referring to shame and guilt, we are speaking of traumatic experiences that must not be identified with the memories of the defeated. There are not only victors and vanquished in history; there are also victims of history, like the indigenous inhabitants of various continents, the Africans deported and sold as slaves, the genocide of Armenians on the fringe of the First World War, or the genocide of the Jews on the fringe of the Second World War, not to forget the Gypsies, the homosexuals, and Jehovah Witnesses, or the Ukrainian genocide in the 1930s. In order to distinguish between the collective memory of losers and that of victims, it is necessary to draw attention to an ambiguity in the term victim itself. It may refer to the victims of wars, defined by their active commitment to a positive cause for which they "sacrifice" their lives, as well as to the violence inflicted on a passive and defenseless victim. There is no sacrifice involved in the case of traumatic memory, a fact which distinguishes it from the traditional forms of heroic memory. Up until recently, these memories could not be addressed by the victims, to say nothing of the perpetrators.

While in some cases such as the Holocaust, a collective memory of victims has slowly been established over the last twenty years, acting also as a model for other victims' collective memories, a collective memory of perpetrators it is still an exception. In such cases, pride and shame interfere and prevent the recognition of guilt. This mechanism is lucidly described by Nietzsche in an aphorism (Nietzsche 1988, 5: 86):

I have done it—says my memory
I cannot have done it—says my pride and remains adamant
Memory, finally, gives in.

The memory of perpetrators, therefore, is always under the pressure of "vital forgetfulness" (Dolf Sternberger). While examples of victims' memory abound, examples of perpetrators' memory were, until recently, practically nonexistent. As easy as it is to remember the guilt of others, it is difficult to remember one's own guilt. This only becomes possible under considerable external pressure. In the post-war German society of the 1950s and 1960s, for instance, there was a strong desire for a closure of memory. Others called attention on the one hand to the Germans' limited capacity for remembering, and on the other to the unrestricted memory capacity of their opponents and victims, insisting that it is not up to the successors of the perpetrators to decide when these crimes are to pass into oblivion.

Half a century and more after the outrageous atrocities of the Holocaust and the criminally begun and conducted Second World War, the long-term effects of traumatic historical events are beginning to be acknowledged by both victims and perpetrators and are addressed in the public social arena. Worldwide, there are now new forms of collective memories in the making, which are centered around concepts such as political recognition, therapeutic restitution, and ethic responsibility. This means that we are witnessing a change in the basic grammar of the construction of collective political memory. Honor, be it triumphant or violated, which had dominated the code of national memory over centuries and had defined the criteria for inclusion and repudiation, is no longer the only touchstone for the selection of memories. On the level of national political memory, remembering had been a way to perpetuate the opposition between triumphant victor and resentful vanquished.

In former times this opposition between victors and vanquished could only be overcome by an agreement of mutual forgetting, as was the case in the treaty of the peace of Westphalia in Germany in 1648, where "perpetua oblivio et amnestia" was the formula to end the Thirty Years' War.

This formula, however, has proven futile when dealing with the opposition between victims and perpetrators after a historical trauma. These two groups are no longer tied together by mutual obligations. The formula of mutual forgetting has therefore been changed into a formula of shared remembering. In changing the formula, the terms forgetting and remembering take on a new meaning. Forgetting and forgiving are no longer connected, because there is no human agent or mundane institution that can assume the authority of redemption. Likewise, remembering and revenge are disconnected, because revenge is no longer seen as a form of empowerment of the mutilated self but rather as a form of disempowerment. In the aftermath of traumatic events, therefore, it is not the political imperative of mutual forgetting, but the ethical claim to shared remembering, that is chosen as a viable foundation for mutual relationships in the future. In this context, the figure of the "moral witness" (Margalit 2002) has entered the stage of history to tell the story of an iniquity where legal persecution is not viable (as in South Africa after apartheid) or remains totally inadequate as in Germany after the Holocaust.

A long-term collective memory of historical trauma does not arise without the cumulative efforts of "memory activists," a political lobby, and economic support. Holocaust museums are now being set up in many places, but where are the museums of the Herero genocide, the Armenian genocide, the Ukrainian genocide, the genocide of the Gypsies, and the attempted extermination of homosexuals? Without the back-up of archives and historical research and without the organization of the respective victims and their successors as a group with a collective identity and a political voice, such a memory is not likely to be formed. The memory of victims is always contested, which means that it has to be established against the pressure of a dominant memory, as is the case, for instance, with the Armenians and the Turks. "A museum devoted to the history of America's wars," writes Susan Sontag, "would be considered as a most unpatriotic endeavor" (Sontag 2003, 94).

1.4   Cultural Memory

On all of its levels, memory is defined by an intricate interaction between remembering and forgetting. Every form of memory that deserves the name, be it individual or collective, is defined by a division between what is remembered and what is forgotten, excluded, rejected, inaccessible, buried. This division is indeed a structural feature of memory itself. It holds true also for the complex architecture of "cultural" memory in a literate society that has devised more or less sophisticated techniques of storing information in external carriers. Cultural memory differs from other forms of memory in that its structure is not bipolar but triadic. It is organized not around the poles of remembering and forgetting, but inserts a third category which is the combination of remembering and forgetting. This third category refers to the cultural function of storing extensive information in libraries, museums, and archives which far exceeds the capacities of human memories. These caches of information, therefore, are neither actively remembered nor totally forgotten, because they remain materially accessible for possible use. One may refer to this intermediary existence between remembering and forgetting as a "status of latency" which in this case arises from the material storage and accessibility of (for the moment) forgotten, unused, and irrelevant information. Within cultural memory, an "active memory" is set up against the background of an archival memory. The active memory refers to what a society consciously selects and maintains as salient and vital items for common orientation and shared remembering. The content of active cultural memory is preserved by specific practices and institutions against the dominant tendency of decay and general oblivion. The perennial business of culture, according to Zygmunt Bauman, is to translate the transient into the permanent, i.e. to invent techniques of transmitting and storing information, which is deemed vital for the constitution and continuation of a specific group and its identity. Monuments perpetuate historical events; exhibitions and musical or theatrical performances create continuous attention for the canonized works of art.

While these active forms of re-creating and maintaining a cultural memory are generally accessible and reach a wider public, the documents of the cultural archive are accessible only to specialists. This part of materially retrievable and professionally interpretable information does not circulate as shared and common knowledge. It has not passed the filters of social selection nor is it transformed by cultural institutions and the public media into a living memory or public awareness. It is important to note, however, that the borderline between the archival and active memory is permeable in both directions. Things may recede into the background and fade out of common interest and attention; others may be recovered from the periphery and move into the center of social interest and esteem. Thanks to this interaction between the active and the archival dimension, i.e. between remembering and forgetting, cultural memory has an inbuilt capacity for ongoing changes, innovations, transformations, and reconfigurations.

The dangers of political memory are spelled out in what Nietzsche wrote about "monumental history": "it entices the brave to rashness, and the enthusiastic to fanaticism by its tempting comparisons" (Nietzsche 1957 [1872], 16). Whereas political memory is defined by a high degree of homogeneity and compelling appeal, cultural memory is more complex because it includes works of art that retain more ambivalence and allow for more diverse interpretations. While the symbolic signs of political memory are clear-cut and charged with high emotional intensity—such as a graffiti on a wall, a slogan on a license plate, a march or a monument—the symbolic signs of cultural memory have a more variegated and complex structure that allows and calls for continuous reassessments and reinterpretations by individuals. Political memory addresses individuals first and foremost as members of a group; cultural memory relates to members of a group first and foremost as individuals. While political memory draws individuals into a tight collective community centered around one seminal experience, the content of cultural memory privileges individual forms of participation such as reading, writing, learning, scrutinizing, criticizing, and appreciating and draws individuals into a wider historical horizon that is not only transgenerational but also transnational. The structure of neither political nor cultural memory is fixed but permanently challenged and contested. Its very contesting, however, is part of its status as lived and shared knowledge and experience.

2   CONCLUSION

There is no need to convince anybody that there is such a thing as an individual memory. Memory attaches to persons in the singular, but does it attach to them in the plural? When Halbwachs introduced the term "collective memory" into the social sciences in 1925, he met with a skepticism that has not fully disappeared. Strictly speaking, wrote Susan Sontag, there is no such thing as collective memory. She refers to the term as "a spurious notion" and insists: "All memory is individual, unreproducible—it dies with each person. What is called collective memory is not a remembering but a stipulating: that this is important, and this is the story about how it happened, with the pictures that lock the story in our minds. Ideologies create substantiating archives of images, representative images, which encapsulate common ideas of significance and trigger predictable thoughts, feelings" (Sontag 2003, 85–6).

The distinction between experiential or existential memory on the one hand and mere representations on the other, is important but more tricky than is at first sight obvious. In many cases, we have no definite way of knowing whether something that we remember is an experiential memory or an episode that has been told us by others and was incorporated into our fund of memories. There are obvious boundaries, of course: The second generation that was born after the Second World War and the Holocaust has no immediate connection to these events. And yet, as trauma-psychiatrists teach us, there are also some indirect and distorted forms of transmission of the traumatic experience from one generation to the other. And where we cannot claim any of these links and channels, individuals may yet adopt and absorb historical events as part of their history and identity which, as we realize more and more, is not confined to the limits of one's biography but may extend into various generations of one's family or the more recent and distant past of one's national history. The rather futile debate over the question of whether there is such a thing as a collective memory or not can be overcome by substituting for the term "collective memory" more specific ones such as "social," "political," and "cultural memory." The point in doing so is certainly not to introduce further abstract theoretical constructs, but to investigate empirically with these conceptual tools how memories are generated on the level of individuals and groups, how they are transformed by media and reconstructed retrospectively according to present norms, aims, visions, and projects. The interdisciplinary project of the memory discourse is to understand better the mechanisms and strategies of the way memories are formed by individuals and groups under specific circumstances, and how they are transmitted and transformed in processes of continuous reconstruction. In this context, the transition from the rhizomatic network of socially interconnected individual memories to more compact and generalized symbolic representations of experience via public media such as books, films, and literature deserve as much attention as the intentional acts of creating a ritual symbolic memory for future generations via memorials, monuments, museums, and rites of commemoration. When elevated to such levels of public attention and obligation, representations of the past can create an appeal for respective groups to absorb them into their self-image not only as historical knowledge but also as a "memory" of the past and incorporate them into one's transbiographical identity.

We must not forget that human beings do not only live in the first person singular, but also in various formats of the first person plural. They are part of different groups whose "We" they adopt together with the respective "social frames" which imply an implicit structure of shared concerns, values, experiences, narratives, and memories. The family, the neighborhood, the peer group, the generation, the nation, the culture are such larger groups to which individuals refer as "We." Each We is constructed through specific discourses that mark certain boundary lines and define respective principles of inclusion and exclusion. To acknowledge the concept of "collective memory," then, is to acknowledge the concept of some "collective identity." There is no question that this concept has been abused in the past and is still conducive to exclusionary and destructive politics. In order to overcome the malignant aspects that this construct is able to generate, it is of little help to deny its reality and efficiency. To contain its problematic potential, it is more efficient to emphasize and maintain the plurality of identities and "memory-systems" within the individual person. They can function as a salutary system of checks and balances to guard against the imperial dominance of one exclusive "collective memory."

REFERENCES

BAUMAN, Z. 1991. *Modernity and Ambivalence*. Ithaca, NY: Cornell University Press.

BECKER, H. A. 2000. Discontinuous change and generational contracts. Pp. 114–32 in *The Myth of Generational Conflict. The Family and State in Ageing Societies*, ed. S. Arber and C. Attias-Donfurt. London: Verlag.

CONNERTON, P. 1989. *How Societies Remember*. Cambridge: Cambridge University Press.

CONWAY, M. A. 1997. The inventory of experience: memory and identity. In Pennebaker et al. 1997.

GIESEN, B. 2004. *Triumph and Trauma*. Boulder, Colo.: Paradigm.

HALBWACHS, M. 1925. *Les cadres sociaux de la mémoire*. Paris: Librairie Felix Alcan, 1st edn.; repr. 1975 with a foreword by F. Châtelet.

—— 1950. *La mémoire collective*, ed. posthumously by J. Alexandre. Paris: Albin Michel. *On Collective Memory*, Eng. trans. and ed. L. A. Coser. Chicago: University of Chicago Press, 1992.

LEWIS, B. 1975. *History—Remembered, Recovered, Invented.* Princeton, NJ: Princeton University Press.

LOCKE, J. 1975 [1689]. Of identity and diversity. In Locke, *Essay Concerning Human Understanding,* ed. P. H. Nidditch. Oxford: Oxford University Press.

MANNHEIM, K. 1952. *Essays on the Sociology of Knowledge.* London: Routledge and Kegan Paul; originally published 1928.

MARGALIT, A. 2002. *The Ethics of Memory.* Cambridge, Mass.: Harvard University Press.

MIDDLETON, D., and EDWARDS, D. 1990. *Collective Remembering.* London: Sage.

NIETZSCHE, F. 1957 [1872]. *The Use and Abuse of History.* New York: Macmillan.

—— 1988. Jenseits von Gut und Böse. In *Gesammelte Werke,* ed. G. Colli and M. Montinari. Berlin: De Gruyter.

NORA, P. 1984. *Les Lieux de mémoire.* Vol. 1: *La République.* Paris: Gallimard.

—— 1986. *Les Lieux de mémoire.* Vol. 2: *La Nation.* Paris: Gallimard.

—— 1992. *Les Lieux de mémoire.* Vol. 3: *Les Frances.* Paris: Gallimard.

NOVIK, P. 1999. *The Holocaust in American Life.* Boston: Houghton Mifflin.

OLICK, J. K. 2003. What does it mean to normalize the past? Official memory in German politics since 1989. Pp. 259–88 in *States of Memory. Continuities, Conflicts, and Transformations in National Retrospection,* ed. J. K. Olick. Durham, NC: Duke University Press.

PENNEBAKER, J. W., and BANASIK, B. L. 1997. On the creation and maintenance of collective memories: history as social psychology. In Pennebaker et al. 1997.

—— PAEZ, D., and RIME, B. (eds.) 1997. *Collective Memory of Political Events. Social Psychological Perspectives.* Mahwah, NJ: Lawrence Erlbaum.

RANDALL, W. L. 1995. *The Stories We Are: An Essay on Self-Creation.* Toronto: University of Toronto Press.

RICOEUR, P. 2000. *La Mémoire, l'histoire, l'oubli.* Paris: Édition du Seuil.

SCHACTER, D. (ed.) 1995. *Memory Distortion: How Minds, Brains, and Societies Reconstruct the Past.* Cambridge, Mass: Harvard University Press.

—— 1999. The seven sins of memory. insights from psychology and cognitive neuroscience. *American Psychologist,* 54(3): 182–203.

SCHUHMANN, H., and SCOTT, J. 1989. Generations and collective memory. *American Sociological Review,* 54: 359–81.

SINGH, A., SKERRETT, J. T., JR., and HOGAN, R. E. 1996. *Memory and Cultural Politics. New Approaches to American Ethnic Literatures.* Boston: Northeastern University Press.

SONTAG, S. 2003. *Regarding the Pain of Others.* New York: Farrar, Straus and Giroux.

TULVING, E. (ed.) 2000. *Memory, Consciousness, and the Brain.* Philadelphia: Taylor and Francis Psychology Press.

VOLKAN, V. D. 1997. *Bloodlines: From Ethnic Pride to Ethnic Terrorism.* New York: Farrar, Strauss and Giroux.

WHITE, H. 1992. Historical emplotment and the problem of truth. Pp. 37–53 in *Probing the Limits of Representation. Nazism and the "Final Solution",* ed. S. Friedlander. Cambridge, Mass.: Harvard University Press.

WILLIAMS, M. S. 1998. *Voice, Trust, and Memory. Marginalized Groups and the Failings of Liberal Representation.* Princeton, NJ: Princeton University Press.

PART IV

IDEAS MATTER

CHAPTER 12

WHY AND HOW IDEAS MATTER

DIETRICH RUESCHEMEYER

THAT ideas matter in politics is beyond question. Knowledge, ignorance, and uncertainty frequently make the difference between success and failure of policies. And in a broader sense ideas can advance social change, as the Enlightenment played a role in the run-up to the French Revolution, or help maintain the status quo, as the doctrine of the divine right of kings to rule did in post-medieval Europe. Yet the importance of ideas compared to other factors shaping social processes has been a matter of debate throughout the history of social thought. Global answers to this question may be inherently elusive; but more detailed questions—perhaps confining themselves to specific developments and circumstances—can elucidate the ways in which ideas make a difference, the conditions that make them more or less effective, and their interactions with other factors that account for social change as well as stability.

It makes sense to delimit this vast subject matter. This chapter focuses on single ideas and idea complexes rather than on the ensemble of ideas commonly understood as symbolic culture. It concentrates on ideas about social and political life and thus largely excludes from consideration the immense bodies of scientific and technical ideas that have transformed economy and society since the industrial revolution and given rise to what is frequently discussed as the information or knowledge society. Furthermore, we are primarily concerned with explicit ideas—

*I wish to thank Zeev Rosenhek for comments on an earlier draft.

with theories of how the economy works for instance, with the proclamation of political ideals, or with considered assessments of threats to valued interests. We will not focus on the taken-for-granted premises of common attitudes and the implicit notions embedded in language and proverbs.[1] At the same time, these more diffuse kinds of ideas may become relevant if this is where the inquiry about how ideas do and do not matter leads us. Ideas about social class, for instance, may be very limited in their impact if they are at odds with understandings of social reality that play down social inequality and that are built into the very language of common discourse (as more generally, one of the conditions shaping the efficacy of ideas is almost certainly how new ideas articulate with various bodies of prevailing ideas). In turn, new ideas may exert very forceful influence if they succeed in shaping these taken-for-granted understandings.

These delimitations do not yet yield a clear definition of the subject of our analysis. However, as this is not a treatise on the philosophy of the mind, I will go only a few steps further toward such a clarification of what is understood here as ideas. We will not equate ideas with all forms of human consciousness. By focusing on explicit ideas about the social world we limit ourselves not only to *expressions* of consciousness but also to reflected expressions in contrast to inchoate emotive reactions to reality. However, while expressions of emotion are not the central subject, we must realize that emotions accompany all forms of perception and reflection, strengthening or softening ideas, sharpening or blurring them, and linking valuation and analysis.

Ideas may be primarily cognitive in character—descriptions of what is the case and tools for understanding how things work. Equally important, ideas can be above all of a normative nature; ideals, values, and norms define what is good and bad. A third category of ideas that is commonly distinguished defines tastes and desires, shaping—together with cognitive and normative ideas—people's preferences. It is important to distinguish these different kinds of ideas, but they are distinct from each other only in an analytical sense. They not only interact with each other but often form stable amalgams. For instance, some theorists of ideology have defined that concept not so much as a distortion of reality (Mannheim 1936) but as a fusion of important cognitive and normative ideas (Parsons 1951; 1959; Geertz 1964). We will be concerned with all three categories, though we will focus especially on cognitive and normative ideas.

Last among these preliminaries, there is the deceptively simple question of who holds a given set of ideas. Can collectivities such as social classes or occupational status groups be carriers of ideas? While methodological individualism rather than

---

[1] Implicit beliefs and value orientations and their relation to established practices have been discussed under the heading of "mentality" or of "habitus" (Bourdieu 1977). Foucault's (1972; 1979) notions of power diffused in the sediments of history and of discourse grounded in social practices make hidden and implicit ideas central to his views. And the "involvement of beliefs in 'lived experience'" play a critical role in Anthony Giddens' "structuration" approach to social theory, which seeks to reconcile agency and structure (Giddens 1979, 183; 1984).

an a priori ontological collectivism seems the position of prudent choice, it is quite possible to arrive at a reasoned attribution of ideas to a social movement, the dominant part of a class, or a defined segment of the political spectrum. This requires collecting—on occasion even just reasonably guessing about—individual expressions, which are then interpreted in the light of the individuals' position in communication networks, the relations of influence and authority, and the antagonisms and solidarities created by interests. In many instances, the participants themselves may well perceive such opinions and views as collective phenomena, as the *faits sociaux* so central to Emile Durkheim's social theory. The attribution of ideas to collectivities is, then, a pragmatic decision contingent on evidence.

1   IDEAS DO MATTER: SOME EXAMPLES

That ideas matter in social and political life is most obvious when it comes to knowledge, false beliefs, and ignorance. An example of considerable consequence comes from macroeconomic policy. In the Great Depression of the 1930s, the pre-Nazi government of Germany worsened the economic slump and increased unemployment when it cut government expenditures in response to declining revenues rather than, faced with unemployment and underused productive capacity, adopting the opposite policy of stimulating demand through budget deficits. The deepening severity of the Depression in Germany is commonly considered a decisive factor in the collapse of the Weimar Republic and the installment of the Nazi regime. That "countercyclical demand management"—increasing demand for goods and services through budget deficits in recessions, while returning to surpluses in boom periods—can optimize the joint goals of employment, growth, and price stability came to be identified with Keynes' (1936) reformulation of macroeconomic theory. That theory was and remains controversial. Yet pragmatically, a policy of countercyclical demand management was successfully adopted during the Depression by several governments, including that of Nazi Germany. It became standard practice after the Second World War, and it continues to be so in spite of the difficult experience with stagnation and inflation in the 1970s and the declining appeal of Keynesianism as a broader policy conception. While we will have to return to the role of other factors shaping macroeconomic policy, it is clear that here is a historical instance where knowledge and cognitive beliefs made a significant difference.[2]

[2] An instance concerning economic knowledge of special contemporary relevance is found in the important discussion of Bockman and Eyal (2002) of the genealogy of neoliberalism's influence in postcommunist Europe. They show that it arose out of a prolonged East–West dialogue that began in the 1920s. It was grounded in transnational networks of economists who analyzed the experience of

Another example also involves cognitive ideas. The views of dominant groups on economic, social, and political conditions and their anticipations about future developments have a decisive effect on constitutional change according to a recent comparative historical study of democratic consolidation. Gerard Alexander (2002) created an ingenious set of hypotheses about when democratic rule becomes consolidated and tested it in the historical trajectories of Spain, France, Britain, Germany, and Italy from before the First World War until after the Second. He postulates—and then shows—that the right's perceptions of political risks to its safety and well-being under democratic or authoritarian rule determine its regime preferences. Because the right had privileged access to the means of coercion, it could decisively block democratic outcomes or support a return to authoritarian government after a period of democratic rule. Consolidation of democracy will come about only if the dominant groups see their interests protected in the future as well as at present. The right hedges on the democratic option if current conditions under democracy are favorable, but the future is uncertain. The right turns away from democracy if it sees its interests better protected under authoritarian rule. And the right gives up authoritarian options and commits to democracy if its assessment of future as well as present risks favors democracy. The perceptions and interpretations of the right, then, have extremely far-reaching effects. This claim stands even if one considers Alexander's model as too stylized and if some of his particular historical assessments were to be successfully contested.

The effective advancement of women's interests during the wave of the women's movement, which started in most rich democracies during the 1960s, relied heavily on ideas and arguments, as did the earlier push for women's voting rights. These are primarily examples of the impact of normative ideas rather than of perceptions and cognitive interpretations of social reality. The normative arguments relied on older ideas of human equality; but they took on a new urgency. This again suggests that other causal factors played a role as well; but the arguments played a significant role in transforming the views of policy-makers and large parts of the populations.

Other examples of normative ideas exerting a strong influence on social change and stability easily come to mind. Consider for instance nationalist ideas developing and buttressing individual obligations to serve and sacrifice in causes defined by nation states or the pronouncements of religious doctrine that shape practices of devotion and authority relations within religious communities.

Can we point to similar examples of ideas that are primarily appreciative in nature, shaping preferences and motivation? Appreciative ideas seem to be most effective in shaping desires through the offer of new experiences and products. Innovation and importation play a major role in the proliferation of consumer desires, but equally or

central command economies. Bockman and Eyal plausibly contrast this account with the prevailing stereotypes that the influence of neoliberal ideas was either the result of an obvious failure of Keynesianism or constituted simply an imposition of Western interests.

perhaps more important are technical innovations and normative changes that make the satisfaction of existing needs and wants more effective and/or more legitimate. Other causal factors, especially status relations, are of great importance for the spread and proliferation of changes in wants and preferences. Appreciative ideas and the dynamics of changing preferences will be treated in this chapter with—a perhaps not too benign—neglect. This in spite of the very considerable importance of the unending increase in desires even and perhaps especially among the most well off, even and perhaps especially in the richest countries.

2   IDEAS DO MATTER: AN ARGUMENT FROM ELEMENTARY SOCIAL THEORY

That ideas matter in social and political life is equally obvious if we consider elementary social theory. A theoretical analysis of action and elementary inter-action constitutes the starting point of the two of most influential theoretical approaches in the social sciences of the past fifty years—the theory of action and social systems of Talcott Parsons, who built his arguments on an interpretation of Max Weber, Emile Durkheim, and the economists Vilfredo Pareto and Alfred Marshall, and rational choice theory, which used elementary economic theory for the analysis of social and political life.

Both theoretical approaches begin with the model of a goal-oriented actor who finds her/himself in a physical and social environment relevant for the attainment of goals. Parsons (1937) insisted that human action cannot be understood without reference to an "internal dimension" of action. This dimension includes the perception and interpretation of the actor's environment, normative orientations, and the development of tastes and preferences.[3] The open space created by the relative indeterminacy of human action in terms of environment and inborn behavior tendencies is "filled" by norms and values, by varying levels of information, interpretation, and analysis, by particular preference structures, as well as by codes of communication. All of these are shaped by collective human creations, though they build on innate foundations. Individuals are not able to produce such orientations

---

[3] In this conception Parsons followed Weber's claim that "meaningful action"—distinguished from sheer behavior conceived as devoid of subjective meaning—must be the elementary building block of social and political analysis. I will neglect here that some social theorists, very prominently for instance Anthony Giddens (1979; 1984), find fault with the centrality of goal orientation in Parsons' theory of action as well as in rational choice theory.

successfully by themselves, though they do add to their change and maintenance. In fact, no single generation is able to create a comprehensive set of such standards, codes, and meanings from scratch, as is obvious when we think of language.

Parsons' conception differs from the strongest (as well as the most simple) version of rational choice theory. This version does acknowledge the importance of the subjective dimension of action by focusing on the rational means–end calculus of actors; but it does so only immediately to close that open space again, attending solely to the rational pursuit of given goals in a well-understood environment; behavior is then shaped by rational and therefore predictable responses to a given environment. Yet while this radically simplified model may have considerable heuristic value in well-understood situations, a more comprehensive approach suitable to a broader variety of situations needs to answer—or make reasonable assumptions about—the same basic questions that led Parsons to speak about an internal dimension of action: How are goals chosen? How are means evaluated? Which understandings of the situation inform the choices? How do norms and values influence the adoption of goals and means? And how do normative orientations themselves come about and change? A comprehensive rational choice theory, then, must surround its core of a rational calculus model with a belt of subsidiary theories. These theories have to deal with needs and wants, cognitive understandings, and normative orientations, inquiring about their causal determinants, the dynamics of their change, and their impact on action. Such theories remain at present incomplete and fragmentary, but they inevitably involve ideas as causally relevant phenomena.[4]

3   GUIDANCE FROM THE HISTORY OF SOCIAL THOUGHT?

The role of ideas has preoccupied thinking about society and history for ages, generating again and again passionate disputes. Can we benefit from this history? The struggle over the role of ideas reached a highpoint with Marx's attack on Hegel's philosophy of history. This has defined the discussion for more than a

---

[4] A glance at historical materialism is instructive here, as it resembles rational choice theory in many ways. Marxist thought always had elements of such subsidiary theories. For instance, it sees needs and wants shaped by people's position in a system of production. Recent developments in Marxist theories of class formation and class action explicitly focus on cultural causal conditions and the role of ideas (Thompson 1963; Gramsci 1975 [1928–37]). I return to Marx's views in the next section.

century. When Hegel opened his teaching at the University of Berlin in 1818, he exhorted his students: "Faith in the power of the mind is the first condition of philosophical studies." And: human beings "cannot think high enough of the greatness and power of the mind." The young Marx turned to Hegel's philosophy in order to get a comprehensive perspective on past history and the future of society. But he soon rejected Hegel's claim that the dialectic of ideas was the key to understanding historical change. He replaced this "idealist" vision with a "materialist" one:

In the social production of their life, men enter into definite relations that are indispensable and independent of their will, relations of production which correspond to a definite stage of development of their material productive forces. The sum total of these relations of production constitutes the economic structure of society, the real foundation, on which rises a legal and political superstructure and to which correspond definite forms of social consciousness. The mode of production of material life conditions the social, political and intellectual life process in general. It is not the consciousness of men that determines their being, but, on the contrary, their social being that determines their consciousness. (Marx 1978 [1859], 4).

This formulation—and its key concepts of substructure, superstructure, and the dependence of consciousness on the relations of production—has become the centerpiece of the Marxist catechism. Yet it deals primarily with the very long run of history. And it is a formulation that dramatizes the contrast to Hegel's ideas. When more specific questions are asked, more complex mechanisms come into view.

That ideas are shaped by the lived experience of groups and classes in distinct social locations remains a central idea. Marx then borrows from the interest psychology and the theory of ideas of eighteenth-century France (e.g. Helvetius) and claims that dominant classes adopt ideas that can serve as a means of domination and as instruments of legitimation, while emergent revolutionary classes seek to define what is necessary to advance their position. This clearly has implications for the efficacy of ideas in class-divided societies: "The class which has the means of material production at its disposal, has control at the same time over the means of mental production, so that thereby, generally speaking, the ideas of those who lack the means of mental production are subject to it" (Marx and Engels 1978 [1845–6], 172).

That this intellectual dominance (and thus the ideas it promulgates) has significant consequences in history is implied even in the formula of substructure and superstructure. The legal and political superstructure and the attendant forms of consciousness maintain the status quo in the face of slow changes in the mode and the relations of production—until fairly sudden developments realign substructure and superstructure. Marx's view of history as shaped by class struggle would lose its dialectic character and the discontinuity of revolutionary turns without that assumption. His insistence that "the mode of production of material life conditions the social, political and intellectual life process" takes aim at the validity and the legitimacy of the "intellectual life process" and at the view that ideas develop autonomously and are the ultimate determinants of the course of history. It is far from denying that ideas have significant consequences, even in the long run.

In the twentieth century, Marxian conflict theory built on these and other complexities in Marx's historical analyses. It emphasized cultural elements in class formation and class action (Thompson 1963) and developed the ideas of cultural hegemony and counter-hegemony (Gramsci 1975 [1928–37]). It also gave political processes a greater degree of autonomy, opening links to the institutionalist realism of Weber's political analysis.

The counter-position was represented in the twentieth century by different versions of Parsonian functionalism and the integration theory of social systems. Beginning with his *Structure of Social Action* (1937), Talcott Parsons made value orientations the strategic entry point for social analysis. This remained so in *The Social System* (1951). Values and norms were emphasized as a key to understanding social life in a methodological sense, not necessarily because they were the causal forces of primary importance. But in his later formulation of "cybernetic hierarchies" governing all systems of action, Parsons (1961) turned from arguments about the strategy of analysis to substantive causal claims. To make this clear requires a brief sketch of this later model.

Parsons distinguished four functional subsystems of social action and societies that deal with (1) adaptation and the generation of resources, (2) goal formation and attainment, (3) integration, and (4) largely latent ultimate orientations required for the maintenance of basic system patterns. In societies, these functional areas correspond to the economy, the polity, the societal community, and the pattern maintenance system linked to culture. These four parts of the model, Parsons claimed, stand in definite relations to each other, relations that can be understood in analogy to cybernetic control mechanisms. Parsons elaborates here a metaphor of Max Weber, who called religious ideas about salvation "switchmen of history" as they direct similar concerns and energies in different directions much as railroad switches send engines and trains to their various destinations (Weber 1958 [1915], 280). In Parsons' model, cultural orientations inform and shape the system of social integration; in the same way, the societal community shapes and controls the polity, and the polity the economy. This "hierarchy of cybernetic control" has an inverted counterpart in a "hierarchy of energy and necessary conditions." As the furnace generates and uses more energy than the thermostat, so the subsystems lower in the hierarchy of control generate and use more resources than those higher in that hierarchy. These formal analogies lead Parsons, at the end of an examination of simple and more complex societies, to a summary statement about the relative importance of ideas and normative orientation:

In the sense, and *only* in that sense, of emphasizing the importance of the cybernetically highest elements in patterning action systems, I am a cultural determinist, rather than a social determinist. Similarly, I believe that, within the social system, the normative elements are more important for social change than the "material interests" of constitutive units. The longer the time perspective, and the broader the system involved, the greater the *relative* importance of higher, rather than lower, factors in the control hierarchy, regardless of whether it is pattern maintenance or pattern change that requires explanation. (Parsons 1966, 113)

This strong statement, which has a counterpart in claims about the relative stability and autonomy of cultural patterns, has found a broad and diffuse following among many defenders of functionalist theory; but it encountered incisive criticism from many theorists who seek to develop Parsons' ideas further. The formal model leads to this conclusion only if one treats the cybernetic metaphor as a valid causal proposition of how social action and the change and maintenance of social systems are determined. Empirically, the claim about the relative importance of normative orders and material interests hardly followed from the preceding evolutionary and comparative sketches.[5] One of the most influential overall assessments of Parsons' theory—that of one of his last students, Jeffrey Alexander (1980–3)—insists that Parsons' theoretical work is, despite its intermittent leanings toward idealist positions, fundamentally multidimensional in character. In his own program, Alexander seeks to strengthen this multidimensionality by integrating Marxian ideas into the overall framework. One of the leading German followers of Parsons' theory, Richard Münch, similarly rejects a causal primacy of culture and the system maintenance component of the social system (Münch 1987).

What can we conclude from this brief excursion in the history of social thought? Contrary to Parsons' early programmatic call to transform disputes about the role of ideas in general by asking more specific questions, thus moving the discussion away from philosophical problems and "into the forum of factual observations and theoretical analysis on the empirical level" (Parsons 1938, 652), the debate is still suffused with ideological inclinations toward broad answers. The left tends to be skeptical about the role of ideas. It sees the autonomous causal power of ideas and ideals contradicted by elementary social and political experience. In this view, the fundamental structures of power and economic advantage stand in the way of realizing ideals no matter how convincing. Maintaining that ideas and ideals are a

---

[5] That the same empirical evidence is open to quite varied interpretations is indicated by Weber's very wording of the "switchmen of history" metaphor, which is part of the same famous essay on world religions that was so important to Parsons' thinking about the role of ideas from the beginning (see already Parsons 1937 and 1938, but also 1966): "Not ideas, but material and ideal interests directly govern men's conduct. Yet very frequently the 'world images' that have been created by 'ideas' have, like switchmen, determined the track along which action has been pushed by the dynamic of interest" (Weber 1958 [1915], 280). Wenzel (1990, 453–5) points out that the cybernetic model reintroduces a dualism of "ideal" and "real" factors that cannot be sustained and that had been overcome in Parsons' earlier insights about the symbolic mediation of all human action. For an ultimately dualist conception of *Ideal-* and *Realfaktoren* in which the content of the "ideal" factors is in the end immune to change, see Scheler (1980 [1926]).

major force shaping social life then comes to be seen as legitimating an unjust world. Ironically, such a skepticism about idealism actually springs itself from an insistence on values and ideals, albeit values and ideals that remain unrealized. Many on the right offer a mirror image of this. Though there is also a materialism of the right, many conservatives are inclined to stress the causal importance of culture. They consider the left's insistence on the realization of ideals as naive idealism. The real world, profoundly shaped by values and realistic cognitive ideas, seems to them thoroughly unjust only if judged by unrealistic yardsticks.

Yet side by side with this continuing ideological discourse we can observe a certain convergence among theorists towards a "multidimensional" perspective, which seeks to move away from one-sided emphases and avoid ideological entanglements. In his valiant attempt to spell out "what sociological theory claims to know in the late twentieth century—100 years into the development of the discipline," Randall Collins presents a "multidimensional conflict theory" as a—perhaps more developed—complement to Alexander's program. (Collins 1987, 74, chs. 4 and 5). Differences among these analysts are in many ways not as radical as conventional views suggest. At the same time, this convergence remains largely at the metatheoretical program level. There is more agreement on problem formulations than on answers. Yet the limited programmatic convergence can be seen as the result of mutual correction of the two dominant traditions. Corresponding in important ways to the arguments from elementary social theory outlined earlier, that convergence offers a broad framework for future investigation.

4   WHAT KINDS OF ANSWERS CAN WE EXPECT?

The controversies generated by the confrontation of idealism and materialism turned on the largest questions: Which factors—ideas or variously defined "material" factors—are more important overall and in the long run? Which general modes describe their interaction? Answers to these broad questions seem beyond reach. What Parsons urged in 1938 still seems a promising way to proceed: the task is to explore more specific, but nevertheless extremely complex questions and to do so by way "of factual observations and theoretical analysis on the empirical level." However, given the limited success of moving in this direction during the last half century, we may well ask what kinds of results we can reasonably expect.

The answers that seem possible are more modest than Parsons appears to have anticipated in 1938. Establishing theoretical generalizations that are plausibly valid across time and space has proved extremely difficult. It is not an accident that Parsons focused on one of the dramatic exceptions—Weber's theoretical sketch of how similar interests in salvation interact with the non-empirical ideas held by the major world religions to engender goals and values of a dramatically different character; this introduced and was supported by his vast, if essayistic comparative analysis of the major world religions.

More likely are partial insights, limited to questions about special kinds of ideas and distinctive social processes, and often also valid only in particular historical domains. Even if sharply focused on the explanation of specific developments, our questions will only rarely find answers that meet textbook specifications of theoretical propositions. Social science does not often produce such hypotheses that have survived repeated empirical tests and that are sufficiently specified to allow predictions. Even the theories of the middle range that Robert Merton advocated two generations ago as a way forward, as well as the recently much discussed "mechanism" hypotheses, rarely meet the textbook requirements for theoretical propositions capable of explanation and prediction, however wide the margins we allow for variation in the outcomes. Reference group theory for instance says something worthwhile about people referring to other social categories and groups when they make cognitive or normative judgments, but it does not tell us which references are taken under which circumstances. Many mechanism hypotheses are similarly underspecified, a fact that earned them the ironic label of "bits of sometimes true theory."[6]

True, there are theoretical insights, which may come from relatively simple empirical findings or even commonsense observations that are sufficient to put unqualified claims into doubt. A (not so simple) example is E. P. Thompson's (1963) study of the constitution of the English working class that denied claims that the conditions of class formation can be read off from objective conditions of material interest and conflict, independent of cultural antecedents. But the research results that we can more commonly expect, derive from reasoned causal explanations of the impact of ideas in one or a few complex cases and are valid only in limited domains, often of unknown extension.

This is true for many areas of research, but it applies with special force to studies that centrally concern ideas. Determining the meaning of ideas inevitably involves interpretation. Such hermeneutic problems are formidable when we deal with explicit and detailed formulations; they become even greater when much less information is available. These problems frequently make a standardization of

---

[6] For the recent revival of interest in mechanisms see Hedström and Swedberg (1998) and earlier Stinchcombe (1991). For the cuttingly funny formulation see Stinchcombe (1998, 267) and Coleman (1964, 516–19). On reference group theory see Merton (1968 [1949]). Ironically, Merton had, in the opening chapters of the same seminal volume, distinguished between "theoretical orientations" of a metatheoretical character and theoretical propositions in the narrower sense. I suggest that the theories of the middle range are actually instances of the former rather than the latter.

inquiry impossible, a fact that often renders survey data of dubious value. Historical studies have to make do, in the absence of such oral information, with even more indirect indications of subjective meanings. Small wonder that many traditional works of this kind simply confine themselves to the study of a few thinkers, either forgoing assertions about wider circles or just claiming representativeness, however great the odds against that.[7]

Studies dealing with the role of ideas will therefore typically involve complex hypotheses about the incidence and the meaning as well as the consequences of ideas, hypotheses that are tested in multiple, non-standardized ways as the investigation proceeds. Many of these hypotheses will not be "portable" beyond the particular context, though some may well meet that standard. However, the complex dialogue between empirical evidence and theoretical surmise that characterizes such studies is often guided by *theoretical frames*. These are not theories in the strict sense. They do not consist of an integrated series of tested theoretical propositions. Rather they set out an approach to the issues in question.

Theoretical frames consist of a number of concepts that clearly define what is to be explained and identify a set of factors relevant for the explanation; they offer justifications for the particular conceptualizations they propose as well as arguments supporting their choice of relevant causal factors; they may explicate certain logical interrelations that are not obvious at first sight; and they may contain also an occasional admixture of specific testable and tested hypotheses. The value of such theoretical frames lies in their usefulness for empirical investigation. While they cannot be judged as true or false in a more immediate sense, their quality nevertheless depends on their adequacy to the realities studied. I submit that much of what we can count as advances in social and political analysis consists of more appropriate theoretical frames for specific problem areas.

In a very broad sense, one could consider the limited convergence on a multidimensional orientation of social and political theory noted above a theoretical frame, but more specific constructions are of greater interest for the questions discussed here. The example of one such focused theoretical frame will make this clear.

Robert Wuthnow opened his powerful study of three of the greatest ideational challenges in the development of Western modernity—the Protestant Reformation, the Enlightenment, and European socialism—by a detailed theoretical frame or, in his more literary choice of words, a "theoretical scaffolding" (1989, 3–15). It begins with the problem of articulation: "Great works of art and literature, philosophy and social criticism, like great sermons, always relate in an enigmatic fashion to their social environment. They draw resources, insights, and inspiration

---

[7] Issues of interpretation and hermeneutics lead quickly into philosophical questions and arguments (see, e.g., Apel 1984). I am here just pointing to pragmatic methodological difficulties. For some ingenious attempts to deal with these see Mohr (1998).

from that environment: they reflect it, speak to it, and make themselves relevant to it. And yet they also remain autonomous enough from their social environment to acquire a broader, even universal and timeless appeal" (p. 3). Next he distinguishes the social and cultural environment, the institutional context, and action sequences within those contexts as components of the conditions of intellectual action. The analysis then focuses on the production of ideas in a community of discourse, on their selection in the wider society, and on the process of their institutionalization that makes resources and channels of communication routinely available and that turns these ideas into a stable feature of a historical period. Finally, for the analysis of the ideas themselves, he distinguishes how the social and cultural environment is perceived and analyzed ("social horizon"), how the new ideas are crystallized and opposed to singled-out features of the status quo ("discursive field"), and how the problems can be resolved by prototypical ideas and actions ("figural action"). Needless to say, this schematic listing can only give a first impression of the theoretical frame that informs this massive study and that is reviewed in its conclusion.[8]

Other examples of theoretical frames that have proved useful in arriving at persuasive explanations of developments or constellations of great interest are not hard to find. Joseph Ben-David, for instance, used a consistent set of analytic ideas in his too little appreciated sketch explaining long periods of stagnation as well as phases of rapid growth in the development of modern science and its applications (Ben-David 1971).

The recourse to theoretical frames may seem open to abuse. The choice of categories and variables could be willful, informed by idiosyncrasy and ideological inclination. And working within the frame could insulate the investigation from contrary ideas. After all, the problems of ideas and their role have, as we have seen, long been the subject of intense ideological disputes. Thus, one might imagine, the discourse could degenerate into a relativism analogous to conflict avoidance in child play: "I'll play in my sandbox, you in yours." But that outcome is hardly necessary. After each explanatory use of a theoretical framework, the results should be—and often are—scanned for anomalies and open questions suggesting revisions of the analytic frame. Equally or perhaps more important, other researchers will insist on such shortcomings, and they are likely to prevail if they do not confine themselves to global claims—that the frame privileges one broad set of factors or another—but demonstrate their point by showing that hypotheses guided by a different theoretical frame can offer better and more comprehensive explanations.

Successful studies aided by such theoretical frames advance our understanding in two ways. First, they give credence to a particular frame, aid in its revision, and lend support to others following a similar theoretical strategy. Second, they themselves offer a reasoned explanatory account of complex historical developments. Once

---

[8] See also Wuthnow (1987) for an overview and evaluation of different theoretical approaches to the study of meaning and culture.

similar developments are explored in other cases, the result could be a more definitive theoretical account of certain kinds of developments.[9] A more modest and perhaps preliminary expectation would be that a number of such historical explanations yield a repertory of possible and likely causal patterns that may be encountered again.

In the remainder of this chapter, I offer a few ideas that could be building blocks for theoretical frames focused on specific problems in the wider field of the role of ideas—on questions about the conditions of impact of ideas, the magnitude of impact and non-impact, as well as to the modes and mechanisms through which ideas make a difference. Some of what follows will take up elements of the earlier grand traditions. Aside from the overall controversies, these contained after all theoretical constructs of great persuasiveness. I think for instance of Parsons' ideas about institutionalization as a mediation between normative as well as cognitive ideas and social processes, or of the role the "division of material from mental labor" played in Marx and Engels' conception of the fundamentals of historical change.[10]

5   How Ideas Matter: Interaction with Other Factors

That the impact of ideas must always be seen in the context of other factors shaping the outcome as well is strongly suggested by the programmatic multidimensional consensus noted above. This virtually obvious maxim may gain a little in complexity if we return to our first example of the role of cognitive ideas, the failure of the last pre-Nazi German governments of the Weimar period to engage in counter-cyclical demand management.

This was not a case of overlooking or neglecting a well-established policy idea. Many German economists saw themselves as largely removed from policy concerns, but a majority adhered to the view that a market economy tends toward optimal equilibria rather than getting stuck in a stable underuse of human and material resources. They therefore were hostile to suggestions that the Great Depression could be ameliorated by the government generating demand. Civil servants in government

---

[9] This anticipation differs from the problematic empiricist hope that theoretical conclusions will emerge simply from an accumulation of empirical findings. The difference lies precisely in the guidance of empirical research by successively revised theoretical frames. If a label were desired for this strategy, a slightly changed version of the old formula of "analytic induction" could serve.

[10] See Marx and Engels (1978 [1845–6]). For some interpretive comments that elaborate the remarks above see Rueschemeyer (1986, 105–6).

were skeptical of deficit financing for similar reasons; in addition, they had to deal with constraints in Germany's international financial situation and feared that "printing money" could make for financial panics in an already panic-prone situation. The most important factor shaping the policy, however, was political. This was driven by the fear of returning to the rampant inflation that had characterized the first years after the First World War. Following the collapse of Imperial Germany, a coalition of labor, business, and government responded to the threat of chaos and political instability with inflationary policies that eventually resulted in the "hyperinflation" of 1922–3. It was this negative policy legacy that was the strongest factor leading to the deflationary policy adopted in 1930–2 (see James 1989).

Even cognitive ideas of considerable potential utility, then, have to meet with complex favorable conditions before they are accepted and used. This is especially true of social and economic ideas, because they typically have normative implications and affect vested interests. They thus are prone to provoke ideological contestation. Hall concludes a comparative analysis of Keynesianism in advanced capitalist countries with a chapter on "The Politics of Keynesian Ideas" (1989, 361–91), in which he offers a theoretical frame identifying three clusters of factors that mediate between a new economic theory and its adoption as a guide to policy: The "economic viability" of economic policy ideas depends on their relation to existing economic theories, the nature of the national economy, and international economic constraints. Their "political viability" is determined by the goals of ruling political parties, the interests of potential coalition partners, and the collective associations with policy legacies. And the "administrative viability" depends on policy inclinations in the relevant agencies and their relative power as well as on their capacities for implementation.

The dynamics of the influence of economic ideas represent of course only a small segment of the very large area of questions concerning the role of different factors shaping the influence of ideas. New normative ideas—values, ideals, and innovations in the normative regulation of life—do not face an altogether different situation in their struggle for acceptance, since it is the rare cognitive assertion about social, economic, and political matters that does not have any implications for the constellation of vested interests and the established moral order. But new normative ideas cannot rely on the appeal of empirical reality claims.

If for no other reason than the vast variety of ways in which new ideas—both cognitive and normative—can relate to established ideas, vested interests, and their bases in the institutional order, the interaction of ideas with other factors shaping their impact is a huge field of inquiry, virtually coextensive with the analysis of social change. At the extremes, it is easy to think of situations that illustrate a near-complete impotence of ideas, even if they strike observers in a different situation as persuasive and powerful, while in other constellations ideas prevail that later witnesses may well find ill-founded and/or morally objectionable. In the following, only a few peculiar issues in the interaction of ideas and other factors will occupy us further.

6   HOW IDEAS MATTER: THE SEQUENCING OF DIFFERENT FACTORS

Commonsense explanations often speak of successful intellectual innovations as "ideas whose time has come." Ideas then matter because powerful supportive factors have already emerged that strongly advance or even guarantee their success. In fact, the ideas themselves may have been shaped by such other factors, as explored in the sociology of knowledge. The role of the ideas themselves may in this case vary between that of a nearly negligible contribution and a causal factor that substantially advances a change which otherwise might remain incomplete or come about only much more slowly.

Women's struggles for equality during the last century and a half provide an example. The idea of a fundamental equality of men and women is of course much older, built in many ways into the universal human condition. Its implications for equal political, civil, and socioeconomic rights, however, had little chance of realization in large-scale agrarian societies. Equal gender rights came onto the agenda of modern societies only when profound changes in the structures of family life, in fertility and mortality, in the relations between work and family, and in the physical requirements of work and warfare removed major obstacles to a vast extension of gender equality. Does this mean that the ideas and the struggles of the women's movements of the late nineteenth century and the last half of the twentieth merely rubberstamped developments that were proceeding anyway? By no means. These ideas involved struggle because gender roles—grounded deeply in the norms of everyday life and in values that have strong popular as well as institutional support—have an amazing staying power even when their macro-structural underpinnings have given way. The ideas of gender equality played an important role in the slow dismantling of male privileges both at the level of the mores governing day-to-day life in diverse subcultures and at the level of politics, legislation, and adjudication. This struggle is not over because of the continuing strength of inherited gender roles; but it is advancing its cause—an impressive demonstration of the relevance of ideas. This is an interesting causal pattern because egalitarian ideas, previously perhaps acknowledged in principle but devoid of a multitude of rights implications that are now sought, are opposed primarily by the staying power of normative ideas about gender, while the macro-structural underpinnings of these gender relations are gone.[11]

---

[11] The ways in which the social structure of agrarian societies blocks gender equality is well established in comparative anthropological studies. For one quantitative cross-societal analysis that also points to war, migration, and the long-term effects of religious myths see Sanday (1981). Rueschemeyer and Rueschemeyer (1990) offer a more extended version of the argument just outlined.

Another instructive instance in which the sequencing of interacting factors shaped the role of ideas concerns cognitive innovation—the transformation of social science in the context of new social problems generated by capitalist development. In can be argued that one major factor instigating the rapid development of empirical social research in Europe at the end of the nineteenth century was social problems that could not be sufficiently understood with the cognitive tools available. "The modern social sciences took shape in close interaction with early attempts to deal with the social consequences of capitalist industrialization" (Skocpol and Rueschemeyer 1996, 3). Once they developed, the new investigations gained influence because of the urgent needs for social diagnosis to which they responded.

One must not, however, think of this too simply as a closed loop between demand for knowledge, its supply, and its subsequent impact. The definition of urgent needs for new insight cannot be taken for granted; it was generated in part by the new social investigations. The supply of the needed information and analysis does not follow automatically from the definition of problems, nor can it be simply understood as a response to well-defined questions. And the influence of the knowledge generated does not follow unequivocally from the identification of the need. Rather, all three phases—demand, supply, and influence—involve complex processes that are shaped by institutional structures, by the location and power of the different interests at stake, and by the knowledge-bearing groups as well as the substance of the knowledge they offered. The project just referred to resulted in a theoretical frame whose outlines can here only be hinted at by pointing to the major actors—state elites in competing nation states that were faced with increasingly divisive class differences and democratizing pressures, the organizational leadership of the major social classes, parties and status groups that occupied a "third position" between capital and labor, and a variety of knowledge generating and knowledge bearing groups and institutions.

7   How Ideas Matter: The Social Construction of Collective Interests

A similar constellation of factors is found in successful political and social movements. These are rarely if ever instigated primarily by a set of ideas. Rather, a complex set of felt problems and emerging openings for change constitute the major conditions for mobilization. Within this context ideas play a critical role offering diagnosis and promising solutions. This seems to apply to working class movements, women's movements, the environmental movement, as well as the great variety of ethnic and national movements. Social and political movements are therefore an eminently promising research site for studying the role of ideas.[12] Here we will focus only on one specific aspect of their role, the social construction of collective interests that are eventually pursued in the movements.

Even if the chances of movements rest on the existence of fairly intense and widespread concerns, the goals actually pursued by the emerging movement do not follow from these concerns. To give just one example, "Communist, social democratic, liberal, Catholic, and even outright conservative organizations have competed with each other for the allegiance of the working class, and all have claimed to represent the best interests of labor" (Rueschemeyer, Stephens, and Stephens 1992, 54). Ideas clearly play a significant role in choosing from the variety of possible trajectories to which an incipient movement may be open. They can have lasting consequences for divided or unified responses to the same broad set of problems, and they decide in large part whether only some issues are addressed while the concerns of parts of the larger potential constituency are neglected.

The way specific ideas gain this influence can be specified further. The exigencies of overcoming the difficulties of moving from widely shared concerns and interests to effective collective action put a premium on small groups of activists and, eventually, on formal organization. This gives disproportionate influence to the organizational leadership, and that "oligarchic" influence does not only constitute a problem for intramovement democracy (which is the way it has found the greatest attention in political sociology); it also shapes the goals actually pursued by the organization and its followers. On the one hand, organization is critical for giving substance and power to an incipient movement; on the other, the same process of organization shapes the specific goals and their justification, their relation to other, broader visions of history and the future, and the choice of means.[13] This is not to deny that the ideas thus generated have to find resonance among the potential constituencies of the movement; but if they do appeal to the implicit ideas represented in these diverse groupings, they do have a chance to spread them along the paths of organizational networks and to transform existing patterns of "consciousness," potentially creating new collective identities.

The simplified model sketched gives some indication of where to locate the generation and promulgation of ideas that play a role in the structuring of social

---

[12] Recent years have seen great advances in this field. On the role of cognitive frames see Snow et al. (1986) and Eyerman and Jamison (1991). More generally, I content myself with two bare references: McAdam, McCarthy, and Zald (1996), and McAdam, Tarrow, and Tilly (2001).

[13] For a more extended discussion of these issues see Rueschemeyer, Stephens, and Stephens (1992, 53–7). Our argument joined modifications of Olson's (1965) theory of collective action and of Michels' (1949 [1908]) theory of oligarchy with considerations of how movements are embedded in the power structure of society, to arrive at a more complex view of the construction of class interests and also of more problematic aspects of collective action. Regarding the latter, we claimed that "from a grass roots point of view, it seems reasonable to speak of an *inherent ambiguity of collective action*" (Rueschemeyer, Stephens, and Stephens 1992, 55).

movements. Yet more than location is at stake. Through their relations of power and influence the organizations and institutions involved constitute springboards for influential ideas.

This points to broader implications. If we look back at Hall's theoretical frame for the politics of Keynesian ideas or at the role of the emerging modern social sciences in interaction with policies addressing social problems by capitalist development, we see in these instances as well how the location in institutions and groups—in government agencies, professional communities, universities, parties, and unions—played a critical role for the efficacy ideas in shaping important outcomes.

8   How Ideas Matter: Structural Protection and the Autonomy of Ideas

Organizational and institutional structures not only nurture ideas and secure their propagation; they also protect and conserve them. This covers a wide range of institutional forms, from small provisions such as the creation and maintenance of libraries to the complex structures involved in the institutionalization of academic inquiry. Such arrangements may protect ideas against simple obliteration; they may keep new ideas from being "nipped in the bud" by the force of tradition and restrain vested interests so as to create an opening for change; and they may shelter innovative ideas against a backlash their impact may have instigated in the wider society, be it for moral or material reasons.

Organizational and institutional structures protect ideas by offering them a separate space from other concerns that are often more pressing and frequently claim higher standing on moral, religious, or simply traditional grounds. This *structural differentiation*, to use the technical language of structural functionalism in which this idea gained prominence, involves normative regulation of the differentiated space itself, giving it a place in the wider social order, and securing this place through influence that elevates its standing, through legal (and ultimately coercive) guarantees, through the provision of material resources, and through a privileged position in grid of communication.

The institutionalization of science—or, more broadly, of academic investigation—in modern societies is a prime example of this structural protection of ideas. This idea entered the mainstream of social theory with the brilliant chapter on "Belief Systems and the Social System: The Problem of the 'Role of Ideas'" in Parsons' *Social System*. The starting point is a fundamental duality in the role of ideas. Their adequacy to reality stands in tension with their impact on social integration and collective identity. At the most elementary level of interaction, "if ego and alter share a distorted belief—about the physical environment or about third parties, if ego corrects his belief to bring it closer to reality while alter does not this introduces a strain into the relations of ego and alter" (Parsons 1951, 328). Parsons' important sketches of the institutionalization of scientific investigation and in particular also of applied science (1951, 335–48,491–2, 494–5, 505–20) found a counterpart in the historically fleshed out treatment of Ben-David (1971) who sought to explain the rise of modern science in Europe after long periods of stagnation in the development of scientific knowledge. He shows how the full institutionalization of scientific investigation was preceded by charismatic movements advocating a new status for science but also how substantial institutional support could develop later in enclaves within more backward societies, relying more on the sponsorship of ruling elites.

Normative and ideological ideas may be similarly shielded from the impact of interests and concerns in society, though this protection is not likely to be as strong and impermeable as the protection of science. We encountered the elements of such protection when we considered the construction of collective interests. Such a stabilization of ideas through organizational and institutional arrangements is the main reason why ideological ideas often have a considerable autonomy vis-à-vis the interests and concerns of their audiences. The several components of the amalgam that is represented by current American conservatism—protection of the material interests of the rich, self-reliant individualism, and a high valuation of market exchange as well as of family and community values, religiosity, and traditional morality—are often explained by long-established popular value traditions. Following the leads of this analysis, however, one should expect that this syndrome of ideas has its grounding at least as much in specific organizations and institutions—in religious seminaries, networks of ministers, repeated political mobilization, secular think tanks, and the associated patterns of elite and mass communication—as in diffuse popular attitudes whose elective affinity defies reasoned expectations of which values are compatible with which others.

Within the spaces of a fairly comprehensive institutional protection, ideas come easily to be seen as more autonomous from other social forces than they are in a broader perspective. In such an arena ideas undergo internal developments undisturbed by extraneous influences and blockages and shaped by their own premises, by logic, and by pertinent insights and findings. If the conditions of this state of affairs are not fully recognized, this can easily become a source of idealistic misunderstandings about the transcendence of ideas and their autonomous efficacy.

In fact, the insulation described may not only protect ideas but also limit their influence. Ideas set aside in such a way may be well preserved, but unless they gain at the same time a certain authoritative standing in society and a privileged place in the lines of communication, their broader influence may be minuscule. In the extreme, ideas may acquire an esoteric character that is cherished as such by its followers. Less extreme patterns seem quite common. In nineteenth-century Europe, critical philology infused biblical studies in universities with a skepticism corrosive of traditional faith, while the ministers trained there were kept from letting this knowledge influence their ministry. More generally, the values held dear in religious doctrine are often formulated in a way that is sufficiently vague and general so as not to antagonize an audience committed to contrary daily routines. This "Sunday sermon" syndrome preserves the values, an effect that must not be underestimated; but as it does so, it fails to structure much actual behavior.

9   How Ideas Matter: Truth and Efficacy

So far, we have not touched on the quality and characteristics of ideas except to distinguish between cognitive, normative, and appreciative ideas. Instead, we have focused on the connection of ideas to social structures and processes. Clearly, however, their qualities, in particular truth, distortion, and falsehood, make a difference.

Intuitively, cognitive ideas that are required for successful action are the most persuasive examples for the claim that ideas matter. Truth and efficacy, however, stand in a complicated relationship. It takes just a moment's reflection that the importance of ignorance and misunderstandings is only the inverse of the role of empirically adequate ideas. For instance, neglecting the collective action problem and its ramifications is at the root of quite a few political misjudgments that block successful action.

That is not where the matter ends, however. Beyond knowledge and ignorance, a powerful role in politics is played by deception and—often willful—illusion. Yet "whoever reflects on these matters can only be surprised by how little attention has been paid, in our tradition of philosophical and political thought, to their significance, on the one hand for the nature of action and, on the other, for the nature of our ability to deny in thought and word whatever happens to be the case" (Arendt 1969, 5; 1968).

Wishful thinking is clearly a powerful mechanism producing illusion. In principle, this is at odds with the chances of successful action; but in many situations and for many people and groups successful problem solving is not the immediate issue. It is then that wishful thinking—motivated by parallel inclinations of many individuals or by mechanisms sustaining group identity and solidarity—comes to the fore. Upsetting troubles can then easily be seen as instigated by outsiders or as the work of the most plausible source of evil—of communist infiltration, the American Satan, the CIA, or the Israeli Mossad. That these examples are obvious and somewhat extreme, should not distract from the fact that the mechanism involved is quite common and can take much more nuanced forms. Such spontaneous and often massive tendencies can be exploited by elites who are bent on deception.

There is no question that intentional deception—outright lying as well as the intentional fostering of mistaken ideas—is endemic in politics. Even if lies that are uncovered are detrimental to trust, the temptation to conceal inconvenient facts is very strong because this seems to maintain trust, morale, and legitimacy. And deception is often effective, especially when it articulates well with existing inclinations toward illusion.

The relations between the consequences of ideas and their cognitive adequacy are quite complex. Lying and delusions are not always disabling even in the long run (though what is disabling depends of course on whose interests are at stake). Withholding knowledge has been defended by the elitist partisans of esoteric knowledge because "a little knowledge can be a dangerous thing" in the minds of the masses. A certain veiling of reality—say about the extent and the dynamics of "deviant behavior"—may protect established norms and values, while realistic descriptions of reality may undermine them. The hope that public lies will always fail in the long run may itself be an idea that is valuable for the protection of civic virtue while its general validity is not unproblematic.

Can simplifications and the attendant distortions be enabling, while an emphasis on complicating inconvenient facts may curtail effective action, especially large-scale collective action? Georges Sorel claimed that ideas, for instance the ideas of Marxism, exerted their greatest social power not as realistic theories but as myths. Vilfredo Pareto, endorsing Sorel's claim, relates this to more fundamental features of social action: "The fact that human behavior is strongly influenced by sentiments in the form of derivations which go beyond experience and reality, explains a phenomenon which has been well observed and elucidated by Georges Sorel, namely, that influential social doctrines (it would be more exact to say the sentiments manifested by social doctrines) take the form of myths" (Pareto 1966 [1916], 246).

10   CONCLUSION: HOW IDEAS MATTER

Quite clearly, ideas matter in society and history. The ultimate answer to why this is the case can be found in fundamental reflections on human social action. How ideas make a difference, however, is a problem that defies comprehensive answers. The reason is simple: Precisely because ideas have pervasive consequences but at the same time interact with other factors, to ask how ideas matter turns on closer inspection into as many problems as the question of how social change and social order come about. As we do not have a general theory of social change and order specific enough to explain what we are interested in (not to mention prediction), we cannot expect a general theory detailing how ideas matter.

What we do have are a number of investigations of the role of ideas in more specific developments and circumstances. Associated with these studies are a number of focused theoretical frames that for the time being constitute the building blocks of advances in the study of the role of ideas.

The theoretical frames we have discussed seem to have an interesting common denominator. It is the way ideas are grounded in groups, organizations, and institutions and the attendant relations of communication and influence that is of decisive importance for their creation, their maintenance, and their impact in society. This focus on organizations and institutions happens to have a fortunate methodological implication: It eases at least to some extent the peculiar difficulties of ascertaining the incidence and meaning of ideas as it tells a little more precisely where to look and as the record of ideas is likely to be better preserved in the context of groups, organizations, and institutions. At several points we encountered the problem that the impact of ideas can only be fully understood if we also consider the ideas of broader audiences, which are likely to be of a more implicit character. However here, too, we may suspect that the strength of these ideas depends to a large extent on their grounding in groups and institutions as well as the codes of everyday life.

If we return from these specific theoretical ideas to the grand discussions of the past, we may conclude that the preceding considerations suggest a certain skepticism about claims for the role of ideas as such. It is not only that their effect seems mediated by the way they are embedded in organizations and institutions. This embedding serves also as selection mechanism, and the very content of ideas is partially shaped by these forms of social grounding and support. This skeptical comment, however, does not endorse the materialist side of the enduring controversy between idealist and materialist claims. Ideas enjoy varying degrees of autonomy in their development, and their impact on social stability and change can be minuscule but also extremely powerful. We are only at the beginnings of a better understanding of the factors that account for the difference.

REFERENCES

ALEXANDER, G. 2002. *The Sources of Democratic Consolidation*. Ithaca, NY: Cornell University Press.

ALEXANDER, J. C. 1980–3. *Theoretical Logic in Sociology*, 4 vols. Berkeley: University of California Press.

APEL, K.-O 1984. *Understanding and Explanation*. Cambridge, Mass.: MIT Press.

ARENDT, H. 1968. Truth and politics. Pp. 227–64 in H. Arendt, *Between Past and Future: Eight Exercises in Political Thought*, enlarged edn. New York: Viking.

ARENDT, H. 1969. Lying in politics: reflections on the Pentagon Papers. Pp. 1–47 in H. Arendt, *Crises of the Republic*. New York: Harcourt Brace Jovanovich.

BEN-DAVID, J. 1971. *The Scientist's Role in Society: A Comparative Study*. Englewood Cliffs, NJ: Prentice Hall.

BOCKMAN, J., and EYAL, G. 2002. Eastern Europe as a laboratory of economic knowledge: the transnational roots of neoliberalism. *American Journal of Sociology*, 108: 310–52.

BOURDIEU, P. 1977. *Outline of a Theory of Practice*. Cambridge: Cambridge University Press; originally published 1972.

COLEMAN, J. S. 1964. *Introduction to Mathematical Sociology*. New York: Free Press.

COLLINS, R. 1987. *Theoretical Sociology*. San Diego, Calif.: Harcourt Brace Jovanovich.

EYERMAN, R., and JAMISON, A. (eds.) 1991. *Social Movements: A Cognitive Approach*. University Park: Pennsylvania State University Press.

FOUCAULT, M. 1972. *The Archeology of Knowledge*. New York: Pantheon.

—— 1979. *Discipline and Punish: The Birth of the Prison*. New York: Vintage.

GEERTZ, C. 1964. Ideology as a cultural system. Pp. 47–76 in *Ideology and Discontent*. ed. D. E. Apter. New York: Free Press. Reprinted pp. 193–233 in Geertz, *The Interpretation of Cultures*. New York: Basic Books, 1973.

GIDDENS, A. 1979. *Central Problems in Social Theory*. Berkeley: University of California Press.

—— 1984. *The Constitution of Society*. Cambridge: Polity Press.

GRAMSCI, A. 1975. *Prison Notebooks*. New York: Columbia University Press; written 1928–37.

HALL, P. A. 1989. *The Political Power of Economic Ideas: Keynesianism across Nations*. Princeton, NJ: Princeton University Press.

HEDSTRÖM, P., and SWEDBERG, R. (eds.) 1998. *Social Mechanisms: An Analytical Approach to Social Theory*. Cambridge: Cambridge University Press.

JAMES, H. 1989. What is Keynesian about deficit financing? The case of interwar Germany. In Hall 1989, 231–62.

KEYNES, J. M. 1936. *The General Theory of Employment, Interest and Money*. London: Macmillan.

MANNHEIM, K. 1936. *Ideology and Utopia*. New York: Harcourt, Brace and World.

MARX, K. 1978. *A Contribution to the Critique of Political Economy*. Excerpted on pp. 3–6 in *The Marx–Engels Reader*, ed. R. C. Tucker, 2nd edn.. New York: Norton; originally published 1859.

—— and ENGELS, F. 1978. *The German Ideology, Part I*. Pp. 146–200 in *The Marx–Engels Reader*, ed. R. C. Tucker, 2nd edn.. New York: Norton; written 1845–6, originally published 1932.

MCADAM, D., MCCARTHY, J. D., and ZALD, M. N. 1996. *Comparative Perspectives on Social Movements: Political Opportunities, Mobilizing Structures, and Cultural Framings*. Cambridge: Cambridge University Press.

—— TARROW, S., and TILLY, C. 2001. *Dynamics of Contention*. Cambridge: Cambridge University Press.

MERTON, R. K. 1968. *Social Theory and Social Structure*, 3rd edn. New York: Free Press; originally published 1949.

MICHELS, R. 1949. *Political Parties*. Glencoe, Ill.: Free Press; originally published 1908.

MOHR, J. W. 1998. Measuring meaning structures. *Annual Review of Sociology*, 24: 345–70.

MÜNCH, R. 1987. Parsonian theory today: in search of a new synthesis. Pp. 116–55 in *Social Theory Today*, ed. A. Giddens and J. Turner. Stanford, Calif.: Stanford University Press.

OLSON, M. 1965. *The Logic of Collective Action: Public Goods and the Theory of Groups*. Cambridge, Mass.: Harvard University Press.

PARETO, V. 1966. *Sociological Writings*, ed. S. E. Finer. New York: Praeger; originally published as *Trattato di Sociologia Generale*, 1916.

PARSONS, T. 1937. *The Structure of Social Action*. New York: McGraw-Hill.

—— 1938. The role of ideas in social action. *American Sociological Review*, 3: 652–64. Reprinted in Parsons, *Essays in Sociological Theory*, rev. edn. Glencoe, Ill.: Free Press, 1954.

—— 1951. *The Social System*. Glencoe, Ill.: Free Press.

—— 1959. An approach to the sociology of knowledge. Pp. 25–49 in *Transactions of the Fourth World Congress of Sociology*. Milan: Stresa. Reprinted pp. 139–65 in Parsons, *Sociological Theory and Modern Society*. New York: Free Press, 1967.

—— 1961. An outline of the social system. Pp. 30–79 in *Theories of Society: Foundations of Modern Sociological Theory*, ed. T. Parsons, E. Shils, K. D. Naegele, and J. R. Pitts. New York: Free Press.

—— 1966. *Societies: Evolutionary and Comparative Perspectives*. Englewood Cliffs, NJ: Prentice Hall.

RUESCHEMEYER, D. 1986. *Power and the Division of Labour*. Stanford, Calif.: Stanford University Press.

—— and RUESCHEMEYER, M. 1990. Progress in the distribution of power: gender relations and women's movements as a source of change. Pp. 106–22 in *Rethinking Progress: Movements: Forces and Ideas at the End of the Twentieth Century*, ed. J. C. Alexander and P. Sztompka. Boston: Unwin Hyman.

—— and SKOCPOL, T. (eds.) 1996. *States, Social Knowledge, and the Origins of Modern Social Policy*. Princeton, NJ: Princeton University Press.

—— STEPHENS, E. H., and STEPHENS, J. D. 1992. *Capitalist Development and Democracy*. Chicago: University of Chicago Press.

SANDAY, P. R. 1981. *Female Power and Male Dominance*. Cambridge: Cambridge University Press.

SCHELER, M. 1980. *Problems of a Sociology of Knowledge*. London: Routledge and Kegan Paul; originally published 1924.

SKOCPOL, T., and RUESCHEMEYER, D. 1996. Introduction. In Rueschemeyer and Skocpol 1996, 3–13.

SNOW, D. A., ROCHFORD, E. B., JR., WORDEN, S. K., and BENFORD, R. D. 1986. Frame alignment processes, micromobilization, and movement participation. *American Sociological Review*. 51: 464–81.

STINCHCOMBE, A. L. 1991. The conditions of fruitfulness of theorizing about mechanisms in social science. *Philosophy of the Social Sciences*, 21: 367–87.

—— 1998. Monopolistic competition as a mechanism: corporations, universities, and nation-states in competitive fields. In Hedström and Swedberg 1998, 267–305.

THOMPSON. E. P. 1963. *The Making of the English Working Class*. New York: Vintage Books.

WEBER, M. 1958. The social psychology of the world religions. Pp. 267–301 in *From Max Weber: Essays in Sociology*, ed. H. H. Gerth and C. W. Mills. Oxford: Oxford University Press; originally published 1915.

WENZEL, H. 1990. *The Ordnung des Handelns: Talcott Parsons' Theorie des allgemeinen Handlungssystems*. Frankfurt: Suhrkamp.

WUTHNOW, R. 1987. *Meaning and Moral Order: Explorations in Cultural Analysis*. Berkeley: University of California Press.

—— 1989. *Communities of Discourse: Ideology and Social Structure in the Reformation, the Enlightenment, and European Socialism*. Cambridge, Mass.: Harvard University Press.

CHAPTER 13

··

DETECTING IDEAS AND THEIR EFFECTS

··

RICHARD PRICE

THIS volume seeks, among other things, to understand to what extent the grounding of politics in particular times, places, and cultures shapes the effort to make universal prescriptions that apply regardless of context. This chapter's particular contribution to this problematique is to address the question of how we even know such ideas and norms—and their effects in politics—when we see them. Such questions have been brought to the fore at the global level in contemporary politics with, among other things, the increasing scope and depth of norms of international law, epitomized by such crystallizing events as the 1998 British arrest of former Chilean dictator Augusto Pinochet, the trial of former Yugoslavian President Slobodan Milosevic at the Hague, and the coming into being of the International Criminal Court (ICC) in 2003. How can you even have universal norms in such a culturally and politically diverse world? Are they indeed really universal, consequential, and how do we know?

Such questions about the role of ideas and norms have a long history in the study of politics from local to global contexts. For skeptics—variously realists, materialists, and often rationalists—ideas do not matter, as power and material interests ultimately drive politics. Others cannot comprehend how anyone could contend that ideas don't matter in politics, given the history of bloody revolutions and wars fought in the name of political ideals. But those convinced of the role of ideas in politics have presented anything but a unified front as to how we are to detect ideas and specify their effects, with a variety of methodological and epistemological positions having been staked out within the social sciences and humanities. Methods include the drawing of causal inferences from statistical correlations and regressions, experimental designs, psychological studies, counterfactual reasoning, and process-tracing which might involve archival research and interviews (Yee 1996). Yee among others has provided a succinct overview of such approaches, concluding that basic inadequacies beset the positivist and interpretivist approaches that have tended to broadly characterize the study of ideas. On the one hand, the behavioralists' and institutionalists' "commitment to empirical analyses of observable behavior that can be tested or falsified renders them reluctant and ill-equipped to analyze the intersubjective meanings and symbolic discourses that give ideas their causal effects," while on the other hand interpretative and discursive approaches "routinely neglect causal analysis by emphasizing instead the interpretation of meanings" (Yee 1996, 102). Over the last decade, however, a number of scholars from different fields have sought to bridge precisely this gap, making an analysis of some of these efforts an appropriate focus for this chapter.

1   CUSTOM, CONSENT, AND CONSTRUCTIVISM

Such questions about the status and role of ideas have long animated central debates in the social sciences and law, and none more importantly than debates in the fields of international relations and international law over the status of international legal norms and their impact on world politics. Despite milestones such as the above in practice, controversies have still abounded over the sources, content, and impact of rules in these and a multitude of other legal developments as well. Without reducing the complexity of these debates, one question in particular will serve as a frequent touchstone for this chapter since it serves as a most fruitful proxy for the problem of the role of international or even universal ideas more generally: how do we know an international norm (such as a customary international law) when we see one? As Tilly and Goodin inquire in the opening chapter to this volume, what sort of evidence is available to answer such questions?

Despite some general agreement among traditional theories of customary law which stipulate that state behavior and expressed legal belief ("*opinio juris*") ought to be taken into account in determining whether a norm has the status of customary law, the details of this question have resisted unambiguous and consistent answers among international lawyers in theory and jurists in practice. International relations (IR) scholars, for their part, have long wrestled with a similar question:

How do we know (robust) international norms when we see them? Given the commonality of these questions, it is no surprise that in the 1990s a push began to integrate scholarship in the fields of international law and international relations.[1] This chapter explores how recent scholarship on norms in international relations, and judicial decisions and international legal scholarship on customary law, might forge a useful synthesis in determining how we know such norms and their effects when we see them.

According to the dominant legal theory of consent, we can identify international legal norms according to the explicit commitments by states to be bound by the rule in question, typically signaled by signing and ratifying a treaty. International norms of importance and consequence have existed, however, that are not confined to treaty norms given explicit consent by all states. International legal scholars and jurists have long recognized that other sources of law exist, including more informal sources such as customary law, though controversies abound as to what exactly counts as a customary rule of law (e.g. Kirgis 1987; Byers 1999; Roberts 2001).

A determination of the status of an international norm as a customary rule of international law constitutes an important threshold in the development of new international standards of conduct, since the concept of a customary norm of international law means that a norm is universal enough that even states that have not explicitly consented to the norm are legally obliged to abide by it. Such determinations are potentially far-reaching indeed given their intrusion upon state sovereignty, though I take heed of the wisdom of cautions against overemphasizing the importance of binding judicial rulings in a realm where they have often been institutionally absent or overridden (Bodansky 1995). Moreover, skeptics have argued that the rules that most scholars and courts have identified as customary law are not universal, and are typically derived from very selective evidence at odds with the majority of actual practice. Further, they have charged that to the extent there are identifiable behavioral regularities, they are not due to obligation and law at all but self-interest (Bodansky 1995; Goldsmith and Posner, 1999). To be sure, even if we can identify norms that qualify as rules of customary law, the skeptics are often right that their effects are less than impressive given the lack of enforcement at the international level. Still, *domestic* courts have employed determinations of international custom for rulings, including perhaps most notably the conviction by a US court of a Paraguayan national of the crime of torture in 1984 in the *Filartiga* case (US Court of Appeals 1980). Such claims of jurists that a norm of universal obligation exists even if not explicitly consented to by all states through a treaty is a fairly stunning claim that ought to be of paramount interest to social scientists seeking to identify international norms in a world of sovereign states: what exactly constitutes such a customary norm of international law? How would

---

[1] See Slaughter-Burley 1993; Slaughter, Tulumello, and Wood 1998; Goldstein et al. 2000; Reus-Smit 2004.

we know a customary rule of international law when we see one? To what extent could it be argued that rapidly emerging new norms such as bans on anti-personnel (AP) landmines, the use of child soldiers, or whaling have already attained the status of other customary norms of international law, such as those prohibiting torture, apartheid, and genocide?

As above, establishing obligations upon states based upon the existence of a customary rule of international law traditionally has required some mix of a demonstration of two requirements: general state practice (norm-conforming behavior), and *opinio juris*—the belief by states that the practice is undertaken as an obligation of international law. Debates about these two requirements not only often run up against more internalized disagreements concerning their relative weight or of what they consist but, indeed, the very notion of international custom making claims of obligation sits ill at ease with the theory of consent that has been the predominant basis of international law. I have addressed elsewhere at length the implications of constructivist international relations scholarship on norms to these debates in legal theory (see also Reus-Smit 2003), arguing that the focus in constructivism upon constitutive effects of norms on actors' interests and identities can resolve theoretical conundrums in international law about how customary norms can be said to exist at all in a world of sovereign states, and that such insights have important implications for legal theories concerning the determinants of customary law (Price 2004). Here I confine myself to a different undertaking: assuming we need to identify some mix of state practice and *opinio juris* to detect a customary norm, I argue that in addition to the kinds of evidence used by courts and legal scholars, such determinations often would benefit from and may require the kind of systematic and close empirical analyses of norms that are the vocational terrain more of social scientists (as laid out below) than of judges or lawyers.

A prominent school of thought that can further our inquiry here is the social constructivist program that has emerged within the subfield of international relations in political science over the last decade. Contrary to materialists like realists who maintain that power and material self-interest explain the important outcomes in world politics, social constructivists contend that norms and ideas constitute power and interests—that is, politics is social, not just material (Wendt 2000). Constructivist scholarship has focused on accounting for norms and their effects, and as such we can to turn to its implications for an area like the laws of war to assess the role of ideas. Realism, long a dominant perspective in international relations, dismisses the role of law or norms and ideas in general as epiphenomenal at the best of times, but especially in time of war. From this view, there has been little need through the course of history to depart from the verity of Cicero's dictum, "*inter arma silent leges*" ("in time of war law is silent"). International law in such times of war indeed has often seemed confined to commenting or debating on the sidelines the legality or illegality of this or that action, sometimes leaving a similarly helpless impression that international rules of law are often not integral to the process of war itself. Constructivist scholarship, however, has focused on understanding not just what a norm is, but researching empirically what it does. Constructivists have also sought to understand not just the regulative but also the productive power of normative and legal discourses, rather than divorcing norms and law on the one hand from power on the other, as has too often been the case in realist, idealist, and some legal approaches. The result of these constructivist turns is an enriched picture of the role of norms. A social construct-ivist perspective on war, for instance, insists that in all but the most absolute of extermination campaigns, war is not the complete absence of norms and law. Rather, in the outbreak, conduct, and ending of hostilities, important aspects of war can be shown to constitute the rule-based conduct of a social institution (Price 1997; Wendt 2000; Scarry 1985).

Those norms manifest themselves in two main ways: regulative effects and constitutive effects, a distinction pioneered by Kratochwil (1989) and succinctly captured in the Katzenstein volume (1996, 5):

In some situations norms operate like rules that define the identity of an actor, thus having "constitutive effects" that specify what actions will cause relevant others to recognize a particular identity. In other situations norms operate as standards that specify the proper enactment of an already specified identity. In such instances norms have "regulative" effects that specify standards of proper behavior. Norms thus either define (or constitute) identities or prescribe (or regulate) behavior, or they do both.

Typically, the norms of warfare that garner the most attention are regulative: the prohibitionary norms that restrain behavior, such as proscriptions against bombing civilians, using chemical weapons, deploying human shields, killing or abusing prisoners of war, and so on. International relations scholarship has dem-onstrated empirically the processes by which such norms are generated and by which they have effects, particularly those aspects of norms that are not captured by positivist or consent-based conceptions of international law, nor the state interest-based accounts of neoliberalism.[2]

The case of the norm against chemical weapons provides an apposite example of how constructivism helps overcome some of the limitations of legal or social scientific positivist conceptions of norms in answering the question: how do we know if a norm really exists? The question of the status of the early chemical weapons taboo has been a perplexing one from the perspective of international law. This is because the underlying epistemological and ontological presumptions of positivist international law do not capture fully the range of important phenomena that constitute norms. Thus, while an entire volume of the monumental studies by the Stockholm International Peace Research Institute (SIPRI) on chemical warfare was devoted to a spirited and utterly thorough defense of the existence of a

---

[2] See Adler 1992; Finnemore 1996; McElroy 1992; Thomas 2001; Tannenwald 2004.

customary norm prohibiting chemical warfare, the volume could muster little to say about the existence of such a norm during the First World War. About this entire period, which witnessed the first massive modern use of chemical weapons, the book was confined to contending in one paragraph that "there was already a widespread belief that such use was contrary to the law of war. This is indicated by the fact that both sides sought to justify their actions by claiming that they were using gas in reprisal" (SIPRI 1973, 103). This claim is interesting both because it points to the critical importance of justifications and violations, thus presciently foreshadowing a key contribution of international relations and legal analysis that was to follow, but also because there was no follow-on to that insight in sustained empirical fashion. It is such empirical follow-up that I argue here is increasingly important for the proper adjudication of cases of customary law, providing an important invitation for a synthesis between social science scholarship and inter-national law.

Another exhaustive legal analysis of chemical weapons concluded of the First World War that while "a dogmatic answer can hardly be given as to the reality of an international norm interdicting the use of gas in warfare ... On the face and in balance it would seem that the evidence shifts the scales toward a conclusion either than no such rule was ever in being, or that if it was it did not survive the war" (Thomas and Thomas 1970, 141). While this conclusion is utterly judicious in its legal caution, it does fly in the face of the fact that the Hague Declaration of 1899 was the crucially important genesis of the modern norm that had lasting effects on the character of that norm (Price 1997). The picture we are driven to derive from such an international legal standpoint then, is an overly static one of a norm existing in the form of the Hague Declaration (or the erroneous denial of its importance or even existence), its disappearance during the chemical warfare of the First World War, and then its reappearance (or birth de novo) in the interwar period. It is difficult if not impossible to reconcile such an approach to norms—you either have a norm or you do not / it either exists full blown or not at all—with periods like the First World War, and indeed with the actual development and practice of norms such as the chemical weapons taboo. Similarly, once such a customary norm is found to exist, claims made on its behalf from the perspective of positivist law render too static a picture of norms. As put in the SIPRI study, "Custom, once established, exists regardless of the contrary wishes of individual states" (SIPRI 1973, 136).

The difficulty here is precisely the same that hamstrings positivist international relations approaches to norms (e.g. Krasner 1983). The latter's mechanical view of the world in which phenomena like norms are treated as variables posits a similar all-or-nothing gambit. The statistical logic of positivism, like the view of legal positivism, leaves little room for numerous incarnations of normative phenomena between the poles of a fully robust, taken-for-granted norm and no norm at all. Courts of law have an obvious practical reason for demanding the all-or-nothing determination that either there is a norm or there is not, while it was on epistemological and methodological grounds that positivist ontology has theorized many norms out of existence in making this move. For these reasons, international legal scholarship in this case at least has had a very difficult time reconciling the existence of a customary norm with its violation.

On the contrary, Kratochwil and Ruggie, in an important article in 1986, argued that it is precisely the counterfactual validity of norms that makes them ill-suited to a full accounting by positivist approaches. A norm may persist, with subsequent consequence, even as it is violated (Kratochwil and Ruggie 1986, 753, 767–8). Traditional positivist and consent-based approaches to international law and international relations that seek to take norms seriously struggle with the phenomena of violations, since the very act of violations from a positivist standpoint means that the norm—which such accounts seek to establish—has been invalidated. But the criteria for identifying a norm for positivist international relations is restricted to brute behavior (compliance or not), from which state interests are imputed; in legal positivism it is state interest manifested in terms of explicit consent of a state, usually in the form of treaty participation. As will be seen below, more subtle indicators are needed for a nuanced appreciation of the phenomena of norms. This can be attained by understanding the role of justifications, but also examining additional empirical indicators that testify to the existence of norms.

An additional contribution of constructivist social science in identifying ideas and norms inheres in the insight that norms do not merely constrain already existing states from pursuing their exogenous interests, but that norms also in part constitute actors and interests. That is, norms do not have solely regulative or restrictive effects, but also productive or constitutive effects. This is indicated in Katzenstein's definition of norms as "collective expectations for the proper behavior of actors with a given identity" (Katzenstein 1996, 5). In terms of our example of norms of warfare, permissive or constitutive norms are those often taken-for-granted conventions which sanction and make possible practices of warfare and identify the legitimate actors authorized to engage in those practices. The intersubjective agreement among states that sanctions murder, for example, is often overlooked as a central practice of war, but it is absolutely central to it. Without it, soldiers would be treated as murderers by both members of their own societies and that of the enemy. But it is because of the shared acceptability of killing legitimate targets in warfare that soldiers who have killed other legitimate targets usually are not treated as murderers, but as heroes or as prisoners of war. The modern soldier is premised upon an intersubjective agreement among states which constitutes the practice of war and its relevant actor identities.

This phenomenon has been brought into sharp relief by the controversies over the Bush administration's treatment of prisoners in its war on terrorism following the terrorist attacks of September 11, 2001: a significant cause of the breakdown of normative restraint has been less a rejection of how to treat prisoners of war than ambiguity as to who gets to count as being defined as a prisoner of war (subject to legitimate killing or respectful treatment as a POW if captured), and who is to be treated as a criminal (legitimately subject to interrogation and criminal sanction). That is, a standard analysis of the Bush administration's abusive handling of the Iraqi prisoners following its war in 2003 might see it as a straightforward violation of a regulative norm, and conclude that the norm has had little restraining effect on the US, bringing the norm's relevance and even very existence into question. But a constitutive analysis would identify more norms more powerfully at work here, insofar as the US has based its position not on the view that legitimate POWS are not deserving of legally protected treatment, but rather that those held are to be conceptualized as terrorists, not soldiers, given the US is waging a war against terror. While I would concur with the considerable legal opinion that this view is mistaken, the point is that the US has not argued it is permissible to abuse prisoners of war (the US has undertaken legal proceedings against those responsible for such abuse), but rather that the US position makes no sense and is not possible without invoking the constitutive effects of norms regarding prisoners of war. Thus, it is only by identifying the "how possible" questions and the constitutive effects of norms that we can understand why the US is not simply slaughtering any and all it deems as hostile regardless of whether they are civilians, soldiers, guerillas, or terrorists, for that—and only that—would be a situation truly devoid of norms.

2   RESEARCH AS A VOCATION

Armed with insights from a social constructivist theoretical account of norms, how is it that a court of law is to find a customary rule of international law? Controversies abound among legal minds concerning how important behavior is supposed to be relative to *opinio juris*, and about how much adherence to each must be exhibited to constitute a customary norm: is "universal" state practice required, or only "general," "persistent," and/or "frequent" state practice? If some formulation of the latter, how many states' participation would constitute a "general" practice of the community of nations, and how many repetitions would count as "frequent" and "consistent"? How many violations would suffice to deny a practice as generally followed?

These questions directly parallel the puzzle of determining the status of norms that has been the subject of much recent debate in the field of international relations; namely, how do you know a robust norm when you see one? To say we know a norm by what it does, as above, is to encounter the problem articulated by Legro that "one can almost always identify a norm to 'explain' or 'allow' a particular effect" after the fact (Legro 1997, 31, 33). The problem for Legro, and indeed for standard social science, is how to avoid tautology and conceptualize norm robustness independent of the very effects attributed to norms, and how to assess norm existence and robustness in the present without the advantage of such hindsight. While thoughtful, Legro's suggestions of durability, concordance, and clarity do not escape this problem (see Price 1998); a more theoretical objection simply finds that what is a problem of tautology for positivist social science is for social constructivists but a recursive instantiation of practices through structures and agents.

As scholars of both law and international relations have argued, no decisive quantitative rule is available to determine definitively the threshold of what amount of state practice among how many states constitutes a settled international norm or rule of customary international law (Chayes and Chayes 1993, 175).[3] The international legal scholar Kirgis has very usefully suggested that a sliding scale seems to operate in determinations of customary law by the International Court of Justice (ICJ) among others. As he put it,

On the sliding scale, very frequent, consistent state practice establishes a customary rule without much (or any) affirmative showing of an *opinio juris*, so long as it is not negated by evidence of non-normative intent. As the frequency and consistency of the practice decline in any series of cases, a stronger showing of *opinio juris* is required. At the other end of the scale, a clearly demonstrated *opinio juris* establishes a customary rule without much (or any) affirmative showing that governments are consistently behaving in accordance with the asserted rule.   (Kirgis 1987, 149)

This formulation is a very useful approximation of both a description of the variation in criteria employed by the ICJ and other courts ruling on cases of customary international law, and a prescription of how to determine customary status. But how is it determined what a state's practice is in behavior and *opinio juris*? It might seem that to establish this would require the kind of sustained empirical analysis that is more commonly the vocation of a social scientist than a judge in a court of international law, a domestic judge in a case involving international legal issues, or an international legal scholar trained more in the interpretation of legal texts than social science research (see also Bodansky 1995). Indeed, in the important *Filartiga* case in which a US court established that torture was a customary norm of international law, the empirical indicators for such a monumental determination were scant and not systematic, at least from the perspective of a social scientist looking to empirically establish a norm (*Filartiga v. Pena-Irala*, US Court of Appeals 1980). As asked by Tilly and Goodin in the Introduction, what

---

[3] Finnemore and Sikkink suggest that no less than one-third of the members of a system are required to constitute a critical enough mass for an emerging norm to lead to a "norm cascade," and that entry into force for treaties is a good proxy to say when a norm exists (Finnemore and Sikkink 1998, 887; on cascades see also Kuran and Sunstein 1999).

kinds of evidence are available for empirical examination of the political processes that constitute developing customary legal norms?

In order to demonstrate concretely how one might practically answer such a question, in what follows I turn to an examination of a particular case: the emergent taboo on the use of anti-personnel (AP) landmines. Would this widely—though not universally—accepted norm constitute a customary norm of international law? In broad strokes, what we would want to ascertain are the emergent *effects* of such norms, such as whether there is a change in general state practice from the use of the dubious weapon as routine, widespread, normal, and uncontroversial to exceptional, restricted, aberrant, and politicized. Here we would look for whether violations are understood and treated by states as breaches of the rule or as recognition of a new rule. Are violations undertaken surreptitiously, in extreme situations only, or as a matter of course? Who decides questions of use—soldiers in the field, commanders, or political leaders? Have the military rules of engagement for deployment of the practice changed? Has the threshold for use been raised to exceptional circumstances for the general practice of states? Do states formally reserve the right to use the weapon under certain conditions, but refrain from using it?

Where would we look for such indicators? Beyond the legal texts usually the staple of courts, we would turn to internal policy documents, military orders, records of the meetings of decision-makers, biographical accounts, statements by government spokespersons, instructions to negotiating teams, statements at international negotiation sessions, and interviews with decision-makers which could all be canvassed to provide evidence to determine the degree to which a nascent norm has been internalized by any given actor. For states that have ratified the treaty and do not use landmines, the assessment is straightforward. But if it is unclear that there are enough such states to claim customary status, then more detailed assessments of the numerous states whose positions are more ambiguous becomes relevant to determine whether they evince sufficient pulls of obligation in their practices and rhetoric. Systematically, one might lay out the following evidence as germane to the task:

I   *Opinio Juris*

    A. *Treaty Status*

        1. Treaty Signature: Has the state signed the AP Landmine Convention?

        2. Treaty Ratification: Has the state ratified the Convention?

        3. Is the level of treaty participation comparable with other norms regarded as customary law, such as prohibitions against torture or slavery?

    B. *General Government Statements*: Evidence to be considered here would include official press releases, speeches by government spokespersons, and statements made by delegates at official conferences and meetings (including United Nations sessions).

1. Has the state upheld or rejected the taboo in official statements? Has there been a shift or inconsistencies in the articulation of official government positions?

2. If the norm has not been rhetorically accepted, are challenges or rejections of the norm directed at the central validity claim of the norm per se, or are they directed at the definitional margins? For example, is the source of resistance what counts as an AP landmine, or timeframes for implementation, as opposed to outright rejection of the idea they ought to be banned?

3. Can the state claim to be a "persistent objector" that has "manifestly and continuously" objected to the central validity claim of an evolving new norm of customary international law proscribing the use of AP landmines?

C. *Reactions to Violations*

1. Accused Parties: What do those accused of the use of mines say in response to allegations? The following scale indicates decreased degrees of rhetorical challenges to the norm: (*a*) rejection of norm; (*b*) no reaction; (*c*) special justifications made; (*d*) denial; (*e*) norm upheld.

2. Accusing Parties: How do they interpret the consequences and significance of violation? (*a*) Are reprisals justified? (*b*) Are accusations of the use of mines being used instrumentally against an opponent? If so, they may provide evidence of the norm since one would only attempt to get mileage out of such accusations if there was such a norm in the first place.

3. Third Parties: How do others respond? (*a*) passive / no reaction; (*b*) condemnation; (*c*) sanctions to enforce norm.

4. Assessment: Are violations understood and treated by the state in question as breaches of the rule or as recognition of a new rule? Does the central validity claim of the norm elicit wide adherence? Do "specially affected states" uphold the validity of the norm? Are challenges on the definitional margins? Are they comparable in effect to reservations attached to other treaties? Are they widespread? Do holdouts repudiate the central validity claims of the norms or accept them (with qualifications)?

II Practices

A. *Production / Export / Possession*

Is there evidence of the influence of a customary norm in these state practices insofar as they contribute to the prescriptive status of illegitimacy? For example, why would a state ban exports if the commodity/activity was to be regarded as routine practice, completely acceptable, and unpoliticized?

(One could keep in mind comparisons to other examples such as the gradual abolition of the slave trade).

B. *Use*

1. Universal. This would be the strictest test of practice: is there universal conformity with the proscription?

2. Violations

   (*a*) Who: (i) States; (ii) Violations by non-state actors in the territory of the state. This could be considered to constitute a criminal act rather than a detraction from international law insofar as only states are recognized as subjects, and the practice is not state practice contributing to custom.

   (*b*) Circumstances: Are AP mines being used routinely in any circumstance of utility, or only in exceptional circumstances such as in the face of threats to territorial integrity / regime viability? (i) Routine; (ii) Surreptitious; (iii) Extreme situations only: what threshold has to be reached to set deployment in motion?

   (*c*) Who Decides? (i) Soldiers in Field; (ii) Commanders; (iii) Renegade Fighters; (iv) Political decision-makers.

3. Reserved Right Not Exercised: Does the state in question formally reserve the right to use the weapon under certain conditions? What are those conditions, and have they been met without use? Who makes the decision to use AP mines, and has this location shifted as a result of the emergence of the taboo?

C. *Assessment*

Is there a change in general state practice from the use of mines as routine, widespread, normal, and uncontroversial to politicized, exceptional, aberrant, and abhorrent? Have there been shifts in the elements of use above even among holdout states? Has the threshold for use been raised to exceptional circumstances for the general practice of states?

3 CONCLUSION

Can we say that ideas move politics, and can we maintain that they do so from the local level to the systemic level of world politics? This chapter has focused on the latter, the most challenging context for identifying ideas and their effects, examining how the fields of international law and international relations identify the existence of the international ideas known as customary law in even the most difficult of contexts, that being war, where ideas are routinely taken to be at their least importance relative to sheer material power. While the absolute universality of such informal ideas and their invariable primacy in driving politics (as opposed to other factors) are more than subject to challenge, so too is the dismissal of such informal norms or "soft law" (Abbott and Snidal 2000, 456), or their understanding in purely functionalist or material interest-based terms. Rather, empirical process-tracing of how such understandings of context insinuate themselves in the practices of actors like states in the international system can plausibly identify the relevance of international ideas for today's political world. And while skeptics are hardly to be dismissed when pointing out the weaknesses of the international system in its ability to enforce norms like customary law, so too are there too many exceptions of compliance with such norms to dismiss them as epiphenomenal (Byers 1999; Reus-Smit 2004). How else indeed are we to make sense of events such as how the British police in 1998 could arrest a former Chilean dictator, at the request of a Spanish magistrate, for the international customary crime of torture— something that is quite difficult to maintain as mere self-interested power politics devoid of the transformative role of ideas that are international in scope?

References

ABBOTT, K., and SNIDAL, D. 2000. Hard and soft law in international governance. *International Organization,* 54: 421–56.

Adler, E. 1992. The emergence of cooperation: national epistemic communities and the international evolution of the idea of arms control. *International Organization,* 46: 101–45.

BODANSKY, D. 1995. Customary (and not so customary) international environmental law. *Indiana Journal of Global Legal Studies,* 3: 1. Available at: http://ijgls.indiana.edu/archive/03/01/bodansky. shtml#top (accessed May 21, 2002).

BYERS, M. 1999. *Custom, Power and the Power of Rules.* Oxford: Oxford University Press.

CHAYES, A., and CHAYES, A. H. 1993. On compliance. *International Organization,* 47: 175–205.

FINNEMORE, M. 1996. *National Interests in International Society.* Ithaca, NY: Cornell University Press.

——and SIKKINK, K. 1998. International norm dynamics and political change. *International Organization,* 52: 887–917.

GOLDSMITH, J. L., and POSNER, E. A. 1999. A theory of customary international law. *University of Chicago Law Review,* 66: 1113–77.

GOLDSTEIN, J., KAHLER, M., KEOHANE, R., and SLAUGHTER, A.-M. 2000. Legalization and world politics. *International Organization,* 54: 385–683.

KATZENSTEIN, P. (ed.) 1996. *The Culture of National Security: Norms and Identities in World Politics.* New York: Columbia University Press.

KIRGIS, F. 1987. Custom on a sliding scale. *American Journal of International Law,* 81: 146–51.

KRASNER, S. 1983. *International Regimes.* Ithaca, NY: Cornell University Press.

KRATOCHWIL, F. 1989. *Rules, Norms and Decisions*. Cambridge: Cambridge University Press.
—— and RUGGIE, J. G. 1986. International organization: a state of the art on the art of the state. *International Organization*, 40: 753–75.
KURAN, T., and SUNSTEIN, C. R. 1999. Availability cascades and risk regulation. *Stanford Law Review*, 51(4): 683–768.
LEGRO, J. 1997. Which norms matter? Revisiting the "failure" of internationalism. *International Organization*, 51: 31–63.
MCELROY, R. 1992. *Morality and American Foreign Policy*. Princeton, NJ: Princeton University Press.
PRICE, R. 1997. *The Chemical Weapons Taboo*. Ithaca, NY: Cornell University Press.
—— 1998. Compliance with international norms and the mines taboo. Pp. 340–63 in *To Walk Without Fear: The Global Movement to Ban Landmines*, ed. M. Cameron, B. Tomlin, and R Lawson. Toronto: Oxford University Press.
—— 2004. Emerging customary norms and anti-personnel landmines. In Reus-Smit 2004, 106–30.
REUS-SMIT, C. (ed.) 2004. *The Politics of International Law*. Cambridge: Cambridge University Press.
—— 2003. Politics and international legal obligation. *European Journal of International Law*, 9: 591–625.
ROBERTS, A. E. 2001. Traditional and modern approaches to customary international law: a reconciliation. *American Journal of International Law*, 95: 757–91.
SCARRY, E. 1985. *The Body in Pain*. New York: Oxford University Press.
SLAUGHTER-BURLEY, A.-M. 1993. International law and international relations: a dual agenda. *American Journal of International Law*, 87: 205–39.
SLAUGHTER, A,-M., TULUMELLO, A., and WOOD, S. 1998. International law and international relations theory: a new generation of interdisciplinary scholarship. *American Journal of International Law*, 92: 367–97.
STOCKHOLM INTERNATIONAL PEACE RESEARCH INSTITUTE (SIPRI) 1973. *The Problem of Chemical and Biological Warfare*. Vol. 3: *CBW and the Law of War*. Stockholm: SIPRI.
TANNENWALD, N, 2004. *The Nuclear Taboo*. Cambridge: Cambridge University Press.
THOMAS, W. 2001. *The Ethics of Destruction*. Ithaca, NY: Cornell University Press.
THOMAS, A. V. W., and THOMAS, A. J. 1970. *Legal Limits on the Use of Chemical and Biological Weapons*. Dallas, Tex.: Southern Methodist University Press.
US Court of Appeals, 2nd Circuit 1980. *Filartiga v. Pena-Irala*. 630 F. 2nd 876.
WENDT, A. 2000. *Social Theory of International Politics*. Cambridge: Cambridge University Press.
YEE, A. S. 1996. The causal effect of ideas on policies. *International Organization*, 50(1): 69–108.

CHAPTER 14

....

HOW PREVIOUS IDEAS AFFECT LATER IDEAS

....

NETA C. CRAWFORD

ARGUMENTATION, the attempt to persuade others with reasons, is one of the signature activities of politics. Even if war, at least temporarily, decides an issue, those who took up the sword must have been persuaded that it was right or prudent to do so. Crucial to the process of persuasion is the content of the argument—the ideas that make sense or don't, that move people to act or leave them unaffected. Many of the ideas that have great power to persuade and mobilize are portrayed as novel—such as Franklin Roosevelt's "New Deal" or Mikhail Gobachev's "new thinking"—and this claim to newness is itself often appealing.

Conversely, while new ideas may prompt innovation, a fixed notion—an *idée fixe*—and the institutions that enact and support it, can prevent change. Thus, Karl Marx could say, "Men make their own history, but they do not make it just as they please; they do not make it under circumstances chosen by themselves, but under circumstances directly found, given and transmitted from the past" (Marx 1978 [1852], 595). Marx and other materialists, reacting against Kant and Hegel's focus on ideas, tended to privilege material forces and constraints. Yet previous ideas are also constraining and disposing—they influence later ideas and help construct the material world.

1   PREMISE, DISCOURSE, INSTITUTIONALIZATION, AND FEELING

Previous ideas may affect later ideas in at least four ways: as the content of formal arguments; as the background discourse; as the organizing principle of institutions and social structures; and through their association with feelings.

In its most direct form, previous ideas become the premises of human reasoning—whether by syllogism or analogy. We could not think in terms of formal logic (syllogism and practical inference) or by analogy without the content of previous ideas available to us. In this instance, actors are often quite conscious of the role of specific previous ideas as the premises for their arguments. Historical analogies are often given in shorthand form, standing in for more complex ideas. For example, "Munich" connotes the dangers of appeasing an aggressor and "Pearl Harbor" of being caught unawares by an unprovoked surprise attack (see Neustadt and May 1986; Khong 1992). The conclusion of analogical argument follow from its premises, e.g. don't appease aggressors.

Of course all arguments occur in a context, within a preexisting discourse that makes the claims intelligible. This background of taken-for-granted beliefs is what Jürgen Habermas (1984) calls the "lifeworld"—"commonsense certainties"—without which we could not understand each other's claims. In this sense, previous ideas are the starting points out of which we make sense of the social and natural world and through which we evaluate new ideas. Similarly, Foucault's articulation of the role of social, scientific, and political discourses, Max Weber's explication of the role of *wertrationalität* or decision-making according to absolute values, and Thomas Kuhn's discovery of the role of scientific paradigms in structuring scientific research, all point to how systems of previous ideas can structure human perception and judgment.[1] In short, because they constitute the language of understanding, previous ideas, as more or less closed discourses, thus affect an individual's receptivity and evaluation of the possibility and legitimacy of later ideas.

Ideas that imply actions to maintain or change the social or natural world must be specified in the form of concrete steps to enact the idea. Previous ideas may thus also affect later ideas when they are institutionalized in the routines and standard operating procedures of organizations and cultures (see Goldstein 1993). Institutionalization requires actors to specify exactly what they mean by an idea and its logical entailments, as well as how they will execute and measure its implementation. During the process of institutionalization there is often room for

---

[1] Foucault 1972; Weber 1961; Kuhn 1955. Also see work in cognitive psychology on schemas, scripts, and frames which function in similar, but more limited ways. See Abelson 1981; and Polletta and Ho, this volume.

disagreement about how to implement the idea, and thus actors may use the original idea as a starting point for their arguments about how to enact a specific idea.

In some cases, the institutionalization of ideas requires creating a new organization, but more often than not, institutionalization occurs within existing organizations. Of course the capacities of already functioning organizations are the result of prior discourses; they have preexisting resources, and off-the-shelf plans, standard operating procedures and routines for addressing both expected and novel situations. Those canned responses themselves are the result of prior beliefs and assumptions about the way the world works and the most effective response to particular situations. Once institutionalized, ideas become part of the social structure that constrains and disposes other social action and the development of new ideas.

Organizations also invent procedures for assessing and organizing new knowledge in the sense that an idea, once institutionalized, becomes the starting point for future investigation and evaluation. Members of the organization see the world through institutionalized beliefs (and feelings), recognize a situation as something that it should address, and use guidelines for data gathering and information processing that are drawn from institutionalized beliefs (and feelings). In this way, through institutionalization, previous ideas come to structure knowledge-making and the concrete practices and resource allocations that become the larger social structure. Resource allocation may even ensure that new ideas that contradict a previous idea are never developed. Thus, the institutionalization of previous ideas helps determine the form and substance of social structures which in turn influences the production of new ideas. In this way, ideas become what Lynn Eden (2004, 3) calls "organizational frames:"

Organizational frames encounter the present and look to the future. At the same time, they embody the past: foundational understandings of organizational mission, long-standing collective assumptions and knowledge about the world, and earlier patterns of attention to problems and solutions. All of this shapes how problems are later defined and how solutions are developed. Once solutions are established as knowledge-laden routines, they enable actors in organizations to carry out new actions, but they simultaneously constrain new actions.

Further, through institutionalization ideas are not only internalized within organizations but externalized, as these ideas are adopted by other organizations and become social norms. Institutionalization is the primary mechanism of path dependency.

Lastly, the discourse and institutionalization of an idea may not only leave a rational trace and shape social structure, but also leave an emotional association. When ideas that humans associate with particular previous discourses or institutions reappear in new context, perhaps under new names, this residue of feeling may be activated, influencing actors' understanding of and receptivity to later ideas and arguments. In other words, when individuals reason by analogy, they may import the feelings associated with the analogy as well as the logical structure and conclusions that follow from it. Although the emotions may have all sorts of effects—for example, from heightening an actors attention to an issue, to causing them to avoid the idea altogether (Crawford 2000; Jasper, this volume)—political scientists essentially neglected their role.

Of course, none of these ways that previous ideas affect later ideas is necessarily separate from the other. These mechanisms and their interaction are illustrated here in the case of the idea of international trusteeship. The idea of trusteeship was first used to transform colonial relations; later trusteeship became the dominant discourse; it was then institutionalized within international organizations and state governments; and the residue of feelings attached to "trusteeship" affects the receptivity of actors to the new ideas and contemporary practices, most especially the idea of transitional administration.

2   THE IDEA OF TRUSTEESHIP

Colonialism is the physical occupation and exploitation of a weaker people by a strong state where the colonized typically have little or no ability to determine their political, economic, judicial, or cultural institutions. The colonizer taxes without representation, organizes the economy to suit its own needs, and the colonized typically go without the due processes of law that would be available in the metropole. All the while the cultural institutions—language, religion, diet, and social practices—of the colonized are both denigrated and replaced with the colonizer's idea of appropriate culture.

But while colonial rule is driven by the logic of exploitation and expropriation, the logic of trusteeship is benevolent and guided development. "Trusteeship ... sanctions the rule of one man over another, in lands that are not his own, so long as the power of dominion is directed towards the improvement of the incompetent and infirm" (Bain 2003, 23). The idea of trusteeship eventually helped to discredit and replace the simple colonial idea that states can acquire other territories and control them for the sole benefit of the colonizer. International trusteeship, as a form of benevolent outside administration, was seen as a route to self-government or independence. The role of trusteeships in the transition to self-rule ended in the early 1990s with the independence of the last Trust Territories.

But the distinction between colonial rule and trusteeship has never been clear-cut. Colonialism was almost always understood by colonizers as both simple expropriation from the weaker by the stronger, and as a benevolent mission to impose the conquerors' religion, civilization, and economic system upon the conquered. For example, in the fifteenth- and sixteenth-century European expansion into the Americas, the Pope granted a right to conquest so long as the conquerors brought the natives out of their presumed barbarism by inculcating them in the Christian faith. Similarly, from the eighteenth century, the influential British parliamentarian Edmund Burke viewed British rule over India in terms explicitly articulated as a trust: "all political power which is set over men, and that all privilege claimed or exercised in exclusion of them, being while artificial, and for so much a derogation from the natural equality of mankind at large, ought to be in some way or other exercised ultimately for their benefit" (quoted in Bain 2003, 36). The French "*mission civilisatrice*" was also about uplift, with the goal of gradual assimilation of the conquered into French civilization. Thus, the notion of some form of responsibility for improvement was part of the colonizing mission, albeit always with the assumption that the colonizer was superior in most or even all respects to the colonized.

3   DISCOURSE AND INSTITUTIONALIZATION

The idea of formal international trusteeship—as opposed to colonial trusteeship—developed in three phases. Trusteeship was formalized as an international responsibility with a corresponding duty of oversight and accountability in a series of nineteenth-century treaties regulating European conquest of Africa, under the League of Nations Mandate system, and following the Second World War, in the UN system. Trusteeship thus gradually became less about the terms of a colonial relationship and more about decolonization through benevolent international intervention.

During their nineteenth-century conquest of Africa, representatives of European governments argued for and recognized responsibility for promoting the general welfare of colonial inhabitants. At the Berlin West Africa Conference of 1884–5, Europeans and Americans linked the conquest with the mission of trusteeship. As the British delegate, Sir Edward Malet, argued, administration of Africa by Europeans should promote the "well being of the native races" (quoted in Gavin and Betley 1973, 131). These sentiments were still alive decades later, as expressed by Britain's Lord Lugard in his explication of what he called the "dual mandate:" "Europe is in Africa for the mutual benefit of her own industrial classes, and of the native races in their progress to a higher plane" (Lugard 1965 [1922], 617). And although, he argued, "British methods have not in all cases produced ideal results, ... I am profoundly convinced that there can be no question but that British rule has promoted the happiness and welfare of the primitive races" (Lugard 1965 [1922], 618).

The discourse of trusteeship was further articulated and institutionalized in 1889–90 when more than a dozen states attending the Conference of Brussels agreed to suppress the Arab slave trade and slavery in Africa, as well as limit the trade in liquor to Africa.[2] Article I of the Brussels General Act said the slave trade would be combated through the "progressive organization of the administrative, judicial, religious and military services under the sovereignty or protectorate of civilized nations," the establishment of "strongly occupied stations" in the interior, the "construction of roads" and railways connecting the coast to the interior, and other means, including the "restriction of the importation of firearms, at least those of a modern pattern, and of ammunition" in areas where the slave trade was ongoing. According to the treaty, this was most of sub-Saharan Africa.[3] Colonizers were also to "diminish intestine [sic] wars between tribes by means of arbitration; to initiate them in agricultural labor and the industrial arts so as to increase their welfare; to raise them to civilization and bring about the extinction of barbarous customs" (Snow 1921, 297). Further, the Brussels Act proposed creating international offices in Brussels and Zanzibar to monitor and coordinate efforts to suppress the trade.

The second landmark in the discourse and institutionalization of the idea of trusteeship was the creation of the League of Nations Mandates system and in the "trustee" powers the League assumed in the Saar Basin from 1920 to 1935 under article 49 of the Versailles Treaty.[4] This opportunity was created when the defeated powers of the First World War—Germany and Ottoman Turkey—lost their colonies in the war. Although some representatives of the victorious powers attending the Paris Peace Conference wanted to simply turn former German and Turkish colonies into their own colonies, participants in the creation of the League of Nations decided after lengthy debate that the captured territory would not be transferred to the victors as it would have been in the past. Further, there was also pressure from pan-Africanists and humanitarian activists to make Africa in particular into an international trust. W. E. B. Du Bois (1965, 9), for example, argued repeatedly in 1918 and 1919 that the "Dark Continent" should be under the benefit of "organized civilization." "This Africa for the Africans could be under the guidance of international organization. The governing international commission should represent not simply governments, but modern culture, science, commerce, social reform and religious philanthropy. It must represent not simply the white world, but the civilized Negro world."

Captured territories that were judged, in the words of Article 22 of the League Charter, "inhabited by peoples not yet able to stand by themselves under the strenuous conditions of the modern world" were placed in the Mandate system where it "should be applied the principle that the well being and development of

[2] The participants included representatives from: Austria-Hungary, Belgium, Britain, Congo, Denmark, France, Germany, Holland, Italy, Norway, Persia, Portugal, Russia, Spain, Sweden, Turkey, the United States, and Zanzibar (Miers 1975, 236–91).

[3] Snow 1921, 294–306; General Act quotes from p. 296.

[4] The League also had administrative roles in Danzig (1920–39) and Upper Silesia (1922–37)

such peoples form a sacred trust of civilization" not simply of individual states.[5] The mandates were organized into three classes according to perceived differences in their level of "development" and "civilization." Class A Mandates—Iraq, Palestine and Transjordan, and Syria and the Lebanon—were thought to have reached a "stage of development" where, with some assistance, they might soon be "able to stand alone." Class B Mandates, located in Central Africa (Togoland, Cameroon, Tanganyika, and Ruanda-Urundi), were "at such a stage, that the Mandatory must be responsible for the administration of the territory under conditions which will guarantee freedom of conscience and religion, subject only to the maintenance of public order and morals, the prohibition of abuses such as the slave trade, the arms traffic, the liquor traffic." Class C Mandates—South West Africa, New Guinea, Nauru, Samoa, and several very small islands located in the Pacific (the Marshalls, Marianas, and Carolines)—were territories that, "owing to the sparseness of their population, or their small size, or their remoteness from the centre of civilisation . . . can be best administered under the laws of the Mandatory as integral portions of its territory, subject to the safeguards above mentioned in the interests of the indigenous population." The nominal aim of the system was the betterment of the inhabitants' lives, with a view toward their gradual assumption of self-determination.

The specific administration of each mandate varied, but the template was that the mandatory power would administer the mandate and the League of Nations would oversee that administration. Three levels of oversight and accountability were institutionalized. First, the League and the mandatory power entered into agreements that specified conditions of governance and articulated goals for improving conditions in the mandate territories. Second, the League's Permanent Mandate's Commission (PMC) required written annual reports and questioned the mandatory power's representatives closely on progress in the mandates on labor conditions, health, education, and the rule of law. And third, the League's proceedings were made public, allowing journalists and activists to use information to challenge conditions in the Mandates and the practices of administrators.

The Mandate system was a genuine innovation in international politics and law, both specifying and expanding the original conception of colonial trusteeship to one of true international responsibility and oversight. As Quincy Wright wrote in 1930:

The system has already resulted in wider recognition of the principle of trusteeship, that dependencies should be administered in the interests of their inhabitants; in the principle of tutelage, that the cultivation of the capacity for self-government is such an interest; of the principle of international mandate, that states are responsible to the international community for the exercise of power over backward peoples even if that responsibility is not fully organized. (Wright 1930, 588)

---

[5] Covenant of the League of Nations, Article 22, paragraph 1.

Ralph Bunche, who later became the chief administrator of the UN Trusteeship system, was a more critical observer of the League Mandate system. His 1934 dissertation compared French administration of its colony, Dahomey (now Benin) with its administration of Togoland, a Class B Mandate. Bunche found that French administration of the mandate was better than their administration of the colony. Exploitation had not disappeared in the Mandate, but periods of forced labor were shorter, the burden of taxation was lighter, political representation of the natives in local administration was greater, education was better and more widely available, and the justice system was fairer.

Yet Bunche thought the Mandate system was flawed in important respects. It lacked both the voice of the native subject and a direct means for the League to investigate the statements of the mandatory powers. In his dissertation Bunche proposed improving the system by including natives directly in the process and by allowing the representatives of the PMC access to the Mandate on a regular basis. Despite these criticisms, like Wright and others, Bunche saw the Mandates system as a progressive institution, moving toward fulfillment of the sacred trust mission articulated in the League Charter.

It is certain that the mandate system will exert an influence far beyond that affecting those areas presently subjected to its provisions. The inexorable force of public opinion will compel, as it has to an extent already, the extension of identical principles to retarded peoples throughout the world, whether they dwell in areas held as colonies and possessions or not. A steady exosmose is carrying these ideas beyond artificial boundaries which originally contained them, and they are having a revolutionary effect on the colonizing nations, great and small.   (Bunche 1934, 143)

The requirement that mandatory powers submit annual reports and the PMC's investigations of public abuse by mandatory powers led to the gradual improvement of conditions in the Mandates. Public accountability for improving conditions, including the gradual implementation of self-rule, became the norm. According to H. Duncan Hall (1948, 188), "The more complete the annual reports became, and the longer and more closely the Commission and the accredited representatives worked together, the more committed the governments were to carrying out the principles of the mandates."

What Bunche found in Togoland was basically the case in other Mandate territories. Some Mandates achieved total independence or at least much greater autonomy. When independence was not the result, there were significant improvements within the Mandates. Specifically, within the Mandate territories, the resort to forced labor decreased, there was greater attention to social welfare and legal rights, and self-determination grew (Callahan 1999; Crawford 2002; Dimier 2004).

The idea and discourse of trusteeship was further institutionalized in the United Nations Charter's Trusteeship system and its Declaration on Non-Self-Governing

Territories. As one of the authors of these chapters of the Charter, Ralph Bunche, then working for the US State Department, was able to institutionalize the innovations in oversight that he had recommended in his dissertation so that the system both built on and extended the mechanisms of oversight and accountability first enacted in the Mandate system. As with the Mandate system, in the trusteeship system there were agreements between the UN and the trustee powers. In addition, more detailed questionnaires were developed to assess trusteeship administration. Further, innovations Bunche regarded as essential—the right for inhabitants to directly petition the UN and the use of "on-the-spot" inspections—were included in the UN system. Bunche became the first administrator of the UN trusteeship system and regarded it as superior to the Mandate system:

The Trusteeship System, like the Mandates System recognizes the international responsibility involved in the administration of the dependent territory placed under it.... The Trusteeship provisions in the Charter deal more positively with the promotion of the welfare of the inhabitants of the territories concerned than did the Mandates system. It calls specifically for the promotion of the advancement of the inhabitants, their development toward self-government or independence, and for the encouragement of respect for human rights and freedom without discrimination.   (Bunche 1947, 59)

Nearly all Mandate powers announced their intention to transfer their Mandates into the trusteeship system, although in the case of Mandate territories under Japanese control in the Pacific the US became the administering power. The US thus administered as "strategic trusts" the Pacific Islands of Palau, the Marshall Islands, the Carolines, and the Marianas. France administered French Togoland and the French Cameroons. Great Britain administered the British Cameroons, Tanganyika, and British Togoland. Australia administered Nauru and New Guinea. Italy administered Somaliland and New Zealand administered Western Samoa. Only South Africa refused to turn its League Mandate territory South West Africa into a UN Trust Territory.

Like Mandates, the trusteeship arrangement was understood to be of limited duration and the administering authority was subject to international oversight and accountability. Further, the goal was self-determination, self-government, autonomy, and eventually sovereignty. The innovations—on-the-spot inspections, direct petitions, and more robust questioning of the trustee power—enhanced the accountability of the trustee power to the UN and indirectly to the inhabitants of the territory. As Ralph Bunche said in 1947, "The principle of Trusteeship involved in the new system is that of third party or international responsibility—not the customary conception of the colonial power itself unilaterally recognizing a moral trusteeship on behalf of its colonial subjects" (Bunche 1947, 58). Oversight by the Trusteeship Council kept the trustee power accountable and administration relatively transparent. The administering authority, as well as other states and international organizations, provided assistance for political and economic development. And the trusteeship system also often helped trust territories conduct their first elections.

The idea of trusteeship was a model for increasing autonomy in all colonies. Specifically, the discourse of trusteeship infused Chapter XI of the UN Charter, the "Declaration Regarding Non-Self-Governing Territories" where the relationship between colonizer and colonized was defined such that the colonizer was understood to be only a temporary steward, acting in the interests of developing the capacities of the colonized. Indeed, the Charter's language echoes the language of the Mandate and trusteeship system:

Members of the United Nations which have or assume responsibilities for the administration of territories whose people have not yet attained a full measure of self-government recognize the principle that the interests of the inhabitants of these territories are paramount, and accept as a sacred trust the obligation to promote to the utmost, within the system of international peace and security established by the present Charter, the well-being of the inhabitants of these territories.

The duties of the colonial power were thus redefined: they must "ensure due respect for the culture of the people concerned . . . develop self-government, to take account of the political aspirations of the peoples . . . promote constructive measures of development" and report on the "economic, social and educational conditions" in these territories. And as with the trusteeship system, administering governments were required to submit annual reports, extending the system of oversight and accountability that characterized the trusteeship system to all colonies. The UN General Assembly established the "Committee on Information from Non-Self-Governing Territories" to monitor implementation of the goals for non-self-governing territories. The discourse of responsible trusteeship and the institutional template of Mandate and trusteeship was thus applied by analogy to all colonies through the UN's efforts to promote decolonization in the General Assembly and in the Committee on Information.

4   TRANSITIONAL ADMINISTRATION AS TRUSTEESHIP OR COLONIALISM

Even as formal colonialism and trusteeship were coming to an end, the United Nations undertook a series of increasingly complex missions—from administering elections and plebiscites, to long-term peacekeeping—that gradually became a new form of what is now called transitional administration. In other words, just as the idea of trusteeship should have been retired, it achieved a new, more controversial (and less institutionalized) life.

The key case in this respect is probably the increasing role the UN took with respect to South West Africa (now Namibia), a former Mandate territory. Only the government of South Africa, which had occupied South West Africa since 1914 refused to designate the territory as a trusteeship. In 1949, South Africa said that its obligations as mandatory power were over. Even as South Africa argued that it had fulfilled the conditions of being a Mandate, South Africa brutally suppressed the independence movement in South West Africa, extracted strategic minerals from the land, and tried to extend South West African style apartheid to the territory. South Africa's refusal to administer South West Africa as a trusteeship started a long battle with the UN General Assembly and in the International Court of Justice, and prompted the increased internationalization of the problem.

In a sense the UN backed into the role of transitional administration through its handling of South West Africa. Between the 1960s and late 1980s, the United Nations assisted the exiled South West Africa People's Organization (SWAPO) liberation movement, and essentially formed a shadow international government for the territory even as South Africa continued to rule South West Africa with growing brutality. In 1967 the United Nations Council for Namibia and in 1976 the Security Council authorized the UN Transitional Assistance Group (UNTAG) to plan for post-independence elections supervised by the UN. For over a decade the UN helped devise plans for the transition to majority rule in South West Africa, and ultimately, when agreement was finally reached that South Africa would exit the territory, UNTAG facilitated demobilization, helped organize the first democratic elections in November 1989, and ultimately helped write a constitution and guarantee independence in 1990.

Following the effort in Namibia, the UN and other ad hoc coalitions of nations set up transitional administrations of varying degrees of comprehensiveness in approximately ten situations.[6] In each case, the UN went beyond the more limited peacekeeping, electoral assistance, and development aid roles it had taken during the cold war. There was a tendency during the 1990s to call this gradual broadening of the UN's role "mission creep" but it was more than that. The extension of the UN's mission from limited to comprehensive intervention was driven by an analysis of the causes of war as defective states or even total state failure.

[6] Cases of transitional administration between 1991 and late 2004 either completed or undertaken by the United Nations and still ongoing at this writing include: Cambodia, 1992–3; Eastern Slavonia, 1996–8; Kosovo since 1999; East Timor, 1999–2002; Sierra Leone, since 1999; Afghanistan since 2002; and Liberia since 2003. Other transitional administrations include: Bosnia and Hercegovina since 1995 under the office of the High Representative; and Iraq from 2003–4 under the US-led Coalition Provisional Authority.

The rationale for greater intervention is evident in a chronological reading of various UN reports during the 1990s. The UN Secretary General's *An Agenda for Peace* (Boutros-Ghali 1992), the *Supplement to An Agenda for Peace* (1995), and the "Report of the Panel on United Nations Peace Operations" (Panel on UN Peace Operations 2000) built on each other and ultimately argue that the only way to bring lasting peace is to repair the defects of the state that had led to war and collapse in the first place. Each report noted a compelling rationale for more complex intervention by the UN to provide and preserve the peace. Peacekeeping missions thus evolved into peace enforcement and peace-building missions, and then to state-building and liberal market democracy-building exercises (see Paris 2004) on the belief that this was the route to stability. Further, the period of transitional administration is often associated with transitional justice—war crimes tribunals and truth commissions—on the assumption that peace and good governance are more likely if the wounds of the past are recognized and hopefully healed through a judicial process or a comprehensive reckoning with the past.

But contemporary transitional administrations are not simply the reincarnation of UN trusteeship. While the core idea of trusteeship—benevolent, if paternalistic, administration of the incapable by the capable outsider—is present in the contemporary institution of transitional administration, some of the safeguards associated with the idea of trusteeship are absent. Specifically, while contemporary transitional administrations share features with traditional trusteeship arrangements, they differ in important respects. For example, these administrations are essentially ad hoc, characterized by a patchwork of oversight by the various UN organizations and individual states or "coalitions of the willing." In addition, accountability by the transitional administrators to either the subjects of administration or to the United Nations is less institutionalized than was characteristic of formal trusteeship or Mandate arrangements.

Finally, the new hybrid transitional administrations, such as the US-led Coalition Provisional Authority in Iraq, have sought accountability neither to the United Nations nor to the citizens of the occupied territory. In the Iraq case, for instance, the idea of trusteeship as including accountability to an international body has been essentially eliminated. Rather, the UN assumed a rather different function with respect to the Coalition Provisional Authority, which had little to do with overseeing the justice or benevolence of the administration even as the United States used the trusteeship and state-building discourse: "A senior American official said the United Nations was playing the role of 'trusted adviser' in getting Iraqis to agree on a plan among themselves [for the composition and structure of Iraq's interim government in 2004]. Others described the United Nations as more than that, a mediator brokering an accord that was beyond the power of the United States to bring about" (Weisman and Hoge 2004).

Yet, even as the list of tasks for UN peace-building expanded to encompass the typical tasks of a functioning government, as Simon Chesterman has noted, there was not a willingness, until recently, to explicitly link transitional administration with the idea of trusteeship.

> One of the many ironies in the recent history of transitional administration of territory by international actors is that the practice is regarded as novel. Attempts to draw analogies either with trusteeships and decolonization on the one hand, or the post-war occupation of Germany and Japan on the other are seen as invitations to charges that the United Nations or the United States is engaging in neocolonialism or imperialism respectively. Within the United Nations in particular, such comparisons are politically impossible.   (Chesterman 2004, 11)

5   THE RESURGENT IDEA OF TRUSTEESHIP

Although most UN officials have shied away from explicitly discussing how its practices might resemble or resurrect either colonialism or trusteeship, others have not been so reluctant. The perceived problem of what to do with a growing number of "weak" or "failed" states, has led some to argue for the return of trusteeship. For more than a decade, scholars, policy-makers, and diplomats across the political spectrum have discussed the possibility of reviving either colonialism or the international trusteeship system. Indeed, just as the last of the former UN trust territories were achieving full independence and the UN Trusteeship Council was closing its doors in November 1994, the call for the return to trusteeship began in earnest. In each case, proponents of trusteeship have had implicitly or explicitly to reckon with the emotional legacy of both colonialism and trusteeship.

For example, the historian Paul Johnson writing under the title "Colonialism's Back, and Not a Moment Too Soon" in the *New York Times Magazine* confused the idea of colonialism with trusteeship when he argued for the return of international trusteeship managed by the "civilized" nations. Johnson's first move is to argue that colonialism was not so bad after all; it was inadvertently beneficial for the colonized. Johnson then argues that a return to external rule would be better than the alternatives. Johnson said, "The Security Council could commit a territory where authority has irretrievably broken down to one or more trustees ... empowered to not merely impose order by force but to assume political functions." The length of the trusteeship, Johnson suggests, would "usually be of limited duration— 5, 10, 20 years ... but a Mandate may last 50 years, or 100" (Johnson 1993, 44).

Others have also raised the idea of a return to trusteeship in respected policy journals. Gerald Helman and Steven Ratner (1992–3) proposed to save "failed states" by reinstituting trusteeship. Richard Caplan in a 2002 *Adelphi Paper* examined UN transitional administrations in the post-cold war era, suggesting that they are "A New Trusteeship." And Martin Indyk (2003, 54), former US Ambassador to Israel writing in *Foreign Affairs*, proposed international trusteeship for Palestine arguing that the "concept of trusteeship has been used to good effect in other places—such as East Timor and Kosovo—where the collapse of order and the descent into chaos have necessitated outside action."

Yet because of its association with colonialism, the idea of trusteeship as embodied in contemporary international transitional administrations has become suspect. "In Eastern Slavonia, Bosnia and Herzegovina, Kosovo and East Timor ... the responsibilities assumed by external actors have been so extensive as to warrant the politically and historically sensitive labels of *trusteeship* and *protectorate*" (Berdal and Caplan 2004, 2). Thus, while the notion of trusteeship was for decades understood as a benevolent and progressive force of external administration as compared to colonial rule, it is now questioned and the term, if not the practice itself, is avoided.

Yet the comparison between new and previous ideas—contemporary transitional administrations and trusteeship—has been used effectively to criticize transitional administration arrangements. Noting the growing number of territories under transitional administration of one form or another, the United Nations official Edward Mortimer has argued that without proper accountability, these institutions have great potential for abuse. Thus, he argues, it might be important to "revive and reform the Trusteeship Council, using it as a mechanism through which the community of nations could effectively exercise its tutelage and responsibility for the interests of those unfortunate peoples who may from time to time find themselves in need of international protection" (Mortimer 2004, 13–14). Mortimer suggests that such a move would be consistent with the UN Charter. "That it smacks of imperialism should not be a decisive objection," argues Mortimer (2004, 14).

[I]nternational administration has imperialistic features whether one likes it or not. It is adopted not as an ideal, but as expedient and seems unlikely to disappear any time soon. The wise course would be to limit the evil by facing up to its true nature and making dispositions accordingly.

Indeed, to the extent that they are ad hoc arrangements, contemporary transitional administrations are deficient when compared to traditional international arrangements of trusteeship as embodied in the League of Nations Mandate system and the UN trusteeship system. As Richard Caplan (2004, 62) argues, "All international territorial administrations lack accountability mechanisms that ensure meaningful independent review and that allow also for significant local input into the review process." Indeed, Jarat Chopra (2000, 27), himself a UN official in East Timor's transitional administration, argues that these arrangements "will be merely another form of authoritarianism unless the transitional administrators themselves submit to a judicious separation of powers and to genuine accountability to the local people whom they serve." Observers such as Mortimer, note that the emotional legacy of trusteeship has hampered clear discussion of the institution of transitional administration:

> Arguments used in the past to justify imperialism—that it spreads "civilization," provides stability, protects minorities, "builds nations," or prepares people for self-government—are all now regarded with skepticism. Do they become more acceptable when deployed to justify rule by an international organization or coalition rather than a single state? If so, it is not obvious why. Undoubtedly, it is this discomfort that explains the general reluctance to codify or institutionalize arrangements for international administration. (Mortimer 2004, 12)

Mortimer's, Caplan's, and Chopra's arguments acknowledge and employ the emotional legacy of the idea of trusteeship. By linking transitional administrations with colonial attitudes, albeit without the accountability of formal trusteeship arrangements, their analysis suggests that by all contemporary standards of sovereignty and democratic principles, contemporary transitional administrations are a step backward. Thus, the idea, discourse, institutionalization, and feeling of trusteeship are used to critique contemporary transitional administrations and to urge their revision.

6   THE LEGACY OF IDEAS: DISCOURSE, STRUCTURE, AND FEELING

The effects of previous ideas on later ideas are perhaps best shown through discourse analysis and process tracing. Colonial missions of civilization and uplift, as well as League Mandates and UN trusteeship were founded on the twin discourses of paternalism and self-determination. These institutions infantalized inhabitants and pushed them into a European-derived mold of a secular, rational, bureaucratic state. Conversely, the system of what became close international oversight of Mandate and trust territories took into account the reality of exploitative occupation by colonizers and trustee administrations, serving as a check on the occupying power.

The idea of trusteeship began as a simple notion of tutelage—the civilized would uplift the barbarian. The discourse of trusteeship evolved into a relationship of benevolent rule and external accountability: trusteeship would both bind the hands of the occupier and bound the scope of its activities. The occupying trust power in a formal trusteeship arrangement was accountable to the United Nations, committed to improve the lot of the occupied, and the people in an international Mandate or trust territory had someone to appeal to besides the occupier. Further, because the aim of trusteeship was self-determination and eventually sovereignty, formal trusteeship limited the duration of occupation. It was a route to improving conditions and to sovereignty, albeit not always or even usually a roadmap to democracy. Thus, trusteeship was and is a paradoxical institution—an infringement on self-determination in order to promote it—under colonialism, a more benevolent form of exploitation, and now sometimes only the least distasteful option out of a set of possible responses to bad governance, continued war, or genocide.

Returning to the conception of trusteeship as a sacred trust, it is useful to think about three elements of the idea as it was institutionalized as formal international trusteeship. International trusteeship involved a duty held by both the trustee power and the international community to protect and improve the life conditions of the subjects of trusteeship. Trusteeship also entailed legal accountability mechanisms for the trustee power, meaning that the trust power was responsible to someone besides themselves. And international trusteeship implicitly entailed a degree of respect for the ability of actors subject to transitional administration to shape their own lives because it granted that the goal was, eventually, self-government.

Much of the attention to transitional administrations focuses on the problems of implementation—such as failures to train police quickly or to establish a new justice system. Yet, the discourse of trusteeship allows observers to frame the key problem of contemporary transitional administration: its paternalism without institutionalized accountability. "Whereas the tyrant merely infringes upon a person's humanity, the paternalist denies it altogether" (Bain 2004, 13). On the other hand, in the short term the alternative to trusteeship or transitional administration might be much worse.

The emotional residue of previous ideas of trusteeship—the distaste that many associate with the institution—may be the strongest direct legacy of the idea. Yet this distaste is regrettable, since the institutionalization of the idea of trusteeship in the rules and standard operating procedures of the UN Trusteeship Council ensured greater accountability and oversight than does the present system of transitional administration. As long as there are transitional administrations, the idea of trusteeship as time-limited comprehensive intervention with accountability provides a standard by which to measure and improve contemporary transitional administrations.

A more diffuse legacy of trusteeship is the way the idea of trusteeship articulated a nascent sense of both civilizational and barbarian identities. The articulation and implementation of trusteeship helped to develop the notion of a particular kind of international society—benevolent—and global governance based on accountability. Trusteeship both promotes and undermines the notion of sovereignty—where that sovereignty is conditional on competence—at the same time that it says the worst forms of exploitation are unacceptable.

REFERENCES

ABELSON, R. 1981. Psychological status of the script concept. *American Psychologist*, 36: 715–29.

BAIN, W. 2003. *Between Anarchy and Society: Trusteeship and the Obligations of Power.* Oxford: Oxford University Press.

——2004. In pursuit of paradise: trusteeship and contemporary international society. *Tidsskriftet Politik*, 7: 6–14.

BERDAL, M., and CAPLAN, R. 2004. The politics of international administration. *Global Governance*, 10: 1–5.

BOUTROS-GHALI, B. 1992. *Agenda for Peace: Preventive Diplomacy, Peacemaking and Peace-keeping.* New York: United Nations.

——1995. *Supplement to an Agenda for Peace.* New York: United Nations.

BUNCHE, R. J. 1934. *French Administration of Togoland and Dahomey.* Ph.D. dissertation, Harvard University.

——1947. The United Nations and the colonial problem. Pp. 51–61 in *Imperialism Ancient and Modern*, Marshall Woods Lectures. Providence, RI: Brown University.

CALLAHAN, M. D. 1999. *Mandates and Empire: The League of Nations and Africa, 1914–1931.* Brighton: Sussex Academic Press.

CAPLAN, R. 2002. A new trusteeship? The international administration of war-torn territories. *Adelphi Paper 341.* London: International Institute for Strategic Studies.

——2004. International authority and state building: the case of Bosnia and Herzegovina. *Global Governance*, 10: 53–65.

CHESTERMAN, S. 2004. *You, the People: The United Nations, Transitional Administration and State-Building.* Oxford: Oxford University Press.

CHOPRA, J. 2000. The UN's kingdom of East Timor. *Survival*, 42: 27–39.

CRAWFORD, N. C. 2000. The passion of world politics: propositions on emotion and emotional relationships. *International Security*, 24: 116–56.

——2002. *Argument and Change in World Politics: Ethics, Decolonization and Humanitarian Intervention.* Cambridge: Cambridge University Press.

DIMIER, V. 2004. On good colonial government: lessons from the League of Nations. *Global Society*, 18: 279–99.

DU BOIS, W. E. B. 1965. *The World and Africa: An Inquiry into the Part Which Africa Has Played in World History.* New York: International Publishers.

EDEN, L. 2004. *Whole World on Fire: Organizations, Knowledge and Nuclear Weapons Devastation.* Ithaca, NY: Cornell University Press.

FOUCAULT, M. 1972. *The Archaeology of Knowledge and the Discourse on Language.* New York: Pantheon.

GAVIN, R. J., and BETLEY, J. A. 1973. *The Scramble for Africa: Documents on the Berlin West Africa Conference and Related Subjects 1884/1885*. Ibadan: Ibadan University Press.

GOLDSTEIN, J. 1993. *Ideas, Interests and American Trade Policy*. Ithaca, NY: Cornell University Press.

HABERMAS, J. 1984. *Theory of Communicative Action*. Volume 1: *Reason and the Rationalization of Society*. Boston: Beacon Press.

HALPERIN, M., SCHEFFER, D., with SMALL, P. L. 1992. *Self-Determination in the New World Order*. Washington, DC: Carnegie Endowment for International Peace.

HALL, H. D. 1948. *Mandates, Dependencies and Trusteeship*. Washington, DC: Carnegie Endowment for International Peace.

HELMAN, G. B., and RATNER, S. R. 1992–3. Saving failed states. *Foreign Policy*, 89: 3–20

INDYK, M. 2003. A trusteeship for Palestine? *Foreign Affairs*, 82: 51–66.

JOHNSON, P. 1993. Colonialism's back—and not a moment too soon. *New York Times Magazine*, 18 April: 22, 43–4.

KHONG, Y. F. 1992. *Analogies at War: Korea, Munich, Dien Bien Phu and the Vietnam Decisions of 1965*. Princeton, NJ: Princeton University Press.

KUHN, T. 1955. *The Structure of Scientific Revolutions*. Chicago: University of Chicago Press.

LUGARD, F. 1965. *The Dual Mandate in British Tropical Africa*. New York: Frank Cass; originally published 1922.

MARX, K. 1978. The eighteenth brumaire of Louis Bonaparte. Pp. 594–617 in *The Marx–Engels Reader*, ed. R. Tucker, 2nd edn. New York: Norton; originally published 1852.

MIERS, S. 1975. *Britain and the Ending of the Slave Trade*. New York: Longman.

MORTIMER, E. 2004. International administration of war-torn societies. *Global Governance*, 10: 7–14.

NEUSTADT, R., and MAY, E. 1986. *Thinking In Time: The Uses of History for Decision-Makers*. New York: Free Press.

PANEL ON UNITED NATIONS PEACE OPERATIONS. 2000. Report of the Panel on United Nations Peace Operations. UN Document No. A/55/405–S/2000/809. New York: United Nations.

PARIS, R. 2004. *At War's End: Building Peace After Civil Conflict*. Cambridge: Cambridge University Press.

SNOW, A. H. 1921. *The Question of Aborigines in the Law and Practice of Nations*. New York: Putnam's.

WEBER, M. 1961. The theory of social and economic organization. In *Theories of Society: Foundations of Modern Sociological Theory*, ed. T. Parsons et al. New York: Free Press.

WEISMAN, R. R., and HOGE, W. 2004. U.S. expected to ask united nations to keep trying for an agreement. *New York Times*, 21 February: A7.

WRIGHT, Q. 1930. *Mandates Under the League*. Chicago: University of Chicago Press.

CHAPTER 15

....

HOW IDEAS AFFECT ACTIONS

....

JENNIFER L. HOCHSCHILD

Practical men, who believe themselves to be quite exempt from any intellectual
influences, are usually the slaves of some defunct economist.

(John Maynard Keynes, 1936)

The truth is always the strongest argument.   (Sophocles, *Phaedra*)

Men freely believe that which they desire.   (Julius Caesar, *De Bello Gallico*)

One does what one is; one becomes what one does.   (Robert Musil, *c.*1930)

WRITERS ranging in era and style from Sophocles and Caesar to Musil and Keynes
have asserted that ideas affect actions. These epigraphs, however, provide more than
eloquent testimony for that assertion. They suggests three ways in which ideas and
actions are linked: ideas can override interests, as Sophocles says, and therefore
change how a person acts; ideas can justify interests, as Caesar says, and therefore
reinforce a person's preferences for action; or ideas can shape a person's understanding of his or her interests, as Musil says, and therefore create a new set of preferred

* My thanks for financial and institutional support to the Radcliffe Institute for Advanced Study,
the Andrew W. Mellon Foundation, the John S. Guggenheim Foundation, and the Weatherhead
Center for International Affairs of Harvard University.

actions. This article explores each of those influences, and considers how much and when ideas affect actions in these distinct ways.

1   "The Truth Is Always the Strongest Argument": Ideas Can Override Interests

The central problem in determining the impact of ideas on actions is causal: How does one distinguish an idea from an action, and then determine which affects the other more than vice versa? One can blur the two concepts by claiming that an idea or set of words *is* an action (as in "I do" while standing with a partner before a minister; see Austin 1975; MacKinnon 1993), or that an action expresses an idea without needing any words (as in voting by raising one's hand). Nevertheless, one cannot analyze the relationship between ideas and actions without first distinguishing them; to do so most sharply, I need to introduce a third term—interests—and then define the three concepts in relation to each other.

Ideas, in this construction, lie in the realm of identity ("who am I, and how am I related to these others?"), morality ("what is right and wrong?"), and causation or interpretation ("how do I understand this phenomenon or process?"). Interests, in this construction, lie in the realm of recognized material or physical desires or drives ("what must I do to get X?"). Actions are intentional behaviors, steps taken to achieve a goal. The most straightforward way, then, to show that ideas affect actions is to posit an idea that would lead to one action *against* an interest that would lead to a different action, and to show that the former action occurs rather than the latter.

That simple, even simplistic construction is surprisingly resonant. It can be framed as false consciousness; people are expected (and hoped) to take a given set of actions based on their interests, but they are persuaded against taking those actions by some set of ideas that obscure their interests or distort their priorities. The failure of voters of the United States to mandate public policies to redistribute more than a tiny fraction of wealth downward is one important illustration. After all, the median level of wealth-holding in the United States is dramatically below the mean level, so the many poor could easily outvote the few rich to establish, for example, a confiscatory inheritance tax. Indeed, thinkers from Aristotle through John Adams feared democracy for just that reason. As Adams put it,

Suppose a nation, rich and poor...all assembled together....If all were to be decided by a vote of the majority, [would not] the eight or nine millions who have no property...think of usurping over the rights of the one or two million who have?...Perhaps, at first, prejudice, habit, shame or fear, principle or religion, would restrain the poor...and the idle...but the time would not be long before...pretexts [would] be invented by degrees, to countenance the majority in dividing all the property among them....At last a downright equal division of everything would be demanded, and voted.

Adams' prediction has not come true; as more and more Americans attained the franchise from the early nineteenth through the mid-twentieth century, inequality in the distribution of wealth rose steadily. It fell in the four decades after the Second World War, but has since risen to prewar levels despite recent increases in voting rights among poor African-Americans, those below age twenty-one, and immigrants.

Arguably US voters' beliefs mistakenly keep them from taking action that would be in their own interests. They may falsely believe that it is hopeless to try to fight the wealthy and powerful (Gaventa 1980), or that they too will someday benefit from permitting the wealthy to keep their assets (Bartels 2005). Or perhaps people permit conceptions of morality to override the impulse to act on their interests; poor Americans may believe that the rich deserve to keep their money just as the poor do (Hochschild 1981), or they may care more about a candidate's religious faith and family values than about his or her tax policy (Brady 2001). Alternatively, they may be tricked by politicians into believing that a policy that helps the wealthy will actually help them (Hacker and Pierson 2005). Whatever the precise explanation, the general point here is that people are taking actions based on ideas of morality, hope, or prudence rather than taking actions that would gratify their interests.

Conceptually similar to false consciousness, but with the opposite normative valence, is the Sophoclean argument that ideas can enable people to rise above their mere interests in choosing what actions to take. This is the argument of Gunnar Mydral, who describes the American dilemma as

the ever-raging conflict between...the valuations preserved on the general plane...[of] the 'American Creed', where the American thinks, talks, and acts under the influence of high national and Christian precepts, and, on the other hand, the valuations on the specific planes of individual and group living, where personal and local interests; economic, social, and sexual jealousies; considerations of community prestige and conformity; group prejudice against particular persons or types of people; and all sorts of miscellaneous wants, impulses, and habits dominate his outlook.

Myrdal was not complacent: "if America wants to make the...choice [admit Negroes to full citizenship] she cannot wait and see. She has to do something big, and do it soon." But he insisted, perhaps strategically, on optimism: "America is constantly reaching for...democracy at home and abroad. The main trend in its history is the gradual realization of the American Creed.... America can demonstrate that justice, equality and cooperation are possible between white and colored people" (Myrdal 1944, xlvii, 1021–2).

Within two decades of the publication of *The American Dilemma*, the United States had desegregated public accommodations and schools (in principle, at least) as a consequence of *Brown v. Board of Education*, and had passed the 1964 Civil Rights Act and 1965 Voting Rights Act. The causes ranged from the pressures of popular political protest through concern that segregation undermined American claims in the cold war—but at least some people responded to the *idea* of the American Creed. Thus federal district judge James McMillan explained in a Senate hearing his ruling that the schools of Charlotte-Mecklenburg, North Carolina, must be desegregated:

I grew up . . . accepting the segregated life which was the way of life of America for its first 300 years. . . . I hoped that we would be forever saved from the folly of transporting children from one school to another for the purpose of maintaining a racial balance of students in each school. . . . I set the case for hearing reluctantly. I heard it reluctantly, at first unbelievingly. After . . . I began to deal in terms of facts and information instead of in terms of my natural-born raising, I began to realize . . . that something should be done. . . . I have had to spend some thousands of hours studying the subject . . . and have been brought by pressure of information to a different conclusion. . . . Charlotte—and I suspect this is true of most cities—is segregated by Government action. . . . The issue is one of constitutional law, not politics; and constitutional rights should not be swept away by temporary majorities.   (quoted in Hochschild 1984, 137)

It seems warranted to accept Judge McMillan's change of heart in the terms that he himself used to explain it (especially given the vilification he received in some quarters); he rejected his and his class's material interests in favor of a more morally resonant understanding of racial segregation, based in part on more accurate knowledge of the true situation and in part on deep convictions about the nation's constitutional core. It is an eloquent statement of how new ideas can override old interests and thus lead to novel actions.

2   "Men Freely Believe that Which They Desire": Ideas Can Justify Interests

The Kantian assumption just discussed, that ideas are most clearly in evidence when they override interests to affect actions, can be relaxed. That is, ideas can influence action by *reinforcing* rather than overriding interests, thereby leading a person to act more vigorously in pursuit of what he or she wanted to do in any case.

Here too there can be varied political or normative connotations of what is analytically the same phenomenon. For example, one can critique the ideology of the American dream by pointing out that it encourages winners in the lottery of life to believe that they deserve their good fortune. The ideology holds that, given a political structure with equal opportunity to advance and reasonably abundant resources, a person's success depends mainly on his or her own talents and efforts. Virtue, in this construction, is associated with success. As a result of this ideology, it is easy for people to come to believe that they are hard-working, talented, and honorable if they single-mindedly pursue wealth. John D. Rockefeller's turn-of-the-century Sunday school address epitomizes the social Darwinist view: "The growth of a large business is merely a survival of the fittest.... The American Beauty rose can be produced in the splendor and fragrance which bring cheer to its beholder only by sacrificing the early buds which grow up around it. This is not an evil tendency in business. It is merely the working out of a law of nature and a law of God."[1] Zora Neale Hurston put the opposite end of this philosophy most simply: "there is something about poverty that smells like death."

Most commentators who reject the ideology of the American dream because it too readily justifies the ruthless pursuit of self-interest are on the political left. But the political right has its own illustrations of how ideas shamefully affect actions by promoting interests while disguising them as something more praiseworthy. Consider affirmative action for affluent African-Americans in colleges, professional schools, and jobs. According to supporters, even well-off blacks suffer from the persistent degradations of racism: they are more likely to be stopped by police or highway patrolmen; their families have less wealth to provide luxuries or a security net; they are presumed to be less intelligent or lazier than their classmates. Therefore affirmative action is warranted to compensate for injustices to them as individuals, to overcome historical and contemporary injustices to their race, and to develop leaders needed by the nation as a whole. To opponents of affirmative action, however, all of this is an elaborate rationale for giving some people an unfair edge in intense competitions. The black daughter of a doctor from Scarsdale is, in this view, using Americans' recent commitment to racial justice to advance her interests, even over the more deserving claims to help from the white son of a coal miner in Kentucky.

I know of no way to determine whether ideas more frequently override interests or reinforce and justify them. The two claims roughly correspond to two disciplines, psychology and economics, and political scientists borrow freely from both. On the one hand, political psychologists such as David Sears and Donald Kinder show how seldom individuals' policy preferences accord with their self-interest in matters such as opposition to mandatory transportation for school desegregation ("forced busing"), government policies on jobs or taxation, or support for a war

---

[1] Ghent 1902, 29. See Piketty (1995) for a fascinating discussion of how this ideology varies across social classes and nations.

(Kinder and Sears 1985, esp. 671–2; Sears and Funk 1990). Psychologically oriented political scientists such as Stanley Feldman similarly point to the importance of values and ideology, rather than self-interest, in structuring political attitudes and policy preferences (Feldman 2003).

Economists, on the other hand, have built a whole discipline around the presumption that knowing a person's material interests permits one to predict how, on average, that person will act in every arena from marriage and racial discrimination (Becker 1976) to preferences for political candidates (Fair 2002) or public policies. In this view, ideas reinforce or even flow rather straightforwardly from interests, and interests lead rather straightforwardly to actions. Some political scientists concur, showing for example that voters do attend carefully to candidates and policy issues linked to their interests, and that they seldom permit countervailing values or ideas to override their interests when they vote (Hutchings 2003).

At the aggregate level, we can again see mixed evidence on the relationship between ideas and interests in producing action. The American Democratic Party draws somewhat more support than does the Republican Party from people with incomes below the median, but the overlap of incomes across the two parties is even more striking. More women than men in the United States endorse affirmative action for women or describe women's rights as "very important" or something that they are "very concerned about," but just as many women as men endorse restrictions on the right to obtain an abortion. Nine out of ten African-Americans vote for the Democratic Party in presidential elections, but a quarter nevertheless describe themselves as "conservative," compared with over a third of whites.[2] In these instances and others, we see evidence both that ideas reinforce interests—which makes it difficult to know how and how much ideas are affecting political action—and that ideas override interests—which makes it clearer that ideas are affecting actions to a considerable degree.

3   "One Does what One Is; One Becomes what One Does": Ideas Create Interests

Another simplifying assumption with which I began now warrants examination. When interests and ideas coincide I have assumed, with Julius Caesar, that the former come first. That is, people have material or physical interests that they reinforce or justify with ideas, the combination of which then produces actions. But

[2] Survey data are from General Social Survey, various years.

what if ideas come first? What if people have conceptions of themselves and the world around them that lead them to conceive of their interests in a particular way? In this view, one does what one is; a person's actions are directed by an understanding of his or her interests, which are *derived from* ideas or conceptions of the self in a particular context.

The claim that ideas create interests underlies arguments ranging from explanations for ethnic conflict, to social movement theory, to behavioral economics, to postmodern linguistic analysis. Ashutosh Varshney, for example, agrees with other scholars that leaders can mobilize ethnic groups in pursuit of the state's (or the resistance movement's) interests, but he argues that ethnic identities and the passion with which people adhere to them must come into existence before any such instrumental manipulation is possible. Identities and passions come first, out of—where? History, culture, religion, family, language, or some combination thereof. Once they are in play, some individuals change their understanding of their own interests to the point where they are prepared to die for even a losing cause; only then is leaders' manipulation possible. As Varshney (2003) puts it, "some goals—national liberation, racial equality, ethnic self-respect—may be deemed so precious that high costs, quite common in movements of resistance, are not sufficient to deter a dogged pursuit of such objectives. The goals are often not up for negotiation and barter; the means deployed to realize them may well be." In short, coming to think of oneself as a member of an oppressed group can lead a person to redefine his or her interests from safety to resistance through a national liberation movement, with an obvious connection to action.

Once an ethnically based struggle is under way and escalating, identities and interests become intertwined. One group's commitment to ethnically based mobilization creates an interest on the part of another group, against which it is mobilizing, in counter-mobilization. But the crucial initial step arguably is a move from a new idea or a renewed commitment to an old idea, to a new understanding of interests.

Even in social movements that fall far short of armed conflict, redefining one's sense of self can change one's definition of interests and subsequent appropriate action. This is the core of the phenomenal impact of Betty Friedan's *The Feminine Mystique* and the consciousness-raising movement that followed it. Once women came to see themselves as an oppressed group, with shared problems caused by institutions and historical practices rather than by their personal failure as wives and mothers, their understanding of their interests changed. They began demanding access to ostensibly male jobs, equal pay for equal work, new policies on divorce and child care, punishment for the new concepts (though old practices!) of marital rape and sexual harassment, and so on. A parallel story can be told with regard to African-Americans developing a sense of linked fate through the course of US history (Dawson 1994), homosexuals redefining themselves from pervert or psychiatric patient to an oppressed group warranting civil rights, or people who could not hear well as they moved from being deaf to "Deaf."

Even something as mild as identification with a political party can produce ideas that change one's understanding of one's interests and eventual political actions. By tracking the same set of voters over time, Paul Goren has found that people choose to identify with the Republican or Democratic Party first, and *then* develop a strong commitment to limited government and traditional family values, or to equal opportunity and moral tolerance, respectively (Goren 2004).

The new field of behavioral economics is full of demonstrations showing how people develop ideas that move their definition of their own interests away from what classical economics would expect. Given a particular frame of reference, they can be easily induced to develop preferences that show how fluidly or "mistakenly" they determine their interests (Kahneman and Tversky 2000). For example, they choose greater certainty over greater gain. Preference reversals occur when individuals are presented with two gambles, one featuring a high probability of winning a modest sum of money (the P bet), the other featuring a low probability of winning a large amount of money (the $ bet). The typical finding is that people often choose the P bet but assign a larger monetary value to the $ bet. This behavior is of interest because it violates almost all theories of preference, including expected utility theory (Slovic and Lichtenstein 1983, 596).

Finally, the claim that ideas create interests and thereby lead to actions is the central premise of the linguistic turn in the social sciences. From this perspective, the whole question of whether and how ideas affect actions is fundamentally misguided because any action—and the very concept of action—emerges from ideas. Without language, ideas, abstractions, comparisons, interpretations, there can be no human action, or at least none that is recognizably human. Consciousness is what turns a baby's instinctive jerks into purposeful grasping, and what turns the adrenalin-based instinct for fight or flight into an emotion and a choice. In short, the materialist framework associated philosophically with Karl Marx and politically with communism and class-based political parties, belongs in the dustbin of history; ideas, not structures, processes, or interests are the motor of history.

As with my earlier discussions of how ideas influence actions, the claim that ideas may lead to a new understanding of interests and therefore to new actions can have multiple political connotations. Consider the question of whether Latinos in the US should think of themselves and be understood as a race rather than an ethnicity. That is the claim of Ian Haney López (1997): "conceptualizing Latinos/as in racial terms is warranted.... The general abandonment of racial language and its replacement with substitute vocabularies, in particular that of ethnicity, will obfuscate key aspects of Latino/a lives." Conceiving of Latinos as a race, he argues, makes much clearer the ways in which they have suffered and still suffer from systematic discrimination and degradation. That clarity, in turn, can lead to political and legal actions to attain rights and resources that will help to overcome group subordination. But Peter Skerry (1999, 83, 97, 118) sees the same move from ethnicity to race as deeply harmful to Latinos. In his view, "the racial lens we have adopted...distorts contemporary policies toward immigrants to the point where some problems are exacerbated, others ignored." If Hispanic immigrants see themselves as an oppressed race rather than a struggling but hopeful new ethnic group in American politics, they will mistakenly define their interests in terms of a "legalistic quick fix," such as litigation or pressure for affirmative action and descriptive representation in legislatures. That focus will draw them away from their really essential interests in obtaining education and jobs, developing community-based security networks, engaging in political mobilization of local communities, and learning English. "Racialization thus makes everything about immigration more intractable." Skerry and Haney López agree on very little substantively, but analytically they are making the same argument: the way that members of a group conceive of themselves will shape their understanding of their interests and their chosen political actions.

One can take a further step by attending to the second clause in the quotation from Musil: it is not just that "one does what one is" as I have been discussing, but also "one becomes what one does." That is, actions may cause ideas, which then cause interests; a person does something, and then searches for a story to explain what her or she is doing or has done. Thus women often join nativist or racist groups in order to spend evenings with their husbands or friends, and only later develop the ideologies and take the actions associated with those groups (Blee 2002). The psychologist Daryl Bem first developed this idea in academic discourse (Bem 1968), but the core insight is as old as the recognition that children taught to take certain actions are likely to develop the personality of the kind of person who would do those acts.

4   MOVING BEYOND "HOW IDEAS CAUSE ACTIONS"

Rather than trying to adjudicate among, or weigh the importance of, the ways in which ideas can cause actions, I turn in conclusion to the more interesting issue of which features of a context shape the relationship between ideas and actions. In broadest compass, there are (at least) three: history, institutions, and leaders.

The role of history is seen most sharply when one considers how ethnic identity can override material interests or shape one's understanding of interests and rights. Most ethnic groups passionate enough to be willing to fight for their autonomy (or for domination) reach back centuries, if not millennia to explain their stance. Consider the Zionists' claim to Eretz Israel, displaced Arabs' claim to the land of Palestine, and Serbs' explanation for the recent war in Kosovo:

As ... Christians are being martyred by their Muslim neighbors for the mere fact of being what they are, it is time to re-visit the history of the Kosovo conflict. Western media consumers may be forgiven for thinking that the history of that conflict starts in 1989, when the Serbs supposedly abolished the autonomy of that hitherto happy and harmonious multicultural province. This is not true, and a truthful account of the problem's background is needed for an informed debate, lest the claims of the Albanian lobbies succeed yet again in imposing a Balkan agenda in Washington that is as offensive to decency as it is inimical to American interests.

Serbia's physical and spiritual heart was in Kosovo. ... Of all Kosovo battles the one that stands out happened on Vidovdan (St. Vitus's Day), June 28, 1389. ... In all those years [since then] the Serbs have celebrated the great battle, not only as a day of mourning but as an event to be remembered and avenged. (http://news.serbianunity.net/bydate/2004/March_24/12.html)

History, as this quotation makes abundantly clear, is not a set of neutral facts and events that occur in succession, but is itself a set of ideas that shape the ideas that lead to action. So invoking history does not resolve the question of how, when, and how much ideas shape actions, but it may provide an analytic starting point for understanding the elements of that relationship in any specific case (see Tilly, this volume).

Political scientists increasingly and usefully interpret the general point that "history matters" through the more precise concept of path dependency, which links change over time to a set of political institutions and practices (see Mahoney and Schensul, this volume). Path dependency can be defined simply as the assertion that "preceding steps in a particular direction induce further movement in the same direction"; from that starting point emerge an array of empirical propositions that help us to understand how and when ideas shape actions. These include the claims that "specific patterns of timing and sequence matter; a wide range of social outcomes may be possible [from a given starting point or in a particular nation]; large consequences may result from relatively small or contingent events; particular courses of action, once introduced, can be almost impossible to reverse; and, consequently, political development is punctuated by critical moments or junctures that shape the basic contours of social life" (Pierson 2000, 251–2).

Thus, for example, one could examine timing and sequence in the legislative introduction of a new policy proposal in order to understand diffusion of a new idea and the circumstances in which it affects a legislator's behavior or the passage of a law. Or one could examine how an idea and its associated actions become more and more deeply embedded in an institution's organization chart and resource allocation, a staff's standard operating procedures (SOPs), or a constituent group's demands—thus showing how a particular course of action, once established, becomes very difficult to reverse (Campbell 2003; Mettler and Soss 2004).

In fact, institutions and SOP's can be thought of as the visible manifestation of the effect of an idea on action; the US Environmental Protection Agency was created and staffed once enough people came to see protection of the environment as a public problem that needed and would respond to a legislative solution. But institutions and established practices can also, conversely, be creators or constrainers of ideas that shape actions. That is, we are now learning that many people who work in the Pentagon or US Justice Department differ from those in the US State Department in their understanding of what is legitimate in international law or under military necessity to obtain information from prisoners of war. Of course, there is a deep causal difficulty here; do people choose to work in the Pentagon (State Department) because they hold a harsher (more lenient) understanding of what is permissible in wartime, or do they develop that view once they work in a given institution? Sorting out that causal question would provide one form of leverage on the question of how much ideas affect actions and vice versa.

Finally, path dependence understood as "increasing returns to an initial investment" (Pierson 2000) is not the only political dynamic through history. Change occurs, sometimes dramatically. Some change can be explained by concepts such as path dependence, institutional channeling, or shared interpretations of history—but not all of it. The study of how ideas affect actions must leave a role for innovation, creativity, inspiration, leadership.

As a discipline, political science does a poor job of understanding sudden transformations because by definition they do not fit well-understood patterns or established covering laws. (No other discipline does any better.) But we have at least some analytic tools that can help to explain when new ideas change actions and when they simply disappear into the vast deep. Concepts such as punctuated equilibrium (Baumgartner and Jones 1993), typologies of leadership (Burns 1979), exemplary biographies (Caro 1974; Branch 1989) or case studies (Birnbaum and Murray 1988), studies of historical periods undergoing major cultural shifts (Rochon 1998), and studies of grassroots mobilization (Payne 1995) can all help us to determine when a leader with a new idea transforms established conventions of action—or at least to understand retrospectively when and how such a break occurred in the past.

A final aphorism: as Victor Hugo tells us, "an invasion of armies can be resisted, but not an idea whose time has come." It is as easy to show that ideas affect actions as it is difficult to specify anything more precise about how, how much, when, and with what political consequences. In that further specification lies work for many political scientists to come.

References

AUSTIN, J. L. 1975. *How to Do Things with Words*. Cambridge, Mass.: Harvard University Press.

BARTELS, L. 2005. Homer gets a tax cut: inequality and public policy in the American mind. *Perspectives on Politics*, 3: 15–32.

BAUMGARTNER, F., and JONES, B. 1993. *Agendas and Instability in American Politics*. Chicago: University of Chicago Press.

BECKER, G. 1976. *The Economic Approach to Human Behavior*. Chicago, Ill.: University of Chicago Press.

BEM, D. 1968. Self-observation as a source of pain perception. *Journal of Personality & Social Psychology*, 9: 205–9.

BIRNBAUM, J., and MURRAY, A. 1988. *Showdown at Gucci Gulch: Lawmakers, Lobbyists, and the Unlikely Triumph of Tax Reform*. New York: Vintage.

BLEE, K. 2002. *Inside Organized Racism: Women in the Hate Movement*. Berkeley: University of California Press.

BRADY, H. 2001. Trust the people: political party coalitions and the 2000 election. Pp. 39–73 in *The Unfinished Election of 2000*, ed. J. Rakove. New York: Basic Books.

BRANCH, T. 1989. *Parting the Waters: America in the King Years, 1954–63*. New York: Simon and Schuster.

BURNS, J. M. 1979. *Leadership*. New York: Harper and Row.

CAMPBELL, A. 2003. *How Policies Make Citizens: Senior Political Activism and the American Welfare State*. Princeton, NJ: Princeton University Press.

CARO, R. 1974. *The Power Broker: Robert Moses and the Fall of New York*. New York: Knopf.

DAWSON, M. 1994. *Behind the Mule: Race and Class in African-American Politics*. Princeton, NJ: Princeton University Press.

FAIR, R. 2002. *Predicting Presidential Elections and Other Things*. Stanford, Calif.: Stanford University Press.

FELDMAN, S. 2003. Values, ideology, and the structure of political attitudes. Pp. 477–508 in *Oxford Handbook of Political Psychology*, ed. D. Sears et al. New York: Oxford University Press.

GAVENTA, J. 1980. *Power and Powerlessness: Quiescence and Rebellion in an Appalachian Valley*. Urbana: University of Illinois Press.

GHENT, W. 1902. *Our Benevolent Feudalism*. New York: Macmillan.

GOREN, P. 2004. *Party Identification and Core Values*. Tempe: Arizona State University, Department of Political Science.

HACKER, J., and PIERSON, P. 2005. Abandoning the middle: the Bush tax cuts and the limits of democratic control. *Perspectives on Politics*, 3: 33–54.

HANEY LÓPEZ, I. 1997. Race, ethnicity, erasure: the salience of race to LatCrit theory. *California Law Review*, 85: 1143–211.

HOCHSCHILD, J. 1981. *What's Fair? American Beliefs about Distributive Justice*. Cambridge, Mass.: Harvard University Press.

——1984. *The New American Dilemma: Liberal Democracy and School Desegregation*. New Haven, Conn.: Yale University Press.

HUTCHINGS, V. 2003. *Public Opinion and Democratic Accountability: How Citizens Learn about Politics*. Princeton, NJ: Princeton University Press.

KAHNEMAN, D., and TVERSKY, A. (eds.) 2000. *Choices, Values, and Frames.* Cambridge: Cambridge University Press.

KINDER, D., and SEARS, D. 1985. Public opinion and political action. Pp. 659–741 in *Handbook of Social Psychology,* 3rd edn., vol. II, *Special Fields and Applications,* ed. G. Lindzey and E. Aronson. New York: Random House.

MACKINNON, C. 1993. *Only Words.* Cambridge, Mass.: Harvard University Press.

METTLER, S., and SOSS, J. 2004. The consequences of public policy for democratic citizenship: bridging policy studies and mass politics. *Perspectives on Politics,* 2: 55–74.

MYRDAL, G. 1944. *An American Dilemma.* New York: Harper.

PAYNE, C. 1995. *I've Got the Light of Freedom: The Organizing Tradition and the Mississippi Freedom Struggle.* Berkeley: University of California Press.

PIERSON, P. 2000. Increasing returns, path dependence, and the study of politics. *American Political Science Review,* 94: 251–67.

PIKETTY, T. 1995. Social mobility and redistributive politics. *Quarterly Journal of Economics,* 110: 551–84.

ROCHON, T. 1998. *Culture Moves: Ideas, Activism, and Changing Values.* Princeton, NJ: Princeton University Press.

SEARS, D., and FUNK, C. 1990. Self-interest in Americans' political opinions. Pp. 147–70 in *Beyond Self-Interest,* ed. J. Mansbridge. Chicago: University of Chicago Press.

SKERRY, P. 1999. The racialization of immigration policy. Pp. 81–119 in *Taking Stock: American Government in the Twentieth Century,* ed. M. Keller and R. S. Melnick. New York: Cambridge University Press.

SLOVIC, P., and LICHTENSTEIN, S. 1983. Preference reversals: a broader perspective. *American Economic Review,* 73: 596–605.

VARSHNEY, A. 2003. Nationalism, ethnic conflict, and rationality. *Perspectives on Politics,* 1: 85–99.

CHAPTER 16

....

MISTAKEN IDEAS AND THEIR EFFECTS

....

LEE CLARKE

TRADITIONAL categories of social analysis presume cognitive and institutional stability. Even scholarship on mental illness and revolutions—domains of thought obviously concerned with disjuncture—are premised on some conception of, respectively, consistent thought processes and established political order. The problem with such an orientation is that it relegates mistake, deception, accident, and disaster (and the like) to a special realm, as if they were anomalous and strange. But they are not. They are, rather, normal and prosaic. Here I concentrate on a special class of mistake, called *misleading ideas*.

Charles Perrow (1999) broke new ground in the study of organizational and technological failures, and how those failures can lead to disaster. The heart of Perrow's analysis is a cross-classification of organizational structure (varying from linear to complex) and technological coupling (varying from tight to loose). Perrow's analysis is undergirded by a pessimism that human-made systems could be error free. He goes much further than the aphorism that because humans are imperfect their systems will necessarily be so, for his analysis points to the kinds of systems whose failure will most likely be catastrophic. Most important for present purposes is that Perrow also analyzes the misleading statements by those who

*For help thanks to James Jasper, Lynee Moulton, Charles Perrow, Patricia Roos, Scott Sagan, and Diane Vaughan.

occupy powerful positions. He unmasks their claims that with sufficient vigilance and resources dangerous systems can be safe.

Lee Clarke (1999) conceptualizes *symbolic plans,* or *fantasy documents,* as plans that are radically disconnected from experience or meaningful expertise. Because of such disconnects fantasy documents are little more than official promises or statements about what officials would like to be able to do rather than actual blueprints for action (which is what operational plans are). Fantasy documents mislead because they are used to over-promise what officials and organizations can deliver.

Diane Vaughan (1996) analyzed the organizational and cultural forces leading to the fateful choice to launch the space shuttle *Challenger.* Production pressures pushed managers to overrule engineers, leading them to neglect copious evidence of impending catastrophe. Additionally, over time NASA personnel convinced themselves that failing system components were not risky. The chief organizational mechanism that facilitated NASA's failure stemmed from the need to reduce uncertainty, a need present in all large organizations. Two specific procedures were operative: relying on a quantification bias (if a risk couldn't be easily counted it did not exist) and routine (the shuttle had not crashed before so why would it crash now?).

Lynn Eden (2004) argues that, at least until the 1990s, military planners and strategists systematically turned away from the problem of nuclear-induced fire. There was solid evidence that fire in urban areas would cause more deaths and property damage than nuclear explosions themselves. But planners mistakenly neglected fire because routines of the organizations responsible for planning set the terms of legitimacy for the kind of information that would be considered relevant. Blast was foregrounded; fire was backgrounded. The effects of that self-deception were significant, because seriously factoring in fire would have changed targeting tactics and strategies, would have lent more ammunition to those arguing that "nuclear winter" made war-fighting ideas insane, and would have given more credibility to arms-control advocates.

From such research, and for theoretical reasons, too, Clarke and Perrow (1996) and Clarke (2005) argue that instabilities, failures, even disasters should be seen as normal, as much a part of everyday life as their opposites. If we jettison the notion that disaster, mistake, and failure are special we can use data about them to understand the wielding of political power, the durability of social networks, or the formation of subcultures. Besides, mistakes, deceptions, lies, and the like are common so treating them as abnormal makes no empirical sense.

People, and the systems they build, make different kinds of mistakes. One way of recognizing a mistake is to look at the degree of consonance between action and proclamation. When the claims do not match action, we are in the realm of mistaken or misleading ideas. To mislead is to guide in a wrong direction. The guidance can be deliberate or inadvertent. An example of the former: Nearly 400 black men were told for forty years by prestigious US government officials, physicians, and nurses that their syphilis was untreatable (Jones 1993). The men were misled about their conditions even after the advent of penicillin *and* knowledge of how syphilis ran its course. An example of inadvertently misleading: Before the 1989 Exxon oil spill in Alaska, major oil companies claimed they could clean up most of the pollution, but in fact that was technically impossible (Clarke 1993). In each of those cases—we could easily generate many more—there was a mismatch between proclamation and action. As a result, the African-American men were misled about their health and their health care, and anyone listening to the oil companies, most importantly Alaskans and regulators, were misled about the safety of the oil transport system in Alaska.

For our purposes here, guiding in the "wrong" direction means moving away from accurately representing the organizing principles of the nuclear war fighting system. There were meaningful contrasts between official representations regarding nuclear war diplomacy in the US, on one hand, and the content of nuclear war fighting plans, on the other. Over time, official talk about how a nuclear war would be conducted diverged sharply from what war planners intended to do in the event of such a war. The talk was, indeed, quite misleading.

I begin with an overview of the history of US nuclear war planning and diplomacy, followed by one of official nuclear talk, then of nuclear war planning. I end with a discussion of the case and draw some conclusions about misleading ideas and deception.

1   Planning and Diplomacy: An Overview

The histories of nuclear war planning and nuclear diplomacy are initially easy to characterize. In the beginning there was *convergence* between the way political leaders *talked about nuclear war fighting* and how generals and planners actually *planned to fight nuclear wars*. Over time, the talk and the plan were increasingly *divergent*. The politicians directed their *talk* toward other, foreign politicians and domestic constituencies and the military war fighters directed their *plans* toward the enemy's (chiefly the Soviet Union's) military forces.

Viewed as a system, the actions of the American nuclear war complex were contradicted by its claims. Simply, action continually pushed in the direction of a first-strike capability while official claims were otherwise. While official rhetoric revolved around the complexities of diplomacy, prevention of nuclear war, and sometimes "limited," fightable nuclear wars, actual war planning was oriented toward launching a first strike. Official rhetoric was more malleable, responding, as all rhetoric does, to different audiences in myriad ways. Operations, on the other hand, entailed a more consistent logic that emphasized a first strike. Official talk and operational behavior had in common that both were organized by the master concept of "deterrence." But the conception of deterrence and how to maintain it held by officials, was not congruent with the conception held by the war planners. Official representations became misleading, over time, leading to the mistaken idea that nuclear strategy was equivalent to conventional strategy.

2   OFFICIAL NUCLEAR TALK: THE RHETORIC OF DETERRENCE

"Never since the Treaty of Westphalia in 1648," said Kenneth Waltz in his 1990 presidential address to the American Political Science Association, "... have great powers enjoyed a longer period of peace than we have known since the Second World War. One can scarcely believe that the presence of nuclear weapons does not greatly help to explain this happy condition" (1990, 744). But, what have been the ideas and policies that have created this happy condition? The official reason for the long peace revolves around stable deterrence. The idea behind deterrence is that one must be sufficiently strong that a potential attacker is too afraid to attack. Maintaining a strong deterrent is omnipresent in the history of official rhetoric about nuclear weapons.

A terminological clarification: Experts distinguish between nuclear declaratory policy and nuclear doctrine. *Declaratory policy* refers to publicly declared words and public documents. *Nuclear doctrine* refers to what planning elites say, privately, to each other about what they will do in a nuclear war. There is a third category, operational behavior, which is what nuclear forces actually do. Declaratory policy is highly public, doctrine is somewhat public, and operations are secret.

There have been variations. The idea of *nuclear* deterrence was meaningless in the immediate moments after the Second World War; nor was there any nuclear doctrine to speak of, for two reasons. One is that at first President Truman did not have effective control over the stockpile. General Kenneth D. Nichols, a close military adviser to President Truman, says that "on June 30, 1948, there were fifty weapons in the stockpile" and that Truman showed no interest in them (Ball 1981, 1; Newhouse 1989, 68). Even top military people charged with planning for war—the Joint Staff Planners—and those charged with assessing broad strategic questions for the Joint Chiefs—the Joint Strategic Survey Committee—"were not cleared for nuclear information until the winter of 1947" (Rosenberg 1982, 28). The second reason is that there had not yet developed any *conception* of how nuclear weapons might be used, or more to the point, how the *threat* could be used.

But in June 1948, the Soviet Union blockaded Berlin, forcing clarification of both nuclear doctrine and declaratory policy. Truman responded to the Soviet provocation by sending two bomber groups to England, clearly implying that they were loaded with nuclear weapons. Truman's response was a hoax, since the aircraft weren't even fitted with the technology to carry atomic weaponry (Rosenberg 1982). But the crisis was important because it threw into bold relief that the United States did not have an official nuclear war policy (Sagan 1989). Political and military elites were prompted to devote more attention to the problem. In 1949 the Soviets detonated a nuclear weapon and there was a Communist takeover in China. One result of these tumultuous times was NSC-68, which was a review of extant military capabilities, external threats, and policies regarding nuclear weapons. Written chiefly by Paul Nitze, NSC-68 recommended a massive military build-up, one that concentrated more on air-delivered nuclear weapons than on ground forces (Eden 1984).

The early 1950s saw the first developed declaratory policy. Eisenhower was the first truly nuclear president, meaning that he had a considerable arsenal at his disposal and that he had to deal with an enemy who also had at least the threat of a nuclear arsenal. It was a time of high international tension, McCarthyism, the "Communist threat," and Sputnik, a time that led Eisenhower to wonder, in a memorandum to Secretary of State John Foster Dulles, in September 1953, whether circumstances of mutual, nuclear inspired deterrence might force the US "to consider whether or not our duty to future generations did not require us to initiate war at the most propitious moment we could designate" (Rosenberg 1983, 33).

The idea (and doctrine) of massive retaliation arose during these years, and policy-makers recognized the strong incentive inherent in a system of nuclear deterrence to strike first. The incentive to strike first emanates from the simple fact that unfired nuclear missiles are vulnerable targets. If deterrence fails—or even looks as though it *might* fail—the operative logic becomes, use them or lose them. By 1954 "massive retaliation" was a publicly proffered policy. The concept had been detailed in an October 1953 national security policy paper, and in Dulles' famous speech of January 1954.

Massive retaliation threatened not only the Soviet Union, but also China and their satellites (Kennedy 1985). If the Soviets, or anyone else, were to strike the United States or Europe with nuclear weapons then the US response would be immediate and overwhelming. And that response would not be proportional to the provocation. Thus the official threat became total annihilation in response to any nuclear attack. Massive retaliation, as a repertoire of official, public talk was directed at both domestic and foreign audiences. Massive retaliation was also a way to instill sufficient fear in Americans that they would ratify massive spending on nuclear weapons (Oakes 1994; Grossman 2001). It was also a worldwide claim that the United States had the technical expertise and the military will to kill large numbers of people (Fischoff 1991).

The 1960s were the years of Robert McNamara who created important new ways of talking about deterrence and declaratory policy. He also had an influence in rationalizing actual war plans. McNamara came from the top corporate position at Ford Motor Company, bringing a respect for rational planning that we would expect of a corporate executive.

McNamara shifted declaratory policy about the utility of nuclear weapons and about US policy toward the Soviet Union. Although Eisenhower had sometimes spoken of nuclear weapons as if they were simply another arrow in the military's quiver—rather than weapons with unique properties—it was sporadic talk unaccompanied by a systematic incorporation of that assumption into official policy. One of McNamara's innovations was to introduce into *public discourse* talk about nuclear war-fighting and limited nuclear war. In June 1962 he declared that the principal goal of US strategy in a nuclear war "should be the destruction of the enemy's military forces, not his civilian population" (Barnet 1981, 26). This was called the "no cities" doctrine and it meant that nuclear targeting could be selective, much as one would try to avoid hospitals and orphanages in conventional attacks.

McNamara's declaratory policy was controversial. Some hailed it as humanitarian because it seemed merciful to disavow the need to incinerate millions of people. Others hailed it because it officially recognized a nagging problem with officially sanctioning massive retaliation: making cities the core of deterrence is irrational and at some point unbelievable. What would happen if the Soviets, for whatever reason, destroyed Manhattan with a nuclear warhead? If US policy were such that it required retaliation against Soviet cities, an attack on US cities would surely follow that retaliation. Since no decision-maker would follow a course of action that would be certain to result in such destruction, massive retaliation for *any* threat was not credible. Or so went the criticism of "massive retaliation."

But others criticized McNamara's "no cities" doctrine as a radical and dangerous departure from US policy, and this is the usual primary reason cited for McNamara soon demurring from it (the other is that it gave the Air Force a justification for a major increase in expenditures).[1] The form of his demurral was to develop an apparently new, apparently more complex policy. As he put it in an interview with Robert Scheer (1982, 216), "we moved from Dulles's strategy of massive retaliation to what was called 'flexible response'." Flexible response allowed the no cities doctrine to be maintained by surrounding it with an apparently more complex

---

[1] There is something to the Air Force point. McNamara was concerned with more than the Air Force's expanding expenditures. McNamara read to Robert Scheer (1982, 216): "This is a highly classified memorandum from me to President Kennedy, dated November 21, 1962. In the memorandum I state, 'It has become clear to me the Air Force proposals are based on the objective of achieving a first-strike capability. In the words of an Air Force report to me, "The Air Force has rather supported the development of forces which provide the United States a first-strike capability".'"

vocabulary. Much more important is that it challenged extant conceptions of deterrence by constructing an image of American policy that was at some variance with the one then prevailing. The theory of deterrence behind "massive retaliation" was blunt and rude—if they worry us we'll hit them hard. The theory of deterrence behind "flexible response," however, sought to convince audiences that the US was a more complex entity, whose motivations and responses would be more uncertain than was the case in the past.

In all this, *stability* in the nuclear stand-off was what the more cautious minds were trying to preserve. If you are playing a first strike game, then it is in your opponent's interest to strike first. But if your first-best option is not to strike at all, and you have a second-strike capability (e.g. invincible submarines), it is in your interest to wait for your opponent to strike first, before striking back. In other words, developing a first-strike capability makes your peace-loving opponents into first-strike opponents, and relying on a second-strike capability makes them into peace-lovers, just like you. If both sides rely on second-strike capabilities, each can afford to wait to be attacked. Each waiting, neither will be, resulting in stable peace. Innovations that threatened nuclear stability—"no cities," "flexible response," or, later, multiple warheads on a single missile—were held to measure against the logic of the nuclear game.[2]

Life after McNamara was more of the same—restatements or refinements of "flexible response." There were no more quantum changes in either declaratory nuclear policy or guidance until the fall of the Soviet Union. James Schlesinger, Nixon's Defense Secretary, announced "a new targeting doctrine that emphasizes selectivity and flexibility" (Barnet 1981, 26). Carter's Secretary of Defense Harold Brown similarly spoke of "countervailing" targeting, which meant specifically targeting Soviet military leadership and command capabilities. Reagan officials drew fire for talking about waging and winning nuclear wars but neither their talk nor their doctrine differed from that which preceded them (the tone, though, was decidedly more aggressive).

Declaratory policy is more public than nuclear doctrine, but the latter is sufficiently public to perform rhetorical functions. Doctrine is more detailed than declaratory policy on targeting, command and control, and specific options (see e.g. Sagan 1989). Those details would probably make most sense to other high-level policy-makers and military planners with responsibility for thinking about such issues. We might say that doctrine is rhetoric directed toward experts and elites— most probably, foreign audiences—while declaratory policy was directed toward general publics—which were most likely domestic audiences. This is not to say that policy and doctrine are or were only talk, or to trivialize them. It is, rather, simply to recognize that they are forms of interaction, since they are necessary and make sense only if one assumes that another actor is listening to the utterances.

[2] See Ball et al. 1987; Freedman 2003; Kaplan 1991; Sagan 1989.

Both nuclear declaratory policy and nuclear doctrine evolved in more "flexible" ways. They represented a diminution in the absolute promise of ultimate annihilation that would be required in response to even a threat of atomic attack. They represented, too, the idea that nuclear wars might be fought as conventional wars had been fought, with both or multiple sides waxing and waning in their efforts and successes. Flexibility employed rational-sounding rhetoric to argue that nuclear war could be limited.

As flexibility replaced annihilation, nuclear diplomacy and nuclear war fighting sounded somewhat less threatening. This, surely, was a mistaken idea. Simply the idea of having alternatives to a tremendous spasm of atomic explosions would suggest less violence, and greater sense. But such rhetorical refinements obscured the incentive to prepare to launch a first, overwhelming strike. That incentive receded from public and semi-public discussion, but it never receded from war planning.

3   NUCLEAR WAR PLANNING

"Those who play pivotal roles in nuclear affairs," bellowed C. Wright Mills (1958) in *The Causes of World War III*, "have no image of what 'victory' might mean, and no idea of any road to victory." Mills seems to have had in mind top-level politicians, drifting toward war by the mere act of preparing for it, and about them perhaps he was right. But he was wrong about the nuclear war planners. Since the bombings of Japan, there has been a shifting network of organizations and experts operating on a definite vision of victory after nuclear war. In its simplest terms the vision consists of the ideas that: (1) nuclear war does not necessarily entail total devastation because (2) the damage can be limited through (3) civil defense measures and sufficient military strength. The United States could win by hitting the enemy hard enough, soon enough, while protecting (some of) its people. I neglect civil defense and concentrate on the issue of "sufficient military strength."

3.1   The Strategic Air Command

Estimates of the nuclear firepower needed to destroy the Soviet Union immediately after the Second World War "postulated the use of anywhere from 20 to 200 bombs" (Rosenberg 1982, 28). By 1948 a war plan was developed that called for "attacks on 70 Soviet cites with 133 atomic bombs" (Rosenberg 1982, 16). Cities were the main targets, largely because warheads couldn't be delivered accurately (airplanes were the delivery vehicles). Planners had to aim for the broadest side of the barn.

The creation of the Strategic Air Command (SAC), and the appointment of General Curtis LeMay as its first commander, were important events in nuclear war planning. LeMay began commanding SAC in October of 1948 with the mandate of ensuring that "the Strategic Air Command was capable of delivering the atomic stockpile on the Soviet Union 'in one fell swoop telescoping mass and time'" (Rosenberg 1982, 29). This was a difficult goal to attain, however, because of insufficient targeting information (and the problem of inaccurate delivery systems). The information deficit was so severe that the CIA had to depend on Nazis and Second World War maps for targeting purposes. In any case, LeMay's imprint on SAC and war planning was substantial. He had witnessed some of the Bikini tests, in the Marshall islands, and realized that with sufficient nuclear weapons and "in conjunction with other mass destruction weapons *it is possible to depopulate vast areas of the earth's surface, leaving only vestigial remnants of man's material works*" (Rosenberg 1979, 67).

SAC's plan, under LeMay, was straightforwardly preemptive. Asked what he would do if it looked as though the Soviets were gearing up for attack LeMay said, "If I come to that conclusion, I'm going to knock the shit out of them before they get off the ground" (in Newhouse 1989, 280).

During the 1950s targeting goals were "contained in a jointly prepared and annually updated short-range war plan known as the Joint Strategic Capabilities Plans" (Rosenberg 1981/2, 8). But it fell to the Commander of SAC to make detailed plans. SAC's annual plan was known as the "SAC Emergency War Plan (EWP) which was submitted to the JCS for review and approval" (Rosenberg 1981/2). In other words the JCS set guidance but the nuts and bolts of nuclear war planning— the targeting and the assumptions that underlay that targeting—were set by SAC.

LeMay created an organization that enjoyed considerable autonomy. Beginning in 1951 LeMay did not even submit his annually updated Basic War Plans as required for JCS review (Rosenberg 1983, 37). Striving for efficiency and a minimum of US casualties, the basic SAC plan was to unleash a mass of death in a single, preventive blow. Or, in the words of a Navy captain who worked on the plan, to leave the Soviet Union "a smoking, radiating ruin at the end of two hours" (Rosenberg 1981/2, 11).

3.2   Technological Changes and Deterrence

The rise of SAC, the development of concepts of mass destruction, and advances in technology urged the rise, development, and advance of actual planning. Beginning in the late 1950s, three documents are key to understanding America's nuclear warplans—the Nuclear Weapons Employment Policy (NUWEP), Single Integrated Operational Plan (SIOP), and National Strategic Target List (NSTL) (Rosenberg 1981/1982).

In January of 1950 President Truman ordered the Atomic Energy Commission to develop the hydrogen bomb (the first H-bomb exploded two years later). In 1955 the US launched its first nuclear submarine and two years later saw the advent of intercontinental ballistic missiles. These events were turning points in the technical capacity to wage nuclear war because submarines could be hidden indefinitely and ICBMs could be launched from across the world, obviating reliance on airplanes to deliver warheads.

These technical advances brought considerable organizational growth, and new ideas about how nuclear weapons might be used. As early as 1950, planners concluded that "the time is approaching when both the United States and the Soviets will possess capabilities for inflicting devastating atomic attacks on each other. *Were war to break out when this period is reached, a tremendous military advantage would be gained by the power that struck first and succeeded in carrying through an effective first strike*" (Sagan 1989, 19).

The threat was clarified in 1957, with the Soviet Sputnik success. The first Sputnik flight, in October 1957, put a basketball-sized satellite into orbit. In November Sputnik II put a dog and a heavier payload into space. While newspapers and pundits saw Sputnik as an indictment of American education and technology, those who knew nuclear weapons saw something quite different. Rather than shoot a dog into space and drop it back on Soviet territory, it was now clearly possible to shoot a nuclear bomb into space and drop it on American territory. These technological developments would make it imperative that war fighters be able to destroy Soviet missiles *before they were fired*.

War planning exercises had confirmed that even a doubling of the target list couldn't "prevent the Soviets launching a strike unless we hit first" (Rosenberg 1981/2, 12). As long as nuclear weapons were the basis of deterrence there would always be a strong incentive to strike first, and quickly. It was not only advances in weapons delivery that fed the nuclear warms race. Simply knowing more about the targets would require more warheads. U-2 overflights of the USSR began in 1956 and by 1959 had identified more than 20,000 targets. David Alan Rosenberg (1981/2, 16), a key military historian, reports that:

To deal with such a huge target complex, SAC, following patterns established in the mid-1950s, continued to plan for a massive combined assault with large-yield thermonuclear weapons on Soviet nuclear capabilities, military forces, and urban-industrial targets. This combination, which became known as the "optimum mix" by 1959, formed the basis for the first SIOP in December 1960.

3.3   1960s: The Single Integrated Operational Plan (SIOP)

Eisenhower presided over a serious organizational battle between the Navy and the Air Force. SAC, part of the Air Force, had controlled nuclear weapons but the nuclear Navy was coming into its own as at least an equal. Indeed in principle, the Navy would have a strategic edge, and therefore be more politically important relative to other services, because submarines—especially submarines powered by nuclear energy—could be made virtually invincible. Eisenhower stepped into the struggle between Navy and Air Force and ordered coordination of the forces. One product of that intervention was the first Single Integrated Operational Plan. As Rosenberg (1983, 7) describes it:

The SIOP aimed for an assurance of delivery factor of 97 percent for the first 200 DGZs [a designated or desired ground zero], and 93 percent for the next 400, well above the goals established by the [National Strategic Targeting and Attack Policy]. To achieve such levels, multiple strikes with high yield weapons were laid on against many individual targets.

Rosenberg (1983, 7) also notes that the SIOP was not much driven by political objectives. "Instead the SIOP was a *capabilities plan*, aimed at utilizing all available forces to achieve maximum destruction. As a result, although it eliminated duplication in targeting, it did not reduce the size of the target list. The plan made no distinction among different target systems, but called for simultaneous attacks on nuclear delivery forces, governmental control centers, and the urban-industrial base." Note how the usual view—that civilian policy drives military strategy—was mistaken.

In August 1960 Secretary of Defense Thomas Gates created the Joint Strategic Target Planning Staff, which was responsible for coordinating nuclear war plans (Sagan 1987). The resulting SIOP used the National Strategic Target List. "The National Strategic Target List," says Sagan (1987, 45), "was developed from a list of more the 80,000 potential targets [this includes China and Eastern Europe] in the Bombing Encyclopedia. This list was analyzed, screened, and finally reduced to 3,729 installations which were determined to be essential for attack" (1987, 44). But the first SIOP, at least, was quite narrow, concentrating only on the initial attack. "Therefore, the foremost object in integrating these forces was to attain the highest probability of success with this initial attack."

The SIOP was designed so the United States would prevail in a nuclear war. Like all plans, it arose to solve a problem, chiefly the problem of the lack of coordination among the armed forces who commanded nuclear weapons. But the very large number of nuclear targets, which would continue to grow, was the result neither of policy nor of the plan itself. Rather, that growth would be required by growth in the number of the enemy's targets and in American ability to detect those targets. In that way, the plan to strike first was propelled by the technology of nuclear war fighting.

The advent of McNamara, as noted, was significant not only for declaratory policy but also for the SIOP itself. "When McNamara was briefed on SIOP-62 on February 4, 1961," reports Rosenberg, "he was disturbed by the rigidity of the plan, the 'fantastic' fallout and destruction it would produce, and the absence of a clear strategic rationale for the counterforce/urban-industrial target mix" (Rosenberg 1983, 6–7). The next month McNamara began reformulating national security policy, especially his "no cities" options.[3]

3.4   1970s and Beyond

From the 1970s to the fall of the Soviet Union there were a few important technical or political developments concerning nuclear war planning, but none that would fundamentally change the logic or organization of preparing to fight a nuclear war.

In 1970 Richard Nixon asked Congress whether "a President, in the event of a nuclear attack, [should] be left with the single option of ordering the mass destruction of enemy civilians in the face of the certainty that it would be followed by the mass slaughter of Americans?" (in Pringle and Arkin 1983, 177). In February of 1971 Nixon gave a foreign policy speech in which he declared "I must not be—and my successors must not be—limited to the indiscriminate mass destruction of enemy civilians as the sole possible response to challenges" (Sloss and Milot 1984, 21). This speech led to a series of studies of targeting practice conducted under Dr. John Foster (then Director of Defense Research and Engineering, and later a member of CIA Director George H. W. Bush's infamous Team B). These studies resulted in the production of NSDM 242 (National Security Decision Memorandum) which was signed by Nixon in January 1974 (Ball 1981). A key part of NSDM 242 renewed attention to targeting a wider range of Soviet military forces (Ball 1981, 2). This emphasis became *possible* because of a technology that was developed in the late 1960s: the Multiple Independently Targetable Reentry Vehicle, the MIRV. MIRVs permitted more than one warhead on a single rocket, and those warheads were, as

---

[3] There was an alternative to all this, but it never gained much military attention. "The creation of the SIOP," writes Rosenberg, "which elevated operational planning to the level of national policy, represented the victory of short term concerns over long term planning. In particular, it effectively killed a major effort within the JCS to redirect U.S. nuclear strategy away from capabilities planning: the Alternative Undertaking. The alternative retaliatory target lists being prepared for the JCS were supposed to require only a fraction of the striking force, and to focus on achieving only the minimum damage necessary to accomplish specific military objectives. Army and Navy sponsors of the project had made no secret of the fact that they hoped those alternative lists might eventually supplant the proposed massive SAC offensive. The lists were not yet completed, however, when the SIOP made them moot" (1983, 70).

the name suggests, capable of independent targeting. It was an ingenious technology because it allowed a fairly easy increase in the power of the nuclear threat.

The advent of MIRVs changed the arms race because their deployment meant that the Soviets would have to increase dramatically the number of their own warheads, simply to counter the new US threat. By 1974 the US had about 25,000 targets for nuclear attack (Ball 1981, 6); the USSR likely had a similar number of targets.

In July 1980, President Carter signed Presidential Directive 59 which changed some aspects of nuclear war-fighting planning.[4] PD 59 ratcheted up the number of targets to 40,000. This increase happened because weapons delivery systems were increasingly accurate. PD 59 emphasized greater targeting of Soviet command and control than was previously the case, indeed making a point of "digging out"— using nuclear weapons to vaporize huge craters in the earth—not only hardened ICBM silos but also leadership relocation centers (Richelson 1983). As well, PD 59 was designed:

To convince the Soviets that no use of nuclear weapons, "on any scale of attack and at any stage of conflict, could lead to victory," the countervailing strategy mandated increased flexibility in war planning, including "the controlled use of nuclear weapons" in hopes of restraining escalation, as well as increased capacity to attack Soviet strategic nuclear and other military forces, national leadership, and command and control targets.   (Ball 1981, 3–4)

PD 59 was also important for another, more mundane reason: by emphasizing command and control targeting it justified the purchase of a super-accurate, hidden missile system, the MX missile.

The Reagan administration's contribution to the nuclear weapons and war-fighting complex was chiefly rhetorical. It introduced the MX missile, but that was Carter's program. The Strategic Defense Initiative channeled money to various parts of the military complex but its fantastic nature meant that it had few implications for actual nuclear war planning.

4   LESSONS

We could tell the story of nuclear war planning and nuclear war diplomacy as a fairly logical progression of abilities: studies were conducted, new information

---

[4] Desmond Ball (1981, 6) points out that in 1977 Carter issued PD 18, which was basically a reaffirmation of NSDM 242, but put it on the shelf for fifteen months "until it was retrieved just prior to the Democratic Convention, revised and up-dated, and formally signed by the president on 25 July as PD-59."

about targets was discovered, new guidance was issued, new plans of attack were constructed. In this story, civilian political leaders set policies and the military developed the technology to carry them out. Such a story would be misleading, so it would be a mistake to believe it (Gamson and Modigliani 1989).

Nuclear war planning and nuclear war talking were poorly coordinated (see Smit, this volume). There was no overarching coordination of the two systems, which allowed each to be driven by different dynamics, with different audiences for their actions and different environmental constraints. The world of nuclear war talk was more flexible, with multiple domestic and foreign audiences for diplomatic speech. The world of nuclear war planning was more closed, and more driven, or constrained, by weapons technology.

Technological advances permitted a much higher degree of accuracy in warhead delivery. With advances in digital circuitry and electronic systems, it became possible to deliver two warheads to within 100 yards of a target. These technical advances had uneven effects on nuclear war talk and nuclear war planning. On talk they would permit the rhetorically defensible position that nuclear war might be fought in a conventional mode. For instance, high-precision delivery systems meant that city-killer "block buster" weapons would be unnecessary. There would be no need, logically, to annihilate most or all of a civilian population when industry, command and control posts, and most other important weapons could be more carefully targeted. Lower yield weapons, too, could be used for destroying targets, which could also limit collateral damage. Public talk about nuclear war fighting could thus more closely resemble talk about conventional wars.

The technical advances in nuclear warheads, warhead delivery systems, and surveillance—matched in the Soviet Union—meant that what politicians could now logically say in public was quite at odds with the effects that more advanced technology would have on actual war planning. That the enemy would have faster, more accurate weapons would greatly increase the pressure massively to release the arsenal, should imminent attack be perceived. The idea of "overkill" changed meaning. Where once it meant that one side in a struggle could kill every *person* several times over, in nuclear modernity it would mean one had the ability to kill the other's *missiles* many times over.

Like all weapons, nuclear warheads are useless if destroyed. But nuclear missiles are singular because of how they compress time. They must be delivered *quickly* or they will be destroyed. And their extraordinary destructive power greatly increases the incentive to prevent an enemy from attacking. Carter et al. point out that "what a Napoleon or Hitler could not accomplish in many months could now, in principle be done by one blow in less than an hour" (1987, 9). Since missiles can travel about 9,000 miles per hour, all targets become highly vulnerable (Carter et al. 1987, 18). This dependence on fast delivery makes it imperative that missiles be used or be lost. If a country is going to have nuclear weapons on the ground, then when those with responsibility for fighting a war develop a sense of imminent attack the warheads must launch immediately. Conventional war-fighting technologies such as tanks, planes, or even armies are more amenable to decentralization than nuclear weapons. Nuclear weapons thus create a very strong incentive to plan to strike first and to strike massively. To do otherwise is to run a very high risk of destruction.

Organizations scholar Chris Demchak argues that "technologically-induced organizational changes will tend to establish a field of choices and condition the way military options are selected by insiders and viewed by outsiders" (Demchak 1995, 4). This logic applies to nuclear weapons. While the technologies are products of human effort they become such overwhelming social facts that they become strong constraints on future action.

Most writings on nuclear diplomacy and nuclear war planning neglect the low degree of coordination in their respective organizational systems, emphasizing instead the one concept that unifies them: deterrence.[5] Doing so creates the impression that there has indeed been a single system. In this telling, high-level politicians set military and diplomatic goals, which in turn propose weapons systems that would meet those goals. All actions are driven by the same conception of deterrence.

But deterrence is a complicated concept, and has served more purposes than a simple view acknowledges. Long ago, Robert Jervis (1976; 1984) brought attention to the problem of misperception in nuclear diplomacy. In particular, the standard view neglects the *symbolic* functions that deterrence has sometimes served. Rather than *driving* talk and choices about nuclear weapons (and defense), the idea of deterrence has been used to justify decisions and actions already made. Ideas about deterrence have legitimated courses of action that were driven by nuclear war-fighting capabilities and technical systems acquisition. The larger point is that deterrence rhetoric was mainly in the public realm. It was directed especially at the Soviet Union, of course, but also toward the American public in an effort to legitimate whatever was the current policy, to secure funds for weapons procurement, or simply for electoral purposes. For example, talk in the Reagan administration, especially in the early 1980s, of a "window of vulnerability" (a term revived from the 1950s) tried to convince people, through the media, that America was open to a Soviet preemptive strike.

Deterrence rhetoric was used misleadingly to try to convince audiences that America's war planning was animated by rational, intellectual considerations. That rhetoric was aimed at misleading domestic and foreign audiences into believing that civilian politicians both were in control of nuclear weapons and understood the technologies they had at their disposal.

It is worth pausing here to point out several major mistakes in the history I've discussed: the neglect by strategists and policy-makers of nuclear winter and

---

[5] See Powers 1982; 1984; Sagan 1989; Sagan and Waltz 1995.

nuclear-generated fire, and the logical problem of maintaining control of the arsenal in hostilities. If either factor were given serious consideration a good bit of nuclear discourse would have looked irrational. The idea of nuclear winter is that even a small handful of large detonations would throw enough debris into the upper atmosphere that the sun would be blotted out for a period of time sufficient to threaten the survival of hundreds of millions of people, and perhaps all of civilization (Powers 1984; Grinspoon 1986). Thus even a first strike launch that drew no response would be suicidal. Such a realization suggests that the rational course of action would be to disarm, or at least draw back to a second-strike force. For if the models that project nuclear winter are valid, then self-deterrence is as important as other-deterrence. But under that condition, the whole project looks like one giant mistake.

The problem of nuclear-generated fire is crucial. As noted, Eden (2004) has shown that military planners systematically ignored fire damage in their estimates of nuclear-generated damage. The organizational production of military blindness said that the only damage that mattered was the damage from blasts. One result of this deeply mistaken idea was that the military requested numbers of weapons at least twice as large as necessary for the amount of destruction they wanted to achieve. Had the knowledge of fire been folded into war plans, the number of necessary warheads would drop, damage estimates would increase, projections of nuclear winter would have been bolstered, and the representation that nuclear war could be controlled would be revealed as a mistake.

One effect of the mismatch between nuclear war planning and nuclear war talk was that the latter was importantly obscured from public view. Had the built-in, all-or-nothing assumptions of planning been more in the public realm, those who tried to persuade us that nuclear wars could be fought like any other could have been challenged more effectively. The notion of a nuclear war that was less-than-Armageddon was long sought after by nuclear planners and policy-makers. It was a notion that was, even in the literal sense of the word, chimerical. The very idea of fighting and winning a nuclear war was misleading.

Planners and policy-makers also failed to make integral to their enterprise the paradox of how to maintain control of a nuclear arsenal when their command, control, communications, and intelligence—3CI—infrastructure would be the first targets of massive attack. It is in the interests of the attacker to destroy the enemy's 3CI, effectively disabling a controlled (because communications and coordination would be gone) second strike capability. This means that the nuclear war would be on auto-pilot as soon as the first weapons were launched. If that were true then a nuclear war could not be controlled, rendering any notions of flexible response, and the like, dangerously mistaken.

Mismatches between proclamation and capability are a specific instance of mistake. Such mismatches are important. It matters whether promises correspond with capabilities, whether talk matches action or capability for action. And it matters whether policy-makers *think* there is such a correspondence. The assumptions that policy-makers, or chief executive officers, make about that correspondence would shape their estimates of the likelihood that their directives would be followed. Those assumptions would also matter for the kind of incentives that policy-makers might put in place to ensure that their policies were implemented. Perhaps most important is that assumptions about the promise–capacity correspondence would matter for whether or not decision-makers would judge certain futures as possible *in the first place*. If possibilities aren't seen as feasible to begin with, consideration of them would be by definition unreasonable, unworkable, perhaps even radical. Most organizations, and their managers, have little choice but to avoid courses of action that are unreasonable, unworkable, and radical. Failing to do so is, indeed, *bad* management. But that can be mistaken.

Were more intellectual attention accorded mistake, deception, and the like, we could develop better theories of why people think and behave as they do. Such phenomena are, as noted, normal rather than special. Social theory that does not include the dark side of society is itself a form of mistake.

References

BALL, D. 1981. Counterforce targeting: How new? How viable? *Arms Control Today*, 11: 1–9.

BALL, H. 1986. *Justice Downwind: America's Atomic Testing Program in the 1950s*. New York: Oxford University Press.

BARNET, R. J. 1981. *Real Security: Restoring American Power in a Dangerous Decade*. New York: Simon and Schuster.

CARTER, A. B., BALL, D., BETHE, H. A., BLAIR, B. G., BRACKEN, P., DICKINSON, H., GARWIN, R. L., GOTTFRIED, K., HOLLOWAY, D., KENDALL, H. W., LEAVITT, L. R. JR., LEBOW, R. N., RICE, C., STEIN, P. C., STEINBRUNNER, J. D., SWIATKOWSKI, L. U., and TOMB, P. D., 1987. *Crisis Stability and Nuclear War*. Ithaca, NY: Cornell University Peace Studies Program, January.

CLARKE, L. 1993. The disqualification heuristic: when do organizations misperceive risk? *Research in Social Problems and Public Policy*, 5: 289–312.

—— 1999. *Mission Improbable: Using Fantasy Documents to Tame Disaster*. Chicago: University of Chicago Press.

—— 2005. *Worst Cases: Inquiries Into Terror, Calamity, and Imagination*. Chicago: University of Chicago Press.

—— and PERROW, C. 1996. Prosaic organizational failure. *American Behavioral Scientist*, 39 (8): 1040–56.

DEMCHAK, C. 1995. Coping, copying, and concentrating: organizational learning and modernization in militaries. *Journal of Public Administration Research and Theory*, 5: 345–77.

EDEN, L. 1984. Capitalist conflict and the state: the making of United States military policy in 1948. Pp. 233–61 in *Statemaking and Social Movements*, ed. C. B. and S. Harding. Ann Arbor: University of Michigan Press.

EDEN, L. 2004. *Whole World on Fire: Organizations, Knowledge, and Nuclear Weapons Devastation*. Ithaca, NY: Cornell University Press.

FISCHOFF, B. 1991. Nuclear decisions: cognitive limits to the thinkable. Vol. 2, pp. 110–92 in *Behavior, Society, and Nuclear War*, ed. P. E. Tetlock et al. New York: Oxford University Press.

FREEDMAN, L. 2003. *Evolution of Nuclear Strategy*, 3rd edn. New York: Palgrave Macmillan.

GAMSON, W. A., and MODIGLIANI, A. 1989. Media discourse and public opinion on nuclear power: a constructionist approach. *American Journal of Sociology*, 95: 1–37.

GRINSPOON, L., Ed. 1986. *The Long Darkness: Psychological and Moral Perspectives on Nuclear Winter*. New Haven, Conn.: Yale University Press.

GROSSMAN, A. D. 2001. *Neither Dead Nor Red: Civilian Defense and American Political Development During the Early Cold War*. New York: Routledge.

JERVIS, R. 1976. *Perception and Misperception in International Politics*. Princeton, NJ: Princeton University Press.

——1984. *The Illogic of American Nuclear Strategy*. Ithaca, NY: Cornell University Press.

JONES, J. H. 1993. *Bad Blood: The Tuskegee Syphilis Experiment*. New York: Free Press.

KAPLAN, F. 1991. *The Wizards of Armageddon*. Stanford, Calif.: Stanford University Press.

KENNEDY, A. 1985. *The Logic of Deterrence*. London: Firethorn Press.

MILLS, C. W. 1958. *The Causes of World War III*. New York: Simon and Schuster.

NEWHOUSE, J. 1989. *War and Peace in the Nuclear Age*. New York: Knopf.

OAKES, G. 1994. *The Imaginary War: Civil Defense and American Cold War Culture*. New York: Oxford University Press.

PERROW, C. 1999. *Normal Accidents: Living With High Risk Technologies*. Princeton, NJ: Princeton University Press.

POWERS, T. 1982. Choosing a strategy for World War III. *Atlantic*, November, 82–110.

——1984. Nuclear winter and nuclear strategy. *Atlantic*, November, 53–64.

PRINGLE, P., and ARKIN, W. 1983. *SIOP: The Secret U.S. Plan for Nuclear War*. New York: Norton.

RICHELSON, J. 1983. PD-59, NSDD-13 and the Reagan strategic modernization program. *Journal of Strategic Studies*, 6: 125–46.

ROSENBERG, D. A. 1979. American atomic strategy and the hydrogen bomb decision. *Journal of American History*, 66: 62–87.

——1981–2. "A smoking radiating ruin at the end of two hours:" documents on American plans for nuclear war with the Soviet Union, 1954–1955. *International Security*, 6(3): 3–17.

——1982. U.S. nuclear stockpile, 1945–1950. *Bulletin of Atomic Scientists*, 38(5): 25–30.

——1983. The origins of overkill: nuclear weapons and American strategy, 1945–1960. *International Security*, 7: 1–71.

SAGAN, S. D. 1987. SIOP-62: the nuclear war plan briefing to President Kennedy. *International Security*, 12: 22–51.

——1989. *Moving Targets: Nuclear Strategy and National Security*. Princeton, NJ: Princeton University Press.

—— and WALTZ, K. N. 1995. *The Spread Of Nuclear Weapons: A Debate.* New York: Norton.

SCHEER, R. 1982. *With Enough Shovels: Reagan, Bush and Nuclear War.* New York: Random House.

SLOSS, L., and MILLOT, M. D. 1984. US nuclear strategy in evolution. *Strategic Review,* 12: 19–28.

VAUGHAN, D. 1996. *The Challenger Launch Decision: Risky Technology, Culture, and Deviance at NASA.* Chicago: University of Chicago Press.

WALTZ, K. N. 1990. Nuclear myths and political realities. *American Political Science Review,* 84: 733–45.

PART V

CULTURE MATTERS

CHAPTER 17

WHY AND HOW CULTURE MATTERS

MICHAEL THOMPSON

MARCO VERWEIJ

RICHARD J. ELLIS

It is hard to imagine a political science that took no account of culture. Ignore culture—all the things we have that monkeys do not[1]—and you have declared humans to be essentially the same as animals. Of course, we *are* animals, and there is much scholarly work on animal behavior, and even on animal social complexity [2], but precious little on their political behavior (beyond the oft-predicted low probability of turkeys voting for Christmas).[3] In other words, it is culture that enables us

[1] For all its flippancy, this is about as good a definition as one can get, and very much in line with Sir Edward Tylor's classic characterization of culture as "that complex whole which includes knowledge, belief, art, morals, laws, customs and any other capabilities and habits acquired by man as a member of society" (Tylor 1871, 1). Since Tylor's time, definitions have proliferated—one study (Kroeber and Kluckhohn 1952) counted 164—and so has disagreement as to what culture is and is not. Among students of political culture, the most widely accepted definition views culture as composed of values, beliefs, norms, and assumptions: that is, mental products (see, e.g., Pye 1968, 218). Such definitions have the virtue of separating the behavior to be explained from the beliefs that are doing the explaining. At the same time, in separating the mental from the social relations and their sustaining transactions, it has the unfortunate tendency of encouraging a view of culture as a mysterious and unexplained prime mover.

[2] E.g. De Waal and Tyack (2003).

[3] The assumption behind this prediction is that turkeys, like humans, are self-interested, and that their interests are self-evident. This is the prevalent "politics of interest" approach: an approach

to *be* political. This means that culture is not contextual to politics; it is essential. All political science, therefore, deals with culture, and so the interesting question is: "How does it do this?"

Some approaches aim to take direct and explicit account of culture: most prominently political and civic culture approaches (Almond and Verba 1963; 1980; Putnam 1993), post-materialism (Inglehart 1977), symbolic interactionism, and the various interpretivist and social constructionist framings. Others try to dodge culture in one of two ways: by contending that, while culture *is* there, it isn't really doing anything; or by pretending that values and beliefs are somehow inherent in individuals (like their fingerprints) rather than emerging from their social interactions. The first dodging is Marxism: culture is a "superstructure" that obligingly positions itself and repositions itself, so as always to render "natural" the current state of the class struggle for control over the means of production.[4] The second dodging is rational choice: with preferences assumed (or, in some way, given or self-evident) the focus is on how people set about getting the things they want, and the deeply political question of how they come to want those things is dismissed (*de gustibus non disputandum*, or some such formula).[5]

Curiously, these culture-dodging approaches are of more interest to a cultural *theorist* than are those that explicitly attempt to embrace culture. The reason is that, since culture is undodgable, each of these culture-dodging approaches is spectacu-

that those who take culture seriously (Schwarz and Thompson 1990, for instance), and who also focus on its relationship to behavior, are deeply dissatisfied with. They are dissatisfied because of this approach's absence of explanatory power: people, we are told, act the way they do because it is in their interests to do so; and, when we ask how we can tell what their interests are, we are told to watch what they do! In taking interests as given (or as self-evident, as with the turkeys and Christmas) the one really worthwhile question—how do people who act in their interests come to know where the interests they act in lie—has been ducked. Had Horatius run away when he saw how hopelessly he was outnumbered, this approach would have us argue that, of course, it was in his interest to run away. But he didn't run away, again, it is argued because it was in his interest not to. Flight and fight, we are being asked to believe, are the same thing!

[4] Ironically, this tension is most apparent in the work of two scholars that have explicitly aimed to reconcile Marxist and cultural analyses: Antonio Gramsci and Pierre Bourdieu. Gramsci (1971) admits that opposing political ideologies exist and argues that these must have some independent influence on society and politics. In the end, however, he maintains that this independent influence of political ideologies mainly serves to reconcile the lower classes to their allotted stations in life. Bourdieu makes a similar claim, namely that reigning systems of classification are but cloaks for class interests. (He calls this "symbolic aggression.") See, e.g., *Homo Academicus* (1988, 204): "Working as an ideology in a state of practice, producing logical effects which are inseparable from political effects, the academic taxonomy entails an implicit definition of excellence which, by constituting as excellent the qualities possessed by those who are socially dominant, consecrates their manner of being and their lifestyle." The main difference between the ideas of Gramsci and Bourdieu is that according to the former "hegemonic political ideologies" pull the wool over the eyes of the lower classes, whereas in the work of the latter our very categories of thought do the pulling.

[5] For instance, in the work of Robert Bates (1988) and David Laitin (1986), culture is not much more than a set of reigning symbols and beliefs that can be manipulated by rational actors to further their own material self-interest. These actors are somehow assumed to be immune to these dominant symbols and beliefs.

larly cultural: that is, everywhere permeated with a distinctive set of beliefs and values. And, as Gabriel Almond (1997: ix–x) has made abundantly clear, not just cultural but political too:

The politics of the Vietnam War and the "cultural revolution" sought to elbow cultural variables aside in the late 1960s and 1970s ... It was argued by the "dependency" school that there was nothing problematic about political values and attitudes. They could be inferred from the international political economy. Good research was defined as that which illuminated and exposed this system of exploitation—a hierarchy of oppression centred in high capitalism in the United States and Europe and extending throughout the globe through the semi-periphery to the periphery. Studies of political attitudes were not only pointless, they were positively harmful, since they attributed solid reality to what were really the products of this exploitative and false-consciousness creating system.

... Rational choice theory in its earlier manifestations also viewed culture and attitudes as unproblematic. All that one required in order to explain social, cultural and political phenomena was rational man, the short-run, hard-nosed calculator, and the mathematics and statistics that he needed in order to make cost-effective choices. The extraordinary success of the public choice movement can only be accounted for by its rigor and parsimony in an age dominated by the reductionist triumphs of physics and biology ... That [rational choice theory's successes] were only partial contributions to the explanation of social and political phenomena is now being generally acknowledged in the "new institutionalism."

Those (like Almond himself) who were struggling to avoid both of these mutually contradictory reductionisms, by taking explicit account of culture, were "whip-sawed in those decades from the dependency left and the rational choice right"[6] (Almond 1997, x).

So here, between these contending social constructions of "the problem," is a deeply political left–right struggle between two theoretical framings, each of which is claiming to *explain* deeply political struggles! A theory capable of explaining that political struggle would be, to put it mildly, a worthwhile step forward in political science.

1   Culture and Behavior: Separate but not Unconnected

An obvious first place to look for such a "meta-theory" is at the various approaches that, unlike Marxism and rational choice, do not try to dodge culture. Are any of

---

[6] *In those decades!* Since then, a variety of political scientists have made great efforts to show that rational choice theory is also compatible with left-wing politics. See in particular Elster (1982).

these up to the task? By and large, as we will see, they are not; they succeed only to the extent that they find their way towards the direction Almond himself has indicated. This is the "new institutionalism": essentially the distinguishing of a small number of different institutional forms, two of which are the markets and hierarchies that were not new even when Adam (Smith, that is) was a lad![7]

The trouble with taking explicit account of culture is that explanation tends to go out the window. Yes, culture and behavior need to be clearly distinguished (and these approaches certainly do that) but so too does the relationship between them, and this vital reconnection is not easily achieved. Beliefs and values justify behavior, and behavior (if perceived to have been successful) confirms beliefs and values. Causality, in other words, runs both ways. Each, therefore, has to be seen as the cause of the other: a common enough state of affairs in the biological sciences that is explained in terms of *viability* rather than the more familiar cause-and-effect. In viability-based explanations (John Maynard Smith 1982 is perhaps the exemplar) particular comings-together—the chicken and the egg, for example—are able to achieve some sort of dynamic stability over time; others are not able to and disappear as quickly as they are formed. If we take this explanatory line then we can enunciate the *rules of the cultural method*. These are negative rules—things to be avoided if we wish to retain explanatory power:

- *Culture as an uncaused cause.* These are explanations of the form: "Why did he do that?" "Because his culture told him to." The invocation of "Asian values," or statements such as "Japan is a high-trust society; the United States a low-trust society," or that "the Judeo-Christian tradition is anthropocentric and can only justify environmental protection as resource management," are examples of this solecism. So too is the "culture wars" formulation (Huntington 1998), in which the culture-carriers—the members of the various blocs: Islamic, Christian, and so on—are pitted against one another because they are Isalamic, Christian, and so on. Though often dressed up in impressive swaths of reasoning, these (like Molière's doctor and his talk of opium's "dormitive properties") simply are not explanations: just elaborate ways of saying "I don't know."[8]
- *Culture as an explanation of last resort.* This is when culture is dragged in only

---

[7] Many would see this dualistic (and, we will be arguing, insufficient) distinction being drawn, for the first time, by Smith himself: markets in his *Wealth of Nations;* hierarchies in his *Theory of Moral Sentiments.* Others would wish to pin its origin on Sir Henry Maine and his celebrated historical transition from *status* (hierarchy) to *contract* (market). However, the distinction is already clearly drawn in the 16th-century satire on hierarchy—*Monkey* (Wu 1942). Seeing this eastern classic as the origin has the added virtue of taking the wind out of the sails of those who argue that the markets-and-hierarchies distinction (indeed, political science as a whole) is West-centric. Indeed Gyawali (2000) pushes the origin back a couple or so millennia: to the various forms of power that are distinguished in Hindu philosophy (thereby enabling critical theorists to claim that the whole caboodle is South Asia-centric).

[8] See, e.g., the contributions to Harrison and Huntington (2001). Other prominent examples are: Fukuyama (1996); Hofstede (2001); and Van Wolferen (1990).

when other explanations—economic, demographic, ecological, organizational, political, and so on—are inadequate.[9] Non-cultural explanations, for instance, are often advanced in relation to environmental matters; indeed they dominate the PRED framing (Population, Resources, Environment, and Development), for example, the "IPAT equation" (environmental Impact equals some multiplication of Population, Affluence, and Technology; Ehrlich and Holdren 1974), and pretty well all the computer-based models that are so relied on in environmental policy-making (and that swallow up so much of the available funding). Such approaches, since they take no account of cognition—seeing *and* knowing—are hopelessly reductionist, and treat people as essentially no different from cattle. They could never, for instance, account for what happened in Greenland during the last mini-ice-age, when the Inuit adapted and prospered and the Vikings stuck to their livestock-rearing and died out. Nor, since they just count heads and take no heed of what is going on in those heads, can these non-cultural approaches give us access to the environmental consequences (and their associated policy implications) of the carnivorous diets of North Americans, say, vis-à-vis the vegetarian diets of, say, Tibetan Buddhists. Yet, were the former to go Buddhist, much of South and Central America would revert from rangeland to carbon-sequestering forest. Who then would claim the carbon credits: Brazil, Mexico, et al. or their northerly neighbor whose citizens had changed their ways; their culture?

• *Culture as a veto on comparison.* The idea here is that each culture (and each subculture) is unique and can only be understood in its own terms. This idea goes back to Wittgenstein's "language games" and is now most firmly entrenched in *interpretive sociology*—most famously in Clifford Geertz's (1973) notion of "thick description." In the last few decades, this assumption has taken social and political science by storm.[10] But, as Harry Eckstein (1997, 27) has observed, thick descriptions, in the absence of any attempts to test and compare, are just "very high-level travel literature." Worse still, the language games that characterize culture, far from being incomparable, are often vigorously engaged with one another: that is how they change! North American carnivorousness, for instance, was succinctly and positively expressed by John Wayne who, when asked how he liked his steak, replied "Just knock its horns off, wipe its ass, and chuck it on the

[9] In the last ten years, this line of reasoning has blossomed again in the study of international relations. For instance, Finnemore (1996); Johnston (1998); Price (1995); Goldstein and Keohane (1993). It is also evident in the "world society literature," which posits that a set of Western, "modern" norms have gained global legitimacy even in regions where it does not make "objective economic" sense to adhere to these values. An overview is Meyer et al. (1997). One drawback of these studies is that they confidently distinguish the "cultural" from the "economic" as well as from the "political." This is problematic given that culture is usually very generically defined as "shared symbols and practices."

[10] This school can be called the hermeneutic or interpretative approach. Two very influential examples are Geertz (1980) and Said (1979). Some other contributions: Dittmer 1977; Edelman 1998; Fernandez 1986; Kapferer 1988; Aronoff 1992; Kubik 1993.

plate." Many of his fellow Americans—those who have moved themselves toward vegetarianism and are now eating much lower on the food-chain—would wish to distance themselves from the Duke's distillation of American manliness. They may not have turned themselves into Tibetan Buddhists, but they are certainly no longer the cultural way they were.[11]

2   How, then, Can We Take Valid Account of Culture?

We can avoid these three pitfalls—culture as an uncaused cause, as an explanation of last resort, and as a veto on comparison—by building cultural theories upon the following bedrock principles:

- Beliefs and values do not just float around, with people choosing a bit of this and bit of that. They are closely tied to distinctive patterns of social relations and to the distinctive ways of behaving that those beliefs and values justify. Theorists of "constrained relativism" refer to each of these mutually supportive comings-together of *cultural biases, patterns of social relations,* and *behavioural strategies* as a "form of social solidarity": a viable (under certain specified circumstances) way of binding ourselves to one another and, in the process, determining our relationship with nature.
- Beliefs and values, therefore (as Durkheim long ago insisted), are not just an explanatory "add-on"; they are essential components of economic, ecological, demographic, organizational, and political explanations.
- We *can* distinguish similarities and differences across cultures, in terms of a small number of universally valid forms of social solidarity. These forms of solidarity are present in all the social entities—nations, firms, churches, and so on—to which the term "culture" is conventionally applied, but they vary in their relative strengths and patterns of interaction. Little is achieved, to draw a chemical analogy, by declaring the various oxides of nitrogen to be incomparably different from one another; progress comes from going inside those molecules and observing that they are all composed of the same elements—nitrogen and oxygen—but in differing proportions and patterns of interaction. In other words, culture, in the conventional sense, *doesn't* matter; what matters is the

---

[11] A perhaps more serious example of this sort of cultural change—it is about racial attitudes—is provided by Stinchcombe (1997).

next level down: the forms of solidarity by which all cultures are both sustained and transformed.[12]

"Cultural biases," we should explain, are much the same as "social constructions of reality" (Berger and Luckman 1967), "models of the person" (Douglas and Ney 1998), and "myths of nature" (Holling 1986): different sets of convictions as to how the world is, each of which, as well as capturing in simple and elegant form some essence of experience and wisdom, renders rational a particular way of behaving in that world.[13] (These cultural biases—or myths of nature, physical and human—are summarized in Figure 17.2 and then illustrated in a "worked example": climate change). A plurality of forms of social solidarity, in consequence, inevitably introduces relativism, but that relativism is not unconstrained because each form of social solidarity is associated with a particular way of organizing social relationships, and there are only a limited number of those. That, at any rate, is what the theory of constrained relativism claims: we can make the world in more than one way but, contra the proponents of post-structuralism, we cannot make it any way we like.[14] More than one, constrained relativists point out, is not automatically infinity; there *are* some numbers in between.

If people and the world could only be one way (as realists, dialectical materialists, and rational choice theorists insist) then anyone who thought otherwise would be suffering from false-consciousness (or, same thing, acting irrationally). Culture, in that case, would be little more than a smokescreen: a means by which those who, for the moment, are exercising control over the means of production can (to mix the metaphor) pull the wool over the eyes of those who, for the moment, are not in control of those means. And if people and the world could be just any old way then, again, culture would not really matter because, with such a cacophony of "voices," all claiming to have got it right, it would all boil down to the question of power: which voices are able, for the moment, to drown out the others?[15]

But if there are only a few voices—three or four or five we will be suggesting[16]— each associated with a particular way of organizing and of acting, and each needing

---

[12] Alter the patterns of interaction of di-nitrogen tetroxide's constituent elements (by increasing the temperature, for instance) and it is progressively transformed into nitrogen dioxide. The same, however, is not true of the other oxides of nitrogen, so the analogy should not be pushed too far.

[13] For an explanation of these myths of nature, and how they relate for the various forms of social solidarity, see Thompson and Rayner (1998).

[14] Nor are all the constraints on the social side. As well as the social construction of nature there is the natural destruction of culture. See Thompson (1988).

[15] Alternatively, it all boils down to a question about the legitimacy of power. If any social construction is as good as any other then there can be no justification for some of them drowning out the others. How to arrange things institutionally so that any emerging power gradients (again mixing the metaphors) are nipped in the bud, becomes the dominant normative concern—as is explicitly acknowledged by many postmodern theorists. For instance, Foucault (1980).

[16] Though we are setting out four solidarities in this chapter, there is in fact a fifth permutation. This corresponds to what (in the Schmutzer–Bandler "impossibility theorem"—see n. 17, about the two sets of discriminators) is called an "all zero" transaction matrix: the seemingly trivial situation in

the others to define itself against, then no one of those consciousnesses is any falser (or any more irrational) than the rest, and drowning-out (since it would destroy the essential plurality) is simply a non-starter. It is because of constrained relativism, therefore, that culture (in the sense of the different social constructions that sustain the different and contending forms of solidarity) matters. Of course, if constrained relativism was impossible (or even implausible) then it would be impossible (or, at least, difficult) to make the case for culture mattering in this crucial way: as one of the three ingredients that make a form of social solidarity viable, rather than as (*a*) an uncaused cause, (*b*) an explanation of last resort, or (*c*) a veto on comparison. Fortunately, the history of social science, being largely a quarrel over what the forms of solidarity *are* (rather than about whether they exist), provides us with some defence against this rejectionist argument. Henry Ford ("History is bunk") may still be right, of course, but the burden of proof, our reading of history suggests, lies with those who maintain that there really is no need to bother ourselves about culture.

3   FROM INSTITUTIONALISM (OLD AND NEW) TO THE THEORY OF CONSTRAINED RELATIVISM

Sir Henry Maine (1861), in his classic text *Ancient Law*, drew a fundamental distinction between two forms of social solidarity: *status* and *contract* (Figure 17.1: Sir Henry Maine). He saw these two ways of binding ourselves to one another (nowadays we call them "hierarchies" and "markets" [e.g. Lindblom 1977]) as the two poles of an historical transition: we used all to be bound by group-based status

---

which there are no transactions at all, and therefore nothing to be accountable or unaccountable about. This socially withdrawn form of solidarity—it is called *autonomy* and is characterized by the hermit—is achieved by those who deliberately distance themselves from the *coercive* social involvement that, in various ways, accompanies all four of the "engaged" solidarities. We are ignoring this fifth solidarity in this chapter so as to keep an already complicated argument a little simpler than it should be. For an explanation of just when and where it is safe to ignore autonomy (and sometimes fatalism too—hence our on the face of it vague talk of "three, four, or five" voices) see the section headed "User-Friendly Cultural Theory" in Thompson, Grendstad, and Selle (1999b). Including this fifth solidarity bumps up the transitions—the arrowheads—from twelve to twenty. Schmutzer (1994) calls the solidarity "the waiting room of history": a place where those on the move between the "engaged" solidarities can pause for a while to recharge their batteries, lick their wounds, change their spots, or whatever. Without that waiting room these transitions would likely be much more difficult and certainly much more tumultuous when they eventually happened.

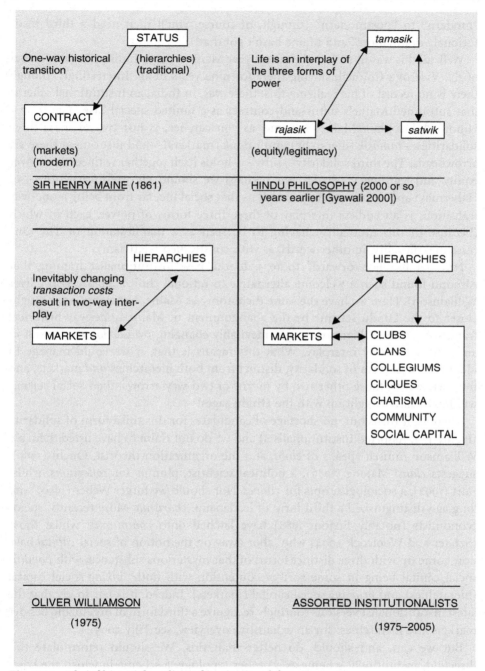

Fig. 17.1 A brief historial outline of institutional framings

relations; now we are bound by individualistic, one-to-one, mutually agreed relationships. So it's "traditional" to "modern," in other much-mouthed words, and if you buy into that then you can easily buy into the next one-way progression:

"modern" to "postmodern" (though, of course, you'll then need a third institutional "destination," and Maine hasn't got that!).

Well, all this was in 1861, and the next year Maine went to India as Legal Member of the Viceroy's Council, staying there for nine years in all. Interestingly, though there is no record of his realizing this, there was, in India, an institutional scheme that subsumed Maine's status-and-contract as a limited special case (Figure 17.1: Hindu Philosophy). Maine's scheme, as you can see, is just two of these three solidarities—*tamasik* (hierarchy) and *rajasik* (markets)—and just one of these six arrowheads. The third solidarity—*satwik*—holds itself together with concerns over equity and legitimacy (shades—or perhaps we should say pre-incarnations—of Habermas) and the six arrowheads tell us that social life, far from being a one-way transition, is an endless interplay of these three forms of power, each of which (because of this mutuality) having to be seen as a manifestation of The One (essential plurality, in other words, as with constrained relativism).

Now let us "fast-forward" to 1975, to the new institutionalist framing that Almond found such a welcome alternative to rational choice (Figure 17.1: Oliver Williamson). Here we have the same dichotomy as Maine, but things are brought closer to the Hindu scheme by the abandonment of Maine's one-way historical transition. With Williamson (1975), inevitably changing *transaction costs* result in an endless two-way interplay. What this means is that, if we could manage to identify a third form of solidarity, distinct from both hierarchies *and* markets, and then relate it to those other two by means of two-way arrows, then social science will finally have caught up with the Hindu sages!

There is, it turns out, no shortage of candidates for this third form of solidarity (Figure 17.1: Assorted Institutionalists) and we do not claim to have listed them all. Williamson himself speaks of *clubs*, and the organization theorist, Ouchi (1980), suggests *clans*. Majone (1989), a political scientist, plumps for *collegiums*, whilst Burt (1992), a sociologist, opts for *cliques*. Nor should we forget Weber (1930) who long ago distinguished a third form of leadership: *charisma*. More recently, socio-economists (notably Etzioni 1988) have latched onto *community*, whilst those (Szreter and Woolcock 2004) who labor away on the notion of social *capital* have now come up with three distinct forms of that mysterious substance, with *bonding* social capital being in some sort of contention with both *linking* social capital (hierarchies) and *bridging* social capital (markets). Indeed, it is fair to say that the latest institutionalist versions routinely recognize a third form of organizing besides markets and hierarchies (for an exhaustive overview, see Tilly 2005).

But we can, and should, do better than this. We should reformulate this threefold, institutional scheme as a proper typology: a scheme in which the types are *mutually exclusive* and *jointly exhaustive*. When we have done that, we find that there is a total of *four* solidarities and twelve arrowheads (Figure 17.2). In other words, we can derive a fourth way of organizing (or solidarity) from the other three. Two steps are involved here:

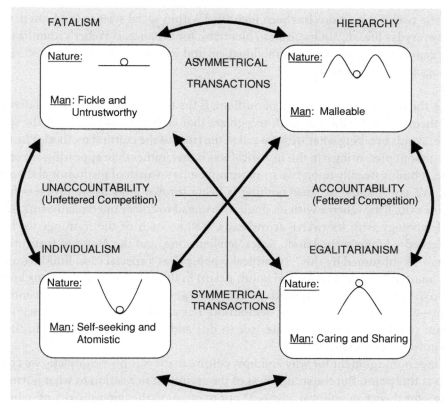

Fig. 17.2 The proper typology according to the theory of constrained relativism

Source: Douglas (1978); Gross and Rayner (1985); Thompson, Ellis, and Wildavsky (1990).

- First, making explicit the two discriminators—*symmetrical* versus *asymmetrical transactions* and *accountability* versus *unaccountability*—ensures the mutual exclusivity of the solidarities. And, by revealing the fourth permutation—which corresponds to fatalism—we ensure joint exhaustiveness.[17]
- Second, by inserting all the arrowheads—there are twelve—we arrive at a fourfold interplay that is *complex*: indeterministic and unpredictable (unlike, say, the Williamsonian scheme in which, if you are tipped out of the market solidarity, you will end up in the hierarchical one, and vice versa). Interestingly, each of

---

[17] The first discriminator is fairly straightforward: symmetry (as in "you scratch my back, I'll scratch yours") versus asymmetry (as in the British Guards officer explaining "I'd expect to be invited to my sergeant's wedding but he wouldn't expect to be invited to mine"). The second discriminator may not be so clear. "You do that and I'll bring the full weight of the law down on you," is an instance of accountability, and so too is the reprimand, "We don't do that sort of thing in this family/regiment/school." Unaccountability is evident whenever we hear the justification, "If I don't do it, somebody else will." The most rigorous treatment of these discriminators is to be found in Schmutzer and Bandler's (1980) cybernetic derivation of the typology.

these twelve transitions has been identified within social science (and often, too, in everyday life). Egalitarianism to hierarchy, for instance, is Weber's *routinization of charisma* (and fatalism to individualism and back to fatalism again is "clogs to clogs in three generations").[18]

This, then, in the most minimal of outlines, is the theory of constrained relativism: the theory that, we have argued, recognizes that culture matters and, at the same time, avoids breaking what we have called the rules of the cultural method. The nice thing about presenting it in this historical way is that, rather than appearing out of the blue, it builds steadily upon two or more millennia's-worth of institutional theorizing. We say "builds" because nothing is being thrown away as we progress from Maine's dualistic scheme with its single arrowhead to constrained relativism's four-fold typology with its twelve arrowheads. Rather, each of the framings we have presented—Maine's, the Hindu Sages', Williamson's, and the Assorted Institution-alists'—is subsumed by this "dynamical typology" as a special case. Building upon the "masters" (both Western and South Asian) in this way—by not declaring any of them wrong but instead pinpointing exactly how and why each of them is not entirely right—also increases the cost of demolition. Reject the theory of constrained relativism (which, of course, you are free to do) and you have rejected all forms of institutional explanation!

Since our argument for why and how culture matters is now complete, we could stop at this point. But the strangeness of the argument in relation to what normally passes for theory in political science,[19] not to mention the unfamiliarity of many of the scholars whose work we have drawn on in setting out our argument, suggest that a quick "worked example" might be in order.

4   THE CULTURES OF CLIMATE CHANGE

Most climatologists agree that by burning fossil fuels and engaging in other forms of consumption and production we are increasing the amount of greenhouse gases that float around in the atmosphere. These gases, in trapping some of the sun's heat,

---

[18] All twelve are set out in Thompson, Ellis, and Wildavsky (1990, 75–8).

[19] No physicist, for instance, would recognize what proponents of rational choice are saying as constituting a theory. The tautology, the conceptual stretching, and the failure to enquire into how it is that actors who are acting in pursuit of their interests come to know what the interests they act in are, would ensure a pretty dismissive response to rational choice in the tough and rigorous world of the physical sciences: "It's so bad it isn't even wrong," as Enrico Fermi once said of one unfortunate physicist's efforts at theory-building!

warm the earth and enable life. The trouble is, some predict, that if we continue to accumulate those gases, over the course of the new century the average temperature on earth will rise and local climates will change, with possibly catastrophic consequences. Will this indeed happen? If so, should we do something about it? And if yes, when? Does global warming put the future of the world at risk? Is time running out? Or should we take our time in order to investigate and evaluate soberly the possible risks of greenhouse gases? There is, as we will see, little agreement on any of those crucial questions: climate change is very much a "contested terrain." In order to understand current conflicts over the prospect of global warming, we find it helpful to sort out this contested terrain in terms of our theory's four forms of social solidarity.

Before we proceed, we need to make a few brief points of clarification. The theory of constrained relativism closely follows the work of Émile Durkheim (1985 [1893]; 1997 [1912]) and Mary Douglas (1970, 1975) in assuming that specific ways of organizing social relations are only viable when complemented by specific ways of perceiving the world that justify these sets of social relations. Thus, its four forms of social solidarity are ways of organizing, perceiving, and justifying sets of social relations.[20] This points to one advantage that the theory has over institutionalist approaches. The latter often capture two or three forms of organizing, but without the distinct ways of perceiving that come with these ways of organizing. The former sets out four ways of organizing that subsumes the two or three forms distinguished in many an institutionalist approach, while also adding a long list of specific norms, beliefs, and perceptions to these organizational types. (Three of them, views of physical nature, human nature, and time will appear below. For the other fifty-seven, see Hofstetter 1998, 55–6.) The theory of constrained relativism does *not* posit that individuals or organizations adhere to a single social solidarity. In fact, it maintains that the life of each individual, and the history of each organization, is an ever-changing amalgam of alternative ways of organizing and perceiving. And it assumes that individual people are able to compare critically the truth-claims of alternative social solidarities, and switch to those they find most compelling (Ellis 1994). Yet, it does postulate that with regard to each public issue four opposing perspectives on what the problem is, and how it should be resolved, always abound—each perspective being articulated by a different set of actors (Coyle and Ellis 1994; Thompson, Grendstad, and Selle 1999a; Verweij and Thompson 2005). This is brought out in the following analysis of the different viewpoints that abound in the current debate over climate change.

- For upholders of the *individualist* solidarity, nature is benign and resilient—able to recover from any exploitation (hence the iconic myth of nature: a ball that, no

---

[20] Indeed, the use of the term "social solidarity" is meant to refer to the Durkheim legacy. In *The Division of Labour in Society*, Durkheim (1997 [1893]) distinguishes between two forms of social solidarity: mechanical and organic.

matter how profoundly disturbed, always returns to stability; Figure 17.2)—and man is inherently self-seeking and atomistic. Trial and error, in self-organizing ego-focused networks (markets), is the way to go, with Adam Smith's invisible hand ensuring that people only do well when others also benefit. Individualists, in consequence, trust others until they give them reason not to and then retaliate in kind (the winning "tit-for-tat" strategy in the iterated Prisoner's Dilemma game: Rapoport 1985). They see it as only fair that (as in the joint stock company) those who put most in get most out. Managing institutions that work "with the grain of the market" (getting rid of environmentally harmful subsidies, for instance) are what are needed.

- Nature, for those who bind themselves into the *egalitarian* solidarity, is almost the exact opposite (hence the ball on the upturned basin; Figure 17.2)—fragile, intricately interconnected, and ephemeral—and man is essentially caring and sharing (until corrupted by coercive and inegalitarian institutions: markets and hierarchies). We must all tread lightly on the Earth, and it is not enough that people start off equal; they must end up equal as well—equality of result. Trust and leveling go hand-in-hand, and institutions that distribute unequally are distrusted. Voluntary simplicity is the only solution to our environmental problems, with the "precautionary principle" being strictly enforced on those who are tempted not to share the simple life.

- The world, in the *hierarchical* solidarity, is controllable. Nature is stable until pushed beyond discoverable limits (hence the two humps; Figure 17.2), and man is malleable: deeply flawed but redeemable by firm, long-lasting, and trustworthy institutions. Fair distribution is by rank and station or, in the modern context, by need (with the level of need being determined by expert and dispassionate authority). Environmental management requires certified experts (to determine the precise locations of nature's limits) and statutory regulation (to ensure that all economic activity is then kept within those limits).

- Finally, there are the *fatalist* actors (or perhaps we should say non-actors, since their voice is seldom heard in policy debates; if it was they wouldn't be fatalistic!). They find neither rhyme nor reason in nature and know that man is fickle and untrustworthy. Fairness, in consequence, is not to be found in this life, and there is no possibility of effecting change for the better. "Defect first"—the winning strategy in the one-off Prisoner's Dilemma—makes sense here, given the unreliability of communication and the permanent absence of prior acts of good faith. With no way of ever getting in sync with nature (push the ball this way or that—Figure 17.2—and the feedback is everywhere the same), or of building trust with others, the fatalist's world (unlike those of the other three solidarities) is one in which learning is impossible. "Why bother?" therefore, is the rational management response.

Time too (which of course is of crucial concern in assessing the risks in climate change) is perceived differently in these social settings.

- Individualistic actors will tend to see the long-term as the continuation of the short-term. Myopically, they insist that doing well in the here-and-now is the best guarantee for doing well later on. "Business as usual" is how complex systems-modelers characterize this individualistic line of action.
- Hierarchical actors—regulators, planners, public-health inspectors, and the like—will tend to be unhappy about all this short-termism (as they call it). While individualists like Henry Ford consider history bunk, hierarchical actors are at pains to anchor their collectivity in it. Hierarchical actors, therefore, can see both the short term and the long term, and do not see the latter as merely the continuation of the former. Development in the here-and-now, they reason, may not be sustainable a decade or two down the road. Their aim, therefore, is to provide a clear description of long-term sustainability and then to intervene in the short-term activities of market actors to ensure that we all arrive safely at that desirable future: "wise guidance," as modelers call it.
- Egalitarian actors will tend to be as distrustful of hierarchies as they are of unfettered markets. The short term, for egalitarians, is severely truncated, and the long term—disastrous if we do not learn the error of our inequitable ways; wonderful if we do—is almost upon us. Radical change now—not business-as-usual and not wise guidance—is what is needed if we are to have a future at all.
- Fatalistic actors, finding themselves marginal to all three active solidarities—individualistic ego-focused networks, bounded and hierarchically ranked organizations, and bounded but unranked groups—see no point in sorting out long terms and short terms this way or that. "If your number's on it," they assure one another, "that's it." Why put yourself to a whole lot of bother over something you can do nothing about?

Now, having set out our theory's predictions about how nature and time are socially constructed within the different forms of solidarity, we can return to the big questions about the risks associated with climate change. Adherents of these different solidarities, not surprisingly, tend to answer these big questions very differently.

1. Those who bind themselves into *egalitarian* settings—often radical environmental groups such as Earth First! (Ellis 1997, ch. 8)—are convinced that corporate greed and power lust are already unleashing catastrophic climate change, and that we must drastically alter our behaviour now, before it is too late. Compromise, for these "deep ecologists," is therefore out of the question:

To avoid co-option, we feel it is necessary to avoid the corporate organisational structure so readily embraced by many environmental groups. Earth First! is a movement, not an organisation. Our structure is non-hierarchical. We have no highly-paid "professional staff" or formal leadership.

The conviction that the problem is serious, imminent, and—if not dealt with quickly—irreversible, supports this egalitarian mode of organization:

> ... our activities are now beginning to have fundamental, systemic effects upon the entire life-support system of the planet—upsetting the world's climate, poisoning the oceans, destroying the ozone layer which protects us from excessive ultraviolet radiation, changing the CO_2 ratio in the atmosphere, and spreading acid rain, radioactive fallout, pesticides and industrial contamination throughout the biosphere. We—this generation of humans—are at our most important juncture since we came out of the trees six million years ago. It is our decision, ours today, whether Earth continues to be a marvellously living, diverse oasis in the blackness of space, or whether the charismatic mega-fauna of the future will consist of Norway rats and cockroaches.

Here (as in Steve Rayner's classic 1982 study of the Workers' Institute of Marxism-Leninism Mao Xedong Thought, in London's Brixton) past, present, and future are compressed in a way that is typical of the egalitarian form of solidarity. All of the past—in this case, six million years of it—has been but a build-up to our present situation; never before have our actions so threatened the viability of the planet on which we depend. Our current choices, moreover, are decisive for all time to come. Make the right decision today—at this "our most important juncture"—and eternal bliss—"a marvellously living, diverse oasis in the blackness of space"—will be our reward. Fail to make that decision and there will be no eternity, save for the "Norway rats and cockroaches."

2. Those who belong to organizations of a more *individualistic* bent—the United States' Cato Institute, for instance, and Britain's Institute of Economic Affairs—see it all very differently. They are skeptical of the diagnosis itself and are convinced that, even if it is correct, the consequences will be neither catastrophic nor uniformly negative. Far from being at a six-million-year juncture, we are, they assert, where we have always been: faced with uncertainties and challenges that, if tackled boldly by a diversity of competing agents, can be transformed into opportunities from which all can benefit. The long term holds no fears for them, because this optimistic short-term bubble, as it moves along, will take care of it all. For that to happen and go on happening, of course, there must be no junctures; at the very least, they must be far enough out into the future for us to not need to worry about them.

Given this social construction of time, individualistically organized outfits prefer a two-pronged approach: the dismantling of junctures within the short-term bubble, and adaptation to any that may exist beyond that bubble. They therefore focus on the lacunae in current climate-change science:

• Clouds, whose formation is poorly understood but which are expected to be more prevalent in a warmer world, would likely reflect more sunlight back into space before it reached the earth's surface.

- Human sources of greenhouse gases are dwarfed by natural sources (volcanoes, for instance, and termites and other wood-digesting creatures)—which means that it is impossible in the short run to say whether any warming (if it is happening) is man-made.
- The climate models that are being used to predict future changes cannot even accurately chart changes that have already occurred.

Looking beyond the short-term bubble, they point out that a carbon-richer climate would increase agricultural productivity, and that, even if the negative impacts did outweigh the positive ones, we would still need to compare the costs of preventing global warming now to the costs of adapting to higher temperatures a few decades hence. Money not spent on preventing climate change, they point out, could be used to tackle other, more pressing environmental and social ills. On top of all that, individualistic organizations, thanks to their myopic construction of time, are open to the view that technological progress and the unpredictable forces of "creative destruction" may soon render today's fuss over climate change irrelevant. The production costs of renewable energy, they point out, have fallen dramatically over the last few decades, and these new technologies—wind, hydro, geothermal, and solar—are rapidly becoming (indeed, in some instances, have already become) competitive with the old technologies of fossil fuels. Their prescriptions, in consequence, dramatically differ from those of the deep ecologists. As Roger Bate, director of the Environment Unit of the Institute of Economic Affairs, concludes:

On the whole, society's problems and challenges are best dealt with by people and companies interacting with each other freely without interference from politicians and the state. We do not know whether the world is definitively warming, given recent satellite data. If the world is warming, we do not know what is causing the change—man or nature. We do not know whether a warmer world would be a good thing or a bad thing.
[The scientific evidence] does not suggest that immediate action for significant limitation on energy consumption is urgently required . . . Until the science of climate change is better understood, no government action should be undertaken beyond the elimination of subsidies and other distortions of the market.

3. This business-as-usual strategy is anathema to the members of the numerous *hierarchical* organizations that have dominated the global warming debate. They are appalled by its short-termism and its accompanying assumption that the myriad and uncoordinated actions of firms and consumers will inevitably be beneficial for the totality. Worse still when this assumption is made across time as well as space—because, hierarchical actors insist, the long-term is never simply the continuation of the short-term. And they are also dismissive of the egalitarian claim that, if only we make the right (and radical) choice today—at this "our most important juncture"—all will be fine for evermore.

In the hierarchical view, each single contribution that households, companies, and even whole countries make to the build-up of greenhouse gases is so small as to be insignificant to these undiscerning actors. Moreover, the consequences lie far into the future and spread across the entire globe: way beyond their temporal and spatial kens. It therefore makes no sense for any household or firm or country unilaterally to reduce its emissions. What we are faced with, therefore, is a "tragedy of the global commons"—and the only conceivable remedy is for all the governments and parliaments of the world to formally agree on the extent to which future emissions should be cut, which countries should do so, how, and when. States should then impose these intergovernmental agreements on the multitude of consumers and producers within their borders.

This is the logic behind the 1997 Kyoto Protocol to the UN Framework Convention on Climate Change. It is espoused by almost all the governments of the world, by UN agencies and the World Bank, as well as by the large mainstream environmental organizations (the ones of which Earth First! is so disparaging). Implicit in their shared commitment is the belief that we can, and should, steer ourselves, in a planned and orderly way, to a rather precisely defined and timed future. The computer models built by the Intergovernmental Panel on Climate Change (and by other proponents of "wise guidance"/ "global stewardship") have been churning out scenarios that supposedly show a variety of future global emissions of greenhouse gases, along with their worldwide ecological and economic impacts, and the costs of attaining these future states. Their business-as-usual scenarios, however, typically account for little rapid technological change (and certainly for no out-of-the-blue, Schumpeterian gales of creative destruction). Other projections that are free of imminent discontinuities—ocean currents changing direction, for instance, or ice caps collapsing catastrophically—reveal that the radical and immediate action advocated by the deep ecologists would be extremely costly and disruptive.

The scenarios, as a result, reproduce the models' hierarchical temporal assumptions as their conclusions: only a gradual and orderly phasing out of greenhouse gas emissions, undertaken by governments and spread out over the next fifty or so years, will see us through. And, as the language in which these conclusions are couched makes clear, these things should be left to the experts:

Studies show that the costs of stabilizing carbon dioxide concentrations in the atmosphere [carbon dioxide being the main greenhouse gas] increase as the concentration stabilization level declines. While there is a moderate increase in the costs when passing from a 750 to a 550 ppm concentration stabilization level, there is a larger increase in costs passing from a 550 to a 440 ppm unless the emissions in the baseline scenario are very low.

In other words, global climate change policy should go neither too fast (as the egalitarian actors would have it) nor too slow (as the individualistic actors would have it). Instead, only those bureaucratic organizations that are both long-lived and far-sighted can determine what that pace should be, and then get all the world's nations to march in step to it.

6 CONCLUSION

We have not laid out the *fatalist* answers to the big questions about climate change because fatalistic actors have better things to do than worry over something they can do nothing about. So what we are left with are three sets of answers to these big questions.

Some will be dissatisfied with this; three, they will protest, is two too many. But those who favor what is called "clumsiness" will point out that elegance—a single set of answers—can only be achieved by silencing two of the voices in the debate. This is something that *cannot* be done (or, at any rate, cannot be done for very long). Moreover, if we *did* manage to do it, we would be discarding all the wisdom and experience inherent in the solidarities we have excluded. On top of that, we would be seriously weakening our democracy by silencing two of the legitimate voices within it.

The solution, therefore, is to resist the urge to go for elegance and to enhance clumsiness instead, seeking out and strengthening all those institutional arrangements in which none of the voices—the hierarchist's calling for "wise guidance and careful stewardship," the egalitarian's insisting that we need "a whole new relationship with nature," the individualist's urging us to "get the prices right," and the fatalist's asking "why bother?"—is excluded, and in which the contestation is harnessed to constructive and noisy argumentation (Verweij and Thompson 2005).

REFERENCES

ALMOND, G. A. 1997. Foreword. In Ellis and Thompson 1997.
—— and VERBA, S. 1963. *The Civic Culture: Political Attitudes and Democracy in Five Nations*. Boston: Little, Brown.
—— —— (eds.) 1980. *The Civic Culture Revisited*. Boston: Little, Brown.
ARONOFF, M. J. 1992. *power and ritual in the israeli labor party*. ARMONK, NY: SHARPE.
BANFIELD, E. C. 1958. *The Moral Basis of a Backward Society*. New York: Free Press.
BATES, R. (ed.) 1988. *Toward A Political Economy of Development: A Rational Choice Perspective*. Berkeley: University of California Press.

BERGER, P., and LUCKMANN, T. 1967. *The Social Construction of Reality.* Garden City, NY: Doubleday.

BOURDIEU, P. 1988. *Homo Academicus.* Cambridge: Polity Press.

BURT, R. S. 1992. *Structural Holes: The Social Structure of Competition.* Cambridge, Mass.: Harvard University Press.

COYLE, D. J., and ELLIS, R. J. (eds.) 1994. *Politics, Policy and Culture.* Boulder, Colo.: Westview.

DE WAAL, F. B. M., and TYACK, P. L. (eds.) 2003. *Animal Social Complexity.* Cambridge, Mass.: Harvard University Press.

DITTMER, L. 1977. Political culture and political symbolism: towards a theoretical synthesis. *World Politics,* 29: 552–93.

DOUGLAS, M. 1970. *Natural Symbols.* London: Routledge.

—— 1975. *Implicit Meanings.* London: Routledge.

—— 1978. Cultural bias. Occasional Paper of the Royal Anthropological Institute (London), 35. Reprinted pp. 183–254 in Douglas, *In The Active Voice.* London: Routledge and Kegan Paul, 1982.

—— and NEY, S. 1998. *Missing Persons.* Berkeley: University of California Press.

DURKHEIM, É. 1985. *The Elementary Forms of Religious Life.* New York: Free Press; originally published 1912.

—— 1997. *The Division of Labor in Society.* New York: Free Press; originally published 1893.

ECKSTEIN, H. 1997. Cultural theory as science, rational choice as metaphysics. Pp. 21–44 in Ellis and Thompson 1997.

EDELMAN, M. 1988. *Constructing the Political Spectacle.* Chicago: University of Chicago Press.

EHRLICH, P., and HOLDREN, J. 1974. Impact of population growth. *Science,* 171: 1212–17.

ELLIS, R. J. 1994. The case for cultural theory: reply to Friedman. *Critical Review,* 7: 541–88.

—— 1997. *The Dark Side of the Left: Illiberal Egalitarianism in America.* Lawrence: University Press of Kansas.

—— and THOMPSON, M. (eds.) 1997. *Culture Matters.* Boulder, Colo.: Westview.

ELSTER, J. 1982. Marxism, functionalism and game theory: the case for methodological individualism. *Theory and Society,* 11: 453–82.

ETZIONI, A. 1988. *The Moral Dimension: Towards a New Economics.* New York: Free Press.

FERNANDEZ, J. W. 1986. *Persuasions and Performances.* Bloomington: Indiana University Press.

FINNEMORE, M. 1996. *National Interests in International Society.* Ithaca, NY: Cornell University Press.

FOUCAULT, M. 1980. *Power/Knowledge: Selected Interviews & Other Writings 1972–1977.* New York: Pantheon.

FUKUYAMA, F. 1996. *Trust.* New York: Free Press.

GEERTZ, C. 1973. *The Interpretation of Cultures.* New York: Basic Books.

—— 1980. *Negara: The Theatre State in Nineteenth-Century Bali.* Princeton, NJ: Princeton University Press.

GOLDSTEIN, J., and KEOHANE, R. O. (eds.) 1993. *Ideas and Foreign Policy.* Ithaca, NY: Cornell University Press.

GRAMSCI, A. 1971. *Selections from the Prison Notebooks.* New York: International Publishers.

GROSS, J., and RAYNER, S. 1985. *Measuring Culture.* New York: Columbia University Press.

GYAWALI, D. 2000. Nepal–India water resource relations. Pp. 129–54 in *Power and Negotiation*, ed. I. W. Zartman and J. Z. Rubin. Ann Arbor: University of Michigan Press.

HARRISON, L. E., and HUNTINGTON, S. P. 2001. *Culture Matters*. New York: Harper-Collins.

HOFSTEDE, G. 2001. *Culture's Consequences*. Thousand Oaks, Calif.: Sage.

HOFSTETTER, P. 1998. *Perspectives in Life Cycle Impact Assessment*. Dordrecht: Kluwer.

HOLLING, C. S. 1986. The resilience of terrestrial ecosystems. In *Sustainable Development of the Biosphere*, ed. W. C. Clark and R. E. Munn. Cambridge: Cambridge University Press.

HUNTINGTON, S. P. 1998. *The Clash of Civilizations and the Remaking of the World Order*. New York: Simon and Schuster.

INGLEHART, R. 1977. *The Silent Revolution: Changing Values and Political Styles Among Western Publics*. Princeton, NJ: Princeton University Press.

JOHNSTON, A. I. 1998. *Cultural Realism: Strategic Culture and Grand Strategy in Chinese History*. Princeton, NJ: Princeton University Press.

KAPFERER, B. 1988. *Legends of People, Myths of State*. Washington, DC: Smithsonian.

KROEBER, A. L., and KLUCKHOLM, C. 1952. *Culture: A Critical Review of Conceptions and Definitions*. Cambridge, Mass.: Harvard University Press.

KUBIK, J. 1993. *The Power of Symbols against the Symbols of Power: The Rise of Solidarity and the Fall of State-Socialism in Poland*. University Park: Pennsylvania State University Press.

LAITIN, D. D. 1986. *Hegemony and Culture: The Politics of Religious Change Among the Yoruba*. Chicago: University of Chicago Press.

LINDBLOM, C. E. 1977. *Politics and Markets: The World's Political and Economic Systems*. New York: Basic Books.

MAINE, H. 1861. *Ancient Law*. London: John Murray.

MAJONE, G. 1989. *Evidence, Argument and Persuasion in the Policy Process*. New Haven, Conn.: Yale University Press.

MEYER, J. W., BOLI, J., THOMAS, G. M., and RAMIREZ, F. O. 1997. World society and the nation-state. *American Journal of Sociology*, 103: 144–81.

OUCHI, W. G. 1980. Markets, bureaucracies and clans. *Administrative Science Quarterly*, 25: 129–41.

PRICE, R. 1995. *The Chemical Weapons Taboo*. Ithaca, NY: Cornell University Press.

PUTNAM, R. D. 1993. *Making Democracy Work: Civic Traditions in Modern Italy*. Princeton, NJ: Princeton University Press.

PYE, L. W. 1968. Political culture. Pp. 218–25 in *International Encyclopedia of the Social Sciences*, ed. D. L. Sills. New York: Free Press.

RAPOPORT, A. 1985. Uses of experimental games. Pp. 147–64 in *Plural Rationality and Interactive Decision Processes* (Lecture Notes in Economic and Mathematical Systems 248), ed. M. Grauer, M. Thompson, and A. Wierzbicki. Berlin: Springer Verlag.

RAYNER, S. 1982. The perception of time and space in millenarian sects: a millenarian cosmology. Pp. 247–74 in *Essays in the Sociology of Perception*, ed. M. Douglas. London: Routledge.

SAID, E. W. 1979. *Orientalism*. New York: Vintage.

SCHMUTZER, M. E. A. 1994. *Ingenium und Individuum*. Vienna: Springer Verlag.

—— and BANDLER, W. 1980. Hi and low—in and out: approaches to social status. *Journal of Cybernetics*, 10: 283–99.

SCHWARZ, M., and THOMPSON, M. 1990. *Divided We Stand: Redefining Politics, Technology and Social Choice*. Philadelphia: University of Pennsylvania Press.

SMITH, A. 2000. *The Theory of Moral Sentiments*. Amherst, NY: Prometheus Books; originally published 1759.

——2003. *The Wealth of Nations*. New York: Bantam; originally published 1776.

SMITH, J. M. 1982. *Evolution and the Theory of Games*. Cambridge: Cambridge University Press.

STINCHCOMBE, A. L. 1997. A proposed fragmentation of the theory of cultural change. In Ellis and Thompson 1997, 105–20.

SZRETER, S., and WOOLCOCK M. 2004. Health by association? Social capital, social theory and the political economy of public health. *International Journal of Epidemiology*, 33: 650–67.

THOMPSON, M. 1988. Socially viable ideas of nature: a cultural hypothesis. Pp. 80–104 in *Man, Nature and Technology: Essays on the Role of Ideological Perceptions*, ed. E. Baark and U. Svedin. London: Macmillan.

——ELLIS, R., and WILDAVSKY, A. 1990. *Cultural Theory*. Boulder, Colo.: Westview.

——and RAYNER, S. 1998. Cultural discourses. Vol. 1, 265–344 in *Human Choice and Climate Change*, ed. S. Rayner and E. L. Malone. Columbus, Oh.: Battelle Press.

——GRENDSTAD, G., and SELLE, P. 1999*a*. Cultural theory as political science. In Thompson, Grendstad, and Selle 1999*b*, 1–23.

————(eds.) 1999*b*. *Cultural Theory as Political Science*. London: Routledge.

TILLY, C. 2005. How and why trust networks work. *Trust and Rule*. Cambridge: Cambridge University Press.

TYLOR, E. 1871. *Primitive Culture: Researches into the Development of Mythology, Philosophy, Religion, Language, Art and Custom*, 3rd edn. London: John Murray.

VAN WOLFEREN, K. 1990. *The Enigma of Japanese Power*. New York: Vintage.

VERWEIJ, M., and THOMPSON, M. (eds.) 2005. *Clumsy Solutions for a Complex World*. Basingstoke: Palgrave.

WEBER, M. 1930. *The Protestant Ethic and the Spirit Of Capitalism*. New York: Scribners.

WILDAVSKY, A. 1987. Choosing preferences by constructing institutions: a cultural theory of preference formation. *American Political Science Review*, 81: 3–21.

WILLIAMSON, O. E. 1975. *Markets and Hierarchies*. New York: Free Press.

WU, C.-E. 1942. *Monkey*, trans. A. Waley. London: Allen and Unwin.

CHAPTER 18

HOW TO DETECT CULTURE AND ITS EFFECTS

PAMELA BALLINGER

For the moment, it remains true that old theories tend less to die than to go into second editions. (Clifford Geertz, *The Interpretation of Cultures*)

How to detect culture and its effects? When asked to write this chapter, the proposed title and its vocabulary of detection, causality, and effects suggested a different way of talking about culture than the one that I—trained as an interpretivist anthropologist in the American school—typically used in my research. Admittedly, a language of clues did not prove unfamiliar to me, though I thought of the task of tracking clues and explaining them in terms of the historical method described by Carlo Ginzburg as, in turn, akin to that of the physician: "indirect, presumptive, conjectural" (1989, 106; see Franzosi, this volume). Writing of history, Ginzburg's query, "But can we actually call a conjectural paradigm scientific?" (Ginzburg 1989, 124) holds equally true for the dominant streams of thought in contemporary American cultural anthropology, powerfully shaped by the interpretivist revolution launched by Clifford Geertz and subsequently elaborated by the reflexive, postmodern critics.

In the last two decades, the traditional custodians of culture have increasingly hedged around and debated their use of the term and concept "culture," with some anthropologists going so far as to suggest that we abandon it altogether or "write against it" (Abu-Lughod 1991). Concomitantly, both within and outside of anthropology the culture concept has increasingly been unloosed from its long-standing anchors—social structure and society. At times, culture has come to acquire enormous (if sometimes implicit) explanatory power, running the risks of analyses that reproduce ideologies of cultural essentialism (Shapiro 1998). Whereas anthropologists have at times become paralyzed by the issue of what culture *is* or what it *does*, practitioners from fields like political science seeking alternatives to their dominant disciplinary paradigms (notably realism) have hesitated less in the face of culture, borrowing from other fields as they produce "culturalist" analyses.[1] These borrowings of anthropological concepts (and to a much lesser degree methods) reflect an important recognition that culture *does* matter (see the preceding chapter). The limitations of such analyses, however, also reveal the need to dig deeper into the scholarly toolbox in order to get at how to locate and "detect" culture.

1   THE CULTURE CONCEPT AT "HOME" AND "ABROAD"

Though culture is one of the defining concepts for anthropology, it remains an essentially contested concept. Raymond Williams contends, culture "has now come to be used for important concepts in several distinct intellectual disciplines and in several distinct and incompatible systems of thought" (1976: 76–7). Even within anthropology, scholars have long debated whether culture is to be understood as a model *of* (that explains behavior) or a model *for* (that explains what people think they are doing, or ought to be doing); whether culture consists primarily in symbols and ideas (the ideational or intellectualist view) or material objects and processes (the materialist position); the degree to which culture determines individual personality and behavior and vice versa; and the relationship between culture and society. This series of long-running theoretical debates over the nature of culture—which consist in various rephrasings of the issue of how to detect culture and its effects—reflects the ways in which, as the anthropological discipline

---

[1] I focus in this essay on what Desch (1998) has labeled the third wave of cultural theories in political science and international security studies, recognizing that interest in culturalist approaches is nothing new within political science.

coalesced intellectually and institutionally in the nineteenth century, its proponents drew on long-standing and not always complementary intellectual traditions for thinking about things such as Culture, cultures, and civilization (Kuper 1999).[2]

The German-born Franz Boas is often credited with the founding of the American school of *cultural* anthropology. Undeniably, anthropologists like Lewis Henry Morgan had sought to place the study of Native Americans on a scientific footing and had virtually invented the field of kinship studies before Boas emigrated to the United States. Yet Boas brought with him and introduced into American anthropology a notion of culture as *kultur*. Directly traceable to the Berlin Society of Anthropology of the 1880s of Rudolf Virchow and Adolf Bastian, this understanding of culture was more broadly rooted in the Romantic celebration of cultures plural embraced by Herder in his rejection of Enlightenment notions of linear progression towards a singular Culture (as refinement and rationality).[3]

For Boas (like the Berlin school that influenced him), every society possessed a unique culture shaped by its historic interaction with the natural environment, as well through its borrowings and exchanges with other cultures. For Boas, culture did not possess the fixed fatalism at that time attributed to race, nor was it something that existed in lesser or greater amounts on a fixed timeline of evolution (from savagery to barbarism to civilization), as Morgan and the unilineal anthropologists of the day contended. Together with the group of students he built up around him, including Alfred Kroeber, Ruth Benedict, and Margaret Mead, Boas argued forcefully that culture, rather than biology, matters most in making us what we are. In doing so, Boas effectively dismantled the unilineal evolutionist framework that had dominated anthropology in its moment of disciplinary formation.

Despite their agreement over what culture was not (i.e. not fixed, like biology), Boas and his followers did not all understand culture in the same way. Boas himself never devoted much attention to theorizing culture and tended to agree with his student Robert Lowie that culture and civilization proved akin to a "planless hodgepodge, that thing of shreds and patches" (in Harris 1968, 353; see also Kuper 1999, 68). Edward Sapir, Ruth Benedict, and Margaret Mead instead thought of cultures as expressing a *Geist* (spirit). Benedict went so far as to distinguish cultures in terms of distinct personality patterns (such as paranoid or ecstatic) that in turn were said to shape the personalities of the individuals comprising that specific culture. In time, this approach became known as the "culture and personality school." During the Second World War and the cold war, scholars working from this perspective produced a wide range of "national character studies" that not only treated culture as if it mapped neatly onto the political boundaries of

---

[2] This discussion reminds us that context also matters, of course, in understanding our own theoretical frameworks.

[3] On Boas and culture, see Stocking (1982, 195–233).

nationhood, but also made questionable leaps from child-rearing habits and socialization processes to assertions about "collective personalities." Despite its intellectual discrediting, many of the assumptions of the culture and personality school continue to underwrite everyday ways of talking about "peoples" and predicting their responses to policy.

In contrast to the culture and personality crowd, Alfred Kroeber (1963) argued that culture resided in material objects (technology, inventions), as well as ideas, language, and ways of doing things. For Kroeber, echoing the French sociologist Émile Durkheim's work on the collective conscience, culture was "superorganic," something larger and independent of either the individual elements that composed it or the actual individuals who belonged to it. Indeed, Kroeber thought that culture, once in place, could survive without any agents or bearers of it. Yet even though Kroeber broke with his teacher Boas in underplaying the importance of the individual to culture (as opposed to the importance of culture on the individual), when he formulated the notion of the superorganic he still revealed his Boasian training through his emphasis on the role of history and diffusion in shaping culture.

After Boas' death, however, Kroeber focused less on these aspects of culture as he entered into a series of long-running theoretical conversations dedicated to rendering the culture concept "scientific." In 1952, he and fellow anthropologist Clyde Kluckhohn produced the volume *Culture*, which sought to separate the wheat of scientific understandings of culture from the chaff of useless, humanistic definitions of culture. Key to Kluckhohn and Kroeber's elaboration of the culture concept was an emphasis on it in terms of symbols, values, and patterns. Kroeber thus downplayed his early focus on culture as embodied in material things (an emphasis that likely reflected his work in founding the anthropological museum at the University of California-Berkeley). Kroeber also entered into dialogue with Kluckhohn's Harvard colleague, the sociologist Talcott Parsons, about the relationship between culture and social structure/action. In a co-written article published in 1958 in the *American Sociological Review*, Kroeber and Parsons further refined the culture concept:

We suggest that it is useful to define the concept *culture* for most usages more narrowly than has been generally the case in the American anthropological tradition, restricting its reference to transmitted and created content and patterns of values, ideas, and other symbolic-meaningful systems as factors in the shaping of human behavior and the artifacts produced through behavior.   (In Kuper 1999, 69)

Kroeber and Kluckhohn thus emphasized the ideational, symbolic aspects of culture, nonetheless keeping in mind the issue of how this model of culture shaped human behavior.

Though Kroeber and Parsons argued for a new science of culture (and a theory of action), the Department of Social Relations at Harvard founded by Parsons would produce a generation of scholars—Clifford Geertz being the most notable for our purposes here—who ultimately would challenge the conviction that anthropological analysis was a scientific, as opposed to humanistic, enterprise. Geertz would do so by taking those very things Kluckhohn, Kroeber, and Parsons stressed in their understandings of culture—its symbolic nature and the focus on meaning—and running with them. Given not only his iconic status within anthropology but also his role as one of the anthropologists most widely read outside of his discipline (including in political science), let us focus on Geertz before turning to more recent anthropological approaches to culture.

Geertz began his scholarly career as a student of development and modernization processes in Indonesia, looking at topics that ranged from cultural ecology analyses of irrigation and (non)modernization (1963a) to the rise of nationalism in "new states" (1963b). Geertz's later incarnation as the interpretivist analyst of the Balinese cockfights and the "ritual state" in Bali and Islam in Morocco signaled a transformation in his approach and held enormous appeal for those scholars (whether historians or political scientists) seeking an alternative to deterministic (and often economistic) explanatory models (Stone 1979, 7–8, 14–19).

In his collection of essays, *The Interpretation of Cultures*, Geertz wrote of culture in semiotic terms, as "webs of significance he [Man] himself has spun," (1973, 5) and as a series of texts. Given this, Geertz urged scholars to *read* (albeit over the shoulders of the native producers of the texts) and suggested that analysis consisted in "sorting out the structures of signification" (Geertz 1973, 9). Geertz thus rejected a cognitivist view that anthropologists should (or ever could) get inside the heads of the natives. Instead, he instructed scholars to focus on culture as a public document. "Ideas are not ... unobservable mental stuff," Geertz writes. "They are envehicled meanings, the vehicles being symbols ... not idealities to be stared at but texts to be read" (1980, 135). The job of the ethnographer lay not just in reading and reinscribing sociocultural discourse but in doing so *thickly*, providing a richly layered description that systematizes the ethnographer's *"interpretations of what our informants are up to, or think they are up to"* (1973, 15). This amounts to a microscopic approach that focuses on local knowledge and theory-infused description.

Geertz himself recognized the methodological problems posed by this microscopic focus. Yet he took anthropologists to task for two strategies typically used for moving from the local/specific to the general: that of reading the micro site as microcosm of a larger entity, and that of treating the specific case as a "natural experiment" (with "primitive" cultures often standing in for "laboratories" because there exists less presumed interference or complexity). In the latter case, Geertz noted,

The great natural variation of cultural forms is, of course, not only anthropology's great (and wasting) resource, but the ground of its deepest theoretical dilemma: how is such variation to be squared with the biological unity of the human species? But it is not, even metaphorically, experimental variation, because the context in which it occurs varies along with it, and it is not possible (though there are those who try) to isolate the y's from x's to write a proper function.   (Geertz 1973, 22–3)

Geertz adds that the business of anthropology qua cultural theory lies not in predicting but, at best, diagnosing and possibly anticipating. He, like Ginzburg, invokes a clinical analogy, comparing the task of cultural interpretation to that of clinical inference. For Geertz, there appears to be little point in trying to write a general theory of cultural interpretation because such a theory would ignore context and thus prove useless. As he sees it, "the essential task of theory building here is not to codify abstract regularities but to make thick description possible, not to generalize across cases but to generalize within them" (Geertz 1973, 26). In stating this, Geertz made a powerful and persuasive case for thick description that attends to the contexts of cultural symbols as enacted in public life and display. Geertz emphasized the trademarks of good anthropology—the fact that one had to "be there," that is, possess experiential knowledge of specific sociocultural contexts, in order to understand the cultural winks and the meanings attributed to them by those doing the winking and witnessing the winking.

Despite the clear strengths of Geertz's approach, one of the many critiques made about it is that it privileges the ideational over the material and it disengages culture from social action. At the theoretical level, Geertz himself warns against these dangers. In his essay "Thick Description," for example, he urges, "Behavior must be attended to, and with some exactness, because it is through the flow of behavior—or more precisely, social action—that cultural forms find articulation" (Geertz 1973, 17). He goes on to add, "If anthropological interpretation is constructing a reading of what happens, then to divorce it from what happens—from what, in this time or that place, specific people say, what they do, what is done to them, from the whole vast business of the world—is to divorce it from its applications and render it vacant." (Geertz 1973, 18).[4]

Geertz, however, does not always realize in practice (i.e. ethnographic accounts of politics such as *Negara: The Theatre-State in Nineteenth Century Bali*) what he preaches in theory. In *Negara*, Geertz argued that in Bali sacred politics ruled. Furthermore, secular and sacred politics proved incompatible. For Geertz, the rituals and pageantry surrounding the state are not code for some deeper structures—they *are* the thing: "because the pageants were not mere aesthetic embellishments,

---

[4] Having said all this, however, Geertz (1973, 30) concludes his essay on "Thick Description" on a note that suggests that at the most we can offer our readings on other cultural texts, texts that consist not so much in (socially and culturally prescribed) actions but in explanations of actions: "To look at the symbolic dimensions of social action—art, religion, ideology, science, law, morality, common sense—is not to turn away from the existential dilemmas of life for some empyrean realm of de-emotionalized forms; it is to plunge into the midst of them. The essential vocation of interpretive anthropology is not to answer our deepest questions, but to make available to us answers that others, guarding other sheep in other valleys, have given, and thus to include them in the consultable record of what man has said."

celebrations of a domination independently existing: they were the thing itself" (1980, 120). Here, the symbolic is action and action symbolic; Geertz thus does attend to behavior, but only behavior and action of a particular sort. Critics of *Negara*, including fellow students of Bali, have raised pointed questions about the messy details of political life (taxation and trade, irrigation, conflict and violence) that disappear from an account that reads life as theater and theater as life (see Kuper 1999, 116–18).

Given all this, the appeal of Geertz to some political scientists might seem surprising. Yet Geertz's focus—if not entirely exclusive—on symbols and symbolic action clearly appealed to many of those political scientists interested in culture. When anthropological authority is cited by political scientists advocating cultural-ism, Geertz is often prominent.[5] This likely reflects Geertz's accessibility and persua-sive, elegant writing style (one of the strengths of what Stone (1979) deemed the "revival of narrative history"). Yet Geertz's emphasis on symbols and representations also proved compatible, at least as he tended to be read or misread outside of anthropology, with prevailing ways of treating culture within political science. "As used by political scientists," argues Alastair Iain Johnston, "... culture is primarily ideational, so as to differentiate it from behavior as the dependent variable ... implicit in some of the terminology is a sense that there is no one-to-one correspond-ence between cultural forms and observable decisions" (1995, 44, fns. 25 and 27 [6]).

The political culture approach, for example, represented one popular way in which some political scientists took account of culture (borrowing ideas from functionalist, symbolic, and structuralist anthropology) from the 1960s on. Many accounts of political culture attend to orientations and opinions, only rarely to behavior (in the form of political participation). While Merelman proposed bring-ing the insights of anthropology (exemplified for him by Geertz) to bear on studies of political culture, his own analysis unsatisfactorily reads cultural products such as the television program *Highway to Heaven* as indicative of American attitudes about political leaders (1989, 489–90). Once again, anthropological approaches become harnessed to a *model for* culture and neglect the *model of* dimension.

The 1980s witnessed another take on culture in the form of what, following the groundbreaking work of Jack Snyder (1997), became deemed strategic culture. Alastair Iain Johnston has usefully outlined the different waves of thinking about strategic culture, with the concept of strategic culture moving from a monolithic notion of single strategic cultures mapping neatly onto "national" cultures to an approach that "leaves behavior out of the independent variable" (Johnston 1995, 41). Such approaches appear almost bizarre to those possessed of a contemporary

---

[5] See, e.g., Johnson (2000); on this issue, refer also to Tilly and Goodin, Introduction to this volume.

[6] See Merelman (1989) for his take on why the materialist approach proves less suited to analyses of political culture; and Desch (1998) on the renewed appeal of culture as an ideational variable in political science analysis.

anthropological sensibility, as do some of the very questions asked by political scientists, beginning with the query "Why respect culture?" (Johnson 2000).

The constructivist approach put forward by Katzenstein et al. (1996) likewise embraced an ideationist view of culture, now understood primarily in terms of norms.[7] Even more problematic were the so-called *solutions* offered by critics of the Katzenstein framework: "A useful definition of culture emphasizes collectively held ideas that do not vary in the face of environmental or structural changes" (Desch 1998, 152). A view of culture as unvarying proves a largely useless one, given that anthropologists have spent the better part of the last three decades going beyond an older view of culture as static and bounded. In addition, Desch proposes his putative "solution" to the shortcomings of the Katzenstein volume as a way in which culture and its specialists (such as anthropologists) might work to "supplement existing theories in national security" (Desch 1998, 166); this would return anthropologists, area studies specialists, and historians to subordinate status as "'fact producers' for the 'analytic narratives' (stylized rational choice depictions) produced by social science 'theorists'" (Lustick 1997, 178).

Another approach that takes culture seriously is the "organizational culture" perspective. In *Imagining War: French and British Military Doctrine Between the War*, Elizabeth Kier takes on a question of traditional interest to students of international politics—how military doctrine develops—and offers a sophisticated and nuanced culturalist response. The limits of Kier's analysis, however, point to the need for ongoing discussion within political science of how to detect culture and its effects. In her study, Kier carefully sifts through various competing explanations for why the British and French militaries clung to defensive doctrines during the 1930s and up to the outbreak of the Second World War. Having done this, she contends that a culturalist perspective best explains doctrinal developments and persuasively argues that interests cannot be presumed as self-evident but rather are socially and culturally constituted.

To some degree, Kier sticks with the (as we have now seen) common view of culture as ideational, as a set of notions about how the world works that become naturalized, seen as obvious and unquestionable (1997, 26; see also 164). Yet these assumptions, in turn, provide ways of "'organizing action'" (1997, 144). Kier here

---

[7] Ted Hopf (1998, 184) distinguishes between conventional and critical variants of constructivism, with work like that of the Katzenstein volume falling under the former category. In contrast, "critical theory aims at exploding the myths associated with identity formation, whereas conventional constructivists wish to treat those identities as possible causes of action. Critical theory thus claims an interest in change, and a capacity to foster change, that no conventional constructivist could make." Hopf further contends that critical, as opposed to conventional constructivist theory focuses on interrogating and unmasking power relationships. These relationships are assumed to include the critical theorists' "own participation in the reproduction, constitution, and fixing of the social entities they observe" (Hopf 1998, 184), a recognition that demands a self-reflexive approach. Rather than specifically discuss here political science work in the critical constructivist mode, such as the volume edited by Weldes et al. (1999), I will incorporate its insights into the subsequent section on "detecting culture."

uses a notion of repertoires, of ways of doing things, that draws explicit on Swidler (1986) and echoes Tilly (1986; 1989). She sees (military) culture as "providing limited means to the organization, not as providing the values that guide action" (Kier 1997, 31). So for Kier, culture *is* more than attitudes or orientation; it also consists in what Swidler deems "a 'tool kit' of symbols, stories, rituals, and world-views, which people may use in varying configurations to solve different kinds of problems" (1986, 273).

In considering how culture organizes action, Kier narrows her focus to what she calls military cultures or, more precisely, military's organizational cultures. Defining organizational culture "as the set of basic assumptions, values, norms, beliefs, and formal knowledge that shape collective understandings" (see Kier 1997, 28), Kier rightly notes that there exist only particular military cultures, not a singular, abstract military culture. She admirably mines a wide range of archival and other documents, including British army manuals and the *Cavalry Journal*, in order to get at the specific military cultures that operated in France and Great Britain in the interwar period.

Kier's argument becomes less convincing, however, when she attempts to wed her self-described interpretivist approach to a language of variables. She argues, for instance, that culture "has an independent causal role in the formation of prefer-ences" and urges the need for research projects "that isolate culture's causal role" (see Kier 1997, 5–6). Such requirements force Kier to ignore important questions about culture (such as the origins of particular military doctrines and repertoires), as well as artificially to isolate out variables in the political scientist's laboratory. Kier's ahistorical approach (to a historical question) enables her, for instance, to maintain that the armies' cultures in both France and Great Britain changed very little or, in her words, "remained relatively static from the late nineteenth century until the outbreak of the World War II" (1997, 144).

Although anthropologists may not agree on culture, most today think of culture as fairly fluid and dynamic, thereby rejecting the old functionalist view of societies and cultures that exist in a kind of "equilibrium." That old view of culture also tended to see it as tightly bounded; cultures mapped onto peoples who, for the most part, mapped onto places. That Kier accepts France and Great Britain as bounded entities as more or less coinciding with nation states may make it easier for her to accept a view of their army cultures as relatively unchanging. Opening up the frame to consider imperial and colonial armies, for example, might raise interesting questions about the effect on those "cultures" of the experience of colonial troops fighting in the European theaters in the First World War. Similarly, expanding the frame might permit discussion of transnational values of class shared by some officers (as so nicely captured by Renoir's film, "La Grande Illusion"). Kier cannot admit such change into her model, however, because she needs her intervening variable (culture) to remain constant in order to demonstrate change in the dependent variable (doctrine) (see Kier 1997, 144).

Kier also makes what, to an anthropologist, seems like a curious distinction between culture(s), genuine and spurious.[8] First, she argues that one common military culture distinguished Great Britain from France, where two competing "cultures" existed. For Kier, the values prevailing in the British situation approximate something like "common sense" whereas "when there are several competing cultures, each culture more closely approximates an *ideology*" (see Kier 1997, 26). Much interpretivist work has demonstrated that culture constitutes a continually contested terrain of politics in which meanings—and power—are challenged, even in situations approaching hegemony.[9] To distinguish a seemingly more consensual cultural terrain from one of "competing cultures" qua ideologies (is there not a shared cultural terrain even here?) seems to imply that some cultures are more genuine than others. Kier further separates out the "instrumental" use of culture from the apparently genuine use of culture. Yet many contemporary anthropologists, in viewing culture as a contested field of power, hold that culture is always instrumental in the sense that there are no contexts innocent or removed from power (as understood in its broadest, rather than a formal sense). Indeed, the "toolkit" metaphor favored by Kier implies that culture proves instrumental quite literally.

In line with this view, one way to detect culture is to examine how, and in what contexts, it is deployed and by whom. In order to keep culture as a causally independent variable, rather than view it as imbricated in a contested field of social relationships, Kier instead argues, "it is important to show that the belief was genuine, and not invoked just to serve other interests. One of the ways of doing this is to show that the actors' beliefs persist despite the fact that continuing to hold those beliefs keeps them from achieving other important goals" (see Kier 1997, 37). Yet doesn't analyzing the construction of interests also require examining how actors within a specific culture view "culture" itself—perhaps indeed as a "weapon" or "resource" in power struggles?[10]

As this discussion here suggests, detecting culture and its effects requires something more (and other) than an attempt to isolate culture as a variable, given the

[8] I use the language of genuine and spurious with irony, since the phrasing itself comes from Edward Sapir and suggests that a previous generation of anthropologists would not have found the distinction problematic.

[9] Even though certain events or ideas may be unthinkable within a particular cultural framework, they do not prove impossible, raising the issue of the degree to which those commonsense views of the world are ever complete. Trouillot has elegantly demonstrated how the successful revolution by black slaves in Haiti proved "unthinkable" at the time of events. He notes, "The Haitian Revolution expressed itself mainly through its deeds, and it is through political practice that it challenged Western philosophy and colonialism" (1995, 89).

[10] Sociologist Lynn Eden's *Whole World on Fire* (2004), a study of why the US military for so long ignored the issue of fire damage effects from nuclear weapons, offers a more effective answer to this question even as it employs an organizational culture perspective frame similar to that of Kier. Eden, however, worries less than Kier does about fitting culture into a framework of variables and uses the term culture much less. Rather, she focuses on organizational frames for knowledge and in doing so demonstrates how particular understandings become powerful (or contested) within certain institutional contexts and for diverse audiences.

limits of some of the best "culturalist" work in political science. This is not to say that anthropologists necessarily have all the answers about how to do that. Traditionally, anthropologists have not given enough attention to the state or formal politics, focusing on small, often face-to-face communities. In a well-known example, Orin Starn has noted how, in Peru, anthropologists "missed" the revolution. Despite their intimate, experiential knowledge of various Andean localities, anthropologists working in the region neither foresaw nor had the tools to understand the rise of the Shining Path movement in Peru.[11] Starn attributes this to "Andeanism," a perspective focused on symbolic and ecological questions that views indigenous culture in terms of continuity and closure against the larger world. In the end, anthropologists were so focused on questions of cosmology or agricultural practices that they failed to notice the peasants' "frequent recourse to action" (Starn 1992, 165).

Considering examples like that of the Andean case, together with discussion of how anthropological concepts have been applied in fields like political science, underscores why culture needs to be treated as something more than just ideas and "worldviews." For as the best cultural analysis reveals, culture becomes embedded at the most basic level, as in the manner of moving and talking, practices of naming, house-building practices, and kinship patterns (not just how people represent descent and connection but how they *live it*). Part of the commonsense quality of culture refers not just to ideas about how the world works that become so taken-for-granted as to appear almost natural (though the potential or the actuality of contestation always remains) but also about ways of being in the world, ways of inhabiting the world that become like second nature. Such an approach reconnects the cultural to the social and the *model for* (the way things are imagined or expected to be) to the *model of* (the way things are).

2 "DETECTING" CULTURE AND ITS "EFFECTS:" SOME THOUGHTS

The traditional means by which anthropologists have studied "culture," as well as "society," has been through field research. For anthropologists, fieldwork often becomes synonymous with participant-observation, the method of "being there" and gaining experiential, detailed knowledge. Anthropologists often pair more formal methods, such as interviewing (particularly the life history method), with the sorts of

[11] Though Starn (1992, 152) does not believe anthropologists should "be in the business of forecasting revolutions," he does criticize his colleagues for failing to pay attention to the kinds of factors that enabled the movement to arise and find support.

informal observations typically recorded in fieldnotes.[12] Johnson and Johnson (1990) discuss the value of both types of methods, noting that their systematic collection of time allocation data contradicted their initial observations about types and amounts of work between the genders among the Machiguenga. At the same time, however, knowledge gained experientially through random visits to households provided data that the anthropologists would never have thought to ask about. The Johnsons thus make a powerful plea for the value of permitting serendipity to enter into the research project (on the importance of flexibility and adjusting the research design to the realities of the field situation, see Hirsch 2003, 41–3).

Yet anthropologists have always used other methods besides the experiential one of being there for getting at culture—including archival research, surveys, and comparative analysis. Years ago, Laura Nader (1988) urged anthropologists to "study up," that is, to take as objects of analysis not just marginalized populations but also those who occupy positions of power. Doing so demands methods other than, or in addition to, participant-observation, given that direct participation in the community in question may not always be possible.

Whether rooted in participant-observation or not, field research entails a considerable commitment of time (and often considerable money, enter the politics of funding). Not coincidentally, the field and hence fieldwork bear agricultural connotations, given that in the English language culture originally referred to the cultivation of land (Williams 1976); digging around in culture, i.e. modern day fieldwork, means getting your hands dirty figuratively (and quite often literally). In order to identify their research communities and define their research plans, anthropologists may initially spend extended periods of time entering into various kinds of social networks, becoming known, and examining the internal cleavages in order to think about the most effective strategies for sampling. (See Hirsch 2003 on implementing this "Needle-in-haystack" method.)

Today, the "field" may range from overlapping physical sites—what Marcus (1995) refers to as multi-sited ethnography—to virtual communities to diasporic communities linked by memories and narratives. Once seen to constitute a localized place, ideas of the field have thus undergone critical examination as scholars take analytical account of processes of deterritorialization and displacement and use them to rethink their assumptions, past and present (Gupta and Ferguson 1997). Yet no matter how the field and cultures are sited (see Olwig and Hastrup 1997), acquiring a detailed, non-superficial understanding of the sociocultural contexts in which things have meaning usually entails a labor-intensive process. And doing so means working within the constraints of power.

---

[12] For various takes on fieldnotes, see the collection edited by Sanjek (1990). Johnson and Johnson (1990, 161) contend, "Fieldnotes provide scientific data to the extent that they contain intersubjectively reliable descriptions of beliefs and behavior of individuals in other cultures; and they are humanistic documents to the extent that they enhance our *understanding* of behavior and beliefs by illuminating their meaning within a cultural context of related meanings."

In writing of different field research stints in Taiwan and the People's Republic of China, Margery Wolf has commented on her different experiences and the different degrees to which she was able to contextualize the information that she recorded. Her first field experience occurred when she accompanied her then-husband, Arthur Wolf, to Taiwan, where they lived with the same family for two years. Here, Wolf became an accidental anthropologist, eventually producing two books drawing upon her experiences in Taiwan. Years later, she carried out a very different project focused on gender inequality in mainland China, with research divided between six different sites at each of which she spent between four and six weeks.

This second research project resulted in a book. Yet Wolf herself admits the limitations caused by her lack of access to the contexts of everyday life. As a foreign scholar working in Communist China, Wolf could only conduct formal interviews and had to do so in the presence of at least one government representative. "Rich as I believe these interviews are," she reflects, "they are frozen in time, individual statements only vaguely anchored in the social and historical context that created them" (Wolf 1990, 351). Wolf admits that she could not get to know her informants in order to observe how they were situated within a variety of social networks. Turning a disadvantage into a strength, Wolf might have focused more on what the constraints on her fieldwork meant in terms of the larger political context and the penetration of state power into the contexts of everyday life, though this was not the focus of her study.

Being explicit about the field situation and the analyst's situation within it (even if the field in question be one defined by archival documents or scholarly discourse) also underscores that detecting culture requires reflexivity. Students of the human sciences have long known that the presence of the investigator invariably impacts the way data are collected; furthermore, all knowledges, including that of the investigator, are invariably situated and partial. In the 1980s, anthropologists interested in reflexivity began to call insistently for a critical ethnography that took account of how, historically, the fieldworker's positioning in a larger field of power—both political (as in a world system marked by inequality and colonialisms) and conceptual (that of the scientist gazing on and studying informants)—had shaped the resulting studies (Clifford and Marcus 1986). This perspective owed much to the interpretivist approach of Geertz, even as it moved beyond and, in some ways, challenged it. Joan Vincent (1991, 47) has argued that this reflexivity be wed to a contextualist approach that "involves understanding ethnography not as aesthetics or poetics, but as a historical phenomenon that must be associated with social, political, and material circumstances." The upshot of this critique has meant extensive rereadings and reinterpretations of the classic ethnographic texts together with a new sensitivity to the conditions of contemporary fieldwork and the need to make explicit the researcher's role and position in that process (part of the politics of knowledge).

Jennifer Hirsch includes a thoughtful commentary on her own positioning in the field. In her case, the field consisted of transnational sites cutting across the borders of the United States and Mexico as she studied sexuality and love among Mexican transnational families. Hirsch discusses, among other things, the importance of certain forms of self-presentation (in this case, as a "proper woman") necessary for her acceptance by informants. While making her research with women possible, this self-presentation necessarily limited Hirsch's ability to conduct one-on-one interviews with men or to be seen as close with members of the Jehovah Witness community. Hirsch makes clear not only the contexts in which she conducted research, however, but also those in which her own understandings and practices (together with those of her informants) are situated. She describes, for example, how she came to rethink her initial ideas about sex and migration (i.e. her own cultural constructs about these issues) on the basis of what her informants found significant and what they did (Hirsch 2003, 281).

In *Birthing the Nation: Strategies of Palestinian Women in Israel*, Rhoda Ann Kanaaneh also meditates on the impact of her hybrid identity (Chinese-Hawaiian-American-Arab/Palestinian) on the research on family planning that she carried out in her native town in the Galilee. Kanaaneh uses her family's experience to illustrate "how diverse and plural the Galilee is, and yet how certain patterns can run through it" (Kanaaneh 2002, 7). Her insider status "both facilitated and circumscribed" (2002, 12) her access and research material, as did her status as a married woman, which permitted her to participate in conversations about sex and contraception. Kanaaneh's informants also had considerable experience with previous researchers and queried her on her methodology, as well as the use to which she would put her research. Whether the researcher be an "insider" (like Kanaaneh) or an "outsider" (like Hirsch), such reflexivity should inform all ethnographic accounts, regardless of their disciplinary origin, and thereby dispense with the fiction of the researcher as a disembodied presence.

Political scientist Michael Barnett's reflexive account of his work as a political officer at the US Mission to the United Nations, Rwanda Desk, reveals how Barnett gradually became an insider on the "terrain" of the UN's institutional culture. As he realized only later, "Not only had I entered the bureaucratic world, but the bureaucratic world had entered me" (Barnett 1999, 179). This identification did not remain at the purely symbolic level but involved Barnett's positioning within a field of interests defined by the institutional culture in which he found himself. This led him to agree with the Secretariat's non-response to the genocide in Rwanda on the grounds that the "needs of the organization overrode those of the targets of genocide" (1999, 184). By reflecting on and placing himself as an actor (not just a neutral observer) in his account of his field research, Barnett gained valuable insights not just into his own response—one of the varied sites in which we detect culture and its effects—but also into the production of indifference within bureaucratic structures. This, in turn, led him to think beyond his "'policy-relevant' recommendations" (1999, 199) to broader questions about the effectiveness of peacekeeping when professionalized or bureaucratized.

Whereas all social scientists face the epistemological and methodological dilemmas posed by the dynamics of studying human populations, those who examine issues of violence confront the additional challenges posed by the ethics of the situation (see Pouligny 2002, 529). Writing of her involvement as both NGO worker and researcher in the study of United Nations peace operations, Beatrice Pouligny stresses, "Invoking my *personal responsibility* as a researcher also means considering the issue of my commitment to the people about whom I have conducted my investigations. Making them not merely 'objects' but also 'subjects' of research entails embarking on a process of participation and partnership" (2002, 536). This also requires careful attention to the ways in which information gathered is used: what forms it takes, the audiences it addresses, whether informants' identities are recognizable, and the degree to which the ethnographer may become complicit with narratives of violence.

Studies of violence have shed considerable light on the ways in which even that violence which appears so "extreme" as to escape explanation reflects specific logics[13]—those of the perpetrators and/or the victims.[14] In acts such as defilement and desecration, perpetrators invert what is sacred, dignified, and human. Obviously, certain aspects of repertoires of defilement suggest some universalities in cultural codes, as in prohibitions against excrement and menstrual waste. Yet other aspects of atrocities that defile the body refer to specific cultural histories, even if the cultural repertoire per se does not necessarily provide the causal explanation for the origin of the violence. For example, when Bosnian Serb soldiers cut off the small fingers and adjacent fingers of Muslim and Croat victims during the conflict in Bosnia, this desecration referred to the Orthodox practice of crossing themselves with three fingers; in addition, it made reference to earlier repertoires of violence employed in the past (the Second World War, the Balkan Wars). In analyzing such

---

[13] On definitions of "extreme" violence, see Sémelin (2002). The reader is also referred to Jane Cowan's (2003) illuminating analysis of what "violent language" meant to minority petitioners and League of Nations officials in the context of bureaucratic procedures to guarantee the minority procedure laid out by the League.

[14] Analyzing culturally patterned forms of violence in former Yugoslavia (such as the blood feud or the cutting off of enemies' noses), Allcock reminds us, "Violence is not necessarily random, arbitrary, meaningless, pathological or antisocial. It may be patterned, directed, significant, normal and constitutive of the social" (2000, 384). At the same time, however, not all violence can be understood in terms of the immediate cultural context and thus analysts also need to be attentive to what Allcock deems exogenous models of violence. The remembrance of such violence obviously draws upon specific cultural practices of narration and memorialization, as well. The Jewish memorial books studied by Kugelmass and Boyarin (1983), for example, demonstrate the ways in which even the unprecedented events of the Holocaust could be incorporated into long-standing frames through which to understand persecution of Jews. And, of course, the Book of Exodus provides the "textual prototype for subsequent 'documentary narrative'—the quintessential *sifrut ha'edut* or 'literature of testimony'" (Young 1988, 20).

forms of violence, defilement appears "the more symbolic since it is physical and material" (Nahoum-Grappe 2002, 555–6); indeed the atrocity "is embraced [by the perpetrators] as having symbolic value" (Allcock 2000, 398). Here, the seeming divide between the symbolic and the material, a reification perpetuated by too many scholars, dissolves. The body symbolizes the collective and yet also belongs to individuals; the act of desecration "*by striking at the real body of the one, destroys the moral space of all*" (2002, 557).

Yet desecration and defilement may also become a tool for protest by victims, as Beğona Aretxaga (1997) has shown for the case of imprisoned female IRA activists who organized a "protest of dirt" in solidarity with male IRA and other Catholic political prisoners in Northern Ireland. Male prisoners had already organized a so-called dirty protest. Refusing to wear prison uniforms after being stripped of their status as political prisoners, the men had remained in their cells, unwashed and amidst their own body wastes. Female prisoners launched a similar protest, one that proved more disturbing to Protestants and Catholics alike precisely because it violated cultural norms about the propriety of women. Not only did the sight of women in their own excrement and menstrual blood break shared cultural taboos, it also challenged the traditional role reserved for women in nationalist discourse as passive (if stoic) supporters of the cause and as providers of sons to the fighting. Furthermore, for Catholics it violated notions of womanhood and motherhood associated with Mother Mary. The women's protest thus drew power from its conscious inversion of cultural norms and strategically used defilement of the body—a form of violence at once symbolic and material—as a means of resistance.

Whether in the form of violence or not, culture is expressed and constituted through practices, i.e. it is embodied—sometimes in the most literal ways possible. Analysts of culture must pay attention not only to formalized or special kinds of practices but also "the little routines that people enact, again and again, in working, eating, sleeping, and relaxing, as well as the little scenarios of etiquette they play out again and again in social interaction" (Ortner 1984, 154). In urging for a reflexive, "sensuous scholarship" that takes account of such embodiment and that calls on scholars to use all their senses, Paul Stoller (1997, 23) moves from his own experiences studying sorcery in Africa to contend,

For ethnographers embodiment is more than the realization that our bodily experience gives metaphorical meaning to our experience; it is rather the realization that, like Songhay sorcerers, we too are consumed by the sensual world, that ethnographic things capture us through our bodies, that profound lessons are learned when sharp pains streak up our legs in the middle of the night.

Political philosopher Howard Adelman learned such painful lessons when he visited a makeshift morgue containing 18,652 corpses in Kigali in 1996. Though he had already co-authored and published a study of early warning and conflict management in regards to the genocide in Rwanda, nothing had prepared Adelman for the sensory experience of genocide itself. This experience has informed his subsequent work on genocide. Not only does the *vision* of those bodies continually revisit him, so does their *smell* for, "once one experiences a genocide, the smells infuse every pore of the body" (1997, 12; on smell and the theorization of genocide, see also Nahoum-Grappe 2002, 555).

Detecting culture requires heeding our senses—listening, hearing, smelling, tasting, feeling—in order to contextualize the realms in which social practices (including those of politics) and their "symbolic" representations operate. In this chapter, I have offered a (necessarily incomplete) historical overview of how scholars have treated culture in order to suggest that in reconnecting (and detecting) the social and the cultural in our analyses, both anthropologists and political scientists may find that "old theories" and "second editions" point to more effective ways of taking account of culture. The new editions of cultural analysis remain to be written.

References

ABU-LUGHOD, L. 1991. Writing against culture. In Fox 1991, 137–62.

ADELMAN, H. 1997. *Knowledge, Aesthetics and Preventing Genocide*. Mimeo., Centre for Refugee Studies, New York University.

ALLCOCK, J. B. 2000. *Explaining Yugoslavia*. London: Hurst and Company.

ARETXAGA, B. 1997. *Shattering Silence: Women, Nationalism and Political Subjectivity in Northern Ireland*. Princeton, NJ: Princeton University Press.

BARNETT, M. 1999. Peacekeeping, indifference, and genocide in Rwanda. Pp. 173–202 in *Cultures of Insecurity: States, Communities, and the Production of Danger*, ed. J. Weldes, M. Laffey, H. Gusterson, and R. Duvall. Minneapolis: University of Minnesota Press.

CLIFFORD, J., and MARCUS, G. (eds.) 1986. *Writing Culture: The Poetics and Politics of Ethnography*. Berkeley: University of California Press.

COWAN, J. 2003. Who's afraid of violent language? Honour, sovereignty and claims-making in the League of Nations. *Anthropological Theory*, 3: 271–91.

DESCH, M. C. 1998. Culture clash: assessing the importance of ideas in security studies. *International Security*, 23(1): 141–70.

EDEN, L. 2004. *Whole World on Fire: Organizations, Knowledge, and Nuclear Weapons Devastation*. Ithaca, NY: Cornell University Press.

FOX. R. G. (ed.) 1991. *Recapturing Anthropology: Working in the Present*. Santa Fe, N. Mex.: School of American Research Press.

GEERTZ, C. 1963a. *Agricultural Involution: The Processes of Ecological Change in Indonesia*. Berkeley: University of California Press.

——1963b. The integrative revolution: primordial sentiments and civil politics in the new states. Pp. 105–57 in *Old Societies and New States*, ed. C. Geertz. New York: Free Press.

——1973. *The Interpretation of Cultures*. New York: Basic Books.

GEERTZ, C. 1980. *Negara: The Theatre State in Nineteenth-Century Bali*. Princeton, NJ: Princeton University Press.

GINZBURG, C. 1989. *Clues, Myths, and the Historical Method*, trans. J. and A. Tedeschi. Baltimore: Johns Hopkins University Press.

GUPTA, A., and FERGUSON, J. (eds.) 1997. *Anthropological Locations: Boundaries and Grounds of a Field Science*. Berkeley: University of California Press.

HARRIS, M. 1968. *The Rise of Anthropological Theory*. New York: Thomas Y. Crowell Co.

HIRSCH, J. S. 2003. *A Courtship after Marriage: Sexuality and Love in Mexican Transnational Families*. Berkeley: University of California Press.

HOPF, T. 1998. The promise of constructivism in international relations theory. *International Security*, 23(1): 171–200.

JOHNSON, A., and JOHNSON, O. R. 1990. Quality into quantity: on the measurement potential of ethnographic fieldnotes. In Sanjek 1990, 161–86.

JOHNSON, J. 2000. Why respect culture? *American Journal of Political Science*, 44: 405–18.

JOHNSTON, A. I. 1995. Thinking about strategic culture. *International Security*, 19(4): 32–64.

KANAANEH, R. A. 2002. *Birthing the Nation: Strategies of Palestinian Women in Israel*. Berkeley: University of California Press.

KATZENSTEIN, P. (ed.) 1996. *The Culture of National Security: Norms and Identity in World Politics*. New York: Columbia University Press.

KIER, E. 1997. *Imagining War: French and British Military Doctrine between the Wars*. Princeton, NJ: Princeton University Press.

KROEBER, A. L. 1963. *Anthropology: Culture Patterns and Processes*. San Diego, Calif.: Harcourt Brace Jovanovich.

KUGELMASS, J., and BOYARIN, J. (eds.) 1983. *From a Ruined Garden: The Memorial Books of Polish Jewry*. New York: Schocken Books.

KUPER, A. 1999. *Culture: The Anthropologists' Account*. Cambridge, Mass.: Harvard University Press.

LUSTICK, I. S. 1997. The disciplines of political science: studying the culture of rational choice as a case in point. *PS: Political Science and Politics*, 30(2): 175–9.

MARCUS, G. 1995. Ethnography in/of the world system: the emergence of multi-sited ethnography. *Annual Review of Anthropology*, 24: 95–117.

MERELMAN, R. M. 1989. On culture and politics in America: a perspective from structural anthropology. *British Journal of Political Science*, 19: 465–93.

NADER, L. 1988. Up the anthropologist: perspectives from studying up. Pp. 470–84 in *Anthropology for the Nineties*, ed. J. B. Cole. New York: Free Press.

NAHOUM-GRAPPE, V. 2002. The anthropology of extreme violence: the crime of desecration. *International Social Science Journal*, 174: 549–57.

OLWIG, K., and HAPSTRUP, K. (eds.) 1997. *Siting Culture: The Shifting Anthropological Object*. London: Routledge.

ORTNER, S. 1984. Theory in anthropology since the sixties. *Comparative Studies in Society and History*, 26 (1): 126–66.

POULIGNY, B. 2002. An ethic of responsibility in practice. *International Social Science Journal*, 174: 529–38.

SANJEK, R. (ed.) 1990. *Fieldnotes: The Makings of Anthropology*. Ithaca, NY: Cornell University Press.

SÉMELIN, J. 2002. Extreme violence: can we understand it? *International Social Science Journal*, 174: 429–31.

SHAPIRO, I. 1998. Can the rational choice framework cope with culture? *PS: Political Science and Politics*, 31(1): 40–2.

SNYDER, J. 1977. *The Soviet Strategic Culture: Implications for Limited Nuclear Operations.* RAND Report [R-2154-AF]. Santa Monica, Calif.: RAND.

STARN, O. 1992. Missing the revolution. Pp. 103–23 in *Rereading Cultural Anthropology*, ed. G. E. Marcus. Durham, NC: Duke University Press.

STOCKING, G. 1982. *Race, Culture, and Evolution: Essays in the History of Anthropology.* Chicago: University of Chicago Press.

STONE, L. 1979. The revival of narrative: reflections on a New Old History. *Past and Present*, 85: 3–24.

STOLLER, P. 1997. *Sensuous Scholarship.* Philadelphia: University of Pennsylvania Press.

SWIDLER, A. 1986. Culture in action: symbols and strategies. *American Sociological Review*, 51: 273–86.

TILLY, C. 1986. *The Contentious French.* Cambridge, Mass.: Harvard University Press.

—— 1989. Collective violence in European perspective. Pp. 62–100 in *Violence in America: Protest, Rebellion, Reform*, ed. T. R. Gurr. Newbury Park, Calif.: Sage.

TROUILLOT, M.-R. 1995. *Silencing the Past: Power and the Production of History.* Boston: Beacon Press.

VINCENT, J. 1991. Engaging historicism. In Fox 1991, 45–58.

WELDES, J., LAFFEY, M., GUSTERSON, H., and DUVALL, R. (EDS.) 1999. *Cultures of Insecurity: States, Communities, and the Production of Danger.* Minneapolis: University of Minnesota Press.

WILLIAMS, R. 1976. *Keywords: A Vocabulary of Culture and Society.* New York: Oxford University Press.

WOLF, M. 1990. Chinanotes: engendering anthropology. In Sanjek 1990, 343–55.

YOUNG, J. E. 1988. *Writing and Rewriting the Holocaust.* Bloomington: Indiana University Press.

CHAPTER 19

....

RACE, ETHNICITY, RELIGION

....

COURTNEY JUNG

THE age of democracy is upon us. Not only do democracies outnumber non-democracies by a factor of two to one at the start of the twenty-first century, but rule by the people has emerged as the single standard of political legitimation.[1] Governments invoke democratic principles, even where the actual practice of representation is inadequate. With the end of the third wave of democratic transitions in 1994, analysts have begun to turn their attention to consolidation, to the chances that these new institutions and norms will prosper and put down roots.[2] The literature on consolidation is focused on the conditions that make democratic survival more or less likely—per capita income, political culture, electoral systems, institutional structure, and racial, ethnic, and religious homogeneity (Przeworski and Limongi 1997; Dahl 1989; Gellner 1983).

This last condition of democratic consolidation is, however, in increasingly short supply. Just as democracy has triumphed as the only game in town, race,

---

* For sage advice on previous drafts, the author thanks Nida Alahmad, Clarissa Hayward, Mala Htun, Patrick Macklem, and Rogers Smith.

[1] According to Freedom House, 61 percent of the countries of the world were electoral democracies in 2003.

[2] Diamond and Plattner 1993; Linz and Stepan 1996; I mark the South African election that ended apartheid in April 1994 as the end of the third wave of democratic transitions. The third wave started with the 1974 overthrow of the Caetano regime in Portugal.

ethnicity, and religion have emerged as central features of political organization and mobilization. In the United States, both parties actively court the vote of ethnic and racial minorities, such as Latinos (Desipio 1998). Concerns over ethnic and religious representation were at the center of the composition of Iraq's Interim Governing Council (Jabar 2004). And in countries like Yugoslavia, Brazil, and India, ethnic, racial, and religious divisions respectively moved to the center of political life in the 1990s (Glenny 1992; Htun 2004a; Chandra 2004). The politics of ethnicity, race, and religion punctuate the political landscape in developed and developing countries, in rural and urban areas, in the East and in the West.

The creeping pervasiveness of democracy, on the one hand, and of racial, ethnic, and religious politics on the other, has generated new concerns among democratic theorists and practitioners. Political scientists and other observers of contemporary politics treat race, ethnicity, and religion as problems. In particular, such social categories are widely considered to threaten the survival of democratic political institutions and the fabric of national society.[3] People organized by racial, ethnic, or religious affiliation express "intense but conflicting preferences" that preclude the development of the type of cross-cutting cleavages that are essential to plural democracy (Dahl 1971; Rabushka and Shepsle 1972, 217). Elections that are nothing but a racial or ethnic census create disincentives for minority participation within the system (Horowitz 1985; 1991). Democratic breakdown is allegedly caused by "ethnic outbidding." Racial, ethnic, and religious politics supposedly create incentives for party leaders to attract support by developing extremist positions that polarize the political spectrum (Rabushka and Shepsle 1972, 67–73; Horowitz 1985, 19).

Concerns for the survival of democracy have led liberal and democratic theorists to propose a variety of solutions to the problems caused by social heterogeneity. What is more, each category seems to have generated a distinct solution, exposing an implicit assumption that race, ethnicity, and religion are groups of different types that pose problems of different kinds.

The Virginia Statute of Religious Freedoms and the US Constitution's non-establishment clause laid out the principle of separation of church and state and, in the line of theorizing that is descended from John Stuart Mill, there is a consensus that the solution to religion is privatization (Mill 1857; 1969 [1874]). Citizens must be free to hold their religious beliefs in their private lives and to practice their religions without interference, but they cannot bring their religious convictions to public and political debate (Rawls 1972; 1985; 1993, xix, 151–4, 220–30). The reason is that religion is an "ultimate commitment" that determines individuals' "highest ideals" as well as their "conceptions of the whole truth" (Macedo 1995, 474–5). It is precisely the comprehensive character of spiritual convictions that puts them in tension with the liberal state and recommends

---

[3] Rustow 1970; Rabushka and Shepsle 1972; Lijphart 1977; 1985; Horowitz 1985; 1991.

their privatization. Democracy cannot process "public reason that can only be appreciated by those who embrace a particular, controversial, comprehensive philosophical or religious system." (Macedo 1999, 9) Religious conviction is fundamentally threatening to a common political dialogue. At least since the heyday of modernization theory, a secular state has been considered an important precondition of democracy (Bhargava 1998; Casanova 1994).

For ethnicity on the other hand, there is a growing consensus that the solution is protection (Kymlicka 1995; Galston 1995; Taylor 1994). Liberal democracies threaten to erase the minority cultures that some of their citizens value and have membership in. Because individuals make sense of the world through the prism of their societal cultures, depriving them of access to such cultures diminishes their capacity to exercise genuinely free choice (Kymlicka 1995). Because individual self-worth is alleged to hang on group worth, withholding group recognition can be a form of oppression (Taylor 1994, 39). Constitutional protection of minority rights has become a condition of access to the European Union (Kelly 2004). Consociational electoral solutions, in which ethnic groups share power, entrench group boundaries in ways that also protect ethnicity, by giving minority populations political standing contingent on cultural group membership (Lijphart 1977; 1985). Consociationalism is the solution that was agreed to in the Dayton Accord that governs postwar Bosnia, and it is the solution envisioned by the US government for postwar Iraq.

For race, however, the solution is "cancellation." The logic behind *mestizaje*, affirmative action, school integration, and multiplying the possibilities of racial identification on the US census in 2000, is to erase race (Prewitt 2004). Most liberal racial policy is aimed at achieving color-blindness (Crenshaw et al. 1995), and many important theorists of race have promoted the ideal of transcending race (Gilroy 2001; Plotke 1995; Sniderman and Carmines 1997). In the US, the 1954 *Brown v. Board of Education* decision to integrate schools, which lay the foundation for subsequent American race policy, challenged the legitimacy of "separate but equal" facilities established by *Plessy v. Ferguson* in 1896.[4] In South Africa, where voting patterns closely mirror racial cleavages, some analysts argue that voters' preferences are based on interests, not race, and conclude therefore that voters are "normal" (Mattes et al. 1999). Mexican national identity was built on the ideal of overcoming racial difference by producing a single Mexican race and, until recently, Brazil was able to trumpet its own triumph over race by pointing to its large mixed race population (Wagley 1972). As Mala Htun (2004b) has argued about gender, race is a class action. That is, there seems to be some consensus that race is a category that forms around a grievance. Once the grievance is redressed, the category, appropriately, disappears. Notwithstanding the frustrating endurance of

---

[4] Bell 2004. By contrast, "separate but equal" would be precisely the recommended solution to ethnicity.

racial discrimination, theorists and practitioners seem agreed that, unlike ethnicity and religion, race might vanish. Public policy should be oriented toward that goal.

1   CONSTRUCTIVISM AND POWER

This typology of solutions is an inadequate response to the challenge that identity politics issues to democratic deliberation. It is inadequate because it fails to take into account the role of power and politics in forging the very categories it seeks to privatize, protect, or cancel. Privatization, protection, and cancellation have the effect of excluding these categories from public deliberation and political contest-ation, and of entrenching the status quo.[5] The constructivist method fleshes out just why these solutions are inadequate, and offers an alternative recommendation for the way politicized race, ethnicity, and religion should be engaged in democratic deliberation. By offering an alternative understanding of what race, ethnicity, and religion are, and of where they come from, constructivism implies a different normative, and not only analytical, approach to thinking about the place of race, ethnicity, and religion in liberal democratic politics.

The widely held view that race, ethnicity, and religion are problematic to democracy flows from primordial assumptions about where such groups come from, how they are constituted, and how they will behave politically. Such groups are taken to be exogenous to the political process, constituted by fundamental differences, and politically immutable (Ordeshook and Shvetsova 1994). Primordi-alists believe that there are some identities that we are simply born into, including race, ethnicity, and religion, and that such groups therefore command a much stronger psychological allegiance, as essentially permanent features of human social organization (Geertz 1963). Democracies have a hard time dealing with these entrenched, and often conflictual social divisions, and with the competing alle-giances of their citizens.

The view that race, ethnicity, and religion are properly subject to different solutions also reveals a primordial logic. They are subject to distinct solutions because each group has a distinct essence. Ethnicity has at its core some unique set of practices and traditions. The reason that ethnicity must be protected is that many people value the practices and traditions that are at the core of ethnicity. The essence of religion is spirituality or belief. It is because faith (or at least much of

---

[5] This reality has long been clear to critical race theorists who argue against color-blindness as an approach to legal theory or as a solution to racial discrimination and oppression (Peller 1995).

Christian faith) can be reasonably construed as a private matter between the individual and her God, that religion can be privatized. Race is subject to cancellation, on the other hand, because its root is evidently physical, yet there is widespread agreement that biological markers of race are either non-existent, or illegitimate as a standard of differentiation. The logic of the solutions derives from primordial assumptions about what race, ethnicity, and religion really are, and from the related proposition that they are different from one another at some essential level.

This is true notwithstanding the fact that the view that such social categories as race, ethnicity, and religion are socially constructed is now commonly held in the social sciences. Yet many analysts continue to treat them as independent variables—a cause rather than a result of politics.[6] They take them as prior and exogenous, for analytical purposes, without taking into account the ways in which those starting points affect where they end up. The field of political science needs systematically to incorporate the study of where identities come from, and how they get constructed politically, into the study of their effects, and into normative political theories of how such categories ought to be accommodated, or not, by democratic society. A constructivist approach to the study of race, ethnicity, and religion, which fully integrates a theory of power into an analysis of the political traction of social categories, demonstrates why privatization, protection, and cancellation are not only politically wrong, but also logically mistaken, as "solutions" to identity politics.

Constructivism stands apart not only from primordial, but also from instrumental theories of identity and groups (Fearon and Wendt 2002). Instrumentalists attend to the individual level of analysis, and they focus on the rational, interest-driven decisions that individuals make in choosing one identity over another (Patterson 1975). Instrumentalists presume people have power over their own behavior, and make free, informed choices (Bates 1983; Laitin 1998). They are particularly interested in the role of ethnic entrepreneurs in mobilizing identity for the purposes of developing or solidifying a power base (Hardin 1995; Fearon and Laitin 1996). They explain the salience of race, ethnicity, or religion as a result of the overt coercive or mobilizing power that elites command over group members (Gourevitch 1998).

Whether they focus on individual decision-making or on elite mobilization however, instrumentalist theories of identity focus attention on what some have called the first "face" of power. Power is an instrument individuals possess, and wield over other actors, to influence outcomes in line with their interests. All people have power over themselves; some people have power over others. Following Dahl, instrumentalists treat power as an empirically verifiable causal relationship (Dahl 1957). Outcomes can be traced to the influence of A over B.

---

[6] Rogers Smith shows that this has been the case with race, for example (Smith 2004, 44–5).

For constructivists however, the second and third faces of power, and most importantly de-faced power, are much more relevant to understanding social outcomes than the power of A over B. Against Dahl, Bachrach and Baratz (1962; 1963) argued that the scope of power is wider than what is suggested by its public face, and that real power is exercised by limiting the public agenda, so that many issues never even become topics of conversation or contention. A decade later, Steven Lukes (1974) took this critique further by exposing a third face of power. Lukes argued that power not only influences the ability of social actors to express their preferences, as Bachrach and Baratz had argued, but that it can also shape the way they perceive and understand their own preferences (though it does not always). This explains why people accept their role in the existing order of things (Lukes 1974, 24).

Although the second and third faces of power issued a challenge to the concept of agents acting freely to influence outcomes, it still preserved an autonomous sphere of true interests and agency. Methodologically, the exercise of power was discernible as a departure from objectively definable interests and authentic action (Gaventa 1980). Power with a face theorists maintained a distinction between free action and action distorted by power. Following Foucault, Hayward argues instead that there is no free action, and that locating a boundary between free and unfree action is itself an exercise of power that privileges as natural, freely chosen, or true, some realm of social action (Hayward 2000, 29; Foucault 1979; 1980). Instead, she argues that power should be de-faced, conceived as a set of boundaries that defines fields of possibility, facilitating and constraining social action in line with norms, conventions, standards, and other institutionalized patterns of interaction (Hayward 2000, 31).

Constructivism shares a deep logic with Hayward's theory of de-faced power. Constructivists explain the salience of social categories as a result of historical processes and practices that forge meaning, and draw boundaries, in particular ways. There is no neutral, or un-constructed sphere of exchange. Constructivists attend to the role of ideas in constructing social life, and are centrally concerned with demonstrating the socially constructed nature of agents or subjects (Fearon and Wendt 2002, 57–8). At the deepest level, constructivism shares with the theory of de-faced power a concern with constitutive, and not only causal explanation. Constructivism is sensitive to the reciprocal relationship between ostensibly dependent and independent variables, through which relations of power sustain or upset existing social configurations.[7] Constructivists proceed on the belief that the fullest account of "how things work" entails unearthing and exposing the ways in which law, or welfare policy, or electoral systems, which often appear to be neutral or rational, contribute to a particular, not neutral, organization and representation

---

[7] Fearon and Wendt (2002, 58) use the example of the master–slave dialectic, in which one cannot exist without the other, to demonstrate the analytical focus of constructivist methodology.

of social reality.[8] They would draw attention to the ways in which such institutions produce, and shape the meaning of, race, ethnicity, and religion, and to their role in making such identities politically salient.[9]

2   RACE, ETHNICITY, RELIGION, AND POLITICS

This background paves the way for a thin, deeply contextualized theory of race, ethnicity, and religion. Constructivism sets forth the proposition that race, ethnicity, and religion (and also class, gender, and sexuality) do not have any essential core that determines their fundamental character.[10] Race does not arise from biology; ethnicity does not arise from culture; religion does not arise from spiritual belief; class does not arise from material conditions.[11] Instead, these categories are constituted by politics, and by the particular historical processes that have organized access to power in ways that forge boundaries of exclusion and selective inclusion. They operate from the outside in. The boundaries constitute the identity; the identity does not constitute the boundary (Butler 1992, 12, 13; Mouffe 1992, 379; Laclau 1994; Sartre 1990).

Therefore, even if there really is no essential racial, religious, or ethnic identity that derives from attributes of birth, once such markers are used to allocate social and economic power, and to bound political inclusion and exclusion, they develop a lived (social, economic, political) reality, with the potential to become political identities. The fact that race, religion, and ethnicity operate from the outside in, and not from the inside out, does not make them any less real, consequential, and sometimes enduring. Constructivists are concerned not with questioning the existence of reality but rather with exploring where reality comes

---

[8] Note here the constructivist roots of both critical legal theory and critical race theory (Crenshaw et al. 1995, xxvi).

[9] As Timothy Mitchell (1992, 1018) argues, "social constructions are not bounded entities with singular identities, but strategies and relations that often exceed their limits, become displaced, reverse themselves, or otherwise elude the descriptive realism that sees them simply as objects."

[10] This is why it is often hard to tell what is race, ethnicity, or religion. Think of the ways in which "Jewishness" appears as race, ethnicity, and religion in different contexts, places, and times. Does the transformation from "Black" to "African-American" imply a move from race to ethnicity?

[11] Adolph Reed (2002, 269–70) argues that race collapses into class, because class has an "essential materially demonstrable foundation" whereas race, "like other categories of ascriptive status has no such essential foundation." We can imagine the reverse proposition—that race is more essential than class because it is rooted in biology. From a constructivist perspective, both would be wrong.

from, given the empirically demonstrable fact that it changes over time and is differently perceived across space. Constructivism is a methodological response to the fact that appeals to essentialism explain very little of social and political significance.

Extended to the political realm, this theory of subjectivity owes an evident debt to the Gramscian concept of hegemony, and in particular to the state's hegemonic production of the terms of its own contestation (Laclau and Mouffe 1985, 151). The concept of hegemony is crucial to theorizing the formation of political identity because it links such identity directly to the hegemonic power—in modernity generally instantiated by the state—and sets limits on what will become an identity with political resonance.[12] If political identities are constituted by prior political relations, and the terms of such relations are set by the hegemonic power of the modern state, then it is the state itself that produces the terms of its own contestation. And if contestation occurs along the lines of inclusion and exclusion already made salient by the state, it predicts the emergence and proliferation of a particular (and not random or infinite) set of political identities in every era.[13]

Only those markers that are employed for the purposes of determining the boundaries of political inclusion, exclusion, and allocation have the potential to develop political resonance. The state, therefore, is not superimposed on a society already divided among competing and incompatible world-views. The state itself plays a crucial role in transforming distinct practices and traditions into social categories. Race, ethnicity, and religion are salient in contemporary politics because differences of skin color, cultural practice, and spiritual commitment have been marked as categories of exclusion and selective inclusion by the state itself. It is as a result of politics that skin color often becomes race, and traditions and practices often become ethnicity, while eye color remains nothing more than eye color. Race, ethnicity, and religion are not exogenous categories of affiliation; they are internal to politics itself.[14]

[12] It is not impossible that some other institution, like a corporation or an international convention, could produce identity. Arguably International Labor Organization (ILO) Convention 169 forged an indigenous identity in the 1990s. Nevertheless, the central role of modern states in determining the boundaries of politics makes it overwhelmingly the case that unless the state is complicit in bounding access around particular markers, such markers will not develop traction. ILO 169 would not have resonated in the absence of a long history of exclusion of indigenous people from full rights in citizenship at the state level.

[13] This argument is not meant to rule out the possibility that race, ethnicity, and religion, or something like them, existed before the full-fledged formation of the Westphalian state. This essay is about the way that social categories get constructed in ways that make them relevant to modern politics, and how they become categories of affiliation with potential political traction. I take that to be a modern phenomenon.

[14] While post-structuralist conceptions of political subjectivity imply that literally anything could develop salience as an identity, the possibilities are in fact limited by the way power is organized. One of the implications is that liberal democrats can relax their concern that allowing political identities free reign to contest politics will expand the range of possible contestations infinitely, and far beyond the capacity of the state to process.

This formulation helps to explain the creation of particular axes of contestation, and why certain forms of contestation are linked to particular political periods. Various theorists have advanced propositions regarding the actual exclusions that have characterized liberal democracy. In his provocative essay "The Dark Side of Democracy," Michael Mann (1999) argues for instance that modern societies governed by liberalism and democracy have always excluded. English democracy began by excluding along already-salient lines of class, differentiating between "the people" (property owners and men of means) and "the populace" (the masses). The class struggle that thereby ensued led eventually to the inclusion of the populace in the definition of the people, and age and gender replaced class as the exclusions that bound the public sphere. Exclusion along ethnic and racial lines did not begin to occur, according to Mann, until the colonial era, and takes particularly pernicious form with the advent of so-called organic democracy. Mann's description of the evolution of exclusions is the type of analysis that would help us to understand, and anticipate the emergence of new political identities and cleavage patterns in different eras.

Charles Taylor (1998, 143–4) also makes an argument about the exclusionary thrust of the democratic appeal to "the people" as a source of legitimation. Democracy works best, he says, when "the people" is a cohesive group that has the capacity to deliberate together to achieve consensus. "To some extent the members must know one another, listen to one another, and understand one another... Democratic states need something like a common identity." Democracy therefore includes a justification for excluding those who appear irreconcilably different. "The exclusion is a byproduct of the need, in self-governing societies, of a high degree of cohesion." Like Mann, Taylor provides an account of the exclusions of democracy, and in particular demonstrates how such exclusions come to be organized along lines of ethnicity, race, and religion.

In these accounts, neither Taylor nor Mann however focuses on the transformative and constitutive role of the discourse of cohesion. But as Anthony Marx (1998) argues in his comparative study of racial mobilization, it is the exclusions themselves that establish the preconditions of political subjectivity. Marx argues that race has been a salient organizing principle of opposition in South Africa and the US, but not in Brazil, because race was a formal marker of exclusion in the former two countries, but not in the latter. Although Brazil is both multiracial and racist, like South Africa and the US, Marx argues that Afro-Brazilians have not mobilized around race to protest their oppression because race has not been marked by the Brazilian state as a formal category of exclusion and allocation.

The modern state then, does not come to a society already divided by the distinct commitments, affiliations, beliefs, and physical attributes of its citizens. Instead the state itself is complicit in producing such divisions.[15] Race, ethnicity, and religion

---

[15] Marx 1998; 2003; Mamdani 1996; 2002; Vail 1989; Young 1976; Comaroff 1987; Jung 2000; 2003.

are not trans-historical psychological phenomena, arising spontaneously as a result of the universal and timeless human need for primary-group recognition; they are contemporary political phenomena.

This is a thin theory because it establishes the deeply contextualized character of such categories as race, ethnicity, and religion, and the concomitant proposition that the contingency with which they are constituted by their political and historical environments prevents reliable aggregation and differentiation. Analysts cannot make many predictions about how they will behave politically.

But this should not be taken to mean that they do not behave politically, or that we cannot say something systematic about the impact, or potential impact of such categories. The constructivist drive to theorize political identities as a cyclical output of politics itself lays the groundwork for reconceptualizing the character of categories like race, ethnicity, and religion as conditions of political agency, the very terms of political engagement. Race, ethnicity, and religion are strategies of contentious politics. When they are mobilized, it is for the purpose of sustaining or challenging particular configurations of power and access.

Constructivists focus attention on the very political process through which a person becomes a subject or agent of a particular type—an African-American instead of a worker, or Catholic instead of Latino. People do not automatically, by fact of birth, have critical capacities. Part of the way we develop such capacities is by constructing identities with social and political meaning and by inhabiting such locations. So, for example, before there could be a Latino political voice, or a "Latino vote" to court, the category of "Latinos" had to be constructed as a group with common interests, a common sensibility, and a history of immigration, conquest, marginalization, etc. It is only with the establishment of this political identity as Latinos that individuals could be bounded by ethnicity to develop political agency and, as a corollary, the critical capacity to contest a particular form of ethnic, linguistic, and maybe even racial discrimination.

The first step in the development of political agency then, is the development of political identity, and political identity does not arise as a fact of birth. It arises as a self-conscious act of political contestation. So it is not, as Benhabib (1992, 214–15) suggests, that only the self that exists prior to her socially constructed political identity will have the capacity for critique. It is instead only once she inhabits the discourses and structures that identify her as a Latina that she will develop the capacity for critique. The choice to identify as a Latina in turn produces a particular narrative of oppression, and a point of critical entry particular to that category of identification.

It is no coincidence therefore, that we can understand the contemporary salience of race, ethnicity, and religion in the same terms that Joan Scott (1999, 30) used to describe the making of the English working class, in her critique of E. P. Thompson's (1963) famous work. She argues that although Thompson set out to historicize the concept of class, to show that it did not arise spontaneously as Marx predicted from material conditions, instead he ended up essentializing it by linking it directly to structural conditions that prefigured politics.

Scott focuses attention instead on the political rhetoric of Chartism, which described "a particular position, the identity of 'working men,' whether antagonistic to, or in cooperation with, masters, the middle classes, shopkeepers or aristocrats" (Scott 1999, 61). It was the concept of class developed through Chartist politics, "as a way of organizing collective identity through an appeal to shared economic, political and 'social experience,'" that constituted the English working class and produced a class identity, in the context of structural conditions that placed millions of people in close proximity in urban slums and on the factory floor. Class developed political meaning as a result of the explicit efforts of political activists to forge the ideology and organizational network that would legitimate and sustain such an identity.

Like class, race, ethnicity, and religion are points of access to political intervention for purposes of upsetting or entrenching the systems of exclusion and selective inclusion through which they are constituted. Transforming such markers into political identities involves active contestation and boundary transgression, as existing power holders resist expansion of the political sphere, and potential contenders try to formulate political identities with greater political leverage. Race, ethnicity, and religion are a political achievement, not an accident of birth. Because identity is a condition of political contestation and a point of access to political agency, race, ethnicity, and religion can be an important weapon in the struggle of the weak against the naturalized order that excludes and marginalizes them (Scott 1985). They are also employed to sustain that order.

3   DEMOCRATIC CONSOLIDATION AND THE POLITICS OF RACE, ETHNICITY, AND RELIGION

What is at stake in the politics of race, ethnicity, and religion is the formation of political identities that grant access to political legitimacy, and from which one can therefore credibly make claims on the state. Such identity is a publicly recognizable structural location that orients political claims and transforms a latent category of people into a group with a sense of common interest and purpose. Such capacity exists to the extent that some markers, like race, gender, class, religion, or ethnicity, have been used to discriminate among people in the allocation of power and resources.

This view of the politics of claim-making, of the intensely political character of the attempt to become a person or group who can make claims, differs significantly from the liberal account of the status of claims. Rawls argues for example that the right to make claims inheres in citizenship in a liberal society. The freedom of liberalism means that citizens "regard themselves as self-originating sources of valid claims." It is only slaves who "are not counted as sources of claims," and this is because they are not free (Rawls 1985, 242–3).

Instead, many people cannot make claims in a liberal society, and their inability to do so does not rest in the fact that they are not free, technically speaking, but rather in the fact that they are denied, or for other reasons cannot locate, a language of political claim-making, a political identity. What liberals imagine as pre-political and automatic, is in fact deeply political. What counts as a language of claim-making is hotly contested precisely because new languages constitute new political actors that may threaten old ones, and challenge the very terms of the existing political debate.

Constructivism is a critical theory of identity formation that goes much further than simply establishing that groups are not natural. It suggests, I think, a much stronger critique of our use of categories like race, ethnicity, and religion than has normally been undertaken, even by constructivists themselves. What is more, taking constructivism seriously has normative implications for political contestation in liberal democracies.

By linking the political salience of race, ethnicity, and religion directly to the way the state itself organizes access to power and membership, constructivism exposes the intrinsically political character of such identities and generates an account of why these markers develop potential political salience. It is within this field of possibility, described by constructivist attention to historical and structural processes that forge meanings of a particular type, that actors behave strategically to influence outcomes in the way instrumentalists predict. Operating within boundaries they do not control, actors organize and mobilize around race, ethnicity, and religion for purposes of maintaining or upsetting existing patterns of access to power. Social categories resonate as political identities when they have been mobilized to operate as explicit political interventions and strategies of contentious politics.

The particular political torque of race, ethnicity, and religion is deeply contextualized, a result of the particular ways in which such markers have been deployed to organize access to power in particular societies. This is why the race card often "trumps" other forms of political identity when it is played in the United States (Mendelberg 2001), but was, until recently, practically mute in Brazilian politics (Marx 1998).

This argument about the character and political leverage of race, ethnicity, and religion has direct implications for the way liberal democracies should treat the politics of identity. If such categories are internal to the political process, liberal democracies should reasonably be expected to open democratic deliberation to the identities and claims the system itself has generated. If such claims are an explicitly political intervention and a strategy of contentious politics, they should be engaged, not privatized, protected, or canceled. They are not a threat to democratic consolidation so much as they are a condition of democratic renewal. When race, ethnicity, and religion arise as salient political identities, they signal some shortcoming of the democratic process. In general we should think of such mobilizations, as Lani Guinier and Gerald Torres (2002) suggest, as a miner's canary—a warning that the poisonous gases of entrenched power threaten the health of democratic society, and that access and membership have been erected on illegitimate and arbitrary foundations.

Democratic consolidation is therefore no more threatened by the politics of race, ethnicity, and religion than it might be by the politics of class or gender. Those categories that gain political salience do so as a result of exclusions and selective inclusions put in place by the political process itself. If they are salient, it is because they have been used to organize access to power. Movements have formed around race, ethnicity, and religion not because people have felt the need to express or defend their primary commitments to these identities, but because these characteristics have served as markers of political inclusion and exclusion. To be democratic therefore, liberalism relies in a fundamental way on the renewal of politics through the contestation of its boundaries.

References

BACHRACH, P., and BARATZ, M. 1962. Two faces of power. *American Political Science Review*, 56: 947–52.

——1963. Decisions and non-decisions: an analytical framework. *American Political Science Review*, 57: 632–42.

BATES, R. 1983. Modernization, ethnic competition and the rationality of politics in contemporary Africa. In *State Versus Ethnic Claims*, ed. D. Rothchild and V. Olorunsola. Boulder, Colo.: Westview Press.

BELL, D. 2004. *Silent Covenants: Brown vs Board of Education and the Unfulfilled Hopes for Racial Reform*. New York: Oxford University Press.

BENHABIB, S. 1992. *Situating the Self: Gender, Community and Postmodernism in Contemporary Politics*. New York: Routledge.

BHARGAVA, R. (ed.) 1998. *Secularism and its Critics*. Delhi: Oxford University Press.

BUTLER, J. 1992. Contingent foundations: feminism and the question of "postmodernism." Pp. 3–21 in *Feminists Theorize the Political*, ed. J. Butler and J. W. Scott. New York: Routledge.

CASANOVA, J. 1994. *Public Religions and the Modern World*. Chicago: University of Chicago Press.

CHANDRA, K. 2001. Cumulative findings in the study of ethnic politics. *APSA-CP*, 12 (1): 7–11.

——2004. *Why Ethnic Parties Succeed: Patronage and ethnic headcounts in India*. New York: Cambridge University Press.

COMAROFF, J. L. 1987. Of totemism and ethnicity: consciousness, practice and the signs of inequality. *Ethnos*, 52: 301–23.

CRENSHAW, K. W., GOTANDA, N., PELLER, G., and THOMAS, K. (eds.) 1995. *Critical Race Theory: The key writings that formed the movement.* New York: New Press.

DAHL, R. 1957. The concept of power. *Behavioral Science*, 2: 201–15.

—— 1971. *Polyarchy: Participation and Opposition.* New Haven, Conn.: Yale University Press.

—— 1989. *Democracy and its Critics.* New Haven, Conn.: Yale University Press.

DESIPIO, L. 1998. *Counting on the Latino Vote.* Charlottesville: University Press of Virginia

DEUTSCH, K. 1961. Social mobilization and political development. *American Political Science Review*, 55: 493–514.

DIAMOND, L., and PLATTNER, M. F. (eds.) 1993. *The Global Resurgence of Democracy.* Baltimore: Johns Hopkins University Press.

FEARON, J., and LAITIN, D. 1996. Explaining ethnic cooperation. *American Political Science Review*, 90: 715–29.

—— and WENDT, A. 2002. Rationalism vs constructivism. in *Handbook of International Relations*, ed. W. Charlsnaes, T. Risse, and B. A. Simmons. London: Sage.

FOUCAULT, M. 1979. *Discipline and Punish.* trans. A. Sheridan. New York: Vintage Books.

—— 1980. *Power/Knowledge*, ed. C. Gordon, trans. C. Gordon, L. Marshal, J. Mepham, and K. Soper. New York: Pantheon Books.

GALSTON, W. 1995. Two concepts of liberalism. *Ethics*, 105: 516–34.

GAVENTA, J. 1980. *Power and Powerlessness: Quiescence and rebellion in an Appalachian Valley.* Urbana: University of Illinois Press.

GEERTZ, C. 1963. The integrative revolution: primordial sentiments and civil polities in new states. Pp. 105–57 in *Old Societies and New States*, ed. C. Geertz, New York: Free Press.

GELLNER, E. 1983. *Nations and Nationalism.* Oxford: Blackwell.

—— 1994. *Conditions of Liberty: Civil Society and its Rivals.* New York: Allen Lane/Penguin.

GLENNY, M. 1992. *The Fall of Yugoslavia: The Third Balkan War.* Harmondsworth: Penguin.

GILROY, P. 2001. *Against Race: Imagining Political Culture Beyond the Color Line.* Cambridge, Mass.: Harvard University Press.

GOUREVITCH, P. 1998. *We Wish to Inform You that Tomorrow We Will be Killed with Our Families.* New York: Picador.

GUINIER, L., and TORRES, G. 2002. *The Miner's Canary: Enlisting Race, Resisting Power, Transforming Democracy.* Cambridge, Mass.: Harvard University Press

HARDIN, R. 1995. *One for All: The Logic of Group Conflict.* Princeton, NJ: Princeton University Press.

HAYWARD, C. R. 2000. *De-facing Power.* Cambridge: Cambridge University Press.

HOROWITZ, D. 1985. *Ethnic Groups in Conflict.* Berkeley: University of California Press.

—— 1991. *A Democratic South Africa?: Constitutional Engineering in a Divided Society.* Berkeley: University of California Press.

HTUN, M. 2004a. From "racial democracy" to affirmative action: changing state policy on race in Brazil. *Latin American Research Review*, 39: 60–89.

—— 2004b. Is gender like ethnicity? Representation of identity groups. *Perspectives on Politics*, 2: 439–58.

INKELES, A. 1966. The modernization of man. In *Modernization: The Dynamics of Growth*, ed. M. Weiner. New York: Basic Books.

INGLEHART, R., and BAKER, W. 2000. Modernization, globalization and the persistence of tradition: empirical evidence from 65 societies. *American Sociological Review*, 65: 19–51.

JABAR, F. A. 2004. Postconflict Iraq: a race of stability, reconstruction and legitimacy. *Special Report*, 120 (May). Washington, DC: United States Institute of Peace.

JUNG, C. 2000. *Then I Was Black: South African Political Identities in Transition*. New Haven, Conn.: Yale University Press.

—— 2003. The politics of indigenous identity: neoliberalism, cultural rights and the Mexican Zapatistas. *Social Research*, 70: 433–62

KALYVAS, S. N. 1998. Democracy and religious politics: evidence from Belgium. *Comparative Political Studies*, 31: 292–321.

KELLY, J. 2004. *Ethnic Politics in Europe: The Power of Norms and Incentives*. Princeton, NJ: University Press.

KYMLICKA, W. 1995. *Multicultural Citizenship*. Oxford: Oxford University Press.

LACLAU, E. (ed.) 1994. *The Making of Political Identities*. London: Verso.

—— and Mouffe, C. (eds.) 1985. *Hegemony and Socialist Strategy*. London: Verso.

LAITIN, D. 1998. *Identity in Formation: The Russian-Speaking Populations in the Near Abroad*. Ithaca, NY: Cornell University Press.

LERNER, D. 1958. *The Passing of Traditional Society*. New York: Free Press.

LIJPHART, A. 1977. *Democracy in Plural Societies: A Comparative Exploration*. New Haven, Conn.: Yale University Press.

—— 1985. Power sharing in South Africa. *Policy Papers in International Affairs* No. 24. Berkeley: Institute of International Studies, University of California.

LINZ, J. J., and STEPAN, A. 1996. Towards consolidated democracies. *Journal of Democracy*, 7(2): 14–33.

LIPSET, S. M. 1960. *Political Man*. Garden City, NY: Doubleday.

LUKES, S. 1974. *Power: A Radical View*. London: Macmillan.

MACEDO, S. 1995. Liberal civic education and religious fundamentalism: the case of God vs. John Rawls? *Ethics*, 105: 468–96.

—— (ed.) 1999. *Deliberative Politics: Essays on Democracy and Disagreement*. New York: Oxford University Press.

MANN, M. 1999. The dark side of democracy: the modern tradition of ethnic and political cleansing. *New Left Review*, 235: 18–45.

MAMDANI, M. 1996. *Citizen and Subject: Contemporary Africa and the Legacy of Late Colonialism*. Princeton, NJ: Princeton University Press.

—— 2002. *When Victims Become Killers: Colonialism, Nativism and the Genocide in Rwanda*. Princeton, NJ: Princeton University Press.

MARX, A. 1998. *Making Race And Nation: A Comparison of South Africa, the United States and Brazil*. Cambridge: Cambridge University Press.

—— 2003. *Faith in Nation: The Exclusionary Origins of Nationalism*. New York: Oxford University Press

MATTES, R. et al. 1999. Judgement and choice in the 1999 South African election. *Politikon*, 26 (2): 235–48.

MENDELBERG, T. 2001. *The Race Card: Campaign Strategy, Implicit Messages and the Norm of Equality* Princeton, NJ: Princeton University Press

MILL, J. S. 1857. *Considerations on Representative Government*. New York: H. Holt and Company.

MILL, J. S. 1969. *Three Essays on Religion*. New York: Greenwood Press.

MITCHELL, T. 1992. Going beyond the state? J. Bendix, B. Ollman, B. H. Sparrow and T. P. Mitchell. *American Political Science Review*, 86: 1007–21.

MOUFFE, C. 1992. Feminism, citizenship and radical democratic politics. Pp. 369–83 in *Feminists Theorize the Political*, ed. J. Butler and J. Scott. New York: Routledge.

ORDESHOOK, P. C., and SHVETSOVA, O. V. 1994. Ethnic heterogeneity, district magnitude and the number of parties. *American Journal of Political Science*, 38: 100–23.

PATTERSON, O. 1975. Context and choice in ethnic allegiance: a theoretical framework and Caribbean case study. Pp. 305–59 in *Ethnicity*, ed. N. Glazer and D. P. Moynihan. Cambridge, Mass.: Harvard University Press.

PELLER, G. 1995. Race-consciousness. In *Critical Race Theory*, ed. Crenshaw et al. 1995.

PLOTKE, D. 1995. Racial politics and the Clinton-Guinier episode. *Dissent*, 42: 221–35.

PREWITT, K. 2004. The census counts, the census classifies. In *Not Just Black and White*, ed. N. Foner and G. Fredrickson. New York: Russell Sage.

PRZEWORSKI, A., and LIMONGI F. 1997. Modernization: theories and facts. *World Politics*, 49: 155–84.

—— ALVAREZ, M. E., CHEIBUB, J. A., and LIMONGI, F. 2000. *Democracy and Development*. Cambridge: Cambridge University Press.

RABUSHKA, A., and SHEPSLE, K. A. 1972. *Politics in Plural Societies*. Columbus, Oh.: Merrill.

RAWLS, J. 1972. *A Theory of Justice*. Oxford: Clarendon Press.

—— 1985. Justice as fairness: political not metaphysical. *Philosophy & Public Affairs*, 14: 223–51.

—— 1993. *Political Liberalism*. New York: Columbia University Press.

REED, A. L., JR. 2002. *You Don't Need a Weatherman to Know Which Way the Wind Blows: Unraveling the Relations of Race And Class in American Politics*. Mimeo., Dept. Political Science, New School for Social Research.

RUSTOW, D. 1970. Transitions to democracy: toward a dynamic model. *Comparative Politics*, 2: 337–63.

SANDEL, M. 1998. *Liberalism and the Limits of Justice*. Cambridge: Cambridge University Press.

SARTRE, J. P. 1990. *Critique of Dialectical Reason*. London: Verso.

Scott, J. C. 1985. *Weapons of the Weak: Everyday Forms of Peasant Resistance*. New Haven, Conn.: Yale University Press

SCOTT, J. W. 1999. *Gender and the Politics of History*, rev. edn. New York: Columbia University Press.

SMITH, R. 2004. The puzzling place of race in American political science. *PS: Political Science and Politics*, 37: 41–5.

SNIDERMAN, P., and CARMINES, E. 1997. *Reaching Beyond Race*. Cambridge, Mass.: Harvard University Press

TAYLOR, C. 1994. The politics of recognition. In *Multiculturalism*, ed. A. Gutmann. Princeton, NJ: Princeton University Press.

—— 1998. The dynamic of democratic exclusion. *Journal of Democracy*, 9(4): 143–56.

THOMPSON, E. P. 1963. *The Making of the English Working Class*. New York: Vintage.

VAIL, L. (ed.) 1989. *The Creation of Tribalism in Southern Africa*. Berkeley: University of California Press.

WAGLEY, C. (ed.) 1972. *Race and Class in Rural Brazil*. New York: Russell and Russell.

WENDT, A., and SHAPIRO, I. 1997. The misunderstood promise of realist social theory. In *Contemporary Empirical Political Theory*, ed. K. R. Monroe. Berkeley: University of California Press.

YOUNG, C. 1976. *The Politics of Cultural Pluralism*. Madison: University of Wisconsin Press.

CHAPTER 20

LANGUAGE, ITS STAKES, AND ITS EFFECTS

SUSAN GAL

AMONG the oldest professorships in political science is the Johan Skytte Chair of Eloquence and Government, established in Sweden in 1622. The title reminds us that in the seventeenth century, as in classical antiquity, oratory and linguistic persuasion were believed to be fundamental to politics. By contrast, despite the increasing influence of post-structuralist notions of discourse, and an abiding concern in the US with the political effects of mass media, the relationship of language to politics has been relatively peripheral in contemporary political science. Linguistic anthropology, communication studies, and cultural studies have more actively taken up what is at stake in the political uses and effects of language. This chapter draws on those fields but also evaluates a growing body of work on the politics of language within political science itself.

My aim is to illustrate how linguistic practices have an impact on politics by choosing three sets of examples that rely on different definitions of "language" and different presuppositions about its functions and organization. Such presuppositions are *ideologies of language* or cultures of language (Silverstein 1979; Schieffelin, Woolard, and Kroskrity 1998). They are ideological in the sense that they provide perspectival views of the relationship between linguistic practices and social life, and reflect the interests and moral commitments of particular social positions. Language ideologies, in this technical sense, are important because they shape the research programs of scholars as much as they guide political activity. They are often unnoticed features of political theory and are embedded in pre-theoretical common sense about the linguistic aspects of political processes.

The first set of examples concerns linguistic nationalism in state systems. What are the effects of state actions on the linguistic usages of their populations; what are the effects of linguistic diversity on states? The evidence concerns patterns of language standardization and the emergence of languages of regional and global communication. Second, I turn to a different definition of language, one based on linguistic practices and their indexicalities. The examples come from the linguistic repertoires and language ideologies of speakers oriented not to states but to global networks that are outside the purview of standardization. Finally, in a third perspective on language, I consider how narratives, frames, and discursive genres of various kinds are used in public events to construct and occasionally subvert popular understandings of political processes. The focus here is on the naturalization of institutional power through linguistic means. Most relevant to these questions is substantive research on dispute settlement and public political performance. This third set of issues raises, in contemporary guise, the classical question of political persuasion.

1 ETHNOLINGUISTIC IDENTITIES IN STATE SYSTEMS

Recent political developments have again highlighted the significance of linguistic issues. Several post-socialist states have broken up, apparently along ethnolinguistic lines; many states, the European Union, and other suprastate organizations must choose among official languages; diasporic migrant populations are increasingly active; and linguistic minorities across the globe are voicing claims for rights and autonomy. These phenomena raise questions (and fears) about the compatibility of linguistic heterogeneity and political unity within a nation-state regime. Similar questions emerged during the rise of post-colonial states in the 1960s.

In response to those earlier changes, political theorists argued that modern states have strong interests in establishing linguistic uniformity throughout their territories. For example, Gellner (1983) stressed the supposed efficiency of a single language of administration, and its unifying and modernizing effects. Hobsbawm (1990) noted that it is usually local elites with a stake in teaching, preaching, and writing in their shared language who organize separatist national movements along linguistic lines against multilingual empires. Anderson (1983) argued that the "imagination" of national communities depends on the coalescence of a single language that can then be used as the vehicle for print capitalism. Newspapers and novels, written in a shared language, sold in regional markets, and read in anonymous simultaneity, create for the masses a sense of national identity and emotional attachment to the nation.

One weakness of these theories was that they implicitly accepted the very assumptions on which linguistic nationalism was built. Their inspiration—like that of linguistic nationalism itself—was the German Romantic notion, exemplified in the writings of Herder and Humboldt (but with deeper roots in European thought) that language constitutes the basis for divisions among different types of people. It does so by expressing the inner spirit or thought of its speakers who, by virtue of a shared referential code—a linguistic unity—constitute a nation and therefore deserve political autonomy over the territory where that language is spoken. In this ideology, the referential function of language is primary; humans are assumed to be inherently monolingual. And the supposedly natural fact of linguistic unity comes to justify and legitimate claims to territorial and political unity (see Bauman and Briggs 2000). In a blunt entailment of this view: if you speak a variant of my language, then your territory should belong to me. Linguistic heterogeneity looms as a political danger when one adopts such presuppositions.

This Herderian ideal—an excellent example of a language ideology—has been enormously influential as an image of centralized politics and socioeconomic progress. Through compulsory and monolingual primary education, general conscription, and increasingly unified, national labor markets, Western European states in the nineteenth century attempted to create the Herderian ideal they simultaneously claimed to have already achieved (Weber 1976). The ideal was exported to the rest of the world through Europe's colonial expansion. Yet the Herderian constellation of one language = one nation = one state = one territory does not exist now, nor has it ever existed as a sociolinguistic reality in Europe, nor in any other part of the globe. Even the most centralized of European states (e.g. France) continue to have linguistic minorities in their periphery. Even some of the smallest (e.g. Norway) have multiple official languages. Nor is multilingualism itself a human oddity. Widespread multilingualism—outside of modern state systems—was characteristic of many areas of North America, the South Pacific, Australia, and parts of native South America, even before European contact, and has continued to be common since. Nevertheless, a state-centered monolingual ideal was justified as a primordial pattern by Europeans and has been the organizing principle of the current world system of nation states. It thus became a sign of "modernity." The political and economic problems of post-colonial states were often blamed on patterns of multilingualism that were stigmatized as the source of disunity and thus a cause of "underdevelopment."

Researchers turned to the linguistic policies and practices of such post-colonial states and tried to understand their problems by modeling multilingual political systems (Zolberg 2001). Attention later turned to post-socialist cases, and European as well as American linguistic minorities. The Council of Europe published its charter on regional or minority languages and called for a future in which each European citizen would communicate in a minimum of two languages in addition to his or her mother tongue. This paradoxically reemphasized Herderian ethno-linguistic identities, while also declaring the desirability of "linguistic diversity," now in the interests of fostering a "knowledge economy." Partly in response, the study of state-sponsored multilingualism gained political urgency.

Much of this newer work has taken a rational choice perspective, and has made two major contributions. First, it has explored language as a commodity that is bought and sold in the form of school curricula, private classes, personal services, lectures, or published texts. This is parallel to work in linguistic anthropology that has stressed the materiality of linguistic practices as objects of exchange and resources for access to upward mobility (Gal 1989; Heller 1988; Irvine 1989). The political scientists go further. They treat languages not only as commodities but also as collective goods, so their spread and restriction are explicable in accordance with economic principles: e.g. free riding, transaction costs, protectionism, and free trade. These studies weigh the incentives, constraints, and costs of choosing an official language, or designating required languages at various levels of education (Pool 1991). What are realistic policy choices for working languages in suprastate contexts such as the European Union, and who should bear the costs of translations (Grin 2003)? Speakers' preferences with respect to language learning are taken to be mainly instrumental. Choices are influenced by speakers' knowledge of the choices of others: The language adopted by the most speakers as a second language has greatest communicative reach and thus becomes all the more desirable (Lieberson 1982). Choices are also constrained by previous investments, e.g. in school systems, or in languages already learned, as well as by elite strategies that exclude those who cannot arrange access.

A second contribution is the notion of a "world language system" which can be modeled by arranging languages in a hierarchy based on the number of first- and second-language speakers each can boast. Predictions about speakers' linguistic repertoires can be made on the basis of such models. In one version, multilingual speakers are seen as the link between "peripheral" languages and "central" ones, which are similarly linked to "supercentral" languages that are in turn linked to the single "hypercentral" language in the world, English (DeSwaan 2001; Van Parijs 2000). The prediction is that speakers learn the languages "more central" than their "own," but not those less so. This produces a "three, plus or minus one" rule. For instance in India: English and Hindi at the national level, a regional language added where appropriate, and a minority language added for speakers whose native language is not the regional one (Laitin 1993). The general logic is also applicable to the European Union, yielding "two, plus or minus one." Speakers learn a national language, upwardly mobile students insist on also learning English. Those who start with English as their home language will have no incentive to learn any others. But those whose home variety is a minority language (or language of migration) will presumably learn three. This pattern resembles the ideal declared by the Council of Europe, and rests on similar economic principles.

Such individual and state strategies have broad political implications. In contrast to religion, race, or ethnicity, state policy cannot be neutral with respect to language for a number of reasons. Government must communicate with its population in some official way, so language cannot be entirely privatized. If there is to be state-supported education, should language teaching be a part of it? Those individuals with access to multilingual education, and thus to several languages, will be more likely—in non-English speaking countries—to enter a regional or global elite, thereby enjoying considerable advantages. Should the cost be publicly funded or should it be borne by individual families?

Furthermore, there are significant inequalities between the citizens of different states on linguistic grounds. Those who grow up speaking a language of wide communication such as English are (invisibly) advantaged since they need not invest in language education at all. Indeed, native English speakers actually benefit from the learning of English by others since it increases the communicative reach of English and hence of their own reading and writings. Should native English speakers be allowed to free ride in this way on the common benefits of English, or should they be required to support financially the teaching of English world-wide? Would such support be seen as linguistic justice or linguistic imperialism (Bhatt 2001)? It is in this policy context, and with the fear that speakers of small languages will be forced to abandon them—either by the logic of rational choice or through coercion—and adopt languages of wider communication, that the issue of "language rights" has taken a prominent place in normative discussions of liberal and democratic theory (Kymlicka and Patten 2003).

Despite important insights, these lines of research are seriously limited by a reliance on named languages—such as Greek, Swahili, Hindi—as units of analysis in model-building, and a neglect of phenomena outside of standardized regimes. I will take up each of these points in turn.

Language labels do not correspond to the linguistic practices of populations but to cultural ideals. Like standards of measurement, *standardized languages* are artfully created social facts. They are made by linguistic experts who engage in corpus building: orthography, vocabulary, literary genres, and grammatical patterns, all in imitation of culturally valued models (such as Latin, Sanskrit), with the goal of enabling the variety to be used in all cultural domains. Institutions such as schools maintain the forms of the standard. Often, the language experts operate with ideologies of linguistic "purity." They try to hide or expurgate the traces of past linguistic relations, dialect chains, contact, and mutual intelligibility that, usually on political grounds, are considered undesirable. The results of these activities are linguistic forms that appear to contrast maximally with other, parallel standards. Very few people speak such "languages." Yet they are assumed to "belong" to speakers who claim what is ideologically construed as a corresponding ethnicity or nationality. This is a form of coercive isomorphism among elites engaged in nation-building.

Standardization is not only a linguistic but also a cultural—or better, an ideological—process, with political consequences. It is not everywhere the same, and need not entail the denigration and elimination of alternative linguistic practices, as the historical case of Sanskrit illustrates (Pollock 2000). Nevertheless, those who today are oriented towards a standardized linguistic regime share certain values. They consider anything other than the standard to be inadequate, even non-language. In contrast to speakers of non-written or "local" linguistic forms, they focus on denotation and correctness. They accept the authority of standard speech, even if they do not speak it, and defer to experts for judgments of correctness on linguistic matters. Speech devalued by expert opinion is taken to be an outward sign of the speakers's ignorance or cognitive deficit. Bourdieu (1991) has used this process of standardization as a key example of symbolic domination and misrecognition. In Bakhtinian (1981) terms, standardization is the process by which the centripetal forces of regimentation and centralization, most often linked to state apparatuses (but sometimes also to churches or other major political institutions) construct unified and ossified languages, in the context of and against the constant innovation and creativity of centrifugal forces. The linguistic diversity that results from these opposed forces operating together is what Bakhtin called *heteroglossia*.

2   FROM STANDARDS TO THE STUDY OF INDEXICAL SYSTEMS

To avoid thinking in terms of named, unified languages, let us take standardization as one of several ideological perspectives, and compare its force and effect to that of contrasting assumptions. So-called "minority languages," "local languages," and "regional dialects" display the underside of standardization. All three categories depend on speakers seeing their own linguistic practices not from their own viewpoint as its practitioners, but from afar, as peripheral to a defining center to which they have been recruited or subsumed, sometimes by force (Keane 1997). Locality itself is a matter of perspective, in this case a perspective on language. The center can be a state, a colonial empire, a missionizing project, a capitalist market. The familiar cultural logic of temporal stages that contrast modernity and tradition is projected onto linguistic forms. The standard language evokes ideals of modernity, including political centralization, national unity, socioeconomic efficiency, and progress. These values emerge simultaneously with nostalgia for the opposing ideals of tradition and authenticity, projected onto the local linguistic forms that modernity supposedly displaces.

One common response of peripheralized elites to these projections is to attempt to gain recognition from the metropole by adopting its ideology and embarking on standardization that tries to rival the language(s) of the center. The attempt is filled with contradictions that divide the minority or regional populations in politically significant ways. Some minority (or non-standard) linguistic forms are selected as a newly recognized (minority) standard. But others are inevitably omitted, thus further stigmatizing many of the speakers whose linguistic practices the (minority) standardizing project was supposed to valorize. Some minority speakers counsel their children to abandon the minority linguistic forms and pay more attention to learning the national language, in the interests of socioeconomic mobility. The elites who are the minority standardizers rely for their livelihood on modern technologies such as textbooks, mass media, and schools, but gain legitimacy with national elites from the traditional authenticity that peripheral linguistic forms and their speakers embody for the modern state and often for heritage tourism. Yet in the minority population overall, those who are most fluent and "authentic" are often socially disadvantaged, hence most concerned with upward mobility, and least committed to using the linguistic forms. Contrary to expectation, then, standardization creates hierarchical heterogeneity, not uniformity.

Ethnographic studies show many of the everyday interactional techniques by which linguistic varieties are demoted in the act of attempting to enhance their value. In translation and teaching, schools directly juxtapose the minority forms— whether defined as "dialects" of the state language, or historically quite divergent varieties—to the state language (Jaffe 1999). The minority variety's difference from the state language is thus emphasized, but in ways that display it as either missing components or having too many of them when the state language is the standard of comparison. The difference becomes iconic of deficiency or excess. It is taken as a flaw of the minority linguistic form and of the speakers onto whom the quality of excess or deficiency is projected (Irvine and Gal 2000). Conflicts among minority elites often involve disputes over what constitutes proof of linguistic knowledge; who is licensed to know best (Hill 1985). Or, there is conflict over the extent to which the boundary with the state language must be policed, and the amount of mixing that should be tolerated (Woolard 1998). Among certain peripheralized populations, for instance Silesian-ethnics in eastern Europe, elites insist that mixing among standard languages is itself the group's characteristic and defining mode of communicative practice.

More radically, some groups oppose the objectification of linguistic practices that is a prerequisite of standardization, indeed of language teaching and of linguistic research itself. This is in part because they hold contrasting language ideologies, ones that define situated efficacy and socially embedded performance— sometimes in sacred contexts—as the most significant aspects of speech. They therefore refuse the "reduction" of speech to writing, the handling of language qua code, the focus on referential function abstracted from usage, and the focus on the link between meaning and form that is the implicit ideology on which diction- aries and grammars are built. Their reasons for opposition are often political. Hopi elders, for instance, argue that teaching Hopi in school, separating it from its uses in order to make it parallel to languages such as English or Spanish, would not only reduce its performative power, but would allow non-Hopi to have access to Hopi language and culture, thereby threatening Hopi sovereignty (Whiteley 2003).

When linguistic practices are in danger of being abandoned, social scientists and now NGOs rush to protect and record the obsolescent language. The rhetoric used to justify this salvage work draws on biological metaphors (e.g. the value of linguistic diversity as parallel to biodiversity; or untapped funds of folk knowledge as parallel to unknown medicinal plants), or on language rights or democratic procedures to decide fairly and justly about language use for groups and individ- uals. Yet, often what requires protection is not a linguistic code but, more radically, a set of presuppositions about the place of linguistic practices in social life that is distinctly at odds with the very forms of documentation and justice that are supposed to provide protection. In short, one would have to destroy the social portion of linguistic practices in order to "save" them. Language rights that presuppose a democratic public sphere in which justice is assured when all lan- guages can be used in equivalent ways for similar purposes, misses the deeper point that language ideologies are themselves diverse and as important to safeguard as the parts of them that non-experts call "languages" (Errington 2003).

Linguistic anthropology has proposed an alternative approach. It starts with the full range of linguistic practices that Bakhtin called *heteroglossia*. This diversity is evident in the linguistic repertoire of any interacting group. It can include several named languages, and always abounds in unnamed genres, registers, varieties, and voicings that mix together what the institutions of standardization try to keep apart. The objects of analysis for this analytic approach are the indexical links between linguistic patterns and social categories. Linguistic features such as the details of pronunciation, lexical collocations, discourse practices, speech routines, genre conventions, all can signal categories of identities, events, spaces, and ethnic or human stereotypes for those who are active in that particular sociolinguistic field. The patterns of indexical links are organized into language ideologies. They are part of the practices, beliefs, and presuppositions that connect the social world to linguistic signs for particular groups of speakers (Silverstein 1979; Gal and Irvine 1995; Duranti 1997). More concretely, as we saw in the Hopi case, language ideologies are folk assumptions about who speaks and should speak how, for what reason and effect, under what circumstances.

By tracing the regional and global circulation of genres, varieties, accents, and the meanings they *index* (i.e. point to and thereby evoke), it is possible to reveal the diffuse, non-state institutions of cultural authority that recognize and validate those meanings, and that are themselves thereby supported. One can map quite a different "world language system" than that visible through the distribution of state-oriented standard languages and the ideologies that regiment them.

Migrants construct images of a global hierarchy of countries, linguistic forms, and options. This partially parallels the hierarchies modeled by rational choice theorists. But the migrants' models are built from a narrower data base and limited social positions. The migrants' view is based on information from mass media and from relatives who have migrated and perhaps returned. As a result, migrants' linguistic responses and abilities do not fit academic models. Albanian speakers in Macedonia are learning English instead of the Slavic state language, whether or not they migrate. Mayan speakers from Central America arrive in the US without knowledge of Spanish, their national language. They are stigmatized in the US as "Hispanic" foreigners. Portuguese migrants in Paris are also stigmatized. Although they are intelligible in French, their speech is recognizably accented as Portuguese. There are no neutral linguistic varieties. Linguistically, at least, the migrants cannot go home again. For when they return to Portugal, they are further stigmatized as arrogant and vulgar when they bring with them traces of their French competence (Koven 2004). These experiences have consequences. Diasporic migrants such as these in the EU as elsewhere, want access to both standard languages for their children. Academic models should include the political implications of foreign accents, the results of informal learning, the social stratification of linguistic forms within standardized languages, and global linguistic hierarchies as constructed from diverse spatial and sociohistorical locations.

A look at some other indexical patterns offers further insights into the creation of communicative networks and the political significance of (non-standard) linguistic practices, especially those that signal contact with "elsewhere." Many young semi-speakers of Basque avoid the language because of the "traditional" identity it indexes, in contrast to Castillian. But they are enthusiastic about pirate radio programs and newspapers that deliberately intersperse Basque and Castilian, taking advantage of the differences and overlaps between them. They identify this kind of word-play with the usage of African-American youth, which then extends to Basque a "modern," even "hip" aura, making it part of a global music and youth scene (Urla 2001). Word-play with English and Swahili operates in a parallel way in Tanzania. To be sure, the English-derived store signs and expressions inter-spersed with Swahili would be rejected as mistakes by English schoolteachers. But schooled correctness is irrelevant within the local Tanzanian context, where what counts is the social indexing of the performer's identity as clever and sophisticated. English forms provide a resource for speakers and writers to create cosmo-politan identities for themselves. By displaying a familiarity with wider circuits of communication, they can contribute materially to creating and activating such circuits (Blommaert 2003).

Another example of a discursive genre that forges transnational communicative linkages is Arabic poetry, sold and circulated on audiotapes throughout the Middle East. Poets comment on life circumstances and exhort their listeners to thought and actions. But it is not Arabic linguistic forms in themselves that create the huge following these tapes enjoy. More important are the poetic genres performed, and the skill of the poets in (re)creating traditional poetry while turning it to contempor-ary uses such as critical commentary on the commodification of poetry itself. It is the poetic form that indexes the poets' and the audiences' identities and political interests (Miller 2002). In all these examples, the institutions that recognize and validate the identities signaled are not state-oriented, standardizing ones such as schools, museums, and dictionaries, but more diffuse ones such as global youth networks, popular media, and far-flung diasporic networks with political potential. It would be interesting to see research on the translation problems that arise inside international advocacy networks that, in a parallel way, mediate among multiple constituencies.

Ideologies of purity contrast with other ideologies, discussed above, that accept and even value the "foreign." They have contrasting implications for the develop-ment of social networks and political linkages. Those valuing purity operate with an impetus to separation, presupposing that linguistic and social difference arise from isolation and firm boundaries. Scholarly frameworks are as implicated in these broad ideological trends as are non-expert frameworks. For example, purist assumptions recall the nineteenth-century linguistic model of branching (Stamm-baum) language change. By contrast, ideologies that value the foreign can incorpor-ate the notion that differentiation arises out of proximity and contact. This happens through mixtures of linguistic practices from different sources that are amalgam-ated into something new. Or it can occur by the replication and "domestication" within one's own speech practices of forms identified as foreign, valued for their aura of distance and power, and deliberately maintained for that very reason (Rutherford 2003).

Young speakers in London high schools create new linguistic forms and identity claims through this second kind of ideology. Their practices are not limited to the varieties of English associated with their own ethnic groups (e.g. Pakistani, other South Asian, or West Indian). They quote or imitate the conventional accents, slang, and genres stereotypically associated with other ethnic groups. The students try on the ethnic identities of others, parodying and echoing fellow students. Over time, they include the enactment and display of others' identities within their own repertoires. The several forms used by any one high school student often evoke the voices of more than one ethnic group, and thereby provide the cultural potential for novel identities and relations among groups. The London-based social identities documented in ethnographic studies carve up the post-colonial world in ways rarely expected on the basis of studies that are limited to standard languages and state-wide politics (Rampton 1995).

3   NATURALIZATIONS OF INSTITUTIONAL POWER

In the discussion of language as a named and objectified unit, I already gave an example of the way in which beliefs about linguistic practices *authorize* other social activities: Within Herderian ideology, the widespread use of what came to be called a particular linguistic form (a "language") enacted and performatively created the ethnic unity it seemed only to describe. Because linguistic practices were seen as independent of human will and hence "natural," the supposed unity of those speaking a single language legitimated claims to ethnic, political, and territorial unity.

This is a crucial political process that works not only for ethnicity and nationalism, but for institutional arrangements generally. Presuppositions about language that are parts of language ideologies systematically work to naturalize social arrangements that seem to have nothing to do with language (see Silverstein and Urban 1996; Gal and Woolard 2001). Participants can interactionally evoke or create a social reality that seems to have been there already; one that interactants seem only to be labeling. This is not the mere enactment or performance of a social category, as in Butler's (1990) conception. Rather, it might well be called the magic of performative ritual, since it actually brings about the social arrangements at issue, and occurs as much in secular as in sacred settings. In this final section, I provide some examples of how performative rituals, when successful, create the impression that current social arrangements are necessary or uniquely justified, thereby legitimating social relations of power.

A simple example is the politics of representation. These are controversies over how some phenomenon is labeled and who is licensed officially and authoritatively to decide on its name and nature. The process has two components. One consists of the public discussion, often taking place in courtrooms and journals, in which professional experts argue over whose jurisdiction encompasses the particular social problem of which the phenomenon is purportedly an example. Such discussions are themselves the means by which the problem is constructed, and the borders of professional jurisdictions are drawn. The analysis of such discussions

in terms of discursive genres and forms of rhetoric is illuminating for an understanding of the linguistic means by which cultural authority is captured. It is also
the way in which moral responsibility and blame are allocated. For instance, once
learning disability has been proposed as the label for a set of phenomena, is it a
pedagogical, a psychological, or a medical issue?

The second component consists of particular incidents of diagnosis. When a
child is categorized as "learning disabled," the consequences for the life of the child
and the family are considerable. Conversation analysts have shown that turn-taking
practices and discursive assumptions taken for granted in psychiatric interviews
and parent–teacher–doctor conferences, combine to produce the child's labeling,
even when parents are providing evidence that would, under other circumstances,
count against it (Mehan 1996). Both aspects of the politics of representation rely on
the discursive genres accepted by professionals and lay people involved. Authoriz-
ing beliefs (i.e. language ideologies) about the relationship of knowledge to specific
linguistic practices make those genres credible. Such discursive genres would
include scholarly journals and their forms of argument and evidence, the practical
experience of teachers, the professional experience of doctors, and the special form
of intimate knowledge that parents can claim concerning their own children. More
obviously political, but with the same general structure, are the debates about what
to call a phenomenon such as abortion. Is it a medical procedure that is the bodily
right of the woman bearing the fetus, or is it "murder"? The political repercussions
are too familiar to detail.

There is some resemblance here to Foucauldian notions of discourse, which he
defined as "practices that systematically form the objects of which they speak"
(Foucault 1972, 49). But Foucault and his many acolytes rarely attend to the
conversational and textual practices that "form the objects," nor to the metadiscourses about language's relation to the social world (language ideologies) that
regiment the particular forms of talk that allow those objects to come into being in
the real-time world of social interaction or textual production. The kind of
performativity that is involved here is more related to Austin's theory of speech
acts, Hymes and Gumperz's ethnography of speaking, and Jakobson's, Tambiah's,
and Silverstein's extension of Peircean semiotics, than to Foucault. A ritual can
transform social reality when it is an *indexical icon*; this means that the action
performs and thereby brings about or seems to demonstrate the self-evident truth
and efficacy of the very relationship or quality that it is seen merely to display.

It is worth emphasizing the contrast between this approach and most discourse
analysis. In the sophisticated form practiced by historians of political thought, the
goal of close attention to language is to recreate the presuppositions with which
political terms made sense to contemporaries, and the ambiguities or controversies that flowed around the terms (Pocock 1960). In the more common and less
fastidious form, discourse analyses are essentially decoding operations. Messages
are assumed to be first and foremost statements about the world, so that a

political discussion, commercial advertisement, or media report is "reduced" to its propositional content and then that content is restated by the analyst. Analyses of messages from those in power consist of attempting to show that the propositional content is misleading in the relevant historical context, or designed to appeal to preexisting prejudices. When messages are judged to originate from the less powerful, their content is labeled as "speaking truth to power." In such simplified views, political communications are "read" as (bad) representations about the world rather than ideologically mediated actions materially located *in* the world and therefore capable of changing it. More abstractly put, most discourse analyses provide critiques of two-way *semantic* relations (word-to-world), rather than three-way *pragmatic* relations (speaker-in-world-with-word). Language ideologies constitute an indispensable fourth term. It is under the aegis of language ideologies—cultural, *metapragmatic* assumptions about the relationship between words, speakers, and worlds—that verbal action in the world is effective (Silverstein 1979).

Dispute settlement is an arena in which discursive practices are efficacious in the performative sense I have been describing. A telling example is the Islamic courts of Kenya, to which Muslim women and men appeal when faced with marital disputes. The form in which troubles can be recounted is set in advance, as is the case in most systems of legal decision-making. But forms of talk are also understood to be indexical of categories of people. In this case the categories are not ethnic but gendered. According to local cultural understandings (language ideologies), to be considered good and proper wives, women should not engage in the speech act of complaining, and certainly not about domestic conflict. A double bind thereby constrains women in lodging complaints: if they do not complain they cannot rectify what they perceive as unfair treatment. If they do complain they undermine their own claims to be the kind of upstanding women who should be treated in ways that preclude complaint. The theoretical point is that women's interactional, linguistic practice is not simply an enactment of something that already exists as a social or cultural fact. On the contrary, it is through the act of complaining, and the way they manage to finesse it, that women performatively create themselves, either as unworthy wives, or, if they are skilled enough, as women who are complaining despite themselves and with justified cause (Hirsch 1995). The complaining storyteller and the events at issue are constructed together. Outcomes are always emergent, contingent, and highly vulnerable to the unexpected actions of others.

Telling stories about an event—as in trials, political speeches, or social science—always involves simultaneously positioning the story itself vis-à-vis other versions, and positioning (constructing) the storyteller as a particular kind of person in the context of the storytelling event. We make ourselves through the stories we tell; and the credibility of our stories is inflected by who we can claim to be (Ochs and Capps 2001). From this dual contextualization is derived the authority and persuasiveness of narratives. In themselves, narratives have well-understood structures and are among the most powerful forms of explanation and of self-justification. But there are no narratives that are free of the interests and biases of the social position from which they are seen to be told. Nor are any free of the conventions (language ideologies) and rival accounts evident in the storytelling context into which they are inserted. We are all in the same situation as the Kenyan women in marital court.

How are reasons and narratives made authoritative? Bakhtin (1981) described it as a process of "ventriloquation," always a borrowing of authority from elsewhere. In today's societies authoritative cultural institutions include science, gods (directly or through quotation of scripture), nations or publics and their needs or desires, personal experience, nature, and law. Speakers characteristically efface themselves, claiming to be merely the mouthpiece through which the culturally accepted authority "speaks." In the case of science, experts ususally adopt a "voice from nowhere" that indexes objectivity, as though they themselves were uninvolved in creating the results they present. By contrast, in speaking the law, one disappears behind specification and minute attention to procedures. Authoritative institutions themselves are created in part through metadiscourses. Major historical examples include the philosophical justifications for republican rather than monarchical government, or the logic of buying and selling previously inalienable property such as labor and land, as in early arguments for capitalism (e.g. Habermas 1989; Hirschman 1997). Importantly, such metadiscourses specify the kind of conventional speech or form of argument that will count as evidence of and support for the new authority. The semiotic techniques by which individuals and governments invoke (ventriloquate) culturally powerful authorities, thereby borrowing their power, seem crucial as subject matter for any discipline claiming to understand the language of politics and the practical processes of political persuasion.

A final example of these points comes from democratic theory, which has shifted from vote-based models to ones that call for opinion-formation and deliberation by an informed and active public (demos) to justify institutional action. Deliberation about opposing views seems to promise the legitimation that voting alone cannot (Kymlicka and Patten 2003). The European Union, by these criteria, seems to have a "democracy deficit" because linguistic diversity, the argument goes, is an obstacle to the formation of a Europe-wide public that, once formed, could be a collective that engages in democratic discussion (Grimm 1995). The EU may well have a democratic deficit, but it is not explicable in these terms. As scholars have noted, "publics" are real social facts, but they are performatively created, much as nations are, but on different grounds. There was no United States of America (and certainly no linguistic uniformity) in the eighteenth century that could ratify the American Declaration of Independence. Writing, signing, publishing, and circulating the document were the acts that created the social unit it was, in retrospect, understood to represent. Similar feats of reflexive, boot-strapping performativity are accomplished for the creation of any public (Warner 2002). It is the institutional organs—including multilingual ones—that the public's existence requires and legitimates that will subsequently assure the public's continuance, if those organs are powerful enough.

On the basis of the research discussed here, it is evident that language is a form of social control as well as a means of reality-construction, thus a crucial part of the exercise of power. But the works reviewed suggest that this formulation is not sufficient. The most fruitful directions of research are those that can specify what aspects and definitions of language are involved; what power, control, and language itself are taken to mean in the sociocultural contexts at issue; and what general processes of semiotics, interaction, performance, and strategizing connect the linguistic practices to political effects.

REFERENCES

ANDERSON, B. 1983. *Imagined Communities*. London: Verso.

BAKHTIN, M. 1981. *The Dialogic Imagination*. Austin: University of Texas Press.

BAUMAN, R., and BRIGGS, C. 2000. Language philosophy as language ideology. Pp. 139–204 in *Regimes of Language*, ed. P. Kroskrity. Santa Fe, N. Mex.: School of American Research.

BHATT, R. M. 2001. World Englishes. *Annual Review of Anthropology*, 30: 527–50.

BLOMMAERT, J. 2003. A sociolinguistics of globalization. *Journal of Sociolinguistics*, 7: 607–23.

BOURDIEU, P. 1991. *Language and Symbolic Power*. Cambridge, Mass.: Harvard University Press.

BUTLER, J. 1990. *Gender Trouble*. New York: Routledge.

DESWAAN, A. 2001. *Words of the World*. London: Polity.

DURANTI, A. 1997 *Linguistic Anthropology*. Cambridge: Cambridge University Press.

ERRINGTON, J. 2003. Getting language rights. *American Anthropologist*, 105: 723–32.

FOUCAULT, M. 1972. *The Archaeology of Knowledge*. New York: Pantheon Books.

GAL, S. 1989. Language and political economy. *Annual Review of Anthropology*, 18: 345–67.

—— and IRVINE, J. T. 1995. The boundaries of languages and disciplines: how ideologies construct difference. *Social Research*, 62: 996–1001.

—— and WOOLARD, K. (eds.) 2001. *Languages and Publics*. Manchester: St. Jerome's Press.

GELLNER, E. 1983. *Nations and Nationalism*. Ithaca, NY: Cornell University Press.

GRIMM, D. 1995. Does Europe need a constitution? *European Law Journal*, 1: 282–302.

GRIN, F. 2003. *Language Policy Evaluation and Europe*. New York: Palgrave.

HABERMAS, J. 1989. *Structural Transformation of the Public Sphere*. Cambridge, Mass.: MIT Press.

HELLER, M. (ed.) 1988. *Codeswitching*. Berlin: Mouton de Gruyter.

HILL, J. 1985. The grammar of consciousness and the consciousness of grammar. *American Ethnologist*, 12: 725–37.

HIRSCH, S. 1995. *Pronouncing and Persevering*. Chicago: University of Chicago Press

HIRSCHMAN, A. O. 1997. *The Passions and the Interests*. Princeton, NJ: Princeton University Press.

HOBSBAWM, E. 1990. *Nations and Nationalism since 1780*. Cambridge: Cambridge University Press.

IRVINE, J. T. 1989. When talk isn't cheap: language and political economy. *American Ethnologist*, 12: 725–37.

——and GAL, S. 2000 Language ideology and linguistic differentiation. Pp. 35–84 in *Regimes of Language*, ed. P. Kroskrity. Santa Fe, N. Mex.: School of American Research.

JAFFE, A. 1999. *Ideologies in Action*. New York: Walter de Gruyter.

KEANE, W. 1997. Knowing one's place: national language and the idea of the local in eastern Indonesia. *Cultural Anthropology*, 12: 1–17.

KOVEN, M. 2004 Transnational perspectives on sociolinguistic capital among Luso-descendants in France and Portugal. *American Ethnologist*, 31: 270–90.

KYMLICKA, W., and PATTEN, A. (eds.) 2003. *Language Rights and Political Theory*. Oxford: Oxford University Press.

LAITIN, D. 1993. The game theory of language regimes. *International Political Science Review*, 14: 227–39.

LIEBERSON, S. 1982. Forces affecting language spread. Pp. 37–62 in *Language Spread*, ed. R. L. Cooper. Bloomington: University of Indiana Press.

MEHAN, H. 1996. The making of an LD student. In Silverstein and Urban 1996, 253–76.

MILLER, F. 2002. Metaphors of commerce: trans-valuing tribalism in Yemeni audiocassette poetry. *International Journal of Middle East Studies*, 34: 29–57.

OCHS, E., and Capps, L. 2001. *Living Narrative*. Cambridge, Mass.: Harvard University Press.

POCOCK, J. G. A. 1960. *Politics, Language and Time*. Chicago: University of Chicago Press.

POLLOCK, S. 2000. Cosmopolitan and vernacular in history. *Public Culture*, 12: 591–25.

POOL, J. 1991. The official language problem. *American Political Science Review*, 85: 495–514.

RAMPTON, B. 1995. *Crossing*. London: Longman.

RUTHERFORD, D. 2003. *Raiding the Land of the Foreigners*. Princeton, NJ: Princeton University Press.

SCHIEFFELIN, B., WOOLARD, K., and KROSKRITY, P. (eds.) 1998. *Language Ideologies*. Oxford: Oxford University Press.

SILVERSTEIN, M. 1979. Language structure and linguistic ideology. Pp. 193–247 in *The Elements*, ed. P. Clyne et al. Chicago: Chicago Linguistics Society.

——and Urban, G. (eds.) 1996. *Natural Histories of Discourse*. Chicago: University of Chicago Press.

URLA, J. 2001. Outlaw language: creating alternative public spheres in Basque radio. In Gal and Woolard 2001, 141–65.

VAN PARIJS, P. 2000. The ground floor of the world. *International Political Science Review*, 21: 217–33.

WARNER, M. 2002. Publics and counter-publics. *Public Culture*, 14: 49–90.

WEBER, E. 1976. *Peasants into Frenchmen*. Stanford, Calif.: Stanford University Press.

WHITELEY, P. 2003. Do "language rights" serve indigenous interests? *American Anthropologist*, 105: 712–22.

WOOLARD, K. 1998. Simultaneity and bivalency as strategies in bilingualism. *Journal of Linguistic Anthropology*, 8: 3–29.

ZOLBERG, A. 2001. Language policy: public policy perspectives. Pp. 8365–73 in *International Encyclopedia of the Social Sciences*, ed. N. Smelser and P. B. Baltes. Amsterdam: Elsevier.

C H A P T E R   2 1

....

THE IDEA OF
POLITICAL CULTURE

....

PAUL LICHTERMAN
DANIEL CEFAÏ

POLITICAL culture is no single thing waiting for researchers to find it in the world. Social scientists construct the category to serve our theoretical agendas and methods of investigation. But political cultures do exist. Political action requires meaning-making, in institutional and everyday settings alike. Those settings may be electoral races, public policy arenas, or judicial proceedings; community service groups, social activist groups, friendship networks, television audiences of mass or niche size, or electronic chat rooms. In all these contexts, individuals or collective bodies communicate and act on claims to resources, opportunities, or recognition—or opinions about what social reality is like, which issues or identities should be public, how state agents or citizens should relate to public issues. Any of these claims or opinions can be political; following many of the works we discuss, we do not restrict "political" to claims on or opinions about the state. *Political cultures* are the sets of symbols and meanings or styles of action that organize political claims-making and opinion-forming, by individuals or collectivities. By culture, we mean patterns of publicly shared symbols, meanings, or styles of action which enable and constrain what people can say and do.

For a contextualist understanding of political culture we turn to recent cultural sociology in the US and pragmatic sociology in France: We define culture as more than a reflection of objective interests or a set of symbolic resources that groups mobilize strategically. In our view, culture structures the way actors create their strategies, perceive their field of action, define their identities and solidarities. Culture is *relatively* autonomous in relation to social structure and social or individual psychology. Throughout this chapter, we situate work congenial to this definition amidst select other approaches, hoping to convey some of the breadth in ideas of political culture circulating in sociology, political science, anthropology, and communication studies, while highlighting especially promising inquiries. Social scientists now face a bewildering array of culture concepts. We hope our way of organizing the presentation may help readers make deliberate choices.

We ourselves needed to make difficult choices: We discuss a relatively few, prominent lines of thinking on political culture, rather than attempting an exhaustive review. We will restrict the chapter to the culture of political action in civil society—the realm of relationships in which people act primarily in their capacity as citizens or members of society, rather than subjects of state administration, or consumers, producers, managers, or owners in the marketplace. Many though certainly not all of the prominent works on political culture have focused outside the state.[1] The bulk of our discussion treats works written by anglophone scholars, or works translated and read widely by them. As the chapter shows, we find that French scholars have taken different paths to some of the same insights as their anglophone counterparts. Contacts between the two worlds of scholarship are increasing;[2] this is an exciting time for students of political culture to become more familiar with parallel inquiries. Emergent research programs on both sides of the Atlantic are showing that while political cultures work differently in different social contexts, they provide enabling and constraining contexts for democratic communication and action.

1   INVENTORIES OF POLITICAL CULTURE: *THE CIVIC CULTURE* AND BEYOND

Many scholars of political culture have drawn insights from Alexis de Tocqueville's observations (1969) on Americans' civic voluntarism and their sense of "self

---

[1] We hasten to add that sociologists increasingly have appreciated that the state is culturally conditioned (for instance: Jasper 1987; Steinmetz 1999), and that it sponsors its own arenas—literally and figuratively—for cultural expression that legitimates its aims and constructs its citizen-subject. For an exemplar, see Berezin's (1997) work on how the Italian Fascist regime used public ritual in hopes of creating an emotional, national community of allegiance to the state. See also Edles (1998).

[2] See, e.g., Lamont and Thévenot (2000).

interest properly understood." Louis Hartz's much-cited thesis (1955) on political liberalism in America highlighted one of the cultural strands woven into Tocqueville's more complex picture. Edward Banfield's case study of a southern Italian village (1958) affirmed Tocqueville's argument with a negative case. Civic association, Banfield held, required the right kind of culture; his Italian villagers failed to act together for the common good because their ethos of "amoral familism" cultivated the pursuit of short-term, individual or familial interest, and the distrust of anyone claiming to do otherwise. Also in Tocqueville's spirit but with a far wider, more systematic reach, *The Civic Culture* (1963) by Gabriel Almond and Sidney Verba stands among the first landmark empirical studies of political culture. A defining statement for American scholars of political culture in the 1960s, it remains a large if ambivalent reference point. Empirically it rested on survey data on values, attitudes, opinions, and beliefs from the United States, England, Germany, Italy, and Mexico. Almond and Verba conceived political culture as a set of psychological orientations—cognitive, affective, and evaluative—toward the political system as a whole. They categorized political cultures into parochial, subject, and participation types: "civic culture" was at once a descriptive and normative concept denoting a system-sustaining mix of all of three.

The study borrowed heavily from the Talcott Parsons' social system theory (Parsons and Shils 1951) with its trio of subjective orientations, emphasis on internalized cultural values, and allegiance to a modernization paradigm of political development. As did its theoretical forebears, *The Civic Culture* imagined close-fitting relationships between political culture and social structure at a social-systemic level, at least in "stable" democracies—in spite of the authors' caution against assuming that the two are always congruent.

Theoretical and normative assumptions have made this classic study liable to powerful criticisms, some of which Almond and Verba (1980) invited into a wide-ranging collection of review essays. Carole Pateman (1980) pointed out that in effect the study affirmed political quiescence as the normal state of affairs. It took as universal the particular, liberal democratic, dominant self-understandings of the postwar US and UK. "Traditionalism" and "familialism" characterized the less-developed political cultures of Mexico or Italy; in the case of Italy, survey research seemed to ratify Banfield's much more local and impressionistic account. Alasdair MacIntyre (1972) challenged Almond and Verba's science of comparative politics to accommodate cultural and institutional differences that complicate comparisons: Did holding an attitude of "pride" in one's government mean the same thing in Italy and Germany? Could cross-national generalizations about political parties hold, when parties may occupy vastly different institutional positions in different nations? Recent moves to reconceptualize culture brought *The Civic Culture* under renewed scrutiny: Margaret Somers (1995) observed that the framework effectively disappeared culture by making social structure and psychological orientations do the real analytic work. We would add that scholarship gets further with culture concepts that help us recognize specific symbolic forms, rather than flat, textureless values, norms, or skills.

While Almond and Verba's abstraction and holism sit uncomfortably with the contemporary tendency to highlight multiplicity and variability in political culture, some contemporary work reinstates their search for the cultural prerequisites of liberal democracy. The inventory spirit of Almond and Verba's work lives on, too. Verba, Schlozman, and Brady (1995) produced an exhaustive survey of Americans' civic skills and practices. Political scientist Ronald Inglehart organized a series of national surveys (1977; 1981; 1990) which suggest that citizens of Western industrial democracies, and especially the highly schooled citizens, increasingly have valorized lifestyle, self-actualization, and a clean environment over material wealth. Cross-national surveys of values and opinions pose some of the same problems of context and interpretation that MacIntyre scored in Almond and Verba's work, though the stable trends Inglehart has found probably suggest at least a little about a great number of people. Sociologist Pierre Bourdieu (1984) critiqued the misleading abstraction and subjectivism in surveys of political opinion, pointing out that the meaning of *holding* an opinion is itself different in different classes. Drawing on French polling data, he interpreted individual survey responses only in relation to other responses by people with different economic and cultural capital within a discursive field of potential opinions. The individual responses become windows on a field that privileges some opinions and some ways of holding opinions over others—rather than indicators of separate, individual, subjective realities. Bourdieu was only one of several prominent theorists whose frameworks bring power back into the study of political culture.

2   POWER COMES BACK: POLITICAL CULTURE IN DOMINATION, RESISTANCE, AND THE FORCE-FIELD OF DISCOURSE

While dissatisfaction with the grand framework behind *The Civic Culture* encouraged some scholars in the later 1960s and 1970s to jettison the culture concept altogether, others found an alternative in cultural Marxism and other, post-Marxist approaches to mass, official, and popular culture. Cultural Marxians departed in significant ways from the bargain-basement reading of Marx, which would treat political culture as static beliefs that dupe people into accepting or misrecognizing the power of the capitalist class. Antonio Gramsci's (1971; 1985) theory of cultural hegemony is one of the most influential, subtle, and misread in the family of Western Marxism.

Gramsci emphasized the social power of articulation—the complicated act of creating a meaningful fit between words or images in some historically specific social context. Gramsci fully understood that words do not reflect reality in a natural or logical correspondence. From a Gramscian viewpoint, political culture is a precipitate of a society's ceaseless articulation processes: In informal and formal settings, everyday conversation and sacred ritual, in popular media and specialized texts, small drops of meaning take shape in dominant currents, or counter-currents of public opinion. And here enters the signal concept of hegemony. "Hegemony" is a summary statement about articulation across a society; it denotes an ongoing state of play in which the most widely circulating, easily articulated definitions of the social world are "dominant," the ones that complement or else do not seriously challenge the interests of the dominant class or groups. Major institutions of the state, and the formal and informal relations of civil society circulate these definitions, giving what we call political culture its main outlines.

To speak of "the hegemonic process" always is to acknowledge the existence of alternative and oppositional articulations, too (Williams 1977). We can call them "political" in that they challenge dominant understandings of the world, whether or not they address the state. These circulate less widely; they may take shape only in people's reception of dominant discourses: Stuart Hall famously demonstrated (1980) that audiences might "decode" a television show in alternative or oppositional ways even when it is "encoded" with dominant discourses that complement the world-views of capitalist elites. In post-Marxist Gramscian scholarship (Laclau and Mouffe 1985), class is no longer the privileged reference point for analyzing cultural hegemony, and a counter-hegemonic project is one that pursues limitless democratization on the basis of a "radical citizen" identity (Mouffe 1992a and b). In this critical ideal, radical citizens respect the democratic aspirations of women, lesbians and gay men, environmentalists, people of color, as well as subordinate classes. Their own identities transmutate continually as claims and counter-claims bring new identities and yet new claims into the arena. Politics is endless.

Some scholars focus more on dominant political culture, the big engines of cultural hegemony. Studies of news programming associated with or influenced by the former Centre for Contemporary Cultural Studies in Birmingham, UK, are a prominent case. David Morley's oft-cited study (1980) of the British *Nationwide* television program, for instance, analyzed the discourse of this widely viewed news show, pointing out that the show worded news events such as labor strikes in terms congenial to management. Yet audience reception of the show varied. The dominant definitions had relatively great or little hold on focus group members' reception of the show, depending on their social backgrounds and experiences; again, the hegemony concept grasps the existence of non-dominant interpretations in conflict with dominant ones. In the US, sociologist Todd Gitlin demonstrated (1980) that news coverage increasingly stigmatized, trivialized, or demonized the growing new left movement against the Vietnam war. These mass-mediated images of flamboyant protestors informed some new leftists' self-understandings, and the nation got the sectarian, sometimes violent left movements that its media had conjured up under a demonizing, hegemonic lens. With the same theoretical imagination, communication scholar Justin Lewis argued (1999) that conventions of news reportage cultivate a commonsense understanding that the US political system hosts a wide range of viewpoints, and in so doing bolsters the power of "corporate center-right interests" even when their stances are not popular.

While recognizing the hegemonic power of mass-mediated discourse and imagery, other scholars emphasize how audiences actively piece together meanings from the media which complement their preexisting social worlds. Conservative Christian women interpret mainstream television portraits of abortion in ways that affirm their own cultural authorities (Press and Cole 1999); lesbians and gay men try to validate their worth without effacing their "otherness" in the forum of TV talk shows (Gamson 1998), even if the corporate-organized forum ultimately undercuts their claims to dignity.

Still other scholars peer more closely into the social worlds that sustain oppositional and alternative political culture. They investigate the local community life cultivated by a communist party (for instance, Kertzer 1990), or the "subaltern counterpublics" (Fraser 1992) of grassroots social movements (Lichterman 1996; 1999), alternative media, or urban enclaves (Melucci 1989; Castells 1983). Historical research finds proto-oppositional readings of everyday social life in the fragmentary, informal, "hidden transcripts" (Scott 1990) of peasants. Eyes peeled and ears to the ground, ethnographers hear signs of class resistance in the popular religion of landless *campesinos* in Nicaragua (Lancaster 1988; see also Comaroff 1985), the local knowledge of coal miners in American Appalachia (Gaventa 1980), or the subcultural clothing and music style of postwar British youth (Hall and Jefferson 1976; Hebdige 1979).

Using "discourse," "practice," "technique," or other terms rather than "culture," scholars influenced by Foucault leave the Marxian orbit and treat culture itself as power, rather than the outer form of an underlying, powerful interest. In one of Foucault's most important insights for students of political culture, identities never inhere in groups. Rather, discourses wield the power to create group identities and subjectivities. Psychiatric discourse creates "the homosexual," for instance (1990); disciplines and techniques of economics, statistics, or criminology call into being a managed, governable population of citizen subjects (Hindess 1996). These disciplines and techniques of "governmentality" cultivate in subjects the control of their own conduct.

Different forms of power produce different opportunities for resistance. Echoing Gramsci's notion of hegemony without its class analysis, Foucault held that to speak of power, even "domination" was always to imply resistance. Power is a relationship in active tension, not a thing that a leader or group *has*. In Foucault's world, there is no exit from the force-field of discourses, disciplines, or techniques—no place beyond "culture," if we are using that term to translate Foucault's concerns—but different kinds of power/knowledge relationships. For Foucaldian scholars, power and resistance to power are instantiated even in the momentary gestures and interactional moves of everyday life: Subordinate groups wield quiet "tactics of resistance" (Certeau 1984) by cutting the corners of proper etiquette. They spoof the dominant pieties with their biting irony and jokes (Wedeen 1999).

Gramscian Marxists depart from simpler concepts of a dominant ideology used handily and self-consciously by class elites to manipulate social subordinates (Ewen 1976; Vanderbilt 1997; Lasch 1979). In the Gramscian perspective, class-based ideologies saturate everyday expression, and people carry them un-self-consciously, even as they contest domination, albeit inchoately. Making a parallel move in a different conceptual world, Foucault bid to "cut off the king's head"(1980)—to analyze the diverse, capillary pathways of power relationships, beyond the static model of authoritative sovereign and consenting subjects. But in either constellation of inquiry, much as they diverge, political culture exists only in relation to (class or group) power, or as a discursive vector or technique *of* power.

3   POLITICAL CULTURE COMES INTO ITS OWN: CULTURE AS A STRUCTURE

Political culture became a more autonomous subject of inquiry again in the 1980s, as sociologists rethought earlier uses of the culture concept. Borrowing from the structuralism of Lacan, Levi-Strauss, and Barthes, social scientists increasingly considered culture as a structure, or a set of structures with an enabling and constraining force irreducible to individual attitudes or institutional power (Smith 1998; Alexander and Seidman 1990). An early statement in this emerging investigation was political scientist Richard Merelman's (1984) argument on the loosely bounded quality of American political culture.

Anthropologist Clifford Geertz (1973) influenced many later researchers to take political cultures as appropriate objects of study in themselves. So we might analyze codes embodied in the drama of Bali's theater state (Geertz 1980), or the ideology of Sukarno's Indonesia (Geertz 1973, 225). We would look not for internalized values nor ideologies that exist only because they convey dominant interests, but "publicly available symbolic forms" through which people experience meaning. Political culture results as both a "model of" the world—a map for locating and defining the social situations—and a "model for" action—a template for mastering and occasionally transforming situations. Geertz's work encompasses a more hermeneutic and a more pragmatist tendency, both of which animate our varied, current repertoire of concepts. Yet there can be tensions between these two, as social anthropologist Adam Kuper (1999, 105) points out: Anthropological (and sociological) participant-observers at least sometimes claim to understand lived action from their subjects' point of view; to "read" social action as a text to be interpreted, on the other hand, is a different enterprise. Kuper argues that Geertz traveled too far towards a purely hermeneutic, even literary project, with a hermetically if artfully sealed notion of culture as a text, divorced from social organization.

Developments roughly parallel to but earlier than Geertz's innovations took place in France. Historians of the Middle Ages such as Georges Duby (1978) and Jacques Le Goff (1985) and of the French Revolution (Furet 1978) conceived of the *"imaginaire"* (Baczko 1984) and *"symbolique"* (Agulhon 1979) and put these cultural structures at the center of their interpretations. Cornelius Castoriadis (1975) argued that society constitutes itself through a "radical imaginary," a cultural template for both alienation and creativity, ideology and utopia. Claude Lefort (1981) combined a sophisticated analysis of political regimes with an understanding of political culture informed by Aristotle's notion of *politeia*, Montesquieu's *esprit des lois*, and Tocqueville's *mores*. Lefort argued that both democracy and totalitarianism depend on the invention of languages, rituals, and symbols; culture does not simply reflect the regime.

4   POLITICAL CULTURE AS SHARED REPRESENTATIONS

One family of inquiries into cultural structure borrows the "late-Durkheimian" (Alexander 1988) notion that political culture is a set of publicly shared representations of what makes a good citizen, or a good society. They share the fundamental insight that words do not reflect underlying ideas or interests transparently. Rather, communication is *structured* from the start by cultural forms that exist somewhat independently of group interests; from this point of view, Gramscians underestimate the enduring power of cultural forms themselves, while Foucault-influenced post-Marxists skip crucial sociological steps by conflating culture and power. Important earlier examples of the "shared representations" approach include

William Sewell's (1980) study of changes in nineteenth-century French discourse, which showed that industrial workers had to invent new "political idioms" to leave the universe of the Old regime corporations. French workers and citizens developed new idioms of the local community (Agulhon 1970), the voluntary association (Agulhon 1977), and the political party (Huard 1996) as well. A recent outpouring of US work conceives shared representations in at least two different ways. One is the concept of "cultural vocabulary," and the other, "cultural code."

4.1   Vocabularies of Politics

One widely read example of this approach to political culture in the US is Robert Bellah and co-authors' *Habits of the Heart*, an interview study of middle-class Americans' moral and political reasoning. Most often, Bellah and his team heard languages of individualism, as when many of their interviewees said that their public commitments depended on "what I can get out of it" or "what feels good to me right now"; less often and more haltingly, Americans articulated their commitments in civic-republican or Biblical language. The authors proposed that an active, democratic citizenry would be hard to sustain over time if Americans' primary cultural vocabulary was so self-oriented; in a preface to a second edition (1996), they observed that Robert Putnam's (2000) much-discussed figures on declining American civic group memberships confirmed their fears.

A society's cultural mainstream holds more than one set or "system" of representations. Rhys Williams (1995) illustrated that social movements draw on different rhetorics of the public good—the good of individual rights or environmental stewardship, for instance. Some representations are politically subordinate or subcultural. Mark Warren (2001), Richard Wood (1994; 1999; 2002), and Stephen Hart (2001) showed that shared religious representations such as those in Catholic social thought can work as political culture, by helping urban social movements construct political claims that are compelling in low-income, minority communities and effective against corporations and local bureaucrats. Wood's comparative research found that the most effective representations were religious traditions which helped activists process ambiguity in their political environments instead of ignoring or trying to transcend it.

All of these studies have discerned vocabularies from qualitative analysis of interviews, ethnographic field notes, or texts. They depend on the analyst's familiarity with a larger cultural or intellectual history behind the groups under study: The Bellah team chose historical, cultural exemplars such as Benjamin Franklin and Walt Whitman to represent strands of American individualism alive in the late twentieth century; French sociologists Boltanski and Thévenot (1991) have pursued a somewhat similar strategy, identifying public vocabularies of moral or political justification as descending from one of six great Western philosophical texts. It is possible, though, to study vocabularies more inductively, and with more quantitative measures. Employing Q-sort methodology, Dryzek and Holmes (2002) gathered samples of statements about democratization from focused discussion groups in each of thirteen post-Communist countries, and then asked a separate set of interviewees in each country to sort the statements. Treating the resulting "sorts" to factor analysis, the researchers reconstructed vocabularies of democratization that they proposed are typical for different countries, and sometimes shared across countries—"socialist authoritarianism," "liberal capitalism," "reactionary anti-liberalism," and more. The methodology may risk atomizing cultural structure into aggregates of individual subjectivities—Bourdieu's critique of under-sociological subjectivism may again apply—but the researchers' knowledge of different national contexts and their commitment to interpretive validity strengthen the argument that these reconstructions plausibly reflect shared representations, and are more than statistical artifacts.

4.2   Codes of Politics

Other researchers in this family of studies would conceive political culture in terms of codes that organize public discourse. Sociologists Jeffrey Alexander (2001) and Philip Smith (Alexander and Smith 1993) identified a set of binary codes in public life that have organized US political debate over the past two centuries. Socialized to these implicit, binary codes, citizens divide up actors, relationships, and institutions into categories of good and evil. Commonly, US legislators affirm "good" political actors by characterizing them as "active, not passive," and "rational, not hysterical"; they ascribe goodness to political relations when they tag them as "open and trusting" rather than "closed and secretive" (Alexander and Smith 1993, 162–3). The codes organize acceptable, communicable speech on *both* sides of a debate. During the Watergate hearings, for instance, both the adversaries and defenders of President Nixon called their own side reasonable and cast the opposing side as irrational or secretive.

The deep cultural codes of society at large, beyond civil society, can structure political debate, too. Linguist George Lakoff and philosopher Mark Johnson (1980) analyze widely shared metaphors in that light. They argue that in everyday thinking, people translate abstract concepts into substances, persons, relationships, or positions in space that we can understand more immediately from experience. So in a society that thinks of argument in terms of war, large parts of political communication consist in trying to "win" an argument by "attacking the opposition," "gaining ground," and putting the "other side on the defensive." These are not natural or purely logical moves, but culturally coded ones. Absent these metaphors, political communication would be organized very differently, as anthropological research on aboriginal Australian and other societies shows (Myers 1991; Brenneis and Myers 1984).

Parallel to students of cultural vocabularies, scholars of binary codes find subordinate or subcultural codes that are patterned and enduring: Ronald Jacobs' study (2000) of media discourse surrounding the Rodney King beating by the Los Angeles Police found codes in the African-American press somewhat different from those organizing depictions of the beating and subsequent riots in mainstream forums. Different sets of codes may organize political debate in other societies; "authoritarian" or "collectivist," as well as democratic codes may propel the terms of national debate in Brazil since the 1990s (Baiocchi 2001).

For analysts of either vocabularies or codes, the question of political culture's relation to social structure makes sense only once the structure of political culture itself is clear. Sociologists close to the shared representations framework have argued (Wuthnow 1989; Swidler 2001) that in the long run, institutional relationships enable some forms of culture to survive and spread while others do not. Swidler has argued (2001) that people may innovate new political culture during periods of great social flux, but that only those forms that "fit" institutionally structured relationships will endure and become commonsensical, tightly entwined with everyday action (Swidler 1986).

4.3   An Alternative from Social Movement Studies: Strategic Framing

The shared representations perspective on political culture contrasts with the notion of "frame" current in American social movements research, and discussed at length in Polletta and Ho's contribution to this volume.[3] Sociologists William Gamson and colleagues' (1982) social-psychological study of responses to injustice was one of the first to introduce Erving Goffman's frame concept to politics researchers. David Snow and his colleagues (Snow et al. 1986; Snow and Benford 1988) and again Gamson (1992) borrowed and significantly reinterpreted Goffman's frame concept, popularizing its use in studies of collective action. By "frames" they meant discursive packages, or ways of communicating about facts and events. In Snow and colleagues' widely cited version, movement groups organize frames strategically, in order to build coalitions and reach target audiences.

---

[3] "Frames and their Consequences" (Ch. 10, this volume) discusses the varied uses of "frame" in social movements research and cites prominent critical reviews of the concept.

This strategic framing perspective helped to make culture prominent in studies of social movements, but at a cost. Some framing studies identified static frames through content analysis, ignoring the flexible back-and-forth of discursive acts, as Steinberg (1999) pointed out; others derived frames from interview talk, although the same interviewees might draw on different vocabularies in their own, everyday settings, as Lichterman (1996) found with environmental activists. Hank Johnston (1991; 1995) made the frame concept more sensitive to narrative form and the texture of everyday experience. Using the frame concept to analyze words and phrases that focus group participants borrow from personal experience, popular wisdom, and media information, Gamson (1992) gave the concept more of a purchase on political culture's sources and textures. Still, the focus group method would neglect moral ambiguities and social identities that are part of the context for communication in natural settings. In some of the most popular usage of the concept, frames are not cultural structures but cultural means for pursuing interests which exist beyond culture.

5   POLITICAL CULTURE AS PERFORMANCE

5.1   Dramas, Arguments, and Narratives

One of the limitations in studying shared codes or vocabularies in the abstract is that we may miss the concrete shape they take in collective action. Dramas, arguments, and narratives are performances addressed to particular publics; they put shared representations in movement. Dramaturgical perspectives have been put forth, famously by Kenneth Burke (1945), and in a variety of social-science veins by sociologists Erving Goffman (1959) and Joseph Gusfield (1981), political scientist Murray Edelman (1964), anthropologist Victor Turner (1974), and very recently by sociologist and cultural theorist Jeffrey Alexander (2004). From this viewpoint, dramatic conventions shape political communication. On stage in politics as in theater, actors play roles and follow scripts as a cast of characters, perform front-stage and backstage actions. They represent to an audience a moral order, with offenders, victims, heroes, witnesses, and experts. Under this analytic lens, social dramas enacted by institutional actors shape a public's perception of social problems, such as the problem of drink-driving (Gusfield 1981), even apart from the "objective" facts of risk or harm. These performances inform policy, as when Yavapai Indians dramatized their opposition to the Orme Dam project in Arizona that threatened their ancestral lands (Espeland 1998).

Narratives, like plays, are performances: Through the conventions of storytelling, political actors communicate claims, opinions, and the very definitions of political issues. Narratives may circulate in mass-mediated discourse, informal sayings, or formal, oral traditions; national monuments and other artifacts as well as people or institutions may communicate them. Narratives are examples of cultural *structure* par excellence, with their convention-governed plots, casts of predictable character types, and genres such as romance or tragedy. Through these conventions, narratives can structure the way a public perceives grievances, imputes motives, defines which issues, characters, or situations are central or peripheral. The Vietnam Veterans Memorial in Washington, DC, is striking in part because its narrative is not typical for a war memorial; it does not tell a romance of heroism and it leaves the "plot" ambiguous (Wagner-Pacifici and Schwartz 1991).

The same events retold with different narrative forms can appear very different and elicit very different senses of propriety or injustice. Ron Jacobs (1996; 2000) used narrative analysis along with attention to the binary codes designating heroic and anti-heroic citizens, to compare retellings of the Rodney King beating in Los Angeles by mainstream and African-American newspapers. Different heroic characters emerged in African-American and mainstream retellings. Narrative analysis can illuminate changes as well as continuities in public culture: Anne Kane (1997) used narrative analysis to follow the transforming meanings of potent symbols during the mass public meetings of the Irish Land War. Terms such as "rent," "land," "landlord," "Ireland," and "constitutional" formed a system of meaning, a coherent discourse, but as the impassioned meetings unfolded, the terms developed new relations to one another, such that landlord actions became "unconstitutional" and Irish land reform a constitutional right. Francesca Polletta (1998*a* and *b*) investigated the narratives that civil rights activists told to new recruits and journalists. She argues that a familiar storyline helped activists make sense of their risky activism: A "force" took over them, they said, compelling them to act spontaneously.

5.2   An Alternative from Social Movement Studies: Collective Identity

The collective identity concept from social movement studies works parallel to these concepts, but with different analytic assumptions. Social movements construct and perform "collective identities," many scholars emphasize, since those identities do not emerge naturally from grievances. Some movement scholars study collective identity in order to understand how activists interpret their social position, given the multiple possibilities (Taylor and Whittier 1992); others want to explain why activists mount more or less radical identities in different arenas

(Bernstein 1997). Activists perform identity and invite publics to identify with them, in die-ins and sit-ins (Lofland 1985), in solemn rituals of protest and arrest (Epstein 1991), or in theatrical disruptions of everyday routine (J. Gamson 1991).

In these studies, movements perform collective identities in response to their social or political subordination, or—in a postmodern scenario—a proliferation of power sources. In scholarship informed by political process or resource mobilization models of social movements, collective identity does not enable and constrain; it crystallizes other social forces and powers that do, or else does strategic work for movement entrepreneurs (Benford 1993). Scholarship indebted to a notion of culture's relative autonomy shows, in contrast, that narratives themselves and not only the forces "behind" them have consequences for action: "Activists' very understandings of 'strategy,' 'interest,' 'opportunity,' and 'obstacle,' may be structured by the oppositions and hierarchies that come from familiar stories" (Polletta 1998b, 424).

6   Emergent Perspectives: Political Culture in Everyday Communication and Action

Studies of political culture as code, vocabulary, drama, or narrative often focus on formal, ceremonial, or mass-mediated contexts, during crisis moments—or else interview situations. Increasingly, studies are examining political culture in ordinary interaction, in the quotidian settings of civil society: local citizens' hearings on environmental issues, volunteer group meetings, social clubs. US students of everyday political culture trace their interest to a larger, linguistic turn in social theory throughout the twentieth century that encouraged sociologists to conceive culture as communication rather than abstract values. For some, the work of Jürgen Habermas (1989; see Cohen and Arato 1992) sparked curiosity about the role that ordinary civic communication plays in sustaining democracy.

A parallel focus on everyday public activities emerged in French sociology in the 1980s. Supplanting the models of Boudon, Bourdieu, Touraine, and Crozier, new perspectives highlighted actor networks (Callon 1989), the ecology of public spaces (Joseph 1984), and the hermeneutics of communication and action (Quéré 1982). These studies benefited from qualitative investigations of interactions and historical events up close; they helped to enlarge anthropological and historical understandings of political cultures (Cefaï 2001), situating them in the contexts of institutional policies, sociability networks, political geography, and collective memory. In this final section we discuss two complementary lines of research on everyday political culture.

6.1   Political Culture as the Implicit Customs of Civic Life

With an imagination for context, we see that vocabularies, codes, dramas, or narratives are themselves always embedded in social settings. Civil society creates and recreates itself as people continue enacting different customary forms of membership in those settings. Different customs of citizenship are themselves meaningful and have their own histories (Schudson 1998); they are not simply derivatives of a group's formally stated purpose or beliefs.

In her study of American civic groups, for instance, Nina Eliasoph (1998; 1996) showed that being a member of a volunteer group *meant* being an upbeat, "can-do" person who carried out tasks efficiently instead of fretting about big social issues. Lichterman found (1995*b*; 1996) that being a member of an environmental activist group could mean being someone willing to make a deeply personalized contribution to the cause, or someone who upholds a communal will and brackets individuality. Groups with different customs had difficulties working together, even when they all affirmed the same "environmental justice" discourse. Researchers have conceptualized customs of group membership within different theoretical traditions, calling them "cultures of commitment" (Lichterman 1996), "civic practices" (Eliasoph 1996; 1998), "cultural models" in the case of Becker's (1999) study of church congregations, or "constitutive rules" in Armstrong's study of lesbian and gay organizations (2002). Each is getting at something like the "group style" (Eliasoph and Lichterman 2003) that a group sustains as it goes about ordinary business. Group styles powerfully shape the meanings and uses of the vocabularies or codes discussed above (Lichterman 1996; Eliasoph 1998; Eliasoph and Lichterman 2003).

Studying group style and representations together illuminates how civic groups measure up to the potentials imputed to them by many theorists of democracy. The volunteer group style shuts down open-ended conversation that ideally characterizes the public sphere; in groups, volunteers avoid discussing what they may worry about in private interviews—that skinheads at the local high school threaten race relations, for instance (Eliasoph 1998). The personalized, self-expressive style of some environmental and queer activist groups (Lichterman 1995*a*; 1996; 1999) encourages public-spirited deliberation—despite social scientists' claims that expressive individualism makes people un-civic-minded or apolitical (Bellah et al. 1985; see also Bennett 1998). In theory, civic participation also teaches citizens how to mobilize relationships and resources for a greater public good (Putnam 1993; 2000; Skocpol 1999).

Yet different group styles promote different ways of shepherding resources and defining ties, and different ways of working with state institutions, apart from group members' religious or political beliefs or social backgrounds (Lichterman 2005). Tallying up "social capital" (Putnam 2000) misses the impact of group style.

6.2   Political Culture as Criticizing, Denouncing, and Claims-making in Public Arenas

Older French scholarship, like its American counterparts, studied static, symbolic codes and legal or political institutions in the abstract, without asking *how* issues or people become public, political, contested in everyday life. Some French scholars have been studying how ordinary citizens and elites create the *res publica* itself, in informal as well as institutional arenas. How do groups and institutions actively define private troubles as public problems? How do they carve out new arenas for dramatizing problems and refocusing law-makers' attention (Cefaï and Joseph 2002)?

To address these questions, Luc Boltanski and Laurent Thevenot (1991) have analyzed "regimes" of public justification with a typology of the logics of rationality and legitimacy—those of domesticity, market relations, technology, civic responsibility, inspiration, or popular opinion. Drawing on these practical logics, actors perform different sorts of "worlds," set up different kinds of relationships, and promote different species of "moral goods." Daniel Cefaï and Claudette Lafaye (2001; 2002) studied a civic association in Paris which opposed the destruction of a neighborhood. They followed the process through which the "destruction" became a public problem, and heard participants in the process invoke different logics and moral goods along the way: Actors interpreted the issue in order to mobilize personal networks of friends; they assessed the *economic* costs of alternative solutions; they proposed *technical* means of guaranteeing the public good; they organized citizen forums to create and mobilize *popular* opinion.

In this action-focused approach to public-making, political cultures structure the ways people launch claims about what should be public rather than private, what publics should consider unjust rather than unremarkable. Researchers also aim to grasp the emotions intertwined with claims to freedom, dignity, equality, justice, or recognition. They focus on ordinary conversation at the supermarket or school gate, in municipal hearings or activist group meetings, and in more formal and less open settings of state agencies or experts' offices, too. Unlike scholarship on "frames" or "ideologies," these researchers are paying attention to the *forms* in which claims circulate and evolve—public rituals, local rumors, legislative debates, for instance—and attention to the *public stages* where they take place. Claims-making follows "grammars of public talk" (Boltanski 1990; Cardon, Heurtin, and Lemieux 1995), sometimes leading to new public issues.[4] In this way recent French scholarship has applied a "pragmatic" approach (see Silber 2003) to understanding the public sphere.

7   CONCLUSION: WHY DOES IT MATTER IF POLITICAL CULTURE IS AUTONOMOUS?

Studies of political culture address enduring theoretical questions about the *res publica* while advancing current debates about civic life. A focus on active meaning-making illuminates the ways people define, challenge, or redefine what will count as "politics" itself. We bid theorists to keep thinking about how political culture shapes and is shaped by social contexts without falling into the traps of functionalism or class-determination-in-the-last-instance, nor lurching the other way toward hermetically sealed cultural systems or analyses that collapse culture and institutional power. We invite more research that can grasp innovation in political culture—strategic or otherwise—without losing the insight that culture itself is structured, and in turn, structures action.

We have taken a stand for concepts that grant the relative autonomy of culture because we think that political culture is one of the conditions of possibility for a democratic society. Almond and Verba were not entirely wrong. Studies of contingent culture can illuminate actors' strategic choices, but cannot tell us why actors perceived those choices to begin with. While political culture is indeed an "idea," it is an idea we need if we want to understand what makes civic groups empowering or disempowering, crucial or irrelevant, as many societies around the globe rewrite their social contracts. Further research on everyday political culture can tell us much more about potentials and predicaments in fast-changing civic arenas.

REFERENCES

AGULHON, M. 1970. *La République au village: les populations du Var de la Révolution à la IIe République*. Paris: Plon.
——1977. *Le Cercle dans la France bourgeoise, 1810–1948: étude d'une mutation de sociabilité.* Paris: Colin.

---

[4] In France, see the historical genesis of political and judiciary "affaires" (Claverie 1998), the invention of "landscape" or "unemployment" as categories of policy (Trom and Zimmermann 2001).

—— 1979. *Marianne au combat: L'imagerie et la symbolique républicaines de 1789 à 1880*. Paris: Flammarion.

ALEXANDER, J. 1988. *Durkheimian Sociology*. Berkeley: University of California Press.

—— 2001. The long and winding road: civil repair of intimate injustice. *Sociological Theory*, 19: 371–400.

—— 2004. Cultural pragmatics: social performance between ritual and strategy. *Sociological theory*, 22: 527–73.

—— and SEIDMAN, S. 1990. *Culture and Society*. Cambridge: Cambridge University Press.

—— and SMITH, P. 1993. The discourse of American civil society: a new proposal for cultural studies. *Theory and Society*, 22: 151–207.

ALMOND, G., and VERBA, S. 1963. *The Civic Culture*. Princeton, NJ: Princeton University Press.

—— —— (eds.) 1980. *The Civic Culture Revisited*. Boston: Little, Brown.

ARMSTRONG, E. 2002. *Forging Gay Identities*. Chicago: University of Chicago Press.

BACZKO, B. 1984. *Les imaginaires sociaux: Mémoires et espoirs collectifs*. Paris: Payot.

BAIOCCHI, G. 2001. *From Militance to Citizenship: The Workers' Party, Civil Society, and the Politics of Participatory Governance in Porto Alegre, Brazil*. Ph.D. dissertation, University of Wisconsin–Madison.

BANFIELD, E. 1958. *The Moral Basis of a Backward Society*. New York: Free Press.

BECKER, P. E. 1999. *Congregations in Conflict*. Cambridge: Cambridge University Press.

BELLAH, R., MADSEN, R., SULLIVAN, W., SWIDLER, A., and TIPTON, S. 1985. *Habits of the Heart*. Berkeley: University of California Press, 2nd edn. 1996.

BENFORD, R. 1993. "You could be the hundredth monkey": collective action frames and vocabularies of motive within the nuclear disarmament movement. *Sociological Quarterly*, 34: 195–216.

BENNETT, L. 1998. The UnCivic Culture: communication, identity and the rise of lifestyle politics. *PS: Political Science and Politics*, 31: 41–61.

BEREZIN, M. 1997. *Making the Fascist Self: The Political Culture of Interwar Italy*. Ithaca, NY: Cornell University Press.

BERNSTEIN, M. 1997. Celebration and suppression: the strategic uses of identity by the lesbian and gay movement. *American Journal of Sociology*, 103: 531–65.

BOLTANSKI, L. 1990. La dénonciation. In *L'Amour et la justice comme compétences*. Paris: Métailié.

—— and THÉVENOT. 1991. *De la justification: Les économies de la grandeur*. Paris: Gallimard.

BOURDIEU, P. 1984. *Distinction*, trans. R. Nice. Cambridge, Mass.: Harvard University Press.

BRENNEIS, D., and MYERS, F. 1984. *Dangerous Words: Language and Politics in the Pacific*. New York: New York University Press.

BURKE, K. 1945. *A Grammar of Motives*. Berkeley: University of California Press.

CALLON, M. 1989. *La Science et ses réseaux: Genèse et circulation des faits scientifiques*. Paris: La Découverte.

CARDON, D., HEURTIN, J.-P., and LEMIEUX, C. 1995. Parler en public. *Politix*, 31: 5–19.

CASTELLS, M. 1983. *The City and the Grassroots*. Berkeley: University of California Press.

CASTORIADIS, C. 1975. *L'institution imaginaire de la société*. Paris: Seuil.

CEFAÏ, D. (ed.) 2001. *Cultures politiques*. Paris: Presses Universitaires de France.

CEFAÏ, D. 2002. Les répertoires d'argumentation et de motivation dans l'action collective. Le cadrage d'un conflit urbain à Paris. Pp. 371–94 in *L'Héritage du pragmatisme*, ed. D. Cefaï and I. Joseph. La Tour d'Aigues: Éditions de l'Aube.

—— and JOSEPH, I. (eds.) 2002. *L'Héritage du pragmatisme: Conflits d'urbanité et épreuves de civisme*. La Tour d'Aigues: Editions de l'Aube.

—— and LAFAYE, C. 2001. Lieux et moments d'une mobilisation collective. L'association La Bellevilleuse, Paris XXe. Pp. 195–228 in *Les Formes de l'Action Collective*, ed. D. Cefaï and D. Trom. Paris: Éditions de l'EHESS.

—— and TROM, D. (eds.) 2001. *Raisons pratiques*. Vol. 12 of *Les Formes de l'action collective: Mobilisations dans des arènes publiques*. Paris: Éditions de l'EHESS.

CERTEAU, M. de. 1984. *The Practice of Everyday Life*. Berkeley: University of California Press.

CLAVERIE, E. 1998. La naissance d'une forme politique: l'affaire du Chevalier De la Barre. Pp. 185–265 in *Critique et affaire de blasphème au siècle des Lumières*, ed. J. Cheyronnaud et al. Paris: Honoré Champion.

COHEN, J., and ARATO, A. 1992. *Civil Society and Political Theory*. Cambridge, Mass.: MIT Press.

COMAROFF, J. 1985. *Body of Power, Spirit of Resistance: The Culture and History of a South African People*. Chicago: University of Chicago Press.

DRYZEK, J., and HOLMES, L. 2002. *Post-Communist Democratization: Political Discourses across Thirteen Countries*. Cambridge: Cambridge University Press.

DUBY, G. 1978. *Les Trois Ordres ou l'imaginaire du féodalisme*. Paris: Gallimard.

EDELMAN, M. 1964. *The Symbolic Uses of Politics*. Urbana: University of Illinois Press.

EDLES, L. 1998. *Symbol and Ritual in the New Spain*. Cambridge: Cambridge University Press.

ELIASOPH, N. 1996. Making a fragile public: a talk-centered study of citizenship and power. *Sociological Theory*, 14: 262–89.

—— 1998. *Avoiding Politics*. Cambridge: Cambridge University Press.

—— and LICHTERMAN, P. 2003. Culture in interaction. *American Journal of Sociology*, 108: 735–94.

EPSTEIN, B. 1991. *Political Protest and Cultural Revolution*. Berkeley: University of California Press.

ESPELAND, W. 1998. *The Struggle for Water*. Chicago: University of Chicago Press.

EWEN, S. 1976. *Captains of Consciousness*. New York: McGraw-Hill.

FOUCAULT, M. 1980. *Power/Knowledge*, ed. C. Gordon. New York: Pantheon.

—— 1990. *The History of Sexuality*, Vol. 1. New York: Vintage.

FRASER, N. 1992. Rethinking the public sphere: a contribution to the critique of actually existing democracy. Pp. 109–42 in *Habermas and the Public Sphere*, ed. C. Calhoun. Cambridge, Mass.: MIT Press.

FURET, F. 1978. *Penser la Révolution Française*. Paris: Gallimard.

GAMSON, J. 1991. Silence, death and the invisible enemy: AIDS activism and social movement "newness." Pp. 35–57 in *Ethnography Unbound*, ed. M. Burawoy et al. Berkeley: University of California Press.

—— 1998. *Freaks Talk Back*. Chicago: University of Chicago Press.

GAMSON, W. 1992. *Talking Politics*. Cambridge: Cambridge University Press.

—— FIREMAN, B., and RYTINA, S. 1982. *Encounters with Unjust Authority*. Homewood, Ill.: Dorsey Press.

GAVENTA, J. 1980. *Power and Powerlessness*. Chicago: University of Illinois Press.

GEERTZ, C. 1973. *The Interpretation of Cultures*. New York: Basic Books.

—— 1980. *Negara: The Theatre State in Nineteenth Century Bali*. Princeton, NJ: Princeton University Press.

—— 1983. Centers, kings and charisma: reflections on the symbolics of power. In *Local Knowledge*. New York: Basic Books.

GITLIN, T. 1980. *The Whole World is Watching*. Berkeley: University of California Press.

GOFFMAN, E. 1959. *The Presentation of Self in Everyday Life*. Garden City, NY: Doubleday.

GRAMSCI, A. 1971. *Selections from the Prison Notebooks*, ed. Q. Hoare. New York: International Publishers.

—— 1985. *Antonio Gramsci: Selections from Cultural Writings*, trans. W. Boelhower, ed. D. Forgacs and G. Nowell-Smith. Cambridge Mass.: Harvard University Press.

GUSFIELD, J. 1981. *The Culture of Public Problems: Drinking-Driving and the Symbolic Order*. Chicago: University of Chicago Press.

HABERMAS, J. 1989. *The Structural Transformation of the Public Sphere*. Cambridge, Mass.: MIT Press.

HALL S. 1980. Encoding and decoding in the television discourse. Pp. 128–38 in S. Hall et al., *Culture, Media, Language*. London: Hutchinson.

—— and JEVERSON, T. 1976. *Resistance through Rituals: Youth Sub-Cultures in Post-War Britain*. London: Hutchinson.

HART, S. 2001. *Cultural Dilemmas of Progressive Politics*. Chicago: University of Chicago Press.

HARTZ, L. 1955. *The Liberal Tradition in American Politics*. New York: Harvest.

HEBDIGE, D. 1979. *Subculture*. London: Methuen.

HINDESS, B. 1996. *Discourses of Power*. Oxford: Blackwell.

HUARD, R. 1996. *La naissance du parti politique en France*. Paris: Presses de Sciences-Po.

INGLEHART, R. 1977. *The Silent Revolution*. Princeton, NJ: Princeton University Press.

—— 1981. Post-materialism in an environment of insecurity. *American Political Science Review*, 75: 880–900.

—— 1990. *Culture Shift in Advanced Industrial Society*. Princeton, NJ: Princeton University Press.

JACOBS, R. N. 1996. Civil society and crisis: culture, discourse and the Rodney King beating. *American Journal of Sociology*, 101: 1238–72.

—— 2000. *Race, Media and the Crisis of Civil Society: from Watts to Rodney King*. New York: Cambridge University Press.

JASPER, J. 1987. *Nuclear Politics*. Princeton, NJ: Princeton University Press.

JOHNSTON, H. 1991. *Tales of Nationalism: Catalonia 1939–1979*. New Brunswick, NJ: Rutgers University Press.

—— 1995. New social movements and old regional nationalisms. Pp. 267–86 in *New Social Movements*, ed. E. Laraña, H. Johnston, and B. Klandermans. Philadelphia: Temple University Press.

JOSEPH, I. 1984. *Le Passant considérable: Essai sur la dispersion de l'espace public*. Paris: Méridiens.

KANE, A. 1997. Theorizing meaning construction in social movements: symbolic structures and interpretation during the Irish Land War, 1879–1882. *Sociological Theory*, 15: 249–76.

KERTZER, D. 1990. *Comrades and Christians: Religion and Political Struggle in Communist Italy*. Prospect Heights, Ill.: Waveland Press.

KUPER, A. 1999. *Culture*. Cambridge, Mass.: Harvard University Press.

LACLAU, E., and MOUVE, C. 1985. *Hegemony and Socialist Strategy*. London: Verso.

LAKOFF, G., and JOHNSON, M. 1980. *Metaphors We Live By*. Chicago: University of Chicago Press.

LAMONT, M., and THÉVENOT, L. (eds.) 2000. *Rethinking Comparative Cultural Sociology.* New York: Cambridge University Press.

LANCASTER, R. N. 1988. *Thanks to God and the Revolution.* New York: Columbia University Press.

LASCH, C. 1979. *The Culture of Narcissism.* New York: Norton.

LEFORT, C. 1981. *L'invention démocratique: les limites de la domination Totalitaire.* Paris: Fayard.

LE GOFF, J. 1985. *L'Imaginaire médiéval.* Paris: Gallimard.

LEWIS, J. 1999. Reproducing political hegemony in the United States. *Critical Studies in Mass Communication,* 16: 251–67.

LICHTERMAN, P. 1995*a*. Beyond the seesaw model: public commitment in a culture of self-fulfillment. *Sociological Theory,* 13: 275–300.

——1995*b*. Piecing together multicultural community: cultural differences in community building among grassroots environmentalists. *Social Problems,* 42: 513–34.

——1996. *The Search For Political Community: American Activists Reinventing Commitment.* Cambridge: Cambridge University Press.

——1999. Talking identity in the public sphere: broad visions and small spaces in sexual identity politics. *Theory and Society,* 28: 101–41.

——2005. *Elusive Togetherness: Church Groups Trying to Bridge America's Divisions.* Princeton, NJ: Princeton University Press.

LOFLAND, J. 1985. *Protest.* New Brunswick, NJ: Transaction.

LOLIVE, J. 1997. La montée en généralité pour sortir du Nimby: La mobilisation associative contre le TGV Méditerranée. *Politix,* 39: 109–30.

MACINTYRE, A. 1972. Is a science of comparative politics possible? Pp. 8–26 in *Philosophy, Politics and Society,* 4th ser., ed. P. Laslett, W. G. Runciman, and Q. Skinner. Oxford: Blackwell.

MELUCCI, A. 1989. *Nomads of the Present.* Philadelphia: Temple University Press.

MERELMAN, R. 1984. *Making Something of Ourselves.* Berkeley: University of California Press.

MORLEY, D. 1980. *The "Nationwide" Audience.* London: British Film Institute.

MOUFFE, C. 1992*a*. Preface: democratic politics today. Pp. 1–14 in *Dimensions of Radical Democracy,* ed. C. Mouffe. London: Verso.

——1992*b*. Democratic citizenship and the political community. Pp. 225–40 in *Dimensions of Radical Democracy,* ed. C. Mouffe. London: Verso.

MYERS, F. 1991. *Pintupi Country, Pintupi Self.* Berkeley: University of California Press.

PARSONS, T., and SHILS, E. 1951. *Toward a General Theory of Action.* Cambridge, Mass.: Harvard University Press.

PATEMAN, C. 1980. The civic culture: a philosophic critique. Pp. 57–102 in *The Civic Culture Revisited,* ed. G. Almond and S. Verba. Boston: Little Brown.

POLLETTA, F. 1998*a*. Contending stories: narrative in social movements. *Qualitative Sociology,* 21: 419–46.

——1998*b*. "It was like a fever . . .": narrative and identity in social protest. *Social Problems,* 45: 137–59.

PRESS, A., and COLE, E. 1999. *Speaking of Abortion.* Chicago: University of Chicago Press.

PUTNAM, R. 1993. *Making Democracy Work.* Princeton, NJ: Princeton University Press.

——2000. *Bowling Alone.* New York: Simon and Schuster.

QUÉRÉ, L. 1982. *Des miroirs équivoques: Aux origines de la communication moderne*. Paris: Aubier.

SCHUDSON, M. 1998. *The Good Citizen*. New York: Free Press.

SCOTT, J. 1990. *Domination and the Arts of Resistance*. New Haven, Conn.: Yale University Press.

SEWELL, W. H., JR. 1980. *Work and Revolution in France*. Cambridge: Cambridge University Press.

——1999. The concept(s) of culture. Pp. 35–61 in *Beyond the Cultural Turn*, ed. V. E. Bonnell and L. Hunt. Berkeley: University of California Press.

SILBER, I. 2003. Pragmatic sociology as cultural sociology: beyond repertoire theory? *European Journal of Social Theory*, 6: 427–49.

SKOCPOL, T. 1999. Advocates without members: the recent transformation of American civic life. Pp. 461–510 in *Civic Engagement in American Democracy*, ed. T. Skocpol and M. Fiorina. Washington, DC: Brookings Institution Press and Russell Sage Foundation.

SMITH, P. (ed.) 1998. *The New American Cultural Sociology*. Cambridge: Cambridge University Press.

SNOW, D., ROCHFORD, B., JR., WORDEN, S., and BENFORD, R. D. 1986. Frame alignment processes, micromobilization and movement participation. *American Sociological Review*, 51: 464–81.

——and BENFORD, R. 1988. Ideology, frame resonance and participant mobilization. *International Social Movement Research*, 1: 197–217.

SOMERS, M. 1995. What's so political and cultural about political culture and the public sphere? *Sociological Theory*, 13: 229–74.

STEINBERG, M. 1999. The talk and back talk of collective action: a dialogic analysis of repertoires of discourse among nineteenth-century English cotton spinners. *American Journal of Sociology*, 105: 736–80.

STEINMETZ, G. 1999. *State/Culture*. Ithaca, NY: Cornell University Press.

SWIDLER, A. 1986. Culture in action: symbols and strategies. *American Sociological Review*, 51: 273–86.

——2001. *Talk of Love*. Chicago: University of Chicago Press.

TAYLOR, V., and WHITTIER, N. 1992. Collective identity in social movement communities: lesbian feminist mobilization. Pp. 104–30 in *Frontiers of Social Movement Theory*, ed. A. Morris and C. Mueller. New Haven, Conn.: Yale University Press.

TOCQUEVILLE, A. de. 1969. *Democracy in America*, trans. G. Lawrence, ed. J. P. Mayer. Garden City, NJ: Doubleday; originally published 1835.

TROM, D, and ZIMMERMANN, B. 2001. Cadres et institutions des problèmes publics: les cas du chômage et du paysage. Pp. 281–315 in *Les Formes de l'Action Collective*, ed. D. Cefaï and D. Trom. Paris: Éditions de l'EHESS.

TURNER, V. 1974. *Dramas, Fields and Metaphors*. Ithaca, NY: Cornell University Press.

VANDERBILT, T. 1997. The advertised life. Pp. 127–42 in *Commodify Your Dissent: Salvos from The Baffler*, ed. T. Frank and M. Weiland. New York: Norton.

VERBA, S., SCHLOZMAN, K., and BRADY, H. 1995. *Voice and Equality: Civic Voluntarism in American Politics*. Cambridge, Mass.: Harvard University Press.

WAGNER-PACIFICI, R., and SCHWARTZ, B. 1991. The Vietnam veterans memorial: commemorating a difficult past. *American Journal of Sociology*, 97: 376–420.

WALZER, M. 1969. *The Revolution of the Saints*. New York: Atheneum.

WARREN, M. R. 2001. *Dry Bones Rattling*. Princeton, NJ: Princeton University Press.

WEDEEN, L. 1999. *Ambiguities of Domination: Politics, Rhetorics and Symbols in Contemporary Syria*. Chicago: University of Chicago Press.

WILLIAMS, R. 1977. *Marxism and Literature*. New York: Oxford University Press.

WILLIAMS, R. H., 1995. Constructing the public good: social movements and cultural resources. *Social Problems*, 42: 124–44.

WOOD, R. 1994. Faith in action: religious resources for political success in three congregations. *Sociology of Religion*, 55(4): 397–417.

—— 1999. Religious culture and political action. *Sociological Theory*, 17: 307–32.

—— 2002. *Faith in Action*. Chicago: University of Chicago Press.

WUTHNOW, R. 1987. *Meaning and Moral Order*. Berkeley: University of California Press.

—— 1989. *Communities of discourse: ideology and social structure in the Reformation, the Enlightenment, and European Socialism*. Cambridge, Mass.: Harvard University Press.

—— 1998. *Loose Connections*. Cambridge, Mass.: Harvard University Press.

PART VI

HISTORY MATTERS

CHAPTER 22

WHY AND HOW HISTORY MATTERS

CHARLES TILLY

Do you suppose that historians labor dumbly in deep trenches, digging up facts so that political scientists can order and explain them? Do you imagine that political scientists, those skilled intellectual surgeons, slice through the fat of history to get at the sinews of rational choice or political economy? Do you claim that political scientists can avoid peering into the mists of history by clear-eyed examination of the contemporary world that lies within their view? On the contrary: this chapter gives reasons for thinking that explanatory political science can hardly get anywhere without relying on careful historical analysis.

Let us begin, appropriately, with a historical experience. Early in 1969, Stanford political scientist Gabriel Almond proposed that the (US) Social Science Research Council use Ford Foundation funds to support a study of state formation in Western Europe. Thus began an adventure. For fifteen years before then, the SSRC's Committee on Comparative Politics had been looking at what it called "political development in the new states." By then, committee members Almond, Leonard Binder, Philip Converse, Samuel Huntington, Joseph LaPalombara, Lucian Pye, Sidney Verba, Robert Ward, Myron Weiner, and Aristide Zolberg had converged on the idea that new states faced a standard and roughly sequential series of crises, challenges, and problems. Resolution of those problems, they argued, permitted states to move on to the next stage en route to a fully effective political regime. In a phrase that reflected their project's normative and policy aspirations, they often called the whole process state- and nation-building. The SSRC committee labeled its crises PIPILD: Penetration, Integration, Participation, Identity, Legitimacy, and Distribution.

Committee members theorized that (*a*) all new states confronted the six crises in approximately this order, (*b*) the more these crises concentrated in time, the greater the social stress and therefore the higher the likelihood of conflict, breakdown, and disintegration, (*c*) in general, new states faced far greater bunching of the crises than had their Western counterparts, hence became more prone to breakdown than Western states had been. The violence, victimization, and venality of new states' public politics stemmed from cumulation of crises. Presumably superior political science knowledge would not only explain those ill effects but also help national or international authorities steer fragile new states through unavoidable crises.

The SSRC scheme rested on one strong historical premise and two weak ones. On the strong side, the theorists assumed that Western states had, on the whole, created effective national institutions gradually, in a slow process of trial, error, compromise, and consolidation. More hesitantly, these analysts assumed both that political development everywhere followed roughly the same course and that the course's end point would yield states resembling those currently prevailing in the Western world.

Since theorists of political development actually drew regularly on Western historical analogies (see, e.g., Almond and Powell 1966), SSRC committee members naturally wondered whether a closer look at Western history would confirm their scheme. It could do so by showing that the same crises appeared recognizably in the historical record, that they occurred more discretely and over longer periods in older states, that later-developing states experienced greater accumulations of crises, and that bunched crises did, indeed, generate stress, conflict, breakdown, and disintegration. In my guise as a European historian, they therefore asked me to recruit a group of fellow European historians who had the necessary knowledge, imagination, and synthetic verve to do the job. (As we will see later, they were also sponsoring a rival team of European historians, no doubt to check the reliability of my team's conclusions.)

Our assignment: to meet, deliberate, do the necessary research, report our results, criticize each other's accounts, and write a collective book. A remarkable set of talented scholars accepted the challenge: Gabriel Ardant, David Bayley, Rudolf Braun, Samuel Finer, Wolfram Fischer, Peter Lundgreen, and Stein Rokkan. We spent the summer of 1970 together at the Center for Advanced Study in the Behavioral Sciences (Stanford, California), frequently calling in critics such as Gabriel Almond, Val Lorwin, and G. William Skinner. We presented draft chapters to each other and a few sympathetic critics in Bellagio, Italy, during a strenuous week the following year. After multiple exchanges and painstaking editing, we finally published our book in 1975.

Before we began the enterprise, I had produced several essays dissenting from the sorts of breakdown theories that formed the midsection of the committee's scheme (e.g. Tilly 1969). Some committee members may therefore have hoped to convert me to the committee's views. Or perhaps secret skeptics within the committee wanted to raise their colleagues' doubts about the committee's political development scheme.[1] In either case, they got more than they bargained for. Looked at closely, the relevant Western European history revealed repeated crises, constant struggle, numerous collapses, far more states that disappeared than survived, and a process of state transformation driven largely by extraction, control, and coalition formation as parts or byproducts of rulers' efforts not to build states but to make war and survive.

In an abortive effort to counter the intentionality and teleology of such terms as "state-building" and "political development," my co-authors and I self-consciously substituted what we thought to be the more neutral term "state formation." The term itself caught on surprisingly fast. Unfortunately, it also soon took on teleological tones in the literature on political change.[2] Contrary to our intentions, students of state formation in Latin America, Africa, the Middle East, or Asia began taking the European experience as a model, and asking why their regions had failed to form proper states.[3] Nevertheless, many readers saw the book as a serious challenge to existing ideas about political development (Skocpol 1985).

What is more, our historical reflections raised the distinct possibility that the processes of state formation were far more contingent, transitory, and reversible than analysts of political development then supposed. Hoping to write the final sentence of the final volume in the SSRC's series of books on political development, I therefore ended my concluding essay with these words:

But remember the definition of a state as an organization, controlling the principal means of coercion within a given territory, which is differentiated from other organizations operating in the same territory, autonomous, centralized, and formally coordinated. If there is something to the trends we have described, they threaten almost every single one of these defining features of the state: the monopoly of coercion, the exclusiveness of control within the territory, the autonomy, the centralization, the formal coordination; even the differentiation from other organizations begins to fall away in such compacts as the European Common Market. One last perhaps, then: perhaps, as is so often the case, we only begin to understand this momentous historical process—the formation of national states—when it begins to lose its universal significance. Perhaps, unknowing, we are writing obituaries for the state.   (Tilly 1975, 638)

I lost, alas, my rhetorical bet: a parallel SSRC group of historians working on direct applications of the crisis scheme to the United Kingdom, Belgium, Scandinavia, the United States, Spain, Portugal, France, Italy, Germany, Russia, and Poland under Raymond Grew's leadership took even longer to publish their volume

---

[1] For hints in that direction, see Verba 1971.

[2] See, e.g., Biggs 1999; Braddick 2000; Corrigan and Sayer 1985.

[3] For critiques, see Barkey and Parikh 1991; Centeno 2002.

than we did. Editor Grew closed his presentation of the book's findings with words more cautious than my own:

Models of political development should not tempt us to explain too much, nor be allowed to stimulate too many ingenious answers before the questions are clear. Today's heuristic device must not become tomorrow's assumption. One of the strengths of these essays is that they do not attempt to create a closed system; another is their recognition of many paths to political survival—and of many higher goals. A next step should be the careful formulation of historical (and therefore not just developmental) problems, followed by the comparison of realities rather than abstractions. The Committee's broad categories of political development, like photographs of the earth taken from space, remind us that familiar terrain is part of a larger system, and urge us to compare diverse features that from a distance appear similar. They do not obviate the need for a closer look.   (Grew 1978, 37)

In short, according to Grew, the crisis-and-sequence scheme may raise some interesting historical questions, but it certainly does not answer them.

Differences between the Tilly and Grew conclusions mark an important choice for historical analysts of political processes.[4] On one side (Grew), we can stress the obdurate particularity of historical experiences, hoping at most to arrive at rough, useful empirical generalizations through close analysis of specific cases. On the other (Tilly), we can use history to build more adequate explanations of politics past and present. Unsurprisingly, this chapter recommends the theoretically more ambitious second course, while heartily agreeing with Grew that it requires expert historical knowledge. Not only do all political processes occur in history and therefore call for knowledge of their historical contexts, but also where and when political processes occur influence *how* they occur. History thus becomes an essential element of sound explanations for political processes.

1   WHY HISTORY MATTERS

Several different paths lead to that conclusion. Here are the main ones:

- At least for large-scale political processes, explanations always make implicit or explicit assumptions concerning historical origins of the phenomenon and time–place scope conditions for the claimed explanation. Those assumptions remain

---

[4] Here and hereafter, "historical" means locating the phenomenon meaningfully in time and place relative to other times and places, "political" means involving at least one coercion-wielding organization as participant or influential third party, and "process" means a connected stream of causes and effects; see Pierson 2004, Tilly 2001a.

open to historical verification and falsification. Example: students of international relations commonly assume that some time between the treaty of Augsburg (1555) and the treaties of Westphalia (1648), Europeans supplanted a web of overlapping jurisdictions with a system of clearly bounded sovereign states that then provided the context for war and diplomacy up to the present.

- In the case of long-term processes, some or all features of the process occur outside the observations of any connected cohort of human analysts, and therefore require historical reconstruction. Example: displacement of personal armies, feudal levies, militias, and mercenary bands by centrally controlled national standing armies took several centuries to occur.
- Most or all political processes incorporate locally available cultural materials such as language, social categories, and widely shared beliefs; they therefore vary as a function of historically determined local cultural accumulations. Example: economically, linguistically, ethnically, racially, and religiously segmented regions create significantly different configurations of state–citizen relations.
- Processes occurring in adjacent places such as neighboring countries influence local political processes, hence historically variable adjacencies alter the operation of those processes. Example: the Swiss Confederation survived as a loosely connected but distinct political entity after 1500 in part precisely because much larger but competing Austrian, Savoyard, French, and German states formed around its perimeter.
- Path dependency prevails in political processes, such that events occurring at one stage in a sequence constrain the range of events that is possible at later stages. Example: for all its service of privilege, the entrenchment of the assembly that became England's Parliament by the barons' rebellion of 1215 set limits on arbitrary royal power in England from that point forward.
- Once a process (e.g. a revolution) has occurred and acquired a name, both the name and one or more representations of the process become available as signals, models, threats, and/or aspirations for later actors. Example: the creation of an elected national assembly in the France of 1789 to 1792 provided a model for subsequent political programs in France and elsewhere.

In all these ways, history matters. In the case of state transformation, there is no way to create comprehensive, plausible, and verifiable explanations without taking history seriously into account.

Apparently political scientists have learned that lesson since the 1960s. Now and then an economist, sociologist, geographer, or anthropologist does come up with a transhistorical model of state transformation.[5] Rare, however, is the political scientist that follows their lead (exceptions include Midlarsky 1999, Taagepera

[5] E.g. Batchelder and Freudenberger 1983; Bourdieu 1994; Clark and Dear 1984; Earle 1997; Friedmann 1977; Gledhill, Bender, and Larson 1988; Li 2002.

1997). To be sure, the historicists could be wrong and the unhistorical modelers right. I hope, however, to persuade you that historical context matters inescapably, at least for all but the most fleeting and localized political processes.

Whether the importance of history seems obvious or implausible, however, depends subtly on competing conceptions of explanation. As a first cut, let us distinguish:

1. Proposal of covering laws for complex structures and processes.
2. The special case of covering law accounts featuring the capacity of predictors within mathematical models to exhaust the variance in a "dependent variable" across some set of differing but comparable cases.
3. Specification of necessary and sufficient conditions for concrete instances of the same complex structures and processes.
4. Location of structures and processes within larger systems they supposedly serve or express.
5. Identification of individual or group dispositions just before the point of action as causes of that action.
6. Reduction of complex episodes, or certain features of those episodes, to their component mechanisms and processes.

In an earlier day, political scientists also explained political processes by means of "7. Stage models in which placement within an invariant sequence accounted for the episode at hand." That understanding of explanation vanished with the passing of political development.

History *can*, of course, figure in any of these explanatory conceptions. In a covering law account, for example, one can incorporate history as a scope condition (e.g. prior to the Chinese invention of gunpowder, war conformed to generalization X) or as an abstract variable (e.g. time elapsed or distance covered since the beginning of an episode[6]). Nevertheless, covering-law, necessary-sufficient condition, and system accounts generally resist history as they deny the influence of particular times and places. Propensity accounts respond to history ambivalently, since in the version represented by rational choice they depend on transhistorical rules of decision-making, while in the versions represented by cultural and phenomenological reductionism they treat history as infinitely particular.

Mechanism-process accounts, in contrast, positively welcome history, because their explanatory program couples a search for mechanisms of very general scope with arguments that initial conditions, sequences, and combinations of mechanisms concatenate into processes having explicable but variable overall outcomes. Mechanism-process accounts reject covering-law regularities for large structures such as international systems and for vast sequences such as democratization. Instead, they lend themselves to "local theory" in which the explanatory mechanisms and

<hr />

[6] See Roehner and Syme 2002.

processes operate quite broadly, but combine locally as a function of initial conditions and adjacent processes to produce distinctive trajectories and outcomes.[7]

2   History and Processes of State Transformation

Across a wide range of state transformation, for example, a robust process recurrently shapes state–citizen relations: the extraction–resistance–settlement cycle. In that process:

- Some authority tries to extract resources (e.g. military manpower) to support its own activities from populations living under its jurisdiction.
- Those resources (e.g. young men's labor) are already committed to competing activities that matter to the subordinate population's survival.
- Local people resist agents of the authority (e.g. press gangs) who arrive to seize the demanded resources.
- Struggle ensues.
- A settlement ends the struggle.

Clearly the overall outcome of the process varies from citizens' full compliance to fierce rejection of the authorities' demands (Levi 1988; 1997). Clearly that outcome depends not only on the process's internal dynamic but also on historically determined initial conditions (e.g. previous relations between local and national authorities) and on adjacent processes (e.g. intervention of competing authorities or threatened neighboring populations). But in all cases the settlement casts a significant shadow toward the next encounter between citizens and authorities. The settlement mechanism alters relations between citizens and authorities, locking those relations into place for a time.

Over several centuries of European state transformation, authorities commonly won the battle for conscripts, taxes, food, and means of transportation. Yet the settlement of the local struggle implicitly or explicitly sealed a bargain concerning the terms under which the next round of extraction could begin (Tilly 1992, chs. 3–4). Individual mechanisms of extraction, resistance, struggle, and settlement compound into a process that occurs widely, with variable but historically significant outcomes. From beginning to end, the process belongs to history.

Consider a second robust process of state transformation: subordination of armed forces to civilian control. Over most of human history, substantial groups

---

[7] McAdam, Tarrow, and Tilly 2001; Tilly 2001b.

of armed men—almost exclusively men!—have bent to no authority outside of their own number. Wielders of coercion have run governments across the world. Yet recurrently, from Mesopotamian city-states to contemporary Africa, priests, merchants, aristocrats, bureaucrats, and even elected officials who did not themselves specialize in deployment of armed force have somehow managed to exert effective control over military specialists.[8]

That process has taken two closely related forms. In the first, the course of military conquest itself brought conquerors to state power. Then administration of conquered territories involved rulers so heavily in extraction, control, and mediation within those territories that they began simultaneously to create civilian staffs, to gather resources for military activity by means of those staffs, and thus to make the military dependent for their own livelihoods on the effectiveness of those staffs. In the process, tax-granting legislatures and budget-making bureaucrats gained the upper hand.

In the second variant, a group of priests or merchants drew riches from their priestly or mercantile activity, staffed the higher levels of their governments with priests, merchants, or other civilians, and hired military specialists to carry out war and policing. In both versions of the subordination process, the crucial mechanisms inhibited direct military control over the supply of resources required for the reproduction of military organization.

As in the case of extraction–resistance–settlement processes, the actual outcomes depended not only on internal dynamics but also on initial conditions and adjacent processes. In Latin America, for example, military specialists who had participated extensively in domestic political control recurrently overthrew civilian rule (Centeno 2002). Military men retained more leverage where they had direct access to sustaining resources, notably when they actually served as hired guns for landed elites and when they could sell or tax lootable resources such as diamonds and drugs. Again, a similar process occurs across a wide range of historical experience, but its exact consequences depend intimately on historical context.

3   SOCIAL MOVEMENTS AS POLITICAL INNOVATIONS

State transformation may seem too easy a case for my argument. After all, since the fading of political development models most political scientists have conducted

---

[8] Bratton and van de Walle 1997; Briant et al. 2002; Creveld 1999; Huters, Wong, and Yu 1997; Khazanov 1993; López-Alves 2000; Wong 1997.

contemporary studies of state changes against the backdrop of explicit references to historical experience. The same does not hold for the study of social movements. By and large, students of contemporary social movements fail to recognize that they are analyzing an evolving set of historically derived political practices. Either they assume that social movements have always existed in some form or they treat social movements as contemporary political forms without inquiring into their historical transformations.

Nevertheless, sophisticated treatments of social movements generally assume a broad historical connection between democratization and social movement expansion.[9] One of the more important open questions in social movement studies, indeed, concerns the causal connections between social movement activity and democratization—surely two-way, but what and how (Ibarra 2003; Tilly 2004, ch. 6)?

Social movements illustrate all the major arguments for taking the history of political processes seriously:

- Existing explanations of social movements always make implicit or explicit assumptions concerning historical origins of the phenomenon and time–place scope conditions for the claimed explanation.
- Some features of social movements occurred outside the direct observations of any connected cohort of human analysts, and therefore require historical reconstruction.
- Social movements incorporate locally available cultural materials such as language, social categories, and widely shared beliefs; they therefore vary as a function of historically determined local cultural accumulations.
- Social movements occurring in adjacent places such as neighboring countries influence local social movements, hence historically variable adjacencies alter the kinds of social movements that appear in any particular place.
- Path dependency prevails in social movements as in other political processes, such that events occurring at one stage in a sequence constrain the range of events that is possible at later stages.
- Once social movements had occurred and acquired names, both the name and competing representations of social movements became available as signals, models, threats, and/or aspirations for later actors.

None of these observations condemns students of social movements to historical particularism. Regularities in social movement activity depend on and incorporate historical context, which means that effective explanations of social movement activity must systematically take historical context into account. Like anti-tax rebellions, religious risings, elections, publicity campaigns, special interest lobbying, and political propaganda, social movements consist of standard means by

[9] Costain and McFarland 1998; Edelman 2001; Foweraker and Landman 1997; Hoffmann 2003; Meyer and Tarrow 1998; Walker 1991.

which interested or aggrieved citizens make collective claims on other people, including political authorities. Like all these other forms of politics, the social movement emerges only in some kinds of political settings, waxes and wanes in response to its political surroundings, undergoes significant change over the course of its history, and yet where it prevails offers a clear set of opportunities for interested or aggrieved citizens.

Consider just two historically conditioned aspects of social movements: their repertoires of claim-making performances and their signaling systems. History shapes the availability of means for making collective claims, from the humble petition received by a Chinese emperor to the *pronunciamiento* of a nineteenth-century Spanish military faction. Those means always involve interactive performances of some sort, preferably following established scripts sufficiently to be recognizable but not so slavishly as to become pure ritual. They therefore draw heavily on historically accumulated and shared understandings with regard to meanings, claims, legitimate claimants, and proper objects of claims.

In any given historical period, available claim-making performances group linking various pairs of claimants, and objects of claims clump into restricted *repertoires:* arrays of known alternative performances. In Great Britain of the 1750s, for example, the contentious repertoire widely available to ordinary people included:

- *attacks on coercive authorities:* liberation of prisoners; resistance to police intervention in gatherings and entertainments; resistance to press gangs; fights between hunters and gamekeepers; battles between smugglers and royal officers; forcible opposition to evictions; military mutinies
- *attacks on popularly-designated offenses and offenders:* Rough Music; ridicule and/or destruction of symbols, effigies, and/or property of public figures and moral offenders; verbal and physical attacks on malefactors seen in public places; pulling down and/or sacking of dangerous or offensive houses, including workhouses and brothels; smashing of shops and bars whose proprietors are accused of unfair dealing or of violating public morality; collective seizures of food, often coupled with sacking the merchant's premises and/or public sale of the food below current market price; blockage or diversion of food shipments; destruction of tollgates; collective invasions of enclosed land, often including destruction of fences or hedges
- *celebrations and other popularly-initiated gatherings:* collective cheering, jeering, or stoning of public figures or their conveyances; popularly-initiated public celebrations of major events (e.g. John Wilkes' elections of the 1760s), with cheering, drinking, display of partisan symbols, fireworks, etc., sometimes with forced participation of reluctant persons; forced illuminations, including attacks on windows of householders who fail to illuminate; faction fights (e.g. Irish vs. English, rival groups of military)

- *workers' sanctions over members of their trades*: turnouts by workers in multiple shops of a local trade; workers' marches to public authorities in trade disputes; donkeying, or otherwise humiliating, workers who violated collective agreements; destroying goods (e.g. silk in looms and/or the looms themselves) of workers or masters who violate collective agreements
- *claim-making within authorized public assemblies* (e.g. Lord Mayor's Day): taking of positions by means of cheers, jeers, attacks, and displays of symbols; attacks on supporters of electoral candidates; parading and chairing of candidates; taking sides at public executions; attacks or professions of support for pilloried prisoners; salutation or deprecation of public figures (e.g. royalty) at theater; collective response to lines and characters in plays or other entertainments; breaking up of theaters at unsatisfactory performances.

Not all British claim-makers, to be sure, had access to all these performances; some of the performances linked workers to masters, others market regulars to local merchants, and so on. In any case, the repertoire available to ordinary Britons during the 1750s did not include electoral campaigns, formal public meetings, street marches, demonstrations, petition drives, or the formation of special-interest associations, all of which became quite common ways of pressing claims during the nineteenth century. As these newer performances became common, the older ones disappeared.

That is where the social movement repertoire comes in. Originating in Great Britain and North America during the later eighteenth century, a distinctive array of claim-making performances formed that marked off social movements from other varieties of politics, underwent a series of mutations from the eighteenth century to the present, and spread widely through the world during the nineteenth and (especially) twentieth centuries. Social movements constituted sustained claims on well-identified objects by self-declared interested or aggrieved parties through performances dramatizing not only their support for or opposition to a program, person, or group, but also their worthiness, unity, numbers, and commitment. (Social movement participants always claim to represent some wider public, and sometimes claim to speak for non-participants such as fetuses, slaves, or trees.) The array of performances constituting social movement repertoires has shifted historically, but from the earliest days it included formation of named special-interest associations and coalitions, holding of public meetings, statements in and to the press, pamphleteering, and petitioning.

Social movement repertoires amply illustrate the importance of history. Although the British–American eighteenth century repertoire brought new elements together, each element had some sort of available precedent. British governments repressed popular, private, non-religious associations that took public stands as threats to the rights of Parliament. Yet they had accepted or even promoted religious congregations, authorized parish assemblies, grudgingly allowed workers' mutual-aid societies that refrained from striking and other public claim-making. Authorities had also long tolerated clubs of aristocrats and wealthy city-dwellers. (The term "club" itself derives from the practice of clubbing together for shared expenses, and thus taking on a resemblance to a knotted stick.) More rarely and indirectly, social movement repertoires also drew on authorized parades of artisans' corporations, militias, and fraternal orders. Adaptations of such parades figured extensively in Irish conflicts from the eighteenth century to the present.[10]

Eighteenth-century innovations broadened those practices in two different directions, converting authorized religious and local assemblies into bases for campaigns and creating popular special-purpose associations devoted to public claim-making rather than (or in addition to) private enjoyment, improvement, and mutual aid. The broadening occurred through struggle, but also through patronage by sympathetic or dissident members of the elite. More generally, the internal histories of particular forms of claim-making, changing relations between potential claimants and objects of claims, innovations by political entrepreneurs, and overall transformations of the political context combined to produce cumulative alterations of social movement repertoires (Tilly 1993).

The formation of the social movement repertoire included substantial losses as well as considerable gains. Many of the avenging, redressing, and humiliating actions that had worked intermittently to impose popular justice before 1800—seizures of high-priced food, attacks on press gangs, donkey-riding of workers who violated local customs, and others—became illegal. Authorities whose predecessors had mostly looked the other way so long as participants localized their actions and refrained from attacking elite persons or property, began to treat all such actions as "riots," and to prosecute their perpetrators. Establishment of crowd-control police as substitutes for constables, militias, and regular troops in containment of demonstrations and marches temporarily increased the frequency of violent confrontations between police and demonstrators. Over the long run, however, it narrowed the range of actions open to street protestors, promoted prior negotiation between social movement activists and police, encouraged organizers themselves to exclude unruly elements from their supporters, and channeled claim-making toward non-violent interaction. Path dependence prevailed, as early innovations in the social movement repertoire greatly constrained later possibilities.

Social movement *signaling systems* similarly illustrate the importance of history. From the start, social movements centered on campaigns in support of or in opposition to publicly articulated programs by means of associations, meetings, demonstrations, petitions, electoral participation, strikes, and related means of coordinated action. Unlike many of its predecessors, the social movement form provided opportunities to offer sustained challenges directed at powerful figures and institutions without necessarily attacking them physically. It said, in effect, "We

[10] Bryan 2000; Farrell 2000; Jarman 1997; Kinealy 2003; Mac Suibhne 2000.

are here, we support this cause, there are lots of us, we know how to act together, and we could cause trouble if we wanted to."

As compared with the many forms of direct action that ordinary people had employed earlier, social movement performances almost never achieved in a single iteration what they asked for: passage of legislation, removal of an official, punishment of a villain, distribution of benefits, and so on. Only cumulatively, and usually only in part, did some movements realize their claims. But individual performances such as meetings and marches did not simply signal that a certain number of people had certain complaints or demands. They signaled that those people had created internal connections, that they had backing, that they commanded pooled resources, and that they therefore had the capacity to act collectively, even disruptively, elsewhere and in the future.

More exactly, from early on social movement performances broadcast WUNC: worthiness, unity, numbers, and commitment. How they broadcast those attributes varied historically, but in early stages the signaling had something like this character:

- *Worthiness:* sober demeanor, neat clothing, presence of dignitaries
- *Unity:* matching badges, armbands, or costumes, marching in ranks, singing and chanting
- *Numbers:* headcounts, signatures on petitions, messages from constituents
- *Commitment:* mutual defense, resistance to repression, ostentatious sacrifice, subscription and benefaction

If any of these elements—worthiness, unity, numbers, or commitment—visibly fell to a low level, the social movement lost impact. This signaling system helps explain two centuries of dispute between authorities and participants over whether pleasure-seekers or vandals had joined a performance, how many of the people present happened to be on the premises for other purposes or out of idle curiosity, how many people actually took part in the performance, and whether the police used undue brutality. Social movement performances challenge authorities and other political actors to accept or reject both a set of claims and the existence of a distinctive collective political actor. But the relevant signaling systems change and vary historically.

4   SOCIAL MOVEMENTS IN HISTORY

With these lessons in mind, let us look more closely at the early development of social movement claim-making. We can usefully begin a history of social movements as distinctive forms of political action in the 1760s, when after the Seven Years War (1756–1763) critics of royal policy in England and its North American colonies began assembling, marching, and associating to protest heightened taxation and arbitrary rule (Tilly 1977). Braving or evading repression, they reshaped existing practices such as middle-class clubs, petition marches, parish assemblies, and celebratory banquets into new instruments of political criticism. Although social movement activity waxed and waned with state toleration and repression, from the later eighteenth century the social movement model spread through Western Europe and North America, becoming a major vehicle of popular claim-making.

In the British Isles, for example, by the 1820s popular leaders were organizing effective social movements against the slave trade, for the political rights of Catholics, and for freedom of association among workers. In the United States, anti-slavery was becoming a major social movement not much later. American workers' movements proliferated during the first half of the nineteenth century. By the 1850s social movements were starting to displace older forms of popular politics through much of Western Europe and North America.

Throughout the world since 1850, social movements have generally flourished where and when contested elections became central to politics. Contested elections promote social movements in several different ways:

- First, they provide a model of public support for rival programs, as embodied in competing candidates; once governments have authorized public discussion of major issues during electoral campaigns, it becomes harder to silence that discussion outside of electoral campaigns.
- Second, they legalize and protect assemblies of citizens for campaigning and voting. Citizens allowed to gather in support of candidates and parties easily take up other issues that concern them.
- Third, elections magnify the importance of numbers; with contested elections, any group receiving disciplined support from large numbers of followers becomes a possible ally or enemy at the polls.
- Finally, some expansion of rights to speak, communicate, and assemble publicly almost inevitably accompanies the establishment of contested elections. Even people who lack the vote can disrupt elections, march in support of popular candidates, and use rights of assembly, communication, and speech.

Once social movements existed, nevertheless, they became available for politics well outside the electoral arena. Take temperance: opposition to the sale and public consumption of alcohol. In Britain and America, organized temperance enthusiasts sometimes swayed elections. American anti-alcohol activists formed a Prohibition Party in 1869. But temperance advocates also engaged in direct moral intervention by organizing religious campaigns, holding public meetings, circulating pledges of abstinence, and getting educators to teach the evils of alcohol. In both Great Britain and the United States, the Salvation Army (founded in London, 1865) carried on street crusades against alcohol and for the rescue of alcoholics without engaging directly in electoral politics. American agitator Carrie Nation got herself arrested thirty times during the 1890s and 1900s as she physically attacked bars in states that had passed, but not enforced, bans on the sale of alcohol. Social movements expanded with electoral politics, but soon operated quite outside the realm of parties and elections.

Anti-slavery action in the United States and Britain (that is, England, Wales, Scotland) illustrates the social movement's rise.[11] Mobilization against slavery and increasing salience of national elections—with slavery itself an electoral issue— reinforced each other in the two countries. The timing of anti-slavery mobilization is surprising. Both the abolition of the slave trade and the later emancipation of slaves occurred when slave-based production was still expanding across much of North and South America. The Atlantic slave trade fed captive labor mainly into production of sugar, coffee, and cotton for European consumption. North and South American slave labor provided 70 percent of the cotton processed by British mills in 1787 and 90 percent in 1838. Although slave production of sugar, coffee, and cotton continued to expand past the mid-nineteenth century, transatlantic traffic in slaves reached its peak between 1781 and 1790, held steady for a few decades, then declined rapidly after 1840.

Outlawing of slavery itself proceeded fitfully for a century, from Haiti's spectacular slave rebellion (1790 onward) to Brazil's reluctant emancipation (1888). Argentina, for example, outlawed both slavery and the slave trade in its constitution of 1853. Between the 1840s and 1888, then, the Atlantic slave trade was disappearing and slavery itself was ending country by country. Yet slave-based production of cotton and other commodities continued to increase until the 1860s. How was that possible? Increases in slave-based commodity production depended partly on rising labor productivity and partly on population growth within the remaining slave population. Slavery did not disappear because it had lost its profitability. Movements against the slave trade, then against slavery itself, overturned economically viable systems.

How did that happen? Although heroic activists sometimes campaigned publicly against slavery in major regions of slave-based production, crucial campaigns first took place mostly where slaves were rare but beneficiaries of their production were prominent. For the most part, anti-slavery support arose in populations that benefited no more than indirectly from slave production. The English version of the story begins in 1787. English Quakers, Methodists, and other anti-establishment Protestants joined with more secular advocates of working-class freedoms to oppose all forms of coerced labor. A Society for the Abolition of the Slave Trade, organized in 1787, coordinated a vast national campaign, an early social movement.

---

[11] d'Anjou 1996; Drescher 1986; 1994; Eltis 1993; Grimsted 1998; Klein 1999, ch. 8.

During the next two decades, British activists rounded out the social movement repertoire with two crucial additions: the lobby and the demonstration. Lobbying began literally as talking to Members of Parliament in the lobby of the Parliament building on their way to or from sessions. Later the word generalized to mean any direct intervention with legislators to influence their votes. British activists also created the two forms of the demonstration we still know today: the disciplined march through streets and the organized assembly in a symbolically significant public space, both accompanied by coordinated displays of support for a shared program. Of course all the forms of social movement activism had precedents, including public meetings, formal presentations of petitions, and the committees of correspondence that played so important a part in American resistance to royal demands during the 1760s and 1770s. But between the 1780s and the 1820s British activists created a new synthesis. From then to the present, social movements regularly combined associations, meetings, demonstrations, petitions, electoral participation, lobbying, strikes, and related means of coordinated action.

Within Great Britain, Parliament began responding to popular pressure almost immediately, with partial regulation of the slave trade in 1788. By 1806, abolition of the slave trade had become a major issue in parliamentary elections. In 1807, Parliament declared illegal the shipping of slaves to Britain's colonies, effective at the start of the following year. From that point on, British activists demanded that their government act against other slave-trading countries. Great Britain then pressed for withdrawal of other European powers from the slave trade. At the end of the Napoleonic Wars in 1815, the major European powers except for Spain and Portugal agreed to abolition of the trade. Under economic and diplomatic pressure from Britain, Spain and Portugal reluctantly withdrew from officially sanctioned slave trading step by step between 1815 and 1867. From 1867 onward, only outlaws shipped slaves across the Atlantic.

Soon after 1815, British activists were moving successfully to restrict the powers of slave owners in British colonies, and finally—in 1834—to end slavery itself. Although French revolutionaries outlawed both the slave trade and slavery throughout France and its colonies in 1794, Napoleon's regime restored them ten years later. France did not again abolish slavery and the slave trade until the Revolution of 1848. With Brazil's abolition of slavery in 1888, legal slavery finally disappeared from Europe and the Americas. Backed aggressively by state power, British social movement pressure had brought about a momentous change.

As of the later nineteenth century, social movements had become widely available in Western countries as bases of popular claim-making. They served repeatedly in drives for suffrage, workers' rights, restrictions on discrimination, temperance, and political reform.[12] During the twentieth century, they proliferated, attached

---

[12] Buechler 1990; Calhoun 1995; Gamson 1990; McCammon and Campbell 2002; McCammon et al. 2001; Tarrow 1998.

themselves more firmly to the mass media, and gained followings in a wider variety of class, ethnic, religious, and political categories. More frequently than before, social movements also supported conservative or reactionary programs—either on their own or (more often) in reaction to left movements. Italian and German fascists, after all, employed anti-leftist social movement strategies on their ways to power (Anheier, Neidhardt, and Vortkamp 1998). As a result of incessant negotiation and confrontation, relations between social movement activists and authorities, especially police, changed significantly.[13]

Regularities in social movements, then, depended heavily on their historical contexts. Eighteenth-century social movement pioneers adapted and combined forms of political interaction that were already available in their contexts: the special-purpose association, the petition drive, the parish meeting, and so on. They thereby created new varieties of politics. Forms of social movement activity mutated in part as a consequence of changes in their political environments and in part as a result of innovations within the form itself on the part of activists, authorities, and objects of claims (Tilly and Wood 2003). Early innovations stuck and constrained later innovations not only because widespread familiarity with such routines as demonstrating facilitated organizing the next round of claim-making, but also because each innovation altered relations among authorities, police, troops, activists, their targets, their rivals, their opponents, and the public at large. When movement repertoires diffused, they always changed as a function of differences and connections between the old setting and the new (Chabot and Duyvendak 2002). Social movement politics has a history.

5   CONCLUDING REFLECTIONS

So does the rest of politics. We could pursue the same sort of argument across a great many other historically grounded political phenomena: democratization and de-democratization, revolution, electoral systems, clientelism, terror, ethnic mobilization, interstate war, civic participation, and more. The conclusion would come out the same: every significant political phenomenon lives in history, and requires historically grounded analysis for its explanation. Political scientists ignore historical context at their peril.

So should political science quietly dissolve into history? Must professional political scientists turn in their badges for those of professional historians? No, at

---

[13] Fillieule 1997; della Porta 1995; della Porta and Reiter 1998.

least not entirely. I would, it is true, welcome company in the thinly populated no man's land at the frontiers of history and political science. But history as a discipline has its own peculiarities. Historians do not merely take serious account of time and place. They revel in time and place, defining problems in terms of specific times and places, even when doing world history. One ordinarily becomes a professional historian by mastering the sources, languages, institutions, culture, and historiography of some particular time and place, then using that knowledge to solve some problem posed by the time and place. The problems may in some sense be universal: how people coped with disaster, what caused brutal wars, under what conditions diverse populations managed to live together. The proposed solutions may also partake of universality: one step in the evolution of humanity, persistent traits of human nature, the tragedy of vain belief. But the questions pursued belong to the time and place, and adhere to the conversation among students of the time and place.

Although we might make exceptions for area specialists and students of domestic politics, on the whole political scientists' analytic conversations do not concern times and places so much as certain processes, institutions, and kinds of events. Let me therefore rephrase my sermon. As the analysis of state transformations and social movements illustrates, political scientists should continue to work at explaining processes, institutions, and kinds of events. To do so more effectively, however, they should take history seriously, but in their own distinctive way.

References

ALMOND, G., and POWELL, G. B., JR. 1966. *Comparative Politics: A Developmental Approach.* Boston: Little, Brown.

ANHEIER, H. K., NEIDHARDT, F., and VORTKAMP, W. 1998. Movement cycles and the Nazi Party: activities of the Munich NSDAP, 1925–1930. *American Behavioral Scientist,* 41: 1262–81.

d'ANJOU, L. 1996. *Social Movements and Cultural Change: The First Abolition Campaign Revisited.* New York: Aldine de Gruyter.

BARKEY, K., and PARIKH, S. 1991. Comparative perspectives on the state. *Annual Review of Sociology,* 17: 523–49.

BATCHELDER, R. W., and FREUDENBERGER, H. 1983. On the rational origins of the modern centralized state. *Explorations in Economic History,* 20: 1–13.

BIGGS, M. 1999. Putting the state on the map: cartography, territory and European state formation. *Comparative Studies in Society and History,* 41: 374–405.

BOURDIEU, P. 1994. Rethinking the state: genesis and structure of the bureaucratic field. *Sociological Theory,* 12: 1–18.

BRADDICK, M. 2000. *State Formation in Early Modern England c. 1550–1700.* Cambridge: Cambridge University Press.

BRATTON, M., and VAN DE WALLE, N. 1997. *Democratic Experiments in Africa: Regime Transitions in Comparative Perspective*. Cambridge: Cambridge University Press.

BRIANT, P., GASCHE, H., TANRET, M., COLE, S. W., VERHOEVEN, K., CHARPIN, D., DURAND, J.-M., JOANNÈS, F., MANNING, J. G., FRANCFORT, H.-P., and LECOMTE, O. 2002. Politique et contrôle de l'eau dans le Moyen-Orient ancien. *Annales. Histoire, Sciences Sociales*, 57: 517–664.

BRYAN, D. 2000. *Orange Parades: The Politics of Ritual, Tradition and Control*. London: Pluto Press.

BUECHLER, S. M. 1990. *Women's Movements in the United States: Woman Suffrage, Equal Rights and Beyond*. New Brunswick, NJ: Rutgers University Press.

CALHOUN, C. 1995. New social movements of the early nineteenth century. Pp. 173–216 in *Repertoires and Cycles of Collective Action*, ed. M. Traugott. Durham, NC: Duke University Press.

CENTENO, M. 2002. *Blood and Debt: War and the Nation-State in Latin America*. University Park: Pennsylvania State University Press.

CHABOT, S., and DUYVENDAK, J. W. 2002. Globalization and transnational diffusion between social movements: reconceptualizing the dissemination of the Gandhian repertoire and the "coming out" routine. *Theory and Society*, 31: 697–740.

CLARK, G. L., and DEAR, M. 1984. *State Apparatus: Structures and Language of Legitimacy*. Boston: Allen and Unwin.

CORRIGAN, P., and SAYER, D. 1985. *The Great Arch: English State Formation as Cultural Revolution*. Oxford: Blackwell.

COSTAIN, A. N., and McFARLAND, A. S. (eds.) 1998. *Social Movements and American Political Institutions*. Lanham, Md.: Rowman and Littlefield.

CREVELD, M. VAN. 1999. *The Rise and Decline of the State*. Cambridge: Cambridge University Press.

DRESCHER, S. 1986. *Capitalism and Antislavery: British Mobilization in Comparative Perspective*. London: Macmillan.

—— 1994. Whose abolition? Popular pressure and the ending of the British slave trade. *Past and Present*, 143: 136–66.

EARLE, T. 1997. *How Chiefs Come to Power: The Political Economy in Prehistory*. Stanford, Calif.: Stanford University Press.

EDELMAN, M. 2001. Social movements: changing paradigms and forms of politics. *Annual Review of Anthropology*, 30: 285–317.

ELTIS, D. 1993. Europeans and the rise and fall of African slavery in the Americas: an interpretation. *American Historical Review*, 98: 1399–423.

FARRELL, S. 2000. *Rituals and Riots. Sectarian Violence and Political Culture in Ulster, 1784–1886*. Lexington: University Press of Kentucky.

FILLIEULE, O. (ed.) 1997. Maintien de l'ordre. Special issue of *Cahiers de la Sécurité Intérieure*.

FOWERAKER, J., and LANDMAN, T. 1997. *Citizenship Rights and Social Movements: A Comparative and Statistical Analysis*. Oxford: Oxford University Press.

FRIEDMANN, D. 1977. A theory of the size and shape of nations. *Journal of Political Economy*, 85: 59–78.

GAMSON, W. A. 1990. *The Strategy of Social Protest*, rev. edn. Belmont, Calif.: Wadsworth.

GLEDHILL, J., BENDER, B., and LARSEN, M. T. (eds.) 1988. *State and Society: The Emergence and Development of Social Hierarchy and Political Centralization*. London: Unwin Hyman.

GREW, R. (ed.) 1978. *Crises of Political Development in Europe and the United States.* Princeton, NJ: Princeton University Press.

GRIMSTED, D. 1998. *American Mobbing, 1828–1861: Toward Civil War.* New York: Oxford University Press.

HOFFMANN, S.-L. 2003. Democracy and associations in the long nineteenth century: toward a transnational perspective. *Journal of Modern History*, 75: 269–99.

HUTERS, T., WONG, R. B., and YU, P. (eds.) 1997. *Culture and State in Chinese History. Conventions, Accommodations and Critiques.* Stanford, Calif.: Stanford University Press.

IBARRA, P. (ed.) 2003. *Social Movements and Democracy.* New York: Palgrave.

JARMAN, N. 1997. *Material Conflicts: Parades and Visual Displays in Northern Ireland.* Oxford: Berg.

KHAZANOV, A. M. 1993. Muhammad and Jenghiz Khan compared: the religious factor in world empire building. *Comparative Studies in Society and History*, 35: 461–479.

KINEALY, C. 2003. Les marches orangistes en Irlande du Nord: Histoire d'un droit. *Le Mouvement Social*, 202: 165–82.

KLEIN, H. S. 1999. *The Atlantic Slave Trade.* Cambridge: Cambridge University Press.

LEVI, M. 1988. *Of Rule and Revenue.* Berkeley: University of California Press.

——1997. *Consent, Dissent and Patriotism.* Cambridge: Cambridge University Press.

LI, J. 2002. State fragmentation: toward a theoretical understanding of the territorial power of the state. *Sociological Theory*, 20: 139–56.

LÓPEZ-ALVES, F. 2000. *State Formation and Democracy in Latin America, 1810–1900.* Durham, NC: Duke University Press

MAC SUIBHNE, B. 2000. Whiskey, potatoes and paddies: volunteering and the construction of the Irish nation in northwest Ulster, 1778–1782. Pp. 45–82 in *Crowds in Ireland c. 1720–1920*, ed. P. Jupp and E. Magennis. London: Macmillan.

McADAM, D., TARROW, S., and TILLY, C. 2001. *Dynamics of Contention.* Cambridge: Cambridge University Press.

McCAMMON, H. J., and CAMPBELL, K. E. 2002. Allies on the road to victory: coalition formation between the suffragists and the Women's Christian Temperance Union. *Mobilization*, 7: 231–52.

————GRANBERG, E. M., and MOWERY, C. 2001. How movements win: gendered opportunity structures and U.S. women's suffrage movements, 1866 to 1919. *American Sociological Review*, 66: 49–70.

MEYER, D. S., and TARROW, S. (eds.) 1998. *The Social Movement Society: Contentious Politics for a New Century.* Lanham, Md.: Rowman and Littlefield.

MIDLARSKY, M. I. 1999. *The Evolution of Inequality. War, State Survival and Democracy in Comparative Perspective.* Stanford, Calif.: Stanford University Press.

PIERSON, P. 2004. *Politics in Time.* Princeton, NJ: Princeton University Press.

della PORTA, D. 1995. *Social Movements, Political Violence and the State: A Comparative Analysis of Italy and Germany.* Cambridge: Cambridge University Press.

——and REITER, H. (eds.) 1998. *Policing Protest: The Control of Mass Demonstrations in Western Democracies.* Minneapolis: University of Minnesota Press.

PORTER, B. 1994. *War and the Rise of the State.* New York: Free Press.

ROEHNER, B. M., and SYME, T. 2002. *Pattern and Repertoire in History.* Cambridge, Mass.: Harvard University Press.

SKOCPOL, T. 1985. Bringing the state back in: strategies of analysis in current research. Pp. 3–43 in *Bringing the State Back In*, ed. P. B. Evans, D. Rueschemeyer, and T. Skocpol. Cambridge: Cambridge University Press.

TAAGEPERA, R. 1997. Expansion and contraction patterns of large polities: context for Russia. *International Studies Quarterly*, 41: 475–504.

TARROW, S. 1998. *Power in Movement: Social Movements and Contentious Politics*. Cambridge: Cambridge University Press.

TILLY, C. 1969. Collective violence in European perspective. Pp. 5–34 in vol. 1 of *Violence in America*, ed. H. D. Graham and T. R. Gurr. Washington, DC: U.S. Government Printing Office.

——1975. Western state-making and theories of political transformation. Pp. 601–38 in *The Formation of National States in Western Europe*, ed. C. Tilly. Princeton, NJ: Princeton University Press.

——1977. Collective action in England and America, 1765–1775. Pp. 45–72 in *Tradition, Conflict and Modernization: Perspectives on the American Revolution*, ed. R. M. Brown and D. Fehrenbacher. New York: Academic Press.

——1992. *Coercion, Capital and European States, AD 990–1992*, rev. edn. Oxford: Blackwell.

——1993. Contentious repertoires in Great Britain, 1758–1834. *Social Science History*, 17: 253–80.

——2001a. Historical analysis of political processes. Pp. 567–88 in *Handbook of Sociological Theory*, ed. J. H. Turner. New York: Kluwer/Plenum.

——2001b. Mechanisms in political processes. *Annual Review of Political Science*, 4: 21–41.

——2004. *Social Movements, 1768–2004*. Boulder, Colo.: Paradigm Press.

——and WOOD, L. 2003. Contentious connections in Great Britain, 1828–1834. Pp. 147–72 in *Social Movements and Networks: Relational Approaches to Collective Action*, ed. M. Diani and D. McAdam. New York: Oxford University Press.

VERBA, S. 1971. Sequences and development. Pp. 283–316 in *Crises and Sequences in Political Development*, ed. L. Binder et al. Princeton, NJ: Princeton University Press.

WALKER, J. L. 1991. *Mobilizing Interest Groups in America: Patrons, Professions and Social Movements*. Ann Arbor: University of Michigan Press.

WONG, R. B. 1997. *China Transformed: Historical Change and the Limits of European Experience*. Ithaca, NY: Cornell University Press.

CHAPTER 23

··

HISTORICAL KNOWLEDGE AND EVIDENCE

··

ROBERTO FRANZOSI

On January 10, 1998, Montereale Valcellina, a small Italian town of some 4000 people nestled at the base of the Friulian Alps, witnessed a most rare event: the conferment of the town's honorary citizenship to Carlo Ginzburg, a historian.

To understand the significance of the event we have to turn back the clock some 400 years, to a time when a most unusual miller—he knew how to read and write and do basic 'rithmetics—walked the streets of Montereale, telling everyone who cared to listen about his religious beliefs. "In the beginning this world was nothing . . . it was thrashed by the water of the sea like foam, and it curdled like a cheese, from which later great multitudes of worms were born, and these worms became men, of whom the most powerful and wisest was God" (Ginzburg 1982, 5–6, 53, 55, 57, 58). Those beliefs, or perhaps more tellingly his readiness to share them with his fellow villagers, would finally lose him his life. Twice tried by the Inquisition for heresy, he was eventually burned at the stake in 1600, the same year as Giordano Bruno.

* I am grateful to Renato Mazzolini for his suggestions on Galileo's work. Ottavia Niccoli, Andrea Del Col, and Carlo Ginzburg were helpful in tracking down some of Ginzburg's work.

It is the story of this miller—"His name was Domenico Scandella, but he was called Menocchio"—that historian Ginzburg masterfully and poignantly tells in *The Cheese and the Worms*, reconstructing it from the records of the Inquisition's trials. It is for his role in putting Montereale on the world's map through a book that has been translated into nearly twenty languages and repeatedly reprinted, that the town was honoring the historian on January 10, 1998.

Ginzburg's historical work, his methodological and epistemological writings, and autobiographical considerations at the margins raise many questions, suggest many points of reflection on issues of historical knowledge and evidence.

1   THE HISTORIAN, THE DOCUMENT, AND THE ARCHIVE

Social scientists conduct interviews, carry out participant observation, or use published, mostly official statistics. Historians tread to the archives. Von Ranke, the "founding father" of modern history, first set the example, some 200 years ago. He spent several years abroad on two tours of European archives (in 1827–31, Vienna, Venice, Ferrara, Rome, Florence, and other Italian cities; and in 1834–7, across Germany, then Paris and London). "A closed archive," von Ranke wrote, "is still absolutely a virgin. I long for the moment I shall have access to her and make my declaration of love, whether she is pretty or not." And closed they were at the time of von Ranke's grand tours—he had to count on Metternich's recommendation to gain access to Italian archives (not the Vatican though!). By the mid-1800s, however, archives across Europe had come under state jurisdiction, and the states, in order to promote the writing of national histories, had not only opened the archives but started funding teams of historians to classify documents properly (Appleby, Hunt, and Jacob 1994, 91–125).

Ginzburg belongs to this Rankian breed of itinerant historians—"In 1961 and 1962 I travelled all over Italy following the traces of the Inquisition archives," he tells us (1993, 80). He portrays his relationship to the archive in more measured terms than von Ranke, but with just as much excitement: "When I was admitted for the first time to the large room which housed in perfect order nearly two thousand inquisitorial trials, I felt the sudden thrill of discovering an unexplored gold mine" (Ginzburg 1990, 157).

For the historian, the physical journey to the archives—a visit to the archives is still a fundamental part of historians' training—parallels another symbolic journey. In Langlois and Seignobos's view, "the journey that the historian takes is one from traces to facts. The document is the point of departure; the past fact is the point of arrival" (1898, 144). "No documents, no history," they put it in lapidary style (1898, 2).

The point: Social scientists "create" their data, as needed, for their own purposes (e.g. testing theories). Historians deal with data created by others, for purposes that are not their own. As Del Col argues, in exploring the limits of Ginzburg's analogies of the historian and the anthropologist, or the historian and the judge, historians cannot interview their witnesses, or ask questions as they wish (1999). They can only listen to voices already there. "The historian has got to be listening all the time," E. P. Thompson wrote. But "if he listens, then the material itself will begin to speak" (cited in Evans 1997, 116). Listening, unfortunately, is not one of social scientists' virtues. If anything, rather than letting the data talk freely, they torture their data until they confess what these contemporary inquisitors want to hear—a widespread practice, known as "data mining" (Franzosi 2004, 230).

2   INTERSECTION OF BIOGRAPHY AND HISTORY

The different types of documents that von Ranke and Ginzburg got out of the same Venetian archives raise an interesting question: Why did one find documents relating to political history and the other, documents relating to the prosecution of ordinary people? Ginzburg himself acknowledges, openly and self-reflectively, the personal motivations that got him into the study of witchcraft, as performed by poor peasant women, and Inquisition trials. No doubt, his research interests on the side of the underdog were shaped by the left-wing culture of his family circle and the fairytale stories of witches he had heard as a child in Abruzzo, where his family had been sent to political confinement by the Fascist regime (Ginzburg 1993, 77–8). Of that, he was quite conscious, and for some time. But then he confesses candidly: "I became conscious only many years later [of something else], when a friend pointed out to me that the choice to study witchcraft and, in particular, the victims of the persecution of witchcraft was not really so strange in a Jew who had experienced persecution. This simple remark left me amazed. How could I have let such an obvious fact escape me?" (Ginzburg 1993, 79).

Ginzburg's identification with the underdog meant looking at history from below. Where other historians—including, perhaps, von Ranke who wrote a *History of the Popes During the 16th and 17th Centuries*—had looked at those same Inquisitorial records to write histories of the institution and histories of the church, a history from above, Ginzburg acknowledges: "I wanted to understand what witchcraft really meant to its protagonists, the witches and sorcerers" (Ginzburg 1982, xix).

In the end, in those Venetian archives, Ranke and Ginzburg both found what they were looking for: Ranke the documentary records of the Venetian ambassadors (known as *relazioni*) he needed for his diplomatic and political history—all the history that matters for him, after all—and Ginzburg his records of oppression for the history that is dear to his heart. Ginzburg (1993, 81–2) shares with us the moment of the discovery of that first document:

I fell into a state of excitement so strong that I had to interrupt my work. While I walked up and down in front of the Archive I thought I had an extraordinary stroke of fortune. I still think so but today this recognition seems inadequate to me. Chance had put in my way a document which was completely unexpected: why (I ask myself) had my reaction been so promptly enthusiastic? . . . [S]ometimes I have chanced to think that the document was there waiting for me and that all my past life predisposed me to come across it. In this absurd fancy there is, I believe, a nub of truth.

Ginzburg (1993, 79) concludes: "That the biography of a historian is not irrelevant for an understanding of his writings, is or should be obvious."

Yet, the process of selection of documents, the process of constitution of evidence is not a purely subjective, personal matter. History intersects with biography, as C. Wright Mills advocated (1959, 4). "The discovery of inquisitorial records as an extremely valuable historical source is a surprisingly late phenomenon," writes Ginzburg (1990, 156). The appreciation of that evidence, its very acceptance as evidence by the historical profession depends upon broader sociopolitical changes. In Ranke's times, what mattered was political history, in a climate of celebration of national histories of the new European states. Inquisitorial documents were "very likely to be treated by a serious historian as a picturesque testimony" (back then, as much as in Ginzburg's time; 1993, 81). But in the 1960s, the rise of social movements, the spreading of Marxist and feminist theories, the new social and intellectual history brought out new concerns. And with new concerns came the need for new types of evidence. In Ginzburg's (in Luria and Gandolfo 1986, 104) words: "the rules of historical method were set up . . . in order to pose specific problems related to specific evidence . . . specific kind of history—political history, ecclesiastical history, institutional history, diplomatic history, and military history. If you start with different problems, you have to look for different evidence." After looking for centuries at history from above, social historians started looking at that same history from below. Once "wanting to know only about 'the great deeds of kings,'" today's historians, "more and more . . . are turning toward what their predecessors passed over in silence, discarded, or simply ignored" (Ginzburg 1982, xiii).

The study of subordinate groups posed serious historiographical and methodological challenges for social historians. The culture of these groups has historically been largely oral, and, therefore, lost. What written records remain—upon which the historian must depend—were "written in general by individuals who were more or less openly attached to the dominant culture. This means that the thoughts, the beliefs, and the aspirations of the peasants and artisans of the past reach us (if and when they do) almost always through distorting viewpoints and intermediaries" (Ginzburg 1982, xv). Such was certainly the case with Ginzburg's inquisitorial records. "Father," the Friulian *benandante* [1] Michele Soppe reminds his inquisitor Fra Giulio Missini of Orvieto, "yes of course I will tell the truth, but I do not understand your way of talking because you are not speaking Friulian" (Ginzburg 1983, 117). But little by little, in giving voice to those silenced by past historians, new and broader types of evidence were admitted, from workers' diaries, ex-slaves' biographies in America, women's letters. Not just texts, but paintings became acceptable evidence. Ginzburg (1981) used those as well in his investigations on Piero della Francesca. [2]

The point: Mills' intersection of biography and history raises disturbing questions: Can objective knowledge be built upon such personal and subjective foundations? Can knowledge transcend the cultural limits of a period? For Ginzburg (1993, 78), "intellectual detachment and emotional participation, rationality and respect for cultural differences, are attitudes which are not only compatible but able to feed each other." Ginzburg, of course, has a vested interest in reassuring his readers. But Appleby, Hunt, and Jacob (1994, 185) approach those same questions by looking at Newton's and Darwin's work and lives and similarly conclude: "objective truth can be produced by deeply subjective people." After all, both Newton and Darwin "were deeply influenced by the political and cultural world in which . . . [they] lived" and by their personal religious, political, racial, or sexual views, yet their science has survived (Appleby, Hunt, and Jacob 1994, 180).

3   NOTHING BUT A STORY

"History is, in its unchangeable essence, 'a tale,'" Trevelyan wrote (1919, 22), expressing a view endlessly repeated, and the historian's "first duty . . . is to tell the story." As stories, historians' narratives possess essential narrative features (no differently from fictional narratives), in particular *coherence* (the story must make sense) and *story point* (what's the point of telling the story? with perhaps its corollary of *teleology*—the

---

[1] Ginzburg has established that between the late 16th and the mid-17th century there lived in the district of Friuli, in the extreme northeast of Italy, certain peasants who called themselves *benandanti*, or "good walkers," who held certain religious beliefs.
[2] See also his article on Warburg and Gombrich (Ginzburg 1990).

entire narrative leading up to an overall story point to which the narrative converges). This writing of history in narrative form is not without consequences; it is not "innocent." It implies both selection and explanation. Certainly, to make a story coherent, historians must select events (or silence certain events and emphasize others); they must decide "to ignore specific domains in the interest of achieving a purely formal coherence in representation" (White 1978, 57).

Of course, there is no escape from being selective. As historians (or social scientists), we could not possibly include in our writing everything that happened in the past (or that surrounds us in social reality). If historians were to do this, they would simply "fail through succeeding" (Danto 1985, 114); fail by producing, not history, but temporal structures with no overall coherence and point, in other words, with no story (Danto 1985, 166). And so would social scientists. A faithful portrayal of social reality would provide no more explanation than what we get by our daily participation and observation of that reality. The selectivity of events to produce coherent stories also implies analysis and explanation (Danto 1985, 251). All stories, true or fictional, must have a beginning, a middle, and an end. And providing that middle between a beginning and an end constitutes an explanation (Danto 1985, 233, 236). In Bloch's (1953, 144) final words: "the historian selects and sorts. In short, he analyzes."

Among storytellers, Carlo Ginzburg is a master. His accounts are gripping. We are made to see and hear the women and men of the Thursday night gatherings of the *benandanti*, from Menichino della Nota, to Paolo Gasparutto, Maria Panzona, and Anna *la rossa*. Menocchio comes back to life before us, with all his stubbornness, with all his need to talk, all his confusion, his fears. Indeed, his family—the caring son and the others who distanced themselves from him and abandoned him—the villagers of Montereale, the puzzled Inquisitors, all come alive. Ginzburg's accounts are also very empathetic. There is no doubt about whose side he is on in these Inquisitorial trials, about his "emotional identification with the defendant." In that sense, Ginzburg is a great social scientist, operating in an interpretative framework (Alford 1998, 72–85) typical of anthropological studies (see his essay on the Inquisitor/historian as anthropologist; Ginsburg 1990) or of ethnographic studies in sociology, where that "emotional identification" goes by the lofty name of "understanding" (*verstehen*).

Ginzburg is a master storyteller in another way: His stories take the reader through the twists and turns of a best-selling detective story. "I am quite diffident of work that presents itself closed, with a concise, easily graspable thesis. If that's the objective, if it's only the conclusion that counts, we might as well get rid of all the preparatory work. I don't believe this attitude is right. I would like to maintain movement and end" (in Colonnello and Del Col 2002, 105).[3] Ginzburg's own detective work of a historian—theorized, as we have seen, in such methodological pieces as "Morelli, Freud and Sherlock Holmes. Clues and Scientific Method" (1980), or betrayed by his favorite use of such nouns as "clue" or "intuition"—is transmitted

---

[3] For a typical example see Ginzburg (1982, 32–3).

through his special way of telling the story as a detective story. Bloch, one of Ginzburg's heroes (1990, viii; Luria and Gandolfo 1986, 91), would have approved that: "The sight of an investigation, with its successes and reverses," he wrote, "is seldom boring. It is the ready-made article which is cold and dull" (1953, 71).

The point: No doubt, history selects, constructs coherent accounts, and offers pat solutions to its readers. But so do the social sciences. Quantitative social science matches theory to statistical results, carefully selects, among hundreds or thousands, the equations with the expected signs of the coefficients, and high significances and R-squares (a practice known as "data mining": Franzosi 2004, 230). And these practices of rigid formalism are further underscored by the increasing rigidification in the format of social science journal articles (Abbott and Barman 1997).

4   SEMANTIC SUBTLETIES? DATA, EVIDENCE, FACTS

Historians talk about facts and evidence. Social scientists talk about data. If such words as "data" conjure up images of science (think of the connection "data and method," methods of data collection, of data analysis), "facts" and "evidence" are more akin to legalistic references. "The lawyer, like the historian, uses evidence," historian Renier (1950, 119) wrote. Facts must be established. Evidence must be evaluated (in relation to an argument). Evidence is such if "it is used as the basis for an inference," we are reminded by George (1909, 14), an Oxford historian, in a chapter titled "What is Evidence?" of a book dedicated to *Historical Evidence*. Ginzburg's (1984, 133, 141–3) work is full of references to clues, proofs, judges; he consciously pursues the metaphor of the historian as judge (1990, 159; 1991), of historical work as detective work (1980). Reliance on evidence, for Ginzburg, provides the defining feature of certain types of disciplines—history, medicine, for instance—where "tiny details provide the key to a deeper reality, inaccessible by other methods" (1980, 11). They define an approach, paradigm, or model of knowledge (variously called evidential, semiotic, or conjectural by Ginzburg) "based on the interpretation of clues" (1980, 12). In the conjectural paradigm, it is the individual, the concrete, and the specific that counts—that particular evidence, that particular clue, not any evidence or clue, in relation to specific types of inference, specific conjectures (1980, 15–16). The scientific paradigm ushered in by Galileo in the early 1600s, on the other hand, is based on considering the common properties of various objects. It abstracts and generalizes. The natural sciences, and later the social sciences, adopted this new paradigm of knowledge.[4] And, of course, when evidence becomes data (*data*, Latin plural of *datum*, meaning "given"), it is taken, rather than given, as granted, as unquestionable facts (Franzosi 2004, 183–7).

Issues of evidence, its sources, and their critical appraisal have dominated methodological historiographical writing over the last two centuries: from the late eighteenth-century German historians of "scientific history," to von Ranke (himself from that tradition, who entrusted upon future historians their enduring "noble dream" of telling the story like it actually happened—*Wie es eigentlich gewesen*); to Langlois and Seignobos (whose 1898 *Introduction aux études historiques* has six of the seventeen chapters, 100 of the 300 pages, with the word critique in the title). All concur that, "Knowledge of all the sources, and competent criticism of them, these are the basic requirements of a reliable historiography" (Elton 1967, 65, 73–83).

For Ranke, the Venetian ambassadors' *relazioni* were exemplary "ideal type" documents ("original narratives of eyewitnesses," primary sources, close to the original events; indeed, purer and uncontaminated, like water at the source!). One hundred and fifty years later and Ginzburg would find his own version of the ideal type document in those same Venetian archives: the records of inquisitorial trials, upon which he would base all his major work (1982; 1983; 1992). "The principal characteristic of this documentation is its immediacy," Ginzburg (1983, xvii) wrote. "Except for the fact that the notaries of the Holy Office translated the testimony from Friulian into Italian, it is fair to say that the voices of these peasants reach us directly, without barriers …" The value of these records is "truly astonishing. Not only words, but gestures, sudden reactions like blushing, even silences, were recorded with punctilious accuracy by the notaries of the Holy Office" (1990, 160).

Yet, both Ranke and Ginzburg may have stretched their case, forgoing their critical habit. Far from being simple, spontaneous eyewitness accounts, von Ranke's *relazioni* are "highly filtered, deeply pondered texts," overburdened with stylistic artifice and strictly adhering to centuries-old stylistic canon (Benzoni 1990, 53). Places, events, and protagonists are seen through the eyes of Venice and the Venetian patrician class. Ginzburg's Inquisitorial records are no less problematic, in spite of Ginzburg's early enthusiasm (Schutte 1976, 306; Del Col 1999).

The point: Historians' "noble dream" of telling the story like it actually happened led to their obsession with truth and objectivity, with its corollary of criticism of evidence. With different dreams of their own—theory-building and generalizing,

---

[4] We find elaborations of this distinction between history and the natural and social sciences among the German philosophers of history of the turn of the nineteenth century, from Rickert to Windelband, who proposed the term "nomothetic" for science, dedicated to the discovery of general laws, and "idiographic," focused on the particular and the individual (see Franzosi 2004, 372 n. 22).

subsuming the historian's particular under general laws—social scientists have been far less concerned with data criticism. As Lieberson (1985, 216) states: "Great attention must be given to evaluating the quality of the data—and this does not appear to be developing at present in social research." The question is: Do our theories rest on solid empirical grounds?

5   THE TELESCOPE AND THE MICROSCOPE

On September 23, 1624, Galileo Galilei wrote a letter to Federico Cesi, founder of the Accademia dei Lincei in Rome, accompanying it with the present of a microscope that he had built: "I am sending to Your Excellency an *occhialino* [5] to see minute things from close up, in the hope that you will find enjoyment from it, like I did. . . . I observed several little animals with great wonder, among which the lice is most horrible, the mosquito and the ring worm are beautiful, and with delight I have seen how house flies and other little bugs are able to walk vertically on mirrors and even upside down. But Your Excellency will be free to observe thousand upon thousand details . . ."

Other than getting some enjoyment out of it, Galileo did not do much with his new invention (in fact, the microscope remained mostly a toy for the enjoyment of the European rich for decades to come; Mazzolini 1997). It had been quite a different story with the telescope, nearly fifteen years earlier. About Galileo's inventing the telescope there is no question. By the summer of 1609, when Galileo heard news of the new device during a visit to Venice, "spyglasses" were already sold in the shops of spectacle makers in many European cities, invented probably only a year earlier in the Netherlands.[6] What Galileo did, and only within a few months of hearing the news, by the end of 1609, was to turn the available 2× to 4× magnification device into a powerful 20× telescope ("far ahead of his nearest competitors;" van Helden 1983, 155). "Because he had won the instrument race, Galileo was able to monopolize the celestial discoveries" (ibid.). And those discoveries came quickly in rapid succession within a year: from the imperfections of the Moon's surface, the multitude of stars, and Jupiter's satellites, to the strange appearance of Saturn and Venus's behavior.

What did allow Galileo "to win the instrument race" and see what he saw? The answer appears to be quite simple: Galileo was not only a great scientist, but a great

[5] It would be a member of the Lincei, the botanist Johann Faber, who changed the name of the new "toy" from *occhialino* to microscope. On Galileo and the microscope, see Mazzolini (1997).
[6] For sure, the first surviving record of the new device is the patent application of a certain Hans Lipperhey, spectacle maker, to the States General of the Netherlands, of October 2, 1608.

craftsman, who knew how to use his hands to make things, one thing being lenses. He put his craftsmanship to good use —something none of his scientific competitors had, at a level that not even the best craftsmen across Europe could match (van Helden 1983, 154). And, perhaps even more importantly, when Galileo pointed his device to the skies, where others just saw "strange spottednesse" on the moon surface, he saw mountains and craters. His knowledge of design and chiaroscuro allowed Galileo to interpret correctly as forms the darker and lighter shades he saw (Edgerton 1984).[7]

The point: "You can see some things, but you can't see everything," Ginzburg acknowledges. When dealing with evidence, there is no passepartout, no single instrument that allows us to see everything. So, use the telescope if you want to see far-away things; use the microscope to see minute things or... use the tool most appropriate to allow you to see what you want to bring into focus. Yet, against such mutually exclusive view of method (the telescope *or* the microscope), Ginzburg (in Luria and Gandolfo 1986, 101; emphasis added) adds: "I am fascinated by the possibility of combining a kind of telescopic attitude *and* a kind of microscopic attitude." In that too, Ginzburg was a master, illuminating with Menocchio's life or the *benandanti*'s rites currents of beliefs cutting through the centuries and through Europe and beyond. He relentlessly pursued the alchemic search for the macrocosm in the microcosm, for *omne omne est*, everything is everything—in the presentation of Ginzburg's (1980, 5) article in *History Workshop*, we read: "it... draws on philosophy, quotes Latin, and ranges across societies and periods in a way which is extraordinary—even shocking—to the English reader." Yet, Ginzburg is pointing here to a different view of method: method not as a specific technique, a specific tool (telescope or microscope, regression or participant observation), where perhaps one tool allows us to see what the other does not; but method as a way of approaching historical and social inquiry.[8]

6   QUALITY VERSUS QUANTITY

As a master storyteller, and one who privileges single individuals, *mentalités*, and culture, Ginzburg is not sympathetic to quantitative historical projects.[9] He makes

---

[7] Similarly, Einstein's view of relativity may have been suggested to him by his practical work on scheduling trains in the Austrian railways at a time where there where no fixed standards of time (Galison 2003).

[8] On these different views of methods, see Franzosi (2004, 273).

[9] Yet, you will not find in Ginzburg's work the vitriolic attacks on quantification of other narrative historians (e.g. Stone, cited in Franzosi 2004, 62, 232).

his preferences quite clear. "A close reading of a relatively small number of texts...can be more rewarding than the massive accumulation of repetitive evidence" (1990, 164). "I believe that intensive analysis of an anomalous case...is infinitely more fruitful" (1993, 81). "The quantitative and anti-anthropocentric approach of the sciences of nature from Galileo on has placed human sciences in an unpleasant dilemma; they must either adopt a weak scientific standard so as to be able to attain significant results, or adopt a strong scientific standard to attain results of no great importance" (1979, 276).

Proponents of quantitative approaches to the study of history, of course, saw it differently, from the French historians of the *histoire sérielle* to the American "cliometricians."[10] In the words of Robert Fogel (Fogel and Elton 1983, 25–6):

Cliometricians [or "scientific," quantitative, historians] want the study of history to be based on explicit models of human behavior. They believe that historians do not really have a choice of using or not using behavioral models since all attempts to explain historical behavior... involve some sort of model. The real choice is whether these models will be implicit, vague, incomplete, and internally inconsistent, ... or whether the models will be explicit, with all the relevant assumptions clearly stated, and formulated in such a manner as to be subject to rigorous empirical verification.

Fogel himself did not just write programmatic statements. He produced some of the exemplary work in quantitative history that would eventually earn him the Nobel Prize in 1993 (shared with Douglass North) "for...applying economic theory and quantitative methods in order to explain economic and institutional change," in the Nobel Committee official motivation for the prize. Indeed, in both his major books on the role of the railways in the development of the American economy (1964) and on slavery as an economic institution (1974, with Engerman), Fogel used economic theory to derive specific hypotheses, that he then tested applying statistical procedures on a wide variety of empirical evidence.

For a while at least, it seemed that the new quantitative history along the social *scientific* model had finally come to rescue history, once and for all, from the quagmire of storytelling (with all its problems of subjectivity, selection, and imprecision—"Do not guess, try to count," Kitson Clark (1962, 14) advised his fellow historians, "and if you cannot count, admit that you are guessing." To the traditional subtle linguistic differences between history and social sciences—data and evidence—the new "scientific" historians added more, and less subtle linguistic differences: theory, models, hypotheses—Ginzburg (1993, 79) tells us that his work did not imply "a specific research hypothesis." And the only one he enter-

---

[10] For an excellent statement of the two approaches to history, see the arguments by two of the champions in the respective traditions, Fogel and Elton (1983).

tained—witchcraft as a form of class struggle—brings us back to the personal, as "an attempt to justify in my own eyes and in those of others, a piece of research lacking true historiographical legitimization."

Yet, by the time of Fogel's Nobel Prize award in 1993, not only Fogel's own work, but more generally quantitative history as well, had come under fire. Fogel's *Time on the Cross* generated a great deal of controversy; his data and method were closely (and repeatedly) scrutinized (Evans 1997, 42). At the same time, "traditional" historians—from Ginzburg, to Bailyn, Elton, Stone, and Schlesinger—had arguments of their own against "scientific" history, namely: That it can only study what is quantifiable, leaving out of the research agenda a great many important historical questions or focusing on trivial, but quantifiable, questions; that their mathematical/statistical representations of historical reality lead to a view of history as variables, rather than as formed by social actors (Franzosi 2004, 282–5). Even quantitative social scientists were raising their voices against the kind of statistical work carried out in the social sciences (Franzosi 2004, 229–32). "There are two things you are better off not watching in the making: sausages and econometric estimates," Leamer (1983, 36) colorfully put it. Quantitative social scientists' noble dream of a search for rigor was slowly turning into a rigid and ritualistic approach to hypothesis testing and to widespread bad statistical practices of "data mining." In Lieberson's (1985, 171) words: " 'Business as usual'...is often nothing more than 'ritualism as usual.' "

The point: The debate quality versus quantity has raged, at times violently, particularly during the 1950s and 1960s, in the social sciences and history. Yet, in many ways, it is a misguided debate. As Elton (Fogel and Elton 1983, 79) retorts: "what he [Fogel] calls traditional history is quite often simply bad, or not very good, history." The same is certainly true for quantitative work (and its critics): no doubt, much of it is simply bad work. And, no doubt, there are questions that are better addressed by quantitative methods and others where a quantitative approach would be hopeless (and not just because we may not have enough data but because we are interested in the subjective meaning of social and historical actors). Ginzburg's questions and work belong here. But his focus on anomalies is not a prerogative of qualitative work or of case studies. In *The Puzzle of Strikes* (1995) I build the arguments chasing after the clues suggested by anomalies: outliers and unexplained residuals. Furthermore, anomalies are such in relation to norms and trends, trends best established by quantitative approaches to history. We know that repertoires of contentious politics changed over time in England or France through the meticulous enumeration of events and the careful mapping of actors and their actions (Tilly 1986; 1995). "I should like to think," Elton (Fogel and Elton 1983, 83) writes about traditional and scientific historians, "that each will go to heaven his own way." I venture to add: may they perhaps go to heaven together.

7   THE LINGUISTIC TURN AND POSTMODERNISM[11]

"Is there ... any specific difference between factual and imaginary narrative, any linguistic feature by which we may distinguish historical and fictional discourse?" Barthes (1970, 153) asked, in a seminal essay on "The Discourse of History." His answer was: "no." Both history and storytelling use similar rhetorical devices and have similar narrative structures. "By its structures alone, without recourse to its content, historical discourse is essentially a product of ideology, or rather of imagination." Unfortunately, that content—historical facts—is more discourse. "The only feature which distinguishes historical discourse from other kinds," Barthes (1970, 145, 153, 155) continues, "is a paradox: The 'fact' can only exist linguistically, as a term in a discourse."

Objectivity and facticity are the results of specific linguistic strategies, of the privileged position of metonymic over metaphoric discourse (White 1978, 81–100, 121–34). By relying on different master tropes in their writings (in particular, metaphor, metonymy, synecdoche, and irony), historians fashion very different kinds of stories out of the same basic material (modes of emplotment), they have provided fundamentally different types of historical explanations (modes of explanation), a metahistory of history. "A historiographical style represents a particular combination of modes of emplotment, argument, and ideological implication" (White 1973, 29). Different authors' historiographical styles are based on somewhat standard, though not rigid combinations of these three different modes of emplotment, argument, and ideological implication.

"*Quod not est in charta non est in mundo*" (what is not in the document is not in the world) had been history's traditional stance with regards to evidence (in Colonnello and Del Col 2002, 158). The postmoderns turned that *realist* position into a nominalist, relativist one. "There is nothing outside the text. ... There has never been anything but writing," Derrida claimed polemically (1974, 158). "Reality," for postmodernists, is something to be put in quotation marks (Appleby, Hunt, and Jacob 1994, 204), the result of "fictions of factual representation" (White 1978, 121), where "historians are the inventors of their documents" (Ricoeur 1984, 110). As Ginzburg (1984, 145) put it: "The insistence on the narrative dimension of historiography ... goes hand-in-hand ... with relativistic attitudes that, *in practice*, tend to annul the distinction between *fiction* and *history*, between purely imaginary narratives and narratives that make truth claims." Texts, including scientific texts, must be viewed as rhetorical artifacts, the result of specific rhetorical strategies, of agreed-upon conventions among members of discursive communities (Franzosi 2004, 222–9). Under the influence of Foucault, knowledge in general is

---

[11] For excellent introductions to the terms of the debate, see Appleby, Hunt, and Jacob (1994) and Evans's (1997) strenuous defence of history against the postmodern attacks.

viewed as the result of a power play between contending groups, but where the most powerful ones have the resources to push for the kind of knowledge they want (or to write history in the way that best represents their interests) (Evans 1997, 191–223; Appleby, Hunt, and Jacob 1994, 198–237). With postmodernists, *both* traditional and scientific historians, *both* human and natural scientists came under threat (Appleby, Hunt, and Jacob ibid.). There may be comfort in numbers, but, as Stone put it, under the influence of postmodernism, "history might be on the way to becoming an endangered species" (cited in Evans 1997, 7).

The point: The postmodernists have had the great merit of alerting us to the linguistic aspects of our scientific writings, have made us aware of the power and interests behind knowledge and science, have highlighted the link between biography, autobiography, and history. But, with their all-out assault on objectivity and truth, they have entrusted upon us a most burdensome legacy, so burdensome that many have simply given up. "Such has been the power and influence of the postmodernist critique of history that growing numbers of historians themselves are abandoning the search for truth, the belief in objectivity, and the quest for a scientific approach to the past" (Evans 1997, 4). "For many historians the notion of evidence is not fashionable . . . It is rejected as an unforgivable positivistic ingenuity" (Ginzburg 1991, 12–3).[12] The real challenge is in an honest pursuit of rigor in the full consciousness of the limits of our science, rejecting a *facile* acceptance of the canons of social scientific writing (not to mention the even more facile acceptance of the attitude that "anything flies"). It is, no doubt, in the realm of pragmatism, of "practical realism," as historians Appleby, Hunt, and Jacob (1994, 247–51, 285) argue, that historians (and social scientists) can overcome the paralyzing doubts brought out by the postmodernist assault on Truth. After all, "as regards . . . truth, the real truth . . . of this truth who knows aught?" (Unamuno 1931, 131).

Teleology: Chance put in my way a historian's work that seemed to contain all the right cues upon which I could graft my discourse on historical knowledge and evidence. Or, perhaps, Ginzburg's work was there just waiting for me, predisposed as I had been by all my past life to come across it. Or, perhaps, if *omne omne est,* I could have gotten there, starting from anywhere . . .

REFERENCES

ABBOTT, A., and BARMAN, E. 1997. Sequence comparison via alignment and Gibbs sampling: a formal analysis of the emergence of the modern sociological article. *Sociological Methodology*, 27: 47–87.

[12] Ginzburg leaves no doubt about his own position on the matter: "I am deeply against every kind of Derrida trash, that kind of cheap skeptical attitude. I think that that is one of the cheapest intellectual things going on. . . . I am deeply against it" (in Luria and Gandolfo 1986, 100).

ALFORD, R. 1998. *The Craft of Inquiry: Theories, Methods, Evidence.* Oxford: Oxford University Press.

APPLEBY, J., HUNT, L., and JACOB, M. 1994. *Telling the Truth About History.* New York: Norton.

BARTHES, R. 1970. Historical discourse. Pp. 145–55 in *Structuralism: A Reader,* ed. M. Lane. London: Cape; originally published 1967.

BENZONI, G. 1990. Ranke's favorite source. Pp. 45–57 in *Leopold von Ranke and the Shaping of the Historical Discipline,* ed. G. G. Iggers and J. M. Powell. Syracuse, NY: Syracuse University Press.

BLOCH, M. 1953. *The Historian's Craft.* New York: Vintage.

CLARK, K. 1962. *The Making of Victorian England.* London: Methuen.

COLONNELLO, A., and DEL COL, A. (eds.) 2002. *Uno storico, un mugnaio, un libro. Carlo Ginzburg, Il formaggio e i vermi. 1976–2002.* Montereale Valcellina: Circolo culturale Menocchio.

DANTO, A. 1985. *Narration and Knowledge.* New York: Columbia University Press.

DEL COL, A. 1999. I criteri dello storico nell'uso delle fonti inquisitoriali moderne. Pp. 51–72 in *L'Inquisizione Romana: metodologia delle fonti e storia istituzionale. Atti del Seminario internazionale, Montereale Valcellina, 23 e 24 Settembre 1999,* ed. A. Del Col and G. Paolin. Montereale Valtellina: Circolo Culturale Menocchio.

DERRIDA, J. 1974. *Of Grammatology.* Baltimore: Johns Hopkins University Press.

EDGERTON, S. Y. 1984. Galileo, Florentine "disegno" and the "strange spottednesse" of the moon. *Art Journal,* 44: 225–32.

ELTON, G. 1967. *The Practice of History.* London: Methuen.

EVANS, R. 1997. *In Defence of History.* London: Granta.

FOGEL, R., and ELTON, G. 1983. *Which Road to the Past? Two Views of History.* New Haven, Conn.: Yale University Press.

FOGEL, R., and ENGERMAN, S. 1974. *Time on the Cross: The Economics of American Negro Slavery.* Boston: Little, Brown.

FRANZOSI, R. 1995. *The Puzzle of Strikes: Class and State Strategies in Postwar Italy.* Cambridge: Cambridge University Press.

——2004. *From Words to Numbers: Narrative, Data, and Social Science.* Cambridge: Cambridge University Press.

GALISON, P. 2003. *Einstein's Clocks, Poincaré's Maps: Empires of Time.* London: Sceptre.

GINZBURG, C. 1979. Roots of a scientific paradigm. *Theory and Society,* 7: 273–88.

——1980. Morelli, Freud and Sherlock Holmes: clues and scientific method. *History Workshop,* 9: 5–36.

——1981. *Indagini su Piero.* Turin: Einaudi.

——1982. *The Cheese and the Worms: The Cosmos of a Sixteenth-Century Miller.* Harmondsworth: Penguin; originally published 1976.

——1983. *The Night Battles: Witchcraft & Agrarian Cults in the Sixteenth & Seventeenth Centuries.* London: Routledge and Kegan Paul; originally published 1966.

——1984. Prove e possibilità. In margine a *Il ritorno di Martin Guerre* di Natalie Zemon Davis. Postfazione. Pp. 129–54 in *Il Ritorno di Martin Guerre: Un caso di doppia identità nella Francia del Cinquecento,* ed. N. Z. Davis. Turin: Einaudi.

——1990. *Myths, Emblems, Clues.* London: Hutchinson Radius; originally published 1986.

——1991. *Il giudice e lo storico: Considerazioni in margine al processo Sofri.* Turin: Einaudi.

——1993. Witches and shamans. *New Left Review,* 200: 75–85.

GEORGE, H. B. 1909. *Historical Evidence.* Oxford: Clarendon Press.

LANGLOIS, C. V., and SEIGNOBOS, C. 1898. *Introduction aux études historiques.* Paris: Hachette.

LEAMER, E. E. 1983. Let's take the con out of econometrics. *American Economic Review*, 73: 31–43.

LIEBERSON, S. 1985. *Making it Count: The Improvement of Social Research and Theory*. Berkeley: University of California Press.

LURIA, K., and GANDOLFO, R. 1986. Carlo Ginzburg: an interview. *Radical History Review*, 35: 89–111.

MAZZOLINI, R. 1997. L'illusione incomunicabile: il declino della microscopia tra sei e settecento. Pp. 197–219 in *Phantastiche Lebensräume, Phantome und Phantasmen*. Marburg an der Lahm: Basilisken-Presse.

MILLS, C. WRIGHT 1959. *The Sociological Imagination*. Oxford: Oxford University Press.

RENIER, G. J. 1950. *History: Its Purpose and Method*. London: Allen and Unwin.

RICOEUR, P. 1984. *Time and Narrative*, trans. K. McLaughlin and D. Pellauer. Vol. 1. Chicago: University of Chicago Press.

SCHUTTE, A. J. 1976. Carlo Ginzburg. *Journal of Modern History*, 48: 296–315.

TILLY, C. 1981. *As Sociology Meets History*. New York: Academic Press.

——1986. *The Contentious French*. Cambridge, Mass.: Harvard University Press.

——1995. *Popular Contention in Great Britain, 1758–1834*. Cambridge, Mass.: Harvard University Press.

TREVELYAN, G. M. 1919. *The Recreations of an Historian*. London: Thomas Nelson and Sons.

VAN HELDEN, A. 1983. Galileo and the telescope. Pp. 149–58 in *Novità celesti e crisi del sapere. Atti del Convegno Internazionale di Studi Galileani*, ed P. Galluzzi. Supplement to Annali dell'Istituto e Museo di Storia della Scienza, Monograph n. 7. Florence: Istituto e Museo di Storia della Scienza.

UNAMUNO, M. de. 1931. *The Tragic Sense of Life in Men and in Peoples*. London: Macmillan.

WHITE, H. 1973. *Metahistory: The Historical Imagination in Nineteenth-Century Europe*. Baltimore: Johns Hopkins University Press.

——1978. *Tropics of Discourse: Essays in Cultural Criticism*. Baltimore: Johns Hopkins University Press.

....

HISTORICAL CONTEXT AND PATH DEPENDENCE

....

JAMES MAHONEY
DANIEL SCHENSUL

PATH dependence is used in quite different and variously well specified ways by scholars interested in the application of history and temporality to the understanding of social and political phenomena. Two examples help to illustrate the breadth of (and perhaps disagreement around) use of this concept.

Jack Goldstone (1998a; 2005) argues that the Industrial Revolution in England was the result of path-dependent process. He contends that "there was nothing necessary or inevitable" about England's breakthrough to modern industrialism (1998a, 275). Rather, the outcome was a product of a number of small events that happened to come together in eighteenth-century England. Perhaps most importantly, the Industrial Revolution depended on the advent of Thomas Newcomen's first steam engine in 1712. Although Newcomen's invention was a bulky, noisy apparatus, it made possible the subsequent creation of more efficient steam engines that dramatically improved the extraction of coal. Efficient coal extraction reduced the price of coal. In turn:

* James Mahoney's research is supported by the National Science Foundation (Grant No. 0093754).

Cheap coal made possible cheaper iron and steel. Cheap coal plus cheap iron made possible the construction of railways and ships built of iron, fueled by coal, and powered by engines producing steam. Railways and ships made possible mass national and international distribution of metal tools, textiles, and other products that could be more cheaply made with steam-powered metal-reinforced machinery. (1998a, 275)

Thus, the sequence of events leading to the Industrial Revolution ultimately depended on the advent of the first steam engine. Yet, Newcomen did not pursue his invention in order to spur an industrial revolution. Instead, he was simply trying to devise a means to pump water from deep-shaft coal mines: the steam engine removed water by turning it into vapor. It was necessary to remove water from the mine shafts because the surface coal of the mines had been exhausted, which had led the miners to dig deeper, which had caused the mines to fill with water. And of course the surface coal of the mines was exhausted in the first place because England was exceptionally dependent on coal for heating. Going even further back, as Goldstone does, England was dependent on coal (rather than wood) because of its limited forest area, its cold climate, and its geology, which featured thick seams of coal near the sea.

Karen Orren's (1991) study of *Belated Feudalism* offers a different kind of example of path dependence, one in which path dependence involves the stable reproduction of a particular outcome. Orren calls attention to the remarkable persistence of status-based labor legislation in the United States. From its inception until well into the twentieth century, the United States legally defined all able-bodied individuals without independent wealth as workers who could be subject to criminal charges for not selling their labor in the marketplace. This "law of master and servant" was originally established in feudal England, but it managed to carry over into the United States, and it then persisted for more than 150 years despite the supposed liberal orientation of American culture.

To explain this path-dependent outcome, Orren emphasizes the key role of American courts in upholding the law. In her view, judges enforced the law because they believed it was legitimate, even though it increasingly clashed with American mores and norms. Specifically, "the judges believed that what was at stake was no less than the moral order of things," and hence upheld the law (1991, 114). Orren emphasizes that American judges did not follow precedent simply because of personal gain (1991, 90). Likewise, she contends that judges did not simply support legislation on behalf of the interests of economic elites, even though the employment legislation clearly benefited employers (1991, 91). Rather, she argues "that the law of labor relations was on its own historical track, and that it carried protection of business interests along for the ride" (1991, 112).

These examples from Goldstone and Orren suggest some of the ways in which social scientists formulate path-dependent arguments. Goldstone's argument shows how path dependence may involve reaction–counter-reaction dynamics, such that an initial event triggers a reaction and thereby logically leads to another quite different event, which triggers its own reaction, and so on, until a particular outcome of interest is reached. By contrast, Orren's argument focuses on a kind of path-dependent sequence in which a particular outcome happens to occur, and then this outcome is subject to self-reproducing mechanisms, causing the outcome to endure across time, even long after its original purposes have ceased to exist. These different uses of path dependence—one to illustrate reaction–counter-reaction dynamics, the other to illustrate self-reproducing dynamics—are both common in the literature, and they are both often regarded as legitimate applications of path dependence.

There are other important differences among scholars who use the concept of path dependence to describe political processes. For example, some scholars believe that path dependence is rare (e.g. Goldstone 1998b; Mahoney 2000), whereas others argue that it is pervasive (e.g. Castaldi and Dosi 2005; Pierson 2000; Somers 1998). Analogously, some scholars see path dependence as a standard mode of analysis used in history, whereas others view the concept as applying more exclusively to arguments in the social sciences. Disagreement over path dependence is quite prevalent, such that even critics of path dependence substantially diverge in their understanding about what is *wrong* with this concept. For example, they assert that the concept gives too much weight to contingent events (e.g. Schwartz 2004), too much weight to deterministic processes (e.g. Huber and Stephens 2001, 3), and too much weight to both contingency and determinism (e.g. Thelen 1999; 2003).

In this chapter, we analyze the different meanings and uses of the concept of path dependence in contemporary academic discourse. Our goal is not to advocate a single, best conceptualization of the term. Rather, we seek to use the array of distinct understandings of path dependence as a means of specifying a number of ways in which historical context matters. We also examine the strengths and weaknesses of different conceptualizations and the trade-offs involved in adopting particular definitions of the concept.

1   DEFINITIONS OF PATH DEPENDENCE

Our discussion focuses on the definitions of path dependence proposed by scholars in economics, political science, and sociology—all three of which have influenced research in political science. In economics, we consider those economic historians who are most responsible for creating and popularizing the term, especially Paul

David, Brian Arthur, Giovanni Dosi, and Douglass North. In political science, we focus on the contributions of Paul Pierson and Kathleen Thelen as well as others affiliated with the "critical juncture" approach, especially Ruth Berins Collier and David Collier.[1] In sociology, we consider the work of several historical sociologists, especially Jack Goldstone, Margaret Somers, and William Sewell. Finally, we also consider certain interdisciplinary travelers such as Charles Tilly.

These scholars are united around the belief that history matters in more profound ways than acknowledged in most social science work. All of them assert that particular events in the past can have crucial effects in the future, and that these events may be located in the quite distant past. Indeed, one of the most distinctive features of path dependence is the idea that the most important effects of a given event may be "temporally lagged"—i.e. not initially felt but clearly visible at a later point in time. Furthermore, scholars of path dependence tend to agree that many leading methodologies—such as mainstream statistical methods and rational choice analysis—can deflect attention away from particular historical events and thereby mischaracterize the causes of important outcomes. In these ways, there is some consensus among scholars who use the concept of path dependence.

At the same time, however, they disagree about the meaning of path dependence in other ways that reflect important disputes about *how* history matters. This disagreement exists across six potentially defining features of path dependent sequences:

- The past affects the future.
- Initial conditions are causally important.
- Contingent events are causally important.
- Historical lock-in occurs.
- A self-reproducing sequence occurs.
- A reactive sequence occurs.

Scholars disagree about whether and in what combination these six conditions must be present for path dependence to exist. For example, they diverge regarding how many attributes should be included in the definition of path dependence. Differences on this issue shape other differences, such as how common one believes path dependence is in the world. Further debates arise when two scholars agree that a particular condition is a necessary condition for path dependence, but disagree whether the condition must be present or absent for the existence of path dependence. These differences reflect profound contrasts in the understanding of path dependence and possibly deep disagreements about the features of history that are most interesting and important.

It bears emphasis that these debates are not merely semantic matters; they intersect with major themes concerning explanation in the social sciences. In

---

[1] In turn, these researchers were influenced by an earlier body of literature on temporal analysis (e.g. Almond, Flanagan, and Mundt 1973; Binder et al. 1971; Lipset and Rokkan 1967).

economics, the work of David and other historians has challenged those scholars who seek to explain events from a universalistic framework, in particular from a neoclassical framework in which efficiency is assumed to drive outcomes in the marketplace. In political science and sociology, path-dependent researchers have questioned prominent modes of explanation that assume "large" outcomes necessarily have "large" causes, that ignore issues of timing and sequence, and that assume rational actors will select outcomes that are optimal for their long-run interests. Research on path dependence has thus sought to put historical analysis on a firmer social-science footing, and in doing so it has focused attention on a host of new explanatory concerns, such as the role of chance, agency, timing, particular events, and the overall methodology of temporality. As Pierson (2000, 251) suggests, "If path dependence arguments are indeed appropriate in substantial areas of political life, they will shake many subfields of inquiry."

Below we will closely examine each of the six potential defining features of path dependence that we list above. We will identify the scholars most prominently associated with each feature, examine their claims, and review and discuss the substantive debates over the place of these features in defining path dependence.

2   THE PAST AFFECTS THE FUTURE

Events that occur in the present are not causally independent from those of the past; instead, as Sewell (1996, 263) puts it, "what has happened at an earlier point in time will affect the possible outcomes of a sequence of events occurring at a later point in time." Drawing on this basic insight, all definitions of path dependence assume that the past affects the future. In some cases, however, scholarly definitions of path dependence stop with this insight; they make the general dimension of "the past affects the future" the only necessary condition for path dependence. This is generally true, for example, of Castaldi and Dosi (2005), Karl (1997), North (1998), Sewell (1996), and Tilly (2005).

A potential problem with this "minimalist" approach to definition is that it leads to a vague conceptualization in which any causal chain could be seen as exhibiting path dependence; every outcome in the social world is, after all, preceded by a series of historical events. Even if scholars were to assume that path dependence occurs only when the "distant past" affects the future, they would still be including a huge range of arguments under the label path dependent. Moreover, this definition provides no distinctive specification of the mechanisms through which the past affects the present.

Most scholars who propose these minimal definitions do so because they are actually interested in a much broader range of temporal concepts and ideas that incorporate more specific insights. For example, Sewell (1996, 264) sees path dependence as one basic component of an "eventful temporality," which includes path dependence alongside other components. In particular, an eventful temporality "assumes that social relations are characterized by path dependency, temporally heterogeneous causalities, and global contingency." Sewell finds the idea that "the past affects the future" important but limited in its utility, and therefore in need of complementary tools to become analytically useful. Similarly, Castaldi and Dosi (2005) formally define path dependence as "history matters," but they discuss the concept in relationship to a very large set of accompanying concepts, including increasing returns, nonlinear dynamics, and chaos. Tilly (Ch. 22, this volume) likewise surrounds his definition of path dependence with an array of ways in which history matters.

In short, all scholars seem to agree that path dependence means that the past affects the future, but they all also agree that this insight is not itself profound. Some scholars choose to define path dependence simply as the notion that the past affects the future, and then employ different concepts in the search for more specific ways in which history matters. Other scholars, however, retain the concept of path dependence as they pursue this search for more.

3   The Causal Importance of Initial Conditions

The next important dimension concerns the causal effect of "initial conditions." Initial conditions are the historically specific configuration of variables at the "beginning"—or perhaps even *before* the beginning—of a sequence of events (Goldstone 1998b). The issue at stake is whether these initial conditions aid in determining the final outcome of a path-dependent sequence. Somers (1998) argues that they do. In her discussion of path dependence, she asserts that "fourteenth-century legal institutions, for example, can be shown under certain initial and subsequent conditions... to be causal factors in the development of nineteenth-century democratic institutions" (768). Here, the particular configuration of variables in the fourteenth century is causally related to an outcome in the nineteenth century. Somers is careful to point out that initial conditions are not the only causal factor—she specifically mentions subsequent conditions as well—but is quite clear that they are one important causal factor in a path-dependent sequence.

By contrast, Arthur (1989, 1994), David (1985), Goldstone (1998*b*), and Mahoney (2000) all argue that initial conditions are not causally efficacious in path-dependent sequences. They make a sharp distinction between initial conditions and the events that immediately follow these initial conditions, arguing that the important causal action corresponds with the immediately following events. Frequently, the language of "critical juncture" is used to characterize this period when important causal processes are launched (see esp., Collier and Collier 1991). In these formulations, critical junctures are periods when a particular option is selected from a range of alternatives, thereby channeling future movement in a specific direction. Through this channeling process, critical junctures narrow the range of possible future outcomes. In essence, then, a new sequence begins with the critical juncture; initial conditions exist prior to the start of this sequence.

Research in the tradition of comparative-historical analysis has generated a number of studies focused on critical junctures. Perhaps most famously, Lipset and Rokkan (1967) hypothesized that European nations evolved contemporary political systems through the resolution of three critical junctures: state–church, party–church, and state–labor cleavages. Collier and Collier (1991) argued that the ways in which Latin American governments pursued the incorporation of labor was a critical juncture that shaped the character of national politics for many decades to come. Subsequently, a number of the Colliers' graduate students published their own analyses using this perspective for political regime outcomes in the Latin American region (e.g. Mahoney 2001; Scully 1992; Yashar 1997).

It is helpful to think of initial conditions as corresponding with the period *before* a critical juncture. Initial conditions may play some causal role in defining a broad range of historically possible outcomes. However, initial conditions do not limit the range of future possibilities that are of particular interest to the investigator. For instance, in Somers' example, unlike what she asserts, initial conditions would leave open the possibility of a case either developing democratic institutions or not developing these institutions. Only once some critical juncture episode has occurred does the sequence track one kind of outcome rather than another. As Goldstone (1998*b*, 834) puts it in his reply to Somers:

Path dependence is a property of a system such that the outcome over a period of time is *not determined* by any particular set of initial conditions. Rather, a system that exhibits path dependency is one in which outcomes are related stochastically to initial conditions, and the particular outcome that obtains in any given "run" of the system depends on the choices or outcomes of *intermediate events* between the initial conditions and the outcome.

We note that the debate between Goldstone and Somers could be simply a semantic difference. What Goldstone and others call "initial conditions" might be viewed by Somers as "antecedent conditions" that come *before* the main sequence of interest (see Collier and Collier 1991). If this is true, the sequence would begin with the critical juncture, not the initial conditions. In other words,

Somers' "initial conditions" might be simply a different terminology for discussing what Goldstone calls "intermediate events."

We further note that Goldstone's language of "intermediate events" is itself somewhat misleading. Goldstone's intermediate events correspond to a critical juncture period. While a critical juncture does occur between initial conditions and a final outcome, it is normally viewed as being closer in time to the initial conditions than to the final outcome. That is, a critical juncture is launched immediately following initial conditions, a point which may still be quite removed in time from the final outcome of interest. In this sense, scholars who reject the claim that initial conditions are causally relevant may still maintain that early events and processes in a sequence are of decisive causal importance. Placing initial conditions outside the confines of the path-dependent sequence therefore becomes an important decision.

4   CONTINGENCY

Many scholars believe that "contingency" is a necessary condition for path dependence. This idea is closely related to the argument that initial conditions cannot predict or explain final outcomes. With contingency, as Goldstone (1998b) notes, there is a stochastic relationship between initial conditions and final outcomes. Contingency is a way of speaking about the unpredictable nature of final outcomes, given some set of initial conditions. In the literature, there are several examples of causally important events that have been viewed as contingent: the creation of the International Typographical Union in the United States (Lipset, Trow, and Coleman 1956), the development of first steam engine in England (Goldstone 1998a; 2005), the introduction of the law of master and servant into the United States (Orren 1991), the death of Martin Luther King Jr. (Isaac, Street, and Knapp 1994), and the emergence of capitalism in Europe rather than China (Wallerstein 1974).

Many scholars link the idea of contingency to critical juncture periods. They argue that the events that characterize a critical juncture period are contingent. In particular, they suggest that the selection of a particular option during a critical juncture represents a random happening, an accident, a small occurrence, or an event that cannot be explained or predicted on the basis of a particular theoretical framework. David (1985) especially emphasizes the idea of chance events or accidents during key choice moments, whereas Arthur (1994) calls attention to small events that are beyond the resolving power of theory. Mahoney (2000) argues that a contingent event need not be random or "small" in scale. Rather, for him, a contingent event is an occurrence that cannot be explained or predicted in light of one or more theoretical frameworks.

Despite these different views on contingency, scholars agree on particular examples of contingency (or at least they have not yet disagreed in writing). For instance, in David's (1985) famous example of typewriter keyboard formats, the selection of the QWERTY format is a contingent event regardless of one's particular definition of contingency. For David, it is contingent because it was selected for non-systematic accidental reasons having to do with the peculiarities of type-bar jamming in early model typewriters. For Arthur, it is contingent because type-bar jamming is a "small event" that cannot be captured by theory. And for Mahoney (2000), it is a contingent event because it cannot be predicted by neoclassical economic theory, which holds that the most efficient technological format will be adopted.

In contrast to Arthur, David, Goldstone, and Mahoney, other scholars do not build the idea of contingency into their definitions of path dependence. For example, Pierson (2000; 2004) holds that one *possible* feature of path dependence is the causal importance of contingent events, but he prefers to view contingency as *not necessary* for path dependence. Likewise, Collier and Collier (1991) suggest that a critical juncture may or may not entail contingency. In making this conceptual move, Pierson and the Colliers avoid one of the more common criticisms of the path-dependent framework: chance plays too large of a role in the beginning of a sequence. For instance, Thelen (1999; 2003) has argued that many of the most important political trajectories are not launched by an initial contingent event. Schwartz (2004) also insists that contingency at the beginning of a sequence is not a helpful approach because it leaves as accidental what are actually the important and systematic origins of institutional outcomes.

On the other hand, the decision formally to exclude contingency from the definition of path dependence is not without problems. For example, following Arthur (1994), Pierson (2000, 253; 2004, 18) summarizes four intriguing consequences of path dependence:

1. Unpredictability: outcomes cannot be predicted on the basis of initial conditions.
2. Inflexibility: shifting to a different path becomes increasingly difficult over time.
3. Non-ergodicity: stochastic factors do not "average out" over time.
4. Path inefficiency: a final outcome may be inefficient relative to previously available options.

It bears emphasis that all of these intriguing consequences, with the exception of inflexibility, require the presence of contingency. Thus, unpredictability and non-ergodicity depend on the analyst assuming that a contingent event occurs; otherwise sequences would be predictable and accidents would be irrelevant. Likewise, inefficiency is generated by a contingent event that allows an inefficient outcome to capture an initial advantage that is reinforced over time. In short, only if path-dependent sequences are marked by contingency do they also exhibit the intriguing features of unpredictability, non-ergodicity, and inefficiency.

5   HISTORICAL LOCK-IN

Whereas many scholars argue that the events that launch a path-dependent sequence are characterized by contingency, these same scholars may assert that subsequent events in the sequence are marked by "historical lock-in." This phrase captures the idea that units may find themselves on paths of development from which they are unable to escape. Indeed, the very notion of path dependence implies at least some degree of this kind of lock-in. Yet, several scholars have been hesitant to include historical lock-in as a necessary feature of path dependence. One major reason why is that historical lock-in suggests a causal determinism in which the destiny of a unit is highly determined by previous events. Scholars who reject this kind of deterministic explanation, but who still seek to use the concept of path dependence, argue that historical lock-in is not inherent to path dependence. Rather, they hold that even under path-dependent circumstances units may and often do change the paths on which they travel (e.g. Crouch and Farrell 2004).

The idea of lock-in has been developed above all by Arthur (1994), who played a leading role in mathematically formalizing the "Polya urn" experiment—an example that in turn influenced Goldstone (1998b), Mahoney (2000), and Pierson (2000). In one version of this experiment, a very large urn initially contains two balls, a red ball and a black ball. One ball is randomly removed and returned to the urn, together with an additional ball of the same color. This process is repeated until the urn is filled. Under these conditions, one cannot predict in advance the final composition of the urn—it could be any proportion of red and black balls. However, as the process of selection takes place, one can predict increasingly well the final composition of the urn. Indeed, after many rounds, the proportion of red and black balls will fall into a stable equilibrium. At this point, the logic of probabilities ensures that a radical shift in the ratio of balls is nearly impossible; lock-in has taken place.

In the Polya urn example, early random events lead to a particular outcome, and then this outcome is stably reproduced over time. Examples from political science suggest that real historical processes may broadly conform to this pattern. For instance, Shefter (1977) argues that patterns of party patronage depend on what happens when parties first make appeals to a mass electorate. If they move toward patronage at that point, they become increasingly locked into patronage as mode of generating support. Likewise, Skocpol's (1999) recent research shows that voluntary associations that happened to develop in the early nineteenth century often managed to persist; by contrast, more recently formed associations face greater difficulty establishing themselves. Skocpol (1992) earlier used a similar logic to help explain the delayed introduction of a general system of welfare in the United States: the presence of Civil War veterans' pensions undercut the development of a constituency in favor of general welfare, which put the country on a path of late development for many welfare programs. Finally, Gerschenkron's (1962) famous study suggests that economic development follows an increasing returns process, in which early industrializers are able to achieve a kind of development that followers cannot easily replicate. Indeed, dependency theorists sometimes argue that late-late industrializers are now locked onto paths of distorted development (e.g. Cardoso and Faletto 1979).

As suggested above, some scholars are skeptical that outcomes are truly locked into particular trajectories of development. They emphasize the possibility of breakpoints within even enduring patterns of development. For example, Sewell's (1996) discussion of temporality calls attention to the possibility of "ruptures" that mark a "surprising break" with established patterns. Likewise, Aminzade (1992) notes that historical sociologists explore forks in the road and bifurcation points that emerge during the course of path-dependent sequences. This emphasis is consistent with frameworks that suggest that critical junctures can be a means through which actors break out of historical lock-in (e.g. Mahoney 2000). Quadagno and Knapp (1992) go so far as to reject explicitly the label path dependence because it "could imply teleological argumentation, and thus undermine the attempt to incorporate temporality and contingency. That is, 'path' could connote determinism and predictability" (503).

There is more general agreement that the causal importance of events is related to their temporal location in a sequence. Early events are more important than later events in determining the final outcome of the sequence, and thereby contribute more to the lock-in of outcomes. This temporal focus does not preclude shifts away from the path, though it does argue that such shifts are increasingly difficult with the passage of time. Such an argument might avoid some of the critiques of determinism to which historical applications of the Polya urn experiment are open.

Among skeptics concerned with the deterministic implications of path dependence, Thelen's (1999; 2003; see also Thelen and Steinmo 1992) work stands out for its concrete suggestions. Notably, she introduces the concept of *layering* to show how outcomes gradually change over time as a result of a series of events that slightly shift developmental trajectories. Although the changes that occur over any short period of time may be marginal, these slight changes can nevertheless accumulate, such that a radical shift in outcome takes place over a long period of time. For example, in Figure 24.1, the initial outcome at time 1 is characterized by features A through E. In each subsequent period, one feature becomes absent (represented

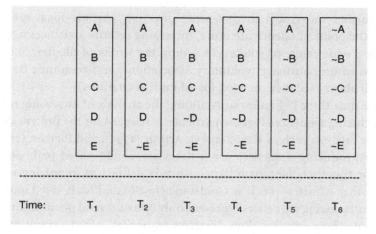

Fig. 24.1 Stylized example of a layering: 80 percent reproduction rate

by the tilde before a letter in the figure). As the figure shows, this pattern of development can culminate in a final outcome that is completely different from the initial outcome. However, because the change was gradual, one might only see the pattern by taking a long historical vantage point.

On the one hand, Thelen's overall vision clashes with the path-dependent image of abrupt moments of transformation followed by long periods of continuity. In her perspective, change and continuity are tightly interwoven such that they occur side by side. On the other hand, the extent of change and continuity necessarily will differ across outcomes. For example, one outcome may be 99.9 percent reproduced across a given unit of time, whereas another may be reproduced at a much lower rate across the same unit of time. Likewise, the unit of time in which change occurs may vary, ranging from short to long intervals. Scholars who include historical lock-in as part of the definition of path dependence study those sequences in which the outcomes of interest are almost entirely reproduced and in which the changes that do occur take place over significant time intervals.

6   SELF-REPRODUCING SEQUENCES

Self-reproducing sequences are those in which a given outcome is stably reinforced over time. The economic model of increasing returns is the archetype of this kind of sequence, in that it is founded on the idea that each step in a particular direction induces further movement in that same direction (Arthur 1994; 1989; Pierson 2000). In the political science literature, increasing returns sequences figure prominently in a wide range of studies, including the works of Shafter, Skocpol, and Gerschenkron on patronage, voluntary associations, and economic development mentioned above (see Pierson 2004 for additional citations).

Here we note three key issues surrounding the analysis of increasing returns and self-reproducing sequences that are particularly relevant for the present discussion. First, some analysts such as David (1985), Arthur (1994), and Pierson (2000) argue that self-reproducing sequences are a necessary condition of path dependence. Indeed, for these scholars, path dependence is defined *as* increasing returns. By contrast, other scholars—such as Goldstone (1998*b*) and Mahoney (2000)—argue that self-reproducing sequences represent only one of several possible kinds of path dependence. These scholars allow "reactive sequences" also to count as examples path dependence. We explore this issue in greater detail in the next section.

Second, based on the existing literature, it appears that increasing returns processes marked by path dependence have two possible end stages: (1) forever increasing returns; and (2) equilibrium.[2] The difference between these two end stages concerns the probability that a given outcome will be reproduced across time. With "forever increasing returns," these probabilities continually increase over time, such that they become closer and closer to one with the passing of each unit of time. In these cases, each and every step down a path makes it more likely that a given outcome will be reproduced. By contrast, with an "equilibrium end stage," the probabilities eventually reach some threshold beyond which further steps do not enhance the likelihood of reproduction. In this case, an increasing returns process gives way to a stable outcome that has a relatively fixed probability of being reproduced (presumably less than one). To our knowledge, path dependence theorists have not conceptualized or addressed this important difference in end stages in any systematic way.

Third, scholars disagree about the mechanisms through which self-reproducing sequences are sustained. Most scholars assume that increasing returns and self-reproduction are driven by the utilitarian considerations of rational actors. In this framework, initial moves in a particular direction increase the benefits of staying the course and/or the costs of shifting direction for rational decision-making actors. However, more sociological approaches suggest a broader range of mechanisms, including functional, power, and legitimation mechanisms (Mahoney 2000; Thelen 2003). In these frameworks, initial moves in a particular direction lead to a self-reinforcing outcome either by increasing the functionality of the outcome,

---

[2] Increasing returns could theoretically be followed by a third end stage, a decreasing returns period, though such a curve would likely produce a shift away from the reproduced outcome, and therefore a break from the path-dependent pattern.

enhancing the power of an elite that supports the outcome, or expanding the legitimacy of the outcome.

Differentiating the specific mechanisms that characterize path-dependent sequences helps bring into focus the theoretical core of many leading works in the field of comparative-historical analysis. For example, Wallerstein's (1974) functional mechanisms appear in his argument that Europe's hegemony in the world economy was reinforced by the global capitalist system itself once Europe initially moved in a capitalist direction. Likewise, Roy (1997) explicitly rejects a utilitarian framework and instead draws on a power-oriented framework to explain the reproduction of the large private corporation in the United States. Finally, Orren's (1991) legitmation assumptions can be found in her argument that the master–servant law was reinforced in the United States through increasing legitimacy within the courts. As these examples suggest, non-utilitarian sociological mechanisms of reproduction are readily found in the empirical literature (see also Mahoney 2000).

7 REACTIVE SEQUENCES

Some scholars include sequences that are not self-reproducing as potential candidates for path dependence. For example, imagine a sequence in which event A leads to event B which leads to event C and so on until event Z is reached. More concretely, consider the event logic though which Ertman (1997) explains the emergence of constitutionalism in Europe (the arrow symbol reads "causes"): peripheral territory within the Roman Empire ⇒ landed elites are weak ⇒ local government structures are strong ⇒ King calls for assemblies ⇒ territory-based assemblies are formed ⇒ constitutionalism develops. These kinds of non-reinforcing sequences are marked by a tight coupling of events in which each event in the sequence is both a reaction to earlier occurrences and a cause of subsequent occurrences. In that sense, the outcome is dependent on each prior event in what forms an overall path. Mahoney (2000, 526) uses the phrase "reactive sequence" to characterize these "chains of temporally ordered and causally connected events."

Reactive sequences might be familiar to those who use causal models as tools for incorporating intervening or mediating variables. While A may connect to Z causally, the mechanisms that link those two variables might be a series of variables themselves, and a full understanding of the relationship between A and Z requires analysis of each step of the process. At the same time, A may connect to Z independently of the mediators, maintaining the direct causal connection between the early variable and the outcome. Scholars who formulate reactive sequence arguments in the path-dependence literature have not explicitly weighed in on the extent to which an initial event exerts a causal impact on a final outcome independent of intervening events. However, they seem to imply that this extent is quite limited. For example, Goldstone (1998a; 2005) implies that the invention of the steam engine led to the Industrial Revolution only or largely because of the intervening events it set into motion.

While no one denies that reactive sequences are present in the world, some scholars argue that they should not be viewed as candidates for path dependence. In particular, Pierson (2000; 2004) argues that the inclusion of reactive sequences opens the concept to far too many sequences, especially given that nearly any non-reinforcing sequence could be construed as a reactive sequence. Hence, Pierson prefers to reserve the label path dependence for only self-reproducing sequences in order to maintain boundaries on the concept. By contrast, Goldstone (1998b) and Mahoney (2000) consider reactive sequences as potential candidates for the designation of path dependence. Recall that these scholars argue that only sequences that are marked by "contingency" may be path dependent. Because the criterion of contingency is highly restrictive, their definition inevitably makes path dependence a quite rare phenomenon. Not surprisingly, therefore, Goldstone and Mahoney are open to considering reactive sequences as potentially path dependent if they meet their other demanding definitional criteria.

Beyond this, there are disputes concerning the actual analysis of reactive sequences. Most of the issues pertain to the nature of the causal linkages between events in a reactive sequence. Because the final outcome of a reactive sequence depends on the occurrence of each prior event in the sequence, one must be certain that each causal linkage in the sequence is valid. For example, as just noted, Ertman (1997) argues that peripheral location in the Roman Empire ultimately breeds the development of constitutionalism. However, this argument depends on the validity of each step in the overall reactive sequence. If any one of these steps proves faulty, the entire enchained argument is called into question. In that sense, reactive sequences often imply a deterministic chain of causation.

These concerns have pushed analysts to explore the way in which narratives are used to establish causality between each event in a reactive sequence. However, narrative remains a rather mysterious mode of causal inference (see Abell 2004). In particular, it is not clear whether it relies on the same logic of inference as variable-centered explanation. Insofar as it does, scholars may be skeptical that narrative provides a compelling basis for establishing firm causal connections in a reactive sequence. By contrast, insofar as narrative analysis relies on a distinctive mode of causal inference, scholars have had difficulty specifying the nature of that mode. These dilemmas might be another reason why some scholars wish to exclude reactive sequences from their definition of path dependence.

8   CONCLUDING DISCUSSION

Why does history matter? One answer, as Tilly's earlier chapter (Ch. 22) suggests, is the existence of path dependence. But the literature on path dependence offers a number of different answers, each suggesting that path dependence must mean something more than just history matters. In this chapter, we have sought to offer an inventory of some of these answers.

A key conclusion that emerges from the discussion concerns the trade-offs involved in employing alternative definitions of path dependence. Perhaps the most basic trade-off is the tension between definitions of path dependence that make the phenomenon common but relatively banal, versus those that make the phenomenon intriguing but quite rare. Definitions of path dependence that stress only the role of antecedent events in shaping subsequent events have the merit of pointing out the ubiquity of path dependence. But these definitions are vulnerable to the charge that they make path dependence into an obvious—even tauto-logical—feature of the world. By contrast, definitions that add the most intriguing features to the concept—such as contingency followed by historical lock-in—are not vulnerable to the charge of obviousness or tautology. However, these defini-tions are open to the criticism of identifying a phenomenon that is at best quite rare in the social and political world.

Interestingly, the success of the concept of path dependence may be related to the fact that some definitions enhance analytic usefulness by defining path dependence in such a way that the phenomenon appears commonplace, whereas others are analytically helpful because they define the concept in a way that calls attention to extraordinary theoretical features. This chapter suggests that the existence of these competing definitions is not inherently problematic; indeed, scholarly analysis may profit from the use of different definitions. Nevertheless, to avoid confusion and enhance rigor, scholars should make their definitional choices and the conse-quences of these choices as explicit as possible.

REFERENCES

ABELL, P. 2004. Narrative explanation: an alternative to variable-centered explanation? *Annual Review of Sociology,* 30: 287–310.

ALMOND, G. A., FLANAGAN, S. C., and MUNDT, R. J. (eds.) 1973. *Crisis, Choice, and Change: Historical Studies of Political Development.* Boston: Little, Brown.

AMINZADE, R. 1992. Historical sociology and time. *Sociological Methods and Research,* 20: 456–80.

ARTHUR, W. B. 1989. Competing technologies and lock-in by historical events. *Economic Journal,* 99: 116–31.

ARTHUR, W. B. 1994. *Increasing Returns and Path Dependence in the Economy*. Ann Arbor: University of Michigan Press.

BINDER, L. et al. 1971. *Crises and Sequences in Political Development*. Princeton, NJ: Princeton University Press.

CARDOSO, F. H., and FALETTO, E. 1979. *Dependency and Development in Latin America*. English Edition. Berkeley: University of California Press.

CASTALDI, C., and DOSI, G. 2005. The grip of history and the scope for novelty: some results and open questions on path dependence in economic processes. In *Understanding Change: Models, Methodologies, and Metaphors*, ed. A. Wimmer and R. Kössler. Basingstoke: Palgrave Macmillan.

COLLIER, R. B., and COLLIER, D. 1991. *Shaping the Political Arena: Critical Junctures, the Labor Movement, and Regime Dynamics in Latin America*. Princeton, NJ: Princeton University Press.

CROUCH, C., and FARRELL, H. 2004. Breaking the path of institutional development? Alternatives to the new determinism. *Rationality and Society*, 16: 5–43.

DAVID, P. A. 1985. Clio and the economics of QWERTY. *American Economic Review*, 75: 332–7.

ERTMAN, R. 1997. *Birth of the Leviathan: Building States and Regimes in Medieval and Early Modern Europe*. Cambridge: Cambridge University Press.

GERSCHENKRON, A. 1962. *Economic Backwardness in Historical Perspective*. Cambridge, Mass.: Harvard University Press.

GOLDSTONE, J. A. 1998a. The problem of the "early modern" world. *Journal of Economic and Social History of the Orient*, 41: 249–84.

——1998b. Initial conditions, general laws, path dependence and explanation in historical sociology. *American Journal of Sociology*, 104: 829–45.

——2005. *The Happy Chance: The Rise of the West in Global Context, 1500–1800*. Cambridge, Mass.: Harvard University Press

HUBER, E., and STEPHENS, J. D. 2001. *Development and Crisis of the Welfare State*. Chicago: University of Chicago Press.

ISAAC, L. W., STREET, D. A., and KNAPP, S. J. 1994. Analyzing historical contingency with formal models: the case of the "relief explosion" and 1968. *Sociological Methods and Research*, 23: 114–41.

KARL, T. L. 1997. *The Paradox of Plenty: Oil Booms and Petro-States*. Berkeley: University of California Press.

LIPSET, S. M., and ROKKAN, S. 1967. Cleavage structures, party systems, and voter allignments: an introduction. In *Party Systems and Voter Alignments: Cross-National Perspectives*, ed. S. M. Lipset and S. Rokkan. New York: Free Press.

——TROW, M., and COLEMAN, J. 1956. *Union Democracy*. New York: Free Press.

MAHONEY, J. 2000. Path dependence in historical sociology. *Theory and Society*, 29: 507–48.

——2001. *The Legacies of Liberalism: Path Dependence and Political Regimes in Central America*. Baltimore: Johns Hopkins University Press.

NORTH, D. C. 1998. *Institutions, Institutional Change, and Economic Performance*. Cambridge: Cambridge University Press.

ORREN, K. 1991. *Belated Feudalism: Labor, the Law, and Liberal Development in the United States*. Cambridge: Cambridge University Press.

PIERSON, P. 2000. Increasing returns, path dependence, and the study of politics. *American Political Science Review*, 94: 251–67.

—— 2004. *Politics in Time: History, Institutions, and Social Analysis.* Princeton, NJ: Princeton University Press.

QUADAGNO, J., and KNAPP, S.J. 1992. Have historical sociologists forsaken theory? Thoughts on the history/theory relationship. *Sociological Methods and Research,* 20: 481–507.

ROY, W. G. 1997. *Socializing Capital: The Rise of the Large Industrial Corporation in America.* Princeton, NJ: Princeton University Press.

SCHWARTZ, H. 2004. Down the wrong path: path dependence, increasing returns, and historical institutionalism. Manuscript, Dept. of Politics, University of Virginia.

SCULLY, T. R. 1992. *Rethinking the Center: Party Politics in Nineteenth and Twentieth Century Chile.* Stanford, Calif.: Stanford University Press.

SEWELL, W. H., JR. 1996. Three temporalities: toward an eventful sociology. Pp. 245–80 in *The Historic Turn in the Human Sciences,* ed. T. J. McDonald. Ann Arbor: University of Michigan Press.

SHEFTER, M. 1977. Party and patronage: Germany, England, and Italy. *Politics and Society,* 7: 403–52.

SKOCPOL, T. 1992. *Protecting Soldiers and Mothers: The Political Origins of Social Policy in the United States.* Cambridge, Mass.: Harvard University Press.

—— 1999. How Americans became civic. Pp. 27–80 in *Civic Engagement in American Democracy,* ed. T. Skocpol and M. P. Fiorina. Washington, DC: Brookings Institution Press and Russell Sage Foundation.

SOMERS, M. R. 1998. We're no angels: realism, rational choice, and relationality in social science. *American Journal of Sociology,* 104: 722–84.

THELEN, K. 1999. Historical institutionalism and comparative politics. *Annual Review of Political Science,* 2: 369–404.

—— 2003. How institutions evolve: insights from comparative historical analysis. Pp. 208–40 in *Comparative Historical Analysis in the Social Sciences,* ed. J. Mahoney and D. Rueschemeyer. Cambridge: Cambridge University Press.

—— and STEINMO, S. 1992. Historical institutionalism in comparative politics. Pp. 1–32 in *Structuring Politics: Historical Institutionalism in Comparative Analysis,* ed. S. Steinmo, K. Thelen, and F. Longstreth. New York: Cambridge University Press.

WALLERSTEIN, I. 1974. *The Modern World System I: Capitalist Agriculture and the Origins of European World-Economy in the Sixteenth Century.* New York: Academic Press.

YASHAR, D. J. 1997. *Demanding Democracy: Reform and Reaction in Costa Rica and Guatemala, 1870s–1950s.* Stanford, Calif.: Stanford University Press.

CHAPTER 25

DOES HISTORY REPEAT?

RUTH BERINS COLLIER
SEBASTIÁN MAZZUCA

HISTORY is typically seen as non-repeating; yet repetition is often considered necessary for making general, explanatory statements in the social sciences. How, then, can political science explain outcomes in a way that does not contradict their fundamentally historical character? This dilemma is a key focus of debate in methodological discussions. It is raised explicitly by contextual political analysis, which, as described in the introduction to this volume, challenges standard forms of explanation that treat cases as repeatable instances of broader phenomena and causal processes.

We will show that to a great extent the dilemma is a false one: its two premises can be rejected. First, history can usefully be seen as repeating. We will argue that even the most radical critics accept some forms of repetition, and these forms are not logically different from those they reject. Assertions of repetition—or "analogies"—involve the creation of analytic categories in relation to which the researcher decides whether two or more cases are instances of the same phenomenon. Such assertions necessarily simplify an obviously complex reality, but simplifications are inescapable. We will examine arguments that reject the use of repetition in description as well as those that criticize explanations of repetition in terms of common causal patterns.

Second, explanation does not require repetition. Explanatory approaches that are usually seen as requiring repetition are those based on correlational arguments.

* We thank David Collier, José María Ghio, and Gerardo Munck

However, repetition is not necessary for correlational approaches, and furthermore such approaches can accommodate context and the unique with techniques that may be more logically consistent than the attempt by contextualists to "ground" general phenomena in particularistic settings.

Does history repeat? We answer this question, which the editors posed for this chapter, in the following way. We consider how political phenomena can be seen as repeating, both in terms of description as cases of the same thing and in terms of common causal patterns. We then review a set of analytic approaches to examine whether and how they treat repetition as a requisite for assessing causal patterns. Before proceeding, however, we offer some conceptual clarifications by analyzing the notions of history, context, and repetition, of which we distinguish three types: replication, recurrence, and reproduction.

1 CLARIFICATIONS: HISTORY, CONTEXT, AND REPETITION

What does it mean to ask "does history repeat?" in a book on "contextual political analysis," and in a section on "history as context"? Three sub-questions arise:

1. What is meant by history in political analysis?
2. What does it mean for history to be context?
3. What does it mean for history to repeat?

1.1 History as Temporal Dimensions

What is history that is not encompassed by the other topics in the present volume: culture, place, technology, and demography? The distinctive feature of history is *time*—a focus on the temporal dimensions of political occurrences and processes.

Time in politics includes four notions. First, history as *period* refers to the fact that political phenomena are located within some socially defined interval of time—world historical time, such as the cold war, or regional historical time, such as the period of import substitution in Latin America. This conception is central to those who ask about the grounding of politics in particular epochs.

Second, history as *conjuncture* refers to a temporal coincidence of a potentially limitless number of forces, actors, structures, and events, including the accidental and the contingent (Aron 1961, 16–17). The limitless nature of these converging elements makes a conjuncture unique. Analysts may call on any array of these to explain or interpret political phenomena. This is typically the conception of history of those who are concerned with the dense detail and particularistic setting in which political phenomena occur.

A third notion is *timing*: the fact that political phenomena may occur in different sequences and with different temporal spreads. Sequence is the ordering of two or more events or processes, such as the ordering of extensive unionization before or after party formation, or of contestation before or after participation (Dahl 1971, 33–40). Temporal spread refers to the distance measured in time between any two components in the sequence.

A fourth temporal idea involves *change over time* and has three variants: the unfolding of a series of different but interconnected events; the longitudinal trajectory of single factors; and the speed of a process or change. *Unfolding* consists of the idea that one thing leads to another, like the successive links of war making, revenue extraction, societal resistance, and constitution writing. Rather than links among multiple phenomena, *longitudinal trajectory* tracks change of a single factor over time, for example GDP or scores on democracy indices. *Speed* measures the time from the beginning to the end of a process, such as the number of years from the first granting of voting rights to universal suffrage.

1.2   Modeling History as Context: Benefits and Limitations

If history matters, is it best seen as context? To answer, it is important to clarify the meaning of context and the temporal dimensions that can be seen as context.

Context is understood as that which "surrounds" a political phenomenon. Therefore context is distinct from the political phenomenon itself, which can be seen either as a single event or process, or as a causal relation. Contextual political analysis is premised on the idea that a consideration of context improves understanding of the political phenomenon of primary interest. To define a context that is specifically historical, the question arises: Which of the temporal notions delineated above may be considered context in the strict sense of surrounding?

Among these notions, longitudinal trajectories provide an example of the insight gained by attention to context. A single observation, like the inflation rate for a specific quarter or the number of strikes in a given year, becomes more intelligible when located within a series of similar data for the preceding and following periods, that is, its temporal surrounding: the time series allows the analyst to assess whether inflation and strike activity are relatively high or low, declining or increasing.

The temporal notion of period provides context not only for a single phenomenon but also for causal relations. The relevance of context in this case centers not only on enhanced interpretation but crucially on its potential to change the nature of a given causal process. Temporal scope conditions are the canonical form of introducing history (period) as context. They limit the period in which causal generalizations hold. For instance, the relationship between export-oriented economic models and economic growth may depend on the period of the world economy: in the 1960s the turn to these economic models caused economic miracles, but in the 1980s it did not.

It is the temporal notion of conjuncture that might seem the most reflective of context, but it actually cancels context in the strict sense of surrounding. Analyses of the conjuncture focus on the effects of the temporal convergence of multiple factors, which may include external forces, long-term internal processes, historical institutional settings, and recent triggering events. However, if factors in this convergence "matter," they are no longer the surrounding of a causal process, but become an integral part of it, namely, the cause.

The general point is that if context is strictly understood as surrounding, its examination cannot be the central research goal but rather should be an auxiliary procedure in the analysis of the political phenomenon located within it. Once its impact is examined, it is thereby incorporated into the political phenomenon of primary interest. Contextual political analysis is thus a "self-liquidating" enterprise, one that can be understood in terms of a paradox. By underestimating context, analysts run the risk of misunderstanding the political phenomena located within it. By attributing direct causal power to context, on the other hand, analysts annul it, since it thereby becomes a "part" of the phenomenon of interest, rather than its "surrounding."

The recent historical turn in the social sciences and the slogan "history matters" must confront this paradox. This turn cannot be a defense of contextual analysis as the ultimate research goal. Examples of historical analysis that most convincingly demonstrate that history matters are those that treat history as cause rather than surrounding. Although above we considered longitudinal trajectory as context, it is more central when analyzed as cause. In Pierson's analysis of "big, slow-moving, and invisible" processes, like proletarianization, longitudinal trajectories may cumulate and have either threshold or distant effects that at some point, for instance, produce critical political realignments (Pierson 2003, 181–6; cf. Stinchcombe 1978, 61–70). Similarly, sequence and speed have entered analysis as causes, while unfolding is a series of causal steps (Huntington 1968, 78–91; Skocpol 1985, 21–6; Shefter 1994, 34; Ertman 1996, 25–8).

1.3 Repetition in History: Replication, Recurrence, and Reproduction

Assertions about repetition are dependent on a set of analytical choices related to concept formation. These include a relatively parsimonious selection of traits, a focus on similarities, and the construction of analytical categories in relation to which cases are seen as instances of the same phenomena. With this in mind, history can be seen as repeating in at least three forms.

Replication can be defined as repetition across different places, and *recurrence* as repetition over time within the same place. Among recent democratization processes, the Greek and Argentine experiences provide multiple instances of replication, as they shared key components of the chain of events leading to the end of authoritarian rule: in both cases an increasingly unpopular military dictatorship sent their countries into an international war, which was a desperate measure to regain domestic support; both countries lost the war, and the defeat precipitated the regime's collapse. A prominent example of recurrence is provided by state-formation in Early Modern Europe. Over the course of the seventeenth century, the Polish monarchs faced recurrent foreign threats, turning time and again to provincial aristocracies in search of financial help to defend themselves. The aristocracies repeatedly ignored the risks and replied by blocking the monarchs' initiatives, and Poland successively lost major portions of its territory to Prussia, Sweden, and Russia.

Both replication and recurrence involve the repetition of discrete phenomena, separated from one another by time or space. However, repetition in history can take the subtler, continuous form of *reproduction*: political institutions, forms of economic organization, and cultural codes are discernible to the observer only to the extent that they have an uninterrupted existence over a considerable span of time. Reproduction is, in a sense, a limiting case of recurrence in that it telescopes to zero the temporal distance between instances of recurrence over time. For instance, trade routes in sixteenth-century Mediterranean Europe constituted a remarkably stable infrastructure of communication among coastal cities and production centers, which generations of merchants and sailors took for granted in their everyday lives. These trade routes, in turn, were associated with ongoing forms of economic organization, like the urban markets of Cadiz and the textile workshops of Venice, where shopkeepers, middlemen, artisans, and consumers showed—and expected from each other—regular and persistent patterns of behavior, including locations and times for transactions, and methods of payment and accounting. These structures and behaviors, then, were continuously repeated over long periods of time.[1]

2   REPETITION AND ITS CRITICS

Observations of repetition in its various forms are commonplace and lie at the center of much social science analysis. Yet they have provoked debate and skepticism. Skepticism takes two forms. Some skeptics reject the possibility of repetition

---

[1] The concept of reproduction and the example of trade routes in the Mediterranean are inspired by the work of Fernand Braudel, especially his concept of *longue durée* (Braudel 1949; 1980).

in history and view assertions of repetition as distorted descriptions of reality. Others accept the possibility of repetition, but reject the existence of systematic patterns of causation that could account for repeated phenomena. The first kind of criticism focuses on problems of *description*; the second, on the *explanation* of repetition. Clearly, the former is more radical than the latter, since it rules out repetition *tout court*, not just causally patterned repetition. To rule out repetition itself, the skeptic has to view statements about repetition as the product of a *false analogy*, an emphasis on superficial similarities that hides deeper contrasts. To rule out the existence of a systematic pattern, the skeptic must conceive of repetition as the product of a *fortuitous coincidence*, a situation dominated by chance rather than by a common causal structure. The false analogy argument blames the analyst for distorting reality; the fortuitous coincidence position considers repetition a random occurrence that is independent from the analyst.

Analyses theorizing repetition in history have explicitly focused on replication and recurrence (either to assert or to reject it), but have generally taken for granted reproduction. Marx and Gerschenkron provide classical examples of attention to these first two forms of repetition. Marx asserted replicating capitalist trajectories and rejected recurrence in his tragedy/farce contrast between the two Bonapartes (1978, 594). Similarly, Gerschenkron (1962) attacked the notion that late industrializers mirror the trajectory of pioneers, at the same time that he hypothesized a common political outcome for latecomers. However, neither Marx nor Gerschenkron problematized reproduction as a form of repetition in history—their historical analyses are populated by capitalist firms, national governments, property rights, trade unions, and political ideologies, the very identification of which depends on the continued existence of core attributes over substantial blocks of time. In more recent debates, both advocates of contextual analysis and adherents to the new historical turn have joined a strong critique of replication/recurrence with a tacit acceptance of reproduction. As we will see, however, reproduction should hardly be considered less problematic than replication or recurrence.

2.1 Legitimate Repetition vs False Analogy

The criticism that statements about repetition in history are distorted descriptions based on false analogies has several variants. This variety is due to the fact that statements about repetition are built on a series of analytical choices made by the observer, and different variants of the critique attack distinct steps in the process of crafting the analogies that underlie statements about repetition.

2.1.1 *Definitional Variants*

The first group of criticisms against repetition is based on the standard claim that historical moments are infinitely complex phenomena, implying that history is a succession of what we have analyzed as conjunctures (Oakeshott 1933, 154). The most serious flaw of this critique is that it rules out repetition in history by definitional stipulation: repetition and history are incompatible notions only because they are defined as antonyms—specifically, phenomena that are not described in their uniqueness are not considered properly historical.

Another problem with this critique is that precisely because historical phenomena in their full detail are inexhaustible, all descriptions of historical processes and events require some form of analytical simplification and selection of attributes. The kind of distortion implicit in simplification/selection affects descriptions that emphasize the unique as well as those that assert repetition.[2] The analytical choice that is distinctive to statements about repetition, then, is not the decision to select, but specifically the decision to select similarities among cases across time and place—similarities that are necessarily few relative to the limitless number of differences that are bracketed. Of course, analogies resulting from these choices may be more or less productive.

Analogies based on the selection of similar attributes are not exclusive to statements about replication and recurrence. They are also the analytical basis of claims about reproduction: to identify enduring institutions, structures, and codes, such claims abstract constant elements from changing ones. The identification of the modern state as an enduring structure is based on the monopoly of violence, while it ignores changes in state functions. Hence, another weakness of the definitional criticism of repetition is that it contradicts the routine acceptance of simplification and selection in assertions of reproduction among social scientists of all persuasions, including historians and contextualists.

Finally, defining history in terms of a limitless number of traits reduces history to conjuncture, the temporal notion that cannot repeat. However history can enter political analysis through other temporal notions, which can repeat depending on the analytical choices made in defining it. A specific world or regional historical period, such as the cold war, which could not recur, may be redefined more abstractly as "strong bipolarity" or "mutual deterrence," and hence could recur.

2.1.2 *Thick Description*

A non-definitional variant of the false analogy critique is a generalization of what Geertz (1973, ch. 1), following Ryle, defined as "thick description" (see also Badie and Hermet 2001, 12–30). For this variant, a focus on similarities implies a superficial description of phenomena (e.g. identical contractions of the right eyelid), which at a deeper level are different entities (a wink versus a twitch). For some contextualists, a corollary of thick description is that any proper understanding of

---

[2] Discussions of "colligatory concepts" in history make explicit the simplifying decisions involved in descriptions of unique historical periods (see Walsh 1974; McCullagh 1978).

a given political phenomenon requires a focus on its unique grounding in its particular institutional or cultural setting.

However, as Geertz recognized, the search for similarities and repetition may not be inappropriate: the "deep" or "thick" is not necessarily unique and unrepeatable. Nor is the unique always relevant for advancing knowledge. The fact that similarities and repetition can be both deep and relevant is clearly shown by Stinchcombe's (1978, 19–21) argument for "deep analogies." One of Stinchcombe's examples is Trotsky's parallel between Bolsheviks and Kadets before the Russian Revolution. Although on the surface Kadets and Bolsheviks were radically different and antagonistic parties, Trotsky pointed to a key shared trait: the high level of commitment by cadres and followers. The commonality is relevant because it helps explain why, in contrast to the Mensheviks, both parties would be able to remain united and increase their support during the Revolution.[3]

In addition, repetition in the form of reproduction is at the core of thick description, despite its emphasis on the unique and distinctive. Although the meaning of externally similar behaviors may not replicate across societies, within a given society the intelligibility of actions, both to participants and to observers, depends on the continuous existence of shared cultural codes—i.e. reproduction over time. To understand each other's actions, members of society resort to a stock of public knowledge that, if not minimally stable, would make communication impossible.

2.1.3 *Homogenization as Repetition within a Case*

A final counter-argument against the false analogy critique relates to issues of case demarcation: the definition of the unit of time or place that is characterized by a given set of attributes. Skeptics who reject repetition across cases face the dilemma that they cannot escape making assumptions of homogeneity—or repetition— across spatial or temporal sub-units within the case they characterize as unique. The attributes selected to characterize a unit may be unique and distinctive, but since any unit can be successively subdivided, the characterization of a unit necessarily involves an implicit or explicit decision to ignore differences across geographical and temporal sub-units within the case, parallel to the way differences across cases are bracketed in the construction of analogies.

Authority in a particular country may be characterized as charismatic. However, a sub-region may obey national rulers on a quite different basis, such as patrimonialism. Such subdividing is limitless. Individuals within any subdivision may not conform to the more general pattern. The same logic applies to temporal units. The

---

[3] The inverse of thick description is not deep analogy but the notion of "system-specific indicators" (Przeworski and Teune 1970, 113–31, esp. 124–30), as it implies that superficially different observations in separate contexts may actually have the same interpretation. Locke and Thelen (1998: 11), for instance, argue that work reorganization in the US has an equivalent meaning, in terms of industrial conflict, to wage flexibilization in Germany. In this example, thin differences hide thick replications.

"lost decade" of the 1980s in Latin America is often thought of as a single period of economic stagnation, regardless of short sub-periods of growth in some countries.

Many repetition skeptics do not recognize the issue of case demarcation and are not explicit about homogenizing choices. Reinhard Bendix is one of the most conspicuous skeptics of repetitions, patterns, and analogies; yet, he characterizes countries and periods, like Soviet Russia or Tokugawa Japan, in terms of uniform cultural and institutional attributes, bracketing in the process numerous temporal and geographic departures from the national patterns (Bendix 1977, 175–211; 1978, 431–49). The point is not that the analytic decision to homogenize a case is wrong, but that it is inescapable for all kinds of analysis. Indeed, like assertions of replication and recurrence, within case homogenization should not be assessed as a mirror of reality but in terms of the insights gained.

Choices about case demarcation are consequential, since distinct theories may be invoked as explanations for differently demarcated units. An example is the growth of the American economy in the twentieth century. Economists trying to explain this growth focus on the long-run pattern, and characterize the rate of change as a linear trend that homogenizes growth over the century. On the other hand, if the temporal focus switches from the long run to the short run, fluctuations become the important outcomes to be explained. Moreover, for explaining growth in the long run, economists not only ignore short-run deviations, but also resort to radically different factors from those explaining yearly or quarterly fluctuations.

2.2   Causal Pattern vs Fortuitous Coincidence

Theories of replication and recurrence as a patterned form of repetition hypothesize one of various causal models. A patterned understanding of replication of democratic transitions, for instance, could see it as the product of parallel internal causes (national economic development), the effect of a common external force (imposition by a global power), or the outcome of diffusion from one case to another (by imitation or competition). Critics are skeptical that systematic patterns actually govern replication or recurrence.

As noted, critics view reproduction as a less disputable feature of social structures and political institutions. However, whether repetition is the effect of a causal pattern or a fortuitous coincidence is a question that is as relevant for reproduction as it is for recurrence and replication. Perhaps because it seems obvious that some structures and institutions reproduce, reproduction is often left unexplained—simply assumed or unproblematically thought of as "historically embedded" (Moore 1966, 485–6). Without an explanation, however, it is not possible to establish if reproduction is the effect of a causal pattern or a fortuitous coincidence. Further, most available explanations of reproduction are identical to explanations of replication and recurrence, and they often embrace a larger and more tentative set of assumptions (Giddens 1979, 4, 80–4, 242–4; 1984, 343–7).

Stinchcombe (1968, 101–29) distinguishes two models for explaining reproduction. The first, based on "constant causes," is the same as explanation of replication and recurrence via parallel internal causes. An example is provided by theories of political institutions as outcomes of the underlying distribution of social power. In these theories, institutional stability is the effect of a recurring balance of power, which remains constant from one period to another.

The alternative model of reproduction resorts to "historical causes." This model posits a separate cause for the origin of an institution and for its stability. Yet, explanations of subsequent stability are no different from those of replication and recurrence—parallel cause, common factor, or a "serial" form of diffusion in which an institution is the outcome of its existence in the previous moment and the cause of its existence in the following one, in an ongoing sequence during the period of its stability.[4] Furthermore, to support serial diffusion, the analyst must rely on economic or sociological notions of agency, either rational expectations or habituation (Cohen 1987, 289–302).

Incorporating reproduction into discussions of repetition, then, helps identify another major dilemma for those who vindicate a greater appreciation for present "imprints" of past events, i.e. enduring historical legacies, and who, at the same time, share a deep skepticism about replication and recurrence of social phenomena (Sewell 1996, 262–4; Somers 1998). In effect, given the prevailing isomorphism among explanations of repetition, including reproduction, skeptics should either be less critical of statements about replication and recurrence, or more critical of assumptions about reproduction—more critical in the sense of providing explicit accounts of reproduction, and, indeed, accounts that are not simply variants of the explanations for the other two forms of repetition.

3 Explanation: Repetition and the Unique

The question of whether repetition is the product of a causal pattern is different from the question of whether the detection of causal patterns requires that phenomena replicate, recur, or reproduce. In the remainder of this chapter we turn to the latter question and examine different explanatory approaches in political

---

[4] The notion of path dependence via self-reinforcing sequence or feedback loop can be subsumed as a variant of this "serial" form of diffusion.

science, assessing their reliance on repetition and their capacity to accommodate the unique case. These approaches can be analyzed in terms of whether they require, permit, or rule out repetition of: (1) initial conditions (or causes) and outcomes; (2) the generative process of actions and events that connects initial conditions and outcomes; and (3) the context in which these are located.

3.1   Correlation

The correlational approach, which includes both small-N comparative method and statistical analysis, subsumes multiple cases under a single generalization by asserting regularities in the relation between initial conditions and outcomes, both seen as variables, X and Y (where X may be a set of variables).[5] In using variables, this approach permits, but does not require repetition of causes and outcomes. Hence it does not rule out analysis of the unique. In the statistical version of this approach, covariation does not require that any two cases have the same score on X and/or Y. The same applies to the qualitative/small-N version, in which outcomes and initial conditions may be arrayed ordinally on a single dimension or located in a typology, often conceived as an intersection of two or more dimensions. Typologies can accommodate the unique since there is no requirement that multiple cases fall into each type.[6] A parallel procedure, the construction of subtypes via successive addition of attributes (democracy, presidential democracy, two-party presidential democracy . . .), can ultimately produce a category for each case.

Critics have charged small-N explanations of macro-political phenomena, like revolution, democracy, or economic reform, with improperly homogenizing cases as replications of the same phenomenon. For critics, these explanations are "invariant models" (Tilly 1995, 1597–601). However, by accounting for similarities among cases the small-N analyst simultaneously explains why they differ from others. Thus, the implicit or explicit difference being explained is at a higher level of generality: not differences among revolutions, but revolution versus non-revolution, or democracy versus authoritarianism, economic reform versus policy continuity. Correlational analysis, then, requires not repetition but a contrast.

At the same time, the correlational approach may involve a requirement about repetition in the context surrounding X and Y. This requirement derives from the

---

[5] While it is commonplace to recognize that correlation does not imply causation, in fact many explanations are built from observations of covariation. By correlational approach we refer to explanatory arguments based primarily on what Goldthorpe (2001) characterized as "robust correlation," in which the analyst has some procedure, statistical or qualitative, for taking into account issues of spuriousness and confounds.

[6] An example is Rokkan's (1970, 132) "Table 5: A 2 × 2 × 2 × 2 Typology of Cleavage Structures and its Fit with the Empirical Cases in Western Europe."

assumption of causal homogeneity, embedded in all correlational explanations: the same causal pattern operates across all cases covered by the generalization (specifically, the same effects follow from the same causes). Thus, if contexts are relevant for the X→Y relation, causal homogeneity assumes they are the same across cases. Alternatively, if contexts are not identical across cases, causal homogeneity assumes that differences among them do not affect the X→Y relation. Correlational approaches, then, commit the analyst to one of two assumptions: contexts repeat, or contexts do not matter.

As skeptics emphasize, the assumption of causal homogeneity is problematic. Even the "law" that a higher price induces a higher supply does not apply universally. As Max Weber and Karl Polanyi noted, in cultures where people consider it inappropriate to buy more goods than those required for everyday subsistence, wage increases past some threshold simply induce people to work less—the price of labor goes up, but the supply goes down.

The correlational approach addresses the potential problems raised by the causal homogeneity assumption and the impact of different contexts in two ways. In both qualitative and statistical analysis, scope conditions may be introduced by restricting the set of cases in an effort to hold context constant (e.g. interwar European regimes). Statistical analysis provides an additional option of introducing time and place "dummies" as control variables. These dummies take the form of specific geographical areas (e.g. region, country, or city) or time periods, defined chronologically or politically (e.g. as specific decades, before/after the fall of Communism, or the cold war period). Both procedures allow the analyst to examine the X→Y relation while removing contextual factors that may affect Y. The statistical approach, however, produces a coefficient for each dummy, which could indicate that the time–place context weighs heavily. Nevertheless, the contextual factors underlying the time or place proxies remain unspecified (what it is about the interwar period, the 1980s, Africa, or northern Italy, for example, that produces an effect on Y). It should be noted that to the extent they can be interpreted and carry substantive meaning, these dummy variables are thereby converted into additional independent variables, and context as surrounding disappears.

3.2 Generative Process with Correlation

Partly to address the limitations of the correlational approach regarding the problem of causation and explanation, many scholars seek to elucidate more closely the process by which a cause leads to an outcome—the "generative process" (Goldthorpe 2001, 8–10). In this section we focus on explanations that view generative processes as necessary supplements to correlational analysis. In the next section we analyze approaches that question or dispense with the correlational approach.

Generative processes have variously been seen as a key for solving the "black box" problem of correlational analysis, as a technique for rejecting the causal status of associations among variables for which no connections in fact exist, as a way to reduce the time-lag between independent and dependent variables, or as a requirement for making the correlation more "understandable" in terms of economic or sociological micro-foundations. In accepting a correlational analysis in which initial conditions and outcomes are seen as variables, and cases are scored on these variables, the two approaches discussed below permit repetition of X and Y. However, they differ in their position regarding repetition of the generative process.

3.2.1   Dynamic Properties

In the Dynamic Properties approach, processes are seen in terms of the dynamic properties inherent in the independent variable X, conceptualized as a typology. Each subtype of X contains a logic of political interaction that sets a specific process in motion. In Sartori's (1976, 131–45) analysis of party systems, for example, parties in the subtype of ideological multipartyism trigger a mechanism of polarization that destabilizes the government and ultimately threatens democratic institutions. The Dynamic Properties approach permits repetition not only in the X→Y relationship, but also in the generative process, understood to be universal across the cases in each subtype. The generative process need not be restricted to a single step, but may involve multiple intervening variables, like the reactive sequences of populist labor incorporation, conservative reaction, ban on party, political stalemate, and military coup (Collier and Collier 1991, 753–4).

3.2.2   Process Tracing

Unlike the "laws of motion" in Dynamic Properties in which intervening steps are seen as variables, Process Tracing seeks to understand the causal connection between specific scores of X and Y through an empirical, case-specific narrative, in which individuals identified by their proper names successively undertake particular actions in ways that can plausibly be seen as set in motion by X and as resulting in Y. The actions and events in this chain do not repeat, as they are narrated at a level in which they are not seen as instances of broader categories. For example, in his account of the origins of constitutional versus absolutist governments in Early Modern Europe, Downing (1992) combines a parsimonious correlational hypothesis, linking regime type to financial pressures during state formation, with a detailed case-by-case study of how specific rulers, like the Great Elector in Brandenburg-Prussia or Colbert in France, undertook particular actions to deal with those pressures.

3.3 Generative Process against Correlations

Two approaches focus on a generative process that does not supply the link between X and Y. The Disruptive Events perspective accepts the generalizations of the correlational approach but focuses attention on the generative processes that, at particular conjunctures, disrupt those generalizations. The Robust Mechanisms approach, on the other hand, makes the greatest break with correlational analysis by rejecting the conceptualization of initial conditions and outcomes as variables. These analytic choices position these approaches quite differently on the issue of repetition in history.

3.3.1 *Disruptive Events*

Like Process Tracing, the Disruptive Events approach views the events that make up the generative process as a unique concatenation of decisions and actions. However, instead of connecting initial conditions to outcomes, events carry the potential to transform the X→Y relation, neutralizing or reversing the effects that initial conditions would have otherwise produced. For Disruptive Events, generative processes may not only explain correlations; they may subvert them (Sewell 1996, 263). Disruptive Events, then, posits a distinct challenge to the form of repetition associated with the assumption of causal homogeneity in correlational analysis. Causal homogeneity breaks down not because of unexplored divergence across cases in terms of contextual conditions—the usual source of concern—but due to the transformative properties of contingent features that may intervene in the process normally linking cause and outcome.[7]

For example, De Gaulle's leadership and the formation of a national unity government, a part of the generative process itself, prevented the breakdown of democracy in France, thereby disrupting the theoretically and empirically established correlation between polarized party systems and democratic collapse.

Unlike other approaches, the phenomenon of interest is unique but the context is seen in terms of regularities. The context of the event is the correlation, and in that sense it can repeat. Indeed, it is the repeatability of the surrounding correlations that makes the event a disruptive force: no repetitive context, no regularities to disrupt.

3.3.2 *Robust Mechanisms*

The key innovation of Robust Mechanisms is the level of aggregation at which it is considered meaningful to classify phenomena as similar or repeating. Individual

---

[7] It should be noted that this approach has a strong tradition in political science, where the role of leadership and decision-making has long been recognized as a creative force overcoming deeper structural processes (Linz 1978). This approach has more recently been introduced in sociology, a discipline which has traditionally placed a stronger emphasis on structure. Sewell (1996) refers to this approach as "eventful sociology."

macro-political episodes of "democratization," for example, are seen as too complex and heterogeneous to be considered as repeating instances of the same phenomenon. The same applies to cases of civil war, revolutions, and other macro-political phenomena that have traditionally concerned comparativists. These episodes are seen as "historical accumulations" of economic, political, and cultural circumstances and institutions, unique to each case. Robust Mechanisms thus advocates a focus on particular episodes, such as Mexican democratization, the American Civil War, or the Russian Revolution (Tilly 2001*a*; 2001*b*, 24–6).

Central to this approach is the identification of repetition at the most basic level of aggregation, the level of mechanisms. Mechanisms are actions and are captured by verbs or derivative nouns (compete/competition, appease/appeasement, threaten/threat, deplete/depletion). Mechanisms—and some combinations or sequences of mechanisms, such as polarization and brokerage—are *robust*, in that they recur widely: they can be detected in diverse spatio-temporal settings and across disparate macro-political process. Indeed, while the same mechanisms need not be compononents of two cases of democratization, they may be shared by quite different macro-processes, for example by both the Mexican Revolution and the collapse of the Soviet Union (McAdam, Tarrow, and Tilly 2001).

It is the repeatability of these mechanisms that, according to Robust Mechanisms, allows for the construction of properly explanatory arguments. Explanation is tantamount to the detection of repetition at this low level of aggregation. Mechanisms are modular components of the larger macro-process, which is conceived as a unique combination of various mechanisms.

In contrast to the Correlation approach, which conditions repetition of X on the repetition of Y, Robust Mechanisms claims that macro-political outcomes do not repeat, but the approach crucially relies on the replicability and recurrence of mechanisms as key causal components in the generation of such outcomes. In other words, whereas the correlational approach only *permits* the repetition of XY, the Robust Mechanisms approach *requires* the repetition of mechanisms, and in that sense makes a stronger identification between repetition and explanation than any other approach.

4   CONCLUSION

In conclusion, we make four points.

First, history can usefully be seen as repeating. We have distinguished different temporal dimensions of history and shown that only one of them definitively does not repeat: the conjunctural notion, which identifies the unique temporal coincidence of a potentially limitless number of factors. Timing and speed, by contrast, may repeat. The same is true of longitudinal trajectory, period, and unfolding, although in order to be seen as repeating, these notions, like all others, may require some abstraction, a recasting at a more general level on the part of the analyst.

Second, to the extent analysts reject repetition in history, they must also reject reproduction of structures and institutions, which is an underlying assumption of most "historically based" analyses: reproduction is a form of repetition and is essentially no different from types that are the target of repetition skeptics.

Third, history is not necessarily context. If history matters, it is not context. The notions of history other than conjuncture may be placed in any position in a causal model, not only context, but also outcome, initial conditions, and generative process. Indeed, history can be shown to matter only if it occupies one of these other positions.

Fourth, standard forms of explanation, like correlation, do not require repetition. Moreover, the correlational approach can accommodate the unique and incorporate context through various logical steps: the introduction of scope conditions, the refinement of typologies, and the creation of subtypes. Other approaches add analysis of a generative process to the correlational approach as a way to deal better with uniqueness. In Process Tracing the generative process is the main channel for introducing case-specific material into the analysis, tracing the generalization governing X→Y through particularistic institutions, actors, and behaviors. Disruptive Events also focuses on a particularistic generative process, as a way to explain the breakdown of generalizations. Disruptive events are the particularistic factor that explains exceptions to X→Y correlations—outliers or "off-diagonal cases."

Political science is an eclectic discipline. Some analytical approaches have the primary goal of generalization; others, of understanding particular cases. Either way, assertions of repetition are useful for political analysis, which cannot be judged only in terms of empirical accuracy but in terms of the insight gained. In the last instance, meeting the standard of empirical accuracy requires point-by-point descriptions of reality—which, as in Borges's tale of Chinese cartographers drawing maps as big as the territory of the Empire itself, hinders understanding.

The use of repetition does not produce a mirror of reality but is a key step in achieving analytical goals. Replication and recurrence are useful in motivating and guiding the search for causal patterns: common or parallel causes or diffusion. Homogenization is an inescapable assumption of repetition for making cases viable analytical units, and reproduction is central for understanding continuity of social life and the endurance of social structures.

REFERENCES

ARON, R. 1961. *Introduction to the Philosophy of History.* Boston: Beacon Press.

BADIE, B., and HERMET, G. 2001. *La Politique Comparée.* Paris: Dalloz.

BENDIX, R. 1977. *Nation-building and Citizenship.* Berkeley: University of California Press.

——1978. *King or People.* Berkeley: University of California Press.

BRAUDEL, F. 1949. *La Méditerranée et le monde méditerranéen à l'époque de Philippe II.* Paris: Colin.

——1980. History and the social sciences: the longue durée. In Fernand Braudel, *On History,* trans. Sarah Matthews. Chicago: University of Chicago Press.

COHEN, I. J. 1987. Structuration theory and social praxis. Pp. 273–308 in *Social Theory Today,* ed. A. Giddens and J. Turner. Cambridge: Polity Press.

COLLIER, R. B., and COLLIER, D. 1991. *Shaping the Political Arena.* Princeton, NJ: Princeton University Press.

DAHL, R. A. 1971. *Polyarchy: Participation and Opposition.* New Haven, Conn.: Yale University Press.

DOWNING, B. M. 1992. *The Military Revolution and Political Change.* PRINCETON, NJ: Princeton University Press.

ERTMAN, T. 1996. *Birth of the Leviathan.* New York: Cambridge University Press.

GEERTZ, C. 1973. *The Interpretation of Cultures.* New York: Basic Books.

GERSCHENKRON, A. 1962. *Economic Backwardness in Historical Perspective.* Cambridge, Mass.: Belknap Press.

GIDDENS, A. 1979. *Central Problems in Social Theory: STRUCTURE, ACTION, and Contradiction in Social Analysis.* London: Macmillan.

——1984. *The Constitution of Society: Outline of the Theory of Structuration.* Cambridge: Polity Press.

GOLDTHORPE, J. H. 2001. Causation, statistics and sociology. *European Sociological Review,* 17: 1–20.

HUNTINGTON, S. 1968. *Political Order in Changing Societies.* New Haven, Conn.: Yale University Press.

LINZ, J. J. 1978. *The Breakdown of Democratic Regimes.* Baltimore: Johns Hopkins University Press.

LOCKE, R., and THELEN, K. 1998. Problems of equivalence in comparative politics: apples and oranges, again. *APSA-CP, Newsletter of the APSA Organized Section in Comparative Politics,* 9 (1): 9–12.

MAHONEY, J., and RUESCHEMEYER, D. 2003. *Comparative Historical Analysis in the Social Sciences.* New York: Cambridge University Press.

MARX, K. 1977. *Capital.* Vol. 1. New York: Vintage Books.

——1978. The eighteenth brumaire of Louis Bonaparte. Pp. 594–617 in *The Marx-Engels Reader,* ed. R. C. Tucker, 2nd edn. New York: Norton.

McADAM, D., TARROW, S., and TILLY, C. 2001. *Dynamics of Contention.* New York: Cambridge University Press.

McCULLAGH, C. BEBHAN 1978. Colligation and Classification in history. *History and Theory,* 17: 267–84.

MOORE, B. 1966. *Social Origins of Dictatorship and Democracy.* Boston: Beacon Press.

OAKESHOTT, M. 1933. *Experience and its Modes.* Cambridge: Cambridge University Press.

PAIGE, J. M. 1999. Conjuncture, comparison, and conditional theory in macrosocial inquiry. *American Journal of Sociology*, 105: 781–800.

PIERSON, P. 2000. Not just what but when: timing and sequence in political processes. *Studies in American Political Development*, 14: 72–92.

—— 2003. Big, slow-moving, and... invisible: macrosocial processes in the study of comparative politics. In Mahoney and Rueschemeyer 2003, 177–207.

PRZEWORSKI, A., and TEUNE, H. 1970. *The Logic of Comparative Social Inquiry*. New York: Wiley.

ROKKAN, S. 1970. *Citizens, Elections, Parties*. New York: David McKay.

SARTORI, G. 1976. *Parties and Party Systems*. New York: Cambridge University Press.

SEWELL, W. H., Jr. 1996. Three temporalities: toward an eventful sociology. Pp. 245–80 in *The Historic Turn in the Human Sciences*, ed. T. J. McDonald. Ann Arbor: University of Michigan Press.

SHEFTER, M. 1994. *Political Parties and the State*. Princeton, NJ: Princeton University Press.

SKOCPOL, T. 1985. Bringing the state back in: strategies of analysis in current research. Pp. 3–43 in *Bringing the State Back In*, ed. P. B. Evans, D. Rueschemeyer, and T. Skocpol. New York: Cambridge University Press.

SMELSER, N. and SWEDBERG, R. 1994. The sociological perspective on the economy. Pp. 3–26 in *The Handbook of Economic Sociology*, ed. N. Smelser and R. Swedberg. Princeton, NJ: Princeton University Press.

SOMERS, M. 1998. "We're no angels": realism, rational choice, and relationality in social science. *American Journal of Sociology*, 104: 722–84.

STINCHCOMBE, A. L. 1968. *Constructing Social Theories*. New York: Harcourt, Brace and World.

—— 1978. *Theoretical Methods in Social History*. New York: Academic Press.

TILLY, C. 1995. To explain political processes. *American Journal of Sociology*, 100: 1594–610.

—— 2001a. Historical analysis of political processes. Pp. 567–88 in *Handbook of Sociological Theory*, ed. J. Turner. New York: Plenum.

—— 2001b. Mechanisms in political processes. *Annual Review of Political Science*, 4: 21–41.

WALSH, W. H. 1974. Colligatory concepts in history. Pp. 127–44 in *The Philosophy of History*, ed. P. Gardiner. Oxford: Oxford University Press.

CHAPTER 26

THE PRESENT AS HISTORY

PATRICK THADDEUS JACKSON

THE Iowa Caucuses, the first electoral test for the eight people then campaigning to be the Democratic Party's nominee for President of the United States, took place on 19 January 2004.[1] After months of speeches, debates, television advertising, and public appearances, Iowa voters were finally able to declare a preference for the candidate of their choice. Around 8:30 p.m., it became apparent from exit polls and preliminary vote returns, that Senator John Kerry would be the victor, followed by Senator John Edwards and then by Howard Dean, the former Governor of Vermont. Shortly after the television news networks "called" the election based on their projections of the final numbers, Dean—as is traditional for an American presidential candidate—appeared before a crowd of his supporters and campaign workers to deliver some brief remarks. "I'm sure there are some disappointed people here," Dean began. "You know something? If you had told us one year ago that we were going to come in third in Iowa, we would have given anything for that." According to the text printed in the next day's *New York Times*, Dean continued:

* For helpful comments and feedback, I would like to thank Holly Jackson, Kiran Pervez, Jennifer Lobasz, Xavier Guillaume, and Benjamin Herborth.

[1] Only six of those people were actually on the ballot in Iowa, however, as Joe Lieberman and Al Sharpton had skipped the contest altogether.

Not only are we going to New Hampshire ... we're going to South Carolina and Oklahoma and Arizona and North Dakota and New Mexico, and we're going to California and Texas and New York. And we're going to South Dakota and Oregon and Washington and Michigan. And then we're going to Washington, D.C. To take back the White House. Yeah.

At the point where the transcript reads merely "yeah," Dean gave a yell, or a call, or a cry. The answer depended on whom you asked. The next day's *Washington Post* described the speech as "an arm-waving, voice-booming appearance that seemed like a victory address" (Harris 2004: 7) while the *New York Times* noted that Dean was "shouting himself hoarse" and displaying "a fierce grin and a red face" (Wilgoren 2004*b*). By the following day, the *Times* was referring to Dean's "guttural concession-speech battle cry" (Rutenberg 2004) while the *Post* reported that Dean had "shocked many Democrats by storming onto the stage in Iowa with arms flailing and face reddening to fire up a huge crowd of younger supporters" (VandeHei 2004*a*: 6), and that Dean had appeared "almost frenzied" and "shrieked his determination to win coming contests" (Broder 2004: 6).

The campaign quickly tried to control the situation. At a press conference the day after the Iowa Caucuses, Dean explained that he had been focused on the campaign volunteers in attendance and not on how his remarks and actions might play on television: "Last night there were 3,500 people there who had worked for weeks in Iowa ... and I thought I owed them the reason they came to the campaign, which was passion" (Wilgoren 2004*a*). The following day he pointed out in speeches that he was "not a perfect person" and sometimes engaged in ill-advised public performances, but that his candidacy was driven by "passion" and that his post-Caucus speech should be understood in that light. Dean even poked fun at himself: "I still have not recovered my voice from my screeching in Iowa" (Nagourney and Wilgoren 2004).

But the speech had already become a media staple, with television stations "replaying it constantly" and late-night talk shows building gags around clips from it (VandeHei 2004*b*: 11). Numerous commentators declared the Dean candidacy to be at an end, as the speech had shown Dean unfit to be president (Kurtz 2004*a*). The *Times* quoted unnamed "advisers" as saying that "they had concluded that the portrayal of Dr. Dean as a candidate unhinged would make it impossible, at least for now, to run advertisements attacking their opponents" (Nagourney and Wilgoren 2004). By the end of the week, the reporters covering Dean had changed their tone dramatically, shifting from a celebration of an unorthodox campaign characterized by its innovative use of the Internet for fundraising to "exploring the psychodrama of Dean vs. Dean ... reasonable moderate or reckless hothead?" (Kurtz 2004*b*: 7).

In the space of a week, Howard Dean had gone from being the presumptive winner of the Democratic primary election to a candidate fighting to stay alive in the polls. Dean had been the clear winner of the "invisible primary"—the campaigning prior to actual elections, in which success is measured through fundraising and public opinion polls—and had received disproportionate media coverage throughout the months before the Iowa Caucuses. He had also collected the most commitments from "superdelegates"—party dignitaries who are appointed by various constituencies rather than being elected at large—and the most prominent endorsements, including the endorsement of former Vice President and 2000 presidential candidate Al Gore (Bernstein 2004: 2–3). But all of that quickly evaporated. Dean failed to win any of the successive electoral contests and withdrew from the race a little over a month later. Dean's post-Caucus speech— dubbed the "I have a scream" speech by many, including by Dean's own pollster (Maslin 2004)—was often cited in the press as a significant moment contributing to his campaign's demise (e.g. Garfield 2004; Stolberg 2004).

Dean's post-Caucus speech, and the rapid production of its meaning, illustrates that the issues of historical interpretation well-known to historians are by no means unique to occurrences taking place in the distant past. The proximity of an occurrence is no guarantee of access to a "true" and unequivocal stream of data that will only subsequently be subject to interpretative controversies. The initial occurrence itself is always mediated by the various combinations of cultural resources that are brought to bear almost at once, as people struggle to make sense of what they have just seen and experienced. This irreducibly historical character of the present extends not merely to the "significance" of some occurrence, but even to the very definition of the occurrence as an "event." What *are* the proper boundaries of Dean's post-Caucus speech? How should it be characterized: red-faced rant, attempt to blow off steam and fire up the troops, public relations gaffe by an inexperienced staff of handlers, or something else? What *did* happen that evening?

Considerations like this direct our analytical attention away from conventional neopositivist causal accounts that seek to disclose cross-case correlations between presumptively stable and unambiguous events (King, Keohane, and Verba 1994). Instead, we should focus on the *cultural politics of "eventing"*: the ways in which occurrences, even present-day or just-recently-past occurrences, come to take on the shape that they have for us at a particular historical juncture. Eventing is logically prior to the study of connections between events, since it is impossible to conduct a study on (for example) the effects of "emotional outbursts" on a candidate's electoral success unless we have first established that Dean's post-Caucus speech was, in fact, an "emotional outburst."

But a focus on eventing also calls into question the whole explanatory strategy of trying systematically to connect events and outcomes so as to generate law-like generalizations, since the contours of an event are never definitively fixed and remain subject to renegotiation. Precisely because the initial experience of an occurrence does not provide anything like a solid core of incontrovertible data that could ground subsequent interpretations, we should be surprised when an occurrence takes on a relatively stable meaning as an "event"—and should seek to explain this outcome instead of simply taking it for granted.

1   PRESUPPOSITIONS

Robert Jervis (1976: 5) suggests that when analyzing how actors perceive situations we should not assume that those actors are any less capable and competent than the social scientists studying them, and notes that both utilize similar methods in order to deal with "uncertain knowledge and ambiguous information." Similarly, Roy Bhaskar (1998: 14) argues that the practices characterizing scientists as they pursue knowledge are similar, at least in form, to the practices characteristic of actors struggling to make sense of their situations: "the properties that scientific activity depends upon ... turn on features that are a necessary condition for any social life at all." This position seems plausible, given that social scientists remain "internal" to their objects of study in a distinctive way: social scientists are always studying situations and objects that are fundamentally like themselves, and are simultaneously observing and engaging in social action.[2] Thus it stands to reason that the ways that social scientists go about making sense of situations might provide some helpful clues as to how sense-making occurs in the course of daily life.

Since the collapse of logical positivism in the mid-twentieth century, philosophers of science have generally agreed with the position that "there is no natural ... demarcation between observational and theoretical propositions," and that observation is therefore in important ways theory-dependent (Lakatos 1978: 99). The sources of evidence that we use to support our arguments are never the unambiguous sources for those arguments. "A source can never tell us what we ought to say ... a theory of possible history is required so that the sources might be brought to speak at all" (Koselleck 1985: 156). This observation applies equally to textual sources, which have their own embedded theoretical presuppositions, and to non-textual sources such as direct personal experience, which are hermeneutically "prestructured" by the expectations and categories that we bring into those experiences. Apprehending the world is never a matter of allowing raw data to impress itself onto a tabula rasa observer, but is always theoretically mediated (Elias 1992, 61–4).

Events and their meanings can therefore never be reduced to some kind of innate dispositional property of the world. Rather, it is the interaction *between* our way of

---

[2] The question of whether this is a strong ontological claim about the distinctiveness of "social" objects, or merely a methodological point about the definition of "the social" with which we ordinarily work, can be safely set aside for the time being. In either case, social scientists always remain, inescapably, social beings—like their objects of study.

interrogating potential sources of evidence and the contents of those sources themselves that leads to conclusions about the character of events. Max Weber forcefully argued that there could be no scientific analysis of social phenomena "independent of specialized and 'one-sided' points of view according to which— expressly or tacitly, consciously or unconsciously—they are selected, analyzed, and structured for representational purposes as objects of research" (Weber 1999: 170). Indeed, it is the value-orientation of the researcher (and of her or his research community) that enables scientific analysis in the first place, by delimiting the empirical field and permitting a focus on particular aspects of the world. Weber further suggested that social scientists always apprehend the world through "ideal-types," which are

formed through a one-sided *accentuation* of *one* or *more* points of view and through bringing together a great many diffuse and discrete, more or less present and occasionally absent *concrete individual* events, which are arranged according to these emphatically one-sided points of view in order to construct a unified *analytical construct* [*Gedanken*]. In its conceptual purity, this analytical construct [*Gedankenbild*] is found nowhere in empirical reality; it is a utopia.   (Weber 1999: 191)

In other words, "a fact is a particular ordering of reality in terms of a theoretical interest" (Easton 1971 [1953]: 53). It is important to keep in mind that both the description of a phenomenon *and* the subsequent analysis or interpretation of that phenomenon are ideal-typical in character, as both derive from the interaction between a conceptual apparatus and the world. This is especially true of "events," which result from processes of "demarcation undertaken for the purpose of uttering particular sentences." Events are plucked out of "dynamic reality" through the insertion of "static boundaries" into the characterization, and have an analytical or theoretical character (Riker 1990: 168–9). Events, and sequences of events are thus generated by a set of theoretical commitments, rather than by the putatively innate character of reality itself.

The analyst's temporal proximity to the phenomenon being analyzed does not mitigate this theoretical character, as scholarly apprehensions of the recent past involve much the same conceptual issues as those presented by the analysis of phenomena at a greater temporal remove. Indeed, there is little compelling reason to suspect that directly experiencing something will provide privileged access to the real character or significance of the thing experienced.[3] While eyewitnesses can

---

[3] I set aside here "spiritual" and other mystical experiences, the distinguishing character of which is that they purport to provide privileged access to the truest nature of things. The problem with such experiences is not that they are necessarily unable to provide what they promise, but that there is no non-tautological way to *evaluate* whether or not they have done so—which is related to the fact that such experiences are, by definition, subjective and thus not capable of being spoken about in an intelligible manner. "What we cannot speak about we must pass over in silence" (Wittgenstein 1974: §7).

provide information that might not be otherwise obtainable, this consideration of *method* (how to gain access to the relevant data) should not be inflated to a *methodological* claim about what kind of data is preferable and what the status of that data is. Eyewitness accounts, especially accounts of contentious events, rarely settle the issue under discussion in a definitive way. Also, memoirs and other first-hand accounts have to be handled with extreme care given the possibility that the writer of the memoir is still fighting old political battles in giving her or his account.

2   HISTORICITY

Matters become even more complicated when we turn from scholarly analysts to ordinary participants. "In fulfilling our responsibilities as competent and professional academics, we must write *systematic texts*; we run the risk of being accounted incompetent if we do not" (Shotter 1993*a*: 25). Such a mode of presentation, whatever its drawbacks,[4] has at least the virtue of spelling out its theoretical presumptions more or less explicitly; much scholarly writing operates with models that provide "an explicit, deductively sound statement of the theoretical argument, separate from a particular empirical context," and that which does not can often be formalized so as to provide such a model (Büthe 2002: 482).

But everyday life is considerably less orderly. People do not tend to operate with the highly abstract conceptual equipment that appears in scholarly accounts (Shotter 1993*b*: 164). Rather, everyday sense-making operates with far more ambiguous schemas, which cannot be exhaustively delineated in advance of their deployment in concrete circumstances (Sewell 1992: 18–19). These schemas are "cultural," in that they consist of "socially established structures of meaning in terms of which people do such things as signal conspiracies and join them or perceive insults and answer them" (Geertz 1973: 12–13)—or observe Howard Dean's post-Caucus speech and understand it as an emotional outburst. As an analytical concept,[5] "culture" directs our attention to those resources of meaning on which

---

[4] In the case of everyday sense-making, the typical scholarly way of writing presents immense problems, inasmuch as it can lead to the mistaken impression that scholarly ideal-typical oversimplifications of public conceptual resources are in fact the same as the resources in question—as though people in their everyday lives actually operated with rigorously demarcated scholarly categories. Scholars of public attitudes, particularly those operating in the Weberian tradition (e.g. Mannheim 1936: 58–9), are very cognizant of the difference.

[5] Designating processes as cultural offers "a view of political phenomena by focusing attention on how and why actors invest them with meaning," and should not be taken as a claim that this is the only way to analyze such processes (Wedeen 2002: 714).

actors can draw in order to establish the boundaries of acceptable action (Ross 1997: 52–3). This focus on "practices of meaning-making" (Wedeen 2002: 714) fore-grounds the *active* character of cultural resources as they are implicated in specific situations.

These cultural resources, or rhetorical commonplaces, constitute a *living tradition*:

What might be called a "living tradition" does not give rise to a completely determined form of life, but to dilemmas, to different possibilities for living, among which one must choose … a "living tradition," in consisting in a set of shared two-sided "topics," "loci," "themes" or "commonplaces," gives rise to the possibility if formulating a whole "ecology" of different and, indeed, unique "positions"—each offering different possibilities for the "best way" to continue and/or develop the tradition.   (Shotter 1993b: 171)

Living traditions contain the cultural resources out of which people make occur-rences meaningful and transform them into events.

In contrast to individualist approaches, whether methodological or phenom-enological (Tilly 1998: 17–18), the resources of meaning highlighted here are not subjective and private, but intersubjective and public in a conceptual or theoretical sense (Laffey and Weldes 1997: 215–16; Tilly 2002: 115). As Wittgenstein (1953: §§152–5) suggests, understanding the meaning of something (in this case, a math-ematical formula)[6] is "not a mental process":

"B understands the principle of the series" surely doesn't mean simply: the formula "$a_n = \ldots$" occurs to B. For it is perfectly imaginable that the formula should occur to him and that he should nevertheless not understand. "He understands" must have more in it than: the formula occurs to him.

Instead of this hypothetical mental occurrence, "understanding" consists in being able to "go on"—in other words, being able to apply the formula in a socially acceptable fashion, which includes the possibility of being corrected if the applica-tion is judged inaccurate (Winch 1990: 58–9). Demonstrating that one knows a formula means applying it correctly (i.e. in a socially acceptable way) in the correct (i.e. socially acceptable) circumstances, a situation that could not arise if formulas existed simply in the privacy of one's own head.[7] Something similar is true of other resources of meaning, even if they are nowhere near as firmly delineated as

---

[6] Mathematical formulas turn out to be a good model for cultural resources in general, inasmuch as many such resources take the form of "schemas" (Sewell 1992: 17–18) or "programs" (Rescher 1996: 38). Of course, the scholarly ideal-typical constructions of such schemas or programs should not be conflated with the actual, improvisational character of lived social experience (Tilly 1998: 52–3).

[7] Contrast this socially focused approach with the introspective "verstehen" approach associated with Dilthey and the hermeneutic tradition of the humanities. "Meaning," in the social-scientific approach that I am advocating here, is intersubjective and connected to appropriate use in a social context, rather than inhering in some transcendental sphere of subjective intent.

a mathematical formula: understanding and using them is irreducibly public and intersubjective.

These considerations suggest that if we want to analyze events we should be attentive to the content of the living tradition of cultural resources on which actors draw in order to make sense of the events in question. It is this living tradition to which scholars implicitly refer when they argue for the importance of "the previous histories and relations of particular interlocutors" (Tilly 2002: 116) implicated in a given episode of sense-making. The availability of particular resources is important in enabling a particular characterization of an event; "all metaphors and all stories are not available to us at each and every moment," and this availability makes a difference (Ringmar 1996: 74). The availability of particular cultural resources is both a logical and an empirical prerequisite of crafting a socially sustainable claim or interpretation; if the appropriate resources are not present, practical and discursive work is required in order to produce and disseminate them in advance of their concrete deployment (McAdam, Tarrow, and Tilly 2001: 47–52; see also Jackson 2006). As Somers (1994: 630) has pointed out, "this is why the kinds of narratives people use to make sense of their situations will always be an *empirical* rather than a presuppositional question."

Beyond the simple question of resource availability, the form of cultural resources is also significant. Cultural resources are *narratives*, which means that they are scripts or plotlines into which particular occurrences can be placed. Narratives are dynamic in that they move a reader/listener/performer from one place to another, unfolding so as to capture the temporality of a developmental process in a way quite foreign to conventional statistical techniques (Abbott and Hrycak 1990: 148–9; Büthe 2002: 484). This narrative character of cultural resources is perhaps most apparent in more or less formalized "scripts" for social interaction (Tilly 1998: 53–5), but is also present in both the most abstract archetypes (e.g. the upstart mortal challenging the gods and failing, condemned by his hubris to a crushing defeat) and the most specific metaphors (e.g. "guttural concession speech battle cry"). Both of these latter figure prominently in the immediate characterization of Dean's post-Caucus speech. Occurrences like those of that evening in Iowa are never just a "pure sequence of isolated events" that have to be subsequently made meaningful (Carr 1986: 24; Heidegger 1962 [1927]: 190–1) but are instead gathered up into sequences with plotlines even as they are experienced in the first place (Carr 1986: 47–8, 89; Somers 1994: 616).

Events, therefore, have "historicity"—an irreducibly historical character—at the very moment of their occurrence. The experience of events is always mediated by the cultural resources which we bring to bear on the experiences at the time; those resources are not created *de novo* each moment, but are in a sense handed down from the past, and form the field of possibilities within which we operate. The field produced by these possibilities may be more or less restricted, ranging perhaps from Orwell's nightmarish world of "newspeak" in which words themselves are tightly controlled to the cacophony of the modern Internet "blogosphere" in which anyone with access to a computer can sound off about virtually any subject.[8] But the historicity of events remains in any case.

3   EVENTING

In much of social science, we focus on the causal explanation of events, trying to ascertain why they occurred or failed to occur. Such explanations take various forms; while traditional strategies involve comparing cases in order to control variance (King, Keohane, and Verba 1994), more recent methodological turns involve the introduction of logical property spaces and "fuzzy set" logic (Ragin 2000) and the increasing prominence of the analysis of *sequences* rather than of putatively solid and stable cases (Abbott 1995). This latter approach is especially prominent in the study of contentious events, where scholars have developed extremely sophisticated techniques for determining the patterns according to which events unfold (McCarthy et al. 1996). Common to all of this work is a methodological disposition to focus on events as discrete happenings taking place outside of the process of conceptualizing them.[9]

But the irreducible historicity of events suggests an alternative way to proceed: instead of working with events as presumptively stable entities, we should focus on the ongoing dynamic process of *eventing* whereby the contours of an event are produced and reproduced.[10] This social negotiation, or "contentious conversation"

[8] A "blog," short for "weblog," is a kind of virtual soapbox from which an author can fulminate about almost anything by posting comments. The net result of the promulgation of blogs is a hyper-abundance of cultural resources available to anyone with a web browser. See http://blog.lib.umn.edu/blogosphere/. This myriad of voices makes analysis more logistically complicated, but does not raise any insoluble theoretical or conceptual problems.

[9] I should stress that this is a *methodological* decision in the Weberian sense: a necessarily partial approach to the study of (social) reality that gains its leverage by deliberately downplaying certain aspects of the phenomenon under investigation. Comparative case study and sequence analysis downplay historicity, and as part of the methodological trade-off gain the ability to make (at least limited) generalizations. I am not convinced that there are absolutely correct and final ways to make such methodological decisions; instead, such trade-offs should depend on the question that one is asking. My advocacy of a different approach here should not be construed as a dismissal of work that proceeds from a different set of methodological principles, but only as an attempt to envision an alternative perspective.

[10] There is another approach to events that also departs from their irreducible historicity: the kind of "effective history," or "history of the present," advocated by Michel Foucault (Foucault 1977: 153). Foucault suggests that interpretations of events in the past (even the recent past) should be specifically and strategically targeted at the production of changes in the present: disrupting facile narratives of origin, denaturalizing arrangements which have come to seem inevitable, and the like. Foucault's

(Tilly 2002: 113–14, 116–18), displays the unusual temporal property that it always takes place *in the present*, even when the event or events that it concerns are held to have taken place in the past. A negotiation about a speech of a few moments or months ago is no different than a negotiation about occurrences decades or centuries in the past, in that in each case the negotiation involves the deployment of the cultural resources available to actors at the point in time when the negotiation takes place, and not necessarily those in existence at the time of the occurrences themselves.

This curious temporality is the origin of "revisionist history," the practice by which the contours of an event are renegotiated using novel cultural resources. Because events have no determinate character outside of the practices that produce and locally stabilize them, they are always available for modification as the living tradition utilized in their interpretation changes. As an example, consider St. Augustine's *post facto* description of his first book in his later work *Confessions* (1992: 68–9). Addressing the God in whom he has only subsequently come to believe, Augustine declares:

I was about 26 or 27 years old when I wrote that work, turning over in my mind fictitious physical images. These were a strident noise in the ears of my heart, with which I was straining, sweet truth, to hear your interior melody when I was meditating on the beautiful and the fitting. I wanted to stand still and hear you and rejoice with joy at the voice of the bridegroom. But that was beyond my powers, for I was snatched away to external things by the voices of the error I espoused, and under the weight of my pride I plunged into the abyss.

In this passage Augustine reads his later understanding and experience of God backwards into his earlier life, lending the earlier occurrences a character that they could not possibly have had at the time. By "emplotting" (Somers 1994: 616) his first book differently, and situating it in a narrative of personal salvation, the very contours of the event are altered—what had been an important step in a career as a rhetor and teacher now becomes a step on his road back to a clearer experience of God, and evidence of a spiritual lack of which he has only recently become aware.[11]

Beth Roy (1994: 186–7) provides a less theologically freighted example of the same phenomenon. In conducting a series of interviews concerning a conflict between Hindus and Muslims in Bangladesh that had taken place several decades in the past, she encountered a strange discrepancy between two of her Muslim sources: "Both

response blends the normative and the empirical in fascinating ways that are somewhat different from the more analytical response to the historicity of events that I propose in what follows. But I do not mean to suggest that the analytic that I propose exhausts, let alone "solves" the problem of historicity.

[11] In fact, Augustine's whole approach to memory and narration has this goal; his general methodology consists of emplotting events within a grand story of salvation (Wills 1999: xiv–xvi, 92–95).

[tellers] placed themselves at the Tarkhania household, for instance, when the haystack was set on fire, but they saw very different fires. Golam [a Muslim peasant farmer] insisted that the Hindus had torched their own structure," while the other interview subject, a Muslim community leader, claimed that Muslims had attacked and burned the Hindu farm. Roy goes on to relate these different versions of the event to the broader social location of the two informants, including the set of cultural resources on which they were drawing to construct their overall sense of the conflict: Golam's was a story about the duplicity of the Hindus, while the Muslim community leader told a story about passions overflowing on both sides and his own efforts to mediate and keep the peace. Here again the very "facts" depend on the perspective adopted and narrated.

Contestation about an event need not take place at such a large remove from the event, however, and it need not take place simply at the level of the individual. On the basis of detailed ethnographic work with a group of copy machine technicians, Julian Orr (1996: 43–5) concludes that "diagnosis is a narrative process," in which techs fit symptoms into familiar stories garnered from work in the field. Orr details the everyday institution of a working lunch during which members of the repair team present otherwise inexplicable symptoms displayed by the machines in their care; the group as a whole then struggles to place the symptoms within a storyline that will make them comprehensible, as well as designating a course of action to be undertaken that afternoon when the repair visit proceeds. Similarly, based on her detailed analysis of extant documents, Jutta Weldes (1999: 102, 117–18) argues that the discussion among US officials concerning what to do about Soviet missiles in Cuba, was a process of narrative contestation involving various ways of characterizing the missiles and the "threat" that they represented.[12]

In all of these cases, we have a present struggle about the contours of an event, the outcome of which affects both the future (by providing a plausible course of action) and the past (by reshaping the division of that past into events and situating those events into plotlines). The narrative contestation disclosed by these analyses is thus a kind of active "presencing" (Heidegger 1962 [1927]: 416–17) of both past and future, in that it selects elements and renders them relevant for contemporary concerns. A focus on this active presencing or eventing keeps agency, understood as the temporal situatedness of actors and the inherently creative aspect of their social actions (Emirbayer and Mische 1998: 973–4), firmly in the foreground of the analysis. Such an analytical move garners both practical–moral and explanatory advantages, in that it simultaneously high-

---

[12] Much recent work in international relations emphasizes that "threats," like "dangers," emerge from socially sustainable narrations of events rather than from putatively intrinsic characteristics of those events themselves (Campbell 1992; Wendt 1992; Wæver 1998).

lights the capacity of actors to have done otherwise that they did (Giddens 1984: 9) and permits a causal analysis of the production of outcomes (Jackson 2003: 236–8).[13]

The key to analyzing eventing in this way is to focus on historically specific configurations or concatenations of factors and mechanisms, rather than looking for law-like generalizations connecting such factors (Katznelson 1997: 99). Different episodes of eventing will have different configurations, and different classes of eventing episodes[14] will most involve different kinds of resources. Delineating these mechanisms and their configuration in a specific situation involves a kind of grounded theorizing in which detailed empirical discussions are brought into dialogue with abstract formulations. But in general, three categories of mechanisms are likely implicated in public episodes of eventing: narrative, audience, and technical considerations (Consalvo 1999: 109–11).[15] Particular combinations of these factors generate the historically specific outcome of any episode of eventing, whatever the particular event in question.

Narrative mechanisms involve those considerations "internal" to the plotline under discussion, including the need to provide some measure of continuity between an event and those events held to precede and follow it. In the case of Howard Dean's post-Caucus speech, the extant plotline before the Iowa occurrences largely involved Dean's "anger," leading to a tendency to characterize moments in terms of a raging disposition. Although Dean and his wife tried to counteract that impression during an ABC television interview several days after the post-Caucus speech (ABC 2004), the previous narration of events imposed certain parameters on those trying to make sense of the new occurrence. These parameters might have been resisted, but this would have required additional effort—effort that was not likely to emerge among journalists working on tight deadlines (Oliver and Myers 1999: 46–7).

Complementing these narrative considerations is the fact that socially plausible stories cannot be promulgated in a vacuum, but must always connect up with cultural resources already present in the relevant audience. The central audience mechanism is therefore something like "resonance," which catches up the extent to which a novel formulation supervenes on and incorporates extant resources. The account of Dean's post-Caucus speech utilized a number of extant resources, ranging from the "tragic fall" archetypal myth to the characterization of Dean as

[13] The kind of analysis that I am sketching here is of course not immune to the temporal dynamics under discussion. The analytical language of mechanisms, actors exercising agency, and the narrative (re)construction of events is itself a historically specific set of cultural resources upon which I am drawing to make sense of a set of situations. To claim that there is anything *definitive* to this kind of analysis would be theoretically inconsistent; like most relational pragmatists, I will settle for the generation of novel and useful insights.

[14] It should go without saying that "episodes" are also ideal-typical theoretical constructs (McAdam, Tarrow, and Tilly 2001: 29–30). But in case it does not, I will say it explicitly.

[15] These three categories are adapted from the work of Stuart Hall on the mass media, although Consalvo helpfully modifies them to highlight the centrality of the technical aspects of representation. See also Jackson and Nexon 2003.

too angry to be "presidential" and the notion that a potential president must look good on television—a cultural resource dating back to the Nixon–Kennedy debates during the 1960 election campaign. The prior production and dissemination of these cultural resources made possible the specific eventing that took place in the press immediately following the speech, in which the image of Dean screaming was emplotted and contextualized for subsequent viewers. The event of Dean's scream was made encounterable as such; viewers could now utilize the visual data as evidence for the accuracy of the very narrative resources that generated the event and its interpretation in the first place.[16]

But was Dean even screaming? It certainly appeared that way on television, and was widely reported that way in the press. But Diane Sawyer, the ABC News reporter who had interviewed Dean during prime time a few days after the incident, pointed out two weeks later that Dean had been holding a special hand-held microphone when he spoke after the Caucus. The microphone was "designed to filter out the background noise. It isolates your voice, just like it does to Charlie Gibson and me when we have big crowds in the morning. The crowds are deafening to us standing there. But the viewer at home hears only our voice" (Sawyer 2004). Here we see the third category of mechanisms playing a role, as technical considerations involving the television medium provide the "raw data" to be formed into an event—but do not do so in anything like a neutral and transparent manner. An additional technical consideration involves the reproducibility and modifiability of electronic imagery; within hours of the speech, clips of Dean speaking set to techno music were circulating around the Internet, and excerpts were readily available for use in various computer applications. There was even a website—www.deangoes-nuts.com—from which people could download remixes of the speech or request the production of special versions (Lee 2004).[17]

Analyzing the cultural politics of eventing requires a detailed tracing of how these mechanisms interact and concatenate to generate a specific outcome.[18] Such an approach preserves agency while recognizing the central importance of context, and may perhaps make us more sensitive to the possibility that an event, however stable it appears at one point in time, always stands capable of renegotiation.

---

[16] Peter Novick (Novick 1999: 144) makes a similar point about "the Holocaust," which only emerged as an event (especially as an event with the focus on the experiences of the victims) in the United States in the mid-1960s. Prior to this time, most survivors were reluctant to discuss their experiences at all, and certainly did not connect them to a broader phenomenon called "Holocaust survivorship." None of this is to say that "the Holocaust didn't happen" or that Howard Dean's post-Caucus speech was grave and quiet; the point is that mere occurrences are *indeterminate*, not that they are simply imagined or that our accounts of them are somehow false—or could be truer.

[17] The website was actually produced by a Dean *supporter*, who was impressed with Dean's exuberance and wanted to share it.

[18] This procedure bears some striking similarities to the position articulated by George Herbert Mead (1959). In recent German sociological debates (e.g. texts collected in Kraimer 2000), this stance is referred to as "reconstructive methodology."

References

ABBOTT, A. 1995. Sequence analysis: new methods for old ideas. *Annual Review of Sociology*, 21: 93–113.

—— and HRYCAK, A. 1990. Measuring resemblance in sequence data: an optimal matching analysis of musicians' careers. *American Journal of Sociology*, 96: 144–85.

ABC 2004. "I'm a human being." Available at: http://abcnews.go.com/sections/Primetime/US/howard_judy_dean_040122-1.html (accessed 5 July 2004).

AUGUSTINE 1992. *Confessions*, trans. H. Chadwick. Oxford: Oxford University Press.

BERNSTEIN, J. 2004. The rise and fall of Howard Dean and other notes on the 2004 Democratic presidential nomination. *The Forum*, pp. 1–13. Available at: http://www.bepress.com (accessed 23 March 2004).

BHASKAR, R. 1998. *The Possibility of Naturalism*, 3rd edn. London: Routledge.

BRODER, D. S. 2004. In N.H., it's suddenly a four-way race. *Washington Post*, 21 January, section A.

BÜTHE, T. 2002. Taking temporality seriously: modeling history and the use of narratives as evidence. *American Political Science Review*, 96 (3): 481–93.

CAMPBELL, D. 1992. *Writing Security*. Minneapolis: University of Minnesota Press.

CARR, D. 1986. *Time, Narrative, and History*. Bloomington: Indiana University Press.

CONSALVO, M. L. 1999. The best of both worlds? Examining bodies, technology, gender and the Borg of Star Trek. Ph.D. dissertation, Department of Media Studies, University of Iowa, Iowa City.

EASTON, D. 1971. *The Political System: An Inquiry Into the State of Political Science*, 2nd edn. New York: Alfred A. Knopf; originally published 1953.

ELIAS, N. 1992. *Time: An Essay*. Oxford: Blackwell.

EMIRBAYER, M., and MISCHE, A. 1998. What is agency? *American Journal of Sociology*, 103 (4): 962–1023.

FOUCAULT, M. 1977. Nietzsche, genealogy, history. Pp. 139–64 in *Language, Counter-memory, Practice*, ed. D. F. Bouchard. Ithaca, NY: Cornell University Press.

GARFIELD, B. 2004. Images that flicker and fade. *Washington Post*, 8 February, section B.

GEERTZ, C. 1973. *The Interpretation of Cultures*. New York: Basic Books.

GIDDENS, A. 1984. *The Constitution of Society*. Berkeley: University of California Press.

HARRIS, J. F. 2004. Kerry scores comeback Iowa victory; Edwards 2nd, Dean and Gephardt lag. *Washington Post*, 20 January, section A.

HEIDEGGER, M. 1962. *Being and Time*, trans. J. Macquarrie and E. Robinson. San Francisco: HarperCollins; originally published 1927.

JACKSON, P. T. 2003. Defending the West: occidentalism and the formation of NATO. *Journal of Political Philosophy*, 11: 223–52.

—— 2006. *Civilizing the Enemy: German Reconstruction and the Invention of the West*. Ann Arbor: University of Michigan Press.

—— and NEXON, D. H. 2003. Representation is futile? American anti-collectivism and the Borg. Pp. 143–67 in *To Seek Out New Worlds: Science Fiction and World Politics*, ed. J. Weldes. New York: Palgrave Macmillan.

JERVIS, R. 1976. *Perception and Misperception in International Politics*. Princeton, NJ: Princeton University Press.

KATZNELSON, I. 1997. Structure and configuration. In *Comparative Politics: Rationality, Culture, and Structure,* ed. M. I. Lichbach and A. S. Zuckerman. Cambridge: Cambridge University PRESS, Pp. 81–112.

KING, G., KEOHANE, R. O., and VERBA S. 1994. *Designing Social Inquiry: Scientific Inference in Qualitative Research.* Princeton, NJ: Princeton University Press.

KOSELLECK, R. 1985. *Futures Past: On the Semantics of Historical Time,* trans. Keith Tribe. CAMBRIDGE, Mass.: MIT Press.

KRAIMER, K. (ed.) 2000. *Die Fallrekonstruktion. Sinnverstehen in der sozialwissenschaftlichen Forschung.* Frankfurt: Suhrkamp.

KURTZ, H. 2004*a.* Press cooking Dean's goose. *Washington Post,* 22 January, online edition (www.washingtonpost.com).

——— 2004*b.* Reporters shift gears on the Dean bus. *Washington Post,* 23 January, section C.

LAFFEY, M., and WELDES, J. 1997. Beyond belief: ideas and symbolic technologies in the study of international relations. *European Journal of International Relations,* 3 (2): 193–237.

LAKATOS, I. 1978. The methodology of scientific research programmes. Pp. 91–196 in *Criticism and the Growth of Knowledge,* ed. I. Lakatos and A. Musgrave. Cambridge: Cambridge University Press.

LEE, J. S. 2004. The revolution will be televised. *New York Times,* 25 January, online edition (www.nytimes.com).

MANNHEIM, K. 1936. *Ideology and Utopia.* San Diego: Harvest Books.

MASLIN, P. 2004. The front-runner's fall. *Atlantic Monthly Online,* available at http:// www.theatlantic.com/issues/2004/05/maslin.htm; accessed 10 May 2004.

McADAM, D., TARROW, S., and TILLY, C. 2001. *Dynamics of Contention.* Cambridge: Cambridge University Press.

McCARTHY, J. D., McPHAIL, C., and SMITH, J. 1996. Images of protest: estimating selection bias in media coverage of Washington demonstrations, 1982 and 1991. *American Sociological Review,* 61: 478–99.

MEAD, G. H. 1959. *Philosophy of the Present.* LA SALLE, Ind.: Open Court Press.

NAGOURNEY, A., and WILGOREN, J. 2004. Contrite Dean tries to recover from his explosive speech. *New York Times,* online edition (www.nytimes.com).

NOVICK, P. 1999. *The Holocaust in American Life.* Boston: Mariner.

OLIVER, P. A., and MYERS, D. J. 1999. How events enter the public sphere: conflict, location, and sponsorship in local newspaper coverage of public events. *American Journal of Sociology,* 105: 38–87.

ORR, J. E. 1996. *Talking About Machines: An Ethnography of a Modern Job.* Ithaca, NY: Cornell University Press.

RAGIN, C. C. 2000. *Fuzzy-Set Social Science.* Chicago: University of Chicago Press.

RESCHER, N. 1996. *Process Metaphysics.* Albany, NY: SUNY Press.

RIKER, W. H. 1990. Political science and rational choice. Pp. 163–81 in *Perspectives on Positive Political Economy,* ed. J. A. Alt and K. A. Shepsle. Cambridge: Cambridge University Press.

RINGMAR, E. 1996. *Identity, Interest and Action.* Cambridge: Cambridge University Press.

ROSS, M. H. 1997. Culture and identity in comparative political analysis. Pp. 42–80 in *Comparative Politics: Rationality, CULTURE, and Structure,* ed. M. I. Lichbach and A. S. Zuckerman. Cambridge: Cambridge University Press.

ROY, B. 1994. *Some Trouble with Cows: Making Sense of Social Conflict.* Berkeley: University of California Press.

RUTENBERG, J. 2004. A concession rattles the rafters (and some Dean supporters). *New York Times*, 21 January, online edition (www.nytimes.com).

SAWYER, D. 2004. The Dean scream: the version of reality that we didn't see on TV. Available at http://abclocal.go.com/wjrt/news/012904_NW_r2_group_deanscream.html; accessed 1 March 2004.

SEWELL, W. H. 1992. A theory of structure: duality, agency, and transformation. *American Journal of Sociology*, 98: 1–29.

SHOTTER, J. 1993a. *Conversational Realities: Constructing Life Through Language*. Thousand Oaks, Calif.: Sage.

——1993b. *Cultural Politics of Everyday Life*. Toronto: University of Toronto Press.

SOMERS, M. R. 1994. The narrative constitution of identity: a relational and network approach. *Theory and Society*, 23: 605–49.

STOLBERG, S. G. 2004. Whoop, oops, and the state of the political slip. *New York Times*, 25 January, online edition (www.nytimes.com).

TILLY, C. 1998. *Durable Inequality*. Berkeley: University of California Press.

——2002. *Stories, Identities, and Political Change*. Lanham, Md.: Rowman and Littlefield.

VANDEHEI, J. 2004a. Dean puts a new face on his candidacy. *Washington Post*, 21 January, section A.

——2004b. Dean tries a self-deprecation strategy. *Washington Post*, 23 January, section A.

WÆVER, O. 1998. Insecurity, security, and asecurity in the West European non-war community. Pp. 69–118 in *Security Communities*, ed. E. Adler and M. Barnett. Cambridge: Cambridge University Press.

WEBER, M. 1999. Die "objektivität" sozialwissenschaftlicher und sozialpolitischer erkenntnis. Pp. 146–214 in *Gesammelte Aufsätze zur Wissenschaftslehre*, ed. E. Flitner. Potsdam: Internet-Ausgabe, http://www.uni-potsdam.de/u/paed/Flitner/Flitner/Weber/index.html.

WEDEEN, L. 2002. Conceptualizing culture: possibilities for political science. *American Political Science Review*, 96: 713–28.

WELDES, J. 1999. *Constructing National Interests: The United States and the Cuban Missile Crisis*. Minneapolis: University of Minnesota Press.

WENDT, A. E. 1992. Anarchy is what states make of it: the social construction of power politics. *International Organization*, 46: 391–425.

WILGOREN, J. 2004a. Dean is subdued. *New York Times*, 21 January, online edition (www.nytimes.com).

——2004b. Little familiar with setbacks, Dean stumbles. *New York Times*, 20 January, online edition (www.nytimes.com).

WILLS, G. 1999. *Saint Augustine*. New York: Viking.

WINCH, P. 1990. *The Idea of a Social Science and its Relation to Philosophy*, 2nd edn. London: Routledge.

WITTGENSTEIN, L. 1953. *Philosophical Investigations*, trans. G. E. M. Anscombe. Oxford: Blackwell.

——1974. *Tractatus Logico-Philosophicus*, trans. D. F. Pears and B. F. McGuinness. London: Routledge.

PART VII

PLACE MATTERS

CHAPTER 27

WHY AND HOW PLACE MATTERS

GÖRAN THERBORN

1 PLACE AND POLITICS

POLITICS begins with place. The Western notion of politics derives from a particular place and the concerns of its inhabitants, from *polis*, the Ancient Greek city(-state). The Roman Empire, for all its territorial extension (from today's Iraq to today's Scotland) was a very place-conscious rule, in which *urbs*, the city (Rome), was the crucial center of power. *Civitas*—whence current key concepts of politics, like citizen(ship/ry), civic, and civil originate, directly or indirectly—was in classical Latin not only a concept but also a designation of place and its inhabitants. *Civitas aureliana*, for instance, was today's German Baden-Baden and French Orléans, *Civitas augusta* today's Italian Aosta. Place was an important notion to classical European social and political theory, such as in Aristotle's *Politics* of the fourth century BCE, and place and motion were key concepts of his *Physics* (Casey 1997; Morison 2002).

The polity with which Aristotle was concerned was the *polis*, the city-state (with an agricultural surrounding), not an empire like that of his pupil Alexander. Book 7 of *Politics* is largely devoted to its ideal location and size, the lay-out of streets and buildings. "[T]he land as well as the inhabitants...should be taken in at a single view" (Aristotle 1988, 164). His main concern is security against enemy assault, so cities should not be built along straight lines, for instance (172); but he also stipulates an elevated site for religious worship and beneath it an *agora* for free men, free of trade, artisans, farmers, and "any such person" (173)

Place politics is not Eurocentric. Ancient Chinese conceptions of government, for instance, were also concerned with place and location. Here the focus was not on the city and empowered male citizens, but on the sovereign ruler, the Son of Heaven, and his mediation between the human and the natural worlds. This central mediation task of kingship, of empire, was tied to a concrete location: the *Ming Tang* (the Hall of Light), which later developed into the central *locus* of imperial power, the "Forbidden City," the imperial Palace City in the center of the capital of the Central Kingdom of the World. The construction of a capital city was a key element of legitimate power, and codified in rules of place-based power in *Kao Gong Ji* (*Code Book of Work*, a Confucian classic from the "Spring and Autumn Period," 6–8 centuries BCE) (Dutt et al. 1994, 31 ff.; Sit 1995, 12 ff.). The rules were spread all over the area of Sinic civilization, stretching from Vietnam to Korea and Japan. They are still very prominent in today's Beijing. The Chinese also developed a more general knowledge about the right place and spatial orientation of construction (*feng shui*, or "geomancy" in Latin English).

In the Americas, pre-Columbian places of power, like Machu Picchu in today's Peru and Tenochtitlán in current Mexico, are still conveying their majestic importance to latter-day tourists.

So much for origins and traditions. But how much of place is there in the current world of broadcasting, globalization, Internet, virtuality? Has place become "abstracted from power," because it is now organized in a "space of flows," and not of places, as Manuel Castells (1996, ch. 6) has argued in a great work? A perusal of the main journals of political science for the new century hardly yields any hint of politics of place, although there are geographers who bring their disciplinary expertise of space to political questions (most recently Jones, Jones, and Wood 2004) and devoted journals like *Hérodote* (situated by Claval 2000; Hepple 2000) and *Political Geography*. Is place becoming something of the past only, or just an academic special interest?

Some reflection will show that place is still crucial today to power and politics, in some respect arguably even more than before. Above all, it matters in three kinds of politics: democratic, military (war), and symbolic. But before entering into hot contemporary empirical issues, let us take a circumspect theoretical look.

2   THE PLACE, THE UNIVERSE, AND THE GLOBE

Place has three decisive aspects of social being. First, it means a fixity in space. A place is a fixed location, a stable spot on a map. This means that place is something you can go to, leave, and return to—after a week, a year, a decade, a century, a millennium. A place can be destroyed and disappear, true, but it is always a good bet that it will be there across the vicissitudes of time, in some shape or other.

Second, place means contiguity. A place is where people can meet, can come and can be close to each other, where buildings can relate, where vehicles meet frequently. In this respect, the importance of place varies, positively with contiguous social ties or with local networks, and negatively with the significance of extra-local networks. Place is the site of face-to-face communication, opposite to letter-writing, calling, and Internet chatting.

Third, place means distinctiveness. A place is something different from another place, from anywhere, and from nowhere. A node is defined only by its connectivity, and a position by its relations; but a place is defined by its characteristics. The Norwegian architectural historian and theorist Christian Norberg-Schulz (1982) has referred to this distinctiveness as "*genius loci*," the spirit of character of place, manifested both in the built environment and in the landscape.

Place matters to the extent that the universal does not. Universal laws rule regardless of place; they rule in all places without distinction. After Aristotle (who accorded a particular priority to place and to the question "where?") universe and space came to obliterate place in Western philosophy and science (Casey 1997). It re-emerged in the mid-1930s in Heidegger's philosophy, to which postmodernist and post-structuralist thought have paid close attention.

In other words, in so far as there are universal laws of social science—of economics, of politics, of sociology—place is irrelevant. Now, social scientists agree to having few if any universal laws. Does that mean that place is recognized as important? Not necessarily, because the non-universal may be specific instead to class, gender, ethnicity, culture, or any other non-place features. American-style identity politics, and studies of it, have hardly highlighted place-based identity (cf. Calhoun 1994).

The global is different. While the universe overshadows all places, the globe reveals them and connections among them. In contrast to the universal, the global denotes interconnection, interaction, interlinkage, as opposed not only to unit isolation but also to boundless universality. And global connectivity further implies global difference, global variability, the very opposite of universalistic invariance.

However, there is a tension between connectivity and variability, and a competition for attention and recognition. The main thrust of global studies has been on connectivity and its consequences of interdependence, influence, and hybridization. Much less analytical energy has been devoted to the global variability of places. The discourse on globalization has focused more on the connection, and less on what is being connected.

Globality, in this sense, has important epistemological consequences, too. In contrast to the one-way gaze of universalism and its privileged vantage-point, globality points to the importance of cross-cultural intercommunication as the infrastructure of the global knowledge of difference and connectivity.

In brief, places have competitors in space, the universe, the network position, flows, processes of connection and linkage, as well as from time, social character, and rational choice. To go further, we had better try to grasp the positive potential of place.

3   PLACE AND SOCIAL ACTION

Politics is a kind of social action, a kind having direct collective implications and involving some choice of course within a wider set of rules. Individual pursuits are not politics. Neither is the adjudication or implementation of rules—tasks of judges and bureaucrats, rather than of politicians or political activists.

Looked at from the general perspective of social action, place may be important for any one or more of five fundamental reasons:

- place is the forming mould of actors;
- place is a compass of meaning to the actions of actors;
- place is the immediate setting in which action occurs, or "takes place";
- place crucially affects the consequences of action;
- and finally (the character of a) place is an eminent outcome of action.

The last aspect means that there is an important feedback loop between place and action. In other words, place is both a crucial explanatory or "independent" variable," an "intermediary" variable of setting or "locale" (Giddens 1994, 118–19), and a significant "dependent" variable. Place is thus an example of the dialectics of structure and agency.

"Place," then, is taken as multiply defined, on a scale ranging from the globe to an office building. One definition is civic-political: being within a certain state, being within a certain political or cultural region, having a particular political or cultural (for instance, religious) history. Another is socioeconomic: having a particular socioeconomic structure (agrarian, industrial, commercial, for example), and being prosperous or poor. Still another we may label sociospatial or geosocial: including geopolitical, geoeconomic, geocultural; being central or peripheral, large or small in social space; or on a continuum of social density, of rurality and urbanity, or of communication, from centrality to isolation. A fourth dimension of place refers to its natural location: for example, coastal or inland, plain or mountainous, and with regard to the quality of the soil and the character of the climate. The first two definitions of place refer to contingent spatial effects from outcomes of past action; the latter two to the intrinsic weight of social and natural space upon social action.

To argue comprehensively and to exemplify adequately these modalities of place significance would require at least a handbook of its own. Within the constraints of this chapter, the approach will be to attempt a systematic outline and a set of illustrations. These are drawn largely, but far from exclusively, from my own work in progress on capital cities.[1]

The capital cities of nation states are of note in this context as places of consequential significance and as places of meaning. Capitals are places where crucial decisions are made, on war and peace, on legislation and taxation, on the final adjudication of crime and litigation. They are places where governments are installed, and where governments lose their power. They are the centers of political debate about the orientation of the country. National capitals are also the locations where decisive reactions to external events have to be made: where ultimata of foreign governments and of fateful organizations like the IMF have to be answered, where pressures and threats from states or transnational corporations have to be either yielded to or resisted. Issues of this sort are decided, not in "global cities" like New York, Los Angeles, or Hong Kong, but in Washington, DC, in Accra, Bangkok, Brasilia, Buenos Aires, Beijing, and other national capitals. Capital cities are places where national differences are made. The capital is therefore often used metaphorically, referring to complex processes of government. "Paris says no"—for instance to an invasion of Iraq—is a way of summing up a whole process of democratic decision-making.

As seats of power, capital cities owe their site to the spatiality of power. Most elementarily, capitals develop with territorial polities—ancient developments in the West (Mesopotamia, Persia) and East Asia (China), but developing very unevenly across the world—and, secondly, with the permanent location of territorial power. The latter phenomenon is also ancient, but disappeared for many centuries in the early European Middle Ages, for instance, and remained rudimentary at least up to the Renaissance. The Central European German *Reich* never managed to get a proper capital in its almost thousand years of existence, until its dissolution in 1806 (Berges 1953; Schultz 1993)—and the capital has been a "problem" in German history at least into the 1990s

3.1   The Formation of Actors

The state you grow up in tends to mold you as a political actor. Your experiences, your successes, defeats, or traumas as a citizen affect your trust or mistrust in institutions and people, your views of government and of politicians. As a Scandinavian in the year 2000 there is a two-thirds chance that you would think that most people can trusted, but if you were Brazilian the probability would only be three in

[1] For a preliminary publication, see Therborn (2002).

a hundred. A good third of Britons had confidence in their Parliament in 2000, but only 7 percent of Macedonians had. The same year, 9 percent of Americans, 17 percent of Poles, 20 percent of Indians, and 96 percent of Indonesians held that army rule would be "good" or "fairly good" for the country (Inglehart et al. 2004, tables A165, E75, and E116).

A classical idea of place molding actors was the urban–rural difference. The United States of America, for instance, were provided with a strong ruralistic, anti-urban message by one of their Founding Fathers, Thomas Jefferson. Appalled by the big cities of Europe, Jefferson held big cities injurious to "the morals, the health and the liberty of man," that is, to the formation of civic actors (in a letter to Benjamin Rush of September 23, 1800, quoted in Yarborough 1998, 84). Big cities have remained in conflict with state politics throughout American history. A recent overview of US local government emphasizes that "one of the most persistent themes in state–local relations has been the conflict between state legislatures and the largest cities" (Berman 2003, 53; cf. Ching and Creed 1997).

More naturalistic but also more vague has been the counter-position of coastal cultural openness and sensuality against inland closure and austerity, a stereotype often invoked with respect to rival cities such as St. Petersburg and Moscow, Barcelona and Madrid, Beirut and Damascus, Shanghai and Beijing, Guayaquil and Quito.

When three eminent American urban scholars, Peter Dreier, John Mollenkopf, and Todd Swanstrom (2001) argue that *Place Matters*, they bring out differences among three Congressional districts, the New York 16th (South Bronx), the Ohio 10th (Westside Cleveland and adjacent suburbs), and the Illinois 13th (a suburbia west of Chicago). What they want to show is the "big difference in the quality of life" between these three metropolitan areas, from poor, staunchly Democratic South Bronx, to affluent, solidly Republican Chicago suburbs, via socioeconomically mixed, politically swinging Westside Cleveland. Economic segregation is making these place differences larger, and the distance between their supply of life chances wider.

Voters in different places of the same country tend to vote differently. Electoral geography was pioneered in France, by André Siegfried just before the First World War, focusing on the regional formation of actors. Territorial effects (ranging from provincial to municipal) could account for 75 percent or more of the party vote variation in eleven of sixteen Western European countries in elections of the 1970s. In Belgium they account for over 90 percent of the variance, and in Austria, Ireland, Sweden, and the UK close to that (Lane and Ersson 1999, 118). Those calculations do not include any controls for other factors, though. If you do control, not only for the social composition of actors but also for constituency characteristics and for political attitudes, little regional variation was found even in Britain (McAllister and Studlar 1992). The more interesting analyses lie between these poles.

Every democratic country exhibits a spatial pattern of voting, with classes, genders, age groups, or religious and secular people, for example, voting differently in different places or regions. But the reasons for this are still controversial among electoral researchers.[2] In this context we shall pay attention to place-voting from the general angles of actor-formation, action-setting, and consequences of action.

Center versus periphery is a spatial dimension of actor-formation, an important cleavage of party systems as well as of voters. In Europe, it was put into focus by the Norwegian political scientist Stein Rokkan (1970; Rokkan and Urwin 1982). The peripheries of a Great Britain centered on the south of England, for example, tend to favor the oppositional left-of-center. The strong north–south polarization in the 1994 Finnish, Swedish, and Norwegian referenda on EU membership combined space and class effects. In favor of EU membership was the affluent, more bourgeois center in the south; and against it was the somewhat less affluent, more working class or small farmer northern periphery.

For the US, Walter Dean Burnham (1970) has argued that the American party system from 1896 to 1932 was hung up on a polarity primarily between an industrial "metropole" in the Northeast supporting the Republicans and "colonial" areas in the West and the South supporting the Democrats. The defeated Confederacy states of the American South established for long a one-party system, throughout the national vicissitudes of the national Democratic label.

But while it has a capacity for hibernation, place politics is not fixed in time. There was, for instance, a significant correlation between the Spanish Socialist vote in 1933 and in the first post-Fascist elections of 1977: strong in Andalucia, Madrid, and Murcia; weak in Castilia-León, Galicia, Navarra, and Aragon (Tezanos 2004, 57). "Critical" elections and gradual sociopolitical processes can change traditions. American politics became more class-based with the New Deal, and class- and culture-based after the end of the Democratic one-party system in the South. Southern culture and traditions still matter, but in different political ways than before (cf. Lind 2003). Indeed, from recent presidential elections a pattern the reverse of the 1896–1920s alignment seems to have emerged. Now Democrats are concentrated in the Northeast (and on the West Coast), while the Republican bases are in the South and the West (Kim, Elliott, and Wang 2004). In France, the regional electoral cleavages going back to mid-nineteenthth century have been reshuffled. In the regional elections of 1986, the right gained even the old left Republican (part of the) south; and in 2004, the left captured Britanny and Vendée in the west, the bastion of the right since the French Revolution.

Since the nineteenth or early twentieth century Western European democratic electoral politics has undergone a process of nationalization, more affected by

---

[2] Recent useful overviews are given by: Johnston and Pattie 2004; Marsh 2002; Johnson, Shively, and Stein 2002.

class and less by locality. However, after the First World War place effects have tended to stabilize. In a few countries, the end of the century saw an increase of the place-formation of voters, in Belgium above all, but also in Italy (Caramani 2004).

Place effects on the formation of political elites have been little studied. But other things being equal (which they rarely are), under democratic conditions—with politicians more rooted in powerful peripheries—the politics of specifically political capitals are likely be less socially cohesive and to be more insulated from economic and cultural elites, as well from popular forces and politicians. To the extent that that is true, it should imply more "log-rolling" or "horse-trading" among legislators. Its governments are more likely to be "governments of strangers" (to borrow a title from a shrewd observer of American public policy—Heclo 1977—who nevertheless paid no attention at all to the peculiar place of Washington). To the extent that it holds, this would imply policy conflict and policy inconsistency, among government incumbents as well as between governments. This sort of capital tends to occur in federal states, with their de-centered domestic politics.

"Total capitals," dominant culturally and economically as well as politically, should be expected (other things being equal) to favor socially and culturally cohesive political elites, and through them more consistent public policies. But the total capital may also harbor—nay, be the center of—all the conflicts of the country. This has certainly been the record of Paris, from the Revolution on. Then at least a common culture or political style may ensue, amidst polarizations of policy. The intellectual character of French national politics and the *pantouflage*, the moving between top positions in the bureaucracy and in business manifest common a Parisian culture of elite schools and literary milieux. But even a centralized country with an overwhelming capital may push provincial power-brokers, "notables," onto the central political stage: as the French Third Republic increasingly did, up to the First World War; and as can still happen, as shown by the current French Prime Minister Raffarin (Corbin 1992, 810 ff.).

The extent to which capital office may be a catapult to national leadership is remarkably small. In so far as there is a capital electoral politics, it may be ill-representative of the country as a whole: that was the case with heavily social democratic Berlin in Wilhelmine Germany, while Paris voted right throughout the twentieth century. Another reason is that an incumbent government tends to be concerned with keeping the capital city under its own control. In Europe, the current French President Jacques Chirac is an exception, in getting to the presidency from being mayor of the capital. In Latin America, though, several capital mayors have recently become presidents, from Tabaré Vázquez in Uruguay to Arnoldo Alemán in Nicaragua.

3.2   Compass of Meaning

Inherent in the distinctiveness of places is their meaning, to inhabitants, to former inhabitants, to visitors, to onlookers, to anyone thinking about them and discussing them. Places vary not only in their size, their topography, their connectivity, or their kind of inhabitants. They have also different meanings, to different people. Places are invested with meaning. As such, places provide compasses of action. Places indicate attachment, belonging, attraction, revulsion; objects of identification, of ambition, and of desire. Their direction of action includes the radiation of meaning by places—such as "global cities" or other sites of power, money, and glory—as well as the pull of place roots. The geographer and architectural theorist Edwatd Relph (1976) distinguishes seven kinds of place-orientation, around the dichotomy of the insider and outsider:

- existential insideness, a close habitual relation;
- empathetic insideness, a reflective relation;
- behavioral insideness, a pragmatically navigating relation;
- vicarious insideness, a relation by identification from afar;
- accidental outsideness, the visitor's look, the tourist gaze;
- objective outsideness, the vision of the deliberately distant observer;
- existential outsideness, alienation from the place.

From historians we have recently learned much about "places of memory," the places where "memory crystallises and takes refuge" (Nora 1984, xvii). "Places," there, are taken in an explicitly metaphorical sense (François and Schulze 2001, 1: 18); the historical inventories include persons, words, inheritance, invested with collective meaning, as well as places (Nora 1984–92; Francois and Schulze 2001).

In order to get at compasses of meaning in a theory of social and political action, we had better take a somewhat different track. In this vein we may focus on:

1. places to be in, to strive to remain in, to go to, or at the very least to follow from afar;
2. places to defend, or to liberate;
3. places to visit: to see; to commemorate; to pay pilgrimage to; alternatively, to avoid;
4. places of discursive reference.

1. *Places to be in.* There are two kinds of places that occupy most of our minds in this respect. One is home—village, town, region—wherever it is. But the positive meaning varies strongly, not only among persons but also over the lifetime of the same person. Centers are the other main kind—centers of action, of wealth, power, and culture.

Comprehensive capital cities—such as Buenos Aires, London, Paris ("the soul of France, its head and its heart": Jordan 1995, 171), Vienna, Cairo, Bangkok, Tokyo, and many others—have this attraction to ambitious people in most walks of life (cf., Charle and Roche 2002). As sites of authority, capital cities also have as a key function to provide compass of meaning to the population of the state. In the Confucian classic on statecraft, the capital should form "a moral yardstick to which his [i.e. the sovereign's] people may look" (Sit 1995, 25). This maxim is echoed more than 2,000 years later in the official 1987 Strategic Long-term Study of Beijing, then characterized as "the nerve center that links the hearts of the people and the Party together... [and as] the 'model district' for guiding the nation in modernisation" (Sit 1995, 321).

Colonial city planning was oriented to conveying the majesty of imperial power. The most ambitious modern example is the construction in the 1910s of a new capital for British India, New Delhi. "First and foremost it is the spirit of British sovereignty which must appreciated in its stone and bronze," one of the two chief architects, Herbert Baker (1944, 219) wrote in a commissioned letter to the *Times* in 1912. To his colleague Edwin Lutyens he stressed that Delhi "must not be Indian, nor English, nor Roman, but it must be Imperial" (Metcalf 1989, 222). A grand imperial design ensued, combining European and Mughal elements, centered on an enormous Vice-regal Palace by Lutyens, flanked by two competing impressive administrative buildings by Baker, up on a hill, at the end of a long and wide avenue-cum-parade ground, Kingsway. Here, as so often, most of the colonial heritage survived decolonization by national recycling. The Vice-regal palace has become the Presidential Palace, and Kingsway has been renamed Rajpath.

The United States built a new capital mainly because of the rivalry among existing cities. From 1774 to 1789 Congress met in eight different places. Washington was laid out by a French engineer, L'Enfant, who had rallied to the American cause and acquired American citizenship. Having grown up in the shadow of Versailles, L'Enfant put forward a daring plan "proportional to the greatness which... the Capital of a great Empire ought to manifest," as he wrote to President Washington (Sonne 2003, 50). L'Enfant soon fell out with the federal commission, but by and large and over time his monumental design for the American capital was realized, with its bipolar political layout, huge diagonals overtowering any civic space (although the Mall has lately become a national rallying-point), and its central Washington Monument.

In Europe a French author in the Age of Absolutism, Alexandre Le Maître in 1682, highlighted three crucial functions of a capital: to be the site of authority; to be the pivot of all exchanges; and to "concentrate the values and the force of a country" (Zeller 2003, 633). An intensive debate about the values and the force of nation represented by competing capitals broke out in Germany with the reunification of the country in 1990. Bonn (the post-Second World War capital of West Germany) and Berlin were invested with very different meanings: Bonn was presented as symbolizing the Western and the European orientation of a post-national Germany, a capital of *Gemütlichkeit*; Berlin was seen as a symbol of German unification and as the normal metropolis of a normal nation, freed of the historical inferiority complexes of the Bonn Republic (Richie 1998: 850 ff.; Keiderling 2004; von Beyme 1991). The vote was close, and cut through traditional party and cultural cleavages. In the end Berlin won with 337 parliamentary votes to 320.

2. *Places to defend or liberate.* Places to defend are often peripheral, which may have been the reason why they were attacked. The Falklands islands at the bottom of the South Atlantic are one of the most peripheral places on the planet from the center of London, but their defense was seen by a large part of the metropolitan population as well as by the government as worthwhile regardless of cost, human and financial. From the other side, opponents as well as supporters of Argentina's then-military regime saw the Malvinas as a natural part of the country, robbed by the British in the heyday of imperialism. To both parties, the value was symbolic only, but high enough to go to war for.

Modern nationalism has led to a remarkable sacralization of national territory, with a great many places that have to be liberated or defended. The Caucasus region has a number of them, and so have former Yugoslavia and the Horn of Africa. Jerusalem/al Qods is not only a sacred place to three religions, but has also become overloaded with contested meanings to two nations in conflict.

3. *Places to visit.* Travel to interesting or beautiful places is ancient, and so is pilgrimage to sacred sites. But places to visit have become much more important in current times. Nation-building has brought national places into focus. "One cannot be fully Indonesian until one has seen Jakarta," Indonesia's greatest writer, Pramoedya Ananta Toer wrote in 1955 (Kusno 2001, 15). Tourism has become a major industry, and tourism politics and policy have become important political tasks. Secondly, there has also evolved a political practice of deliberately investing places with heavy symbolic meaning, as sites of commemoration. This is most developed in Europe, mainly with reference to events of the Second World War and the Nazi terror. Former concentration camps and death camps, like Buchenwald and Auschwitz, and former Jewish ghettoes in many cities have become meaningful places to visit.

Places may also have a meaning of repulsion, places not to be visited. The German war cemetery of Bittburg was such a place in the eyes of many, on the occasion of an official visit there by President Reagan and Chancellor Kohl, because SS men are also buried there. Every time a senior Japanese politician visits the Yasakuni shrine in Tokyo there is a Chinese protest, because Japanese war criminals have been laid at rest there.

4. *Places of discursive reference.* Places of meaning may orient our minds and discourse. The little Belgian town of Waterloo, where Napoleon was fatally beaten in 1815, has become synonymous with defeat to such an extent that it has entered the world of late twentieth-century pop hits. "Munich" in international politics stands for accommodation to violent dictators, after the British and French Prime Ministers

agreed to Nazi German demands on Czechoslovakia in a summit in 1938. "Vichy" (the small-town site of the pro-German government of France in 1940–4) in European political discourse denotes collaboration with an occupying enemy (cf. Watkins 2004). "Pearl Harbour" in American politics means perfidious attack, and "Sèvres" in Turkish discourse refers to splitting the country (after the Paris suburb where the Ottoman empire was subjected to a humiliating peace treaty in 1920). In Chile during the left-wing government of Allende in the early 1970s, right-wing graffiti painted the name of "Jakarta," the Indonesian capital, where an anti-communist massacre—of probably more than half a million people—was unleashed in 1965.

3.3   Settings of Action

Almost all social action, except for telephonic or electronic communication, takes place somewhere, in some local setting. Capital cities are settings of power, exercise, and contest, truly "landscapes of power" in a phrase that Sharon Zukin (1991) uses primarily to refer to New York. A famous case of city planning as a setting for political action is the transformation of Paris in the third quarter of the nineteenth century. It was carried out for Emperor Napoleon III by his prefect, Baron Hauss-mann. There were several reasons for changing old, rapidly grown Paris; above all hygienic ones, as the city had become very insalubrious. Imperial aesthetics was also an important concern. Whatever the controversial priority order, a major task of Haussmann was to make government power safe from rebellion by the people of densely populated, labyrinthine east-central Paris. By time of the June 1848 violent repression of insurrectionary Paris, barricades had been put up eight times since 1827; and twice revolutions had succeeded, in July 1830 and February 1848. The solution was to raze a number of poor neighborhoods, to open up a set of big boulevards, difficult to barricade and easy to move troops in, and to locate army barracks close to places of popular gathering. Most affected by this strategic plan were the areas between what are now the Places de la République and de la Nation on the Right Bank, and on the Left from the new Boulevard Saint Michel to Mount St. Geneviève (Jordan 1995). As a counter-insurgency strategy all this was hardly successful, and did not prevent the revolutionary Paris Commune of 1871, but the setting of urban life in Paris had been lastingly transformed.

In the colonial cities, racial segregation was the primary rule, as manifestations of power and for reasons of security, epidemic as well as political (Georg and de Lemps 2003). The most ambitious governors built new European cities outside indigenous ones, as the French governor Lyautey did in Morocco (Abu-Lughod 1980; Rabinow 1989), or as the British did in New Delhi, which was laid out spaciously as a tree-shadowed garden city just opposite the crowded Old Delhi. Like other cities of the British Empire, it also had its layout segregated not only between the rulers and the natives, but also between the military "cantonments" and the administrative "civil lines." Not quite 5 percent of the new city area was intended as "Native Residential" (Hussey 1950, 263). These colonial military cantonments or "Defense Colonies" still contribute to the configurations of urban life in cities of Bangladesh, India, and Pakistan.

But capitals can also be or provide spaces of civic representation. A powerful citizenry is manifested in a civic space, a public space where people can meet as citizens and as individuals with varied tastes. The ancient Greek *agora* and the Roman forum are classical examples. The tradition was revived by the autonomous High Medieval cities of Europe, in particular along the city belt from Italy to the Low Countries. Italian Siena's *Piazza del Campo* is arguably one of the most beautiful examples (cf. Rowe 1997, ch. 1), but it may be followed by the *Grande Place* of Brussels. In the Americas, the Boston Common (Hackett Fischer 2000) is perhaps a paradigmatic example. But all colonial Latin American cities had and still have a central square where people met and assembled. True, it was also used for displays of power, such as military parades, and in Hispanic America it was often called *Plaza de Armas* (Place of Arms).

Security considerations seem to render futile the idea of the architects of the new Berlin government quarter, Schultes and Frank, of a "Federal and Civic Forum" between the Chancellors's Office and the parliament building, although there is still some open, accessible space there. The civic space of Chandigarh, the capital of Indian Punjab and later also of the Indian state of Haryana, was laid out by the great modernist architect Le Corbusier, relating the three branches of government through open squares, provided with abstract civic sculptures. The insecurity situation—with the Punjabi Chief Minister assassinated in the 1990s—has led to a closing off to the public of the whole governmental area. However, in democratized Seoul, the area in front of City Hall has been changed from just a traffic circus to a lawn accessible to pedestrians where people gather, for small outdoor concerts as well as for expressing political opinion.

The classical Chinese concept of political space was in a sense the opposite of the civic one, centered on a closed space of power, the imperial palace as the "Forbidden City." On its south side, was an opening onto an outer court for petitions and for public announcements (Sit 1995, 56 ff.). The Javanese *kraton* or royal palace was laid out on the basis of similar principles, as a closed, central site of power, with a public space (*alun-alun*) for royal announcements and for public celebrations and festivities (Tjahjono 1998, 90). In Muslim cities the mosques and their large courtyards are places of assembly, but of members of the *umma* (the religious community) rather than of a political citizenry, who were usually facing an overtowering, fortified site of power, from the Red Fort of Mughal Delhi to the Topkapi of Ottoman Istanbul. But sometimes the Muslim city could include a big central square, a *meidan*, in front of a palace or and/of the main mosque. In this respect, the center of Isfahan resembled that of Lima or Quito, with a meeting-place and a place of public recreation. In other respects, the East as well as the West Asian cities were dominated by private, family space, of compounds around a walled-in courtyard connected only by meandering alleys, very different from the Ancient European street grid that was later exported to the Americas.

Another kind of political space is the space for political rallies. Nationalism was the first major wave of popular mobilization, and it could often make new use of absolutist parade grounds: the *Champs de Mars* in Paris, where the Revolution held its first mass rallies; or the *Heldenplatz* in Vienna, the "Heroes Square" in front of the imperial palace, where the coming of the First World War in 1914 and of Adolf Hitler in 1938 were fêted. The Communist rulers paid serious attention to places of mass rally. In Moscow the old Red Square outside the Kremlin was a natural site, focused by the Lenin Mausoleum of 1924. The East Germans tore down the war-damaged imperial castle to make room for a large rallying-point, the *Marx-Engels-Platz.* Mao Zedong and the Chinese comrades were duly impressed by Red Square upon their visit to Moscow in 1950, and set upon enlarging the Tian An Men, just south of the imperial Forbidden City, into the largest political parade ground in the world (Webb 1990).

The world religions have also realized the significance of places of mass assembly, as manifested by the place around the *Kaaba* in Mecca or outside the church of St. Peter in Rome.

The settings of voting behavior may be viewed in various ways. At one end, there is the structural context, presumably perceived by the voter. For instance, according to British census polls for the period of 1991–2001, the percentage voting Conservative or Labour varied strongly with the structural socioeconomic disadvantage of the neighborhood. In the most advantaged areas 77 percent of the "higher service class" of professionals and managers voted Tory, and 68 percent of skilled manual workers; whereas in the least advantaged neighbourhoods 48 and 19 percent did, respectively (Johnston et al. 2004, table 4.).

From another angle, the setting of voting is social interaction, local campaigning, groups or networks of political discussions. There is no unanimity among electoral specialists on the importance of these interactive effects, but they clearly exist (Huckfeldt and Sprague 1995; Whiteley and Seyd 2003).

3.4   Places and Consequences of Action

"Being in the right place at the right time" (or "in the wrong place at the wrong time") are well-known words of wisdom, applying to sexual as well as to political life. In politics, it applies both to aspiring leaders and, especially, to ordinary people. When police and military round-ups are being made, you had better not be in the wrong place. Otherwise you may, in present times, land in Guantánamo or in some other concentration camp. In order to make a successful bid for power, you have to be in the right place at the decisive moment

Wars, geopolitical or world systems, and democratic elections are all examples of the importance of place for consequences of action. And capital cities are by definition the place where consequential state action is taken.

Maps have always been crucial to modern warfare. Why? Because it is crucial to locate where your enemy is, what possibilities of movement he has, and where to hit him hardest. Knowing where to do battle, and when, is a key demand on a successful commander. Recent supposedly "precision bombing" has raised the stakes, rather than making place trivial.

To stay, in the face of encirclement, and fight was a fatal mistake of the Nazi Germans in Stalingrad and of the colonial French at Dien Bien Phu. The decision of the US Clinton administration in the 1990s to concentrate military interventions in the Balkans—where Secretary of State Albright was well connected—and to leave Rwanda to its fate, made possible the genocide of Tutsi people by Hutu people, and substituted Croatian and Albanian ethnic cleansing for Serbian in the former Yugoslavia. But it did bring about the desired regime toppling in Serbia. The decision of the Bush administration to make war in Iraq has been successful in "regime change," but again at the cost of large-scale destruction and killings, of about 12,000 to 13,000 civilian Iraqis according to estimates reported by CNN on September 8, 2004. A large part of the death and destruction does not seem to have been intended, but followed from the violent logic of the place, which the bombers and invaders never bothered to learn about. To both US governments, the dynamics of place seems to have been fatally neglected.

In the heyday of inter-imperialist rivalry about a century ago, a geographical theory of politics and power, *geopolitics*, was developed by Rudolf Kjellén (the Swedish professor of geography and political science who coined the term), Harold Mackinder (Oxford geographer and LSE Director), and Friedrich Ratzel (the German geographer). States struggling for space was their common vision, and spatial parameters of this big-power rivalry their main concern (Heffernan 2000). The characteristic confluence of the emerging academic discipline of geography, the climate of Social Darwinism, and the peak of intra-European imperialist rivalry, carried forward by the German Nazis, discredited the idea of geopolitics for a while after the Second World War. But the thesis by Frederick Jackson Turner of the sociopolitical importance of the American frontier and of its closing around 1890 is also an influential example of geopolitical thought. De facto, the cold war strategists on both sides were clearly very geographically conscious, in negotiating and pressuring their respective territorial "spheres of influence."

Geopolitics made an interesting comeback in the 1990s. It did so intellectually, in a culturalist mutation: as part of a postmodern geography, focusing on imaginations of space, on bodies in places, and on non-state politics, by institutions, cities, or movements of resistance to power (Agnew 1999; Ó Tuathail and Dalby 1998; Soja 1996). It did so politically, in a more direct return to classical strategic geopolitics as part of a new assertiveness of American world power. The most eloquent and significant example is Zbigniew Brzezinski (1997), National Security Adviser to President Carter and a key architect of the Islamic counter-revolution in Afghanistan.

To Brzezinski, control of Euarasia is the "chief geopolitical prize" for the United States, and the decisive strategic question to be addressed is how that "preponderance on the Eurasian continent" can be sustained (1997, 30). The answer is sought in seeing Eurasia as a "grand chessboard" on which the struggle for global primacy is played. The approach is explicitly geopolitical, as "geographic location still tends to determine the immediate priorities of a state" (38). The key units are "geostrategic players"—"the states that have the capacity and national will to exercise power or influence beyond their borders in order to alter . . . the existing geopolitical state of affairs" (40)—and "geopolitical pivots," "states whose importance is derived . . . from their sensitive location" (41).

In this neoclassical as well as in classical geopolitical thought, state actors are shaped by their place in the world, but the main emphasis is on the risks and the opportunities for state power that the control—by ego or by alter—of places and territories offer, and on the best strategies of states under given geopolitical conditions. A more economic than military–political view of geopolitics, befitting a Japan-centered perspective, is provided by Rumley et al. (1998). A less imperial, more objective view of contemporary geopolitics is given by its American academic doyen, S. B. Cohen (2003, 3) as "the analysis of the interaction between geographical settings and perspectives, and international politics."

Place also matters in the world system of Immanuel Wallerstein (1974), his associates, and followers. Economic and social development, in this influential perspective, is not primarily a matter of individual countries taking off. They follow from a world system of division of labor, established by Western European powers in the sixteenth century, and the location of countries within it: in the advantaged core, in the exploited periphery, or in the intermediate semi-periphery. The dynamics of the systemic logic may be argued about, but world system analysis is a prominent example of place-matters analysis.

World system analysis is basically a kind of geoeconomics, both related to and rivalling geopolitics. The recent "global cities" perspective gives this global geoeconomics an urban twist. Here commanding and pace-setting action is portrayed as being concentrated into a hierarchy of "global cities," headed by London and New York (Sassen 1991; Taylor 2004). In this perspective, states—and their capacity to tax, to control borders, and to wage wars—tend to disappear from view, being of secondary significance at most. Places matter in this view to the extent that they are the sites of transnational corporate headquarters, in particular of firms of business services. Washington, DC, then appears as a "medium"-sized "global command center," similar to Amsterdam (Taylor 2004, 90).

In most electoral democracies, the decisive thing is not just how many votes you get. It matters also, and sometimes crucially, where you get your votes. Above all, this is important in the Anglo-Saxon first-past-the-post system, which in theory always and in practice sometimes can produce an elective majority for a party backed by a minority of voters. Most recently, this was the case in the US in 2000, when the Electoral College of state representatives elected George W. Bush President of the United States with 47.9 percent of the votes against 48.4 percent for Al Gore. In American history a minority President had been inaugurated three times before, but all in the nineteenth century (John Quincy Adams in 1824, Rutherford Hayes in 1876, and Benjamin Harrison in 1888). In 1951, Winston Churchill and the British Conservatives won a very consequential election, opening a thirteen-year period of Tory rule, with less votes than the Labour Party, 48.0 to 48.8 percent, yielding a seat majority of 51.4 to 47.2 (Flora 1983, 151, 188).

Electoral strategists in countries with this electoral system are, of course, always primarily preoccupied with "swing" constituencies or, in American presidential elections, swing states.

The electoral importance of place also means that the drawing up of electoral districts has become a major political art. In its (normal) biased form it has even been given a name, "gerrymandering," after the early nineteenth-century governor of Massachusetts, Gerry, who according to a contemporary cartoonist, created salamander-like constituencies. In most, but far from all American states this is a partisan task, carried out by the majority of the state legislature where the votes are cast.

3.5   Places as Outcomes of Action

Places are not fixed in time, in spite of their inherent inertia. They may go up and down in terms of population and of relative centrality or prosperity. Some of these changes are governed by nature: by volcanoes and earthquakes, by climate changes, by the wanderings of fish shoals, by the silting of rivers. But most tend to be outcomes of human action, by the discovery/exploitation or the depletion of natural resources, by the building and obsolescence of transport routes (mountain passes, bridges, canals, ports, and railways, for example), by policies of territorial exploitation, neglect, or support, or by direct place construction or destruction.

About eighty years ago, a British historian (Cornish 1923) tried to grasp the location of what he called *The Great Capitals*, by which he meant "Imperial" capitals or capitals of "Great Powers." Most important in his view was their location as the "Storehouse" of the wealth of the empire; secondly, there was transport connectivity, "Crossways"; and thirdly, considerations of war, "Strongholds." Under these constraints, the fact that the foreign relations of the empire are conducted from the capital propels the capital into a "Forward position," relatively close to the exterior. More often than not the national capital is the most cosmopolitan, or the most "globalized" part of the nation.

However, the place of the capital is not determined only by national dimensions. Capital cities are made up of a triangle of relations: between the local and the national, the national and the global, and the global and the local. As places they constitute the habitat of a local population with their everyday needs and habits. Like all places, capital cities have their *genii loci*, their local "spirits of place," given by their location, and their local social and political relations. The river and the hill provide the parameters of Prague, the sea and the islands of Stockholm and Helsinki, for instance. Local Washington is actually largely black and poor, very different from the national and the global radiations from the White House, the Pentagon, and Capitol Hill. In Helsinki, the City Council has determined the sites of national buildings and monuments, separating the Republican Parliament from the ex-imperial government area, for instance. In many other countries, from the UK to China, the capital city is largely directly under central government control.

While Cornish is a good starting-point, situating social action in natural settings, later experience testifies to other springs of capital action as well. This is seen most easily and clearly in the modern history of deliberately created capitals.

Why have new capitals been constructed, as alternatives not only to remaining in the historical place but also to moving to some other city in existence, an ancient political practice?

Starting with St Petersburg, begun in 1703, officially a capital (or "throne") city in 1712, with the transfer of the imperial court to it, and continuing up to the first years of the twenty-first century, we may distinguish a limited set of reasons for such major political displacement.

St Petersburg was a product of monarchical absolutism, and its rationale was reactive modernization. The founding of a new capital was part of an effort from above to modernize the country, then conceived more in cultural than in economic terms. From its "forward" location at the western edge of the empire, St Petersburg was built as a fortified gateway to more developed Western Europe, and as a vanguard of Russian modernization. Dutch city planning, Italian architects, and French culture were resorted to for this purpose, and made possible by a massive use of coerced labor (Lemberg 1993; Jangfeldt 1998; Tjekanova et al. 2000; Zeller 2003, 666 ff.). The modernist thrust of Tsar Peter I was to remain unrivalled for a long time. Edo/Tokyo was already a major city, perhaps the largest in the world in the eighteenth century, although it became the imperial capital only with the Meiji Restoration of 1868 (Seidensticker 1985, ch. 1). Ankara was also in existence, although at a modest level, before chosen as the capital of Turkey in the 1920s (Sen and Aydin 2000).

Chronologically, Washington was the next novel capital. It was to set a pattern for the rest of the white settlements of the British Empire as well as for the USA. The main picture of this capital history is one of places of political exchange.

The location of US capital cities were often bargaining chips in political games, or interest compromises. The federal capital owes its site on the Potomac to a deal brokered by Alexander Hamilton, whereby the union took over all public debt in exchange for Northern support for a Southern site for the capital (Cummings and Price 1993, 216 ff.). The world had experienced the founding of new capitals before in modern times. But the conception of a specifically political center, separated from the economic and demographic one—which was then Philadelphia—was new, although adumbrated in the role of the Hague in the Dutch United Provinces as the meeting village of the Estates-General. It set an American pattern, followed already in 1797 when the state government of New York moved to Albany and in 1799, when that of Pennsylvania went to Lancaster. In 1857, Abraham Lincoln put together an infrastructural package of railway and canal construction with a relocation of the Illinois capital to Springfield (Johannsen 2000, 186 ff.). An anti-urban animus has played a significant part in the widespread American practice of making relatively small cities state political capitals, from Albany, New York, and Harrisburg, Pennsylvania, to Sacramento, California, via Lansing, Michigan, and Springfield, Illinois (cf. Dye 1988; Berman 2003).

The Washington principle of territorial political balance was followed in Canada in 1867, when Queen Victoria conferred capital status to the town of Ottawa, on the border of Anglophone Ontario and Francophone Quebec. It was further followed in Australia, placing the capital Canberra between the major capitals of the states of Victoria and New South Wales; in New Zealand, placing the capital Wellington between the North and the South Island; and in South Africa, where the capital functions were divided between the government in Transvaal Boer Pretoria, parliament in Anglo Cape Town, and the Supreme Court in Boer Oranje Bloemfontein. But the US anti-urban animus did not spread.

The new capitals of recent times have a different rationale. The most spectacular is Brasilia, built in the late 1950s on the high plateau wilderness of interior Brazil. Brasilia was built as a project of national development, opening up a previously undeveloped interior. Owing to its master planner (Lucio Costa) and its master architect (Oscar Niemayer), Brasilia has become an icon of mid-twentieth-century urban modernity, daring and controversial (cf. Kubitschek 1975; Holston 1989)

The Nigerian move from Lagos to the new Abuja, while spatially similar to the Brazilian move to Brasilia was more motivated by reasons of ethnic balance and political security. Lagos, the inherited colonial capital, was de facto a mainly Yoruba city, and as such impregnated by one the three major ethnicities of multiethnic Nigeria. The official criteria for choosing a new capital for Nigeria were as shown in Table 27.1.

The relocation was actually decided by a military dictatorship, under mounting pressure from popular protests as well as from assassination attempts. It should not be assumed that these official criteria were de facto strictly abided by. Nevertheless, at least they provide an insight into an important contemporary political discourse on place.

In recent years, there has been a growing concern in several parts of the world with too much centrality, with overgrown capitals suffering from congestion and overpopulation. The most advanced example is in Malaysia, where the capital is moving to a new city, Putrajaya, already well under way—with a palatial Prime Minister's Office and a nearby large mosque as their most impressive constructions. The Malaysian capital move is also related to a vision of electronic information

Table 27.1 Official criteria for choosing the Nigerian capital

Criterion	Proportional weight
Centrality	22
Health and Climate	12
Land Availability and Use	10
Water Supply	10
Multi-Access Possibility	7
Security	6
Existence of Local Bldg. Materials	6
Low Population Density	6
Power Resources	5
Drainage	5
Soil	4
Physical Planning Convenience	4
Ethnic Accord	3

Source: Eyinla 2000, 250

development—both similar to and different from the Brazilian interior develop-ment program with Brasilia—and includes the building of a parallel high-tech city, Cyberjaya.

The current Korean president is committed to locating out of Seoul for similar reasons. There is a parliamentary decision supporting the move, and the selection of a preliminary site by mid-2004, but this is still on the drawing board. Discussions along the same lines are being held in several Asian countries: China, Japan, Indonesia. But plans may get stuck, as in Argentina in the 1980s, or the realization stalled, as in Tanzania or Côte d'Ivoire.

4   PLACES IN HISTORY AND TODAY

While increasingly mobile, human beings still locate themselves in places, fixed, contiguous, distinctive. Places mold actors, structuring their life chances, providing them with identities and traditions of social and political action. Places direct actors, by attraction or repulsion, providing compasses of action, contribute to the meaning of life by orienting civic action, supporting action, subject action, consuming action, celebration, remembrance, mourning, non-action. Social action almost always takes place in a specific location. Places are strategic sites of action, very much affecting outcomes of success, victory, and power—and their opposites. The creation, development, or destruction of places form an important part of political agendas.

Are these effects and implications of place mainly a legacy of the past, largely being overcome in the current age of electronic networking and global satellite communication? The evidence is ambiguous, but three conclusions seem to be warranted. First and foremost, place has not disappeared, but is still important. Secondly, it is less important than a century ago. Thirdly, the evidence for a recent major change is flimsy, and most probably untenable.

Institutions of formal education clearly mitigate the effects of place of birth, although the latter still weighs heavily on your channels to schooling. Faster means of transport (automobiles, airplanes, fast trains) have made distances shrink. There is currently as much inter-national migration as a century ago, but it is today much easier to keep up ties to places of origin—by satellite TV, telephone, e-mail, and bank remittances—than previously. Intra-national migration, on the other hand, has increased enormously, in Africa, Asia, and Latin America. Place voting declined before the First World War, but little after, and some very recent tendencies of Europe and America go both up and down.

Geopolitics was always controversial, its relevance always contested. But it is a noteworthy sign, that it has recently staged a discursive comeback. Military technology is undoubtedly much less place-dependent than previously. Intercontinental nuclear missiles make up the aces, rather than defensive or controlling locations. More doubtful is whether current concerns with "global governance" have moved beyond the "great games" of rival imperialisms 100 years ago, and its interimperial conferences, like that in Berlin of 1884.

The cities versus state literature remains within the field of place. The gist of this business-focused literature is the emphasis on central or "commanding" places versus others. The current tendencies towards a regionalization of trade and of interstate cooperation point to a mounting significance of place and contiguity. The European Union, the NAFTA, the Mercosur, the ASEAN, the Asian extensions of ASEAN to the east (China, Japan, and South Korea) and recently to the west (India), the African Union: all indicate an increasing importance of place, albeit a move from nation state to region. The classical centre–periphery distinction, with regard to all kinds of action, does not seem to be disappearing.

While there is some (contradictory) evidence of a diminishing importance of place in the formation of actors and in affecting the consequences of action, no such tendency can be detected with respect to place as the meaning of action. Places of meaning are invented all the time. A noteworthy example is the Garden of Diana of Wales put up in Revolutionary Republican Havana in the late 1990s. While there is no hard quantitative evidence, it seems plausible that the number of meaningful places is increasing. There is in any case quite an entrepreneurship around to invent such places.

This is being written in the shadow of American elections. In 2000, the US presidential election was decided in Miami-Dade county, in 2004 in the state of Ohio. Few spots of the planet are likely to be unaffected by who wins the legitimate power of the United States.

REFERENCES

ABU-LUGHOD, J. 1980. *Rabat: Urban Apartheid in Morocco*. Princeton, NJ: Princeton University Press.

AGNEW, J. 1999. The new geopolitics of power. Pp. 173–93 in *Human Geography Today*, ed. D. MASSEY, J. ALLEN, and P. Sarre. Cambridge: Polity Press.

ARISTOTLE 1988. *The Politics*, ed. S. EVESON, trans. B. Jowitt. Cambridge: Cambridge University Press.

BAKER, H. 1944. *Architecture and Personalities*. London: Country Life.

BERGES, W. 1953. Das Reich ohne Hauptstadt. Pp. 1–30 in *Das Hauptstadtproblem in der GESCHICHTE*, ed. Friedrich-Meinecke-Institut. Tübingen: Max Niemeyer Verlag.

BERMAN, D. R. 2003. *Local Government and the States*. Armonk, NY: M. E. Sharpe.

BEYME, K. von 1991. *Hauptstadtsuche*. Frankfurt: Suhrkamp.

BRZEZINSKI, Z. 1997. *The Grand Chessboard*. New York: Basic Books.

BURNHAM, W. D. 1970. *Critical Elections and the Mainsprings of American Politics*. New York: Norton.

CALHOUN, C. 1994. *Social Theory and the Politics of Identity*. Oxford: Blackwell.

CARAMANI, D. 2004. *The Nationalization of Politics*. Cambridge: Cambridge University Press.

CASTELLS, M. 1996. *The Rise of the Network Society*. Oxford: Blackwell.

CASEY, E. C. 1997. *The Fate of Place: A Philosophical History*. Berkeley: University of California Press.

CHARLE, C., and ROCHE, D. (eds.) 2002. *Capitales culturelles Capitales symboliques: Paris et les expérience européennes*. Paris: Publications de la Sorbonne.

CHING, B., and CREED, G. M. 1997. Recognizing rusticity: identity and the power of place. Pp.1–38 in *Knowing Your Place: Rural Identity and Cultural Hierarchy*, ed. B. Ching and G. M. Creed. London: Routledge.

CLAVAL, P. 2000. *Hérodote* and the French Left. In Dodds and Atkinson 2000, 239–67.

COHEN, S. B. 2003. Geopolitical realities and United States foreign policy. *Political Geography*, 22: 1–33.

CORBIN, A. 1992. Paris–province. Pp. 777–823 in *Les lieux de mémoire III :1 Les Frances*, ed. P. Nora. Paris: Gallimard.

CORNISH, V. 1923. *The Great Capitals: An Historical Geography*. London: Methuen.

CUMMINGS, M. C., JR., and PRICE, M. C. 1993. The creation of Washington, DC. In Taylor et al. 1993, 213–29.

DODDS, K., and ATKINSON, D. (eds.) 2000. *Geopolitical Traditions*. London: Routledge.

DREIER, P., MOLLENKOP, J., and SWANSTROM, T. 2001. *Place Matters: Metropolitics for the Twenty-first Century*. Lawrence: University Press of Kansas.

DUTT, A., COSTA, F., AGGARWAL, S., and NOBLE, A. 1994 *The Asian City: Processes of Development, Characteristics and Planning*. Dordrecht: Kluwer.

DYE, T. R. 1988. *Politics in States and Communities*. Englewood Cliffs, NJ: Prentice Hall.

EYINLA, B. M. 2000. From Lagos to Abuja: the domestic politics and international implications of relocating Nigeria's capital city. In Sohn and Weber 2000, 239–68.

FLORA, P. 1983. *State, Economy, and Society in Western Europe, 1815–1975*. Vol. 1. Frankfurt: Campus.

FRANÇOIS, E., and SCHULZE, H. 2001. *Deutsche Erinnerungsorte*, 3 vols. München: C. H. Beck.

GEORG, O., and DE LEMPS, X. H. 2003. La ville européenne outre-mer. Vol. 2: 279–544 in *Histoire de l'Europe urbaine*, ed. J.-L. Pinol. Paris: Seuil.

GIDDENS, A. 1994. *The Constitution of Society*. Cambridge: Polity Press.

HACKETT FISCHER, D. 2000. Boston Common. Pp. 125–43 in *American Places*, ed. W. E. Leuchtenburg. Oxford: Oxford University Press.

HECLO, H. 1977. *Government of Strangers*. Washington, DC: Brookings Institution.

HEFFERNAN, M. 2000. On the origins of European geopolitics, 1890–1920. In Dodds and Atkinson 2000, 27–51.

HEPPLE, L. 2000. Yves LACOSTE, *Hérodote* and French radical geography. In Dodds and Atkinson 2000, 268–301.

HOLSTON, J. 1989. *The Modernist City: An Anthropological Critique of Brasilia*. Chicago: University of Chicago Press.

HUCKFELDT, R., and SPRAGUE, J. 1995. *Citizens, Politics, and Social Communication*. Cambridge: Cambridge University Press.

HUSSEY, C. 1950. *The Life of Sir Edwin Lutyens*. London: Country Life.

INGLEHART, R., BASÁÑEZ, M., DÍEZ-MEDRANO, J., HALMAN, L., and LUIJKS, R. (eds.) 2004. *Human Beliefs and Values*. México: Siglo XXI.

JANGFELDT, B. 1998. *Svenska vägar till Sankt Petersburg*. Stockholm: Wahlström & Widstrand.

JOHANNSEN, R. W. 2000. Illinois old capitol. Pp. 185–99 in *American Places*, ed. W. E. Leuchtenburg. Oxford: Oxford University Press.

JOHNSON, M., SHIVELY, P., and STEIN, R. M. 2002. Contextual data and the study of elections and voting behaviour: connecting individuals to environments. *Electoral Studies*, 21: 219–33.

JOHNSTON, R., and PATTIE, C. 2004. Electoral geography in electoral studies: putting voters in their place. Pp. 45–66 in *Spaces of Democracy*, ed. C. Barnett and M. Low. London: Sage.

JOHNSTON, R. K., JONES, R., SARKER, PROPPER, C., BURGESS, S., and BOLSTER, A. 2004. Party support and the neighbourhood effect: spatial polarization and the British electorate. *Political Geography*, 23: 367–402.

JONES, M., JONES, R., and WOODS, M. 2004. *An Introduction to Political Geography*. London: Routledge.

JORDAN, D. 1995. *Transforming Paris: The Life and Labour of Baron Hauussmann*. New York: Free Press.

KEIDERLING, G. 2004. *Der Umgang mit der Haupstadt*. Berlin: Verlag am Park.

KIM, J., ELLIOTT, E., and WANG, D.-M. 2003. A spatial analysis of county level outcomes in US presidential elections 1988–2000. *Electoral Studies*, 22: 741–61.

KUBITSCHEK, J. 1975. *Por Que Construí Brasilia*. Rio de Janeiro: Bloch Editores.

KUSNO, A. 2001. Violence of categories: urban design and the making of Indonesian modernity. Pp. 15–50 in *City and Nation. Rethinking Place and Identity*, ed. M. P. Smith and T. Bender. New BRUNSWICK, NJ: Transaction.

LANE, J.-E., and ERSSON, S. 1999. *Politics and Society in Western Europe*, 4th edn. London: Sage.

LEMBERG, H. 1993. Moskau und St. Petersburg: Die Frage der Nationalhaupstadt in Russland: Eine Skizze. Pp. 103–13 in *Hauptstädte in europäischen Nationalstaaten*, ed. T. Schieder and G. Brunn. Munich: Oldenbourg.

LIND, M. 2003. *Made in Texas*. New York: Basic Books.

MCALLISTER, I., and STUDLAR, D. 1992. Regional voting in Britain: territorial polarisation or artefact? *American Journal of Political Science*, 3: 168–99.

MARSH, M. 202. Electoral context. *Electoral Studies*, 21: 207–18.

METCALF, T. R. 1989. *An Imperial Vision: Indian Architecture and the British Raj*. Oxford: Oxford University Press.

MORISON, B. 2002. *On Location*. Oxford: Clarendon Press.

NORA, P. (ed.) 1984–92. *Les lieux de mémoire*, 7 vols. Paris Gallimard.

Norberg-SCHULZ, C. 1982. *Genius loci: Landschaft, Lebensraum, Baukunst*. Stuttgart: Klett-Cotta.

Ó TUATHAIL, G., and DALBY, S. (eds.) 1998. *Rethinking Geopolitics: Towards A Critical Geopolitics*. London: Routledge.

RABINOW, P. 1989. *French Modern*. Cambridge, Mass.: MIT Press.

RELPH, E. 1976. *Place and Placelessness*. London: Pion.

RICHIE, A. 1998. *Faust's Metropolis*. London: HarperCollins.

ROKKAN, S. 1970. *Citizens, Elections, Parties*. Oslo: Universitetsforlaget.

—— and URWIN, D. 1982. *The Politics of Territorial Identity*. London: Sage.

ROWE, P. G. 1997. *Civic Realism*. Cambridge, Mass.: MIT Press.

RUMLEY, D., CHIBA, T., TAKAGHI, A., and FUKUSHIMA, Y. (eds.) 1998. *Global Geopolitics and the Asia-Pacific*. Aldershot: Ashgate.

SASSEN, S. 1991. *The Global City*. Princeton, NJ: Princeton University Press.

SCHULZ, U. (ed.) 1993. *Die Hauptstädte der Deutschen*. Munich: C. H. Beck.

SEIDENSTICKER, E. 1985 *Low City, High City*. San Francisco: Donald S. Ellis

SEN, F., and AYDOIN, H. 2000. Ankara: Vom Dorf zur Hauptstadt. Pp. 161–81 in A. Sohn and H. Weber (eds.), *Hauptstaädte und Global Cities an der Schwelle zum 21. Jahrhundert*. Bochum: Winkler.

SIT, V. F. S. 1995. *Beijing*. Chichester: Wiley.

SOJA, E. W. 1996. *Thirdspace: Journeys to Los Angeles and Other Real-and-Imagined Places*. Oxford: Blackwell.

SOHN, A., and WEBER, H. (eds.) 2000. *Hauptstädte und Global Cities an der Schwelle zum 21: Jahrhundert*. Bochum: Winkler.

SONNE, W. 2003. *Representing the State: Capital City Planning in the Early Twentieth Century*. Munich: Prestel

TAYLOR, J., LENGELLÉ, J. G., and ANDREW, C. (eds.) 1993. *Capital Cities: Les Capitales*. Ottawa: Carlton University Press.

TAYLOR, P. J. 2004. *World City Network*. London: Routledge.

TEZANOS, J. F. 2004. El PSOE en la democracia. *Temas para el debate*, 117–18: 55–60.

THERBORN, G. 2000. *Die Gesellschaften Europas 1945–2000*. Frankfurt: Campus.

——2002. Monumental Europe: the national years. *Housing, Theory and Society*, 19, 1: 26–47.

TJAHJONO, G. 1998. Palace and city. Pp. 90–3 in *Indonesian Heritage: Architecture*, ed. G. Tjahjono. Singapore: Editions Didier Millet.

TJEKANOVA, O., URUSOVA, G., and PRIJAMURSKI, G. 2000. *Det kejserliga St: Petersburg*. Jyväskylä: Gummerus.

WALLERSTEIN, I. 1974. *The Modern World Systems*. New York: Academic Press.

WATKINS, S. 2004. Vichy on the Tigris. *New Left Review*, 28: 5–17.

WEBB, M. 1990. *The City Square*. London: Thames and Hudson.

WHITELEY, P., and SEYD, P. 2003. How to win a landslide election by really trying: the effects of local campaigning on voting in the 1997 British general election. *Electoral Studies*, 22: 301–24.

YARBOROUGH, J. M. 1998. *American Virtues: Thomas Jefferson and the Character of a Free People*. Lawrence: University Press of Kansas.

ZELLER, O. 2003. La Ville Moderne. Vol. 2: 595–860 in *Histoire de l'Europe urbaine*, ed. J.-L.Pinol. Paris: Seuil.

ZUKIN, S. 1991. *Landscapes of Power: From Detroit to Disneyworld*. Berkeley: University of California Press.

CHAPTER 28

....

DETECTING THE SIGNIFICANCE OF PLACE

....

R. BIN WONG

"PLACE" is difficult to define. Even more difficult is establishing criteria for its significance in political processes. Unless we can detect the significance of place in political processes and outcomes, spatial specificities easily reduce to idiosyncratic features with little if any analytical relevance. This chapter first briefly reviews some of the challenges faced in defining place and offers a few examples of the significance some analysts have assigned to place. It proposes a strategy for detecting different features to what initially seem to be similar situations, in order to suggest how an attention to place can help us explain variations in political outcomes when many features of the situations would lead us to expect the same kinds.

1 SOME PROBLEMS AND POSSIBILITIES FOR ANALYZING PLACE

....

All political processes are empirically grounded in some place, but much analysis of both processes and outcomes in political science proceeds without close specification of place. Key explanatory variables are usually assumed to be constant across place. This does not necessarily mean that processes and outcomes are assumed to be universal. It does however mean that political processes and outcomes are usually thought to fall into a few possible groups.

To suggest that place influences either political processes or outcomes could mean that analysts have in mind one or more specific traits of a situation that can influence the object of study. For instance, features of a place can matter to political behavior because of ecological characteristics or social characteristics. Charles Tilly's (1964) classic study of the 1793 counter-revolution in western France's Vendée demonstrated how protests in this part of France against the Revolution were reactions to urbanization broadly conceived with attendant changes in the commercial economy and efforts by the state to extend its reach; an intensive analysis of archival data from southern Anjou shows a series of differences between those places that supported the Revolution and those that did not, including characteristics of farming families and their production, the conditions of the weaving industry, and the structure of towns and roles of the bourgeois who lived in them.

Another French example, considerably more urban than Tilly's and published three decades later by the late Roger Gould (1995), shows how the spatial bases of social organization for major Paris political protests in the mid and late nineteenth centuries changed with the physical changes made to the urbanscape by French architects and administrators. In 1848 workers of a common craft or trade lived in the same neighborhood; in addition to sharing a workplace they shared recreational space at cafes and cabarets. Two decades later, the building of major boulevards destroyed neighborhoods and pushed workers to newly incorporated municipal frontiers where workers of different trades lived amidst other kinds of people who joined them on the basis of neighborhood ties to resist the government and form the Paris Commune of 1871. The organization of urban space of course matters to political conflicts and social movements in other parts of the world as well, whether we move to medieval Flanders or contemporary Beijing (Boone 2002; Zhao 1998).

Place can mean several things in the analysis of political processes and outcomes. It can refer both to a set of substantive traits such as natural environment and ecology, social structures and organizations, or belief systems and popular culture, and also to relational features linking one place to others of an economic, political, cultural, or social variety; relational features link places in some mix of horizontal and vertical ways—the market exchange norm of neoclassical economics would be the horizontal ideal and the bureaucratic integration of political space from an administrative center would be a vertical norm of spatial relations. Notions of place in different analyses of political processes and outcomes can be quite different from each other. Particular elements of place involve subjects treated separately in other sections of this volume, including "ideas," "culture," and "history."

Thomas Gieryn (2000) has offered a taxonomy of three kinds of place. First, place is a "geographic location" ranging in scale from rooms in a building to a planet in the solar system. Second, it is a "material" form, created by people's activities. Third, place is a "symbolic" form, given subjective meanings and personal value by people who recognize it as more than just a geographic location or site of activities. For Gieryn all three elements of place need to be present for a space to meet his criteria of a "place." While this strategy has the advantage of defining place so that it cannot be reduced to some subset of its component elements, it also has a couple of possible disadvantages. First, Gieryn restricts the concept of place to only those spaces that agents themselves label and recognize, yet one could well imagine cases where either locational or material features of place matter to political processes and outcomes without the space being invested with symbolic value by the actors themselves. Second, the analyst often wants to be able to compare places—to evaluate their connections or to sort through their similarities and differences as possible indicators for how political processes will unfold and what kinds of outcomes are most likely, irrespective of the different personal meanings of place that actors in different settings create.

Gieryn's three elements of place each has its own range of subjects that are sometimes joined together in particular research efforts. The kinds of themes raised for place as a symbolic form include places of commemoration and memory, as well as religious sites. Powerful agents often control or expect to control sites rich in symbolic significance—governments forge many sites of commemoration, while religious establishments typically manage important sacred sites. Places with symbolic value are also sites for competition and contention, in particular those rich with symbols of political power and authority, such as Tiananmen in Beijing, where the 1989 democracy demonstrations were the most recent large-scale challenge to the state (Esherick and Wasserstrom 1990). When looking at places rich in symbolic significance, the particular histories and memories associated with each are distinct, but they all act as stages on which celebrations and competitions occur. How these celebrations or competitions fit into larger political processes and the kinds of outcomes that obtain cannot be anticipated from characteristics of the place itself. Rather it is the situating of the symbolic form of place in a larger context that shapes political possibilities.

In contrast, when we think about the other two kinds of place highlighted by Gieryn's definition, geographic and material, differences in the nature of place can help us anticipate characteristics of political processes and outcomes. Paying attention to place as an explicit category, rather than looking separately at the varied elements that go into making a particular place, makes sense because it points us to clusters of features that jointly define conditions that otherwise would not be recognized as related, let alone as necessarily important to explaining political processes and outcomes.

I turn to geographical and material aspects of place in the next sections, and in a final section I sketch a strategy for detecting different features of what initially seem to be similar situations, in order to suggest how attention to place can help explain variations in outcomes when many features of the situations would lead us to expect the same kinds of political outcomes. The places to be examined—China as a whole and Europe as a whole—are far larger than those usually considered in analyses addressing place. But I shall apply the same principle that is usually applied on smaller spatial scales of distinguishing among places according to certain key features that some of them share and others do not. For both small-scale social conflicts and larger-scale political processes I will suggest that the relative importance of interest-based negotiations and belief-inspired choices varies among places, and that examples of very broad contrasts can be drawn from Chinese and European experiences as historically distinct and separate sets, each composed of its own similar places.

2   PLACE AS A GEOGRAPHICAL LOCATION

Most analyses of political processes and outcomes for which we can identify some kind of place compare or contrast places that are related to each other. For instance, G. William Skinner (1977) has argued that the relative importance of fiscal and military responsibilities in late imperial Chinese local administration varied with the location of the county post on the administrative hierarchy—counties nearer the center were richer and expected to yield more taxes, while those on the peripheries had greater military defense responsibilities; I have suggested that the relative importance of officials and local elites in financing and managing certain types of granaries and schools varied according to the economic wealth of a county and thus its geographic location: the richer the county, the more likely officials relied on elites to take on these kinds of public responsibilities (Wong 1997a). Certain political and economic traits of space vary systematically and thus make location an important predictor of the traits a particular place will have. More complex analyses of political space have been made for the study of Europe, many of them inspired by Stein Rokkan's analyses of Europe's changing territorial structure, including studies of national states as well as the territorial systems that predated the construction of these states (Flora 1999). Some studies of European state-making stress the particular ways in which space is defined in the process of modern state formation (Biggs 1999). Studies of Asian state-making cases have both shown the difficulties of moving from older conceptions of space to newer notions brought in from Europe, and argued that cartography was used to map space and assert territorial control much as they were in European cases (Winichakul 1994; Hostetler 2001).

At least two features of place as geographical locations deserve our attention. First, the traits of place that matter here can be both substantive and relational: substantive because certain aspects are rooted in place such as the real or potential use of a navigable river and relational because they depend on flows of people, ideas, or resources to and from different points. Second, the Chinese examples just given stress hierarchical types of space but many spatial schemes are more horizontal in character—economic exchange between major regional markets, or diplomatic relations among states of roughly similar capacities and intentions.

3   PLACE AS A HUMAN PROJECT AND AS A POLITICAL OBJECT

The examples given above stress the ways in which geographical location, in terms of the particular resources of the location or its relation to other places, shapes what human activity is likely to produce politically, economically, and socially. Place in Gieryn's sense of material form highlights the creation of place by human activities.

Geographer John Agnew has recently offered an analysis of Italian politics, especially since the Second World War, with explicit and central attention to place largely in the sense of Gieryn's material form. For Agnew (2002, 217), "Politics is structured through the places people make in their transactions with one another—local, regional, national, and wider." People are related to each other through networks, which have defined territorial dimensions. "In other words, it is by means of the social experiences and institutional opportunities of the places they inhabit that people construct the reasons and emotions that either encourage or inhibit particular identities and interests" (Agnew 2002, 218). For Agnew place defines a range of locations where politics occur; specific places are socially constituted by the human activities that flow through networks of interaction.

Some places are clearly defined contiguous physical spaces like a European coffee house or Chinese teahouse. The European place is a site for Jurgen Habermas's (1989) eighteenth-century public sphere where urban people gather to discuss political issues involving their rulers, while Chinese teahouses of the same period more commonly hosted conversations about marriage proposals and commercial possibilities (Wang 2000). Other places take on their meaning from their position in larger geographical spaces given human definition by social connections of one kind or another. Chinese worshipping at a common Buddhist temple, or at one of several temples belonging to a particular sect, shared places that could serve as sites for believers to engage not only in religious rituals, but to mobilize for protests against local officials or organize to pursue a common project such as irrigation works. Europeans whose churches formed a focal point for local community were also subordinated to religious hierarchies within which their priests or pastors participated. Chinese religious places were more autonomous. In contrast, political hierarchy was far more developed in China, creating bureaucratically defined spaces and places on scales far beyond the most successful early modern European state-makers.

James Scott (1999) has identified important features of places that are subjected to outside political control, a feature common to all places larger than a city-state. In order to rule, states must create legible locales; in order to make places understandable, they have to collect and order limited amounts of information that allow them to exert control. The cost of such legibility is the state's inability to monitor let alone manipulate effectively the far larger amounts of information that are generated by people in the course of constructing their daily spaces and filling them with activity. There is an information asymmetry generated by state efforts to create legible locales. As a result, local knowledge that makes particular places work and survive is beyond the grasp of state representatives. The gap between local practices and central understandings sets boundaries to what states can effectively do to rule despite their aspirations to be more controlling; Scott suggests ways in which specific locales are distinct if not unique, and thus that place matters greatly to understanding how political processes unfold and what outcomes obtain. Scott stresses the general situation of "seeing like a state" and the very local particularities of specific cases. In between these two extremes we might be able to characterize relations between central states and locales according to the strategies of each to cope with the challenges and opportunities the other poses. In other words, to what extent do states recognize the limits created by their desires for legibility, and how does their understanding of the problem affect their strategies of rule? How do local people create spaces for their own practices that can go on unimpeded by the state?

Consider again China. One of the long-standing strategies of Chinese states in late imperial as well as contemporary times has been to expect local governments to interpret general directives in ways that reflect local conditions. When thinking of making policy changes, the central government has often begun by creating experimental cases to observe outcomes, both intended and unintended. Finally, Chinese central governments also evaluate local initiatives and consider their potential relevance to larger numbers of places. For their part, local Chinese leaders and common people, today as in the past, usually aim to keep their activities from attracting notice of a government they know to be too distant to maintain routine surveillance. Upsetting this stable accommodation of incomplete knowledge since 1949 have been moments of mass political movements when the government makes demands of people throughout society and pressures them to conform in behavior and supply information that confirms state priorities, be these economic targets during the Great Leap Forward or political reorganization during the Cultural Revolution.

4   PLACE IN HORIZONTALLY AND VERTICALLY STRUCTURED SPACE

Relations between places can be either hierarchical, horizontal, or some mix of the two. The political examples just recounted above are clearly vertically linked with the locales having their own distinct, more horizontal sets of linkages to define them as places. Economic examples based on markets are also both horizontal and vertical. Social protests and movements have been related to a combination of economic and political changes, first in European history and then elsewhere. For instance, E. P. Thompson's (1971) classic study of the moral economy of the English crowd depicts the competing world-views of protestors seeking to protect their customary claims on local food supplies in times of dearth, against merchants and officials aiming to ensure the continued movement of grain from producing areas to consuming areas. For Thompson, a new capitalist market ideology accompanied the commercial penetration of the countryside by merchants supported by the government. Later scholarship raised the importance of "community" rather than "class" to explain the actions of protestors, leading to some work that showed what types of places were more likely to be sites for contention over food supply issues than others. Historian John Bohstedt (1983) found more violent actions in industrial towns than in market towns, which he attributed to the disruptive effects of industrialization and urbanization. Geographer Andrew Charlesworth (1993) has put popular disturbances into regional contexts and identified the kinds of local networks of solidarity that made protests possible. Place matters in terms of the kinds of social networks that are possible and these vary through space.

One could expect contests over food to be a more general diagnostic for commercial penetration of rural areas and the formation of central governments wishing to promote economic integration to support urbanization and industrialization. Yet if we turn to conflicts over food in China we do not find the same sequence of large-scale changes. In Chinese cases as well, contests over food supplies were a kind of conflict particular to certain kinds of economic and political conditions—supply instabilities, people with expectations of both merchants and officials to ensure their local needs, and a willingness and ability to protest when others did not act as those threatened with insufficient food deemed proper. In

Europe, as the institutional capacities of commerce and the productivity of agriculture made possible the more effective supply of grain and bread to consumers close to and far from points of production, people became less likely to block grain shipments or demand cheaper bread; they accepted the fact that money was needed to buy bread in a market economy and therefore organized to secure wages they deemed desirable. More generally, through much of the research on changing forms of collective action attending the development of capitalism and the formation of national states in the nineteenth century, there has been a focus on how people are able to express interests and bargain with economic and political authorities (Wong 1997*b*: 209–29). When we compare protests over food supplies in China and Europe, important differences emerge regarding the capacities of participants to bargain.

5   TYPES OF BARGAINING AND STRATEGIES
OF CONTROL

The key differences are not due to the likely use of coercive force, which of course limits the abilities of participants to bargain, but which exists everywhere. Rather, the differences reside in the ways that competing interests are linked to the expression of beliefs and ideology.

While E. P. Thompson may have exaggerated the degree to which a "moral economy" of popular protest contrasted with a political economy of commercialization, people were clear about articulating their immediate interests and these interests differed from those of officials who supported the formation of larger food supply markets. Central governments in England and France supported the "free" flow of food. Central government officials in the Chinese empire in contrast were ambivalent about free flows of grain. In general they supported movements of grain according to supply and demand conditions, but they simultaneously believed that people, urban and rural, throughout the empire should enjoy subsistence security against harvest shortfalls. The different interests of officials and the people they ruled were subordinated to a common ideology asserting political responsibility for subsistence security.

This submersion of interests under paternalistic beliefs applied more generally to political process in late imperial China to suggest a larger contrast between the general Chinese and European situations. The Chinese did not move to interest-based negotiations in political practice that could be distilled at the level of political principles into social contract theory. Instead, the Chinese affirmed a set of Confucian principles and expectations of paternalist support. When elites or common people found themselves in situations where their interests diverged from those of the state, they usually sought ways to avoid officials, their scrutiny, or their demands. They could succeed in this general approach because the imperial state lacked the bureaucratic capacity to reach systematically and routinely into the villages spread across a vast agrarian empire. As a result, officials, elites, and common people did not develop strategies of negotiation.

Political processes in nineteenth-century China and Europe were very different. The absence of much interest-based negotiations in late imperial China made possible Chinese government reliance on methods of social control conceptualized and acted upon in major ways at a later time in European history. Chinese officials and elites pursued a Confucian cultural hegemony that defined the categories through which people understood social responsibilities and political possibilities. These practices undermine a conventional view of belief-centered technologies of social control that span the state and a broader domain of politics outside the government. Based on an examination of European evidence such technologies of social control have often been identified as initially distinctive features of the West, especially during the twentieth century, in Foucault's concepts of "discipline" and "governmentality" and by scholars using Gramsci's notion of "hegemony." The European state's nineteenth-century efforts at cultural education strike analysts as a key feature of the modern state (Lloyd and Thomas 1997). Such moves handicap our abilities to detect the significance of place because they fail to look seriously at what exists outside Europe before Europeans arrive as major influences, or to consider the possibilities that political activities deemed to be features of modern Europe existed in other contexts before they became part of European politics.

6 INTERESTS AND BELIEFS

The contrast of Chinese and European political processes in terms of the conceptual salience of interests and beliefs suggests that some important features of the specificity of a particular place to political processes might be predicted according to the relative importance of interests versus beliefs in defining relations between political actors. Places where the explicit articulation of interests looms large are likely those in which democratic engagements and outcomes are also more likely. In contrast, places where interests are obscured by statements of belief can either be ones that encourage people to satisfy their interests indirectly or places where threats of coercion make public acceptance of dominant beliefs necessary.

For instance, the processes and outcomes of social movements in North American and Western European contexts have generally differed from those in China. Social movements in Western settings have typically pushed particular interests and achieved specific goals, such as the vote, first for women and then for blacks. Social movements are tied to interest-group politics and occupy a space in democratic politics, as James Morone has demonstrated for the US case (Morone 1998). In China social movements have protested government actions, such as signing the Versailles Peace Treaty at the conclusion of the First World War, but these movements did not produce institutional reforms because the sets of policies and institutions that make this possible do not exist. Moreover, the communists developed distinctive abilities to mount movements both before and after they came to power in 1949. Communist-led social movements after 1949, most visibly the Great Leap Forward and the Cultural Revolution, submerge interests beneath the rhetoric of political belief reinforced by threats of coercion. Social movements thus differ according to place within American and Chinese settings. One diagnostic of the differences turns on the relative salience of interests and beliefs.

Interests and beliefs figure more generally in political processes associated with citizenship and nations. Citizenship is often conceived in one of two ways. On one hand, citizenship is a relationship between the state and individuals based on a negotiated bundle of rights and responsibilities; on the other hand, citizens are members of a nation who believe in a shared past and aspire to a common future. The distinction does not mean of course that people who pursue interests do not have beliefs, nor that those who express beliefs do not also have interests. Rather, the distinction is intended to characterize relations among actors rather than attributes each of them may have. When actors engage each other on the basis of interests, they negotiate. When they interact according to beliefs, acts of persuasion become more salient.

People pursuing interest-based negotiations and those following belief-inspired actions, like the governments they engage, are aware of and sometimes connected to larger political networks than people in these same places were in earlier times. "Places" change because of the influence of ideas and institutions originating elsewhere. But new possibilities do not necessarily mean previous ideas and institutions suddenly lose meaning or stop having consequences. Changes in discourse can largely reframe existing interests in new rhetoric, recast political action in terms of new beliefs, or some combination of the two so that people perceive their relations to others in new ways. These are acts of translation creating new meanings for the participants, the significance of which for political processes and outcomes depends on how differently they wish to act and can act. Place becomes no less specific for its connections to other areas; instead the characteristics of place are changed by their connections. For instance, the concept of "citizen" was introduced into Chinese political discourse in the late nineteenth century and became associated with ideas about revitalizing people to serve the nation more effectively in the early twentieth century. "Citizens" had duties to the nation but little was said about "rights" before the First World War. "Citizens" were those individuals who recognized the changed nature of their obligations to society and addressed their concerns to their government. In principle these new "citizens" believed they had the same concerns as their government for national salvation. They did not imagine themselves to be pursuing interests distinct from those of the state, as they hoped it would act. Twentieth-century governments in China, however, have wanted their citizens to be loyal subjects committed to the patriotic tasks set for them by the state. We can compare the Chinese case with others by first asking how state and subject relate in terms of interests and beliefs. We can thus gain a sense of the relevance of place to political processes and outcomes. Searching for ways to delve beneath the common elements of twentieth-century discourse to consider how concepts are translated to new semantic contexts and into political practice means addressing place as significant to both processes and outcomes.

Some places are more likely to be sites of negotiation based on interests, while others are more likely to be situations where belief-based acts of persuasion are common. In reality the spectrum between two extremes of relations conducted according to interests or beliefs has an array of possibilities. To look more closely at "interests," the successful pursuit of interests and negotiated compromise by both citizens and their governments depends on the quality of knowledge each party has. In some instances it is difficult to predict outcomes based on the amount of knowledge someone seeking to act on his interests can muster; alternatively, actors can decide they will tolerate a certain level of uncertainty because the costs of procuring additional information is deemed too expensive. In democracies and under authoritarian regimes officials face related problems of seeking to make policy decisions with incomplete knowledge about the impacts their decisions will have. Both citizens and their governments face challenges that derive from incomplete knowledge.

7   POLITICAL PROBLEMS OF PLACE

Place varies according to how the challenges of incomplete knowledge are expressed and addressed. Information on choices can be asymmetric and this can influence the decisions people make—some Russians voting in the 1990s favored the return of the Communists, not because they were necessarily better but they were more predictable than the people who replaced them. People had more confidence in the expected values of Communist rule than they did in the relatively untried alternatives associated with considerable chaos.

Rational choice axioms work best when people conceive issues as interests and thus can calculate choices. When issues are cast in terms of beliefs, explicit choice sets are often reduced and actors engage each other more through acts of persuasion and coercion and efforts at escape. Or so it might seem. One can, for instance, distinguish political situations in which citizens can negotiate with their governments about their interests on a routine basis from the very different situation in which people have no rights and no abilities to engage authorities directly, and instead utilize what James Scott has called the "weapons of the weak" (Scott 1985). The weak reject tacitly the claims and demands of the hegemonic powers, on occasion quietly expressing counter-hegemonic beliefs of their own; they sometimes work as slowly as they can, misreport information when they find it safe to do so, and generally protect their own interests, not through negotiation but through the rejection of authority as legitimate. The contrast between these situations and those under democratic regimes, however, becomes less obvious when we see that both individuals and corporations in the United States engage in tax fraud, perhaps more often than they seek to change taxation policy through open processes of negotiation.

If political relationships among governments and their subjects (and in modern times their citizens) vary according to the ways in which interests and beliefs get used by different actors, we have at least a partial guide to some of the kinds of places in which political processes take place, often with different outcomes despite certain other similarities. Other chapters in this volume argue for the importance of contextual explanations as an alternative to either general covering law-type propositions or the opposite extreme of contingent constructions. In their introduction to the volume Charles Tilly and Robert Goodin counsel us to look for "mechanisms" that work in specific situations. We might discover similar mechanisms lead to different outcomes in different places. I am suggesting that the mechanisms at work in a particular process like a contest over food supplies may be very similar at the most local level, but as we add larger contextual frames, we can detect how place makes a difference to the outcomes of what appear initially to be similar events. Rather than expect similar political processes to be at work everywhere or to the contrary to argue that all processes are situated in their own particular genealogical sequences, we could find ways of identifying what is similar and different about various places and armed with that knowledge track larger and smaller political processes of democratization, social identity formation, social movements, and protests.

REFERENCES

AGNEW, J. 2002. *Place and Politics in Modern Italy*. Chicago: University of Chicago Press.
BIGGS, M. 1999. Putting the state on the map: cartography, territory, and European state formation. *Comparative Studies in Society and History*, 41: 374–405.

BOHSTEDT, J. 1983. *Riots and Community Politics in England and Wales, 1790–1810*. Cambridge, Mass.: Harvard University Press.

BOONE, M. 2002. Urban space and political conflict in late medieval Flanders. *Journal of Interdisciplinary History*, 32: 621–40.

CHARLESWORTH, A. 1993. From the moral economy of Devon to the political economy of Manchester, 1790–1812. *Social History*, 18: 205–17.

ESHERICK, J. W., and WASSERSTROM, J. N. 1990. Acting out democracy: political theater in modern China. *Journal of Asian Studies*, 49: 835–65.

FLORA, P. (ed.) 1999. *State Formation, Nation-Building, and Mass Politics in Europe: The Theory of Stein Rokkan*. Oxford: Oxford University Press.

GIERYN, T. 2000. A space for place in sociology. *Annual Review of Sociology*, 26: 463–506.

GOULD, R. 1995. *Insurgent Identities: Class, Community, and Protest in Paris from 1848 to the Commune*. Chicago: University of Chicago Press.

HABERMAS, J. 1989. *The Structural Transformation of the Public Sphere*. Cambridge, Mass.: MIT Press.

HOSTETLER, L. 2001. *Qing Colonial Enterprise: Ethnography and Cartography in Early Modern China*. Chicago: University of Chicago Press.

LLOYD, D., and THOMAS, P. 1997. *Culture and the State*. Routledge.

MORONE, J. 1998. *The Democratic Wish: Popular Participation and the Limits of American Government*, rev. edn. New Haven, Conn.: Yale University Press.

SCOTT, J. C. 1985. *Weapons of the Weak: Everyday forms of Peasant Resistance*. New Haven, Conn.: Yale University Press.

——1999. *Seeing Like a State*. New Haven, Conn.: Yale University Press.

SKINNER, G. W. 1977. Cities and the hierarchy of local system. Pp. 275–351 in *The City in Late Imperial China*, ed. G. W. Skinner. Stanford, Calif.: Stanford University Press.

THOMPSON, E. P. 1971. The moral economy of the English crowd in the eighteenth century. *Past & Present*, 50: 76–136.

TILLY, C. 1964. *The Vendée*. Cambridge, Mass.: Harvard University Press.

WANG, D. 2000. The idle and the busy: teahouses and public life in early twentieth-century Chengdu. *Journal of Urban History*, 26: 411–37.

WINICHAKUL, T. 1994. *Siam Mapped: A History of the Geo-Body of a Nation*. Honolulu: University of Hawaii Press.

WONG, R. B. 1997a. Confucian agendas for material and ideological control in modern China. In *Culture and State in Chinese History*, ed. T. Huters, R. B. Wong, and P. Yu. Stanford, Calif.: Stanford University Press.

——1997b. *China Transformed: Historical Change and the Limits of European Experience*. Ithaca, NY: Cornell University Press.

ZHAO, D. 1998. Ecologies of social movements: student mobilization during the 1989 prodemocracy movement in Beijing. *American Journal of Sociology*, 103: 1493–529.

CHAPTER 29

SPACE, PLACE, AND TIME

NIGEL J. THRIFT

THIS chapter is an attempt to review and synthesize work that is currently going on in human geography and other areas of social science which addresses the questions of space, place, and time as cultural processes of spatial and temporal formation. It is not a comprehensive review by any means. That would involve negotiating so many different topics that include space and time in some shape, form, or dimension—from the many and various templates provided by electoral geography, including gerrymandering and various forms of pork barrelling, through the ambitions of socialist planning and now capitalist forms of market integration like logistics and geodemographics which, with more or less ideological fuss, attempt to forge space and time into a predictable set of places within which predictable subjects can be forged, to the variegated pattern of all manner of riots and protests, all the way from the small, spontaneous demonstration to the coordinated mayhem of many global protests—that I would rapidly run out of space, as well as severely testing the reader's attention span.

Instead, what I want to do is point to some of the key *questions* that arise when space and time are treated not just as passive dimensions which have to be transcended but as constitutive elements of the work of political relation. In turn, I will argue that treating space and time as *active* constituents of political relation points towards new kinds of politics which are not just derivative of political forces but represent new and vibrant political terrains and gains. In other words, my intention is to help to galvanize political theory and practice, in the sense that I want to both rematerialize them and simultaneously make them open to more.

To this end, the chapter is in three main parts. In the first part, I will discuss the nature of space and time as a constituent rather than a secondary part of social process through a brief history of contemporary geography. Given the constraints of space, the subsequent parts of the chapter provide two synoptic cuts into the active spatial and temporal nature of contemporary politics and political process. Thus, in the second part of the chapter, I will discuss how space and time intervene in the practice of politics via a discussion of the new forms of territory that are now making themselves known. Amongst other issues, I want to concentrate on the topic of scale. I want to argue that little and large are becoming outmoded terms that no longer make much sense. It is difficult to make out what they might mean. Other terms are becoming current which, though they lack clarity, may well prove more incisive. Then, in the third part of the chapter, I will consider the new kinds of *politics of credence* that have been able to heave in to view which rely on the manipulation of the micro-fabric of space and time in order to maximize an affective bounty, and which should surely be given more attention by political theorists than has so far been the case. In a sense, these affective politics form a fresh political territory. Finally, I offer some brief conclusions.

Throughout the chapter, my concern will be to demonstrate three main things. The first is the continuing importance of political *invention*. There is no reason to believe that the political sphere is any more devoid of innovation than any other sphere of human life, all the way from the invention of democracy through the invention of the nation state, to the invention of the network of network institutions and standards of governance that characterize a good part of the world today. Then, second, that politics cannot therefore be assumed to have a stable content. Though this has become something of a truism, still it is important to state again that the study of politics cannot be reduced to what constitutes political discourse at any particular time. Politics escapes stable categorizations. Third, I will want to argue, very much in the spirit of this *Handbook*, that contextual political analysis is the only meaningful form of political analysis and that this principle should be engrained in the practices of political theory. One reason is a simple operational point. The conduct of contemporary politics takes place at many sites, not all of which are labeled "political" but many of which have political intent nonetheless. Barry (2001, 205) describes this process of displacement thus:

While they may be crucial in the contemporary configuration of government, the development of technical standards, environmental regulations and intellectual property law are, with a few exceptions, conducted between technical specialists, bureaucrats and industrial lobbyists. In these circumstances, the oppositional politics of a technological society are displaced elsewhere, emerging, often unexpectedly, at the many sites of scientific and technical practice: the laboratory conducting animal experiments; the construction site of a road or dam; the experimental farm; the psychiatric ward; or the polluting chemical plant. In a technological society, students of politics need to focus their attention not just on the formal centres of political authority but on the many sites where political action comes to circulate. It is from such sites, as Ulrich Beck has suggested, that politics may come to *flood* across many other fields.

The other reason is an ethical point: the alternative to contextual political analysis too often enshrines particular unacknowledged political geographies which simply mirror the concerns of the powerful and institute a deadly dynamic of *forgotten places* which act as a kind of suppressed repressed in ways that are increasingly untenable, not least because many of these forgotten places have found ways to deliver scattered but deadly reminders of their existence. This is a point I will return to in the concluding part of this chapter.

1   THE NATURE OF SPACE AND TIME

There are certain field disciplines which have had to grapple more than most with the issue of site, disciplines like archaeology, anthropology, and geography. For a long time, these disciplines occupied something of a marginal position. They often seemed to other disciplines to be caught in the intellectual doldrums—hopelessly empirical gatherers of facts, out of touch with grand theoretical currents. Though this was never true, it was the case that these disciplines had their difficulties in belonging to the mainstream of social science. One of the reasons for this was that their relationship with theory was fraught: theory seemed to act as a means of washing away the detail which they considered to be both a constitutional impera- tive and a means of living. Then, the knowledge that they had gathered (very often as artefacts) was caught up in imperial missions, often with their own geometries of power. Many theories often seemed, in both their ambition and scale, uncannily to repeat that mission. One more problem was provisionality. To many writers in these disciplines it was clear that the events that they studied were not caught in some determinate aspic but could have gone many ways, sometimes indeed on a whim. And, in turn, out of the turning points of these events (insofar as these could ever be identified) vast new chains of events followed. This had been a favorite debate of history but with geography added in the story became not just more complex but also more difficult to represent. And finally, they had developed methods of close study of communities which, from ethnography to fieldwork, forced them to cope with detail as other than an incidental illustration. Detail was not a form of contingency. It was not a means of stirring in uncertainty. It was something that had to be taken into theory as the speaking of the world. In turn, these disciplines had therefore been forced to factor space and time into their writings right from the start. Space and time were not frames. They were the means by which it became possible to listen to and teach ourselves to them. For a time, this seemed to mean that these disciplines occupied an uneasy ground, one in which either vast cosmologies were spun from the smallest details or micro-studies were constructed whose motivation was simply to illustrate grand theoretical categories. But that has changed.

The case of geography is an interesting example of this process in action.[1] Geographers began reimporting theory into their discipline in the revolutionary 1960s, and so in the main that theory took the guise of Marxism. But it soon became clear that such a simple act of importation would not do. Such grand theory suffered from a chronic lack of fit in that it seemed to explain everything but only by denying any other kinds of differences other than the ones it had pre-legislated, differences which were apparent to geographers on a daily basis in their work (Massey and Thrift 2003). Through the 1970s, 1980s, and 1990s there has been an often painful period of rewriting of theory so that it is able to go with the spatio-temporal grain of the world. This involved initially promiscuous but then increasingly selective acts of theoretical importation and synthesis, resulting in a sophisticated theoretical discourse carried out in journals like *Society and Space*. This discourse has involved an increasing range of political imperatives that have each made their mark on theory, from feminist claims through work on ethnicity and identity through to current work on how the claims of entities like animals can be given a voice. And, most encouragingly, it has involved an increasingly interdisciplinary focus as the spatial turn across the social sciences has given the theoretical writings of geographers a constituency and has begun to produce a true interdisciplinary conversation, not least with political scientists intent on rematerializing their discipline. For example, most recently a fascinating strand of work has grown up around the prospect of doing ethnographies of networks. Starting in conventional sociological territory with the ideas of networks as connections between individuals traced out through interviews, there are now attempts to understand networks as simultaneously other forms of subjectivity and forms of analytical commitment. The interesting question then becomes what terms should we use to describe this subjectivity, and why does it describe itself as a network? What new forms of advocacy has it engendered? What productive effects, intended and unintended, does this modality of presentation have? And what might an ethnography of such an object consist of?[2]

---

[1] State-of-the-art reviews can be found in Anderson et al. (2003); Duncan, Johnson, and Schein (2004); and Thrift and Whatmore (2004).

[2] Cf.: Riles 2001; Bornstein 2003; Holmes 2000; Fortun 2000; Ong and Collier 2004.

What this and other examples show is that, across the social sciences, we can see space and time taking on a number of roles. First, they stand for particular ambitions. So, they stand for those who want to see the world as a tapestry of spaces and times which may enshrine difference or equally may result from structured processes (such as the accumulation of capital) which may themselves still produce difference, wittingly or unwittingly. Of these diverse spaces and times, perhaps the most striking addition of late is a global sense of place which is simultaneously a process of homogenization and diversification of identity. Then, they stand for those in these disciplines who want to work with a notion of societies as made up of a diversity of material things which are part and parcel of how societies go forward and not just incidental transmitters of "culture," as found in areas as diverse as actor–network theory, the sociology of science, studies of material culture (taking in studies of consumption, in particular), and so on. Such an approach sees material things as constitutive. For example, items like the passport are not seen as just representative of the state but as means by which the state has been able to come in to existence and continues to reproduce its many selves (Torpey 2000). Then, they stand for those who believe that the singularity of the event is not just a unique empirical formation but can be theoretically investigated by using new theoretical infrastructures, such as found in the work of Deleuze. In turn, such work has pointed to the ways in which the background assumptions about what will turn up are changing, producing a new arena of political attention; attention itself. And, finally, they stand for those who want to take the apparatuses by which space and time is built up seriously. That might mean taking up the political ramifications of all manner of communications media in the construction of empire,[3] or it might mean more fully taking in the burgeoning literature on speed (Dillon 1996) as it has moved on from crude characterizations like time–space compression or Virilio-like hyperbole, or it might mean considering the politics of space and time as a politics in its own right, from the gradual standardization of space and time through the actions of a vast number of international committees through to the politics of milliseconds that have occupied those designing the various versions of the Internet.

To summarize the story so far. Space and time are no longer seen as a passive backdrop to human endeavor. Rather, they are seen as the stuff of human endeavor, resulting in a background which is our assumption about how the world is, a background of spaces which can be measured out and times which turn up on time which are a part of the spread of industrialized modes of spatial and temporal production that can be held responsible for the vast swathes of urban space which have been added to the world in the last fifty years and which now, seen from space, light up large parts of the world. Lefebvre took this vast urbanized space as evidence that space was increasingly produced in much the same way as factories produce

---

[3] A topic which had an early progenitor in political history in the work of Harold Innis.

cars. And he believed that something was being lost as a result which could only be regained by isolated acts of resistance. That something was place.

In turn, we can argue that this longing for something lost has led to much of the language of *place* that we so often deploy today. In geography, place is a beginning and an end. It is one of those words—rather like "political"—that sets off a flurry of expectations, most of which are never fully satisfied, in the same way that nostalgia is never what it used to be. Roughly speaking, however, we can argue that geographers usually mean place to signify spaces that are loaded with an extra significance, that are "sticky" in some way. Usually this stickiness takes three forms. First, it can be taken to have a phenomenological twist: place is a way of conveying something like a Heideggerian background and can, in line with this theoretical lineage, resonate according to the way in which embodied presentation in practices is more or less aligned and so produces a more or less authentic sensory experience. Second, it can be taken to convey the ways in which spaces do not only operate in the present in a world of immediate cause and effect, but can also appeal to what Nora (1996) calls a second register of cultural propriety that has been carefully constructed through numerous projects, many of whose founding impulses have been long forgotten and yet whose symbols still retain grip. In other words, place acts as the symbolic overlay over space, producing a meaningful landscape of signs nurtured over time and producing spaces of cultural significance which may be elevated or mundane, but which are always sites about which people care and which they will want to invest in. Then, finally, place can be taken to be a set of refrains which circulate among spaces producing rising and falling intensities, gradually establishing a territory which may be permanent or fleeting but which always demands that notice be taken.

2   THE LANGUAGE OF TERRITORY

The sheer variety of concerns that can be placed under the rubric of space, place, and time should give us some pause for thought: one of the difficulties—and opportunities—of the turn to space and time in politics is that it considerably broadens what can be regarded as political, as it takes in complexities which have often heretofore been brushed over as second order. Politics is understood as made up of a whole series of zones and sites which may suffer all kinds of rigidities and instabilities in practice but are still often represented as homogeneous in public discourse. This is particularly the case so far as the geography of politics is concerned, where it is often claimed that smooth and well-connected zones called territories exist which on closer inspection turn out to be anything but. Rather that claim tends to be part of a continuing effort of rhetorical-cum-material integration.

That said, in many ways, for a contextual political analyst an abiding concern must still be with territory and in this section I want to consider the practice of territorialization in more detail. It certainly cannot be denied that boundary-making in order to produce territory is a key element of human political behavior and has been the backbone of war and other kinds of state-making down the ages (Mann 1993). But, in recent times, it has become clear that many different kinds of political spaces now vie for existence, only one of which is the nested hierarchical territory of the nation state—which in any case is a relatively recent invention in most parts of the world. In this second section, I therefore want to consider other kinds of space/time/place that are now coming to constitute a kind of permanent political shadow world as a result of the institution of new kinds of political *machine*, technologies of government that utilize a range of techniques to produce collective arrangements of bodies, artefacts, instruments, and discourses which go to make up what we call persons and institutions of various kinds, and which are therefore political right from their inception (Barry 2001; Mitchell 2002). These machines have a number of important characteristics, of which I will mention four.

1. They are orderings, not orders. They are continually on the move, deriving and demonstrating new variations which are as likely to accrete as cancel each other out. They modulate and feed back in a continuous loop, rather than simply pass on commands.
2. They are increasingly technological in nature, the result of the degree to which political knowledge has become systematized in networks of devices which require technological capacity to operate and discriminate. Most particularly, we can point to the use of computer software to encapsulate scientific methods that have recast the old arts of patrol, diagnose, cross-reference, and survey, thereby beginning to produce something like *continuous government* which will act as a kind of politics by default. Two main methods of working toward this continuous government are currently in operation. The first of these is profiling, simulations of the likes and dislikes of citizens that present a recurring problematic for and solution to government (Elmer 2004). The second is track and trace, the attempt continuously to track citizens' spatial routines, producing what might be called a real-time census in which the state of citizens can be continually updated (Thrift 2004*b*). These new virtual arts of "dataveillance" are bent on reconstructing the citizenry in and as a series of "oligoptic" (Latour 1999) electronic spaces within which they will be able to be reconstructed as surveilled and therefore re-cognizable as governmental objects in the classic Foucauldian sense. Thus, side-by-side with the growth of pastoral modes of government bent on fashioning the self, a development which has been the focus of so much comment of late (Rose 1996), we can see a brute technological

utilitarianism of standardization and extension and sheer scaling up of the arts of government continuing to develop.

3. These machines demonstrate the increasing irrelevance of thinking in terms of scale. What is "big" and what is "small" are increasingly muddled up. "Little" things count just as much as "large" (Thrift 1999), to the extent that the distinction becomes suspect. Interestingly, such a conception chimes with the work of Gabriel Tarde who always argued that such a distinction between "smaller" interactions and "bigger" social structures was suspect. Thus Tarde was insistent that,

It is always the same mistake that is put forward: to believe that in order to see the regular, orderly, logical pattern of social facts, you have to extract yourself from their details, basically irregular, and go upwards until you embrace vast landscapes panoramically; that the principal source of any social co-ordination resides in a very few general facts, from which it diverges by degree until it reaches the particulars, but in a weakened form; to believe in short that while man agitates himself, a law of evolution leads him. I believe exactly the opposite.   (Tarde 1999, cited in Latour 2002, 124)

4. These machines operate as means of constituting new kinds of spatiality and temporality which can reset these qualities by redefining agency. In particular, the construction of all manner of spaces and times which rely on increased information gathering and communications abilities is allowing "territories" to be constituted in different ways than formerly. This latter point deserves greater elaboration.

I want to point to three developments in particular. To begin with, it is possible to argue that the spaces of the powerful are changing shape. Thus, it has been argued that the art of government of a good part of the world is now divided between machines that work across territorial space rather than within it. The work of three authors, though it clearly exaggerates the strength of the tendency, still makes the point. Thus, Slaughter (2004) argues that a global system of governance is now coming into existence, one which relies on the proliferation of a series of transgovernmental networks which routinely cross national borders and, in a number of ways, form relatively closed worlds of governance but of global extent. These networks challenge the idea that governance has to rely on continuous and contiguous territories to exert influence. Rather, as exercised by these new transgovernmental institutions, "the core characteristic of sovereignty would shift from autonomy from outside interference to the capacity to participate in transgovernmental networks of all types" (Slaughter 2004, 34). In turn, we might see citizens increasingly cast by and out of interlocking governmental spaces, being formed in a variety of ways by a variety of networks in "a world in which sovereignty means the capacity to participate in co-operative regimes in the collective interest of all states" (Slaughter 2004, 270). As Slaughter points out, such a move may mean an overall increase in state power, even as national states become "disaggregated." Barry (2001) has argued much the same thing by reference to the case of the European Union as a characteristic example of a new form of proto-governance in which an ambition to become a set of more or less homogeneous zones which maximizes qualities like mobility and skills is in the end achieved by a kind of bricolage, dependent on the widely varying ambitions and powers of a set of different cross-border institutions which do not add up but still produce momentum. Finally, Keane (2003) goes farther still. Like a number of recent "cosmopolitical" authors (e.g. Beck 2000), he wants to identify an emergent form of global governance—he calls this "cosmocracy"—in which worldwide webs of interdependence have thickened to the point where they have produced a radically new way of doing political power:

These chains of interdependence are oiled by high-speed, space-shrinking flows of communication that have a striking effect: they force those who wield power within the structures of cosmocracy to become more or less aware of its here–there dialectics. The power structures of cosmocracy are constantly shaped by so-called "butterfly effects", whereby single events, transactions or decisions somewhere can and do touch off a string of (perceived) consequences elsewhere within the system. Those who wield power know not only that "joined-up government" is becoming commonplace—that governmental institutions of various function, size and geographic location, despite their many differences, are caught up in a thickening, fast-evolving webs of bilateral, multilateral and supranational relations...Cosmocracy stands on the spectrum between the so-called "Westphalian" model of competing sovereign states and a single, unitary system of world government. It functions as something more and other than an international community of otherwise sovereign governments. It is not understandable in terms of the nineteenth century idea of balance-of-power politics. It is also wrong to understand it as a two-tiered, proto-federal polity that has been formed by the gradual pooling of the powers of territorial states under pressure from arbitrage pressures and cross-border spillovers. Cosmocracy is a much messier, a far more complex type of polity.   (Keane 2003, 98)

To follow on, much the same thing can be seen to be happening in other political registers. For example, in the cultural register, it is possible to argue that so-called global civil society (Keane 2003) is producing notions of identity and citizenship which stray outside the conventional bounds of subjectivity, producing new maps of the political subject. Through all manner of networks and technologies, subjects are becoming strung out across space and time in ways which cut across conventional political territories and constitute new ones which may still look to the older political frameworks for certain resources and allegiances, but also add new things into the mix. Indeed it is possible to argue that much "cultural" globalization is actually experimentation with novel forms of circulating citizenship which are able to take in and make claims of many places at once. In turn, these forms of citizenship demand new forms of political narrative and institution that, over time, can become new forms of political subjectivity, replete with their own needs and demands, longings and belongings, which no longer necessarily correlate with bounded territories (Amin, Massey, and Thrift 2003).

Then, to end this section, it is possible to argue that space and time are being constructed in new ways, producing new forms of the political and politics. In particular, the conduct of politics now relies on greater speed. It is not necessary to sign up to a notion of a "dromocratic" revolution (Virilio 1996) to see that politics now uses the speed afforded by modern communications technologies to work in new and not always beneficial ways. Thus, the dictates of speed have lead to the installation of a new round of metrics—"hyper-metrics"—which measure the world in millimetres and milliseconds, courtesy of new technologies like GIS and GPS. Then, information-gathering processes become semi-automatic (Manovitch 2001). They rely on continuous operation through modulated loops rather than true interruptions. Content therefore often becomes incidental to the main business of feeding the machine. And, last, information-gathering relies on active intermediation by the media. Each event is increasingly caught up with a media double which, seen as a historical event, is probably best likened to writing about the event, but writing that is often more present than the event itself (Greenhouse 1996). The results, at least, are clear. For example, the media use visual rhetorics which convey a heightened sense of the event but, at the same time, lead to an appreciation of those events which is severely attenuated. In the United States, to take one instance, attention to news is often tuned out of a public sphere increasingly run by private concerns and taken up by a larger and larger number of types of media with an increasingly problematic effect on "the right to inform" (Mindich 2004). The result is that many US citizens have no news habit and, as a result, have increasingly thin political knowledge, the result not so much of "dis-information" as "un-information."

3   THE LANGUAGE OF AFFECT

In this final section, I want to look forward to another way of framing political spaces which has come to seem more and more important, perhaps in part because of the increasing hold of uninformation in many parts of the world, namely affect. It is difficult to deny the extraordinary importance of affect in political life, as a means of thinking the political and framing and obtaining credence. From its rhetorical usages which were regarded as so important in the ancient and medieval traditions through its current rhetorical incarnation as the flurries of anxiety that are let loose by concentrated press and media attention to concerns over identity, from the waves of anger and rage that are marshalled and directed by armies to the moods that can seemingly sap the spirit of nations (Ekstein 1989), from the barrage of moral standards based around notions of the healthy body politic that often seem to typify modern government to the kind of gleeful amorality typical of so many imperial adventures, affect is intimately connected with the political and with the exercise of politics. In turn, generating affect relies on manipulating *space*. Indeed there are many who would argue that space is the touchstone of affect, since it is involved at every point of its generation: in the welling-up of the body, in the business of interaction between bodies and other bodies, and between bodies and things, in the structuring of performative environments so that they are more likely to touch off one affect than another, in the ways in which affect seems to spread within and between populations like an epidemic, in the various resonances with other affects which can set off new rounds of emotional investment, and so on.

In the literature, affect covers a wide variety of meanings of what constitutes affect. It can mean the bubbling up of drives, the ways in which embodiment takes shape in interaction, how the contours of the face not only convey but work up emotions, or the more general Spinozan notion of the active outcome of an encounter, which may be greater or lesser forces of existing (cf. Thrift 2004a).

In turn, the discovery of affect has produced new means of framing the political and politics. Specifically, we can point to three main reworkings which have occurred since the end of the nineteenth century, each of them related to the others. The first is that of attention. It would be possible to argue that gaining and keeping attention is now one of the key modern political battlefields: keeping populations concentrated on a shifting multiplicity of issues, each of them given momentary affective weight, is a massive task which occupies several global institutions. In turn, the history of modern politics has to take in the moments when new kinds of political appeal made possible through sheer gut impact became possible. In particular, there is the developing technology of film, and the corresponding theory of film as a means of producing cognitive shocks which are sufficiently large that they constitute a new nervous system born in parallel with it (Crary 1999; Taussig 1992). Then, there is the parallel development of systems of knowledge of making symbols a/effective, taking in the discovery of mass media advertising, the history of totalitarian symbols like the swastika, taken ownership of by the Nazis and subsequently irredeemable in many parts of the world (Quinn 1997; Heller 2000), the iconic status of many modern brands (Lury 2004), and current attempts to produce messages that can be tagged to specific population segments and spaces. Finally, there is the admixture of politics and the institution of media celebrity, producing hybrid figures like Ronald Reagan and Arnold Schwarzenegger who know how to project potential, even though their politics might seem to amount to something quite different.[4]

---

[4] Of course, affective symbols are hardly the mantle of just the powerful. They are also routinely deployed in all forms of counter-politics, especially where life is concerned, as if strong affective response must constitute the answer. For example, the environmental, the "pro-life," and the animal rights movements will often make what are purely affective appeals, in which one emotionally charged image stands proud as a kind of proof which requires no other argument.

The second impact is on how to characterize the nature of contemporary democracy (Berlant 2002; Marcus 2002). Here I will again concentrate on three themes. To begin with, modern democracies function at least in part through the ability of leaders and parties to project persuasive affective messages, most especially through the apparatuses of presentation and communication provided by the gamut of the modern media,[5] which can generate anxiety or fear or optimism or hope or other "habits" that are an integral part of political thought (Marcus 2002). Indeed some authors (e.g. Nolan 1998) have argued that these democracies now function through an "emotivist ethos" which makes appeals to the therapeutic self of the citizen, in part because affect provides a common language in increasingly pluralist polities, in part because it provides new and potent means of state legitimation, and, in part, because subjects are increasingly formed through knowing affective practices (such as therapy and ideas of feeling the pain of victimhood) which they come to expect to see echoed in public life. Then, it is quite clear that many democracies around the world systematically exclude various groups. The affective firestorms that are periodically unleashed by the media may be one of the only ways in which these groups can gain access to any kind of public voice by feeling the pain of the supposed victim, but they do so at the cost of increasing those groups symbolic negativity and their association with sub-personhood. For example, as Berlant (2002) points out, in the United States, politics has been based on the appearance of white maleness, the possession of property, and the capacity to feel pain. Making claims outside this system is nearly always associated with finding the smallest available site of consensus (such as the vote) and organizing around it, producing a "formal vestibularity" which promises that "nothing will change except for the better life that can be already imagined" (Berlant 2002, 169).

Mention of imagination brings us to the third impact, which is that of hope. Hope is a forward-looking affect, one which assumes a future time and space which will consist of circumstances in some way better than those of the present. Thus, hope is an integral part of most political action, but it is only quite recently that this drive into the future, usually made up of indeterminate and ill-formed wishes and longings as much as it is of determinate political programmes, has started to be given the full attention it surely deserves. The rediscovery of the writings of Ernst Bloch and other "practical utopianists" give us the beginnings of a window on to this part of political life, as do many writings of political anthropology which document the survival of hope, even in situations of extreme conflict or oppression. In turn, they open on to imagined political landscapes of longing for different

---

[5] Of course, this appeal to affect is hardly new—witness the savage sophistication of so much Nazi politics—but I think it is possible to argue that it has massively intensified through the proliferation of the media and the creation of subjects who are primed to think in this way.

futures which, though they may often be inchoate, are surely important. Most particularly, they show the vital importance of particular spaces in generating particular politics of time future as well as time past through their ability to produce affects like hope as well as anxiety. In other words, spaces act as conveyors of political aspirations, pulling the past into the future but also, every now and then, helping to spark off new combinations of needs and demands which act to shape a future quite different from the past.

4   CONCLUSIONS: POLITICS AS PROCESS IN PROCESS

So what conclusions can we draw from the different arguments and instances cited so far? First, that political theory is actively changed by the addition of space and time. Some have made the argument that political theory has chiefly proceeded as though politics took place in an absolute Newtonian space and time, when what is needed is a recourse to something approximating a relative Einsteinian space and time. The result would be that the spatial assumptions underlying such entities as rights discourses can be foregrounded and used to position and chasten them so that, in turn, a ground for compromise and concession might be set out in which rights would come with a generic proviso for conditionality (Dimock 2002). Others have argued that what is needed is a whole set of different figures of space and time, refrains which through structured accretion gradually set up different political landscapes. Yet others want to reveal a world made up of a patchwork of polities proceeding at different rates and running to different rhythms. Whatever the case, it seems that these different solutions are symptomatic of a widespread turn to a political theory which can work with more nuanced moral spaces, which realizes that there is no absolute space of rights but still gives full weight to disagreement.

Second, and in turn, such a spatial turn produces a post-colonial world that cannot be reduced to one map or one political force or one cause but consists of a cross-cutting and constantly shifting dynamic map of concerns, disagreements, and struggles. Yet a spatial reductionism of a familiar kind still crops up routinely in certain kinds of political theory,[6] a reductionism that very often echoes the concerns of the powerful, if only in counterpoint, in revolving around a remarkably few

---

[6] This reductionism is not restricted to the right. For example, on the left there are currently those intent on discovering an immanent multitude, a recent case in point of the recovery of this persistent tendency being found in the work of Hardt and Negri (2004).

"central" places which it is assumed constitute the whole world. Overwhelmingly, that means that the world of political theory is still a world seen from just a few places which is concerned only with the places that those places have on their agenda. For example, it is very often assumed that the key political conundrum in the world today is those countries which have most recently borne the footprint of US involvement (Afghanistan, Iraq) or of US strategic interests (Israel, Palestine, Saudi Arabia, Iran). Every now and then other places make it on to the agenda, usually as a result of an atrocity which involves US or allied citizens. This is the standard "colonial present" (Gregory 2004). But this is not good enough. Perhaps I can make my point indirectly to begin with. It is always worth recalling that first realization, common to many of those who venture into the field, that here are peoples who share few of the political concerns that you have always taken as holy writ. Very often, they do not point in the same political directions or have the same political predilections. That same lack of what has been accepted as a cardinal political orientation can be extended to many forces in the world, forces for whom the United States is just one amongst many political compass points. On the grander scale, think only of the diversity of strategic concerns that preoccupy all the other colonial presents that inhabit the world: China's colonization of Tibet, and its Hanification of many other parts of its empire. Russia's continual fight with separatist movements and its calculated interference in Georgia and the Ukraine. Indonesia's colonization of Irian Jaya. Then think of the myriad of border conflicts and skirmishes, too many of them to mention. And this is before we get to the vast number of proto-nationalist movements, terrorist combines, and just bands of young thugs still searching for an ideology. From these places of struggle, the world just looks different.[7]

Then, third and finally, this realization of diversity and difference makes it possible to become attuned to or imagine all kinds of new politics of credence which might hitherto have been overlooked or regarded as trivial, a lively addition to the politics of moral spaces that has been enunciated by authors like Campbell and Shapiro (e.g. Campbell 1999). I want to end this piece by briefly considering some of these ethico-spatial politics.

The first of these is the enunciation of an agonistic politics of disagreement (Ranciere 1999) which has processes of learning rather than resolution at its heart. Such a politics is less concerned with mapping out determinate political pro-grammes and more concerned with learning to grow together, whilst all the time retaining different political interests (Stengers 2002). It is, if you like, a politics of resolute irresolution.

The second kind of politics is one that is trying to burrow down into the affective layers of politics by concentrating on those small spaces of time between action and

---

[7] This is why, of course, the general connections between contextual political analysis, political geography, and area studies must be kept up.

cognition in which affect forms and has its say. This so-called "neuropolitics" (Connolly 2002; Thrift 2001; 2004b; 2004c) is intent on lighting the shadowy political pathways through which people come to care or hate. It therefore acts like a layer cake, slipping down into and taking hold of action by galvanizing several layers of expression, each with their own "speeds, capacities and levels of linguistic complexity" (Connolly 2002, 45).

Such a political ambition can be linked to the third kind of politics of credence which was a constant in twentieth-century political thought and is now being revived. This politics concentrates on the everyday as a primary political substrate. Tracing a path from Baudelaire through the surrealists to writers like Lefebvre and de Certeau, as well as through another quite separate path which takes in both pragmatism and the work of Agnes Heller (e.g. Bennett 2001; Dumm 1999), it argues for a politics of spaces that are briefly opened up to other ambitions, practices, and interpretations, a politics of small gains that enliven the textures of everyday life and can act as expressive jumping-off points into other political dimensions. In summary, these might all be described as politics of what Bhabha (2003) calls "the cultural front," an area of intermediate living in which a range of expressive potentials can be nurtured and brought forth via the contiguity of what might be quite different time and space frames. As such, they represent a means of maneuvering minoritarian formations in from the margins of the concerns of conventional political bodies. Bhabha (2003, 31) links the discovery of this political zone to Gramsci, though, no doubt, many other avatars might well be invoked:

A cultural front is not necessarily a political party; it is more a movement or alliance of groups whose struggle for fairness and justice emphasizes the deep collaboration between aesthetics, ethics and activism. A cultural front does not have a homogeneous and totalizing view of the world, it finds its orientation from what Gramsci describes as "the philosophy of the part (that) always precedes the philosophy of the whole, not only in its theoretical orientation but as a necessity of real life". Today, as we are offered the stark choices of civilizational clash— between Faith and Unfaith, or Terror and Democracy—it is illuminating to grasp something that demands an understanding that is less dogmatic and totalizing, a philosophy of the part, a perspective that acknowledges its own partiality "as a necessity of life."

Let me conclude. Space, place, and time are not just incidental to contextual political analysis. Rather, they are central moments in the process by which the political is formed and reckoned and the practices of politics are able to roam and multiply. They are the means by which what may be a large number of fragmentary and discontinuous possibilities are actualized in particular events. Thus the poetics of space, place, and time, quite literally form the ethical horizon of the political and politics, a latent world which both forms a background and provides the means to produce foregrounds (Vesely 2004). They are the very stuff of politics.

REFERENCES

AGAR, J. 2004. *The Government Machine: A Revolutionary History of the Computer*. Cambridge, Mass.: MIT Press.

AMIN, A., MASSEY, D., and THRIFT, N. J. 2003. *Recreating the Political*. London: Catalyst.

ANDERSON, K., Domosh, M., Pile, S., and Thrift, N. J. (eds.) 2003. *The Handbook of Cultural Geography*. London: Sage.

BARRY, A. 2001. *Political Machines: Governing a Technological Society*. London: Continuum.

BECK, U. 2000. *World Risk Society*. Cambridge: Polity Press.

BENNETT, J. 2001. *The Enchantment of Modern Life*. Princeton, NJ: Princeton University Press.

BERLANT, L. 2002. Uncle Sam needs a wife: citizenship and denegation. Pp. 144–74 in *Materializing Democracy*, ed. R. Castronovo and D. D. Nelson. Durham, NC: Duke University Press.

BHABHA, H. 2003. Democracy de-realized. *Diogenes*, 50: 27–36.

BORNSTEIN, E. 2003. *The Spirit of Development: Religious NGOs, Morality and Economics in Zimbabwe*. London: Routledge.

CAMPBELL, D. (ed.) 1999. *Moral Space*. Minneapolis: University of Minnesota Press.

CONNOLLY, W. 2002. *Neuropolitics: Thinking, Culture, Speed*. Minneapolis, University of Minnesota Press.

CRARY, J. 1999. *Suspensions of Perception*. Cambridge, Mass.: MIT Press.

DILLON, M. 1996. *The Politics of Security*. London: Routledge.

DIMOCK, W. C. 2002. Rethinking space, rethinking rights: literature, law and rights. Pp. 248–66 in *Materializing Democracy*, ed. R. Castronovo and D. D. Nelson. Durham, NC: Duke University Press,.

DUMM, T. L. 1999. *A Politics of the Ordinary*. New York: New York University Press.

DUNCAN, J. S., JOHNSON, N., and SCHEIN, R. (eds.) 2004. *The Companion to Cultural Geography*. Oxford: Blackwell.

EKSTEIN, M. 1989. *Rites of Spring: The Great War and the Birth of the Modern Age*. London: Macmillan.

ELMER, G. 2004. *Profiling Machines: Mapping the Personal Information Economy*. Cambridge, Mass.: MIT Press.

FORTUN, K. 2000. *Advocacy after Bhopal*. Chicago: Chicago University Press.

GREENHOUSE, C. J. 1996. *A Moment's Notice: Time Politics Across Cultures*. Ithaca, NY: Cornell University Press.

GREGORY, D. 2004. *The Colonial Present*. Oxford: Blackwell.

HARDT, M., and NEGRI, A. 2004. *Multitude*. Harmondsworth: Penguin.

HELLER, S. 2000. *The Swastika*. New York: Allworth Press.

HOLMES, D. R. 2000. *Integral Europe: Fast Capitalism, Multiculturalism, Neofascism*. Cambridge: Cambridge University Press.

KEANE, J. 2003. *Global Civil Society?* Cambridge: Cambridge University Press.

LATOUR, B. 1999. *Paris: Ville invisible*. Paris: Institut Sythelabo.

—— 2002. Gabriel Tarde and the end of the social. Pp. 117–32 in *The End of the Social*, ed. P. Joyce. London: Routledge.

LURY, C. 2004. *Brands*. London: Routledge.

MANN, M. 1993. *The Sources of Social Power: The Rise of Classes and Nation States, 1760–1914.* Cambridge: Cambridge University Press.

MANOVITCH, L. 2001. *The Language of New Media.* Cambridge, Mass.: MIT Press.

MARCUS, G. E. 2002. *The Sentimental Citizen.* University Park: Pennsylvania State University Press.

MASSEY, D., and THRIFT, N. J. 2003. The passion of place. In *A Century of British Geography,* ed. R. J. Johnston and M. Williams. Oxford: Oxford University Press.

MINDICH, D. T. Z. 2004. *Tuned Out: Why Americans Under 40 Don't Follow the News.* New York: Oxford University Press.

MITCHELL, T. 2002. *Rule of Experts: Egypt, Techno-Politics, Modernity.* Berkeley: University of California Press.

NOLAN, J. L. 1998. *The Therapeutic State.* New York: New York University Press.

NORA, P. 1996. *Realms of Memory,* 3 vols. New York: Columbia University Press.

NORRIS, P. 2003. *Democratic Phoenix.* Cambridge: Cambridge University Press.

ONG, A., and COLLIER, S. (eds.) 2004. *Global Anthropology.* Malden, Mass.: Blackwell.

QUINN, M. 1997. *The Swastika: Constructing the Symbol.* London: Routledge.

RANCIERE, J. 1999. *Disagreement.* Minneapolis: University of Minnesota Press.

RILES, A. 2001. *The Network Inside Out.* Ann Arbor: University of Michigan Press.

ROSE, N. 1996. *Thinking Our Selves.* Cambridge: Cambridge University Press.

SCOTT, J. C. 1999. *Seeing Like a State.* New Haven, Conn.: Yale University Press.

SLAUGHTER, A. M. 2004. *A New World Order.* Princeton, NJ: Princeton University Press.

STENGERS, I. 2002. Interview. In *Hope,* ed. M. Zournazi. London: Pluto Press.

TARDE, G. 1999. *Les Lois Sociales.* Paris: Editions Decouverte.

TAUSSIG, M. 1992. *The Nervous System.* New York: Routledge.

THRIFT, N. J. 1999. It's the little things. In *Contemporary Geopolitics,* ed. K. Dodds and D. Atkinson. London: Routledge.

—— 2001. Afterwords. *Environment and Planning D: Society and Space,* 18: 213–55.

—— 2004a. Intensities of feeling: towards a spatial politics of affect. *Geografiska Annaler,* 86B: 57–78.

—— 2004b. Remembering the technological unconscious by foregrounding knowledges of position. *Environment and Planning D: Society and Space,* 22: 461–82.

—— 2004c. Summoning life. Pp. 81–103 in *Envisioning Human Geographies,* ed. P. J. Cloke, P. Crang, and M. Goodwin. London: Arnold.

—— and WHATMORE, S. J. (eds.) 2004. *Cultural Geography,* 2 vols. London: Routledge.

TORPEY, J. 2000. *The Invention of the Passport.* Cambridge: Cambridge University Press.

VESELY, D. 2004. *Architecture in the Age of Divided Representation.* Cambridge, Mass.: MIT Press.

VIRILIO, P. 1996. *The Art of the Motor.* London: Verso.

SPACES AND PLACES AS SITES AND OBJECTS OF POLITICS

JAVIER AUYERO

1 GLOBAL SCENES OF CONTENTIOUS POLITICS IN AND OVER SPACE AND PLACE

Tehran Pars, Iran, 1970s

When we got out of the house that night, I saw something that I hope nobody will ever see again. The whole neighborhood had been surrounded by the soldiers who had sneaked in quietly and stopped anyone from turning a light on.... Yes, they had brought four bulldozers. They forced everybody out of their homes, and then started to demolish them. In one house, a whole family including children went up on the roof top, and said "we won't come out." But the agents destroyed the house. The man fell and the house collapsed on him. And the woman, as soon as she saw this, fainted and dropped her child from her hands.

The scene could have taken place in a shantytown of Buenos Aires or in a *favela* of Rio de Janeiro where state agents routinely raze poor enclaves, particularly but not exclusively those deemed "out-of-(urban)-place". This particular one occurred in Javadieh in Tehran Pars, Iran, during the 1970s. The cited squatter is referring to a specific episode within the wave of state action against illegal housing that started in 1974 and ended in 1977. During the 1970s, and much like their counterparts in Quito, Lima, and dozens of other Latin American cities, thousands of poor Iranian families invaded lands and subsequently demanded security of tenure, services (electricity, running water, sewer systems), and improvement of their dwellings from the state. By the summer and autumn of 1977, writes Asef Bayat (1997, 46), "the squatter areas had emerged as battle grounds. The municipality's demolition squads, escorted by hundreds of paramilitary soldiers, as well as dozens of bull-dozers, trucks, and military jeeps, raided the settlements to destroy illegal dwellings and to stop their further expansion." State repressive action was, Bayat continues, "normally carried out at night, when collective resistance against demolition was very difficult—when the residents were either in bed or away from their shelters. The municipal agents would ask people to come out of their dwellings and the bulldozers would wreck the shacks and shanties, leaving behind the rubble of tin plates, car tires, and mud bricks" (ibid.). Contention over urban space was never ending: after state troops and officials were gone, "squatters would reappear on the ruins of their wrecked shelters and try once again to put together the rubble to resurrect their homes. 'If they demolish even for 50 times [sic], we will rebuild again,' said a shantytown dweller" (1997, 48).

Beijing, China, 1989

When I got up in the morning, I saw students in Beijing Teacher's were already marching at the campus stadium. I wanted to know what was happening in People's University. I went there by bicycle. At the time that I arrived, students of People's University had gone north to meet students from Beijing University. I then followed. By the time that I met with students of People's University they had already joined with students from Beijing University and moved back again. I then rode back to the Friendship Hotel intersection and watched. There were police lines there and students from Northern Communication were stopped by them on the south side. When the big troops [of students] arrived, with the efforts from both sides, the police line soon collapsed.... As soon as students pushed policemen aside, I rode back to Beijing Teacher's to see what they were doing. I saw that students were sitting on the sidewalk outside their university. I passed the message: go quickly in Chegongzhuang direction, students from other universities are coming.

Place-specific details aside, the frantic back-and-forth described in the above testimony could have come from a Seattle protester or a Bolivian rioter. This one comes from a student called the "liaison man" by sociologist Dingxing Zhao. Not formally movement organizers, liaison men were students who "wanted to see more of the demonstration" and who ended up providing crucial coordination, riding their bicycles from one university to another during the 1989 Beijing student movement. The very ecology of Beijing's Haidian district in or around which most universities are located, one at a short distance from the next, facilitated liaison men's spatial practices, as well as the rapid communication and diffusion of dissident ideas (Zhao 1998).

Santiago del Estero, Argentina, 1993

Personnel from the different precincts . . . as a preventive measure, carried out movements to simulate a stockade . . . covering the surroundings of the Government House. . . . After a while, demonstrators from different unions started to arrive through various routes. [Most of the protesters] were concentrated on the main square [in front] of the Government House, and the rest were located at the back of the building. . . . The protest atmosphere increased [and] some sectors were already trying to go forward, over the police stockade that was holding the crowd back with enormous efforts . . . [T]hey started to throw blunt objects (bricks, sticks, bottles, etc.) at the police personnel and the building as they started to move forward. [After the tear gas] the demonstrators withdrew but came back in new groups. . . . When there was finally physical contact between the demonstrators that were angrily struggling to get closer to the Government House and the police personnel the situation was almost untenable. . . . When faced with the seriousness of the facts, and given the lack of elements for riot control, we started the retreat . . . [T]he protesters started to enter the House of Government through different places, throwing incendiary bombs into the building . . . they destroyed everything they found on their way: chairs, tables, glasses, windows, documents, etc. [. . .] An estimated number of 1500 protesters, following the same actions that were taken in the Government House . . . moved towards the Courthouse that is located a few meters away from the House. The police personnel were overwhelmed and the building is more vulnerable because of the existence of large windows with glass and multiple entrances.

This excerpt comes from the report written on the hot night of December 16, 1993 by a police agent in Santiago del Estero, Argentina. That day, the city witnessed what the *New York Times* (Dec. 18, 1993, p. 3) called "the worst social upheaval in years." Three public buildings—the Government House, the courthouse, and the legislature—and nearly a dozen private residences of local officials and politicians were invaded, looted, and burned down by thousands of public workers and residents of Santiago. State and municipal employees, primary and high school teachers, retired elderly, students, union leaders, and others demanded their unpaid salaries and pensions with arrears of three months, protested against the implementation of structural-adjustment policies, and voiced their discontent with widespread governmental corruption.

Miami, United States, 2003

Activist Lisa Fithian arrived in Miami weeks before the November 17, 2003 meeting of the Free Trade Area of the Americas. She has been involved in planning protests around the world, from Cancún to Seattle and Prague. She was there to scrutinize the city: "My eye is trained," she said, "I walk through a city, and I see a parking garage, and I think, That'd be a great place to drop a huge banner, or I see an open restaurant, and I think, That'd be a good place to escape if things get crazy. Sometimes places will tell me what they want." (*New York Times Magazine*, Nov. 16, 2003, p. 60)

2   THE PLACE OF SPACE IN THE STUDY OF POLITICS

Squatters in Iran, students in China, police agents in Argentina, and activists in the United States know it well: Space, whether as a terrain to be occupied, an obstacle to be overcome, or as an enabler to have in mind, matters in the production of collective action. Space is sometimes the site, other times the object, and usually both the site and the object of contentious politics.

For the past decade, following the pioneering works of Foucault (1979; 1980) and Lefevbre (1991), geographers and social theorists have been making calls to incorporate "space" in our understandings and explanations of social phenomena.[1] Space has been "reasserted" in contemporary social theory and analysis (Soja 1989), to the extent that, by now the proposition that "the social and the spatial are inseparable and that the spatial form of the social has causal effecticity" (Massey 1994, 255) is widely accepted among geographers and sociologists. "[S]ociety," writes geographer Doreen Massey (1994, 254), "is necessarily constructed spatially, and that fact—the spatial organization of society—makes a difference to how it works." This means that the spatial should be approached not merely as a product of social processes, that is, space as "socially constructed," but also as part of the explanation of those processes, that is, the social as "spatially constructed." Massey tells us (1984, 4):

Spatial distributions and geographical differentiation may be the result of social processes, but they also affect how those processes work. "The spatial" is not just an outcome; it is also part of the explanation... [it is important] for those in [the] social sciences to take on board the fact that the processes they study are constructed, reproduced and changed in a way which necessarily involves distance, movement and spatial differentiation.

Despite the widely shared reassertion of "the interpretive significance of space in the historically privileged confines of contemporary critical thought" (Soja 1989, 11),

---

[1] See, e.g., Soja 1989; Pred 1990; Massey and Allen 1984; Massey 1994; Harvey 1989; Giddens 1984; Gottdiener 1985; Agnew 1987.

research on contentious politics has been surprisingly slow in acknowledging the geographic constitution of contentious action. In a comprehensive review, geographers Martin and Miller (2003) note that among social movement researchers, for example, the absence of attention to the geographic structuring of collective action remains a significant gap. In another insightful article devoted to thematization of space as one of the "silences" in the study of contentious politics, William Sewell, Jr. (2001, 52) acknowledges that, "[M]ost studies bring in spatial considerations only episodically, when they seem important either for adequate description of contentious political events or for explaining why particular events occurred or unfolded as they did. With rare exceptions, the literature has treated space as an assumed and unproblematized background, not as a constituent aspect of contentious politics that must be conceptualized explicitly and probed systematically." In sum, space- and place-related dynamics usually are part of the descriptions of contentious politics, but "rarely play significant part in analysts' explanations of what is going on" (Tilly 2000, 5).

In an issue of the journal *Mobilization* specifically dedicated to the dissection of the place of space in the analysis of protest activity, Martin and Miller (2003, 149) argue that space and place are "both context for and constitutive of dynamic processes of contention." As in any other social process, contention takes place in particular geographical contexts and this spatial constitution affects the way in which this "sit(e)-uated" (Pred 1990) collective practice operates.

Truth be told, spatial sensibilities have been around since social sciences' inception. A case in point is *The Communist Manifesto*, where Marx and Engels highlight the spatial concentration of workers as an essential precondition for the mobilization of the industrial proletariat:

But with the development of industry the proletariat not only increases in number; it becomes concentrated in greater masses, its strength grows, and it feels that strength more. The various interests and conditions of life within the ranks of the proletariat are more and more equalized, in proportion as machinery obliterates all distinctions of labour, and nearly everywhere reduces the wages to the same low level.   (Marx and Engels 1998 [1848], 45)

Spatial amassing in factories leads not only to an increasing force of the working class as a political actor but also to a shared understanding of that mounting collective might.[2] Space, Marx and Engels believed, matters as both the material and symbolic basis for collective action. In what reads as an anticipation of the "time–space compression" argument made by David Harvey (1989), *The*

---

[2] S. Smith (1987, 60) makes a similar argument about the 1917 Russian Revolution in Petrograd: "No fewer than 68 percent of the city's workforce worked in enterprises of more than a thousand workers—a degree of concentration unparalleled elsewhere in the world. The concentration of experienced, politically aware workers in large units of production was critical in facilitating the mobilization of the working class in 1917."

Communist Manifesto encapsulates both the enabling and constraining dimensions of physical space. While "miserable highways" hindered the "union of workers"—and thus their collective action—during the Middle Ages, the railways facilitate joint action during the inception of industrial capitalism:

Now and then the workers are victorious, but only for a time. The real fruit of their battles lies, not in the immediate result, but in the ever expanding union of the workers. This union is helped on by the improved means of communication that are created by modern industry, and that placed the workers of different localities in contact with one another. It was just this contact that was needed to centralize the numerous local struggles, all of the same character, into one national struggle between the classes. But every class struggle is a political struggle. And that union, to attain which the burghers of the Middle Ages, with their miserable highways, required centuries, the modern proletarians, thanks to the railways, achieve in few years. (Marx and Engels 1998 [1848], 46)

Feagin and Hahn (1973) provide a by now classic example of the way in which space has been part of the description of protest, in their case ghetto revolts, mainly in terms of the role played by segregation and "ghetto encapsulation." Collective behavior approaches have also paid some attention to the spatial dimensions of riots (McPhail 1971; 1991; 1992; Miller 1985). As Miller (1985, 249) argues, "assembling processes" are more likely to occur in some cities than in others. Residential segregation, population density, city size, types of residential dwellings, presence or absence of barriers to street-level communication (railroads, rivers, highways, etc.) are major elements in the "immediate interaction environment" (McPhail 1971, 1072) in which riots take place. Urban history has also been attentive to the role of space in contentious episodes. Historians of France, to cite one last example, are very familiar with the spatialization of insurrectionary processes: see, for example, Gould's (1995) path-breaking work on the macro-level ecological dimensions of insurgent identities, and Farge and Revel's (1991) detailed description of the "vanishing children" Parisian revolt.

Space and place, contemporary social scientists agree, should become part of the understanding and explanation of contentious politics. In this brief chapter I highlight the presence of a working consensus among social scientists and geographers regarding the recursive relation between physical and symbolic space and contentious politics: *space and place constrain and enable (and are constrained and enabled by) contentious politics.* This structured and structuring dimension of space and place is best summarized by William Sewell, Jr. (2001, 5) when, referring to two particular cases of contentious politics (social movements and revolutions), he points out that they are not only "shaped and constrained by the spatial environments in which they take place, but are significant agents in the production of new spatial structures and relations." Below, I survey four main areas around which analysts have been working towards geographically contextualized interpretations and explanations of contentious politics. These are: (1) space as a repository of social relations; (2) built environment as facilitator and obstacle in contentious politics; (3) mutual imbrication between spatially-embedded daily life and protest; (4) spaces as meaningful arenas, i.e. space as place.

3   SPACE AS DEPOSITORY

Analyses sensitive to the difference that geography, as a container of durable social relations, makes in the operation of social processes—from counter-revolutionary activity (Tilly 1964) to political culture (Putnam 1994) to forms of rule (Geertz 1981) to political and ethnic violence (Roldán 2002; Varshney 2002)—have been a staple in the social sciences. Geographers, in particular, have paid sustained attention to this dimension. A case in point is Routledge's (1993) work on the peasant-based Chipko movement that surfaced in India in 1972 in response to ecological destruction, an analysis highly sensitive to issues of physical and symbolic environment as well as space as a container of social relations.

Wendy Wolford's (2003) penetrating analysis of the contextual dynamics surrounding individual decisions to join the Brazilian Movement of Rural Landless Workers (MST) provides an example of an approach to space as a repository of social relations (see also Wright and Wolford 2003 for an expanded, fine-grained treatment of the genesis and development of the movement). Wolford compares two different groups within the MST movement: a group of former family farmers in Santa Catarina, in southern Brazil, and a group of former rural plantation workers in the estate of Pernambuco, in the Brazilian embattled northeast. Wolford's question—"Why do people decide to join the MST?"—receives a geographically based theoretical answer (spatial contexts are embedded with specific social relations critically important to the choices concerning participation in collective action), and an empirical one:

In southern Brazil, small farmers who decided to join MST were tied into a spatially expansive form of production that they valued as part of a broader community. Family and community ties that were forged and re-forged through everyday practices working on the land helped to lower the threshold for participation in MST. In the northeast, on the other hand, MST found it very difficult to mobilize new members because social ties on the sugarcane plantations were too weak to facilitate mobilization and the culture of private property and hierarchy made MST's methods of land occupation appear illegitimate.   (Wolford 2003, 159)

4   SPACE AS BUILT ENVIRONMENT

Although not focused on geographic differences, McAdam's (1982) now classic work on the genesis and development of the civil rights movement also hints at the relevance of the spatial dimension in the organization of insurgency—in his case, pointing at rural isolation and at the system of racial domination as impediments to activism. The sheer physical distance built into the working of the sharecropping system was, together with racial violence, an obstacle to collective action inhibiting an essential ingredient in joint politics: co-presence. Crucial in popular contention (Tilly 2003), co-presence is both enabled and constrained by the built environment: "Because it is largely the networks of roads, city streets, canals, ports, railways, and airports that govern movement through space, the built environment is a major determinant of the time-distance constraints ['the length of time required for persons, objects, or mediated messages to get from one place to another'] under which social movements operate" (Sewell 2001, 60). A conclusive empirically grounded statement on the impact that the built environment had on counter-revolutionary activity in rural areas can be found in Tilly's 1964 classic.

Zhao's ecological analysis of the genesis and development of the Beijing student movement illustrates another point about the physical environment: it makes possible or hampers the likelihood of contention *and* molds its form. As Zhao (1998, 1495) puts it:

Almost all campuses in Beijing are separated from the outside by brick walls with only a few entrances guarded by the university's own security forces. During the 1989 Beijing student movement, no police or soldiers had ever gone inside campuses to repress students...the existence of campus walls was important for the development of the movement.

Another example of the ways in which the physical environment, by shaping social interactions, has an impact on the unfolding of contentious politics comes from the Nepal's Movement for the Restoration of Democracy (MRD) analyzed by Routledge (1997). During 1990, and partially encouraged by the success of democratic protest in Eastern Europe, the principal oppositions parties of Nepal launched the MRD to demand "the dismantling of the panchayat system, the restoration of parliamentary democracy, and the reduction of the kings's powers to those of a constitutional monarch" (Routledge 1997, 74). Activists consciously utilized the urban topography of Patan, the city that served as the base of operations of the underground leadership of the movement. Many squares in Patan were used by militants as meeting places given that, being linked by a "labyrinthine web of streets, the squares afforded a protected space out of the purview of the government" (1997, 78). Patan's narrow streets, furthermore, "prevented any mass deployment of government forces, or the deployment of armed vehicles, while aiding the escape of activists from the police. The interconnected network of backstreets that traversed the town enabled activists to avoid the main streets, and to move unhindered from one end of Patan to the other, or from Patan to Kathmandu without detection" (ibid.). Urban geography, in other words, provided activists with the free and safe spaces that, according to Sewell (2001, 69) are "a sine qua non of social movements."[3]

Contentious politics takes places in physical space; activists take advantage or put up with spatial constraints. The Beijing "liaison men" were not an exception in their deployment of spatial practices. The Nepali MRD provides another example of the relevance of spatial practices in contentious politics. The chief location of MRD activity was the capital, Kathmandu, and the surrounding towns of Patan, Kirtipur, and Bhaktapur where, geographer Paul Routledge tells us, the MRD enacted two different spatial forms of protest: the "pack" and the "swarm":

Concerning the tactics of the swarm, numerous demonstrations were conducted within urban spaces . . . movement slogans calling for the end of the panchayat regime and a return to democracy. By temporarily occupying streets and squares, Nepalis articulated, both physically and symbolically, their resistance to the regime. During the demonstrations, packs of students initiated spontaneous corner demonstrations whereby small groups of students would assemble at a strategic location within the city, shouting anti-government slogans, burning effigies of the king, and distributing movement literature; then disperse if the police arrived and reassemble at another location. Often many of these corner demonstrations would be held simultaneously at various locations so as to stretch police capabilities of deployment. Various diversionary tactics were employed by activists (e.g. running through the streets with *mashals* [burning torches]) to draw police attention away from movement meeting sites.   (Routledge 1997, 76)

The highly theatrical disruptions of public space organized by ACT UP such as kiss-ins, die-ins, etc. (Brown 1997) or the public performances carried out in the midst of a highly repressive context by the Mothers and Grandmothers of Plaza de Mayo in Argentina (Arditti 1999; Bouvard 1994) provide other illustrations of spatial practices deployed by social movements. During the last decade, to provide one last example, the road-blockade became a widely shared spatial practice throughout Latin America adopted by different groups to make diverse sorts of claims—from the unemployed in Argentina to the indigenous peoples in Ecuador and Bolivia (Svampa and Pereyra 2003; Barrera 2002; Sawyer 1997).

---

[3] For a conceptual dissection of the term "free space" see Polletta (1999)

5   SPATIAL ROUTINES

The embeddedness of contentious politics in local context gives protest its power and meaning. Existing scholarship insists on the rootedness of collective action in "normal" social relations, on the multifarious ways in which joint struggle takes place embedded, and often hidden in the mundane spatial structures of everyday life (Rule 1988; Roy 1994; Auyero 2003). As Sewell (2001, 62) puts it: "The sites and the strategies of contentious political movements are shaped in various ways by the spatial routines of daily life. Contentious events often arise out of spatial routines that bring large numbers of people together in particular places." In other words, daily spatial routines (rounds to the market, strolls in the local square, etc.) shape the emergence and form of contentious politics.

Likewise, contentious politics, "develops its own particular spatial routines with their own histories and trajectories" (Sewell 2001, 62). These routines, as Tilly's notion of "repertoire of contention" captures well, shape subsequent collective struggles. Understood as the set of practices by which people get together to act on their shared interests, the notion of repertoire invites us to examine patterns of collective claim-making, regularities in the ways in which people band together to make their demands heard, across both time and space (see also Tarrow 1996). "Repertoires," Tilly asserts (1995, 25), "are learned cultural creations, but they do not descend from abstract philosophy or take shape as a result of political propaganda; they emerge from struggle." This collective struggle takes place, literally in space as becomes clear when Tilly enumerates some of the things protesters learn: "People learn to break windows in protest, attack pilloried prisoners, tear down dishonored houses, stage public marches, petition, hold formal meetings, organize special-interest associations. At any particular point in history, however, they learn only a rather small number of alternative ways to act together" (1995, 26).

Blackouts are frequently adopted as forms of expressing dissatisfaction against a certain government or policy, from Argentina (a massive turning out of lights in the capital was a highly successful collective act of protest against the perceived widespread corruption of the neoliberal presidency of Menem) to Nepal. In this last case, we can view the organization of the blackout as a crystal-clear summation of the extant continuities between a spatialized organization of daily life and the public contestation of/in space. Writes Paul Routlege (1997, 77):

Although the blackouts were called by the movement leadership, the communication of the action was conducted by city residents. Residents relayed the message of the action from rooftop to rooftop across Kathmandu. ... Traditional Newar houses within the city consist of only three, four or five storeys. The upper storey opens out onto a porch (*kaisi*) which is used for various rituals. One of these—the flying of kites during the Mohani festival as a message to the deities to bring monsoons to an end—involves symbolic communication. The porches are also used for more secular activities such as the drying of clothes and talking with neighbours. By informing their neighbours of the blackout protests from their rooftop porches, residents utilised a cultural space that was already important for both community and symbolic communication. In so doing, a space of interwoven meanings was produced. The rooftops acted as a place for the performance of religious rituals, daily activities, and resistance. The latter was facilitated by the propinquity of low elevation of the city dwellings, and the fact that they were out of the purview of government forces.

6   MEANINGFUL SPACES: PLACE

In an article devoted to exploring the existing links between the head of the Hindu-nationalist Shiv Sena party, Bal Thackeray, and anti-Muslim riots, *New Yorker* contributor Larissa MacFarquhar (1997) mentions the campaign launched by the Bharatiya Janata Party (BJP) to reconstruct a temple at a crucial moment in the rise of Hindu Radicalism. Her description exemplifies how certain meaningful arenas can become both context *and* stake in contentious politics; how *place* as a web of meanings located in space matters in politics (see Tuan 1977; Agnew 1987). The campaign, MacFarquhar describes, "focussed on a mosque in Ayodhya, a small city in the northern state of Uttar Pradesh. The mosque was built on what was said to have been the site of Lord Ram's birthplace. Some Hindus maintained that there had been a Ram temple on the site which was destroyed by the Moguls to make way for the mosque in 1528. The BJP decided that the mosque was an unendurable insult to Hindus and had to be removed." In September 1990, as close to 100,000 Hindus stormed the mosque, thirty people died when the crowd was stopped by the police. Years later, "three hundred thousand Hindus gathered at the temple grounds and, this time, were not restrained. The mosque was destroyed, and across the country the worst communal violence since Partition ensued" (MacFarquhar 2003, 52).

Places are sites and objects of contentious politics. Collective actions swirl around physical locations with preexisting meanings. Joint struggles can also modify the symbolism of certain settings. As Sewell (2001, 65) asserts:

The 1963 March on Washington gathered on the Mall in front of the Lincoln Memorial for the obvious symbolic reason that Lincoln had been the author of the Emancipation Proclamation. But the success of the March had the unintended consequence of changing the meaning of the Mall, of making it henceforth the preeminent site for national protest marches, beginning a long series of gigantic demonstrations ranging from marches against nuclear energy, to gay right marches, to the Million Man March.

Much the same could be said about the symbolic reconfiguration of space sometimes produced by ethnic violence. As Veena Das observes: "Each riot leaves its own signature . . . the violence against the Sikhs in 1984 in Delhi or against the Tamils in 1983 was a traumatic experience for the entire Sikh and Tamil communities because the violence penetrated into spaces that had been considered relatively immune. In contrast, the Hindu–Muslim riot in 1987 in Delhi remained confined to the walled city, a traditional area in which riots have occurred with some regularity" (1990,11). Communal conflicts of the kind analyzed by Brass (1996), Roy (1994), Amin (1995), and others also point to the relevance of symbolically charged space as not only the locus of contention but as its object. As Das (1990, 11) points out: "The control of sacred spaces and their protection continues to be an important symbol around which communal conflicts tend to be organized."

7   Tasks Ahead

Contentious politics does not unfold, to quote geographer Doreen Massey, "on the head of a pin, in a spaceless, geographically undifferentiated world" (1984, 4). As my admittedly uneven survey shows, space and place are increasingly seen as crucial explanatory dimensions in the study of contentious politics. What sorts of questions does a spatial approach to politics lead us to ask? First, how is protest or social movement activity affected by the dominant social, political, cultural, and/or economic relations in a certain region? For example, does the fact that patronage is a prevailing informal way of doing politics in certain places of the world affect the form that collective action takes in such regions? Second, how does physical space affect the origins and course of joint action? For example, do certain types of city layouts favor, discourage, or preclude certain types of contentious politics? How is co-presence, a crucial dimension in social movement activity, affected by, say, suburban life? How are protest tactics influenced by the geographic isolation of a particular community? Third, how and why do particular forms of making claims and/or expressing grievances tend to recur in time and others tend to disappear after a short use? How are recurring forms of protest rooted in habitual, everyday practices? For example, how do particular types of routine survival strategies used by the urban poor impact on the type of actions adopted during subsistence crises? And last, how and why do certain sites acquire the character of meaningful places in the aftermath of collective action? What are the concrete processes of meaning-making at work in, say, the transformation of an otherwise ordinary street corner into a popular memorial that reminds those passing by of either heroic or regrettable contentious experiences?

Geographers and social scientists agree in that contentious politics should be seen both geographically structured and geographically structuring collective practices. Contention, in other words, takes place in extant geographies and creates new ones. Despite existing theoretical agreements, there is still much empirical research to be done on the difference space and place make in the origins, dynamics, and outcomes of politics. Let's get to work.

REFERENCES

AGNEW, J. 1987. *Place and Politics.* Boston: Allen Unwin.

AMIN, S. 1995. *Event, Metaphor, Memory: Chauri-Chaura 1922–1992.* Berkeley: University of California Press.

ARDITTI, R. 1999. *Searching for Life: The Grandmothers of the Plaza de Mayo and the Disappeared Children of Argentina.* Berkeley: University of California Press.

AUYERO, J. 2002. The judge, the cop, and the queen of carnival: ethnography, storytelling, and the (contested) meanings of protest. *Theory and Society*, 31: 153–89.

——— 2003. *Contentious Lives: Two Argentine Women, Two Protests and the Quest for Recognition.* Durham, NC: Duke University Press.

BARRERA, A. 2002. El movimiento indígena ecuatoriano: entre los actores sociales y el sistema político. *Nueva Sociedad*, 182: 90–105.

BAYAT, A. 1997. *Street Politics: Poor People's Movements in Iran.* New York: Columbia University Press.

BOUVARD, M. G. 1994. *Revolutionizing Motherhood: The Mothers of Plaza de Mayo.* Wilmington, Del.: Scholarly Resources.

BRASS, P. 1996. *Riots and Programs.* New York: New York University Press.

BROWN, M. 1997. Radical politics out of place? The curious case of ACT UP Vancouver. Pp. 152–67 in *Geographies of Resistance*, ed. S. Pile and M. Keith. London: Routledge.

DAVIS, D. 1999. The power of distance: re-theorizing social movements in Latin America. *Theory and Society*, 28: 585–638.

DAS, V. (ed.) 1990. *Mirrors of Violence: Communities, Riots, and Survivors in South Asia.* Oxford: Oxford University Press.

FARGE, A., and REVEL, J. 1991. *The Vanishing Children of Paris.* Cambridge, Mass: Harvard University Press.

FEAGIN, J., and HAHN, H. 1973. *Ghetto Revolts: The Politics of Violence in American Cities.* New York: Macmillan.

FOUCAULT, M. 1979. *Discipline and Punish.* New York: Random House.

——— 1980. *Power/Knowledge*, ed. C. Gordon. New York: Pantheon.

GAMSON, W. 1990. *The Strategy of Social Protest*, 2nd edn. Belmont, Calif.: Wadsworth.

GEERTZ, C. 1981. *Negara.* Princeton, NJ: Princeton University Press.

GIDDENS, A. 1984. *The Constitution of Society.* Berkeley: University of California Press.

GOTTDIENER, M. 1985. *The Social Production of Space*. Austin: University of Texas Press.

GOULD, R. 1995. *Insurgent Identities: Class, Community, and Protest in Paris from 1848 to the Commune*. Chicago: University of Chicago Press.

HARVEY, D. 1989. *The Condition of Postmodernity*. Cambridge, Mass.: Blackwell.

LEFEBVRE, H. 1991. *The Production of Space*. Oxford: Blackwell.

MCADAM, D. 1982. *Political Process and the Development of Black Insurgency, 1930–1970*. Chicago: University of Chicago Press.

——Tarrow, S., and Tilly, C. 2001. *Dynamics of Contention*. Cambridge: Cambridge University Press.

MACFARQUHAR, L. 2003. The strongman: where is Hindu-nationalist violence leading? *New Yorker*, May 26: 50–7.

MCPHAIL, C. 1971. Civil disorder participation: a critical examination of recent research. *American Sociological Review*, 36: 1058–73.

——1991. *The Myth of the Madding Crowd*. New York: Aldine de Gruyter.

——1992. *Acting Together: The Organization of Crowds*. New York: Aldine de Gruyter.

MARTIN, D., and MILLER, B. 2003. Space and contentious politics. *Mobilization*, 8 (2):143–56.

MARX, K., and ENGELS, F. 1998. *The Communist Manifesto*. London: Verso; originally published 1848.

MASSEY, D. 1984. Introduction: geography matters. In Massey and Allen 1984, 1–11.

——1994. *Space, Place, and Gender*. Minneapolis: University of Minnesota Press.

——and Allen, J. (eds.) 1984. *Geography Matters!* Cambridge: Cambridge University Press.

MILLER, D. 1985. *Introduction to Collective Behavior*. Belmont, Calif.: Wadsworth.

PILE, S. 1997. Introduction: opposition, political identities and spaces of resistance. In Pile and Keith 1997, 1–32.

——and Keith, M. (eds.) 1997. *Geographies of Resistance*. London: Routledge.

POLLETTA, F. 1999. "Free spaces" in collective action. *Theory and Society*, 28: 1–38.

PRED, A. 1990. *Making Histories and Constructing Human Geographies*. Boulder, Colo.: Westview.

PUTNAM, R. 1994. *Making Democracy Work*. Princeton, NJ: Princeton University Press.

ROLDÁN, M. 2002. *Blood and Fire: La Violencia in Antioquia, Colombia, 1946–1953*. Durham, NC: Duke University Press.

ROSENTHAL, A. 2000. Spectacle, fear, and protest: a guide to the history of urban space in Latin America. *Social Science History*, 24 (1): 33–73.

ROUTLEDGE, P. 1993. *Terrains of Resistance: Non-violent Social Movements and the Contestation of Place in India*. Westport, Conn.: Praeger.

——1997. A spatiality of resistance: theory and practice in Nepal's revolution of 1990. In Pile and Keith 1997, 68–86.

ROY, B. 1994. *Some Trouble with Cows*. Berkeley: University of California Press.

RULE, J. 1988. *Theories of Civil Violence*. Berkeley: University of California Press.

SAWYER, S. 1997. The 1992 Indian mobilization in lowland Ecuador. *Latin American Perspectives*, 24 (3): 65–82.

SEWELL, W. H. 2001. Space in contentious politics. Pp. 51–88 in *Silence and Voice in the Study of Contentious Politics*, ed. R. Aminzade et al. Cambridge: Cambridge University Press.

SMITH, D. 1987. Knowing your place: class, politics, and ethnicity in Chicago and Birmingham, 1890–1983. Pp. 277–305 in *Class and Space: The Making of Urban Society*, ed. N. Thrift and P. Williams. London: Routledge.

SMITH, S. 1987. Petrograd in 1917: the view from below. In *The Workers' Revolution in Russia, 1917: The View from Below*, ed. D. D. H. Kaiser. Cambridge: Cambridge University Press.

SOJA, E. 1989. *Postmodern Geographies: The Reassertion of Space in Critical Social Theory.* London: Verso.

SVAMPA, M., and PEREYRA, S. 2003. *Entre la Ruta y el Barrio: La Experiencia de las Organizaciones Piqueteras.* Buenos Aires: Biblos.

TARROW, S. 1996. The people's two rhythms: Charles Tilly and the study of contentious politics. *Comparative Studies in Society and History*, 38: 586–600.

THOMPSON, E. P. 1993. *Customs in Common.* New York: New Press.

TILLY, C. 1964. *The Vendée.* Cambridge, Mass: Harvard University Press.

——1995. Contentious repertoires in Great Britain. In *Repertoires and Cycles of Collective Action*, ed. M. Traugott. Durham, NC: Duke University Press.

——2000. Spaces of contention. *Mobilization*, 5: 135–60

——2003. Contention over space and place. *Mobilization*, 8: 221–6

TUAN, Y. F. 1977. *Space and Place.* Minneapolis: University of Minnesota Press.

VARSHNEY, A. 2002. *Ethnic Conflict and Civic Life: Hindus and Muslims in India.* New Haven, Conn.: Yale University Press.

WOLFORD, W. 2003. Families, fields, and fighting for land: the spatial dynamics of contention in rural Brazil. *Mobilization*, 8: 157–72.

WRIGHT, A., and WOLFORD, W. 2003. *To Inherit the Earth: The Landless Movement and the Struggle for a New Brazil.* Oakland, Calif.: Food First Books.

ZHAO, D. 1998. Ecologies of social movements: student mobilization during the 1989 pro-democracy movement in Beijing. *American Journal of Sociology*, 103: 1493–529.

CHAPTER 31

··

USES OF LOCAL KNOWLEDGE

··

DON KALB

LOCAL knowledge has become global business. In the last two decades, transnational banks and corporations have begun to pride themselves on posters at airports of their global reach and simultaneous talent for local solutions. Governments, from big poor states such as India to small rich countries like Belgium, indulge in decentralizing their authority and capacities to local levels ostensibly to make their bureaucrats respond to local needs as expressed in local knowledge. Big city administrations delegate discretionary powers to districts and neighborhoods for the same purpose. Western development and aid programs to poor countries are insisting on the need to incorporate the local knowledge of villagers in project design and implementation. Most miraculously, the International Monetary Fund and the World Bank, among the world's most insulated and expert-driven administrations, have since the mid-1990s been pleading consistently for the inclusion of local knowledge in research and policy-making. Local knowledge and the puzzle of how to discover and how to use it, clearly has become a favorite of expert seminars worldwide.

This *must* carry multiple oxymoronic qualities. Local knowledge is notoriously hard to define, but any definition includes the following properties: it is relational, situated, practical, dynamic, positional, unevenly distributed, and often communicated orally or bodily.[1] It concerns forms of knowledge generated and situated

---

[1] Bourdieu 1990; Ellen 1998; Geertz 1983; Goody 1987; Ginzburg 2002; Long and Long 1992; Appfel-Marglin and Marglin 1990; Scott 1990; 1998; Sillitoe 1998.

within complex local life-worlds; it refers to the know-how of dealing with local complexity and exigency. As they meet with the administrative logic, formal rationalism, "project life," and "audit cultures" of large-scale modern bureaucratic or expert organizations the outcome is inevitably a contradictory brew. The contemporary dream of global experts to codify what are thought to be local knowledges into a universal "Knowledge Bank," something the World Bank according to some should eventually become, and then combine this with a repository of freely downloadable "best practices," is a utopian project of truly Enlightenment proportions; but it is not hard to see why it is doomed to fail.[2] The reasons are theoretical and ontological. But they can also be read from a wealth of recent analyses and stories such as the following one by the development specialists Allan and Martin Rew (forthcoming).

The Eastern India Rainfed Forest Program, amply sponsored by the British Department for International Development and spearheading the effort to incorporate local knowledge, had a program for "participatory tree planting". It had noted the large chunks of unused soil around villages on the Chottanagpur plateau, West Bengal. Focus groups and other modern "participatory" techniques to explore local ideas had led to a consensus among representatives from several villages: local inhabitants wanted cashew trees. The assumption was that cashews could add considerably to the diversification and security of local incomes. There seemed to be full "buy in" by local leaders and the experts thought it was an entirely rational and appropriate preference. After planting the cashews, astonishingly, the trees were all but neglected. There was hardly any interest in cultivating and harvesting them. Instead, various border conflicts with adjacent villages emerged over territories that turned out to have been historically contested. By planting trees on them villages within the program had at once gained an edge in this contestation over land in relation to villages outside the program. Development workers had not previously been aware of such historical and hidden disputes; no one had told them. The tree-planting program had apparently been manipulated in order to resolve such disputes in the favor of some villages over others. Even more basically, village people seemed to have opted for the trees because nothing else appeared to be on offer; and they thought it was not smart to decline a gift. But in all probability they had never really intended to do forest work, harvest the cashews, and turn themselves into cash-croppers for the international food industry. Sure, they

---

[2] The "Knowledge Bank" idea resembles the earlier Human Relations Area Files project which was meant to catalogue local cultures and make them available for large-scale comparative analyses in anthropology and other social sciences. Few analysts ever made use of it and it has largely gone into oblivion. A different issue is the collection of indigenous knowledges concerning landscape, flora, and fauna as is done by Michael Warren's Center for Indigenous Knowledge for Agriculture and Rural Development at Iowa State University; see www.iiitap.iastate.edu/cikard. For the debate on local farmers' knowledge and the need for its incorporation in development see Chambers, Pacey, and Thrupp (1989) and Scoones et al. (1996). Local agricultural knowledge is an altogether different theme than local social and political knowledge as discussed in this chapter.

worked their rice paddies to provide for some basic nutrition and gain some local prestige. But the men were essentially seasonal migrants and informal worker-peasants, certainly no farmers. They were not prepared to transform their livelihoods entirely because some development organizations plus accompanying consultants had for once put an eye on them. Neither the British development workers nor the Indian experts, in spite of all their modern participatory techniques and sincere pledge to build on local knowledge, had understood that these people were not farmers at all.

Pace the "Knowledge Bank" fantasy, the story warns us against treating local knowledge as a thing in itself that is shared locally, can be discovered, registered, and codified, depending on correct methods and proper translation. Since Kuhn (1962), Feyerabend (1975), Latour (1986; 1993), and others, we are aware that Western science itself is more an institutionalized social practice, guided by history, interest, and politics, than a disembodied set of portable methods and universal laws; the human sciences even more so than others. Local knowledge certainly far surpasses Western formal knowledge in its contingent, flexible, and political nature. Local knowledge is by definition embedded knowledge, a set of situated, embodied, and practical insights into dynamic and shifting social relations and institutions of production and reproduction; including all the often hidden divisions, suppressions, and misrecognitions that such wisdom inheres. It is also suffused by habits, preferences, duties, and virtues that stem from its social and practical character, and that change if circumstances demand. It is first of all knowledge for place-based social survival and as such deeply political. It is knowledge, in James Scott's words, that serves as a weapon for the weak, even though it will regularly favor first of all the strong among the weak (as gender specialists are most systematically aware of). Indeed, it is both object and provisional outcome of continuous formal and informal contestation.

Knowledge, therefore, may not be the right word for it: relational and practical learning would be a better framing. Also, the prefix local has become increasingly problematic. As institutional securities on the ground over the last decades have continually been deepened by global process ("the disappearance of the peasantry, the end of the welfare state, the end of development, postfordism, globalization, etc.") and local actors have been forced to improvise and regroup in response, they often have done so by building, expanding, engaging, or imagining connections in space. Their understandings have necessarily followed suit. Much of local knowledge nowadays reflects a keen awareness of global conditions and practices, albeit from very specific and utilitarian vantage points (Moore 1996). Anthropologists such as Ann and Norman Long (1992) have called attention to these "knowledge interfaces." And Arjun Appadurai (1996), Ulf Hannerz (1992; 1996), Daniel Miller (1997), and I (Kalb 2002; 2004), among others, have emphasized the various ways in which global "scapes" have been folded into and appropriated by contemporary local communities.

But this has never been just a one-way, top-down flow of knowledge, as is well illustrated by the current effort of large-scale administrations to incorporate and work with local knowledge. On the contrary, the reverse way has been traveled just as often. James Scott has even argued that "formal order ... is always ... parasitic on informal processes, which the formal scheme does not recognize, without which it could not exist, and which it alone cannot create or maintain" (1998, 310). He shows that high-modernist designs, such as Prussian forestry, Stalinist agricultural collectivization, or the urban modernism of Le Corbusier could in the end only function by allowing local actors to make junctions between plan and practice. Like the East India Rainfed Forest Program, the *Normalbaum* that was developed on the Prussian feudal estates, one of the key inventions in the development of scientific forestry, became a failure for the lack of recognition of its wider habitat, human as well as natural (Scott 1998). Scott emphasized the distinction between *techne* and *metis* (practical know-how) and argued that without incorporating or rather leaving space for the latter, formal technocratic knowledge creates failed or unsustainable outcomes.

This is also true outside the proverbially complex world of agricultural and human habitats. High modernist industrialism, for example, often stymied local invention and led to local stagnation in the next round. Competitive alternatives to Fordist and Taylorist mass production emerged in industrial districts worldwide by making full use of local knowledges of materials, processes, markets, as well as industrial relations and community relations and turning them into new skills to be transferred to the next cohorts of local actors (Sabel and Zeitlin 1985). The same happened with organizational forms: Japanese, East Asian, and post-socialist industrialists recombined the latest global paradigms of industrial organization with local forms, networks, and knowledges, creating distinctive and powerfully competitive local capitalisms[3]—which are now, paradoxically, often threatened with homogenization by IMF or European conditionalities as core capitalisms become impatient with the obstacles put in their way.

Local knowledge, therefore, is always locked in a dialectical relationship with the actions of accumulated capital and coercion. By definition, such power wielders come armed with formal "universal" knowledge, and with the intention to turn local knowledge into new, reproducible, and exploitable formats for their own advantage. It is therefore not so much its local quality that makes local knowledge distinctive, but rather its embedded, relational, practical, and contingent form of knowing and learning, as against formal deductive reasoning.

This definition implies that incorporation into the canon, however, is necessarily problematic. Apart from ontological reasons, there are also strategic reasons to despair about the "Knowledge Bank" and similar designs for incorporating local knowledge in formal bureaucratic and technical systems. Consider how local knowledge comes to be

[3] Sayer and Walker 1995; Grabher and Stark 1997; Storper and Walker 1989; Storper 1997.

known to non-local publics. Meeting an external expert who comes to tap your local knowledge, first, and then helping him or her to turn it into what global civil society-speak would call a "local consensus," is a highly consequential, power and interest-laden event: there is by definition something serious at stake, something that will lead to gain or loss for some, both materially and in relation to self-respect and dignity. Local knowledge as we know it is thus by definition generated in an unequal, tension-ridden, and contingent event of social interaction. The transcripted, filtered, and polished outcome of that event is what we will finally get to know as local knowledge. Without this production sequence we would never hear about it. Experts are minimally the midwives of local knowledge, but sometimes rather the godfather or godmother. What experts often tend to reify as a thing called local knowledge can thus better be seen as the contingent product of a complex and dynamic field of power relationships, both among locals as well as between locals and their external interlocutors. It is a negotiated project or program rather than an empirical fact. And the program is by definition interest driven: it is always part of radical emancipatory and democratic projects on the one hand, or expert, administrative, or corporate driven interests on the other, and sure they sometimes overlap.

1   RADICAL DEMOCRATIC PROJECTS

Radical academic work in political anthropology and sociology, as well as cultural studies and social history, since the 1960s regularly sought to restore or reconstruct "the voices of the poor," the agency of the powerless, and the weapons of the weak from a reconstructed Marxist, feminist, or post-structuralist/culturalist starting point. Their efforts reflected the emergent vocabularies of contemporary (new) social movements that criticized the achievements and governmentalities of liberalism, communism, social democracy, or nationalism. Beyond the modern gods of economic growth, "development," and bureaucratic redistribution, social movements often coined what were seen as more cultural or identity based claims for the recognition of alternative modernities. The new studies were closely affiliated. Their objective was to capture the culturally suffused political will and moral economies of dependent populations in their moments of resistance to domination. They showed that rulers as well as ruling orthodoxies in historiography and social science systematically sought to disqualify such "insubordination" as backwardness, fanaticism, the in itself not very meaningful byproduct of stress caused by social change and social differentiation, anomie, deviance, or—classically—as a misguided belief in irresponsible and charismatic leaders.

Also, academic research was bent on differentiating the moral visions of the rank and file within local movements and protest-events from the post-hoc interpretations of established leaderships, such as social democrats in Western Europe, communists in Eastern Europe or East Asia, and nationalists in India and other post-colonies. Victorious movements had often retrospectively repressed more radical or alternative popular possibilities.

The keyword was borrowed from Antonio Gramsci: "the subaltern." It referred at once to classes—suppressed and dependent, also in their cultural and political productions—and to meanings, hinting at their un-obvious difference and distance from ruling orthodoxies and their hidden and unrealized alternative potentialities. In other words, it did precisely what the Marxist concept of class had failed to do in a convincing way, and it did so by leaving actual locations, relations, and contents open. Local knowledge became a symbol for a methodology that sought to wrest a relational and contextual account of the emergent visions of justice that underlay collective action, rituals, myths, rumors, stories, everyday practices, and other events from sources often produced by the dominant, though supplemented and enriched by local and participatory techniques (such as ethnography, oral history, etc.) as well as theory and comparison.

In contrast to the consultants who are currently seeking local knowledge to help ease, legitimate, or bolster the interventions of the powerful, all of this academic work was keenly aware of the contingency and embeddedness of the provisional judgments of subalternity. There was no idea of local knowledge that had merely to be registered, codified, and stored. Rather, it had to be read between and behind the lines of local practice; it had to be recovered; it was often softly spoken, and not necessarily with one voice, or even a clear voice, to paraphrase Gerald Sider (1986). It could also be silenced by circumstance and be held in stock for a while, only to come powerfully to the surface when times required or allowed so. In this vein—I am just giving some examples from an impressive body of literature—Barrington Moore (1978) showed why and how miners in the Ruhr had a distinct idea of how industrial society had to be ordered and which social rights had to be respected by ruling classes; and why they became rebellious when such rights lay under fire. Erhard Lucas (1976) showed why the political outlooks of iron workers in Solingen and other small iron making places in the *Bergische Land*, even though firmly on the left, were quite radically different from Moore's miners and why they left the miners alone in their post-First World War rebellion. John Foster (1974) explained why textile workers in Oldham easily married over status distinctions while Tyneside shipyard workers stuck with their own groups, and how such marital behavior was part and parcel of wider political perceptions. E. P. Thompson (1963) in England and Ranajit Guha (1989) in India explained why recurrent local rebellions of workers and peasants in Lancashire and Bengal were certainly no "rebellions of the belly" but a fight for the recognition of their specific moral economies. Guha also showed that local visions of alternative social orders were not necessarily secular, as so much of social science or nationalist history believed they had to be or at least had to become. In India, upland *Adivasi* protest was regularly framed in millenarian visions of the return of a god-king from a golden past. This was not restricted to the colonies. Shoemakers and cigar makers in proto-industrial rural zones in the southern Netherlands also derived strong and dissenting moral visions from Social Catholicism (Kalb 1997), as did groups of miners in the Ruhr and, later, Polish workers organized in the Solidarity union (Ost 1990). Jean and John Comaroff (1991a,b) described how black migrant workers in the South African Bantustans imported the Zionist church from African-American communities in Chicago to radicalize local Methodism and nurture a strong vision of a just kingdom to critique apartheid, exploitation, and dispossession. Kakar (1996) showed how violent *Hindutva* supporters indulged in "chosen traumas" in the context of a failing and partly criminal local state and depressed regional economy in Hyderabad, India. This was all shown to be local knowledge par excellence: causations of particular insights and convictions always started from the social particularities of place, from the modes of local rule and its insertion in wider systems of power and exchange, and from the unequal everyday relationships of local social survival. Subaltern knowledge, of course, made use of written and codified sources and traditions—religions as well as secular and critical trad-itions—but its meaningful reality (its use, its "parole") was an enacted and per-formative one, firmly embedded in the exigencies of local life.

In one aspect, though not in another the work of James Scott (1990) realized the potential of this perspective to the full. Scott focused on "everyday forms of resistance," making a distinction between "public and hidden transcripts." He argued that open and organized resistance had historically been the exception rather than the rule among subaltern classes. The absence of open and organized dissent, however, did not necessarily mean the absence of dissent or alternative moral perceptions. People would fake consent in public, adhere to prescribed rituals of obedience, and then in private and everyday life mock the powers that be, vote with their feet, and develop repertoires of shared knowledge of how to suffer less and profit more. Scott described a plethora of such hidden transcripts in various human societies and finally concluded that there was little evidence histor-ically and comparatively of a robust cultural hegemony by elites over subaltern classes, or even cultural hegemony at all. Local, private, everyday knowledge was by definition sheltered, distinct, and subversive.

In his notion of hidden transcripts, Scott took the idea of local knowledge to its logical conclusion: the local and the everyday harbored by definition important secrets about the independent insights, judgments, and strategies of common people. If you wanted to know what local people thought about their circumstances and the social order they lived in, you had to go local, have a beer, drink *chai*, and in particular stay with the family (which he saw as the most intimate site, and the most impenetrable for power-holders). But in another respect, he lost the sense of how local knowledge came about, how it functioned, and what it could signify. Scott, in his more theoretical passages, was not very interested in the *particular* social relations of rule, production, and reproduction, in which hidden transcripts emerged. He worked on a much higher level of abstraction: the essential subaltern as it were. The hidden transcript, consequently, became universal and free-floating rather than situated. It tended to become the full property of its possessors rather than the tentative speech acts of its users or the emergent ethos of local social relationships. While strong on the hidden aspect of the radical project of local knowledge, Scott in the end lost sight of that other defining moment: the relational, contingent, and situated nature of it.

Thus, all societies in his vision became a specimen of the hierarchical agricultural civilizations from which he drew most of his examples; even contemporary industrial workers in the West could be approached with the tools derived from them. He thereby overlooked the intricate ways in which local life worlds could internally be shaped and stratified according to the logics of overarching power, in modern societies perhaps even more so than in premodern ones. Small-scale and intimate worlds are never just independent in their social constitution but often rather a product of wider logics of rule and accumulation. They are never just themselves, as Scott realized so powerfully in his later work. And while this may not prevent people from having some private thoughts of their own, and even sharing them with friends, it does prevent them from doing so under conditions of their own choosing. Wider hierarchies and centralized logics of rule and accumulation do impose on local and intimate life sharp strictures, silences, and forms of repression and exclusion in which local actors become more than merely complicit. Such wider hierarchies become easily internalized in the local, and localities often become more focused on their own pecking orders, the daily fights of excluding some and including others, than on shared and generalized contempt for the rulers up there. Scott, though aware of the danger, envisioned the local too much as a sociologically sheltered and culturally egalitarian or intimate sphere; hence his celebration of the family. And he thought liberal democratic societies were most protective of such shelters.

Not surprisingly, there is an important debate connected to this about the nature of what Gramsci (1991) called hegemony and Foucault called governmentality (Burchel, Gordon, and Miller 1991), and the ways to study it. Scott has been criticized for working with a problematic concept of cultural hegemony that assumes perfect equivalence of meanings and outlooks among subalterns vis-à-vis the powerful if it has to be present. Rather, it has been argued by political anthropologists such as Roseberry (1994), Smith (2004), and Gledhill (2000), harking back to aspects of Gramsci (Williams 1976; 1977; 1980), and Hall (Morley and Chen 1996), that hegemony is a relational moment rather than an idealist one. It is not first of all about consensus, imposed or negotiated, but rather about historic power blocs that shape social relations in ways that exert particular pressures and set certain limits on achievable social forms. It is about social relationships and spaces of negotiation and autonomy within systems of domination more than about culture in the idealist sense. Thus, local, everyday, and subaltern knowledge, while not necessarily subservient to orthodoxy, can never simply ignore the wider relational fields of power: rather *it is entirely shaped within it*, and it is by definition forced to speak the language developed by it if it wants to be heard at all, as Roseberry has insisted (1994). In modern societies, moreover, there is an impressive array of institutions, from very immediate ones such as the family, to (on a first look) more distant ones like education, the media, the welfare state, and the law, that help people to continually habituate and internalize such authorized languages and orthodoxies. Foucault and Gramsci seem stronger now than Scott's radicalization of the local and the everyday once made us believe.

The local, however, does retain a peculiar force. It does indeed not lie in the supposed independence and the depth of its hidden knowledge but in the particularity and contingency of the social relationships in which that knowledge is situated, generated, used, put to work. It lies, in the language of Henri Lefebvre (1991) and David Harvey (2000), in the particular dialectic of the production of space and the making of place. The first, a large-scale process of the creation of human spaces for accumulation—cities, regional, national, transnational landscapes; the second, an intimate as well as public process of inhabiting, appropriating, claiming, and contesting place. The two are closely intertwined. In *Expanding Class* (1997) I explore this dialectic in the case of Eindhoven, the Netherlands. I show that Eindhoven, headquarters of Philips electronics, emerged in the later nineteenth century out of the dynamics of an export oriented and light manufacturing landscape. The flexibility that gave the region its dynamism, arose from what I called flexible familism: a practice that stemmed from worker-peasant families in need of extra cash bringing in their daughters to work next to male family members on textiles, cigars, and lamp-bulbs. In the course of time, labor market positions and statuses of fathers who could bring in several disciplined daughters were strengthened vis-à-vis those who could not. For employers in a peripheral location, competing with more advanced producers on the European market this greatly enhanced their flexibility to deal with periodic fluctuations in demand or with short-term price erosion. The reserve army enjoyed systematic social protection from the family, so to say. This locational advantage attracted further cycles of capital investment and ultimately led to a world famous light manufacturing site, featuring in the 1930s the largest radio factory in the world and in the 1950s and 1960s one of the biggest manufacturing complexes in Europe. In distinction to earlier explanations why worker protest was absent here—Catholicism, traditionalism, paternalism—I show that Philips and other manufacturers gradually discovered the local knowledge of how children were socialized for exploitation by an implicit alliance between large employers and parents; and how the city itself, the set-up of its neighborhoods, its social housing, its proportions and densities, its leisure, education, and social services became, step by step, geared to the requirements of an expanded flexible familism, as private and public rulers, further exploring local knowledge learned more and more about the preconditions of their own success. There was indeed a local secret to be discovered: it was about the displacement of class to gender and generation and hinged on the question of how and to what extent parents could be seduced to help capitalists exploit their daughters without breaking the family bonds. The emerging implicit contract between capitalists and parents involved jobs, housing, pensions, and other social services. It perverted love and care with exploitation and duty, and made courting between the sexes difficult and stressful even though it often turned out to be the only realistic option for escape. In 1930 the ILO complimented Philips for its excellent local knowledge and rare corporate responsibility, and offered it as an example of socially acceptable capitalist governance.

2   CORPORATE, ADMINISTRATIVE, AND EXPERT DRIVEN PROJECTS

What then is the difference between Philips and the Eastern India Rainfed Forest Program in their dealings with local knowledge? It is about the interests that guide formal rationalities: Philips could discover local knowledge, in particular the logics that tied parents and children to electronics production and to each other, because this knowledge touched at the heart of its own long-term self-interest and because its self-interest was—for the time being—firmly anchored in the locality and its key relationships, in fact an active and experimental force in shaping it. In contrast, the Eastern India Rainfed Forest Program failed to discover that local inhabitants were not farmers at all because its rationale and self-interest were to plant trees, not to support mobile populations with mixed occupations and multiple sources of income, nor even exploit them and derive a profit or prestige from that. Moreover, it could not spend ten or more years experimenting with forms of local intervention to learn about the upland localities and develop a whole social services department based on it, as Philips did in Eindhoven (or Ford in Detroit). Its objective, determined in Delhi or London was to plant trees on unused soils and its employees were supposed to help spend its budget in a short timespan and with a maximal number of planted hectares as the outcome. While Philips was in a very material sense "interested" in local knowledge and local populations, the Eastern India Rainfed Forest Program was not.

Thus, administrative, corporate, and expert driven projects to discover local knowledge and incorporate it in the formal orders of modern bureaucracies should not necessarily be shallow. What they discover and will do with it depends on the interests behind it and, consequently, on the nature, duration, and intensity of its local entanglements. Partial overlap of local and global interests or bargaining between actors can facilitate (partial) discovery of local knowledge and (partially) successful incorporation and implementation[4].

IKEA, for instance (*Financial Times*, Sept. 15, 2004) seems to have understood some of the mechanisms that force parents to exploit their children in the carpet-making belt of Uttar Pradesh, India, and is developing ways to prevent that from happening. Why? In its effort to attract home-working rug-makers in the villages— and to reduce its production costs by entering into a specialized zone with among the lowest wages on earth—it discovered that many households were tied to local entrepreneurs by extensive debt and loan systems. If such debts accumulated in the course of keeping a household with young children afloat, parents saw no other chance than stepping up home production by engaging their children (thus again contributing to overall depressed wage levels). IKEA, in a bid to tie households into its own producer networks, started to offer women workers a small wage supplement to be invested in a mutual fund. In pressing times, mothers, thus, were entitled to small loans. This prevented them from turning to local sharks and drift into debt-peonage. It also enabled them to keep their children at schools— some of which were sponsored by IKEA. IKEA's interests, thus, were served well. In addition, its record of corporate responsibility could be advertised for public relations in the West. Of course, IKEA would never study local knowledge to explore the possibilities for union organizing or other structural openings for lifting the region's 300,000 carpet-making households out of poverty. On the contrary, it regularly warned that rising expectations could force it to move elsewhere. But partial overlap of interests did enable it to discover and roll back the webs of debt bondage.

Local knowledge has recently become global business. But this is not so much because of such partial convergence of hard material and production-based interests between global and local actors as in the Philips and IKEA cases. It is for reasons that are rather ideological, even though deeply rooted in the exigencies of organizing neoliberal governance as a globally hegemonic paradigm. The reasons are threefold: (1) the increasing legitimacy-deficit of governments, global administrations, and corporate actors as they intervene in local life worlds; (2) the mobilizations of local and global civil society; and (3) the severe curtailment of independent academic research, on the one hand, and the proliferation of expert and consultancy assignments for social scientists on the other. These conditions combine to push for "participation," "accountability," "responsibility," and "citizenship" (among others) as serious concerns for governmental and corporate administrations (see, e.g., Cooke and Kothari 2001; Muller and Neveu 2002; Nuijten 2004). These recent

---

[4] Compare Charles Tilly (2003; 2005) who argues that the extension of states into trust networks through time leads to bargaining and, in the European experience, to democratization. Democratization is supposed in turn to turn sheltered spheres and knowledges into public ones.

global logos serve as a substitute for substantive democracy as their practical meanings are often defined by large-scale administrations, sometimes in dialogue with experts from (highbrow) civil society-interrogators. The conditions and the logos now lend increased urgency for administrations to deal with local knowledge in order to facilitate acceptance—"buy in" is the codeword—by local constituencies. This has non-trivial consequences for methods and meanings.

Consider a programmatic statement by James Wolfensohn, then President of the World Bank: "We are realizing that building development on local forms of social interchange, values, traditions and knowledge reinforces the social fabric. We are starting to understand that development effectiveness depends in part on 'solutions' that resonate with a community's sense of who it is" (quoted in Frankland 2003, 301). Behind the lines one hears Putnam's social capital and the anthropologists' emphasis on community and identity, which both mean to say that global administrations like the World Bank seek a decidedly enlightened and responsible role.

Here is how the enlightened role worked out in a dam building project by AES Corporation, the largest power producer in the world, at Bujagali falls, Uganda, a project partly financed by the World Bank. British Consultants were hired by the Ugandan government to do the required Environmental Impact Assessment, which included "the effects on culture and objects of cultural value" (Frankland 2003, 302). The consultants as well as AES first floated the (incorrect) idea that the dam could well mean free electricity for everyone and jobs to many; then they did a survey among a sample of the local population, the result of which indicated that a majority of local people saw no overriding problem with the dam and looked forward to the benefits; next they interviewed the local ancestral head of the clan that "owns" Bujagali falls and who runs the Bujagali shrine—a tourist attraction—Namamba Budhagali, who insisted that he had to perform rituals for which AES would have to pay. Finally, after some very profitable rituals the Chief decided that the shrine could be relocated at the cost of $ 20,000 to be paid to him personally. Frankland (2003) reports that local politicians immediately put forward two further claims of ownership of the shrine. Before long, scores of local actors began claiming monetary compensations. And they were actually getting them, because the dam had to be built, the decision had long been taken, very substantial loans were waiting, and AES had not for nothing budgeted seed and goodwill-money during the incubation period of the project.

The message is, indeed that consultancy and expert activity surrounding corporate and governmental interventions in local life worlds is rarely meant to deepen local democracy or to generate reliable insights into local knowledge. It is intended to facilitate swift and smooth implementation of large-scale interests defined elsewhere. It serves to help administrations to achieve critical "buy in" of potentially obstructive actors. Not surprisingly, this often causes serious strategic trouble—the monetary inducements everywhere associated with "buy in" are regularly accompanied by corruption and may lead to local rebellions against corporations, authorities, and local beneficiaries; but it also causes ontological and conceptual trouble for the quest to gather and incorporate local knowledge. In this case, as in many others, local culture became for all practical purposes defined, reduced, and reified as an object—the shrine and its warden. Next, in this case as well as in others, a Western conception of individual property rights was projected onto it. The consultants as well as AES's panel of experts had not reached far beyond what Western tourists would have expected and learned. A "meltdown of meaning," as Johan Pottier (2003) calls the phenomenon.

This is not an extreme case of global actors intentionally getting local knowledge wrong for the sake of accumulation. By assuming that local communities are by and large homogeneous and can be represented by elected or delegated individuals, as has become common in Western democracies, global actors like mining corporations in New Guinea or Shell in Nigeria have regularly helped to create new local power structures that are perceived as largely illegitimate in local eyes. Western conceptions of property or of family and kinship, too, often stand in the way of a deeper understanding of local structures and local knowledge. Canadian and Australian mining corporations in New Guinea used to hire consultants to "map" local family lineages in order to determine which individuals were entitled to compensations for allowing "their" soil to be exploited. But kinship here, as in large parts of Africa, was traditionally a flexible instrument to include people in systems of work, exchange, and reproduction, not a "thing" to be represented in a written document that would form the basis of exclusive property claims and compensations. It resulted in the wholesale destruction of local trust. Deep suspicion, local rebellions against both the mines and the profiteers, and protracted periods of armed tension have been the consequence of such "consultant understandings" of local knowledge in both Nigeria and New Guinea: revolts against the meltdown of meaning (Silitoe and Wilson 2003).

The question of method deserves a final word. While anthropological methods—fieldwork, participant observation, ethnographic interviews, local histories and archives, and the ethnographic report for representing the findings—are the proverbial tool to discover local knowledge, modern administrations, as we have seen do not find it easy to deal with such approaches. Understandably so, since bureaucracies rely on formal knowledge and formal procedures and have built their own reputations and the reputations of their staff on the prestige of context-free, anonymous, calculable, transferable, and "transparent" forms of knowing. Ethnographic methods and insights, like their subject and basic material, do not easily fit in such grids: the definitive reason to doubt the viability of the "Knowledge Bank" or similar efforts. Perhaps the best illustration is the fate of the "participatory poverty assessments" that the World Bank has been doing since c.1995. Participatory poverty assessments make use of local focus groups in order to gather qualitative material on local situations of poverty in non-Western countries

(Campbell and Holland 2005; Campbell 2005). They are the World Bank's answer to the critique on expert-driven quantitative representations of poverty, the effort to include "the voices of the poor." Tellingly, the material gathered is labeled "subjective" as against objective. And in the process of synthesizing it with the quantitative material from household surveys into a national report it is step by step transformed into just another quantitative survey of how many people think they are poor according to their own definition or not. Clearly, if the administrative objective is counting the poor, focus groups are not likely to teach researchers anything beyond that goal, even though local knowledge may hide a host of clues of why people are withheld from securing more satisfying livelihoods. Typically these assessments employ economists rather than anthropologists. Local knowledge of situated social relations is first conceptualized as mere subjective meaning and then turned into things and numbers. Despite loudly proclaimed good intentions, what modern administrations, even the most enlightened ones, take as local knowledge is still often at best a rather contradictory brew; at worst it sometimes differs little from the mechanisms of corruption or exploitation.

References

APPFEL-MARGLIN, F., and MARGLIN, S. A. (eds.) 1990. *Dominating Knowledge: Development, Culture, and Resistance*. Oxford: Clarendon Press.

APPADURAI, A, 1996. *Modernity at Large: Cultural Dimensions of Globalization*. Minneapolis: University of Minnesota Press.

BOURDIEU, P. 1990. *The Logic of Practice*, trans. R. Nice. Cambridge: Polity.

BURCHEL, G., GORDON, C., and MILLER, P. 1991. *The Foucault Effect: Studies in Governmentality*. Chicago: University of Chicago Press.

CAMPBELL, J. forthcoming. Theory and method in the study of poverty in East Africa. *Focaal—European Journal of Anthropology*, 45.

——and HOLLAND, J. forthcoming. Development research: convergent or divergent approaches and understandings of poverty. *Focaal—European Journal of Anthropology*, 45.

CHAMBERS, R., PACEY, A., and THRUPP, L. A. (eds.) 1989. *Farmers First: Farmer Innovation and Agricultural Research*. London: Intermediate Technology Publications

COMAROFF, J., and COMAROFF, J. 1991a. *Of Revelation and Revolution*: vol. 1, *Dialectics of Modernity on a South African Frontier*. Chicago: University of Chicago Press.

——1991b. *Of Revelation and Revolution*: vol. 2, *Christianity, Colonialism and Consciousness in South Africa*. Chicago: University of Chicago Press.

COOKE, B., and KOTHARI, U. (eds.) 2001. *Participation: The New Tyranny*. London: Zed Books.

ELLEN, R. 1998. Reaction to Sillitoe. *Current Anthropology*, 39: 238–9.

FEYERABEND, P. K. 1975. *Against Method: Outline of an Anarchistic Theory of Knowledge*. London: New Left Books.

FOSTER, J. 1974. *Class Struggle and the Industrial Revolution: Early Industrial Capitalism in Three English Towns*. London: Weidenfeld and Nicolson.

FRANKLAND, S. 2003. The still waters of the Nile. In Pottier et al. 2003, 298–321.

GEERTZ, C. 1983. *Local Knowledge*. New York: Basic Books.

GINZBURG, C. 2002. *Clues, Myths and the Historical Method*. Baltimore: Johns Hopkins University Press.

GLEDHILL, J. 2000. *Power and its Disguises: Anthropological Perspectives on Politics*. London: Pluto Press.

GOODY, J. 1987. *The Interface Between the Written and the Oral*. Cambridge: Cambridge University Press.

GRABHER, G., and STARK, D. (eds.) 1996. *Restructuring Networks in Post-Socialism. Legacies, Linkages and Localities*. Oxford: Clarendon Press.

GRAMSCI, A. 1991. *Prison Notebooks*, ed. J. A. Buttigieg. Vol.1. New York: Columbia University Press.

GUHA, R., and SPIVAK, G. C. (eds.) 1989. *Selected Subaltern Studies*. New York: Oxford University Press.

HANNERZ, U. 1992. *Cultural Complexity: Studies in the Social Organization of Meaning*. New York: Columbia University Press.

——1996. *Transnational Connections: Culture, People and Places*. London: Routledge.

HARVEY, D. 2000. *Spaces of Hope*. Berkeley: University of California Press.

KAKAR, S. 1996. *The Colors of Violence: Cultural Identities, Religion and Conflict*. Chicago: University of Chicago Press.

KALB, D. 1997. *Expanding Class: Power and Everyday Politics in Industrial Communities, The Netherlands, 1850–1950*. Durham, NC: Duke University Press.

——2002. Afterword: globalism and post-socialist prospects. Pp. 317–35 in *Post-socialism*, ed. C. Hann. London: Routledge.

——2004. Time and contention in the "great globalization debate." In Kalb et al. 2004, 9–48.

——PANSTERS, W., and H. Siebers, H. (eds.) 2004. *Globalization and Development: Key Issues and Debates*. Dordrecht: Kluwer Academic.

KUHN, T. S. 1962 *The Structure of Scientific Revolutions*. Chicago: University of Chicago Press.

LATOUR, B. 1992. *Laboratory Life: The Construction of Scientific Facts*. Princeton, NJ: Princeton University Press.

——1993. *We Have Never Been Modern*, trans. C. Porter. Hemel Hempstead: Harvester Wheatsheaf.

LEFEBVRE, H. 1991. *The Production of Space*, trans. D. Nicholson-Smith. Oxford: Blackwell.

LONG, N., and LONG, A. (eds.) 1992. *Battlefields of Knowledge: The Interlocking of Theory and Practice in Social Research and Development*. London: Routledge.

LUCAS, E. 1976. *Arbeiterradikalismus. Zwei Formen von Radikalismus in der deutschen Arbeiterbewegung*. Frankfurt: Verlag Roter Stern.

MILLER, D. 1997. *Capitalism: An Ethnographic Approach*. Oxford: Berg.

MOORE, B. 1978. *Injustice: The Social Bases of Obedience and Revolt*. London: Macmillan.

MOORE, H. 1996. Introduction. In *The Future of Anthropological Knowledge*, ed. H. Moore. London: Routledge.

MORLEY, D., and CHEN, K.-H. (eds.) 1996. *Stuart Hall: Critical Dialogues in Cultural Studies*. London: Routledge.

NUIJTEN, M. 2004. Governance. In Kalb et al. 2004, 103–30.

OST, D. 1990. *Solidarity and the Politics of Anti-Politics: Opposition and Reform in Poland since 1968*. Philadelphia: Temple University Press.

POTTIER, J. 2003. Negotiating local knowledge: an introduction. In Pottier et al. 2003, 1–29.

—— Bicker, A., and Silitoe, P. (eds.) 2003 *Negotiating Local Knowledge: Power and Identity in Development*. London: Pluto.

REW, A., and REW, M. forthcoming. Quality at some point became quantity: flawed participatory and other poverty assessments from Northern Orissa. *Focaal—European Journal of Anthropology*, 45.

ROSEBERRY, W. 1994. Hegemony and the language of contention. Pp. 355–66 in *Everyday Forms of State Formation: Revolution and the Negotiation of Rule in Modern Mexico*, ed. G. M. Joseph and D. Nugent. Durham, NC: Duke University Press.

SABEL, C., and ZEITLIN, J. 1985. Historical alternatives to mass production: politics, markets and technology in nineteenth century industrialisation. *Past and Present*, 108: 133–74.

SAYER, A., and WALKER, R. 1992. *The New Social Economy: Reworking the Division of Labor*. Oxford: Blackwell.

SCOONES, I., THOMPSON, J., and CHAMBERS, R. 1996. *Beyond Farmer First*. London: Intermediate Technology Publications.

SCOTT, A. J., and STORPER, M. (eds.) 1986. *Production, Work, Territory: The Geographical Anatomy of Industrial Capitalism*. London: Allen and Unwin.

SCOTT, J. C. 1990. *Domination and the Art of Resistance: Hidden Transcripts*. New Haven, Conn.: Yale University Press.

—— 1998 *Seeing Like a State*. New Haven, Conn.: Yale University Press.

SIDER, G. M. 1986. *Culture and Class in Anthropology and History: A Newfoundland Illustration*. Cambridge: Cambridge University Press

SILLITOE, P. 1998. The development of indigenous knowledge: a new applied anthropology. *Current Anthropology*, 39: 223–52.

—— and WILSON, R. A. 2003. Playing on the Pacific ring of fire: negotiation and knowledge in mining in Papua New Guinea. In Pottier et al. 2003, 241–72.

SMITH, G. 2004. Hegemony: critical interpretations in anthropology and beyond. *Focaal—European Journal of Anthropology*, 43: 99–120.

STORPER, M. 1997. *The Regional World: Territorial Development in a Global Economy*. New York: Guilford Press.

—— and Walker, R. 1989. *The Capitalist Imperative: Territory, Technology and Industrial Growth*. Oxford: Blackwell.

THOMPSON, E. P. 1963. *The Making of the English Working Class*. London: Gollancz.

TILLY, C. 2003. *Contention and Democracy in Europe, 1650–2000*. Cambridge: Cambridge University Press.

—— 2005. *Trust and Rule*. Cambridge: Cambridge University Press.

WILLIAMS, R. 1976. *Keywords: A Vocabulary of Culture and Society*. London: Fontana.

—— 1977. *Marxism and Literature*. Oxford: Oxford University Press.

—— 1980. *Problems in Materialism and Culture: Selected Essays*. London: Verso.

PART VIII

POPULATION MATTERS

CHAPTER 32

WHY AND HOW POPULATION MATTERS

DAVID LEVINE

THE Black Death, in the words of Fernand Braudel (1984, 314–15), was a "headlong tumble into darkness—the greatest drama ever registered in European history." Braudel's colleague, Robert Fossier (1987, 1), claims that the Black Death was "the turning point in the history of the world, from which Dante's heirs went out to conquer new continents over the next four centuries." Despite its horrendous toll, the Black Death pales in comparison with the so-called "Columbian exchange." There would initially appear to be parallels between the European Black Death and the holocaust wreaked among the "virgin populations" in the New World when, within a century after European contact, only 10 percent of the aboriginal population remained in both Peru and Mexico. What is more, the European structures of political, social, and cultural life adapted to the regime of epidemic mortality rather than being overwhelmed and ultimately destroyed by it.

The Black Death arrived in Europe in 1348; its first visitation killed roughly half the population. The impact of plague mortality was electrifying, bewildering, and terrifying. Petrarch, who lived through the first fury of the pandemic and lost his lover and many friends, asked the basic question 550 years ago:

When will posterity believe that there was a time when, without combustion on heaven or earth, without war or other visible calamity, not just this or that country but almost the whole earth was left uninhabited ... empty houses, deserted cities, unkempt fields, ground crowded with corpses, everywhere a vast and dreadful silence?

A full world was emptied. There was no effective method of protection which made the plague so much more frightening. It destroyed all bonds of community in a maelstrom of fear and loathing.

This new mortality regime, a recurring cycle of pestilential fury, became the spectre haunting Europe. Yet for those living in the shadow of the Black Death, life went on; the struggle for mastery took place in new circumstances which often inflected the course of change. The politics of class relations in feudal England, the politics of state formation in Renaissance Tuscany, and the politics of religious life in early modern Germany took place in the context of demographic transformation but, as I will argue, changes in population composition and vital rates identify pivotal transformations in social life though these experiences can only be understood by placing them in context and by finding non-demographic explanations for them. Of course, causal arrows also flowed in the other direction: changing forms of behavior modified social systems.

In contrast to the post-Columbian devastation that nearly destroyed aboriginal populations and led to the complete reorganization of polities and societies in the New World, in the Old World the impact of the Black Death was nowhere near so catastrophic. But it was hardly uneventful. Half the European population died when it was first exposed to the plague; thereafter, for almost 300 years, the plague was an unwanted—and occasionally deadly—part of the European experience. The plague became endemic; sometimes its recurrence was national, but often it was local and highly virulent. This unpredictability dominated the historical experience of all who lived through this terrible period. Indeed, the "domestication" of epidemic mortality in late medieval Europe is, in this comparison, its most outstanding characteristic. The "domestication" of plague stretched social fabrics. It radically changed how people negotiated with cultural systems of inherited meaning in new circumstances as well as how they responded to the deployment of political force in a situation that revised the relative powers of contending parties. After the onset of the new mortality regime, neither belief nor power could be carried out in old, traditional ways; new methods were developed that reflected the impact of plummeting population levels on the organization of social and political relationships. Dramatic reductions in population levels meant that there were fewer surviving workers whose previously abridged freedoms had been the key to feudalists' ability to hold sway over them. For feudalists, their pie was getting smaller because rents as well as services became difficult to collect and also because there were many fewer people who owed them tribute; but, additionally, their control itself was being challenged in novel ways. For the state, the slipping grasp of its intermediaries posed key problems regarding its own legitimacy as well as its day-to-day control over the polity—and its tax revenues. Plummeting levels of survival gave a poignant edge to the jeopardy of survival itself and, in so doing, raised questions about the Church's claims to intercede on survivors' behalf with the ultimate arbitrator of life-after-death. However, to look at the changing configuration of both political power and cultural beliefs in this way telescopes processes that were resolved contingently, in historical time. Indeed, the immediate political response to the decline of population was a class solidarity on the part of the feudalists while the existential questions surrounding survival and salvation were understood within inherited cultural structures and systems of belief.

Systems of power were stretched but did not immediately break apart in response to the Black Death. Demographic decline took place both dramatically with the outbreak of plague in 1348/9 and then persistently for generations thereafter as the empire of epidemic disease kept the European population under its influence. The decline of population—in terms of overall population totals and also of the jeopardy of individual survival—was a crucial factor in determining the context in which struggles for mastery took place. Collective and individual strategies could not be oblivious to this brute fact. Yet, like the long-terms trends in climate—and these six generations lived in colder, wetter conditions than the ten generations who had lived before them, after the year 1000—demographic forces created the changing conditions of living in both natural workplaces and socially created polities. Neither feudalism, nor the Tuscan city-states, nor Christendom buckled under the pressure of catastrophic levels of mortality. Yet, none survived intact; each bore the imprint of living in the shadow of death. The decline of feudalism, the rise of the Renaissance Florentine state, and the divisions within Christendom were worked out in new circumstances that were dominated by the precipitous decline in the number of people. The contingency of these resolutions makes it evident that even such a momentous, radical demographic event like the Black Death was not, by itself, a crucial determinant of historical change. But if we deny the independence of the demographic variable, we cannot gainsay its importance.

1 THE BLACK DEATH AND THE END OF FEUDALISM IN ENGLAND

The English state apparatus and the feudal system of landholding joined forces in the wake of the Black Death when it seemed that a dearth of labor might send its cost skyrocketing. Everywhere, across Europe, "From Spain to Norway, princes, parliaments and city magistrates vied with each other to regulate wages" (Genicot 1966, 706). It seems that, in the short term, the landlords' political response to the decline in laborers was effective. However, in the longer term, feudal oppression disappeared, but landlords did not (Jones 1975, 941). The salience of this point emerges clearly when we look at the social experience of feudalism in the aftermath of the Black Death in England.

Even before the Black Death there had been landlord petitions seeking aid from the royal courts in improving their legal position against fugitive villeins. Thus, feudal lords had long experience of relying on the state to enforce class solidarity amongst themselves. Confronted with the imminent collapse of their familiar world, the governing elite—king, magnates, and gentry—coalesced under the umbrella of state authority, compelling individuals to stand by their obligations. After the Black Death, legal reforms that were largely oriented toward disciplining the working classes provided an overt and explicit governmental tool for the constitutional exercise of upper-class solidarity (Palmer 1993, 12, 141, 213). The English state's involvement in the direct enforcement of labor discipline "had the effect of unifying the discontent, because the target of resentment was no longer the individual lord alone but also the local officials of the government" (Hilton 1985, 62).

The state apparatus and the feudal system of landholding had joined forces in the wake of the Black Death when it seemed that a dearth of labor might send its cost skyrocketing. Almost as soon as the plague reached England's shores, the 1349 Ordinance of Laborers was proclaimed. Less than two years later, the next Parliament enacted the 1351 Statute of Laborers because

a great part of the people, and especially of workmen and servants, lately died of the pestilence, many seeing the necessity of masters and great scarcity of servants will not serve unless they may receive excessive wages, and some rather willing to beg in idleness than by labour to get their living.

The sudden opportunity that the plague mortality gave to surviving laborers—to secure higher wages or to demand personal and tenurial freedom—catalyzed the political nation. Similar laws were enacted in other countries, but what distinguished the Ordinance and Statute of Laborers was that in England the landlords closed ranks and vigorously enforced these laws. In the changed conditions which developed after the massive depletions caused by the Black Death, landlords had thus used the political relationship inherent in feudal tenures to protect themselves from the new realities of the marketplace. The implementation of labor legislation reflected the constellation of political forces centered in Parliament, describing the gravitational orbit of social relations in the fields and forests of the countryside. From a bottom-up perspective, there was little evidence that the landlords were willing to give up their extra-legal powers conferred by the laws of villeinage: indeed, "the real significance of the labour laws lies not so much in their actual application as in the threat they posed to the interests and rights of all those—about a third of the total population—that made their livelihood by selling their services on the open market" (Ormrod 1996, 158).

The immensely heavy mortality caused by the Black Death may have been more purgative than toxic because the surplus population had been so great before 1348, but the recurrent visitations of the pestilence created unprecedented contradictions between the interests of feudal landowners and the dependent population. These contradictions were not resolved immediately. The trickle of feudal rents and incidental payments demanded from villeins did not immediately cease as might be expected in a situation in which labor became scarce. The first appearance of the plague was followed by a long series of poor harvests leading to high prices which provided employers some flexibility in dealing with their laborers' demands for higher wages. If seigneurial incomes seemed to maintain themselves, it was largely because wages were traditionally "sticky." Or, to look at this matter from another perspective, as R. H. Hilton suggests, "there was a general seigneurial reaction between the first plague [1348] and the 1370s, showing itself in the successful depression of wages below their natural level and in a relative increase in revenues from land" (Hilton 1983, 40–1). The bumper harvest of 1375 ended a long cycle of poor yields and high prices that masked the changing terms of trade between land and labor. But because wages remained "sticky," workers were kept in line for a generation after the first visitation of the plague. However, the new conditions of the later 1370s meant that the landlords' Indian summer came to an abrupt end. This economic factor played a crucial part in mobilizing resentment against both land-lords and tax collectors which would explode in 1381.

If the "seigneurial reaction" was not completely successful it was not for want of trying on the part of the upper classes. In the century after the Black Death eight pieces of labor legislation were passed by the English Parliament which all had the aim of fixing rates of pay, enforcing contracts of employment, making work compulsory when offered (at fixed rates of pay), and even trying to require migrant workers to carry a kind of internal passport (Clark 1983). These severe demands proved to be unenforceable because it was impossible to create and to sustain the kind of surveillance network that would carry out the letter of the law. The feudalists' failure reflected both their reluctance to buck the economic currents of the time and the plebeians' ability to move with them. It has been estimated that wage levels rose three- or fourfold in the century after the Black Death.

The Indian summer of demesne farming was, therefore, quickly followed by the winter of the feudalists' discontent. The Peasants' Revolt of 1381 must be situated in this transition:

the root cause of the Revolt . . . is to be found in the persistent attempts made by manorial lords and employers of all degrees to halt changes which no power on earth could check or halt, still less reverse. If there had been no attempt to interfere with these changes there would have been no Revolt. . . . when everyone in authority, wherever one turned for work, seemed to be in a conspiracy to snatch back all the advantages and opportunities that surviving the pestilence afforded to even the humblest labourer, then the king's foreign gambles, his everlasting proddings and probings for money, and his newfangled taxes, proved to be more than ordinary men and women were prepared to put up with.   (Bridbury 1992, 37)

Something had had to give. In the event, seigneurialism withered away as the social relations of production were defeudalized across the length and breadth of the English countryside.

Seen in the perspective of this long-standing experience of feudal exactions and their newly acquired knowledge regarding the economic benefits of freedom, the competition for labor gave the unfree population an unparalleled opportunity to seek out a better life elsewhere. In the words of a 1376 Commons petition:

above all and a grater mischief is the receiving of such vagrant labourers and servants when they have fled from their master's service; for they are taken into service immediately in new places, at such dear wages that example and encouragement is afforded to all servants to depart into fresh places, and go from master to master as soon as they are displeased about any matter. For fear of such flights, the commons now dare not challenge or offend their servants, but give them whatever they wish to ask, in spite of the statutes and ordinances of the realm.

The Peasants' Revolt of 1381 is intimately linked with the death rattle of feudalism but changes in the level of population or the supply of land could alter the supply and demand axes but, by themselves, are insufficient to explain the character of political struggle. This is because the power of feudal lords was not solely related to such economistic measures. Their powers were economic as well as social, political, and juridical. And, these powers were backed up by their monopoly on military force which was cloaked in its mantle of parliamentary legislation.

The Peasants' Revolt was of short duration and most of the action was localized in the home counties, around London. It was provoked by the king's third poll tax in four years—its lesson "so far as contemporaries were concerned . . . [was] that taxation did not have to be onerous to be thought intolerable." The Great Revolt of 1381 stopped the "fiscal experiments" (i.e. Poll Taxes) and "put an end to large expenditures on war. Effective war with France practically ceased" for a generation. The 1381 Revolt reversed the drift of fiscal policies which had, since the reign of Edward I (1271–1307) enabled the crown to wage war by extracting ever-higher taxes from the population.The fusion of state and seigneurial powers gave the English Rising its historical importance. It was, above all, a revolt against feudalism. In the words of one contemporary: "the supreme and overriding purpose of the revolt was the abolition of villeinage and all that went with it. This was the heart of the matter" (Fryde 1991, 237, 252, 259–60).

In the later fourteenth century the changing terms of trade between now scarce labor and now plentiful land made a mockery of the earlier state of affairs so that the cost, as it were, of villeinage would have become painfully obvious. Moreover, it should not be forgotten that the manorial lords' immediate response to their declining incomes had been to turn the feudal screw ever tighter. Thus it is appropriate to note that there was a spatial dimension to the Peasants' Revolt and the attempted reimposition of strict seigneurial controls which raised tensions in the highly manorialized south and east where demesne production for the market was most firmly entrenched and where labor services were least likely to have been commuted into cash payments. In these fluid circumstances the indignity of villeinage would have been exacerbated by the increasingly heavy economic penalties attached to it.

Villeins struck out against their servitude and resisted feudal exactions. The quantitative extent of such flight is not really crucial because if some fled then the others bargained from a much stronger position. Furthermore, such mobility was probably more characteristic of the smallholders and cottagers than the substantial villeins who were the central core of the manorial tenantry. In the Huntingdonshire manor of Broughton, for example, fifty-six of ninety-six tenements had acquired new tenants between 1380 and 1400. Now, obviously, this was a matter not only of old tenant families dying out and/or migrating but also of new ones taking up vacant holdings. So, it would appear that before 1400 the population had not dwindled to such an extent that there was no longer a demand for manorial holdings. But, in contrast to earlier periods, what is unusual about the end of the fourteenth century is that it had now become the tenants—most often the smaller ones—who were exercising choice by switching masters. The feudal lords of Broughton were no longer able to use their monopsony control over land to regulate the mass of the population. And, this state of affairs was acceptable to the lords because what they now had come to prize, even above their feudal rights which were vanishing before their very eyes, was their need to maintain an income flow and their capital base—by whatever means necessary.

A century ago, J. Thorold Rogers wrote that the "solid Fruits of victory rested with the insurgents of June 1381 . . . the perils had been so great and the success of the insurrection was so near that wise men saw that it was better silently to grant that which they had stoutly refused in Parliament to concede" (quoted in Hilton 1950, 2). Eight years later, in fact, the parliamentary regulations of 1389 recognized that the new conditions of peasant mobility and labor shortage had put an end to the reign of custom. This statute enacted that wages were to be promulgated locally, twice a year. Such flexibility was previously unknown. It was a frank acknowledgment that market relations and seigneurial controls could no longer coexist.

2   PLAGUE, RENAISSANCE, AND THE RISE OF THE FLORENTINE CITY-STATE

The Black Death attacked the northern and central Italian communes with a spectacular ferocity. The best evidence comes from Tuscany. As Giovanni Boccaccio wrote in the *Decameron* about the first visitation of plague in Florence, as a result of which "it is reliably thought that over a hundred thousand human lives were extinguished within the walls of the city":

> this scourge had implanted so great a terror in the hearts of men and women that brothers abandoned brothers, and in many cases wives deserted their husbands. But even worse, and almost incredible, was the fact that fathers and mothers refused to nurse and assist their own children, as though they did not belong to them.

Florence's population fell from roughly 120,000 in 1338 to under 50,000 in 1351. By the time of the 1427 *Catasto* the city's population was enumerated at 44,068, an overall decline of 69 percent. In the rural area surrounding Florence, losses were similar. The population of Prato, a mid-sized Tuscan commune thirty kilometers northwest of Florence, seems to have begun a slow decline in the generation before mid-century but thereafter the fall was precipitous: if its enumerated population in 1427 is taken as an index of 100 then Prato's total in 1298–1305 was 424.3. In the countryside of Prato the overall decline was rather less dramatic—from an index-figure of 266.6 at the beginning of the fourteenth century down to 100 at the time of the 1427 *Catasto*. In the smaller Tuscan towns of Pistoia, Pisa, Arezzo, Volterra, and San Gimignano, where there was also an initial halving of the taxable hearths in 1348/9, the later fourteenth century was a period of prolonged decline. Later figures suggest a population as little as one-quarter the size of its pre-plague levels.

Siena, Florence's prime rival for power in Tuscany, seems to have been the most grievously wounded Tuscan city, if we are to lend credence to the chronicle of an employee in the *Biccherna* [the city's accounting office] who suggests an urban death rate of 84 percent. His own experience was profoundly searing:

> Father abandoned child, wife husband, one brother another; for this illness seemed to strike through the breath and sight. And so they died. And none could be found to bury the dead for money or friendship. Members of a household brought their dead to a ditch as best they could, without priest, without divine offices. Nor did the [death] bell sound. And in many places in Siena great pits were dug and piled deep with the multitude of dead.... And I, Agnolo di Tura, called the Fat, buried my five children with my own hands.

Across the Sienese *contado*, the governing council recognized that "decrease is unequal. Some have decreased moderately, others immensely, still others have been completely wiped out." In 1353, for example, the male population of the commune of Sassoforte had fallen to 31 percent of its pre-plague level; the neighboring commune of Montemassi suffered at least a 73 percent death rate among adult males (Bowsky 1964, 17–25).

The historians of these demographic relations note that "In the thirteenth century, these secondary Tuscan towns had competed vigorously against one another, and also against Florence. Their subsequent steep demographic decline *allowed* Florence to consolidate its economic and political hegemony and to assume the status of a regional metropolis" (Herlihy and Klapisch-Zuber 1985, 60–72; my emphasis). This suggestion that there was a direct connection between the generalized demographic crisis and the particular Florentine response is questionable. To be sure, wealth became more highly concentrated in the Florentine *reggimento* and this inequality became more pronounced in the century after the Black Death, but a more relevant factor was the Florentines' arrogation of political and military power over the whole Tuscan economy. The Arno city prospered at the expense of its lesser rivals: Pisa, Lucca, Pistoia, Prato, Volterra, Cortona, Arezzo, and Siena as well as the smaller towns like San Gimignano, Colle, and Certaldo.

The hegemony of Florence created a distinctively "early modern" state-formation that was based on the way in which Tuscan society's unequal distribution of wealth narrowed the inner-circle of the plutocracy and seemingly ended the social mobility which had been so pronounced in Florence up to the time of the Black Death. The super-rich, who were about to embark on an orgy of palace-building in Renaissance Florence, could often trace their descent back generations to a rustic migrant who came to the Arno city in search of the legendary wealth of its gold-paved streets. The first Medici, for example, was mentioned in the Florentine archive in the twelfth century—probably the younger son of a minor gentleman, a rural notary, or a rich peasant who came from the Mugello Valley where the family continued to maintain extensive ties. In 1216 the *arriviste* moneylender Bonagiunta de' Medici became a member of the communal council. His descendants would rise and fall again in an oscillating spiral of social mobility that was a microcosmic example of the vast social movements that were changing the texture of Western society. Others could trace their lineage back to an even older ruling class whose landed patrimonies were thoroughly imbricated with their involvement in the early modern worlds of commerce, banking, and industry.

The Renaissance Florentine upper-class was characterized by the immense spread of each lineage's wings; the branching process was effusive. Florence, like other centers of the commercial revolution, was run by vast cousinages which drew the upper classes—landed and mercantile—into labyrinthine kinship alliances. Perhaps the most graphic illustration of the success of this family strategy was the urban tower which combined a feudal regard for security and sanctuary with a clannish regard for kith and kin. The skyline of Florence was spiked with about 150 towers in the mid-twelfth century when the magnates exercised almost uncontested, centrifugal authority. By 1200 it seems that there were more than 200 of these five- or six-storey buildings in a city that could not have had more than about 25,000 inhabitants. The communal city of the early thirteenth century was a battlefield, scarred by feuds and vendettas. In this regard, Florence was similar to other Tuscan cities but the slow accretion of power in the hands of the communal authorities was paralleled by both the demise of these fortifications and the gradual restriction of patrician violence.

The public sphere was defined in the process of clarifying the boundary line between the authority of the state and the influence of the patrician families. One of the first acts of the *primo popolo* in the 1250s was to begin a systematic campaign against the towers of the magnates which was to continue for nearly a century until their military functions were destroyed (Becker 1960, 432). Even without their fortified residences, upper-crust Renaissance Florentines continued to maintain strong roots in their neighborhood; their residences clustered in districts where their ancestors had lived for centuries (Kent 1977). The Florentine patricians were gradually weaned from a politics of faction and vendetta; their domestication almost imperceptibly brought them into the civic polity. The early Renaissance elite was thus an almost differently constituted species from the feudal magnates of the *dugento*; in place of a born aristocracy, the members of the later elite were characterized by their multiple indentities—lineage continued to be important but so, too, were class relations, patron–client networks, neighborhood connections, ritual and religious brotherhoods, business associations, and political alliances. Leonardo Bruni, an early fifteenth-century chancellor, made this point in his *Panegyric*, when he claimed that "the city itself stands in the center, like guardian and lord, while the towns surround Florence on the periphery, each in its own place."

Perhaps the key moment in the transformation of Florence from a late-medieval commune into the capital city of a territorial state took place when the super-rich became stockholders in the funded debt which funneled energies of the upper classes into public service (i.e. "civic humanism"), slowly drawing them away from destructive factional battles that had plagued the commune since its earliest days. The creation of a funded debt also allowed the Florentine state to find a secure source with which to pay for its military adventures thereby extending its control over both Tuscan territory and its own citizens. From its beginnings in the pre-plague troubles of the 1340s, the massive decline in population provoked by the Black Death was paralleled by the astonishing growth in the funded debt: one million florins in the 1360s, three million florins in 1400, and eight million by the 1450s (Becker 1967, 2: 233). There was, it would seem, an inverse correlation between population size and the growth of the public debt. It was as if the purgative mortality of the Black Death created a new series of strategies—strategies that were based on communal solidarity rather than older, narrow concerns with lineage.

Public life in early Renaissance Florence clustered around the funded debt. Florence was well on the way to becoming a giant corporation in which the middling and affluent citizenry had invested a very substantial portion of their patrimony. In contrast to the communal polity, which was a material body that had no center of gravity, the *monte* became "the heart of this body which we call city... every limb large and small must contribute to preserving this heart as the guardian fortress, immovable rock and enduring certainty of this salvation of the whole body and government of your State", as legislators of the 1470s wrote. Anything adversely affecting the welfare of the republic "perforce dealt a cruel blow to the private fortunes of the citizenry, for in fact the two had become inseparable" (Becker 1967, 2: 162). The growth of the *monte* indicates the trajectory by which the state had become the largest consumer of capital; a rentier class had become both stockholders and officeholders; even their daughters' dowries were incorporated into movements of the financial octopus. In this way, the decentered polity of the commune was superseded by a joint-stock public company, the Renaissance State. This shared stake was a prime factor in the creation of a more recognizably modern vision of the state whose sovereignty overrode the individual interests of its members.

In the interest of promoting social harmony as well as business-as-usual in the post-plague era, the Florentine state had inserted itself into the organization of the economy. For the capitalist, the main impact of this new development was that the creation of the funded debt guaranteed a fixed return on investments; for the workers, the growth of new institutions—welfare, policing, food supply, and building projects—created a more predictable environment. The elite Florentines who invested in culture, building, and decorative arts during the Renaissance did not only do so because the city was experiencing hard times but also because its economy was precociously modern. Human capital was highly prized. A nascent welfare state—a corporate economy—was being made under civic aegis. The middling sort involved themselves in fraternal institutions devoted to both piety and material aid. Indigents, orphans, and undowered daughters of the respectable, the infirm, the sick, the elderly, and those whose poverty forced them to live below their station all benefited. A strong mercantilist policy successfully guided this expansion, through a program of direction and protection.

The Florentine corporate economy subjected the worker to numerous regulations but it also stabilized the relations between labor and capital. Perhaps this was not a level playing field but it was far better than the free market of the pre-plague era when laborers, working full-time, were unable to earn enough to feed a family of four on a diet consisting solely of bread. After the mid-century crisis, it seems that workers could consume meat, "even the better kinds—veal, lamb, and sausage," and still exercise their leisure preference (Goldthwaite 1985, 343). Stable food prices, low rents, political order, social stability, an organized labor market, a fluid occupational structure, and a premium placed on individual talent all contributed to put the elite of the working class in early Renaissance Florence on the threshold of social respectability. It wasn't much, but it was much better than was available to plebeians anywhere else in Renaissance Europe. It was granted at a price—the effervescence of the popular culture of spontaneous festivals, dancing, singing, tavern life, and popular heresy were made the object of surveillance in reaction to the menace of the many-headed monster of plebeian insurrection.

After the Ciompi insurrection of 1378, the state's apparatus of surveillance was overhauled; the *Otto di Guardia* was a carefully selected tribunal of eight citizens who had wide-ranging powers of repression and played a significant role in changing the captious everyday life of communal Florence into the ordered social ecology of the Renaissance state's capital. It was "an offensive coming from above" as "the courts and the organization of police by the Mid-Quattrocento became instruments, at the disposal of the Florentine patriciate for solving problems and conflicts with his or her social inferiors." Another policing apparatus, the *Ufficiali di Notte* [Officers of the Night] was created in the early fifteenth century to maintain surveillance through a network of spies, informers, and full-time *balestrieri* and *berrovarii*— over matters of private morality, sexual deviance, and child abuse. These new disciplinary institutions guided social behavior into acceptable channels. Anticipating later policies of benign neglect or repressive tolerations, the intra-class squabbles, tavern brawls, and street fights among the plebs were largely beneath the concern of the magistracy which was, in contrast, much more alert when they came upon actions that smacked of sedition (Cohen 1980, 82–9, 127, 157–9, 167, 180, 194, 208).

A kind of welfare absolutism took shape as the continued respiration of the Renaissance social system came to depend on a working population whose daily bread was subsidized as part of a institutional complex made up of hospitals, orphanages, dowry funds, workhouses, and welfare schemes. The independence of the small towns in Tuscany withered, the countryside was de-industrialized, and risk-avoidance came to dominate the rural economy. Taxation and military might enforced this process that sucked the life-blood out of the provincial peasantry and the small-town artisans for the benefit of the few hundred family-clans of the Florentine *reggimento* and their provincial brokers (Benadusi 1995).

3   PESTILENTIAL FURY, CULTURAL DESPAIR, AND THE RE-CREATION OF RELIGIOUS IDENTITIES

The Roman Catholic Church was, arguably, the most proactive state-formation in medieval Europe; but, in the wake of the Black Death, it became a reactive force. In a certain sense, doctrinal hardening had a logic of its own. But when we stand back from the particularity of these intellectual currents, it is impossible not to be impressed by the fact that a society in crisis found its outlet in readily accessible building blocks of intolerance. The mendicant orders led this bloodthirsty campaign. Since their inception at the beginning of the thirteenth century during the Albigensian Crusades against the Cathars in Languedoc, these inquisitors had tried to co-opt popular religious culture and guide it along orthodox channels. It was, indeed, their guiding belief that the crooked timber of humanity could be reformed so that something entirely straight would be built from these raw materials. In directing this sedulous quest for conformity the friars, who were missionaries, polemicists, preachers, and inquisitors, had created a stack of kindling which was waiting to be ignited. These fires of rage were sparked by the pestilential fury of the Black Death. The sedulous quest for conformity was perverted in the course of the fourteenth century into something altogether more frightening—first, the scapegoating of identifiable groups like lepers and Jews and then, second, the displacement of these hatreds onto a much less obviously identifiable group of witches.

For a beseiged Church whose secular powers had become profoundly insecure in the wake of the Black Death, witchcraft came to be seen as a competing source of magical power. And, in this regard, it is interesting to quote Peter Brown's observation that accusations of witchcraft often occur when

two systems of power are sensed to clash within the one society. On the one hand, there is articulate power, power defined and agreed upon by every one (and especially by its holders!): authority rested in precise persons; admiration and success gained by recognised channels. Running counter to this there may be other forms of influence less easy to pin down: inarticulate power: the disturbing tangibles of social life; the imponderable advantages of certain groups; personal skills that succeed in a way that is unacceptable or difficult to understand. Where these two systems overlap, we may expect to find the sorcerer.   (Brown 1972, 119)

The most famous example of late medieval witch-finding is provided by the case of Joan of Arc who grew up while the kingdom of France was in complete chaos, during the 1420s. French disarray was so complete that wolf packs frequently entered Paris, either through breaches in the ramparts or unguarded gates. The reign of the mad King Charles VI (1380–1422) had witnessed the disintegration of social authority. This dislocation was given a vicious twist by internecine feuds and factional murders among the ruling elite. England's triumphant victory at Agincourt and their subsequent alliance with the Burgundians proved to be pyrrhic victories. In the 1420s, a puppet-regime sponsored by the English occupied Paris and most of northern France. France was beset by factional fighting, financial collapse, military defeat, English scorched-earth warfare, pillaging and looting on the part of unemployed soldiers who joined forces in free-booting bands of routiers and écoucheurs, and seething peasant discontent. Ground rents in the heartland of the Île de France were only 10 percent of their level a century earlier—before the wars and the plague. The French countryside was quadruply oppressed from "the genocide that had been perpetrated . . . by bacilli, economic crisis, brigandage, and the English" (Ladurie 1987, 62, 56). The great bread-basket of the Île de France had been almost deserted:

From the Loire to the Seine, and from there to the Somme, nearly all the fields were left for many years, not merely untended but without people capable of cultivating them, except for rare patches of soil, for the peasants had been killed or put to flight.... We ourselves have seen the vast plains of Champagne, Beauce, Brie, Gâtinais, Chartres, Berry, Maine, Perche, Vexin, Norman and French, Caux, Senlis, Soissonais, Valois, as far as Laon and beyond, as far as Hainault, absolutely deserted, uncultivated, abandoned, devoid of all inhabitants, overgrown with brushwood and brambles.   (Quoted in Warner 1991, 34)

Joan of Arc emerged in the late winter of 1429 as France's unlikely savior; she rallied a flagging cause and this intervention ultimately helped the Valois kings to turn the tide of the Hundred Years' War and the reunification of France. Yet once the Maid of Lorraine had provided the energy that enabled the Valois to turn the tide, she was cast aside and left to face the trumped-up charges of heresy by which her English captors sought to snuff out her seemingly magical powers. It was one of those ironies of history that Joan of Arc's trial occurred too soon, so that her judges could not make the charges of witchcraft stick, no matter how hard they tried. In the end, the illiterate farm-girl was overwhelmed by their scholastic logic although they had to settle for a judgment of guilt-by-heresy rather than being able to find her "guilty" of witchcraft. Joan's trial was, of course, political theater; the court's decision was known in advance and the only jeopardy that was attached to the proceedings was related to Joan's steadfast parrying of her inquisitor's relentless questioning (Sullivan 1999).

The doctrine of witchcraft which emerged in the half-century following Joan's trial amalgamated five separate elements into a coherent system: an interest in magic and sorcery was transmuted into the legal concept of black magic through which harm was inflicted on others; the witch sold her/his soul to the Devil in order to gain extraordinary earthly powers; for witches, copulation with the Devil was a rite of initiation and was most frequently linked to females; individual witches were joined together in secret societies; and these leagues were assembled over large distances because, it was argued, the witch's magical powers included the ability to fly. There seems to be little doubt that this coherent doctrine was knit together from both popular fantasies and the fabrications of deluded scholars (Cohn 1975).

The Black Death intensified the contradictions of early modernization by pointedly emphasizing the ambiguous relationship between the clergy and the *saeculum*. The path to salvation may have been prepared by Christ's Passion and the suffering of the Virgin Mary but the massive fact of death was so unpredictable and sweeping in its impact that no one was secure, gave it a personal immediacy and provided the context in which this interpretative search for meaning took place. This drift towards "atomization" was part of a privatization of piety in which the "basic Christian unit tended to become the individual or the family, the privileged place of initiation to elementary religion, to the essential sacraments and daily observance (prayers and fasts)" (Verger 1987, 150). This shift towards the privacy of the introspective self was part of a more general movement in spatial organization as specialized functions, more rigidly defined, replaced undifferentiated areas. This ideal which was "not without parallels to the authorities' vision of the ideal society: more hierarchy, more segregation, stricter regimentation, and closer monitoring of individual behavior" (Contamine 1988, 504).

There is a danger of making an anachronistic assessment of the pre-Reformation Church's vitality from the way in which its public in Germany melted like April snow in the wake of Luther's stand at the Diet of Worms in 1521. Fifteenth-century Germany was pervaded by a "mood of restlessness, of expectancy, of indefinable anxiety" (Dickens 1974, 12). This turbulent, anxious, often violent piety has been called *Frömmigkeit*, which was focused upon the massive uncertainty concerning the appropriate measures to ensure salvation that flourished in the post-plague period. Apprehensive and impatient spirituality was symptomatic of the fears that haunted those who lived in the shadow of the Black Death. Martin Luther was a child of these times. But he rose above them by giving the characteristic *Frömmigkeit* a radically new theological answer to the quest for salvation.

The building-blocks for Luther's novel interpretation of Christian salvation had already been set in place. Martin was the child of an odd couple—a restless entrepreneur and a determined *hausfrau* who seems to have invested her aspirations to regain lost status in her son—status she lost with her marriage to an uneducated peasant. Endowed with immense inner discipline, as a young man Luther had been educated in the most advanced schools of the day. The Young Luther grew up in world that was in despair about salvation and everything in his upbringing drew him more deeply into the vortex of despair engendered by these common concerns—in fact, four of his siblings had died from the plague. But though the Young Man Luther may have achieved success in his chosen calling, he was unsatisfied. Indeed, so far as we can tell, he lived most of his monastic years in a state of existential uncertainty. Hans Luder, the father, had judged Martin Luther to be disobedient but had later accepted his son's career choice—but this was a small matter compared to the sure and certain knowledge that God-the-Father judged Martin Luther to be unworthy of his saving grace. This, in a nutshell, was the predicament that Martin Luther—son and sinner, professor and theologian, believer and churchman—faced squarely. It was a predicament that Luther shared with his contemporaries. It was a predicament that could not be resolved by recourse to accepted practices and received doctrines.

Between his entry into the monastery in 1505 and the fateful day in October 1517, when he posted the "Ninety-Five Theses" on the door of the Castle Church in Wittenberg, Martin Luther found himself in a double bind. On the one hand he tried, with all his might and extraordinary intellectual powers, to understand how he could make himself worthy of God's saving grace while, on the other hand, knowing that the decision was not his to make (von Rohr 1962, 61–74). And, like others, the harder he tried, the less success he met in resolving this Sisyphean task. As he said, "My own situation was this: however blameless my life as a monk, I felt myself standing before God as a sinner with a most uneasy conscience; and I could not believe God would be appeased by any satisfaction I could offer. I did not love but hated this just God, who punishes sinners..." Luther's genius, then, was to propose a wholly new problematic—or, more correctly, he proposed that the original human anthropology found in the Pauline Epistles of the New Testament was the only guide for humans groping for salvation.

In place of the scholastic goal of the monk, the mystic, and the pilgrim who all endeavored to become like God through their wholesale identification with the divine, Luther's reinvented anthropology removed the possibility that humans could earn their own salvation through the traditional combination of good works, contrition, penance, and indulgences. For this reason, there was no need to inquire endlessly into one's motivations or to minutely subdivide sins because simple faith in Christ's grace was the answer to the problems of sin, death, and salvation that vexed contemporaries. Thus, Luther argued, humans had to trust absolutely and unconditionally in the goodwill bestowed upon them by Christ's crucifixion. They had to have faith because they could only be saved by faith, and by faith alone. Justification by faith alone, justification through the unearned imputation of Christ's merits to the sinner formed the flywheel of Luther's theology. Everything else was irrelevant. Everything else was just obfuscation. With that, the entire sacramental edifice—and the accompanying state-formation—that had been built up by the Roman Catholic Church was denied legitimacy.

There were many critics of the fifteenth-century Church, but none was able to gain the public hearing that accompanied Luther's censures. The reason for his unique powers must be connected to his tremendous skill as a polemicist, skills that were aided and abetted by the radical enlargement in the information technology of the times. Luther was an accomplished philosopher and a revolutionary theologian, but what his audience saw—and identified with—was an anguished, pious, suffering Christian. Martin Luther grasped their existential confusion of living in the wake of the Black Death and rendered an intelligible response to his contemporaries' shared sense of *Frömmigkeit*. As one of Luther's young students wrote to his mother, faith in the pure light of the Gospel superseded the "*fantasey, zauwberey, Teüffels gespennszt*, and *Aberglawben*" (fantasy, magic, heresy, Devil's ghosts, and superstition) of her protective charms, fasts, pilgrimages, confession, festivals, vigils, rosary prayers, and endowed masses. For such people, the Reformation was a form of enlightenment that drove the old religion's burdensome superstitions not only out of the mind's eye but also dispelled them from their streets and away from their homes. (Ozment 1975, 83–82) When Reformation Protestants wrote their autobiographies it is clear that they had come to regard the plague as a punishment instituted directly by God which inspired widespread fear and temporarily dissolved religiously-sanctioned social order.

Luther's radical simplification of Christianity—his call to return to the purity of the gospels—struck a responsive chord among his fellow Augustinians, university faculty, wandering students, and especially the massive numbers of lumpen-clergy who were employed in the memorial celebrations of the Mass which had proliferated as the recurrent visitations of the Black Death sent a series of shudders through all ranks of society. The key figures of the German Reformation all acknowledged that they owed their "theological quickening" to Luther who was virtually unknown in 1517 but had become famous by 1521. For them, as for Martin Luther himself, this was not an evolutionary transformation but rather a mutation. Friendship networks tied these men together even before the publication of Luther's "Ninety-Five Theses." These connections proved to be of crucial importance in the transmission of Protestantism by the first-generation evangelic-als who were mostly younger than Luther—who was himself in his mid-thirties. (Hillebrand 1968) The youth of the first-generation evangelicals draws our attention to a strand in the sociology of revolution in which the radicalization of these discontented intellectuals was related to the difficulties they faced in achieving social mobility as their numbers grew much faster than the positions available to them. This disparity not only accelerated the process of political change by increasing their downwards social mobility but also heightened their resentment.

The three phases of the Reformation—the sermon movement, the reformation of the liturgy, and abolition of the Mass—spread successively across southwestern Germany in five, seven, and nine years, respectively. The evangelical spokesmen were most successful in the fragmented interstices of the southwest—a land full of imperial cities, dwarf towns, and knights' fiefdoms—where social and political order was being continuously negotiated. The intensity of commercial contacts in this region created a fertile seed-bed for the transmission of new ideas, too. Along the main roads which criss-crossed this region, the Word resonated back-and-forth between the nodal towns from where it was carried afield to remote villages. The key figures were the preachers—many of whom were clandestine and itiner-ant, but a surprisingly large number were regular clergy and especially the *Pradi-kanten* (foundation preachers) whose charisma, knowledge, and word-spinning skills could be legendary. Reformation sermons were unconventional. They broke with tradition by calling for the active participation of the audience in contrast to the passivity of the traditional believers who had only been called upon to bear witness to the miracles of the Eucharistic transformation. They often preached outdoors, too. Hedge-preachers, frequently known as the eponymous *Karsthans* (roughly translated as "Jack Hoe" with the meaning of something like "jack of all trades" and/or "man of the people") tended to promote the gospel of social unrest and, not surprisingly, the Habsburg administrators hounded them out of their territories as did the Bavarians. The printing presses, too, played a considerable role in transforming the "largely inarticulate sentiments of uneasiness, insecurity, longing for reform into clearly defined issues capable of arousing consent or dissent..." These could now be made objects of public debate. The "most important accomplishment of this mass medium may have been the instantaneous and relatively uniform instruction of a widespread stratum of supporters of the principal reformers" (Kohler 1986, 157, 171).

In a few short years, between 1517 and 1525, European society was jolted by the German struggle with the Roman Papacy. These years had been pregnant with alternative possibilities as the the Emperor Charles V's military victories over the French in Italy, culminating in the Battle of Pavia in 1525, seemed to have put the Habsburgs on the brink of establishing a Holy Roman Empire throughout the heartland of Europe. But the Habsburgs' imperial state-formation was lost to eternity; this pathway was blocked by the upsurge of social, religious, economic, and political turmoil in the German lands—turmoil was multi-faceted and included a Knights' War in 1522/3 and a Peasants' War in 1525/6. It is only partially correct to say that Germany imploded and entered a state of political involution as a result of the Habsburgs' failure. The Renaissance process of territorialization prevented the consolidation of a centralized imperial state; yet the persistence of the hundreds and hundreds of princedoms, city-states, bishoprics, and institutional oddities that continued to retain state-like functions prevented the disintegration of the Old Reich into an archipelago of independent polities.

The Old Reich was "Europe's hollow center." Its flawed but functioning constitution became steadily more refined after 1525 in the protections it purported to offer the weaker states by protecting them from encroachment—or, at least, outright takeover—by their stronger neighbours. This constitutional structure not only provided a constant source of tension but also, paradoxically, varying coalitions which balanced disparate forces to maintain an equilibrium. An equilibrium that was as much the product of discord as accord (Walker 1971, 12–13).

Early modern Germany did not become fragmented because it was static; it became static because it was fragmented. The fragmentation of the Old Reich was its characteristic hallmark, and when we search for the mechanism that set Germany on this course, Martin Luther's overarching presence is unavoidable. Living in the shadow of the Black Death, Martin Luther transformed the late medieval discourse on piety by mastering the novel possibilities of communication that were made possible by the new technology of printing. His pamphlets were best-sellers and his message galvanized political discourse by redirecting it in ways that he defined. His impact was electric. Martin Luther constructed a gospel of social harmony in an age of uncertainty; he insistently connected the preservation of public authority with its private manifestations, most especially the patriarchal domination of the *hausvater. Herrschaft* was thus imbricated within the reproduction of everyday life: the father was the ruler of his household in the same way that the ruler was the father of his land.

4   BACTERIOLOGICAL HOLOCAUSTS AND RECOMBINANT SOCIAL STRUCTURES

In the Europe of the plague-dominated centuries, old characteristics were recombined into new structures. The "bacteriological holocaust" set the context in which feudalism declined, the Renaissance state rose, and the Reformation spread. But, as the comparison with the Columbian impact on the aboriginal population of the Americas makes evident, the Black Death in Europe had a relatively limited impact. In considering the implications of the Black Death it is crucial to emphasize the point that it was a recurrent pandemic. Its real devastation was not just the result of its initial encounter with a virgin population but, rather, the way in which its repeated attacks precluded a quick recovery. It seems to have been akin to a "biological die-off" in which an ecological space was cleared, enabling mutations to develop in relative freedom. However, the plague-mortality regime did not—in and of itself—cause the Peasants' Revolt, Renaissance state-formation, or religious Reformation. Demographic events—even ones as massive as the Black Death—do not act alone nor in a vacuum. Rather, demographic forces acted more as an unpredictable triggering mechanism than as an independent variable.

So, finally, one is led to wonder if there was—and might again be—a threshold level of demographic disaster. If the 90 percent mortality of the Amerindians brought about near-complete collapse, can one say that a 50 percent reduction in population (such as occurred in Europe with the initial occurrence of the Black Death) was inadequate to the task? Or do we need to balance the demographically disastrous impact of European germs with the contemporaneous importation of European arms, armies, and techniques of production (Diamond 1997)? In the absence of Europeans—as opposed to Europeans' germs—can we be so sure that the Amerindian societies' "near-complete collapse" would have been so complete? Could we argue, then, that anything short of annihilation would spare structures of political organization and systems of understanding? Certainly, the European experience of living in the shadow of the Black Death would suggest that social structures are so powerful that they are capable of survival (and mutation) in conditions of extremity.

Instead of exploring demographic effects and evidence across their full range of application, this chapter treated an extreme case—the Black Death—in detail, in order to dramatize the profound connections between demographic processes and social life at large. The key point that has been made is that new demographic parameters were not, in themselves, determinative; rather, they changed the relative powers of contestants whose struggles not only made use of inherited systems of organization and symbolic understanding but also made use of them in novel ways. Population processes and perceptions of demographic structures were intimately linked with ways in which social organizations were imagined. In closing this discussion, let me briefly treat one example of this: in the late eighteenth century it was widely believed that the English (and Irish) population was stationary—or maybe even declining. But, the census enumerations of 1801 and 1811 contradicted this gloomy vision and substantiated Thomas Robert Malthus' recent prognostications that current welfare policies were aiding and abetting the growth of the wrong sort of people in the population. Quite clearly, the impact of vulgar Malthusianism on social policy was electric; at a stroke it altered the parameters of debate and, somewhat later, was a crucial ingredient in completely changing the perception of social welfare. Demographic "facts" were subject to arithmetic logic so that demographic "evidence" changed the way that men understood their political options.

In addition to changing the allocation of welfare, this new, Malthusian perspective on contemporary demographic forces led to a dramatic revision in the perception of Empire: in conditions of stable or declining population—such as was imagined in the pre-census period—it was feared that investment and proactive involvement in imperial projects would not have been feasible as the defeat in the American war of independence seemed to prove. However, the new statistical parameters led early nineteenth-century Britons to be significantly more enthusiastic in responding to the demands of empire. Patrick Colquhoun's *Treatise on the Wealth, Power and Resources of the British Empire* scotched any lingering gloomy apprehensions, leading the most sanguine imaginations of the day to anticipate a new, glorious chapter in the accession of population, territory, and power (Colley 2004). And the benefits worked both ways in a virtuous circle: the empire not only provided a repository for the out-migration of the Malthusian "lesser sort" but also provided a demand for British goods. And, of course, the empire was a resource injecting gobs of capital into the hands of those who controlled the British political economy. Infusions of capital largely underwrote the burgeoning demand for industrial products as well as these consumers' demand for more traditional goods like houses, clothing, furniture, and crockery. The latest historiography on the Industrial Revolution has forced us to recognize that it was just as much about consumer demand and consumer durables as it was about self-acting machinery and steam power. In making sense of these new frontiers of possibility, contemporaries realized that it was not just the actual growth in numbers that mattered; but, rather, it was their perception of that growth which led to radical, new policy initiatives as well as a reconfiguration of the structures in which politics took place.

Population matters to political processes, then, not as an "exogenous" force like cosmic rays, but as a constitutive element of social life. Anyone who treats fluctuations in fertility, mortality, nuptiality, morbidity, or migration as if they occurred outside of politics or prior to politics misses one of demography's great contributions to social analysis: the demonstration that even subtle alterations in social arrangements translate immediately into demographic effects such as shifts in household composition and life expectancy. Such effects, furthermore, reshape human capacities, propensities, and opportunities for political action. The intimate connection between demographic shifts and variations, on one side, and variation in life experiences, on the other, makes demographic effects and demographic evidence crucial to the explanation of political processes.

REFERENCES

BECKER, M. B. 1960. Some aspects of oligarchical, dictatorial and popular *Signorie* in Florence, 1282–1382. *Comparative Studies in Society and History*, 2: 421–53.
—— 1967. *Florence in Transition*, 2 vols. Baltimore: Johns Hopkins University Press.
BENADUSI, G. 1995. Rethinking the state: family strategies in early modern Tuscany. *Social History*, 20: 157–78.
BOWSKY, W. M. 1964. The impact of the Black Death upon Sienese government and society. *Speculum*, 39: 1–34.
BRAUDEL, F. 1984. *The Perspective of the World*. London: Fontana/Collins.
BRIDBURY, A. R. 1992. *The English Economy from Bede to the Reformation*. London: Boydell Press.
BRITNELL, R. H. 1990. Feudal reaction after the Black Death in the palatinate of Durham. *Past and Present*, 128: 28–47.
BROWN, P. 1972. Sorcery, demons and the rise of Christianity. In *Religion and Society in the Age of St. Augustine*. London: Faber and Faber.
CLARK, E. 1983. Medieval labor law and English local courts. *American Journal of Legal History*, 27: 330–53.
COHEN, S. K., JR. 1980. *The Laboring Classes in Renaissance Florence*. New York: Academic Press.
COHN, N. 1975. *Europe's Inner Demons*. New York: Basic Books.
COLLEY, L. 2004. *Captives. Britain, Empire, and the World, 1600–1850*. New York: Anchor Books.
CONTAMINE, P. 1988. Peasant hearth to papal palace: the fourteenth and fifteenth centuries. In *A History of Private Life*, vol. 2, *Revelations of the Medieval World*, ed. G. Duby. Cambridge, Mass.: Harvard University Press.
DIAMOND, J. 1997. *Guns, Germs, and Steel*. New York: W. W. Norton.
DICKENS, A. G. 1974. *The German Nation and Martin Luther*. London: Edward Arnold.
FOSSIER, R. 1987. Introduction. In *The Cambridge Illustrated History of the Middle Ages, 1250–1520*, ed. R. Fossier. Cambridge: Cambridge University Press.
FRYDE, E. 1991. Royal fiscal systems and state formation. In *The Agrarian History of England and Wales*, Vol. 3, *1348–1500*, ed. E. Miller. Cambridge: Cambridge University Press.
GENICOT, L. 1966. Crisis: from the Middle Ages to modern times. In vol. 1 of *The Cambridge Economic History of Europe*, ed. M. M. Postan. Cambridge: Cambridge University Press.
GOLDTHWAITE, R. 1985. *The Building of Renaissance Florence*. Baltimore: Johns Hopkins University Press.
HERLIHY, D., and KLAPISCH-ZUBER, C. 1985. *Tuscans and their Families*. New Haven, Conn.: Yale University Press.
HILTON, R. H. 1950. *The English Rising of 1381*. London: Lawrence and Wishart.
—— 1983. *The Decline of Serfdom in Medieval England*. London: Macmillan.

HILTON, R. H. 1985. Peasant movements in England before 1381. In *Class Conflict and the Crisis of Feudalism*, ed. R. H. Hilton. London: Hambledon Press.

HILLEBRAND, H. J. 1968. The spread of the Protestant Reformation of the sixteenth century: historical case-study in the transfer of ideas. *South Atlantic Quarterly*, 67: 127–54.

JONES, A. 1975. The rise and fall of the manorial system: a critical comment. *Journal of Economic History*, 32: 938–44.

KENT, F. W. 1977. *Household and Lineage in Renaissance Florence.* Princeton, NJ: Princeton University Press.

KOHLER, H.-J. 1986. The *Flugschriften* and their importance in religious debate: a quantitative approach. In *"Astrologi hallucinati": Stars and the End of the World in Luther's Time*, ed. P. Zambelli. Berlin: W. de Gruyter.

LADURIE, E. L. R. 1987. *The French Peasantry 1450–1660.* Berkeley: University of California Press.

ORMROD, W. M. 1996. The politics of pestilence: government in England after the Black Death. In *The Black Death in England*, ed. W. M. Ormrod and P. G. Lindley. Stamford: Watkins.

OZMENT, S. 1975. *The Reformation in the Cities.* New Haven, Conn.: Yale University Press.

PALMER, R. C. 1993. *English Law in the Age of the Black Death, 1348–1381.* Chapel Hill: University of North Carolina Press.

SULLIVAN, K. 1999. *The Interrogation of Joan of Arc.* Minneapolis: University of Minnesota Press.

VERGER, J. 1987. Different values and authorities. In *The Cambridge Illustrated History of the Middle Ages, 1250–1520*, ed. R. Fossier. Cambridge: Cambridge University Press.

VON Rohr, J. 1962. Medieval consolation and the young Luther's despair. In *Reformation Studies*, ed. F. H. Littell. Richmond, Va.: John Knox Press.

WALKER, M. 1971. *German Home Towns: Community, State, and General Estate, 1648–1871.* Ithaca, NY: Cornell University Press.

CHAPTER 33

··

THE POLITICS OF DEMOGRAPHY

··

BRUCE CURTIS

THIS chapter is concerned with the politics of demographic knowledge both in terms of its political conditions of possibility and its practical utility. Demographic knowledge is inherently a political and administrative knowledge. This is so because it is based on conventions for establishing equivalences among human subjects and events, for attributing identities to them, and for locating them in time and space. As with other sciences, demography abstracts from the immense complexity of the empirical world. It classifies and equates qualitatively different phenomena to construct "populations," whose features are represented numerically (Desrosières 1998). It seeks to identify quantitative regularities and variations. It characterizes populations in terms of their internal features through concepts such as the population profile. It attempts to identify the dynamic features of change in populations and to inform decisions about policy. Well-developed demographic knowledge makes it possible to isolate and identify individuals, to locate them in historical trajectories, and to categorize and group them together to form sub-populations.

On the basis of the simplifications that it works on empirical phenomena, demographic knowledge facilitates practical action by a wide variety of agencies and interests, both public and private. In the wealthy countries at least, routinely generated knowledge about individuals has increased massively in the last half century and continues to proliferate. New information technologies augment dramatically the possibilities for recording, storing, transmitting, and manipulating details about the activities of individuals. Such technical capacities are conjugated with elements of scientific, political, and administrative infrastructure to make it possible to identify individuals reliably, to characterize them more and more thoroughly, and to form them into population segments according to the most diverse interests (Caplan and Torpey 2001; Headrick 2000). Apparently mundane devices and practices, many of them originating in the 1960s and 1970s, such as the credit card, the inscription of bar codes on objects, and the mapping of territories into postal codes, lay the groundwork for extensive interventions (Eaton 1986; Gandy 1993; Torpey 2000). Governments, for instance, commonly sell or make freely available demographic and other census information about citizens grouped according to their postal codes. Those interested can map average income, occupational categories, family size, property ownership, or even the possession by households of electronic devices. Mass market retailers can construct "market basket data," tracking what items their customers purchase together and, if customers order by mail, or pay by credit card, or offer their postal code when asked, can track consumption patterns across geographic and population segments. Where a particular kind of retail store is likely to succeed, or what kinds of remedial programs a public school might need to offer, or where it would be most efficient to locate a hospital, may thus be anticipated. Political authorities concerned to combat "terrorism" can construct profiles of the population segments from which problematic activities arise and locate them geographically, or follow the geographic movements of individuals, in principle before terrorist acts occur.

These technical capacities have no inherent valence, beyond the fact that, conceptually, they abstract individuals from the complexities of their lives and subject them to a process of simplification: they may be used for good or ill (for a contrasting view, Scott 1998). That the Canadian government requires every beef farmer to attach a tag to every beef cow and to keep a record of its history means that (if the system works) tainted meat can be traced to its source and the public health protected. The systematic tracking of surgical outcomes can lead to better medical procedures; recording the drug regimens of the elderly and relating these to health records might lead to the discovery and elimination of dangerous drug interactions. Exhaustive recording of the spending habits of welfare recipients can prevent them from supplementing inadequate government support payments by casual employment. Profiling members of a population by ethnic origin can support racist policing activities. The point is that all these capacities depend on elementary conventions that treat people and objects as fundamentally equivalent, that identify individuals in ways that make it possible to distinguish amongst them, and that locate them in time and space.

Well-established conventions allow demographers and others who use knowledge of population to make claims and to engage in debate without the debilitating necessity of constantly revisiting basic assumptions. Yet knowledge conventions are agreements among interested parties, and so constitute political arrangements.

Some conventions are so elementary that their political character can be revealed only by revisiting the debates and conflicts that surrounded their establishment. That every person enumerated in a census shall have the same weight as every other person in the resulting population total is a case in point. For much of the pre-history of demography, attempts at "numbering the people" had no interest in identifying all people individually. It was not technically possible to do so in any case before individuals were marked in some way that distinguished them reliably, such as the adoption of distinct names (Lefebvre-Teillard 1990). Those whom it was important to identify by political or religious authorities for most of recorded history have been those who could pay taxes or tithes, or perform military service, or who had a right to live within the walls of a town, within the confines of a manor or parish (Biller 2000; Buck 1977). In feudal societies, lords and serfs were as different as dogs and horses; that they were equivalent was barely conceivable. The social identities of the vast majority of individuals were of no consequence: for practical purposes they were subsumed under those of lords and masters, priests and heads of households (Behar 1998).

Demography embodies the political conventions of democracy and the historical development of both demography and democracy have been uneven (Lenoir 1995; 2000). In point of fact, the central demographic concept, "population" is itself a democratic concept. It assumes the existence of some sort of fundamental equality or equivalence among all human bodies (Curtis 2002). Armed with the democratic notion of population, modern demographers can now speak of the population of ancient Rome or of South America before European contact, but the notion would have been unintelligible to people in those places and times. Earlier political and religious authorities sometimes used the word "population," but meant something different from it than do modern demographers. For instance, in Europe, as the modern state system was taking shape in the wake of the Reformation, authorities became interested in knowing the forces of the state, but this concern was with "populousness," rather than with a population composed of fundamentally equivalent atoms (Poovey 1998). One of the forces of the state was the body of the people; a comfortable, flourishing, sturdy people made a strong state. Increasing populousness was an index of wise government; calculations of the strategic possibilities for advantage in the competition and conflict among states were related to national wealth and populousness. Yet neither the conceptual apparatus nor the institutional capacity existed to make it possible to know what demographers now call the population.

Conflicts between the Catholic Church and Protestant sects in Europe led to the creation of parish registers of baptisms (not births), marriages, and deaths in many countries. Registration was influential in naming individuals and, in cases such as the administration of the Poor Law in Elizabethan England, in binding individuals to the parish of their birth. For most of Europe before the nineteenth century, however, the information in parish registers was never centralized to create measures of population. Nonetheless, the infrastructure provided by state churches in Protestant Europe in the eighteenth century made it possible for authorities to conduct some of the first censuses in which named individuals were enumerated as populations. The abstract notion of the soul, the Protestant belief that each soul's personal acquaintance with the divinity was significant, religious uniformity, and the administrative framework of the parish made the eighteenth century Swedish census one of the first to embody a modern conception of population, but it remained an exception (Dupâquier and Dupâquier 1985). The modern conception of population was propelled especially by the American and French Revolutions.

The French Revolution led to attempts to homogenize social, political, and economic relations in the new republic and to centralize administration. The introduction of civil status in the early 1790s was intended to eliminate all effective differences among citizens and it was accompanied by an effort to standardize people's names. State agencies replaced the church as the keepers of registers of vital events. In conjunction with projects for dividing France into the standardized administrative units of departments, cantons, and communes, for standardizing weights and measures, and for a geometric survey, such initiatives caused the individual to stand forth clearly in its relation to political authority.[1] Subjection to the political authority of the state, rather than to the divine authority of the church, came to be the element shared by all citizens. By the first years of the nineteenth century, schemes abounded in France for naming and numbering houses and streets according to a systematic plan, and for according each citizen an identity number and card, tying each to a specific house (Denis 2000). On the other hand, the American Revolution was especially significant in the formation of demographic thinking by establishing the principle of representation by population for the new federal government and by requiring the execution of a decennial census, the first of which was held in 1790.

While the conceptual and administrative possibilities for constructing populations, and hence demographic practice, existed at the end of the eighteenth century in Europe and America,[2] it was generally only from the mid-nineteenth century, when census making became a regular state practice, that nominal enumeration and the equivalence of each human body were accepted conventionally. Even then, the partial development of democratic relations retarded matters. Until 1860 in the United States, for instance, slaves were counted only as 60 percent of a white person and even after the establishment of nominal enumeration were numbered but not named (Anderson 1988; Cohen 1982). In European settler colonies, members of aboriginal populations were often either ignored, or enumerated haphazardly.

Demographic knowledge thus embodies the elementary political conventions of democracy and depends on particular kinds of administrative organization. More-

---

[1] Bourguet 1988; Brian 1994; Nordman 1989; Woolf 1984.
[2] For Italy and England: Patriarca 1996; Higgs 1989; Glass 1973; Drake 1972.

over, while the elementary convention of individual human equivalence is firmly established in national censuses of population, it is a convention that may change in the future. Attempts, again in the United States, to make the fetus a person with legal rights while still in the womb may mean that what the census now counts as one person may at some future time be counted as more than one.

Other demographic conventions are subject to more or less constant renegotiation, and still others change in keeping with shifting political, administrative, medical, moral, or other interests. For example, changing medical classifications of disease may change reports of causes of death and hence our understanding of the impact of disease on society and history. Groups may come together to demand that they be identified in particular ways in a census, or that they cease to be identified. Governments concerned with affirmative action programs may introduce new identifiers to the census. To take another example, the displacement of most births from the mother's home to the hospital obstetrics ward in the industrial countries led to a changed convention for reporting place of birth in civil registers. Reports of world population by the United Nations have been repeatedly revised retrospectively, and population agencies in individual countries not infrequently revise their own past population reports.[3]

All these changing conventions have practical consequences in terms of what it is possible to know and to do with demographic information. Yet these conventions do not simply reflect conditions in the world that demography seeks to know. They shape and reshape that world actively; such is the nature of any scientific engagement with the world. A notable characteristic of demographic knowledge is that it is provisional, subject to continual refashioning, both in relation to the past and in relation to the future. Understandings of past demographic conditions are altered on the basis of changing conventions in the present. Predictions about future demographic conditions depend upon past understandings. Applying a changed definition of being employed or being retired to a past census may alter understandings of the causes and timing of capitalist industrialization, or of the networks of social dependency that conduce to a long life. Late or delayed registration of births or deaths may lead to retrospective alterations of reported birth or death rates (Emery 1983). Altered conceptions of who belongs to a given population may transform our understanding of the distribution of wealth or disease. All these provisional accounts are inextricably bound up with conflicts over how members of a population came to be where they are, what characterizes the world they inhabit, and what the future portends for them (Anderson 1993).

Other conventional arrangements characterize the execution of the periodic census of population, the leading source of demographic knowledge. Individuals must be located on an enumeration grid to be included in a census, but those to be enumerated are physically mobile, and the degree of mobility of members of

---

[3] Cole 2000; Coleman 1982; Emery 1993; Keilman 2001.

different populations varies historically. Work and residence are increasingly separated for many; college and university students reside away from their parents; other people perform military service and reside in barracks at home or abroad. Migrant workers live and maintain themselves on a day-to-day basis in one place but reproduce themselves as members of households in another. Migrants commonly cross geopolitical boundaries and so does the income they earn. Again, in the wealthy industrial countries, professionals increasingly commute to work, and married couples may work in different cities, meeting only on weekends. The children of divorced parents may live in separate households. For the middle classes in North America and parts of northern Europe, summers may be spent in the countryside, winters in the city.

Yet censuses embody the conventional fiction that individuals occupy single spaces within a defined territory; the technology of census-making is intolerant of multiple locations. There are two main methods for binding individuals to spaces in order to produce an enumeration grid. Censuses based on the *de jure* principle assign individuals to some place where they have some sort of right to be. Censuses based on the de facto principle place individuals where they were believed to be physically at the moment of enumeration. Censuses commonly modify these two principles in practice, but the technical differences have political implications. Both methods discipline members of populations in the sense of tying them to spaces within an enumeration grid and of holding them in those spaces for purposes of investigation and administration. Where people are held to be has consequences for individuals, in terms of eligibility for and practical delivery of social services, for instance. Distributing individuals differently across political territory has implications for the recognition of political rights, the distribution of political representation, the planning of administrative initiatives, and the construction of social imaginaries more generally.

Thus, for instance, if a *de jure* census embodies the principle that individuals properly belong in the place they were born, or where their parents live if they have themselves yet to establish an independent household, the claims of displaced persons to a right to return to their homeland, or the demands of migrants to a city or state for access to education and health care may be more easily denied by authorities. Debates about which regions of a nation are flourishing and which declining will be affected if a *de jure* census reassigns individuals from the place in which they live and work to some other place. If a system of representation by population prevails, the political weight of regions will be affected by the method of census enumeration. For instance, in late nineteenth- and early twentieth-century Canada, where ethnic and religious conflict surrounded issues of the relative size and growth rates of urban and rural, Protestant and Catholic, English and French groups, the adoption of a *de jure* enumeration plan shaped both the distribution of electoral seats and images of ethnic/religious pride. The period was one of extensive out migration from rural French Canada to the Canadian cities and the American factory towns. Under the *de jure* principle, migrants were assigned to their parents' residences in the countryside. The electoral weight of the countryside was increased and ethnic-religious activists could claim that French Canadian identity flourished best in a rural situation under the guidance of the Catholic clergy (Curtis 2001).

De facto censuses, by contrast, most commonly attempt to locate individuals in the place where they happened to be physically at some moment of enumeration: where they slept on the night before census day, for instance. Unlike the *de jure* model (which is in fact a system of registration), the de facto model aspires to a more empirical version of the location of individuals in time and space. Yet it also inevitably stylizes the distribution of individuals and the character of social relations. Where individuals cross administrative boundaries in commuting between home and work, they may be enumerated at home, yet the bulk of their effects on the market, the environment, and productive activity will occur elsewhere. The tax base of cities may be affected negatively, or epidemiological investigations of disease clusters may miss the consequences of dangerous working conditions, if deaths and births are recorded where people sleep but not work.

Many censuses mix de facto and *de jure* principles, for instance by locating wage earners where they were on enumeration day and treating their dependents as if they had been there too. The children of migrants born in a country may be counted as citizens there while their parents are not. The same children may have the right to citizenship, and hence to be enumerated in two countries. The point is that demography is based on practices that work complex forms of discipline upon the empirical existence of potential members of population. It is clear that censuses do not in any simple sense reflect or capture the lived realities of physical location for members of an enumerated population. They model these realities in keeping with more or less clearly articulated conceptions that are tied to more or less well elaborated objectives. They identify individuals and groups and tie them to particular kinds of spaces. Such identifying practices subsequently become the grounds for further investigation and action. Again, conceptual simplification is an inevitable element in all sciences; yet all simplification has the potential for doing violence to social complexity. Demographic modernization theories, for instance, took dramatically simplified conceptions of the relations between changing fertility rates and capitalist industrialization as a justification for promoting ill-conceived birth control policies in developing countries (Greenhalgh 1996).

A further element of complexity is added by the fact that demography has a tenuous relationship with empirical observation. Civil registers may be affected by reporting practices that produce culturally acceptable, rather than exhaustive accounts of births, marriages, and deaths. Census enumerators rarely, if ever, actually observe directly more than a small portion of an enumerated population and usually cannot witness other reported events or activities. Some censuses are indeed conducted by political authorities demanding that residents of a territory remain inside their houses until enumerators come to observe them. Yet technical difficulties surround even this tactic, unless the population to be enumerated is small and densely settled, for there is the issue of enumerating the enumerators. They cannot be in their houses at the same time as they are enumerating other people. Usually both *de jure* and de facto censuses rely on the evidence of selected informants as to the physical locations of people at the moment of enumeration, as to who is entitled to be in a given place, and other information.

Such informants are typically described as "head of household" and in most modern censuses the head of household has been held to be male. Those not clearly attached to a household will tend not to be enumerated, and the interests that heads of households have will shape the information provided to census-makers. Informants may have the most diverse interests imaginable in presenting particular kinds of accounts of their household. They may not wish to reveal that some family members have moved out or sleep out, or that fugitive sons have any connection with them, or that pension-receiving parents have died. Some descriptions of their household may threaten their access to services, as when welfare agencies exclude single mothers from benefits under a "man in the house" rule. Informants and census-makers may not understand the purpose of the census in the same way. In any case, censuses are commonly reports of the reports of others about third parties, and where informants are invited to report on events that happened last night or last week or last month, they are exercises in oral history as well. Demographic analysis relies on numerical accounts of social relations and processes that are only as good as the theoretical conceptions that shape them are sound, and the conventions of observation and reporting that underlie them are consistent and coherent (Hindess 1973).

In part because of the difficulties of comprehensively enumerating those who are not in stable households, because of the expense of attempting to send out enumerators to canvass large populations, and because of the development of statistical sampling techniques, some national governments have substituted the sample survey for the every-person enumeration. In this method, typically, some number of territorial segments of a mix considered to approximate the general distribution of population are enumerated intensively, and perhaps repeatedly, estimates of likely error are constructed, and the results are extrapolated to the territory as a whole. As with attempts at every-person enumerations generally, this method depends on a foreknowledge of the population, through the classification of territory into typical population densities and profiles, before sampling and extrapolation take place. However, it tends to be better able to capture mobile elements of population at lesser cost than do other methods, and in any case, modern census-makers do not aim for a perfect census, but for one that will suffice for administrative, political, and scientific purposes (for an explicit statement, see Hansen et al. 1953).

Yet the sample survey models population and redistributes individuals in ways that have consequences for state finance and political representation, and it encounters political opposition in some countries precisely for this reason. In the United States for the 2000 census, conservative forces effectively prevented the adoption of the sample survey on constitutional grounds and earlier attempts to correct the 1990 census by using statistical technique to compensate for forms of undercounting were also defeated. The sample survey method would have yielded higher population totals for urban areas and for the inner cities by virtue of its better capture of transients and migrants. The cities, which tend to elect more liberal representatives, would have acquired greater political weight and greater entitlements to state funding as well. The representations of population constructed by demography have political, administrative, technical, and scientific implications.[4]

Censuses and similar practices identify elements of population and social events in the strong sense of connecting them to identities. They classify and categorize individuals and groups, as well as objects and activities. Assigning individuals and groups to membership in occupational, religious, social class, racial, and ethnic categories affects their life chances and shapes political and administrative initiatives (Urla 1993). Some methods of identifying elements of population are residues of past conflicts and projects that have come to be taken for granted, yet even these typically point to ways in which states represent themselves to their own citizens and others (e.g. Arel 2002). Other methods of identification turn out to be matters of life and death for those identified: being known as a Tutsi on one's identity card in Rwanda in the 1990s; being categorized as an enemy alien in First World War Canada or in Second World War United States; being categorized as a Jew in 1940s France or Poland, or the Soviet Union of the 1980s.[5]

How national governments characterize citizens and how they represent social relations and conditions may influence national identities. For instance, some national governments are concerned to present class relations as a matter simply of the distribution of income in which no sharp cleavages or distinctions appear; others attempt to relate class difference to all forms of wealth; and others still treat class as a matter of occupation. Portrayals of social class relations and the related phenomena of income, occupation, and employment status vary among countries, but have also been changing within countries. Nineteenth- and early twentieth-century censuses commonly mixed status and occupational indicators, describing some people's occupations, for instance, as "carpenter," "farmer," or "labourer," and others' as "gentleman," "widow," or "retired." Early English censuses classified occupations in terms of the materials with which people worked: here, the census manager was a medical doctor interested in connecting occupational exposure to substances with types and rates of disease (Higgs 1991). Twentieth-century English censuses, by contrast, reported on social class in broad categories that roughly corresponded to a tripartite classification of upper/middle/lower that originated

---

[4] Anderson and Fienberg 1999; Choldin 1994; Draga 1999; Parsons 1972.
[5] Abramson 2002; Aly and Roth 2004; Behar 1998; Labbé 1998; Uvin 1994; 2002.

out of eugenic concerns with falling fertility in the dominant classes (Donnelly 1997; Szreter 1984). While the English classified occupations in keeping with this hierarchical notion, French occupational classifications retained the logic of an earlier craft organization of industry (Topalov 2001). When social benefits came to be tied to occupational classification in France, some workers came together to demand recognition in new categories; such was the case with the internally very diverse group that came to be known as *cadres* (roughly, middle managers) (Boltanski 1982). Dramatic differences in the representation of social conditions are sometimes produced by changes in the logic of classification: the decision in England to remove "housewife" from the category of those actively employed led to a sudden increase in the portion of the population officially considered to be dependent (see also Deacon 1985).

Race, an eminently political concept, and ethnicity have been treated in widely different ways as well. The four countries most concerned with racial classification historically have been the United States, Israel, apartheid South Africa, and Brazil, yet each has dealt with the substance of such classifications differently (Nobles 2002). The United States and Brazil, for instance, share a common heritage with respect to African slavery, although the foreign slave trade lasted longer and was more extensive in Brazil, which was the last country in the western hemisphere to abolish slavery. Yet, in contrast to the situation in the United States, after abolition there was no legal or effective racial segregation in Brazil. Here, the census took up difference not in terms of blood or inheritance, but rather in terms of categories of colour and for much of the twentieth century, state policy championed colour mixing (not from liberal motives, but because mixing was thought to produce superior whiteness). In the United States, by contrast, difference was taken up through conceptions of blood, with the belief being that one drop of "Negro" blood made a person a Negro. Brazilian demographers refused until the 1970s to consider relating "colour" to social condition; American demographers introduced the category "mulatto" in the mid-nineteenth century in an effort to prove that race mixing led to a shortened lifespan. Public opposition in France in the early twenty-first century, by contrast, led to the abandonment of a project to attempt to relate ethnicity to socioeconomic condition on the grounds that such a link would lend itself to discrimination or racism (Blum 2002).

While nineteenth- and early twentieth-century American census enumerators were often invited to assign people to a racial category by visual inspection, extremely elaborate and labyrinthine initiatives were employed in apartheid South Africa in an attempt to bolster the fiction of racial differences. Census classifications could sometimes be contested, but how one was classified had dramatic consequences in terms of where one could work, live, go to school, with whom one could have sexual relations, marry, and so on (Bowker and Star 1999). In Israel, by contrast, the relevant social distinction is between Jew and non-Jew; Jews are defined as part of the nation, other categories of population are treated as "other." Jews are enumerated in terms of place of birth, which is an effort to avoid differences of sect, while all other groups are identified by religion, which appears on individual identity cards (Goldscheider 2002). Meticulously detailed historic census records in Nazi Germany made it possible for bureaucrats to identify and to locate those defined as "Jewish" in pursuit of policies of "racial purity" (Aly and Roth 2004).

Censuses are implicated in the practices known as "making up people," whereby individuals or groups react to the ways in which they are represented or excluded (Hacking 1986; Porter 1986; Poovey 1995). At times, those categorized may adopt the census's portrayal of them as part of their identity, either wholeheartedly or for strategic reasons. In Canada, for instance, to facilitate affirmative action policies in regard to government employment, censuses have begun to identify some individuals as members of "visible minorities." Some of those placed in the category use their membership to demand preference in hiring decisions. Others reject the category as discriminatory, especially since the "visibility" in question is not in any simple sense one that involves sight. Other ways of engaging with categories are also possible. Individuals may demand to be recognized as a census grouping, as with Hispanic Americans. Individuals may parody the census's demand that they identify themselves. In several English-speaking countries, informal campaigns encouraged respondents to offer "Jedi Knight" (from the movie Star Wars) as their religious affiliation. In England in 2001, Jedi Knight passed the statistical threshold for recognition as an official religion.

The consequences of census-making for identity formation have been debated extensively in the case of British imperial censuses in India. Influential work by Bernard Cohn suggested that the British project of governing India went forward in part through the translation of Indian social relations and conditions into forms of knowledge comprehensible to English rulers. These simplifications subsequently formed the basis of policy-making. Cohn claimed that censuses imposed alien religious categories on the Indian population, often against its struggles of resistance. Yet once these categories were normalized through their incorporation in discourse and practical policy, people began to live their lives and to understand themselves in terms of them. Later attempts to change imposed categories were opposed by those now contained in them (Cohn 1987; 1996). Taking Cohn further, a number of other writers suggested that differences of caste and religion before British imperialism were minor forces in regions of India. Caste and religion were operative, but social divisions were relatively fluid, localized, and modified in keeping with particular empirical circumstances. They did not constitute general and systematic relations of domination. It was claimed that censuses of population, especially from the later nineteenth century, codified widely varied differences of caste and religion from minor elements in lived social relations and elevated them into basic organizational principles and cleavages (Appadurai 1993; Bayly 1999).

Critics suggest that while Cohn captured well one dynamic of rule that involved demographic categories, in keeping with other historians of colonial India he neglected important dimensions of the relations between colonial and pre-colonial political circumstances. The tendency of the literature was to present systematic knowledge of population as a European project and to represent the imperial census-making projects as a break with earlier Indian practices. Later work, however, suggests that administrative knowledge at least of populousness was produced in many parts of the Indian subcontinent under the Mughal Empire, and it employed caste-based categories. However, these administrative enquiries were locally bounded and did not lead to the kinds of abstraction that synthesizes people into a population. Nonetheless, the suggestion is that English census-makers in India relied upon Indian informants and managers for the elaboration of census categories. Census managers drew on their own ways of categorizing population, and their own political and economic interests, in shaping the representations produced through the census. The late nineteenth century imperial censuses of India were thus hybrid objects, drawing selectively upon prior social relations and divisions, systematizing and simplifying these, and ensconcing them as organizational categories in social and political administration (Smith 1985; 2000; Peabody 2001; Guha 2003).

In sum, demography is a political knowledge both in its basic form and in its applications. It depends upon a set of political conventions that equate individuals and groups and that tie them to particular locations within territories. The processes of simplification, abstraction, and aggregation involved in constructing demographic knowledge create powerful new possibilities for configuring and reconfiguring social relations and processes in keeping with a great variety of interests. Demography can participate in rational social planning, in the identification of the environmental circumstances that surround disease clusters, in revealing the effects of social changes on the ages at which women have children. It can also participate in projects of genocide, "ethnic cleansing," or eugenics, by classifying individuals and locating them in space.

REFERENCES

ABRAMSON, D. 2002. Identity counts: the Soviet legacy and the census in Uzbekistan. In Kertzer and Arel 2002a, 176–201.

ALY, G., and ROTH, K. H. 2004. *The Nazi Census: Identification and Control in the Third Reich.* Philadelphia: Temple University Press.

ANDERSON, B. 1993. *Imagined Communities.* London: Verso.

ANDERSON, M. J. 1988. *The American Census: A Social History.* New Haven, Conn.: Yale University Press.

—— and FIENBERG, S. E. 1999. *Who Counts? The Politics of Census-Taking in Contemporary America*. New York: Russell Sage Foundation.

APPADURAI, A. 1993. Number in the colonial imagination. Pp. 314–39 in *Orientalism and the Postcolonial Predicament*, ed. C. A. Breckenridge and P. van der Veer. Philadelphia: University of Pennsylvania Press.

AREL, D. 2002. Language categories in censuses: backward- or forward-looking? In Kertzer and Arel 2002*a*, 92–120.

BAKER, K. M. 1990. *Inventing the French Revolution*. Cambridge: Cambridge University Press.

BAYLY, S. 1999. *Caste, Society and Politics in India from the Eighteenth to the Modern Age*. Cambridge: Cambridge University Press.

BEHAR, C. 1998. Qui Compte? "Recensements" et statistiques démographiques dans l'Empire ottoman, du XVI au XXe siècle. *Histoire et Mesure*, 13: 135–45.

BILLER, P. 2000. *The Measure of Multitude: Population in Medieval Thought*. Oxford: Oxford University Press.

BLUM, A. 2002. Resistance to identity categorization in France. In Kertzer and Arel 2002*a*, 121–47.

BOLTANSKI, L. 1982. *Les cadres: La formation d'un groupe social*. Paris: Minuit.

BOURGUET, M.-N. 1988. *Déchiffrer la France. La statistique départementale à l'époque napoléonienne*. Paris.

BOWKER, G., and STAR, S. L. 1999. *Sorting Things Out: Classification and its Consequences*. Cambridge, Mass.: MIT Press.

BRIAN, É. 1994. *La mesure de l' État: Administrateurs et géomètres au XVIIIe siècle*. Paris: Albin Michel.

BUCK, P. 1977. Seventeenth-century political arithmetic: civil strife and vital statistics. *Isis*, 68: 67–84.

CAPLAN, J., and TORPEY, J. (eds.) 2001. *Documenting Individual Identity: The Development of State Practices in the Modern World*. Princeton, NJ: Princeton University Press.

CARTER, S. B., and SUTCH, R. 1996. Fixing the facts: editing of the 1880 U.S. Census of Occupations with implications for long-term labor-force trends and the sociology of official statistics. *Historical Methods*, 29: 5–24.

CASSEDY, J. H. 1969. *Demography in Early America: Beginnings of the Statistical Mind, 1600–1800*. Cambridge, Mass.: Harvard University Press.

CHOLDIN, H. M. 1994. *Looking for the Last Percent. The Controversy over Census Undercounts*. New Brunswick, NJ: Rutgers University Press.

CLARK, A. K. 1998. Race, "culture" and mestizaje: the statistical construction of the Ecuadorian nation, 1930–1950. *Journal of Historical Sociology*, 11: 185–211.

COHEN, P. C. 1982. *A Calculating People: The Spread of Numeracy in Early America*. Chicago: University of Chicago Press.

COHN, B. 1996. *Colonialism and Its Forms of Knowledge: The British in India*. Princeton, NJ: Princeton University Press.

COHN, B. I. 1987. The census, social structure and objectification in South Asia. Pp. 224–54 in *An Anthropologist among the Historians and Other Essays*. Delhi Oxford University Press.

COLE, J. 2000. *The Power of Large Numbers: Population, Politics and Gender in Nineteenth-Century France*. Ithaca, NY: Cornell University Press.

COLEMAN, W. 1982. *Death is a Social Disease: Public Health and Political Economy in Early Industrial France*. Madison: University of Wisconsin Press.

CURTIS, B. 2001. *The Politics of Population: State Formation, Statistics, and the Census of Canada, 1840–75*. Toronto: University of Toronto Press.

——2002. Foucault on governmentality and population: the impossible discovery. *Canadian Journal of Sociology*, 27: 505–33.

DEACON, D. 1985. Political arithmetic: the nineteenth century Australian census and the construction of the dependent woman. *Signs*, 11: 27–47.

DENIS, V. 2000. Entre Police et Dèmographie. *Actes de la recherche en sciences sociales*, 133: 72–8.

DESROSIÈRES, A. 1985. Histoire de formes: statistiques et sciences sociales avant 1940. *Revue française de sociologie*, 26: 277–310.

——1991. How to make things which hold together: social science, statistics and the state. Pp. 195–218 in *Discourses on Society*, ed. P. Wagner, B. Wittrock, and R. Whitley. Dordrecht: Kluwer.

——1998. *The Politics of Large Numbers*. Cambridge, Mass.: Harvard University Press.

——2001. How real are statistics? Four possible attitudes. *Social Research*, 68: 339–55.

DONNELLY, M. 1997. Statistical classifications and the salience of social class. Pp. 107–31 in *Reworking Class*, ed. J. R. Hall. Ithaca, NY: Cornell University Press.

DRAGA, K. 1999. *Sampling and the Census: A Case Against the Proposed Adjustments for Undercount*. Washington, DC: American Enterprise Press.

DRAKE, M. 1972. The census, 1801–1901. Pp. 7–46 in *Nineteenth-century Society: Essays in the Use of Quantitative Methods for the Study of Social Data*, ed. E. A. Wrigley. Cambridge: Cambridge University Press.

DUFFIN, J. 1997. Census versus medical daybooks: a comparison of two sources on mortality in nineteenth-century Ontario. *Continuity and Change*, 12 (2): 199–219.

DUNAE, P. A. 1998. Making the 1891 Census in British Columbia. *Histoire sociale/Social History*, 31 (62): 223–41.

DUPÂQUIER, J., and DUPÂQUIER, M. 1985. *Histoire de la dèmographie: La statistique de la population des origines à 1914*. Paris: Librairie Académique Perrin.

EATON, J. 1986. *Card Carrying Americans*. Totowa, NJ: Rowman and Littlefield.

EMERY, G. 1983. Ontario's civil registration of vital statistics, 1869–1926: the evolution of an administrative system. *Canadian Historical Review*, 64: 468–93.

FUCHS, R. G., and MOCH, L. P. 1995. Invisible cultures: poor women's networks and reproductive strategies in nineteenth-century Paris. Pp. 86–107 in *Situating Fertility: Anthropology and Demographic Inquiry*, ed. S. Greenhalgh. Cambridge: Cambridge University Press.

FURSTENBERG, F., STRONG, D., and CRAWFORD, A. 1979. What happened when the census was re-done: an analysis of the recount of 1870 in Philadelphia. *Sociology and Social Research*, 63: 475–503.

GANDY, O. H. 1993. *The Panoptic Sort: A Political Economy of Personal Information*. Boulder, Colo.: Westview Press.

GLASS, D. V. 1973. *Numbering the People. The Eighteenth-century Population Controversy and the Development of Census and Vital Statistics in Britain*. Farnborough: Saxon House.

GOLDSCHEIDER, C. 2002. Ethnic categorizations in censuses: comparative observations from Israel, Canada, and the United States. In Kertzer and Arel 2002a, 71–91.

GREENHALGH, S. 1996. The social construction of population science: an intellectual, institutional, and political history of twentieth century demography. *Comparative Studies in Society and History*, 38: 27–66.

GUHA, S. 2003. The politics of identity and enumeration in India c.1600–1900. *Comparative Studies in Society and History*, 45: 148–167.

HACKING, I. 1986. Making up people. Pp. 222–36 in *Reconstructing Individualism: Autonomy, Individuality, and the Self in Western Thought*, ed. T. C. Heller, M. Sosna, and D. E. Welbery. Stanford, Calif.: Stanford University Press.

HANNAH, M. G. 2000. *Governmentality and the Mastery of Territory in Nineteenth-century America*. Cambridge: Cambridge University Press.

HANSEN, M. H., HURWITZ, W. N., et al. 1953. The accuracy of census results. *American Sociological Review*, 18: 416–23.

HEADRICK, D. R. 2000. *When Information Came of Age: Technologies of Knowledge in the Age of Reason and Revolution, 1700–1850*. Oxford: Oxford University Press.

HIGGS, E. 1989. *Making Sense of the Census: The Manuscript Returns for England and Wales, 1801–1901*. London: HMSO.

——1991. Disease, febrile poisons and statistics: the census as a medical survey, 1841–1911. *Social History of Medicine and Allied Sciences*, 43: 465–78.

——1996. A cuckoo in the nest? The origins of civil registration and state medical statistics in England and Wales. *Continuity and Change*, 11 (1): 115–34.

HINDESS, B. 1973. *The Use of Official Statistics in Sociology. A Critique of Positivism and Ethnomethodology*. London: Macmillan.

HIRSCHMAN, C. 1987. The meaning and measurement of ethnicity in Malaysia: an analysis of census classifications. *Journal of Asian Studies*, 46: 555–82.

KATEB, K. 1998. La gestion statistique des populations dans l'empire colonial français: le cas de l'Algérie, 1830–1960. *Histoire et Mesure*, 13: 77–111.

KEILMAN, N. 2001. Data quality and the accuracy of United Nations population projections, 1950–95. *Population Studies*, 55: 149–64.

KERTZER, D. I., and AREL, D. (eds.) 2002a. *Census and Identity*. Cambridge: Cambridge University Press

————2002b. Censuses, identity formation, and the struggle for political power. In Kertzer and Arel 2002a, 1–42.

LABBÉ, M. 1998. "Race" et "nationalité" dans les recensements du Troisième Reich. *Histoire et Mesure*, 13: 195–223.

LEFEBVRE-TEILLARD, A. 1990. *Le Nom: droit et histoire*. Paris: Presses Universitaires de France.

LENOIR, R. 1995. L'invention de la démographie et la formation de l'État. *Actes de la recherche en sciences sociales*, 95: 36–61.

——2000. Savoirs et sciences d'état: généalogie et démographie. *Actes de la recherche en sciences sociales*, 133: 96–7.

NOBLES, M. 2002. Racial categorization and censuses. In Kertzer and Arel 2002a, 43–70.

OWEN, R. 1996. The population census of 1917 and its relationship to Egypt's three nineteenth century statistical regimes. *Journal of Historical Sociology*, 9: 457–72.

PARSONS, C. (ed.) 1972. *America's Uncounted People* Washington, DC: National Academy of Sciences.

PATRIARCA, S. 1996. *Numbers and Nationhood: Writing Statistics in Nineteenth-Century Italy*. Cambridge: Cambridge University Press.

PEABODY, N. 2001. Cents, sense, census: human inventories in late precolonial and early colonial India. *Comparative Studies in Society and History*, 43: 819–50.

PEREZ, L. 1984. The political contexts of Cuban population censuses, 1899–1981. *Latin American Research Review*, 19: 143–61.

POOVEY, M. 1995. *Making a Social Body: British Cultural Formation, 1830–1864*. Chicago: University of Chicago Press.

—— 1998. *A History of the Modern Fact: Problems of Knowledge in the Sciences of Wealth and Society*. Chicago: University of Chicago Press.

PORTER, T. 1986. *The Rise of Statistical Thinking 1820–1900*. Princeton, NJ: Princeton University Press.

PORTER, T. M. 1996. *Trust in Numbers. The Pursuit of Objectivity in Science and Public Life*. Princeton, NJ: Princeton University Press.

PRÉVOST, J.-G., and BEAUD J.-P. 1994. Models for recording age in 1692–1851 Canada: the political-cognitive functions of census statistics. *Scientia Canadensis*, 18: 136–51.

ROSE, N. 1991. Governing by numbers: figuring out democracy. *Accounting, Organizations and Society*, 16: 673–92.

SCOTT, J. C. 1998. *Seeing Like a State: How Certain Schemes to Improve the Human Condition Have Failed*. New Haven, Conn.: Yale University Press.

SMITH, R. S. 1985. Rule-by-records and rule-by-reports: complementary aspects of the British imperial rule of law. *Contributions to Indian Sociology*, NS 19.

—— 2000. Between local tax and global statistic: the census as a local record. *Contributions to Indian Sociology*, NS 34: 1–35.

STARR, P. 1987. The sociology of official statistics. Pp. 7–57 in *The Politics of Numbers*, ed. W. Alonso and P. Starr. New York: Russell Sage Foundation.

—— 1992. Social categories and the liberal state. Pp. 154–79 in *How Classification Works: Nelson Goodman among the Social Scientists*, ed. M. Douglas and D. Hull. Edinburgh: Edinburgh University Press.

SZRETER, S. 1984. The genesis of the Registrar-General's social classification of occupations. *British Journal of Sociology*, 35: 522–45.

TOPALOV, C. 1998. L'individu comme convention: Le cas des statistiques profesionnelles du XIXe siécle en France, en Grande-Bretagne et aux États-Unis. *Genëses*, 9: 98–101.

—— 2001. A revolution in representations of work: the emergence over the 19th century of the statistical category "occupied population" in France, Great Britain and the United States. *Revue française de sociologie*, 42 (Supplement): 79–106.

TORPEY, J. 2000. *The Invention of the Passport: Surveillance, Citizenship and the State*. Cambridge: Cambridge University Press.

URLA, J. 1993. Cultural politics in an age of statistics: numbers, nations, and the making of Basque identity. *American Ethnologist*, 20: 818–43.

UVIN, P. 1994 Violence and UN population data. *Nature*, 372: 495–6.

—— 2002. On counting, categorizing, and violence in Burundi and Rwanda. In Kertzer and Arel 2002a, 148–75.

WALTERS, W. 1994. The discovery of "unemployment:" new forms for the government of poverty. *Economy and Society*, 23: 265–90.

WEISS, A. 1999. Much ado about counting: the conflict over holding a census in Pakistan. *Asian Survey*, 39: 679–93.

WOOLF, S. 1989. Statistics and the modern state. *Comparative Studies in Society and History*, 31 (July): 588–604.

WOOLF, S. J. 1984. Towards the history of the origins of statistics: France, 1789–1815. Pp. 81–194 in *State and Statistics in France 1789–1815*, ed. J.-C. a. W. Perron and S. J. Harwood. Amsterdam: Academic.

WORTON, D. A. 1998. *The Dominion Bureau of Statistics: a History of Canada's Central Statistical Office, 1841–1972*. Montreal: McGill-Queen's University Press.

ZEMAN, S. A. B. 1990. The four Austrian censuses and their political consequences. Pp. 31–9 in *The Last Years of Austria-Hungary*, ed. M. Cornwall. Exeter: University of Exeter Press.

CHAPTER 34

POLITICS AND MASS IMMIGRATION

GARY P. FREEMAN

POPULATIONS shape polities and are shaped by them. States seek to monitor, manage, and improve populations via census enumerations, the recording of births, deaths, and marriages, and the administration of social surveys (Curtis, this volume), the construction of ethnic, racial, and socioeconomic categories (Kertzer and Arel, this volume; Sanders 2002), control of internal migration and settlement (Curtis, this volume), and various social welfare and policing measures. States may also try to affect the size or rate of growth of populations. High or low fertility rates can have political implications if they provoke fears of societal decline or too rapid growth by specific groups. Attempts to regulate the reproductive behaviors of citizens achieve mixed or unintended results (United Nations 2004). Numbers can be abruptly added or subtracted by military force, but in rule-bound political systems with stable borders the most feasible and politically salient source of population change is migration. This chapter deals exclusively with politics and mass immigration in Western democracies.

Modern European societies have been modified more by the departure of residents than the entry of newcomers. In the seventeenth and eighteenth centuries immense numbers of settlers, colonial administrators, soldiers, priests, and prisoners left Britain, France, Spain, Portugal, the Netherlands, and other countries for the New World (Moch 2003). The United States, Canada, Australia, and New Zealand developed into classic countries of immigration, as did to a lesser extent countries in South America and southern Africa. In the nineteenth and early twentieth centuries another huge flow of humanity (perhaps 55 million) from west and east Europe moved mostly into the Americas and Australasia (Stalker 2000, 4; Hatton and Williamson 1998, 3).

Since the middle of the twentieth century, however, all Western democracies have become de facto if not willing migrant destination countries. Economic and demographic trends suggest this turn of events will persist. Differences in real wage rates between the West and other parts of the world are large. Fertility rates in the West are generally at or below replacement, whereas they are much higher in the sending regions (Stalker 2000, 21–5, 135–7). This latest mass migration, with its predominantly East–West and South–North trajectories, represents an epoch-defining reversal of the direction of flows for European countries and a substantial increase in pressures for entry and a change in the sources of migrants for traditional immigration countries (Massey et al. 1998).

International migration, therefore, constitutes a key context for contemporary politics in the liberal democracies.[1] The governments and electorates of the democracies are profoundly ambivalent about immigration and implement contradictory policies that produce inconclusive outcomes. On the one hand, a restrictive impulse leads Western states to seek to limit and control migration. Restriction is driven by desire, fear, and prejudice. Western states and their citizens desire to preserve material and political privileges, fear public disorder and insecurity, and exhibit prejudice against ethnically and culturally dissimilar peoples who are thought to undermine social cohesion and traditional ways of life. Hostile public opinion, acts of violence and discrimination, alarmist media, a tightening net of national and regional regulations, and the emergence of extreme-right parties exploiting anti-immigrant anxieties testify to the heat the issue generates. Desire, fear, and prejudice produce an unseemly siege mentality at the core of Western democratic capitalism.

But there is another side to this story. The struggle to preserve economic privilege and national sovereignty takes place in the context of constitutions, laws, political cultures, and economies that defeat efforts to exclude migrants. Founded on respect for individual rights, liberal states encourage individual initiative, prosper through the productivity of free markets, and avoid intrusive regulation of private behavior. Efforts to control immigration run aground amidst these contradictory values and the institutions that embody them. At the same time that migration is viewed with dread by many citizens, it is considered fortuitous and

---

[1] Although migration constitutes a context of Western politics, Western states helped create it. Just as out-migration from Europe was often involuntary, current immigration is in part a result of the actions of Western states. Their colonial policies spawned post-colonial migrations. Their military interventions produce refugee flows. Trade and investment in the "developing areas" contribute to new migration streams. Furthermore, some migrants are actively recruited and others respond to favorable labor market signals in the West.

welcome by many others. An impressive impulse toward inclusion coexists along-side that of restriction.

For some, mass migration is not simply a contextual feature of politics in the liberal democracies, but a manifestation of a fundamental reordering of global relations that challenges the viability of traditional nation states. Looking at immigration control and immigration incorporation, I explore the following questions. Can national states deal effectively with this new migration context so that they control migration rather than being controlled by it? Can the liberal democracies absorb ethnic and religious minorities without becoming more frag-mented and contentious societies? Will states fashion distinct reactions to mass migration or will they be driven by its imperatives toward broadly similar policies? Does the European Union constitute a forum within which its members can create a supranational immigration regime?

1   IMMIGRATION CONTROL

National states and the laws and institutions they create are the main constraints on migration worldwide and in their absence migration flows would be both different and larger (Zolberg 1981). Nevertheless, the most striking characteristic of immi-gration policy in Western societies is the large "gap" between rigorous laws and tough rhetoric, on the one hand, and glaring evidence of the failure of these laws and the emptiness of this rhetoric, on the other (Cornelius, Tsuda, Martin, and Hollifield 2004, 4). A substantial disparity between the efforts to regulate migration and outcomes is undeniable. The immigration halt in the labor-importing Euro-pean countries in the 1970s was followed, not by the exit of temporary guest workers, but their settlement and reunion with old and new family members. Rather than declining, the size of the foreign populations in Western countries stabilized or grew considerably throughout the 1980s (OECD 1991, 124; 1999, 264). Large numbers of illegal migrants testify to the cracks in protective walls. In 2002 there were an estimated three million unauthorized workers in the fifteen member states of the European Union and nine million undocumented immigrants in the United States. Over three million migrants were legalized after 1986 in the United States and around a million and a half in the 1990s in five amnesties carried out in France, Greece, Italy, Portugal, and Spain (*Migration News*, September 2002; Miller 1999, 36–41).

Nonetheless, it is gross oversimplification to declare flatly that "controls have failed" or that traditional state sovereignty is a thing of the past. Gaps between intentions and outcomes are common in all areas of public policy and are not necessarily signs of failure. The democracies differ in their determination to master immigration and some are better situated and equipped by location and history than others. Brochmann (1999a, 299–302) identifies "preconditions of control" such as economic and political geography, immigration history, and labor market structure that create diverse migration contexts for states. To paraphrase Tolstoy, one might say that all immigrant destination states are unhappy, but each is unhappy in its own way.

The failure of control policies may temporarily reflect the issue's novelty (Alink, Boin, and t'Hart 2001) and that new immigration countries had to start from scratch erecting control apparatuses (Sciortino 1999). From a somewhat longer perspective, states are enhancing their "mechanisms of control" (Brochmann and Hammar 1999), developing an impressive arsenal of new institutions, tactics, and technologies that involve devolution of policy to sub-state and private actors and externalizing efforts to reduce migration pressures at their source (Guiraudon and Lahav 2000; OECD 2004, 67–72).

Migration and migration control policies take numerous forms—organized refugee resettlement, on-site asylum seeking, unauthorized entry and work, visa-overstaying, permanent settlement, and temporary entry for tourism, business, study, or work. Dealing with refugee resettlement, legal immigration for permanent settlement, and visas for temporary entry is much less challenging than preventing unauthorized entry or work. Managing asylum seekers may be the most difficult of all given the legal, moral, and political constraints operating on states, especially with respect to deportation (Gibney and Hansen 2003). Studies that focus on specific types of migration may yield more credible conclusions than work that generalizes about immigration *tout court* (Meyers 2004, 17).

Despite these qualifications a sizable gap between interests and outcomes remains. One set of explanations links this to processes of globalization. For some the integration of a world market for goods, services, and finance leads necessarily to global and regional markets for labor. Capitalist economies require both skilled and unskilled migrant workers to fill vacancies and maintain competitiveness. Anti-immigration backlash persuades national states to mount protectionist barriers, but they cannot succeed in the long run (Stalker 2000, 1–10; Sassen 1999). For others, the uneven performance of immigration control regimes is rooted in the emergence of transnational institutions and values devoted to the protection of human rights. These sensibilities sustain forms of "postnational membership" (Soysal 1994, 3) that extend "rights across borders" (Jacobson 1996) and make traditional modes of national citizenship increasingly obsolete. The global market facilitates growing numbers of "transnational migrants" who are "embedded in multi-layered social fields" in two or more countries and, hence, regularly engage in practices both inside and outside the bounds of territorial states (Levitt, DeWind, and Vertovec 2003, 567). Work from the globalization perspective contributes usefully to our understanding of contemporary migration processes, but risks underestimating the continuing primacy of national states and overlooking the ways states express and channel transnational trends.

The chief alternative to globalization is the model of "embedded realism" (Hansen 2002) based on domestic politics. Joppke (1998, 15–20) memorably identified "self-limited sovereignty" as the source of the immigration policy gap. Governing elites, bureaucrats, and courts interpret restrictive policies as incompatible with national laws and constitutions. The groups and parties that organize around immigration are not as resrictionist as typically implied. In the traditional immigration countries, powerful interests that benefit directly from immigration mobilize to support open policies and typically override the less organized objections of popular opinion (Freeman 1995; Betts 1999; Veugelers 2000).

Immigration politics in Europe is more contentious. Anti-immigration parties and volatile electorates narrow the scope for liberal policies (Betz and Immerfall 1998). Lacking long traditions of immigration, there is a smaller reservoir of positive experience and sentiment upon which to draw. Restrictive policies and a rancorous political discourse lead to a widespread perception that "Fortress Europe" is closed to migrants. Such epithets mislead in important ways, however. While they capture the ugly tone of the worst of the rhetoric, they fail to credit the willingness of European states to grant migrants access to welfare, permanent residence, and citizenship. This openness derives as much from immigration-friendly domestic laws and interests as from abject policy failure.

Significant elements in all the democracies want to control migration and to prevent the entry of those deemed unwanted. They are not always willing, however, to pay the price more effective controls entail in terms of expenditures, limits on liberties, and interruption of tourism and business. There are other interests that support the admission of certain classes of migrants from whom they expect to benefit economically and fiscally. In the early 1990s Messina (1994) laid out a compelling case that the unhappy aftermath of the guest worker era made the resumption of labor recruitment schemes in Europe a political non-starter. Scarcely a decade later, however, these states compete to attract highly skilled temporary migrants whose creativity and special talents they covet. Two countries reputed to be among the most anti-immigration in Europe—Germany and the United Kingdom—are leading the way even though the bulk of new skilled workers must necessarily come from outside Europe. Perception of a severe demographic crisis feeds support for migration as a means to slow down, if not reverse population decline and aging. Migration is frequently championed as a means to stabilize the finances of old-age pension systems by improving dependency ratios. Evidence that only continuous immigration on a colossal scale can do any more than ameliorate these problems fails to put the idea to rest (UN 2001).

There is a good deal to be said for both transnational and domestic perspectives on immigration. Rather than follow this debate into what may become a theoretical cul-de-sac, scholars should explore the interaction between the global and the national. Although global and regional changes are challenging traditional modes of sovereignty, individually and collectively states are fighting back. Beset by similar external pressures, national states develop distinct immigration control regimes that reflect long-standing institutional and cultural idiosyncracies. Moreover, the extensive cooperation on immigration and asylum in the European Union does not prevent member states from steering policy to their own purposes.

A recent survey concludes that the immigration policies of the receiving states exhibit broad and impressive similarities (Meyers 2004, 173–5). Nonetheless, the settler societies diverge in important ways from European states (Freeman 1995; Cornelius, Tsuda, Martin, and Hollifield 2004) and among themselves (Freeman and Birrell 2001). With respect to Europe, Hammar's landmark study concluded that "policy divergence has come to an end; instead, there is now a trend towards policy convergence" (1985, 292). Fourteen years later, however, Brochmann observes that "the process of harmonization witnessed in today's Europe can be more precisely labeled *conditional convergence*" (1999*a*, 333). Persisting variations across liberal states reflect cultural, historical, and institutional differences that shape national reactions to immigration (Joppke 1999). Dual nationality and asylum issues have a particular resonance in Germany due to its unfortunate history, while in post-imperial Britain dual nationality is a non-issue and asylum politics is fixated on costs. Immigration politics in Germany and France reflect different traditions of nationhood (Brubaker 1992; Hollifield 1992). In Scandinavia immigration is folded into discourses on the welfare state (Hammar 1999; Brochmann 1999b). The new countries of immigration in Southern Europe are more tolerant of illegal migration than their northern neighbors (Geddes 2003, 149–72).

At first glance, the evolution of immigration and asylum policy in the European Union seems to support the thesis of eroding sovereignty. The abolition of internal borders, steps toward common policies on asylum, external borders, and immigration, and the 2004 transfer of immigration and asylum to the Community pillar suggest a dramatic march towards supranational immigration policies. Such a conclusion is problematic, however. Are the successes or failures of the movement toward common immigration and asylum policies more impressive? Certainly a great deal has been accomplished and there is more cooperation over migration, and a more central role for EU institutions, than just a few years ago. On the other hand, each step forward has been tortuous (van Selm and Tsolakis 2004). Although the Commission takes a leading role in formulating multilateral approaches, critical decisions remain in the hands of the Council, which is to say the member states. Cooperation has been directed more to enhanced control than enhanced movement. National decision-makers have not so much been directed by Brussels as they have "escaped to Europe" (Geddes 2000) in order to find policy-making venues that shield them from national parliaments and courts (Guiraudon 2000*b*).

The new migration context poses serious challenges to liberal democratic states which have not yet demonstrated the capacity to deal adequately with them. Nonetheless, states continue to assert their prerogatives to control their borders, and when they agree to delegate authority to regional regimes such as the European Union their intent is to obtain national objectives more effectively than they can on their own. Changes at the global or regional level are real, but their impact is transmitted through nationally specific processes. Few systematic comparisons of the receiving states exist but the available evidence suggests that states operate nationally distinct immigration regimes, even inside the EU. The development of reliable indicators of immigration policies to facilitate judgments about the extent of convergence based on more than intuition is a major research imperative.

2   IMMIGRANT INCORPORATION

None of the European states set out to become multi-ethnic immigrant societies, nor did the traditional countries deliberately undertake to accept mass immigration from the Third World. Had they posed the option to voters directly they would surely have heard a resounding "no." Nonetheless, by 1999 there were an estimated 11.8 million foreigners in France, Germany, Italy, the Netherlands, Norway, Sweden, and the United Kingdom. They constituted 8.9 percent of the German population and 5.6 percent of the French (MPI 2004). Twelve million Muslims, mostly of immigrant origin, lived in the European Union in 2001 (*Migration News*, May 2001). The sources of migration to the traditional countries have shifted sharply, and permanently, to Asia, Latin America, and Africa.

Incorporating immigrant minorities from diverse cultural backgrounds is a challenge for Western polities on the order of their accommodation of the industrial working classes a century earlier. Large and growing Muslim communities, in an era of Islamic fundamentalism and fears of terrorism, pose a special test for which there is practically no precedent (Lewis 1994, 14). Whether Muslims en masse adopt the norms and accept the cultural compromises required of democratic citizens or be the agents of a "clash of civilizations," peaceful or otherwise, is an open question (Huntington 1996). The traditional immigration countries have been absorbing immigrants for generations, but even they are dealing with inflows at near historic levels and under novel conditions. In the past they generally aspired to assimilation such that migrants melted into the native population. More recently, they have experimented with either formal (Canada, Australia) or informal (the United States) multiculturalism, an approach that legitimates retention of elements of cultural difference. The European states often ignored issues of incorporation during the first decades of mass migration on the assumption that their migrants were temporary. Once settlement was undeniable, they began to patch together incorporation schemes. Only France embraced a strong version of cultural assimilation. Other states either flirted with cultural and social exclusion (Germany) or opted for some variant of multiculturalism.[2]

Joppke and Morawska (2003, 10) argue that infatuation with official multiculturalism is on the wane although "de facto multiculturalism has become a pervasive reality in liberal, immigrant-receiving states." They detect the emergence of a strong inclination to return to a middle ground of integration that rejects both exclusion and assimilation. Of the traditional societies only Australia has significantly contracted its multicultural commitments (Freeman and Birrell 2001; Castles 1992). In Europe, however, there is something of a stampede towards more assertive integration measures. The most striking indicators of this are "integration contracts" that mandate acquisition of host country language and knowledge of local history and political institutions as requirements for resident visas, naturalization, or the receipt of social benefits. These have been adopted in states with widely varying approaches to incorporation.

Germany long refused to admit that immigrants might be permanent and, therefore, had no incentive to impose assimilationist measures that might have been counter-productive to the process of return. By 2003 both government and opposition had turned around and submitted integration bills to mandate language classes with examinations as a condition for receipt of welfare and unemployment benefits. Austria adopted similar legislation in 2004 (*Migration News*, January 2004). France, the European country with the strongest predisposition to try to assimilate immigrants, has experienced some of the most intense cultural conflicts. In 2003 reception and integration contracts were established to require acquisition of French and completion of civics courses in return for a residence permit. Nevertheless, France has made numerous practical concessions to multiculturalism (Schain 1999). As Islamic fundamentalism began to preoccupy the government, efforts were made to coopt the Muslim community through the creation of a national representative council even though this meant recognizing the legitimacy of an ethnic minority.

Sweden and the Netherlands were early enthusiasts of multiculturalism that are now stressing economic integration over cultural matters and placing more responsibility on immigrants to adapt (Hammar 1999). In their early multicultural

---

[2] A variety of typologies purport to sort out these frameworks. They focus primarily on such matters as terms of membership and whether migrants are dealt with individually or as groups. These attempts at theoretical generalization are vitiated by the unsystematic, ad hoc, and incoherent incorporation measures states employ (Koopmans and Statham 2000; Entzinger 2000). For a critical review of work employing the rubrics of race and ethnicity in the European context, see Bovenkerk, Miles, and Verbunt (1991); on the United States, see King (2000).

phase, both countries went "beyond a plea for tolerance...[toward] the public affirmation of difference as socially desirable" (Geddes 2003, 102). Fears that such policies hamper successful adaptation and increase social distance between migrants and natives led to a new Dutch policy in 1994 that emphasized equal opportunity for individuals rather than groups and instituted a program in Dutch values and language (Entzinger 2003). Sweden followed a similar track. After 1985 concern that multiculturalism was not working stimulated a move toward placing more emphasis on Swedish language and culture (Geddes 2003, 121; Hammar 1999). Britain devised a model of multiculturalism that bore little resemblance to the practices of other European states (Favell 1998), but recent events indicate that it too is reconsidering the necessity of integration. A White Paper on migration and citizenship speaks of "integration with diversity," stresses the importance of common values and the need for newcomers to speak English, and proposes allegiance oaths for new citizens (Home Office 2002).

Although scholars debate whether formal citizenship is any longer required to enjoy most of the rights of citizens (Soysal 1994; Hansen and Weil 2001; Bauboeck 1994), genuine integration of immigrant minorities must include access to citizenship. In the traditional immigration societies citizenship is relatively easily available (Aleinikoff and Klusmeyer 2000; Schuck 1984), but there is wide variation in the relative openness of European citizenship policies, many of which have recently been altered (Çinar, Davy, and Waldrauch 1999). Howard (2003, 22) concludes that "it is still too early to speak of a convergence process within the countries of the EU" and identifies a pattern of "durable divergence" instead. Hansen (1998, 760) agrees "there is no clear direction to policy change in Europe, and that one can at most speak confidently of a liberal harmonisation of naturalisation in North-Western Europe." He points out, however, that "with the exception of Austria, Luxembourg, and Greece, all second-generation migrants have a right to acquire citizenship either at birth or by the age of 21."

The study of incorporation could be advanced if scholars moved outside the purview of formal integration policies to explore the impact of regulatory regimes not directed specifically at migrants. Political science has failed to link the study of comparative political economy and the welfare state to immigration both because immigration specialists have not employed the insights of these cognate fields and because the latter have largely ignored immigration. Labor market policies that feature in the varieties of capitalism literature, for example, are critical to the fates of migrants and migration is a central factor determining the human capital endowments of capitalist labor forces (Engelen 2003; Portes 1995). An unprecedented characteristic of migration today is that the main countries of destination are rich welfare states. Whether migration is eroding the political consensus on which the welfare states rest or is a means of rescuing them from financial ruin is a key question for students of the democracies (Guiraudon 2000a; Bommes and Geddes 2000; Ireland 2004).

6   CONCLUSION

Demographic change has notable implications for polities but it is not a prominent interest of political scientists. Among the factors affecting population change migration is the most important and the most subject to political manipulation. Political science has recently mobilized its resources to analyze immigration, but the sub-field is still a marginal and relatively undeveloped enterprise within the discipline. This chapter explored just one aspect of the subject, migration into the Western democracies in the last forty years. I argued that liberal states are torn in their approach to immigration and this indecision is reflected in policies that are an incoherent mix of aggressive restriction and active and passive acceptance. This situation may be unstable, and over time one or the other impulse could win out. The more ardent advocates of immigration can point to numerous forces pushing Western societies toward their future as multicultural countries of immigration— intensifying trade, technological change, demographic imbalances between sending and receiving areas, the rights revolution, European integration, and the coming of age of a post-materialist generation for whom tolerance is a bedrock principle. Skeptics point out the paucity of successful multicultural societies, note the deeply entrenched human propensity for national and ethnic conflict, and generally view the current situation as an unprecedented social experiment on a grand scale that may yet devolve into a cauldron of cultural and religious animus. At present, ostentatious efforts by governments to control unwanted migration, however ineffective they may be, are necessary to purchase public willingness to go along with the renewed recruitment of skilled migrants and reformulated programs to integrate existing immigrant communities.

REFERENCES

ALEINIKOFF, T. A., and KLUSMEYER, D. (eds.) 2000. *From Migrants to Citizens*. Washington, DC: Carnegie Endowment for International Peace.

ALINK, F., BOIN, A., and T'HART, P. 2001. Institutional crises and reforms in policy sectors: the case of asylum policy in Europe. *Journal of European Public Policy*, 8: 286–306.

BAUBOECK, R. 1994. *Transnational Citizenship*. Aldershot: Edward Elgar.

BETTS, K. 1999. *The Great Divide*. Sydney: Duffy and Snellgrove.

BETZ, H.-G., and Immerfall, S. (eds.) 1998. *The New Politics of the Right*. New York: St. Martin's Press.

BOMMES, M., and GEDDES, A. (eds.) 2000. *Immigration and Welfare*. London: Routledge.

BOVENKERK, F., MILES, R., and VERBUNT, G. 1991. Comparative studies of migration and exclusion on grounds of "race" and ethnic background in Western Europe: a critical appraisal. *International Migration Review*, 25: 375–91.

BROCHMANN, G. 1999a. Controlling immigration in Europe. In Brochmann and Hammar 1999, 297–334.

—— 1999b. Redrawing lines of control: the Norwegian welfare state dilemma. In Brochmann and Hammar 1999, 203–32.

—— and HAMMAR, T. (eds.) 1999. *Mechanisms of Controls.* New York: Oxford University Press.

BRUBAKER, W. R. 1992. *Citizenship and Nationhood in France and Germany.* Cambridge, Mass.: Harvard University Press.

CASTLES, S. 1992. The Australian model of immigration and multiculturalism: is it applicable in Europe? *International Migration Review,* 26: 549–67.

ÇINAR, D., DAVY, U., and WALDRAUCH, H. 1999. Comparing the rights of non-citizens in Western Europe. *Research Perspectives on Migration,* 2: 8–11.

CORNELIUS, W. A., TSUDA, T., MARTIN, P. L., and HOLLIFIELD, J. F. (eds.) 2004. *Controlling Immigration.* Stanford, Calif.: Stanford University Press.

ENGELEN, E. 2003. How to combine openness and protection? Citizenship, migration, and welfare regimes. *Politics & Society,* 31: 503–36.

ENTZINGER, H. 2000. The dynamics of integration policies: a multidimensional model. Pp. 97–118 in *Challenging Immigration and Ethnic Relations Politics,* ed. R. Koopmans and P. Statham. Oxford: Oxford University Press.

—— 2003. The rise and fall of multiculturalism: the case of the Netherlands. Pp. 59–86 in *Toward Assimilation and Citizenship,* ed. C. Joppke and E. Morawska. Houndmills: Palgrave.

FAVELL, A. 1998. *Philosophies of Integration: Immigration and the Idea of Citizenship in France and Britain.* London: Macmillan.

FREEMAN, G. P. 1995. Modes of immigration politics in liberal democratic states. *International Migration Review,* 29: 881–902.

—— and Birrell, B. 2001. Divergent paths of immigration policy in the United States and Australia. *Population and Development Review,* 27: 525–51.

GEDDES, A. 2000. *Immigration and European Integration: Towards Fortress Europe?* Manchester: Manchester University Press.

—— 2003. *The Politics of Migration and Immigration in Europe.* London: Sage.

GIBNEY, M., and HANSEN, R. 2003. Deportation and the liberal state: the forcible return of asylum seekers and unlawful migrants in Canada, Germany and the United Kingdom. Working Paper No. 77. Geneva: UNHCR.

GUIRAUDON, V. 2000a. The Marshallian tryptich reordered: the role of courts and bureaucracies in furthering migrants' social rights. In Bommes and Geddes 2000, 72–89.

—— 2000b. European integration and migration policy: vertical policymaking as venue shopping. *Journal of Common Market Studies,* 38: 251–71.

—— and LAHAV, G. 2000. A reappraisal of the state sovereignty debate: the case of migration control. *Comparative Political Studies,* 33: 162–95.

HAMMAR, T. 1985. *European Immigration Policy.* Cambridge: Cambridge University Press.

—— 1999. Closing the doors to the Swedish welfare state. In Brochmann and Hammar 1999, 169–201.

HANSEN, R. 1998. A European citizenship or a Europe of citizens? Third country nationals in the EU. *Journal of Ethnic and Migration Studies,* 24: 751–68.

—— 2002. Globalization, embedded realism, and path dependence: the other immigrants to Europe. *Comparative Political Studies,* 35: 259–83.

—— and WEIL, P. (eds.) 2001. *Towards a European Nationality.* London: Routledge.

HATTON, T. J., and WILLIAMSON, J. G. 1998. *The Age of Mass Migration.* New York: Oxford University Press.

HOLLIFIELD, J. F. 1992. *Immigrants, Markets, and States.* Cambridge, Mass.: Harvard University Press.

HOME OFFICE, UK 2002. *Secure Borders, Safe Haven.* London: HMSO.

HOWARD, M. M. 2003. Foreigners or citizens? Citizenship policies in the countries of the EU. Paper presented at the European Union Studies Association Conference, Nashville, 27–9 March.

HUNTINGTON, S. P. 1996. *The Clash of Civilizations and the Remaking of World Order.* New York: Simon and Schuster.

IRELAND, P. 2004. *Becoming Europe: Social Policy and Immigrant Integration in Germany and the Low Countries.* Pittsburgh: University of Pittsburgh Press.

JACOBSON, D. 1996. *Rights Across Borders: Immigration and the Decline of Citizenship.* Baltimore: Johns Hopkins University Press.

JOPPKE, C. (ed.) 1998. Immigration challenges the nation-state. Pp. 5–46 in *Challenge to the Nation-State.* New York: Oxford University Press.

—— 1999. *Immigration and the Nation-State.* Oxford: Oxford University Press.

—— and MORAWSKA, E. 2003. Integrating immigrants in liberal nation-states: policies and practices. Pp. 1–36 in *Toward Assimilation and Citizenship,* ed. C. Joppke and E. Morawska. Houndmills: Palgrave.

KING, D. 2000. *Making Americans.* Cambridge, Mass.: Harvard University Press.

KOOPMANS, R., and STATHAM, P. 2000. Migration and ethnic relations as a field of political contention: an opportunity structure approach. Pp. 13–56 in *Challenging Immigration and Ethnic Relations Politics,* ed. R. Koopmans and P. Statham. Oxford: Oxford University Press.

LEVITT, P., DeWIND, J., and VERTOVEC, S. 2003. Transnational migration: international perspectives. *International Migration Review,* 37: 565–75.

LEWIS, B. 1994. Legal and historical reflections on the position of Muslim populations under non-Muslim rule. Pp. 1–18 in *Muslims in Europe,* ed. B. Lewis and D. Schnapper. London: Pinter.

MASSEY, D. S., ARANGO, J., HUGO, G., KOUAOUCI, A., PELLEGRINO, A., and TAYLOR, J. E. 1998. *Worlds in Motion.* Oxford: Clarendon Press.

MESSINA, A. M. 1994. Political impediments to the resumption of labour migration to Western Europe. *West European Politics,* 3: 31–46.

MEYERS, E. 2004. *International Immigration Policy.* New York: Palgrave.

MILLER, M. J. 1999. The prevention of unauthorized migration. Pp. 20–44 in *Migration and Refugee Policies: An Overview,* ed. A. Bernstein and M. Weiner. London: Pinter.

MOCH, L. P. 2003. *Moving Europeans: Migration in Western Europe Since 1650,* 2nd edn. Bloomington: Indiana University Press.

MPI (Migration Policy Institute). 2004. Stock data (foreigner). Available at: http://www.migrationinformation.org/ GlobalData/charts1.cfm.

OECD 1991. *Continuous Reporting System on Migration (SOPEMI).* Paris: OECD.

—— 1999. *Trends in International Migration: SOPEMI.* Paris: OECD.

—— 2004. *Trends in International Migration: SOPEMI 2003.* Paris: OECD.

PORTES, A. (ed.) 1995. *The Economic Sociology of Immigration.* New York: Russell Sage Foundation.

SANDERS, J. 2002. Ethnic boundaries and identity in plural societies. *Annual Review of Sociology*, 28: 327–57.

SASSEN, S. 1999. *Losing Control? Sovereignty in an Age of Globalization*. New York: Columbia University Press.

SCHAIN, M. 1999. Minorities and immigrant incorporation in France. Pp. 199–223 in *Multicultural Questions*, ed. C. Joppke and S. Lukes. Oxford: Oxford University Press.

SCIORTINO, G. 1999. Planning in the dark: the evolution of Italian immigration control. In Brochmann and Hammar 1999, 233–60.

SCHUCK, P. 1984. The transformation of immigration law. *Columbia Law Review*, 84: 1–90.

SOYSAL, Y. 1994. *Limits to Citizenship: Migrants and Postnational Membership in Europe*. Chicago: University of Chicago Press.

STALKER, P. 2000. *Workers Without Frontiers*. Boulder, Colo.: Lynne Rienner.

United Nations (UN) 2001. *Replacement Migration*. New York: UN.

—— 2004. *World Population Policies, 2003*. New York: UN.

VAN SELM, J., and TSOLAKIS, E. 2004. The enlargement of an "area of freedom, security and justice:" managing migration in a European Union of 25 members. Policy Brief #4. Washington, DC: Migration Policy Institute.

VEUGELERS, J. W. P. 2000. State–society relations in the making of Canadian immigration policy during the Mulroney era. *Canadian Review of Sociology and Anthropology*, 37: 1–16.

ZOLBERG, A. R. 1981. International migrations in political perspective. Pp. 3–27 in *Global Trends in Migration*, ed. M. M. Kritz, C. B. Keely, and S. M. Tomasi. New York: Center for Migration Studies.

CHAPTER 35

POPULATION CHANGE, URBANIZATION, AND POLITICAL CONSOLIDATION

JEFFREY HERBST

SOMETIME between 2004 and 2007, in a city, most likely in China or India, a child will be born and there will be more residents of cities than of rural areas for the first time in human history. This is a remarkable development: In 1950, only 30 percent of the world's population lived in urban areas. In contrast, it is estimated that 60 percent of the world's population will be in cities by the year 2030. Indeed, during the period 2000–30, urban population growth (totaling 2.1 billion) will account for almost all of total population growth worldwide (amounting to 2.2 billion), as the rural areas will be demographically stagnant. Urban populations are projected to grow at roughly twice the rate of total world population (1.8 percent versus 1 percent) and will double in about thirty-eight years (UN 2002a, 1, 4).

While a sense that cities are getting bigger and demographically more important has been palpable for many years, the full political implications of the historic population shift to the urban areas has not been understood, or even analyzed. Most of the studies that have focused on urban politics have examined implications for poverty and political mobilization within cities (e.g. Nelson 1979) or as a setting for ethnic politics (e.g. Varshney 2001) or to study the changing urban–rural balance of power (e.g. Bates 1981; Lipton 1977). Few works discuss the evolution of national political systems within the context of an increasingly urbanized society. Even William H. McNeill's (1990) erudite monograph *Population and Politics since 1950*, the only work whose title focuses on the subject at hand, largely focuses on the political implications of growing numbers of people in history, not the particular problem of the more recent radical change in the spatial mix of populations. What the changing composition of the rural/urban population mix means for state consolidation in the developing world, in particular, has been less examined. Yet, especially in Africa and Asia, where the greatest urbanization will occur in the next few years, it is the cities where the state is most evident and the rural areas where the state is weakest. Indeed, a central problem in the poorest developing countries is that the state is present in only the urban areas. That people are increasingly moving to urban areas, or being born into permanent urban populations, where the state is at its most powerful, is a seminal development that will have many profound effects on politics in the developing world in the years to come.

A focus on the political implications of urbanization is also helpful given how much attention is devoted to globalization. How countries react to international pressures is obviously a critical subject, especially given the volatility of financial markets, increasing integration of trade, and availability of foreign investment. The Internet, the ability of money to move anywhere instantly, and the global media, among many other forces, have led some to conclude that geography is no longer relevant. However, the continual movement to the cities, and the increasing number of people who know of no other life than the urban one they were born into, suggests that location within a country is still critically important. Indeed, in the next fifteen years, hundreds of millions of people will vote with their feet and indicate that, despite the ability of money to cross great distances instantly, it is crucial to their life chances to be in a particular place.

This chapter will begin to explore the political implications for state consolidation in developing countries in the historically unprecedented situation that most populations everywhere will be located primarily in urban areas. It focuses on the opportunities and challenges that urbanization poses for two critical aspects of state consolidation: building the coercive apparatus of the state itself and the popular control of public coercion through the establishment of democracy. Urbanization is of such world-historic significance that it will undoubtedly take many years to explore fully. However, some trends are observable now, especially as urban populations steadily, and seemingly inexorably continue to rise.

1   THE POPULATION REVOLUTION

It is ironic that Thomas Malthus (1986), who first published his famous *Essay on the Principle of Population* in 1798, is much the most famous scholar of population and politics, even if his predictions were, in fact, wrong. Malthus was concerned about the tendency of all populations to increase beyond their capacity to feed themselves. However, population growth as he was writing was below 0.6 percent a year and it would not be until 1804 that the world is estimated to have had one billion people. Population growth would later accelerate as growth rates passed 1 percent in the 1920s and peaked at about 2.04 percent in the late 1960s. Correspondingly, after taking millennia to reach one billion, the world added a second billion by 1927 and probably took to only 1974 to double again to four billion (United Nations 1999, 3–5). In the United Nations medium-fertility scenario, the world population stabilizes at 11 billion in 2150 (UN 1998, ix) although there is obviously enormous uncertainty surrounding that number.

The total numbers themselves are daunting and perhaps overwhelm the critically important spatial story. One of the most important manifestations of the growth of world population is the growing importance of the urban population.

On a global basis, the rate of urban population growth over the period 1950–2000 has been almost a full percentage point higher (2.68 versus 1.75) than total population growth. This demographic momentum combined with the projected rate of growth of urban populations in the future will cause city-dwellers eventually to outnumber rural populations in most places. In what the United Nations calls the "more developed regions" populations were primarily urban (54.9 percent of total population) even in 1950, but in the "less developed regions" only 17.8 percent of all people were then in the urban areas. By 2000, the percentage of people in rich countries in urban areas was 75 percent; however, the really important development was the more than doubling of the percentage urban population in poorer countries to 40 percent. By 2030, the developing countries are projected further to converge on the urban reality of developed countries with 56 percent of their populations in urban areas compared to 83 percent in developed areas (UN 2002a, 4). Put another way, in 1950, rich countries were three times as urban as poor countries while in 2030 they will be only 1.5 times as urban.

More specifically, the dramatic urbanization between 1970 and 2030 is largely an African and Asian affair. As Table 35.1 demonstrates, Latin America was already mostly urban in 1970. Africa and Asia, on the other hand, will go from having roughly one-third of their populations urban in 2000 to over half in 2030. Africa has had the highest urbanization rate for several decades, albeit from a very low base. Asia, driven in part by the massive urbanization of China, has also had a very high urban growth rate.

Table 35.1 Percentage urban in major world areas

	1970	2000	2015	2030
World	36.8	47.2	53.7	60.2
Africa	23.1	37.2	45.3	52.9
Asia	23.4	37.5	45.9	54.1
Europe	64.6	73.4	76.3	80.5
Latin American and Caribbean	57.6	75.4	80.5	84.0
Northern America	73.8	77.4	81.1	84.5
Oceania	71.2	74.1	76.1	77.3

Source: UN 2002*b*, 30.

Indeed, the growth of the urban population is so region-specific that Africa and Asia will account for almost 85 percent of the increment in the world's urban population between 2000 and 2030, as opposed to absorbing 66 percent of the increment in urban population between 1950 and 2000. All other areas of the world will see their percentage of the world's urban population decline. This is most notable in Europe, which will only have about 11 percent of the world's urban population by 2030, as opposed to more than one-third in 1950 (UN 2002*b*, 31, 33).

The growth of urban areas is generally most commonly depicted in the development of megacities, those with populations of over 10 million. In 1950, there was only one such city (New York) while in 2015, twenty-one cities are projected to be truly gargantuan. Not only are there more very large cities but they are getting much bigger: The New York of 1950, unquestionably the largest city of its time, would only be the sixteenth largest in 2015. Finally, the overwhelming number of the very large cities will be in what is now the developing world. Only Tokyo, New York, Los Angeles, and Osaka will be amongst the megacities in 2015 (UN 2002*b*, 8).

However, while megacities are the most dramatic indication of the increasing urban basis of the majority of mankind, they are not, in fact, the most important parts of the evolving urban hierarchy.

Table 35.2 shows where the incremental population has gone in the last fifteen years and is projected to go in the medium-term. Megacities do not absorb that much of the increment, in large part because very few countries are large enough to have one city of ten million people.[1] Rather, and most importantly, it is cities and towns of less than 500,000 and then cities of 1–5 million that will absorb

---

[1] For instance, the fifty-three countries on the African continent have a median population of only 8.7 million. Calculated from World Bank 2003.

Table 35.2 Where will the additional people live?

Annual Population increase	1975–2000	2000–2015
World (millions)	79.6	76.7
Of which will live in cities (millions)	52.8	67.2
Of which live in:		
Developed countries (millions)	6.6	3.8
Developing countries (millions)	46.2	63.4
Of the increase in the developing countries:		
Percentage that will live in cities of more than 10 million	9.5	11.1
Percentage that will in cities of 5–10 million	5.3	8.8
Percentage that will live in cities of 1–5 million	20.6	25.7
Percentage that will live in cities of 500,000 to 1 million	7.9	6.7
Percentage that will live in cities of less than 500,000	44.2	42.0

Source: UN 2002b, 86

approximately two-thirds of the population increment. The sheer number of these types of cities in the developing world make them more likely destinations than the larger but relatively infrequent agglomeration of more than 10 million people.

Another way to look at the issue is to examine "primate" urban areas, those cities with the largest urban population in a given country. Out of the 114 primate cities worldwide with populations over 750,000, just over half (61) experienced declines in their percentage of the urban population between 1975 and 2000 even though it is likely that almost all contained absolutely more people. Between 2000 and 2015, such declines will become more general: 101 out of the 114 primate cities will see their share of the urban population reduced, although usually by 4 percent or less. As the United Nations has noted, "the declining level of primacy of most primate cities with populations of at least 750,000 inhabitants indicates that, as the overall levels of urbanization of countries increase, there is a greater diversification of the urban system and the largest cities tend to see their preponderance eroded by the growth of medium-sized and smaller urban areas."[2] Put another way, urbanization is becoming so prevalent that people do not even have to move to the primate city in order to get the full advantages of city life. Thus, while in a large number of countries, one city may not be as dominant, urban life is for the first time in human history the norm across the world.

[2] Data in this paragraph and quote from United Nations 2002b, 104.

2   POLITICAL IMPLICATIONS OF THE NEW URBANIZATION

The formal authority of the state is almost always associated with urban areas. The common shorthand of saying "Berlin argues" to indicate Germany's preference or "it is the view in London" to describe the opinion of the United Kingdom, are simply some of the most banal indications that the offices and buildings that define a state are always in urban areas and that the capital is always amongst the most important city centers. Quite often the capital is the most important city: for instance, in all but four African countries (Benin, Cameroon, Malawi, and South Africa) the capital is the largest single city and capitals are "almost invariably the fastest growing cities in African states" (Griffiths 1994, 162).

More generally, whatever the overall strength of the state, it is generally considered to be strongest in the urban areas. As Huntington noted many years ago of very poor countries, "The city is still but a small growth in society as a whole, but the groups within the city are able to employ their superior skills, location, and concentration to dominate the politics of the society at the national level (Huntington 1968, 74). In contrast, the rural areas, where populations are sometimes spread over significant distances far from the capital, are seen as areas of political vacuum. For instance, Gledhill notes that in Mexico, "The hills are associated with wildness, violence, and political freedom, the plains with docility, pacification, and susceptibility to repression, a contrast which contains an element of truth" (Gledhill 1988, 317). Similarly, the idea of the anarchic northern frontier that presented the opportunity to escape from the state, is an integral part of old Russian political mythology (Scheffel 1989, 115). In Southeast Asia, the divide between center and periphery is also often pronounced: "In many senses, the capital *was* the state, and its power radiated from center to the periphery" (McCloud 1995, 71; emphasis in the original).

Perhaps more importantly, in recent years physical control of the capital has been the defining feature of internationally recognized governments. As developing countries proliferated after the Second World War, the international community was faced with a problem of recognition: it understood that many governments did not control their own territory and were not viewed as legitimate by their populations. In addition, coups displaced some governments. How then was it possible to recognize who was the legitimate government of the day without going through the time and expense (not to mention violations of sovereignty) that would be associated with determining the actual legitimacy of rulers or the amount of territory they actually controlled? This problem came to a head with the first coup in West Africa when Togolese President Olympio was killed in a military revolt on January 13, 1963. There was significant sentiment to condemn the coup because African leaders were obviously afraid that the same fate might be visited upon them. However, after a brief period of ostracism, Togo was allowed to re-enter normal diplomatic relations with other African countries and to sign the Charter of the Organization of African Unity (*West Africa* 1963, 597).

The OAU said, in effect, that if an African government is in control of the capital city, then it has the legitimate right to the full protection offered by the modern understanding of sovereignty. Thus, Olympio's killers were recognized as the legitimate government of Togo because they controlled Lomé, not because they were perceived by the Togolese as legitimate or because they physically controlled the territory of the country. As a result, in subsequent decades, even if a developing country did not have physical control over its own territory, by the rules of the international community, it could not be challenged by other domestic groups or by outsiders. In fact, large countries such as Ethiopia, Zaire, and Angola at various times did lose control of parts of their territories to opponents but the international community always recognized whoever controlled Addis, Kinshasa, and Luanda as the unquestioned leaders of those territories. Thus, Mobutu was recognized as the ruler of Zaire even though he controlled little more than Kinshasa and its environs for the last years of his rule and continued to be recognized as the leader while the forces of Laurent Kabila marched through the country in late 1996 and early 1997. Kabila was only recognized as the legitimate ruler when he captured Kinshasa on May 17, 1997. Nor is this rule limited to Africa. For instance, the government of Hamid Karzai in Afghanistan can hardly be described as having a monopoly on legitimate violence throughout its territory yet it is seen as the sovereign government of the day. Similarly, many of the other recognized governments in Central Asia do not have real control over their territories yet their claim to sovereignty is unquestioned.

This decision rule has been popular with the international community. Physical control of the capital is the easiest indication of political presence for outsiders to discern. It would have been far more difficult for the international community to have recognition rest on measures of popular support or administrative presence throughout a country. Finally, states have relations with other states. The decision rule that territorial control or popular legitimacy was irrelevant therefore meshed nicely with the operational code of international diplomacy. There has been some fraying of this rule in recent years, notably as continental organizations and the international community are increasingly reluctant to recognize military officers that overthrow democratically elected governments even if they control the capital. However, clearly illegitimate authoritarians (e.g. Robert Mugabe in Zimbabwe) who control the capital are still recognized as the government of the day by the international community.

2.1   Improving Prospects for State Consolidation

As a result of the association between the state and urban areas, the most obvious implication of the dramatic change in the urban/rural balance is that an extraordinary number of people are moving to where the state is strongest, and are therefore voluntarily coming under greater state authority. States in the developing world, no matter what their baseline strength, will be able to have more people within their physical reach in the next few years, not because of anything that leaders have done but simply because people worldwide are moving to the capital city and other urban areas that are the places most conducive to state control. After millennia where the challenge of states across the world was to expand territorially in order to capture the population, the people are now coming to the state. The result will be a potential strengthening of the state's capacity to control, if not to serve, its populations.

However, the movement of more people toward urban centers, including the capital does not automatically mean more powerful states. Robert Kaplan's (1994) description of the chaos of West African urban areas is undeniably accurate for some places, even if many of the specific predictions he made ten years ago have not occurred. For states to consolidate, they still must make the right choices about governance and institutional structures. The implications of increased urban populations for states is that if they make the right decisions, more people will immediately come under their sway. In the short term, the increasing urban populations will cause numerous problems, notably the overload on social services and explosion in crime that Kaplan persuasively described. However, in the long term, the movement of people poses an extraordinary opportunity for states to consolidate their control over populations while doing relatively less to broadcast power over territory than was the case in the past.

2.2   Changing Poles of Opposition

While urbanization may help state consolidation in countries where governments make good choices, it also has the potential to affect the particular challenges that states face when trying to build the monopoly on legitimate violence. Much of developing country politics has been described as a conflict between cities and the rural areas. The decision rules adopted by the international community with regard to state recognition described above were developed in a world where a basic challenge for states was that they did not have control over the majority of their citizens who lived in the rural areas. Of course, there will continue to be significant rural populations in Africa and Asia, and the rest of the developing world, and it will probably continue to be the case that the very poorest people will be found in the rural areas.

However, as populations continue to migrate to the cities and permanent urban populations grow, the tension between city and rural areas may lessen as the countryside becomes more demographically marginal to the state. Rather, the continuing wave of urbanization and the diversification of places that people are migrating to holds out the possibility that conflict between cities will become an increasingly important schism in the future. As noted above, migration to cities has become so great that the primate city in most countries has a declining share of the urban population. The growth of cities between one and five million and especially the very significant increase in populations of towns and cities of less than 500,000, raises the possibility that conflict between cities, or different forms of urban agglomerations, may become an increasingly central part of national politics for many nations. As South Africa urbanizes, for instance, the future of conflict may be between Johannesburg, with its dependence on natural resources, and Cape Town, with its coastal position and primacy in some financial services, rather than the traditional division between blacks and whites that had an important spatial dimension. The tension between the cities on China's coast that are doing phenomenally well and those in the interior that are doing less well is also increasingly apparent. Similarly, many West African nations whose capitals are on the coast will find that interior urban agglomerations are becoming increasingly important. Mosul also played a central role in focusing Kurdish opposition to the Hussein government in Baghdad.

Ethnic challenges to the state may become especially severe if those opposed to the government of the day can look to a regional city as the embodiment of their hopes for greater ethnic homogeneity, or as an economic and political challenger to the capital itself.[3] Indeed, just as movement of people to the capital may help the state, movement to non-primate cities may strengthen the hand of those who challenge the state by making it easier to rally their forces. It is not inevitable that the growth of non-primate cities threatens national authorities; the exact dynamics are still dependent on the decisions that leaders make. However, it may now be easier for challengers to the state to coalesce if they have a regional city that can serve as the site for political mobilization.

The rules that the international community has created that equate control of the capital with sovereign authority may not be as helpful if leaders are confronted with challenges that are more directly centered on large and growing regional cities. It may have been reasonable to argue that a new state could not be expected to control its entire hinterland and therefore control of the capital was the defining characteristic of sovereignty. However, the loss of control of a non-primate city is a more striking departure from the norm of uniform territorial control that is supposed to define sovereignty and may throw into doubt the legitimacy of the capital's rule.

[3] I am grateful to Christopher Clapham who suggested this idea to me.

Indeed, the international community may be more accepting of challenges to the state based in large regional cities because of globalization. One of the defining features of the changing international political economy is that flows of money, information, and culture no longer have to go through the gates that national authorities have established. Rather, money and information flow directly to consumers through the Internet or advanced financial services. Thus, as non-primate cities grow, they will be able to access the international economy in a relatively easy manner and attempt to match their population growth with increasing ties to the outside world. In a well-functioning country with good governance, such a development would be extremely positive because it would mean a diversification of urban opportunities and help in absorbing the massive numbers settling in the cities. However, in a poorly functioning country, the international community may have more ties with a regional city, especially if it is located in a region rich with natural resources, than in the capital where political stagnation and corruption will have alienated foreign governments.

It is not a paradox that urbanization may make political consolidation easier but may also facilitate the mobilization of populations who challenge the state. Larger city populations are a potential boon to both state-makers and those who want to destroy their state because more people are within their reach. What matters most is the decisions that leaders make to bind their countries together. Indeed, insightful leaders will use the new opportunities posed by urbanization to build their states. Leaders who fail to understand the dynamics of urbanization may fail sooner because there will be challengers who are able to garner followers easier than in the past.

2.3   Urbanization and Democratization

The political implications of urbanization go beyond simply how many people the state will likely be able to control. One of the most important challenges that states face today is how to consolidate their power while becoming more democratic. Indeed, an unprecedented number of poor states are attempting to become democracies at what are historically low per capita incomes and while their control of their own territory is problematic. Nigeria, Afghanistan, Mozambique, and many other developing countries may be very poor and their states limited in their geographic reach but in addition to state consolidation, they are also, in varying ways, facing the challenges of democratization. To build a state and to build a democracy at once may, in some cases, be paradoxical because state consolidation involves in part increasing the physical power of the state, while democratization tries to reign in the state's coercive abilities by giving more power to the citizenry.

Urbanization affects the dual process of state consolidation and democratization and may make the simultaneous implementation of both processes less problematic. One of the critical problems that reflect the failings of both a state and its democratic system is the weaknesses of political parties. Many political parties in the developing world are little more than vehicles for charismatic politicians and have no programmatic base. Their ability to mobilize citizens, especially in the rural areas, is limited and they can hardly be considered to be transmission belts of democracy between people and the distant state. Political parties in the developing world are weak in part because states are weak: in settings where rural areas are administratively far from the state it is extraordinarily expensive and difficult to establish branches of political parties outside the capital. Some rural residents may also not see the point of participating in political parties if the state is irrelevant to their everyday lives.

The continual rise in the urban population means that political parties will, almost by definition, find it easier to connect with their constituents, campaign for more votes, and be more of a reality for a greater percentage of the voting population. It has been notoriously difficult to create "green parties"—those that explicitly represent rural populations—in many developing countries. As the people come to the capital and other major areas, they will inevitably energize political parties. States must still design political institutions appropriately if they are going to have successful democracies and the reigning in of the state's coercive power is inevitably a long and difficult process. However, that both states and political parties could be helped by urbanization gives some hope that the historically unprecedented attempt to build both states and democracies at the same time can be helped by the shift in population distributions.

Beyond the potential empowerment of political parties, it is not unreasonable to expect that urbanization will lead to the empowerment of a greater share of the population and therefore also potentially aid processes of democratization. At the most basic level, the urban population has always exercised disproportionate power in developing countries because of the threat of the urban riot (Bates 1981). As urbanization increases, there will be proportionately more people who have the option of the protest or, in countries where democracy has only been partially institutionalized the organized protest may not be as repressed as before. Such protests are important, especially when organized elections may not have been institutionalized fully or when there is substantial belief that such elections can still be rigged.

In an increasingly urban world, the disproportionate power that city-dwellers have will almost by definition be less of a political problem. Urban bias—the accumulation of advantages that results from the location of clinics, schools, roads in urban areas as well as subsidies on foreign grown foodstuffs that are disproportionately consumed by urban populations—has been one of the scourges of development. For most of the last fifty years, too many resources have been devoted to urban areas where too few people live. As populations become increasingly urbanized, they will essentially be moving to (or growing up in) areas that are relatively well-serviced and therefore the "goods" that constitute urban bias will increasingly be spread over more and more people. There is always, of course, the possibility that states could even further increase the urban bias so that the asymmetries between the portion of the population that is urban and goods provided remains steady, but this seems unlikely given the international pressure to ameliorate urban bias. Also, so much is currently going to so many urban areas that it would be hard for the disproportionate benefits to continue to track the growing city population.

Finally, urbanization may directly influence the design of the voting system, one of the critical choices that states have to make when deciding how their democracy will function: For instance, the choice of voting systems has long been cast as a choice between two basic types of system. One is plural systems where people vote for representatives within a defined constituency. Such systems provide a territorial link between voters and the representative that they elect (and who therefore knows what territorial space she represents). There are also proportional representation systems where people vote for parties and then representatives are appointed to legislatures on the basis of their party's share of the vote. In the purest form, a proportional representation system does not allow any kind of territorial link between the voter and the representative because people cast their ballots for parties.[4] As populations become increasingly urbanized, the appeal of systems that provide clear territorial links between people and their representatives becomes less important because the most important territorial aspect of plural systems in the developing world is that they provide the rural areas with a distinct voice. While it could still be argued that different cities need to be represented differently, the strongest arguments in favor of plural systems of representation had to do with the advantages provided to rural areas when a representative knew where her constituents lived because politics was so inherently urban that rural areas would, it was thought, otherwise lose out.

3   CONCLUSION

Urbanization per se does not necessarily lead to positive or negative developments in politics. The continual movements of people to the cities in the poorer parts of

[4] See, e.g., the debate between Joel D. Barkan (1995) Andrew Reynolds (1995).

the developing world have encouraged some authors, notably Kaplan (1994), to stress the growing crisis of urban services and crime in cities. These problems are undoubtedly significant. However, put in a different time frame the historic movement of people to the cities, and the increasing number of people born into permanent urban populations, presents opportunities as well as dangers to states. No matter how disorganized and chaotic major cities in the poorer parts of the developing world appear to outsiders, these areas are actually amongst the easiest for a state to control and could be the vanguards for democratization. At the very least, more and more people will be in areas that states are likely to control than was the case only a few decades ago. There are also many other implications for national politics that will slowly but surely become apparent as the dominance of urban populations becomes an inescapable fact of political life in more and more countries.

References

Agnew, J. 2001. *Reinventing Geopolitics*. Heidelberg: Dept. of Geography, University of Heidelberg.

Anderson, B. 1991. *Imagined Communities: Reflections on the Origin and Spread of Nationalism*. London: Verso.

Barkan, J. D. 1995. PR and southern Africa: elections in agrarian societies. *Journal of Democracy*, 6: 106–16.

Bates, R. H. 1981. *Markets and States in Tropical Africa*. Berkeley: University of California Press.

—— 1983. *Essays on the Political Economy of Rural Africa*. Cambridge: Cambridge University Press.

Boone, C. 2003. *Political Topographies of the African State*. Cambridge: Cambridge University Press.

Bratton, M., and Van de Walle, N. 1997. *Democratic Experiments in Africa*. Cambridge: Cambridge University Press.

Diamond, J. 1997. *Guns, Germs and Steel*. New York: Norton.

Gledhill, J. 1988. Legacies of empire: political centralization and class formation in the Hispanic-American world. Pp. 302–19 in *State and Society*, ed. J. Gledhill, B. Bender, and M. T. Larsen. London: Unwin Hyman.

Gottmann, J. 1973. *The Significance of Territory*. Charlottesville: University of Virginia Press.

Griffiths, I. L. 1994. *The Atlas of African Affairs*, 2nd edn. London: Routledge.

Herbst, J. 1990. Migration, the politics of protest, and state consolidation in Africa. *African Affairs*, 89: 183–203.

—— 2000. *States and Power in Africa*. Princeton, NJ: Princeton University Press.

Huntington, S. P. 1968. *Political Order in Changing Societies*. New Haven, Conn.: Yale University Press.

Iliffe, J. 1987. *The African Poor*. Cambridge: Cambridge University Press.

Kaplan, R. D. 1994. The coming anarchy. *The Atlantic*, 273 (2): 44–76.

Lijphart, A. 1999. *Patterns of Democracy*. New Haven, Conn.: Yale University Press.

LIPTON, M. 1977. *Why Poor People Stay Poor: Urban Bias in World Development.* Cambridge, Mass.: Harvard University Press.

McCLOUD, D. G. 1995. *Southeast Asia: Tradition and Modernity in the Contemporary World.* Boulder, Colo.: Westview Press.

McNEILL, W. H. 1990. *Population and Politics since 1750.* Charlottesville: University Press of Virginia.

MALTHUS, T. R. 1986. *An Essay on the Principle of Population,* 7th edn. Fairfield, NJ: August M. Kelley.

MAMDANI, M. 1996. *Citizen and Subject: Contemporary Africa and the Legacy of Late Colonialism.* Princeton, NJ: Princeton University Press.

MANN, M. 1986. *The Sources of Social Power,* Vol. 1. Cambridge: Cambridge University Press.

MURPHY, A. B. 2002. National claims to territory in the modern state system: geographical considerations. *Geopolitics,* 7: 193–214.

—— 2004. Territorial ideology and international conflict. Pp. 280–96 in *The Geography of War and Peace,* ed. C. Flint. Oxford: Oxford University Press.

NELSON, J. M. 1979. *Access to Power: Politics and the Urban Poor in Developing Nations.* Princeton, NJ: Princeton University Press.

NIJMAN, J. 2001. Visualising a new metageography: explorations in world-city space. Pp. 113–28 in *The Territorial Factor,* ed. G. Dijkink and H. Knippenberg. Amsterdam: Vossiuspers.

O'LOUGHLIN, J. 2001. Political geography of world cities. Pp. 97–112 in *The Territorial Factor,* ed. G. Dijkink and H. Knippenberg. Amsterdam: Vossiuspers.

REYNOLDS, A. 1995. PR and southern Africa: the case for proportionality. *Journal of Democracy,* 6: 117–24.

ROKKAN, S. 1975. Dimensions of state formation and nation-building: a possible paradigm for research on variations within Europe. Pp. 562–600 in *The Formation of National States in Europe,* ed. C. Tilly. Princeton, NJ: Princeton University Press.

SANDBROOK, R. 1982, *The Politics of Basic Needs: Urban Aspects of Assaulting Poverty in Africa.* London: Heinemann.

SCHEFFEL, D. Z. 1989. "There is always somewhere to go . . ." Russian old believers and the state. Pp. 109–20 in *Outwitting the State,* ed. P. Saklník. New Brunswick, NJ: Transaction.

SHUE, V. 1998. *The Reach of the State: Sketches of the Chinese Body Politic.* Stanford, Calif.: Stanford University Press.

SIMON, D. 1992. *Cities, Capital and Development: African Cities in the World Economy.* London: Bellhaven.

SPEARS, I. S. 2004. States-within-states: an introduction to their empirical attributes. Pp. 1–14 in *States-within-States,* ed. P. Kingston and I. S. Spears. New York: Palgrave Macmillan.

STEVENSON, R. F. 1968. *Population and Political Systems in Tropical Africa.* New York: Columbia University Press.

United Nations (UN) 1998. *World Population Projections to 2150.* New York: UN.

—— 1999. *Population Growth, Structure and Distribution.* New York: UN, Division of Economic and Social Affairs.

—— 2002a. *World Urbanization Prospects: The 2001 Revision, Data Tables and Highlights.* New York: UN.

—— 2002b. *World Urbanization Prospects: The 2001 Revision.* New York: UN, Department of Economic and Social Affairs.

Varshney, A. 2001. *Democracy, Development and the Countryside: Urban–Rural Struggles in India* 2nd edn. Cambridge: Cambridge University Press.

—— 2001. Ethnic conflict and civil society: India and beyond. *World Politics*, 53: 362–98.

West Africa. 1963. No more African groups. June 1.

Whittlesey, D. 1939. *The Earth and the State.* New York: Henry Holt and Co.

Winichakul, T. 1994. *Siam Mapped.* Honolulu: University of Hawaii Press.

Wong, R. B. 1997. *China Transformed.* Ithaca, NY: Cornell University Press.

World Bank 2003. *World Bank Africa Database on Cd-Rom, 2003.* Washington, DC: World Bank.

CHAPTER 36

POPULATION COMPOSITION AS AN OBJECT OF POLITICAL STRUGGLE

DAVID I. KERTZER
DOMINIQUE AREL

IN RECENT years various strands of social theory have converged to raise the issue of how modern national states represent their populations and, in doing so, divide them into a variety of categories that take on political importance. These involve both inquiries into the evolution and nature of states and state power, and theorization about the nature of identities and resistance from below to the exercise of state power.

James Scott, whose *Seeing Like a State* has been influential in this movement, cites the recommendation given by an adviser to Louis XIV in 1686, urging that he authorize a census of his subjects:

Would it not be a great satisfaction to the king to know at a designated moment every year the number of his subjects, in total and by region, with all the resources, wealth & poverty of each place; [the number] of his nobility and ecclesiastics of all kinds, of men of the robe, of Catholics and of those of the other religion, all separated according to the place of their residence?... [Would it not be] a useful and necessary pleasure for him to be able, in his own office, to review in an hour's time the present and past condition of a great realm of which he is the head, and be able himself to know with certitude in what consists his grandeur, his wealth, and his strengths?   (Scott 1998, 11)

If knowledge is power, there is no greater power than the creation of knowledge. And with numerous theorists seeing the rise of the modern nation state as linked to a new relationship between rulers and the ruled, one that is no longer mediated through intermediate institutions such as guilds or corporate religious communities, the counting and categorization of each member of the population becomes central. As Foucault (1991, 99–100), whose work has been one of the main spurs to this line of inquiry, put it: "The perspective of population, the reality accorded to specific phenomena of population, render possible the final elimination of the model of the family." In Foucault's view, "the population is the object that government must take into account in all its observations and *savoir*, in order to be able to govern effectively in a rational and conscious manner."

As Scott points out, reading the population in this way can only be made possible through radical simplification. Such simplification is not only necessitated by the very complexity of humanity and the social world, which could never be represented in any other way, but also, as Scott maintains, the observations made by state agents are a product of the limited number of objectives that the state has in dealing with its population. "[U]ntil the nineteenth century," Scott (1998, 23) argues, "the most prominent of these were typically taxation, political control, and conscription." In the latter part of that century, however, modern states discovered a new realm in their midst: "the social" (Holquist 2001, 111). Represented as an organic body, but generated by a full accounting of the individuals who composed it, the social developed into a new site of state intervention, in furtherance of its domestic and foreign policy objectives. The state's capacity to intervene, irrespective of the nature of the regime (whether democratic or totalitarian), rested on the degree to which the state rendered its population "legible."

As the Sun King's counselor recognized, there was no more basic way for the state to know its population than through the conduct of a general census. (An idea, one should add, that caught fire with Marshal Vauban, Louis XIV's principal war minister, who undertook the conduct of amazingly detailed household censuses in military cities). Something of the sort was expressed by another Frenchman, writing almost two centuries later, when Pierre-Joseph Proudhon, his anarchist streak clearly on display argued: "To be governed is to be under surveillance, inspected, spied on, superintended, legislated, regulated, restrained, indoctrinated, preached at, controlled, appraised, assessed, censored, commanded... To be governed is to be noted, registered, enumerated, accounted for, stamped, measured, classified" (in Caplan and Torpey 2001, 1). Indeed, state authorities have long encountered resistance to the taking of censuses, as people recognized that the state's interest in enumerating them bespoke an assertion of power that might not be to their benefit. The fact that such censuses were commonly undertaken, previous to the nineteenth century, in order to make tax collection and conscription more efficient, did nothing to encourage popular support for these efforts.

While the first regular national census was undertaken in the United States in 1790, regular European secular national censuses initially began under the impetus of the vast Napoleonic effort to extend the state's gaze over its population. In 1801, France's prefects received instructions from the new Bureau de Statistique of the Ministry of the Interior: "Delve deeply and with care into all that pertains to the population," they were told, for "no material is more deserving to fix the gaze of an administrator" (in Cole 2000, 6). In that year, too, the first French national census was taken, to be repeated every five years. By the last quarter of the century, most states in Europe were holding regular censuses.

With the wave of enthusiasm for national statistics identified with the Belgian Adolphe Quetelet, and the holding of regular international congresses of statisticians throughout Europe in the mid-nineteenth century, the frenzy of interest in the collection of national statistics, including censuses, was linked to a deep faith in the power of such numbers to speak for themselves. Thus in 1860 the new Statistical Society of Paris passed a resolution to make clear that "statistics is nothing else than the knowledge of the science of facts." And the society's statutes proclaimed that, as such, statistics "ought to provide the basis upon which society is governed" (Porter 1995, 79–80).

The state's interest in "simplifications," as theorized by Scott necessitated the creation of specific social categories. As it turned out, if the statistics "spoke for themselves," the categories that produced them did not. Take the basic category of who is to be counted in the first place. Should a census count all those actually residing on a state's territory, only those formally registered, or only citizens? And if residence is to be the criterion, how does one separate a transient migrant from a permanent one? Modern states continue to apply different criteria to assess the boundaries of their population to be counted (Arel 2002), and far from being apolitical scientific markers, census categories reflect political choices.

In their exploration of "the social," states have sought to collect information utilizing a number of socioeconomic categories, such as age, sex, and occupation. Notwithstanding the variation in how they are defined, there is general agreement about the desirability of using these types of categories. Less obvious, however, has been the role of *cultural identities* in the production of state statistics (Kertzer and Arel 2002). A case in point is the so-called "racial" marker. The category of race appeared on the American census—and in colonial censuses—because it was deemed a "self-evident component of human identity" (Nobles 2002, 50). And yet, long after the "naturalness" of race was utterly discredited, it nonetheless remains a central category of the American and several other censuses. The category of (ethnic) nationality has similarly long been recognized as self-evident in the eastern half of

Europe, while rejected on philosophical grounds by the other half. What matters in a census is determined by political interests and prevalent discourse.

Confronting the social has meant a struggle to represent a population utilizing certain identity categories, such as race, language, ethnic nationality, ethnic origins, religion, and caste. While there are many bureaucratic means through which such categorization is enacted, a case can be made that none is more important than the regular national census. This is so because in the popular imagination, the census is seen as a powerful, perhaps the ultimate means of group recognition.

The census also holds a powerful sway over the political analyst. Notwithstanding a general acceptance that identities are constructed, social scientists who rely on census data for their statistically based inquiry rarely pause to consider the implications of constructivism over the production of data. While the collection of data itself is subject to a rigorous scientific methodology, how the data are framed responds to political imperatives. Put differently, the categories used to gather census data are inherently part of the process of creating and re-forming political identities. The census becomes a political battleground not due to a vitiation of what should be a technical exercise, but rather because of its fundamental role in representing groups. For this reason, in considering here how population composition becomes an object of political struggle, we will limit our own consideration in the remainder of this chapter to battles over the census.

1   THE AGENTS OF CATEGORY CONSTRUCTION

The metaphor of the "gaze" of a modernizing state conjures up an image of unilateral imposition of census categories on a powerless population. This paradigm has been most prevalent in studies of colonial censuses. The most influential case here has been that of colonial India, where according to some scholars, the British imposed a categorization scheme based on European notions of religion and of "caste" that proved to have huge consequences for the social and political history of South Asia. Bernard Cohn (1987), the most influential contributor to this line of work, pointed out how fluid and localized were both religious and caste identities. Indeed, the very categories of "religion" and "caste," it could be argued, were European inventions. Bringing together a vast variety of localized beliefs and practices and unifying them under the label of "Hinduism," to be considered as a "religion" like Christianity, for example, had huge social consequences.

Similarly, Cohn argued, the European concept of caste captured a highly localized and complex phenomenon of social division and was used by the colonial rulers to divide the vast Indian population into a fixed number of ranked castes. This, in turn, had a powerful impact on developing Indian society, both in offering categories on which government policies could act, and in providing people with identities of a sort they had not previously had. Confronted with the task of pigeonholing everyone in these categories, and having to struggle with the instructions for how to do so, the mass of educated local enumerators, operating in a sea of illiterate peasants, came to view "India" as composed of a population divided into just such categories.

But the view of these totalizing identities as a top-down imposition of colonial authorities has been challenged by Peabody (2001), who offers evidence that the British colonial censuses of the nineteenth century were in fact influenced by pre-existing cultural and political practices. Examining the enumeration of households carried out in the western Rajasthani kingdom of Marwar in the seventeenth century, he finds that two centuries before the British began their census-taking, the authorities of this Indian kingdom were already dividing households into caste categories. These were important to the pre-colonial state because different rates of taxation pertained to the households of different castes, and caste councils were employed as a mechanism for the collection of some of these taxes.

In this context, Peabody found that in the very earliest British colonial censuses, in the 1820s, people were divided into caste categories, and that "the drive to minutely classify the population in terms of numerous castes did not typically emanate from higher-ranking officials in the colonial bureaucracy, but from lower-level [Indian] administrative officials who were actually collecting the data in the field" (2001, 830). In examining tax enumerations of the Mughal Empire, Guha (2003, 153) concurs that the "differential demands on various groups were themselves calibrated to the power, numbers, and status of communities that had an existence independent of the registers and tax-rolls." The gaze of the colonial state was in fact shaped by the gaze of pre-colonial local administrators.

The history of the American census also challenges the paradigm of top-down category creation. For nearly two hundred years, the ever changing category of "race" was the preserve of state officials. Not only were non-whites excluded from the process of defining the category, but the determination of race in each individual's case was left to the census-taker (Nobles 2002). With the passage of the civil rights legislation in the mid-1960s, however, the collection of statistics on race became essential to buttress policies of affirmative action. This new linkage between racial category and political benefits led to a democratization of the process of determining which races were to be included in the category.

There are few more dramatic instances of this process than the addition of the question on Hispanic origin to the 1970 US census. The questionnaires for the census were already at the printer—absent such a question—when a Mexican American member of the US Interagency Committee on Mexican American Affairs demanded that the question be included. In an apparent attempt to curry favor with a growing political constituency, President Nixon ordered that the question be added to the long form that year. Since 1980 it has been on the short form, the result of strong lobbying by Hispanic organizations (Choldin 1986; Yanow 2003).

One striking result of the American state's preoccupation with identity categories was on display in the 2000 census, when 80 percent of all households were asked to fill out a short form, containing, other than their names, only five questions for each household member. Two of these questions were aimed exclusively at pigeonholing each individual into an ethnic/racial category (the other three were: relationship to household head, sex, and age). Not a single question was asked on the individual's job, education, place of birth, or even marital status, yet everyone in the United States was asked if he or she was "Spanish/Hispanic/Latino," and for his or her "race."

The Indian and American cases suggest that the boundaries between state and society may be blurred when it comes to establishing who exactly is categorizing whom. In British India, census planners had to rely on local administrators, who themselves often relied on traditional ways of counting people according to social status. The colonial gaze may thus have resulted from a far greater degree of cooptation than previously acknowledged. Even when the target population is totally excluded from the process of categorization, as African-Americans were for a long time, one should not assume that the state acted as a unified agent. Nobles (2002) notes how the category of "mulatto" was introduced in the 1850 US Census as a response to demands from ethnologists who wanted to prove that mixed races were biologically inferior (lower life expectancy, etc.). Before racial census politics entered the arena of public campaigns in the 1960s–70s, it nonetheless involved diverse players from the Census Bureau, Congress, governmental agencies, and the portion of society that had full civic rights. Who was doing the counting, and the criteria employed, have to be viewed as a political process involving various agents. The inclusivess and transparency of the process necessarily depended on the degree of openness of the state itself.

2   THREE MODELS OF LINKING STATE-RECOGNIZED IDENTITY CATEGORIES TO POLITICAL POWER

Arel and Kertzer (2004) have distinguished three models in which states divide populations into identity categories as a way of allocating political resources: the Affirmative Action, Territorial Threshold, and Power-Sharing models. Insofar as censuses are employed to make these distinctions, they become political battle-grounds, for the central institutions of government may be at the mercy of the resulting counts, and the benefits enjoyed by individuals may be linked not only to their own identification, but to the relative strength of their identity category's number in the census.

2.1   The Affirmative Action Model

In the *Affirmative Action Model* the state distinguishes an identity category whose members are to be the beneficiaries of special benefit programs, justified as a way of making up for past discrimination against those in the category. Such is the category of "scheduled" tribes and castes used in the Indian census, as well as the category of "American Indian" in the United States census.

Once again, the Indian case is illuminating. British Imperial censuses painstak-ingly listed and enumerated the myriad "castes" of the realm, but the practice was dropped by post-independence leaders on the grounds that it "reinforced casteism" (Jenkins 2001). An exception was however made for the lower castes. In order to fight past discrimination, the government instituted policies of "positive" discrim-ination to ensure a fair representation of these groups in the public sector.

With a variety of benefit programs available today to members of these so-called "scheduled" tribes and castes, including land ownership, the struggle to be identified with such a category has reversed the process of Sanskritization noted by earlier scholars, which involved those identifying with a particular caste adopting behavior characteristic of higher castes in an effort to claim higher status for their caste (Kertzer 1988, 112–14). Now, individuals with identities in castes not previously eligible for special benefit struggle to be recognized as members of an identity category enjoying such benefits. Reviewing the period between the 1971 and 1981 censuses of India, Guha (2003, 162) writes: "The numbers involved are striking. Hundreds of thousands of people—the majority functionally illiterate—could devise, communicate, and im-plement an identity strategy in the ten years between two censuses."

A similar trend of "ethnic renewal," which Nagel (1995, 949) defines as the "adoption of a nondominant ethnic identity" by someone formerly identifying with a dominant group, can be observed among American Indians. Between 1960 and 2000 the number of people identifying as American Indian on the US census nearly quintupled to its current total of 2.5 million (excluding, for the 2000 census, an additional 1.6 million who listed Indian and another "race"). This increase far exceeds reasonable expectations of natural growth, reflecting a general rise in ethnic pride in American society, as well as "a strategy to acquire a share of real or putative land claims awards or other possible ethnically-allocated rewards (such as scholar-ships, mineral royalties, employment preference)" (Nagel 1995, 956).

In the reward-driven affirmative action model, census politics operates at two levels. The first is the composition of the list of privileged groups, with a built-in incentive for new ethnic entrepreneurs to clamor for the inclusion of their putative group. The second is the determination of individual membership in the privileged group, particularly when land rights and restricted access to specific occupations are at stake. Although the registration of individual members is not done by the census, which after all is a confidential undertaking aimed at generating aggregate statistics, respondents time and again tend to view the census as an official act legitimating their professed identity (Darrow 2002). In this view, the census does not count what is out there, it selectively *recognizes* groups calling for recognition.

2.2   The Territorial Threshold Model

In the *Territorial Threshold Model*, political privileges and political power are assigned to members of a particular identity category based on their having attained a given statistical threshold on a particular territory. The prized threshold is that of a presumed majority. The principle at work here is one that has been dear to nationalist movements since the nineteenth century. As Gellner (1983, 1) put it, "Nationalism is a political principle which holds that the political and the national unit should be congruent." Where those sharing a particular "national" identity are in the majority, in this view, the "nation" should also have power over the state. This principle can also be employed to allocate power in more peripheral areas within larger states. Insofar as the territorial model is invoked, the actual results of censuses are crucial in determining the boundaries of such units of devolved power, and in determining whether the existing power-holding national or ethnic group in fact continues to have a majority of the population, the rationale for this allocation of power in the first place.

A typical example comes from Pakistan, which in the 1960s decided to reorganize government along provincial lines, dividing the (then western part of the) country into provinces each of which was identified with a particular ethnic group presumed to be holding a clear demographic majority in the given province: Punjabis in Punjab province, Sindhis in Sindh province, Baluchis in Baluchistan province, etc. Each province was then assigned a quota of government jobs and contracts, government revenue, university admissions, and the like, all linked to the demographic weight of the province. This system has made the census politically sensitive, for two reasons. First, in those provinces where it was no longer clear that the politically authorized ethnic group actually held the majority—as in Baluchistan—the ethnic count was potentially destabilizing. Second, all provinces had a strong interest in seeing that its own population was maximized in the count, and that no overcount took place in any other province. It was for such reasons that the 1991 decennial census kept being postponed, finally taking place only in 1998.

Every census enumerator had to be accompanied by a soldier, and the published results which stated that the ethnic proportions had not changed in nearly twenty years, appeared improbable (Weiss 1999).

A variation of the model obtains when the exercise of collectively defined rights hinges on the attainment of a certain statistical plateau, not necessarily a majority. The classic case here is that of language rights, particularly the right to minority-language schooling, whose linkage to the census was pioneered by Austro-Hungary (Brix 1982). Much of the monitoring work done since the 1990s in Eastern Europe by European organizations is based on the premise that whenever there is a concentration of speakers of a given language, they should have access to a reasonable number of services in their language, beginning with public education. The census is used as a tool to document these claims, and it can quickly become a site of contestation when such concepts as "territory," "language," and "concentration" are translated into categories. How should "language" be ascertained (and what is the difference between a language and a dialect?)? What should be the threshold for a sufficient "concentration"? And on which territory should the threshold apply? Answers to these questions generally tend to favor the interest of the majority.

2.3   The Power-sharing Model

In the *Power-sharing Model* political offices and other positions under political control are allocated according to a formula among members of two or more identity categories. Harmony among members of different such groups is maintained by this agreed-upon division of spoils and of power. Such a division is almost always justified along the lines of actual numerical divisions within a population, so that, for example, where those identifying with three different identity categories are of equal number, the positions they are allocated should be equal in number and influence. Similarly, where those in an identity category claim a fifth of the population, they should by this principle be allocated a fifth of the political positions in play. The classic example of the power-sharing model is Lebanon, where following a civil war an autonomous region under the Ottoman empire was established, with power to be shared proportionately by members of different religious sects. Under the French Mandate, from 1920 to 1943, this system was further expanded and institutionalized.

By the time of independence in 1943, a system was established in which the president was to be a Maronite Christian, the prime minister a Sunni Muslim, and the president of parliament a Shia Muslim. Membership of parliament was allocated according to the ratio of six Christians for every five Muslims. All this was based on a 1932 census, taken by the French, showing 54 percent of the population to be Christian and 46 percent Muslim. These results have been contested ever since, as they were contingent on citizenship criteria that favored Christian groups (Maktabi 1999). Because a new census would certainly show that the Christians lacked a majority, no new census could be taken. In a modest bow to demography, in 1958 the ratio of Christians to Muslims mandated for employment in the Lebanese civil service was changed from 6:5 to 6:6 (Baaklini 1983). Clearly, however, the political system enshrined by the power-sharing model is inherently unstable, at the mercy of changes in population ratios, making the census politically explosive.

3   SOVIET ETHNOGENESIS AND THE THREE MODELS

The Soviet Union and following its breakup, the Russian Federation, have been unusual in incorporating all three of the above-listed models into their political system. The use of ethnic—or "nationality"—categories to divide and evaluate the population of Russia predated the founding of the USSR. In the last decades of the nineteenth century demographic analysis of the country's population was largely in the hands of military statisticians, who disaggregated the population into component ethnic groups, each assigned various qualitative traits. Best of all were the ethnic Russians, and establishing an ethnic Russian majority often became a high priority in military planning. As one such specialist focusing on Central Asia, put it at the time, increasing the size of the ethnic Russian population through colonization would make it possible "to influence strongly the transformation of the physiognomy of the entire country" (in Holquist 2001, 120). The first census of the Russian empire took place in 1897, and involved a tremendous effort of ethnic categorization, with 230 groups initially recognized, later simplified into 120 identity categories. Census authorities had to confront the fact that in many parts of the empire people had no idea of what their nationality label was supposed to be. The first Soviet census in 1926, came up with a similar list—based on intensive consultation with ethnographers—yet their work was not easy, for they had to introduce a precise, limited list of identity categories where, out there in the social world there was but a mass of flux and indeterminacy (Blum and Mespoulet 2003).

What was most distinctive about the Soviet state was the use of these nationality categories as a basis for creating a vast system of territories that were each identified with particular nationalities, and in which various political, economic, and cultural benefits would flow to those of the privileged nationality. In such localities and especially in the republics, the use of ethnic quotas ensured various advantages to members of the titular groups, in terms of positions of political power, economic privileges, admission to schools and universities, use of language, and promotion of "cultural" programs (Martin 2001).

Tellingly, following the collapse of the Soviet Union the new Russian Federation preserved the Soviet system of nationality-linked republics and autonomous areas. Firmly in control of their ethnic territory and liberated from Soviet restrictions on publicly airing national grievances, titular elites became preoccupied with producing numbers that would sanction the legitimacy of their rule, namely, obtaining a numerical majority in their "homeland." In the 2002 Russian census, the most publicized case in this Territorial Threshold contest involved the Tatars of Tatarstan who feared that the possible recognition as a separate nationality of a group previously counted as Tatars (the Kryashens, Tatar-speaking Christians), would prevent them from obtaining the majority that had eluded them in the 1989 Soviet census.

But the Russian Federation also continued the Soviet practice of following an affirmative-action model with respect to a variety of small, indigenous communities, most notably the "Peoples of the North" (Slezkine 1994), but extending more generally to what a 1999 law called "small-numbered peoples." Those who fit into such identity categories, which by law could not surpass 50,000 people, were deemed to enjoy special rights such as fishing quotas, military exemption, and control over the sale of lands. A conflict arose in some cases between the workings of the territorial model and the affirmative-action model, as can be seen in the ethnic republic of Altai in Siberia. Seeing others obtain benefits as small-numbered people, a variety of small traditional communities sought such benefits by asserting their "indigenous" identities. However, Altai authorities at the republic level saw such identity assertion as a threat to their own power, for the multiplication of such groups drained the pool of "Altais" and so risked undermining the claim of an Altai majority in the Altai republic.

The Russian Federation has also incorporated a power-sharing model as a means of dealing with problems of conflict in the mountainous Caucasus republic of Dagestan, bordering Chechnya. In the Soviet Union, Dagestan was a rare "national territory" (in this case, an "autonomous republic") that was not named after a titular ethnic group. Soviet state-builders promoted a composite "Dagestani" identity from an array of mountainous peoples, and local elites strove to present this common identity in their dealings with Moscow. Internal politics, however, was driven by a complex interaction between several groups whose ethnic identity had been recognized by the Soviet census.

The weakening of central control in the 1990s, made this intra-Dagestani competition far more sensitive. In order to deal with incipient ethnic strife, Dagestan chose to devise a complex power-sharing formula dividing positions and benefits among fourteen identity groups (but in fact tending to favor the top two groups, as in Lebanon). Yet the revised affirmative action policy risked splintering one of the dominant groups, the Avars into several "small numbered people," a development that was deemed unacceptable for the maintenance of the status quo in Dagestan. Moreover, the 2002 census in showing that an adjustment of the rank-ordering of the nationalities was in order, has posed the kind of threat to systems that follow the power-sharing model previously experienced in Lebanon.

4   CONCLUSION

Political actors and scholars alike, often deplore the fact that a census has been "politicized." But this assumes that the categorization of a population can be detached from politics. For that to be true, one has to take the view that cultural categories or identities are objective realities that can be discovered and documented, with the use of a proper methodology. This assumption is the fallacy of primordialism, namely, the notion that group identities are ontological entities that are formed outside of social and political processes. Yet what we have learned from the vast constructivist literature is that identities are contextual, and that the context, social and political, determines their saliency. There is little doubt that the Kryashen of Tatarstan feel both Kryashen and Tatar to different degrees. The debate is which of the two identities has greater salience in a post-Soviet context where the Russian state is open to the recognition of new nationalities. The census is not an instrument that can objectively give an answer to this question. It should rather be seen as an arena where this battle over identity saliency takes place in a changing political context.

The decision to categorize the composition of a population along cultural markers, and the formulation of these categories are political choices. The affirmation of an identity by an individual on the census, within the repertoire offered, is also a matter of choice, dependent on a variety of factors such as status, material incentives, and the degree to which an identity is felt to be significant. A state uses the census to "gaze" at the composition of its population. The gaze of the researcher, however, is on the myriad of political choices that are inherent in a census operation. What remains theoretically disputed is the extent to which a state in this exercise of "simplifications," can actually *create* salient identities. What is clear is that the representation of cultural categories on a census is an object of political struggle, explicitly or implicitly.

References

AREL, D. 2002. Demography and politics in the first post-Soviet censuses: mistrusted state, contested identities. *Population*, 57: 801–28.

—— and KERTZER, D. I. 2004. Counting, identity categorizing, and claiming political rights: nationalities and the struggle for power in the 2002 Russian census. Available at www.watsoninstitute.org (accessed Nov. 30, 2004).

BAAKLINI, A. I. 1983. Ethnicity and politics in contemporary Lebanon. Pp. 17–56 in *Culture, Ethnicity, and Identity: Current Issues in Research*, ed. W. C. McCready. New York: Academic Press.

BLUM, A., and MESPOULET, M. 2003. *L'anarchie bureaucratique: Statistique et pouvoir sous Staline*. Paris: Editions La Découverte.

Brix, E. 1982. *Die Umgangssprachen in Altösterreich zwischen Agitation und Assimilation. Die Sprachenstatistik in den zisleithanischen Volkszählungen*. Vienna: Hermann Böhlaus Nachf.

CAPLAN, J., and TORPEY, J. (eds.) 2001. *Documenting Individual Identity: The Development of State Practices in the Modern World*. Princeton, NJ: Princeton University Press.

CHOLDIN, H. M. 1986. Statistics and politics: the "Hispanic issue" in the 1980 census. *Demography*, 23: 403–18.

COHN, B. 1987. The census, social structure and objectification in South Asia. Pp. 224–54 in Cohn, *An Anthropologist amongst the Historians and other Essays*. Delhi: Oxford University Press.

COLE, J. 2000. *The Power of Large Numbers: Population, Politics, and Gender in Nineteenth-century France*. Ithaca, NY: Cornell University Press.

DARROW, D. 2002. Census as a technology of empire. *Ab Imperio*, 4: 145–76.

FOUCAULT, M. 1991. Governmentality. Pp. 87–104 in *The Foucault Effect*, ed. G. Burchell, C. Gordon, and P. Miller. Chicago: University of Chicago Press.

GELLNER, E. 1983. *Nations and Nationalism*. Ithaca, NY: Cornell University Press.

GUHA, S. 2003. The politics of identity and enumeration in India c. 1600–1990. *Comparative Studies in Society and History*, 45: 148–67.

HOLQUIST, P. 2001. To count, to extract, and to exterminate. Population statistics and population politics in late imperial and Soviet Russia. Pp. 111–44 in *A State of Nations: Empire and Nation Making in the Age of Lenin and Stalin*, ed. R. G. Suny and T. Martin. Oxford: Oxford University Press.

Jenkins, L. D. 2001. Categorizing and counting on the census. Pp. 89–107 in Jenkins, *Identity and Identification in India: Defining the Disadvantaged*. New York: Routledge.

KERTZER, D. I. 1988. *Ritual, Politics and Power*. New Haven, Conn.: Yale University Press.

—— and Arel, D. (eds.) 2002. *Census and Identity: The Politics of Race, Ethnicity and Language in National Censuses*. Cambridge: Cambridge University Press.

MAKTABI, R. 1999. The Lebanese census of 1932 revisited: who are the Lebanese? *British Journal of Middle Eastern Studies*, 26: 219–41.

MARTIN, T. 2001. *The Affirmative Action Empire: Nations and Nationalism in the Soviet Union, 1923–1939*. Ithaca, NY: Cornell University Press.

NAGEL, J. 1995. American Indian ethnic renewal: politics and the resurgence of identity. *American Sociological Review*, 60: 947–65.

NOBLES, M. 2002. Racial categorization and censuses. In Kertzer and Arel 2002, 43–70.

PEABODY, N. 2001. Cents, sense, census: human inventories in late precolonial and early colonial India. *Comparative Studies in Society and History*, 43: 819–50.

PORTER, T. M. 1995. *Trust in Numbers: The Pursuit of Objectivity in Science and Public Life*. Princeton, NJ: Princeton University Press.

SCOTT, J. C. 1998. *Seeing Like a State*. New Haven, Conn.: Yale University Press.

SLEZKINE, Y. 1994. *Arctic Mirrors: Russia and the Small Peoples of the North*. Ithaca, NY: Cornell University Press.

WEISS, A. M. 1999. Much ado about counting: the conflict over holding a census in Pakistan. *Asian Survey*, 3: 679–93.

YANOW, D. 2003. *Constructing "Race" and "Ethnicity" in America*. Armonk, NY: M. E. Sharpe.

PART IX

TECHNOLOGY MATTERS

CHAPTER 37

....

WHY AND HOW
TECHNOLOGY
MATTERS

....

WIEBE E. BIJKER

TECHNOLOGY matters. Bicycles were instrumental in the political and social emancipation of women (Bijker 1995); photo and film technology induced a subtle form of apartheid (Wajcman, this volume); nuclear arms and energy shaped, for example through the non-proliferation treaty, international relations since the 1950s (Smit, this volume); the low-hanging overpasses on Long Island discourage since the 1920s the presence of buses on the parkways, thus preventing public transport access to the prestigious Long Beach public park (Winner 1980).

Politics matters too, to understand technology's development. The refrigerator got its hum (i.e. is now driven by electricity rather than gas) because of the political power play between American electricity and gas utilities in the 1920s (Cowan 1983); gender politics resulted in the contraceptive pill rather than the male pill (Wajcman, this volume; Oudshoorn 2003); the technical development of anti-ballistic missile systems can only be understood by analyzing the dynamics of the international political relations between the US and the USSR (Smit, this volume); the Long Island overpasses are *deliberately* low, because of the racial and social segregation policy that its designer, Robert Moses, maintained: "Poor people and blacks, who normally use public transit, were kept off the roads because the twelve-foot tall buses could not handle the overpasses" (quoted in Winner 1980, 23).

Technology matters: it matters to people, planet, and profit; it also matters to policy-making and politics; and it should thus matter to political studies. In this chapter I will argue why this is the case, and what consequences this may have for political studies.

Before arguing why and how technology matters to politics, it seems prudent to define what I mean by "technology" and "politics." Although the next section will offer a preliminary answer to that question, my central argument in this chapter will be that technology and politics cannot be defined in simple and neat ways: both can be very different things in different contexts. Worse, their "definitions" are interdependent: technology and politics constitute each other to an important degree—as two sides of the same coin. The implication of this argument is that the answers to the "why" and "how" questions about technology's influence on politics are closely tied together; and that these answers are also closely tied to answering, vice versa, about politics' influence on technology. It only makes sense, I will argue, to discuss the relation between technology and politics in a contextual way, related to specific circumstances. General statements, such as "all technology is political" or "all politics is technological" may be true, but not very helpful.

1   WHAT IS TECHNOLOGY?

Although an important argument in this chapter will be that the boundaries between technology and science, society, politics, etc. are contingent and variable, we have to start somewhere. It is helpful to distinguish three different layers of meaning in the word "technology." At the most basic level, "technology" refers to sets of physical objects or *artefacts*, such as computers, cars, or voting machines (and note the gender bias; Wajcman, this volume). At the next level, it also includes human *activities*, such as in "the technology of e-voting," where it also refers to the designing, making, and handling of such machines. Finally and closest to its Greek origin, "technology" refers to *knowledge*: it is about what people know as well as about what they do with machines and related production processes. Using "technology" in these three meanings, allows us to be more specific than when employing "technology" as a container concept at macro level, as for example in: "Political modernization . . . embraces today changes in politics and government in individual countries and states derived from major shifts in technology" (Graham 2001, 9963).

These three layers comprise the most common meanings of technology. For my discussion of the role of technology in politics, and especially in political theories, this is not enough however. It is important to recognize that—within these common meanings of technology—different *conceptions* of technology can be used. These concepts differ in the (often implicit) underlying assumptions about technology's development and about technology's relation to other societal domains. I will distinguish two conceptions: the standard and the constructivist concepts of technology.

1.1   Concepts of Technology

The standard image of science and technology was the dominant view of technology among students of technology and society until the 1980s, and is still widely held by citizens, politicians, and practitioners. In the standard image of science, scientific knowledge is objective, value-free, and discovered by specialists. Technology, similarly, is an autonomous force in society and technology's working is an intrinsic property of technical machines and processes.

Some of the implications of these standard images are positive and comforting. Thus, for example, scientific knowledge does appear as a prominent candidate for solving all kinds of problems. In the domain of political thought, this naturally leads to technocratic proposals, where technology is viewed as a sufficient end in itself and where the values of efficiency, power, and rationality are independent of context. The standard view accepts that technology can be employed negatively, but in this view the users are to be blamed, not the technology. Not surprisingly, the standard image also leaves us with some problems. For some questions, for example, we do not yet have the right scientific knowledge. An adequate application of knowledge is, in this view, a problem too. The role of experts is problematic in a democracy: how can experts be recognized by non-experts; how can non-experts trust the mechanisms that are supposed to safeguard the quality of the experts; and, finally, how can experts communicate their esoteric knowledge to non-experts? In the realm of technology, an additional problem is that new technologies may create new problems (which, it is hoped, in due time will be solved by still newer technologies). The most pressing problem, however, relates directly to the central issue of this chapter. It is best explained by introducing "technological determinism."

The standard conception of technology implies a technological deterministic view of the relation between technology and society. Technological determinism, then, comprises two elements: it maintains that (1) technology develops autonomously, following an internal logic which is independent of external influences; and that (2) technology shapes society by having economic and social impacts. Technological determinism thus implies that technology does *not* matter much to politics, nor to political theory. The little relevance that technology, in a technological deterministic view, has for politics only relates to its societal impact. After all, if technology's development is really autonomous, it cannot be subject to "outside" control in the form of policy-making or political debate. Technology's blessings and curses then just happen "out of the blue," and politics can only hope to anticipate these developments and effects, and prepare society for it (Winner 1977). Applied to, for example, the nuclear arms race: "In our bleakest moments, the nuclear world has seemed to be a technological juggernaut out of control, following its own course independent of human needs and wishes" (MacKenzie 1990, 383). A classic reaction to this diagnosis was—at least in retrospect—the establishment of the Office of Technology Assessment attached to the US Congress in 1972 (Bimber 1996). I shall return to this below.

However, technological determinism is not only politically debilitating—it is also empirically wrong. Especially since the 1980s, many historical and sociological case studies have shown that technology *is* socially shaped (MacKenzie and Wajcman 1999). In the case of the nuclear arms race, and more specifically the technical development towards increasing missile accuracy, the empirical argument against technological determinism is clear-cut: "An alternative form of technological change exists, which is no less progressive (on some conventional criteria, such as its use of novel inertial sensors, it is more so), but where progress has a quite different meaning. Its institutional base is civil and military air navigation, where extreme accuracy is little prized, but reliability, producibility and economy are" (MacKenzie 1990, 385). This empirical work in the history and sociology of technology has led to an alternative conception of technology: the constructivist view. In the 1970s and 1980s detailed empirical research on the practices of scientists and engineers led to the formulation of a constructivist perspective on science and technology. This work by sociologists, historians, and philosophers became known under the banners of "sociology of scientific knowledge" (SSK) and "social construction of technology" (SCOT).[1]

Social shaping models stress that technology does not follow its own momentum, nor a rational goal-directed, problem-solving path, but is instead shaped by social factors. In the SCOT approach "relevant social groups" are the starting point for the analysis. Technical artefacts are described through the eyes of the members of relevant social groups. The interactions within and among relevant social groups can give different meanings to the same artefact. Thus, for example, to union leaders a nuclear reactor may exemplify an almost perfectly safe working environment with very small chances of on-the-job-accidents compared to urban building sites or harbors. To a group of international relations analysts, the reactor probably represents a threat because of its potentially enhancing nuclear proliferation, while for the neighboring village the risks of radioactive emissions and the benefits of employment may strive for prominence. This demonstration of interpretative flexibility is a crucial step in arguing for the feasibility of any sociology of technology—it shows that neither an artefact's identity, nor its technical "success" or "failure," are intrinsic properties of the artefact but subject to social variables.

---

[1] See, e.g., Collins 1985; Collins and Pinch 1998; Bijker, Hughes, and Pinch 1987; Bijker and Law 1992.

In the second SCOT step, the researcher follows how interpretative flexibility diminishes, because meanings attributed to artefacts converge and some artefacts gain dominance over others—and in the end, one artefact results from this process of social construction. Here, key concepts are "closure" and "stabilization." Both concepts are meant to describe the result of the process of social construction. "Stabilization" stresses process: a process of social construction can take several years in which the degree of stabilization slowly increases up to the moment of closure. "Closure," a concept stemming from SSK, highlights the irreversible end point of a discordant process in which several artefacts existed next to each other.

In the third step, the processes of stabilization described in the second step are analyzed and explained by interpreting them in a broader theoretical framework: why does a social construction process follow this course, rather than that? The central concept here is "technological frame." A technological frame structures the interactions among the members of a relevant social group, and shapes their thinking and acting. It is similar to Kuhn's concept of "paradigm" with one important difference: "technological frame" is a concept to be applied to all kinds of relevant social groups, while "paradigm" was exclusively intended for scientific communities. A technological frame is built up when interaction "around" an artefact begins. In this way, existing practice does guide future practice, though without logical determination. The cyclical movement thus becomes: artefact → technological frame → relevant social group → new artefact → new technological frame → new relevant social group → etc. Typically, a person will be included in more than one social group, and thus also in more than one technological frame. For example, the members of the Women's Advisory Committees on Housing in the Netherlands are included in the technological frame of male builders, architects, and municipality civil servants—this allows them to interact with these men in shaping public housing designs. But at the same time many of these women are included in the feminist technological frame, which enables them to formulate radical alternatives to the standard Dutch family house that dominates the male builders' technological frame (Bijker and Bijsterveld 2000). Extending this concept, Lynn Eden has used "organizational frames" to explain why the US government, in its nuclear armament planning, concentrated on blast damage and systematically underestimated, and even ignored damage from mass fire (Eden 2004). (Pre-empting what I shall argue below, her study also shows that to understand state politics, it is often necessary to delve into the politics of agencies, services, and private companies—distinctions between "kinds" or levels of politics do not match the practice of politics, and one should therefore be careful to use such distinctions in methodologies and theories.)

Before I start using the constructivist conception of technology to address the questions why and how technology matters, there is one other issue to discuss: which technologies are we considering anyway?

1.2   Specific Technologies?

The thrust of my argument below will be that *all* technologies matter to politics and to political theory—from the dams in India to the space shuttle in the US, from Internet to public housing, and from guns to voting machines. Some technologies however are, at first sight, different because they are explicitly *meant* to play a political role, and thus have been studied by political scientists. The use of new communication and Internet technologies to improve upon democratic processes is the most recent example (Hague and Loader 1999). Hacker and Van Dijk (2000, 1) define digital democracy as "a collection of attempts to practice democracy without the limits of time, space and other physical conditions, using information and communication technologies or computer mediated communication instead, as an addition, not a replacement for traditional 'analogue' political practices." The term "digital democracy" is meant to highlight that it is not an altogether different form of democracy, breaking with all established practices in particular times and locations (as suggested by the term "virtual democracy"), or a naive reliance on direct democracy (such as in "teledemocracy"), or something identical to previous experiences with radio and television (such as the term "electronic democracy" would suggest), or only occurring in and through the Internet (as suggested by the term "cyberdemocracy").

The impact of digital technologies on democracy (and hence on politics and political science) is often overstated when presented as a solution to current problems of political legitimacy (e.g. by Barber 1984). But it is also underestimated when the implied fundamental change in political practices is not recognized.

From way back politics is a matter of verbal skills, management capacities and the art of negotiation. It is a collective routine of talkers and organizers. In digital democracy this routine would transform into a practice of people working primarily as individuals at screens and terminals, clicking pages, reading and analyzing information and posing or answering questions. It is likely to become a routine of technical and symbolic-intellectual skill instead of a practical-organizational and verbal-intellectual one.   (Dijk 2000, 31)

This would have quite different consequences for different models of democracy. In answering the question how technology matters to politics, I will continuously stress the importance of the specificity of different technologies, contexts, and political systems: what works in the US does not automatically work in Europe, what works in India does not necessarily work in the US. Van Dijk (2000) does exactly that, when he discusses the different ways in which digital democracy may take shape when seen in the context of Held's (1996) models of democracy; Hagen (2000) does the same by following the discussions on digital democracy in different *national* political cultures.

In some cases, technology matters in politics because it explicitly and deliberately is "politics by other means." Most obviously this is the case for military technology

(Smit 2005). Since the Truman doctrine of "containment," the cold war nuclear strategies, and Reagan's impenetrable "peace shield" of the Strategic Defense Initiative, "the key theme of closed-world discourse was global surveillance and control through high-technology military power. Computers made the closed world work simultaneously as technology, as political system, and as ideological mirage." (Edwards 1996: 1) Also many sophisticated forms of contemporary political and social control in civil society are rooted in the development of technologies. Much contemporary control is better symbolized by manipulation than by coercion, by computer chips than by prison bars, and by remote and invisible filters than by handcuffs or guns. An increase in technical sophistication of these control technologies often implies being more covert, embedded, and remote; often involuntary and occurring without the awareness or consent of its subject (Fijnaut and Marx 1995; Lyon 2003).

In other cases, technology matters to politics because it has become so highly politicized that hardly anyone would think of ignoring or disputing this political dimension. Nuclear power is a clear example. The fact that nuclear power reactors may be operated in such a way that they produce weapon-grade fission material makes them political in an almost trivial sense. But there is much more involved. For example, this possibility of producing weapon-grade material need not be an explicit political decision, but can be designed into the reactor. In the case of France, this resulted in producing weapon-grade plutonium before the government had decided to build an atomic bomb:

Flexibility in the basic principle of the gas-graphite reactors meant that they could produce both plutonium and electricity. How well they did one or the other depended on the specific design. But the fact that they could do both made possible the production of weapons-grade plutonium in Marcoule's reactors before the government officially decided to build the atomic bomb. This flexibility also made it possible for the [the French Atomic Energy agency] CEA to demand plutonium from [the French national electricity producer] EDF's reactors: thus technologies could not only enact political agendas but also make possible new political goals.   (Hecht 1998, 334)

A link between nuclear technology and politics exists, in addition to the military connection, also in the role of nuclear energy in general economic policy and in the national self-image. Hecht (1998, 335) concludes about the first French "civil" nuclear project:

The EDF1 (reactor) was important not because it itself would produce economically viable electricity but rather because it constituted the first step in a nationalized nuclear program that would enact and strengthen the utility's ideology and industrial contracting practices. In this instance as in many others, EDF1's technical characteristics were inseparable from its political dimensions. Had EDF1 failed to function properly, or had engineers and workers been unable to garner adequate operational experience from the reactor, the plant would have failed both technically and politically.

Nuclear power can also be argued to be an "inherently political technology" in that it presupposes an authoritarian, if not totalitarian state (Winner 1986). No government can, anymore, dream of delegating a decision about installing nuclear power to a group of engineers, arguing that nuclear technology is merely a neutral technology. Such a decision now is generally recognized to be political, necessarily involving discussions about societal risk, public health, and international relations.

However, the example of nuclear energy also shows the difficulty of arguing that one technology is more political than another. Surely, not everyone accepts the argument that a nuclear state would inevitably become a closed and totalitarian police-state; certainly, some engineers still believe that a decision about installing nuclear power is best made on the basis of technical-economic arguments, uncorrupted by politics. And, for that matter, also guns and weapons have been called neutral and apolitical: it is the shooter who is political, not the technology. On the other hand, arguments about the importance for the national economy and for the national identity have been made for other technologies than nuclear power too—for example about railway infrastructures and biotechnology (Dunlavy 1994; Gottweis 1998), or about dams as "Temples of Modern India."[2] Other technologies have been labeled political that would—at first glance—not be so. Classifications such as the International Classification of Diseases are powerful technologies: "embedded in working infrastructures they become relatively invisible without losing any of that power" (Bowker and Star 1999: 319). The bicycle was political, in the hands of suffragettes.

At the end of this section in which I reviewed technologies that seemed specifically relevant to politics, I thus can only conclude that all technologies matter to politics and political theory—all "artefacts have politics" (Winner 1980). This does not merit, however, general and abstract statements about the relation between politics and technology. The other lesson from the previous discussion of "political technologies" is that all technologies matter differently. Before I review the various answers to this question about the nature of the relation between technology and politics, however, the notion of politics need to be unpacked as well.

2   WHAT IS POLITICS?

Technological determinism induces, I argued, passivity; political determinism may do so as well. The latter then refers to the view that "what happens is a result of decision making by a state. Sometimes a particular person (the President, perhaps)

---

[2] Jawaharlal Nehru, cited by Roy 1999. Arundhati Roy's essay on the Narmada dams is recommended reading for all students of politics and technology.

or a collectivity (the 'political-military elite,' perhaps) is seen as representing the state. But in all cases, the form of explanation is the same. The state is conceived of as akin to an individual, rational human decision maker. It has a goal, and chooses means...to fulfill that goal" (MacKenzie 1990, 395). In this section I shall not attempt to give a comprehensive review of the various meanings of "politics": that would, in a handbook like this, be like carrying water to the sea (or coals to Newcastle). Rather, I want to remind readers that "politics" and "democracy" have just as rich a spectrum of different meanings in different contexts as "technology" does: only by recognizing this richness, can we reap the potential fruits of studying the relation between technology and politics. Instead of reviewing political scientists on this matter—for those analyses I refer the reader to the other parts and volumes of this handbook—I shall discuss how students of science, technology, and society have conceptualized politics in their work.

The basic point is well summarized in MacKenzie's reaction to the political determinism mentioned above. Whether to explain the choice between counter-force or counter-city strategies, between building missiles or bombers, or between extreme accuracy or more destructive power: "In explaining each, I have always had to disaggregate 'the state,' identifying the often conflicting preferences of its different parts such as different armed services and even subgroups within these services. So the state should not be thought of as unitary. I have also typically had to disaggregate 'decision,' identifying instead various different levels of policy process, each leading perhaps to a result, but not necessarily to any overall coherence" (MacKenzie 1990: 396). Such then is the agenda for this section: to disaggregate the notions of politics and democracy as used in technology studies. (I limit myself to technology studies; similar cases, arguments, and concepts can, however, also be found in studies of *science* and politics.[3])

Politics may refer then, first, to the political system of modern democracy. The functioning of knowledge, transparency, and accountability in a "civil epistemology of the modern democratic polity" as founded in the political philosophies of Jefferson, Paine, Priestley, and De Tocqueville receives, for example, a new emphasis when the role of technology is highlighted:

The belief that the citizens gaze at the government and that the government makes its actions visible to the citizens is, then, fundamental to the democratic process of government. The shift from the projection of power through pomp and splendor to the projection of power through actions which are either literally technical or at least metaphorically instrumental is, in this context, responsive to the taste Tocqueville ascribes to democratic citizens for "the tangible and the real." The political significance of acting technically in the democratic field of action lies precisely in the supposed anti-theatricality of technology. (Ezrahi 1995, 162)

---

[3] See, e.g., Bal and Halffman 1998; Collins and Evans 2002; Guston and Keniston 1994; Guston 2000; Guston 2001; Halffman 2002; Jasanoff 1990; Nowotny, Scott, and Gibbons 2001; Jasanoff 2004.

Technology is thus seen as producing and upholding a modern democratic concept of visible power whose exercise appears publicly accountable to the large public. I will return to discussing politics at this general level of political culture, but will first investigate the implications of this "civil epistemology of the modern democratic polity" for the role of knowledge and expertise in politics.

Politics is then, second, also knowledge and expertise, especially in a modern society that is so thoroughly technical and scientific. And because technical expertise has traditionally been a male domain, politics thus is also sexual politics— mirroring the gendered character of technology itself (Wajcman 2004). Another important issue is how to relate expert knowledge to political deliberation. One answer to this question is technocracy. The label "technocrat" was fairly neutral until the Second World War, but then acquired a derogatory ring. In the wake of the French Revolution, engineers and scientists had built technocracy on a radical distinction between politics and technology: "universalistic science and conflicted politics were to go their separate ways, and the fact-value distinction given institutional form. By this apparent separation of means (technology) and ends (politics), the technocrats hoped to configure the relationship of the state to its citizens in amoral terms, and return authority over the technological life to the bureaus where they served as administrators" (Alder 1997, 302). But after 1945 this backfired on the technical elite: the term "technocrat" came to mean "someone who had breached a boundary, who had moved from his area of expertise into the domain of political decision making. The dangers inherent in breaching this boundary were considerable; first and foremost among them was the capitulation of democracy to technocracy" (Hecht 1998, 28). Technocracy, in this view, meant the replacement of politicians by experts—financial and administrative experts as much as technical and scientific. Discussions about technocracy seem to have faded out since the 1960s. In other settings and in other vocabularies, however, the politics of expertise and the role of expertise in politics still are—or are again—central issues. The first relates to the role of scientific advisers in politics and regulation; the second is linked to recent experiments on democratization of technology.

Politics thus is, third, scientific advice. Scientific and technical advisers play such a dominant role in the politics of our modern society that they have been dubbed "the fifth branch," in addition to the classic three branches of the state and the fourth branch of civil service (Jasanoff 1990). The politics of regulatory science, or more precisely the boundary work between science, technology, regulation, and politics has become a focal point of research (Bal and Halffman 1998; Halffman 2002). This work employs a methodological focus on boundary work (Gieryn 1983; 1999): the work that is done by scientists, policy-makers, civil servants, and politicians to distinguish politics from technology and then to relate the two again in specific terms. The ontological foundations of these studies of boundary work are completely opposite to the basic assumptions underlying technocracy. Where technocracy was based on the positivistic assumption that technology and politics are fundamentally different things and can be distinguished clearly, these boundary studies work on the constructivist assumption that technology and politics are *made to be* different, resulting in different distinctions depending on the specific contexts. This constructivist perspective also allows an explanation of the "paradox of scientific authority" in our modern knowledge society, which is directly relevant to politics and political theory: on the one had we live in a "technological culture" in which science and technology are the all-pervasive constituents of the societal fabric, including political institutions and politics; on the other hand we see that the authority of engineers, scientists, doctors, and experts-in-general is not taken for granted anymore. What are the implications for political decision-making, how do advisory institutions such as the US National Academy of Sciences or the Dutch Health Council succeed in giving scientific advice to politics without being able to claim an intrinsic, time and context independent authority? These bodies of scientific advice maintain their scientific authority by continuous boundary work, and not because of some intrinsic institutional characteristic of their institution or of their position between politics and science/technology (Hilgartner 2000; Bal, Bijker, and Hendriks 2002).

The fourth meaning of politics I want to discuss is again related to expertise, but now to the expertise of non-scientists and non-technologists. This is an important issue when democratization of politics is translated into the need to increase public participation. This focus on participation was dominant in technology studies in the 1990s, and is still an important issue. Its origins date back to the controversy studies in the 1970s (Nelkin and Brown 1984; Nelkin 1979; Nelkin and Pollak 1979), industrial democracy studies in the 1980s (see below), and of course to a more general questioning of established democratic institutions in the 1980s and 1990s (Bijker 2002). Much of this work refers to Barber's (1984) plea for a "strong democracy." The most explicit argument, formulated in what almost could be called a blueprint for a new society, can be found in Sclove's *Democracy and Technology* (1995). When public participation in politics of technology is argued for, the question is pertinent whether this public does have the necessary technological expertise to assess the various alternatives. The question of expertise of the lay participants in democratic processes is an almost irresolvable one when viewed from a positivistic perspective—hence the technocratic solution of delegating such decisions to technical experts.

From a constructivist perspective this is different. Constructivist analyses of scientific knowledge and technical expertise, as I argued above, have shown that such expertise is not intrinsically different from other forms of expertise. The conclusion, then, is that groups of non-scientists and non-engineers have other forms of expertise, rather than no expertise, and that the label "layperson" as opposed to "expert" is not appropriate (Bijker 1997). This does not preclude the possibility that such groups of participants do acquire scientific and technical expertise, as has been documented for patient groups in AIDS research, and for women users in architectural and urban design (Epstein 1996; Bijker and Bijsterveld 2000). Recently, philosophers of technology have drawn upon the pragmatist John Dewey, "whose early articulation of the problems of combining participation and representation remain pertinent today" (Feenberg 2001, 140). Already in the 1920s, Dewey argued for radical changes in democratic institutions to accommodate them to what he called "the machine age." Dewey (1991, 15–16) specified the general public as consisting of "all those who are affected by the direct consequences of transactions to such an extent that it is deemed necessary to have those consequences systematically cared for." Does Dewey's definition of public lend support to pleas for more direct democracy and citizens' participation? Or does it, rather, stress the need to focus on the process of political deliberation: "What characterizes the range of Western democratic politics for Dewey is not a specific fixed institutionalized form, like free elections or a parliament of representatives. Democracy, we read in Dewey, is precisely the constant flux and experimentation with different political forms that are spurred by the contestation existing ones elicit and which construct different collectives and articulations among them" (Gomart and Hajer 2003, 56–7). To the political participation by groups of "other experts" I will return below, in the context of sub-politics.

A fifth meaning of politics—but it will be clear by now that my various disaggregates of politics are overlapping and intertwined—focuses on large technical projects. Many of the current political controversies are related to decisions about such large projects—from infrastructural works such as airports, railway lines, or water works to large plants such as powers stations or waste facilities. Because large parts of the general public are affected by these plans, the cry for public participation is loud. At the same time, the worry that NIMBY (Not In My Back Yard) effects will hamper political decision-making up to the point of damaging the public cause, is equally pertinent (Gerrard 1994; Piller 1991). Also studies that do not explicitly focus on the participation question, typically highlight the political dimensions of large technical systems.[4] As Thomas Hughes, arch father of the historical studies of large technological systems, observes: these technologies "give rise to binding nuclei for a host of dependent political and economic interests. Interwoven with political and economic interests of particular kinds, technology is far from neutral" (1983: 318–19). And he concludes about his three historical case-studies of electricity distribution: "In Chicago, technology dominated politics; in London, the reverse was true; and in pre-World War I Berlin there was coordination of political and technological power" (Hughes 1983, 461–2).

Yet another important way of relating politics to technology is through industrial democracy. Work in the 1980s linked action research for labor unions with broader perspectives on social democracy and democratization of society: "democratiza-

---

[4] See, e.g., Abbate 1999; Hughes et al. 2001; Summerton 1994; Mayntz and Hughes 1988; Hughes and Hughes 2000.

tion must now be seen as the primary strategic goal of the labour and social, movements. It is the precondition for further social advance. Moreover, it seems... to be the only viable response to the industrial challenge of effecting a rupture with Fordism, and the immediate political challenge posed by the New Right" (Mathews 1989, 220). Initially, much of this work was directly tied to democracy at the shop floor, but Mathews does relate this to broader democratization strategies, associating workers and citizens as agents of social change. In the 1990s the focus continued to shift to this wider societal perspective (Sclove 1995).

The seventh meaning of politics I want to discuss transcends the previous perspectives on industrial and direct democracy, and returns us to the macro level of society and political culture. Politics in Ulrich Beck's (1986; 1992) "risk society" acquires a very different meaning as compared to classic political theory. Marx's and Weber's concepts of "industrial" or "class society" now have to be substituted, Beck argues, by the concept of "risk society." The central political question is not anymore about the production and distribution of wealth, but about risk: "How can the risks and hazards systematically produced as part of modernization be prevented, minimized, dramatized, or channeled? Where they do finally see the light of day in the shape of 'latent side effects,' how can they be limited and distributed away so that they neither hamper the modernization process nor exceed the limits of that which is 'tolerable'—ecologically, medically, psychologically and socially?" (Beck 1992, 20). The role of technology is here specifically analyzed in the light of the risks it causes. Especially the risks associated with ionizing radiation, pollution, and genetic engineering are central: their often irreversible harm, their being invisible to the unarmed human eye, and their causes being only identifiable through scientific knowledge (and thus being open to social definition and construction) require a reassessment of politics in the risk society. The distribution of risks now determines social and power relations, instead of the distribution of wealth, as was the case in class society.

This must have implications for our conception of politics: "A central consequence... is that risks become the motor of the *self-politicization* of modernity in industrial society; furthermore, in the risk society, the *concept, place and media of politics* change" (Beck 1992, 183, italics in original). In the industrial society, the citizen was partly *citoyen*, using the democratic rights in arenas of political deliberation and decision-making, and partly *bourgeois*, defending private interests in the fields of work and business. Correspondingly, a differentiation had occurred between the political and the technical systems in industrial society. Negative effects in one system were compensated in the other: "Progress replaces voting. Furthermore: progress becomes a substitute for questions, a type of consent in advance for goals and consequences that go unnamed and unknown" (Beck 1992, 184). The social inequalities of the class society, the high development of production forces and scientification of society, and the dramatic and negative global effects of technology yield a radical transformation of the relation between the political and the non-political: "the concepts of the political and the non-political become blurred and require a systematic revision.... On the one hand established and utilized rights limit freedom of action *within* the political system and bring about new demands for political participation *outside* the political system in the form of a *new political culture* (citizens' initiative groups and social movements)" (Beck 1992, 185, italics in original). Societal change is not debated in parliament or decided by the executive government, but created in the laboratories and industries of micro-electronics, nuclear power, and genetic modification. These technological develop-ments thus loose their political neutrality, though at the same time continue to be shielded against parliamentary control: "Techno-economic development thus falls between politics and non-politics. It becomes a third entity, acquiring the precar-ious hybrid status of a *sub-politics*" (Beck 1992, 186). Politics is thus spreading into society, and is being "displaced" from the centers of traditional political power into a polycentric system. For a stable development of a future democratic structure of the new risk society these sub-politics need to be supplemented with new political institutions (Beck 1997; 1993; Dijk 2000).

Now that I have deconstructed both technology and politics into a variety of context-dependent meanings, let us turn to the core question: how and why does technology matter to politics, how do the "two" relate?

3   WHY AND HOW DOES TECHNOLOGY MATTER?

I shall review various answers to the questions why and how technology matters to politics and to political theory, even though several of these answers have already been given implicitly in the previous sections. I will start with the general question of the relation between technology and political culture, then turn to the specific field of technology assessment.

3.1   Technology and the Political Culture of Democracy

One way in which technology has been considered to matter to politics and political theory, is in quite general terms about the relation between technology and modernization. A central claim of modernization theories is that technological development and economic, social, and cultural change go together in coherent ways (Inglehart 2001). Arch fathers of modernization theory such as Karl Marx, Emile Durkheim, and Max Weber took their starting point in the Industrial Revolution and the way in which it had transformed Western European societies and politics. Subsequent work linked modernization to development by asking questions about the differential impact of technological development on politics outside Europe and North America (Graham 2001). In the 1990s, this style of political studies could observe that "yet another revolution in technology linked to information technology, the growth of knowledge based industries, and the globalization of economic processes produced major realignment in politics and economics" (Graham 2001, 9964). These studies have led to new theories about modernization that combine the observation of the shift from mass production to knowledge-based industries, with an analysis of structural economic policies, the creation of market economies worldwide, and fundamental changes in political institutions of state and society. At this general level of modernization theory, the relation between technology and democratization is also questioned, as for example in: "The emergence of postindustrial, or 'knowledge' society, favors democratic institutions, partly because these societies require highly educated and innovative workers, who become accustomed to thinking for themselves in daily job life. They tend to transfer this outlook to politics, undertaking more active and more demanding types of mass participation" (Inglehart 2001, 9970). One answer, thus, is that technology matters to politics, because it has shaped the modern state and its political and democratic institutions. But can this be made more specific?

Another way in which technology matters to politics and shapes politics is by setting the conditions for political discussion and development. I intend this in a most comprehensive way. Technology basically shapes the political world, from the language and the metaphors, to the economic boundary conditions and the communication technologies. The technology of computers not only controlled the vast networks that were central to the globalist aims of the cold war, but also provided the apocalyptic vocabulary and metaphors in which the foreign policy was formulated. This technology "constituted a dome of global technological oversight, a *closed world*, within which each event was interpreted as part of a titanic struggle between the superpowers" (Edwards 1996, 1–2). In this case, technology mattered to politics because it helped to shape its very aims and means; at the same time it was also an object of politics and technology policy.

In the case of computers and the cold war, technology and politics thus co-evolved as two sides of the same coin. This "co-evolution" or "co-production" of technology and politics (or society) is a common phrase in current technology studies (Jasanoff 2004). It needs to be made more specific to do real explanatory work however. One way to do that is to use Hecht's concept of "technopolitical regime:" these are grounded in state institutions (such as CEA and EDF; see above) and consist "of linked sets of individuals, engineering and institutional practices, technological artifacts, political programs, and institutional ideologies acting together to govern technological development and pursue technopolitics (a term that describes the strategic practice of designing or using technology to constitute, embody, or enact political goals)" (Hecht 1998, 56–7). This concept allows us to describe the interaction between politics and technology in a quite specific way. CEA's technopolitical regime involved the production of weapons-grade plutonium and thus helped to create France's de facto military nuclear policy. EDF's regime positioned its reactors deliberately in counterpoint to CEA's technopolitics, and thus created France's nuclear energy policy. In similar vein, the concept "technological frame" has been used to describe in detail the interaction between Barcelona politics and the technology of town planning and architecture (Aibar and Bijker 1997). The difference between the two concepts is that the technopolitical regime is connected to state institutions in which a variety of social groups are acting, while a technological frame is linked to one relevant social group that may be dispersed over a variety of societal institutions. It is important to recognize that both are analysts' concepts describing the relation between technology and politics; the actors involved may think quite differently about this relationship. In the case of the struggle between France's CEA and EDF, Hecht describes how EDF even deliberately and strategically tried to separate politics from technology, to take a "technocratic pose" (Alder 1997), and to create a technological determinist interpretation in which there was such a thing as a single best technology that should be adopted without political deliberation.

Another way in which technology matters to politics, is by shaping the means of political debate: the arena, the communication links, the agenda. Such a perspective can, of course, be applied to analyzing eighteenth-century politics and the technologies of architecture (think of an analysis of the plans of parliamentary buildings and the layout of meeting rooms), mail correspondence, and messenger communication; but most current research focuses on the relation between digital technologies and politics (Bimber 2003). Most experiments with digital democracy are conceived and experienced "as a means of reviving and reinvigorating democratic politics which for a variety of reasons is perceived to have lost its appeal and dynamism" (Tsagarousianou 1998, 168). Such experiments started in the 1980s to challenge the monopoly of existing political hierarchies over powerful communication media, to amplify the power of grassroots groups to gather and distribute critical information, and to organize political action. Then other initiatives followed by local authorities to improve contact with citizens, to upgrade the delivery of services and information, and to encourage citizen participation in public affairs (Tsagarousianou, Tambini, and Bryan 1998). Both American and European local authorities created experimental "digital cities," hoping that new information and communication technologies would help to resuscitate declining citizen participation in political life and give new vigor to local politics.

These digital city experiments use very different definitions of (digital) democracy: they ranged from mainly deliberative to more plebiscitary models, and from grassroots self-organization and empowerment to public information provision-centered projects. Interesting questions regarding the access to political debate are raised by these experiments:

Who will carry the cost of rendering the network services accessible to the public? Will the right to access be complemented by ensuring that citizens develop the competence to use the services available to them and overcome, often socially conditioned, and class, gender, age and ethnicity-related, aversion to and distance from the technology and skills necessary? How are the rights to free speech/expression and concerns over the abuse of the city network balanced?   (Tsagarousianou 1998, 171)

It will be clear that answers to these questions will be very different, depending on the national and, indeed, local political culture. In the American libertarian civic tradition a key goal may be to encourage the formation of citizens' groups and initiatives. In a traditionally left-wing Italian region the focus may be on securing the network access as a public good and the implementation of citizens' rights. An English digital city experiment may be designed as a means for economic regeneration. Taking stock of how these digital technologies matter to politics is a sobering experience. Behind the rhetoric of digital democracy often the main activity is the dissemination of information of which the agenda and content are controlled by the governmental authority. "In spite of the discourses of interactivity which underlie most 'electronic democracy' initiatives, most of them have in practice been executive-initiated, top-down and mostly based on giving more access to information. Politics in this form remains more of a model of convincing through the dissemination of information than of communication and discussion" (Tsagarousianou 1998, 174).

3.2   From Technology Assessment to Precaution

Technology assessment, often abbreviated as TA is one concrete way in which politics has been dealing with technology since the 1970s. Technology matters to politics in our modern societies because, as I argued above, these technologies do shape so pervasively our societies and cultures. The term "TA" is also used when non-political actors such as firms, consultancies, or health care agencies want to evaluate and assess the promises or profits and the potential costs and risks of new technological options. I will restrict myself to the public, political use of TA.

The beginning of TA, under that name, is marked by the US Technology Assessment Act of 1972, which assigned to the Office of Technology Assessment a mission of providing neutral, competent assessments about the probable beneficial and harmful effects of new technologies. Breathing a rather technological determinist view, the law explained as its rationale that: "it is essential that, to the fullest extent possible, the consequences of technological applications be anticipated, understood, and considered in determination of public policy on existing and emerging national problems" (quoted by Bimber 1996). The agency's role was seen as an "early warning device," providing foresight about the possible positive and negative consequences of technological developments. It could build on early sociological studies of the societal effect of technology, such as by Ogburn (1946), and on early management approaches to handling technological uncertainties, such as by the RAND Corporation (Yearley 2001). By the mid-1980s the original exclusive emphasis on being expert witness to parliaments by providing scientific reports, the concept of TA, "was complemented with an interest in linking up more closely with decision making, or at least contributing to setting an agenda. Public debates about energy and environmental issues helped to make this aspect of TA more prominent" (Yearley 2001, 15512). TA has become an important ingredient of government technology policy. In the 1990s and into the twenty-first century, TA also started to add participatory approaches to the expert-based methodologies. In some European countries (Denmark, the Netherlands) forms of public participation have now been institutionalized, especially for TA's agenda setting role. Largely independent of this development of public TA, in the 1980s TA for specific technology sectors also became institutionalized—the clearest examples are the, in many countries legally required Environmental Impact Statements, and the field of medical technology assessment.

All varieties of TA combine forms of anticipation and feedback, joining, so to speak, "writing a history of the future, supported by judgments of experts and by social-science insights and data, and informing action or preparation for action" (Yearley 2001, 15513). This combination creates the fundamental "anticipation and control dilemma:" at an early stage of a technology's development, it still is so malleable that it can be controlled and changed but its impact cannot be anticipated; and when the impact becomes clear, the technology has become so obdurate that it is difficult to control (Collingridge 1980). This increasing obduracy of technology has been conceptualized in different ways: technological systems acquire "momentum" (the exemplar is the large-scale electricity distribution system; Hughes 1983); and technologies acquire "path dependency" when they incorporate investments, users, other technologies, etc. (a well-known example is the QWERTY keyboard; David 1985). This obduracy of technology is socially constructed, and helps to include the societal impact of technology into constructivist technology studies (Hommels 2005). Constructive Technology Assessment is meant to offer a political and managerial solution to the anticipation and control dilemma. It builds on societal experiments with the introduction of new technologies; it mixes private and public actors, provides occasion for societal learning about new technologies, and results in feedback into further design and development (Rip, Misa, and Schot 1995). The critical question can be raised whether such efforts can escape the boundaries set by the rationality of the dominant power structure: "Rationalization in our society responds to a particular definition of technology as a means to the goal of profit and power. A broader understanding of technology suggests a very different notion of rationalization, based on responsibility for the human and natural contexts of technical action." Feenberg (1995, 20) then proposes to call this "subversive rationalization," "because it requires technological advances that can be made only in opposition to the dominant hegemony."

Closely linked to technology assessment—and an obvious way in which technology matters to politics, i.e. as object of that politics—is technology policy. But what can this be? To foster technological innovation—with its emphasis on change—is not a natural role for governments: "In all well-ordered societies, political authority is dedicated to stability, security and the status quo. It is thus singularly ill-qualified to direct or channel activity intended to produce instability, insecurity and change" (Rosenberg and Birdzell 1986: 265). It has also been argued that in a free market economy, the only justifiable role for technology policy would be to perform technology assessments (Freeman and Soete 1997). Nevertheless, technology policy in a broader sense is increasingly seen as an important responsibility of government (Branscomb 1993). It is now also realized that a technology policy that merely focuses on the supply side is not enough, and that research and innovation policies to address the demand side need to be added (Branscomb 2001). Since the 1990s the concept of "national system of innovation" is increasingly used, both in innovation studies and in policy discourse. This results in stressing the coherence of political, cultural, managerial, and institutional characteristics in determining the innovative capacity of a country.[5] Thus technology policy is being broadened to incorporate insights from technology studies as well as other social sciences.

Conceptualizing modern society as a risk society, as I described in the previous section, has implications for the ways in which technological developments are assessed in politics. Let me briefly retrace the way in which politics handled risks before the 1990s. Probabilistic risk assessment had been developed in the early 1970s as a reductionistic engineering technique to estimate the risk of a system's failure resulting from the mishap of single parts or sub-systems. The so-called "reactor safety study" of the US Atomic Energy Commission of 1975 used this technique and concluded that citizens were more likely to be killed by a falling meteorite than by an accident with a nuclear power plant. With this risk conception, it made sense that politics would, in a technocratic fashion delegate the management of risks to experts. The Three Mile Island nuclear plant accident of 1979 then violently questioned this solution. According to technical analysis, this accident could never have happened. It thus "brought to public and sociological attention an incipient schism between the state, its technological experts and citizens" (Rosa and Freudenburg 2001, 13357). This was further aggravated by a series of psychometric

---

[5] See, e.g., Dosi et al. 1988; Nelson 1993; Miettinen 2002; Elzinga 2004.

studies that showed the discrepancies between public and expert interpretations of risk, for example: a systematic underestimation of risks to which one is routinely exposed, an overvaluation of novel or possibly catastrophic risks, and an under-valuation of risks to which one is exposed by own choice. This caused a problem for policy-makers: "If they base regulations on expert judgments—that is, keyed only to the statistical probability of harm—policies may be unpopular or even sub-verted, whereas basing policies on the public's apparent preferences threatens to make regulations arbitrary, unscientific, or too costly" (Yearley 2001, 13361). More-over, social constructivist analyses have shown that expert risk estimates cannot be equated with "real" risks anyway (Wynne 1992).

A key element in how technology matters to politics in our high-tech risk society is the uncertainty of scientific knowledge, technological risks, social-eco-nomic parameters, and cultural values and priorities. There is a variety of ways to characterize these uncertainties.[6] But they all lead to describing a world where "in the sorts of issue-driven problems characteristic of policy-related research, typically facts are uncertain, values in dispute, stakes high and decisions urgent." Such a world needs what Funtowicz and Ravetz (2001, 19) have called "post-normal science." This label refers to the non-normality of current politics, technology, and science: "In 'normality,' either science or policy, the process is managed largely implicitly, and is accepted unwittingly by all who wish to join in. The great lesson of recent years is that that assumption no longer holds. We may call it a 'post-modern rejection of grand narratives', or a green, NIMBY politics. Whatever its causes, we can no longer assume the presence of this sort of 'normality' of the policy process."

A striking new development, which may well turn out to be a focal point of how politics and technology matter to each other in the next decade, is the precaution-ary principle. Probably the most cited version of the precautionary principle is the one in the Rio declaration: "Where there are threats of serious or irreversible damage, lack of full scientific certainty shall not be used as a reason for postponing cost-effective measures to prevent environmental degradation" (UN 1992). This provides a way for politics to handle technologies under highly uncertain condi-tions: the principle allows interfering, even when it is not clear what the risk exactly is. It implies a shift from prevention of clear and manifest dangers towards precautionary action to avoid hypothetical risks. A wealth of literature has de-veloped since, that translates this principle into various precautionary approaches (Klinke and Renn 2002; EEA 2001). The interpretation and implementation of the precautionary principle inevitably will vary, according to legal and scientific doctrines, and to the openness of political culture. This is possibly also its weakness. The precautionary principle has an intuitive appeal but lacks broadly shared conceptual clarity. It may be depicted as a "repository for a jumble of adventurous beliefs that challenge the status quo of political power, ideology and

---

[6] See, e.g., Funtowicz and Ravetz 1989; Wynne 1992; Asselt 2000.

civil rights" (Golding 2001, 11962; see also O'Riordan and Jordan 1995). Nevertheless, I think that developing the precautionary approach may offer a prudent next step in the evolution of politics' dealing with technology: it may help to sail between the Scylla of the illusion of a technocratic, rational politics and the Charybdis of political bankruptcy in the light of paralyzing uncertainty about new technological developments. Implementing the precautionary approach will help politics (in all its various meanings) to avoid the pitfalls of technocracy and technological determinism because it integrates constructivist views of science and technology into technology assessment and political deliberation and decision-making.

4   IMPLICATIONS FOR POLITICAL STUDIES

The previous review may be summed up by the slogan that "all technology is political and all politics is technological." I have shown how this slogan is based on a variety of empirical studies of technology and politics, and how it translates into specific theoretical interpretations of the relationship between technology and politics. I will not try to summarize this rich variety, further exemplified by the subsequent chapters in this volume, in general statements. Rather, I will formulate some "lessons" for political *studies*.

The first reason to pay attention to technology in political studies is that such a focus on the technological in society will reveal aspects of politics that remain unnoticed otherwise. Only through an analysis of the "nuts and bolts" of missile technologies and the intricacies of accuracy tests can we fully understand US foreign policy since the 1950s. Only through an analysis of the details of nuclear reactor design and its implications for the proportion of fissile material in nuclear waste can we understand French atomic weapon politics. And I have argued that this applies to *all* technologies—from bicycles to public housing, from electricity distribution to railways—because we live in a "technological culture:" a society that is constituted by science and technology. "It is too weak a position even to see technology and politics as interacting: there is no categorical distinction to be made between the two" (MacKenzie 1990, 412–13).

A second, more specific reason to study technologies is that they shape political concepts and discussions. (The same applies, of course, vice versa: politics shapes technology; but that is not the point here.) New forms of communication and information technologies are changing people's ideas about democracy and practices in public arenas. But, again, only a detailed analysis of the technical intricacies of, for example, Internet search engines will reveal that this medium, originally hailed for its open and non-hierarchical character, is now increasingly structured by commercial interests that consequently will also shape digital democracy projects in specific ways. It is important to actively render such influences of technology visible, because the more successful technologies are, the more they get black-boxed and entrenched in society. The most pervasive and influential technologies are often the least visible and thus most immune to political deliberation.

Thirdly, more strategic lessons can be drawn from studying technology—lessons that relate to the practice of political studies. A focus on technology helps to recognize the boundary work that fuels practical politics. Distinctions, problem definitions, identities: they are all actively constructed by the actors involved, rather than found in nature or society as intrinsic properties. Classification is a balancing act and technology assessment is boundary work.

The bottom line, then, is that technology should matter to political studies because it matters to politics. And technology matters to politics because our world is pervasively technological. Such are the—quite simple—answers to the "why" question of this chapter. There is no such simple answer to the "how" question however, or it would be the constructivist adage: context matters. Technology matters to politics in as many different ways as there are contexts of politics and contexts of technology.

REFERENCES

ABBATE, J. 1999. *Inventing the Internet*. Cambridge, Mass.: MIT Press.

AIBAR, E., and BIJKER, W. E. 1997. Constructing a city: the Cerdà Plan for the extension of Barcelona. *Science, Technology & Human Values*, 22: 3–30.

ALDER, K. 1997. *Engineering the Revolution: Arms and Enlightenment in France, 1763–1815*. Princeton, NJ: Princeton University Press.

ASSELT, M. B. A. von. 2000. *Perspectives on Uncertainty and Risk: The PRIMA Approach to Decision Support*. Dordrecht: Kluwer Academic.

BAL, R., BIJKER, W. E., and HENDRIKS, R. 2002. *Paradox van wetenschappelijk gezag: Over de maatschappelijke invloed van adviezen van de Gezondheidsraad, 1985–2001*. Den Haag: Gezondheidsraad.

BAL, R., and HALFFMAN, W. (eds.) 1998. *The Politics of Chemical Risk: Scenarios for a Regulatory Future*. Dordrecht: Kluwer Academic.

BARBER, B. R. 1984. *Strong Democracy*. Berkeley: University of California Press.

BECK, U. 1986. *Risikogesellschaft: Auf dem Weg in eine andere Moderne*. Frankfurt: Suhrkamp Verlag.

——1992. *Risk Society*. London: Sage.

——1993. *Die Erfindung des Politischen: Zu einer Theorie reflexiver Modernisierung*. Frankfurt: Suhrkamp Verlag.

——1997. *The Reinvention of Politics*. Cambridge: Polity Press.

BIJKER, W. E. 1995. *Of Bicycles, Bakelites and Bulbs*. Cambridge, Mass.: MIT Press.

—— 1997. Demokratisierung der Technik—Wer sind die Experten? Pp. 133–55 in *Aufstand der Laien. Expertentum und Demokratie in der technisierten Welt*, ed. M. Kerner. Aachen: Thouet Verlag.

—— 2002. The Oosterschelde Storm Surge Barrier: a test case for Dutch water technology, management and politics. *Technology & Culture*, 43: 569–84.

—— and Bijsterveld, K. 2000. Women walking through plans—technology, democracy and gender identity. *Technology & Culture*, 41: 485–515.

—— Hughes, T. P., and Pinch, T. (eds.) 1987. *The Social Construction of Technological Systems*. Cambridge, Mass.: MIT Press.

—— and Law, J. (eds.) 1992. *Shaping Technology / Building Society*. Cambridge, Mass.: MIT Press.

Bimber, B. 1996. *The Politics of Expertise in Congress: The Rise and Fall of the Office of Technology Assessment*. Albany: State University of New York Press.

—— 2003. *Information and American Democracy*. New York: Cambridge University Press.

Bowker, G. C., and Star, S. L. 1999. *Sorting Things Out: Classification and its Consequences*. Cambridge, Mass.: MIT Press.

Branscomb, L. M. (ed.) 1993. *Empowering Technology: Implementing a U.S. Strategy*. Cambridge, Mass.: MIT Press.

—— 2001. Technological innovation. In Smelser and Baltes 2001, 15498–502.

Collingridge, D. 1980. *The Social Control of Technology*. London: Frances Pinter.

Collins, H. M. 1985. *Changing Order: Replication and Induction in Scientific Practice*. London: Sage.

—— and Evans, R. 2002. The third wave of science studies: studies of expertise and experience. *Social Studies of Science*, 32: 235–96.

—— and Pinch, T. J. 1998. *The Golem: What You Should Know About Science*, 2nd edn. Cambridge: Cambridge University Press.

Cowan, R. S. 1983. *More Work for Mother*. New York: Basic Books.

David, P. 1985. Clio and the economics of QWERTY. *American Economic Review*, 75: 332–7.

Dewey, J. 1991. *The Public and its Problems*. Athens, Oh.: Swallow Press; originally published 1927.

Dijk, J. Van. 2000. Models of democracy and concepts of communication. In Hacker and Dijk 2000, 30–53.

Dosi, G., Freeman, C., Nelson, R., Silverberg, G., and Soete, L. (eds.) 1988. *Technical Change and Economic Theory*, 2nd edn. London: Pinter.

Dunlavy, C. A. 1994. *Politics and Industrialization: Early Railroads in the United States and Prussia*. Princeton, NJ: Princeton Univversity Press.

Eden, L. 2004. *Whole World on Fire: Organizations, Knowledge, & Nuclear Weapons Devastation*. Ithaca, NY: Cornell University Press.

Edwards, P. N. 1996. *The Closed World: Computers and the Politics of Discourse in Cold War America*. Cambridge, Mass.: MIT Press.

Elzinga, A. 2004. Metaphors, models and reification in science and technology policy discourse. *Science as Culture*, 13: 105–21.

Epstein, S. 1996. *Impure Science: AIDS, Activism and the Politics of Knowledge*. Berkeley: University of California Press.

European Environment Agency (EEA) 2001. *Late Lessons from Early Warnings: The Precautionary Principle 1896–2000*. Copenhagen: EEA.

EZRAHI, Y. 1995. Technology and the civil epistemology off democracy. In Feenberg and Hannay 1995, 159–71.

FEENBERG, A. 1995. Subversive rationalization, technology, power and democracy. In Feenberg and Hannay 1995, 3–24.

—— 2001. Looking backward, looking forward: reflections on the twentieth century. *Hitotsubashi Journal of Social Sciences*, 33: 135–42.

—— and HANNAY, A. (eds.) 1995. *Technology and the Politics of Knowledge*. Bloomington: Indiana University Press.

FIJNAUT, C., and MARX, G. T. 1995. *Undercover*. The Hague: Kluwer Law International.

FREEMAN, C., and SOETE, L. 1997. *The Economics of Industrial Innovation*, 3rd edn. Cambridge, Mass.: MIT Press.

FUNTOWICZ, S., and RAVETZ, J. 1989. Managing the uncertainties of statistical information. Pp. 95–117 in *Environmental Threats*, ed. J. Brown. London: Belhaven Press.

—— —— 2001. Post-normal science: science and governance under conditions of complexity. Pp. 15–24 in *Interdisciplinarity in Technology Assessment. Implementation and its Chances and Limits*, ed. M. Decker. Berlin: Springer.

GERRARD, M. B. 1994. *Whose Backyard, Whose Risk: Fear and Fairness in Toxic and Nuclear Waste Siting*. Cambridge, Mass.: MIT Press.

GIERYN, T. F. 1983. Boundary-work and the demarcation of science from non-science: strains and interests in professional ideologies of scientists. *American Sociological Review*, 48: 781–95.

GIERYN, T. F. 1999. *Cultural Boundaries of Science*. Chicago: University of Chicago Press.

GOLDING, D. 2001. Precautionary principle. In Smelser and Baltes 2001, 11961–3.

GOMART, E., and HAJER, M. A. 2003. Is that politics? For an inquiry into forms in contemporaneous politics. Pp. 33–61 in *Social Studies of Science and Technology*, ed. B. Joerges and H. Nowotny. Dordrecht: Kluwer Academic.

GOTTWEIS, H. 1998. *Governing Molecules: The Discursive Politics of Genetic Engineering in Europe and the United States*. Cambridge, Mass.: MIT Press.

GRAHAM, L. S. 2001. Political modernization: development of the concept. In Smelser and Baltes 2001, 9963–5.

GUSTON, D. 2000. *Between Politics and Science*. Cambridge: Cambridge University Press.

—— 2001. Boundary organizations in environmental policy and science (Special Issue). *Science, Technology & Human Values*, 26: 399–500.

—— and KENISTON, K. (eds.) 1994. *The Fragile Contract: University Science and the Federal Government*. Cambridge, Mass.: MIT Press.

HACKER, K. L., and DIJK, J. VAN. (eds.) 2000. *Digital Democracy*. London: Sage.

HAGEN, M. 2000. Digital democracy and political systems. In Hacker and van Dijk 2000, 54–69.

HAGUE, B. N., and LOADER, B. 1999. *Digital Democracy*. London: Routledge.

HALFFMAN, W. 2002. *Boundaries of Regulatory Science: Eco/toxicology and Aquatic Hazards of Chemicals in the US, England and the Netherlands, 1970–1995*. Amsterdam: University of Amsterdam.

HECHT, G. 1998. *The Radiance of France: Nuclear Power and National Identity after World War II*. Cambridge, Mass.: MIT Press.

HELD, D. 1996. *Models of Democracy*, 2nd edn. Cambridge: Polity Press.

HILGARTNER, S. 2000. *Science on Stage*. Stanford, Calif.: Stanford University Press.

HOMMELS, A. M. 2005. *Unbuilding Cities*. Cambridge, Mass.: MIT Press.

Hughes, A. C., and Hughes, T. P. (eds.) 2000. *Systems, Experts and Computers: The Systems Approach in Management and Engineering, World War II and After.* Cambridge, Mass.: MIT Press.

—— Allen, M. T., and Hecht, G. 2001. *Technologies of Power.* Cambridge, Mass.: MIT Press.

Hughes, T. P. 1983. *Networks of Power: Electrification in Western Society, 1880–1930.* Baltimore: John Hopkins University Press.

Inglehart, R. 2001. Sociological theories of modernization. In Smelser and Baltes 2001, 9965–71.

Jasanoff, S. 1990. *The Fifth Branch: Science Advisers as Policymakers.* Cambridge, Mass.: Harvard University Press.

—— (ed.) 2004. *States of Knowledge: The Co-production of Science and Social Order.* New York: Routledge.

Klinke, A., and Renn, O. 2002. A new approach to risk evaluation and management: risk-based, precaution-based and discourse-based strategies. *Risk Analysis,* 22: 1071–94.

Lyon, D. 2003. Surveillance technology and surveillance society. Pp. 161–83 in *Modernity and Technology,* ed. T. J. Misa, P. Brey, and A. Feenberg. Cambridge, Mass.: MIT Press.

MacKenzie, D. 1990. *Inventing Accuracy.* Cambridge, Mass.: MIT Press.

—— and Wajcman, J. (eds.) 1999. *The Social Shaping of Technology,* 2nd edn. Buckingham: Open University Press.

Mathews, J. 1989. *Age of Democracy: The Politics of Post-Fordism.* Oxford: Oxford University Press.

Mayntz, R., and Hughes, T. (eds.) 1988. *The Development of Large Technical Systems.* Boulder, Colo.: Westview Press.

Miettinen, R. 2002. *National Innovation System.* Helsinki: Edita.

Nelkin, D. (ed.) 1979. *Controversy: Politics of Technical Decisions.* Beverly Hills, Calif.: Sage.

—— and Brown, M. S. 1984. *Workers ar Risk.* Chicago: University of Chicago Press.

—— and Pollak, M. 1979. Public participation in technological decisions: reality or grand illusion? *Technology Review,* 81: 55–64.

Nelson, R. R. (ed.) 1993. *National Innovation Systems.* New York: Oxford University Press.

Nowotny, H., Scott, P., and Gibbons, M. 2001. *Re-thinking Science: Knowledge and the Public in an Age of Uncertainty.* Cambridge: Polity Press.

O'Riordan, T., and Jordan, A. 1995. The precautionary principle in contemporary environmental politics. *Environmental Values,* 14: 191–212.

Ogburn, W. F., Adams, J., and Gilfillan, S. C. 1946. *The Social Effects of Aviation.* Boston: Houghton Mifflin.

Oudshoorn, N. 2003. *The Male Pill.* Durham, NC: Duke University Press.

Piller, C. 1991. *The Fail-Safe Society.* Berkeley: University of California Press.

Rip, A., Misa, T. J., and Schot, J. (eds.) 1995. *Managing Technology in Society.* London: Pinter.

Rosa, E. A., and Freudenburg, W. R. 2001. Sociological study of risk. In Smelser and Baltes 2001, 13356–60.

Rosenberg, N., and Birdzell, L. E. 1986. *How the West Grew Rich.* New York: Basic Books.

Roy, A. 1999. *The Greater Common Good.* Bombay: India Book Distributors.

Sclove, R. E. 1995. *Democracy and Technology.* New York: Guilford Press.

Smelser, N., and Baltes, P. B. (eds.) 2001. *International Encyclopedia of the Social & Behavioral Sciences.* Oxford: Elsevier Science.

Summerton, J. (ed.) 1994. *Changing Large Technical Systems.* Boulder, Colo.: Westview Press.

TSAGAROUSIANOU, R. 1998. Electronic democracy and the public sphere: opportunities and challenges. In Tsagarousianou, Tambini, and Bryan 1998, 167–78.

—— TAMBINI, D., and Bryan, C. 1998. *Cyberdemocracy.* London: Routledge.

United Nations (UN) 1992. *Rio Declaration on Environment and Development.* New York: UN.

WAJCMAN, J. 2004. *TechnoFeminism.* Cambridge: Polity Press.

WINNER, L. 1977. *Autonomous Technology.* Cambridge, Mass.: MIT Press.

—— 1980. Do artifacts have politics? *Daedalus,* 109: 121–36; reprinted in Winner 1986, 19–39.

—— 1986. *The Whale and the Reactor.* Chicago: University of Chicago Press.

WYNNE, B. 1992. Uncertainty and environmental learning: reconceiving science and policy in the preventive paradigm. *Global Environmental Change,* 2: 111–27.

YEARLEY, S. 2001. Sociology and politics of risk. In Smelser and Baltes 2001, 13360–4.

CHAPTER 38

....

THE GENDER
POLITICS OF
TECHNOLOGY

....

JUDY WAJCMAN

MAINSTREAM political analysis has traditionally been concerned with behavior, institutions, and structures, rather than the politics of technology. Machines, artefacts, and things have generally been treated as background context, rather than dealt with even-handedly alongside persons, institutions, and events. By contrast, science and technology studies emphasize the way material resources, artefacts, and technology make society possible. As Latour (1991, 103) expresses it: "technology is society made durable."

This approach avoids both technological determinism and social determinism. That is, the view that technology is an external, autonomous force affecting society or, conversely, concentrates exclusively on the social shaping of artefacts, neglecting how technologies themselves alter social relations (MacKenzie and Wajcman 1999). In other words, science and technology studies no longer think of technology and society as separate spheres influencing each other: technology and society are mutually constitutive. Such an approach contributes to an understanding of social and political change by exploring how technologies and new forms of social life are co-produced. Society itself is built and bound together with objects and artefacts. Science and technology studies, then, draw attention to the neglect of technology or materiality in much social and political theory.

One way of expressing this is in terms of the power of objects. The conceptions of power that prevail in the social sciences tend to neglect this form of power (with the important exception of military technology). Writers such as Lukes (1974) and Held (1995) define power in terms of the capacity of social agents, agencies, and social institutions. For example, technology does not figure as one of Held's seven key "sites of power," which he defines as an interaction context or institutional milieu through which power operates to mold people's life-chances and effective participation in public decision-making (1995, 173).[1] Even Foucauldian influenced writers, leaving aside Foucault's classic metaphor of the "panopticon," limit their discussion of power relations to social technologies.

This neglect is not surprising given that when technical systems are completely integrated into the social fabric, they become "naturalized," disappearing into the landscape. Take, for example, the way seemingly innocuous technologies such as photography and film assume, privilege, and construct whiteness. Dyer (1997) describes how it is extremely difficult to film black and white faces in the same film and do equal justice to both. Each requires a completely different handling of lighting, make-up, and film developing. The variation in filming conditions means that when black and white actors are portrayed together, one groups tends to lose out, and systematically it is black actors who are technologically short-changed. Dyer traces this bias in the use of film techniques to the film industry's origins in the US and Europe. From the mid-nineteenth century, experiments with the chemistry of photographic stock, aperture size, length of development, and artificial light all proceeded on the assumption that what had to be got right was the look of the white face. By the time of film (some sixty years after the first photographs), technologies and practices were already well established and shaped subsequent uses. So the very chemistry of photography represents a subtle form of technological apartheid.

While race relations and ethnicity are still relatively unexplored in science and technology studies, there is now a substantial body of work examining the ways in which technological objects may shape and be shaped by the operation of gender interests. Feminists have identified men's monopoly of technology as an important source of their power; women's traditional lack of technological skills as an important element in their dependence on men. A key issue has been whether the problem lies in men's domination of technology, or whether technology itself is inscribed with gender power relations. Reflecting current conceptualizations of the relationship between technology and society, described in Bijker's chapter (Ch. 37, this volume), feminist technology studies have now adopted a mutual shaping framework in which technoscience is both a source and consequence of gender relations.[2] In other words, gender relations can be thought of as materialized in technology,

[1] The seven sites are the body, welfare, culture, civic associations, the economy, violence and coercive relations, regulatory and legal institutions.

[2] See Berg 1996; Faulkner 2001; Lie 2003; Sorensen and Stewart 2002; Wajcman 2004.

and masculinity and femininity in turn acquire their meaning and character through their enrolment in working machines. I call this "technofeminism" (Wajcman 2004) and in this chapter will demonstrate that such a perspective on technology adds a new dimension to political analyses of gender difference and sexual inequality.

1   TECHNOLOGY AS MALE CULTURE

What role does technology play in embedding gender power relations? Let us begin with the traditional conception of what we take technology to be. We tend to think about technology in terms of industrial machinery and cars, for example, over-looking other technologies that affect most aspects of everyday life. The very definition of technology, in other words, has a male bias. This emphasis on technologies dominated by men conspires in turn to diminish the significance of women's technologies, such as horticulture, cooking, and childcare, and so repro-duces the stereotype of women as technologically ignorant and incapable (Stanley 1995). The enduring force of the identification between technology and manliness, therefore, is not inherent in biological sex difference. It is rather the result of the historical and cultural construction of gender.

Indeed, it was only with the formation of engineering as a white, male, middle-class profession that "male machines rather than female fabrics" became the modern markers of technology (Oldenziel 1999). During the late nineteenth cen-tury, mechanical and civil engineering increasingly came to define what technology is, diminishing the significance of both artefacts and forms of knowledge associated with women. The rise of engineering as an elite, with exclusive rights to technical expertise, involved the creation of a male professional identity based on educational qualifications and the promise of managerial positions, sharply distinguished from shop-floor engineering and blue-collar workers. It also involved an ideal of manli-ness, characterized by the cultivation of bodily prowess and individual achieve-ment. The discourse about manliness was mobilized to ensure that class, race, and gender boundaries were drawn around the engineering bastion.

It was during and through this process that the term technology took on its modern meaning. Whereas the earlier concept of useful arts had included needle-work and metalwork as well as spinning and mining, by the 1930s this had been supplanted with the idea of technology as applied science. At the same time, femininity was being reinterpreted as incompatible with technological pursuits. The legacy of this relatively recent history is our taken for granted association of technology with men.

We thus need to understand technology as a culture that expresses and consolidates relations amongst men. Feminist writing has long identified the ways in which gender–technology relations are manifest not only in institutions but also in cultural symbols, language, and identities. Men's affinity with technology is integral to the constitution of subjectivity for both sexes. A classic example is the archetypal masculine culture of engineering, where mastery over technology is a source of both pleasure and power for the predominantly male profession (Hacker 1989; Faulkner and Lohan 2004). Engineering is represented as the very epitome of cool reason, as a detached, abstract activity, the antithesis of "feminine" feeling. This resonates with today's dominant image of IT work, the young, white, male "nerds" or "hackers" who enjoy working sixteen-hour days. Indeed, it is rare to see a female face among the dot.com millionaires. The "cyber-brat pack" for the new millennium—those wealthy and entrepreneurial young guns of the Internet—consists almost entirely of men. Writers such as Castells (2001), who eulogize about the counterculture hacker origins of the Internet, fail to notice that the culture of computing was predominantly the culture of the white American male (Star 1995).

This is not to imply that there is a single form of masculinity. Sexual ideologies are remarkably diverse and fluid, and for some men technical expertise may be as much about their lack of power as the realization of it. It is indubitably the case however that in contemporary Western society, the hegemonic form of masculinity is still strongly associated with technical prowess and power (Connell 1987). Feminine identity, on the other hand, has involved being ill-suited to technological pursuits. Different childhood exposure to technology, the prevalence of different role models, different forms of schooling, and the extreme gender segregation of the job market all lead to what Cockburn (1983, 203) describes as "the construction of men as strong, manually able and technologically endowed, and women as physically and technically incompetent". Entering technical domains has therefore required women to sacrifice major aspects of their gender identity.

A recent report comparing six countries, including the US, found that women are generally under-represented among graduates in the information technology, electronics, and communications-related subjects, despite the fact that they form the majority of university graduates overall (Millar and Jagger 2001). In the US, for example, women are particularly under-represented among graduates in computer and information science (34 per cent) and engineering (21 per cent) (National Science Foundation 2004). At the doctoral level, in computer and information science, women are but 19 per cent, and only 17 per cent in engineering. The exception is the biological sciences, where women continue to be well represented.

This bias in women's and girls' educational choices has major repercussions because employment in the information technology, electronics, and communications sector is graduate intensive. It is reflected in women's low participation in these occupations across the US economy, which declined from 37 per cent in 1993 to 28 per cent at the start of the twenty-first century. Where women are relatively well represented is in the lower status occupations, such as telephone operators, data-processing equipment installers and repairers, and communications equipment operators. By contrast, male graduates are heavily concentrated among computer system analysts and scientists, computer science teachers, computer programmers, operations and systems researchers and analysts, and broadcast equipment operators. These sexual divisions in the labor market mean that women are largely excluded from the processes of technical design that shape the world we live in.

2   MALE DESIGNS ON TECHNOLOGY

Feminists have demonstrated that this marginalization of women from the technological community has a profound influence on the design, technical content, and use of artefacts (Cockburn and Ormrod 1993; Cowan 1983; Lerman, Oldenziel, and Mohun 2003; Lie 2003; Oudshoorn 1994; Wajcman 1991). Technological systems implicitly place men's experiences and men's investments at the centre, without acknowledging their specificity. The corollary is the simultaneous denial of other realities such as women's. A criticism of mainstream science and technology studies has been that in its concern to identify and study the social groups or networks that actively seek to influence the form and direction of technological design, it has overlooked the effects of structural exclusion on technological development. The sociotechnical networks that actor-network theory, for example, is interested in are networks of observable interactions. As a result, agents in these studies are most commonly male heroes, big projects, and important organizations, in what Star (1991) has described as a "managerial or entrepreneurial" model of actor networks. While this theory perceives that artefacts embody relations that went into their making, and that these relations prefigure relations implied in the use and non-use of artefacts, it is less alert to the inevitable gendering of this process.

A technofeminist analysis widens the lens to show how preferences for different technologies are shaped by a set of social arrangements and institutions that reflect men's power and resources in the wider society. A classic example is the routine use of women's bodies as the prime site for biomedical practices and experimentation. "Biomedical scientists and traditional philosophers have encouraged us to assume that women's bodies are simply closer to nature, and consequently easier to incorporate into biomedical practice," while the male reproductive system is, by nature, more resistant to intervention (Oudshoorn 2003, 8). The contraceptive Pill was developed for use by women, rather than men because male scientists were defining women's bodies as more malleable than men's and reproduction as women's responsibility.

Although the technical feasibility of male contraceptives was demonstrated as early as the 1970s, scientists, feminists, journalists, and pharmaceutical entrepreneurs questioned whether men and women would accept a new male contraceptive if one were available. The belated emergence of the male pill reflects changes in gender politics rather than representing recent scientific breakthroughs.

Let us take the example of the wired house as a further illustration of the gender politics of design. One of the great paradoxes of domestic technologies is that, despite being universally promoted as time and labor saving, these technologies have been singularly unsuccessful in lessening women's domestic load (Cowan 1983; Bittman, Rice, and Wajcman 2004). We might have hoped that the electronic home would achieve the wholesale elimination of household labor. The smart houses occupied by the very affluent display what high-technology dwellings might offer the family of the future. Magazines like *Wired* and futuristic films present home networking as the backbone infrastructure of the twenty-first-century lifestyle. But it seems that the designers and producers of the technological home, such as the MIT "House of the Future" have little interest in housework.[3] Home informatics is mainly concerned with the centralized control of heating, lighting, security, information, entertainment, and energy consumption in a local network or "house-brain" (Berg 1994). Prototypes of the intelligent house tend to ignore the whole range of functions that come under the umbrella of housework. The target consumer is implicitly the technically interested and entertainment-oriented male, someone in the designer's own image. The smart house is a deeply masculine vision of a house, rather than a home, somewhat like Corbusier's "machine for living." The routine neglect of women's knowledge, experience, and skills as a resource for technical innovation in the home is symptomatic of the gendered character of the process. So too is the slant in research effort toward technologies that absorb time (home entertainment goods such as television and CD players) rather than save time (such as dishwashers and washing machines) (Hamill 2003). The space-age design is directed to a technological fix rather than envisioning social changes that would see a less gendered allocation of housework and a better balance between working time and family time. The wired home may have much to offer but democracy in the kitchen is not part of the package.

Electronic games are another domain in which the gender politics of technology are played out. In fact video games began at one of the places where computer culture itself got started. The first video game was Space War, built at MIT in the early 1960s (Turkle 1984). Many of the most popular games today are simply programed versions of traditional non-computer games, involving shooting, blowing up, speeding, or zapping in some way or another. They often have militaristic

---

[3] See http://architecture.mit.edu/house_n.

titles such as "Destroy All Subs" and "Brute Force" highlighting their themes of adventure and violence, and the most ubiquitous electronic toy is called "Game-boy." Given that it is predominantly young men (often computer hackers) who design games software, it is hardly surprising that their inventions typically appeal to male fantasies, and reinforce a particular brand of masculinity.

This is not to imply that women are passive victims of technologies. A crucial point is that the relationship between technological and social change is funda-mentally indeterminate. The designers and promoters of a technology cannot completely predict or control its final uses. Technology may well lead a "double life," "one which conforms to the intentions of designers and interests of power and another which contradicts them—proceeding behind the backs of their architects to yield unintended consequences and unanticipated possibilities" (Noble 1984, 325). Rather than conceive of users as passive consumers, science and technology studies scholars have increasingly focused on how users interact with artefacts to become agents of technological change (Oudshoorn and Pinch 2003).

A good illustration of how this double life might operate, and how women can actively subvert the original purposes of a technology, is provided by the diffusion of the telephone. In studies of the American history of the telephone, Fischer (1992) and Martin (1991) show that there was a generation-long mismatch between how the consumers used the telephone and how the industry thought it should be used. The people who developed, built, and marketed telephone systems were predomin-antly telegraph men who assumed that the telephone's main use would be to replicate that of the parent technology, the telegraph. Although sociability (phoning relatives and friends) was and still is the main use of the residential telephone, the telephone industry resisted such uses until the 1920s, condemning this use of the technology for "trivial gossip." Until that time the telephone was sold as a practical business and household tool. When the promoters of the telephone finally began to advertise its use for sociability, this was at least partly in response to subscribers' insistent and rural women's innovative uses of the technology for personal conversation.

3 MOBILIZING IN CYBERSPACE

Interest in these issues has been heightened, and the terms of the debate changed by the rise of the mobile phone and the Internet. Contemporary feminist commentary has been much more positive about the possibilities of new information and communication technologies (ICTs) to empower women and transform gender relations. Indeed, early concerns about women being left out of the communications revolution now seem misplaced. A proliferation of mobile phones, the Internet, and cyber-cafés are providing new opportunities and outlets for women. This is particularly the case for middle-class women in highly industrialized countries who are better placed than other groups of women to take advantage of these technologies. Around the world, although women still account for a lower proportion of Internet users than men, their share is rapidly rising. While the early adopters of the Internet were overwhelmingly men, recent data from the US show no gender difference in Internet use (NTIA 2002). China, a country where Internet take-up is relatively recent, shows how rapidly change can occur. Over a five-year period from 1997, the proportion of Internet users who were female rose from 12 to 39 per cent (CNNIC 2002).

A recurring theme in the literature on ICTs is the fear that the globalization of communications will lead to homogenization, and reduce sociability and engagement with one's community (Sunstein 2001). For example, writers such as Putnam (2000) link ICTs with the earlier form of communications technology—television—as contributing to the loss of civil society and the rise of individualization. However, all the signs are that new electronic media can help to build local communities and project them globally. The expansion of cyberspace makes it possible for even small and poorly resourced NGOs to connect with each other and engage in global social efforts. These political activities are an enormous advance for women who were formerly isolated from larger public spheres and cross-national social initiatives. "We see here the potential transformation of women, 'confined' to domestic roles, who can emerge as key actors in global networks without having to leave their work and roles in their communities" (Sassen 2002, 381). Just as the car increased women's mobility and capacity to participate in public space, so the new media have expanded women's horizons and capacity to connect with networks and campaigns to improve their conditions. To this extent, women are reinterpreting the technologies as a tool for political organizing and the means for creation of new communities.

The highly innovative Million Mom March, held on May 14, 2000, provides an example of the role of electronic space as a crucial force for new forms of civic participation. Bimber (2003) argues that it was the abundance of information and communication technologies that enabled a group of politically inexperienced women to take on the massively resourced National Rifle Association and organize the largest rally in the US history of gun control. While marches have long been a feature of mainstream politics, relying on established political activists, this march of over 100,000 did not fit this pattern. It took place outside the influence of the traditional organizational structure and policy framework for gun control lobbying. The women began their campaign by registering the "Million Mom March" as an Internet domain name. The organization primarily existed in cyberspace, communicating via electronic mail and using the website to built up support and distribute information. The campaign reframed gun policy as a motherhood and family issue: that mothers and others concerned with the health of children should care about gun control. "This reframing, along with low-cost communication techniques and, eventually, coverage by mass media, proved enormously successful at mobilizing citizens not engaged in the traditional contest over crime and the Second Amendment. This fact made the Million Mom March unusual, not only in the gun control arena but more generally in the history of political marches" (Bimber 2003, 164). Communication technologies did not in themselves determine this political action, but they certainly facilitated the formation of new political connections.

4   CYBERFEMINISM

This is not the only way that women have been seizing the opportunities provided by ICTs to shrug off the constraints of their traditional roles. The emergence of cyberfeminism has given voice to a new stream of gender theory that embraces utopian ideas of cyberspace being gender-free and the key to women's liberation. Cyberfeminists claim that the Internet provides the technological basis for a new form of society and a multiplicity of innovative subjectivities. According to Plant (1998), for example, digital technologies facilitate the blurring of boundaries between man and machine and male and female, enabling their users "to choose their disguises and assume alternative identities." Identity exploration challenges existing notions of subjectivity and subverts dominant masculine fantasies.

The idea that the Internet can transform conventional gender roles, altering the relationship between the body and the self via a machine, is a popular theme in postmodern feminism. The message is that young women in particular are colonizing cyberspace where, like gravity gender inequality is suspended. In cyberspace, all physical, bodily cues are removed from communication. As a result, our interactions are fundamentally different because they are not subject to judgments based on sex, age, race, voice, accent, or appearance but are based only on textual exchanges. In *Life on the Screen*, Turkle (1995) enthuses about the potential for people "to express multiple and often unexplored aspects of the self, to play with their identity and to try out new ones ... the obese can be slender, the beautiful plain, the 'nerdy' sophisticated." It is the increasingly interactive and creative nature of computing technology that now enables millions of people to live a significant segment of their lives in virtual reality. Moreover, it is in this computer-mediated world that people experience a new sense of self that is decentered, multiple, and fluid. In this respect, Turkle argues, the Internet is the material expression of the philosophy of postmodernism.

Like many other authors, Turkle (1995, 314) argues that gender-swapping, or virtual cross-dressing, encourages people to reflect on the social construction of gender, to acquire "a new sense of gender as a continuum." In a similar vein, Stone (1995) celebrates the myriad ways that the interactive world of cyberspace is challenging traditional notions of gender identity. Complex virtual identities rupture the cultural belief that there is a single self in a single body. Stone's discussion of phone and virtual sex, for example, describes how female sex workers disguise crucial aspects of identity and can play at reinventing themselves. She takes seriously the notion that virtual people or selves can exist in cyberspace, with no necessary link to a physical body. Our relationship to technology and technical culture, then, are pivotal to the discourse of gender dualisms and gender difference.

The most influential feminist commentator writing in this vein is Donna Haraway (1985; 1997). She argues that we should embrace the positive potential of technoscience, and is sharply critical of those who reject technology. Famously, she prefers to be a "cyborg"—a hybrid of organism and machine parts—rather than an ecofeminist "goddess." She notes the great power of science and technology to create new meanings and new entities, to make new worlds. She positively revels in the very difficulty of predicting what technology's effects will be and warns against any purist rejection of the "unnatural," hybrid entities produced by biotechnology. Genetic engineering, reproductive technology, and the advent of virtual reality are all seen as fundamentally affecting the basic categories of "self" and "gender."

For Haraway, technoscience is a cultural activity that invents Nature, and constructs the nature–culture axis as a classificatory process. This has been the key mechanism for constituting what women are. For feminists then, the collapse of these oppressive binaries—nature/society, animal/man, human/machine, subject/object, machine/organism, metaphor/materiality—is liberating. With the advent of cyber-technology, women gain the power to transcend the biological body and redefine themselves outside the historical categories of woman, other, object. The laws of nature and biology as the basis for gender difference and inequality, have finally lost their authority. The cyborg creature—a human-machine amalgam—fundamentally redefines what it is to be human and thus can potentially exist in a world without gender categories. For Haraway, rupturing the ontological divide between living organisms and dead artefacts necessarily challenges gender dualisms.

Haraway's treatment of femininity and masculinity, and nature and culture as inherently relational, highly contexualized concepts is not unique to post-structuralism. Rather, it echoes the way gender has come to be theorized over the past two decades within feminist theory. It also reflects the increasing preoccupation in social science with the body, sexuality, and the role of biomedical technologies—technologies for the body. In studies of childbirth and contraception, in-vitro fertilization, cosmetic surgery, and genetic engineering, feminists have argued that there is no such thing as the natural, physiological body. One consequence of this work is that the conventional distinction between sex (natural) and gender (social) has been thoroughly contested and deconstructed. Technologies, like science are now seen as contributing to the stabilization of meanings of the body. With the rise of modern science, bodies have become objects that can be transformed with an increasing number of tools and techniques. Modern bodies are made and remade through science and technology; they too are technological artefacts (Clarke 1998). The cyborg metaphor has been widely adopted within feminist studies to capture this idea: that sexed bodies and gendered identities are co-produced with technoscience.

5   MATERIAL RELATIONS

Feminist theories of the woman–machine relationship have long oscillated between pessimistic fatalism and utopian optimism. The same technological innovations have been categorically rejected as oppressive to women and uncritically embraced as inherently liberating. While there was a tendency in early second-wave feminist writing to treat women as passive victims of technological change, postmodern cultural theories such as cyberfeminism too often see the digital revolution as offering unlimited freedom. Both the virtuality of cyberspace and the prosthetic possibilities of biotechnologies spell the end of naturalized, biological embodiment as the basis for gender difference. While such work has stimulated important new insights into the gender power relations of technology, it risks fetishizing the new. Such a discourse of radical discontinuity has echoes of technological determinism. Technology itself is seen as liberating women, as if these new technologies are an autonomous, gender-neutral force reconfiguring social relations. Digital technologies, like older technologies are malleable and contain contradictory possibilities, but they also reveal continuities of power and exclusion, albeit in new forms.

Recent feminist writing within science and technology studies, technofeminism, eschews both the lingering tendency to view technology as necessarily patriarchal and the temptation to essentialize gender. Moreover, it points to the connections between gender inequality and other forms of inequality, that come into view if we examine the broader political and economic basis of the networks that shape and deploy technical systems. In particular, this means tying together the material realities of a technology's production and use.

Much of the triumphalism about digitization rests on the assumption that we are living in a post-industrial consumer-based society. There is a widespread belief that production is no longer the organizing principle of contemporary society. The focus has shifted to information, consumption, culture, and lifestyle. However, production has not disappeared, but is being carried out in strikingly novel forms on an increasingly global basis. Much low-skilled assembly-line work has moved offshore to the third world and is predominantly performed by women rather than men. The quintessential product and symbol of the new age, the computer is often manufactured in precisely this fashion. For a young woman in the West, her silver cell phone is experienced as a liberating extension of her body. The social relations of production that underpin its existence are invisible to her.

As material objects, mobile phones have to be mass produced in factories. Furthermore, along with other electronic devices, such as laptops they require the scarce mineral Coltan. One of the few places where this can be found is Central Africa, where it is mined under semi-feudal and colonial labor relations, to provide raw product for Western multinational companies (Agar 2003). The sharp rise in the price of Coltan on global markets has local effects, accentuating exploitation and conflict among competing militias, with the very specific consequences for women that military conflict brings—namely, rape and prostitution. A mobile phone then is a very different artefact depending upon a person's place within the sociotechnical network.

6   CONCLUSION

Understanding the place of new technologies from a political perspective requires avoiding a purely technological interpretation and recognizing the variable outcomes of these technologies for different social orders. Technologies embody and advance political interests and agendas and they are the product of social structure, culture, values, and politics as much as the result of objective scientific discovery. They can indeed be constitutive of new gender dynamics, but they can also be derivative and reproduce older conditions. The electronic revolution has coincided with massive social transformations associated with increasing emancipation of women worldwide, economically, culturally, politically. The old discourse of sex difference has been made increasingly untenable by the dramatic changes in technology, by the challenge of feminism, and by awareness of the mutating character of the natural world. For all the diversity of feminist voices, there is a shared concern with the hierarchical divisions between men and women that order the world we inhabit. The process of technical change is integral to the renegotiation of gender power relations. But technology is not a surrogate for political action—neither in the past, nor in the future. Revolutions in technology do not create new societies, but they do change the terms in which social, political, and economic relations are played out. Science and technology embody values, and have the potential to embody different values. The recognition that gender and technology are mutually constitutive opens up fresh possibilities for feminist scholarship and action.

REFERENCES

AGAR, J. 2003. *Constant Touch: A Global History of the Mobile Phone.* Cambridge: Icon Books.

BERG, A. J. 1994. A gendered socio-technical construction: the smart house. Pp. 165–80 in *Bringing Technology Home: Gender and Technology in a Changing Europe*, ed. C. Cockburn and R. F. Dilic. Milton Keynes: Open University Press.

——1996. *Digital Feminism.* Report No. 28. Dragvoll: Senter for Tenologi og Samfunn, Norwegian University of Science and Technology.

BIMBER, B. 2003. *Information and American Democracy: Technology in the Evolution of Political Power.* Cambridge: Cambridge University Press.

BITTMAN, M., RICE, J., and WAJCMAN, J. 2004. Appliances and their impact: the ownership of domestic technology and time spent on household work. *British Journal of Sociology,* 55: 401–23.

CASTELLS, M. 2001. *The Internet Galaxy.* Oxford: Oxford University Press.

CLARKE, A. 1998. *Disciplining Reproduction: Modernity, American Life Sciences, and "the Problems of Sex."* Berkeley: University of California Press.

CNNIC. 2002. 11th Survey Report. Available at: www.cnnic.net.cn.

COCKBURN, C. 1983. *Brothers: Male Dominance and Technological Change.* London: Pluto Press.

——and ORMROD, S. 1993. *Gender and Technology in the Making.* London: Sage.

CONNELL, B. 1987. *Gender and Power.* Cambridge: Polity Press.

COWAN, R. S. 1983. *More Work for Mother: The Ironies of Household Technology from the Open Hearth to the Microwave.* New York: Basic Books.

DYER, R. 1997. *White.* London: Rouledge.

FAULKNER, W. 2001. The technology question in feminism: a view from feminist technology studies. *Women's Studies International Forum*, 24 (1): 79–95.

——and LOHAN, M. 2004. Masculinities and technologies. *Men and Masculinities*, 6 (4): 319–29.

FISCHER, C. S. 1992. *America Calling: A Social History of the Telephone to 1940.* Berkeley: University of California Press.

HACKER, S. 1989. *Pleasure, Power and Technology.* Boston: Unwin Hyman.

HAMILL, L. 2003. Time as a rare commodity in home life. Pp. 63–78 in *Inside the Smart House*, ed. R. Harper. London: Springer.

HARAWAY, D. 1985. A manifesto for cyborgs: science, technology, and socialist feminism in the 1980's. *Socialist Review*, 80: 65–108.

——1997. *Modest_Witness@Second_Millennium. FemaleMan©_Meets_Oncomouse™.* New York: Routledge.

HELD, D. 1995. *Democracy and the Global Order.* Cambridge: Polity Press.

LATOUR, B. 1991. Technology is society made durable. Pp. 103–31 in *A Sociology of Monsters: Essays on Power, Technology and Domination*, ed. J. Law. London: Routledge.

LERMAN, N. E., OLDENZIEL, R., and MOHUN, A. P. (eds.) 2003. *Gender and Technology: A Reader*. Baltimore: John Hopkins University Press.

LIE, M. (ed.) 2003. *He, She and IT Revisited: New Perspectives on Gender in the Information Society*. Oslo: Gyldendal.

LUKES, S. 1974. *Power*. London: Macmillan.

MACKENZIE, D., and WAJCMAN, J. 1999. *The Social Shaping of Technology*, 2nd edn. Milton Keynes: Open University Press.

MARTIN, M. 1991. *"Hello Central?" Gender, Technology, and the Culture in the Formation of Telephone Systems*. Montreal: McGill-Queen's University Press.

MILLAR, J., and JAGGER, N. 2001. *Women in ITEC Courses and Careers*. London: Women and Equality Unit, DTI.

NATIONAL SCIENCE FOUNDATION. 2004. *Women, Minorities, and Persons with Disabilities in Science and Engineering*. NSF04–317. Arlington, Va.: Division of Science Resources Statistics.

NATIONAL TELECOMMUNICATIONS AND INFORMATION ADMINISTRATION (NTIA). 2002. *A Nation Online: How Americans Are Expanding their Use of the Internet*. Washington, DC: US Department of Commerce.

NOBLE, D. 1984. *Forces of Production: A Social History of Industrial Automation*. New York: Knopf.

OLDENZIEL, R. 1999. *Making Technology Masculine: Men, Women and Modern Machines in America*. Amsterdam: Amsterdam University Press.

OUDSHOORN, N. 1994. *Beyond the Natural Body: An Archaeology of Sex Hormones*. London: Routledge.

—— 2003. *The Male Pill: A Biography of a Technology in the Making*. Durham, NC: Duke University Press.

—— and PINCH, T. (eds.) 2003. *How Users Matter: The Co-construction of Users and Technology*. Cambridge, Mass.: MIT Press.

PLANT, S. 1998. *Zeros and Ones*. London: Fourth Estate.

PUTNAM, R. D. 2000. *Bowling Alone: The Collapse and Revival of American Community*. New York: Simon and Schuster.

SASSEN, S. 2002. Towards a sociology of information technology. *Current Sociology*, 50: 365–88.

SORENSEN, K., and STEWART, J. (eds.) 2002. *Digital Divides and Inclusion Measures: A Review of Literature and Statistical Trends on Gender and ICT*. Trondheim: NTNU.

STANLEY, A. 1995. *Mothers and Daughters of Invention*. New Brunswick, NJ.: Rutgers University Press.

STAR, S. L. 1991. Power, technologies and the phenomenology of conventions: on being allergic to onions. In Law 1991, 26–56.

—— (ed.) 1995. *The Cultures of Computing*. Oxford: Blackwell.

STONE, A. R. 1995. *The War of Desire and Technology at the Close of the Mechanical Age*. Cambridge, Mass.: MIT Press.

SUNSTEIN, C. R. 2001. *Republic.com*. Princeton, NJ: Princeton University Press.

TURKLE, S. 1984. *The Second Self: Computers and the Human Spirit*. London: Granada.

—— 1995. *Life on the Screen: Identity in the Age of the Internet*. New York: Simon and Schuster.

WAJCMAN, J. 1991. *Feminism Confronts Technology.* University Park: Pennsylvania State University Press.

——2004. *Technofeminism.* Cambridge: Polity Press.

CHAPTER 39

....

MILITARY TECHNOLOGIES AND POLITICS

....

WIM A. SMIT

There must be more—and more adequate—military research in peacetime. It is essential that the civilian scientists continue in peacetime some portion of those contributions to national security which they have made so effectively during the war. (Vannevar Bush, 1945)

In the councils of government, we must guard against the acquisition of unwarranted influence, whether sought or unsought, by the military-industrial complex...Yet, in holding scientific research and discovery in respect, as we should, we must also be alert to the equal and opposite danger that public policy could itself become the captive of a scientific-technological elite. (President Dwight D. Eisenhower, Farewell Address, 1961)

IN HIS 1852 article on "The Eighteenth Brumaire" Karl Marx wrote: "Men make their own history, but they make it not of their own accord or under self-chosen conditions, but under given and transmitted conditions." To what extent does this observation for politics and policy-making hold when we view current weaponry and military technological developments as such conditions? And, to what extent have weaponry and military technology shaped political analysis, or in what way have they themselves become a subject of political analysis? Technology, in particular military technology matters indeed, in various ways, as this chapter will show.

From the beginning of human civilization, around 5000 BC, military relationships, in interplay with the three other basic (organizational) sources of power[1] distinguished by Michael Mann in his masterpiece on social power (Mann 1986–93), have been important in structuring and shaping human social relations. Military power, in its turn, was influenced by technological change, as was the case with many other human activities like agriculture, transport, sailing, communication, and later, industrial production. For instance, innovations in chariot design just after 2000 BC helped to change the balance of power in Eurasia, whereas the chariot's superiority, in its turn, was finally ended by a metallurgical revolution around 1200–1000 BC that developed cheap iron tools, weapons, and body armor (Mann 1986, 162, 179–89). However, military technology is only one element in warfare. At least as important is military organization and tactics (Mann 1986, 100, 162–5, 199–203, 453–8; McNeill 1982).

Still, through the centuries the way wars have been fought has been greatly influenced by science and technology (McNeill 1982). New technologies can change the balance of warfare, though in due time they are usually copied by other parties. Inventions like gunpowder, artillery, and rifles revolutionized warfare, though often more by a prolonged cumulative effect, taking many decades of development if not more than a century (McNeill 1982, 83). Individual scientists, for centuries, have advised the military on specific problems: Archimedes reportedly helped the tyrant of Syracuse in devising new weaponry against the Romans in 212 BC; Leonardo da Vinci supplied us with a variety of drawings of new armaments; and, since the emergence of "modern" science in the sixteenth and seventeenth centuries, many prominent scientists, including Tartaglia, Galileo, Newton, Descartes, Bernouilli, and Euler have devoted some of their time and intellect to helping solve military problems. Subsequently, the Industrial Revolution and its inventions impacted the military as well,[2] e.g. through the transition from sailing ships to vessels propelled by steam engines, through the railway system providing a (sometimes dedicated) transport infrastructure for the military, but also by the introduction of mechan-

---

[1] These are: ideological, economic, and political relationships. Mann locates the four basic power sources in *overlapping networks of social interaction*. "They are also *organizations, institutional means of attaining human goals*. Their primacy comes not from the strength of human desires for ideological, economic, military, or political satisfaction but from the particular *organizational means* each possesses to attain human goals, whatever these may be ... The four sources of power offer alternative organizational means of social control" (Mann 1986, 2–3, italics in original).

[2] The military were often not eager to adopt new technologies, as noted, for instance by McNeill (1982, 224): "The ritual routine of army and navy life as developed across centuries discouraged innovation of any kind. Only when civilian techniques had advanced clearly and unmistakably beyond levels already incorporated into military and naval practice, did it become possible to overcome official inertia and conservatism." See also Douglas (1985) and Van Creveld (1989, 223).

ized (mass) production techniques for manufacturing military equipment.[3] The early twentieth century and First World War years also saw the rise of autocars and tanks propelled by internal combustion motors.

With the rise of modern national states holding, at least formally the monopoly of the legitimate use of (military and police) force, military power became an integral part of the state (Tilly 1990; Mann 1993, ch. 3). That warfare and military developments greatly impacted on national states may be evident from the fact that eighteenth-century Great Powers were at war in 78 percent of years and nineteenth-century ones in 40 percent (Tilly 1990, 72; Mann 1993, 412). The accompanying adoption of new military technologies had a series of indirect but profound political effects such as (*a*) promoting new forms and levels of extraction by states, including the classic ratchet effect by which taxes rise dramatically during wars but almost never return to their pre-war levels; (*b*) creating state bureaucracies; (*c*) altering the experience of, and access to weapons and military experience in the general population (Tilly 1990).

The scope of this chapter, however, will be narrower than these broad issues and focus specifically on military technological change and its relation with both politics and political analysis. By an in-depth analysis of military technological innovation since the Second World War, we will show that this relation actually represents an *entwined evolution* (or co-evolution) of military technology, politics, and political analysis. The co-evolutionary nature of this process is not typical of the post-Second World War period, but a general feature of the interplay between military (as well as civil) technological change and societal developments. The *content* of such co-evolutionary processes, however, will differ between periods and for different technologies. This approach, in a modest way, matches Mann's analysis of the interplay and transformation of "overlapping networks of social interaction" that represent his four sources of social power.

The reason for focusing on the post-Second World War period is that the Second World War produced a dramatic change in the way scientists became involved in military matters and military technological innovation. Science and scientists in great numbers were mobilized for weapons innovation in a highly organized and concentrated effort. In the USA these scientists contributed, mainly under the auspices of the newly established Office of Scientific Research and Development (OSRD), to the development of a variety of new technologies, including the atomic bomb, radar, the proximity fuse, and penicillin (Rhodes 1986; Baxter 1968). The decisive contribution of scientists to these war efforts implied a fundamental shift in the role of science and technology in future military affairs. This is exemplified by the advice of the wartime director of OSRD and US science policy adviser Vannevar Bush (1945; 1980, 6) to the President, quoted at the start of this chapter.

---

[3] Actually, armament manufacturers responding to needs and requirements from the military, developed manufacturing methods, that in their turn spilled over to the civilian sector (Smith 1985).

His advice stood in sharp contrast to Thomas Alva Edison's suggestion, many years before, during the First World War, to the Navy, that it should bring into the war effort at least *one* physicist in case it became necessary to "calculate something" (Gilpin 1962, 10).

For the first time in history military research and development (R&D) became a large-scale organized and institutionalized process even in peacetime, indeed on a scale not seen before; it was legitimized as well as fueled by the climate of the cold war. In the decades following the Second World War, weapons generations succeeded each other in a rapid process of "planned obsolescence". The R&D was carried out in national laboratories, the defense industry, laboratories of the military services, and at universities to varying degrees in different countries. In 2000 an estimated 54 billion dollars was spent on military R&D by NATO countries and Russia.[4] At the same time these huge efforts of weapons innovation became politically controversial (see Section 2 below).

Whereas developing *"command technology,"* defined by McNeill as "seeking deliberately to create a new weapons system surpassing existing capabilities" (McNeill 1982, 173–4) has occurred at times in the past few centuries, it remained exceptional until about 1880, when an arms race developed, in particular on warship technology (McNeill 1982, 279–85; Mann 1993, 496–7). The era after the Second World War is distinct for several reasons: not only would it be more apt now to speak of "command *science* and technology," but also the scale, speed, and organizational complexity of the innovation process, as well as the breadth of science and technologies involved, have become so tremendous that one may really speak of a revolution of the weapons innovation process.

This organized and systematic pursuit of military R&D for weapons innovation interacts in a threefold way with politics and political analysis:

- Weapons innovation and military technology have become a subject of politics and policy-making, both nationally (military R&D and weapons acquisition) and internationally (e.g. arms control agreements and laws of war).
- Weapons innovation and its interaction with national and international security have become a subject of political analysis (as it is for other fields, including studies on technology development and its societal impact).
- Military and dual use technology developments as well as their impacts are complex phenomena, influenced by many factors which are not under the control of policy-makers. But, being relevant for many policy issues these developments, as well as studies on their dynamics constitute at least a context of importance for politics.

---

[4] During the period 1991–6, after the end of the Cold War, the amount spent annually on military R&D decreased by about 10 billion dollars and then stabilized at a level of about 54 billion dollars (SIPRI 2003, 405–6).

These three types of interaction will be elaborated in the following sections. It will be shown that there is not a "one way impact," neither from military technological developments on politics and political analysis, nor vice versa. The influence is one of mutual shaping, a process which may be characterized as the *co-evolution* of military technology and both politics and political analysis (compare Rip and Kemp 1998; Moors, Rip, and Wiskerke 2004; Geels 2004).

1   WEAPONS INNOVATION AND MILITARY TECHNOLOGY BECOME A SUBJECT OF POLITICS

1.1   The Institutionalization of Military R&D and Weapons Innovation

Following Vannevar Bush's advice, an extensive and broad military R&D program started—or better, was continued—after the end of the Second World War. It included atomic weapons research, the development of (long range) missiles and aircraft, nuclear propelled submarines, military electronics, and chemical weapons. Moreover, it also provided substantial military funding of basic research at many elite universities, like MIT, CalTech, Carnegie Mellon, Stanford, and Johns Hopkins, based on the idea that basic science was a main source for new military technologies (Smit 1995*a*). Later, its utility for defense was doubted, succinctly phrased by the Secretary of Defense Charles E. Wilson in the mid 1950s: "Basic research is when you don't know what you are doing" (Kevles 1979, 383). The pervasive influence of military-funded R&D also led to a wide involvement of university faculty through advisorships to the US Department of Defense, military laboratories, or the defense industry, that is, involvement in politics on military technology.[5] Well-known is the JASON group in the USA, consisting of excellent scientists, forming a "second generation" advisory pool for the military, often advising through "Summer studies" (Kevles 1979, 402). In particular during the Vietnam War, in the 1960s and 1970s, such university–military links became highly controversial (Kevles 1979; Dickson 1984).

---

[5] Gilpin 1962; York and Greb 1982. For scientists involved in French atomic policy, see Weart 1979; Goldschmidt 1980. For the Soviet Union, see Holloway 1994. For the UK, see Arnold 2000.

1.2   The Need for Control

Next to US governmental support for the development of new weapons (including the hydrogen bomb—a thousand times more destructive than the uranium and plutonium bombs dropped on Hiroshima and Nagasaki, respectively), already by the end of the Second World War concern arose about other countries possibly obtaining nuclear weapons, in particular the Soviet Union, but also (industrialized) Western European countries like France and Sweden (and later also West Germany). The issue of preventing the proliferation of nuclear weapons was born. Concerns both about the actual use and about the spread of atomic weapons had already been raised from 1944 by a number of scientists involved in the US Manhattan Project. These scientists, including Niels Bohr, Leo Szilard, and a number of physicists drawing up the so-called Franck report (June 1945) urged for openness and international control of the further development of atomic energy after the war, rather than pursuing a futile course of secrecy by the USA (Hewlett and Anderson 1990).

In 1946 the USA submitted the Baruch Plan, based on the Acheson–Lilienthal Report, for international control of atomic energy to the United Nations. The terms were unacceptable to the Soviet Union because the United States would keep its nuclear weapon monopoly for some time to come. The counter-proposal by the Soviet Union—the Gromyko Plan—in its turn was unacceptable to the USA (Goldblat 1982, 13–14; Hewlett and Anderson 1990, 530–619). Thus the first attempt at arms control foundered. From then on the proliferation of nuclear weapons started, first the Soviet Union, then Great Britain, France, and China, and later India, Israel, South Africa,[6] and Pakistan. It implied the start of a technological arms race between East and West not only on nuclear weapons, but on all kinds of weaponry that resulted from the new institutionalized, science-based search for advanced military technologies, including missiles, missile defense systems, military satellites, anti-satellite weapons, nuclear submarines, anti-submarine systems, precision-guided weapons, sensors, chemical and biological weapons, C^3I (Command, Control, Communications and Intelligence) technologies, and so on.

1.3   Arms Control on the Political Agenda

Though the first attempt at arms control foundered, arms control has been on the international political agenda since. A machinery of bilateral (USA–Soviet Union), trilateral (USA–UK–SU), and multilateral (usually under the aegis of the United

---

[6] On 24 March 1993, South Africa's President F. W. de Klerk disclosured that South Africa had developed and produced nuclear weapons in the late 1970s but had dismantled and destroyed them before joining the Non-Proliferation Treaty in 1991 (SIPRI 1994).

Nations) negotiations on a variety of arms control issues came into being. Though often troublesome, these negotiations have resulted in quite a number of arms control agreements (see, e.g., Goldblat 1982 and SIPRI Yearbooks), including limitations on the number of nuclear weapons and delivery vehicles, or dealing with nuclear weapon-free zones, restrictions on nuclear weapons tests, non-proliferation, prohibition of chemical and biological weapons and of "environmental modification techniques," non-militarization of outer space, and conventional arms limitations in Europe. Such agreements aimed at least formally at curbing the "quantitative" and "qualitative" (i.e. technological) arms race, which had actually already been foreseen by a number of scientists (and warned against) by the end of the Second World War. One difficulty that emerged time and again was that the proclaimed goals of such agreements were undermined or circumvented—intentionally or not—by the development of new military technologies. Moreover, in many cases technologies and equipment could be used for both civil and military activities. For instance, uranium enrichment plants may produce nuclear fuel for nuclear power plants, but also highly enriched uranium for a nuclear bomb (Krass et al. 1983; Albright, Berkhout, and Walker 1997). Chemicals used in the civil sector may also be "precursors" of chemical weapons. The *dual use* character of such technologies makes it hard to control their spread to other countries (Brauch et al. 1992). We will further elaborate on this issue in Section 3 below.

By now it may have become evident that the strongly institutionalized and organized military technological innovation since the Second World War has strongly influenced (the focus of) politics and policy-making, for instance by transforming traditional national and international security issues (see also Section 2). At the same time these huge weapons innovation efforts, in their turn, were facilitated and supported, and sometimes constrained ("arms control") through these evolving political processes, showing the co-evolutionary character of these developments. Military technology was put on the (international) political agenda, becoming itself the subject of politics.

National governments often sought to obtain nuclear weapons and missiles not only for purely military reasons. National pride and prestige and influence were additional critical factors in obtaining these weapons, as was the case with Great Britain (Arnold 2000) and France (Goldschmidt 1967; Scheinman 1965). It was not only politicians who pushed the technology. Scientists and engineers from military laboratories, the defense industry, and universities were often influential in getting political support for the new military technologies they advocated. So much that politicians sometimes felt captives of this scientific-technological elite, as exemplified by the Eisenhower quote at the beginning of this chapter.[7]

---

[7] See also York 1971, 9–14; Killian 1977, 237–9.

2   WEAPONS INNOVATION AND ITS EFFECTS

2.1   Scientists and Engineers Enter the Scene of Political Analysis

Traditionally, the study of weapons and military technology focused on their impact on war-fighting and gaining victory and in a number of cases, on subsequent wider societal effects. It was the domain mainly of (military) historians.[8] Not surprisingly, after the Second World War, the breed of scholars involved has changed related to the interweaving of politics and the organized, continuous, and high-pace innovation of military technology in peacetime (fueled by the Cold War).

First, scientists and engineers, many of whom had been involved in the development of nuclear weapons entered the scene. For one, they were moved by moral concerns about the weapons of mass destruction they had developed. They also became concerned about the huge military R&D effort and the resulting weapons which in their view might cause a rapid *decrease* rather than an *increase* of national (and international) security (see, e.g., York 1971, 228). For instance, nuclear missiles, once launched by the adversary would leave only very brief decision time—tens of minutes, or even less—to react. A mere warning—false or not—that the adversary had launched its nuclear missiles might trigger nuclear war. The risk of a preemptive strike by an adversary put pressure towards a nuclear policy of "use them or lose them," thus worsening "crisis instability" (Ball and Richelson 1986).

Using their inside knowledge of the workings of new military technologies, these natural scientists and engineers were able to open up the "black box" of technology and make thorough and extensive impact studies on national and international security and on arms control. These studies pointed out, for instance, that the anti-ballistic missile (ABM) systems, consisting of many land-based anti-missile missiles, as proposed by the USA in the 1960s would actually stimulate the Soviet Union to deploy even more nuclear missiles to saturate the US defense system. Also, a similar ABM system by the Soviet Union would trigger the USA to deploy multi-warhead missiles (MIRVs—Multiple Independently Targetable Re-entry Vehicles). These missiles, carrying up to twelve nuclear warheads, could thus saturate the capabilities of the Soviet ABM interception missiles. Actually, the development and deployment of MIRVed missiles by the USA *preceded* a possible Soviet ABM system. As the then US Defense Secretary, Robert McNamara wrote (quoted in Allison and Morris 1975, 118):

---

[8] See, e.g., McNeill 1982; Parker 1988; Van Creveld 1989. For an excellent and critical review of studies on the history of military technology see Hacker (1994), which includes a wealth of references; see also Roland (1985; 1993).

Because the Soviet Union *might* [emphasis in original] deploy extensive ABM defenses, we are making some very important changes in our strategic missile forces. Instead of a single large warhead our missiles are now being designed to carry several small warheads...Deployment by the Soviets of a ballistic missile defense of their cities will not improve their situation. We have *already* [emphasis added] taken the necessary steps to guarantee that our strategic offensive forces will be able to overcome such a defense.

This weapons innovation "dynamic" was aptly encapsulated by Jerome Wiesner, former science adviser to President John F. Kennedy, as "we are in an arms race with ourselves—and we are winning." In the 1990s, when the USA continued its efforts to develop anti-satellite (ASAT) technology capable of destroying an adversary's satellites, Wiesner's words could rightly have been paraphrased as "we are in an arms race with ourselves—and we are losing." For the irony here is that it is the US military system that more than any other country's defense system, has become dependent on satellites (for communication, early warning, weapons guidance, reconnaissance, eavesdropping, and so on), would be highly vulnerable to a hostile ASAT system. The most likely route, however, for hostile countries to obtain the advanced ASAT technology would not be through their own R&D, but through the *proliferation*, that is, diffusion of US ASAT technology once it had been developed. Thus the USA would very likely decrease rather than increase its own security by developing ASAT technology.

Many of the early and later "impact assessments" of weapons innovations assessed their potential for circumventing or undermining existing international agreements that aimed at halting the arms race, like the Anti-Ballistic Missile (ABM) Treaty (1972) and the accompanying Strategic Arms Limitation Agreements (SALT 1972), the SALT II Treaty (1979), and a Comprehensive Test Ban Treaty (CTBT 1996). Natural scientists, with their inside technological knowledge, also contributed to developing and assessing verification technologies that made arms control agreements politically acceptable (Gilpin 1962; Tsipis, Hafemeister, and Janeway 1986).

In addition, assessments were made, both by independent scientists and governmental agencies, of the potential for civil technologies to spill over into military applications: for in such cases, countries could, under the guise of developing civil technologies make all the preparations needed for developing nuclear, chemical, or biological weapons (Krass et al. 1983). These "dual-use" technologies could be a route to the proliferation of weapons, for instance by lowering the threshold for obtaining those weapons without formally violating the Non Proliferation Treaty (1971), the Comprehensive Test Ban Treaty (1996), the Biological Weapons Convention (1972), or the Chemical Weapons Convention (1993). The *Arms Control* readings (York 1973) from the Magazine *Scientific American* provide an instructive sample of early defense technology assessments.

2.2 Military Technology, Arms Control, National and International Security

Next to the scientists and engineers, policy and defense analysts became involved in studies on the impact of new military technologies on arms control and national and international security. "Think tanks" and dedicated defense/political/arms control research institutes came into being, such as Rand Corporation and the Brookings Institution in the USA, the International Institute for Strategic Studies (London), and the Stockholm International Peace Research Institute (SIPRI) to name a few.

Related to the new "reality" of nuclear weapons, the new breed of analysts developed new military-political doctrines for the USA and NATO, including Massive Retaliation and MAD (Mutual Assured Destruction) to deter the Warsaw Pact both from attacking NATO countries and from using nuclear weapons. New doctrinal concepts were introduced like "massive retaliation," "preemptive first strike," "nuclear threshold," and "flexible response" (Ball and Richelson 1986; Freedman 2003; Schelling 1966). These new doctrines, in turn entered politics (and the military). Subsequently, US military R&D, (nuclear) weapons acquisition, and the US military posture were geared to support such doctrines (Enthoven and Smith 1971).

Other analysts focused on international arrangements for arms control and on the required verification of such agreements (see e.g. Stanford Arms Control Group 1976). Also the innovations from systematic military R&D on conventional weapons, in particular from the 1960s (e.g. precision-guided weapons, sensors, and electronic warfare) triggered studies of their impact on military doctrines (see, e.g., Holst and Nerlich 1977; Alford 1981).

One may conclude that the new military technologies resulting from the systematic pursuit of weapons innovation have profoundly transformed both the (inter-) national security situation and the study of these security issues. Here again we see a co-evolution of weapons innovation processes, focus and content of political analysis, and politics.

2.3 Dynamics of the Technological Arms Race

A plethora of studies have appeared on the *dynamics* of the technological arms race (see, e.g., Gleditsch and Njølstad 1990), including the nature of military R&D and the weapons acquisition process.[9] Many of them dealt with what President Eisen-

---

[9] See, e.g., Long and Reppy 1980; York 1971; Allison and Morris 1975; Brooks, 1975; Greenwood 1975.

hower in his much-cited farewell address called the military-industrial complex, later extended to include the bureaucracy as well. Such studies belong to what has been called the bureaucratic-politics school or domestic structure model (Buzan 1987, ch. 7), in contrast to the action–reaction models (Buzan 1987, ch. 6), which focus on interstate interactions as an explanation for the dynamics of the arms race. A third approach, the technological imperative model (Buzan 1987, ch. 8) sees technological change as an independent factor in the arms race, causing an almost unavoidable advance in military technology, if only for its links with civil technological progress—though a link whose importance is under debate (see Section 3). To some extent, these studies might be considered as complementary, focusing on different elements in a complex pattern of weapons development and procurement. For instance, the "reaction" behavior in the interstate model might be translated into the "legitimation" process of domestically driven weapons developments.

A number of these studies originated from a concern about the weapons innovation process being "out of control." However, what does it mean to "bring weapons innovation under political control?" On the face of it, the concept seems obvious but it actually needs elaboration. In national politics there is often no consensus on the kinds of armament that are desirable or necessary.[10] Those who say that politics is not in control may actually mean that developments are not in accordance with their political preferences, whereas those who are quite content with current developments may be inclined (though not necessarily) to say that politics is in control. Neither position is analytically satisfactory. But neither is it satisfactory so to say that politics is in control simply because actual weapons innovations are the outcome of the political process, which includes lobbying of defense contractors, interservice rivalry, bureaucratic politics, arguments over ideology and strategic concepts, and so forth, as Greenwood (1990) has suggested. Rather than speaking of control, one should ask whether it would be possible to influence the innovation process in a systematic way, or to steer it according to some guiding principle (Smit 1989). This implies that the basic issue of "control," even for those who are content with current developments, concerns whether it would be possible to change their course *if this were desired*. This issue will be further discussed in the next section.

[10] For instance, where the anti-nuclear weapon movement rallied against nuclear weapons because of their apocalyptic character, others have argued based on the same apocalyptic character, that "modern weaponry has made war too dangerous for nuclear powers to use as an instrument of policy" (Wright 1965, 1514–9; see also Roland 1995).

3   TECHNOLOGY AS A "CONTEXT" OF POLITICS AND POLICY-MAKING?

3.1   The Co-evolution of Technology and Society

In Sections 1 and 2 above, we showed the close interaction between military technological innovation (as institutionalized since the Second World War), politics, and political analysis characterized as a process of co-evolution. The picture of a new technology, originating from an "autonomous" technological development, having its (long term) impact on society is a distorted picture of the complex interactions between technological and societal developments.[11] Insights from Science and Technology Studies show that technological developments are not independent or decoupled from societal developments, but that the two are closely entwined (Bijker, Hughes, and Pinch 1987; Bijker and Law 1992). Indeed, those developments are better described as a process of *co-evolution* or *co-production* (Rip and Kemp 1998; Moors, Rip, and Wiskerke 2004; Geels 2002; 2004).

The stirrup, invented around the turn of the fifth–sixth century and entering the European scene in the early eighth century, turned out to be a revolutionary and decisive factor in war fighting at the time. The new (military) technology, by formidably enhancing the charge of knights not only implied superiority on the battlefield. In the centuries following, as argued by White (1962), it also catalyzed the transformation of the social and political structure of Europe into the feudal system (see also Roland 2003). Whereas its short-term effects (superiority on the battlefield) might have been foreseen (and were actually recognized, for instance by the Frankish king Charles Martel, around AD 732), this certainly is not the case for its long-term effect (the rise of the feudal system), which actually resulted from the co-evolution of technology and society. The general phenomenon of "co-evolution" is also evident from cross-cultural studies of the development and impact of specific technologies, like the stirrup in Europe and Asia, or the clock in China and Europe (Landes 1983). Likewise, in his social history of the machine gun Ellis (1993) has shown the intricate interweaving of weapons innovation with social, military, cultural, and political factors.

Here we have part of the answer to the question relating to the quotation from Marx at the start of this chapter. In the long term, weaponry inherited from the past provides an important and given context—i.e. *not self-chosen* conditions—for politics and policy-making that cannot easily be changed, at least not in the short term. This "given context" is actually equivalent to the long-term evolving *socio-technical landscape* in a *co-evolutionary multi-level approach* of technological

---

[11] See for these complex interactions, Jasanoff et al. (1995).

innovation (Rip and Kemp 1998; Moors, Rip, and Wiskerke 2004; Geels 2002; 2004). Landscapes, at the macro level in this approach encompass material and immaterial elements: material infrastructures, political cultures and coalitions, social values, world-views, and paradigms. They are beyond the direct influence of actors and evolve over time, partly through accumulating developments at the lower levels. In this approach, the meso-level is the level of *socio-technical regimes* which describe the dominant practices, rules, and assumptions in techno-logical innovation processes. The micro level (or *niche level*), describing individual actors (including organizations) and local practices in technology developments, often is a source for initiating change at the higher levels. A basic feature of this analytical model for understanding technological innovation is the interaction between the levels in this multilayered structure of co-evolutionary sociotechnical change.

If the weaponry context inherited from the past cannot easily be changed, what about current (and future) military technological developments? The co-evolu-tionary multilevel model implies that we have given only part of the answer to Marx's issue, as the reader may also have sensed from Section 1, which dealt with military R&D and weapons innovation as a subject of politics. The process of co-evolution implies that politics may influence (military) technological develop-ments, but also that such influence often will be limited.[12] We now return to the issue of "control," in the previous section reformulated as the capability to change the course of military technology and weapons innovation. We will discuss two main aspects of relevance to the question of control, namely (*a*) the role of socio-technical networks, and (*b*) the issue of dual-use technology and the integration of civil and military technology.

3.2   Socio-technical Networks

We have emphasized the interweaving of technological and societal developments, coined as a "seamless web" (Bijker, Hughes, and Pinch 1987). Taking into account this seamless web character and at the same time be able to analyze the intertwined social and technological processes, an approach in terms of "socio-technical net-works" (both as analytical tool and as a representation of the dynamics of techno-logical developments) appears to be useful (Elzen, Enserink, and Smit 1996; Smit 1995*b*). In the multilevel approach these networks are to be located and operate in the border area of the niche and regime level.

---

[12] Politicians may overrate their influence and actually be deluded by an "illusion of agency," though possibly a "productive illusion" (Deuten and Rip 2000).

Such types of networks are closely related to the *policy network* concept as defined, for instance, by Marin and Mayntz (1991). In their concept the actors (i.e. corporate or collective actors, rather than individuals) are *interdependent*, though formally *autonomous*, whereas these actors are *linked laterally* (or horizontally) rather than vertically (Marin and Mayntz 1991, 15–16). These networks, therefore, deal with *inter-organizational* arrangements and interactions (see also Rhodes and Marsh 1992). The interactions typically have the characteristics of negotiation: often there is no central decision-making or power centre (Van Waarden 1992), but rather a multitude of such centers. The interactions among actors are characterized by the exchange of what Callon (1992) has called *intermediaries*, which include money, artifacts, know-how, raw materials, information, military strategic considerations, etc. Such intermediaries are "recombined" by network actors in different ways—ways that are typical of or actually typifies an actor.[13] The main features of sociotechnical networks are, first, the existence of a relatively stable pattern of interactions among the actors—networks show *resilience* (Elzen, Enserink, and Smit 1996)—and, second, their common involvement in some particular technological development, for instance a specific military technology or weapons system (e.g. the European Fighter Aircraft; see Smit, Elzen, and Enserink 1998). The various actors attribute (different) "functions" to the network, depending on their interests and perspectives. These attributed functions (or "meanings" of a network), which will overlap, actually form a bridge between "structure" and actor perspectives (Van Waarden 1992). Therefore, a main advantage of the network approach is that, while it recognizes the importance of structure, it leaves room for individual initiative and strategic actions by corporate actors (Smit 1995*b*, 77). The network approach also implies a shift in traditional policy analysis of "guidance, control and evaluation" (Kaufmann, Majone, and Ostrom 1986) from a top-down, linear, and rational approach, to conceiving it as a problem of co-ordination, including "orchestration of network interactions," "self-regulation" (Smit 1995*b*), and possibly the renewing of institutional settings, that is, new forms of "governance" (Rhodes 1997). Sociotechnical networks, therefore, are a well-suited entrance to study the issue of *governance* in (military) technological developments.

---

[13] Rather than characterizing actors independently from the network, they may be identified by the way they are processing intermediaries or by the role they play in the interaction processes. For instance, a governmental agency in a regulatory role may want to influence the behaviour, that is, the actions of other organizations within the network (for instance, through "gentlemen's agreements" or covenants regarding environmental issues). To this end it processes intermediaries in a way characteristic of regulatory purposes. The actor characteristics may thus be identified by looking at the actor's actions and role within the network.

3.3   Military Socio-technical Networks and Governance of Weapons Innovation

Sociotechnical networks in weapons innovation and its associated military R&D differ in one respect from those of most other technologies, in that there is only one (type of) customer for the end product—that is, the state.[14] Moreover, only a specific set of actors comprises the socio-technical networks of military technological developments, including the defense industry, military laboratories, the military, the defense ministry, and the government. The defense ministry, as the sole buyer on the monopsonistic armament market, has a crucial position. In addition, the defense ministry is heavily involved in the whole R&D process by providing much of the necessary funding, or by refunding successful independent R&D carried out by the defense industry (as is usual in the USA). Yet the defense ministry, in its turn, is dependent on the other actors, like the defense industry and military laboratories which provide the technological options from which the defense ministry may choose. One particular feature is the lengthy road—often ten to fifteen years—of developing new weapons systems, which implies that it will be hard to halt or even redirect a system when much investment has already been put in. Influencing weapons innovations by politicians, therefore, requires a continuous process of assessment, evaluation, and (re-)directing efforts, starting at the early stages of the R&D process. Just striving for "technological superiority," one of the traditional guiding principles in weapons development, will lead to what is seemingly an autonomous process. Seemingly, because technology development is never truly autonomous. The network approach and the character of military technological innovation show that whereas no single actor within the network can fully control military technological developments, these may still be influenced by any of the actors, including political actors, though an actor's influence will be constrained by the objectives and actions of the other network actors.

Military sociotechnical networks generally represent a "closed world" (compare Edwards 1996). Still, the networks' environment may influence military technological developments. A case in point is anti-personnel (land-)mines (APMs), used in military conflicts in many countries including Cambodia, Vietnam, and Angola, which have disabled and still disable annually an estimated 10,000 civilians (SIPRI 2002), for many years after military conflicts have ended. Actions by both the

---

[14] Weapons systems, of course, may also be exported to other national states. In case of multinational defense companies and international collaboration, the national states involved will all be customers. Some civil industries, like nuclear power and telecommunications in the past, showed considerable similarities in market structure—monopolies or oligopolies coupled with one, or at most a few dominant purchasers. They were also highly regulated, and markedly different from the competitive consumer goods sectors.

International Campaign to Ban Landmines[15] and the International Committee of the Red Cross have resulted in the international APM Convention, prohibiting the use, stockpiling, production, and transfer of APMs. In addition, the concern about civilian victims triggered the development of new designs for remotely delivered mines, including mechanisms for self-destruction or self-neutralization after a given timespan of, for instance, thirty days.

Likewise in the early 1990s, when dedicated blinding laser weapons were still under development, assessments, particularly by the International Committee of the Red Cross (ICRC 1993) and the Human Rights Watch organization, designated them as "inhumane weapons." This "external" interference in weapons development contributed to the 1995 Protocol IV of the "Inhumane Weapons" Convention (the CCW of 1981), prohibiting both the use and the transfer of Blinding Laser Weapons. Since the USA agreed to the Blinding Laser Protocol, the Pentagon has cancelled several blinding laser weapon programs.

In conclusion, the analysis above shows that there is room for governance of military technological developments, both from within and from outside the socio-technical networks. Thus, the second part of the answer addressing the Karl Marx quotation at the beginning of this chapter is that technology development is not an autonomous process that "drives history" (Smith and Marx 1994) or in itself fully determines the "given conditions" referred to by Karl Marx.

3.4   Controlling Dual Use Technology and the Integration of Civil and Military Technology

As mentioned in Section 1, technologies having both military and civil applications complicate efforts to prevent the proliferation of advanced weaponry, in particular nuclear, chemical, and biological weapons of mass destruction, (long range) missiles, but also militarily relevant space and computer technology.[16] Under the guise of developing or purchasing civil technologies, countries may lower the technological threshold for actually acquiring advanced weaponry. In the years following the Second World War, the recognition of this "dual use" problem, combined with

---

[15] In the fall of 1997 the International Campaign to Ban Landmines and its coordinator Jody Williams were awarded the Nobel Peace Price.

[16] Proliferation may occur not only to national states but also to terrorist organizations. The existence of suppliers' networks, like the one around Dr. Abdul Qadeer Khan—the "father of the Pakistani nuclear bomb"—trading illegally in sensitive nuclear and missile technology and materials also implies a risk of selling these goods to terrorist organizations (*Arms Control Today* 2004). Likewise, fissile material or even nuclear weapons from poorly protected stockpiles in Russia might appear on the black market. Also nuclear technologists out of job, e.g. from Russia, looking for employment elsewhere, may represent a risk of the spread of sensitive nuclear know-how.

the strained East–West relations, resulted in the establishment of the Coordinating Committee for Multilateral Export Controls (COCOM, in 1949) as the major framework of the USA and its allies for export controls. Whereas under this regime "dual use" was viewed as a negative feature, which complicated export controls, by the end of the cold war in 1989 a profound change in the discourse on dual use technology occurred. Rather than a negative feature, the dual use aspect of technology was viewed as something that should be promoted and pursued, as it might solve the twin problem of maintaining a high-tech defense technology base restrained by limited budgets, and improving a country's economic competitiveness by a more efficient allocation of R&D funds. From this perspective, the civil and military contexts and activities for developing technology should be integrated where possible, rather than separated by a technological and bureaucratic divide between military and civil applications. In particular the military wanted to profit more from progress in civil technological areas where civil R&D had taken the lead, as is the case with information and communication technology.

In practice, the systematic integration of civil and military technological developments meets many obstacles, including differences in governmental influence and regulations, goals (national security versus commerce), market structure, standards and specifications ("milspecs"), sensitivity to costs, different product cycles (years in the commercial versus decades in the military sector), and different industrial and technological "cultures" (see, e.g., Alic et al. 1992). Molas-Gallart (1997) distinguished four different (interaction) mechanisms through which technologies may cross the border between civil and military applications, emphasizing the organizational aspects of dual use transfer and pointing to the obstacles for each of them. Though such transfers do occur, the "transferred" technologies are often not optimized to the requirements of the "receiving" sector.[17] They may, however, cause problems for controlling the spread of militarily sensitive technology. It has been argued that in case of "ambiguous" civilian R&D—i.e. R&D with evident serious implications for the proliferation of military technology—where possible, the development of alternative technological options should be chosen. The possibility of such alternative R&D options has been shown by Schaper et al. (1992) and Smit (1998) for R&D of inertial confinement fusion (of relevance for designing thermonuclear weapons) and of laser isotope separation (of relevance for producing enriched uranium or plutonium for nuclear weapons), and also by Altmann (1994) arguing for specific constraints on R&D of beam weapons and electromagnetic guns. The previous discussion on (governance in) sociotechnical networks implies that the possibility of effectively (re-)directing such research is more promising in cases where the ambiguous R&D under consideration requires large

---

[17] For the strained civil–military relationship in the development of dual use technology, see Smit (1998), who provides examples from micro-electronics, nuclear reactors, lasers, and guidance and navigation technology.

(governmental) funding, provided that the willingness to do so exists. For in such cases the (governmental) supplier of funds will have a stronger position in the network by its control over one of the resources that are necessary for the continuation of the R&D project (see also Smit 1990).

One difficulty in the governance of dual use technological developments—or in governing either the integration or separation of civil and military technology—not mentioned so far is that, whereas at face value the distinction between civil and military technology seems obvious, from an analytical point of view it appears that such a distinction, and therefore the concept of dual use technology, is less clear. Te Kulve and Smit (2003) have shown that rather than an intrinsic feature of the technology itself, the civilian, military, or dual use character of a technology is often the result of its shaping within sociotechnical networks. That is, not only the shaping of the technology but also the (dual use) meaning attached to it, depends on its institutional and cultural context. Moreover, "dual use" is a *dynamic* concept, implying that the civil, military, or dual use meaning attached to a technology may change, for instance during the development of the technology in interaction with changes in the number and nature of the actors involved in its sociotechnical network (Te Kulve and Smit 2003). Therefore, from the perspective of "early warning" for military applications, a continuous monitoring of technological developments, especially in new areas like nanotechnology and genetic engineering, seems to be in place.

4 CONCLUSION

Military power, next to ideological, economic, and political relationships, has been designated by Michael Mann as one of the four basic sources of social power. The interplay of these four alternative means of "organizational means of social control," has structured and shaped social relations since human civilization evolved. In its turn, these "organizational means" transformed over time in both their form and their content. One factor that has, at times substantially transformed military power is technological development. Another factor is new military organization and tactics, often shifting the balance of warfare. A third factor is the emergence of national states, where military power was transformed through an intricate interplay with the institutional structuralization of the emerging national state.

This chapter has focused on the role of military technological change, emphasizing the co-evolution of military technology and society. Through an in-depth analysis of military technological innovation since the Second World War, this was narrowed down to focus on the close interaction between the new and unprecedented systematic and organized weapons innovation process that emerged from the Second World War and developments in both politics and political analysis. It was shown that this interaction actually represents an *entwined evolution* (or co-evolution) of military technology, politics, and political analysis. Weapons innovation and its associated military R&D have strongly influenced (the focus of) politics and policy-making, for instance by transforming traditional national and international security issues. At the same time the huge weapons innovation efforts, in turn, became a (controversial) subject of politics and policy-making. Weapons innovation and its accompanying military R&D were facilitated and supported, and sometimes constrained ("arms control") through the very political processes which they themselves helped to transform, showing the co-evolutionary nature of these developments. Political analysis, in interaction with a transforming political situation, underwent change as well. New (military) doctrinal concepts were developed and, in addition, natural scientists entered the scene of political analysis, for instance on arms control (and verification) issues. Both in their turn influenced military technological developments.

The co-evolutionary transformation of military technology, politics and political analysis since the Second World War has been explicated in this chapter mainly by pointing at the transformation of national and international security issues in relation to the "technological arms race" and weapons proliferation. In the period after the cold war additional security issues have come to the fore, for instance related to international terrorism. In addition to concerns about the proliferation of current weapons technologies to terrorist groups, developments in (new) technological domains (e.g. genetic engineering, nanotechnology) with possible weapons applications (dual use technologies) also raise concern.

The issue of political control of weapons innovation, including the "technological arms race" which in this chapter is reformulated as the capability to change the course of military technology and weapons innovation, has been discussed from a co-evolutionary multilevel perspective. From this perspective, military technologies inherited from the past are part of a slowly evolving sociotechnical landscape, constituting a kind of context for (but also being influenced by) sociotechnical developments at the lower—"meso" and "niche"—levels. It has further been argued that at these lower levels the approach from a sociotechnical network perspective is particularly suited for dealing with governance issues of weapons innovation and dual use technology. This applies as well to developments in (new) technological domains, like genetic engineering and nanotechnology.

In conclusion, first, this chapter has hinted at the broad issue of (ever transforming) military power as one of the four basic sources of social power. Second, it has provided the "co-evolutionary framework" for studying the interaction between military technological change, politics, and political analysis. Third, it has offered the still somewhat rudimentary tool of the "sociotechnical networks approach" for both studying and influencing military technological change.

REFERENCES

ALBRIGHT, D., BERKHOUT, F., and WALKER, W. 1997. *Plutonium and Highly Enriched Uranium 1996: World Inventories, Capabilities and Policies.* Oxford: Oxford University Press for SIPRI.

ALFORD, J. (ed.) 1981. *The Impact of New Military Technology.* Adelphi Library 4. Aldershot: Gower for IISS.

ALIC, J., BRANSCOMB, L. M., BROOKS, H., CARTER, A. B., and EPSTEIN, G. L. 1992. *Beyond Spinoff: Military and Commercial Technologies in a Changing World.* Boston: Harvard Business School Press.

ALLISON G. T., and MORRIS, F. A. 1975. Armaments and arms control: exploring the determinants of military weapons. *Daedalus* 104 (3): 99–129.

ALTMANN, J. 1994. Verifying limits on research and development. Case studies: beam weapons, electromagnetic guns. Pp. 225–33 in *Verification After the Cold War— Broadening the Process.* ed. J. Altmann, T. Stock, and J.-P. Stroot. Amsterdam: Free University Press.

Arms Control Today. 2004. A sprawling nuclear black market. *Arms Control Today,* 34 (2): 23.

ARNOLD, L. 2000. *Britain and the H-bomb.* New York: St. Martin's Press.

BALL, D., and RICHELSON, J. (eds.) 1986. *Strategic Nuclear Targeting.* Ithaca, NY: Cornell University Press.

BAXTER, J. P. 1968. *Scientists Against Time.* Cambridge, Mass.: MIT Press; originally published 1946.

BIJKER, W. E., HUGHES, T. P., and PINCH, T. 1987. *The Social Construction of Technological Systems.* Cambridge, Mass.: MIT Press.

——and LAW, J. 1992. *Shaping Technology / Building Society.* Cambridge, Mass.: MIT Press.

BRAUCH, H. G., VAN DER GRAAF, H. J., GRIN, J., and SMIT, W. A. (eds.) 1992. *Controlling the Development and Spread of Military Technology.* Amsterdam: Free University Press.

BROOKS, H. 1975. The military innovation system and the qualitative arms race. *Daedalus,* 104 (3): 75–97.

BUSH, V. 1945. *Science—The Endless Frontier.* Charter Document for the U.S. National Science Foundation. Washington, DC: Government Printing Office. Reprinted: New York: Arno Press, 1980

BUZAN, B. 1987. *An Introduction to Strategic Studies.* Basingstoke: Macmillan.

CALLON, M. 1992. The dynamics of techno-economic networks. Pp. 77–102 in *Technological Change and Company Strategies,* ed. R. Coombs, P. Saviotti, and V. Walsh. London: Academic Press.

DEUTEN, J. J., and RIP, A. 2000. Narrative infrastructure in product creation processes. *Organization,* 7 (1): 69–93.

DICKSON, D. 1984. *The New Politics of Science.* New York: Pantheon.

DOUGLAS, S. J. 1985. The Navy's adoption of radio, 1899–1919. In Smith 1985, 117–73.

EDWARDS, P. N. 1996. *The Closed World: Computers and the Politics of Discourse in Cold War America.* Cambridge, Mass.: MIT Press.

ELLIS, J. 1993. *The Social History of the Machine Gun.* London: Random House; originally published 1976.

ELZEN, B., ENSERINK, B., and SMIT, W. A. 1996. Socio-technical networks: how a technology studies approach may help to solve problems related to technical change. *Social Studies of Science*, 26: 95–141.

ENTHOVEN, A. C., and SMITH, K. W. 1971. *How Much is Enough? Shaping the Defense Program, 1961–1969*. New York: Harper and Row.

FREEDMAN, L. D. 2003. *The Evolution of Nuclear Strategy*, 3rd edn. London: Palgrave Macmillan.

GEELS, F. W. 2002. Technological transitions as evolutionary reconfiguration processes: a multi-level perspective and a case-study. *Research Policy*, 31: 1257–74.

——2004. *Technological Transitions and System Innovations: A Co-evolutionary and Socio-Technical Analysis*. Cheltenham: Edward Elgar.

GILPIN, R. 1962. *American Scientists and Nuclear Weapons Policy*. Princeton, NJ: Princeton University Press.

GLEDITSCH, N. P., and NJØLSTAD, O. (eds.) 1990. *Arms Races: Technological and Political Dynamics*. London: Sage.

GOLDBLAT, J. 1982. *Agreements for Arms Control*. London: Taylor and Francis for SIPRI.

GOLDSCHMIDT, B. 1967. *Les Rivalités Atomique*. Paris: Fayard.

——1980. *Le Complexe Atomique: Histoire politique de l'Energie Nucléaire*. Paris: Fayard.

GREENWOOD, T. 1975. *Making the MIRV*. Cambridge, Mass.: Ballinger.

——1990. Why military technology is difficult to constrain. *Science Technology and Human Values*, 15: 412–29.

HACKER, B. C. 1994. Military institutions, weapons, and social change: towards a new history of military technology. *Technology and Culture*, 35: 768–834.

HEWLETT, R. G., and ANDERSON, O. E. 1990. *The New World: A History of the United States Atomic Energy Commission*. Berkeley: University of California Press.

HOLLOWAY, D. 1994. *Stalin and the Bomb*. New Haven, Conn.: Yale University Press.

HOLST, J. J., and NERLICH, U. (eds.) 1977. *Beyond Nuclear Deterrence: New Arms, New Aims*. London: Macdonald and Jane's.

ICRC (International Committee of the Red Cross) 1993. *Blinding Weapons*. Reports of the meetings of experts convened by the ICRC on battlefield laser weapons 1989–1991. Geneva: ICRC.

JASANOFF, S., MARKLE, G. E., PETERSON, J. C., and PINCH, T. (eds.) 1995. *Handbook of Science and Technology Studies*. London: Sage.

KAUFMANN, F.-X., MAJONE, G., and OSTROM, V. (eds.) 1986. *Guidance, Control and Evaluation in the Public Sector*. Berlin: Walter de Gruyter.

KEVLES, D. J. 1979. *The Physicists: The History of a Scientific Community in Modern America*. New York: Vintage Books.

KILLIAN, J. R., Jr. 1977. *Sputnik, Scientists, and Eisenhower*. Cambridge, Mass.: MIT Press.

KRASS, A. S., BOSKMA, P., ELZEN, B., and SMIT, W. A. 1983. *Uranium Enrichment and Nuclear Weapon Proliferation*. London: Taylor and Francis for SIPRI.

LANDES, D. S. 1983. *Revolution in Time*. Cambridge, Mass.: Harvard University Press.

LONG, F. A., and REPPY, J. (eds.) 1980. *The Genesis of New Weapons*. New York: Pergamon.

MANN, M. 1986–93. *The Sources of Social Power*. Vol. 1: *A History of Power from the Beginning to A.D. 1760*. Vol. 2: *The Rise of Classes and Nation-States, 1760–1914*. Cambridge: Cambridge University Press.

MARIN, B., and MAYNTZ, R. (eds.) 1991. *Policy Networks*. Boulder, Colo.: Westview.

MᴄNᴇɪʟʟ, W. H. 1982. *The Pursuit of Power: Technology, Armed Forces, and Society since A.D. 1000*. Chicago: Chicago University Press.

MᴏʟᴀS-Gᴀʟʟᴀʀᴛ, J. 1997. Which way to go? Defence technology and the diversity of dual-use technology transfer. *Research Policy*, 26: 367–85.

MᴏᴏʀS, E. H. M., Rɪᴘ, A., and WɪSᴋᴇʀᴋᴇ, J. S. C. 2004. The dynamics of innovation: a multi-level co-evolutionary perspective. Pp. 31–56 in *Seeds of Transition*, ed. J. S. C. Wiskerke and J. D. van der Ploeg. Assen: Royal Van Gorcum.

Pᴀʀᴋᴇʀ, G. 1988. *The Military Revolution: Military Innovation and the Rise of the West 1500–1800*. Cambridge: Cambridge University Press.

RʜᴏᴅᴇS, R. 1986. *The Making of the Atomic Bomb*. New York: Simon and Schuster.

RʜᴏᴅᴇS, R. A. W. 1997. *Understanding Governance*. Buckingham: Open University Press.

—— and Marsh, D. 1992. New directions in the study of policy networks. *European Journal of Political Research*, 21: 181–205.

Rɪᴘ, A., and Kᴇᴍᴘ, R. 1998. Technological change. Vol. 2: 327–99 in *Human Choice and Climate Change*, ed. S. Rayner and E. L. Malone. Columbus, Ohio: Battelle Press.

Rᴏʟᴀɴᴅ, A. 1985. Technology and war: a bibliographic essay. In Smith 1985, 347–79.

—— 1993. Technology and war: the historiographical revolution of the 1980s. *Technology and Culture*, 34: 117–34.

—— 1995. Keep the bomb. *Technology Review*, 98: 67–9.

—— 2003. Once more into the stirrups: Lynn White, Jr., medieval technology and social change. *Technology and Culture*, 44: 574–85.

Sᴄʜᴀᴘᴇʀ, A., Lɪᴇʙᴇʀᴛ, W., Sᴍɪᴛ, W. A., and Eʟᴢᴇɴ, B. 1992. New technological developments and the non-proliferation regime: redirecting and constraining R&D; the case of Laser Fusion, Laser Isotope Separation, and the use of Highly Enriched Uranium. In Brauch et al. 1992, 121–38.

Sᴄʜᴇɪɴᴍᴀɴ, L. 1965. *Atomic Energy Policy in France under the Fourth Republic*. Princeton, NJ: Princeton University Press.

Sᴄʜᴇʟʟɪɴɢ, T. C. 1966. *Arms and Influence*. New Haven, Conn.: Yale University Press.

SIPRI. 1994. *SIPRI Yearbook 1994*. Oxford: Oxford University Press.

—— 2002. *SIPRI Yearbook 2002: Armaments, Disarmament and International Security*. Oxford: Oxford University Press.

—— 2003. *SIPRI Yearbook 2003: Armaments, Disarmament and International Security*. Oxford: Oxford University Press.

Sᴍɪᴛ, W. A. 1989 Defense technology assessment and the control of emerging technologies. Pp. 61–76 in *Non-provocative Defence as a Principle of Arms Reduction*, ed. M. ter Borg and W. A. Smit. Amsterdam: Free University Press.

—— 1990. Controlling military technological innovation—the role of verification. Pp. 53–70 in *Unconventional Approaches to Conventional Arms Control Verification*, ed. J. Grin and H. van der Graaf. Amsterdam: Free University Press.

—— 1995a. Science, technology, and the military: relations in transition. In Jasanoff et al. 1995, 598–626.

—— 1995b. A framework for a sociology of assessing and intervening in technology development. *European Review*, 3 (1): 73–82.

—— 1998. Ambiguous civilian R&D: preventing destabilizing military applications. Pp. 273–92 in *Conversion of Military R&D*, ed. J. Reppy. London: Macmillan.

SMIT, W. A., ELZEN, B., and ENSERINK, B. 1998. Coordination in military socio-technical networks: military needs, requirements and guiding principles. Pp. 71–105 in *Getting New Technologies Together*, ed. C. Disco and B. van der Meulen. Berlin: Walter de Gruyter.

SMITH, M. R. 1985. Army ordnance and the "American system of manufacturing," 1815–1861. Pp. 39–86 in *Military Enterprise and Technological Change*, ed. M. R. Smith. Cambridge, Mass.: MIT Press.

——and MARX, L. (eds.) 1994. *Does Technology Drive History? The Dilemma of Technological Determinism*. Cambridge, Mass.: MIT Press

STANFORD ARMS CONTROL GROUP 1976. *International Arms Control: Issues and Agreements*, ed. J. H. Barton and L. D. Weiler. Stanford, Calif. Stanford University Press.

TE KULVE, H., and SMIT, W. A. 2003. Civilian–military co-operation strategies in developing new technologies. *Research Policy*, 32: 955–70.

TILLY, C. 1990. *Coercion, Capital and European States, AD 990–1990*. Oxford: Blackwell.

TSIPIS, K., HAFEMEISTER, D. W., and JANEWAY, P. (eds.) 1986. *Arms Control Verification*. Washington, DC: Pergamon-Brassey's.

VAN CREVELD, M. 1989. *Technology and War*. New York: Free Press.

VAN WAARDEN, F. 1992. Dimensions and types of policy networks. *European Journal of Political Research*, 21: 29–52.

WEART, S. R. 1979. *Scientists in Power*. Cambridge, Mass.: Harvard University Press.

WHITE, L. 1962. *Medieval Technology and Social Change*. Oxford: Oxford University Press.

WRIGHT, Q. 1965. *A Study of War*, 2 vols. Chicago: University of Chicago Press.

YORK, H. 1971. *Race to Oblivion*. New York: Simon and Schuster.

——(compiler) 1973. *Arms Control*. Readings from *Scientific American*. San Francisco: Freeman.

——and GREB, A. 1982. Scientists as advisers to governments. Pp. 83–99 in *Scientists, the Arms Race and Disarmament*, ed. J. Rotblat. London: Taylor and Francis.

....

CHAPTER 40

TECHNOLOGY AS A SITE AND OBJECT OF POLITICS

....

SHEILA JASANOFF

TECHNOLOGY. A composite of Greek *technē* (skill) and *logos* (study of), the term as normally defined exudes utility and resists abstraction. It is, as most dictionaries tell us, simply the use of established scientific principles to solve practical problems. It is no more than the extension of our normal capabilities to achieve what most of us desire anyway: to alleviate pain and misery; ease work; increase wealth; overcome physical and temporal barriers to action; and open up previously inaccessible worlds to human insight and exploration. Technology allows our species to acquire the bodies and minds, the environments, and the entertainments that we collectively aspire to; through it, we fashion the lives that our imaginations have rendered desirable. Technology, so viewed, is instrumental and mechanistic. It realizes visions, but seems itself to remain value-free. It is an extension of the self, a productive force, the ultimate enabler, but for all that a tool, subject to ideas and ideals that originate elsewhere, outside the sphere of the technological. Where, then, in technology's ambit do we find the spaces of the political?

Myths offer instructive points of departure. As dreams have their obverse in nightmares, so the narrative of technology as a liberating and empowering force has its jarring counterpoint in stories of error, failure, and loss of control. Technology, in these darker accounts, not only enables but also constrains. It produces unforeseen harms, sets up obstinate hierarchies, channels and manages possible forms of life, and subordinates human capabilities to its own impersonal, destructive logics of rationality and domination. Unmanaged technology, we are constantly reminded, can give rise to disorder and misrule. Four powerful myths have crystallized around these not unconnected fears. They represent technology, in turn, as *unavoidable risk*, as *immutable design*, as *dehumanizing standard*, and as *ethical constraint*. Through these four lenses, and the events and reflections that each opens onto we can map the politics of technology as it is enacted and experienced in the contemporary world.

Icarus, son of Greece's legendary artisan Daedalus embodies the age-old figure of technology as risk. Icarus inherited his father's daring but neither his foresight nor his wisdom. Daedalus escaped from captivity in Crete with wings ingeniously crafted of feathers and wax, but Icarus fell to his death when he flew too near the sun, whose heat melted the wax and destroyed his wings. In a tragic modern inversion of the myth, the US space shuttle Challenger exploded in 1986, killing all seven crewmembers aboard, when its stiff rubber O-rings failed to seal in the streaming hot gases during a launch in the unexpected cold of a late January morning in Florida (Vaughan 1996). Molten wax, nonresilient O-rings: both testify to the dangers of reaching for superhuman heights with less than perfect understanding of the instruments at the explorer's disposal.

For technology as design, we may turn again to Daedalus, father of Icarus, the master builder who conceived the Cretan labyrinth, a maze so difficult to penetrate that it safely held the half-human, half-bull Minotaur, although it also prevented the escape of the youthful victims ritually led in to satisfy the monster's inhuman appetites. It took a woman's ingenuity and a man's hardihood, Ariadne's ball of string unwound by Theseus, to end the Minotaur's dominion and bring the victor back out alive. But escape is not nearly so easy from the construct that, following Jeremy Bentham (1995 [1787]), Michel Foucault (1995) conceived as modernity's most characteristic architectural achievement: the Panopticon, the circular, transparent building from whose central watchtower a single guard could hold a community of prisoners within a web of permanent surveillance.

Fast forward to the twentieth century, where Aldous Huxley's 1932 novel *Brave New World* provides the canonical myth of technology as an instrument of standardization. Here we find humanity's craving for safety and order driven to pathological extremes. Huxley's world is one from which suffering in its grosser forms has been banished. But in exchange for freedom from hunger and illness, fear and pain, lost too are the powers of creativity, empathy, and self-fulfillment that liberal societies see as the cornerstones of lives worth living. In this controlled society, people themselves are graded and sorted into classes whose capacities are carefully tailored to the functions they perform. Reason crowds out emotion; the system's logic overrides its members' desire for self-expression. Many have deplored this transformation of the human from godlike inventor to cog in the machine as one of modern technology's worst unintended consequences (Bauman 1991; Habermas 1984; Ellul 1964).

Finally, for technology as ethical transgression, the story that has haunted the Western imagination like none other for nearly two centuries is Mary Shelley's *Frankenstein*. Written in 1816 by a girl of nineteen, the tale of the Swiss scientist who built from inanimate matter a being he could not control has become the quintessential fable of technological over-reaching. The Frankenstein myth was infused with new life when, in 1997, Ian Wilmut's research group at Scotland's Roslin Institute announced the birth of Dolly, a sheep created from a mammary gland cell of a six-year-old ewe, and hence genetically identical to her "mother." The announcement refuted biologists' long-held belief that cells in adult bodies, human or animal, were fixed into specialized roles that could not be altered. Real life appeared once again to reprise the elements of myth, as technology reversed the expected course of nature, created a hitherto unknown kind of living thing, and by foreshadowing similar manipulation of human beings, seemed to outstrip the moral intuitions and rule-making capacity of elected lawmakers.

These four framing narratives are not, of course, wholly independent of one another. Fear of technology's harmful consequences is intimately linked, for instance, to concerns about ethical violations. The charge of "playing God" applies as much to acts that are perceived to contradict the natural order of things (e.g. cloning humans) as to acts of managerial ambition which through lack of adequate foreknowledge, misfire and expose society to disproportionate harms.[1] Similarly, to the extent that technology orders or designs the physical and psychological parameters of human existence, it does so through sometimes forcible processes of standardization that demarcate normal social identities and behaviors from those regarded as deviant or abnormal (Hacking 1999; Foucault 1978).

Each of the four narratives provides a rationale for a lively politics of technology, although as we shall see each has also given rise to its own distinctive conceptual dialectic, articulated through specific constellations of political actors, controversies, discourses, and forms of action. Common to all four as well is that disputes in each center on the ambiguous figure of the technical expert. Appearing in force on the political scene since the late eighteenth century (Golan 2004), experts are primarily charged with providing assurances that it is safe to live with the powers unleashed by technology. But experts also operate as lightning rods for controversy in every area of contested application: weaponry, surveillance, polling, medical intervention, transportation, energy use, and communication, to name some of the most significant. All of these politically charged technologies raise questions about the competence, foresight, interests, and wisdom of experts (Jasanoff 1995; Nelkin 1992). They also cast doubt on the possibility of democratic rule in

---

[1] E.g. Carson (1962) on the disastrous environmental impact of persistent organic pesticides.

societies where technically trained elites perform so much of the everyday work of governance (Price 1965).

1   THE POLITICS OF RISK

On any day in 2005 at any major airport in the United States, an anthropologically inclined onlooker would have observed a strange ritual. Lines of slow-moving, ticketed passengers, loaded down with bags and packages of varying colors and contours, walk up to a conveyor belt and start divesting themselves of assorted items under the watchful eyes of uniformed guards: laptop computers are removed from their cases, pockets emptied of anything metallic, belts removed, coats and scarves piled into plastic trays, bags and packages put on the belt, and most bizarre of all, shoes and boots taken off in preparation for the owners' awkward passage through the rectangular arch of a metal detector. On the other side of the barrier, the process reverses itself, as pocket and briefcase contents are returned to their places, jackets and coats donned again, and shoes put back on stockinged feet. Speeded up, the anthropologist might think, it would make a hilarious cartoon sequence of people going through apparently meaningless motions—and so it would if only the stakes were not so grave.

The increased intensity of airport security screening around the world is, of course, a response to the terrorist attacks of September 11, 2001, in New York and Washington, in which nineteen young Islamic militants destroyed the twin towers of the World Trade Center and parts of the Pentagon, killing themselves and some 3000 others in the process. But why must all those shoes come off, and why especially in the United States? One man's actions at the turn of the twenty-first century changed the conditions of travel for 688 million passengers a year on US domestic airlines. Richard Reid, a Briton with ties to the Al Qaeda organization held responsible for the 9/11 attacks, boarded an American Airlines flight in Paris on December 22, 2001, with enough explosives to destroy the plane packed into his shoes. His attempt to light the fuse that would have converted his shoes into bombs was foiled in time, but the episode turned every shoe worn by every airline passenger into a suspected weapon, and hence (unless exonerated as containing no metal) a target of special screening, regardless of the costs in time, inconvenience, and embarrassment for passengers or in added demands on overworked security personnel.

The instant transformation of that most mundane of civilian artifacts, the shoe, into an object of military interest—a potential weapon—underlined the sociologist

Ulrich Beck's (1992) argument that the global spread of science and technology has spawned a "risk society," in which everyone regardless of social class or standing, is exposed to incalculable, possibly catastrophic threats that do not lend themselves to rational control. Technologies earlier seen as safeguards against risk (shoes to prevent injury or infection, for example) can suddenly reveal themselves as sources of unexpected danger. The sweeping in of so many million shoes into the purview of airport surveillance systems also points to a fact about risk that social psychologists have noted for some time: that people are particularly concerned about risks that arouse dread—through their unfamiliarity, scope, or uncontrollability (especially of new technologies)—and they will in consequence spend more to control low-probability, high-consequence events than they will to regulate more ordinary hazards like bicycling accidents, that may in the aggregate cause greater damage to lives or property (Slovic et al. 1980; 1985).

Politically, these observations have played into two quite different responses to the governance or management of risk; these may be labeled the *technocratic* and the *democratic*. Grounded in a positivistic commitment to the view that risks are determinate probabilities of harm, and a corresponding faith in the power of experts to calculate these probabilities correctly, the technocratic approach seeks to insulate the process of risk analysis as far as possible from the distorting influence of plebeian politics (Breyer 1993; NRC 1983). The calculation of probabilities, termed risk assessment, is deemed a matter for experts; the choice of acceptable risk levels and control policies is relegated to a later stage of risk management, in which public values are permitted to come into play. Key to implementing this strategy is a commitment to formal assessment methods and rigorous review by experts, followed by a quantitative comparison of the costs and benefits of risk reduction, so as to arrive at the most rational (understood as most economically efficient) regulatory outcomes. This normative preference for efficiency entails additional prescriptions that bear on the relations between experts and the public in risk decisions: that experts should be considered more trustworthy than laypersons when disagreements arise about the severity of risk (Sunstein 2002; 2005); that benefits from reducing one risk should be offset against the costs of others that might thereby be increased (Graham and Wiener 1995); and that more should be done to communicate risks properly to the public, so as to bring their perceptions in line with those of experts.

Western governments throughout the last third of the twentieth century took pains to ensure that their citizens would not, on the basis of uninformed opinions and unfounded fears, reject technological innovations that the state's own experts had deemed safe or bearable. To this end, governments made considerable investments in the public understanding of science and technology. Democratic states were particularly committed to this policy, because technology for them was not merely an engine of wealth creation but also, as in grand nation-building projects like the atomic bomb or the Apollo mission, a potent instrument of self-legitimation (Ezrahi 1990). To the skeptical citizens of modern democracies, such technological successes offer a compelling demonstration that the state is acting effectively on their behalf. But to appreciate the successes as successes, states recognized, citizens must be taught to perceive the risks and benefits of technology in the same way as experts. Programs to enhance the public's scientific understanding aimed to fulfill this pedagogical mission, but these efforts encountered both political and conceptual difficulties (Wynne 1995).

If the technocratic approach to risk management recommends sealed-off spaces for expert deliberation, the democratic response seeks rather to enlarge the role of public participation in decision-making about risk.[2] Opponents decry this trend as misguided populism: an overreaction to singular, self-contained cases of mismanagement, like the transmission of "mad cow" disease to humans through poor agricultural practices in Britain in the 1980s; or a working out of the erroneous principle that the people's preferences should prevail in democracies regardless of the facts found by experts (Sunstein 2002); or the application of an extreme relativizing tendency in the sociology of knowledge that places lay experience on a par with specialized expert knowledge (Collins and Evans 2002). At stake in the move to democratize risk management, however, is not a new form of class warfare between experts and laypeople, the epistemic haves and have-nots of modern knowledge societies, but rather a struggle over who should assess the purposes of technology and with it the meaning of lives worth living.

Supporting this analysis are numerous studies that reveal risk to be a deeply constructed phenomenon, a function in part of long historical and cultural legacies that predispose societies to regard some harms as worth enduring and others not.[3] European welfare states, for example, have judged the threats to social solidarity flowing from grossly inequitable distributions of risks, as well as the potential public costs of compensation for faulty predictions, to be less tolerable than has the neoliberal United States (Rosanvallon 2000). To this disparity may be attributed the European Union's embrace of the precautionary principle as a normative basis for health, safety, and environmental regulation in the 1990s (Tickner 2003), a stance that US politicians and analysts committed to the expert discourse of risk assessment dismissed as unscientific, protectionist, or a sign of weakness and insecurity (Sunstein 2005; Kagan 2003). Embedded in well-entrenched regulatory institutions and practices, these disparate orientations to risk may be taken for granted by those within the system, and indeed be accepted as part of the natural order of things until comparative analysis reveals the cultural specificity of some of the underlying premises.[4]

---

[2] CEC 2002: UK House of Lords 2000; NRC 1996.
[3] Jasanoff 1986; 2005; Douglas and Wildavsky 1982; Douglas 1966.
[4] Jasanoff 2005; Vogel 1986; Brickman, Jasanoff, and Ilgen 1985.

Advocates of the democratic approach also point out that, when experts and laypersons disagree about risk governance, they are not necessarily focusing on the same object of inquiry. While experts are chiefly concerned with the probability of deterministic failures in technological systems, publics may care more about issues of purpose and responsibility (Irwin and Wynne 1996). Put differently, experts and publics (and even different expert communities[5]) frame risks differently, with consequent differences in the questions asked and the explanations deemed satisfactory. Mathematical formulations, the preferred discourse of expert risk analysis, fail to address lay concerns for metaphysics and morality. What new ontologies are technologies bringing into the world (e.g. robots, anti-depressants, genetically modified crops), and how desirable are they (Haraway 1991)? Who benefits from technologies that might malfunction and cause catastrophic harm? What mechanisms are in place to compensate those who may suffer from technological breakdowns? A costly mistake like "mad cow" disease operates in this context to reinforce legitimate public concerns about the reliability of expertise, as well as about institutional irresponsibility at the highest levels of governmental or corporate power. Far from operating according to what the sociologist Brian Wynne has termed the "deficit model"—which represents the lay citizen as a technically illiterate, emotionally undisciplined actor—the public emerges in the light of this analysis as capable of sophisticated and reflective institutional analysis, and possibly better able than acknowledged experts to evaluate the implications of technological design for democratic governance (Irwin and Wynne 1996; Wynne 1995).

The dismissive label "populist" also denigrates the experiential knowledge, or lay expertise (Collins and Evans 2002; NRC 1996) that various publics bring to the assessment of risks. Such knowledge stems in part from people's close personal acquaintance with actual, rather than ideally imagined uses of technology; exclusion of this kind of knowledge cannot be considered innocent from the standpoint of decision-making, since it not infrequently leads to disaster (Jasanoff 1994; Wynne 1988). Experiential knowledge, too, is often buried within organizational frameworks that impede its free flow or effective use and uptake by those in power.[6] Expert risk analyses may fail to take account of such stickiness until after bad events have occurred. Nation states can be seen in the light of these observations as particularly complex organizations that command distinctive means of framing technological risks and producing and testing public facts. These "civic epistemologies" (Jasanoff 2005), or patterned ways of generating politically relevant knowledge provide a further argument for broadening expert risk deliberations so as to accommodate a polity's preferences for culturally specific forms of reasoning, proof, and argument.[7]

[5] Cf. Eden (2004) and Jasanoff (2005; 1986).
[6] Power and Hutter 2005; Eden 2004; Vaughan 1996; Short and Clarke 1992; Clarke 1989; Perrow 1984.
[7] See also Antony, this volume.

2   THE POLITICS OF DESIGN

The labyrinth and the Panopticon—the one dark and inward-leading, the other transparent and outward-gazing, but both equally confining—appropriately capture the power of technology to design the conditions of life. Both imaginings, moreover, make clear how intimately technological design is bound up with projects of governance writ large. Daedalus was not a free agent; he served King Minos of Crete, so well in fact that the king eventually imprisoned him to keep him from seeking another master. Bentham, the quintessential utilitarian conceived the Panopticon as an efficient means for the state to control disorderly prison populations with the least investment of resources. Indeed, incorporating normative principles into the design of buildings and other material objects has proved to be an efficacious means of regulation at every scale of social organization, from global to smallest local.

That "artifacts have politics" (Winner 1986) is widely acknowledged. Langdon Winner offered as an example the famously low underpasses designed by Robert Moses for New York's suburban highways, supposedly in order to keep busloads of black day-trippers away from white residential enclaves. Social exclusion was in this way built into the design of urban infrastructure. Feminist theoreticians and historians have pointed to the gendered implications of technological design, whether to exclude women from some lines of work or to insert them more deeply into traditionally female gender roles (Wajcman 1991; Cowan 1983). More generally, the French philosopher of technology, Bruno Latour calls attention to the regulative capacity of all sorts of mundane artifacts, such as the speed bump, or "sleeping policeman," which serves in lieu of a human traffic controller (Latour 1992). Through their very materiality, technologies exert power; once in place, they cannot easily be redesigned or removed. The question of paramount concern for democratic politics, then, is whose design choices matter. Who in fact designs technologies?

In the most optimistic accounts, it is the users of technology who have the final say. Technologies, according to this view are socially constructed by various stakeholder groups: thus, consumer preferences ultimately control whether bicycles will have ten speeds or cars come equipped with anti-lock brakes (Bijker, Hughes, and Pinch 1987). Objecting that this account unduly privileges the social at the expense of the material, proponents of actor-network theory have argued that non-human actants also participate in the making of design, offering resistances that human actors must overcome in order to make a technology function (Callon 1986). Others, however, dismiss both streams of constructivist analysis as perpetuating the myth of market liberalism while ignoring the complex macro-political economy of global manufacturing. Aided by compliant experts, sovereign states and their official sub-units have historically invested huge resources in promoting specific technological designs, especially in the areas of military technologies and their offshoots in the fields of computers and information technology (Edwards 1996;

MacKenzie 1990), and latterly also in biomedicine. Under totalitarian rule, this partnership of science and technology with the state can lead to such practical and ethical disasters as Soviet agriculture and Nazi medicine (Bauman 1991; Proctor 1988); but even in liberal democratic nations non-transparent alliances between experts and their political masters can produce "closed worlds" of discourse (Eden 2004; Edwards 1996; Gusterson 1996), underwriting virtually invisible, publicly inaccessible, and from the standpoint of human welfare, highly questionable choices in the development of technology.

Corporations emerged in the nineteenth century as equally important players in the politics of design, with their own stables of experts, whose capacity for inventiveness the law turned into economically useful "intellectual property." By the end of the twentieth century, the power of corporations to disseminate their techno-normative design choices around the globe surpassed that of many nation states (Noble 1976; 1977). In a world so dominated by the military-industrial complexes of developed nations, and by the monopoly power of companies like Microsoft or MacDonald's, end-users have little latitude to criticize, let alone shape basic design choices. Even the Internet, once hailed as the architectural framework for a genuinely free exchange of ideas and information, a quintessential "technology of freedom" (de Sola Poole 1983), seemed to be turning under corporate dominance into a space for controlled communication and closely held ownership of thought (Lessig 2001).

Against this backdrop, the politics of technological design has taken shape between the theoretical ideal of *participation* and the practical possibilities of *resistance*. Despite calls for greater democratization of design choices (Sclove 1995; Winner 1986), dethroning experts in the pay of capital has not proved easy and resistance remains the more readily available means of political expression. In one celebrated, late twentieth-century example, Monsanto, the leading US producer of agricultural biotechnology announced its intention to develop a technique of gene modification that would render the seeds of staple crops sterile by design, and hence unusable from year to year. If carried through, this project might have affected millions of poor farmers who, having planted their fields with Monsanto's seeds, would have had to return to the company for new seeds each year. In this case, a development activist organization, the Rural Advancement Foundation International, later known as the ETC Group launched an extremely effective campaign against Monsanto's so-called "terminator technology," forcing the company to back down. The result, in effect, was the abandonment of a trajectory of product development that would, by novel technological means, have shifted control of seed fertility from farmers to a corporate patent holder. For the most part, however, corporate design choices remain shielded from early public review under a tacit social contract that grants confidentiality to the innovation process and leaves it to the market to determine the acceptability of already realized technologies.

Multinational institutions created in the aftermath of the Second World War have become another rallying point for the politics of resistance, especially as reflected in worldwide contestation over the goals, methods, and processes of development (Stiglitz 2002). The rise of an anti-globalization movement, represented in force at the World Trade Organization's third ministerial conference in Seattle in November 1999, put questions of public and corporate accountability at the head of the international political agenda, with a specific focus on issues of technological design. Protest centered in part on large-scale projects of environmental and social engineering, such as the construction of high dams to meet power and irrigation needs in many parts of the developing world. Planned and carried out on a wave of enthusiasm for modernization, these dams became by the later decades of the twentieth century symbols of ill-conceived technological design in many newly independent nations. Not only had the expert designers failed to take account of the dams' long-term environmental consequences, but as protest movements dramatically demonstrated, they had also ignored the impacts on the lives of people made landless and homeless through these massive relocation projects (Khagram 2004; Hall 1990). As the armies of the dispossessed gained voice and visibility (Roy 1999), even impersonal global institutions like the World Bank were forced to reconsider their development policies and become more open to inputs from below (Goldman 2005).

Given that slightly more than half the developing world's labor force still consisted of farm workers around the turn of the century, it is perhaps not surprising that improving agricultural technologies surfaced as a prime objective for development experts. The Green Revolution of the 1960s showed that scientific techniques could be applied to producing significantly higher-yielding grain varieties, with the possibility of reducing hunger worldwide. But success in raising yields did little to alter underlying problems of poverty and inequality, and political discourse fifty years later remained stubbornly divided over whether the revolution had succeeded in its normative, as opposed to its technical goals. In local contexts, where the lines between rich and poor often solidified, the Green Revolution spawned numerous acts of resistance, employing what the political scientist James Scott (1976; 1985) evocatively termed "weapons of the weak."

On the larger canvas of globalization, the failure to eradicate poverty, guarantee food security, and prevent environmental harms led many critics to challenge the Green Revolution and its successor, the Gene Revolution promised by modern agricultural biotechnology, as continuing impositions of hegemonic Western power and violence on the developing world.[8] Pulling up genetically modified plants from research plots around the world became the modern analogue of an earlier era's smashing of mechanized looms. The instinctive response from governments and their expert advisers, then and now, was to decry these demonstrations

---

[8] Shiva 1997; Visvanathan 1997; Mies and Shiva 1993; Nandy 1988.

as senseless, backward-looking acts of vandalism. Critics blamed public ignorance of science, radical environmentalism, and media hype—in short anything but a shortfall in democratic institutions—for these demonstrations. Mechanisms for proactively involving an emerging global public in design decisions affecting the majority of the world's population, as in the case of agricultural biotechnology eluded the imagination of ruling elites.

3   THE POLITICS OF STANDARDIZATION

Certain design features are favored more by those in power than others. Chief among these is the strategy of simplification, through which the complex jumble of human identities and behaviors can be rendered, in James Scott's term, "legible" and therefore manageable (Scott 1998). The instruments most commonly used for this purpose are classification and standardization (Bowker and Star 1999; Desrosières 1998). The former sorts things into categories that produce legibility and meaning; the latter ensures that the categories so created are filled with similar entities, permitting valid comparisons and the treatment of like as like. It would be difficult to navigate the social structures of modernity without relying on standard categories defined by technical experts. For anything to circulate productively in the world—persons, goods, currency, services, scientific claims, technological artifacts—people and institutions need to know the exact parameters of what is being exchanged. Equally, standards provide the foundation for building safety and trust, without which one could not effectively operate elaborate, spatially dispersed technological systems. And yet classification and standard-setting inevitably entail costs: the creation of senseless or meaningless categories, the reduction of complexity, the elimination of ambiguity, and the sometimes forcible pigeonholing of persons and things into categories in which they do not belong (Bauman 1991).

The relationship between technology and standards has been variously conceived, but whatever the conception the implications are always profoundly political. In technological worlds, humans may become both cognitively and physically the extensions of impersonal machines, with consequent loss of autonomy, individual personality, and freedom of thought and expression.[9] Technologies of mass communication, in particular, not only vastly expand the sphere of public deliberation, but through their power of reproduction actually construct the masses,

---

[9] Habermas 1984; Noble 1976; Ellul 1964.

pressing people into shared and reductive ways of thought (Lessig 2001; Benjamin 1968). At the same time, film and more particularly television have privatized the domain of visual expression and communication, disrupting ancient social bonds and promoting the phenomenon that the political scientist Robert Putnam (2000) dubbed "bowling alone." Yet, for all its alienation and atomization, a public whose members have learned to read and think alike can still be led to destructive ideologies and fundamentalisms. The marriage of state power with print capitalism underpinned, in Benedict Anderson's view, the rise of nationhood as a specific form of "imagined community" with all its potential for destructive mass mobilization (Anderson 1991).

The social sciences and associated technologies of the modern era are at once a response to and an instrument of state power. Techniques such as cost–benefit analysis and risk assessment permit states to justify actions taken on behalf of their citizens, just as they allow citizens, reciprocally, to hold the state accountable for arbitrary actions (Porter 1995; Jasanoff 1986). Through bottom-up action, citizens may even be able to use social science methods to make their problems visible to otherwise uncaring states (Skocpol 1992). The objectivity that these methods claim can guard against egregious abuses of authority, and yet as shown through comparative analysis, such objectivity itself is a cultural construct that can clothe exercises of power in a spurious rationality unless its intellectual foundations are available for democratic reexamination and critique (Jasanoff 2005). Like the mass media, the social sciences, too, have the power to *make* populations by specifying how to group people into standard categories for the diagnosis and treatment of social ills. As Foucault's writings preeminently demonstrate, the social sciences and technologies serve in this way as the instruments of a new biopower, through which the organization and control of life begin to feature as the stuff of politics (Foucault 1978). Wielded not only by governments but by other expert state-like institutions, such as hospitals, schools, and prisons these biosciences and biotechnologies transform people's subjective ways of understanding themselves, producing what the philosopher Ian Hacking has called new "social kinds" (Hacking 1999; 1995). The eye of external power converges in these institutions with the inner eye of psychological self-perception to produce, in effect, disciplined and self-regulating societies.

It is no surprise, then, that in a period of multiple and overlapping standardizations politics frequently takes the form of individuals asserting themselves against political forces that would rather treat them as members of manageable populations. Briefly put, the conflict so posed is between an *epidemiological* and a *clinical* gaze: the former operating through statistics, numerical aggregation, formal models, and general patterns of cause and effect; the latter wishing to restore to view the individual, the particular, the non-repeatable, and the unique (Desrosières 1998; Epstein 1996). The locus for such confrontations is often the courts, the only institutions of modernity that routinely hold their doors open for the airing of individual grievances against the objectifying and standardizing impulses of the regulatory state. Yet even here through disputes about the qualifications of experts representing the two standpoints, the imperial, population-focused, epidemiological gaze has to some degree successfully appropriated the discourse of science as its own, and so has extended its reach at the expense of the humbly clinical (Jasanoff 1995).

4   THE POLITICS OF ETHICAL CONSTRAINT

Mary Shelley's *Frankenstein* won a new etymological lease on life in the final years of the twentieth century, when British advocacy groups attached the label "frankenfoods" to the products of the new agricultural biotechnologies, thereby implicitly characterizing them as monstrous hybrids unfit for human consumption. Behind the catchy media rhetoric and sometimes lurid imagery, there lurked a growing set of concerns about the ontological implications of the new technologies, particularly those based on the mid-century revolutions in genetics and molecular biology. Could technology populate the earth with entities we would rather not see proliferate, or even come into being? Could developments against nature still be counted as progress? Almost overnight in the 1990s, especially after the birth of the cloned sheep Dolly, the distinction between the *natural* and the *unnatural* became a matter for high politics. Governments of most industrial nations recognized that the legitimacy of their biotechnology policies would depend on navigating that boundary with at least as much circumspection as had previously been invested in decisions about physical safety and risk.

If the politics of risk contains at its core an effort by the state to convert lay citizens to the viewpoint of experts, then the politics of ethical constraint has sought by contrast, to turn lay intuitions into matters of expert judgment. In pursuit of this goal, industrial democracies from the 1980s onward began experimenting with institutions and procedures that would convey formal ethical advice to decision-makers. The appearance of public ethics commissions as a new institutional form provided one salient marker of this development (Jasanoff 2005). Another was the diversity of procedural formats through which national governments sought to extract ethical intuitions from citizens and translate them into principled bases for formulating law and policy. These experiments with citizen juries, consensus conferences, inquiry commissions, referenda, and ethics councils reached a kind of apogee in 2003 with the UK government's nationwide debate on public attitudes to the commercialization of genetically modified crops. Entitled

GM Nation? the event entailed the most comprehensive mobilization of an entire polity ever undertaken around a bioethical question. Differently composed and possessing different formal powers, the varied responses to the problem of bioethics nonetheless had one object in common: they all sought to remove ethical judgment from the domain of the private and the subjective and to transmute ethics itself into a new kind of expertise that states could muster in promoting innovative technologies.

As interesting as the spread of the new expert discourse of bioethics, was the exclusion of some topics from the domain of ethical deliberation. Under US law, for example, intellectual property decisions remained firmly black-boxed within the technical framework of legal interpretation, resisting attempts to recast decisions about the ownership of biological organisms or materials into the language of ethics. Famously, in its 1980 decision in *Diamond v. Chakrabarty* the US Supreme Court ruled that living organisms were patentable under law and that ethical concerns had no place to play in this determination. Manipulation of the human genome and of stem cells taken from embryos aroused enormous passion and generated intense ethical debate in many countries; the manipulation of plant and animal genomes, however, provoked little discussion with rare exceptions, as when the Chicago-based artist Eduardo Kac inserted a jellyfish gene into a rabbit embryo to make an animal that glowed green under ultra-violet light. Interesting, too, was the boundary silently drawn between decisions that were felt to be about risk and those that were seen to involve an ethical component. The national bioethics commission appointed by US President Bill Clinton, for instance, could not reach an ethical consensus on the rights and wrongs of human cloning, but it did conclude that cloning "to create a child would be a premature experiment that would expose the fetus and the developing child to unacceptable risks" (NBAC 1997).

5   CONCLUSIONS

Surveying the landscape of democratic politics since the second half of the twentieth century, one must conclude that the genie has definitively escaped from the bottle: technology, once seen as the preserve of dispassionate engineers committed to the unambiguous betterment of life, now has become a feverishly contested space in which human societies are waging bitter political battles over competing visions of the good and the authority to define it. In the process, the virtually automatic coupling of technology with progress, a legacy of the Enlightenment, has come undone. Uncertainty prevails, both about who governs technology and for whose benefit. No matter which way one looks, the frontiers of technology are seen to be at one and the same time, frontiers of politics. Settling these regions—making them at once technically tractable and socially habitable—requires the simultaneous activation of society's cognitive, instrumental, and normative capacities in a complex dynamic of co-production (Jasanoff 2004).

Technology as a site and object of politics displays itself clearly in four linked yet separate aspects: as risk; as design; as standard; and as ethical constraint. On each front, as we have seen, politics has played out as a dialectic between competing propositions. In the case of risk, debate has centered on the degree to which technocratic faith in expert assessments or guarantees of safety should take precedence over democratic concerns for institutional accountability and the equitable distribution of technology's burdens and benefits. Controversies over technological design have crystallized around the appropriate timing of public involvement—whether it should be meaningfully participatory, far upstream in the manufacturing process, or rather expressed through resistance after a product or system is already on the market or in the theater of war. Opposition to technology's standardizing logic has pitted the statistician's epidemiological gaze against the clinician's sensitivity to interindividual variability and predilection for case-centered explanations. And the search for new ethical constraints in the wake of the biological revolution, has activated debates about the right way to draw the boundary between the natural and the unnatural in a period when the stuff of life increasingly also serves as the stuff of politics.

Weaving through all four sites of political engagement is the figure of the technical expert, that invisible yet ubiquitous ordering agent of modernity. In ever expanding areas of governance, it is the expert more than the legislator or the corporate executive who determines how lives should be lived, individually and collectively. The very meaning of democracy, therefore, increasingly hinges on negotiating the limits of the expert's power in relation to that of the publics served by technology. Are experts accountable, to whom, on what authority, and what provision is there for the injection of non-expert values on matters that fall in the gray zones between conjecture and certainty? By addressing these questions, the politics of technology has tacitly taken up a central challenge of contemporary representative democracy, one left too long untouched by classical political theory.

Two hundred years ago, documents were written that still underpin the legitimacy of modern states. These national constitutions allocated responsibility among the branches of government and specified the protected rights and liberties of individual citizens. They checked untrammeled power and made space for creative fashionings of the self. Today, it is not so much these written texts as the architecture of complex technological systems that performs the constitutional functions of enabling and constraining civilized forms of life—especially on a global scale. By examining the resulting dispensations of artifacts, nature, and society we come closer to understanding how technologies can be scaled to enhance, rather than oppress the human faculties that dreamed them. The politics of technology is the play and the ploy through which today's citizens can assert control over potentially dangerous extensions of their ambitiously inventive selves.

REFERENCES

ANDERSON, B. 1991. *Imagined Communities*, 2nd edn. London: Verso.

BAUMAN, Z. 1991. *Modernity and Ambivalence*. Ithaca, NY: Cornell University Press.

BECK, U. 1992. *Risk Society: Towards a New Modernity*. London: Sage.

BENJAMIN, W. 1968. The work of art in the age of mechanical reproduction. In *Illuminations: Essays and Reflections*, ed. H. Arendt. New York: Schocken Books.

BENTHAM, J. 1995. *The Panopticon Writings*. London: Verso; originally published 1787.

BIJKER, W., HUGHES, T., and PINCH, T. (eds.) 1987. *The Social Construction of Technological Systems*. Cambridge, Mass.: MIT Press.

BOWKER, G. C., and STAR, S. L. 1999. *Sorting Things Out: Classification and Its Consequences*. Cambridge, Mass.: MIT Press.

BREYER, S. 1993. *Breaking the Vicious Circle: Toward Effective Risk Regulation*. Cambridge, Mass.: Harvard University Press.

BRICKMAN, R., JASANOFF, S., and ILGEN, T. 1985. *Controlling Chemicals: The Politics of Regulation in Europe and the United States*. Ithaca, NY: Cornell University Press.

CALLON, M. 1986. Some elements of a sociology of translation: domestication of the scallops and the fishermen of St. Brieuc Bay. Pp. 196–233 in *Power, Action, and Belief*, ed. J. Law. London: Routledge and Kegan Paul.

CARSON, R. 1962. *Silent Spring*. Boston: Houghton Mifflin.

CLARKE, L. 1989. *Acceptable Risk? Making Decisions in a Toxic Environment*. Berkeley: University of California Press.

COLLINS, H. M., and EVANS, R. 2002. The third wave of science studies: studies of expertise and experience. *Social Studies of Science*, 32: 235–96.

COMMISSION OF THE EUROPEAN COMMUNITIES (CEC) 2001. *European Governance: A White Paper*, COM (2001) 428. Brussels, July 27, available at http://europa.eu. int/eur-lex/en/com/ cnc/2001/com2001_0428en01.pdf.

COWAN, R. S. 1983. *More Work for Mother: The Ironies of Household Technology from the Open Hearth to the Microwave*. New York: Basic Books.

DE SOLA POOL, I. 1983. *Technologies of Freedom*. Cambridge, Mass.: Harvard University Press.

DESROSIÈRES, A. 1998. *The Politics of Large Numbers: A History of Statistical Reasoning*. Cambridge, Mass.: Harvard University Press.

DOUGLAS, M. 1966. *Purity and Danger: An Analysis of Concepts of Pollution and Taboo*. London: Routledge and Kegan Paul.

——and WILDAVSKY, A. 1982. *Risk and Culture*. Berkeley: University of California Press.

EDEN, L. 2004. *Whole World on Fire*. Ithaca, NY: Cornell University Press.

EDWARDS, P. 1996. *The Closed World: Computers and the Politics of Discourse in Cold War America*. Cambridge, Mass.: MIT Press.

ELLUL, J. 1964. *The Technological Society.* New York: Vintage.

EPSTEIN, S. 1996. *Impure Science: AIDS, Activism, and the Politics of Knowledge.* Berkeley: University of California Press.

EZRAHI, Y. 1990. *The Descent of Icarus: Science and the Transformation of Contemporary Democracy.* Cambridge, Mass.: Harvard University Press.

FOUCAULT, M. 1978. *The History of Sexuality,* Volume 1. New York: Pantheon.

—— 1995. *Discipline and Punish: The Birth of the Prison.* New York: Vintage.

GOLAN, T. 2004. *Laws of Men and Laws of Nature: The History of Scientific Expert Testimony in England and America.* Cambridge, Mass.: Harvard University Press.

GOLDMAN, M. 2005. *Imperial Nature: The World Bank and Struggles for Social Justice in an Age of Globalization.* New Haven, Conn.: Yale University Press.

GRAHAM, J., and WIENER, J. (eds.) 1995. *Risk versus Risk.* Cambridge, Mass.: Harvard University Press.

GUSTERSON, H. 1996. *Nuclear Rites: A Weapons Laboratory at the End of the Cold War.* Berkeley: University of California Press.

HABERMAS, J. 1984. *The Theory of Communicative Action.* Vol. 1: *Reason and the Rationalization of Society.* Boston: Beacon Press.

HACKING, I. 1995. *Rewriting the Soul: Multiple Personality and the Sciences of Memory.* Princeton, NJ: Princeton University Press.

—— 1999. *The Social Construction of What?* Cambridge, Mass.: Harvard University Press.

HALL, P. 1990. *Great Planning Disasters.* Berkeley: University of California Press.

HARAWAY, D. 1991. *Simians, Cyborgs and Women: The Reinvention of Nature.* New York: Routledge.

HUXLEY, A. 1932. *Brave New World.* London: Chatto and Windus.

IRWIN, A., and WYNNE, B. (eds.) 1996. *Misunderstanding Science? The Public Reconstruction of Science and Technology.* Cambridge: Cambridge University Press.

JASANOFF, S. 1986. *Risk Management and Political Culture.* New York: Russell Sage Foundation.

—— (ed.) 1994. *Learning From Disaster: Risk Management After Bhopal.* Philadelphia: University of Pennsylvania Press.

—— 1995. *Science at the Bar: Law, Science and Technology in America.* Cambridge, Mass.: Harvard University Press.

—— (ed.) 1997. *Comparative Science and Technology Policy.* Cheltenham: Edward Elgar.

—— (ed.) 2004. *States of Knowledge: The Co-production of Science and Social Order.* London: Routledge.

—— 2005. *Designs on Nature: Science and Democracy in Europe and the United States.* Princeton, NJ: Princeton University Press.

KAGAN, R. 2003. *Of Paradise and Power: America and Europe in the New World Order.* New York: Knopf.

KHAGRAM, S. 2004. *Dams and Development: Transnational Struggles for Water and Power.* Ithaca, NY: Cornell University Press.

LATOUR, B. 1992. Where are the missing masses? The sociology of a few mundane artifacts. Pp. 225–58 in *Shaping Technology/Building Society,* ed. W. E. Bijker and J. Law. Cambridge, Mass.: MIT Press.

LEACH, M., SCOONES, I., and WYNNE, B. (eds.) 2005. *Science and Citizens: Globalization and the Challenge of Engagement.* London: Zed Books.

LESSIG, L. 2001. *The Future of Ideas: The Fate of the Commons in a Connected World.* New York: Random House.

MacKenzie, D. 1990. *Inventing Accuracy: A Historical Sociology of Nuclear Missile Guidance*. Cambridge, Mass.: MIT Press.

Mies, M., and Shiva, V. 1993. *Ecofeminism*. Halifax: Fernwood.

Nandy, A. (ed.) 1988. *Science, Hegemony and Violence*. Tokyo: United Nations University.

National Bioethics Advisory Commission (NBAC) 1997. *Cloning Human Beings*. Washington, DC. Available at: http://www.georgetown.edu/ research/nrcbl/nbac/ pubs/ cloning1/cloning.pdf (accessed April 4, 2005).

National Research Council (NRC) 1983. *Risk Assessment in the Federal Government: Managing the Process*. Washington, DC: National Academies Press.

——1996. *Understanding Risk: Informing Decisions in Democratic Society*. Washington, DC: National Academies Press.

Nelkin, D. (ed.) 1992. *Controversy*, 3rd edn. Newbury Park, Calif.: Sage.

Noble, D. F. 1976. Social choice in machine design: the case of automatically controlled machine tools, and a challenge for labor. *Politics and Society*, 8: 313–47.

——1977. *America By Design: Science, Technology and the Rise of Corporate Capitalism*. Oxford: Oxford University Press.

Perrow, C. 1984. *Normal Accidents: Living with High Risk Technologies*. New York: Basic Books.

Porter, T. M. 1995. *Trust in Numbers: The Pursuit of Objectivity in Science and Public Life*. Princeton, NJ: Princeton University Press.

Power, M., and Hutter, B. (eds.) 2005. *Organizational Encounters with Risk*. Cambridge: Cambridge University Press.

Price, D. K. 1965. *The Scientific Estate*. Cambridge, Mass.: Harvard University Press.

Proctor, R. N. 1988. *Racial Hygiene: Medicine Under the Nazis*. Cambridge, Mass.: Harvard University Press.

Putnam, R. 2000. *Bowling Alone*. New York: Simon and Schuster.

Rosanvallon, P. 2000. *The New Social Question: Rethinking the Welfare State*, trans. B. Harshav. Princeton, NJ: Princeton University Press.

Roy, A. 1999. *The Greater Common Good*. Bombay: India Book Distributors.

Rueschemeyer, D., and Skocpol, T. (eds.) 1996. *States, Social Knowledge, and the Origins of Modern Social Policies*. Princeton, NJ: Princeton University Press.

Sclove, R. 1995. *Democracy and Technology*. New York: Guilford.

Scott, J. C. 1976. *The Moral Economy of the Peasant*. New Haven, Conn.: Yale University Press.

——1985. *Weapons of the Weak: Everyday Forms of Peasant Resistance*. New Haven, Conn.: Yale University Press.

——1998. *Seeing Like a State*. New Haven, Conn.: Yale University Press.

Shelley, M. 1994. *Frankenstein*. Ware: Wordsworth; originally published 1816.

Shiva, V. 1997. *Biopiracy: The Plunder of Nature and Knowledge*. Toronto: Between the Lines.

Short, J. F., and Clarke, L. (eds.) 1992. *Organizations, Uncertainties, and Risk*. Boulder, Colo.: Westview Press.

Skocpol, T. 1992. *Protecting Soldiers and Mothers: The Political Origins of Social Policy in the United States*. Cambridge, Mass.: Harvard University Press.

Slovic, P. et al. 1980. Facts and fears: understanding perceived risk. Pp. 181–214 in *Societal Risk Assessment: How Safe is Safe Enough?*, ed. R. Schwing and W. A. Albers, Jr. New York: Plenum.

——1985. Characterizing perceived risks. Pp. 91–125 in *Perilous Progress*, ed. R. W. Kates et al. Boulder, Colo.: Westview.

STIGLITZ, J. E. 2002. *Globalization and Its Discontents.* New York: W. W. Norton.

STOKES, D. E. 1997. *Pasteur's Quadrant.* Washington, DC: Brookings Institution.

STOREY, W. K. 1997. *Science and Power in Colonial Mauritius.* Rochester, NY: University of Rochester Press.

SUNSTEIN, C. 2002. *Risk and Reason: Safety, Law, and the Environment.* Cambridge: Cambridge University Press.

——2005. *The Law of Fear.* Cambridge: Cambridge University Press.

TICKNER, J. A. (ed.) 2003. *Precaution: Environmental Science and Preventive Public Policy.* Washington, DC: Island Press.

UNITED KINGDOM, HOUSE OF LORDS SELECT COMMITTEE ON SCIENCE AND TECHNOLOGY 2000. *Third Report: Science and Society.* Available at: http://www.parliament.the-stationery-office.co. uk/pa/ld199900/ldselect/ldsctech/38/3801.htm (accessed April 4, 2005).

VAUGHAN, D. 1996. *The Challenger Launch Decision: Risky Technology, Culture, and Deviance at NASA.* Chicago: University of Chicago Press.

VISVANATHAN, S. 1997. *Carnival for Science: Essays on Science, Technology and Development.* Delhi: Oxford University Press.

VOGEL, D. 1986. *National Styles of Regulation.* Ithaca, NY: Cornell University Press.

WAJCMAN, J. 1991. *Feminism Confronts Technology.* University Park: Pennsylvavia State University Press.

WINNER, L. 1986. Do artifacts have politics? Pp. 19–39 in Winner, *The Whale and the Reactor.* Chicago: University of Chicago Press.

WYNNE, B. 1988. Unruly technology. *Social Studies of Science,* 18: 147–67.

——1995. Public understanding of science. Pp. 361–88 in *The Handbook of Science and Technology Studies,* ed. S. Jasanoff et al. Thousand Oaks, Calif.: Sage.

——1996. Misunderstood misunderstandings: social identities and public uptake of science. In Irwin and Wynne 1996, 19–46.

PART X

OLD AND NEW

....

CHAPTER 41

DUCHAMP'S URINAL:WHO SAYS WHAT'S RATIONAL WHEN THINGS GET TOUGH?

....

DAVID E. APTER

The main factor in the matter is really the system in which they subsist, not the conscious will of individuals, who may indeed in many cases be carried along by the system to positions they would never have arrived at by deliberate choice. (Pareto 1966, 269)

1 BACKGROUND

....

PARETO's is the dominant view even to this day. Indeed, it is one that I share mostly but not completely. However, there is another side to the coin—one that over time (given the nature of modern politics) seems to me more and more immediately relevant. That is the role of discourse as discourse in the preservation and alteration of political systems including what might be called languages of action (Mitchell

1983).[1] In the age of modernism, sacrificing for higher principles can just as well lead to burnings at the stake as it did in the age of Savonarola. In effect, people can talk themselves into anything—and that goes for people everywhere. The purpose of this discussion is to consider how, why, and when discourse can play this role.

Before doing so I want to consider very briefly why so obvious a factor as discourse, what people say to each other and to themselves, is not more central to political analysis, as compared to systemic approaches. It is not that discourse is entirely ignored, of course. But as a major concern in political and social and political analysis, it definitely takes a back seat. This despite the fact that at major universities there are institutes, research centers, whole industries aimed at understanding what affects political attitudes and shapes beliefs. The tendency is to treat such matters behaviorally and instrumentally, however, rather than subjecting them to substantive interpretation. The more general interest is on questions of the intertwining of propaganda and political advertising with the education of citizens, or on instances when differences in views affect political elections or policy outcomes, or on when they result in conflict. Certainly there is concern about when the pursuit of interests makes for the enrichment or the banalization of values (political beliefs as patriotic gore), and also about how populist manipulation associated with political campaigns affects parties, elections, and leadership—not to speak of when and how political beliefs can at some times represent deep convictions and at others more momentary reactions. These and many other questions are matters of political and social scrutiny.

Furthermore, the way that loyalties are currently manipulated to become matters of not only affiliation but also identity, makes them less matters of choice and more like endowed convictions that pre-cook what constitutes relevant information. Hand-me-down reactions substitute for knowledge, and off-the-cuff judgments for interpretation. Insofar as one believes that democracy requires an informed citizenry, the existing emphases on studying attitudes, belief systems, and political predispositions using relevant measurement techniques would appear to be more than satisfactory.

---

[1] The term discourse can be used in several ways. It can refer to the grammar and the rhetoric of language. It can constitute the ways people interact in terms of exchanges of meaning. It can take a more political turn as a mode of negotiation or confrontation. It can be treated as a system in and of itself, of which linguistics is the more general framework, representation the particular mode of expression, and interpretation the context of meaning. More instrumentally it can be used to establish moral and other boundaries by establishing defining qualities which can denigrate, demonize, and dehumanize those designated as "negative others," pariahs, brutes, human beings becoming merchandise, or it can glorify, humanize, etc. Political discourse as a weapon tends to establish binaries, good and evil empires, for example. Here discourse will refer first to how people interpret their social and political conditions by means of recounting or narrativizing their experiences, an empirical matter, and second as an analytical framework providing categories of the analysis of the way narrativizing generates political power.

The problem is that such emphases, important as they are, do not deal with the power of discourse itself, the uses of political language, and the power of interpretation to affect people's judgment in important ways. On such matters, political theory remains descriptive rather than analytical, despite efforts to categorize and periodize the relationship between belief systems and the mobilization of opinion and of political groups. Even the best such analyses, like that of Putnam (1973) or earlier Converse and others, which give a more-or-less down-on-the-ground view of what people think, wind up as relatively Olympian.

There is a difference between distributional empirical analysis and contextual understanding of people's reactions to and understanding of events on the ground. One needs to be able to move from people as individual units to the ways their own understanding of what is to be done lead them to form themselves into groups, transform organization into institutions, and what such jurisdictions as nations and states come to mean. We need to know what makes for interpretative benchmarks (disjunctive historical punctuation marks, wars, major depressions, revolutions, regime changes) by means of which "mentalities" are redefined and periodized.[2] We need to be able to connect on a deeper level the relationship between shifts in public policy and the actions of proponents and opponents, whose discourse itself and the instrumental use they make of it enables them to control or transcend their immediate circumstances. The focus in this regard is on the uses of narrative as stories told by individuals which, as they become collectivized, become a framework for interpretative analysis.

By emphasizing discourse and the role of interpretation I want to examine such questions as, "When does cultural and ethnic diversity produce conflict, sometimes murderous, and when do multicultural communities live in relative harmony?" And in terms of the last question, "To what extent does poverty create the conditions under which ethnic, religious, ideological, and other differences can be fabricated, manipulated and—in the name of principles of justice or rights—become a means to self-interest and political corruption?" (Benhabib 1996). One also wants to know when political exhortations fall on more-or-less deaf ears, and when there is wider receptivity—not least of all in terms of how people can turn the ordinariness of daily life into political drama.

One cannot begin to deal in depth with such questions here of course. But it is possible to examine them with a view to identifying what such analysis might require. And in any case, given the range of circumstances and ambiguities most of what might be true of one situation might also be true of another, but with vastly

---

[2] With respect to such movements there is already an enormous literature, both analytical and using case materials (Smelser 1969). In these terms I want to use discourse theory as a way to deal with the problematic of collective action, that is, "joint action in pursuit of common ends," a definition that raises the question of how such action evolves out of individual actions (Tilly 1978; 1984; McAdam 1982; Tarrow 1994). It is a problem for which systemic analysis can only take us so far (Tilly 1984; Arrow 1963; Olson 1965; Green and Shapiro 1994).

different outcomes. As for systemic hypotheses such as "the greater the gap between rich and poor, the greater the degree of social and political polarization therefore the greater the chance of political conflict or contestation" (which one might consider a fairly commonsense idea) is empirically more dubious, since no one-to-one relationship between degrees of poverty and political conflict can be established any more than with degrees of social suffering or perceived injustices. There are too many contingencies and concrete variations on established themes (Soule and Olzak 2004; Apter 2001). Similarly, cultural differences that become explosive may appear to result from age-old rivalries that on closer inspection turn out to be new conflicts in old battle dress. Some areas such as the Balkans, the Caucasus, parts of Africa, and so on appear to be perpetually embattled; but historically they show a much more mixed picture, ranging from conflict to accommodation and from virtually rigid exclusivist boundaries to high degrees of social and political interaction. Similarly with religions, which can be ecumenical or monopolistic or both. And of course a great deal will depend on political institutions and their responsiveness to needs. In some cases democracy is successful in easing political tensions; in other cases it intensifies such tensions. Injunctions in the name of cultural traditions easily translate into collective claims and become part of the great debate between individual versus collective representation, including how much of the one is necessary to enhance the other. Much will also depend on the degree to which some minority communities themselves maintain closed boundaries, accepting economic interaction with a host society but resisting social interaction. In any case, while cultural diversity can work in many different ways, it is not "difference" that makes the difference but the way differences are coded, ritualized, narrativized, and textualized. The point is that although such questions are subject to a great deal of debate many plausible factors can be mobilized case by case. And a great deal depends on the discriminatory qualities and powers built into and deployed by interpretative languages.

There are a variety of systemic theories that are being used to explain how people define the terms of their existence, their ideas of causes and consequences, according to real or perceived grievances, individually and collectively. Among these rational choice theory is perhaps the most generalized. It has certain difficulties, however. For example it is difficult to derive the individual from the collective (Olson 1965; Arrow 1963). But it can serve to explain such matters as affiliations and identities, immigration and emigration, citizenship and affiliation, as well as such matters as ideological preferences and language shifting (Laitin 1989). Other theories point to more instrumental factors, as in the work of Amartya Sen (1984). Some purport to explain ethnic poverty (referring to ethnic groups among which poverty appears resistant to remedial efforts) less as a result of than a cause of poverty (Easterly and Levine 1997)—an idea that seems to work in the few cases where it applies, but leaves out the many cases where it does not. What systemic theories are good at doing is establishing a logic of probabilities. But there remains a gap between the predisposition towards an event and its actual occurrence. On such matters there are long-standing and continuing debates (Tilly 1984; King, Keohane, and Verba 1994).

In these terms one might say that discourse theory is simply a step towards closing the gap—a way of suggesting what can transform a possibility into a reality. It can best be used in a context of case studies and particularly cases that are somewhat deviant, highlighting the exception rather than the rule in order to cast light on the rule itself. One reason why this is so is because for the most part, what people do tends to naturalize events and normalize what should be problematic. For example who would doubt that over time people will resist reconsidering the terms and meaning of the system of which they are part, while some by deliberate choice, will act to change it? Similarly, it is to be expected that each generation will see things differently and such changes are bound to be socially and politically abrasive; that what is considered progress by some will be considered erosion and decline by others. It is also obvious that the process of mediating past and present will go through periods of normalcy and social trauma. Moreover, normalcy tends to be associated with a shrewd and common universe of discourse in which the terms are pretty much shared. But "normalcy" as a social condition may of course hide all kinds of festering sores which, redefined as injustices at a later time can become politically significant. Behind American "normalcy" when cities were safer to live in and schools more stable teaching environments was hidden the plight of black Americans, ethnic poverty, and economic discrimination.

In any case, most contemporary efforts to deal with the kinds of questions indicated above assume a common universe of discourse dominated by bargaining, exchange, rewards, and constraints by means of carrot and stick policies, not to speak of costs and benefits, price and quantity. Such approaches by their very nature cannot be wrong. What most people do most of the time is amenable to such analysis. It is less convincing, although admittedly still useful in dealing with those circumstances where people will try to trip up systems by defying their configural boundaries, roles and rules, norms and structures. They are less good at accounting for anxiety, outrage, or rage—or at understanding how certain passionate commitments elevate, in the name of outrage, outrageous principles that become all consuming.[3] It is when these become more important than interests that the rules of bargaining and exchange change—something we see in more extremist political movements, manifested not least in violence and terrorism.

---

[3] I myself have studied groups and interviewed members of the Popular Front for the Liberation of Palestine in Damascus whose hatred of Jews was the central principle of their existence, their conversation, a kind of morbidity. In the course of research in Africa, Latin America, and Europe I have also encountered hate groups whose intensity (and indeed the entire structuring of their lives, the networks they share, the language they use) is entirely internal and internalized while directed with peculiar ferocity at those they dislike.

We have posed these questions for a purpose, to draw attention to a body of knowledge that is concerned with such topics but in a very different way from conventional political analysis. In fact, the analysis of language and discourse in politics has in the past several decades become a central feature of critical theory, but not by political scientists. Appearing under various names and guises—structuralism, post-structuralism, political phenomenology, discourse analysis—that have themselves become objects of controversy (not least of all in the so-called "culture wars") and quite often derision. Whatever the merits of such debates, those of relevance here concern themselves in some fashion with what Jerome Bruner (1991) has referred to as the "narrative construction of reality"—a way of analyzing how people interpret events in which they participate as well as the political perspectives they draw from these.

It is that aspect of politics that I want to examine here, where the emphasis is on the narrative reconstruction of reality. I want to explore how events are endowed with meanings, the importance in this regard of context, and the kinds of categories that might be useful for so doing. The purpose of such an enterprise is to examine how in these terms discourse becomes a source as well as a means of political power (Bhabha 1990).

2   DISCOURSE AND SYSTEM

In this sense the present emphasis is less on strong structural configurations than on actions (not least violent ones) aimed at systemic amendment and alteration. We want to know better how to "read" political actions in terms of what Geertz (1973) has called "social texts." We want to see, both analytically and empirically, how the quotidian can be transformed into the exceptional by means of an accumulation of ordinary events and experiences that suddenly cohere differently, to make a different sense. And the starting point for such analysis is talk, that is the common articulation of immediate experiences, first in intimate settings such as the familial and then moving out to more public ones, neighborhoods, clubs, political groups, parties, movements, and so on. It is by means of such amalgamating intersubjectivities that arguments are built up and expressive rationalities formed, especially those that embody a certain generosity or preference for one or other set of ideas and offer ensembles of relevance in the events themselves (Cefaï 2001). Making a narrative out of one's private condition is the starting point for such shared exchanges. These in turn provide privileged understanding of actual circumstances, identities, a sense of affiliation, and more particularly where one stands in relation to power (whether one exercises it, is its beneficiary or victim). Such narratives then provide an interior understanding that makes for consociation, what will be called "discourse communities."

The shift from individual narrative to collective stories does not happen by itself. It requires agents, more-or-less exceptional political figures who gain substance in the act of collectivizing and who are able to articulate publicly what have previously been more private or local thoughts. In short, they need to be good storytellers in the sense that they provide drama and excitement by touching on people's actual experiences and circumstances and by so doing enable those people to see themselves in a different light. When by this means new clienteles are mobilized, discourse becomes central in the formation of collective power—whether inside the system or outside it.

Depending on the richness of the narrative, the extent to which it is germane to people's experiences and prevailing social moods, the mobilizing discourses can take different forms that appear to make the most sense in the context of the moment, whether conservative or radical, orthodox or revolutionary. Their specific content forms concrete systems, providing an improving consequence over the past and a logic of outcomes for the future. It is in this sense that discourse enables individuals to change their views and in so doing alter the way they see their lives and institutions. Hence, if "system" configures political and social behavior, "discourse" and interpretation alters system.

The emphasis here is on the transformation from the ordinary to the exceptional. Conventional institutions, even those that embody representative principles of government, are in this sense always subject to review. There is always a radical project. What divides people according to the terms of prejudicial categorical imperatives can be the fine-tuning of ethical sensibilities vis-à-vis race, ethnicity, and gender as well as class, colonialism, and forms of mental apartheid that have led to injustices, discrimination, and common and punitive discrepancies. It can be the reduction to the primitive: violence, terror, torture, the debasement of lives and property.

3   DISCOURSE AND POLITICS

Discourse analysis seems to be against the grain of most contemporary political analysis, and to some extent it is. This is particularly so as political science became a science, that is, when it became both systematic and systemic. One might say that in its earlier modes its science was based on the configuring properties of laws and institutions and their combination in the original and enabling properties of constitutions. The instrumentalities, law, law-making, legislative and executive bodies, administrative structures, and the dynamics of party politics and electoral systems, as well as constraints on executive power, represented democracy as both a model and a standard against which to judge all other systems.

In this regard political science has been about discourse and is itself a discourse. Not least of all it is a story, an evolutionary narrative of the political good cast in the form of a "history of ideas" about the refinement and development of political mechanisms which over time constitute a stable self-sustaining "system"—a kind of moving equilibrium model—in which executive accountability and checks and balances coincide with equity in balancing by means of power and money. In terms of the political science discourse democratic ideas and influences will triumph over others in a story of continuous struggle and unfinished accomplishment (Pagden 1987). The sub-text is the refinement of political sensibilities, of humanity as the embodiment of rights and obligations in laws and procedures, which make their appearance as a result of the give-and-take of politics, that is to say the consequences of the mutual reinforcement of the procedural and the institutional. It is a narrative of the Enlightenment, civil and emancipatory, rationality triumphing, democracy as transcendental overcoming of monopolistic religious and political beliefs to emerge into the light of the open society (Smith 1997). As an evolution of institutions democracy is thus universalized as a system, only temporarily reversible, and despite variations in concrete practices its underlying premises constitute a one-size-fits-all set of principles with structural variations according to time, place, and manner—and the more difficulties encountered along the way, the more heroic the struggle to arrive there (Shapiro 1986).

But of course such a narrative contains a good deal of wishful thinking. Obviously such an evolution is and has been reversible, and many times. Its counter-revolutions have been religious and political, the more radical forms of the latter providing a critical discourse and a logic within its own evolutionary narrative. Moreover, instead of the economic and the political balancing each other, with the political market rectifying inequities of wealth in the economic market and the economic market diluting the concentration of power in the political one, they quite often reinforce one other to produce conditions where the discourse is applied from above to achieve compliance from those on the bottom or where the discourse from the bottom becomes radicalized. Here the discourse of development has produced both Marxist and liberal modes of interpretation, with many varieties and offshoots.

Paradoxically enough, as Marxism and other radical discourses have for the time being virtually disappeared, perhaps the greatest threat to the democratic discourse today is the revival of those most powerful of reinterpretative discourses, whose claims are increasingly posed in religious-ethical terms, their power deriving not least of all in conversionary and monopolistic impulses. Combine such ethical with redemptive claims, and institutional political discourses begin to change their meaning as well as their sources of power.

All the more so since as a discourse religion involves the most intimate aspects of personal life, indeed the meaning of life itself, an ascetic component defined as moral virtue, an esthetic component embodied in religious language. Redemptive truths, spoken through the political persona as mediator between the divine and man, the word as revelatory, as orality, reverberating in the sonorority of chants, accompanied by sanctifying gestures, and as texts: all become self-reinforcing sacred objects, their meanings subject to exegesis. Public space is a pulpit, a stage, a theater, a place of worshipful performance, complete with intertwined panoplies of conse-cration, homilies, the lives of saints, demons, Tantric figures, as the case might be. The sacramental miniaturization of the throne of god offers politics the earthly simulacrum for the heavenly cosmos, and narratives of suffering and overcoming. In Christianity it is the stations of the Cross; in Islam, the battles of Mohammed; in Judaism, exile, depatrimonialization, repatrimonialization, and so on.

In turn discourse in these terms has concrete organizational consequences: splits, denominational conflicts, the urge to monopolize god, to proselytize, interpreting texts to power the political in the name of religion with all its claims to loyalties. By combining fantasy and fiction with events shrouded by subsequent and selective recounting, the assertion and ritualization of truth values is the foundation of orthodoxies.

Of course religious discourse has no monopoly on such matters. The same applies as well to discourses that claim reason as the foundation of doctrine, from the Enlightenment to Marxism, and it frequently surrounds even the most pragmatic of contemporary interest politics. In this sense doctrinal discourses, both religious and political share certain characteristics. Each can be flammable. Each invokes its heroes, its fictionalized history. Each has its own calvary and eschat-ology—George Washington's winter, Lenin in exile, Mao's internal exiles and eternal returns. A host of political leaders can be included: Peron in Argentina; "Che" in Cuba (and elsewhere in Latin America); Nkrumah in Africa; not to speak of the host of Islamic fundamentalists who today have so successfully hijacked decolonization and anti-imperialist struggles and hitched their secular political goals to the star of ecclesiastical redemption. Indeed, the revival of mythical events by means of religious discourses serves up self-authenticating pedigrees that in connecting past and present, do so in ways that redefine a moral as well as political evolution. In this respect religious beliefs are modes of discourse that can be both explicitly anti-political and entirely political, all at the same time. In these respects too politics is at something of a disadvantage because in the last analysis it confronts a here-and-now reality that religion does not.

So it is that even here-and-now politics, so practical and instrumental at one level, can at another produce its own myths and magic. Its narratives endow terrain, place, and persons with identities that take on their own sacral characteristics. Nations especially are the result of founding myths and transcending stories, with their own equivalents of the stations of the cross. Leaders, especially radical ones that have been imprisoned or exiled by authorities, become Odysseus-like accumulating an aura of wisdom through wanderings. Others, more oracular use their exile to make cosmocratic claims to political truths—a Lenin for example, not to mention many putative third world descendants. These acquired characteristics make light of the secular accomplishments of Western democracy in part because of real discrepancies between principles and practices—discrepancies that seem to be systemic in character rather than simply because of repugnant politics. By turning the less advantaged into political victims, a condition is established for defining discrimination and a logic is provided for compensatory action and systemic alternatives, quite often justifying the use of political violence in the transition. In this way particular discourses can alter the terms of engagement between people in and between different parts of the world.

In this sense discourse as politics is not simply reactive. Interpretation incorporates political imagination and creativity. So too violence becomes a particular form of liberating expressive action. Fascism claimed an intrinsically liberating, cleansing power through its love affair with danger, death, and dying. Doctrine in this sense derives from acts that make people afraid, or otherwise cause them to sit up and take notice. Nothing is more theatrical and in this sense political than the funerals of victims, the chants of followers in the procession, the howls of remorse and anger (Hollier 1988).

More dispassionately, one might want to consider terrorism or other forms of violence diagnostically, as symptomatic of some larger ill. In this sense it is there, not only to be "read" as a "text" but as a source of information about how to provide ameliorative rather than retaliatory action, especially where the perpetrators do not themselves appear to be political extortionists but have some broader principles in mind. However, where principles are raised over interests, neither amelioration nor retaliation is likely to achieve a satisfactory result. For it is more and more often the case that violence as a discourse creates its own system, its own networks and interior goals (Apter 1999). In this sense too inversionary discourses are things in themselves with a momentum of their own. Indeed, if they were to succeed in achieving their ostensible goals they would lose their *raison d'être*. That is why so often the real goals of many such movements are quite different from their ostensible ones. When violence as a discourse creates its own objects, to win would be to lose. With the politics of the deed, the old anarchist slogan, the act itself represents the unification of the symbolic and the concrete; the more shocking the act, the greater the impact. Indeed, the smaller a violence-prone group, the more intense its hatred for some representational enemy, the more totally preoccupying such hatred becomes until it is absolutely central to one's whole being. In this respect what may be seen as a liberating project is itself a straitjacket. By the same token the choreography of violence can become virtually an art form, itself a radical mode of recontextualization.

4   DISCOURSE AS SYMBOLIC CAPITAL

Which brings us to the expressive side of political action as symbolic capital. In virtually every political confrontation there is an artistic component, the expressly symbolic referent, dress and costume, the esthetics of weaponry, songs, poems, architecture, etc. The arts of war and peace are expressions of art itself, the latter not at all separate from politics. In these terms the power of art as an expression of politics as well as being a mode of discourse has long been recognized. Indeed, the American and French Revolutions, for example, created whole symbolic iconographies, while claiming connections with the classical antique world (Ozouf 1976; Chartier 1991; Darnton 1984). In African and Asian polities, the discourses included claims to authentic pedigrees of ancient civilizations. As for Islam, just as in the Middle Ages "rendering to Caesar" became irrelevant so too in the Muslim world there was a single overarching, all-embracing political community rather than a doctrine of two swords, sacred and secular. In all these different discourses, language and social text intertwine, and so does art whether in a context of religion or politics, visuality as well as performance making up a truly significant dimension of the expressive or symbolic side of power (Alexander 2004). Hence, memory, myth, and the various forms of their representation as power are both a consequence of discourse and a product of the creativity, culture, and art that go into it. How and in what form is always site- and situation-specific. Moreover, discourse creation also involves discourse-shifting, each such shift invoking a change in cultural repertoires (Bauman 1973).

To illustrate what I mean, I will take as an example of such discourse-shifting a specific event that in effect changed the course of the discourse on modern art— particularly art that became increasingly non-representational, just before and after the First World War. Doctrines such as Cubism, Dadaism, Russian Constructivism, and Italian Futurism were political in the sense that they were bound up with war and revolutions, and as such fundamentally engaged with politics both as disaffiliation and as affiliation with radical movements. In broader terms art movements of these kinds were part of a larger and radical discourse that took many forms, some of them quite surrealist in their own right.

The period was one of particular ferment and this was reflected in terms of discourse. Democratic claims, rights to self-determination, intertwined with radical transformation and revolutionary art forms requiring new modes of under-standing—new views of social and political context, but also color, form, seeing altogether. In this sense much of modern art was deliberately subversive, and politics was explicitly joined with art not only in posters, manifestos, and Agitprop, but street theater demonstrations, posters, staged confrontations with authorities: a political choreography, politics as theater.

The point is that the symbolic is always an articulated affinity between art and politics, with the creativity of the symbolic radiating outwards in movements going from centers to peripheries, and at many levels and guaranteed to cause outrage, both politically for and politically against. Which brings me to the now famous and humorous example which provides the title of this chapter—Duchamp's urinal. Politically trivial in itself, it was an event that came to have an enormous impact on the discourse of modern art and its canon. In 1917, the year is not irrelevant since it marked American entry into the First World War, the artist Marcel Duchamp who some would argue was to become the most influential figure in twentieth century art as well as the least political of artists, submitted an upside down porcelain urinal signed R. Mutt for exhibition at the First Annual Exhibition of Independent Artists in New York. Although the show was not supposed to be juried, and Duchamp himself was one of the twenty-one members of the board of directors, it was rejected, setting off a storm of controversy. The controversy itself served as a kind of lightning rod for those with differing views about art. The upside-down urinal became an icon for those for who passionately believed that academic art had become obsolete, just as the old world had become obsolete in the light of the horrific consequences of the war.

Some referred to the urinal as the Madonna of the Bathroom; others saw it metaphorically as a Buddha, a Madonna, a Fountain. The debate was not least about whether the functional had intrinsic aesthetic properties, and whether by turning it upside down this most functional of objects became something else. In any case it served as a redefining moment for the discourse on art—a debate that not only continues to this day and one in which Duchamp long after his death continues to figure. For our purposes the example illustrates the following points. One is the importance of the discourse itself. Second is the importance of discourse shifting in relation to context and interpretation. Third, it shows how interpretative action is a consequence of both. (As for the urinal itself: when is it a urinal, top down, bottom up, or no matter what, and when is it something else?)[4]

---

[4] For those who would like to see this "urinal-fountain" it is on permanent exhibition at the Centre Pompidou in Paris. As for Duchamp himself, he gave up art for chess, a game whose only object is to win on the basis of rational choices. But even as a chess fanatic he never lost his sense of "context." Impeccably dressed for the occasion he had himself playing chess with a naked woman. And chess, after all, has its dark and light pieces.

5   DISCOURSE AND CHANGE

Which brings us back to the question of discourse and change. Symbolic inter-ruptions can serve as seismic shifts that manifest themselves in long-cycle tenden-cies. Or they can serve as punctuation marks demarcating points in a narrative of long-cycle alternations. One might go further and say that all politics is a combin-ation of long-cycle contexts combined with short-cycle events. This is as true for democracies, where the past is continuously being evoked as a measure for the present, as it is for other kinds of societies not least those that might be called "honor and revenge" systems in which long-nursed grievances erupt in sporadic, vengeful tit-for-tat outbreaks.

But long-cycle changes are certainly at work in the United States, a context of narratives more and more mutually hostile and cumulative, memory building on memory to the point that previous events, the Civil War and its aftermath for example, begin to combine with other long-cycle changes in American society triggered by short-cycle events like the civil rights movement of the 1960s together with its anti-war discourses and claims to racial equality. These are very much present in the polarized politics of America today. If for some the 1960s represented the end of post-Second World War optimism, the discourses of its largely gener-ational and radical mobilization challenged conventional practices in the name of deep principle, dividing and offending parts of the political community in ways many found and still find disturbing. To upset long-standing and discriminatory racial patterns, to elevate gender issues, to decry patriotism in terms of war in Vietnam meant turning conventional practices and discourses upside down. It is one thing to make the top of a urinal its bottom, but when the discourse community itself such as it is or was is being overturned, it means the world is coming apart.

One response to long-cycle change is deep anxiety, if not hatred of all that challenges conventional boundaries, sexual, racial, or political. Nor is it surprising that such feelings have found their way into religious revivalism and evangelical fundamentalism. Both offer the promise, and indeed the authority to put what's wrong in the world right. Combined with other factors—not least the political truculence that manifested itself in political party realignments, including the virtual desertion by the South from the Democratic Party—these are some of the long-cycle changes manifested in the dominant political discourse of the day, where the center has moved so far to the right that the United States is now in some ways a different country. These discourse shifts not only register the deep divides in the voting population, but are manifested in the interpretive context of contemporary issues such as the price of oil, the level of unemployment, how to deal with terrorism, or the war in Iraq. In this sense, although one might say that how people interpret politics and vote depends on how they see the issues of the day, that in turn depends on where they stand in relation to the longer-cycle changes.

6   MEANING AND CONTENT

In these regards one might also say that to explain political life and action context is everything. It gives meaning to events. It creates an aura of understanding. It is a basis of competing views. It leads to factions. Interpretation goes together with opinion, public and private. It forms mutually hostile groups or cooperative coalitions. Context frames meaning. Meaning creates context. Change the one and you change the other. Some contexts are broad and inclusive like religion or nationalism, each of which is subject to a kind of meaning-mitosis, division into sects, ideological fractions. In this sense each provides a framework and a language for the interpretation of the here-and-now, even as it resonates with the before and after.

This kaleidoscopic quality would suggest that, like Duchamp's "fountain" contextual analysis is more art than science, more subjective than objective, less subject to structural rules, impossible to quantify, and lacking in empirical and methodological precision. It is at best a residual of social science, a way of handling certain kinds of contingencies after all other explanatory approaches have been exhausted. One might call attention to context and with it interpretation as analysis of the last instance.

It is not only in the name of science that context and interpretation are placed in this category. If the most realistic way of coming to understand complex political and social phenomena is by means of theories that examine the institutions, structures, and terms that delimit the free scope of human action (and of course such structural limitations will vary in terms of which kinds of configural theories one selects), they are also altered by political actions that break the mold. All political and social life is bounded. It is subject to limitations. Finding what those limits are—whether in predominantly economic terms, or different forms of social structure, or the rationality rules of market competition—is one of the main purposes of configural or structural forms of analysis. And nibbling away at their limits is what a good deal of political action is about, not only in terms of particular and rectifying issues, but in more generalized terms, principles, ethics, and theory.

Which brings me to the role of subjectivity. As a topic it is outside the scope of this essay, as it is from most political science inquiry. However, this does not mean it is irrelevant. In discourse terms, the matter of collectivizing actions and events is a process of "objectivizing" the subjective. One way to do this is in terms of ranked preference, scheduled priorities, attitudes and beliefs that can be surveyed as social facts, thereby establishing profiles, evaluative criteria that enable comparisons through time and between systems. Another is simply to assume a common rationality, an approach that decontextualizes all cultural and other differences between groups to establish a common standard of motivated action. The best example is rational choice theory, which has developed highly generalized models that lend themselves to formalization, the most analytically powerful of which provide rationality universals that hold under any variety of circumstances, the more impervious to particularities the better (Green and Shapiro 1994).

That these dominant tendencies will remain so is not due to some preference to orthodoxy but to the way in which the logic of science applies to human affairs. The present emphasis while in no way challenging such tendencies, suggests that just as scientific inquiry answers questions so it raises new ones—some of which lie beyond their theoretical scope. It is in this sense that discourse, by examining both concrete events and how people come to understand them according to one or other discourse, reverses that logic emphasizing context, interpretation, and indeed the role of meaning in politics. It emphasizes theoretically what has been considered residual by rational choice and other systemic theories. In this sense the broad question to be dealt with is whether or not it is possible to square the circle between the individual and the collective, the objective and the subjective in ways that open up new dimensions of theoretical and empirical research. It is this possibility that I now want to explore.

7   THE INDIVIDUAL AND THE COLLECTIVE

One might demur that all these matters, context included are simply matters of opinion and can be treated as such. In which case the proposed emphasis is unnecessary at best and to be treated as such. Hence it becomes important to connect the discussion so far with a structural and systemic analysis of what is often considered the ultimately configuring process, namely the political economy of development. Meaning may become important in an historical or cultural context, especially if it provides for a logic from which political consequences follow. It is in establishing such logic that political leaders find their openings, especially those whose narrative abilities (whether oracular or revelatory, or historical and analytical) appear to offer that interpretative authenticity on which to base their authority (Kojeve 1969).

Context in this sense can take the form of historical memory, retrieved again and again to become a social ethos and a cultural mystique, as Pierre Nora (1997) and others have illustrated so well in the case of France. Or it can be a much more bread-and-butter affair, developmental, a matter of material well-being. Favoring discourse, however, does not mean giving short shrift to systemic concerns. Take for example a problem I have been working on for many years: the relationship between development (and more particularly globalization), the changes it brings about in social and institutional structures, and the differential ways people respond to these changes. It is a commonplace that development (or better, economic growth) is essential if societies are to provide greater opportunities for more and more people. It is also a commonplace that improved economic development creates the political conditions favorable to democracy. (In these terms China might be the most interesting example to watch.) But suppose development in this sense turns out to be a two-edged sword, sometimes producing such desired consequences and sometimes not. Suppose, that is, that it can also produce structural conditions that not only undermine opportunities for most people, but produce deep fissures in society, fundamental social cleavages. So much so that the results speak of a politics of negative rather than positive pluralism, where social life continues to become more complex, but under worsening conditions that politically breed factionalism, localism, separatism, mutual hatred, and so greater political unrest and propensities to violence (Apter 2001).

In my own experience in many less developed parts of the world, particularly those in which I have done research, the impact of technologically advanced global development on the labor force has been to favor capital-intensive industry even where labor is cheap, thus driving people out of agricultural pursuits and into urban areas where they become not simply unemployed but marginalized, indeed functionally superfluous.

Meanwhile in these same areas, those engaged in capital-intensive industry and the administrative and governmental networks on which further economic and social growth depend—those who come to constitute a functionally significant elite—live in an entirely different universe, in terms of wealth, schooling, knowledge, and training and in their social settings, including neighborhoods, clubs, and institutional networks. In this sense one can recall the logic of Marx's polarization hypothesis but with a huge difference. For Marx the changes in the mode of production would produce changes in the relations of production in which a value-creating proletariat would become sufficiently aware (that is, conscious) of its economic role and eventually expropriate those who controlled property and wealth. With modern globalization, a proletariat is a rapidly waning force, and the dynamic of globalized capitalism is to increase wealth by means of information-based technologies, resulting in capital- rather than labor-intensive industries. The result is quite opposite to what Marx predicted, and more like the view of certain anarchists like Bakunin—i.e. a growing body of those more-or-less permanently unemployed and marginalized, and whose conditions of life are perpetually at risk, to an extent that survival requires changing the rules rather than abiding by them.

I use Marx loosely, of course, but do so in order to underscore the fact that his is a still relevant structural critique of global capitalism in terms of its dynamics or dialectic. If his original projections of class struggle were based on crucially faulty value and wealth-creation assumptions, he certainly recognized early the importance of innovation, information, and technology in the productive process, including the impact on social formations and classes. His emphasis on working class consciousness as the power of repossession was not wrong as much as insufficiently right in terms of certain dynamics.

But there is a sense that the underlying logic of Marx's critique of capitalism, its form rather than its substance, is still valid. That is, the way he connected development processes to conditions of radical possibility still hold. For Marx not any consciousness would do but the kind rooted in the particular conditions of life, itself the foundation for transforming what he regarded as conditions of possibility into realized opportunities. Since Marx a variety of theories, drawn from many fields and by scholars of whom many had only the most remote connection to Marx, have portrayed "consciousness" in a similar manner—but have built on it terms of language, signs, codes, iconography, aspects that make possible the interpretation of political life.

Later Marxists and neo-Marxists began paying more and more attention to the extent to which objective processes structure consciousness and individual and collective meaning, not least in terms of unreason, the doctrinal irrationalities of Fascism. By so doing they opened the door to a wide spectrum of theories of political consciousness, from Lukacs to the Frankfurt School, from linguistics to French structuralism and post-structuralism, all of which created a body of ideas quite appropriate to but independent of political science analysis.

8   NARRATIVES AND TRANSFORMATION

To recapitulate, what we are calling "discourse theory" emphasizes the way people interpret their circumstances and act accordingly. It represents a particular way of looking at an even more particular subject, in a still more particular role. Located at the intersection of the economic and social the actual conditions of both serve as the raw materials for both individual and collective narration, which in turn becomes a mode of interpretation.

What first appears as an "objective" condition becomes, in the mind's eye, subjective: a story both unique to the self and familiar a thousandfold. Collective or civic life is concerned with this thousandfold commonality. It is both authorial and autonomous. I have referred to such transformations as discourse-shifting that transforms the subjective into the objective (but it is more than that). Just how such transformations occur is, as I have tried to show, both simple and complex. At its most simple the subjective is made "objective" as a collective story, which becomes "subjective" when one listens to it, absorbs it, and becomes part of the story one's self.

Such transformations happen all the time. And it gives instrumental substance to political acts. Every political speech, ceremony, celebration, parade, "happening" as a public occasion has an instrumental purpose (Combes 1984; Hamon and Rotman 1987). The effectiveness of each lies in creating its own text while engaging listener, reader, audience as part of a public text—a process of incorporation. It is the way the "marketplace of ideas" manifests itself on a workaday basis. Ideas count in this sense not as some abstract philosophical debate between representatives of the higher canon, but in the down-to-earth of what can be called the "imaginary real"—what one comes to consider as validated by experience, if only by a stretch of the imagination.[5]

As already suggested, the term "discourse" is being used in two ways: as an approach or framework with theoretical ambitions applied to (and this is its second meaning) discourses as employed on the ground in the form of recounted events. The recounting in narrative form is itself empirical. Narratives are "read" discursively when, as theory, the discourse includes appropriate analytical categories that enable us to examine empirically when and how people make stories out of events, both individually and collectively. Collective stories come to have political consequences when as myths they purport to be history, when as history they are reinterpreted as theories, and when as theories they make up stories about events. So regarded, theories that become stories create fictive truths. In politics, truth-telling and storytelling are part of the same process by which people interrogate their past in order to transform the future. The degree to which they do so will vary with time, place, and circumstance (Apter 1993). As for narrative itself, it is a process, a way of organizing human experience. It creates the frames of meaning that themselves represent systems of conceptual order. Political discourse consists of such frames as they both represent and order the exercise of power—including principles of hierarchy, representation, and accountability. Evolving in the form of narrative interpretations of events and ideas, logical and mythic, political discourse establishes criteria and contexts for comparing and evaluating political systems.

In this sense, whatever the content of such discourses the narrative process is never innocent. Even where discourses appear to emerge from circumstances and events spontaneously, they have to be carefully crafted so as not to appear contrived. Thus the importance of agents able to convert chance into condition, contingencies into system, and negative circumstances into positive outcomes— and above all to locate and combine myth and logic and channel outlet-seeking

---

[5] A good example is the famous storming of the Bastille in the early days of the French Revolution, an event much celebrated and regarded as a decisive revolutionary event and a symbol of revolutionary justice. In fact, the Bastille was defended from the "mob," which itself consisted of only about 800 people by a tiny garrison, mainly Swiss. As for the large numbers of persecuted prisoners presumed to have been held inside, they consisted of "four forgers, two lunatics, and a dissipated young noble." This small harvest of freedom did not prevent the attackers from cutting off the head of the governor of the Bastille, and parading it on the head of a pike through the streets of Paris (Cobban 1985, 149–50).

grievances onto which people can place their anger. And, when the extraordinary is constituted as common sense, powers of interpretation do not yield mere knowledge but insight—a form of higher truth. So considered, the interpretative process enables people within the group to be considered as exceptional and exempt from ordinary rules.

All this is, of course, very abstract. But there is nothing abstract about the process and the actual empirical activity involved. Inquiry begins with the actual ways and circumstances in which individuals begin to recount their own stories, how they become systematized, collectivized, and formed into master narratives. In these regards a distinction can be drawn. On the one hand is the more instrumental rationality of politicians, with their natural propensity to truck, bargain, and exchange virtually anything for votes, and to appeal to sufficient self-interested others for not only their favor but also their money. On the other hand, politician-agents speak with the voice of higher authority, words sacralized as Texts, the capitalized version referring to authoritative writings of sainted figures, canonized or not, laying down proper modes of belief, conduct, and relationships, public and private. (That formulation might suggest a too-clear distinction between the saint-politician and the secular-politician, the one corresponding to virtue the other to sin. In fact a good many politicians who are clearly sinners consider themselves to be saints; which is where the rub comes in.[6])

9   DISCOURSE TRADITION

We turn now to a pedigree for the kind of political discourse theory favored here. The ideas I have been using are drawn, somewhat arbitrarily from a wide variety of theorists few of whom agree with one another. We can broadly distinguish them in terms of three main traditions, the philosophers of language including such forebears as Peirce, Sassure, and Wittgenstein and whose later representatives constitute a very large group, including linguists like Roman Jacobson, Noam Chomsky, and Umberto Eco. A second group might be considered phenomenologically inclined, including sociologists like Basil Bernstein, Erving Goffman, and Herbert Garfinklel, philosophers like Alfred Schuetz, John Austin, Paul Ricoeur,

---

[6] Renan (1927, 52–3) makes the point that neither Socrates nor Jesus ever wrote down their thoughts. Plato was one of two interpreters who in effect created the Socratic texts, while the various versions of the Gospels did the same for Jesus. One could make almost the same argument for Mao, a good many of whose writings were speeches written down and rewritten to form their own body of authorized gospels.

and Ernest Gellner (1964). A third group consists of anthropological structuralists such as Claude Levi-Strauss, Mary Douglas, and Jack Goody, and those more inclined to social constructivism such as Clifford Geertz and Victor Turner. As for historians, those more inclined to "reconstructionism" such as Robert Darnton, Pierre Nora, Le Roy Ladurie, and Francois Furet are what might be called "historical contextualists." Finally there has been the rediscovery of the relationship of literary analysis to politics in the contribution of such figures as Kenneth Burke, W. J. T. Mitchell, Roland Barthes, Hayden White, Stephen Greenblatt, Frederic Jameson, and Terry Eagleton, and of course in particular Foucault (1979) and Baudrillard (1981) whose concerns range from neo-Marxist structuralism to the analysis of symbolic forms.

These are only a small sample of those who today are part of or indebted to structuralism, post-structuralism, social constructivism, as lines of inquiry into social action. If one part of the task of social analysis is to try and establish determinate boundaries that configure the range of options and choices open to individuals, the other is to examine how individuals alter the boundaries that delimit their options and possibilities. One might also say that such varied and different theoretical emphases have at times produced in academia groups as deeply divided on analytical grounds as political and social groups are on ideological or religious ones. However, despite the fact that they vary so widely, what makes them of interest here is how they approach the problem of fictive accounting or to put it somewhat differently, the role of the imaginary real that in people's minds comes to constitute truth.

To take a few examples, Levi-Strauss (1955, 428–44) laid out the structural properties (or better, the isomorphic ordering) of myth and theory in which narratives took the form of logical binaries whose congruities literally composed the order of the universe by establishing rules of inter-mediation: between man and the cosmos, men and women, kin and family, earth and sky, land and water, and so on. Others more interested in theories of semiotics saw the ordering process in terms of codes and codex, signs and signification, and Eco's "sign production."

Hayden White (1987) refers to the narrative process itself as "the poetic troping of the facts." Terry Eagleton (1991) refers to "drenched signifiers," that is, images and metaphors so symbolically powerful that they become incentives to action. Foucault (1979) examines discursive codes that establish authority and power, which for Francois Furet (1979) constitute non-scientific representational strategies leading to a structure of time, or time consciousness. Paul Ricoeur (1967) emphasizes discourse as sin, confession, and purification as negative poles for overcoming projects, individual first and collective later. Henri Lefebvre (1986) deals with space as terrain and jurisdiction as agora—a theater of intersection between addressor and addressee. For Baudrillard (1981) discourse produces symbolically dense miniaturized versions of state and society whether encampments, staging areas, fortresses, neighborhoods, or any space that can form a symbolic moral center, the actions of which constitute what Guy Debord (1987) referred to as "spectacle." Most important to this discussion is Bourdieu's (1977) concern with symbolic capital, in contrast to economic capital and indeed as a substitute for it. Although his use differs from mine, for both of us a good deal of the point of discourse analysis is about how such capital forms. In examining its mythic and logical components, we come to understand its role as a source of power in and of itself, and the conditions under which it waxes and wanes. In this sense words and actions, and the narratives in which they are expressed are what Durkheim (1938) called "social facts." The hope is that by examining how people interpret their circumstances we will be able to explain better what prompts them to act collectively, how they navigate difficulties by circumventing or transcending negative social and political circumstances. It is an approach that reveals itself best under conditions of confrontation and conflict, where people are more inclined to say what they do, and do what they say. So considered, although discourse theory is a product of many different concepts and categories and thus prove to the charge of eclecticism, it can also be given systemic properties.

10   RISK

The preference here is for a view of different theories and interpretative schemes as options. Like changing the lenses on a camera, one can use different approaches to see different aspects of the complex phenomenon that is political life. Whatever the analytical approaches, however, the starting point is a hypothesis, as explicit as possible, and the clear identification of the empirical field within which that hypothesis is to be examined. Particularly where one is concerned with narrative, interpretation, and symbolic expression in a context of retrievals, the mobilization of memory, and the transformation of these into prescriptive strategies, at a minimum one needs to gather information about what people do, what people say they do while doing it, what people say about what they are saying, and what people say about what they are doing. These are best obtained by interviews in depth and over time—a political ethnography.

This brings me to the kinds of social and political realities that constitute the stuff of ordinary life, the raw materials of which become the basis for individual and collective narratives. These are connections between discourse as a process and the circumstances under which the narrative process becomes politically significant. To repeat, the analytical problem is the gap between what is structurally determined, and what in structural terms becomes the "transformational contingent."

Here one wants to know what triggers such contingencies and how to examine the circumstances that make for one rather than another. In my own experience if there is one common denominator that underlies most political and social situations where the transformational contingent becomes important, it is risk, the structural conditions that make for it, and the ways people have of coping or dealing with it, not least by the interpretation their own conditions in terms of it.

Of course there are many kinds of risk. There is immediately present danger, in which an individual feels hunted or threatened, whether from the well-known or unknown. There is collective risk, as when in the process of global development those previously employed in—and indeed who were considered the foundation of—the old industrial process become victims of the new, with its capital intensive, innovative, information based, scientific, and technological modes of production, shaping investment strategies with policies based on short-term timeframes. The old labor force is increasingly redundant. Labor in this sense stops being a resource and becomes simply irrelevant. Risk in these terms means displacement, depatrimonialization, a condition of marginality becoming more permanent. Risk, then, is one thing for those who are functionally significant (those elites that constitute the knowledge and technology community) and quite another for those who become functionally superfluous. For the first, rationality is based on abstract as well as concrete information drawn from a variety of sources and translatable into systems. For the functionally superfluous, risk is immediate. Basic survival is at stake on a more-or-less daily basis. Where the first uses risk in a context of power, the second is subject to risk on a basis of powerlessness, one consequence of which is to become violence-prone—to create the conditions of power in a search for prey, the victim becoming the hunter. It is this latter which results in crime, individual and organized, what Angelina Peralva (2001) in her study of violence in the *favelas* of Brazil has called the "spiral of criminality."

Under such circumstances including real physical dangers, survival depends on immediate recognition of threats, with action a function of learned experience. In this sense risk-proneness requires *metaphorical thinking*. The this-is-the-that within the communicated morphologies of associative learning, i.e. *x* is *y*. As a mode of quick recognition and perceptive immediacy, under circumstances of random dangers, one is required to make instant decisions. Metaphorical thinking in this sense is a highly developed cognitive mode and is fundamental to the storytelling process. Narrative, especially that which defines a project of overcoming, a way of transcending the immediacy of risk, tends to pile metaphor on metaphor. It is here that discourse becomes virtually a thing in itself.

For example, in the hands of political storytellers metaphors become consensually validated through *mimetic narration*. It is this that endows political storytelling with a certain magical quality—the ability to cast a spell over the listeners. There is something risk-assuaging in listening to some major political figure who is both agent and agency, giving voice by means of a mythic recounting of one's daily condition, its past and its future. A good agent in this sense uses the *retrieval* of past events to provide a logic which *projects* transcending outcomes. Plundering the past for metaphorically vibrant examples, what happens is a kind of personal transmigration to the collective in which memory purports to be history and history is validated as memory. Narrative in these terms serves simultaneously to collectivize the individual and to individualize the collective.

Risk is not of course the basis of all such narrativizing. A good deal of it is based on rethinking, on the search for new and better political solutions. But new and better means defining some negative pole to be transcended. Political myth is invariably a logical and rationalistic project based on what originally were metaphorically dense and patterned master narratives of loss (loss of patrimony, loss of innocence, etc.). The purpose of the narrative is gain, the overcoming of obstacles by means of struggles. By way of a sequence of critical moments of failure, hesitation, and despair, it affirms steadfastness in the ongoing journey, so that despite any continuing precariousness of the situation, the eventual miracle will be achieving the object of the quest.

11   DISCOURSE COMMUNITIES

Which brings us to political narratives themselves. They not only form into texts, but a *mythical* denouement will require a *logical* explanation, an argument showing how and why the desired outcome, often millennial is a product of a higher truth, revelatory or epistemological or both. Transformed into logic, mythic events then become foundational for a body of self-evident truths. In this regard conviction is based on an explicit combination of myth and logic, or better a *mytho-logic* that, in the telling contains more than meets the eye. Then even when apparently unvarnished and transparent, encoded words will convey interior meaning to knowing listeners. Individuals are transformed from members to initiates, complicit in the collective insight.

It is in the context of shared narratives that people convey their individual experiences to the collective fund, a contribution that validates the first by the general "truths" of the second. It is by means of such acts of conveyance that an individual joins a *discourse community*. Gaining access to collective experience in this way provides not only an affiliation but also a method of interpretation and a form of capital—*symbolic capital*.[7] Unlike economic capital based on assumptions

---

[7] The concept of symbolic capital derives from Bourdieu (1977) although this usage varies from mine.

of market rationality—a "natural propensity to truck, barter, and exchange"—symbolic capital embeds rationality within the discourse itself. Among its starting assumptions are a natural propensity to make stories out of experiences and a similar propensity to require logical explanation, the first providing the basis for the second. Different from economic capital and its logic of exchange, symbolic capital constitutes a fund from which individuals can for their personal enhancement, draw down more than they put in, especially in terms of moral sustenance. They are thereby empowered to transcend their own deficiencies with acts that may surprise even themselves. By the same token, *interests* are raised to the level of *principles*, *demands* to the level of *rights*, and members of the collectivity become less and less likely to engage in a politics of negotiation. The discourse so generated is itself a form of sociation. The more shared experiences take on narrative form; the more collectivized the group, the more the discourse community will also become empowered as a political movement. Moreover, in such mobilized discourse communities affiliation is cemented by continuous recounting, while mimetic repetition and incantation endows certain terms with esthetic familiarity, like music adding tonality and resonance. Spectacle counts, and there is a theatrical, often an operatic quality to the speeches, meetings, exhortations which fill a public space. But unlike opera or theater, the line between audience and stage is blurred. Insiders are not differentiated from outsiders. What is shared is insight and revelation, and these in turn define obligation. In the most powerful discourse communities whether ostensibly sacred or secular, a "theological" foundation is established, with the discourse community reconstituting itself as a "chosen people" (Apter and Saich 1994).

12   AGENCY

Of course such processes do not happen by themselves. They require agents. So crucial is agency in the formation of symbolic capital and the creation of discourse communities that it requires further discussion. It is by means of agents that people are enabled to talk and think collectively about how to transcend their predicaments. Agents create narratives. As individuals they authenticate themselves by the way they articulate collective memory and by speaking they open the way to creative alterations.[8] In present terms, agents can be very diverse in character. They may for

---

[8] One might ask whether or not this emphasis is overblown and whether the emphasis on agency adds much to Weber's concept of charisma, with its twin implications of a gift of grace and correspondingly, the suspension of conventional norms in favor of those prescribed the agent.

example include politicians who assume saintly proportions by transforming self-interested claims and actions into higher principles and by so doing not only enhance their endowments as politicians but as a community investiture.

Which is where the role of both social and written texts enter the picture. Agents differ from more ordinary storytellers insofar as they become makers of texts. The political accomplishment is to create those texts that become authoritative. They partake of the sacred when they appear to transcend ordinary convictions and common sense (Khosrokhavar 2001). Agents by this means transform self-interest into collective principle. Their tools are speaking and writing. Their power derives from the way they combine orality with textuality and in a certain sense, magic with logic, myth with theory. By so doing they re-present the here and now. They give a sense of urgency for the future. Theirs is a culmination of the past whose logic is a self-validating project that takes the form of a master narrative.

In this sense agents are above all activists. They are intellectual entrepreneurs. The more inversionary a movement the greater the space in which as mytho-logicians they can offer themselves as political cosmocrats, "revelators" with sacral pretensions, self-styled philosopher-kings, or thinker politicians. What they are among other things is *bricoleurs*. Their raw materials are events of everyday life as lived and culled from public memory and with the reality of experience. They plunder earlier memories, those "stockpiled" in the form of narratives that consti-tute a fund, a cultural reservoir, for the making of social texts on which the agent can draw. Improvising, expropriating, and transforming such raw materials into organized and coherent lessons, agents are to some extent teachers who embody the master narrative. Performance counts.

Agents in this sense are actors. With words and gestures, the body itself signifies the moving mover who decodes the common condition. Required too is political imagination, an ability to project appealing and logical outcomes and with both ingenuity and political creativity. Typically, agents are boundary-setting. They define jurisdictions, ritualize the boundaries between them, and in more radical persuasions, seek to transform these into some defined break, a past and a future, a disjunction between what is and what ought to be, and by so doing they create a new political cosmos in which people can relocate themselves. Grafting logic onto myth and myth onto logic, they translate the common despondency into some-thing that offers a promissory note for the future. They do these things by telling stories, creating narratives and embodying them in texts both mythic and logical, that create a moral basis for responsibility and obligation. Moreover they make use of appropriate occasions, terrains to take possession of public space, fora, *agoras*.

In present terms, however, charisma suffers from the same defects as culture, or ideology; like them an overkill category, the term has been used loosely—so much so that it has almost come to mean anyone with a political personality able to attract followers.

Place is crucial, for terrain so endowed with significance becomes sacred, a boundary, a moral redoubt, a simulacrum, a miniaturized version of a larger space, a microcosmic terrain standing for the whole jurisdictions waiting to be conquered.

Agents, then, use narrative as myth, invoking the past in the form of appropriate mythic retrievals, using these as the evidence for logical exegesis, defining the future as the ineluctable consequence of the past—the present the purpose of all relevant previous history, and the validation of space in terms of time. The metaphors may also contain the metonymies giving novel projects a pedigree (so for example the legacy of the Jacobin revolution in the Bolshevik). Antecedents served up as comparisons are then confirmed by logic. In this sense, narrative is based in historicity, logic leads to systemicity, thereby becoming ahistorical—colonizing the future (Apter 1987).

There are a number of characteristic patterns associated with agency. One is the ability to turn lived experiences into stories, each of which possesses some benchmark state of grace that transforms into positives social negatives, like loss, suffering, struggle that are intrinsically dramatic. Exceptional circumstances, tragedy, suffering, torture, betrayal, murder, and death are made to serve as promontory events each of which provides a quotient of insight, knowledge, or shrewdness. Struggle develops recognized qualities attached to collective identity. In this sense socially constructed but imaginary realities are embodied in compelling "truth" narratives accompanied by a suitable pageantry that stands for boundaries—borders and trangressions; affiliations, loyalties, and apostasies; terrains, jurisdictions, and betrayals; insiders, outsiders, and strangers in the midst—all of which distinguish the good from the bad citizen. By such relevant markers appropriate clienteles are identified (ethnic, religious, racial, kin, clan, and class). Out of grievances and aspirations arise redeeming surrogates who personify negativized others, Genet's thief or homosexual, Fanon's (1961) colonial African, Foucault's (1979) madman or prisoner, and so on.

Along with such markers go ritual endowments, insignia, votary paraphernalia, flags, and uniforms choreographed in theaters of the absurd, and such solemn occasions as the mass, the parade, the funeral. As Mamphnela Ramphele (1996, 107) put it, in South Africa "History is often reinterpreted, reenacted and represented in a manner that is intended to shape social memory in the political speeches and other ceremonial acts that are part of political funerals. Symbols in the form of flags, T-shirts, and other memorabilia find space for defiant display." All manner of votary ceremonies can become relevant—candlelight parades, pistols on belts, whips in hand, or the massed formations of guns—with technology, speed, the magic within the terrifying logic of power. In the right circumstances and given the right events, almost anything can indeed be endowed with symbolic intensification.

13 CONCLUSION

It should be clear that we have proposed discourse theory as more than an addendum to political science. As such it can serve as a way of unpacking more conventional omnibus categories already in use (belief system, ideology and culture, etc.). Those have suffered "overkill": by explaining too much, they explain too little (Eagleton 1991). Our deepest concern is with how and why at times, words can kill. How does ecclesiastical belief lead to murder in the cathedral? How much was Nazi ideology the cause of the Holocaust? When do ethnicity, religion, language, or other differentiating social criteria that establish exclusivity define so definitively "others" that they become part of a process of negative exchange, the most extreme consequences of which can include genocide?

Which brings us back to the original concern with context and indeed to Duchamp's "fountain." That event can be said to have constituted a break in the commonsense as well as the professional analysis of what constitutes art. Out of it came not one but many discourses, so much so that one can argue that more than anyone else Duchamp became a primary agent in the contemporary understanding of artistic endeavor. Moreover, by transforming found objects into "ready-mades" and making "art" out of commonplace household objects he redefined that totally instrumental mechanism of rational choice, the art market. Which while this might constitute a certain irony also suggests the connection between discourse and rationality, that is, the ability to redefine what is rational, if not the rules of the game then the game itself. The example of Duchamp suggests something else that is often overlooked in the analysis of politics: the extent to which successful discourse shifts embody both creativity and entrepreneurship. In tandem they work to redefine the fit between private experience and public awareness of what that experience means. One consequence of this, and it is a continuing concern, is how then to turn the political power so generated into appropriate structures that frame contingency, institutions that function to satisfy social and political needs, and relatively efficient procedures to accomplish both. It is here that the fit between private experience and public awareness become critical. For if the discrepancies between them become too obvious what happens all to often is that the discourse becomes a smokescreen for the arbitrary use of force. Nor are democracies exempt from this. One reason why so many so-called democracies are only so in name, facades for political manipulation and corruption in so many parts of the world (and elections merely an opportunity for manipulation), is precisely because the gap between the discourse and the realities on the ground become redefined as cause and effect—democracy seeming to cause structural contradictions that undermine values and corrode representative institutions and corrupt procedures, then democracy becomes not only a poor version of itself but a travesty. It this condition which today allows counter-discourses to continue to flourish, and not least of all, especially in the absence of socialist or other rationalistic discourse, creates the moral space for religious revivalism and other doctrinal alternatives to fill what becomes a discourse vacuum, providing redemptive programs that are both concrete and practical, and steps along the road to political purity. To the extent that such discourses become both monopolistic and punishing, the source and justification for violence, almost any belief is possible and any idiocy plausible, even if it is only for the moment.

I have tried to make the case that discourse theory is, for political analysis a way of understanding those aspects of politics that have to do with context and meaning. I have also tried to suggest categories that can be used empirically, and by means of which theory so derived can reconstitute structure. I propose these remarks as a possible residential addition to the main edifice of political analysis, to make what is now residual more central—not as a substitute but as a supplement to more conventional models, an appropriate amendment if one accepts the importance of the symbolic aspects of power. By examining the dialectic nature of symbolic capital, for or against the state, one can reveal what more conventional analysis both ignores and disguises in the name of rational action. In these terms discourse theory can be placed at one end of a continuum where rational choice is at the other. However, where rational choice theory emphasizes rationality rules, discourse theory emphasizes the meaning behind those rules.

Politics may be considered a chess game, all wins and losses. But in politics no game brings finality. Events have a way of finding themselves recapitulated, whether as memory, vindication, revenge, or projection. How many victories come back to haunt the winner? How many political victories turn out to be Pyrrhic? As for rationality, not even cracking the genetic code solves the mystery of life itself. No reductionism can in the last analysis explain the bouts of madness that so often accompany the quotidian of politics. Configurational theories can do only so much. In hindsight, systemic inevitability is something of an illusion. How many significant events that looked inevitable, proved on closer inspection not to be so? And how many political systems that failed might just as easily have succeeded? A cool theory like rational choice which reduces politics to a flat plane, is not much good at explaining what makes the retrospectively irrational appear rational in its moment. It does not do very well with politically hot events. In this sense, like the scientists who observe the stars and planets or the biologists who read the codes of life itself, social and political scientists, for all their emphasis on theory have only scratched the surface in trying to understand that extraordinary complex human political being for whom (one might say) context is all.

References

ALEXANDER, J. 2004. From the depths of despair: performance, counterperformance and "September 11th." *Sociological Theory*, 22: 88–105.

APTER, D. E. 1987. *Rethinking Development*. Newbury Park, Calif.: Sage.

—— 1993. Yan'an and the narrative reconstruction of reality. *Daedalus*, 122: 207–32.

—— 1999. La apothéose de la violence politique. In *Faut-il s'Accommoder de la Violence?* ed. T. Ferenszi. Paris: Editions Complexe.

—— 2001. Structure, contingency and choice. Pp. 252–87 in *Schools of Thought*, ed. J. Scott and D. Keates. Princeton, NJ: Princeton University Press.

—— and SAICH, T. 1994. *Revolutionary Discourse in Mao's Republic*. Cambridge, Mass.: Harvard University Press.

ARROW, K. 1963. *Social Choice and Individual Values*, 2nd edn. New Haven, Conn.: Yale University Press.

BAUDRILLARD, J. 1981. *Simulacres et Simulation*. Paris: Editions Galilee.

BAUMAN, Z. 1973. *Culture as Praxis*. London: Routledge and Kegan Paul.

BENHABIB, S. 1996. *Democracy and Difference*. Princeton, NJ: Princeton University Press.

BHABHA, H. K. (ed.) 1990. *Nation and Narration*. London: Routledge.

BOURDIEU, P. 1977. *Outline of a Theory of Practice*. Cambridge: Cambridge University Press.

BRUNER, J. 1991. The narrative reconstruction of reality. *Critical Inquiry*, 18: 1–21.

CEFAÏ, D. 2001. *Cultures Politiques*. Paris: Presses Universitaires de France.

CHARTIER, R. 1991. *The Cultural Origins of the French Revolution*. Durham, NC: Duke University Press.

COBBAN, A. 1985. *A History of Modern France*. Harmondsworth: Penguin.

COMBES, P. 1984. *La Littérature et Le Mouvement de Mai 68*. Paris: Seghers.

DARNTON, R. 1984. *The Great Cat Massacre*. New York: Basic Books.

DEBORD, G. 1987. *La Société du Spectacle*. Paris: Editions Gerard Lebovici.

DURKHEIM, E. 1938. *The Rules of Sociological Method*, trans. S. Solvey and J. Muellet. Glencoe, Ill.: Free Press.

EAGLETON, T. 1991. *Ideology*. London: Verso.

EASTERLY, W., and LEVINE, R. 1997. Africa's growth tragedy: policies and ethnic division. *Quarterly Journal of Economics*, 112: 1203–50.

FANON, F. 1961. *Les Damnes de la Terre*. Paris: Maspero.

FOUCAULT, M. 1979. *Discipline and Punish*, trans. A. Sheridan. New York: Random House.

FURET, F. 1979. *Penser La Révolution Française*. Paris: Gallimard.

—— and OZOUF, M. (eds.) 1989. *A Critical Dictionary of the French Revolution*, trans. A. Goldhammer. Cambridge, Mass.: Harvard University Press.

GEERTZ, C. 1973. *The Interpretation of Cultures*. New York: Basic Books.

GELLNER, E. 1964. *Thought and Change*. London: Weidenfeld and Nicolson.

GREEN, D., and SHAPIRO, I. 1994. *Pathologies of Rational Choice*. New Haven, Conn.: Yale University Press.

HAMON, H., and ROTMAN, P. 1987. *Generation*, 2 vols. Paris: Editions du Seuil.

HOLLIER, D. (ed.) 1988. *The College of Sociology (1937–9)*, ed. B. Wing. Minneapolis: University of Minnesota Press,

KHOSROKHAVAR, F. 2001. *L'Instance du sacré*. Paris: Les Editions du Cerf.

KING, G., KEOHANE, R., and VERBA, S. 1994. *Designing Social Inquiry: Scientific Inference in Qualitative Research*. Princeton, NJ: Princeton University Press

KOJEVE, A. 1969. *La Notion de l'autorité*. Paris: Gallimard.

LAITIN, D. 1989. Linguistic revival: politics and culture in Catalonia. *Comparative Studies in Society and History*, 31: 297–317.

LEFEBVRE, H. 1986. *La Production de l'Éspace*. Paris: Editions Anthropos.

LEVI-STRAUSS, C. 1955. The structural study of myth. *American Journal of Folklore*, 78 (270): 428–44.

McADAM, D. 1982. *The Political Process and the Development of Black Insurgency*. Chicago: University of Chicago Press.

MITCHELL, W. J. T. (ed.) 1983. *The Politics of Interpretation*. Chicago: University of Chicago Press.

NORA, P. (ed.) 1997. *Realms of Memory*, 3 vols. New York: Columbia University Press.

OLSON, M., JR. 1965. *The Logic of Collective Action*. Cambridge, Mass: Harvard University Press.

OZOUF, M. 1976. *La Fête Révolutionnaire*. Paris: Editions Gallimard.

PAGDEN, A. 1987. *The Languages of Political Theory in Early-Modern Europe*. Cambridge: Cambridge University Press.

PARETO, V. 1966. *Sociological Writings*, ed. S. E. Finer. London: Pall Mall Press.

PERALVA, A. 2001. *Violence et démocratie*. Paris: Editions Balland.

PUTNAM, R. 1973, *The Belief Systems of Politicians*. New Haven, Conn.: Yale University Press.

RAMPHELE, M. 1996. Political widowhood in South Africa: the embodiment of ambiguity. *Daedalus*, 125 (1): 99–117.

RENAN, E. 1927. *The Life of Jesus*. New York: Modern Library.

RICOEUR, P. 1967. *The Symbolism of Evil*. Boston: Beacon Press.

SEN, A. 1984. *Resources, Values and Development*. Cambridge, Mass.: Harvard University Press.

SHAPIRO, I. 1986. *The Evolution of Rights in Liberal Theory*. Cambridge: Cambridge University Press

SMELSER, N. J. 1969. *Social Change in the Industrial Revolution; An Application of Theory to the British Cotton Industry*. Chicago: University of Chicago Press.

SMITH, R. 1997. *Civic Ideals*. New Haven, Conn.: Yale University Press.

SOULE, S. A., and OLZAK, S. 2004. The politics of contingency and the Equal Rights Amendment. *American Sociological Review*, 69: 473–97.

TARROW, S. 1994. *Power in Movement*. Cambridge: Cambridge University Press.

TILLY, C. 1978. *From Mobilization to Revolution*. Reading, Mass.: Addison-Wesley.

——1984. *Big Structures, Large Processes, Huge Comparisons*. New York: Russell Sage Foundation.

WHITE, H. 1978. *Tropics of Discourse*. Baltimore: Johns Hopkins University Press.

——1987. *Content of the Form: Narrative Discourse and Historical Representation*. Baltimore: Johns Hopkins University Press.

THE BEHAVIORAL REVOLUTION AND THE REMAKING OF COMPARATIVE POLITICS

LUCIAN PYE

THE generation that came to political science right after the Second World War was most fortunate for that was an exceptionally exciting time in the discipline. The shock waves of the "behavioral revolution" that had been initiated at the University of Chicago during the interwar years were bringing new life to a discipline that had long been mired in the study of constitutions and institutional structures. The Chicago school, led by Charles Merriam, Harold Gosnell, Quincy Wright, and Harold Lasswell shifted the focus of study onto dynamic processes, the play of power, and free reign to use all the methods and concepts of the other social sciences (Almond 2002). The products of the Chicago department, who included Gabriel Almond, William T. R. Fox, V. O. Key, David Truman, Herman Pritchett, Ithiel Pool, Alexander George, and many more were bringing the behavioral revolution to departments across the country.

The behavioral approach had many dimensions, but four were of defining importance. First, there was an emphasis in methodology upon quantification and the statistical analysis of data-sets (Hempel 1965). Second, there was an equally strong emphasis upon political psychology and political culture (Lasswell 1930). Third, was the recognition that all political acts involve choices by specific agents or decision-makers. Fourth, there was an uninhibited exploiting of the concepts and findings of the other social sciences: in sociology this involved in particular the works of Talcott Parsons, Max Weber, and Emile Durkheim; the key anthropologists included Clyde Kluckhohn, Margaret Mead, Ruth Benedict, Cora Dubois, and Geoffrey Gorer, all of whom had contributed their professional skills to the war effort; from psychology the works were above all those of Freud and Erik Erikson; and rather later in the game there was from microeconomics the model of optimizing behavior that in time became the basis for rational choice theory, but initially there were the works in political economy of Kenneth Arrow, James Buchanan, Gordon Tullock, and Mancur Olson (Olson 1965).

What was exceptional about the behavioral revolution was that all these diverse concepts and approaches were easily integrated and there was little inner tension or clashes. No particular approach sought hegemonic status. As a graduate student one might do objective statistical work one day and on the next you might be into depth psychology. Freud's model of the unconscious was just as objectively solid as, say, the balance of power theory in international relations. One used whatever was the most useful in dealing with the particular problem one was seeking to solve.

Above all one was given by one's mentors a vivid sense of exactly where the frontiers of knowledge were, and thus one could position oneself to take the next step with confidence that you were actually advancing knowledge. The University of Chicago school had set the pattern of using the city of Chicago as a laboratory for testing propositions about political processes and behavior. Now other places and times could be used as the evidence for comparative findings about the workings of politics. The goal was usually what was thought of as the scientific method of testing generalized hypotheses (Hempel 1965). Different scholars, however, had different ambitions. Some wanted to show that their particular case was unique and distinctive, while others sought to make their case studies representative of general findings.

Change was the theme of the day not just within the discipline of political science but also in the larger political world. The end of European colonialism had produced a host of new states that soon had profound implications for the study of comparative politics. Before the Second World War comparative politics consisted of little more than the descriptive analysis of the constitutional arrangements of the handful of major powers, and the study of the dominant ideologies of the day—Fascism, Nazism, Communism (Friedrich 1937). Now there was suddenly a multiplicity of new states. Initially there was uncertainty as to what this meant for the discipline, and therefore it was left to economists to take the lead. To the amazement of political scientists, the economists were uninhibited in talking about backward states with stagnant economies and modernizing states with dynamic economies based on self-sustaining growth. Political scientists after the horrors of Nazism and the two world wars of the twentieth century, thought it proper to discard the concept of "progress" as outdated nineteenth-century thinking. However, it was soon clear that the leaders of the new states welcomed the economists and looked down on political science as having nothing useful for them. It also became clear to political scientists that a bland descriptive approach would not do for there was something disgraceful about saying, "Every country has its distinctive culture. We happen to have cultures that make us rich and powerful, while you have cultures that leave you poor and weak." It was the leaders and intellectuals of the emerging nations who spoke of their desires for economic development and social and political modernization. From India to Communist China, from Southeast Asia to Africa the common theme for public discourse was the need for economic development and modernization. Political science had to get into the game and offer assistance for national development if it was to be relevant to the contemporary world. It would be historically wrong to believe that Western political scientists imposed the idea of modernization on the developing world. It was they who first wanted development. It would be equally wrong to suggest that political scientists of the day expected modernization to take place easily with only a few bumps in the road. Although the concept of the failed states only came later, there had been awareness that some countries would have a difficult time with nation-building. My decision to study Burma in 1958 was initiated by my concern that although Burma had many objective factors that should have given the Burmese advantages in national development—the country had an educated leadership, it was not overpopulated, the average rice farm was 22 acres, compared to the half- and quarter-acre farms in Japan and China, and it was endowed with valuable natural resources— I judged that it was likely to have serious problems with development because of cultural factors (Pye 1962).

1 THE STRESS BETWEEN UNIVERSAL AND CONTEXTUALIZED KNOWLEDGE

By the early 1960s a troublesome problem arose that pulled behavioralism in two different directions. On the one front there was the striving for generalizable findings that would place the discipline on more solid scientific foundations. On the other front the emphasis on empiricism meant respecting the particular and hence a stress on contextualization. Lasswell long believed that generalized knowledge and empirical analysis were two parts of the same process (Lasswell 1963). At the time there was little awareness that some of the theorizing about the nature of science was setting the stage for undermining the power of science and opening the slippery slope to postmodernism. Karl Popper (1972) came up with the vivid distinction between the hard sciences, which being highly deterministic could be thought of as being like the study of "clocks," while the human sciences because of the role of choice, purpose, and decision should be studied as "clouds" (see also Almond 1990, ch. 2). Popper further weakened the concept of science by arguing that science is advanced not by proof of propositions but by the falsification of propositions—what seems to be true may just be waiting further research that will falsify it. Scientific knowledge thus was seen as having weak foundations because of the potential for future falsification. Thomas Kuhn (1962) further weakened the position of logical positivism as being the right road to a deterministic science by suggesting that science advances not by building on the work that has gone before but by periodic radical changes in paradigms—as in the jump from Newtonian to Einsteinian physics. In sum, developments in the philosophy of science put into question the goal of making political science emulate physics and the hard sciences. Given the propensity for academic pendulums to swing from extreme to extreme, it would not be long before some political scientists began to deny the possibility of any form of objective science since everything is governed by the choice of subjective paradigms.

At the same time the commitment to utilize the concepts and findings of all the social sciences pulled political science toward greater respect for identifying and describing the particular and the unique. For example, with respect to political sociology it was initially possible to operate in terms of typologies of systems, but with greater detail in the empirical work it became clear that there were significant differences within the categories, and thus political systems could not be readily categorized. The case with respect to anthropology was much the same: as a first step one could set up categories of cultures, but with more careful analysis the differences became more critical, and hence research into comparative political cultures moved steadily toward identifying what might be unique and distinctive in each culture. Generalized typologies became the starting point of detailed research and not its conclusions.

2   AREA STUDIES AND POLITICAL SCIENCE

Another factor that brought change to the field of comparative politics was that as the newly trained comparativists went into the field they discovered that there were other Western scholars who had already been there. These were the area specialists who had deeply immersed themselves in the cultures, history, and languages of the various societies. With a command of the languages and traditions of the non-Western cultures they had knowledge that had to be respected.

The integrating of such knowledge was not easily accomplished for the area specialists saw the new comparative politics researchers as people intruding into their domain, and with little right to sit at their table. Most area specialists were humanists and thus they believed that skill in understanding the foreign society required years of work so one could intuitively appreciate a different culture. One only had a right to speak about a distant country if one had gone to the trouble of learning that country's language. The relationship was also complicated when area specialists were attacked for being political advocates of their respective countries (Samuels and Weiner 1992). It started with China specialists being attacked as being unnecessarily sympathetic to the Chinese communists, and it of course became much more serious with the passions over the Vietnam War.

At the purely scholarly level the immediate post-Second World War degree of tension between comparativists and area specialists gradually receded. Political scientists found that they could benefit from the work of area specialists and thus the two could be partners and not rivals (Pye 1975). A force in bringing the two together was the decision of the federal government and the leading foundations, that Americans needed to know more about the outside world and thus arrangements were established that diverted funds to the various area associations dealing with Asia, Africa, Latin America, and the Middle East. Political scientists were soon active and effective competitors for such field research funds.

3   MODERNIZATION THEORY AND THE COMMITTEE ON COMPARATIVE POLITICS

Work on political development and modernization theory in the 1950s and early 1960s was thus greatly assisted by the support of the major foundations for work on the newly emerging states. Organizationally political science benefited by the Social Science Research Council's decision to establish the Committee on Comparative Politics which was first chaired by Gabriel Almond and then by this author. The Committee sought to advance the field of comparative politics by supporting the work on comparative political development in the new states. Through its conferences and publications the Committee stimulated debates about social and political change which resulted in the evolution of modernization theory, a theory which was based on a combination of Talcott Parsons' social systems, Harold Lasswell's political psychology, and Gabriel Almond's structural functionalism.

However, by the late 1960s and 1970s developments largely outside of political science began to cause trouble for the Committee's work. First, there were the disruptions on campuses caused by the passionate divisions over the Vietnam War. Work in the entire field of political development came under attack as critics charged that modernization theory was nothing more than a form of ideology in support of America in the cold war.

Modernization theory did expose itself to criticisms because its exponents failed to indicate the timeframe appropriate for testing its validity. Were we talking in terms of changes over a few years, a few decades, even centuries? Certainly it had to be several decades, indeed perhaps a century or more. And where the theory dealt with the effects of the socialization process, the timeframe would have to be a matter of at least two if not three generations. Too often people seemed to assume that the changes suggested by the theory should happen almost instantaneously, and certainly during a single administration. The Committee on Comparative Politics did make an effort to clarify the time dimension basic to the modernization process. The Committee members spent a summer workshop at the Center for Advanced Study in the Behavioral Sciences in Palo Alto working on the consequences of developing states experiencing in different sequences five critical problems. These "developmental crises" as they came to be called were national identity, legitimacy, participation, penetration, and distribution (Binder et al. 1971). Thus, if the state apparatus "penetrated" the society before legitimacy was established the result would be repressive rule; participation without first establishing national identity would result in tribal politics; distribution without first resolving participation and identity would produce corruption. There was no attempt to establish any particular sequence as being theoretically the proper one. The goal was only to sensitize scholars to the consequences of different sequences. The Committee did seek to broaden the scope of modernization theory by trying to work with historians from Europe and the United States (Tilly et al. 1976; Grew et al. 1978). The effort did not last long enough to overcome the historians' focus on the unique and the specific and the political scientists' attraction to universal and abstract generalizations.

Work on modernization was losing its momentum as the discipline of political science began to fragment, with the parts going off in different directions. Instead of the united front of the early behavioral revolution, there were now competing, and indeed feuding elements. No longer was there a clear sense of where the frontiers for the advancement of knowledge lay. New fashions came along, such as rational choice, but there was no hegemonic approach. The comfortable living together of different approaches that characterized the behavioral revolution at its height was replaced with feuding sects (Almond 1990).

Modernization theory was somewhat vindicated with the collapse of the Soviet Union, and of Communism more generally. It was also vindicated by the economic and democratic successes of the East and Southeast Asian states. Moreover, key elements of modernization and development theories have been revived under the new "in" political science topics of "globalization" and "transitions to democracy." Globalization posits the same general historical movement towards modernity that was basic to development theory. Needless to say, globalization theory puts greater emphasis upon the powers of the profit motive than scholars of the early 1950s thought reasonable, since they had personally in their own lives chosen to ignore "profit maximization" in favor of the less monetarily rewarding careers in academia.

Much the same can be said about the relationship of current interest in "transitions to democracy" and earlier work on democracy and political development. In the past we tended to mute our support of democracy as the goal of development, partly because we did not want to bring the cold war into the advancement of objective political science. Now it is possible to be far more open about the goal of democracy, not the least because it is the people in developing countries who openly want to achieve democracy, and less a sense of the West imposing democracy on them.

The fact that current interest in "globalization" and "transitions to democracy" can benefit from earlier work on political development and modernization suggests that knowledge in political science is indeed cumulative. Thomas Kuhn's theory about paradigm shifts to the contrary notwithstanding, we do operate in a discipline in which we are constantly in debt to those who went before. Some may say that modernization theory "collapsed" (Gilman 2003, ch. 6), but it can be argued that the very act of recognizing its flaws has made the theory even stronger. What cannot be denied is that the excitement of the earlier days has passed and cannot be recaptured. Unfortunately when one reviews all the comings and goings in the discipline it is hard to spot any development that seems to have the potential for capturing the enthusiasms of a generation of political scientists the way the behavioral revolution and political modernization did in their time. There seems to be a perverse form of balance of power at work in the discipline so that if any approach shows signs of creative life and promise, the practitioners of other theories are quick to gang up and pick holes in the potential new leader.

It is also a fact that our sophistication in the philosophy of science is such that no matter what approach is being used there always seems to be a gap between what political scientists aspire to as the ideal in methodology and what we end up with as standard practices. The more ambitious our aspirations for the discipline as a science the more frustrated and disappointed we become. Skepticism is so easy to come by that Alasdair MacIntyre (1971) has questioned whether "a science of comparative politics is possible?" He argues that any grand, abstract generalization such as those basic to any science is not possible when it comes to the diverse complexities of political systems and cultures. The difficulties in coming up with abstract generalizations that are truly illuminating and not trite truisms has broadened the appeal of work that focuses on the concrete and the specific. The result has been a revival of respect for descriptive analysis—what Clifford Geertz (1973) has called "thick description"—and the practice of comparative histories or "analytic narratives" (Bates et al. 1998). The problem of the distinctive and specific also arises in trying to use sample survey questionnaires in different cultural contexts. The cultural contexts can change the meaning of the questions.

The combination of these problems has given rise to the call for contextualization in all forms of comparative analysis. If the goal is to compare total systems then the historical context of each must be respected and analyzed. If the approach calls for the use of surveys, then attention must be given to the cultural and linguistic contexts that will give different meanings to the questions being posed. The concerns of contextualization are such as to pull the discipline towards greater respect for what is distinctive and specific and away from broad generalizations. There is now a need to show respect for what was not long ago dismissed as "mere description." Fortunately the vineyard that political scientists work in is very large, and thus there is space for people to follow all manner of methodological approaches and substantive focuses for their studies. We need to respect diversity and to recognize that different scholars have different talents, and hence will be comfortable in employing different approaches and in seeking answers to different questions.

References

ALMOND, G. A. 1990. *A Discipline Divided: Schools and Sects in Political Science.* Newbury Park, Calif.: Sage.
—— 2002. *Ventures in Political Science.* Boulder, Colo.: Lynne Rienner.
BATES, R., GREIF, A., LEVI, M., ROSENTHAL, J.-L., and WEINGAST, B. 1998. *Analrytic Narratives.* Princeton, NJ: Princeton University Press.
BINDER, L. et al. 1971. *Crises and Sequences in Political Development.* Princeton, NJ: Princeton University Press.
FRIEDRICH, C. J. 1937. *Constitutional Government and Politics.* New York: Harper.
GEERTZ, C. 1973. Thick description: toward an interpretive theory of culture. Ch. 1 in Geertz, *Interpretation of Cultures.* New York: Basic Books.
GILMAN, N. 2003. *Mandarins of the Future: Modernization Theory in Cold War America.* Baltimore: Johns Hopkins University Press.
GREW, R. et al. 1978. *Crises of Political Development in Europe and the United States.* Princeton, NJ: Princeton University Press.
HEMPEL, C. G. 1965. *Aspects of Scientific Explanation.* New York: Free Press.
KUHN, T. S. 1962. *The Structure of Scientific Revolutions.* Chicago: University of Chicago Press.
LASSWELL, H. D. 1930. *Psychopathology and Politics.* Chicago: University of Chicago Press
—— 1963. *The Future of Political Science.* New York: Atherton Press.

MacIntyre, A. 1971. Is a science of comparative politics possible? Ch. 23 in *Against the Self-Images of the Age*. New York: Schocken Books.

Olson, M., Jr. 1965. *The Logic of Collective Action*. Cambridge, Mass.: Harvard University Press.

Popper, K. R. 1972. *Objective Knowledge: An Evolutionary Approach*. Oxford: Clarendon Press.

Pye, L. W. 1962. *Politics, Personality and Nation Building: Burma's Search for Identity*. New Haven, Conn.: Yale University Press.

—— (ed.) 1975. *Political Science and Area Studies: Rivals or Partners*. Bloomington: Indiana University Press.

Samuels, R. J., and Weiner, M. (eds.) 1992. *The Political Culture of Foreign Area and International Studies*. Washington, DC: Brassey's.

Tilly, C. et al. 1976. *The Formation of Nation States in Western Europe*. Princeton, NJ: Princeton University Press.

Name Index

Subject Index

Lightning Source UK Ltd.
Milton Keynes UK
UKOW05f2110200917
309579UK00004B/197/P

9 780199 548446